INTERNATIONAL BUSINESS

INTERNATIONAL BUSINESS

Challenges in a changing world

JANET MORRISON

*Formerly Senior Lecturer and Programme Leader for
Undergraduate and Postgraduate International Management
Degrees, University of Sunderland Business School, UK*

palgrave
macmillan

First published 2009 by
PALGRAVE MACMILLAN

Palgrave Macmillan in the UK is an imprint of Macmillan Publishers Limited,
registered in England, company number 785998, of Houndmills, Basingstoke,
Hampshire RG21 6XS

Palgrave Macmillan in the US is a division of St Martin's Press LLC,
175 Fifth Avenue, New York, NY 10010.

Palgrave Macmillan is the global academic imprint of the above companies
and has companies and representatives throughout the world.

Palgrave® and Macmillan® are registered trademarks in the United States,
the United Kingdom, Europe and other countries.

ISBN-13: 978–1–4039–4563–1
ISBN-10: 1–4039–4563–2

This book is printed on paper suitable for recycling and made from fully
managed and sustained forest sources. Logging, pulping and manufacturing
processes are expected to conform to the environmental regulations of the
country of origin.

A catalogue record for this book is available from the British Library.

Library of Congress Cataloging-in-Publication Data

Morrison, Janet.
    International Business : challenges in a changing world / Janet Morrison.
        p. cm.
    Includes bibliographical references.
    ISBN 978–1–4039–4563–1 (alk. paper)
1. International business enterprises. 2. Globalization—Economic aspects.
    3. International trade. 4. Competition, International.
I. Title.
HD62.4.M677 2009
658'.049—dc22

                                                        2008030086

10 9 8 7 6 5 4 3 2 1
18 17 16 15 14 13 12 11 10 09

Printed and bound in China

All maps © Maps in Minutes™, 2007

Contents in brief

Contents

part 4   **Managing in the global environment**   **315**

part 5   Global issues and IB   471

List of figures and tables

Figures

Tables

List of plates

About the author

Janet Morrison, now retired, was a senior lecturer in strategic and international management at Sunderland University Business School in the UK, where she enjoyed a long career in teaching, research, curriculum development and course administration. She taught international business modules at undergraduate and postgraduate levels, including International Business Environment, Management in a Global Environment, Japanese Business and the Social and Cultural Environment of International Business. She was programme leader for undergraduate international business degrees and the MBA in International Management.

Janet's academic background goes back to her first degree (in political science and history) at Mary Washington College of the University of Virginia in the US (now the University of Mary Washington), followed by a master's degree from the University of Toronto in Canada and, later, a law degree from the University of Newcastle-upon-Tyne in the UK. She also studied in Chicago and Nagoya in Japan.

Her published research includes articles in a range of areas, including corporate governance, Japanese business and corporate social responsibility. She is the author of *The International Business Environment* (2006), first published by Palgrave Macmillan in 2002 and now in its second edition.

Acknowledgements

I would like to thank my husband Ian for his steadfast encouragement and support. I would also like to thank all those involved at Palgrave Macmillan for their help at every stage of this project. In particular, warmest thanks are owed to my editor Ursula Gavin and development editor Catherine Travers. I am grateful to the (anonymous) reviewers of draft chapters for their many suggestions and comments, which have been invaluable. Many teachers and students I have been fortunate to know, as well as many businesspeople who feature in this text, have provided inspiration galore, at least some of which will, I hope, rub off on readers.

All maps in this book are copyright © Maps in Minutes™, 2007, and are reproduced with kind permission. The country data presented in Appendix 2 is used with kind permission from *The Statesman's Yearbook* (www.statesmansyearbook.com).

Preface

This book provides a lively, informative and stimulating introduction to international business for business and management students. Based on nearly 30 years of teaching experience, it is designed to offer a substantial, but readable, academic foundation as well as to encourage readers to adopt a critical perspective.

International business now touches the lives of everyone across the globe, in ways not always easy to fathom. Moreover, events and trends, which once unfolded gradually, are now racing ahead with breathtaking speed, testing even experienced managers. Understanding the 'how' and 'why' of current trends is becoming ever more urgent for tomorrow's managers and decision-makers, as global and local impacts become increasingly intertwined. Bearing in mind these needs, this book has three major aims:

- To unlock the processes and players that drive international business, together with their impacts on societies and their physical environments.
- To guide the student through the strategy formulation and decision-making processes which take place in the international arena in a wide variety of international business contexts.
- To encourage a critical approach to the issues and events that arise in business contexts across the globe.

This text is designed for business studies and management degree courses at undergraduate level, as well as MBA and masters degree courses. The choices of degree courses and curriculum options for undergraduate and postgraduate students have never been wider, from general management courses to those with a specialist focus, such as marketing or HRM. International business has become a vital component of all these courses, combining a broad geographic coverage with a range of functional and disciplinary perspectives. This book's integrative approach spanning core disciplines makes a valuable contribution to the curriculum, complementing specialist modules. It is engagingly written and includes clear explanations, making it readily accessible to a range of students, including those for whom English is a second language.

Approach

International business encompasses all types of business organization, all parts of the globe and all aspects of business activity, yet international business textbooks to date have tended to limit their coverage in one or more ways. Most are economics and finance oriented, taking only passing account of societal, ethical and environmental implications. Most focus on the US, for its leadership role in global business and enterprise values and culture. In contrast, this book takes a broader approach, in terms of perspectives and geographical focus:

✓ **Multidisciplinary approach**: Economic concepts and analysis are presented alongside political, social, ethical and legal analysis, to give a richer picture, as well as a more solid foundation for strategy formulation. Concepts and theories are presented and discussed in terms of both business and society implications. Throughout the text, attention is drawn to the tension between economic, social and ethical considerations in international business operations.

✓ **Truly international outlook**: US, European and Japanese firms are placed in the broad international context, providing the reader with a balanced view of current trends towards multiple centres of business activity. The rise of developing and transition economies is highlighted as a trend which is shaping the competitive environment in virtually all industries. The case studies and vignettes reflect these changing centres of gravity, featuring key emerging economies such as China and India, and also a wide range of other locations in Asia, Africa and Latin America. From Azersun, an agricultural firm in Azerbaijan, to Weg Electric in Brazil, national and global influences are clearly analysed in a vast array of differing locations.

✓ **Diversity of business perspectives**: In today's world, the competitive landscape comprises a range of players, from small private enterprises to large multinationals and state-owned organizations. The numerous case studies feature examples of all these types of organization and, importantly, how they interact in practice.

✓ **Diversity of social and cultural perspectives**: The growing variety of economic players mirrors a diversity of social and cultural perspectives in today's business world, which is another of the book's themes. Ownership structures, management practices and employee relations are all affected by national environments and corporate history. Understanding these differing ways of doing business is essential for the international manager.

✓ **Focus on global issues**: Global issues are highlighted throughout the book, with systematic analysis from a business perspective in Part 5. The ecological environment, human well-being and development issues are now seen as being central to strategy and operations. This book provides a coherent presentation of corporate social responsibility (CSR), including underpinning theories and strategic implications. CSR approaches in a range of developing countries and diverse cultural environments are provided, to meet the growing needs of international managers for CSR commitment, followed up with effective policies and practices.

Content

This text balances environmental analysis, strategy and management, inviting critical reflection on their interrelationships. It is divided into five parts, each with a broad focus designed to fit into a systematic overall plan. As the map of the book shows, each part forms a logical foundation for the one which follows. The final part forms the conclusion, examining global issues in the business context.

An overview of the content of each chapter is given below.

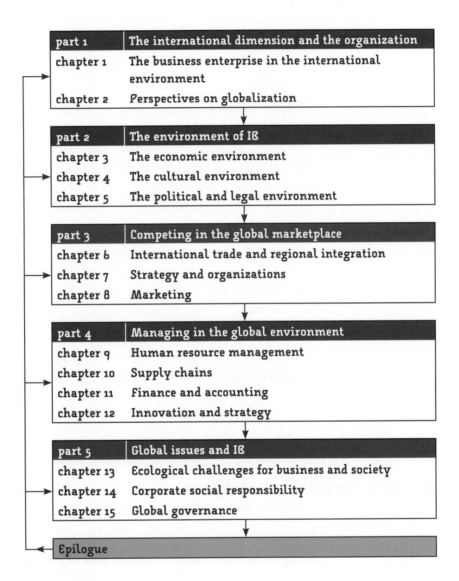

part 1	The international dimension and the organization
chapter 1	The business enterprise in the international environment
chapter 2	Perspectives on globalization

part 2	The environment of IB
chapter 3	The economic environment
chapter 4	The cultural environment
chapter 5	The political and legal environment

part 3	Competing in the global marketplace
chapter 6	International trade and regional integration
chapter 7	Strategy and organizations
chapter 8	Marketing

part 4	Managing in the global environment
chapter 9	Human resource management
chapter 10	Supply chains
chapter 11	Finance and accounting
chapter 12	Innovation and strategy

part 5	Global issues and IB
chapter 13	Ecological challenges for business and society
chapter 14	Corporate social responsibility
chapter 15	Global governance

Epilogue

Part 1 The international dimension and the organization

The opening chapters introduce the internal and external aspects of the business and its international environment, together with an overview of international trends:

- **Chapter 1: The business enterprise in the international environment**
  This introductory chapter presents the key features of the business organization, including ownership, entrepreneurial aspects and decision-making structures. The business is also placed in its international context, giving an overview of the international business environment and identifying key players.

- **Chapter 2: Perspectives on globalization**
  Globalization and internationalization are considered as broad trends in international business. Key theories and patterns of foreign expansion of markets and production are explained. The chapter invites a critical perspective on globalization, together with an examination of its impacts on societies across the globe.

Part 2 The environment of IB

These chapters look in turn at three key dimensions of the international environment:

- **Chapter 3: The economic environment**
  This chapter explains the key concepts of macroeconomics and illustrates them with a range of examples. National economic systems are identified and contrasted, emphasizing the ways in which businesses function in these differing national contexts. Patterns of economic development are explored, with their implications for international business.

- **Chapter 4: The cultural environment**
  Cultural dimensions, including theories of culture, are used to profile national cultures in the context of business operations and markets. Organizational culture, particularly in the context of internationalization, is examined. This chapter casts light on how culture change is taking place across the globe, as economic development and urbanization are leading to changes in societies and lifestyles.

- **Chapter 5: The political and legal environment**
  The contours of political systems and their claims to legitimacy are examined, including varying types of democratic transition, and their impacts on business. Issues of political and legal risk are examined, as these factors are taking on greater relevance for international businesses as they expand more widely.

Part 3 Competing in the global marketplace

In these chapters, we turn to strategy formation and implementation in the international competitive environment, focusing on theory and practice:

- **Chapter 6: International trade and regional integration**
  Basic concepts and trade theories are examined, highlighting the most recent trends in international trade and their impact on international business.

- **Chapter 7: Strategy and organizations**
  This chapter looks at the firm in the competitive environment, examining how it designs strategy to gain competitive advantage, and what organizational structures will help (or hinder) its successful internationalization.

- **Chapter 8: Marketing**
  The focus here is specifically on the ways in which marketing contributes to the firm's achievement of its goals internationally. Although a global marketing strategy might be thought essential for the global business, national differences have challenged marketing strategists, enlivening the competition between local and global products.

Part 4 Managing in the global environment

These chapters each focus on a specific specialist business function, highlighting the international dimension:

- **Chapter 9: Human resource management**

  Focusing on international human resource management (IHRM), this chapter examines how HRM planners accommodate local workplace values and practices as organizations expand into a range of locations. Co-ordinating diverse practices and maintaining a focus on strategic goals are challenges for HRM internationally, especially in the context of a growing array of working and organizational relationships.

- **Chapter 10: Supply chains**

  The importance of inter-organizational networks in international operations is highlighted. Internationalization of production has transformed manufacturing, from global sourcing to assembly and distribution. As much manufacturing has shifted to low-cost environments, quality management and transport have become key factors in the new competitive landscape.

- **Chapter 11: Finance and accounting**

  The text now turns to the function of finance and accounting in strategy and practice. Global financial markets are clearly explained, highlighting implications for businesses in their corporate financing and operations. Accounting standards and practices are discussed in the context of internationalization and gradual harmonization of national practices.

- **Chapter 12: Innovation and strategy**

  Innovation is universally recognized as key to competitive strategy, but how can managers 'make it happen'? The chapter looks at strategies and policies which foster innovation in the international context, taking into account national differences in innovation systems and their legal implications.

Part 5 Global issues and IB

Finally, the major challenges which businesses face in the twenty-first century are highlighted. The three chapters bring together themes of business impacts in societies and environments from earlier chapters, providing an overview and synthesis, as well as a critical perspective:

- **Chapter 13: Ecological challenges for business and society**

  These include pollution, climate change and environmental degradation, all of which are impacting on strategy and policies for the future. For managers, therefore, environmental assessment and changes in management practices are becoming primary considerations.

- **Chapter 14: Corporate social responsibility**

  CSR considerations now pervade international business activities, in both production and markets. The main theories are set out and evaluated in the context of the changing views of the role of companies in societies. Corporate governance and differing national cultures are taken into consideration.

- **Chapter 15: Global governance**

  This chapter brings together the themes of globalization and rule-making institutions which are increasingly shaping the markets in which international firms operate. Firms have long since become accustomed to dealing with governments and regulators, but in the new environment, networks, relationships and co-operation among governmental and corporate players are redefining the regulatory frameworks within which businesses operate. These changes create both opportunities and challenges for international businesses in a changing competitive environment.

Features

This book is packed with carefully thought-out features to aid understanding, provide real-life applications and stimulate thought and discussion. In particular, it includes an outstanding set of case studies and vignettes and two useful appendices – an atlas section complete with full colour maps, and an extensive list of country data.

It is easy to navigate, with each part of the book clearly distinguishable by a characteristic colour. There is a range of handy quick reference tools, for example a list of abbreviations at the start of the book, a glossary at the end, and appendices showing maps and country data.

An outline of each of the book's features is given below, and the guided tour of the book provides an at-a-glance summary.

At the start of each chapter

- **Chapter outline and learning objectives**: On the opening page of each chapter you will find an outline of the main sections, along with learning objectives, setting out what the student can expect to gain from the chapter in terms of knowledge and applications.
- **Introduction**: Each chapter introduction begins with a short vignette, highlighting a key theme using a topical example so that the material in the chapter is instantly contextualized and its relationship with real-world events firmly established. The vignette is then followed by an overview of the material to be covered in the ensuing chapter.

Throughout each chapter

- **On-page glossary**: For quick reference, key concepts and terms are defined in the margins at the points in the text where they are introduced. (They are also listed in the Glossary at the end of the book.)
- **Web checks**: References to relevant websites appear in the margins, providing an entry point to the range of online resources available. The web checks also offer guidance on navigating the websites they refer to.
- **Pause to reflect**: Throughout the chapter, readers are invited to look critically at the material and apply concepts and principles in differing contexts by answering questions posed by the pause to reflect feature.
- **Figures and tables**: The figures and tables serve to aid learning and present data trends. Figures are generally presented where topics are introduced, in the belief that a visual diagram showing links among a number of

elements is a useful learning aid. A full list of these features is provided at the beginning of the book.

- To recap...: Each main section finishes with a box highlighting its main points. These crystallize students' understanding of the key points and should provide a handy reference point.

Case studies

Reflecting the international outlook of the book, these are drawn from an exceptionally diverse range of geographical locations, spanning all continents and all stages of development. They also cover a broad spectrum of company types.

Each case study is followed up by a set of questions to check learning, prompt discussion and encourage students to apply the concepts they have learned to real-world situations, encouraging an active, problem-based approach to learning. The case studies have also been designed to encourage students to see the links between the different topic areas covered in the book. The text contains three types of case study:

- Full case studies (CS): Each chapter contains two full case studies – one within the main part of the chapter and the other at the end. They illustrate and explore specific chapter themes as well as interactions with other relevant issues.
- Strategic crossroads (SX): These are shorter vignettes with a narrower focus than the longer cases.
- Country focus (CF): There are two country focus features per chapter, each presenting a snapshot of key areas of the business environment in a specific country and also offering a glimpse of relevant companies, both domestic and foreign, showing the challenges they face and how they are meeting them. Each country focus is accompanied by a map of the relevant country, with key centres of population and other features highlighted.

A full guide to all the case studies is provided. This consists of a series of grids providing an overview of the main areas covered by each case study. For case studies (CS) and strategic crossroads (SX) features, the headings reflect strategy, business functions and CSR. For country focus (CF) features, the headings reflect environmental dimensions and development issues.

At the end of each chapter

- Conclusions: Each chapter's concluding section presents the main threads of the discussion succinctly, showing how the chapter's main points relate to each other and to the overall themes. Each conclusion highlights both strategic and environmental dimensions for international business.
- Review questions: These are set out in two sections before the closing case study of the chapter. Part A contains questions which test students' grasp of knowledge and concepts. Part B questions invite more critical thinking and assessment of the material in the chapter. The Part B questions can be used for group discussion or individual study.
- Further research: In addition to references, suggestions for further reading are given at the end of chapters. These are additional avenues to follow,

offering more in-depth elaboration of the material, or presenting different critical perspectives. These recommendations provide a window on some of the key contributions to scholarship in this field, including those from Michael Porter, Paul Krugman and Joseph Stiglitz.

At the end of the book

- **Appendices**: The book contains two appendices providing students with valuable reference points and context for geographical and economic information:
    - **Appendix 1** is an atlas section (including capital cities)
    - **Appendix 2** provides detailed geographical, social and economic data for countries throughout the world in tabular format, for convenient, at-a-glance reference.
- **Glossary**: The glossary contains all the key concepts and terms featured in the margins.
- **References**: Every chapter contains many references to source material. References in the text are listed at the end of the book. References in case studies and country focus boxes are listed at the end of the feature box itself. Many references cite important scholarship in the area of international business, both theory and empirical studies. Theories are necessarily presented only briefly in the text, and following up these sources with further reading will greatly enhance understanding of their points of view.
- **Index**: The index is presented in three sections: the index of business organizations, the index of people and the subject index.

Finally, it is appropriate to note here that the book contains an abundance of cross-references, to both content on specific topics and relevant case study and country focus boxes. They are inserted to highlight links which offer further illumination to readers, and also to show the substantive links among topics in different chapters.

Companion website

International Business: Challenges in a changing world is accompanied by extensive online materials, accessible to lecturers and students at **www.palgrave.com/business/morrisonib**.

This companion website is packed with valuable features to aid teaching and learning, including **free access to selected articles from the *Journal of International Business Studies***.

Journal for International Business Studies **zone**
Adopters of *International Business: Challenges in a changing world* will have free access to a unique journal zone, offering:

- An introductory section for students with guidance on how to get the most out of journal articles
- Free access to a selection of articles from the *Journal of International Business Studies*
- Author-written supporting commentary explaining the background to each article, defining key terms and making links with relevant sections of the textbook
- Critical thinking questions and guideline answers.

In addition to the unique journals zone, the following password-protected online materials have been carefully designed to support lecturers in delivering their IB course:

- PowerPoint lecture slides for each chapter including relevant figures and tables. The slides can be customized by lecturers to suit module needs
- Lecturer manual including:
  - Suggested answers and discussion guidelines for questions in the book
  - Discussion guidelines for web-based assignments and synthesis/reflection questions provided on the website (see further details below)
  - Sample course outline giving suggested course structure for a range of course lengths
  - Sample end-of-module exam paper
- Testbank including multiple choice questions and short answer questions for each chapter, to use as a resource for creating end-of-module assessments
- VLE-compatible cartridge of the above materials, enabling them to be loaded direct into BlackBoard, WebCT or Moodle learning platforms
- Regular updates section giving details of recent events and their impact on the case studies included in the book.

Students will be able to check and expand their learning using the following features:

- Multiple choice questions for each chapter to self-test and check understanding
- Web-based assignments for each chapter to develop research skills and provide further examples of how theory applies to practice
- Synthesis and reflection questions for each part of the book to encourage consideration of the interrelationship between different areas and promote critical thinking
- Expanded searchable glossary of key terms for quick reference
- Annotated web links and RSS feeds to relevant sites and articles
- Country data table in electronic format, which can be manipulated and reordered by different categories.

This book's truly international and contemporary approach and coverage, together with its outstanding pedagogical features and clear explanations, offer a fresh and engaging IB course which we hope will offer an enjoyable and enlightening path through the subject for lecturers and students alike.

Guided tour of the book

Chapter outline listing the main areas covered

Learning objectives outlining what students will gain from the chapter

Mini-vignette to provide real-world context by highlighting a key theme using a topical example

Introduction giving an overview of the material in the chapter

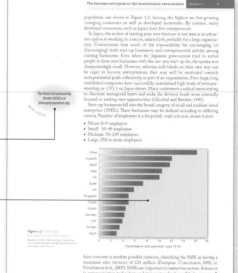

On-page glossary defining key concepts and terms

Web check directing readers to relevant online materials

Graphs to illustrate key trends

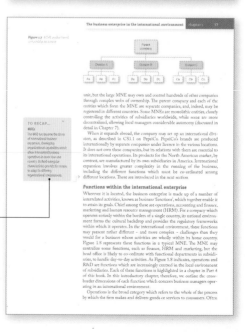

Pause to reflect inviting readers to look critically at the material

To recap... highlighting the main points in each section

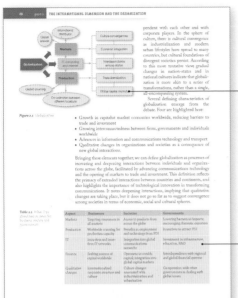

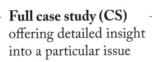

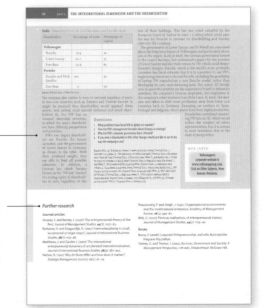

Strategic crossroads (SX)
providing a focused
case study

Diagrams and tables
to summarise key
information and
concepts

Country focus (CF)
offering a snapshot of a
specific country

Conclusion showing
how the main points in
the chapter interrelate

Review questions
designed to test students'
grasp of knowledge and
invite critical thinking

Full case study (CS)
offering detailed insight
into a particular issue

Further research
directing students to
more in-depth
information

List of abbreviations

ACP	African, Caribbean and Pacific (countries)
Apec	Asia-Pacific Economic Cooperation
Asean	Association of Southeast Asian Nations
BIS	Bank for International Settlements
BPO	business process outsourcing
CEO	chief executive officer
CFO	chief financial officer
COO	chief operating officer
CPI	consumer price index
CSR	corporate social responsibility
ECJ	European Court of Justice
ECB	European Central Bank
EPZ	export processing zone
EU	European Union
FDI	foreign direct investment
FSA	Financial Services Authority (UK)
FTSE	Financial Times Stock Exchange (index)
GATT	General Agreement on Tariffs and Trade
GDP	gross domestic product
GM	genetically modified
GNI	gross national income
GRI	Global Reporting Initiative
HIV/Aids	human immunodeficiency virus/ acquired immunodeficiency syndrome
HKSE	Hong Kong Stock Exchange
H	human resource
HRM	human resource management
IASB	International Accounting Standards Board
IEA	International Energy Agency
IFRS	international financial reporting standards
IGO	inter-governmental organization
IHRM	international human resource management
IJV	international joint venture
ILO	International Labour Organization
IMF	International Monetary Fund
IP	intellectual property
IPCC	Intergovernmental Panel on Climate Change
IPO	initial public offering
IPR	intellectual property rights
ISP	internet service provider
IT	information technology
JIT	just-in-time
LNG	liquefied natural gas
LSE	London Stock Exchange
M&A	merger and acquisition
MDG	Millennium Development Goal
Mercosur	Mercado Común del Sur (Southern Common Market)
MFN	most favoured nation
MNE	multinational enterprise
Nafta	North American Free Trade Agreement
Nato	North Atlantic Treaty Organization
NGO	non-governmental organization
NHS	National Health Service (UK)
NYSE	New York Stock Exchange
ODA	official development assistance
OECD	Organisation for Economic Co-operation and Development
Opec	Organization of Petroleum Exporting Countries
PPP	purchasing power parity
R&D	research and development
RTA	regional trade agreement

SBU	strategic business unit	UNEP	United Nations Environment Programme
SEC	Securities and Exchange Commission (US)	US	United States of America
SME	small and medium-sized enterprise	USDA	United States Department of Agriculture
TQM	total quality management		
UK	United Kingdom	VER	voluntary export restraint
UN	United Nations	WEF	World Economic Forum
UNDP	United Nations Development Programme	WHO	World Health Organisation
		WTO	World Trade Organization

Guide to case study and country features

These grids are designed to provide a handy reference point showing the key themes addressed in the case studies. Case studies (CS) and strategic crossroads (SX) features have been grouped together in the first grid, with subject coverage reflecting strategy, business functions and CSR. Country focus (CF) features are presented in the second grid, with subject coverage highlighting environmental dimensions and development issues.

Case Studies and Strategic Crossroads

Chapter	Case study (CS) and strategic crossroads (SX) boxes	International strategy	Culture	Supply chains	Organization and governance	Marketing	HRM	Innovation	CSR	Finance	Page number
1 Introduction	SX1.1 McDonald's	●			●					●	11
	SX1.2 Ericsson	●		●	●						15
	CS1.1 PepsiCo	●	●			●					20
	CS1.2 Volkswagen	●	●	●	●		●		●		35
2 Globalization	SX2.1 Puma	●	●			●					45
	SX2.2 Dyson	●		●				●			56
	CS2.1 Nokia	●	●		●			●			50
	CS2.2 IBM/Lenovo	●	●		●			●			73
3 Economic environment	SX3.1 Samsung		●		●					●	84
	SX3.2 Aviation Valley	●			●			●			104
	CS 3.1 Heineken	●	●	●	●			●			99
	CS 3.2 Wal-Mart	●	●	●	●		●		●		113
4 Cultural environment	SX4.1 Chugai-Roche	●	●		●			●			138
	SX4.2 Arab media	●	●			●					150
	CS4.1 Citigroup S. Korea	●	●				●				140
	CS4.2 DIY goes global	●	●		●	●					152
5 Political and legal environment	SX5.1 ABC Learning	●	●							●	179
	SX5.2 YouTube	●	●			●		●		●	182
	CS5.1 Online gambling	●	●			●			●		172
	CS5.2 Royal Dutch Shell	●		●	●				●	●	190
6 International trade and regional integration	SX6.1 China/Africa trade	●	●						●		204
	SX6.2 Kenya's EPZs	●			●					●	224
	CS6.1 Boeing/Airbus	●		●	●			●		●	216
	CS6.2 Textile industry	●		●					●		233
7 Organizations and strategy	SX7.1 Weg Electric	●		●				●			250
	SX7.2 ABB	●			●						256
	CS7.1 Unilever	●			●	●		●			259
	CS7.2 Nissan	●	●		●	●				●	272

Chapter	Case study (CS) and strategic crossroads (SX) boxes	International strategy	Culture	Supply chains	Organization and governance	Marketing	HRM	Innovation	CSR	Finance	Page number
8 Marketing	SX8.1 Hispanic media	●	●			●					290
	SX8.2 Children's advertising		●			●			●		308
	CS8.1 P&G	●	●		●	●		●			300
	CS8.2 McDonald's	●	●	●		●					312
9 HRM	SX9.1 GECAD	●					●	●			338
	SX9.2 Austrian banks	●	●				●			●	349
	CS9.1 L'Oréal	●				●	●		●		335
	CS9.2 Indian outsourcing	●	●				●	●			352
10 Supply chains	SX10.1 Bosch	●		●				●			369
	SX10.2 Maersk	●		●	●						386
	CS10.1 Toyota	●		●		●	●	●			378
	CS10.2 Dell	●		●	●	●					390
11 Finance & accounting	SX11.1 APP Indonesia	●			●				●	●	403
	SX11.2 Chinese accounting		●							●	428
	CS11.1 Mittal Steel	●		●						●	417
	CS11.2 Cadbury Schweppes	●		●		●				●	431
12 Innovation	SX12.1 Martek Marine	●						●			439
	SX12.2 Amadeus	●	●			●		●			449
	CS12.1 Kodak	●			●	●		●			462
	CS12.2 Pharmaceuticals	●	●			●		●	●		468
13 Ecology	SX13.1 Whole Foods Market	●	●			●			●		502
	SX13.2 Huhtamaki	●				●			●		507
	CS13.1 BP	●			●		●		●		495
	CS13.2 Green cars	●				●			●		511
14 CSR	SX14.1 Accenture	●							●	●	528
	SX14.2 Anglo American	●			●				●		544
	CS14.1 GrupoNueva	●	●		●			●	●		530
	CS14.2 Nike	●		●					●		548
15 Global governance	SX15.1 Product Red	●				●			●		556
	SX15.2 Chinese internet		●						●		586
	CS15.1 Gazprom	●		●	●				●	●	578
	CS15.2 Microsoft	●				●		●	●	●	590

Country Focus

Chapter	Country focus	Region	Economic environment	Social and cultural	Trade and competitiveness	Political and legal	Development issues	Page number
1 Introduction	CF1.1 Japan	E. Asia	●	●	●			23
	CF1.2 Venezuela	S. America	●			●	●	29
2 Globalization	CF2.1 USA	N. America	●	●	●			47
	CF2.2 India	S. Asia	●	●	●	●	●	61
3 Economic environment	CF3.1 UK	N. Europe	●			●		92
	CF3.2 Romania	C. Europe	●	●			●	108
4 Cultural environment	CF4.1 Turkey	S. Europe/Asia	●	●	●		●	125
	CF4.2 Mexico	N.America	●	●			●	146
5 Political & legal environment	CF5.1 Russia	E. Europe/Asia	●			●		163
	CF5.2 France	Europe	●			●		175
6 International trade and regional integration	CF6.1 Germany	Europe	●		●			200
	CF6.2 Brazil	S. America	●		●		●	221

Chapter	Country focus	Region	Economic environment	Social and cultural	Trade and competitiveness	Political and legal	Development issues	Page number
7 Organizations and strategy	CF7.1 Poland	C. Europe	●		●		●	245
	CF7.2 South Korea	E. Asia	●	●		●		265
8 Marketing	CF8.1 China	Asia	●	●			●	286
	CF8.2 South Africa	S. Africa	●		●		●	293
9 HRM	CF9.1 Vietnam	Asia	●	●	●		●	327
	CF9.2 Sweden	N. Europe	●	●		●		341
10 Supply chains	CF10.1 Spain	S. Europe	●	●	●			362
	CF10.2 Slovakia	C. Europe	●		●		●	373
11 Finance & accounting	CF11.1 Hong Kong	E. Asia	●	●	●	●		409
	CF11.2 Dubai	Middle East	●	●			●	421
12 Innovation	CF12.1 Singapore	Asia	●	●	●			445
	CF12.2 Switzerland	Europe	●		●	●		455
13 Ecology	CF13.1 Egypt	N. Africa	●	●			●	480
	CF13.2 Australia	Australasia	●		●			490
14 CSR	CF14.1 Nigeria	C. Africa	●	●			●	518
	CF14.2 Myanmar (Burma)	Asia	●	●		●	●	524
15 Global governance	CF15.1 Kazakhstan	W. Asia	●			●	●	559
	CF15.2 Burkina Faso	W. Africa	●	●	●	●	●	568

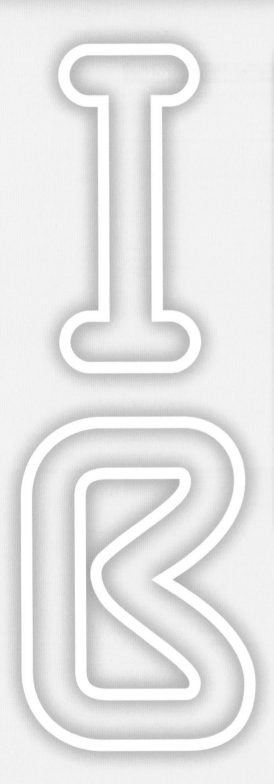

The two chapters in this part form an introduction to the book as a whole, focusing on the business organization in the international environment.

Chapter 1 presents an overview of the international environment, highlighting the differing levels, from local and national, to regional and international. The discussion focuses on the main identifying features of the business organization, including ownership and decision-making structures, as they adapt in differing geographical contexts. It is emphasized that the multinational enterprise (MNE), central to international business activities, covers a variety of organizations, large and small, which will feature throughout the book. A theme of the chapter is that growing interactions between organizations, governments and societal players are resulting in a broader view of the business organization in society.

This theme is pursued in Chapter 2, which looks at varying perspectives on globalization, often argued to be the defining characteristic of our times. We critically debate the nature of globalization, highlighting trends in globalized production and markets. The discussion takes an overview of globalized production, contrasting the key features of foreign direct investment (FDI) and other modes of international operations. The chapter analyses their impacts on societies and the environment, and considers the roles of governments and firms in the wider stakeholder context.

chapter 1

The business enterprise in the international environment

chapter 2

Perspectives on globalization

part 1	The international dimension and the organization
chapter 1	The business enterprise in the international environment
chapter 2	Perspectives on globalization

part 2	The environment of IB
chapter 3	The economic environment
chapter 4	The cultural environment
chapter 5	The political and legal environment

part 3	Competing in the global marketplace
chapter 6	International trade and regional integration
chapter 7	Strategy and organizations
chapter 8	Marketing

part 4	Managing in the global environment
chapter 9	Human resource management
chapter 10	Supply chains
chapter 11	Finance and accounting
chapter 12	Innovation and strategy

part 5	Global issues and IB
chapter 13	Ecological challenges for business and society
chapter 14	Corporate social responsibility
chapter 15	Global governance

Epilogue

chapter **1**

THE BUSINESS ENTERPRISE IN THE INTERNATIONAL ENVIRONMENT

chapter outline

learning objectives

▷ To highlight the ways in which the international dimension in business activities is distinctive from national and local enterprises
▷ To appreciate the role of the entrepreneur and entrepreneurship in the international environment
▷ To gain an overview of the ways in which enterprises organize and adapt when they expand internationally
▷ To gain an understanding of the key players in the international environment with which businesses interact

Introduction

In cities around the world, companies such as McDonald's and Starbucks have become familiar sights, having successfully expanded from their American roots. They are finding, however, that countries vary considerably in their receptiveness, and that new competitors, many with local backgrounds, are crowding onto the scene. Café Coffee Day, an Indian chain founded in 1996, has enjoyed rapid expansion in India, where coffee shops are growing in popularity among the under-21s, who make up half of India's billion-plus population. Exemplifying the confidence of firms in today's emerging economies, Café Coffee Day is now expanding into other Asian countries, Europe and the Middle East. Meanwhile, Starbucks, having been in China since 1999, is keen to enter India, but has run into objections from the Indian government, as well as from Asian business partners guiding its proposed Indian venture. These companies represent two contrasting themes which are central to this book. First, firms from emerging markets are becoming more international in their horizons; and, second, differences in national business environments are still influential forces in international business.

Whatever its background, the business that seeks to expand internationally faces new challenges as well as new opportunities. Its internal organization, culture and strategy are likely to owe much to its home environment, but as it expands internationally, it is also influenced by the foreign environments in which it operates as well as developments in the broader international environment. Seizing business opportunities abroad involves taking on new risks. This chapter aims to provide insight into the organizational aspects of international business activities in the context of these diverse environmental influences.

The chapter begins with an introduction to the international business in its environment. The first section highlights the distinguishing features of the international business and outlines the key dimensions of the international environment. We then look at how businesses grow from small beginnings to become large organizations spanning continents. Businesses are typically started by an enthusiastic founder, whose entrepreneurial skills contribute to its success. Entrepreneurship is therefore a vital ingredient. The following section examines the ways in which the firm develops as an organization, with greater complexity and attention to specialized functions. Internal roles and governance acquire important legal dimensions, which are outlined in the following section.

The multinational enterprise (MNE) has become the driver of international business. The dynamics of the MNE are likely to change as its organization becomes international. In particular, interactions with other organizations and adaptation to the changing environment present challenges for international managers. The following sections introduce each of these types of interaction. Co-operation between firms has become a key feature of international business, creating relations between firms. Similarly, the international environment presents an array of both governmental and non-governmental players, which impact on MNEs. They include national and regional authorities, as well as formal and informal international organizations. A summary of these key players, in addition to providing an overview, forms a reference point for later chapters, in which their impacts will be analysed in specific contexts.

Café Coffee Day's website is www.cafecoffeeday.com. Starbucks' website is www.starbucks.com.

WEB CHECK

plate 1.1 The outdoor café has become a popular aspect of city life around the world.

International business in a changing environment

Businesses everywhere seek to provide goods, services, or a combination of both, to customers, at prices they are willing to pay. The presence of many businesses providing similar products or services creates a market in those products, where producers and sellers compete with each other to persuade potential customers to buy their products over those of their rivals. Increasingly, we see foreign firms competing alongside local and national firms for customers, as businesses become more aware of the potential for international expansion. In this section, we identify the characteristics of international business and the dimensions of the international environment which they must confront as they expand beyond national borders.

What distinguishes international business?

International business: Any business activity across national borders, including exporting and importing, manufacturing, service provision and retailing; also refers to the organization itself which engages in cross-border business.

International business refers to any business activity which spans more than one country. This is a broad definition, covering all types of business activity and a variety of organizations, large and small. The essential characteristic is that the organizations involved in the transaction are located in different countries.

A common way of classifying businesses is according to their geographic scope, which may be local, national or international. They are presented in Figure 1.1, which features four main aspects in which these types of business differ: organization, market, sourcing and communications.

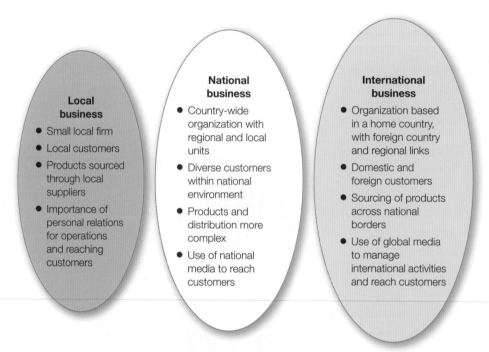

Local business
- Small local firm
- Local customers
- Products sourced through local suppliers
- Importance of personal relations for operations and reaching customers

National business
- Country-wide organization with regional and local units
- Diverse customers within national environment
- Products and distribution more complex
- Use of national media to reach customers

International business
- Organization based in a home country, with foreign country and regional links
- Domestic and foreign customers
- Sourcing of products across national borders
- Use of global media to manage international activities and reach customers

Figure 1.1 Comparison of the local, national and international business

The local business is closely identified with a local community. The local market, where commercial activity is based mainly on face-to-face relations, is a model with which we are all familiar. The business which operates exclusively in a local community gains a clear picture of products to suit customers' needs, the profile of likely customers, and the prices they are willing to pay. For example, a local bookseller will provide a selection of children's books in a community where there are many young families. The bookseller may decide to expand to an adjoining region, or to diversify the range of products, offering, for example, DVDs and computer games. These are typical ways for a small business to grow, sometimes aiming to become national in scope. As it grows, its organization changes, along with its market and communications. Organizational changes which adapt to changing markets and environments are key to understanding the distinction between a purely local business and a national or international one.

The domestic business oriented to its national domestic market is a familiar phenomenon everywhere. Expansion within national boundaries may be relatively manageable, depending on the size of the country. All parties are likely to speak the same language and use the same currency. Transactions are within a single legal system, and transport links are usually part of a national system. The risks are fairly foreseeable and manageable. It is not surprising that nationwide businesses serving domestic markets have become a mainstay of the business landscape. From banks to supermarkets, these are the types of businesses with which people are most familiar. They provide employment and wealth creation, and profits are directed back into the local economy. Hence, strong domestic businesses are perceived as traditional indicators of a country's prosperity. If they wish to carry on expanding, however, national firms sooner or later contemplate branching out abroad.

As Figure 1.1 shows, the firm which expands from its home country must establish links abroad. We tend to think of trade – the export and import of all types of goods across national borders – as exemplifying international business. But service providers, too, expand abroad. They include financial services, IT services, distribution and transport. Thanks to improvements in transport and communications technology, the international dimension has become routine everyday business for firms all over the globe. However, dealing in different currencies presents risks, and cross-border transport links might involve numerous intermediaries. Nonetheless, industries such as manufacturing, traditionally national in orientation, have become transformed by the ability to shift production and sourcing to alternative locations with relative ease. Retailers have also expanded internationally, opening branches outside their home countries, or acquiring ongoing businesses in other markets. The global retailer, like the global manufacturer, has become a reality. The growth of global media, such as the internet and satellite television, has facilitated communications in global markets. However, many complications remain for the unwary. As the next section shows, persisting differences in national environments both present opportunities and pose obstacles.

Going international
What are the pitfalls for the national company hoping to expand internationally? How can they be minimized? Give an example of a company you are familiar with, which has succeeded in going international. Do you know of any that have struggled? How did they go wrong?

PAUSE TO REFLECT

Dimensions of the international environment

The business which goes international enjoys greater prospects for expansion than would be possible within local or national markets. Even Café Coffee Day, with over 500 outlets in India, is expanding overseas. Seeking markets or conducting operations in new locations requires an understanding of new environments which are largely unfamiliar, especially in businesses where cultural preferences loom large. Advances in communications and transport tempt firms into thinking that internationalization has become simple, and, in many ways, it has. But national boundaries are still important in many aspects of the economic, political, legal and cultural environment. These are explored in detail in Part 2 of this book. Here, we take an overview of these key dimensions of the international environment.

As Figure 1.2 indicates, in each of the dimensions, there are national, regional and international influences. Distinctive national institutions, economies and cultures shape the business environment of a country. As countries differ widely, the firm with international aspirations must assess carefully what types of activity it wishes to carry out abroad and which national envi-

Figure 1.2 Dimensions of the international environment

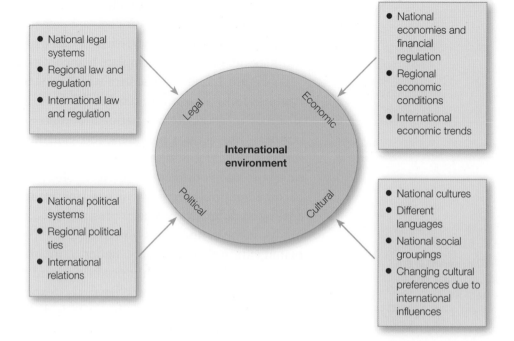

- National legal systems
- Regional law and regulation
- International law and regulation

- National economies and financial regulation
- Regional economic conditions
- International economic trends

International environment

Legal   Economic   Political   Cultural

- National political systems
- Regional political ties
- International relations

- National cultures
- Different languages
- National social groupings
- Changing cultural preferences due to international influences

ronments will be most advantageous. At the same time, countries are becoming increasingly integrated in regional and international ties, such as political and trade relations. Therefore, even the business which remains local or national in its orientation is influenced by events and trends in the wider environment. Opportunities and challenges take in both national and international factors, as the next section reveals.

Comparing local, national and international businesses
Think of a business enterprise in each of these categories, with which you are familiar. Compare them in terms of organization, customers and products.

PAUSE TO REFLECT

Entrepreneurship goes global

Entrepreneur: Individual who, having identified a new business opportunity, assembles the necessary resources and creates a new business.

Entrepreneurship: Attributes associated with business start-ups, including identifying opportunities, pursuing innovative ideas, and willingness to undertake manageable risks. These may be nurtured in any business, be it large or small, a start-up or an established firm.

Businesses often start life as the bright idea of an individual entrepreneur who has the ambition, persistence – and funding – to turn it into a reality. The entrepreneur is usually defined as a person who, having identified opportunities and accessed the necessary resources, creates a new business (see Zimmerer et al., 2007). Entrepreneurship is broader in scope: it certainly includes identifying opportunities, but it encompasses existing businesses which reorient themselves to become more entrepreneurial, for example providing new products and services.

Levels of entrepreneurial activity in a country are an indication of the vibrancy of the economy, and research shows a correlation between overall entrepreneurial activity and economic growth (Global Entrepreneurship Consortium, 2007). Every country sees its potential entrepreneurs as the key to healthy businesses in the future, but country environments differ considerably in their conduciveness to entrepreneurial activity. In a survey of 60 countries, the Global Entrepreneurship Consortium measured the level of entrepreneurial activity within each country. Early stage entrepreneurs, including owners of new businesses, as a proportion of the adult working population, are shown in Figure 1.3. Among the highest are fast-growing emerging economies as well as developed economies. By contrast, many developed economies, such as Japan, have few entrepreneurs.

In Japan, the notion of starting your own business is not seen as an attractive option to working in a secure, salaried job, probably for a large organization. Governments bear much of the responsibility for encouraging (or discouraging) both start-up businesses and entrepreneurial activity among existing businesses. Even when the Japanese government tried to entice people to form new businesses with the one-yen start-up fee, the uptake was disappointingly small. However, whereas individuals on their own may not be eager to become entrepreneurs, they may well be motivated towards entrepreneurial goals collectively, as part of an organization. Even large, long established companies have successfully maintained high levels of entrepreneurship, as CF1.1 on Japan shows. Many underwent a radical restructuring to eliminate managerial layers and make the division heads more externally focused on seeking new opportunities (Ghoshal and Bartlett, 1995).

Start-up businesses fall into the broad category of small and medium-sized enterprises (SMEs). These businesses may be defined according to differing criteria. Number of employees is a frequently used criterion, shown below:

- Micro: 0–9 employees
- Small: 10–49 employees
- Medium: 50–249 employees
- Large: 250 or more employees

Sales turnover is another possible criterion, classifying the SME as having a maximum sales turnover of £24 million (European Commission 2000, in Hutchinson et al., 2005). SMEs are important in numerous sectors. Advances in communication technology and transport make it possible for even small manufacturing firms to export their products globally. Even in the retail

The Global Entrepreneurship Monitor (GEM) is at www.gemconsortium.org.

WEB CHECK

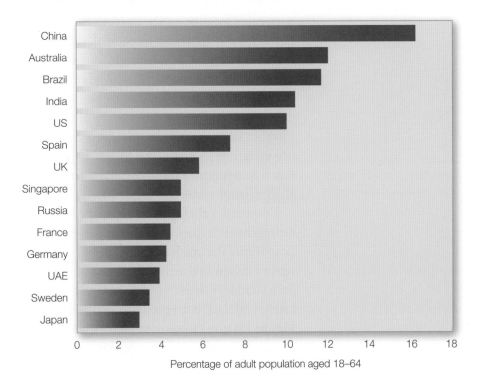

Figure 1.3 Early stage entrepreneurial activity, 2006

Source: Global Entrepreneurship Consortium (2007) *Global Entrepreneurship Monitor 2006*, at www.gemconsortium.org

Percentage of adult population aged 18–64

WEB CHECK

The OECD's Centre for Entrepreneurship, SMEs and Local Development (CFE) contains a wealth of information and reports. It can be accessed by going first to the OECD homepage at www.oecd.org. Under *Browse by departments*, click on *CFE*.

Franchise: A commercial agreement by which a business (the franchisee) is allowed to use the brand, products and business format of another business (the franchisor), in return for payment of agreed fees between the two parties.

sector, once thought to be the bastion of local businesses, SMEs are able to reach consumers in many countries, particularly in specialized markets such as luxury goods (Hutchinson et al., 2005). These companies tend to be highly entrepreneurial and make use of networking opportunities – attributes which larger companies, rather set in their ways, have difficulty emulating. Hence, flexible and innovative SMEs can enjoy competitive advantages.

Alternatively, the SME may be a franchise business, benefiting from the reputation of a well-known brand. Under a franchise arrangement, a business, the 'franchisee', agrees to terms set by the owner of the brand, the 'franchisor', to run the business as a separate enterprise. A franchise can be defined as:

> a contractual agreement between two legally independent companies whereby the franchisor grants the right to the franchisee to sell the franchisor's product or do business under its trademarks in a given location for a specified period of time. (Lafontaine, 1999)

The franchisee pays the franchisor a percentage of the revenues as a royalty for the right to use the brand and for backup services. The franchise arrangement has traditionally been popular for businesses such as fast-food chains, hotels and car rental companies, but it has recently enjoyed growing popularity in newer types of services, such as spas. It is estimated that one in every seven jobs in the US economy is in franchised businesses (Swann, 2005). McDonald's, featured in SX1.1, is perhaps the most well-known example of expansion by franchise businesses, but retailers such as Body Shop and l'Occitane have also grown internationally by use of the franchise. Café Coffee Day is also a franchise operation. A franchisee may take on more than one outlet and cover a larger geographical area, giving scope for entrepreneurs aiming to build larger businesses.

It was once assumed that the entrepreneur would focus initially on a particular locality, concentrating on building business reputation and brand familiarity. If that was successful, then expansion into national and international operations might follow. The timescale for such developments to unfold could be many years. Today's global entrepreneur has an altogether different outlook. Many entrepreneurs now look to start a business and expand it rapidly in a short space of time. In the fast-moving environment of internet companies, Google grew from a start-up to a multimillion dollar organization in just a few years. Entrepreneurial businesses that see themselves as operating internationally from the outset are known as born-global firms (Knight and Cavusgil, 2004) (see further discussion in Chapter 12).

Born-global firm: Entrepreneurial firm which adopts a global focus and commitment to international operations from the start.

Companies that expand rapidly run the risk of creating a 'bubble' of expectations, which may be difficult to sustain, especially in periods of economic downturn. The crash of many global internet companies in 1999–2000 represents a lesson in the management of expectations. Firms which were founded on a sound business model and innovative capacity were able to survive. Has today's global entrepreneur learned the lessons of the dot-com bubble? Figure 1.4 gives a guide to factors which determine long-term success. While innovative ideas and the backing of financial sources are necessary in the

Figure 1.4 The global entrepreneur

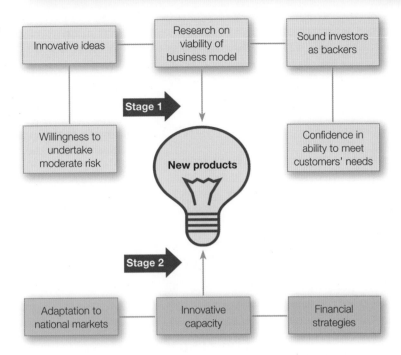

early stages, the needs of the business evolve. Remaining entrepreneurial is a challenge, as new technology is quickly superseded, and products may become obsolete in a matter of months, rather than years, as in previous eras. Hence, the ability to sustain innovative capacity and to raise finance from multiple sources will be crucial to long-term success. Adaptation to local markets also becomes more central to strategy as the company diversifies its range of products to different consumers. The successful business will soon find that competitors are coming up with similar offerings, aiming to capture a slice of any new market, as shown in SX1.1. Hence, competitive pressures can intensify for a business in this second stage, and innovative capacity will help to keep it ahead. As companies grow and become more complex organizations, it can become difficult to maintain the entrepreneurial and innovative culture which inspired their early days (Ghoshal and Bartlett, 1995).

TO RECAP...

Entrepreneurship

Entrepreneurs combine a range of attributes which all businesses need to some extent, whether they are start-ups or established organizations. These include enthusiasm and drive to attain goals, willingness to take manageable risks, innovative ideas and agility in adapting to changing markets.

STRATEGIC CROSSROADS

1.1

Will more franchises deliver super-size profits for McDonald's?

McDonald's, the fast-food chain, was the pioneer of franchising in the US in the 1950s, and has become the world's most widely known example of franchising. However, although the bulk of the company's restaurants are franchise businesses, many, especially outside the US, are owned and managed directly by McDonald's. These wholly owned businesses have been a cause of concern due to weak financial performance. Of a global total of 30,000 restaurants, 8,000 (27%) are owned and operated by McDonald's. Of the company's 13,500 restaurants in the US, only 15% are company owned, whereas in Europe, the percent-

age is 38%. In the UK, its 770 company-owned restaurants saw a 71% fall in profits in 2003.

Consumer concerns over healthy eating have affected sales at McDonald's outlets generally. Furthermore, a growing number of new and innovative competitors have attracted consumers away from McDonald's typical menus. The company set about a recovery strategy designed to deliver new healthier menus and refurbished premises. The revitalization programme has been enjoying success in the US, where franchise arrangements predominate, but its design and implementation have not been so successful in other parts of the world. Should the company therefore convert the wholly owned businesses to franchises, in order to improve performance? One of McDonald's major shareholders has asked for just such a strategic shift, but has met resistance from McDonald's management.

McDonald's has pointed out that the strength of its brand lies in its being directly involved in the business in the same way as its franchisees. It would lose this 'hands-on' involvement if it became a pure franchisor. In addition, it points out that its company-owned restaurants operate in countries which lack enforceable franchise laws, such as China and Brazil. However, the company introduced a new plan in 2006 which does represent a shift in strategy. It announced plans to sell 1,500 loss-making restaurants run by the company to local entrepreneurs in 20 countries. These would be 'developmental licensees', a type of franchise whereby the entrepreneur invests the capital to open the outlet, in contrast to McDonald's standard franchise arrangement, under which McDonald's owns the land and builds the restaurant. The developmental licensees would be provided with marketing and supply chain support from McDonald's. The hope is that these new entrepreneurial businesses will compete more effectively. However, their success will depend not just on the efforts of the new owners, but on the company's ability to meet consumers' increasingly discerning tastes in all its markets.

Questions

◆ What reasons lie behind the comparative success of McDonald's franchise outlets over the company-owned ones?
◆ How does the developmental licence fit in with McDonald's overall revitalization programme?

Sources: Grant, J., 'Investor urges McDonald's to sell off restaurants', *Financial Times*, 14 November 2005; Buckley, N., 'McDonald's benefits from healthy menus', *Financial Times*, 14 October 2004; Grant, J., 'McDonald's to expand licensees', *Financial Times*, 25 January 2006; Grant., J., 'McDonald's revamp gives platform for improvement', *Financial Times*, 22 April 2006.

WEB CHECK

McDonald's website is www.mcdonalds.com.

The global entrepreneur
It is arguable that entrepreneurship is more crucial for success in international business than for success at national level. Why?

PAUSE TO REFLECT

Cross-border enterprises: their internal environment

As a firm's international activities expand, its organization becomes more widely ramified and complex. In this section, we focus on the firm itself, beginning with the features of the company, which is the most common form of business enterprise globally. Much terminology relating to companies is introduced in this section, which might seem rather daunting, but familiarity with their meanings is necessary to understand and discuss companies' activities around the world. In this discussion, we refer to the general principles relating to companies worldwide, bearing in mind that companies are subject to the legal environment in particular countries where they are located. We then look at the types of company which feature most often in international business. Chief among these is the multinational enterprise (MNE), which has evolved as business horizons have expanded.

Roles inside the company

To begin a business, a person need only start trading, but without preliminary research and planning, the business stands little chance of success. The sole trader, being personally liable for all the firm's activities, will soon find that it makes sense to set up the firm as a separate legal entity by forming a registered company. The corporate form offers significant benefits. From a legal and accounting standpoint, the company is a separate entity from its founders. Another important factor is that there are tax advantages to trade as a company rather than as a self-employed individual. Even small family-based businesses tend to form companies through a formal process of 'incor-

Registered company: Entity formed through registration with national authorities, which enjoys legal status separate from the owners and limited liability for the company's obligations.

poration'. Companies are commonly referred to as 'firms', although, strictly speaking, firms are unincorporated businesses. The legal owners of a company are its shareholders, and the company's share capital in total is referred to as its equity. The owners of the business typically become the new company's first shareholders. In buying into the company, shareholders are providing the necessary capital to fund the business. Their liability, known as 'limited liability', extends to this investment, shielding them from the debts of the firm. As the company grows, managers may well be brought in to take over some of the tasks of the owner/managers who started the business. Those who take part in the management of the company are ultimately answerable to the shareholders for their actions. The company may also need to borrow money, and the company's creditors, too, have an interest in the company, in that they will expect to be repaid and receive interest. A typical company will rely on both equity and debt financing (discussed in detail in Chapter 11).

As a business grows, management roles take on more formal contours. The main roles are shown in Figure 1.5. Directors have overall responsibility for the business, although they need not take an active part in management. If the company is a small one, the owners, for example the founding family members, may take all the major decisions. In the small business, the roles of owners, managers and directors are wrapped up in the same people. However, as companies grow larger, these roles tend to be separated. As Figure 1.5 shows, directors have key responsibilities. They may appoint a chief executive officer (CEO), who is answerable to them, and they, in turn, are answerable to the shareholders. Other senior managers report to the CEO. Directors, managers and shareholders all have different perspectives, and tensions are likely to emerge. Shareholders may hold shares as a financial investment, with little interest in management, but many shareholders actively seek to influence strategy. Directors may take little interest in the day-to-day running of the business, leaving this role to professional executives and other salaried managers. However, directors, whether active or not, bear responsibility for how the business is run. Much of the discussion in this book focuses on these different roles and how they interact in real companies.

A company is registered in a particular location, usually a country, and it must adhere to that country's laws in respect of company formation. A company with a presence in several countries must also comply with the relevant legal requirements in its various locations, not merely its home country. In the US, company registration is a matter for the 50 individual states, the state of Delaware being the most popular because of its highly developed

Equity: Total shares in the registered company.

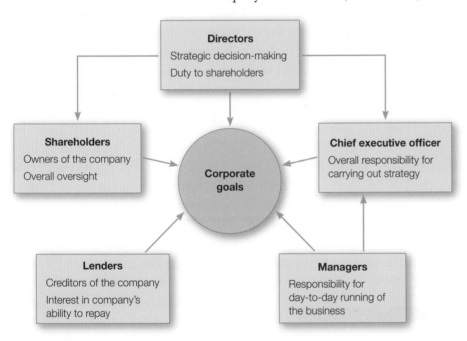

Figure 1.5 Roles within the public company

corporate law framework. In the European Union (EU), company law has been a preserve of the different national systems, but it is now possible to incorporate as a *societas europaea* (SE), or European company, or for a company registered in a member country to convert itself into an SE. In 2006, Allianz, the German insurance company, became the first large European company to do so. An advantage is that a company with subsidiaries in several EU countries can, for some purposes, operate a single system throughout its organization, rather than having to cope with different national laws for each of its subsidiaries. On the other hand, the new European company legislation does not extend to taxation, accounting, or directors' liability, which are still subject to national laws. A perceived advantage for large German companies is the reduction in board size, from a rather unwieldy 20 to 12. However, despite registering as SEs, German companies are compelled to maintain the two-tier corporate governance structure, discussed below.

A registered company normally begins life as a private company, and, if successful, considers becoming a public company several years later. The main distinction between public and private companies is that shares in public companies are traded freely on stock exchanges, while shares in private companies are not, remaining in the hands of 'insiders'. Public companies are subject to more regulation, for example the disclosure of accounts and other financial information. Small family firms tend to be private companies, whereas larger national and international businesses tend to be public companies. The distinction can be illustrated by comparing two American fast-food chains, McDonald's and White Castle. White Castle is a private company which has been owned and managed by the same family (now the third generation) since its founding in 1921. Its menus, which feature mainly hamburgers, have hardly changed since then, and none of its 400 outlets is outside the US. McDonald's is a public company which has expanded internationally, and its menus have adapted to differing national tastes.

Some large businesses choose to remain private. Two of the major international credit card companies, Master Card and Visa, have long been private companies, both seeking to go public in 2007. Their rival, American Express, by contrast, has been a public company for most of its existence. When a company becomes listed as a public company on a stock exchange, inviting investors to subscribe for its shares, the process is known as an initial public offering (IPO), or 'flotation'. The company's shares can then be traded on the exchange. Only a small portion of the public company's capital needs be offered for sale. Companies are often controlled by dominant investors, such as the family or descendants of the founder, who own or control the majority of the shares, even in public companies. An example is the Swedish company, Ericsson, discussed in SX1.2.

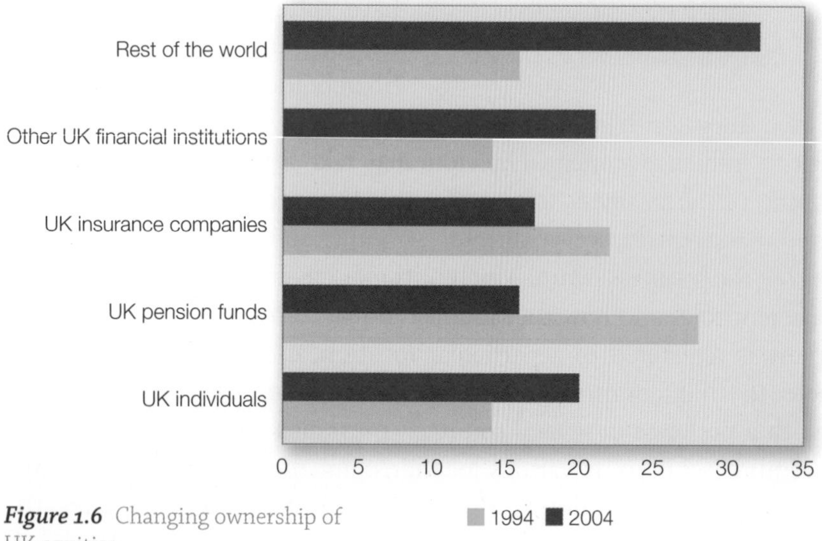

WEB CHECK

For information on the SE, go to the EU's homepage at http://europa.eu, which forms the Gateway to the EU. Click on *Internal Market*, then *Summaries of legislation*, followed by *Businesses in the Internal Market*.

Private company: Registered company in which shares are not tradable; subject to lower levels of public disclosure of information than the public company.

Public company: Registered company in which all or a portion of shares are tradable, usually on a stock exchange; subject to a high level of public disclosure of corporate information.

Initial public offering (IPO): Process by which a company becomes a public company, inviting prospective investors to subscribe for its shares for the first time.

Figure 1.6 Changing ownership of UK equities

Source: *Financial Times*, 22 June 2005

■ 1994   ■ 2004

Businesses which are mainly national in scope tend to have mainly domestic shareholders. As companies become international, they attract investors from other countries. Shareholders in large public companies are typically other companies and institutional investors such as pension funds. Shareholder profile may change over the years, as the example of the UK illustrates. In 1963, 54% of UK shares were in the hands of individuals, but this percentage declined between the 1960s and the 1990s, as domestic pension funds increased their investments in equities. As Figure 1.6 shows, individuals and pension funds owned 48% of the market in 1994, but by 2004, both these groups had reduced their holdings, partly because they decided to diversify internationally. By the same token, holdings of overseas investors nearly doubled between 1994 and 2004. Managers of UK companies, therefore, are now looking at a wider range of shareholders, who are likely to have divergent ideas on company strategy.

A state or governmental authority may own whole companies or a block of shares. If its stake is over half, it will have effective control, but a lower stake will still give it considerable influence. An example is the block of Volkswagen shares owned by Lower Saxony, which is discussed in CS1.2. When a government sells off a stake in a state-owned company, it is said to be 'privatized', as private investors are invited to subscribe. The company thus created is a public company. Typically, the government offers a portion of the shares in an IPO, but retains a sizable stake under state control. This has been the pattern in the French government's privatizations of utilities companies. For example, 30% of Gaz de France was offered to the public (see CF5.2).

Privatization: The process of converting a state-owned entity into a company in which private investors are invited to buy shares.

TO RECAP...

Public and private companies

The private company's shares are kept within a small circle of owners and cannot be traded on a stock exchange. The public company's shares are traded on one or more stock exchanges, although the proportion of shares 'floating' in this way varies, and in many public companies, there is a core of established shareholders.

STRATEGIC CROSSROADS

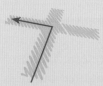

1.2

Ericsson adapts its traditional strengths to a changing environment

Ericsson is one of Sweden's most famous industrial companies, accounting for 15% of the country's exports. One in 10 Swedes owns shares in it directly, and many more indirectly through investment funds. Still, under the company's dual share system, the shares held by these ordinary shareholders carry almost no voting rights, whereas two Swedish shareholders, one of them the holding company of the Wallenberg family, who own less than 10% of the shares, monopolize the voting rights and have effective control of the company. Traditionally, Ericsson's senior executives are recruited from within the company, contributing to a conservative strategic outlook. From its engineering base, it grew to become the world's largest supplier of telecommuncations networks. Serving growing telecoms markets might be thought to ensure continuous demand, but, in fact, global demand for telecoms equipment took a downturn at the start of the new millennium, plunging Ericsson into crisis. A new chief executive, the first 'outsider' in more than 60 years to head Ericsson, faced a tough task to turn round the company.

How did the bright prospects of the start of the new millennium go wrong? A major setback was caused by shrinking investment by telecoms operators. Telecoms operators, who had incurred debts by investing heavily in third-generation (3G) licences, were compelled to rein in capital spending. Competitive pressures came from Chinese manufacturers who were able to undercut the Swedish company on price and made inroads in European markets. Ericsson suffered severe losses between 2001 and 2003, bringing it to the brink of disaster and causing it to reduce the number of employees from 107,000 to 47,000. It needed nothing short of a major strategic rethink, having seen its share price fall from a peak of SKr230 in March 2000 to just SKr3 in September 2003.

The company has traditionally relied on equipment sales as its main source of revenue. It embarked on a cost-cutting programme, shifting manufacturing of its products to China. Realizing that it would have to compete with Chinese technology companies to win European business, its chief executive stresses that it now seeks not simply to provide products, but to view the operator's network as a whole, making products fit end to end. The company is therefore enlarging its services division, and was pleased to win a contract in 2005 to manage an entire 3G network in Italy. While the services division is set to grow, the company does not see a major shift in its business model, which is dominated by equipment sales. Its mobile handset joint venture with Sony can fit into this broader strategic perspective of providing more of an end-to-end solution for customers. The company seemed to have weathered the crisis, largely due to strong demand for second generation GSM networks in Africa, the Middle East and Latin America. The gradual roll-out of 3G networks has also boosted sales. However, shareholders were jolted by a profits warning late in 2007, suggesting that order books were not as healthy as they had thought. Ericsson thought it had learned the lesson that no business can afford to become complacent in the changing global environment. The CEO has come under renewed pressure to show the leadership skills which he displayed to turn the company around following the bleak days of 2003.

Questions

◆ What were the causes of the crisis at Ericsson?
◆ How has the company managed to turn the business around, and what are the lingering risks?

Sources: Brown-Humes, C., 'Ericsson rings up the wrong numbers', *Financial Times*, 29 April 2002; Brown-Humes, C., 'Ericsson sets sights on better times ahead', *Financial Times*, 7 October 2003; George, N., 'Ericsson back from the brink', *Financial Times*, 29 May 2005; Odell, M., 'Ericsson weak in Europe', *Financial Times*, 1 February 2006; Ibison, D., 'Ericsson chief starts to feel a different type of chill', 25 October 2007.

WEB CHECK

Ericsson's homepage is at www.ericsson.com. Click on *investors* for corporate information.

Who controls the company?
How are the following types of company likely to differ in terms of culture and strategy? In your view, which are most likely to develop successful international strategies?
● the private company ● the state-owned company
● the public company in which a single family exerts control
● the public company with diverse shareholders, none owning more than 10% of the equity

PAUSE TO REFLECT

The multinational enterprise (MNE)

Companies which do business in multiple geographical locations can be referred to in several different ways. 'Multinational corporation' (MNC) and 'transnational corporation' (TNC) are often used to refer to an organization which does business across national borders. TNC is the preferred term of the UN and its agencies. On the other hand, much international business research, such as that of John Dunning, adopts the term multinational enterprise (MNE). MNE is adopted here for the reason that the notion of 'enterprise' seems preferable to 'corporation' in capturing the multiplicity of relations which make up the modern international business. The MNE can be defined as 'an organizational entity or system of cross-border relational interactions' (Dunning, 1993b: 38). This definition reflects the view that, although based on the corporate form, it is more helpful to view the international business as a set of relations between linked organizations than as a single organization (Ghoshal and Bartlett, 1990). The MNE is thus a co-ordinator of dispersed activities and relations.

As an MNE grows in size and geographical reach, it may acquire subsidiaries abroad, often by buying existing businesses. Typically, the parent company is located in the home country, with subsidiaries located in foreign locations. The MNE may eventually develop a multi-tiered structure, whereby a division is itself a parent company owning a number of subsidiaries (see Figure 1.7). The parent company as a legal entity remains the basic

Multinational enterprise (MNE): An organization or set of organizational relations co-ordinating business activities across national borders.

Figure 1.7 MNE multi-tiered ownership structure

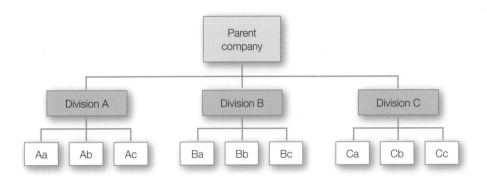

unit, but the large MNE may own and control hundreds of other companies through complex webs of ownership. The parent company and each of the entities which form the MNE are separate companies, and, indeed, may be registered in different countries. Some MNEs are monolithic entities, closely controlling the activities of subsidiaries worldwide, while some are more decentralized, allowing local managers considerable autonomy (discussed in detail in Chapter 7).

When it expands abroad, the company may set up an international division, as described in CS1.1 on PepsiCo. PepsiCo's brands are produced internationally by separate companies under licence in the various locations. It does not own these companies, but its relations with them are essential to its international operations. Its products for the North American market, by contrast, are manufactured by its own subsidiaries in America. International expansion involves greater complexity in the running of the business, including the different functions which must be co-ordinated among different locations. These are introduced in the next section

Functions within the international enterprise

Wherever it is located, the business enterprise is made up of a number of interrelated activities, known as business 'functions', which together enable it to attain its goals. Chief among these are operations, accounting and finance, marketing and human resource management (HRM). For a company which operates entirely within the borders of a single country, its national environment forms the cultural backdrop and provides the regulatory frameworks within which it operates. In the international environment, these functions may present rather different – and more complex – challenges than they would for a business whose activities are wholly within its home country. Figure 1.8 represents these functions in a typical MNE. The MNE may centralize some functions, such as finance, HRM and marketing, but the head office is likely to co-ordinate with functional departments in subsidiaries, to handle day-to-day activities. As Figure 1.8 indicates, operations and R&D are functions which are increasingly centred in the local environment of subsidiaries. Each of these functions is highlighted in a chapter in Part 4 of this book. In this introductory chapter, therefore, we outline the cross-border dimensions of each function which concern business managers operating in an international environment.

Operations is the broad category which refers to the whole of the process by which the firm makes and delivers goods or services to consumers. Often

Figure 1.8 Business functions in the international context

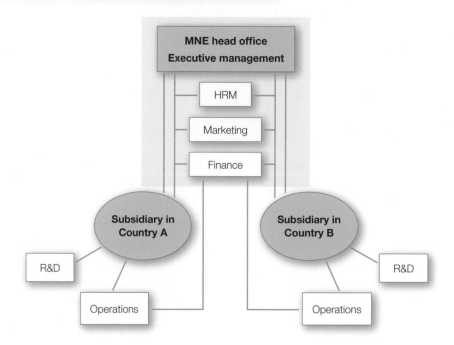

International operations: Process by which the firm makes and delivers its goods or services across national borders.

Accounting and finance for international businesses: Budgeting, costs and raising finance, any or all of which arise in more than one country, and involve more than one regulatory authority.

this takes the form of a production process, such as manufacturing. Production processes have become transformed by computing and information technology, and, hand in hand with these advances, production networks have become international operations across national borders. For example, components may be sourced from a range of countries, adding to the complexity of planning and control of operations. Global sourcing may permit economies of scale in an operation, and also reduce costs (discussed in Chapter 10).

Determining costs and budgeting are aspects of the accounting and finance function, specifically management accounting. Finance is the broad area which concerns the processes by which the company raises money for its activities, and financial reporting specifically concerns disclosure of financial information about the company to shareholders and the general public. Accounting and finance for international business may involve a number of different countries. Financial regulation is traditionally a matter for national governments, and disclosure requirements differ markedly between countries. Some demand a high level of transparency, requiring companies to disclose full details about their finances, ownership and directors. In others, little of this information needs to be made public. With growing cross-border business activity, there have been moves towards international accounting standards, the aim being to achieve greater consistency (see the discussion in Chapter 11). It is also true that pressures have grown for greater transparency on the part of companies. These pressures emanate in part from businesses who seek full and accurate information about foreign business partners as necessary in order to reduce risk in cross-border transactions. There are also pressures from a wider international public, an increasing proportion of whom are affected by movements in capital markets, for example through pension fund investments. We live in a world in which advances in communications technology make possible wide dissemination of information, and as powerful economic players, MNEs are increasingly called on to explain how they finance and manage their businesses, information which they have traditionally kept out of the public domain.

Marketing and HRM are functions which are sensitive to cultural and social dimensions in particular environments. Marketing concerns the variety of activities which enable the business to satisfy customers' needs for goods and services at prices they are willing to pay. Market research provides information to the firm on product attributes, the characteristics of consumers and the comparable offerings of rival firms. International marketing seeks to reach consumers in more than one market. Markets differ significantly from country to country, in terms of both products themselves and marketing approaches which are likely to win over consumers to buy the product (discussed further in Chapter 8). While companies with strong global brands such as Coca-Cola once put their faith in global advertising campaigns, they have now opted for local marketing strategies designed to reflect local tastes and values.

Similarly, while a large company will have a central HRM department, it is likely to devolve many aspects of HRM policy to local managers. HRM is the function which concerns the people who work for the company; international HRM (IHRM) focuses on HRM activities in the MNE's various locations. An MNE's central HRM department may well determine policies on recruitment, reward systems, training and employee relations, but in all these areas, local managers are likely to be given authority to adapt policies to the local environment (discussed in Chapter 9). Moreover, legal requirements relating to employment and industrial relations differ from country to country. For example, part-time workers in some countries are treated as merely 'casual', and have few rights, whereas in others, their position is akin to that afforded a full-time employee (see CF1.1 on Japan). Recalling the discussion above on MNE structures, it should be noted that in foreign operations, workers are likely to be employed by a foreign subsidiary or an independent subcontractor, and not by the MNE directly. Nonetheless, companies are coming under pressure in ways similar to those noted in relation to financial disclosure above. Able to access information on global operations, consumers are bringing pressures to bear on global companies such as Nike and Gap in respect of employment practices in foreign locations where the products they buy are manufactured.

Seeking new knowledge and applications is referred to as research and development (R&D). R&D lies behind new products and services and new ways of delivering them. In some industries, such as pharmaceuticals, R&D is crucial, as earnings are directly linked to markets for new drugs. Large MNEs have traditionally conducted their R&D activities in their home countries, but they are increasingly shifting to decentralized research units in numerous international locations. There are two main factors behind this shift. The first is that research breakthroughs often come from smaller, more entrepreneurial units rather than large bureaucratic organizations. Hence, GlaxoSmithKline, the pharmaceutical company, now has six dispersed research centres, each with a particular focus. The second factor is that, while researchers used to be clustered in the advanced economies, developing countries such as India and China are now gaining rapidly in research expertise. Local companies are benefiting, but, in addition, foreign investors are attracted to the pool of skilled researchers available at salaries considerably lower than those in the advanced economies. Bearing in mind that wages are the chief component of R&D spending, many companies, including General Electric (GE) and Microsoft, have set up R&D centres in China.

International marketing: Function by which an organization assesses and meets the needs of consumers outside its home market, for its products.

International HRM (IHRM): Process and activities of people management which involve more than one national context.

Research and development (R&D): Science and technology directed towards new and improved products and processes.

GE provides extensive information about its R&D on its website. Go to the homepage at www.ge.com, and from there, click on *innovation*.

WEB CHECK

TO RECAP...

Business functions in the international business

All the key business functions (accounting, operations, HRM, marketing and R&D) present choices between centralized and decentralized decision-making and control. Costs and local legal requirements must be taken into account, as well as the opportunities to benefit from local skills in, for example, R&D.

Case study 1.1:
PepsiCo's path to internationalization

PepsiCo is known across the world for its most famous brand, Pepsi, which was the name it gave its carbonated cola, invented in 1898. This was 12 years after the invention of Coca-Cola, and the two companies have been competing fiercely ever since. Both brands became symbols of American culture, and for both companies, Americans' seemingly inexhaustible thirst for cola products was the recipe for growing sales. However, as the American market matured, the companies evolved divergent strategies. Coke remained focused on carbonated beverages, seeking to expand in international markets.

By contrast, PepsiCo looked mainly to its home market, but diversified its product offerings. It bought Frito-Lay, the snack business in 1965, beginning its long history of diversification, to reduce its dependence on cola drinks. In 1993, it launched a bottled water, Aquafina, and in 1998, it acquired Tropicana, a juice brand, placing it in a good position to benefit from rising consumer demand for healthier drinks. In 2001, it acquired Quaker Oats, the cereals and snacks business, following the collapse of Coke's negotiations to buy the company, revealing divisions on strategy within Coke's board. With Quaker Oats came Gatorade, the market leader in energy drinks, further diversifying PepsiCo's portfolio of companies. Aquafina water and Gatorade drinks have seen rises in sales, helping PepsiCo to offset declining sales of sugary carbonated drinks in North America, where consumers have become concerned about health and obesity. Although Coke has belatedly launched new products for health-conscious consumers, Pepsi's established brands have had a sizable head start. It owns six of the 15 largest selling brands sold in US supermarkets, giving it considerable bargaining power when dealing with large retailers such as Wal-Mart. Soft drinks currently account for only 20% of Pepsi's sales, whereas they account for 80% of Coke's sales. PepsiCo's market capitalization of nearly $99 billion overtook Coke in 2005.

North America continues to be PepsiCo's most lucrative market, but it is increasingly focused on international expansion. Its international activities are managed by a separate division, PepsiCo International, which is responsible for both beverage and snack products outside North America. They are not produced by wholly owned subsidiaries, but by local companies licensed by PepsiCo to produce these products for local markets. Increasing international sales have also helped to offset weakness in the American soft drinks market. International revenues are now more than a third of the PepsiCo group total of $10 billion, and international profits account for 22% of a total of $6.1 billion (see figure). Still, PepsiCo International's CEO says: 'Ninety-five per cent of the world's population is outside North America, so we should be generating more than a third of our sales there' (Ward, 28 February 2005). India, China and Russia have been the fastest growing overseas snacks markets, while the Middle East, China and Argentina have seen the fastest growth in beverages. Pepsi trails behind Coke in most international markets. Both companies see emerging markets as the brightest prospects for growth, but both, too, are aware that they could suffer from anti-American sentiment. PepsiCo

executives feel their brands are perceived as less 'American' than Coke or McDonald's. Some, such as Walker's crisps in the UK, are perceived as local by consumers. Both PepsiCo and Coke have suffered setbacks in India, as seven states banned their beverages in 2006, on the grounds that levels of pesticides were too high. The companies denied these allegations, suspecting that anti-American sentiment might have been a factor.

PepsiCo's new CEO, Indra Nooyi, was appointed in 2006. As an Indian and a woman, she represents a break with corporate tradition. She is keen to keep up the pace of international expansion. PepsiCo, like Coke, has set its sights on China's 1.3 billion consumers, but in fact the strongest growth here has been in bottled water, juice and tea, where local producers dominate the market. The two US companies have opted to concentrate on their carbonated drinks in China, but this segment has declined from one-third to about 21% of the Chinese market since 1999, while branded water has risen 37%. This trend suggests that consumers are becoming more discerning in all markets.

Figure
PepsiCo's operating profit by division

Source:
Financial Times,
28 February 2005

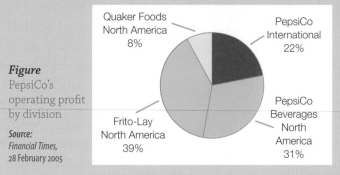

In response, as in the period of PepsiCo's initial diversification, the company is looking to adapt its products to changing consumer tastes. Its snacks have traditionally been of the salty and fatty varieties, and consumers now seek less fattening, healthier alternatives. A healthier range of products, such as low-fat baked snacks, is therefore being promoted by Frito-Lay. From 2005 to 2006, the group increased its spending on marketing of healthier snacks from 20% of its media spending to 50%, reflecting its changing strategy. In 2004, PepsiCo introduced a voluntary labelling system on its products, to inform consumers on various health criteria such as fat content. The group's North American revenues saw the proportion coming from healthier products increase from 36% in 2004 to 40% in 2005. The new healthier brands, as well as increased sales of non-carbonated drinks, are now seen as the best prospects for growth in the North American market.

The company is also eyeing the European market, as here, too, consumers are turning to healthier options. In 2006, it considered buying the French group, Danone, whose bottled water, dairy products and cereals would complement its product portfolio. However, suggestions of a takeover met with a frosty response from French politicians, largely due to the association of the brand with American fast-food culture.

Questions

1   How has PepsiCo's diversification strategy proved to be advantageous in comparison to the strategy of Coca-Cola?
2   What trends in consumer preferences has PepsiCo sought to satisfy?
3   How internationalized do you feel PepsiCo has become?
4   Describe PepsiCo's current strategy in both its home market and international markets.

Sources: Ward, A., 'Diversifying PepsiCo puts fizz in global earnings', *Financial Times*, 13 July 2005; Ward, A., 'Coke gets real: the world's most valuable brand wakes up to a waning thirst for cola', *Financial Times*, 22 September 2005; Ward, A., 'Pepsi to promote "healthier" snacks', *Financial Times*, 9 February 2006; Ward, A., and Wiggins, J., 'Paris fears PepsiCo's thirst for their icon', *Financial Times*, 21 July 2005; MacDonald, N., 'Pepsi seeks to rebuild as "cola war" looms', *Financial Times*, 4 July 2005; Ward, A., 'A better model? Diversified Pepsi steals some of Coke's sparkle', *Financial Times*, 28 February 2005; Johnson, J., 'Ban on Coca-Cola and Pepsi extends across 7 Indian states', *Financial Times*, 11 August 2006; Wiggins, J., 'Pepsi plans expansion through takeovers', *Financial Times*, 26 April 2007.

How effective are
centralized functions?
Looking at HRM, marketing and R&D, what
are the advantages of decentralization for the
MNE with operations in a number of different
countries? What are the pitfalls?

PAUSE TO REFLECT

Corporate governance

A company's decision-making structures and processes at the highest level are referred to as its corporate governance. These structures are influenced by the cultural environment of the company's home country, as well as by its corporate history. In particular, corporate governance systems represent different views of the company's role in society. In the US and the UK, corporate governance is generally perceived to be based on a goal of maximizing shareholder value. In other countries, notably Japan, Germany and other European countries, the wider view of stakeholder interests is taken into account. The tension between these groups of interests is one of the main themes of international management, as the case studies in this book reveal. A critical discussion of the issues occurs in Chapter 14. At this stage, we identify the concepts and principles, and highlight the main issues.

Governance systems

Governance systems which fall into the US and UK tradition, known as the 'shareholder model', tend to have a single-tier board of directors. The company's CEO and other senior executives who are employed by the company are its executive directors, but modern corporate boards also include independent, so-called non-executive directors. Whereas they may be genuine 'outsiders' who are independent of company ties, in practice, many have personal ties with the company, such as retired executives. The appointment of genuinely independent directors is now seen as indicative of best practice, and is a legal requirement in many countries. It is also recommended that the offices of CEO and chairman of the board be held by different people, to avoid possible conflict of interest. Non-executive directors may themselves be directors of other companies, often affiliates or subsidiaries, or they may represent major shareholders.

In contrast, the two-tier board exists in 18 of the EU's member states. Known as the 'stakeholder model', it formalizes inputs from stakeholders, mainly employees. This participation of stakeholders in corporate decision-making at the highest level underpins the concept of 'co-determination' which prevails in Germany (Tuschke and Sanders, 2003). The supervisory board takes the major decisions, such as a decision to acquire another company. Employee representatives, usually trade unions, take a proportion of the seats on the supervisory board. This proportion is typically one-third

Corporate governance: A company's decision-making structure and processes at the highest level, by which its directors are responsible to its owners and other stakeholders.

Executive directors: Officers employed by the company, who are in charge of day-to-day management.
Non-executive directors: Officers who sit on the board as independent directors, not employed in management positions.

WEB CHECK
PepsiCo's home page is www.pepsico.com. Click on investors for corporate information.

of the seats. In Germany, it is one-third in companies with over 500 workers, and one-half in companies with over 2,000. The company's managers form the second tier, the management board. While the management board focuses on enterprise matters, the supervisory board takes a broader view of the interests of the company as a whole. The final case study in this chapter highlights corporate governance at Volkswagen, where Porsche is increasing its stake and control.

The single-tier board has become the norm in corporate governance structures outside Europe, although their corporate cultures may differ from that of the shareholder model. Japanese corporate governance combines the structures of single-tier systems with a focus on stakeholders, especially employees, as the major driving force of the company. As Japan becomes more market oriented, however, Japan's companies are undergoing changes, as CF1.1 shows. MNEs in emerging economies have tended to adopt opaque governance structures, often insider dominated.

As companies become more international in their ownership and activities, they interact with a variety of other organizations and come under pressure to consider a wide range of interests. We have mentioned employees as important stakeholders, but the concept covers a range of other interests, as the next section highlights.

Stakeholders

Stakeholder refers to a broad range of organizations and interests which influence the company and which the company influences (Freeman, 1984). It is helpful to distinguish between primary and secondary stakeholders, as shown in Figure 1.9. Shareholders and employees are primary stakeholders, playing direct roles in the company, while national and regional institutions are secondary stakeholders: the latter may be influential in terms of policies and regulation, but they are external to the firm. A trade union, which negotiates pay and conditions on behalf of a workforce, is clearly a stakeholder. Its actions may have a direct impact on the firm, for example in calling a strike. However, its organization is independent of the company, and it acts as an agent on behalf of employees. As noted above, trade union representatives have an important role to play in corporate governance in many countries. Also influential are suppliers and customers of the company, which may have long-standing relations with the management, and with whom there is day-to-day communication and exchange of information. These affiliated firms may also merit a seat on the board, and are clearly stakeholders. In some countries, such as Japan, their relational ties may be so close that they are perceived as 'insiders', although they are employed by separate companies.

Impacts of the company on communities and the environment are becoming increasingly

Stakeholder: Individual, organization or interest which affects the company or is affected by it.

Figure 1.9 Executive managers and company stakeholders

important for MNEs to take into account. It is arguable that, although it is rather vague to speak of a whole society as being a stakeholder, it is nonetheless appropriate. The company's interactions with communities in which it operates are tangible impacts of the company's activities, for example the presence of a factory. Residents close to the factory are certainly affected by it, but may well have no formal dialogue with the company. If the company takes a stakeholder approach to its role, it sees community relations as essential to achieving corporate goals. Stakeholder management is now seen in the context of the international company's role in the many societies in which it operates. Stakeholder interests form part of a broader philosophy of corporate social responsibility (CSR), which views the company as having not just an economic role and responsibilities, but also social, legal and ethical responsibilities. (These issues are discussed in detail in Chapter 14.) Many of the companies featured in our case studies, such as Ericsson, provide CSR reports on the investor relations pages of their websites, indicating the growing prominence of social dimensions in the broader corporate governance picture. Co-operative relations with business partners are another type of stakeholder relationship, as the next section indicates.

Corporate social responsibility (CSR): The approach of the business enterprise which takes in economic activities, legal obligations and social responsibilities.

COUNTRY FOCUS 1.1 – JAPAN

Electronics industry spearheads Japanese economic recovery

Japan is held up as a model of successful industrial development. As the first Asian country to industrialize, its example has been particularly relevant for other Asian countries seeking similar economic success. In the aftermath of the Second World War, Japanese companies, with government help and guidance, set about rapid expansion which brought export success, particularly in Western markets. Its consumer electronics industries and car manufacturers led the way. Japanese companies became world leaders in televisions and audio products, famous for their technological excellence and innovative features. Behind these achievements was a system of employment which engendered high levels of employee commitment and guaranteed full-time employees a job for life. Japan's new affluent middle class, secure in their jobs, fuelled consumer demand for the latest products. Company names familiar to modern consumers, such as Sony, Hitachi and Toshiba, are still market leaders, but they have undergone many changes from the heady days of rapid economic growth. Nowadays, they are seen in the context of competition against more recent Asian rivals, such as South Korean and Chinese companies. How fit are Japan's companies to compete in the new environment?

From 1990 onwards, Japan's economy suffered a prolonged period of recession, with depressed consumer spending and stagnant industries. At the same time, the later industrializing countries of East Asia were experiencing rapid economic growth. Japanese companies, with their high cost base, had become uncompetitive, but restructuring whole workforces seemed impossible in the Japanese context, as workers were effectively guaranteed a job for life. A 'lost generation' of graduates in the 1990s were unable to find jobs which utilized their skills, and found themselves in lowly paid jobs with no employment security. Companies needed new creative talent, but had to cut back on recruitment. Restructuring came about gradually, relying on early retirement plans and recruitment freezes.

Companies began hiring employees on short-term contracts, without the traditional long-term guarantees, bringing about cultural changes in the workplace. Workers can now expect to change jobs as corporate needs change, and they must adapt to a system of promotions based on merit rather than on seniority. A growing use of part-time workers and other 'non-regular' workers has brought about labour flexibility. In the five years from 1997, the number of full-time workers fell by 4 million to 34.6 million, while the number of part-time workers rose from 966,000 to 2.5 million. Significantly, too, the number of temporary workers hired out by agencies also rose, from 257,000 in 1997 to an estimated 2 million in 2004. By 2007, non-regular workers accounted for 33% of the workforce (see Figure 1). There is a worrying divide between employees in regular employment, which includes manufacturing industries, and workers in non-regular employment. Temporary and casual staff earn only about 40% of the wages of full-time workers, and this group is dominated by young people and women workers. While manufacturing wages recovered from 2002, other sectors saw continuing decline. The Japanese government is now hoping that consumer spending will take off, spurring economic growth.

Japanese companies are now more competitive than they were in the 1990s, and looking to meet the rising global demand for new digital electronics. While Japanese companies were at the forefront of the liquid crystal display (LCD) innovation, many sought cost reductions by forming alliances with Asian competitors. This turned out to be a strategic mistake, as they transferred key technology to rivals, who were able to catch up and capture market share. Now, Japanese companies are regaining lost ground. They are meeting surging demand for new digital cameras and DVD recorders, choosing to manufacture most of these digital consumer products in Japan. Utilizing their depth of skill in high-quality picture-making, they feel able to compete with rivals in South Korea and Taiwan. Toshiba has developed a new flat panel TV which provides clear colour, low electricity usage and reduced materials costs. The company feels this technology will be hard for others to copy, giving

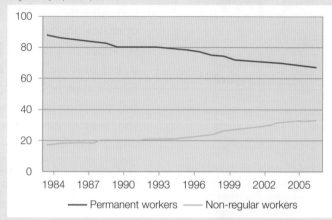

Figure 1 Proportions of permanent and non-regular workers in Japan, 1984–2007

Source: The Economist, 'Sayonara, salaryman', 5 January 2008

them competitive advantage in the growing LCD market (see Figure 2). However, as the digital sector develops, standardization of components is leading to lower prices, making it more difficult for Japanese companies to generate profits.

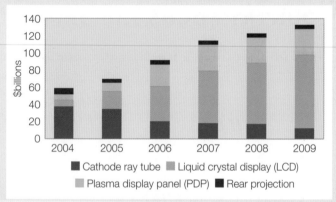

Figure 2 Global projected revenues in television sets

Source: Financial Times, 11 May 2006

Success in the electronics industry is reviving Japan's manufacturing base and contributing to the country's economic growth. Japanese consumers are regaining their taste for new high-tech products, which their manufacturers are eager to satisfy. Japanese mobile phone operators were the first to introduce camera phones, and there is growing demand in Japan for PCs with TV tuners. Sony and Toshiba are rising to the challenge of improving the picture quality of the TV in the PC. These companies have come through the restructuring of the 1990s and now have more flexible labour forces. Commentators point out that Japan's system of lifetime employment and seniority pay were not cast in stone, but were products of the circumstances which occurred in the post-war era, when the economy enjoyed strong growth and full employment.

Recovery from the long period of economic downturn has been largely due to the painful changes Japanese companies have undergone, but recovery also depends on Japanese workers regaining their zest for spending on consumer products, which has been slow to accelerate in Japan's changing work environment.

plate 1.2 Companies specializing in picture technology stand to gain in a world increasingly focused on screens.

Questions

◆ What problems have Japanese companies had to overcome in order to regain competitiveness in global markets?
◆ Why is the electronics industry one of Japan's best hopes for renewed economic growth?
◆ Assess the impact of changes in employment patterns on Japanese society.

Sources: Pilling, D., 'A wageless recovery: Japan's economic growth has failed to boost workers' pay', *Financial Times*, 10 November 2004; Pilling, D., 'Japanese in danger of "creating a sub-class of poorly paid"', *Financial Times*, 24 Janauary 2004; Nakamoto, M., 'Second chance: the digital revolution is reviving Japan's electronic industry', *Financial Times*, 6 August 2004; Pilling, D., 'A country finding its way back to normality', *Financial Times*, 12 October 2005; Emmott, B. (2005) 'Mission accomplished', *The Economist: The World in 2006*; *The Economist*, 'Still work to be done', 1 December 2007; *The Economist*, 'Sayonara, salaryman', 5 December 2008.

WEB CHECK

Information on Japan in the regional and international environment can be found by going to the OECD's home page at www.oecd.org. Click on *Browse by country*, and then on *Japan*. Sony's corporate website is www.sony.net. Here you can go to *Investor Relations* and *Corporate Social Responsibility*.

The organizational environment

Enterprises in today's environment are able to take advantage of unprecedented opportunities to share knowledge and experience. For MNEs with subsidiaries in various locations, these ties can help to build necessary local knowledge, as well as links with local companies. Links include both formal and informal channels, shown in Figure 1.10. While networks are informal and fluid, alliances and joint ventures are more formal. Note how these ties overlap. Companies A and B have an alliance, while the two are joined by C in an informal network. Companies A and C have formed a formal joint venture, Company D, in which each has a 50% stake. Each of these arrangements will be discussed in turn.

Figure 1.10 Alliances, networks and joint ventures

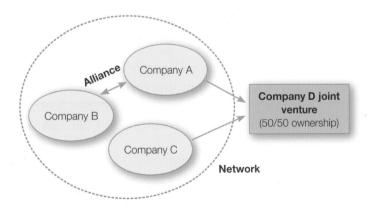

Alliance: Co-operative arrangement between two or more different organizations for a particular purpose, which offers benefits to participating organizations while retaining their individual identity.

Alliances and joint ventures

Alliances generally involve the sharing of knowledge, technology and assets for some common purpose. The MNE, or one of its subsidiaries, may forge links in networks of many types, from suppliers of components to R&D. A company which sells products in consumer markets may have an agreement with an allied company to offer services to consumers, such as finance or after-sales service, which are complementary to its business. For example, co-operative agreements between companies in R&D, whereby they pool resources and skills, can facilitate greater progress than separate R&D departments working on their own (Narula and Duysters, 2004). Medical research and research in emissions reduction are two examples where progress has been greater as a result of combined forces. While we tend to think of competition between organizations as out-and-out rivalry in all respects, the newer view of alliances to achieve corporate goals represents a modification on the traditional concept of inter-firm rivalry (Osborn and Hagedoorn, 1997). It is true that some types of alliance may have the effect of being anti-competitive, but alliances referred to here offer benefits to both organizations and consumers. For the individual companies involved, the prospect of getting their new products into the market more quickly than would have been possible with a stand-alone R&D unit justifies the 'co-operate to compete' approach (Jorde and Teece, 1989).

Joint venture: A formal arrangement between two or more organizations, which may be based in different countries, which results in the formation of a new entity in which each invests.

A joint venture is a type of strategic alliance consisting of a formal arrangement between two or more organizations to set up a new entity, in which each of the partners has an ownership stake. In Figure 1.5, Companies A and C form Company D. The joint venture company is likely to be registered in the country where the new venture is to take place. Typically, one of the partners is local and one is a foreign investor. Starbucks' proposed entry into the Indian market, highlighted in the opening vignette, involved two Asian partners, one an experienced Indian retailer and the other the operator of Starbucks franchises in Indonesia. The partners may be companies, government bodies, international agencies or individuals. The joint venture could also be between two companies in different countries for a project, such as an infrastructure project, in a third country. The joint venture has proved to be a popular vehicle for many types of international business, from large infrastructure projects to retailing. Its main attraction is that it facilitates the blending of a host partner's local knowledge with the capital and expertise of an outside investor. It has been successfully used in many developing countries where there is a need to attract outside capital. The success of the joint venture depends in large part on whether the partners are able to forge a smooth working relationship, avoiding the tensions which are likely to arise in a joint enterprise between members of different organizations with contrasting corporate cultures. Joint ventures have been the norm for foreign companies investing in China, as shown in CS1.2.

Networks

Networks: A broad category of both intra-firm and inter-firm links. They may involve individuals, teams and whole organizations.

Networks may be both intra-firm and between companies (the latter is shown in Figure 1.10). Again, the traditional picture of the business landscape as inhabited by autonomous companies, each acting independently, has been superseded by a more complex picture, in which organizational boundaries are blurred. The network may comprise individuals or teams of staff, working in different locations. For example, a design team for a new product may involve not just design specialists, but engineers and marketing specialists. They may well be working in different locations, but are able to work on a new project through the internet. In such a scenario, these participants could be employed by different organizations, for example a specialist design company. The interdependence fostered in networks represents another example of the ways in which co-operative arrangements can form part of an organization's competitive strategy (Hakansson and Ford, 2002).

Network arrangements have the benefit of flexibility, and allow the co-ordination of specialist inputs, spread over different locations. SMEs are well placed to network in informal ways. Often, they are run by enthusiastic owners/managers personally, and make links through friends and family ties, trade fairs and exhibitions. It should be remembered, however, that they can add to the complexity of projects and raise issues of ownership. It may be difficult to ascertain where legal obligations fall, and if there is a failure at some stage in a project, there could well be delays and economic loss. In this event, contractual responsibilities need to be clear, which is not always the case in networks. Indeed, a network is often an informal arrangement with no legal standing in its own right. This is less critical with intra-firm networks than with inter-firm ones. For a large multi-locational company, the internal network provides an opportunity for cutting across departmental boundaries and innovatory working arrangements.

TO RECAP...

Alliances, joint ventures and networks

Organizations may benefit from alliances which afford them opportunities to form co-operative links for a particular purpose with or without the need to take an ownership stake. The joint venture involves taking a stake in a new entity, often with a foreign partner familiar with the environment and business practices in the location where the new venture is planned. Networks offer opportunities to share ideas and information at all levels of an organization, and, thanks to modern communications, can extend across the globe.

Co-operate or go it alone?
For the company seeking international links short of the radical step of acquiring a foreign company, what possibilities should be explored in terms of alliances, networks and joint ventures?

PAUSE TO REFLECT

Key organizational players in the international business environment

So far, we have focused on a variety of organizational roles and stakeholder interests relevant in international business. We now shift the focus to key players in the international environment, recalling the national, regional and international influences shown in Figure 1.2. Lines of interaction of the MNE and other organizations are shown in Figure 1.11. Direct roles in business activities are indicated by solid lines, and indirect roles, through influence and dialogue, are indicated by broken lines. As Figure 1.11 shows, the MNE is at the hub of a network of relations, both direct and indirect. For the international business, large or small, managing these interactions successfully is crucial to achieving its goals. We look at them in turn.

National governments

A national government enjoys the ultimate authority for the enactment and implementation of laws and policies within its country's geographical territory. This ultimate authority is usually referred to as its 'sovereignty', ensuring that there is no higher authority within its territory. It may also delegate lawmaking powers to regional or local authorities within its territory. Laws

National government: Formal institutions by which sovereign lawmaking authority is exercised in a country.

Figure 1.11   MNE interactions

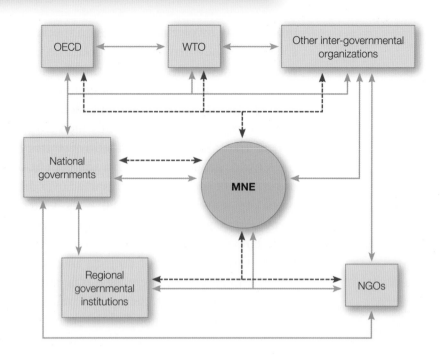

and policies emanating from all these governmental authorities may impact both directly and indirectly on the businesses which operate within their borders, whether foreign or domestic. Indirectly, governments are responsible for lawmaking and implementation in numerous fields relevant to business: planning, employment, health and safety, taxation, subsidies for particular industries, import duties, environmental protection and competition law.

In addition, most governments have in place machinery for the regulation of company affairs, financial services and accounting regulation. Unlike private economic players, a government has the power of compulsion (Stiglitz, 1989), and, if it sees the need, it can use coercion to enforce its will. No private organization can simply impose a universal tax on individuals and use the money raised for purposes it thinks fit. Whereas businesses engaged in private enterprise are accountable to their owners, governments, in principle, have a view to the national interest of the country, although in practice, governing elites sometimes act in predominantly self-interested ways. Governments may be direct players in economic life through owning and controlling companies. Government policies towards foreign investors, such as tax advantages, may be welcoming. Alternatively, they may adopt a more critical attitude towards foreign investors, as Starbucks, PepsiCo and other foreign investors have found in India.

In some countries, state ownership is spread across many industries. In France, for example, there has been a high level of state ownership in industries such as electricity (Electricité de France) and telecommunications (France Télécom), whereas in the US, private ownership predominates. These two countries are both democracies, but they represent contrasting models of the role of government in society. On the one hand, a large public sector in the national economy may be seen as socially beneficial, while, on the other, it may be seen as stifling and burdensome for the individual citizen. Privatization of state industries, opening them up to market forces and inviting private investors, is gradually taking place in many countries, including France. The EU has pursued a policy of requiring national governments to open up industries, such as utilities, to competition, and it has also legislated against governments subsidizing their own domestic companies.

Running counter to this trend, some states have pursued policies of nationalization, bringing enterprises under state control which had previously been in private hands. There have been significant moves towards nationalization of oil and gas industries in three major producing countries: Russia, Venezuela and Bolivia (see CF1.2 on Venezuela and CF5.1 on Russia). These moves seem to be signalling a trend towards more assertive policies by national governments over energy resources. The pros and cons of state ownership raise sensitive issues in international business, with repercussions far beyond the parties concerned. Private investment had been key to developing the oil and gas assets in these countries, and, in response, foreign companies have invested heavily. An abrupt change of policy on the part of governments is unsettling not just for the companies involved, but for the business environment generally. (A critical discussion of these issues can be found in Chapter 15.)

TO RECAP...

Role of national governments

National governments play both direct and indirect roles. They act directly when they own or control companies. Indirectly, they are responsible for legislation which provides regulatory frameworks and standards within which businesses operate in the national environment.

COUNTRY FOCUS 1.2 – VENEZUELA

An uncertain future for foreign multinationals in Venezuela

Venezuela is the world's fifth largest oil producer, generating huge revenues from growing demand and rising oil prices. Oil accounts for 90% of the country's export earnings. Yet oil wealth has brought neither the prosperity nor the stability that Venezuelans had hoped for. Tensions between the multinational oil companies which operate in its oilfields and the Venezuelan government under its radical nationalist president, Hugo Chávez, have resulted in stoppages, lost production and deteriorating relations since Chávez took office in 1999. President Chávez rose to prominence on a wave of populist and anti-American fervour. Relations with business interests within the country have been turbulent, as he has embarked on radical reform of property rights. Above all, he has been eager to assert Venezuelan sovereignty over its natural resources. As a result, the large MNEs that have invested in its oil industry have encountered increasingly hostile policies.

During the 1990s, when oil prices were low, Venezuela welcomed the large oil companies, eager to benefit from their technical abilities to explore and develop oilfields. Venezuela is estimated to have the largest reserves of extra-heavy crude oil in the Western hemisphere. The companies benefited from favourable terms such as low royalty payments to the state. Now, however, the government feels that the companies are enjoying a windfall, and that the state should renegotiate these terms, to recoup what the government feels should be its rightful share. It is estimated to have clawed back some $5.4 billion from international oil companies. It has raised taxes and required foreign energy companies to convert 32 operating contracts into joint ventures with the Venezuelan state-owned oil company, Petróleos de Venezuela (PDVSA), in which it would hold the majority stake. Some companies agreed the new terms, but others, such as ExxonMobil, refused and sold its stake in the affected oilfield. The government took control of two oilfields operated by Total and Eni, the French and Italian companies, after they failed to agree to see their operations converted to joint ventures, and Eni has threatened to sue PDVSA for a unilateral termination of its contract. A new hydrocarbons law was passed in 2001, raising taxes on new projects. A consequence of the uncertainty and nationalist policies has been loss of production, as shown in the figure.

Other multinationals have been served bills for back taxes that are alleged to be due. IBM and Microsoft came under pressure as the Venezuelan tax authority examined alleged tax irregularities. Venezuela's tax authority has had difficulty in trying to establish a tax-paying culture in the country, and targeting large multinationals for a crackdown is seen as a signal of the new policy of 'zero tax evasion'. Mobile phone companies – Nokia, Ericsson and Siemens – and the carmaker Honda were also affected.

The government's targeting of large multinationals has played well with populist sentiments at home, and the Chávez government has channelled large sums of oil revenues into social spending, including healthcare and schools. However, it has been disappointing in its delivery of other tangible benefits

plate 1.3 Not far from the modern buildings symbolizing oil wealth, poor living conditions are signs of the divisions in Venezuelan society.

to raise living standards for the poor. Nearly a third of the population suffer from poverty, defined as having less than $2 a day. Most of the country's population is urban, and there is a pressing need for investment to create jobs. However, investment has been disappointing, and foreign investors have been discouraged by the political risk.

Oil company executives argue that national oil companies lack the technology to exploit oil reserves effectively, and that PDVSA has not invested in infrastructure sufficiently, although the country's exports are almost totally dependent on oil. On the other hand, working with governments is essential in the oil industry as government-owned companies control an estimated 72% of the world's oil reserves. The balance of power between governments and the large oil companies has shifted over the years. The companies were dominant in the 1960s, but a wave of nationalizations sent the pendulum swinging the other way in the 1970s. Since then, the technological know-how of the companies has given them a dominant position, which now seems to be ebbing away. In a world of growing energy concerns, co-operation between governments and multinationals is probably the best means of striking a balance. Relations with the US, which is only a six-day tanker voyage from its oilfields, are particularly crucial for Venezuela. It supplies 11–14% of US oil imports, and US refineries are designed specifically for processing Venezuelan crude. PDVSA wholly owns five refineries in the US, and its subsidiary, CITGO, partly owns four others. Chávez has threatened to cut off oil supplies to the US and divert them to China, but this move, in addition to repercussions for US interests, would be damaging for Venezuela. China's refineries are not equipped to handle Venezuelan crude, and transport costs would rocket.

Venezuela has benefited from surging demand for oil, but, like other resource-rich states, it could be vulnerable to global economic downturn. Its failure to diversify its economy could weaken its long-term economic health. Politically, Chavez suffered a setback late in 2007, when he failed to obtain a majority in a national referendum he had called to make constitutional changes which would give him greater executive powers. The proposed changes also included a provision remov-

Figure Potential losses of oil production due to geopolitical conflict or nationalism, 2000–06

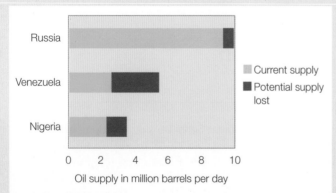

Oil supply in million barrels per day

Source: Financial Times, 5 May 2006

ing limits on the number times he could stand for re-election. It was felt that poverty and poor social welfare were causes of this rebuff by the electorate. Tellingly, 44% of voters did not vote. A lesson seems to be that improving social conditions is necessary for stability. Revenues from oil are the main source of funding for social programmes. A rebuilding of relationships between the government and multinational companies could serve both the country's interests and those of investors.

Sources: Webb-Vidal, A., 'Chavez quickens drive to wrest oil revenues', *Financial Times*, 28 April 2006; Lapper, R., 'Why investors are deaf to the Latin American march of the populists', *Financial Times*, 6 April 2006; Webb-Vidal, A., 'Peasants "unlikely to reap rewards of Venezuela land reform', *Financial Times*, 13 January 2005; Hoyos, C., 'Big oil groups to accept Caracas demands', *Financial Times*, 16 December 2005; Boxell, J., and Morrison, K., 'A power shift: global oil companies find new rivals snapping at their heels', *Financial Times*, 9 December 2004; Lapper, R., and Webb-Vidal, A., 'Businesses count the cost of Chavez's survival', *Financial Times*, 11 February 2003; United Nations (2005) *Human Development Report 2005* (New York: United Nations Development Programme); Lapper, R., and Mander, B., 'Brought to book', *Financial Times*, 5 December 2007.

Questions

◆ What are the causes of MNEs' complaints against the Venezuelan government?

◆ To what extent are these complaints justifiable?

◆ What advice would you give to MNEs wishing to do business in Venezuela at present?

WEB CHECK

For information about Venezuela, go to the World Bank's website at www.worldbank.org. Go to *Countries*, and then *Venezuela*.

Government for better or worse

Consider the government of the country in which you live. Look at each of the following areas, and assess whether or not governmental policies and laws are serving businesses and consumers well. What changes would you recommend?

● Taxation ● Health and safety at work ● Environmental protection ● Corporate governance

PAUSE TO REFLECT

Regional institutions

The post-war period has seen a proliferation in regional groupings of states, mainly originating from the wish to promote free trade among the states within the region, whereby business can buy and sell goods and services across national borders unfettered by barriers to trade such as import duties. Such groupings include the EU, the North American Free Trade Agreement (Nafta) and the Association of Southeast Asian Nations (Asean; discussed further in Chapter 6). Agreements which started as essentially free-trade agreements, however, have taken on other dimensions, and, in the case of the EU, have led to considerable economic and political integration. Enlargement in 2004 saw 10 new member states, converting the 'EU 15' to the 'EU 25', as shown in Figure 1.12. The number grew to 27 in 2007. Fifteen of the EU's member states are members of the eurozone, benefiting from the single currency for interstate transactions. The EU, therefore, has acquired a governance role akin to that of national governments described above. For a number of industries, the legal and regulatory frameworks are derived from European institutions, together with administrative apparatus to implement them. Much environmental law in EU member states, for example, originates with the EU Commission, while national governments, such as that of the UK, have rather lagged behind in this area of legislation.

Figure 1.12 The European Union and eurozone

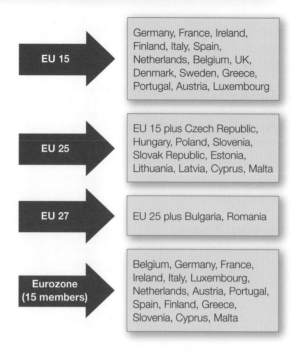

EU 15 →	Germany, France, Ireland, Finland, Italy, Spain, Netherlands, Belgium, UK, Denmark, Sweden, Greece, Portugal, Austria, Luxembourg
EU 25 →	EU 15 plus Czech Republic, Hungary, Poland, Slovenia, Slovak Republic, Estonia, Lithuania, Latvia, Cyprus, Malta
EU 27 →	EU 25 plus Bulgaria, Romania
Eurozone (15 members) →	Belgium, Germany, France, Ireland, Italy, Luxembourg, Netherlands, Austria, Portugal, Spain, Finland, Greece, Slovenia, Cyprus, Malta

Businesses are often inclined to see protective legislation as a hindrance, and such legislation emanating from regional structures seems more remote than that of national legislatures. On the other hand, the EU has been responsible for opening up markets, whereby states are barred from discriminating against goods and services from other member states. The EU framework has advanced well beyond that of other regional groupings in creating governance structures, and thus acquiring a degree of compulsion akin to that of a state. However, its legitimacy is not universally accepted, and states have not given up their sovereign authority in key areas such as taxation, social security, education and defence. As noted above, EU company registration is in its infancy. On the other hand, much domestic company and employment law in member states is derived from EU directives.

TO RECAP...

Regional institutions in the EU take on a number of policy dimensions once reserved for national governments. These regulatory frameworks, increasingly important for cross-border business, are facilitating business expansion across the EU.

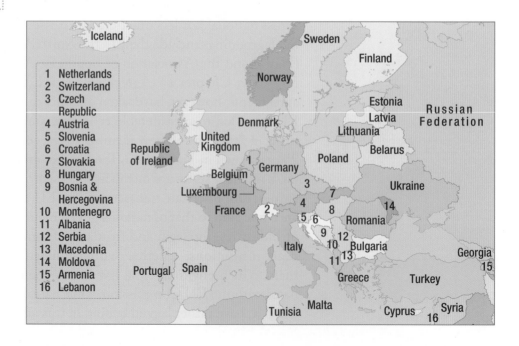

1 Netherlands
2 Switzerland
3 Czech Republic
4 Austria
5 Slovenia
6 Croatia
7 Slovakia
8 Hungary
9 Bosnia & Hercegovina
10 Montenegro
11 Albania
12 Serbia
13 Macedonia
14 Moldova
15 Armenia
16 Lebanon

International organizations

Relations at international level rely on co-operation between sovereign states. There are a number of international organizations which provide governance structures in particular areas of global concern. These global issues are analysed more fully in the Part 5. Here, we highlight the main organizations whose influences will become apparent in the following chapters.

Growing interaction between states has led to co-operative frameworks and guidelines at international level, known as inter-governmental organizations (IGOs). Many set standards for cross-border businesses. An example is the International Labour Organization (ILO), which sets labour standards at international level. The United Nations (UN), with its 200 member states, is the most nearly universal inter-governmental organization. The UN itself was formed in the immediate post-war period, when the foremost thoughts in people's minds were the need to preserve peace and prevent future wars. Since its inception, however, the UN has seen the need to take a lead in social, economic and cultural issues, and particularly in developing countries, which form the majority of its member states. Most of the multilateral treaties which form the basis of international law stem from institutions connected to the UN. States commit themselves to adhering to these obligations and enforcing them among their citizens, individuals and businesses alike. Hence, growing institutional and governance frameworks at international level are beginning to mirror those at national level.

For international business, the World Trade Organization (WTO) is one of the most influential of the inter-governmental organizations. Its chief goal is to facilitate the opening of trade between over 150 member states, through the negotiation of multilateral trade agreements. It also provides a system for the settlement of trade disputes where member states are alleged to be in breach of existing agreements.

While it was once thought that the WTO would mainly focus on the major trading nations, the importance of trade to all nations – whether large or small, developed or developing – has led to much broader awareness and participation in its activities.

Informal organizations also abound at international level. They facilitate co-operation and dialogue among governments, and some have taken on an authoritative rule-making role. An example is the Organisation for Economic Co-operation and Development (OECD), formed in 1961. It was originally conceived as an organization bringing together the rich countries of the world. It now has 30 members, and its numbers continue to grow. In practice, the OECD now covers many global issues which concern developing and developed countries alike. It carries out a great deal of research and gathers statistics worldwide. It has grown in authority as it has widened its range of topics, which now extend beyond economic issues to the environment and society. The G7 countries comprise the leading industrialized democracies (Canada, France, Germany, Japan, Italy, the US and the UK). They have been joined by Russia recently, becoming known as the G8. Their regular meetings highlight global issues, such as the environment and security, and can lead to co-operative initiatives, such as aid to poor developing nations (discussed in Chapter 15).

Inter-governmental organization (IGO): Grouping of representatives of sovereign states formed to foster international co-operation to tackle particular global issues.

The OECD's home page is www.oecd.org. The WTO's is www.wto.org. The UN's home page is www.un.org, which acts as a gateway to the many UN agencies and programmes.

WEB CHECK

Non-governmental organizations (NGOs): Voluntary organizations formed by private individuals for particular shared purposes, usually independent of government.

Also instrumental in nurturing awareness of global issues with local impact have been the many non-governmental organizations (NGOs) which have been set up. They cover a wide variety of organizations and issues. Many are civil society organizations run by private individuals. Some exist to provide technical services, while others are geared towards publicizing and campaigning on particular global issues. Most NGOs perceive their roles as influencing governments and stepping in to fill gaps in government welfare activities. Many do vital humanitarian work which is supported by states. Although most are independent of governments, however, some are sponsored by governments as tools of government policy, leading to some confusion and ambiguity in their perceived status (Halliday, 2000). NGOs have been active in promoting change in particular spheres, such as the environment and labour standards, increasingly working with businesses and governmental organizations.

TO RECAP...

International structures

International organizations may be formed and sustained by co-operation between governments of sovereign states, who agree to abide by their goals. The UN and its many associated agencies are examples. Numerous international associations and organizations also exist independent of government. Many are voluntary associations entered into by businesses wishing to see across-the-board standards and practices.

Conclusions

☐ International business entails greater complexity in both organization and strategy than the national or local firm. Businesses seeking to expand internationally find that a diversity of national environments presents a host of challenges, extending across economic, political, legal and cultural dimensions. Businesses which are entrepreneurial and international in their thinking from the outset are often better placed to take advantage of new opportunities, particularly in the internet and high-tech sectors, than established companies dominated by their home-country culture. SMEs increasingly play vital roles in international business.

☐ There is no single model or optimal size of the international firm. The MNE covers a range of possible organization and ownership structures. While it is generally the case that the MNE is a public company with international shareholders, many MNEs remain home-country dominated, with prominent shareholders, including governments. The company's shareholder profile and the size of dominant stakes affect its strategy and culture. The company's corporate governance system is linked to its ownership and is the chief determinant of how major decisions are taken. These systems vary in their openness to outsiders and in the transparency of their processes, but, in general, pressures for greater transparency intensify as companies become more internationalized. Similarly, companies now take greater account of stakeholder interests, extending their perspective to social and environmental issues, both globally and in national environments.

☐ MNEs increasingly interact with other players in the international environment. Co-operative alliances and networks are facilitated by advances in communications technology and open up new opportunities, especially in emerging markets. For many companies, the international joint venture offers an opportunity to benefit from the know-how of a local partner. National governments play a crucial role, directly and indirectly, for domestic and foreign businesses within their borders. Interaction and co-operation between governments have led to a range of international frameworks which impact on international business. MNEs are thus involved in a range of relations with government and civil society players. Managing stakeholder relations, both national and international, is key to international business success.

MNE responses to external influences

To what extent, in your view, do MNEs risk losing sight of their primary role of achieving enterprise goals, when seeking positive relationships with both business partners and the other key players in the international environment, highlighted in this chapter?

PAUSE TO REFLECT

Review questions

Part A: Grasping the basic concepts and knowledge

1. In what ways is the international business enterprise distinctive from a local or national business? What new risks are posed for the business which 'goes international'?

2. Why are entrepreneurs important in a national economy? What is their role in international business?

3. Why would a business decide to form a registered company?

4. What are the principal characteristics of the public company, which distinguish it from the private company?

5. How is the MNE structure well suited for international expansion?

6. Looking at the key functions in the international business organization, which are likely to be concentrated in the firm's head office, and which in foreign subsidiaries?

7. Explain the differing models of corporate governance which prevail in different countries.

8. What is the role of the independent 'non-executive' director on a company board?

9. Explain the position of the stakeholder in a company, and distinguish between primary and secondary stakeholders, giving examples.

10. What advantages are offered by the strategic alliance in internationalization?

11. Why does the joint venture make sense for a company thinking of developing an international presence?

12. In what areas does national legislation play a crucial role in the regulation of business?

13. In what ways do governments play a direct role in international business? In which countries is this role expanding, and why? (See CF1.2 on Venezuela.)

14. Explain the role of an inter-governmental organization.

15. Why has there been a growth in international organizations at government level, and are they an aid or hindrance to businesses?

16. How has the NGO evolved as a player in the international environment?

Part B: Critical thinking and discussion

1. Entrepreneurs are generally acknowledged to be innovators and wealth creators. However, as Figure 1.3 shows, there are significant differences between countries in the proportion of people involved in start-ups. What are the causes of these differences, and what can government authorities do to encourage more entrepreneurs?

2. In what ways do ownership profile and control influence a company's culture and strategy? Give some examples from the case studies and strategic crossroads boxes.

3. Give some examples of stakeholders in international businesses. In what ways do companies take account of their interests, or fail to?

4. National governments often seek to shape business behaviour and intervene in the business environment to achieve national economic goals. What such activities by governments are mentioned in this chapter, and are they justified?

Case study 1.2: Volkswagen struggles to get back on the road

Volkswagen, Europe's largest carmaker, is seen as a symbol of German industrial strength, but it has also come to illustrate the negative side of German industry, including labour inflexibility and corporate governance problems. The company has a long history of engineering excellence, in both car and components manufacturing. Unlike other motor manufacturers, it manufactures many of its components in-house in Germany. While this is beneficial for quality control, it is expensive, particularly in the context of Germany's high labour costs. German automotive workers enjoy the highest earnings per hour of any in the world. As the figure shows, VW's labour costs per hour differ between eastern and western regions, and are much higher in Germany than in Portugal. German employees benefit from both a strong system of job security and a corporate governance system based on co-determination, by which employees representatives take half the seats on their company's supervisory board. In the case of VW, these seats are all taken by the powerful labour union, IG Metall. VW's system of co-determination also includes a works council, which plays a direct role in employment matters. Falling profits and loss of competitive position have forced VW's management to embark on a cost-cutting strategy, but it has found it difficult to reduce its labour costs, even though it estimates that the company's factories are 20% overstaffed.

In 2004, VW reported its third annual drop in profits. Worryingly, the company suffered setbacks in two major markets, the US and China, where it had had strong performance hitherto. It sustained losses in the US market in 2004 and 2005, partly because of the weakness of the US dollar, but, as the head of its US operations has pointed out, the company was also to blame. New models and better marketing should help to boost sales, but he has also suggested that cost savings could be found by buying components locally for its Mexican factory. VW has long been a market leader in China, where it has two factories, operated as joint ventures with the Shanghai Automotive Industry Corporation (SAIC). These factories manufacture VWs under licence for the Chinese market, which has been growing rapidly. However, new entrants such as General Motors, Hyundai and Honda have crowded into this booming market, and VW has seen its dominant position slipping away. Moreover, SAIC has benefited from technology transfer in its VW joint ventures. In moves that could have long-term consequences for the global motor industry, SAIC and Chery Automobile of China are both planning to set up manufacturing joint ventures in China and the UK, to produce cars for other markets. These developments would give the Chinese manufacturers a competitive presence in global markets which they have not had in the past, and would exert pressures on European manufacturers, including VW, in their home markets.

A programme of cost savings was embarked on in 2005. Agreement was reached with the labour unions for a wage freeze, and there are plans for restructuring, which would see job losses of perhaps 20,000. Agreement with the union would ensure that these losses are voluntary, and a new agreement to allow workers to retire at 58 will help to reduce the overcapacity.

Figure Labour cost per hour

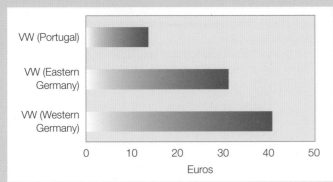

Euros

Source: Financial Times, 7 November 2006

Table Ownership structure of Volkswagen and Porsche, 2006

Shareholders	Percentage of votes	Percentage of capital
Volkswagen		
Porsche	27.4	20
Lower Saxony	20.7	15
Free float	51.9	65
Porsche		
Porsche and Piëch families	100	50
Free float	0	50

Source: Financial Times, 17 November 2006

The company also wishes to turn to external suppliers of parts in low-cost locations such as Eastern and Central Europe. It might be assumed that shareholders would applaud these moves, and, indeed, most outside investors and small shareholders do, but VW has an unusual ownership structure, in which the major shareholders have differing perspectives and priorities.

VW's two largest shareholders are Porsche, the luxury carmaker, and the government of Lower Saxony in Germany, as shown in the table. With their combined weight, they are able to fend off possible takeovers. In addition, a German law, which became known as the 'VW law', limited the voting rights of shareholders to 20%, regardless of the size of their holdings. This law was ruled unlawful by the European Court of Justice in 2007 – a ruling which could pave the way for Porsche to increase its shareholding and thereby take over the company.

The government of Lower Saxony and IG Metall are concerned about the long-term future of Volkswagen, and particularly about jobs in the region. Early in 2008, the German government bowed to the court's decision, but maintained support for the position of Lower Saxony and the trade unions in VW, which could thwart Porsche's designs. Porsche, which is the world's most profitable carmaker, has faced criticism that it is in a position to use VW's engineering resources to its own benefit, including the possibility of having VW manufacture a new Porsche model, rather than developing its own manufacturing base. The union, IG Metall, uses its powerful position on the supervisory board to defend its members, the company's German employees, but employees in the company's other locations have little voice. In 2006, the decision was taken to shift some production away from lower cost countries back to Germany, dismaying car workers in Spain, Portugal and Belgium, where plants have been highly productive.

Porsche has considered converting VW into an SE, which would reduce the number of union representatives, but it is certain to meet resistance, due to the clash of perspectives.

Questions

1 What problems have beset VW in global car markets?
2 How has VW's management brought about changes in strategy?
3 Why has VW's corporate governance been criticized?
4 If you were a shareholder in VW, what changes would you like to see in the way the company is run?

Sources: Milne, R., 'Volkswagen chooses to swim against the current', *Financial Times,* 7 November 2006; Milne, R., 'VW chief resigns in midst of bid battle', *Financial Times,* 8 November 2006; 'That's all, Volks', *Financial Times,* 17 November 2006; Milne, R., and Mackintosh, J., 'Shield for corporate Germany or a family affair?' *Financial Times,* 27 September 2005; Mackintosh, J., and Milne, R., 'VW reviews viability of parts facilities', *Financial Times,* 14 September 2005; Griffiths, J., 'China looms in rear view mirror', *Financial Times,* 1 March 2005; Mackintosh, J., 'VW changes strategy to revive sales', *Financial Times,* 10 January 2006; Milne, R., 'VW's Piëch fights off the critics', *Financial Times,* 4 May 2006; Milne, R., 'VW to replace chairman Piëch in shareholder deal', *Financial Times,* 21 January 2006; Williamson, H., and Milne, R., 'Germany protects part of "VW law"', *Financial Times,* 17 January 2008.

WEB CHECK

Volkswagen's corporate website is www.volkswagenag.com. Click on *Other Subjects,* then *Investor Relations.*

Further research

Journal articles

Alvarez, S. and Barney, J. (2007) 'The entrepreneurial theory of the firm', *Journal of Management Studies,* **44**(7): 1057–63.

Barkema, H. and Drogendijk, R. (2007) 'Internationalising in small, incremental or larger steps?', *Journal of International Business Studies,* **38**(7): 1132–48.

Matthews, J. and Zander, I. (2007) 'The international entrepreneurial dynamics of accelerated internationalisation', *Journal of International Business Studies,* **38**(3): 387–403.

Nelson, R. (1991) 'Why do firms differ and how does it matter?', *Strategic Management Journal,* **12**(2): 61–74.

Rosenzweig, P. and Singh, J. (1991) 'Organizational environments and the multinational enterprise', *Academy of Management Review,* **16**(2): 340–61.

Witt, U. (2007) 'Firms as realizations of entrepreneurial visions', *Journal of Management Studies,* **44**(7): 1125–40.

Books

Burns, P. (2008) *Corporate Entrepreneurship,* 2nd edn, Basingstoke: Palgrave Macmillan.

Steiner, G. and Steiner, J. (2005) *Business, Government and Society: A Management Perspective,* 11th edn, Maidenhead: McGraw-Hill.

chapter 2
PERSPECTIVES ON GLOBALIZATION

learning objectives

▷ To evaluate contrasting views on globalization and its transformational effects on businesses and societies
▷ To gain an overview of the means by which organizations expand internationally, in both markets and production
▷ To appreciate leading theories of internationalization and foreign direct investment (FDI)
▷ To examine critically the impacts of globalization on societies

Introduction

Impending closure of a car components factory in the province of Cádiz in Spain in 2007, by its American owner, Delphi, led to a wave of protests at the site, supported by political leaders, including the Spanish prime minister and the EU Commission president. The workers' trade union organized a two-day general strike, which paralysed business and transport across the region, achieving global media attention. In the end, the factory closed, affecting not just the 1,600 employees, but an estimated 4,000 people in the region who depended on Delphi for business. By 2008, Delphi had relocated to Morocco, where wages are one-fifth of Spanish levels. Scenarios like this have become commonplace, and are closely identified with globalization, the topic of this chapter.

Delphi's website is
http://delphi.com.

WEB CHECK

Almost every aspect of modern life is shaped to some extent by processes of globalization. With relative ease, the consumer can enjoy worldwide travel, the internet and access to goods and services from around the world. For international businesses, three features stand out: the need to think about markets in numerous countries in a 'joined-up' way; the importance of global brands; and the imperative to seek the most advantageous location for production of their products. This chapter will examine all these aspects of globalization, but it aims also to look critically at the various processes taking place behind the scenes, as it were, including their impact on societies, highlighted in the opening vignette. Discourse on globalization sometimes takes the form of presenting arguments of those who support it, weighed against objections put forward by those who oppose it. That approach tends to rest on the assumption that we are confronted with a single global phenomenon. The approach adopted here, in contrast, looks at globalization as a number of strands which, when unbundled, exhibit different effects in different contexts.

The chapter begins by identifying the core features of globalization. It highlights the distinctions between the globalization of markets and of production, the latter having progressed to a greater extent than the former. Key theories of internationalization are examined from the perspective of the firm, focusing on trends in the expansion of markets and international production. As these processes encompass more and more countries, particularly developing countries, globalization's impact on societies raises issues

for businesses and governments. These issues are explored in the remainder of the chapter. It emerges that, while benefits such as new jobs in manufacturing are bringing wealth to countries which have received significant FDI, industrialization has been a mixed blessing, often associated with poor working conditions and environmental pollution. Workers in manufacturing jobs in high-cost countries are among the most vulnerable to the effects of globalization, challenging firms and governments in the developed world to adapt to global competition.

plate 2.1 Mobile phones are now part of everyday life for people the world over, such as this user in India.

What is globalization?

It has become commonplace to observe that we all now live in a globalized world, transforming the way we live and work. Aspects frequently highlighted include global media and telecommunications, global brands, worldwide production and integrated financial markets. At the forefront of these phenomena are MNEs, benefiting from the opening of markets across the globe, and from advances in computing and internet technology, which make it possible to link far-flung activities in global networks.

In his book, *The Lexus and the Olive Tree*, Thomas Friedman (1999: xvii) describes the world as 'being tied together into a single globalized marketplace and village', driven by 'the spread of free-market capitalism to virtually every country in the world' (p. 8). This picture of a thoroughly globalized world, sometimes referred to as one of 'hyperglobalization', has become rather contentious. Taking issue with the hyperglobalizers, some academics have argued that the extent of globalization has been exaggerated and that, in fact, markets and organizations function more along national and regional lines (Rugman and Verbeke, 2004).

Globalization: Increasing and deepening interactions between individuals and organizations across the globe.

Somewhere between these two approaches is the view adopted here, that global processes are taking place, but that these processes can be differentiated, proceeding more rapidly in some spheres than in others, and also differing in intensity and effects from place to place (Ietto-Gillies, 2003). These processes are depicted in Figure 2.1. Global capital markets and growing economic integration vary significantly between countries. Trade and economic integration have surged ahead in the developed world and in some developing countries, but countries in much of Africa have seen little benefit. Some globalization theorists predicted the demise of the nation-state, but national economies and national governments remain important players. They have undergone changes, however, as they have become more interde-

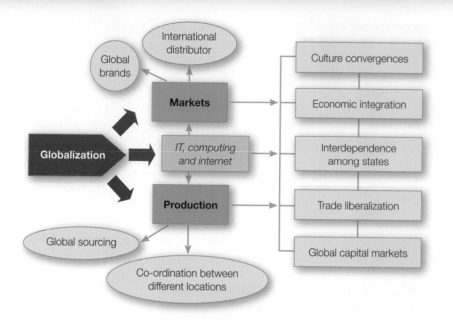

Figure 2.1 Globalization

pendent with each other and with corporate players. In the sphere of culture, there is cultural convergence as industrialization and modern urban lifestyles have spread to many countries, but cultural foundations of divergent societies persist. According to this more tentative view, gradual changes in nation-states and in national cultures indicate that globalization is more akin to a series of transformations, rather than a single, all-encompassing system.

Several defining characteristics of globalization emerge from the debate. Four are highlighted here:

- Growth in capitalist market economies worldwide, reducing barriers to trade and investment
- Growing interconnectedness between firms, governments and individuals worldwide
- Advances in information and communications technology and transport
- Qualitative changes in organizations and societies as a consequence of new global interactions.

Bringing these elements together, we can define globalization as processes of increasing and deepening interactions between individuals and organizations across the globe, facilitated by advancing communications technology and the opening of markets to trade and investment. This definition reflects the primacy of extended interactions between countries and continents, and also highlights the importance of technological innovation in transforming communications. It notes deepening interactions, implying that qualitative changes are taking place, but it does not go so far as to suggest convergence among societies in terms of economic, social and cultural spheres.

Table 2.1 What does globalization mean for business, society and government?

Aspect	Businesses	Societies	Governments
Markets	Targeting consumers in all markets	Access to products from across the globe	Lowering barriers to imports; encouraging domestic exporters
Production	Worldwide scanning for production capacity	Benefits in employment and technology from FDI	Incentives to attract FDI
IT	Intra-firm and inter-firm IT networks	Integration into global communications networks	Investment in infrastructure, education, R&D
Finance	Seeking sources of capital worldwide	Openness to outside capital; integration into global capital markets	Interdependence with regional and global financial systems
Qualitative changes	Internationalized corporate structure and culture	Culture changes associated with industrialization and urbanization	Co-operation with other governments in dealing with global issues

The implications of globalization for business, society and government are highlighted in Table 2.1. For businesses, organizational structures and culture evolve with the changes taking place in their operations, markets and finance. For governments, greater interaction leads to interdependencies, implying that governments have less scope for autonomous policies. However, national policies are clearly influential: investment in education and technology facilitates strong domestic industries as well as attracting FDI. From a society perspective, consumers benefit, as do workers in sectors which have become integrated into the global economy. However, these benefits may well not reach all in a society. Moreover, new industrial and urban environments often have a downside of poor living and working conditions, as well as environmental pollution. These are examined in detail in a later section.

Globalization of markets

In 1983, Theodore Levitt published an article entitled 'The globalization of markets', in which he predicted the merging of existing national markets for goods into a single global market, where standardized consumer products are sold in the same manner everywhere, the tastes and preferences of consumers everywhere having become irrevocably homogenized (Levitt, [1983] 1995). Peering into the future, he saw global companies, such as Coca-Cola and McDonald's, leading the way, although at the time he wrote the article, many markets were closed to outsiders and nearly a third of the world's population lived under communism.

By 1990, when McDonald's opened in Moscow and communist governments were crumbling, it looked as if Levitt's predictions of the globalization of markets might be coming true. But the picture had changed by the late 1990s: global brands were losing their lustre; consciousness of cultural roots was on the rise; and the large global companies were facing serious competition from smaller agile competitors. However, we should not be too hasty to conclude that Levitt simply got it wrong. The companies he highlighted have grown into even larger global organizations, expanding into many more countries. Levitt's article drew attention to the fact that global companies are in a position to co-ordinate activities across continents, leading to greater efficiency and economies of scale. The trend that Levitt failed to foresee was the persisting diversity of consumers and markets. MNEs have undergone shifts in strategy, away from the one-size-fits-all view of markets towards local responsiveness. A paradox of globalization has been that technology has not only facilitated the efficient delivery of standardized products, it has facilitated ranges of customized products for different markets.

The growth of global markets, as Levitt foresaw, has been most pronounced in sectors which rely on a standardized product or service for all customers. These are mainly in industrial products such as microchips and engine components; commodities such as agricultural produce, oil and other fuels; shipping; telecommunications and financial products. However, markets for consumer products in which tastes and preferences are influenced by culture have not become as homogenized as envisaged by Levitt.

Consumers now have more choice than ever. In previous eras, the local company provided goods and services produced locally for people in its own

TO RECAP...

Global transformations

Globalization's hallmarks are increasing and deepening among organizations and individuals across the globe. However, there are differing views on the extent of the changes taking place. The hyperglobalization view of convergence towards a global system has been somewhat blunted by the evidence of fragmentation in markets and societies, as well as nation-centric policies of governments. The less radical view sees global transformations taking place in businesses, governments and societies through increasing interactions and evolving changes.

Globalization of markets: The melding of national markets into a single global market; applies to standardized products, such as industrial goods and commodities, but for most consumer products, national markets remain distinct.

Globalization of production: A trend in manufacturing industries, in particular, of shifting operations to countries where conditions and environment are more advantageous for the firm than they are in its current location; usually involving cost reductions.

TO RECAP...
Globalized markets
Although the modern MNE is not likely to come up with a model of the global car which is a hit with all consumers in all markets, it is certain to have a global marketing strategy, targeting particular markets with products from its portfolio which it has reason to believe will be suited to needs and tastes in each market.

Developed country: Country whose economy has become industrialized and technologically advanced.

Developing country: Country in the process of industrialization and building technological capacity.

Transition economy: Economy which is shifting from state planning to market orientation.

geographic area, and enjoyed a stable market in which it had knowledge of local tastes and spoke the same language as consumers. A trickle of foreign imports did not disturb it unduly, as these were too expensive for most people. The position in many markets, especially in advanced economies, is now reversed. Imports of standard products are often cheaper than the local equivalent. Domestic manufacturing companies may struggle to compete with multinationals, which benefit from economies of scale and greater resources. Three main factors are at work: falling tariffs and other trade barriers; falling transport costs; and the shift of production to lower cost locations. These factors, underpinned by new technologies, are all facets of globalization. The successful company in today's world is able to source components globally and deliver finished products to diverse markets, providing consumers in each with products adapted to their tastes at competitive prices. The globalization of production, therefore, has been crucial to market success.

Globalization of production

A more recent trend than expanding markets has been the shift from home-country production of goods, particularly manufactured goods, to production in other countries. Products may be destined for consumers in the home market, the host market or other parts of the world. Companies may co-ordinate the sourcing of materials, components and know-how from many countries to produce a complex product like a car. By breaking down the manufacturing process into its separate stages, each phase takes place in the most advantageous location. Hence, research, design, sourcing of components and assembly of the final product may all take place in different locations, co-ordinated through high-tech networks.

In particular, manufacturing of mass-produced goods has largely shifted to low-cost countries. Every country has economic conditions which attract different types of business. The differences which are particularly relevant for production decisions are associated with levels of economic development. These are discussed in the next chapter, but for present purposes, it is useful to identify the broad groupings:

- Developed countries are those whose economies have become industrialized and technologically advanced, with high levels of income and prosperity. These are mainly in North America and Europe, with the addition of Japan in Asia.
- Developing countries cover a wide range of countries in the process of change from economies based on agriculture and natural resources to industrial production. For labour-intensive industries, those countries with abundant numbers of low-cost workers are said to enjoy comparative advantage over high-wage economies.
- The transition economy refers to the countries moving from communist or state-planned systems to market-based systems. Many have become industrialized during communism, but they overlap with developing countries in many respects, as they are now focusing on economic growth to generate the wealth needed to bring the prosperity of the developed countries.

Emerging economy or market: Fast-growing developing or transition economy.

A further category which is often used is the emerging economy or market. This term refers to fast-growing developing and transition economies, which attract foreign investors and offer prospects of expanding consumer markets. The main emerging markets are India (developing), Brazil (developing), Russia (transition), and China (both developing and transition).

As with national differences between markets, differences between countries and regions come into play in the location of production facilities and the forms those operations take. These are called 'location-specific advantages', or just 'location advantages'. For example, India has nurtured a strong IT capacity, and has attracted global companies outsourcing IT and related services. India's economic development has most often been compared with that of China, where export-oriented manufacturing industries have flourished, mostly in mass-produced goods, from textiles to standardized consumer electrical goods. Both countries offer location-specific advantages: China offers abundant cheap labour, and India, skilled labour for knowledge-intensive industries. However, each is looking to diversify, as India is broadening its policies to attract manufacturing FDI (highlighted in CF2.2), and China is seeking to move up the value chain, to more high-tech activities. As the world's two most populous countries, each with populations of over a billion, they are also, potentially, the world's largest markets. Not surprisingly, therefore, many companies eye the market potential they offer, in addition to their location-specific advantages in production.

TO RECAP...

Globalized production

Globalization of production allows companies to break down the manufacturing process into its separate stages, each in the most advantageous location. MNEs see developing countries as attractive locations for operations which depend on abundant low-cost labour.

Globalization: myth and reality

In what respects does it make sense to speak of globalization of markets? Why has globalization of production proceeded more rapidly than globalization of markets?

PAUSE TO REFLECT

Methods of internationalizing operations

Foreign direct investment (FDI): Investment by an organization in a business in another country with a view to establishing production in the host country.

Greenfield investment: FDI which involves the investor in setting up an operation from scratch in a new location.

A variety of arrangements have been adopted by firms wishing to internationalize some or all of their operations. Figure 2.2 depicts these options in terms of the degrees of internationalization and ownership. Foreign direct investment (FDI) involves ownership and control of foreign operations, including setting up a subsidiary in a greenfield site – greenfield investment – and outright purchase of a company in the desired location. Because these involve a high degree of ownership and control, they appear on the right in Figure 2.2. Similarly, they involve deepening international commitment, and are therefore at the top of the figure. FDI also includes joint ventures where the ownership stake is sufficient to give management control, thus positioning joint ventures at the midway point in the figure. A company not wishing to own foreign operations may license a foreign company to produce goods to its requirements and bearing its trademarks. This type of arrangement can broadly be described as 'outsourcing'. Involving no equity stake, it ranks at the lowest point on the ownership axis. In recent years, outsourcing has become a popular choice, largely because it offers an enticing combination of cost savings and a relatively modest, initial capital outlay as compared to FDI. Some companies

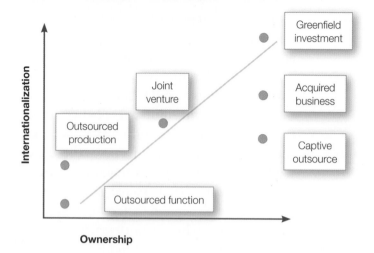

Figure 2.2 Methods of internationalizing operations

seeking the advantages of outsourcing, but with the control that comes with ownership, set up a subsidiary specifically to carry out an outsourced function, such as a call centre. This 'captive' outsourcing operation thus falls under FDI, as it is owned by the investor. Each of these internationalization methods will now be discussed in turn.

Outsourcing

Outsourcing: Shifting of an operation or process by one organization to another, under a contractual agreement, usually designed to reduce costs for the organization shedding the activity.

Outsourcing is a broad term which covers any contractual arrangement by which an organization (the client company) obtains goods or services it needs from another organization (the outsourcing company), rather than providing them itself in-house. Both the outsourcing contractor and the client company may be in the same country, but it is the growth in cross-border outsourcing which is highlighted as an indicator of globalization.

A company may outsource some or even all its manufacturing process to one or more other firms. When it outsources the entire process, it becomes, in effect, a 'virtual' manufacturer. The manufacturing may be carried out under an agreed licence, by which the manufacturers are allowed to legally use the trademark of the client company. The licence may also provide for oversight of the process with respect to quality. Typically, these arrangements are adopted by companies in the developed world to make use of outsourced manufacturing in developing countries with a view to exporting the products to their home consumers or consumers in other developed markets. Contract manufacturers have prospered from outsourcing, growing into large, co-ordinated operations, able to shift factory production among different locations to achieve economies of scale (Buckley and Ghauri, 2004).

Nike is an example of outsourced manufacturing. It contracts for its trainers and other sports goods to be made by hundreds of companies in foreign locations, mainly in China and Indonesia. The attraction of these locations is their abundance of workers available for relatively low-skilled manufacturing jobs at wages a fraction of what they would be in the developed world. In all, some 660,000 workers are employed to make products bearing the Nike logo, almost all by independent companies subcontracted to Nike (see CS14.2).

Nike and other companies have been criticized for the 'sweatshop' conditions which occur in the factories producing their products, raising

CSR issues for management. Critics point to the fact that health and safety, environmental and employment law in developing countries give only weak protection, and enforcement is patchy. Moreover, governments are not likely to raise regulatory barriers which might discourage future investment. Puma, a rival of Nike, featured in SX2.1, has made use of monitoring by NGOs to satisfy consumer concerns over poor conditions in outsourcing factories.

STRATEGIC CROSSROADS

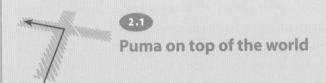

2.1

Puma on top of the world

Figure
Percentages of Puma's global revenue by region

Source: Financial Times, 4 August 2006

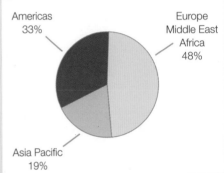

When Italy lifted the football World Cup in 2006, there were celebrations in the town of Herzogenaurach, Germany. Puma, the sportswear company sponsoring Italy, could celebrate a triumph for their brand. Adidas, also based in the town, sponsored the largest number of teams, including France, the runners-up. Puma sponsored all five African teams in the finals of the competition, using the logo, 'United for Africa', looking ahead four years, when Africa will host the finals. Puma's marketing, which cost a fraction of the marketing budgets of its larger rivals, Adidas and Nike, is indicative of the fresh approach of its entrepreneurial CEO, Jochen Zeitz, who took over the company in 1993. Then, the company was losing money, and its products were more likely to be found in discount stores than in the kit of sports personalities. He was 29 at the time, becoming Germany's youngest chief executive. His twin strategy to revive the company involved cutting costs and building the brand. Production was moved out of Europe to Asia. He is aware that his competitors, who also outsource in Asia, have faced criticisms for sweatshop conditions in sportswear manufacturing, but he points to the fact that Puma uses independent NGOs to monitor conditions, and has had no complaints for years.

Zeitz has transformed Puma into a global brand by focusing on sports lifestyle, rather than getting leading athletes to wear its products, as Nike and Adidas have done. It aimed to add a fashion element, to excite the consumer, paying less attention to matching competitors' products head on. Puma now has annual sales of €2 billion, and enjoys the highest profit margins in the industry. It has added two other headquarters, one in Boston, USA, and one in Hong Kong. Its workers come from all over the world. Zeitz says of Puma: 'We are a global company now, no longer German. I mean, can you imagine, when I got here we had what was called an "export manager" and he couldn't speak English' (Milne, 12 June 2006). As indicated in the figure, the Americas and Asia together now account for a slightly larger proportion of Puma's revenue than Europe, the Middle East and Africa.

The Puma brand today relies in large measure on trends in fashion, which can be ephemeral and are notoriously hard to predict. The leaping cat logo has become widely recognized, but Adidas and Nike are also seeking to win over consumers with exciting new products. Adidas has hired Stella McCartney, the fashion designer, to design new sportswear. Puma's potential in sports fashion caught the attention of PPR, the French group which owns Gucci and other upmarket labels, as well as large retailers. Having taken a 27% stake in Puma, PPR is contemplating taking it over, with a view to exploiting the growing luxury sports sector. Puma would gain from increased capital investment, helping to boost its sports products as well as luxury fashion products. In the past, Zeitz has been sceptical about mergers, but the backing of a strong luxury and retailing group should strengthen Puma's competitive position.

Questions

◆ How did Puma manage to recover its profitability?
◆ What is distinctive about Puma's brand strategy in global markets?

Sources: Birchall, J., 'US group targets a wider market', *Financial Times*, 4 August 2005; Milne, R., 'Giant leap forward for the sportswear outsider', *Financial Times*, 12 June 2006; Garrahan, M., 'Adidas earns its sell-faster fashion stripes', *Financial Times*, 3 May 2005; Milne, R., 'World Cup puts Puma out in front', *Financial Times*, 4 August 2006; Milne, R., 'Puma ponders next step in luxury sport sector', *Financial Times*, 11 April 2007.

WEB CHECK

Puma's corporate home page is http://about.puma.com, where there is information about investor relations and CSR.

Business process outsourcing (BPO): The shifting of particular business functions or processes to a specialist company, usually for cost savings.

Offshoring: Contracting out of a business process to another country, the main motivation usually being to benefit from its low-cost environment.

Business process outsourcing (BPO) has become common, usually due to the cost savings envisaged. For client companies, the rationale is that any function which is not core to its business can be shifted to an outside provider. In addition to IT services, back-office administration, call centres and help lines are candidates for outsourcing. The outsourcer is usually a specialist in the particular activity, and is able to achieve economies of scale, as it serves other customers as well. The client organization may well feel that handing these functions over to experts will give managers more time to focus on the company's main business. Outsourcing IT and accounting has thrived, and, as these are largely technical processes, they lend themselves to outsourcing. Outsourcing of HR functions has become popular, following BP's example in 1999. Its programme proved to be rather ambitious and had to be scaled back, but it has proceeded on an incremental basis since then. The outsourcing company may be in the same geographical region as the client company, but shifting functions abroad to a lower cost location, which is often called offshoring, is also taking place.

The term offshoring is applied to the contracting out of a function specifically to a low-cost country. The practice has grown dramatically, particularly in the services sector (UN, 2005). India has been a popular offshore location for companies from the US and the UK. In addition to call centres, Indian outsourcing companies now offer a range of back-office services to international companies. Offshoring has come to have negative connotations, implying that cost is the only factor in the decision to outsource and that the firm will inevitably cut jobs in the home country. Neither of these implications may apply to a particular outsourcing decision, but both are closely linked to the phenomenon in general. Not all outsourcing is offshoring. HR and public sector outsourcing in the UK, for example, have tended to go to specialist domestic companies. In an ironic twist, half a million workers in India's state-owned banks went on strike in 2006, in protest at the outsourcing of back-office tasks to the country's own private outsourcing companies, which have prospered through offering just these services to global MNEs.

plate 2.2 Football has become popular in Africa, boosted by hosting the World Cup in 2010.

Outsourcing is sometimes criticized for its alleged transferring of jobs from advanced economies to cheaper locations, contributing to an international division of labour. It is argued that, while the company and its shareholders benefit, the employees in the home country lose out, as their jobs migrate to lower cost locations. In fact, the situation is much more complex than the critics suggest. Cost savings can be ploughed into upgrading the skills of workers, who are then able to take on more skilled jobs. The most vulnerable workers are in low-skilled jobs in which the tasks are not dependent on being in the same location as the consumer. Researchers, however, face difficulties in quantifying the number of lost jobs. Millions of US jobs were lost due to the shift of manufacturing to East Asia and Mexico in the 1980s. It is estimated that the loss of jobs due to outsourcing is of a much lower magnitude, estimated at 473,000 in 2004 (Luce and Merchant, 2004).

Of greater significance has been the political impact of occurrences like large factory closures due to a shift to foreign production. When a community loses a large employer, there may be considerable effects, as the closure can adversely affect all aspects of the local economy, including retailers and providers of services of all types, from building to leisure centres. On the other side of the coin, outsourcing is likely to be seen by the host country as beneficial. It brings in jobs and rising demand for consumer goods and services which bring prosperity to communities. However, the new jobs may not be very secure. Outsourcers continually seek cheaper locations elsewhere, leading to accusations that a downward spiral, or 'race to the bottom' will ensue. The same phenomenon is also associated with FDI, although to a lesser extent, as these investors have a greater stake in the local economy.

TO RECAP...

Outsourcing

Outsourcing offers a means by which a company can contract out almost any of its activities, from a single process such as a call centre to an entire production chain, to another company, often across national borders. Business process outsourcing is also popular, yielding cost savings, but outsourcing has acquired negative connotations as it is perceived to be linked with loss of jobs in the home country.

COUNTRY FOCUS 2.1 – THE USA

What has happened to American manufacturing jobs?

The traditional picture of American manufacturing is that of the blue-collar worker on the assembly line in one of the many car factories in the Detroit area of Michigan, known as 'Motown'. However, Motown and other large swathes of American manufacturing have declined into 'rust-belt' areas, their industries uncompetitive in today's global economy. From 2000 to 2005, Michigan, with a total population of 9.9 million, saw the disappearance of 218,000 manufacturing jobs, mostly in the car industry, with knock-on effects in the local economy. For the state's inhabitants, this translated into a median fall in household income of 19%, the largest fall in the US. A senior economist at the Federal Reserve Bank described Michigan as a 'basket case' (Cameron et al., 2005).

The plight of General Motors (GM) and its subsidiary, Delphi, is indicative of the industry's problems, and reflects those of America's traditional blue-collar workers in general. In 1999, GM floated off its components operations in a new public company, Delphi. Although Delphi became independent of its former parent, most of its sales were to GM, and its 180,000 workers, who were unionized, brought with them the generous terms of GM employment contracts, including pensions and retirement healthcare, which weigh on company finances. For every vehicle GM produces in North America, $2,200 in costs goes into healthcare and pensions, more than the cost of raw materials. Moreover, GM and Delphi guaranteed wages and benefits, so that, when orders fell and there was no work, the company had to continue paying full wages and benefits to laid-off workers, in a 'jobs bank'. Delphi sank to losses of $2.8 billion in 2004. In the same year, its unfunded pension and retirement healthcare liabilities reached $10.4 billion. In 2005, it filed for protection under Chapter 11 of the US bankruptcy code, becoming the biggest US manufacturer ever to file for bankruptcy. The company could continue to operate, but it needed urgently to renegotiate its labour contracts.

Generous pensions and healthcare packages were a feature of US industries during their heyday in the post-war period. In contrast to European countries which have some form of universal national health provision, the US model has been that the state provides only minimal safety-net provision, and that large employers and insurance schemes shoulder the main burdens. These costs have grown dramatically, as Figure 1 shows. GM is America's largest private purchaser of healthcare, spending $4.8 billion in 2006, to cover healthcare of 1.1 million people. They include employees, dependants and retired employees (who number 432,000).

Figure 1 Percentage changes in US employment costs (civilian workers)

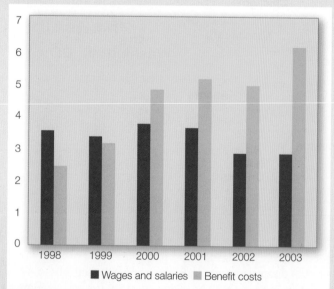

- ■ Wages and salaries ■ Benefit costs

Source: Financial Times, 20 January 2004

The trend is now for companies to scale back these benefits, but workers may be left feeling vulnerable. Low-income workers who do not work for large companies with health schemes are increasingly unable to afford the rising costs of insurance schemes. A worrying consequence is the growing number of workers with no health cover at all, which has increased by 6 million since 2000, reaching 45.8 million in 2006. These people are at risk from treatable illnesses, and could see long-term effects on their quality of life and ability to work.

Figure 2 US market share of major car manufacturers

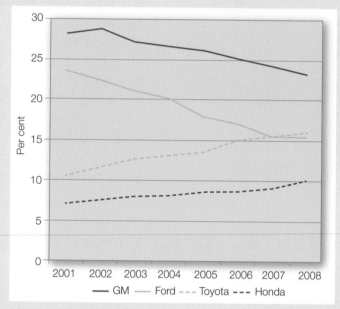

- ── GM ── Ford --- Toyota --- Honda

Source: Financial Times, 18 January 2008

As Figure 1 shows, wages rose at only 2.9%, but benefit costs rose at over 6% in 2003. For workers in companies with health cover, inter-generational tension is emerging. Current workers may face wage cuts to pay for health bills of retired workers. Current workers know they will not enjoy equivalent benefits when they themselves retire. Furthermore, stagnating wages for low-skilled jobs contrast sharply with the income growth of the richest Americans. The differential between the earnings of chief executives and the average American was 26 in 1973. In 2004, it was 300.

The past 20 years have seen the growth of car factories in the US owned by the Japanese companies, Toyota, Honda and Nissan, as well as the Korean company, Hyundai. These new competitors have eaten into American manufacturers' market share, as Figure 2 shows. The foreign manufacturers bypassed the traditional 'old economy' regions of Michigan and Ohio, going to southern states such as Alabama and Tennessee, often aided by FDI incentives from local governments. Their workforces are not unionized, and they do not enjoy the lavish benefit packages.

Delphi's CEO says: 'What is happening at Delphi [is] simply a flashpoint, a test case, for all the economic and social trends that are on a collision course in our country and around the globe' (Simon, 22 May 2006). Delphi hopes to restructure its way back to profitability, partly by rewriting its labour contracts. It is diversifying into high-tech businesses. Its new satellite radio has proved popular, and it is a world leader in this market. The company has attracted private equity investors (see Chapter 11 for an explanation), and is emerging from bankruptcy. It has announced plans to sell or close all but eight of its 28 US plants, and to shift manufacturing to overseas locations, highlighted in the opening vignette of this chapter. The closures will be a further blow to the communities in Michigan, where car and components factories have dominated the local economy for decades. The mayor of Lansing, Michigan, is philosophical. His community has seen the death of a way of life. Looking to the future, he says: 'The theme of my government is going to be "diversify, diversify, diversify"' (Chaffin, 25 November 2005).

Sources: Chaffin, J., 'GM workers see the good life fizzle away', *Financial Times*, 25 November 2005; Cameron, D., Drohan, M. and Ward, A., 'Job cuts mean fresh blow to heart of US car industry', *Financial Times*, 25 November 2005; Roberts, D., 'America's dilemma', *Financial Times*, 13 January 2006; Luce, E., 'Out on a limb', *Financial Times*, 3 May, 2006'; Simon, B., 'Motown blues', *Financial Times*, 19 September 2005; Mackintosh, J., 'How the wheels fell off at General Motors', *Financial Times*, 10 January 2005; Simon, B., 'A generation of working-class Americans under pressure', *Financial Times*, 22 May 2006; Simon, B., 'End of the road for thousands of car workers', *Financial Times*, 23 June 2006; Simon, B., 'Delphi aided by $2.5 equity deal', *Financial Times*, 19 July 2007; Simon, B., 'Stalled in Detroit', *Financial Times*, 18 January 2008.

Questions

◆ In what ways are the problems at GM and Delphi illustrative of the problems for manufacturing workers in the US generally?
◆ In the quote from Delphi's CEO, what trends is he referring to?
◆ Assess the strengths and weaknesses of Delphi's 'survival plan'.

WEB CHECK

Delphi's home page is http://delphi.com.
GM's home page is www.gm.com. Click on *Investors* and also *Retirees*.

Foreign direct investment (FDI)

FDI can be defined as investment by an organization in a business in another country, with a view to establishing production in the host country. The organization aims to gain control over this foreign production. There are various methods it can use to achieve its goals. It may simply buy a foreign business, becoming the new owner. Assuming the business is a going concern, production continues under the new owners, who are likely to have new ideas on how to manage the business more efficiently. Alternatively, the company may take the bolder step of buying a greenfield site in the foreign location and setting up a production unit to its own specification. This process will be longer and more complex for the company, but it will benefit from a unit designed specifically for its purposes and to its own specifications, and where its own technology can be incorporated from the outset. The greenfield option is often seen as the ideal, but this type of strategy is a high-risk one. In particular, it involves dealing directly with authorities in the host country for numerous permissions and services. As these processes are likely to be quite different from those in the home country of the investor, communication difficulties, delays and costs could mount before the project comes on stream. SX2.2 on Dyson, later in this chapter, provides an example of this type of investment. The Dyson factory in Malaysia had been operating for two years before production was shifted there entirely.

A less radical type of investment is through the joint venture, whereby the investing company joins up with a partner organization in the host country to form a new organization, specifically designed for the investment envisaged. The joint venture combines the advantages of the host partner's local knowledge and expertise with the know-how and capital of the investing company. Clearly, success depends largely on whether the partners share the same goals and how well the partners knit together in practice. In some countries, such as China, joint ventures have predominated, as the retention of an element of local control has been government policy. It is only in recent years that Chinese authorities have allowed foreign investors to own more than 50% of a joint venture. In general, joint ventures may be preferred in locations where the investing company has little local knowledge and experience of business practices, and where the cultural environment is very different from that of its home country.

A key aspect of FDI is the control which the investing company exerts over the overseas production. The joint venture involves give and take between partners, whereas the greenfield investor and the investor who has bought an existing company have the control which goes with ownership of their new assets. In all these cases, the investor establishes relations within the host environment. Hence, the investment is termed 'direct'. CS2.1 on Nokia illustrates expansion by FDI, transforming Nokia into a global company.

By comparison, investors who wish neither to have their products manufactured abroad nor to own and control foreign assets may still wish to invest overseas, for example by buying shares in a foreign company which seems to have good growth prospects. This type of investment is called portfolio investment, and is a financial investment only, not aimed at running the business. However, distinctions between the different types of investment may become blurred. A company may acquire a wholly owned subsidiary overseas, and leave the existing management to run the business, whereas another company may acquire only a minority stake in a foreign company's equity and proceed to exert control. The acquisition by Renault of a 37% stake in Nissan in 1999 is an example. New management introduced by Renault carried out radical changes, signifying a shift in control to the French company. It should also be remembered that ownership of shares in itself involves a role in decision-making, and even a stake of under 10% may be looked on as worthy of a seat on the board of directors. An investor may acquire such a stake with a view to raising it in future, or even making a takeover bid. Key theories, discussed in the next section, help to provide a clearer overall picture of the links between location, ownership and control in the growth of international businesses.

Portfolio investment: Financial investment in an overseas company without a view to obtaining control over management decision-making.

TO RECAP...

FDI options

FDI, entailing a significant ownership stake and management role in foreign operations, involves deeper interactions with the host location than either outsourcing or portfolio investment. Investing in a greenfield site is slower than acquiring a foreign company in the same type of operation. For the company with little experience of the foreign environment, the joint venture is an obvious entry mode, but its success depends heavily on a smooth relationship between the investor and the local partner in the host country.

Case study 2.1:
Nokia keeps competitors at bay

The global mobile phone market, although relatively young, has matured rapidly, presenting both opportunities and challenges for handset makers and network operators. The growth of Nokia, the Finnish conglomerate which shifted its strategic focus to mobile phones in the early 1990s, coincides with the growth of the market itself. Nokia became the biggest maker of mobile phones in 1998, and has maintained its position as market leader (see figure), even during the downturn in the telecommunications sector from 2001 to 2003. Even so, it has often found itself outmanoeuvred by competitors, responding belatedly to changing consumer trends, and having to sacrifice profit margins in order to hang on to market share. With the departure in 2006 of key executives who had guided the company for over a decade, could changes in strategy be taking place?

Nokia has prided itself on the quality of its product portfolio, which has been the strength of its brand. It spends more on R&D than any other handset maker, investing particularly in software development and handset innovations. While many of its competitors outsource manufacturing, Nokia manufactures 70–80% of its phones itself. It has been confident that the strength of its brand and the quality of its products would enable it to maintain both high market share and high profit margins, but costs and changes in its markets have caused managers to rethink.

In Western Europe, which has been Nokia's main market, consumers have been looking for eye-catching, innovative products. Samsung, with its folding clamshell models, and Sony Ericsson, with its larger colour screens and camera phones, have combined style with reasonable price, making inroads into Nokia's market share. Nokia seemed to be caught without attractive products in these segments, and although it has fought back with new models, it has had to cut prices, damaging margins. The company's revenues peaked in 2000, at €30.4 billion. In that year it sold 128 million phones. Revenues in 2003 were €29.5 billion from sales of 179 million phones.

Was Nokia becoming out of touch with what consumers were wanting? It seemed not to appreciate the importance of style in

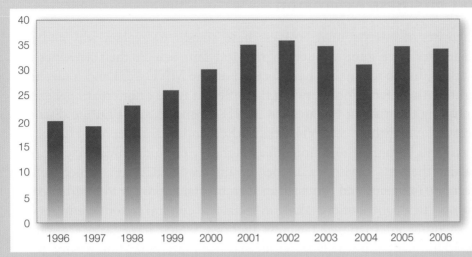

Figure Nokia's percentage share of the global mobile phone market

Sources: *Financial Times*, 7 May 2004; 28 January 2005; 28 June 2006

Regional German officials were dismayed by the decision, especially as the plant had received €88 million in subsidies and research grants. They intended to hold Nokia responsible for the retraining and job-seeking activities for the sacked workers.

Nokia is by far the most successful company in Finland, accounting for 20% of the country's exports, and employing 22,400 people in Finland. The Nokia brand enjoys extraordinary customer loyalty in its home market, where it has had a market share as high as 93%. This share slipped to 80% in 2003, as domestic retailers found that even highly loyal Finnish customers preferred Samsung's colour-screen models and clamshell designs. Nokia's corporate culture has been highly homogeneous and closely knit, most of its executives being long-serving and Finnish. But the company has become global in its geographic reach. Some head-office functions, such as finance, have moved to New York, and New York is the location of the new enterprise solutions division. Following the restructuring, its new board still has only four non-Finnish members out of 12. Some Finns are concerned that the company might move away, particularly because of high Finnish taxes. On the other hand, some would argue that a more diverse perspective is just what is needed if Nokia is to maintain its position in global markets.

the consumer's mind. More generally, the company had failed to adjust its strategy for the fragmentation which was occurring in the market. It was being attacked by Samsung at the high end of the market, Sony Ericsson in the middle range, and Siemens at the lower end, where the basic entry-level phone is the key product. A corporate restructuring followed in 2004, in which two new business units were created. The multimedia division focuses on the high-end consumer products, including advanced imaging, music and gaming. The 'enterprise solutions' division aims to serve the business 'smart' phone market. Thus, these specialist units are now separate from its mainstream mobile phone business. The company is now focusing on emerging markets such as China and India, but in these very competitive markets for basic phones, margins are tight. Nokia's handset sales in China grew by a third in 2006, helping the company to claim 35% of China's mobile phone market. This impressive performance reflected the company's drive to attract new subscribers with low-cost handsets.

In 2008, Nokia announced it was closing its German plant in Bochum, with the loss of 2,300 jobs, and moving production to Romania, where wages are one-tenth the levels in Germany.

Questions

1 Why did Nokia miss consumer trends, belatedly having to match competitors' offerings?
2 How do you explain Nokia's continuing dominance of the mobile phone market?
3 Assess Nokia's current competitive position in global markets, particularly the likelihood of retaining its large market share.
4 To what extent is Nokia a global company?

Sources: Brown-Humes, C., 'Nokia chases growth with major shake-up', *Financial Times*, 27 September 2003; Brown-Humes, C. and Budden, R., 'Not so mobile', *Financial Times*, 7 May 2004; George, N., 'Nokia answers the call for fresh leadership', *Financial Times*, 20 December 2004; Odell, M. and Munter, P., 'Pivotal figure hands over in a period of great change', *Financial Times*, 10 October 2005; George, N., 'Nokia wins back market share to bolster top spot', *Financial Times*, 28 January 2005; Munter, P., 'Buoyant Nokia beats forecasts', *Financial Times*, 21 April 2006; Song, J., 'LG hopes phone will sweeten its outlook', *Financial Times*, 28 June 2006; Dickie, M., 'Nokia cultivates China lead', *Financial Times*, 12 December 2007; Anderson, R. and Williamson, H., 'Nokia to shift German jobs to Romania', *Financial Times*, 16 January 2008.

WEB CHECK

Nokia's home page for corporate information is http://nokia.com/aboutnokia, where there is information on investors and CSR.

New economic geography of manufacturing

For a company wishing to manufacture a standard consumer product (such as basic mobile phones), compare the advantages and disadvantages of FDI and outsourcing production. Does the particular FDI entry mode matter, for example acquisition of a business, greenfield investment or joint venture?

PAUSE TO REFLECT

Theories of international business expansion

Theorists of international business have sought to explain why and how businesses have gone about geographical outreach in their activities and markets. In the main, they have focused on the MNE, FDI and trade, highlighting the interactions between the different types of international expansion. Key theorists in the areas of MNE expansion and FDI are discussed below. Among the most influential early theorists are Stephen Hymer and Raymond Vernon, who is noted for his theory of product life cycle. Scandinavian theorists devised a model of internationalization, which reflects Vernon's influence and provides an incremental approach to internationalization. Their contribution, taking in social and cultural factors, contrasts with most other international business theories, which have been economics-based. Influential in the latter group has been internalization theory, which analyses the MNE in the context of FDI. John Dunning incorporated this approach in his paradigm of ownership, location and internalization, known as the eclectic (or OLI) paradigm. His is the most comprehensive theoretical explanation with specific focus on FDI.

Early theories of FDI

Stephen Hymer sought to explain how FDI differed from portfolio investment. Writing in the 1960s, he observed the relatively new phenomenon of firms establishing production facilities abroad. Why would they undertake such an apparently risky strategy, given that they would be competing against local firms in the host country, who had inherent advantages of local knowledge? While portfolio theorists had focused on the financial capital that foreign investors contribute, Hymer found that FDI involved bringing in a range of other resources, including technology, managerial skills and marketing skills. These resources were not likely to be evident in the domestic businesses in developing countries, and hence these countries possessed location advantages. In addition, as these resources were specific to the firm, they could be said to be ownership advantages. The foreign firm was able to organize production more efficiently and was therefore able to compete against local firms. However, the fact that a firm possesses advantages over other firms in any particular type of activity does not necessarily imply that it should set up its own enterprises in other countries. It could choose instead to license a local manufacturer to make the product. The key to FDI, he argued, was the ability to exert control over the advantages, giving the owner monopoly power, and this could only be exploited in situations of market failure. In emphasizing the need to gain market power as central to FDI, Hymer underestimated other factors such as transaction costs, and tended to confuse location and ownership advantages (Yamin, 1991). However, his attempts to predict the future effects of the growth of multidivisional companies show remarkable insight. Writing in the 1970s, Hymer foresaw that by 2000, the large MNEs, with highly developed centralized structures, would be able to co-ordinate international production in locations across the globe. Although differing local circumstances would seem to indicate the need for decentralized decision-making, it was likely that developing countries would

Location advantages: Factor endowments of a particular country or area within a country, which offers specific benefits to the potential foreign investor.

Ownership advantages: Resources specific to the firm, such as technology, managing skills and marketing skills.

become 'branch-plant countries', being restricted in their scope for independent activity and the ability to pursue their own goals (Hymer, 1975: 55). Conflicts, he felt, were possible 'between national planning by governments and international planning by corporations' (Hymer, 1975: 60). These are issues which we recognize today as central to the globalization debate, but which had not been identified as such in Hymer's day.

Another early theorist of international production is Raymond Vernon, whose theory of the product life cycle is relevant both to theories of FDI and international trade. Here we look specifically at its importance to theories of FDI, leaving his contribution on international trade to Chapter 6. Writing in the 1960s, Vernon ([1966] 1999) took the perspective of US companies, who enjoyed innovatory superiority to competitors in both products and processes. These could be considered ownership advantages, although Vernon was concerned more with location than organizational matters.

Figure 2.3 Product life cycle

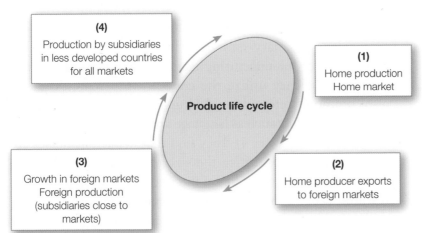

Vernon envisaged the life cycle of a new consumer product originating in the US, such as a washing machine or television. Initially, the product is produced in the US for American consumers (1), as shown on the right in Figure 2.3. Proceeding clockwise, the next step in the cycle is export of the product to countries with a similar level of consumer demand, such as European countries (2). As the product becomes more widespread and standardized, however, and imitators start to produce similar products, the need to reduce costs becomes paramount. At the same time, foreign markets for the product expand, and the firm decides to site production in a foreign location by establishing a subsidiary there (3). Not only will production be near the new markets, but labour costs will be reduced. In the final stage of the product cycle, subsidiaries are established in less developed countries, from which they export to the new markets and even back to the home country (4).

Vernon's theory was limited in the factors it took into account, and it assumed that all innovation stemmed from US firms. The life cycle envisaged by his theory spanned a rather longer period than one would encounter today: now, an innovative product may become standardized and widely distributed in a matter of months, rather than years. Production in a low-cost location is now envisaged from the outset, serving all markets simultaneously, as firms are keen to maximize returns, knowing that the product may well be superseded by new technology in a short space of time. Despite these limitations, however, the life cycle theory offered a new explanation of foreign production and was innovative in showing the links between trade and FDI.

TO RECAP...

Early theories of FDI

Hymer identified the importance of location and ownership advantages in the FDI decision-making process. Vernon's product life cycle theory, while US-centric, is noteworthy for its insight in showing how innovative products become standardized and cheaper over time. Production moves to lower cost locations, from which they are exported to all markets.

Theory of incremental internationalization

Scandinavian theorists have devised a model of incremental internationalization, based on their research in the 1970s on selected Scandinavian companies (Johanson and Wiedersheim-Paul, 1999). Like Vernon's, this model envisages a series of stages in the process and sees the use of exports as the initial entry mode into international markets. However, this research focuses on the organizations themselves, highlighting how the knowledge which they gain about foreign markets and operations in each stage impacts on their future commitments in those markets (Johanson and Vahlne, 1999). The stages they envisage move from export via an independent agent, to the establishment of a sales subsidiary and then to the establishment of a production or manufacturing facility in the foreign location (Figure 2.4). They utilize the concept of 'psychic distance', also commonly referred to as 'cultural distance', which focuses on cultural factors such as language and education (see further discussion in Chapter 4). They find that, while businesses are often advised to prioritize the size of the potential market, decisions in the early stages of internationalization tend to be towards those countries which are culturally proximate to their own, such as countries in the same geographical area or ones which share the same language.

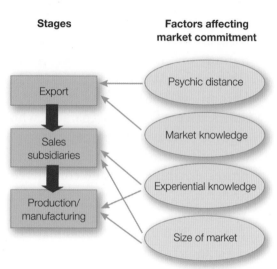

Figure 2.4 Incremental internationalization

The entire process involves incremental adjustments which take account of the changes experienced by the firm and changes which it finds in the environment. CS2.1 on Nokia provides an illustration of this process. As it shows, the company has focused on markets close to home, only entering the large emerging markets of China and India much later. Gaining knowledge of the new market is a major factor in its success (or failure). Much of this knowledge is objective, and can be transmitted by conventional teaching and learning. However, the knowledge that is gleaned through working with new partners, known as 'experiential knowledge', is the key to success (Barkema et al., 1996). This type of knowledge is based on evolving relations between individuals, and is particularly important in management and marketing. These theorists conclude that the better the firm's knowledge of the market, in both objective and experiential knowledge, the deeper will be the commitment to that market.

Dunning's eclectic paradigm

Eclectic paradigm: Dunning's theory of FDI, based on ownership advantages, location advantages and internalization.

In his eclectic paradigm, John Dunning (1993a) sought to construct a general theory explaining foreign-owned production, drawing on contributions of earlier theorists, including theorists of MNEs and international trade. He called the paradigm 'eclectic', as it brought together concepts from diverse research strands, which included ownership advantages (O), location advantages (L) and internalization theory of the MNE (I), to form the OLI paradigm. The paradigm covers all forms of foreign production by firms in all countries. It views the three elements as conceptually distinct, although in practice they interact with each other (see Figure 2.5). First, the firm contemplating foreign production will have ownership

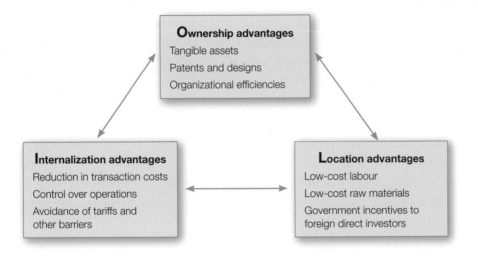

Figure 2.5 Dunning's eclectic paradigm

advantages unique to itself. These are ownership-specific assets which give it advantages over other firms, home or abroad. They may be tangible, for example new products, or intangible, for example know-how. They may be capacities and abilities to generate innovations, as well as the innovative products themselves. Included are property rights in patents, research capacity (including skilled staff), financial know-how, ability to realize economies of scale, and marketing and management skills. Ownership advantages are likely to occur in particular countries, where there are high levels of technological skills, from which all the country's firms are able to benefit.

The firm which possesses O advantages could choose to sell them or sell the right to use them. A company which licenses a foreign firm to manufacture its patented product does the latter. Alternatively, it could seek to add value by exploiting them itself, realizing the advantages of internalization. Dunning drew on internalization theory, which examined why firms would choose to own and control value-added activities rather than rely on the market. Firms are likely to perceive that cost benefits will arise in their cross-border activities if they own or control them through organizational means, thus internalizing the activity and reducing transaction costs which would otherwise arise. The greater the firm perceives its O advantages to be, the greater its incentive to internalize their use. For example, ownership advantages are critical to a company such as Dyson, featured in SX2.2 below. Hence, its own designs and patented products are kept in-house.

Apart from avoiding transaction costs, the firm may wish to internalize activities for other reasons: it may fear that suppliers of products or services will not produce to the right quality or to contract specifications; it may wish to control market outlets; it may wish to control conditions of sale; or it may wish to avoid tariff barriers imposed by governments. The firm may also fear that its technology will be transferred to rivals or potential rivals, as in the joint venture operations of Volkswagen highlighted in CS1.2. As these considerations show, there are many risks associated with foreign production, making the case for internalization look compelling.

The final element, location advantages, highlights comparisons between the home country and possible host countries. Factors which the firm takes into account in looking for L advantages include: resource endowments; costs of labour, materials and energy; presence of support services; and investment incentives which might be offered by governments. If the company is looking to sell its products in the foreign location, then market size and characteristics are also important.

The eclectic paradigm provides an analytic framework designed to explain 'what is' in terms of foreign value-added activities, rather than the normative issues of 'what should be' (Dunning, 1993a: 76). Nonetheless, it does consider MNE strategies and strategic goals. It argues that:

> at any given moment of time, a firm is faced with a configuration of OLI variables and strategic objectives to which it will respond by engaging in a variety of actions relating to technology creation, market positioning, the formation of corporate alliances, organizational structures, political lobbying, intra-firm pricing, etc. These actions, together with changes in the value of exogenous variables it faces, will influence its overall competitive position. (Dunning, 1993a: 87)

The OLI paradigm serves chiefly as an aid to assess the costs and benefits of foreign production, but its concepts can be helpful in looking at the broader issues of the impacts of MNE activity in host countries. Dunning himself delved into the economic consequences of FDI and the behaviour of MNEs, particularly economic development (Dunning, 1993a, Chapter 10). He predicted that the outward FDI of a country's firms would vary in type and level with the country's level of development. A general trend is that firms of all countries will become internationalized over time. Moreover, today's developing economies will probably embark on international expansion at an earlier stage in their development than did the early industrializing countries. However, recalling the elements of globalization listed above, we would now probably take a broader view of the effects of FDI, extending beyond the economic, to include social, political, cultural and environmental impacts.

> **TO RECAP...**
>
> **The OLI paradigm**
>
> Dunning's eclectic paradigm forms a framework for evaluating FDI from the perspective of the firm, focusing on ownership, location and internalization advantages. While location and ownership advantages had been highlighted by earlier theorists, the addition of internalization advantages based on transaction cost analysis, added a new element to form a more comprehensive framework.

STRATEGIC CROSSROADS

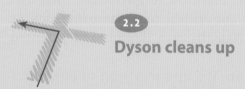

2.2
Dyson cleans up

James Dyson, the British inventor and entrepreneur, has become known mainly for his distinctive bagless vacuum cleaners, whose brightly coloured plastic shapes stand out among the more staid models of competitors. For Dyson Appliances, the company he founded in Malmesbury in England in 1993, success in the British market led to expansion in Europe, where Dyson claims a fifth of the market by value. Perhaps his most stunning achievement has been to capture 20% of the American market in 2005, after only two years' endeavours. Here, Dyson fronts his own advertisements for the product, but attributes his success more to the technology than marketing. He feels that the dual cyclone technology sells the machines, even though prices are more than double that of competitors' machines. The Dyson machine has also been a success in Japan, where consumers are noted for being especially hard to please. The model designed for the Japanese market is small and light, ideal for small apartments, and is equipped with a powerful digital motor. He is planning to enter the Chinese market, which is perhaps ironic, as China is the preferred location for most of the world's manufacturers of household appliances.

As an entrepreneur, Dyson has never lacked confidence, but he faced serious obstacles in getting his inventions off the ground, coming close to bankruptcy several times. From an engineering background, he worked for five years, from 1979 to 1984, to perfect his new vacuum cleaner, going through over 5,000 prototypes. He tried to sell it to large manufacturers, but was turned down by Philips, Electrolux and Black & Decker. He formed his own company, of which he is the sole shareholder, and has protected his inventions with patents. Still, he has had to fight numerous legal battles with Hoover, which has a similar machine. During hard times, he had sold technology rights to his machines in the US and Japan, and had to buy them back before he could launch in these markets.

In 2002, Dyson took the step many engineering companies before him have taken, shifting production to Asia, where he set up a factory in Malaysia. Two years later, all production was shifted to the new factory, resulting in the loss of 800 jobs in Malmesbury. Many in Britain were dismayed over the move, but cost reductions of 30% in Malaysia gave Dyson the budget to expand in the US. A local council leader said of the move: 'We have good employment here, but what we need is a balance; we have lots of service sector jobs but the Dyson manufacturing jobs were vital to that balance' (Marsh and Pickard, 2002). Dyson still employs 1,200 people in R&D and design in Malmesbury. He is unrepentant, blaming the government for failing to give sufficient incentives for innovation and doing too little to promote design and engineering in schools: 'The government is trying but we have a cultural problem with manufacturing because our schools tell us that if we do not study we will end up in a factory' (Guthrie, 2004). In the past 30 years, British manufacturing jobs have halved, now representing only 12% of the workforce. Dyson feels the answer is to develop added-value manufacturing: 'If that's the model for modern Britain, that's OK.' He goes on to say, however, that he fears the entire sector will be driven offshore: 'It absolutely could happen. But we're a British company, I'm British, I like living here. I just hope the government makes life easier, not more difficult' (Eaglesham, 2005).

Questions
- At what points in the growth of Dyson's business did it face strategic crossroads?
- What factors influenced the company's choice of direction at these crucial junctures?
- Do you agree with Dyson's predictions on the British manufacturing sector generally?

Sources: Marsh, P. and Pickard, J., 'Dismay at job losses as Dyson shifts production to Malaysia', *Financial Times*, 6 February 2002; Urquhart, L., 'Carpets of US moving into Dyson's sights', *Financial Times*, 30 June 2002; Guthrie, J., 'Dyson rails at cultural spanner in the works', *Financial Times*, 1 October 2004; Eaglesham, J., 'Dyson seeks to brush up industry's image', *Financial Times*, 19 November 2005; Guthrie, J. and Roberts, D., 'A Brit who cleaned up', *Financial Times*, 26 February 2005.

WEB CHECK

Dyson's website is www.dyson.co.uk.

Theories of internationalization
In light of companies you know and those featured so far in this book, which of the theories presented here best explains the internationalization process?

PAUSE TO REFLECT

Changing patterns of FDI

FDI inflows: Value of FDI which flows into a recipient country from all foreign investors.

FDI outflows: Value of all foreign direct investments made by a country's firms over a period, usually a year.

FDI stock: Accumulated value of all foreign investments within a country.

Among the key features of globalization identified above are growing economic integration; interconnectedness between organizations; and the growing importance of IT, advanced communications and transport. Although economic integration through trade has been occurring for centuries, it is only in the post-war period that FDI has grown dramatically, outstripping growth in trade. FDI is measured in terms of 'inflows' and 'outflows'. FDI inflows represent the aggregate value of FDI into a recipient country from all foreign investors, usually referred to as an annual sum. FDI outflows are the aggregate value of the foreign direct investments made by a country's firms over a period, usually a year. FDI stock refers to the accumulated value of all foreign investments within a country, which represents flows over a number of years. In Figure 2.6, we can see the strong growth in inward investment stock. Healthy inflows suggest that the country offers location advantages or a large market which is best serviced by locating in the country. The investor may also serve other regional markets as a 'bloc', such as the EU. Large outflows suggest that the country's companies are competing successfully on the global stage. Some countries, most notably Japan, have strong outflows, but little inward investment, as its policy environment has discouraged inward investors.

Figure 2.6 Growth in value of global FDI stock

Source: UN, *World Investment Reports 2005 and 2007* (Geneva: UN)

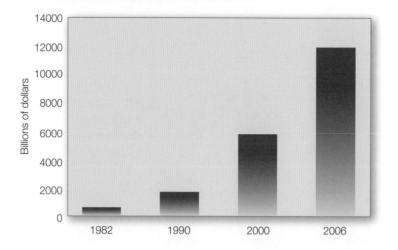

Japan's rather insular perspective is unusual. The trend has been for countries, both developed and developing, to become more open to FDI.

Destinations of FDI

Most of the developed world has attracted high levels of FDI, as Figure 2.7 shows. A major factor is that foreign investors seek to set up production in or near their largest markets, which tend to be in the advanced economies of North America and Europe. Another factor is that mergers and acquisitions of businesses make up as much as half of all FDI, and that deals between very large companies, so-called 'mega-deals', tend to be between MNEs in the developed countries. These have been facilitated in recent years by the growth in debt financing and the active role of private equity groups and hedge funds in corporate financing and acquisitions (discussed further in Chapter 11). An earlier peak, in the late 1990s, saw a number of such deals, including the ExxonMobil merger and the merger of GlaxoSmithKline. With a downturn in the availability of credit late in 2007, such deals became more difficult to finance. FDI flows to developed countries have been influ-

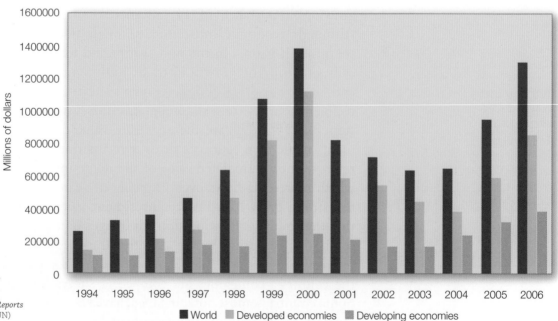

Figure 2.7 FDI inflows, 1994–2006

Source: UN, *World Investment Reports 2004, 2005 and 2007* (Geneva: UN)

enced by government trade policies which set limits on imports. Large foreign manufacturers have been able to circumvent the restrictions by setting up production in the country of their target consumers. Japanese motor manufacturers successfully pursued this strategy in the US, and have reaped the benefits in terms of American market share (see CS10.1 on Toyota).

FDI grew strongly in the late 1980s, at an annual rate of 26%, while world exports grew at 15% (Dicken, 2003: 52). After a decline in the early 1990s, FDI surged again until 2000, but declined in the new millennium, affected by the global economic downturn (see Figure 2.7). Flows resumed growing again in 2004, to both developed and developing countries. Their impressive growth in developed countries has stemmed largely from mergers and acquisitions, combined with high stock market values.

FDI flows to the developing world have been rising steadily since 2004. Two factors can be highlighted. First, companies are seeking opportunities for production efficiencies and market growth in the developing world. This has led to an FDI boom, in which greenfield investments are prominent. A few very successful developing economies have received the bulk of FDI. China is the largest recipient, and India, Mexico and Brazil are also attracting large flows. Second, the rise in prices of many commodities, such as oil and minerals, has benefited countries rich in these natural resources, many of which are in the developing world. Resource-rich African countries have gained, seeing FDI flows double between 2004 and 2006. Countries rich these resources, including Angola, Equatorial Guinea, Nigeria and Sudan, have all benefited from foreign investment, and account for half of all the FDI flows to Africa. Apart from these sectors, FDI flows to Africa are low, reflecting weak industrial and technological environments.

FDI flows to developing countries drive economic growth, encouraging many governments to actively court foreign investors. In China, overseas investors have been welcomed, providing capital and modern technology. Technology transfer and the acquisition of management expertise gleaned from foreign investors can also benefit the growth of indigenous businesses. On the other hand, governments may display ambivalence towards foreign investors, particularly if an industry is perceived as 'strategic'. The Indian government has been lukewarm towards FDI, accounting in large part for India's low inward flows (see CF2.2). Recently, Chinese authorities have been reluctant to allow takeovers of domestic firms by foreign companies in industries such as construction and banking, indicating a possible cooling in sentiment towards foreign investors. At the same time, Chinese companies are branching out to become internationalized themselves, as the closing case study in this chapter shows.

Outward investors

MNEs have been at the forefront of the globalization processes described in this chapter. As large companies have internationalized, companies of all sizes have followed their example. Total MNEs numbered 37,000 globally in the early 1990s, with 170,000 foreign affiliates. By 2006, their number had climbed to 78,000, with 780,000 foreign affiliates (UN, 2007a). Particu-

TO RECAP...
Destinations of FDI
The gap between FDI flows to developed and developing countries seems to be closing, as global competitive pressures lead companies to seek lower cost locations. However, flows are directed mainly towards a few major developing countries, most notably China, while many poorer countries in the developing world have attracted little FDI, unless they are endowed with keenly sought natural resources.

Figure 2.8 Number of MNEs based in developed, developing and transition economies

Source: UN, *World Investment Report 2007* (Geneva: UN)

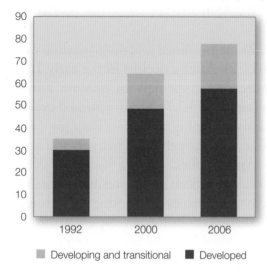

larly notable has been the increase in the number of MNEs based in developing countries, shown in Figure 2.8.

MNEs based in the developed world represented 84% of total outflows in 2006 (UN, 2007a). Looking back, in the 1950s and 60s, half of all FDI flows originated in the US. In the 1970s, Japanese and European firms started investing abroad, resulting in the decline in America's share of the total to about one-third. As MNEs from developing countries expand internationally, they are becoming active in FDI. Recall Dunning's observations above on the likely increase in outward FDI from developing countries. While it hardly existed in 1980, these outflows had reached $174 billion in 2006, 14% of the world's total, giving developing countries 12.8% of global FDI stock. Figure 2.9 indicates that Asian firms account for the bulk of this growth. The transition economies of the CIS (Commonwealth of Independent States, which includes the Russian Federation and countries which were part of the former Soviet Union) are internationalizing, particularly in the oil and gas industries (see CS15.1 on Gazprom and CF15.1 on Kazakhstan). Much of this FDI is in the form of merger and acquisition (M&A) activity with firms in other developing countries, as well as with firms in developed countries. The acquisition of IBM's PC business by Lenovo of China, which features in CS2.2, falls into this category. The takeover in 2006 of a Canadian nickel mining company by the Brazilian company Companhia Vale do Rio Doce (CVRD, now known as Vale) is also indicative of the growing importance of natural resources in the global economy. Vale is the world's leading producer and exporter of iron ore, and has enjoyed huge profits due to growing demand, particularly from China.

Many outward investors, such as those in the CIS, are wholly or partially state owned. These 'national champions' often target emerging markets where they invest in resources to build market share. French companies, including many state enterprises, have been particularly acquisitive internationally. In 2005, French companies spent $115 billion on purchases of

Figure 2.9 FDI outflows from developing and transition countries

Source: UN, *World Investment Reports, 2005, 2006 and 2007* (Geneva: UN)

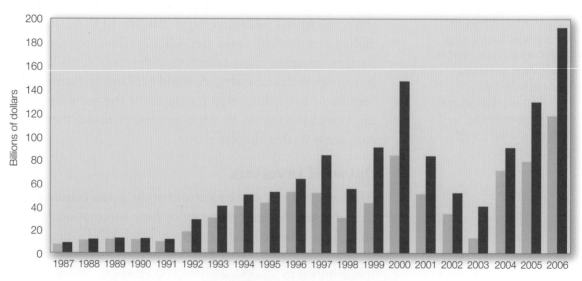

TO RECAP...
Outward investors in FDI
The world's outward investors are predominantly large MNEs, which may be owned by private investors or states. While historically most outward investors have been from the developed world, MNEs from developing countries are increasingly expanding through FDI, both in developed and developing countries.

foreign companies, overtaking the US (Betts, 2006). Takeovers by state-controlled companies may be viewed with ambivalence in host countries. The US blocked a proposed takeover of Unocal, the US oil company, by CNOOC, the Chinese national oil company, in 2005; and Unocal then merged with Chevron. Governments have welcomed foreign investors who wish to build greenfield projects or take over ailing businesses, but today's MNEs are often looking for quick returns and market share. In this competitive environment, almost any business can become an attractive target for an ambitious MNE with money to spend. As CF1.2 on Venezuela highlighted, foreign investors and governments are now thinking of the broad implications of each investment project, taking into account interactions with numerous potential stakeholders. FDI has thus become a sensitive issue. The governments of both Poland and India, for example, have expressed objections to the expansion of global retailers in their markets, for fear of adverse affects on local retailers. However, both have given the go-ahead to Tesco and others to build hypermarkets.

COUNTRY FOCUS 2.2 – INDIA

'Made in India' comes of age

India is well known for its software development expertise, call centres and back-office services. However, its international reputation in services has not been matched by its manufacturing industries, in which it compares poorly with China, the global leader in mass manufacturing. China's industrialization has fuelled impressive economic growth of 9–10% per annum for over a decade, while next door in India, the view took hold that India could happily bypass the traditional models of building development on manufacturing. Economic development resting on services was the chosen route, playing to the country's strengths and leading to more high-value industries. The growth rate of India's economy has hovered around 6–7%, but growth in employment has remained only 1% per annum, contributing to problems of unemployment and poverty. Recently, a re-examination of the country's strategy has been taking place, to focus more on manufacturing.

Like China, India is home to over a billion people, but India's population is much more youthful than China's. Nearly a third of India's population is under 15, whereas in

China, 22.5% of people are under 15, which makes China demographically more like countries in the developed world. For Indian policy-makers, job creation in manufacturing would seem an obvious policy goal, but FDI is needed. Flows are now growing, but are still well behind flows into China (see figure). Government policy has been a factor: the government has been reluctant to liberalize state-owned industries, and heavy-handed bureaucracy is a deterrent to enterprise. India has a high level of illiteracy: only 61% of the adult population has basic literacy, which is on a par with some of the least developed countries in Africa. By comparison, 91% of Chinese adults are literate. In addition, India's weak infrastructure, a major factor for manufacturing companies, has suffered from underinvestment and compares poorly with China, with its better roads and ports.

Figure A comparison of FDI inflows to India and China

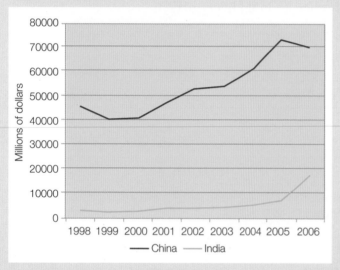

Sources: UN, *World Investment Reports 2004, 2005 and 2007* (Geneva: UN)

In some respects, India would seem to have significant location advantages over China. Most of the business community is English-speaking. It is a democracy with an established independent legal system, albeit one that is slow and cumbersome. It also provides protection for intellectual property rights (IPR), such as patents, which are important for the protection of innovations. The business climate in India is now changing, as manufacturing moves more into the limelight. Will India belatedly enjoy its own industrial revolution?

In fact, 'made in India' already enjoys a reputation in manufacturing, in engineering-based industries and in those in which software plays an important part. The conglomerate Mahindra & Mahindra (M&M) has looked to modernize and internationalize its operations. It has prioritized advanced technology and innovation, and devoted resources to product development. Its tractor business, a domestic market leader, has set up production in the US and China, hoping to make gains in world markets. In a joint venture with Renault in 2002, it launched the Scorpio, a new sports utility vehicle, which has proved

popular with India's affluent middle class. Development costs for the Scorpio were only $120 million, one-fifth what they would have been in the West. In addition, working with component suppliers which were much cheaper than those in Europe or Japan helped to keep costs down, enabling the plant to make a profit even on a relatively small-scale operation. The president of its automotive unit says the Scorpio has 'broken the myth of economies of scale' (Merchant et al., 2005).

Similarly, Bajaj Auto is seeking to become a global force in small motorcycles and scooters. Now the fourth biggest producer, behind three Japanese companies, Bajaj is demonstrating how the use of advanced manufacturing techniques can pay off in terms of quality and sophistication of the product. Whereas an Indian company could well base its strategy on using large numbers of poorly paid workers, Bajaj has taken the view that this route is counterproductive in terms of quality products and international expansion. It has reduced its workforce by half, although this has entailed making sizable compensation payments, as required by India's labour laws. Its sales have benefited from the huge size of the domestic market, 7–8 million, which is second only to China's, which is 11–12 million. The company aims to build up its non-India sales to 30% of its output, partly by increasing exports, and partly by building plants outside India. It has plans to build factories in Indonesia and Nigeria.

By focusing on its strengths in engineering and services, India is building a manufacturing base which is distinctive, and the signs are emerging that more manufacturers are seeing the advantages of India as a location. The government now intends to bring in reforms to attract more foreign investors. Multinationals which have long thought of China as the logical location for their operations are now thinking again. The chief executive of an Indian textile company, Gokal Das Exports, says that even in an area such as textiles, where China has a huge lead, his company can compete: 'We have the skills where the Chinese are weak: high quality design and software, the ability to interact with western customers in English and a managerial talent pool which has a very flexible and cosmopolitan mindset' (Luce and McGregor, 2005). M&M's chairman is similarly upbeat. Referring to the novel by Salman Rushdie, he compares his own company to the birth of India, both 60 years old: 'We're both Midnight's Children and today, outrageously ambitious' (Merchant, 2006).

Questions

◆ Why has India prospered in IT and services, while failing to develop manufacturing industries?

◆ What factors have played a part in the success of the companies featured in the case study?

◆ Assess India's prospects for attracting FDI in manufacturing in the future.

Sources: UNDP (2005) *Human Development Report 2005* (New York: UNDP); UN (2005) *World Investment Reports 2004 and 2005* (Geneva: UN); Luce, E. and McGregor, R., 'A share of the spoils: Beijing and New Delhi get mutual benefit from growing trade', *Financial Times*, 24 February 2005; Wolf, M., 'On the move: Asia's giants take different routes in pursuit of economic greatness', *Financial Times*, 23 February 2005; Wolf, M., 'What India must do to catch up with and possibly outpace China', *Financial Times*, 25 February 2006; Marsh, P., 'Effort to transport domestic success', *Financial Times*, 26 January 2006; Johnson, J., 'Back to the future: India is gaining belated credibility as an emerging export train', *Financial Times*, 30 November 2005; Merchant, K., Marsh, P. and Johnson, J., 'A transformation led by improving factory efficiency', *Financial Times*, 30 November 2005; Merchant, K., 'Indian heir renews his inheritance', *Financial Times*, 3 July 2006.

WEB CHECK

Mahindra & Mahindra's website is www.mahindra.com.
Bajaj Auto is www.bajajauto.com.

FDI perspectives
From a country perspective, inward FDI can be seen as an opportunity or a threat. To what extent do you think this is an accurate statement? Give examples to support your views.

PAUSE TO REFLECT

Impact of globalization on societies

In this section, we unbundle the strands of globalization, assessing their impact on societies. Economic impacts are possibly the most obvious, but other impacts, including technological, cultural and environmental, while rather more qualitative, also have long-term effects. Although we tend to view countries as a whole, it should be borne in mind that some groups in a country may gain while other groups – and the ecological environment – may be worse off. Whether changes bring benefits or detriments depends in large part on the position of the vantage point being discussed. A further point should be stressed: governments play an important role in determining how wealth is distributed. Resources may be channelled to benefit all in society, paying for improved education and health, but often excluded groups miss out. Oil-rich developing countries, such as Nigeria, Angola and Equatorial Guinea, are examples. They have benefited from oil revenues, but the majority of their populations remain poor, with limited access to healthcare and education.

Both country focus features in this chapter highlighted processes identified with globalization. In the case of the US, prospects are bleak for those who have lost their jobs in American car manufacturers. Conversely, workers in newer factories built by foreign investors, such as the Japanese, have good prospects. In India, jobs and prospects for technology workers are rosy. However, prosperity has not trickled down to the poor, rural sections of society, who have little education and little hope of obtaining jobs in the sectors which are thriving. It is suggested that, by attracting more FDI, India should follow the Chinese example and become more integrated into the global economy. However, it should be remembered that China, too, has a rural hinterland which has seen little of the benefits of FDI. We look first at the economic impacts of globalization.

Economic impacts

In the opening vignette, we highlighted the plight of Delphi workers in southwest Spain. Globalization of production has been a catalyst for industrialization in many parts of the world. In the example of the Delphi factory, the jobs were located in Spain largely to benefit from lower costs than in the US. Soaring American costs, however, continued to plague the company, sending it into bankruptcy. Spanish workers were justifiably fearful that their jobs would go to Morocco, where costs were lower and employee safety protection weak. Globalization has brought foreign enterprises into less industrialized regions of the developed world, but its greatest impact has been in developing countries where industrialization is now taking off.

Development, economic growth and new prosperity have come to the countries which have opened their doors to foreign investors and outsourced production. Advances in IT and computing have benefited countries with the technological capacity to seize opportunities. The outsourcing of services is bringing business to countries where costs are low, while advanced economies are seeing the migration of many activities to cheaper locations. Developing countries are becoming integrated into production networks. Moreover, this expansion has been rapid. Between 1985 and 2001, the number of countries receiving FDI tripled (UN, 2001: 4). By the late 1990s, nearly half of all the world's manufacturing jobs were in developing countries (UNDP, 1998). However, the benefits of this expansion have been unevenly distributed. Inequality remains high, both within countries and between countries (World Bank, 2006). In this section, we examine to what extent the observable trends are due to globalization or other factors.

Effects of globalization can be seen in the wage differentials for highly skilled and less skilled work. Industrialization is boosting wages for factory workers in developing countries which have attracted manufacturing FDI, opening a gap between these workers and rural inhabitants who cannot access the new jobs. In developed economies, highly skilled workers able to seize opportunities in the high-tech sectors have seen wage rises, while less skilled workers, who are in the majority, have seen declining wages. Globally, wages in skill-intensive industries are going up more quickly than in low-skilled industries (Dollar, 2004: 26).

We look now at how these trends impact on inequality within specific countries. From the 1990s, the period when globalization strongly gathered pace, income inequality increased in several major industrialized

Figure 2.10 Share of the top 1% of earners in gross income in selected industrialized countries

Source: ILO (2004) *A Fair Globalization* (Geneva: ILO)

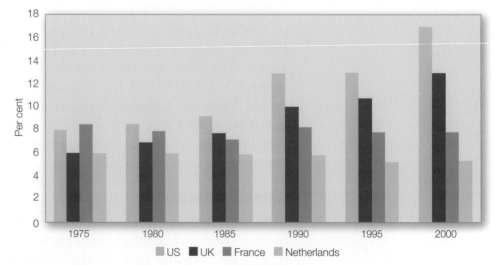

economies, as well as major developing countries such as China (Dollar, 2004). In China, the shift from a national health service to a market approach has exacerbated inequalities, leaving the poorest with limited access (UNDP, 2005). A good test for inequality is to consider the top 1% of a country's earners and see what percentages of the gross income in the country they receive. The share of the top 1% rose in the US from 8% in 1975 to 17% in 2000, as Figure 2.10 shows. It also rose significantly in the UK. Narrowing inequality in France is exceptional, and has been interpreted as a result of the government's strong social welfare policies (Kanbur and Lustig, 1999). Growing inequality is documented in a survey of 73 countries, spanning the last two decades (UNDP, 2005). Of the 73 countries surveyed, 53, representing more than 80% of the world's population, have seen growing inequality, while 9, representing only 4% of the world's population, have seen narrowing inequality.

Governments are in a position to redress inequalities through policies and spending priorities. There is a distinction between equality of opportunities and equality of outcomes (World Bank, 2006). It is the former which most would feel is preferable, implying that investment in education, which enables people to obtain jobs, is preferable to social security payments to the unemployed who lack relevant skills. But governments face difficult choices: they can raise taxes to pay for education and social programmes, but if they impose high rates of taxation, they risk discouraging business investment. A general trend has been the lowering of corporation tax, offering a location advantage to foreign investors. France has reduced inequality through generous social programmes, but social costs fall heavily on businesses, and the government remains concerned that inward FDI flows are only about half the amount of its outward flows (Hollinger, 2005).

Globalization held out the hope that, as economic integration progressed, developing countries would catch up with the developed world. But in the international division of labour, market forces favoured some countries and groups within countries, while adversely affecting others. The income gap between rich and poor countries has increased in the last decade (World Bank, 2006). Adjusting for difference in the cost of living, in 1990, the average American was 38 times richer than the average Tanzanian. By 2005, the American was 61 times richer (UNDP, 2005). Developing countries which have attracted significant FDI and outsourcing have seen increased growth rates and reduced levels of poverty. Even so, to catch up with the high-income countries, India would have to sustain its present growth rates until 2106, which is unlikely (UNDP, 2005). Prospects for the least developed countries, including most of sub-Saharan Africa, are bleak. Economies in sub-Saharan Africa have stagnated, and average incomes were lower in 2005 than in 1990. These countries have suffered from high levels of external debt and dependence on primary commodities, particularly agricultural products (see discussion in Chapter 15). They have also been adversely affected by trade barriers which protect agriculture in industrialized countries.

Inequalities in the world economy reflect many factors at work besides those associated with globalization. These other factors include geography, history (including war and other conflicts), social divisions and the ways in

TO RECAP...

Economic impacts of globalization

Globalized production has led to waves of industrialization, generating manufacturing jobs and related development in regions and countries favoured by FDI and outsourcing. Workers in the new manufacturing regions have benefited, as have skilled workers in technology-intensive sectors. Less fortunate have been low-skilled industrial workers in high-cost countries, as these industries have tended to migrate to low-cost countries.

which political and economic power are exercised in different countries. These are factors which also influence the distribution of wealth *within* countries. It might be argued that national policy-makers should focus their efforts on the situation within their borders and ignore inequalities between countries, which are not really their responsibility. However, in this era of greater inter-connectedness and interdependence, the growing perception of both ordinary citizens and policy-makers is that policies in one country can affect others. For example, the lowering of trade barriers by industrialized countries on agricultural produce from developing countries would benefit poor countries in their efforts to gain shares of global wealth. We will return to these issues in the Chapter 6 on trade and Chapter 15 on global governance.

Globalization's winners and losers
Looking at both globalization of markets and production, to what extent is it inevitable that there are winners and losers from these processes? Are there ways of helping the apparent losers to catch up, without adversely affecting the winners?

PAUSE TO REFLECT

Spillover effects: Opportunities for local firms to benefit from FDI, gaining technological competence which generates new local businesses and technological capacities.

Diffusion of technology

In the previous section, we found that levels of technology within industries and countries are important determinants of participation in the global economy. Developing countries which attract foreign investors hope for spillover effects from technology transfer which will spur their own innovative capacity. Such effects might be links between the investor company and local suppliers, with whom technology might be shared. The local supplier may eventually be able to develop technology independently, thereby helping to contribute to the country's economic development. A risk is that local businesses, unable to compete with the foreign investor, will be crowded out. Joint ventures are also a source of technology transfer, discussed in more detail in Chapter 12. For now, the point worth noting is that gains for the host country depend on several factors. Opportunities to acquire education and relevant skills may be fostered by its government, encouraging the growth in innovative capacity. In addition, entrepreneurial qualities will contribute to the ability of local companies to absorb and exploit technology, as CS2.2, on IBM and Lenovo, illustrates. In a joint venture, the local partner may gain both innovative and managerial expertise in order to launch its own technology and brands.

Also important are government policies in attracting inward investors. Most governments would like to attract the latest technology, in order to ensure the greatest benefit from technology transfer. They are also keen to attract higher value activities such as R&D, for which they require a pool of highly educated scientists and engineers. Singapore has been successful in this respect, attracting the research activities of MNEs (see CF12.1). By contrast, in countries which attract outsourced manufacturing, these low-skilled and lowly paid jobs may offer few spillover effects. Moreover, the outsourcing company offers little in the way of long-term commitment to the location. MNEs in Asia are able to shift production to cheaper locations as they emerge. Southeast Asian economies which industrialized in the

Figure 2.11 Number of internet users per thousand people

Source: UNDP (2007) *Human Development Report 2007–2008* (Basingstoke: Palgrave Macmillan)

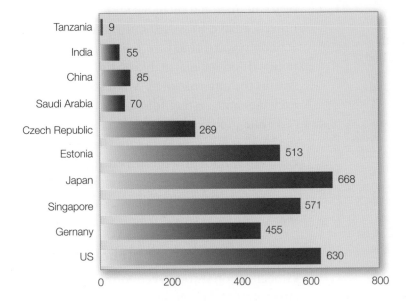

1980s have seen much low-skilled manufacturing shift to China in recent years as their economies could no longer compete with China. As Chinese costs rise, production has shifted to other Asian countries, such as Vietnam (see CF9.1).

Global networks offer opportunities for co-ordinated operations, distribution, marketing and even R&D in different locations. As noted above, however, the benefits of high technology flow to countries with the relevant infrastructure and widespread access to computers and the internet. Those in rich countries benefit the most. As Figure 2.11 shows, there are huge discrepancies in levels of internet access between rich and poor countries. Note also the position of Estonia, a small, middle-income country which has promoted high-tech enterprises and internet use. There are also disparities within countries. India presents a dramatic contrast between the regions where high-tech investment is concentrated and regions where it is non-existent, with the result that India's overall figure for internet use is very low.

Global financial markets

In another strand of globalization, many countries have opened their doors to foreign financial investors. Financial liberalization also involves openness and ease of transactions within national financial systems. These measures, in turn, attract more foreign investors. The revolution in IT and the internet has facilitated instantaneous transactions, at the heart of global financial flows. Paperless transactions and round-the-clock trading in financial markets have become a reality. At the same time, innovations in financial instruments bring new ways to invest, and a new breed of investor and fund manager. These investors can have a rather speculative approach to investing. They seek short-term gains, which often present themselves in emerging markets, such as Southeast Asian countries and Latin America. In the 1990s, emerging markets thus attracted capital flows. However, such flows can be volatile: rapid surges in capital inflows can be followed by swift exits. The effects on host economies can be devastating, as evidenced by the Asian financial crisis of 1998. With hindsight, financial liberalization should have been backed up by sound national financial and banking systems, but many of these countries proved unable to withstand the roller coaster of global markets. Indonesia's economy was ruined by the collapse in its currency in 1998, which led to political and social instability. The crisis also led to considerable soul-searching within the International Monetary Fund, which has oversight of the global exchange rate system (discussed further in Chapter 11).

While global capital markets allow investors new opportunities to internationalize their investments, the volatility of capital mobility brings significant risks, both for the investor and host countries which seek to attract these funds. Financial markets, often highlighted for the extent to which they have become globalized, offer a stark lesson that globalization brings increased risks as well as potential gains.

Culture change and globalization

Globalization through economic integration has implications for the cultural environment, but these are more qualitative and more difficult to assess than economic effects, such as rising incomes. Culture is a very broad heading, which will be examined in detail in Chapter 4. For now, it is useful to distinguish between two of culture's many aspects:

1. Values and a sense of belongingness arise from traditional social groupings to which people belong (such as national cultures).
2. Changes in economic activity associated with industrialization impact on lifestyle and behaviour.

It is suggested by some authors that the second aspect will inevitably predominate, destroying traditional cultures as people's lifestyles change. These processes, when combined with other aspects of globalization, imply a trend towards cultural convergence, as diverse national cultures will melt away (Ohmae, 1995). It is useful to look at the extent to which Ohmae's predictions are turning into reality.

Industrialization and urbanization are changing people's lives in similar ways, no matter where they are. The most significant cultural change is the shift from an agricultural way of life to life in a city, often in a factory environment. Wages may be better and more regular than agricultural work, but factory conditions may be poor, and workers may have to move a long way from their families. These changes took place gradually over more than a century in North America and Europe, whereas they are happening rapidly in today's industrializing countries, largely driven by FDI.

Michael Porter (2000) suggests that there is 'increasing convergence of opinion around the globe on what it takes to be prosperous'. He sees these

plate 2.3 Workers streaming into the factory at the start of the day – a sight becoming familiar around the world, as industrialization spreads.

values centring on a productivity culture. Societies which have deeply rooted traditional values, beliefs and behaviours undergo transformation as notions of productivity, competition and wealth creation take hold. For individuals, this means a shifting to wage labour, moving to cities and leaving kinship ties behind in the rural environment.

Converging economic values and lifestyles, however, are not the whole story, just as economic culture is not synonymous with culture as a whole. Many aspects of culture, including language, symbols, family values and religion, national and local cultures, do still matter to people. What is more, the (real or imagined) fear that they may be threatened by globalization serves to invigorate their followers. These diverse value systems can and do mix with a modern economic culture, as Asian societies show (Tu, 2000).

Environmental impacts

Environmental degradation is an urgent global issue, for businesses, governments and individuals alike. Not all environmental problems in today's world can be blamed on current globalization processes. A major cause of environmental degradation historically has been industrialization, which, for two centuries, has brought economic benefits, but at a cost to the environment. Forests are felled to make way for factory development, as well as for the roads necessary to connect the factory to distribution channels. Factory processes produce pollution of the air, land and water. We now consider factory owners to be responsible for the outcomes of their operations, but this is a relatively new idea. Earlier industrialization paid little heed to environmental outcomes, which has been a major factor contributing to current global problems.

The current wave of industrialization is taking place in the context of globalization. It can be distinguished from earlier eras in several ways. First, its impacts are much more widespread: all countries now aspire to be industrial powers. Moreover, industrial complexes are so large, both in spatial dimensions and outputs, that environmental impacts have more harmful consequences for both ecosystems and humans. Second, it is taking place at breakneck speed by historical standards. That speed is driven by MNE global production strategies above all. Third, scientific knowledge and monitoring are now much more advanced than in previous eras, enabling the effects of pollution, including geographic spread, to be accurately tracked.

Thanks largely to FDI, Guangzhou in China has become a powerhouse of export-oriented manufacturing, producing almost every type of consumer product from refrigerators to shoes for global markets. The landscape has been transformed by vast factories and stark dormitories for migrant workers. These contrast with the luxury condominiums, gated communities and new golf courses for the nouveaux riches, which have also sprung up. All suffer from the pollution of the Pearl River. Streams have turned black and the atmosphere is thick with pollution. One resident says about the way it was before the factories: 'The environment was great. There was no ash in the sky. But the people were poor … Nowadays, at least we have money – not as much as you westerners – but when we've got enough, we'll sort out the environment' (Mallet, 2006). Of course, global environmental problems, already advanced, are not so easy to arrest. Global warming, thinning of the ozone layer, loss of biodiversity, depletion of natural resources: these are all aspects of environmental deterioration associated with industrialization and urbanization (discussed further in Chapter 13).

Government industrial policies and regulations could promote environmental protection, but governments in developing countries are inclined to subordinate environmental concerns to goals of economic development. Attributes of consumer society such as affordable cars, good roads and cheap air travel enable people to be far more mobile than earlier generations. These aspects of globalization, taken for granted in the developed world, are increasingly coming within the reach of middle-class consumers in the industrializing countries. However, the environmental consequences of greenhouse gas emissions and the depletion of energy resources raise the question of whether our lifestyles will need to change to a more sustainable level of consumption if future generations are to enjoy an equivalent quality of life. These issues are addressed in Part 5.

MNEs and social impacts

Liberalization in national economies in the last two decades has allowed MNEs to enter previously closed markets and to expand in other markets. The former category includes China and the former communist countries of Central and Eastern Europe. The latter category includes India and Latin American countries. One has only to look at the plight of one of the few remaining closed economies, North Korea, where famine is still a major problem, to see the perils of a closed economy combined with an authoritarian government.

In 2006, 73 million workers were employed in foreign affiliates of companies based in other countries (UN, 2007a). This is three times the number in 1990, and represents 3% of the global workforce. China, with the largest

> **TO RECAP...**
>
> **Environmental impacts of globalization**
>
> Globalized manufacturing has fostered industrialization and economic development in many developing countries, but environmental concerns have tended to be of low priority. Environmental degradation, transborder pollution and concerns over the depletion of natural resources have become global issues.

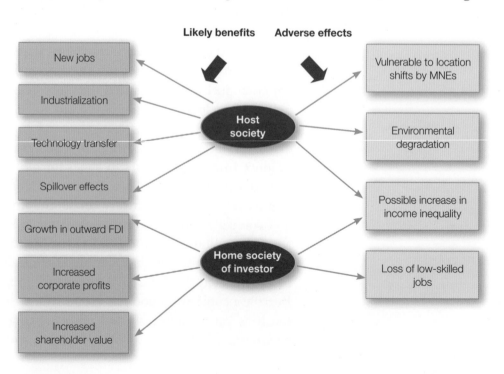

Figure 2.12 Globalized production and social impacts

number, is home to 24 million workers employed by foreign affiliates, up from 5 million in 1991. Still, these workers account for only 3.2% of China's total workforce. In some small countries, such as Ireland and Singapore, the proportion of workers employed by affiliates of foreign MNEs is half the total workforce. Foreign MNEs employed 5 million people in the US in 2006, whereas US MNEs employed 9 million people in foreign locations.

Perspectives on social impacts differ between host societies and home societies. Figure 2.12 summarizes the major social impacts of globalized production. MNEs exist to keep their owners happy. They require a steady flow of profits in order to stay in business and provide a return for investors. Globalization of production and global financial markets have generated handsome profits and paid gratifying dividends to shareholders. As Figure 2.12 shows, these benefits mainly flow to the home society of the MNE. On the other hand, when the MNE shifts production to low-cost locations, its shareholders might applaud, but it faces criticism at home. Outsourced production and FDI have contributed to greater efficiencies, economies of scale and reductions in costs. The competitive environment in most sectors has become intense. As the case studies and strategic crossroads features in this chapter have shown, manufacturing in low-cost environments has become imperative for companies wishing to compete in global markets. Host societies have benefited from the job creation and industrialization, but the consequent urbanization and environmental problems have raised questions about how these processes could be better managed, and who should be responsible for oversight. Growing inequality in society, as Figure 2.12 indicates, is the one impact which is likely to be shared by both the host society and home society of the MNE.

Inequality exists to some extent in all societies, and is often more pronounced in traditional as opposed to modern societies, in which people enjoy greater social mobility. The current concern with inequality has focused specifically on the role played by globalization (Kanbur and Lustig, 1999). In particular, the role of markets can be highlighted. Governments are increasingly aware of the effects of market forces within their borders and beyond. They seek the benefits of economic integration, but they are aware that markets favour some workers, regions and sectors, and not others. The economist and former US Treasury Secretary Larry Summers has said: 'Market forces … have tended to pay everyone more like salespersons – on the basis of what they produce' (Atkinson, 2000). Political debate has ensued, focusing on the social consequences and the extent to which governments should take responsibility. As we saw in Chapter 1, CSR and stakeholder approaches take the view that companies themselves bear responsibility for social impacts. Companies now have growing levels of engagement within the societies in which they operate. These interactions implicitly acknowledge that the company's success and local communities' gains go hand in hand. Shareholders who take a short-term view might be disappointed, but, in the long term, shareholders wish to see sustainable value creation, implying that social aspects of the company's operations matter as much as economic ones.

TO RECAP...

MNEs and social impacts

MNEs are becoming more aware of the social impacts of their operations and investment in both home and host societies. Engagement in host communities can help to bring wider benefits than just economic gains. In home countries, too, MNEs are increasingly taking a stakeholder approach to social impacts, viewing the company as part of local communities.

Conclusions

◻ Globalization has 'shrunk' the world, in that distance is no longer a major obstacle for those wishing to communicate or do business across the globe. Interconnectedness across national boundaries engulfs individuals, business organizations and governments. For businesses, the question of where to locate the production of goods or provision of services, once assumed to be the home country of the company, now offers choice among many potential contenders in different parts of the world. There is also abundant choice in the means for organizing production, including outsourcing, joint ventures and FDI. The MNE has thus been able to build and co-ordinate operations in numerous countries, benefiting from location advantages. Similarly, whereas the home country was once considered the key market in which to sell their products, even young companies are now looking to markets across the globe. For the consumer, there is an unprecedented choice of products to buy, as well as unprecedented access to information, goods, entertainment and services via the internet. Nonetheless, while the means of delivering goods and services have become globalized, national markets remain divergent.

◻ For societies, MNE strategies of shifting production have brought jobs and opportunities for technology transfer to a wide range of countries. The developed world has attracted foreign investors wishing to locate near their largest markets, and now it is the turn of emerging economies. There are differing perspectives on these developments. Low-skilled workers in advanced economies are vulnerable, as MNEs are shifting low-skilled operations to lower cost locations such as China. Developing countries which have attracted significant FDI have seen rising incomes in manufacturing industries, as well as spillover effects of technology transfer. Development is uneven, however, and concerns over global inequalities and environmental degradation are being linked to globalization. Businesses and governments are recognizing that policies and strategies should be broadened beyond solely economic goals, to include qualitative impacts on societies.

MNEs and social impacts
MNEs are responsible to their owners to achieve efficiencies and generate profits. Why should they be concerned about the social outcomes of their globalized operations?

PAUSE TO REFLECT

Review questions

Part A: Grasping the basic concepts and knowledge

1. What are the differing theories of globalization and its impacts?
2. To what extent have we witnessed globalization of markets? Give examples.
3. What is meant by globalization of production?
4. What advantages are offered by outsourcing as an international strategy? Are there drawbacks? Explain.
5. Consider the case for and against offshoring, from the point of view of the company seeking to relocate particular functions, and the country providing the services.
6. Why is the growth in FDI indicative of globalization?
7. Contrast the benefits and drawbacks of greenfield investment and acquisition of an existing business.
8. Outline Vernon's product life cycle theory. What insights does it offer which remain helpful in the current environment?
9. To what extent do the theories of incremental internationalization contribute to our understanding of the internationalization process? Give examples.
10. Explain each of the types of advantage highlighted by Dunning in the eclectic paradigm. In what ways does his theory represent an advance on those of earlier theorists?
11. What are the benefits of inflows and outflows of FDI for a national economy? Give examples of countries with large inflows and those with large outflows.
12. How has the position of developing countries evolved in terms of FDI?
13. Who has benefited from global financial markets, and why? Why are they considered a 'mixed blessing' for emerging markets?
14. Why are the environmental impacts of globalization becoming a global issue, and not just a local one?
15. How do the social impacts of globalization impact on the MNE?

Part B: Critical thinking and discussion

1. Outsourcing production offers cost advantages to the company, especially in mass-produced manufactured products, but often incurs a 'backlash' of criticism. What are the specific objections voiced against this strategy, and what are the arguments in favour?
2. In the debate on globalization, to what extent do you agree with those who argue that national and regional differences remain important determinants?
3. Assess the winners and losers from globalization, including countries, companies and groups in societies.
4. Globalization is associated with increasing inequality. This is one of the arguments often highlighted as a negative impact. Assess the evidence on the basis of current trends, deciding whether this criticism is justified.
5. Should MNEs concern themselves with the adverse social impacts of globalization? If so, what should they be doing in terms of changing their global strategy?

IBM stunned the world in 2004 by announcing that it had sold its personal computer (PC) business to Lenovo, a Chinese company little known outside China. The takeover even attracted the attention of the US Congress, whose Committee on Foreign Investment in the US was needed to clear the deal, as a takeover by a Chinese company in the technology sector could raise questions of national security. For both companies, the takeover represented a dramatic change of strategy. IBM's reputation was built on its hardware expertise, and it was now selling off its entire PC business. Lenovo was an entrepreneurial Chinese PC producer, which had built up a market share of 30% in China, but had little presence elsewhere. It paid $1.75 billion for IBM's PC business, making this the largest ever overseas acquisition by a Chinese company. Overnight, Lenovo became a global company.

IBM, as its name, International Business Machines, reflects, has traditionally viewed its core business as hardware, but changes in direction over the years have led it more into software and services provision. Its mainframe computer business, which had been successful in the 1970s and 80s, waned in the 90s, as PCs surged in popularity. In the 1980s, the company built up a PC business, but one with little of its own technology: it used processors from Intel, software from Microsoft and outsourced manufacturing. In this very competitive market, it was failing to make profits, as Dell and Hewlett-Packard steamed ahead (see Figure 1). The logical move was to sell the PC business, in order to concentrate on higher value activities, mainly for business customers. Its hardware division has focused on the top-end server market, adding features and adapting technology from its mainframe computers. The resurgence of its mainframe computers, newly engineered and designed to run Linux open-source software, is also proving successful.

In services, IBM aims to capture swathes of the outsourcing sector, offering all types of BPO, including logistics support, call centres, human resources and more. This sector, however, has become crowded, as smaller flexible companies with lower costs, such as Wipro from India, compete for work. IBM's management now see the company's strategy as moving towards large BPO projects, its 'business process transformation services'. The company will need to change its culture from a product and

Case study 2.2:
IBM and Lenovo: a tale of globalization

software orientation to one of service provision, which will require greater flexibility and more of a solutions approach than its traditional hardware business. Reflecting its new outsourcing orientation, the company has reorganized and shed 13,000 jobs, mainly in Europe, moving departments to lower cost locations: human resources to Hungary and payroll functions to Romania.

IBM has retained strong ties with its former PC business, through an equity stake and licensing agreements for its patents and designs. It owns 19% of Lenovo's shares, and it allowed Lenovo to use the IBM brand name on its products for five years. One of IBM's greatest successes had been the ThinkPad notebook computer, with its iconic black casing, which continues to be sold by the new owners under the Lenovo brand. Lenovo is increasing the range of products offered under the ThinkPad brand, to cater for small and medium-sized businesses. For Lenovo, the IBM brand was a step towards building its own global brand. It can point to Samsung in South Korea, an Asian company which has gained a reputation for innovative products backed by a strong brand. However, Lenovo dropped the IBM brand name two years ahead of schedule due to customers' acceptance and recognition of the Lenovo and Think trademark.

Lenovo's strength has been in producing computers for the Chinese market. Founded only in 1984, the company's success can be mainly attributed to its entrepreneurial founder and now chairman, Yang Yuanqing, who, as part of the deal, had to step down as CEO, to make way for the new CEO, who was the former head of IBM's PC division. The new head of human resources has also come over from IBM.

Lenovo has ambitions to challenge Dell and Hewlett-Packard, particularly on price and products designed for emerging markets. It can put to good use its experience in designing low-cost machines for the Chinese market. Its expertise in procuring low-cost components will give it an advantage, especially important as procurement costs account for 70–80% of total revenues in this sector. It can use its new economies of scale to further lower procurement costs. It also aims to target small business users in developed economies, which had never been a priority for IBM.

Can Lenovo's performance match its global ambitions? In the first two years after the takeover, it introduced its own branded products outside China, and increased its revenues fourfold. It now has significant sales outside China (see Figure 2). However,

Figure 1 Market share of worldwide PC shipments

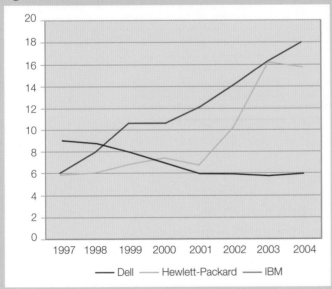

Source: Financial Times, 26 August 2005

Figure 2 Lenovo turnover ($14,500 millions), 2007

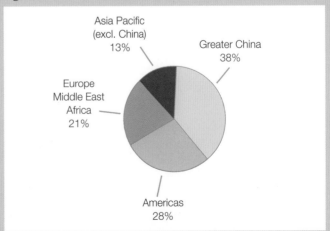

Source: Lenovo, Financial information, www.lenovo.com

the huge organizational and logistical changes have taken their toll, net profits in 2005 falling to just $22 million, a fifth of the previous year's. Doubts revolve mainly around the fact that a relatively young company with no experience outside its domestic market has acquired a global company three times its size. There are the cultural differences between the acquired business, a rather bureaucratic division of a large American MNE, and the new entrepreneurial Chinese owners, whose management team before the takeover had an average age of 28. The chief financial officer says: 'It's not a difference between Chinese and Americans, but really between an entrepreneur company and a well-established multinational company' (Dickie, 30 September 2005).

For Lenovo, complexities of supply chains, products and technology have been difficult to manage, especially as the new headquarters in New York and the Chinese workforce are 12 time zones apart. For other Chinese companies eyeing international expansion, the success of Lenovo would be an example to follow. Lenovo's failure would send a strong signal that, despite energy and ambition, they might not yet have the management skills to take on leading MNEs in established markets. By 2007, the company had made progress towards restructuring the business, and felt confident to launch new products aimed at the global consumer PC market, taking on rivals Dell, Hewlett-Packard and Acer (of Taiwan). New IdeaPad notebooks will be launched in the US, France, China, India, Russia and other markets.

Questions

1   Critically assess the changes in strategy that have taken place at IBM, both before and after the sale of the PC business.
2   What aspects of globalization are highlighted in the case study?
3   Analyse the acquisition of IBM's PC business by Lenovo in terms of ownership-specific advantages and location-specific advantages.
4   Assess Lenovo's prospects in competition with established rivals.

Sources: London, S., 'Is Big Blue fading again?', *Financial Times*, 9 May 2005; Dickie, M. and Lau, J., 'IBM brand loyalty holds key for Lenovo', *Financial Times*, 9 December 2004; London, S., 'A global power made in China', *Financial Times*, 9 November 2005; London, S., 'Your rules and my processes', *Financial Times*, 10 November 2005; Morrison, S. and Roberts, D., 'Error message: slowing growth at Dell', *Financial Times*, 26 August 2005; Dickie, M., 'Lenovo targets small business', *Financial Times*, 30 September 2005; Waters, R., 'IBM repackages its brain power', *Financial Times*, 11 July 2006; Taylor, P., 'Lenovo shifts strategy with move into consumer PC sector', *Financial Times*, 3 January 2008.

WEB CHECK

Lenovo's website is www.lenovo.com. Click on investor relations. IBM's website is www.ibm.com/investor.

Further research

Journal articles

Dunning, J. and Pitelis, C. (2007) 'Stephen Hymer's contribution to international business scholarship: an assessment and extension', *Journal of International Business Studies*, **39**(1): 167–76.

Books

Bhagwati, J. (2004) *In Defense of Globalization*, New York: OUP.
Dunning, J. (1988) *Explaining International Production*, London: Unwin.

Dunning, J. and Mucchielli, J.-L. (eds) (2002) *Multinational Firms: The Global-Local Dilemma*, London: Routledge.
Held, D. and McGrew, A. (2007) *Globalization/Anti-Globalization*, 2nd edn, Cambridge: Polity Press.
Scholte, J. (2005) *Globalization: A Critical Introduction*, 2nd edn, Basingstoke: Palgrave Macmillan.
Stiglitz, J. (2002) *Globalization and Its Discontents*, London: Allen Lane.

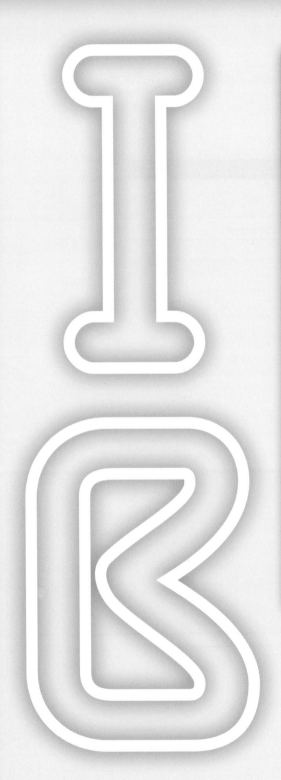

The three chapters which make up Part 2 focus on different dimensions of the business environment. Chapter 3 concerns the economic environment, with particular focus on national economies. The key concepts used by economists to describe and compare economies are introduced, showing their implications for business. Differing models of national economic system are contrasted, highlighting varieties of capitalist development in developed, developing and transition economies. Evolving regional integration is examined in the context of continuing diversity in economic systems. These differences are pursued in Chapter 4, on the cultural environment. Here, facets of culture, including values, language and religion, are placed in the context of differing national cultures, drawing on key culture theories. With this foundation, the chapter moves on to discuss organizational culture and its implications for international business. For firms in the international arena, understanding and engaging with business partners and consumers in multiple cultures is becoming core to business success. Many of the key cultural dimensions, such as individualism and collectivism, translate into political and legal systems, which are the subject of Chapter 5. In this chapter, characteristics of political systems are identified, together with the broader political culture in diverse national environments. While transitions to democracy and moves towards the rule of law are proceeding in many countries, instability abounds, in both political and legal spheres, creating political and legal risks for business. Furthermore, these risks are often most acute in developing and transition economies, which offer some of the greatest potential for enterprise growth. A trend is the growing legal and political co-operation at international level, which is bringing a further environmental factor into play for international business.

chapter 3
THE ECONOMIC ENVIRONMENT

learning objectives

▷ To become familiar with concepts and tools used by economists for comparing national economies
▷ To identify the differences between divergent economic systems, including their market openness, social perspectives and the role of the state in economic life
▷ To assess the prospects and opportunities of the world's developing and transitional economies
▷ To gain an overview of regional integration in the global economy
▷ To highlight the challenges faced by the least developed economies

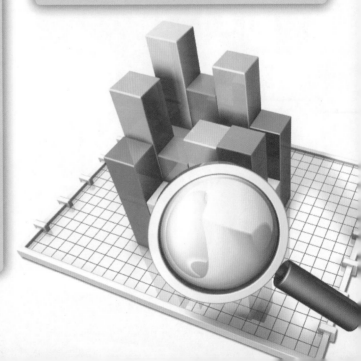

Introduction

Hungary's prime minister, Ferenc Gyuresany, enjoyed victory in elections in 2006, but his happiness was short-lived. He was forced to admit to a party meeting that, in order to win votes, he had lied to the electorate 'morning, noon and night' about the public finances (Wagstyl, 2007). He had claimed they were sound when in fact there was a massive deficit due to unchecked public spending. Protests, riots and demonstrations erupted outside Parliament, plunging the country into the worst upheaval since the uprisings against communism. The public's disillusionment contrasted sharply with the euphoria which greeted EU admission in 2004. To deal with mounting deficits, Gyuresany was compelled to bring in austerity measures, but these were met with more hostility. Doctors, pensioners and students all joined in protests, objecting to new fees and reduced benefits. Meanwhile, opposition leaders pressed for a referendum aimed at voting the prime minister out of office. The example of Hungary highlights two influential factors in the economic environment, which form themes for this chapter. They are, first, the role of government in economic policy; and second, the importance of the social and political context of economic activities.

plate 3.1 Government economic policies impact on consumers' spending decisions and also on perceptions of their country's political leaders.

National economies are changing along with changes in the global economy, discussed in the last chapter. Chief among them is globalization, which is associated with several interrelated processes. Liberalization is opening more and more economies to outside investors, while the spread of market economies is bringing competition and private enterprise to economies formerly closed or semi-closed. Nonetheless, the single market predicted by hyperglobalization theorists is still a long way off. National economies are showing considerable exuberance in embracing markets, both at home and outside their borders. At the same time, interdependence, another aspect of globalization, is linking national economies in webs of relations with other countries. Chief among these trends has been regional integration, particularly within Europe, although national economic diversity remains a reality.

The chapter begins with the basic concepts used by economists to measure and compare national economies. The role of government policy is highlighted, and developed further in the section on public finances. We then turn to the underlying characteristics of different types of economic system: the planned economy, the liberal market model, the social market model and Asian economic models. For international business, the different types of economy create quite different environments. We then turn to the transition and developing economies, which are of growing interest to MNEs in terms of global strategy, given their potential for global production and new markets. Next, regional integration is examined in respect of its impact on national economies and contribution to globalization. Finally, the chapter focuses on the plight of the poorest developing countries and their prospects of economic growth.

For information on Hungary's economy and society, see the OECD's website at www.oecd.org, and click on *Hungary* in the country list.

WEB CHECK

Comparing national economies as a whole

The national economic environment forms the backdrop of most business activity, whether local, national or international. A nation, rather like a household, can be rich or poor, growing in prosperity or lagging behind. National economies are analysed both in overall terms – macroeconomics – and at the level of individual enterprises – microeconomics. Utilizing the concepts and tools of both disciplines, economists can gain a detailed picture of economic activity at all levels. Numerous indicators give a picture of the relative health of an economy and how it compares with others. These data aid policy-makers and businesses alike (see Huo and McKinley, 1992). These comparisons show global trends and divergences. The key economic indicators are highlighted in this section.

Macroeconomics: Study of whole economic systems, in particular, national economies.

Microeconomics: Study of economic activity at the level of individuals and enterprises.

Size and income comparisons

The national income of an economy may be measured as gross national income (GNI), which is the total income from all the final products and services produced within its borders, including the income which its residents earn from employment and investments abroad. It is usually calculated on an annual basis. This is the broadest measure of a national economy, and is an indicator used by international bodies, such as the World Bank and IMF, to assess national prosperity. GNI includes gross domestic product (GDP), which is the value of total economic activity within an economy, including both domestic and foreign producers.

Gross national income (GNI): Total income from all final products and services produced within a country; includes foreign income earned by the country's residents.

Gross domestic product (GDP): Value of the total economic activity within an economy, including domestic and foreign producers.

GNI and GDP can be presented as total sums for an entire economy. The world's largest economies appear in Figure 3.1. The US is by far the biggest economy. Given China's fast rate of growth, it is overtaking France and the UK, which both have slower growth rates.

GNI and GDP can also be calculated taking population into account, which gives us GNI or GDP per capita, or per head. The per capita figure is a better indication of the nation's economic prosperity for comparative purposes. GNI per capita is the gross national income divided by the coun-

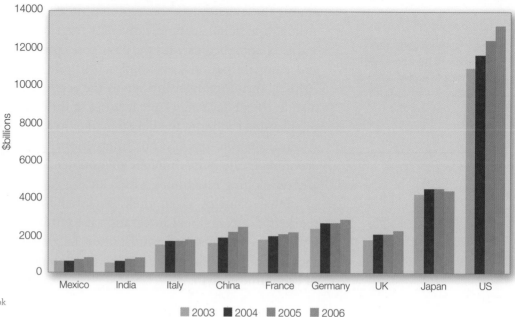

Figure 3.1 GDP of selected countries, 2003–06

Source: IMF (2006) IMF Economic Outlook database, www.imf.org

try's population at mid-year. For these purposes, a country's population is defined as all residents within its borders, regardless of whether they are citizens. Local currencies are converted into US dollars. As an example, China and France in 2004 had a similar GNI, both about $1,400 billion. France, with a population of 60 million, had a GNI per capita of $22,400, while China, with a population of 1.2 billion, had a GNI per capita of $1,000 (World Bank, 2004). A comparison of the GDP of the two countries showed a similar divergence: France had a GDP per capita of $29,410, while China's was $1,100. These comparisons, however, can be misleading, as the equivalent of $1,000 in China will purchase far more of the necessities of life than the same sum in France. Hence, adjustments to achieve purchasing power parity (PPP) are made to take account of the cost of living in different countries. The adjustments for PPP are sometimes referred to as 'real' income.

GDP per capita adjusted for PPP is often used for country comparisons, using the US as the benchmark. Looking at the two examples again, we now find that France had a GDP per capita of $27,600. The fact that the PPP adjustment has produced a somewhat lower figure indicates that the cost of living in France is higher than in the US. Chinese GDP (at PPP) per capita rose to $5,000, indicating that the cost of living in China is much lower than in the US. These adjusted figures give a more accurate picture of the disparity between the two countries. China's GDP as a whole, if calculated according to PPP, would make it the world's second largest economy.

Countries may be classified as high income, middle income or low income. As Table 3.1 shows, the high-income countries are mainly the industrialized economies. They represent 81% of global GDP (World Bank, 2004). The largest category, middle-income countries, includes those which are developing and industrializing. Many of these countries, such as Nigeria and Venezuela, are rich in natural resources, and many have seen growth in FDI. Low-income countries, concentrated in Africa and South Asia, are mainly agricultural, although India presents a mixed picture. Despite high-tech industries and industrialization in some areas, the country is overwhelmingly rural (see CF2.2).

Table 3.1 Selected high-, middle- and low-income countries

High income (GNI per capita of $10,066 or more)	Middle income (GNI per capita of $826–10,065)	Low income (GNI per capita of $825 or less)
Australia, Bahrain, Denmark, France, Germany, Italy, Japan, S. Korea, New Zealand, Norway, Slovenia, Spain, Sweden, Switzerland, United Arab Emirates, UK, US – 39 countries in total	Argentina, Belarus, Bolivia, Brazil, Bulgaria, Chile, China, Croatia, Czech Republic, Egypt, Estonia, Indonesia, Iran, Jordan, Kazakhstan, Malaysia, Mexico, Poland, Russian Federation, Saudi Arabia, Thailand, Venezuela – 91 countries in total	Afghanistan, Angola, Bangladesh, Cambodia, Congo, Ethiopia, Ghana, India, Kenya, N. Korea, Nigeria, Pakistan, Somalia, Sudan, Tanzania, Uganda, Vietnam, Zambia – 61 countries in total

Source: UNDP (2006) *Human Development Report 2006* (Basingstoke: Palgrave Macmillan).

Levels of economic development

The middle- and low-income groups, which comprise most of the world's countries, represent different types of economic activity as well as varying degrees of wealth and prosperity. Many factors are involved, including geography, natural resources and sociocultural environment. Every economy can be profiled according to three types of economic activity, or sectors:

- Primary, which includes agriculture, mining and fishing
- Secondary, which is manufacturing and industrial production
- Tertiary, which consists of services such as IT.

Economic development: Process of change in economic activities and organizations of a country.

When we speak of a country's economic development, we refer to its processes of change in economic activities and organizations, which are bringing about wealth creation and prosperity. The traditional pattern of economic development follows the three sectors in the order listed: from a mainly agricultural to an industrial society, and finally shifting to services. The UN classifies 24 countries as high-income, developed economies (see Table 3.2). For these countries, manufacturing industries have given way to services as sources of income. Developing countries form the largest group in the UN's classification, 137 countries. In the main, these countries are following the traditional pattern of economic development, embarking on industrialization from a mainly agricultural base. There are some variations, however. Countries with significant natural resources, including oil and gas reserves, focus on exploiting these resources, often with the aid of FDI, rather than building manufacturing capacity. Some developing countries are aiming to move directly from agriculture to service-based economies. An example is Jordan, which is a middle-income, developing country. Indeed, the service sector is growing in most economies, developed and developing (World Bank, 2004).

The UN uses a separate category for Central and Eastern Europe and the Commonwealth of Independent States (CIS). These countries are 'transition' economies, making the transition from a communist planned economy to a market-based economy. Many had industrial infrastructure, although in need of modernization. Hence they fall somewhere between the high-income industrialized countries and the developing economies. They are mainly in the middle-income group of countries in Table 3.1. Finally, there are 50 countries which are classified as the least developed countries. These countries are mainly agricultural and roughly coincide with the low-income countries in Table 3.1. There are some apparent anomalies, however. Kenya, India and Nigeria are developing countries, but remain in the low-income group in Table 3.1. In these countries, for various reasons, development has not as yet brought the rise in living standards which they had hoped for. Nigeria, despite its oil wealth, has suffered from social and ethnic divisions and political instability. Kenya, which has made progress in economic development, has suffered setbacks from ethnic strife which erupted following disputed elections in December 2007. India is now enjoying buoyant economic growth, but poverty remains a problem.

Table 3.2 Selected developed, transition, developing and least developed countries

Developed	**Australia, Belgium, France, Germany, Greece, Ireland, Italy, Japan, S. Korea, New Zealand, Norway, Spain Sweden, UK, US**
Transition (Central and Eastern Europe and CIS)	Albania, Bulgaria, Croatia, Czech Republic, Estonia, Hungary, Kazakhstan, Latvia, Lithuania, Poland, Romania, Russian Federation, Slovakia, Slovenia, Ukraine
Developing countries	Angola, Argentina, Bangladesh, Bolivia, Botswana, Brazil, Cambodia, Cameroon, Chad, Chile, China, Cuba, Ecuador, Ghana, India, Indonesia, Iran, Jordan, Kenya, N. Korea, S. Korea, Kuwait, Malaysia, Mali, Mexico, Nigeria, Pakistan, Turkey, Uganda, United Arab Emirates, Venezuela, Vietnam
Least developed countries	Afghanistan, Bangladesh, Burkina Faso, Cambodia, Chad, Ethiopia, Haiti, Malawi, Mali, Mauritania, Senegal, Somalia, Sudan, Tanzania, Togo, Uganda, Zambia

Source: UNDP (2006) *Human Development Report 2006* (Basingstoke: Palgrave Macmillan)

Differing rates of growth

Percentage growth in GDP or GNI from year to year is a measure of growth in the economy. Economic growth promotes prosperity, providing jobs for growing populations and fuelling consumer demand. Every economy has ups and downs associated with the business cycle, which is the movement of economies over a period of time. The country may enjoy economic boom, with high levels of production satisfying high levels of demand at home and abroad. When demand eventually falters, growth slows. Diversified economies are more able to weather downturn in demand. The economy may slow, even stagnate, growing at 1% or less. A sharp slowdown in growth is a recession, and, in extreme cases, it may slump into depression, as in the Great Depression of 1929. The effects of cyclical ups and downs can be softened through monetary policy tools such as raising or lowering interest rates. Raising interest rates increases the cost of borrowing, tending to dampen lending. This move is helpful if the economy is growing more rapidly than is sustainable. Lowering interest rates eases lending, giving a boost to a stagnating economy.

High rates of growth, which could be 10% or more, occur during periods of rapid industrialization, or in the wake of a discovery of rich natural

Economic growth: An economy's increase in total income over time, usually shown as an annual percentage change.

resources. In the last decade, Southeast Asia has enjoyed rapid growth, but Asian countries vary in their stages of development. Japan enjoyed high growth rates during its post-war industrialization, but its economy stumbled in the 1990s, and growth is rising again in the new millennium (see CF1.1). Other Southeast Asian economies, such as South Korea and Taiwan, saw similar growth and slowdown (see SX3.1). They have now been overtaken by China's rapid growth, which started to accelerate with the opening up of the economy to market forces in 1980. Since then, growth has been in the 9–10% range (see Figure 3.2). The oil-rich former communist state of Azerbaijan enjoyed 25% growth in its economy in 2006, thanks mainly to FDI from major oil companies.

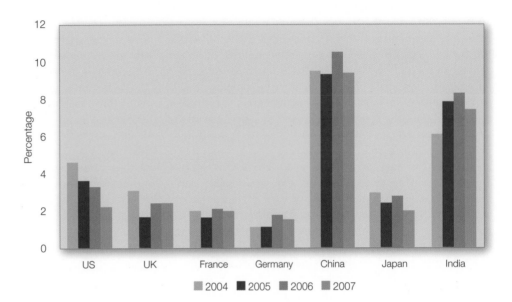

Figure 3.2 Economic growth in selected countries

Source: The Economist Economic Indicators (2007), www.economist.com/indicators

Sustainable growth is needed to provide future jobs and prosperity, but rapid growth is seldom sustainable in the long term. Growth slowed in most countries in 2007, as Figure 3.2 highlights. At present, there is concern that the Chinese economy is 'overheating'. Chinese demand has led to price rises in raw materials and energy in world markets. A dramatic slowdown in the Chinese economy would have global consequences. MNEs worldwide now look to China for both low-cost production and growing consumer demand, as illustrated in CS3.2 on Wal-Mart. China's high levels of energy consumption and growing levels of pollution could indicate that its current level of growth is not sustainable.

Growth tends to slow as countries become industrialized and per capita GDP rises. A slowing of growth in the developed countries in 2007 has had impacts in other countries, as rich countries are major importers of products globally. The post-communist transition economies of Central and Eastern Europe (discussed later in this chapter) are now enjoying growth rates of around 4%, thanks in part to their location advantages for FDI.

TO RECAP...

Economic growth

National economies need to grow to create jobs and generate wealth. High growth rates tend to occur in economies whose economic development is 'taking off', for example through rapid industrialization. Growth rates tend to slow as economies mature, but maintaining momentum is important to create jobs and remain competitive.

STRATEGIC CROSSROADS

3.1

The Samsung empire untamed – for now

Consumers across the world tend to think of Samsung as synonymous with mobile phones and flat-screen televisions. It is the world's largest computer chip and flat-screen producer. Yet in its home country of South Korea, Samsung represents a highly diversified conglomerate, its businesses spanning the construction industry, retailing, insurance, hotels and credit cards, in addition to the famous Samsung Electronics. It even runs a Disneyland-style theme park called Everland, which became the centre of a real-life corruption scandal. Although Samsung's success may be a source of pride to Koreans, they have rather a love–hate relationship with the company. This is partly because it has tentacles in so many aspects of consumer life. In addition, the company represents the strength of the family-dominated chaebol, which harks back to South Korea's period of rapid economic development.

Gone are the days when the country enjoyed 8% annual growth rates. The current rate of growth is about 4.6%. Following the Asian financial crisis of 1998, foreign investors acquired ailing businesses cheaply, destroying much of the power of the chaebols. The state introduced market reforms, opening up the country, once known as the 'hermit kingdom'. Samsung, which survived the financial crisis better than other chaebols, is still family controlled. Its ownership structure is dominated by the Lee family through cross-shareholdings in affiliated companies. Lee Kun-hee, the group chairman, known as the 'emperor', has attempted to secure the succession of his son, Lee Jae-yong, the largest shareholder in Samsung Everland, which is the key Samsung holding company. Lee Kun-hee had himself inherited the group from his own father. Mr Lee launched a public relations campaign to make Samsung a 'more loved company', partly in an effort to smooth succession, but this effort seemed to backfire when government regulators began pursuing financial irregularities.

The South Korean government has attempted to dilute the power of the chaebol through limiting cross-investment. Two Everland executives were prosecuted and found guilty of aiding the chairman in the illegal transfer of shares to members of his family. A further scandal erupted in 2008, when it was alleged that the company had amassed billions of dollars in secret funds used to bribe government officials, known as the slush funds scandal. The secret funds also seemed to have been channelled into the purchase of some $64 million-worth of modern art, including Roy Lichtenstein's work, *Happy Tears*, bought by a mystery buyer at an auction for over $7 million in 2002. The scandal has shaken the art market in South Korea, as well as deepening suspicion about the activities of the Lee family.

South Korea has transformed itself from an agrarian economy to the world's eleventh largest economy in the space of a single generation, arguably creating a disjointedness between society and the economy, of which Samsung's turmoil is an example. An authority on corporate governance has said: 'The deep-rooted desire for inheritance is making Samsung do many things that hurt its reputation as a global business group' (Fifield and Song, 2005). Samsung Group, which accounts for about 15% of the South Korean economy, has been credited with playing a crucial role in the country's economic development, a model 'tiger' economy. However, traditional loyalties and market reforms can clash. The strength of the founding family in Samsung is not easily tamed, but, on the other hand, they are not shedding 'happy tears'.

Questions
- ◆ Why is Samsung the target of criticism from both public opinion and regulators in South Korea?
- ◆ How does Samsung exemplify the disjointedness between society and the economy?

Sources: Fifield, A. and Song Jung-A, 'Saga of the son tarnishes Samsung reputation', *Financial Times*, 12 October 2005; Song Jung-A, 'Samsung executives sentenced', *Financial Times*, 5 October 2005; Fifield, A., 'Citizens turn restless in the "republic of Samsung"', *Financial Times*, 10 June 2005; Fifield, A., 'S Korea tries to reassure foreign investors', *Financial Times*, 7 April 2006; Song Jung-A, 'Court upholds convictions of Samsung pair', *Financial Times*, 20 May 2007; Song Jung-A, 'S Korea scandal adds to pop art cachet', *Financial Times*, 9 February 2008.

WEB CHECK

For corporate information on Samsung, go to www.samsung.com/us.

Beyond the boom

Expectations run high in today's developing economies, as modern consumer lifestyles beckon. When criticized for breakneck expansion by those in the developed world, they are likely to accuse critics of wishing to 'pull up the ladder'. What are the risks faced by today's developing economies in terms of their own sustained growth, and why is there concern in other countries?

PAUSE TO REFLECT

Inflation: a national and global phenomenon

Inflation: The persistent rise in the general level of money prices.

Rapid economic growth is often associated with inflation, which is the 'persistent rise in the general level of money prices' in an economy (McAleese, 2001: 294). Inflation which spirals out of control is known as 'hyperinflation', and is a cause of financial crisis. Latin American countries have been prone to hyperinflation. Deflation is the persistent fall in prices, which is uncommon. Japan in the 1990s is an example of deflation, associated with economic stagnation. The rate of inflation is expressed as a percentage rise or fall in prices with reference to a particular point in time. Every country has a consumer price index (CPI), representing prices of key goods and services purchased by the average consumer. The movement of the rate of inflation is based on the rises and falls in this index.

Prices paid by consumers for products and services, and by businesses for raw materials and energy, are sensitive issues in the national economy. The general rule is that inflation rises if demand is tending to exceed potential supply. Economists refer to the gap between the actual level of economic activity and the potential level that it can sustain as the 'output gap'. If the economy is operating at the limits of its sustainable capacity, inflation tends to occur, whereas if output is below potential, there is scope for non-inflationary growth. However, estimating potential in an economy is somewhat inexact, and has become more problematic as the world's economies have become more integrated. Recent years have seen several trends across the world's major economies. These include falling prices of imported manufactured goods from Asia, from appliances to clothes and shoes. Also, because of new technology and cheaper production, audio-visual equipment has fallen in price, costing less than a quarter in 2004 of what it cost in 1987. Low-cost airlines have slashed the cost of air travel. However, rising oil prices have impacted on transport costs. Rising demand is also sending up prices of minerals and metals, as seen in CS3.1 on Heineken. Inflation is also occurring in global food prices (see Chapter 15). Inflation is therefore becoming a global, as well as national, issue.

The 1970s was the last period when inflation was a serious problem in the developed world, largely because of oil price shocks. Inflation reached 25% in European countries in 1975. While no country is immune from global markets, the extent of their impact depends partly on national factors, such as dependence on imports that are rising in price; the gains from rising prices received for exports; and the extent to which the economy is integrated into the global economy.

Comparing inflation from country to country is difficult, as national consumer indexes differ in what they take into account. Owner-occupier housing is not taken into account in the eurozone, whereas it is in the US. The US index looks at 'core inflation', which leaves out energy and food, while the European CPI includes both. Figure 3.3 provides a rough comparison among key economies. It indicates that inflation in China is relatively high, raising the possibility that prices of manufactured exports will be affected. This could lead to inflation in the US, its biggest customer, but before that happens, producers will see their profit margins squeezed. Within the eurozone, the target inflation figure set by the European Central Bank

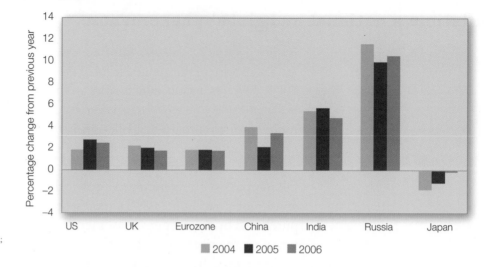

Figure 3.3 CPI inflation

Sources: Financial Times, 8, 30 November 2004;
30 November 2005; 24 May 2006

The home page of the European Central Bank (ECB) is www.ecb.int. A range of financial information is available on this site.

TO RECAP...

Inflationary pressures

Inflation reflects both national and global factors. As economies become more integrated, inflationary pressures are felt globally. Rising commodity and fuel prices have been caused largely by increased demand from the rapidly developing countries such as China. Falling prices of manufactured products, thanks to shifts to low-cost locations, are starting to reverse, as the higher costs of production and higher wages in developing countries impact on prices.

(ECB) is 2% or under. Annual inflation across the 15 countries of the eurozone seemed by edging above this target in 2007. Inflation in the US would be higher if energy and food were included, which is what some economists recommend (Cecchetti, 2006). Here, rising property prices were accompanied by high levels of personal borrowing: consumers have gone on shopping sprees, confident in the belief that their houses were increasing in value. A fall in property values in 2007, combined with rising debt among householders, sent shockwaves through the American economy.

Inflationary pressures abound in the global economy, impacting on national economies in different ways. Rising energy and metal prices reflect rampant demand in developing countries, especially China, and also instability in some of the resource-rich regions. Food price inflation has taken place globally, especially due to rising demand from the growing middle classes in the emerging economies such as China and India (see Chapter 15 for a further discussion). Falling prices of manufactured products, thanks to shifts to low-cost locations, are starting to reverse, as the higher costs of production and higher wages in developing countries impact on prices. As most countries import food, fuel and manufactured goods, to a greater or lesser extent, many governments are concerned about the impacts of inflation on their national economies.

Businesses, consumers and governments wish to see price stability in the economy, which is generally interpreted as being consistent with inflation in the 0–2% range. In every country, central policy-makers, usually in its central bank, have various tools at their disposal to control inflation. Chief among these is altering interest rates up or down. Raising interest rates indirectly reduces demand. It can also attract outside financial investors looking for attractive interest rates. However, raising interest rates could well dampen growth in the economy, and, hence, policy-makers face a delicate balancing act. Within the eurozone, the ECB sets an interest rate applicable across the 15 countries. However, as Figure 3.2 showed, growth has been weak in both France and Germany. The ECB raised interest rates three times in 2006, but for member states with weak growth, these rises may not be appreciated. The US Federal Reserve, which governs interest rates in the US, also raised interest rates slightly in 2006, but reduced them in 2007, as the economy seemed to be taking a downturn.

Focus on specific aspects of national economies

In this section, we look at aspects of the national economy which provide a fuller picture of economic activity. They are: employment and productivity of the workforce; balance of payments, which reflects trade with other countries; and inequality, which indicates to what extent economic benefits are reaching all in society.

Employment and productivity

The proportion of people in work and the hours they work can provide insight into the business environment in a country. The proportion of the population in work is high in the US, at over 50%, while in the EU it is around 43%. This discrepancy, in part, reflects demographic trends. Population growth in Europe is slow, only 0.4% per annum, while the US population is growing at 1.2%. In Europe, the proportion of the population of working age is dwindling, and the proportion of pensioners is rising, as life expectancy improves. Attractive early retirement schemes have been common in Europe, but, as longevity increases and health costs rise, governments are now shifting to policies which encourage people to work longer. Workers in the US work longer hours than their European counterparts, over 1,800 hours a year, compared to 1,500 in Europe. However, working long hours does not make a nation's workers more productive than those with shorter hours. Labour productivity can be measured by taking an index of hours worked per person, divided into an index of output. Comparisons can thus be made between countries. Looking at Figure 3.4, we find that labour productivity has risen in the US and Germany, but declined in the UK, Japan and France.

If a country's growth in labour productivity is disappointingly low, it could be because technology is not up to date. Key to improving labour productivity is the use of computers and effective management of staff. Political leaders have cause to be concerned if a productivity gap emerges between their country and competitors. Raising labour productivity is a factor in raising economic growth, as shown in Figure 3.5. Attracting FDI is a means

Labour productivity: Calculation which divides output by the hours worked per person.

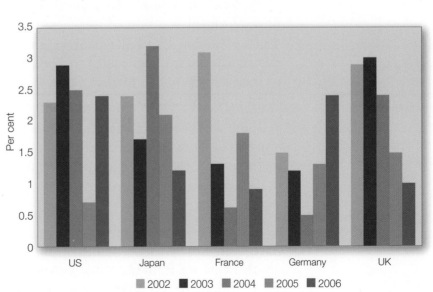

Figure 3.4 Annual growth in GDP per hour worked

Source: OECD (2008) Databases at SourceOECD, oecd.org

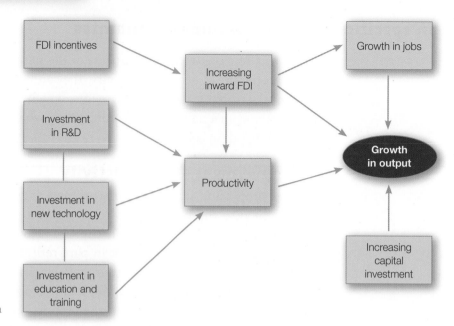

Figure 3.5 Productivity and growth

of achieving both aims, but persuading foreign companies to invest can be difficult if the pool of skilled workers is small. Hence, improving education and skills levels will attract investors, as well as leading to improvements in productivity across the board.

Employment policies and costs of labour are other important factors for businesses. In France, some relaxation of the 35-hour maximum working week has been introduced. The government attempted to introduce more flexible contracts to encourage the employment of younger workers, but scrapped the idea following violent street protests. Germany, known for high labour costs and inflexible labour laws, has seen initiatives taken by companies such as Volkswagen (featured in CS1.2) and Siemens. They have restructured workforces, frozen wages and brought in longer hours. In 2004, Siemens presented their staff in North Rhine, Westphalia, with a stark choice: increase working hours from 35 to 40 hours per week with no extra pay, or half the jobs would shift to Hungary. The resultant deal with the trade unions became an example for other large German companies to follow (Atkins and Williamson, 2004).

Tackling unemployment is another limb of government policy. Rising unemployment is a sign of weakness in the economy and can undermine social cohesion. Unemployment as an economic phenomenon refers to people who are able and willing to work, but cannot find a job. It is expressed as a percentage of the total workforce. The ILO's definition of unemployment covers two groups:

- Those without a job, but who have actively sought work in the last four weeks and can start work in the next two weeks
- Those who are out of work, but have found a job and will be starting it in the next two weeks.

Structural unemployment: Loss in jobs due to changes in technology or shifting of operations to another location.

Unemployment can have many causes. Structural unemployment occurs when changes in technology result in a loss of jobs. It also occurs where jobs have been lost when an industry shifts operations to another region or another country. Both these phenomena have occurred in American manufacturing jobs. American rates of growth and productivity have been impressive, nonetheless, and unemployment has been relatively low overall. However, as CF2.1 on the US indicated, particular regions have suffered from manufacturing decline, and manufacturing wages have not risen in line with output and profits.

Youth unemployment is especially worrying, as it may indicate too little investment in job-creating industries and weak skills training. As Figure 3.6 shows, France, Italy and in particular Poland have high levels of youth unem-

Figure 3.6 Unemployment in selected countries, 2006

Source: UNDP (2007) *Human Development Report 2007–2008* (Basingstoke: Palgrave Macmillan)

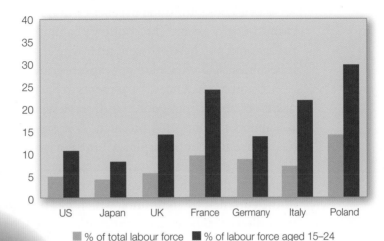

■ % of total labour force   ■ % of labour force aged 15–24

ployment. Poland has both the highest unemployment in the EU and the highest youth unemployment, at 29.6%. It is not surprising that Poles were the largest group from the 10 new EU member states in 2004 to seek work abroad, when youth unemployment was over 40%. Their departure leaves worrying gaps for companies in Poland seeking qualified workers (Cienski, 2006) (see SX3.2). In many countries, regional disparities in unemployment are a concern for policy-makers. If a whole industry collapses and nothing takes it place, long-term unemployment results. There is also the phenomenon of underemployment, whereby people capable of full-time substantial jobs are doing casual and low-skilled work, with little job satisfaction or prospects. Education and retraining go some way towards helping the unemployed to acquire skills needed, but governments also aim to attract new industries into areas of high unemployment, which can act as a catalyst to regeneration. In turn, these measures should generate growth. However, as CF3.1 on the UK shows, regional disparity in growth is likely to remain.

For developing countries, job creation and economic growth go hand in hand. Labour shortages and unemployment can co-exist, where there are people willing to work, but without the relevant skills. These shortfalls in skilled workers can act as a dampener on growth. Hong Kong, Singapore and South Korea are examples of countries with policies which have generated high-skilled jobs to meet the needs of new industries. The challenge is greater in China and India, which are much larger and more diverse, suffering in part from the fact that some regions have lagged behind others. Targeted growth strategies to boost regions which have received little investment can lead to more job creation and foster social stability.

Tackling unemployment

Advise policy-makers in the following two situations:
● Country A in Europe is suffering from 20% unemployment in a specific region, due to the demise of manufacturing jobs. The workers who have lost jobs are mainly semi-skilled workers in their thirties and forties
● Country B, a developing country, is suffering from 40% unemployment in rural areas, particularly among workers in the 18–24 age group. FDI has brought manufacturing jobs to some cities, but, with costs and wages rising, these jobs are becoming scarcer

PAUSE TO REFLECT

TO RECAP...

Unemployment

Unemployment is disheartening for the individual who cannot find a job, for society and for the national economy. Policies which governments can adopt are:
● Encourage start-up businesses
● Encourage investment in domestic industries
● Improve education and skills training
● Target the above three policies particularly in regions of high unemployment

Balance of payments

All countries desire to build lucrative trade relations with other countries, exporting products to world markets and importing products which will benefit their own consumers and businesses. A country's **balance of payments** is the total credit and debit transactions between its residents and those of other countries over a specific period, usually a year. Its current account is made up of two parts: the merchandise trade account, for trade in goods; and the services account, for trade in services, also including profits and interest earned from overseas assets. The country's capital account is for transactions such as the sale and purchase of assets, including shares. When countries are compared, it becomes clear which are net exporters and which are net importers.

A country's balance of payments reflects the competitiveness of its businesses in exporting goods and services, as well as the demand from its consumers for imported products. If it exports more goods than it imports, it has a current account surplus. China is a good example, as Figure 3.7 indicates. This is largely because its manufacturers enjoy cost advantages over other countries (although these costs are rising). They are aided by the exchange rate of the currency, the renminbi, which has been pegged to the US dollar, rather than allowed to float in money markets (see Chapter 12). China could revalue the renminbi, but this would make its goods more expensive in export markets. As it is, there is a trade imbalance with its biggest customer, the US. Note from Figure 3.7 that the US has a huge trade deficit, amounting to over 6% of GDP. The US would ideally like to export more to Chinese consumers.

Balance of payments: The total credit and debit transactions between a country's residents and those of other countries over a given period.

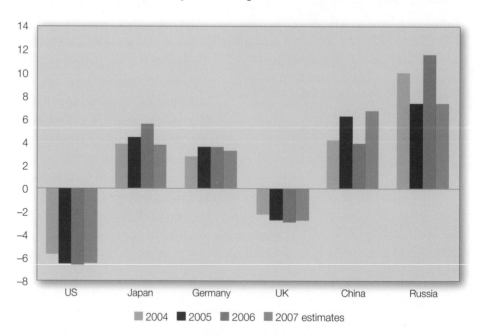

Figure 3.7 Current account balances (as percentage of GDP)

Source: The Economist Economic Indicators (2007), www.economist.com/indicators

Countries may use various policy instruments in this situation, such as import tariffs or quotas (discussed in Chapter 6). However, most of the world's countries are now integrated into multilateral trade agreements, such as those overseen by the WTO, which deter protectionist measures in the interests of open markets. On the other hand, countries do subsidize their own producers in some sectors, particularly agriculture. These protectionist policies can have distorting effects in world markets.

Income inequality: The extent to which the members of a population do not all enjoy equal shares in the country's income.

A country with a current account deficit might be concerned that its producers are not very successful in exporting, probably reflecting high costs of production. This is the UK's position in respect to merchandise trade, while it enjoys a surplus on trade in services. On the other hand, German exporters have been highly successful despite high costs in Germany. (Germany is featured in CF6.1.)

Inequality

In all societies, there are some people who have greater power, wealth or status than others. In traditional societies, distinctions are often based on kinship, customs or religion. The inequality referred to here concerns economic measures, which may focus on income, wealth or consumption. Inequality is greater to the extent that the population do not all enjoy equal shares. Greater wealth or income may well be combined with higher status in the traditional sense – royal families are likely to be wealthier than ordinary citizens. However, when looking at economies, only economic measures of inequality are taken into account. A commonly used measure of income inequality is the Gini index. A Gini coefficient is derived for each country, a value of 0 representing perfect equality, and a value of 100 representing perfect inequality. Looking at the proportion of income earned by each fifth (quintile) of the population is also indicative of the degree of inequality.

The proportion of income earned by the top 20% can be compared to that of the lowest 20%, as shown in Table 3.3. The table also gives Gini coefficients for a selection of countries, as set out in the UN's *Human Development Report*. Some countries provided no data (for example all Middle Eastern countries), and some data are not up to date, but they do give an indication of differences between countries. Of the advanced economies, the US is more unequal, suggesting a link with more market-oriented policies. Latin American and African countries are among the world's most unequal, due to the concentration of land and economic wealth in a few hands. Poverty, social tensions and political instability are associated with these high levels of inequality. Economic

Table 3.3 Inequality measurements for selected countries

Country	Gini coefficient	Share of the richest 20%	Share of the poorest 20%	Year
US	40.8	45.8	5.4	2000
Japan	24.9	35.7	10.6	1993
Sweden	25	36.6	9.1	2000
Germany	28.3	36.9	8.5	2000
Hungary	26.9	36.5	9.5	2001
China	44.7	50	4.7	2001
Brazil	59.3	63.2	2.4	2001
Mexico	49.5	39.4	4.3	2002
India	32.5	43.3	8.9	1999
Nigeria	43.7	49.2	5	2003
South Africa	57.8	62.2	3.5	2000

Note: Gini coefficient, 0 = perfect equality, 100 = perfect inequality

Source: UNDP (2006) *Human Development Report 2006* (Basingstoke: Palgrave Macmillan)

growth can be accompanied by growing inequality, as successful businesses, and their staff, reap greater rewards. China is less unequal than Mexico and Brazil, but the top 20% of the population account for half the national income.

The degree to which inequality is a concern for policy-makers depends partly on a society's values. Rich rewards for those at the top of the corporate ladder can be an incentive to workers lower down. Similarly, entrepreneurs who create business empires from humble beginnings, such as Bill Gates, are admired. The American dream is premised on equality of opportunity, implying that anyone, whether born into a rich or a poor family, can, with hard work, become rich. Research suggests that, although 80% of Americans believe this to be true, upward mobility is, in fact, something of a myth. The likelihood of Americans remaining in the same economic bracket as their parents is higher than anywhere else in the developed world (Luce, 2006). In other countries, such as Japan, huge discrepancies between executive pay and that of other workers are frowned on as damaging to the company and society. There are certainly very rich Japanese business executives, but most of us could not name them. They keep rather low profiles and are not household names, even in Japan. In Chapter 2, we found that inequality has been growing over the last two decades in many countries, suggesting that globalization is a factor (although not the only factor). CF3.1 on the UK, which follows, confirms this view. Countries which prioritize social welfare, such as Sweden and Germany, have lower levels of inequality. Land reform in some countries, such as Taiwan, has broken up large holdings, resulting in greater equality of wealth.

TO RECAP...

Inequality

Countries vary in the degree of inequality in the distribution of income and wealth among their populations. They also vary in their attitudes to this inequality. Highly unequal societies are likely to have problems of poverty and social instability. Governments may design policies which aim at redistribution, such as land reform and social welfare programmes.

COUNTRY FOCUS 3.1 – THE UNITED KINGDOM

Two-speed Britain

Following 1997, when the Labour Party took over the reins of government after 18 years of Conservative rule, the British economy enjoyed its longest period of sustained growth in recent history. Growth averaged 2.7% per annum from 1997 to 2005, making it the envy of other European countries. Levels of unemployment fell, and Britain attracted record flows of inward

FDI. Its flexible labour market and relatively open, business-friendly environment have attracted foreign investors, allowing the economy to benefit from the forces of global competition. However, behind the headline statistics, there lies an unevenness among different regions of the country. Two-speed Britain resembles a north–south divide, as shown in the figure. In northern areas, older industries such as mining and manufacturing have almost disappeared. Manufacturing was 20% of national income in 1997, and is below 15% today. The large-scale manufacturing which remains is all foreign owned. Annual private sector growth in the northeast was 1.3% between 1997 and 2003, while private sector growth in the same period in London was 4% and in the southeast, 3.5%.

When the Labour Party took office, public services and infrastructure were suffering from years of underinvestment. Schools and hospitals were in need of upgrading. Income inequality, having risen rapidly in the 1980s, when the Conservative prime minister Margaret (now Baroness) Thatcher was in power, levelled off when John Major, her successor, was in power. The new Labour government aimed to reduce inequality by policies designed to tackle poverty. Labour pledged to invest in public services and create a modern welfare state. Its reforms on employment, however, continued a Conservative theme, which was to restrict out-of-work benefits, through a welfare-to-work policy. Those out of work would need to search for work or go on training programmes: it promised a mixture of 'work for those who can, security for those who can't' (Timmins, 2005). The new government aimed to alleviate poverty, by striking out at the causes of poverty. It targeted poor pensioners and poor families with children. In particular, it aimed to provide better conditions for children in deprived areas, through nurseries and other facilities.

When Labour came to power, regional differences in prosperity were greater than in any European country or the US.

Figure Public and private sector average annual percentage growth in selected regions of the UK, 1997–2003

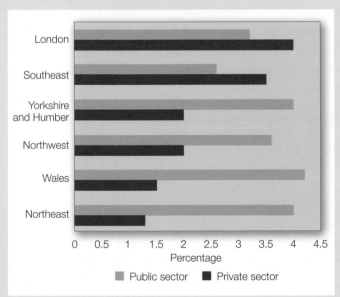

Source: ONS; *Financial Times,* 20 September 2006

The government aimed to spread economic opportunities in northern England, Scotland and Wales. After two years of relative austerity, the new government embarked on dramatic increases in public spending. Public spending rose from 37.4% of national income in 1999–2000 to a planned 43.1% in 2007–8. Healthcare and education benefited above all. The major recipients were in poorer regions, where public sector employment was highest. Barnsley in Yorkshire had seen the death of the coal industry between 1985 and 1993, resulting in the loss of 20,000 jobs. The election of the Blair government brought hope that new policies would renew the town. The Sure Start programme in a new children's centre, funded by the national government, offered new educational opportunities for children of poor families. Health initiatives, such as the Health Action Zone, were aimed at improving health in deprived areas. Numerous initiatives from central government brought in funds, although not necessarily on programmes that local leaders felt were the best way to spend the money. Phil Coppard, chief executive of Barnsley council, said: 'Suddenly an amount of money will drop out of the sky on you and you can have it if you can spend it. There is an awful lot of that, particularly from the Home Office. There is no communication – they are forever launching stuff. It still goes on' (Giles and Wilson, 2006).

While the spending has resulted in improvements in educational opportunities and health, there are critics who question how long-lasting the effects will be. It was clear in 2006 that the public spending bonanza would soon be over, as the government was compelled to deal with the budget deficit. Some of the health initiatives have been swept away in the restructuring of the National Health Service. Meanwhile, Barnsley's Sure Start managers were worried that the public funding on which it depends will be cut back. A worry for community leaders is that private sector enterprises seem to have been squeezed out, as the availability of public sector jobs dampened entrepreneurial inclinations. Private sector jobs which have sprung up in the northeast and Yorkshire have largely been back-office service jobs and call centres, which are vulnerable to being offshored by the forces of globalization. The economic problems faced by Barnsley remain, despite the spending on public services.

While surging public expenditure has been an equalizing force, the gap between regions has become wider. Globalization has been a factor. Business and financial services have flocked to London and the southeast, while regional economies have seen declines in manufacturing industries on which their prosperity had been based. In addition, despite efforts to reduce income inequality, inequality remains roughly the same as it was during the Conservative era, seeing huge rises for the top 0.5% and below-par gains for the bottom 5%. Income inequality became greater than it was in 1979. In the globalized economy which Britain has become, the haves in the booming service economy are growing richer, while the have-nots in yesterday's industries face a bleak prospect as manufacturing migrates to low-cost locations. It is perhaps ironic that the south produced the success stories which the Labour government had hoped would emerge in the less prosperous regions.

Questions

- ◆ Why has the regional divide persisted, despite the targeting of public spending and public sector jobs in the poorer areas?
- ◆ What have been the effects of globalization on the British economy?
- ◆ In your view, what policies would be needed to reduce inequality and boost regional employment?

Sources: Stephens, P., 'Another country: with Blair has come confidence in an embrace of the world', *Financial Times*, 22 September 2006; Giles, C., 'A tale of two valleys', *Financial Times*, 19 September 2006;

Giles, C., 'Forgotten Britain: how widening disparities blight a star performer', *Financial Times*, 20 March 2006; Giles, C. and Wilson, J., 'Gone north: state largesse brings help and hope but little change', *Financial Times*, 20 September 2006; Timmins, N., 'Spending power: how Labour has taken the welfare state to a higher plateau', *Financial Times*, 20 April 2005.

WEB CHECK

Information on the UK economy can be found under the country list on the OECD's website at www.oecd.org.

Some more equal than others

What does equality of opportunity consist of? Almost all societies aim for equality of opportunity in education, by providing universal access for at least a few years of schooling. In some, it is felt that even university tuition fees should be provided by the state. What should the state aim for: equality of opportunity or equality of outcomes? To what extent is either of these aims practicable?

PAUSE TO REFLECT

Public finances

National governments play a crucial role in the economic environment, demonstrated in the example of Hungary at the start of this chapter. They take in large amounts of money, mainly through taxation and other charges, and they spend large sums of public money on a huge variety of activities, from agriculture to voting systems. While businesses often complain about the tax burden, they benefit in many ways. They may benefit directly through grants, subsidies or other financial accommodation under numerous specific programmes. Indirectly, they benefit from a workforce educated and trained in relevant skills through public funding. Where governments are less inclined to spend public money on services such as healthcare, the burden may fall directly on business, as CS3.2 highlights. Governments must perform a delicate balancing act. There are constant pressures to increase spending on health, education and the environment, but, with limited resources, they must prioritize.

Government spending

In a sense, the government can be seen as a household on a large scale, and good housekeeping principles of keeping spending within the limits of revenues would seem to apply. However, there is a crucial difference between governments and households, in that individuals in need of cash cannot simply demand more money from an employer and expect to receive it, whereas governments can raise taxes and legally compel residents to pay them. Governments must estimate what they will receive from taxes and other sources in any given year; they cannot be sure. Similarly, they commit funds to public spending programmes, but costs may rise and the money must be found. Hence, government finances may go into debt. The budget balance for any country is the extent to which public spending exceeds receipts. In the UK, this is known as the 'public sector borrowing requirement' (PBSR). The debt that accumulates over the years is referred to as the 'national debt'. Both the national budget balance and national debt can be expressed as a percentage of GDP. When national debt grows to large proportions, it can pose a problem for government finances, but the extent to which national debt and budget deficits are problems depends largely on the particular country. If economic growth is strong, it is arguable that deficits are not so serious, as receipts are rising. However, this approach rather flies in the face of good housekeeping principles, and should receipts fail to reach expectations, as sometimes happens, budget cuts may have to be made.

Budget deficits are a fact of life in many countries, as Figure 3.8 shows. Within the EU, the Economic and Monetary Union (EMU) specifies that the budget deficit should not exceed 3% of GDP. This is known as the 'growth and stability pact'. Twelve of the EU's 27 members are in breach of the stability pact, and five of them are also members of the eurozone. Notably, France and Germany, both key economies in the eurozone, have been in breach since 2002. This gloomy state of public finances in Europe reflects various factors, including tax revenues below forecast levels, increasing welfare costs, increasing costs of healthcare and the rising pension costs of an ageing population. Japan has shared many of these problems, and, as Figure 3.8 suggests, is trying to control spending. Its government is also proposing raising taxes and raising funds through privatizing the post office. The US saw a growing deficit in 2006, largely because of increased spending on the armed forces and national security.

National budget balance: The extent to which public spending exceeds receipts from taxes and other sources.

Figure 3.8 Budget deficits in selected countries (as percentage of GDP)

Source: The Economist Economic Indicators (2007), www.economist.com/indicators

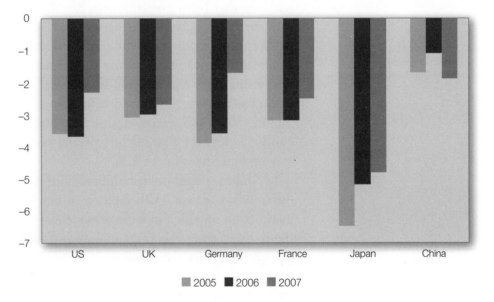

Decisions about where to direct public spending are taken by governments on the advice of experts in government departments which oversee the spending programmes. All government departments will make a case for increases, but, given the limitations on resources, there will be winners and losers. In Britain, the Labour government elected in 1997 went on a public spending spree, as described in CF3.1. Health was the main beneficiary, seeing rises of 10% annually (equivalent to over 7% allowing for inflation).

WEB CHECK

The OECD home page at www.oecd.org has links to sites bringing together statistics and reports on health and social welfare issues.

TO RECAP...

Public spending priorities

All governments face pressures on public spending, social welfare programmes being particularly sensitive. Generous public provision in areas such as health and pensions is having to be restructured in many countries, because of rising costs and ageing populations.

Direct and indirect taxes: Direct taxes are paid by individuals and companies on their earned and unearned income. Indirect taxes are incurred for goods and services at the point of delivery.

By 2005, health spending had doubled since the party took office. However, it is estimated that much of this money was absorbed by administration and other costs, resulting in only a 4% annual increase in output for the first five years (Wallace, 2004).

A difficulty which governments face is that of rising costs to meet existing commitments such as pensions, social security, education and healthcare. Roughly half the UK government's spending is on health and social services, and spending on education is 13%. Any government which tries to rein in spending by cutting back on these programmes is likely to find its reforms unpopular with the electorate. In many countries, structural reforms are being attempted to bring public spending down to a sustainable level, but reforms such as raising the pension age and reducing employment protection rights are not popular. The fall of the SPD coalition in Germany in 2005 can be partly attributed to opposition to market reforms. However, the new coalition government of Angela Merkel is facing the same balancing act (see CF6.1).

Taxation

National governments rely on taxation to raise revenues for public spending. Taxation can be used as a means of redressing inequality in society, in that taxation of the rich can be channelled to fund social programmes for the poor. This policy is known as 'redistribution'. Taxation has become an issue in the global competitive environment, as countries have used both low rates of tax and simplified systems to lure foreign investors. Governments impose both direct and indirect taxes. Tax on income, both earned and unearned (such as that from investments), is a direct tax. Individuals pay income tax on their earnings, as do businesses which are not incorporated. A company is liable to corporation tax, while its employees are liable to income tax on their remuneration. Rates of income and corporation tax are traditionally progressive, rising with the increase in income. However, the debate about introducing a 'flat rate', discussed below, is now gathering steam. Indirect taxes include VAT and excise duties on petrol. In addition, governments may choose to impose charges for specific purposes, such as the environmental levy on businesses in the UK.

MNEs may operate in numerous different countries, each of which has a different tax regime. Although, in principle, they are liable to pay tax in the jurisdiction in which income arises, there are legitimate ways to shift liabilities to those where tax rates are low and away from those with high tax rates. For governments, the taxation of MNEs has become somewhat frustrating, as the tax 'take' is relatively low for the amount of economic activity generated. Drafting rules in order to increase tax revenue can be counterproductive. Taxing statutes in the UK have grown in size and become almost impossibly complex, even for experts. Simplifying the system has been urged by business leaders.

Figure 3.9 shows that EU tax rates are generally falling, especially among newer members. Some countries have sought to attract FDI by both their low rates of tax and a simplified system known as the 'flat tax'. Such a system in its pure form involves a single rate of tax for all personal and corporate

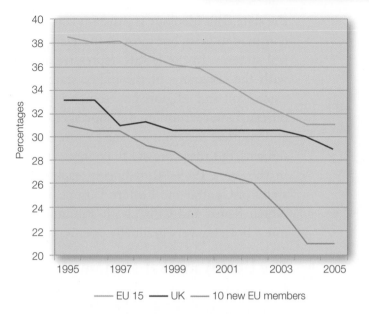

Figure 3.9 Top rates of corporation tax

Source: Financial Times, 3 October 2005

income. Most deductions and allowances are eliminated in the interests of simplicity. Estonia was the first country to adopt such a system, followed by other countries in Central and Eastern Europe, as highlighted in CF3.2 on Romania. Most countries have a graduated system of taxation, which imposes higher rates on individuals or companies with higher income. Many in Western Europe argue that a flat tax system, while welcome to the rich, would be detrimental to the poor and middle-income households. Businesses in the UK have argued that the government should adopt both rate cuts and a simpler system. Research published in 2005 found that a reduction of 10 percentage points in the rate of tax would boost annual growth by one or two percentage points (Lee and Gordon, 2005). Such a step would involve a loss of tax revenues, at least in the short term, making it unlikely to win government favour.

> **TO RECAP...**
>
> **Taxation in perspective**
>
> National governments use the design of national taxation systems to reflect policy goals. High taxes are associated with the aim of providing for greater social spending. Lighter taxation on businesses acts as an attraction for FDI investors.

Diverse economic systems

National economic systems reflect values that are rooted in the cultural and political life of the country. These values may change over time, and changing values interact with changes occurring in economic activity. The dominant economic system in today's world is capitalism, which is based on principles of market exchange. Most of the world's countries are market economies to a greater or lesser extent. At the opposite extreme is the planned economy, where supply is monopolized and controlled by the state. In this section, we look first at the planned economy and then at the different hues of capitalist market economy.

The planned economy

Planned economy: Economic system in which the supply and price of goods and services are controlled by central planning authorities of the state.

The planned economy is state dominated. Supply and pricing of goods and services are controlled by state authorities. Every sector in the economy is run by a state agency, according to a central plan. The Soviet Union, or Union of Soviet Socialist Republics (USSR), was based on the Marxist-Leninist ideology of the Communist Party, whose party leaders effectively controlled the state. This ideology is a distant cousin of the many socialist parties which continue to exist, but most of these are democratic parties in pluralist political systems. In the USSR, repressive authoritarian political rule combined with the apparatus of the police state, denying the people basic rights of expression and religion, not to mention civil and political rights. In the end, bureaucracy, corruption and shortages of basic consumer goods led to social and political instability in the 1980s. Efforts were made to introduce liberal reforms, but these proved to be ineffective. The monolithic edifice crumbled in the years 1989–90, falling in each of the Soviet republics and satellite states of Central and Eastern Europe. Planned economies which remain are North Korea and Cuba, both communist dictatorships and closed economies. Both are very gradually opening their economies to market forces.

The liberal market economy

Capitalism rests on freedom of enterprise for all within the society. In principle, in a liberal market economy, people are free to engage in business without interference from the state, allowing the market in particular goods and services to determine supply and demand, together with prices. The values associated with capitalism are liberal values of individualism, freedom to pursue one's personal goals, and minimal state interference. The role of the state in the liberal economic perspective is one of enabling rather than acting directly as an economic player. The state plays an important role in establishing a legal framework in which the market can operate, and its regulatory and judicial system provides oversight. Among these legal safeguards are:

- Legal protection of private property, enforceable in an independent court system
- Fairness in the operation of markets, ensuring that market-distorting restrictions such as price-fixing do not subsist
- Competition law, ensuring that monopolies and cartels are curtailed.

The US and the UK are usually grouped together as exemplifying this liberal market model, as shown in Figure 3.10. It is often referred to as the 'Anglo-Saxon' model. Ireland, Canada and Australia are also in this broad

TO RECAP...

The planned economy

Planned economies under the control of state apparatus have tended to be inefficient, leading to shortages and, ultimately, to social unrest. The break-up of the Soviet Union marked the end of the last large planned economy.

Liberal market economy: Capitalist economic system, in which supply and demand, as well as prices, are determined by free markets for goods and services.

Figure 3.10 Differing models of capitalism

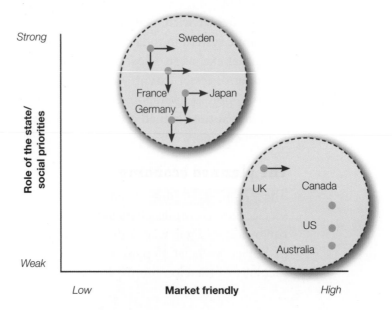

grouping. They share a view of the state as limited to intervening where necessary to ensure fairness in markets. Although we tend to think of American capitalism as the product of its entrepreneurs, the state played an important supporting role in the US during the nineteenth century, particularly in the area of transport (Kozul-Wright, 1995). For example, linking the Atlantic and Pacific by rail was a mammoth public–private endeavour, swallowing federal grants of $68 million – a huge commitment in the 1860s. By contrast, a significant role for the state in social spending did not materialize. Elements of the welfare state exist in the US, but mainly as a 'safety net'. In particular, there is weak employment protection and limited benefits for unemployed people. The welfare state is more developed in Britain. Britain also invested in state-owned industries such as utilities, although a wave of privatizations shifted the economy more towards market forces in the 1980s. This is indicated by the arrow in Figure 3.10. The British economy is therefore somewhere between the American model and the social market model of other European states.

Case study 3.1: Heineken seeks refreshing changes

Heineken, the Dutch brewing company, has found itself drawn into global competitive pressures in beer markets which are compelling it to make changes in its markets, products and its organization. The world's fourth largest brewer by volume, it faces stiff competition from its three large rivals, all of which have grown through mergers and acquisitions. Anheuser-Busch (maker of Budweiser) is America's largest brewer, and is now facing renewed competition from second ranking SABMiller, Miller Brewing of the US having been taken over by South African Breweries in 2002. Third ranking Inbev was formed by a merger between Belgian Interbrew and Brazilian Ambev. Heineken, with its roots in the Netherlands, is just over 50% owned by the Heineken family, which makes it less likely to be a takeover target itself, but also restricts its scope for making strategic acquisitions in the manner of its larger competitors. With profit growth stagnating, Heineken was reorganized in 2003, with a view to responding more quickly to market pressures. The new CEO said: 'I have changed the way [Heineken] is managed ... from a northern European way to a more Anglo-Saxon approach, because we measure ourselves against companies that are mostly managed that way' (Bickerton and Wiggins, 2006). The change is to a 'model that rewards individual responsibility' (Bickerton and Wiggins, 2006). A 13-member executive committee replaced the 36-member management group which had relied on consensus decision-making, holding back the company in a period of rapid consolidation. An outcome of these changes is that regional executives can now make quicker decisions on acquisitions in key markets.

While it does not aspire to overtake the other big brewers in volume sales, Heineken, like its rivals, is compelled to look for growth in emerging markets, such as Eastern Europe, Russia and China. In North America and Western Europe, changing lifestyles and drinking habits have seen consumers shifting away from beer towards wine and spirits, as Figures 1 and 2 show. Spirits are now the favourite alcoholic beverage among 21–27-year-olds in the US, especially the flavoured versions of their products, with vodka brands leading the way. Spirits companies have been successful in winning over women customers with enticing new flavours. Their approach is that social changes are leading to consumers 'drinking less but better' (Wiggins, 2005). This is bad news for the large brewers, who are turning to emerging markets to make up the shortfall. China is now the world's fastest growing beer market, with Russia not far behind. Russia accounted for 5% of the world beer market in 2003, but by 2009, it is expected to be the world's third largest, ahead of Germany and Brazil. The large brewers have moved quickly to acquire brewers in Russia. Heineken now owns a number of Russian breweries, giving it 14% of the Russian market and making it the third largest producer in Russia.

In addition to seeking acquisitions, Heineken is looking at innovation to provide growth. The new management focus on individual initiative is encouraging a more risk-taking approach. While rivals have introduced flavoured beers, Heineken has so far

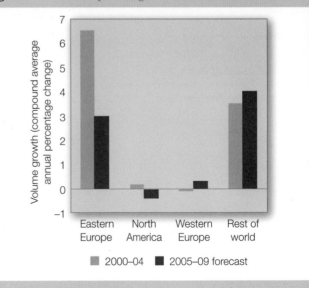

Figure 1 Beer consumption in global markets

Figure 2 Spirits consumption in global markets

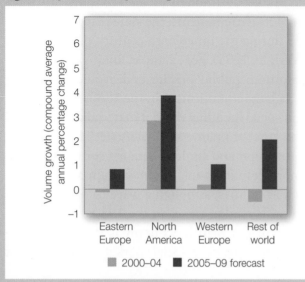

Volume growth (compound average annual percentage change)

■ 2000–04   ■ 2005–09 forecast

Eastern Europe   North America   Western Europe   Rest of world

Source: Financial Times, 19 August 2005

plate 3.2 Leisure activities such as going to bars and restaurants with friends are popular aspects of social life – and also a growth area for international business.

refrained, putting its faith in its flagship Heineken brand, which accounts for 20% of its sales. To win back customers in the US, it launched Heineken Premium Light, a low-alcohol beer, which became its first extension of the Heineken brand. In France, it has launched Heineken Small, a 15 cl bottle, designed to appeal to women drinkers.

Packaging has been one of the company's areas of innovation and marketing strategy. Spending more on packaging than rivals, it has been taken aback by the rising cost of raw materials. In particular, aluminium has risen in price nearly 50% since 2003, as part of the general boom in metal prices. Aluminium, which is robust, light and easy to recycle, has been fast replacing steel cans in the beverage industry, as in other consumer products. Having pioneered its use, Heineken chose aluminium for its new sophisticated slim bottles designed for nightclubs and bars. Rising aluminium prices have caused the company to search for cost savings elsewhere. This is just one aspect of

its continual programme of cost savings, which have included closing breweries and centralizing purchasing. Heineken now announces savings targets in advance, even when it is not clear where the savings will be made. This is a departure from the more traditional management approach that the company used to have. The new CEO says: 'It is that tension that an organisation needs. It pushes people to go that extra mile, out of the comfort zone' (Bickerton and Wiggins, 2006).

Heineken will need all the ingenuity it can muster, in both products and markets. The slim aluminium bottle has also attracted the attention of Anheuser, which used it for a version of its premium brand, Michelob, aimed at the younger consumer. Beer has had an image problem in the past, as downmarket and uninteresting. Consumers have turned to wines and spirits, as well as speciality and craft beers. The large brewing companies must seek out both new markets and new ways to refresh sales in mature markets.

Questions

1 What changes are taking place in global drinking habits?
2 Looking at the quotation in the first paragraph, in what ways have changes in Heineken's management made it more 'Anglo-Saxon'?
3 To what extent are the changes at Heineken giving it a competitive edge on its larger rivals?
4 Why does the future look sparkling for the global brewing companies in emerging markets?

Sources: Wiggins, J., 'Drink in the pink: distillers lure the affluent while beer finds fresh thirst in emerging economies', *Financial Times*, 19 August 2005; Bickerton, I. and Wiggins, J., 'Change is brewing at Heineken', *Financial Times*, 9 May 2006; Grant, J., 'Anheuser addresses beer's worrying image problem', *Financial Times*, 29 November 2005; Wiggins, J., 'Heineken seeks new route to young drinkers', *Financial Times*, 31 October 2005; Bickerton, I., 'Raw materials costs hit Heineken profits', *Financial Times*, 7 September 2006; Tieman, R., 'All wrapped up and going just about everywhere', *Financial Times*, 2 November 2005.

WEB CHECK

Heineken's website is www.heineken.com.

The market model for all?
Advocates of the liberal market model acknowledge a role for the state, but prefer to see state intervention only in limited circumstances. Are they thus admitting that, in practice, markets do not serve public welfare goals? Explain your reasoning.

PAUSE TO REFLECT

The social market economy

The social market model of capitalism combines market values with social priorities. The social market economy takes a more positive view of the role of the state than the more liberal market economies, prioritizing social and welfare programmes. The social market economies can be loosely grouped together, as depicted in Figure 3.10 above. While all assign a stronger role to the state than the more liberal market economies, they differ in how they view the state's role in practice. Welfare state policies and state guidance (and often ownership) of key enterprises are both present, but in differing strengths. Employment protection is another area in which these countries differ. As indicated with arrows in Figure 3.10, these countries are undergoing changes, weakening the state's role and becoming more market friendly. Different strains are present in the political climate of each of these countries. The traditional social democratic parties tend to prioritize social justice, and the more liberally inclined parties tend to emphasize market reforms.

Nordic countries are usually held up as welfare state models. High levels of taxation notwithstanding, Sweden can point to a record of healthy economic growth and budget surpluses (see CF9.2). The Nordic states consistently come near the top of the world competitiveness league composed by the World Economic Forum (WEF) (see Chapter 6). Besides economic indicators, the WEF criteria include technological competence and innovation, and the quality of public institutions. These countries also come near the top of the UNDP's Human Development Index, reflecting priorities given to preventive medicine and education (UNDP, 2005).

Other European countries, in both northern and southern Europe, are also social market economies, but with less emphasis on the universal welfare state than the Nordic countries (Sapir, 2005). France and Germany are often grouped together as exemplifying a 'Rhineland' model of capitalism. In these countries, employment protection is prioritized, supported by strong trade unions. It will be recalled from Chapter 1 that German corporate governance is based on co-determination, formalizing employee representation on corporate boards. France and Germany have embarked on market reforms and privatization, cutting back the role of the state. These economies have had years of weak growth and budget deficits, combined with high unemployment. Relatively high social costs and inflexible labour markets have been a deterrent to investors. However, the availability of skilled workers is an attraction, as is the appeal of eurozone integration and proximity to large markets. All are having difficulty funding social spending commitments. Impetus for market-oriented reforms is coming from the EU Commission and also from competitive pressures in the business environment. Potential investors are comparing these economies with the new EU members, where lower wages and lower rates of tax present economic advantages.

Asian models of capitalism

Finally, we look at Asian models of capitalism, exemplified by Japan, South Korea, Singapore and Taiwan. These countries have had differing paths of economic development, but the state played a key role in all of them. They share a strong cultural environment, imbued with Confucianism, and a strong sense of nationhood and society. Traditional kinship ties have blended with capitalist forms to create distinctive varieties of capitalist development, where family enterprises based on cultures of loyalty and commitment have formed the model, even among firms that are not family based. Japan's economy has rested on a blend of relational ties between governments, politicians and business leaders, known as alliance capitalism (Gerlach, 1992). The other Southeast Asian countries, too, have emphasized relational ties over pure market forces (Prasad and Ghauri, 1995). However, as SX3.1 showed, tensions remain. These economies have demonstrated that traditional social values can blend with economic values prevalent in capitalism. Their example tends to suggest that capitalism can flourish in countries outside the individualist cultures of the earlier capitalist economies.

Alliance capitalism: Capitalist market model which rests heavily on relational ties among firms, through cross-shareholding and personal ties.

TO RECAP...

Asian capitalism

Asian economies have evolved market models which reflect national cultures. They generally provide lower levels of public spending on social welfare than the European social market economies, but assign a positive role to the state in both society and economic activities.

A good place to do business?

Businesses are sometimes accused of wanting the best of all worlds. They welcome government aid for enterprises and R&D, and they appreciate state provision of universal healthcare, education and social security. At the same time, they want lower taxes and less government intervention and regulation. What should the foreign investor look for in the economic environment of possible locations? Which of the developed market economies described in this section wins out in terms of a good place for doing business, and why?

PAUSE TO REFLECT

Transition economies

Transition economy: A country which is changing its economy from a state-planned system to a market-based one.

Transition economy covers a wide range of countries which are in the process of transforming their economies from state-run planned systems to market-based systems. As they are opening their economies to outsiders, they have generally benefited from globalization, through growing flows of FDI and outsourced production. In this section, we look at the main groups of transition economies, beginning with the former Soviet Union and its satellite states of Central and Eastern Europe, which embarked on market reforms following the collapse of their communist regimes in 1989–90.

Economies of Central and Eastern Europe

These 29 economies represent a rather disparate group of countries. They can be divided into three main subgroups:

1 Central Europe and the Baltic states which gained EU membership in 2004 – Czech Republic, Estonia, Hungary, Latvia, Lithuania, Poland, Slovakia, Slovenia.

2 Countries in southeast Europe, of which two (Bulgaria and Romania) joined the EU in 2007. Others are waiting to join – Croatia, Albania, Bosnia-Herzegovina, Macedonia, Turkey, Serbia, Montenegro.

3 Nations of the former Soviet Union, which have had rather turbulent economic fortunes in the aftermath of communist regimes – Russia, Armenia, Azerbaijan, Belarus, Georgia, Kazakhstan, Kyrgyzstan, Moldova, Tajikistan, Turkmenistan, Ukraine, Uzbekistan.

States in the first group have made significant progress towards stable market economies. They have enjoyed economic growth, averaging 5.3% in 2006, which is slightly less than the 5.6% growth of 2005. This rate compares favourably with the EU 15 states, but their GDP per capita remains well below levels in Western Europe. Largely because of their low costs, they have attracted substantial FDI, much from Western Europe (see Figure 3.11). Many new investors, including SMEs, have set up in these countries, confident that EU membership ensures a stable regulatory environment. SX3.2 on Aviation Valley illustrates an example. A further temptation to investors has been their low tax rates, and, in some cases, the flat tax. In motor manufacturing, the new members' share of EU output has increased to 20%. Portfolio investment is also good. The driving force in these states is integration into the EU-wide economy. As wage levels rise, retailers and service providers, both domestic and international, are eager to satisfy growing consumer demand. All these countries now have functioning multi-party democracies with constitutional safeguards. Their public finances, however, have posed substantial challenges. They have reduced the role of the state, largely through privatizations, but many suffer from budget deficits as a result of generous public spending. Reducing welfare spending and dealing with unemployment are still unfinished business. They still struggle with poor infrastructure, corruption and poor public services.

States in the second group, the countries of southeast Europe, have also seen good growth in GDP, at 4.9%. These countries, particularly Romania, as featured in CF3.2, have also attracted FDI, benefiting from lower costs than the EU 10 accession states. Still, they feel they are losing out on much potential investment, particularly greenfield manufacturing plants, which are locating in the EU 10 states. They aspire to EU membership, achieved by Bulgaria and Romania in 2007. Chief among the criteria which must be met are a functioning market economy and democratic government. Corruption and weak legal systems have been weaknesses in their case for EU member-

Figure 3.11 FDI flows to selected countries in Central and Eastern Europe

Source: UN (2007) *World Investment Report 2007* (Geneva: UN)

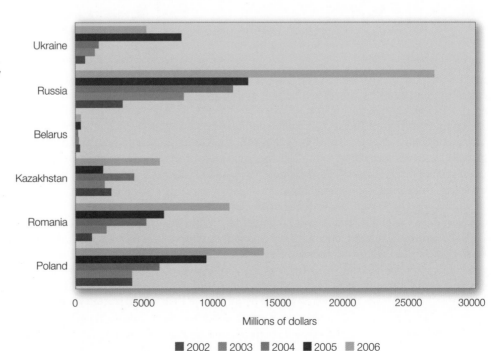

■ 2002 ■ 2003 ■ 2004 ■ 2005 ■ 2006

ship. This group of states includes those affected by the turbulent break-up of Yugoslavia in the wars of 1991–95. These countries are keen to catch up with economic reforms, but they are still poor countries by EU standards, with GDP per capita only a tenth of Western European levels.

The third group comprises the nations that made up the Soviet Union. These countries are also making the transition to market economies, but their strong state traditions and powerful state-controlled enterprises have hampered market developments. In the early 1990s, Russia allowed market forces to run rampant, particularly through ill-conceived privatizations in the natural resources sectors, which resulted in growing power in the hands of a few rich 'oligarchs', with little institutional framework or oversight (Hunter, 2003). This was disastrous for the Russian people, watching GDP fall 42% from 1990 to 1998 (Maddison, 2001). Hyperinflation and financial collapse shook the country in 1998. Since then, the state apparatus has reasserted its authority, reining in the power of the oligarchs, but the result has been a growth in state power. This has been the case especially in the important energy sector, which is a major source of wealth (see CF15.1 on Kazakhstan). Some of the former Soviet republics have introduced the forms of democracy, but entrenched political establishments have made democratic reforms problematic, contributing to an unstable political environment for potential investors. Democratic grassroots movements have sprung up in Ukraine and Georgia, harbouring aspirations for Western-oriented reforms. Resource-poor countries such as Belarus and Tajikistan have benefited from the presence of energy exporters, but profits are concentrated in entrenched establishments, and poverty is widespread. In all the states in this third group, there remain problems of poverty and weak public institutions.

WEB CHECK

The transition economies are profiled individually on the World Bank's website at www.worldbank.org. Click on individual countries.

TO RECAP...

Post-communist transition

Former communist states have privatized state-owned industries and opened their economies to market forces, to varying degrees. The eight former communist countries which joined the EU in 2004 have become functioning market economies, although problems of corruption and cumbersome bureaucracy remain. These problems also affect southeast European countries. In the former Soviet republics, the state continues to play a strong role.

STRATEGIC CROSSROADS

3.2

Aviation Valley attracts high flyers

A remote wooded valley in the southeast of Poland may seem an unlikely location for a high-tech cluster of enterprises to spring up, but, thanks to the vision of its founders, Aviation Valley is building engineering and R&D capacity to compete globally. Located on the border with Ukraine, this is one of the poorest areas in the enlarged EU. Its remoteness is exacerbated by Poland's notoriously poor road links, which partly explains why this region has received only $2 billion in FDI in the entire 15 years since the end of communism. Located in this region, WSK Rzeszow, an aircraft engine parts company, has gone through a number of metamorphoses. During communism, it produced parts for Russian MiG fighters. As a state-owned company, WSK was overstaffed and inefficient. It was forced to produce all component parts itself, in a vertically integrated process, which was expensive and wasteful. Moreover, it had to meet social obligations such as providing sports and holiday

facilities for employees, which numbered 11,000 at its height. With the fall of communism, more than half the staff had to be dismissed, and its attention shifted to Western export markets. In Poland's market reforms, it was privatized and later sold to US conglomerate, United Technologies Corporation (UTC) in 2002. UTC also owns Pratt & Whitney aircraft engines and Sikorsky helicopters.

WSK is now a more streamlined, less bureaucratic company, thanks in part to UTC's emphasis on Japanese-inspired quality management and lean manufacturing methods. The president of WSK came up with the idea of bringing together a group of companies in the aviation industry into a technology cluster, naming it Aviation Valley. His aim was to create a cluster of components suppliers which would also attract R&D enterprises. On the benefits of clusters (discussed in more detail in Chapter 7), Michael Porter (1998: 205) says that they 'capture important linkages, complementarities, and spillovers of technology, skills, information, marketing and customers' needs that cut across firms and industries'. Aviation Valley started with 20 members and has grown to 40, including the local University of Technology. Alongside local companies there is a

German aviation parts company. Other outside investors in aviation and technology are now coming in. The advent of low-cost airlines has helped greatly in overcoming the problems of a poor road network. For companies in Aviation Valley, access has become easier with the advent of Ryanair, which began flights to the region in 2005.

A major attraction of Aviation Valley has been the availability of a qualified workforce at wages one-seventh of those in Germany. Companies are working with universities and schools in the region, helping to train engineers and researchers for jobs in local firms. Such initiatives, while rare, will help to stem the stream of Poland's highly qualified young people leaving the country for better paid jobs elsewhere.

Aviation Valley's directors realize that long-term advantage will depend on quality products supported by cutting-edge R&D. In this way, the cluster will benefit companies which, in isolation, would be unable to compete globally. The Valley took a booth at the Paris Air Show, which would have been impossible for any of the firms individually. Aviation Valley's director says: 'We have to build up a significant research and development capacity so that we can maintain our foothold in the industry' (Wagstyl, 2005).

Questions
- What are the specific benefits of the industrial cluster in the Polish context?
- In what ways can Aviation Valley benefit Poland's economy?

Sources: Maitland, A., 'A call for substance over appearance', *Financial Times*, 10 July 2006; Cienski, J., 'Aviation Valley's high-tech cluster prepares for take-off', *Financial Times*, 23 November 2005; Porter, M. (1998) 'Clusters and competition', in *On Competition* (Boston, MA: Harvard Business Review Press); Wagstyl, S., 'Solid growth may still fail to dent unemployment', *Financial Times*, 23 November 2005.

WEB CHECK

The home page of Aviation Valley is
www.dolinalotnicza.pl/pl.
A variety of information is available.

PAUSE TO REFLECT

FDI flows to Central and Eastern Europe
Assess the advantages and disadvantages for foreign investors in the following transition economies, in terms of their economic environment:
● Poland ● Romania (see CF3.2) ● Russia

China's market reforms

The liberalization process in China started in 1980. At that time, the country was poor and mainly agricultural. Its GDP per capita at PPP was only one-twentieth that of the US. By comparison, Japan's GDP per capita in 1950, at the start of its development surge, was one-fifth that of the US. Economic development through market forces was the goal of China's leaders, but within parameters determined by the authorities. Foreign direct investors were welcomed, particularly in the export-oriented enterprise zones. Since then, the Chinese economy has grown rapidly, mainly through the thriving private sector. It is estimated that private and foreign-owned enterprises generate 52% of GDP (Wolf, 2006a). China's growing numbers of entrepreneurs and private start-up companies are an encouraging sign of vibrancy in the economy. They have thrived even though they have faced greater restrictions and received less state help than state-owned enterprises. It is arguable that the direct role played by its bureaucratic leadership, while responsible for market reforms, has mainly benefited state industries and foreign investors, rather overlooking the innovative and creative role that SMEs are playing. New jobs and rising wages are creating a new consumer-led revolution, as increasingly affluent Chinese acquire the trappings of new middle-class lifestyles. Wage rises in manufacturing are averaging over 10% a year, as shown in Figure 3.12. Adding to the increased costs of raw materials and energy, they are creating pressure on export prices.

Growth rates in China have been in the region of 9% for two decades. While some have argued that this is an unsustainable level, the country's leadership has not shown any desire to curtail growth. The 2005 five-year economic plan highlighted two important concerns. These were the need to increase per capita GDP and to increase energy efficiency. These two aims give us some indication of the role of market reforms, suggesting that the goal is not to create a capitalist system, but to use capitalist means for creating prosperity within the existing state structure. Looking at the first concern, widespread disparity in income and quality of life exists across this vast country. State systems of health, education and housing have been dismantled in the enthusiasm for market reforms. The withdrawal of state support has been exacerbated by the huge disparities between incomes in the prosperous coastal cities, where manufacturing is concentrated, and poor rural areas. Social tensions, sometimes erupting into unrest, are common. Manufacturing firms have relied on migrant labour, but some are moving inland from coastal areas, to reduce labour costs (see Chapter 10).

The second concern raised in the five-year plan was the need to improve energy efficiency, recognizing the potential impact that China's growing pollution could have on growth. It was estimated that environmental damage from pollution could cost the country the equivalent of 3% of economic output annually. The Environmental Protection Administration has said: 'Although [China's] brand of high consumption, high pollution and high-risk development has had a certain historical use, our economy has now hit a bottleneck for resource and energy use' (McGregor, 2006). Nonetheless, the quest for imports of energy and raw materials has prompted Chinese leaders to look for long-term deals with suppliers all over the world, including African governments (see SX6.1). Chinese MNEs are also flexing their muscles in international markets, making acquisitions which are strategically advantageous.

While China's economy, on the surface, seems mainly market-oriented, there are numerous shortcomings that cast doubt on the depth of its market

Figure 3.12 Chinese annual wages in manufacturing
Source: *Financial Times*, 12 July 2006

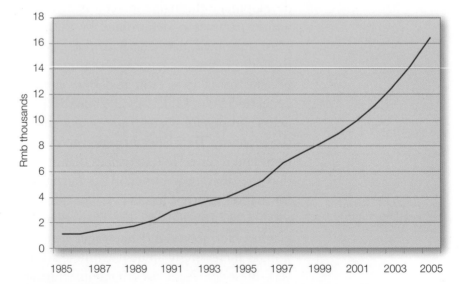

WEB CHECK

See the World Bank's
website on China,
www.worldbank.org.

TO RECAP...

China's market reforms

In two and a half decades, China has made huge strides in opening its economy to market forces, particularly foreign investment in manufacturing industries. Weaknesses remain, nonetheless, in property rights protection, the extent of state interference and weak legal institutions.

mechanisms. It is estimated that only 14% of China's fixed assets are in private hands (de Jonquières, 2006). Private property rights, while recognized, remain weak and vulnerable to state interference. Patents and other intellectual property rights are poorly enforced. Government restrictions on content apply to media and internet companies. Governance in Chinese companies is well below the principles of transparency and accountability that are expected in MNEs globally. For example, 'non-tradable' shares, often held by central and local governments, make up about two-thirds of the common shares in China's 1,350 listed companies. These inside investors effectively control their companies (Tucker, 2006).

After over two decades of strong growth, China's GDP per capita in 2005 was still only one-sixth that of the US, the same as Japan in 1961 and South Korea in 1982, although the last two countries had experienced only about a decade of growth. There remain contradictions between the market-led economy and the power of China's communist-dominated bureaucracy (Pei, 2006).

China's capitalism

Contrast China's market reforms with those in the post-communist transition economies. How are the conflicts between open markets and party-dominated bureaucracy likely to be resolved in the future?

PAUSE TO REFLECT

Regional integration

Most countries develop ties with their neighbours. Sometimes they lead to conflict, but more often, they lead to economic benefits for both. Obvious advantages of doing business with neighbours are that transport and communication costs are less than with distant firms. Often, historical and cultural affinities mean that businesses in neighbouring countries have an inherent understanding of each other's values and behaviour. Ties therefore develop on a firm-to-firm basis, as businesspeople build relations with regional firms. This piecemeal approach can be contrasted with formal steps taken by governments to design agreements, such as trade agreements, with other countries. Having the legal status of treaties, these regional trade agreements can bring down trade barriers, making it easier for cross-border transactions. Hence regional integration develops along both formal and informal lines. While we live in an era of globalization, it is perhaps ironic that regional integration is also thriving. It can be argued that, as global forces become more powerful, countries can form a counterbalance by grouping together with others in the region (Castells, 2000). However, regions differ in the extent of their integration and in the goals of their member states.

What is a region? A region may be a formal grouping of geographically adjacent countries, or it may simply refer informally to a group of adjacent countries. Asia, for example, is a region which is becoming more integrated economically, but there is no single trade pact which unites these countries. Asean is a grouping of Southeast Asian countries, but does not include either Japan or China, the two big powers in the region. On the other hand, economic ties, including FDI and joint ventures, are rapidly growing among Asian countries, spurred by Chinese growth. Japanese and Taiwanese companies are some of the biggest investors in China. Within Europe, the EU comprises 27 members (see Figure 1.12), and there is a lively debate on how far enlargement should go. Potentially, the EU could have 33 member states, which some feel would make it unwieldy. It would also be very disparate. Nafta is a trade agreement comprising three countries only, the US, Canada and Mexico. This trade grouping is dominated by the US, and efforts to extend it to a Free Trade Area of the Americas have floundered.

Trade theorists sometimes speak of world trade being dominated by the 'triad' of three large trade 'blocs': North America, Europe and Japan (Rugman and Verbeke, 2005). In fact, the growth of China has made it more realistic to speak of Asia as the third bloc. Regional trade agreements involve varying degrees of commitment to common trade regimes (examined in detail in Chapter 6), but, in general, they do not venture into deeper economic and political ties, and these regions remain economically diverse. The exception is the EU, which, starting as a trade pact, has developed a considerable life of its own.

TO RECAP...

Regional integration
Both formal and informal processes are building ties among countries and businesses in geographic regions. Regional links have strong attractions for businesses, as there is likely to be cultural understanding between neighbours and transport costs are relatively low.

COUNTRY FOCUS 3.2 – ROMANIA

Romania open for business at last

Romania's overthrow of communist rule in 1989–90 was the most violent of the uprisings in Central and Eastern Europe. Hope turned to disappointment in the 1990s, as a succession of governments perpetuated the ills of the past, allowing corruption to become entrenched and failing to pursue economic reforms. Unlike other post-communist states, Romania seemed stuck in a time warp. The state remained all-powerful, and the business climate was corrupt and uncertain. Inflation reached a peak of 55% in 1999. The 1990s were seen by many Romanians as a lost decade.

Economic reforms began in earnest in 2000, when the Social Democratic government began privatizations and attempted to bring budget deficits under control. These reforms gathered pace with a new coalition government which came to power in 2004, led by the Alliance for Justice and Truth. Reforms were given impetus by the prospect of EU accession. There was still much to do, especially as problems with corruption and bloated bureaucracy remained. The new finance minister has said that the state should act 'more like a referee than like a player in the economy' (Condon and Fak, 2005). The new government promised to clean up corruption and reduce the role of the state, to give a level playing field for business. In an attempt to boost FDI, one of its first moves was to bring in a flat 16% tax on both personal income and corporation profits.

Figure Romania's GDP growth

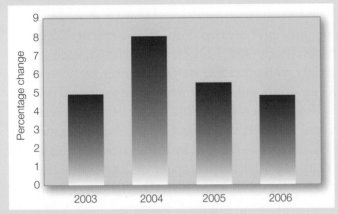

Source: Economist Intelligence Unit data, www.economist.com/indicators

The new government announced in 2004: 'We can finally speak of a transition' (Condon, 23 February 2005). In October of that year, the EU declared Romania to be a 'functioning market economy'. In September 2006, the country was assured of accession in January 2007, along with Bulgaria. These countries are poor in comparison with the 10 accession countries of 2004, which are themselves poor in comparison to the EU 15 countries. Romanian GDP per capita is just $5,080, a quarter of the EU 15 average. One-third of employment is in the declining agricultural sector. GDP growth has been similar to that of other Eastern European countries, in the 5% range, except in 2004, when it was 8% (see figure). The spike was due to a bumper harvest which followed a disastrous drought in 2003. Privatizations have brought in FDI, but these are one-off, and there is a fear that new owners will slim down workforces in the new companies. The other main source of FDI has been in low-skilled outsourced manufacturing in textiles and shoe-making. It is feared that this type of production is likely to move east in due course. Remittances from Romanians working abroad have been significant for years. By 2006, there were an estimated 2 million Romanians working in EU countries, out of a population of 22 million. The country desperately needs to create new jobs, to stem the flow of Romanians to other parts of the EU. MNEs and domestic start-ups are competing for educated professionals, and jobs are becoming better paid. Romania's education system, inherited from the communist era, stresses science education, and, combined with IT training, provides the country with highly skilled workers, an attraction for foreign investors.

A successful foreign investor in Romania has been Renault, owner of the Dacia Logan saloon. This ultra-cheap car was designed for developing countries, but its popularity has surpassed even the most optimistic forecasts, leaving its Romanian factory unable to cope with demand. While the car's popularity with domestic consumers has been understandable, its demand in other European countries, such as France and Germany, has come as a pleasant surprise to the company. The car is now being assembled in far-flung locations, including Morocco, Columbia, Russia and Iran.

Among entrepreneurs, Dan Ostahie is an outstanding example. He watched his sister emigrate to the US in 1992, where she works for Oracle. Of his graduating class of 44 in electronics and communications from Bucharest Polytechnic University, 70% went abroad, but he decided to stay at home and start a business selling televisions. In the beginning, he could only afford old discarded sets which he first had to repair. A decade later, at the age of 38, he is a multimillion-aire, and his company, Altex, is now the country's largest retail chain of electronics and home appliances. While his own energy was key to his success, he had a piece of good fortune, in the privatization of the banking sector, which led to a boom in retail lending. His first consumer credit deal was in 2002, and after that, sales rocketed. The company is now expanding in Serbia and Bulgaria. He says that at the time of his graduation, he wanted to emigrate: 'The dream was to go to the US.' However, as one of Romania's richest young entrepreneurs, he is probably thinking: 'Who needs the American dream?'

In its *Doing Business Report* in 2006, the World Bank ranked Romania second in improvements made to encourage business. This is indicative of the strides taken by the former communist state. Still, the EU has listed nine critical areas to address, including corruption, judicial independence, social security, border security, state aid and environmental protection. The government is reducing bureaucratic interference and state aid, but many powerful interests dating from the 1990s, in both business and politics, remain intact, casting a gloomy shadow over attempts to rid the country of corruption. The receipt of €30 billion from the EU between 2006 and 2012 will test how effective reforms have been in ensuring accountability and transparency in public finances. Expectations are tinged with a hint of scepticism. The new foreign minister says: 'What Romania needs at the moment are people who are determined to rebrand the country' (Condon, 23 February, 2005).

Questions

◆ How successful is Romania's economic transition to date?
◆ How can Romania prevent the emigration of its workers?
◆ Why is there still cause to be sceptical about Romania's economic prospects for the future?

Sources: World Bank (2006) *Doing Business Report 2006*, www.ebrd.com; Condon, C., 'EU hopes spur new revolution', *Financial Times*, 23 February 2005; Mackintosh, J., 'Renault's Romanian success boosts profits', *Financial Times*, 29 September 2005; Guha, K., 'World Bank praises pro-business reforms in many African countries', *Financial Times*, 6 September 2006; Condon, C. and Fak, A., 'A big effort to make up for lost time', *Financial Times*, 23 February 2005; Condon, C., 'How to be a multimillionaire', *Financial Times*, 23 February 2005; Gallagher, T., 'Europe opens the door to an unreformed Romania', *Financial Times*, 2 October 2006.

WEB CHECK

Information on Romania's economy is located on the country page of the World Bank's site, www.worldbank.org.

The European Union

While the European Union (EU) began with a trade agreement, the Treaty of Rome in 1956, successive treaties have extended its remit and led to deepening integration among members. It has not always been smooth sailing, and the EU is currently debating basic issues on its future direction: how should it be organized in the twenty-first century, and how far should enlargement go? The EU's core principles are freedom of movement for goods, capital, people and services. Trade and FDI have flourished, each of the member states trading mainly with other EU states. However, services, which represent 70% of the EU economy, are not yet open across national borders. A long-awaited services directive has been difficult to negotiate against a backdrop of strong national interests. In respect of the free movement of people, only three of the EU 15 states – the UK, Ireland and Sweden – allowed workers to enter freely from the 10 accession states of 2004. The others all applied restrictions, due to last for up to seven years. Restrictions for Bulgarians and Romanians have also been imposed following their accession, including restrictions in the UK.

The 15 EU states which have become members of the eurozone have committed themselves to deeper economic integration, but their economies have not converged as had been expected. The single currency, the euro, is the most visible sign of integration, bringing to an end currency risk among member countries. They are required to keep national public finances under control, and to keep budget deficits within 3% of GDP. These economies have generally not enjoyed the growth rates that they had hoped for. While Ireland and Spain enjoyed +4% growth in 2004 and 2005, these growth rates have fallen back. France and Germany have had weaker growth and relatively high unemployment. Public spending has been difficult to control, and budget deficits in excess of the stability pact limit have persisted. The ECB determines interest rates for the whole of the eurozone, but fiscal policy, including taxation, is still a matter for national authorities. Taxation rates differ, therefore, from quite low rates in Ireland to relatively high rates in Germany. As Figure 3.9 showed, the 10 new EU countries of 2004 have tended to use low-tax policies as a location advantage. Slovenia, Cyprus and Malta have joined the eurozone, and others wish to follow.

The EU has also had problems balancing its own budget. The new members are relatively poorer countries than the EU 15, accounting for only 15% of EU GDP. These countries are net recipients of EU funds, and the EU 15 are net contributors. From its early days, the organization paid generous subsidies to farmers, through the Common Agricultural Policy (CAP). Although this budget has been whittled away, agricultural spending still accounts for over a third of all EU spending (see Figure 3.13). Regional aid in the form of 'cohesion' funds also takes a large share of the budget. Most of this money is now going to the eight poor member states to the east, acting as an effective transfer of funds from rich to poor states. Budget negotiations tend to bring national self-interest to the fore. Poorer members attempt to gain as big a slice of the cake as they can, while the countries which are net contributors are increasingly questioning the EU budget burden. These richer countries have had slower growth rates and budget

WEB CHECK

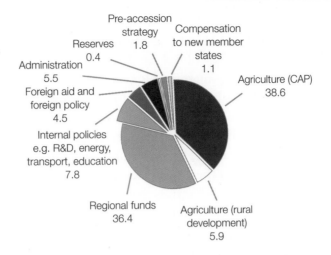

Figure 3.13 EU budget 2005, percentages of total, €116.5bn
Source: Financial Times, 13 December 2005

Pre-accession strategy 1.8
Compensation to new member states 1.1
Reserves 0.4
Administration 5.5
Foreign aid and foreign policy 4.5
Internal policies e.g. R&D, energy, transport, education 7.8
Regional funds 36.4
Agriculture (rural development) 5.9
Agriculture (CAP) 38.6

deficits, and their representatives are under pressure at home to reduce spending. Populations of the rich countries of the EU 15 are now less willing than in the past to fund motorways and other projects in Eastern Europe, especially as the new EU states are attracting FDI to fuel growth rates of 5%, twice the rate of the 'old' EU of 15.

The divergence of national interests which has emerged in the enlarged EU is perhaps indicative of strains within the differing perspectives of capitalism in the EU. All members except the UK and, to a lesser extent, Ireland, subscribe to a social market model of capitalism. The free-market perspective prefers market solutions for poorer regions, accepting that some inequality is inevitable, whereas the social market model aims to use funding aid to promote social justice. On the European stage, this latter aim entails richer countries giving financial support to the poorer nations and regions to raise the general level, ultimately strengthening European unity. The Netherlands, the largest per capita net contributor to the EU budget, along with France, voted 'no' to the new constitution for an enlarged EU, indicating a resurgence of national self-interest. As both states are social market systems, the signs are that social values at home do not necessarily translate to the wider European project.

TO RECAP...

EU economic integration

With continuing enlargement, the EU has embraced diverse economies and differing levels of economic development. Aims to achieve a single market in goods, capital, people and services have faltered, with differing perspectives of national self-interest of member states. Within the eurozone, differing financial systems remain in place, and budget deficits are a concern. The EU's finances are themselves stretched, especially in light of demands from new poorer member states.

The least developed economies

Fifty countries fall within the UN's category of least developed economies. Most are agricultural economies, dependent on fragile lands and volatile commodities markets. A few are in Asia, including Afghanistan, Bangladesh and Cambodia, but the vast majority are in Africa. Poverty, illiteracy and disease are major challenges in these countries, making it difficult to stimulate economic development. Another feature that most share is poor governance. Most of these countries were former colonies, which, having achieved independence, looked to build democratic political systems and foster national identity, as well as promote economic development. However, ethnic tensions and conflict, including civil wars, have hampered nation-building and economic activity. Many are termed 'fragile states', indicating that fragmented loyalties, often to clans or tribes with local power bases, hold more sway than central government institutions. Most of these fragile states are in sub-Saharan Africa, a region which is recognized by the UN as having the lowest levels of human development. The UN's Millennium Development Goals include halving the proportion of people living in absolute poverty from the 1990 level by 2015 (discussed in Chapter 15). This goal looks increasingly unattainable in sub-Saharan Africa.

Africa is home to 13% of the world's population, and is growing in population at a quicker rate than any other continent – nine times quicker than Western Europe. Yet it generates only 3% of world GDP, with a per capita income of only 5% of the high-income countries. Although African countries were at the same income level as Asian countries 30–40 years ago, since then, Asian countries have forged ahead, raising incomes and reducing poverty, while African countries have disappointed in both respects. The countries of Africa present a mixed picture. Those rich in natural resources, including oil and minerals, have benefited from the wealth generated, but this wealth has often been concentrated in the hands of elites and not found its way to improving conditions for whole populations. Ethnic divisions, weak governance and corruption have been widespread problems.

The poorest countries of sub-Saharan Africa have been the focus of programmes devised by the world's richest countries, comprising aid and debt relief. Official aid has been channelled to sub-Saharan Africa for over four decades. Financed through the IMF and World Bank, this aid has been aimed essentially at reducing the level of extreme poverty (discussed in Chapter 15). The aid has been substantial, amounting to $435 billion. In Mozambique, it has amounted to about one-quarter of GDP, and in Uganda, one-tenth. In these countries, the aid has been reasonably well administered. Mozambique has achieved growth in income per head of 4.3% between 1990 and 2001. Ghana is another relative success, achieving growth of over 4%. The aid has been directed mainly towards health and education, but a rethinking currently underway is looking at the wider issues of development needs. These are explored in Chapter 15.

TO RECAP...

The least developed countries

These countries have struggled to achieve sustained economic growth, due to a range of factors, including political instability, poor governance, social and ethnic conflict and corruption. High levels of poverty and disease make economic activities difficult to sustain. Aid from rich countries, as well as foreign investors, offers prospects for development.

Conclusions

- National economies diverge in their activities, size and organizations. The rich countries of the developed world, mainly in America and Western Europe, enjoy the highest levels of GDP per capita. The earliest to industrialize, these high-income economies are now mainly service based and reliant on high-tech sectors. Joined by Japan in the 1970s, developed states share concerns about competitiveness in the global economy. All face the public spending pressures of ageing populations, and rising costs of healthcare. Attracting and retaining FDI becomes difficult in these high-cost environments, and manufacturing jobs have tended to migrate to lower cost developing economies. On the positive side, large markets and good infrastructure in the developed countries provide location advantages for international business strategists.

- Divergent models of economy have emerged as more countries have become industrialized. Alongside the liberal economic model of the UK and US, there has evolved the social

market model prevalent in European countries, which takes a more state-oriented approach to social welfare. Although there is no specifically Asian model of capitalism, Asian countries tend to share a view of the state as guiding economic development, although not acting in a strong welfare role. China is now the world's largest developing economy, and also a transition economy, progressing from state planning to market institutions. Its high growth rate owes much to FDI and the burgeoning domestic private sector. Despite strong growth, China still has much to do to raise levels of prosperity for all the population.

- MNEs have also beaten paths to the post-communist transition economies of Central and Eastern Europe. Many of these countries have seen the fruits of market reforms, in the shape of EU membership, and their low costs make them attractive for foreign investors. But corruption and uncertain legal environments continue to cloud their prospects. The former Soviet republics, including Russia, offer even greater rewards, but higher risks from the growing role of the state. Some of the world's least developed economies are attracting attention for their natural resources, but the gains from extraction industries could prove short-lived. For these – and other – developing countries, improved governance and enterprise structures are needed to assure sustainable growth.

> **Global versus national**
> As has been seen in this chapter, there is much economic data available comparing national economies, which MNEs can assess in terms of the best environments for their operations and markets. Globalization therefore accentuates national economic differences, making them more, rather than less, important. Do you agree or disagree with this view, and why?

PAUSE TO REFLECT

Review questions

Part A: Grasping the basic concepts and knowledge

1. What is the significance of GNI and GDP in comparing economies?
2. Cite two examples of countries from each of the following categories: developed; transition; developing countries; and least developed countries. Explain how the structures of their economies contrast.
3. What is economic growth, and what are the reasons for differing growth rates among national economies?
4. Explain what is meant by inflation and how high inflation is damaging in an economy.
5. What can governments do to reduce high levels of unemployment?
6. Why is inequality a concern of governments?
7. Budget deficits have been acute among some EU countries, but governments have struggled to bring them under control. Why?
8. What are the characteristics of the planned economy? Why have planned economies failed?
9. Contrast the liberal market economy with the social market model. Why are countries with social market models taking steps towards more liberal market reforms?
10. The Asian economies are often grouped together. How are they similar and how are they different from one another?
11. What is a transition economy, and in what respects does it differ from a developing economy?
12. How have the post-communist transition economies diverged from each other? What problems still cloud the business environment in these countries?
13. Discuss the ways in which China's market reforms have made progress in economic development, and the factors which cast a shadow over its sustainability.
14. What is meant by regional integration?
15. What are the principles on which the EU rests? Why has progress been slow in bringing them into practice?
16. What are the problems of the least developed countries which hold back economic development? What are the solutions?

Part B: Critical thinking and discussion

1. Looking at two countries which have high growth rates at present, explain why they are growing strongly, and what their prospects are for continued growth. Next, look at two countries with low growth rates, explaining why growth is weak and what their prospects of upturn are.
2. How have businesses benefited from economic integration within the EU? Contrast those in the EU 15 with those in the 12 recent accession states.
3. Assess the priorities of the EU's budget. What is the justification for richer countries subsidizing development in the poorer countries? Do you agree with this policy, and why?
4. Assess the impact of globalization on differing national economies: a developed economy; a developing economy; and a transition economy.

Case study 3.2: Wal-Mart's great leap forward

Wal-Mart is the world's largest retailer, but this American retailing giant is finding life at the top hard at home, and even harder abroad. In 1962, Sam Walton, Wal-Mart's founder, devised a business model which seemed to guarantee continued growth: employ lowly paid staff (called associates) to sell low-cost, mass-market products predominantly aimed at America's low-income groups. By the end of the 1990s, the model was starting to look tarnished, as consumers became more diverse and demanding, and employee relations started to deteriorate. The supermarket sector, once the domain of national chains, has now gone global. In the UK, Tesco forges ahead both at home and abroad, its sales growing faster abroad than at home. Wal-Mart, by contrast, has concentrated on the US, but with sales growth at home slowing, it belatedly looked abroad. Wal-Mart has looked to changes in strategy and organization to boost sales at home, as well as compete in global markets. Currently, the US accounts for 80% of its profits, but it hopes to increase global profits from the current 20% to 30%.

From its southern headquarters of Bentonville, Arkansas, the company built its chain of over 3,000 supercenters. These large 'big box', warehouse-type stores are mainly in out-of-town locations. Wal-Mart's core customers are mainly low-income groups, often rural, in tune with the company's southern roots. The company's pricing policy, 'everyday low prices', has encapsulated its strategy. Initially a food retailer only, non-food ranges, such as clothing and appliances, were added only in 1988. Its worldwide sourcing, benefiting from economies of scale, has brought in low-cost textiles and appliances, particularly from China.

Rising fuel and utility prices have affected the spending of Wal-Mart's core low-income customers. In contrast, its chief competitor, the northern-based chain Target, which caters for more affluent and urban customers, has been less affected by

plate 3.3 Retailing has gone global, with the advent of large stores such as hypermarkets, which are now expanding in emerging markets.

rising fuel prices. Wal-Mart has traditionally relied on its suppliers to carry out market research, which has provided a rather piecemeal picture of what its customers want. It has recently started a more customer-focused approach, doing its own surveys of customer preferences. It found that, of customers who shop frequently at Wal-Mart, nearly a third focus only on food, with its low profit margins, ignoring the non-food products, with their higher profit margins. This research led to the conclusion that wider appeal was needed, to attract more diverse consumers and to entice them to spend in all departments.

Traditionally a highly centralized company, Wal-Mart is attempting to decentralize its decision-making, giving more voice to local management. Divisional heads and regional managers had all been based in Bentonville. A decision was taken to move these managers out to local offices, joining them up by video conferencing periodically. The divisional heads now have a degree of autonomy, in order to meet local customers' needs. Wal-Mart's localization strategy, through the 'store of the community' policy, allows store managers to have more say in the selection of goods on offer. For example, where there are many Hispanic consumers, Hispanic brands are now on offer.

Wal-Mart executives have been concerned that higher profit growth is needed in the US to offset higher costs. Wal-Mart is the largest private employer in the US, employing 1.4 million people. Working for such a large organization, low-wage workers might be expected to be unionized. However, the company refuses to recognize the grocery workers' trade union. Wal-Mart's business practices and employee relations have generated considerable adverse publicity. Healthcare has been a bone of contention. The company offers no comprehensive healthcare. It has healthcare insurance schemes which its employees must pay for to obtain cover, but premiums are too expensive for many, resulting in the poorest relying on Medicaid, which is the government-supported safety net for the poorest citizens. The company has faced a number of legal challenges in its employment practices. A sex discrimination lawsuit has been lodged by its women workers. Going back to 1998, this lawsuit is on behalf of 1.6 million women in 30 states, and is by far the largest sex discrimination case ever heard in the US. The company also faces legal action in the US for

allowing subcontractors to hire illegal immigrants as cleaners. Abroad, it is accused of allowing sweatshop conditions in its contract suppliers in China, Indonesia, Bangladesh, Nicaragua and Swaziland. While a number of companies, such as Nike, use independent monitors, Wal-Mart uses its own monitors of factory conditions, adding to the company's damaged reputation. Its environmental record also causes concern, as the company has repeatedly fallen foul of the Environmental Protection Agency for waste from its stores.

Since the late 1990s, Wal-Mart has sought to expand internationally. Its remaining international retail units are shown in the figure. Its purchase of Asda in the UK in 1999 has been its most successful acquisition. It also entered the difficult supermarket environment in Germany, where the 'hard' discounters such as Aldi and Lidl have grown to 40% of the market. While Wal-Mart's global logistics should have guaranteed economies of scale to enable it to compete, the 85 stores struggled to make profits, losing out to the established discounters. It also encountered

Figure Number of retail units of Wal-Mart International, 2006

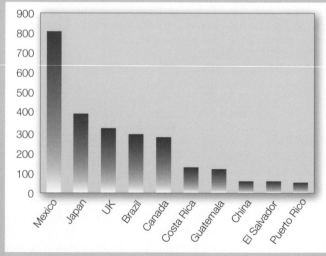

Source: *Financial Times*, 29 July 2006

problems with Germany's strong trade unions. Wal-Mart sold these shops to the Metro chain in 2006. Its attempts to win over Japanese consumers have also faltered, its subsidiary Seiyu struggling to make profits. South Korea was also a formidable challenge, and here, the 16 loss-making supermarkets were also sold in 2006.

Wal-Mart has now moved on to China, where it competes against a number of other Western hypermarket players, such as Tesco and Carrefour. Here, Wal-Mart is seeking to replicate its model with burgeoning ranks of wage-earning consumers, also hoping to offer them its own credit card. The bank backing the scheme is substantially owned by state entities and non-tradable shares, as is common in China. In a further move, Wal-

Mart, known for its anti-union stance in the US, has allowed trade unions to set up branches in its Chinese outlets, and has also allowed the Chinese Communist Party to set up a branch in one. While this may seem ironic, the partnership between the Chinese Communist Party and Wal-Mart has a logic: the company seeks profits in the world's largest and fastest growing market, while China's leaders wish to keep an eye on this mighty investor. This latest chapter in Wal-Mart's localization strategy might not go down very well, however, with shareholders back home in Bentonville.

Questions

1　Assess Wall-Mart's strategy and organizational changes in its US operations.
2　Wal-Mart's international expansion, to date, has not been an unqualified success. Are its prospects better for its great leap into China, and why?
3　In what ways does Wal-Mart epitomize twenty-first-century capitalism, including its good and bad aspects?

Sources: Roberts, D., 'Wal-Mart launches drive to polish its image', *Financial Times*, 14 January 2005; Birshall, J., 'Wal-Mart faces sweat-shop lawsuit', *Financial Times*, 14 September 2005; Birchall, J., 'Wal-Mart tries to halt mass suit', *Financial Times*, 8 August 2005; Birchall, J., 'Supermarket sweep: how the world's biggest chain aims to swap tired for tidy', *Financial Times*, 10 November 2005; Weismann, G., 'Why Wal-Mart decided to pack its bags in Germany', *Financial Times*, 29 July 2006; Birchall, J., 'Trouble in store', *Financial Times*, 29 April 2006; 'Whale-Mart', *Financial Times*, 5 April 2007.

WEB CHECK

Wal-Mart's corporate website is http://investor.walmartstores.com.

Further research

Journal articles

Child, J. and Tse, D. (2001) 'China's transition and its implications for international business', *Journal of International Business Studies*, **32**(1): 5–21.

Pryor, F. (2006) 'Economic systems in developing nations', *Comparative Economic Studies*, **48**(1): 77–99.

Rosefielde, S. (2007) 'The illusion of westernisation in China and Russia', *Comparative Economic Studies*, **49**(4): 495–513.

Books

Albert, M. (1993) *Capitalism vs. Capitalism*, New York: Four Walls Eight Windows.

Baimbridge, M., Harrop, J. and Philippidis, G. (2004) *Current Economic Issues and EU Integration*, Basingstoke: Palgrave Macmillan.

Chakrabarti, S. (2003) *Transition and Economic Development in India*, London: Routledge.

Goldstein, A. (2007) *Multinational Companies from Emerging Economies*, Basingstoke: Palgrave Macmillan.

Krugman, P. (1990) *The Age of Diminished Expectations*, Cambridge, MA: MIT Press.

Mavrotas, G. and Shorrocks, A. (2007) *Advancing Development*, Basingstoke: Palgrave Macmillan.

O'Brien, R. and Williams, M. (2007) *Global Political Economy*, 2nd edn, Basingstoke: Palgrave Macmillan.

OECD (2004) *Understanding Economic Growth*, Basingstoke: Palgrave Macmillan.

Don't forget to check the companion website at **www.palgrave.com/business/morrisonib**, where you will find web-based assignments, web links, interactive quizzes, an extended glossary and lots more to help you learn about international business.

chapter 4
THE CULTURAL ENVIRONMENT

learning objectives

▷ **To appreciate the differing facets of culture as they impact on business interactions**
▷ **To identify and apply culture theories in differing business contexts**
▷ **To highlight the differences in organizational cultures, and how they affect business activities across national borders**
▷ **To understand the processes of culture change taking place across the globe, along with their implications for business**

Introduction

The harshest winter weather for five decades struck China early in 2008, just as people's thoughts turned to returning to home villages for celebration of the lunar New Year. This annual event, comprising over 2 billion journeys, is the world's largest annual movement of people – larger even than the annual pilgrimage (the haj) to Mecca for Muslims. China's industrial production relies on tens of millions of migrant labourers from rural areas working in factories concentrated in the coastal regions. For these workers, accustomed to living in crowded dormitories near their factories, a trip back to their home villages to see families is precious. But snow and icy conditions brought travel chaos, leaving hundreds of thousands of people stranded at airports and in railway stations, some for several days, before eventually giving up in dismay. The government did keep some trains moving, but these were pressed into transporting vital coal to power stations to keep China's all-important industries running. The government has considered introducing staggered holidays for workers, but no other date has the same meaning for the Chinese. For China's leaders, national pride in the Beijing Olympics was sharply jolted when pictures of thousands of stranded, angry workers flashed across the world's media. Bad weather can strike anywhere, but the extreme upheaval witnessed in China highlighted the tensions in Chinese society and strains on cultural bearings which have resulted from breakneck economic growth.

Culture influences just about every aspect of a business enterprise, including its products, the ways its staff communicate with each other and the values and goals of the organization. Culture is also a crucial ingredient in the organization's relations with other firms and their employees, with customers and with an array of stakeholder groups. While we are usually very aware of quantitative issues, such as price, in business transactions, the impact of culture, in matters such as feelings of trust and ease of communication, are more qualitative and less obvious. They are, nonetheless, equally important, especially if a long-term business relationship is envisaged. With global communications and cross-border business opportunities growing all the time, the cultural environment becomes ever more challenging. As highlighted in Chapter 2, globalization has paved the way, but it is still people of divergent cultural backgrounds who drive production, transactions and markets.

plate 4.1 Bright red lanterns greet the Chinese New Year, a time for family reunions and celebrations.

We begin by looking at culture's many facets, including values and behaviour, which distinguish one culture from another. Looking next at the roots of culture, we focus on key determinants: national cultures, social groupings, religion and language all play a part. A number of culture theories, which help in explaining and comparing cultures, are then explored. These concepts are applied to the business context, starting with a discussion of organizational culture. Enterprises in today's world are becoming more conscious of their own cultures, realizing the need to be adaptable in interactions with other organizations and with stakeholders in differing national environments. National environments are not static or monolithic, but constantly evolving and diverse. Lastly, we look at culture change in different countries and regions. These changes are shaping the global competitive environment. Changes in work, lifestyles and economic activity have profound effects on societies, as the opening vignette shows. MNEs have played a role in bringing about these changes, and are also responding to changing needs in societies, from both workers and consumers.

Culture's many facets

Culture: Shared, learned values, norms of behaviour, means of communication and other outward expressions which distinguish one group of people from another.

Culture encompasses all aspects of human communication, values and behaviour. This very broad range of phenomena has been studied particularly by anthropologists, who have provided guidance on the characteristics of culture, which allow them to draw 'maps' of different cultures. Anthropologists highlight two important characteristics of culture. First, it is essentially social: it is about shared values, symbols and behaviour, which other people in the same group recognize, and whereby they communicate, both in languages and by nonverbal communication. Second, it is learned, rather than innate. It is acquired through socialization processes, beginning from birth and continuing throughout life. We acquire culture largely without being aware of the process (Hall, 1976). Culture can thus be defined as shared, learned values, norms of behaviour and means of communication within a group, which, together with outward expressions, impart a sense of belonging and identity to members of the group and distinguish it from other groups.

The four main facets of culture, therefore, are values, behaviour, communication and outward expressions (see Figure 4.1). They may vary in significance from culture to culture. In some, behavioural patterns may be

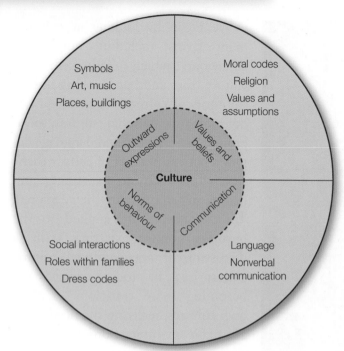

Figure 4.1 Facets of culture

paramount, while in others, shared values are the 'glue' which binds the group together. We look at each in turn:

1 *Values, beliefs and assumptions* which members of a group share are some of the most powerful facets of culture. They relate to the way in which we see the world, views of right and wrong, good and evil, what is beautiful and what is ugly (Hofstede, 1994). They also determine a person's status in society. The role of the individual, the position of the family in society, and the role of the sexes are all derived from values and assumptions. Assumptions also cover ways of thinking, such as differing views of time. This world picture can stem from religion (discussed in the next section), or it may stem from a secular ideology, such as communism or nationalism.

2 *Norms of behaviour* are closely related to a group's values and beliefs. For example, if, as in Confucianism, the duty of filial loyalty is paramount, the child who steps out of line is frowned upon. In a society, norms of behaviour may be enforced informally, by society's pressure to conform, or by a legal system reflecting shared values. There may be conflict between the two. A son may know that his father has committed a crime, but would not tell the legal authorities because of a sense of loyalty to his father. It can be the other way around, too. In the period of the Cultural Revolution in China, 1966–76, members of families turned on their parents, resulting in considerable cultural turmoil (Leys, 1978: 47). Recently, Confucianism has been restored to a position of respect in China, although within a broader framework of communist ideology.

When people in a society adopt routine behaviours, such as bowing in Japan, each time the gesture is made, the culture is reinforced. Conversely, Japanese businesspeople in a Western corporate environment are likely to offer a handshake rather than bow, or even both. The sight of a Western person bowing while the Japanese offers a hand, while outwardly comical, can be deeply embarrassing. One should not be misled by the adoption of behaviour to accord with business partners. The Japanese person is likely to see this as merely a means to smooth relations, leaving Japanese cultural values and assumptions intact. Negotiation between Western and Asian businesspeople therefore relies heavily on each side gaining as much of an understanding as possible of the other's culture (Buckley et al., 2002).

3 *Communication* includes formal language and nonverbal communication. Fundamental to culture, they are the means by which learning and interaction among members of a group take place, as well as communication with those outside the group. These have become sensitive issues for businesses, as cross-border transactions increase the need for cross-cultural communication.

4 *Outward expressions* of culture have perhaps become more significant in recent years, facilitated by the growth of global media. A few of the many

possible outward expressions of culture are art, music and buildings. For businesses, as for other organizations in society, symbols and logos identify the firm, projecting an image of its values.

The springs of culture

In this section we look at some of the origins and expressions of cultural differences. Understanding differing perspectives, some of which have long historical roots, is an aid to understanding people from different cultures when we encounter them in business situations. It is also an aid to designing products and services for diverse groups.

Nations

When we think of differing cultures in the business context, we are usually referring to national cultures. Although this is rather an imprecise term, it is the most frequently used classification in business and management research. Used with caution, it can be a helpful way of identifying cultural differences among peoples, although it has its limitations, as this chapter will show.

The nation is a group of people whose distinctive culture binds them together with a sense of common identity, language, shared history and usually a historical homeland. A nation is synonymous with a 'people'. Having recognized the French-speaking province of Québec as a 'distinct society' in 1995, the Canadian parliament recognized it as a 'nation within a united Canada' in 2006. This move was rather bittersweet for the Québécois: while they were pleased with the recognition of their nationhood, many aspire to the independence which befits a nation. Native American tribes, who were the indigenous peoples of America, had all the defining characteristics, and were often called 'nations'. Nowadays, the term 'nation' commonly means 'nation-state', which denotes a legal territorial entity. Unlike Québec or the Native American tribe, the nation-state is a sovereign entity. The tribe occupies territorial lands, enjoying some degree of autonomy, but only that which is delegated by the US government. Consider the following quote from a Native American Yakima Indian, whose tribe signed a treaty with the US government in 1854, which confined them to a reservation just over half the size of their tribal lands:

> They [the US government] gave us dual citizenship in 1924. How can a little teeny stupid 150-year-old government grant citizenship to a Yakima Indian who has been here for eight million years? (Terkel, 1980: 178)

Nation-states are often referred to simply as states, as in the member states of the EU. Modern nation-states may be home to multiple cultures. Some are indigenous cultures, which, although nearly wiped out by colonial powers, remain significant in some countries, particularly in Latin America (see CF4.2 on Mexico). A major source of diversity is migrants who form their own communities, perpetuating their own subculture within a society. As Figure 4.2, shows, of the world's 200 countries, 110 are home to cultural minorities amounting to more than 25% of the population. This diversity may create tensions, especially if minority groups are disadvantaged, adversely

TO RECAP...

Facets of culture

Facets of culture may be grouped under four headings: values and beliefs; norms of behaviour; communication; and outward expressions. Together, they form a distinctive cultural profile which people in cultural groups share, whether they be a whole nation, a family or an organization.

National culture: Culture, including a sense of identity and belonging, which distinguishes and unites people, linking them to a territorial homeland, usually a nation-state.

Subculture: Culture which distinguishes a minority grouping in a state where a different national culture is dominant.

Social cohesion: Shared sense of belonging to a society despite cultural differences.

affecting social cohesion. On the other hand, diversity plays a positive role. Employees from divergent backgrounds bring a variety of perspectives to organizations, which can be of benefit, especially if strategists have their sights on the international stage.

Figure 4.2 Cultural diversity: percentage of population from cultural minorities within countries

Source: UNDP (2004) *Human Development Report 2004* (New York: UNDP)

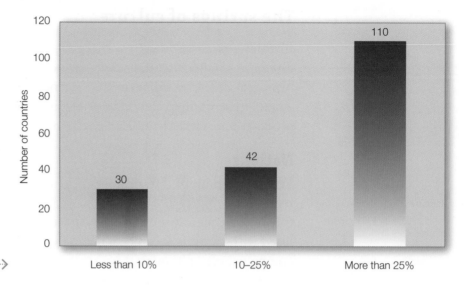

TO RECAP...

National culture

Shared language and history create strong feelings of belonging associated with national culture. Nation-states tend to have a predominant national culture, but most also have minority cultures within their borders, largely arising from migration.

Social and ethnic groupings

Culture may spring from a variety of social groupings which overlap to some extent with national cultures. A kinship group, a village or a region may be a focus of identity, bearing the hallmarks of a distinctive culture. An ethnic group has many of the characteristics of a nation. The group has a shared history and mythology, often semi-historical tales passed down through the ages which impart a sense of continuity between past and present (Anderson, 1991). In fact, myth, folklore and history can become blurred (Smith, 1991). While language, religion and customs are the outward signs of these ethnic communities, their strength derives equally from a strong subjective sense of belonging, a sense that can still exist even when a people has become sepa-rated from its homeland. The diaspora communities, such as Armenians and Jews, are an example. The states of sub-Saharan Africa were mostly constructed in the colonial era, with little regard for ethnic identity, hoping that a kind of civic territorial patriotism would hold them together. These states, however, tend to be home to numerous ethnic groupings, with tensions and conflicts simmering beneath the surface. The fostering of new political communities which aim to create a common sense of identity has been difficult in a context of strong existing ethnic cultures, and is one of the challenges facing African states.

Ethnic grouping: People drawn together by a sense of common identity, a sense of belonging and a shared history, including a belief in common descent (real or mythical).

TO RECAP...

Social and ethnic groups

Language, religious beliefs, kinship and ethnic ties create a diversity of social groups, leading to separate cultural identities. They are often the focus of tension within society.

Who am I?
We might answer this question by stating our name, and perhaps the country we call home. A Japanese person might answer with the name of the organization he or she works for. How would you answer this question? How does self-identification fit into an overall picture of a person's culture?

PAUSE TO REFLECT

Religions

Religion can be a powerful cultural force. Thousands of religions exist, and they may be found in any type of social environment, from agricultural communities to modern urban settings. It might be thought that secular values associated with capitalism would supplant religious values as societies develop economically. What seems to have happened, however, is that economic values and religious beliefs exist side by side. Research by Pew Global Attitudes Project (2002) shows that, although religion has relatively few active adherents in many Western societies, it is of major importance in the US and in many developing countries, as shown in Figure 4.3. For this research, respondents indicated whether religion plays a 'very important role in their lives'. The US seems to stand alone among developed countries, in that 59% of respondents agreed with the statement. Also of note is the fact that in Italy and Poland, both closely associated with Roman Catholicism, religion has fewer strong adherents than in the US. By contrast, religion is extremely important to people in the developing countries highlighted here, especially in Africa.

The Pew Global Attitudes Project is at http://pewglobal.org.

WEB CHECK

Figure 4.3 The importance of religion in people's lives

Source: Pew Global Attitudes Project, 2002, at http://pewglobal.org

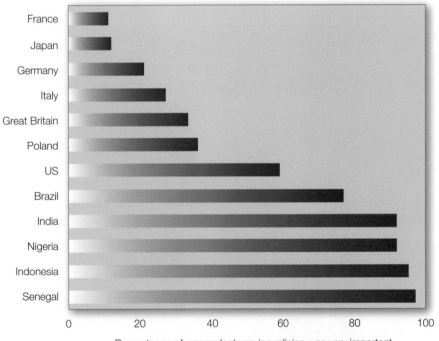

Percentages of respondents saying religion was very important

Major religions are shown in Figure 4.4. It should be noted that most include a number of subgroups, as explained below. 'Indigenous' is a vast category covering some 300 million people and hundreds of religions. Three of the world's major religions are Asian in origin: Buddhism, Confucianism and Hinduism. These are also some of the oldest, and there has been some intermingling among them. In Figure 4.4, the term 'Chinese traditional' includes Confucianism. Together with the other two major Asian religions, their adherents are about one-quarter of the world's population. Buddhism has been highly influential, not just in India, where it was founded, but also in China and Japan. The basis of the religion is the Buddha's teaching, which rests on the 'eightfold path', by which the individual travels ultimately to

Buddhism: Asian religion based on the teachings of Buddha.

Confucianism: Ancient Chinese ethical and philosophical system based on the teachings of Confucius.

Hinduism: Polytheistic religion whose followers are concentrated in India.

nirvana. The teachings have been disseminated through various sects, which together attract some 5 million followers. Similarly, Confucianism rests on the teachings of its founder, Confucius. This ancient religion dates from the 5th century BC. The religion is most important for its moral precepts, which have been highly influential in China, Japan and Korea. They emphasize 'filial piety' and family values, which have carried through to the social and economic organizations in these countries.

Hinduism is the third of the Asian religions, and the oldest. It is a poly-theistic religion, involving the worship of many gods, whereas the other two are monotheistic religions which recognize only one god. Hinduism is concentrated in India, where it has been profoundly influential on Indian culture. The caste system of rigid social stratification derives from Hindu beliefs, and, although officially abolished at the time of Indian independence, is still a factor in Indian society.

The oldest of the world's monotheistic religions is Judaism. In common with Christianity and Islam, Judaism was founded in the Middle East, and its holy sites rub shoulders with sites which are also sacred to these other important religions. Prescriptive rules are important for followers of Judaism, particularly dietary rules and rules related to the preparation of food in the kosher tradition. For this reason, it is often helpful for Jewish people to live in communities where there are kosher shops to cater for their needs. The world's 14 million Jews tend to see the modern state of Israel as essentially their homeland, because of its historical and spiritual significance for all Jews.

The two largest religious groupings in the world are Christianity and Islam, both monotheistic. Christianity numbers some 2.1 billion followers, or about 33% of the world's population, as shown in Figure 4.4. Christians believe that Jesus Christ is the son of God, and their sacred scripture is the Bible. Historically, splits have occurred in Christianity, springing from differing interpretations of the Bible. The split between the Orthodox Church and the Roman Catholic Church occurred in the eleventh century. The Roman Catholics have become by far the most numerous group of Christians, partly because of the spread of Catholicism through the colonization of Latin America by Spain and Portugal. Its clerical hierarchy, notions of sainthood and the position of the Pope as head of the church are important aspects of Christianity for Catholics, but were the source of dissent within the Church which led to the breaking away by Protestant groups in the sixteenth century. Protestants have themselves fragmented into various churches, such as Methodists, Lutherans and Baptists. A recent trend is the growth of evangelical Christianity, through newer churches independent of the established denominations. In America, there are estimated to be 70 million evangelicals, whose organizations are growing in wealth as well as converts (Wallis, 2005). Besides their growing influence in the US, they have spread their missionary activities to many countries, notably in Latin America and Africa.

Islam is the world's second most practised religion after Christianity, with 1.3 billion followers. It is a monotheistic religion, whose followers worship

Polytheistic religion: Religion based on belief in numerous gods or other deities.

Monotheistic religion: Religion based on belief in one god.

Judaism: Ancient monotheistic religion, predominant in the modern state of Israel.

Christianity: Monotheistic religion based on belief in Jesus Christ, whose teachings are in the Bible.

Islam: Monotheistic religion based on the teachings of the prophet Muhammad, as revealed in the Koran; followers are referred to as Muslims.

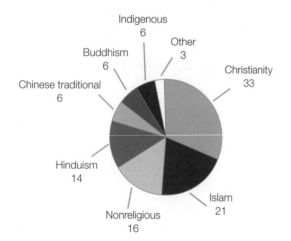

Figure 4.4 World religions, as percentages of world population, 2005

Note: Percentages add up to more than 100% because of overlap among adherents

Source: World religions data, http://www.adherents.com

Allah. Founded by the prophet Muhammad in the seventh century, Islam has also split into different sects, notably Sunni and Shi'ite, varying in their religious leaders and in their interpretation of the sacred text, the Koran. The Koran is the source of law for Muslims, and Sharia law covers all aspects of life. Tension between the sects of Islam and between traditional and reforming elements has caused instability within the followers of Islam. CF4.1 on Turkey shows these possible sources of conflict in Muslim society.

Most of the world's states are officially secular, tolerating the practice of all religions in theory, even though, where there is a dominant religion, minority religions can suffer discrimination. Just as most states are now multicultural to some extent, most are also home to diverse religions. More than 150 states (although not the US) have ratified the International Covenant on Economic, Social and Cultural Rights, which recognizes the right of all people to practise the religion of their choice. Most states have also enshrined religious freedom in their constitutions. The US Constitution, with its Bill of Rights (dating from 1791), became a model which other countries have broadly adopted in modern written constitutions.

TO RECAP...

Religion in the world

Religion is a primary source of values and beliefs for a large portion of the world's people. Depth of religious belief and practice ranges from those who are nominally of a particular religion, but are not active adherents, to those who devote their entire lives to serving religious goals. Some religious establishments and hierarchies wield considerable economic and social power, in addition to their spiritual and moral roles.

A comprehensive survey of world religions is provided on the Adherents website, www.adherents.com.

WEB CHECK

COUNTRY FOCUS 4.1 – TURKEY

Turkey between past and future

Istanbul's vibrant marketplace, the Grand Bazaar, was a thriving trade and cultural hub between East and West in the mid-fifteenth century, before Columbus discovered America and before the birth of capitalism in northern Europe. It was also at the crossroads of Christian and Islamic cultures.

Turkey's Ottoman rulers conquered a vast empire, straddling Asia and Europe. From the remains of the sprawling Ottoman Empire emerged the modern Republic of Turkey, dating from 1923. The new republic became a focus for Turkish identity and culture, as well as the Turkish language, one of the world's 10 main language groups. Characterized by a secular, westward-looking government, Turkey developed economically and politically into a modern democratic state which is now in the frame for EU membership. It would become the first mainly Muslim country in the EU and the most populous; its population of 72 million set to overtake that of Germany in 2015. It would also be the poorest EU state, as shown in the figure comparing GDP per capita in Turkey with EU member states.

Reflecting its history, Turkey is a land of contrasts – between rich and poor, urban and rural, as well as between reforming and conservative Muslims. In the western cities, such as Istanbul, the wealthy business elite have prospered, dominated by a handful of powerful family companies. These thriving urban areas are highly westernized. The countryside, by contrast, is steeped in conservative Muslim values. Here, the wearing of the hijab (traditional Muslim headscarf) is common. Turkey's large poor population presents some of the greatest challenges for the government. Unemployment at 11% demands that more jobs need to be created, but the weak education system hampers efforts. The average Turkish child receives only four-and-a-half years of state education. Liberalization measures, mainly since the 1980s, have opened up the country to more diverse market forces, including FDI. At the same time, people have moved to the cities in search of work. This migration to the cities has been a major change taking place in Turkish society. The urban population, 45% of the total population in 1980, is now estimated to amount to 70%. The new city dwellers, fresh from rural areas and often living in shanty towns on the outskirts of cities, have tended to retain traditional Muslim values and dress. In addition, Turkey has a minority Kurdish population concentrated in the south-

east. Kurds make up 20% of the total population. They have their own language and culture. High unemployment and tribal conflict within the Kurdish community contribute to social instability.

The diverse cultural environment presents a contrasting picture of a rather inward-looking, conservative Muslim society on the one hand, and a modern, market-oriented consumer society on the other. The party currently in power, the Justice and Development Party (the AKP) is a Muslim political party and Recep Tayyip Erdogan, the prime minister, is a devout Muslim from a provincial background. It is ironic that this conservative government is steering Turkey towards economic and social change.

The push for EU membership has come from the outward-looking business community, conscious of the economic potential, particularly in FDI and tourism, that this vast country presents. Given its relatively high unemployment, Turkey needs job-creating FDI, which EU membership would generate. It is well placed to attract FDI, as its wage levels are low by European standards. It has been home to numerous vehicle manufacturing plants built by global motor manufacturers. It has also built up the textile sector, becoming a major textile exporter. However, in the global environment, it is competing with China, which has even lower wage levels. Geographic location is in Turkey's favour, as transport to European markets is much cheaper from Turkey than from China, but its weak educational system raises doubts that it can provide the skilled workforce that foreign investors now seek.

A home-grown business, Aksa, part of a large Turkish industrial group, provides a good example to other businesses of what can be accomplished. Aksa is the world's largest producer of acrylic fibres, a wool-like fibre used in clothing and carpets, as well as industrial uses such as brake linings. It faces stiff competition from China, whose equivalent firms are increasing production 15% per year, and where labour costs are a quarter those in Turkey. Aksa is meeting the threat by developing new, more advanced fibres, through increased spending on R&D. Its high-tech plant in Yavlova is reckoned to be the world's most efficient. Here, machinery and raw materials are the main costs, employee expenses being small proportionately. One-third of Aksa's output is of high-grade fibres. Mustafa Yilmaz, the managing director of Aksa, is well aware that Chinese rivals are also developing new technology, but he is confident that new weather-resistant textiles for use in outdoor furniture and yacht sails will offer technological advantage over Chinese rivals.

The investment climate in Turkey has improved, but economic and social divisions within the society remain a source of potential instability. Erdogan points to the extraordinary progress Turkey has made in modernization and reform in a short space of time. He sees Turkey's role as bridging cultural diversity within the enlarged EU, highlighting 'the significance of Turkey as a facilitator for bringing together cultures and civilisations – helping to spread universal values to a broader geography' (Erdogan, 2005).

Figure GDP per capita of Turkey and selected EU member states

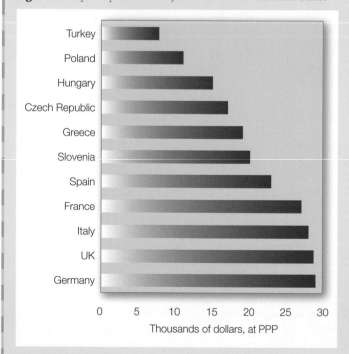

Source: Financial Times, 5 October 2004

Questions

◆ What cultural influences continue to be important in Turkey?

◆ What social and cultural changes are taking place in Turkey?

◆ Assess the positive and negative factors in Turkey's case for EU membership.

Sources: Gardner, D., 'Turkish delight', *Financial Times*, 4 September 2005; Boland, V., 'Turkey is becoming a re-religious society', *Financial Times*, 5 October 2004; Marsh, P., 'Out to compete with Chinese', *Financial Times*, 16 December 2004; Boland, V., 'A country more comfortable with itself', *Financial Times*, 29 November 2005; Boland, V., 'Has enthusiasm for Europe been misplaced?', *Financial*

Times, 28 June 2006; Boland, V., 'Overcrowded, under-funded and uninspiring', *Financial Times*, 28 June 2006; UNDP (2005) *Human Development Report 2005* (New York: UNDP); Erdogan, R., 'Turkey's historic journey', in *The Economist: The World in 2006*.

WEB CHECK

Find out about development and society in Turkey on the World Bank's website, www.worldbank.org, by going to *Turkey* under *Countries*.

Diverse societies

To what extent is your home-country environment diverse, in terms of ethnic groupings, different language groups and multiple religions? How have businesses responded to this diversity in terms of employment and consumer products? How would you respond to those who argue that catering for cultural subgroups is socially divisive, and that assimilation to mainstream culture will go further in building social cohesion?

PAUSE TO REFLECT

Language and communication

How we communicate with others and how we expect others to respond are facets of culture derived heavily from values and attitudes. Language and patterns of behaviour differ across cultures, posing obstacles for business relations.

Language and nonverbal communication are acquired very early on in life. There are many thousands of languages spoken in the world, and there are many others which have been lost, as speakers dwindled in number. In most countries, there is a dominant language, which is taught in its public schools and which forms the gateway to employment in the country's organizations. Members of minority cultures may face a dilemma: schools offer the official language, but their native language is spoken at home. Research suggests that bilingual education is preferable in these circumstances, providing a well-balanced educational experience, as well as the ability to build a fulfilling career in either language environment (UNDP, 2004).

The world's most widely spoken languages are given in Figure 4.5. As can be seen, Mandarin Chinese tops the list, but many other languages are also spoken in China. Written Chinese is an ancient language, used not just by Mandarin speakers, but also understandable to speakers of other Chinese languages, as well as Koreans and Japanese people. They would have difficulty communicating orally, but they would understand the written words and be able to look them up in dictionaries. Despite differing national cultures, therefore, language is thus another cultural tie among them, in addition to their common Confucian heritage.

As Figure 4.5 shows, the numbers of English speakers jumps dramatically, rising to 34.6%, if speakers of English as a second language are taken into account. The same phenomenon can be seen with other languages. There are

Figure 4.5 The world's most widely spoken languages
Source: Financial Times, 26 August 2005

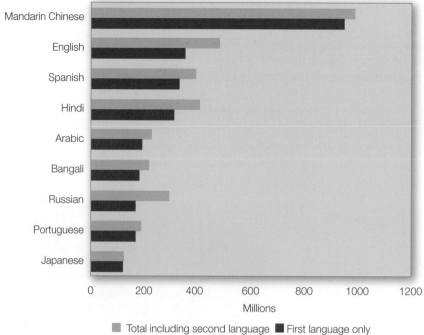

Nonverbal communication:
Gestures and facial expressions
which convey meaning within a
particular linguistic context.

some 400 languages in India, and Hindi is commonly used for intercultural communication, as well as being the language of government. However, English is also used by people in India to communicate with each other when neither speaks English as a first language. The number of speakers with Russian as a second language is 75.9% more than first-language speakers, accounted for by the dominance of Russian in the countries of the former Soviet Union and satellite states. Increasingly, English is seen as the language of business, and there is now a global boom in teaching and learning English.

Language exists in a cultural context. A machine translation package can translate language as linguistic code alone, whereas in real life, language is always in context (Hall, 1976: 90). In every culture, nonverbal communication also plays a part. There are many types of this unspoken communication, such as facial expressions or gestures of the hand or head which carry meanings in specific cultures and contexts. The same gesture may have different meanings in different cultures. Silence, too, carries meaning. The Japanese person, rather than saying 'no' to an idea, which might seem impolite, will remain silent, to convey disapproval. Cultures which are rich in nonverbal communication may pose difficulties for the uninitiated.

Hall distinguishes between high-context and low-context communication at opposite ends of a continuum. The high-context communication is 'one in which most of the information is either in the physical context or internalized in the person' (Hall, 1976: 91). Explicit words are not so important. The example Hall gives is of twins who have grown up together. They are able to communicate more economically than two lawyers in a courtroom setting, who express everything they wish to say. The low-context communication is like that of the two lawyers: most of the information is in the actual words. Asian languages tend to be at the high-context end of the spectrum, while English is a low-context language. In high-context cultures, distinctions between insiders and outsiders are important, and bonds are strong, whereas these categories matter less in low-context cultures. Business situations

High-context culture: Culture in which information is conveyed nonverbally, often relying on personal understandings of meanings.
Low-context culture: Culture in which information is conveyed predominantly by explicit expression.

involving people from high- and low-context cultures can be fraught with misunderstanding. Hall's conclusion was that people from high-context cultures find it harder to adapt when asked to step outside their own system: they move to the bottom of the context scale. Hence those from low-context cultures need to be prepared to be more explicit about every detail than they would normally be. However, in these situations, subtlety is needed, to avoid 'talking down' to that person (Hall, 1976: 92).

In high-context societies, personal relations are paramount, in business as well as in families. In family businesses, the senior members of the family have a patriarchal role, and are owed respect by those more junior. Even if the younger members feel that the firm's strategy is wrong, they are not free to express their views. Such disruption to the perceived natural order of things would cause disharmony in the organization. Asian societies typify this kind of culture. For the Asian businessperson, it is of utmost importance to cultivate personal relations with other people. An example in the Japanese context is given in SX4.1. In that case, the key to cementing the alliance was the rapport between the two companies' executives. Only in this way can trust be nurtured. The Chinese concept of guanxi captures this notion. Guanxi relates to personal relations, and is closely connected with China's Confucian heritage. Hierarchical relationships within the family, in which younger members owe loyalty to their superiors, are the basis for the reciprocal ties which exist in business and society generally. Without good personal relations, business transactions are unlikely to succeed (Dana, 2000). On the negative side, however, making the right personal contacts sometimes amounts simply to paying the right people, for example, for regulatory approvals. Practices akin to bribery would be considered corrupt in many countries, not to mention illegal.

In low-context cultures, explicit communication is more important than interpersonal ties. These societies are associated with individualism, whereas high-context cultures are associated with collectivist values. These dimensions are examined in the next section. In business relations, the low-context cultures place more emphasis on legalities of relations, including contractual obligations. Although the need for harmonious personal relations is appreciated, these are considered secondary to the formal legal terms. As a result, conflicts can arise in cross-border business transactions. The westerner may well feel that a joint venture is mainly a question of foreseeing potential problems, with provision for penalties and other legal redress included in the formal document. However, for the non-western partner, the success of the venture relies more on how well the individuals who are co-ordinating operations get on with each other, both at work and socially. If their relations are smooth, any problems can be resolved at the personal level.

Guanxi: Personal relations which establish trust and mutual obligations necessary for business in China.

Intercultural communication

Assume that a retailing company from the UK is wishing to set up a store on a greenfield site in Poland, with a view to further expansion. What language policy should it adopt, and why? Should it:
• Rely essentially on English, assuming that the Polish will speak English, and getting in agency interpreters for specific situations only
• Hire bilingual English–Polish staff, to act as links with suppliers and authorities
• Hire local Polish staff who speak some English and are familiar with how things are done in Poland

PAUSE TO REFLECT

TO RECAP...

Language and culture
Language is intimately linked to the culture of a people, and the world's thousands of languages are testament to immense cultural diversity. Although English predominates in the world of business, local languages aid firms in building relations and understanding of differing business locations. Of relevance is the difference between high-context cultures, in which personal relations are paramount, and the more impersonal context of low-context cultures.

Culture theories

Variations between different cultures have been extensively researched, leading to theories which help us to see coherence within cultures and divergences between them. These theories strive to impose some systematic overview of cultural orientations or dimensions. Hall's theory of low- and high-context cultures is one of these. The three theories introduced in this section are rather broader in aim, seeking to map how entire value systems underlie the way of life of homogeneous groups of people. The authors featured here are Kluckhohn and Strodtbeck, Hofstede and Trompenaars. The latter two theorists wrote with specific reference to organizational culture and management practices, while the first two were influential in identifying value orientations which later theorists drew on.

Value orientation theory

The basic value system of a group of people includes normative elements, such as what constitutes good behaviour, as well as aesthetic elements, such as what is pleasing to the eye. Importantly, it also includes ways of viewing the nature of things, how people see 'what is' or 'what is natural', which connect to the group's vision of what ought to be. Kluckhohn and Strodtbeck (1961: 10) started from an assumption that 'there is a limited number of common human problems for which all peoples at all times must find some solution'. They singled out five problems common to all groups:

- *Human nature orientation* – human nature may be viewed as neutral, innately evil but alterable, innately good, or a mixture of good and evil.
- *Relationship with nature* – differing cultures see nature in three possible ways. It may be a force to which they are subjugated or a force to be mastered, (the US is an example of the latter). A third possibility is that people see themselves as working in harmony with nature (for example Japan).
- *Time orientation* – past, present and future all present time problems for a people. Some societies give value preference to the past, as in ancestor worship traditional in Asian societies. Others, such as Americans, look to the future as better than the present.
- *Activity orientation* – being, being-in-becoming and doing are the three possible orientations. In most societies, one finds all three. The being orientation stresses what the person is, rather than what he or she can accomplish. Being-in-becoming stresses activity which has as its goal development of the self. The doing orientation stresses activity as a good in itself: for the American, just 'getting things done' is an accomplishment.
- *Relationship with people* – for some groups, particularly traditional societies, kinship, or a 'lineal' orientation, which continues across the generations, is of primary importance. An emphasis on the group suggests a 'collateral' orientation (referred to as 'collectivist' by other authors), while an emphasis on the individual is its opposite.

Kluckhohn and Stroedbeck stressed that in any society, there are differing solutions within each of these five areas. For example, a society may have a strong lineal and collateral orientation, as well as a focus on the past, but, over time, individualism and a focus on the future may emerge as economic development proceeds. Although dating from the 1950s, the concepts they

TO RECAP...

Value orientation theories

These culture theories focus on the differing orientations shown by cultures to basic relationships with other people and nature, as the basis for analysis and comparison.

identified have a striking relevance to culture change in modern societies. Warning against rigid or deterministic classification, these authors emphasized that most societies are a mixture of differing orientations, and that they change over time. They also highlighted that people can gradually become assimilated into a different culture.

Hofstede's cultural dimensions

Hofstede's theory of cultural dimensions provides a framework for classifying national cultures. It is helpful in understanding culture in numerous contexts, including the family, organizations of all types and societies as a whole. Hofstede (1994) identified four cultural dimensions which he tested empirically through research in over 50 countries. He later added a fifth, time orientation (Hofstede, 1996). A drawback of his research was that it was limited to employees of a large company, IBM. However, Hofstede stressed that respondents were from a broad cross-section of society. The five cultural dimensions can be described briefly as follows:

- *Power distance* – the extent to which people in the society accept the unequal distribution of power. In countries where power distance is large, power is concentrated in the top echelons of the country or the organization, and subordinates feel they have little power or influence in decision-making. Where it is small, power is distributed more evenly: those at the top are responsive to subordinates' views, and ordinary people feel they have a voice in decision-making.
- *Individualism* – the value of the individual person as an autonomous, self-motivated actor. In countries with high individualism, people are seen as setting their own goals and taking responsibility for their own actions. At the opposite pole are collectivist cultures, where the group takes precedence over the individual, and collective goals predominate. The collectivity could be the family, the organization or the state.
- *Uncertainty avoidance* – the ways in which people respond to the uncertainties of life. In countries with a high ranking, people feel anxious about what lies ahead, whether at work or in other social settings. In countries with low uncertainty avoidance, people have lower levels of anxiety and appear to be easy-going. Appearances may be deceptive, however. People in high ranking countries tend to be more expressive and emotional, whereas in the low ranking countries, people are not so expressive of their feelings. They may feel stress in uncertain situations, without showing it.
- *Masculinity* – the degree of assertiveness and competitiveness in a society, associated with gender roles. Countries which rank high in masculinity are more aggressive and acquisitive, while in more feminine countries, people are more caring, co-operative and concerned with quality of life.
- *Time orientation* – the perspective on time that a group shares. In some cultures, people take a short-term perspective, thinking mainly of current preoccupations and relations. In societies with a long-term perspective, the day's preoccupations are seen in the context of a longer time frame.

Some of Hofstede's findings for specific national cultures appear in Figure 4.6. From these, it is possible to group similar cultures together over a number

Figure 4.6 Hofstede's cultural dimensions

Sources: Hofstede, G. (1994) *Cultures and Organizations: Software of the Mind* (London: HarperCollins); Hofstede, G. (1996) 'Images of Europe: past, present and future', in Joynt, P. and Warner, M. (eds) *Managing Across Cultures: Issues and Perspectives* (London: Thomson) pp. 147–65

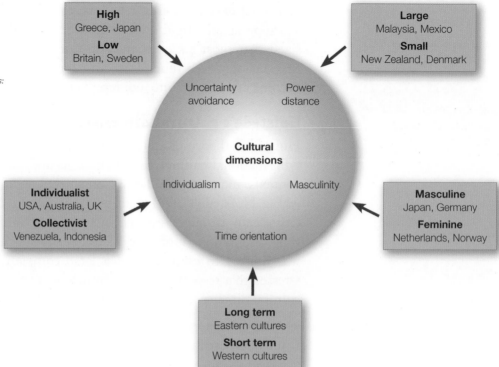

of dimensions. Countries with large power distance and collectivist cultures include Latin American and Asian countries, while small power distance and individualism predominate in northern European and English-speaking countries. For uncertainty avoidance, there are less clear patterns. Lower rankings include northern European countries, but high uncertainty avoidance seems to be rather country specific. Japan has relatively high uncertainty avoidance, medium power distance and medium individualism, but it is the top ranking country in masculinity. These findings would tend to confirm Japan's pre-eminence for its consensus-driven management style. Its high masculinity score suggests a strongly competitive approach by its companies in international business, but, in terms of Japanese society, the relatively weak position of women. South Korea also ranks high in uncertainty avoidance, but ranks among the more feminine countries. As shown in CS4.1, Citigroup found South Korean employees resistant to changes and also prone to labour unrest, both relatively common phenomena in countries with high uncertainty avoidance. Noisy protests were wrongly interpreted simply as a sign of aggression inviting confrontation, when they actually reflected fears for job security and employee welfare – values which are prioritized in feminine cultures. In this context, co-operative measures would be more fruitful than confrontation.

Hofstede's theory of cultural dimensions has been highly influential in international business and management research. Its strength has stemmed largely from its comprehensive nature: the theoretical framework can be applied to any country, as well as any context within a country, such as families, organizations or government. Another benefit is that it quantified cultural differences, allowing comparisons to be easily made between countries. On the other hand, Hofstede's correlation linking individualistic cultures with economic development, perhaps understandable in 1970, now looks problematic.

TO RECAP...

Hofstede's cultural dimensions

Hofstede's five cultural dimensions allow us to draw a picture of the ways in which a social group, from a family through to a whole society, deals with the situations which arise in everyday life. While criticized for its limitations, it seems to have withstood the test of time, providing insight into differences between national cultures.

Trompenaars' relational dimensions

Trompenaars (1994) sought specifically to present a theory of cultural dimensions designed to guide managers in organizations. He drew on the concepts of earlier theorists, applying them to practical situations which confront the international manager. For example, he provided practical tips for doing business in individualist or collectivist cultures. Trompenaars began with the approach of Kluckhohn and Strodtbeck, looking at the range of problems that every culture must deal with. These he grouped under three headings: relationships with people, attitudes to time, and attitudes to the environment. He set out five orientations under relationships with people, which are reminiscent of Hofstede's cultural dimensions. These are:

- *Universalism versus particularism* – the universalist culture emphasizes social codes, while the particularist culture emphasizes personal relationships.
- *Individualism versus collectivism* – the individual may be a primary focus of value or subordinated to group values.
- *Neutral versus emotional* – interactions with others may be objective and instrumental (in neutral cultures), or involve emotional expression (emotional cultures).
- *Specific versus diffuse* – specific relations focus on a particular transaction such as a contract, while diffuse relations involve the whole person.
- *Achievement versus ascription* – a person may be judged on achievements accomplished, or on status and connections.

Each of the above dimensions presents a dichotomy. While these should be seen as relative rather than absolute categories, they can be helpful in understanding different cultures, particularly in a business context. For example, Asian organizations are likely to take a collectivist approach, to emphasize personal relationships (particularist), and to be diffuse rather than specific in focus. Western organizations are likely to take a rule-governed approach (universalist), be more individualistic, focus on a particular transaction (specific), and keep interactions at an objective level (neutral). Trompenaars offered a framework designed to help managers deal with the problems presented by globalization. Companies wish to expand internationally, but must adapt their organizations and products to local cultures. He said: 'The internationalisation of business life requires more knowledge of cultural patterns' (1994: 4). His research and theory contribute to an understanding of how these patterns impact on businesses in practice.

TO RECAP...

Trompenaars' theory

Focusing on cultural dimensions, which highlight patterns of orientation to relations and attitudes, this theory seeks to provide a practical guide to managers in differing cultural environments.

Applying culture theories

Consider the national cultural environment with which you are most familiar. To what extent do Hofstede's cultural dimensions paint a helpful picture of the national culture? What are the limitations of this, and other, culture theories?

PAUSE TO REFLECT

Business and culture

Business relations across national borders, whether within the same organization or between organizations, rely on understanding and communication across cultures. A starting point is the organization itself. As we will see, organizational culture plays a crucial role in cross-border business.

Organizational culture

Hofstede observed that any group of people, varying in size from a family to a whole society, has a distinctive culture. He demonstrated how national cultural characteristics permeate all a national culture's organizations. It would be a mistake, though, to view national culture in a determinist way. The national culture forms a backdrop for the organization, but the role of the founder and managers are important in instilling values and norms of behaviour that will specifically help it to achieve its goals, or, indeed, hold it back from fulfilling its potential (Barney, 1986).

The outward signs of an organization's culture include its logo and brands, its guiding mottos and mission statement, traditional formal occasions which recall its history, office layout and the design of its website. These outward expressions give the organization its distinctive identity. However, its culture runs deeper, touching its underlying values, ways of thinking and principles which guide and unite members. The large organization evolves its own language, which acts as a bond between workers in different departments and different locations. This organizational language distinguishes members instantly from outsiders. Organizational culture can be defined as the values and practices of an organization in its relations with its full range of stakeholders. For business enterprises, it is common to refer to organizational culture as 'corporate culture'. The elements of organizational culture are shown in Figure 4.7. Hofstede's research (1999: 389) found that national cultures differ mainly at the level of basic values, and organizational cultures differ more at the level of practices. It should be remembered that an organization such as a business represents only a part of a person's life. Our national cultural values are deeply rooted, formed during early childhood, and have taken a grip long before we join organizations. We may also change organizations during our working careers. Organizational cultures are therefore more transitory, and can be managed to some extent by changing practices. In Figure 4.7, systems of communication and procedural formalities, for example, can be changed, while values and history are more deeply rooted.

Organizational or corporate culture: Values and practices of an organization in relations with its stakeholders.

Figure 4.7 Organizational culture

Source: Adapted from Hofstede, G. (1999) 'The business of business is culture', in Buckley, P. and Ghauri, P. (eds) *The Internationalization of the Firm* (2nd edn) (London: Thomson) pp. 381–93

Hofstede (1999) identified six basic dimensions of organizational culture which highlight differing management practices:

- *Process-oriented versus results-oriented cultures* – process-oriented cultures are more technical and bureaucratic, while in results-oriented cultures, all are concerned more with outcomes.
- *Job-oriented versus employee-oriented cultures* – in the job-oriented culture, concern for the employee extends only to matters directly related to work. In the employee-oriented culture, the employee's overall well-being is taken into account.
- *Professional versus parochial cultures* – in the professional culture, staff are identified mainly by their professional expertise, while in the parochial culture, what matters is the organization they work for.
- *Open system versus closed system cultures* – in the open system, people communicate easily with those inside the firm as well as newcomers and outsiders. In the closed system, barriers to communication exist in all these respects. The research found that this dimension closely reflected national cultural differences, those with small power distance being more open.
- *Tightly versus loosely controlled cultures* – in the tightly controlled culture, matters such as formalities and procedures are strictly controlled, while in loosely controlled cultures, a more relaxed approach prevails. Much depends on the industry: a research laboratory is more tightly controlled than an advertising agency.
- *Pragmatic versus normative cultures* – the pragmatic culture adopts a flexible approach towards dealing with outsiders, including customers, while the normative culture is more rigid in its dealings.

These differing practices, such as open or closed systems, are intermingled with values, and may well reflect national cultural dimensions. For example, Japanese companies exemplify an employee-oriented approach: the member of staff may be so imbued with dedication to the company that it becomes more important in life than his or her real family. Companies which are struggling to compete may identify cultural weaknesses which are affecting performance. For example, the firm may have a closed system and reliance on formal procedures, which act as a barrier to innovation. Managers in this situation would need to change the practices and culture. In large MNEs, there may be subcultures specific to particular units, giving rise to possible clashes. Again, managers face a challenge building a corporate culture across the organization which will aid it in achieving its goals. This task entails balancing the need for commonality across the different units with the need to adapt practices to local cultures in the firm's foreign affiliates.

TO RECAP...

Organizational culture

Organizations differ in their values, norms of behaviour, language and level of formality. Large organizations may evolve subcultures in different units. A unifying corporate culture across different units is an aid in achieving overall goals, but adaptations are needed in differing locations.

Organizational cultures with national roots

Link the following characteristics of organizational culture with countries in which they are likely to occur, stating your reasons:
- All procedures governed strictly by the rule book
- Open, relaxed communication among employees of all levels
- Emphasis on strong corporate identity, reinforced with highly visible symbols
- Hierarchical, with detailed job descriptions

PAUSE TO REFLECT

Rooted in the home culture?

Many MNEs are steeped in the home culture of the firm. Their managers and investors are likely to be nationals of their home country. For these firms, cultural distance, identified by internationalization theorists, can be a major obstacle (see Chapter 2). Cultural distance can be defined as the degree to which a firm is unfamiliar with the culture of a foreign business location, whether a market or possible production location (Kogut and Singh, 1988; Ghemawat, 2001). Some firms adopt a more international approach in their organization and outlook, although top management is still probably based in the home country. The pull of national culture is strong, even among firms that appear to be highly internationalized. Differing outlooks can be placed on a continuum ranging from ethnocentric at one extreme to polycentric at the other.

An ethnocentric organization is wholly imbued with its home national culture, assuming the validity of its own values and ways of doing things. When it acquires foreign subsidiaries, it is likely to give little authority to local employees in foreign locations. Its strategy is likely to be dominated by executives in its head office, who are nationals of the home country (Perlmutter, 1995). The polycentric organization is open to other cultures, and is likely to be more responsive and adaptive to local cultures in its international operations. The polycentric company is not stateless: its legal status and governance connect it to its home country. However, it wears its national culture lightly, and its managers adopt an outward-looking orientation. This approach is often associated with smaller countries, where, because their domestic market is limited, managers are impelled into wider markets more quickly than those in larger countries. Switzerland, featured in SX4.1, is an example. In international business, a polycentric approach, which is more flexible and adaptable to local differences, is likely to have a competitive advantage over the more inflexible approach of ethnocentric firms.

It has been predicted, particularly by hyperglobalizers, that truly global companies would evolve into essentially 'placeless' organizations, not rooted in any single country. This prediction now seems to have been rather overstated. Research by Pauly and Reich (1997) shows that national differences remain vitally important in the operations of MNEs. They looked specifically at Germany, Japan and the US, which accounted for 75 of the world's top 100 firms in 1995. Seeking to assess the strength of the home country as a company's centre of gravity, they looked for indicators which would provide concrete evidence of the influence of national culture. The three they focused on were the influence of national institutional and ideological background on firms' internal governance, financing structures and location of R&D. Pauly and Reich (1997: 5) found that 'the domestic structures within which a firm initially develops leave a permanent imprint on its strategic behaviour'. These leading MNEs were dominated by the outlook of home investors and ownership structures, which their managers viewed as their key relationships. Since this research, international investment has grown, and it might now be argued that companies have become more international in their view of stakeholders. However, as Figure 4.8 shows, the boards of American, German and Japanese companies have fewer foreign directors

Cultural distance: In the business context, the degree to which a firm is unfamiliar with the culture of a foreign business location.

Ethnocentrism: Perspective of individuals and organizations completely imbued with their own culture, to the exclusion of differing cultures.

Polycentrism: Perspective of individuals and organizations which recognizes their own culture as one among many, and strives to understand differing cultures.

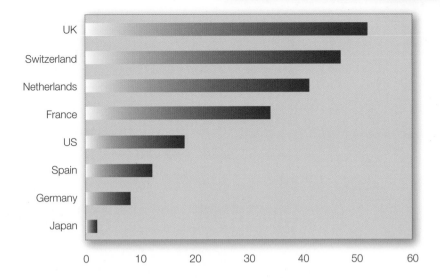

Figure 4.8 Percentage of foreign directors on the boards of the largest MNEs in selected countries
Source: UN (2004) *World Investment Report 2004* (Geneva: UN)

than those of the other countries shown. Firms in smaller economies are more likely to be outward focused than those in larger economies.

The UN annually assesses how internationalized the world's 100 largest MNEs have become. It calculates a ranking for a transnationality index, which is based on the average of three ratios: foreign assets to total assets, foreign sales to total sales and foreign employment to total employment. The 10 top ranking companies for transnationality appear in Table 4.1, followed by a selection of five other large companies generally perceived as global; all but one of the firms which are the most transnational are from smaller countries, while the firms which are the largest in terms of assets are less transnational. The five other MNEs listed are some of the world's largest companies. All have risen somewhat in their transnationality rating over the previous two years, but remain low in the ranking overall. Toyota creeps up over 50% (from 47.3% in 2005) and General Electric has risen from 43.2% in 2005 to 50.1% in 2007.

It is notable that some of the large American MNEs with low transnationality, such as Ford, General Motors and Wal-Mart, have struggled to retain competitiveness in global markets. Toyota, also ranked relatively lowly, at 64th, seems to have been more competitive globally. This might suggest that Japanese companies have been more flexible in localizing their strategies. Another explanation is that Japanese companies have been well placed, geographically and culturally, to take advantage of investment possibilities in Asia, where some of the world's fastest growing economies are located. It should also be noted that companies can alter their outlooks and strategies. Radical reappraisal of strategy is often triggered by weakening financial performance. Japanese companies, as noted in CF1.1, restructured in the 1990s, when their domestic economy was in the doldrums. It is thus arguable that they have evolved towards more polycentric organizations as they restructured. Coca-Cola of the US is another example. Prompted by flagging sales, it shifted its strategy to become more locally responsive, adapting products, brands and advertising to local tastes in different countries.

TO RECAP...

Company perspective

Companies, like individuals, seem to acquire enduring perspectives and values early in life. Companies with a polycentric outlook are often from smaller countries, while many of the world's largest companies are less transnational. For the ethnocentric company, shifting strategy towards a more international outlook is likely to involve becoming more polycentric in outlook.

Table 4.1 Transnationality rankings of companies

Trans-nationality ranking	Company	Home economy	Industry	Trans-nationality index (%)
1	Thomson Corp.	Canada	Media	97.2
2	Liberty Global	US	Telecommunications	96.5
3	Roche Group	Switzerland	Pharmaceuticals	90.5
4	WPP Group	UK	Business services	87.8
5	Philips Electronics	Netherlands	Electricals and electronics	87.4
6	Nestlé	Switzerland	Food and beverages	86.8
7	Cadbury Schweppes	UK	Food and beverages	86.7
8	Vodafone	UK	Telecommunications	82.4
9	Lafarge	France	Mineral products	81.9
10	SABMiller	UK	Consumer goods/brewer	81.1
Selected others				
64	Toyota Motor Corp.	Japan	Motor vehicles	51.6
70	General Electric	US	Electricals and electronics	50.1
79	Ford Motor Co.	US	Motor vehicles	47.6
85	General Motors	US	Motor vehicles	42.9
96	Wal-Mart Stores	US	Retailing	25.0

Source: UN (2007) *World Investment Report 2007* (Geneva: UN)

STRATEGIC CROSSROADS

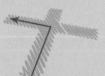

4.1
Flexible approach builds value for Chugai–Roche alliance

The partnership between Chugai Pharmaceutical of Japan and Roche, the Swiss pharmaceutical giant, presents a model of co-operation which enables both companies to achieve their own distinctive corporate goals. Japan is the world's second largest market for medicines after the US. Chugai Pharmaceutical has been successful in over-the-counter and prescription drugs in its home market, and has also acquired operations in the US. It was an early pioneer of R&D in biotechnology, and has good prospects of innovation in this area, which is growing more rapidly than the industry as a whole. Its research ranges from treatments for lung cancer to rheumatoid arthritis. However, entering the new millennium, Chugai's outward-looking CEO was concerned that it lacked the resources for further R&D development. He sought a non-Japanese partner, one who would understand and appreciate Japanese culture, as well as allow Chugai to pursue its research. The idea of a straightforward takeover was not appealing because, in

Japan, it is normally a strong company which acquires a weak one, implying management failure. In fact, Chugai *was* a strong company. The solution came from Switzerland, in the form of Roche Pharmaceuticals, whose CEO was impressed with Chugai's research record.

The deal between the two companies was talked through by the two CEOs personally, and its success is largely down to the good personal relations between the two. In 2002, Roche bought just over 50% of Chugai's shares. Roche had had a Japanese subsidiary, Nippon Roche, for 100 years, which Chugai took over, easing the pain of being taken over. Roche left Chugai's management in place, and took just three seats on its board. Chugai's CEO says of the deal: 'People were a little sceptical. Many have a psychological barrier about being owned. It also required courage by western management to rely on a Japanese company. These worries and concerns were made obsolete by us being open, keeping trust, having a process' (Jack, 2006). This broad 'hands-off' approach has allowed Chugai to carry on its research into biological drugs, linking into Roche's international network of research and marketing. With the support of Roche behind it, Chugai has now risen from 11th to third largest pharmaceutical company in Japan.

As a highly internationalized Swiss company, Roche was well placed to forge this alliance. Founded in 1896, it embarked on international expansion the following year, setting up subsidiaries in Germany and Italy. Within 10 years, it had subsidiaries in 10 countries, including tsarist Russia. Roche now has 70,000 employees in 150 countries. Given the limited size of the Swiss market, only 7 million people, Roche, like other Swiss companies, had to look abroad for opportunities. It generates 99% of its sales outside Switzerland. Its alliance with Chugai, while providing opportunities in the Japanese market through Chugai's distribution network, is more about seeing research into new drugs come to fruition.

Questions

◆ Why has the alliance between Chugai and Roche been successful?
◆ What lessons can be learned by other Western companies seeking Japanese alliances?

Sources: Hall, W., 'Punching well above its weight', *Financial Times*, 14 May 2003; Gapper, J., 'Swiss science rises above the crowds', *Financial Times*, 21 July 2005; Jack, A., 'A model experiment in Japan', *Financial Times*, 21 April 2006.

WEB CHECK

The home page of the Roche Group is www.roche.com. For the link to Chugai's home page, click on *countries*, *national websites*, *Asia* and then *Japan*.

Changing cultures in the modern world

This section looks at how cultures are changing in some key respects. These are economic development, urbanization, the role of women and the impact of multicultural societies.

Culture change and economic development

Culture changes which come with economic development stem from the shift from rural to urban environments, reflecting changes in the ways people make a living. Family-oriented economic activity, which prevails in agricultural areas, provides a strong social network as well as cultural roots. Although conditions are often poor for people who migrate to industrial areas, the prospect of paid employment holds out the hope of improved living conditions. One migrant to the industrial area of Guangzhou from rural Hunan in China says: 'Living conditions in the village are much better, but there is no money there' (Mallet, 2006). The feeling of attachment to a rural family home has been strong in Asian countries, as highlighted in the opening vignette of this chapter.

Better educational opportunities and the prospect of rising salaries and standard of living characterize societies enjoying economic development. Accompanying these improvements are changing lifestyles in modern consumer societies, with their acquisitive and materialistic values. In this sense, there does seem to be a convergence in capitalist development. Countries in both Christian and Islamic traditions have seen secularization accompany capitalist development, as CF4.1 highlighted in respect of Islamic culture. In Asian countries, Confucianism as a traditional influence stresses the value of education as a means of rising in society. This influence has proved beneficial in the modern context, as education is perceived as imperative for acquiring new skills and technology. The Confucian influence has also persisted in Asian organizations, as CS4.1 shows.

TO RECAP...

Culture change and economic development

Change from a predominantly agricultural society to an industrial, urbanized one involves a shifting orientation from a family-oriented lifestyle to a more individual-oriented one. Salaried work in a commercial organization, which typifies capitalist market economies, is associated with materialist, secular values. Nonetheless, traditional values have an enduring influence, greater in some societies than in others, contributing to diverse consumer and organizational cultures.

Citigroup, the world's largest financial services group, took the bold step of acquiring a South Korean bank, KorAm, in 2004. In its home market of the US, Citigroup seemed to be losing its competitive edge, and foreign acquisitions seemed the next logical move. South Korea was chosen because it was on the way to recovering from financial crises of the past, and it represents a large potential market. The KorAm Bank, with its 238 consumer branches, seemed a suitable acquisition. It was formed 21 years previously by a joint venture between local companies and the Bank of America. The purchase of KorAm Bank was Citigroup's largest purchase ever outside the US and Mexico. The new entity formed was Citibank Korea, becoming Korea's sixth largest lender. Korean was the designated language for the new offshoot. The head of Citigroup's corporate banking arm in Korea acknowledged that the task of integrating the two very different businesses and cultures would be difficult: 'once you get out of the US, particularly when issues of culture and language become paramount, it's a matter of demonstrating that we can do it' (Guerrera and Ward, 2004). KorAm's chief executive, in post since 2001, retained his position in the new bank. Having previously worked for Citigroup for two decades, he was well placed to bridge the cultural gap between the two companies.

To integrate the two banking systems and cultures, 'gap analysis' was used. For each difference between the two banks, the aim was to choose the best. However, highlighting gaps was not necessarily the best way to bring people together, and the new owners clearly had the upper hand in deciding which practice to choose. Integrating the IT systems was a mammoth undertaking, and it suffered from delays due to labour disputes. The parent company decided to change the reward system of the Korean branches. Branch managers had been accustomed to being more generously rewarded for lending than for taking in deposits. This was the opposite of Citigroup's policies, which paid greater rewards for attracting deposits. The policy was therefore reversed, causing some resistance from staff, accustomed to the old ways. The new bank also reduced the authority of bank managers to assess risk based on their own experience, giving more authority to the top managers' assessment of economic trends.

The US parent company also seemed to underestimate the cultural hurdles. Six months after the takeover, KorAm's workers came out on strike for a better wage deal and a pledge of no redundancies. The bank is still determined to impose its own compensation practices, but it has become embroiled in labour disputes. Indeed, labour relations are one of the country's most serious threats to competitiveness. Although only 12% of the South Korean workforce are union members, their influence extends beyond their actual numbers. Companies, rather than the state, are the traditional source of most welfare benefits in South Korea. It is for this reason that workers are so vociferous and aggressive in seeking to protect jobs and wage levels. As a leading trade union official says: 'if you are sacked, you suddenly become an orphan ... Job insecurity is a serious problem' (Song, 2005). South Korean

Case study 4.1:
Testing times for Citigroup in South Korea

workers also fear that their jobs could migrate to low-cost China. Corporate leaders warn that frequent strikes and excessive wage demands in sectors such as manufacturing will deter investors, as evidenced by South Korea's mixed record of FDI inflows (shown in the figure). Flows to South Korea fell in 2005 and 2006, contrary to global trends.

Figure South Korea's FDI inflows

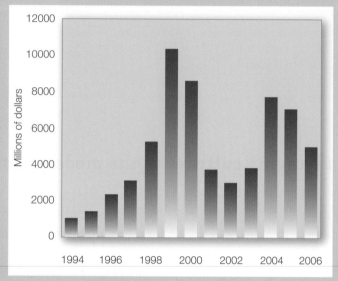

Sources: UN, *World Investment Reports, 2004, 2005, 2007* (Geneva: UN)

Poor labour relations tend to tarnish foreign companies' reputation within the country. One experienced foreign manager advises that noisy protests are simply part of the Korean culture – a means of expression in this still developing society. Raucous, banner-waving demonstrations are signs of deep-seated fears for job security, not indications of hostility or unwillingness to work together. But adopting a confrontational approach to unions, or attempting simply to impose company policy, makes it difficult to build good relations with employees.

Many foreign companies have found both the competitive environment and the cultural challenges testing. Wal-Mart and Carrefour pulled out, and other well-known names such as McDonald's and Coca-Cola have struggled. Citigroup expected a bumpy transition period. Its country manager for Korea said: 'When two rivers meet in the Amazon ... they flow beside each other for 10 miles before eventually merging.' Despite the fact that Citigroup derives 40% of its income from outside the US, the CEO acknowledges it has had problems, saying: 'I am very conscious that we are still too US-centric a company ... We need to be more international' (Wighton, 2005).

Questions

1   What difficulties has Citigroup faced in building market share in South Korea?
2   What issues within the two organizations have held up the integration process?
3   In your view, what mistakes has Citigroup made in integrating the two organizations?
4   What recommendations would you give to Citigroup for any future acquisition in Asia?

Sources: Wighton, D., 'Road to growth: Prince insists Citigroup still has the skills to make its size tell', *Financial Times*, 8 August, 2005; Wighton, D., 'Citigroup chief settles in for the long haul', *Financial Times*, 1 October 2004; Guerrera, F. and Ward, A., 'Adding spice to life at Citigroup', *Financial Times*, 18 October 2004; Song, J., 'The biggest threat to competitiveness', *Financial Times*, 17 November 2005; Song, J., 'Concern at the power of unions', *Financial Times*, 1 December 2004; Han, S., 'Citigroup falters in South Korea', *International Herald Tribune*, 18 August 2005; UN, *World Investment Reports 2004, 2005, 2006* (Geneva: UN).

WEB CHECK

Citigroup's website is www.citigroup.com.

Urbanization

Moving from a rural area to a city represents a radical shift in way of life, not just economically, but also in terms of social and cultural implications. Whereas rural life is mainly agricultural, reliant on unwaged work and dominated by family ties, life in a city is usually among people who are unrelated and work is in a formal organization for a wage. Urbanization is the process of transformation from a rural to an urban environment. It is particularly associated with the industrialization of production. In the Industrial Revolution in Britain (late seventeenth and early eighteenth century), the new factories were in the cities, where both living and working conditions were often unhealthy. While, in theory, sanitation and clean water should have been easier to provide in an urban environment, these developments were slow to materialize.

Urbanization: The process of large-scale shift from a rural to urban environment.

Urbanization is now taking place across the globe. In the developed world, over 80% of people now live in cities. These cities have long since left behind their origins as industrial centres. In the twentieth century, they became a magnet for immigrants, giving rise to immigrant community subcultures. Cities are being transformed again, as globalization and modern technology generate wealth, particularly in financial services and the media. Besides employment in newer sectors, a city's abiding attraction is a vibrant lifestyle, with amenities such as entertainment, restaurants and bars, as well as shopping areas. However, there remain problems of urban poverty in many older inner cities, as businesses (and people) move out to leafier areas. Designing modern cities which are pleasant and healthy places to live is a challenge for both the older cities and their newer counterparts in developing countries.

Figure 4.9 Projected growth of urban and rural populations in less and more developed regions of the world

Source: UN (2007) World Urbanization Prospects, The 2007 Revision, www.un.org/esa/population/unpop

The year 2008 is a landmark, when the world's urban population overtakes the rural population. Urbanization in the developing world is taking place more quickly and on a larger scale than experienced in earlier periods of urbanization, as Figure 4.9 shows. In London, the UN estimates that it took 130 years for the population to jump from 1 million to 8 million. In Dhaka in Bangladesh, it took just 37 years, and in Seoul, South Korea, it took 25 years (Harvey, 2006a). Almost all the growth in urban populations between 2005 and 2030 is occurring in less developed regions, where cities are growing rapidly, often in a haphazard way. As in earlier eras, infrastructure for basic needs such as clean water and sanitation lag behind. More than a quarter of the developing world's urban population, amounting to 560 million people, lack access to sanitation and clean water (UNDP, 2006). The percentage of the urban population living in slums stood at 40% in the Asia Pacific region in 2005, and 61% in Africa. More people live in the slums of Mumbai in India than in the whole of Norway.

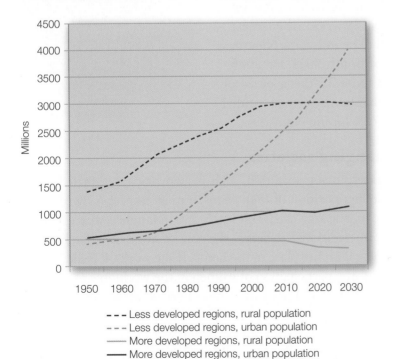

--- Less developed regions, rural population
--- Less developed regions, urban population
—— More developed regions, rural population
—— More developed regions, urban population

Figure 4.10 Growing cities in the developing world

Source: UN (2005) World Urbanization Prospects, The 2005 Revision, www.un.org/esa/population/unpop

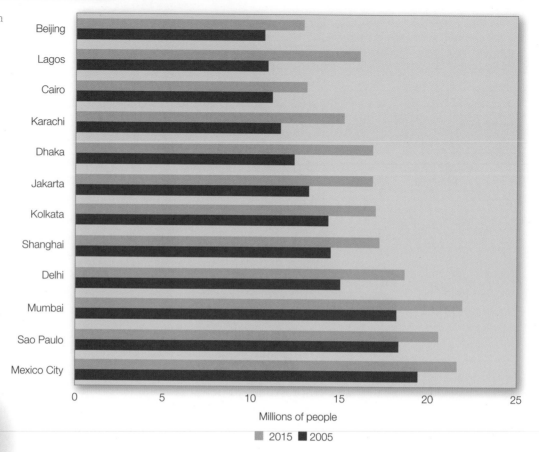

Millions of people

■ 2015 ■ 2005

The UN's urbanization website is www.unhabitat.org. Here there is a wealth of information on urbanization trends and projects across the world.

WEB CHECK

TO RECAP...

Divergence in urban life

Whether in the developed world or the developing world, people see the city as offering opportunities for a better life, but the reality, especially in the developing world, is likely to be poor and unhealthy conditions, even if employment is available. The growth of cities in the developing world is now a major challenge for authorities and businesses.

In contrast to earlier eras, rapid urbanization in today's world suffers from pollution from motor vehicles. Air pollution and toxic rivers add to the health problems, especially among slum dwellers (see a further discussion in Chapter 13). Figure 4.10 shows the projected population in 2015 of the fastest growing cities in the developing world. The largest growth is expected to be in Lagos, Nigeria and in the cities of South Asia. By 2015, there are expected to be 22 'mega-cities' of over 10 million inhabitants in the world; 17 of these will be in developing countries.

The urban–rural divide

Developing societies typically exhibit an urban–rural divide, as salaried work in the cities surges forward, while agricultural employment shrinks, leading to poverty in rural areas. What steps can be taken by governments to bring about more even development?

PAUSE TO REFLECT

Women and changing societies

In a hierarchical society or organization, each person has a designated place. Hence, for someone in a position of high status, utmost respect is owed, often reflected by the type of language used. This is the case in families, where a father is owed deference. In traditional societies, the role of women is likely to be constrained, in keeping with her place in the home. If she works, it is likely to be in the family business. The participation of women in the workforce of different countries is shown in Figure 4.11. As can be seen, in societies where traditional values predominate, the proportion of women working is low. Of the countries shown, the highest rate of participation of women in work is in Sweden, a relatively egalitarian society. Sweden also has well-developed provisions for the care

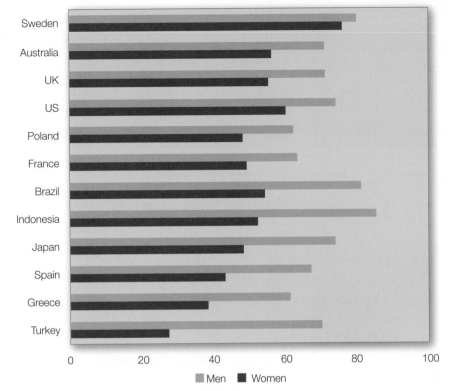

Figure 4.11 Comparison between percentages of men and women in the adult labour force (selected countries)

Note: The percentages are proportions of the total population aged 15 and over who are able to work or are actually working. Hence, people classified officially as unemployed within the country are included

Source: UN Department of Economic and Social Affairs (2005) UN Statistics Division, http://unstats.un.org

of children, which make it feasible for mothers to go out to work. In countries where such provisions are limited or expensive, women are more likely to stay at home to look after children, whether by choice or necessity.

Economic participation is only one of the ways in which the role of women is changing. Research for the World Economic Forum assesses the gender gap in three other areas, in addition to economic participation. They are educational attainment, political empowerment, and health and survival indicators. Its results, shown in Figure 4.12, rate countries from 0 to 1, where

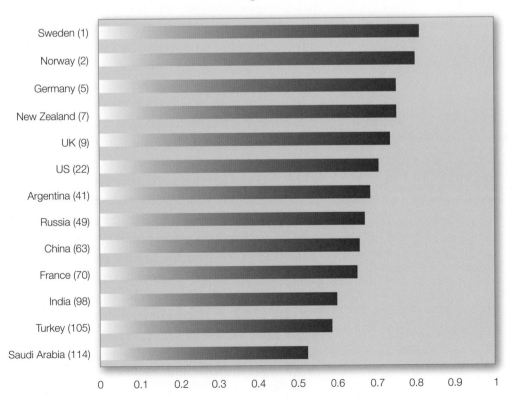

Figure 4.12 The global gender gap (ranking in brackets)

Source: World Economic Forum (2006) *The Global Gender Gap 2006 Report*, www.weforum.org

TO RECAP...

Women in changing societies

As economies develop, women are more likely to be in paid employment outside the home. However, inequalities in educational opportunities, health, wages and political representation are continuing issues in most societies.

Immigration: The movement of people into a country.

Emigration: The movement of people out of a country.

Refugee: A person forced to leave his or her own country, for any of a number of reasons, including natural disaster and civil war.

Remittances: Money sent back to home countries by migrant workers.

1 represents equality between women and men. The smallest gap is in Sweden, while the largest is in Saudi Arabia, indicating the strong prevalence of traditional values in relation to women's roles. Looking at the position of France, half of French women are employed in the economy, but their attainment under the four criteria is only 0.65 that of men. A reason for this lowly ranking is that there are very few women in the legislature, government or higher executive posts in business. The US is also ranked relatively lowly for the same reasons, whereas in Sweden, women occupy half the seats in the national assembly.

Multicultural societies

Most of the world's societies are home to people of different cultural backgrounds. Two main causes are immigration and the presence of indigenous peoples in countries which have been taken over by outsiders, often through past colonization. While we tend to think mainly of immigration as indicative of the movement of people, it should not be overlooked that, in many countries, for example those in Latin America, there are significant numbers of indigenous people, often discriminated against, who are now becoming more politically active, as shown in CF4.2 on Mexico. African-Americans, in both North and South America, although not indigenous (their ancestors were traded as slaves), have also suffered discrimination, both in terms of civil rights and equal opportunities.

Emigration covers a range of motives and types of people. Many are refugees from conflict or natural disaster. The vast majority, however, are those who simply seek a better life abroad. Globalization has facilitated mobility, through more transportation links and cheaper travel. However, administrative obstacles to migration have actually increased. The massive migration of people to the New World that took place in the latter part of the nineteenth century and the early years of the twentieth century occurred in an environment of relatively open borders. Nowadays, most countries impose administrative restrictions on immigrants, and those who enter must have documents showing a valid reason, such as joining families already in a country. Nonetheless, unofficial migration flourishes.

Migrants from poor to rich countries send much of the money they earn to their relatives in the home country. Remittances, which are sums of money sent back home, are important in the economies of many poor countries, amounting to 10% or more of GDP. However, the World Bank warns that, while they aid development, they are no substitute for national policies and have little impact on poverty reduction. Its researchers found that for each 1% increase in the ratio of remittances to GDP, the portion of the population living in poverty was reduced by only about 0.4% (López and Fajinzylber, 2006). (See CF4.2 on Mexico for a further discussion of remittances.) Many migrants, even if they take only temporary work, eventually settle, bringing up families. In these cases, the flow of remittances decreases, as the new country becomes their home. Figure 4.13 sets out the countries with the highest proportion of foreign-born people living within their borders. Not surprisingly, these are in the developed world, and the New World countries of Australia, Canada and the US are among the most popular.

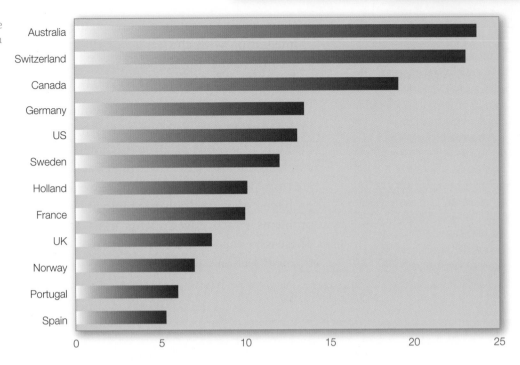

Figure 4.13 Foreign-born people as percentage of total population
Source: Financial Times, 18 May 2006

A number of recognized approaches to multiculturalism can be highlighted around the globe. They are assimilation, the cultural melting pot and cultural pluralism:

Assimilation: Process by which a minority culture gradually acquires the language and culture which predominates in a country.

1 Assimilation involves the minority adopting the language and culture of the dominant culture. France has adopted this policy, but it should be borne in mind that the historical context plays a part. French colonies were looked on as essentially overseas France, and thus assimilation was a logical approach. Recent problems of unrest in French cities and suburbs, where North African immigrants are concentrated, suggest that the policy might need rethinking. Problems of poverty, poor education and unemployment in Muslim communities are partly to blame. Some 20 million Muslims are living in Europe, making up 5% of the population. However, many Muslim communities are only partially integrated into local cultures.

Cultural melting pot: A mixture of cultures to form a new and distinctive culture, often in a new setting, such as the 'settler' societies of the US and Australia.

2 The cultural melting pot is where cultures, old and new, mix to form a new culture. The US has prided itself on this approach, but separateness and cultural pride are still evident. Hispanic immigrants have come mainly from Mexico, but also from other countries in Latin America and the Caribbean. Many are illegal immigrants, having no official right to reside in the US. They often seek informal and low-paid work, and are sometimes perceived as a threat by local people, concerned that their jobs could be at risk from these unofficial workers. The concept of the melting pot probably reflected an earlier historical era, when the US was still in a process of nation-building and all were welcome.

Cultural pluralism: The recognition of separate cultures within a society.

3 Cultural pluralism accommodates a degree of cultural separateness, not seeking to impose the dominant culture of the country. Nonetheless, certain ground rules apply, as in any pluralist society. Any subculture must abide by the laws of the land, accepting that other cultures also have a right to exist. This type of approach may pose problems, such as how far to accommodate faith schools or extend bilingual education. But, ideally, it

TO RECAP...

Multiculturalism

Most societies are multicultural to some extent. While the existence of cultural minorities is sometimes seen as divisive, forcing people to abandon their own cultures in the interests of assimilation is now seen as contrary to best public policy, as well as contrary to human rights. Cultural pluralism recognizes separate cultures within a basic framework of non-discrimination and equal opportunities.

allows people to retain a sense of cultural community while to some extent integrating with the values of the dominant culture. The approach also accords with cultural liberty as a human right, which has been recognized in international law (UNDP, 2004).

Under all three approaches, social cohesion depends on equal opportunities in education and employment. Most countries have legislated against discrimination, but often enforcement is weak. In this respect, businesses can take the lead with CSR policies. Often, children from minority groups are from poor backgrounds and are weak in school, partly because of language problems. Poverty, high unemployment and social exclusion are recurring problems which governments must address, as CF4.2 on Mexico shows. These issues also impact on businesses, especially in the developing world, as the next section addresses.

COUNTRY FOCUS 4.2 – MEXICO

Mexico struggles to heal divided society

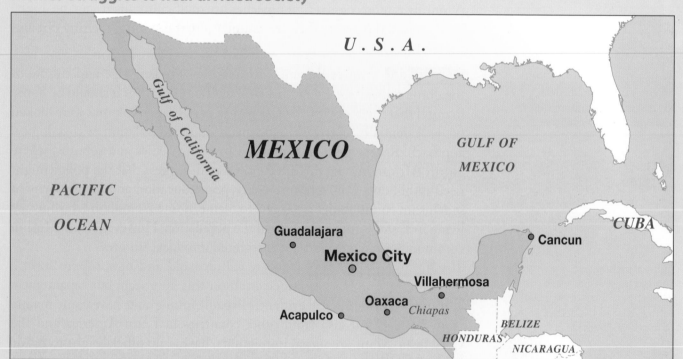

On the face of it, Mexico is in an advantageous position in today's global economy. It is a major oil producer. It enjoys privileged access for its exports to the US, the world's largest consumer market. It attracts flows of FDI that poorer developing countries can only dream of. It also has a recent history of relatively stable democratic government, unlike some of its Latin American neighbours to the south, giving it an institutional basis for economic growth and prosperity. However, while wealth is being created, benefits are not feeding through sufficiently to make the big improvements needed in Mexico's largely poor and divided society.

Mexico is home to more indigenous people than any other country in Latin America. These inhabitants are the descendants of diverse cultures and languages, including the Mayans, Aztecs, Zapotecs and Mixtecs. Although Spanish is the official language, there are still 62 living indigenous languages, Náhuatl (Aztec) and Maya accounting for nearly 4 million speakers between them. Estimates of numbers of indigenous inhabitants vary. Until 2000, the Mexican government's census counted only speakers of indigenous languages, but in that year, it began taking into account 'indigenous groups', giving a more accurate picture of self-identification. Their number is estimated to be about 10 million, or 10% of the total population, up from 5 million in 1980. They form the majority of the population in the states of Campeche, Chiapas, Oaxaca and the interior of Yucatán.

Official policy in relation to these indigenous peoples has been one of assimilation with the dominant Spanish culture, in which their languages and cultures are not officially recognized. Indeed, so great has been the intermingling that 60% of the population are reckoned to be part-indigenous in ancestry. However, the core indigenous groups have retained their heritage and languages. For decades, they have lagged behind in social development, suffering from widening gaps in education, income and quality of life as compared with the non-indigenous population. Moreover, complaints of discrimination and environmental degradation of their lands have accentuated their sense of being second-class citizens. Only in the past 15 years have self-awareness and self-identity been growing, given impetus by political activism. A crucial watershed year was 1994, the year Mexico joined Nafta. This was the year of the Zapatista rebellion in Chiapas, a political uprising seeking self-rule, in which 150 people died. Following these traumatic events, the needs of indigenous peoples became part of the national agenda.

The government of Vicente Fox and the National Action Party (PAN), elected in 2000, promised increased spending on health and education for indigenous people. It did not go so far as autonomy, but it marked a change in policy from assimilation to multiculturalism. A new National Commission for Development of Indigenous Communities was set up. Its head has stated: 'The indigenous don't want to be completely assimilated – they want their rights, their lands, their languages and their autonomy to be respected' (Smith, 2006). Still, in a report commissioned by the World Bank, Hall and Patinos found that progress has been disappointing. They found that levels of extreme poverty (defined as having less than $1 a day to live on) among indigenous people decreased from 70.8% to 68.5% between 1992 and 2002, compared with a decrease from 18.7% to 14.9% among the non-indigenous population. While these decreases are welcome, progress is disappointing. Moreover, there is a stark contrast between mainly indigenous and non-indigenous communities. In 2002, a person living in a municipality where 10–40% of the population is indigenous had an average income of 46% of that of a person in a non-indigenous municipality. Where the indigenous population was over 40% in the municipality, income was only 26% of that in a non-indigenous municipality. Hall and Patinos bleakly conclude that this finding reflects weak educational attainment, cultural obstacles and plain discrimination. An indigenous person can expect only 4.6 years of elementary schooling, compared with 7.9 years in the non-indigenous population. As Figure 1 indicates, in both education and basic services, such as drinking water and sanitation, there are still significant gaps.

Mexico's poor often seek work in the US, where average GDP per capita is six times that of Mexico. Remittances from the estimated 25 million Mexicans in the US rose from $7 billion in the year Fox took office to $25 billion in 2005. While this may look like a success story, it constitutes a concern on both sides

Figure 1 Comparisons between Mexico's indigenous and non-indigenous population

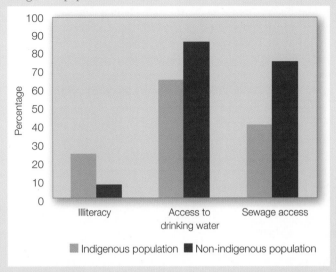

Source: Hall, G. and Patinos, H. (2005) *Indigenous Peoples, Poverty and Human Development in Latin America: 1994–2004* (Basingstoke: Palgrave Macmillan)

of the border. Immigrants make better wages in the US than they would at home, but their status is precarious, and they are disadvantaged in education, health and social services. Meanwhile, Oaxaca and Chiapas, where indigenous Mexicans predominate, are becoming depopulated. Remittances are helping to build houses, roads and other infrastructure, but they are of little use in ghost towns. Typically, ties of second-generation Mexicans to home villages weaken: they remain in the US, and remittances could well dry up. Mr Fox tried and failed to achieve an agreement with the US on guest worker status for Mexicans. Investment and employment opportunities at home in Mexico are needed, but these are very thin in the predominantly rural indigenous states.

FDI inflows have soared to $18.3 billion in 2004 and $17.8 billion in 2005 – the highest in Latin America. The benefits have flowed mainly to the *maquiladoras* (assembly plants) in the free-trade zones in the north of the country, created by Nafta, where manufacturing serves consumer markets in the US, the destination of 90% of Mexico's exports. Much of this

Figure 2 Economic growth in Mexico and the USA: annual

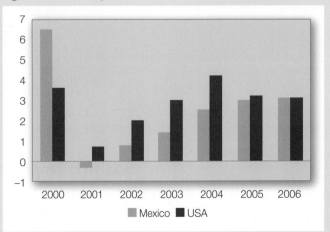

Source: OECD Statistics, http://stats.oecd.org

industry is low skill, relying on cheap labour. Many of these jobs have been lost to China, which, in 2003, displaced Mexico as the biggest exporter to the US. *Maquiladora* clusters are now learning that high-tech products are a surer way to create competitive advantage. However, these new industries are still vulnerable because of their dependency on the US market. Any downturn in US consumer spending is immediately felt in Mexico. The US downturn in 2001 had this effect, leading to almost no growth in Mexico, as Figure 2 shows. GDP growth in Mexico averaged a disappointing 1.4% in the period 1990–2003.

Investment in job creation in the rest of the country, particularly rural areas with high unemployment, has been disappointing. Mexican farmers have seen their livelihoods suffer because of imported subsidized maize from the US under Nafta rules. Oil revenues have provided about one-third of central government funds, but Mexico's oil is running out, and the country could be forced to import oil by 2015. The state-owned oil company lacks the expertise to exploit deep reserves under the sea, and is barred by the constitution from engaging in joint ventures with private companies, which could provide the necessary expertise.

The presidential election of 2006 saw a closely fought contest between Felipe Calderón, a Harvard-educated economist, representing the ruling PAN, and the charismatic politician, Andrés Manuel López Obrador of the Democratic Revolutionary Party (PRD), whose campaign focused on helping the poor, who, he argued, had not seen the benefits of globalization and economic integration with the US. His populist emotional style of politics was directed particularly towards the downtrodden indigenous people whom he has long championed, along with the poor of Mexico City, where he had been mayor. Obrador was widely predicted by the polls to be heading for victory, reflecting widespread disillusionment evident in Mexican society. In the end, Calderón won 35.9% of the votes cast, and Obrador, 35.3%. However, his coming so close to victory was a signal that Mexico's political voices are becoming more diversified, reflecting the divisions within its society.

plate 4.2 The border between Mexico and the US is symbolic of the barriers posed for poor people seeking opportunities for a better life in the US.

Questions

◆ Summarize the grievances of Mexico's indigenous peoples against the Mexican authorities.
◆ Why has Mexico made so little progress in creating jobs and prosperity, despite benefiting from globalization?
◆ Is Mexico on the way to achieving social stability through recognition of cultural diversity, or creating potentially divisive forces, as in the past?
◆ Assess the advantages and drawbacks of Mexico as a location for an FDI investor.

Sources: Authers, J., 'Mexico learns only the biggest survive', *Financial Times*, 13 October 2003; Thomson, A., 'Mexican economy seeks extra spice', *Financial Times*, 1 February 2006; Lapper, R., 'Benefits of stability are ploughed back into the country', *Financial Times*, 21 June 2006; Thomson, A., 'Mexican candidate takes fight to the streets', *Financial Times*, 1 August 2006; Lapper, R., and Thomson, A., 'Calderón poised to seal win in Mexico', *Financial Times*, 4 July 2006; Yoshioka, H. (2006) *Language or Identity: The Measurement of Indigenous Population in the Mexican Census*, (Princeton: Office of Population Research); Smith, G., 'Doors are opening for Mexico's Indians', *Business Week*, 22 March 2006; Hall, G. and Patinos, H. (2005) *Indigenous Peoples, Poverty and Human Development in Latin America* (Basingstoke: Palgrave Macmillan).

WEB CHECK

For information about Mexico, go to the World Bank's website, www.worldbank.org. Click on *Mexico* under *Countries*.

Cultural diversity

In what ways can businesses combine business success and social development in minority communities, either indigenous or immigrant?

PAUSE TO REFLECT

Business implications

Changing societies and cultural diversity pose both challenges and opportunities for international business. Management research has tended to focus on national cultures as the key determinant, taking a rather simplistic view of cultural dimensions. However, nationality is only part of the story and, for many people, may not be their main source of cultural identity. For many, ethnic grouping at a subcultural level is more important in their lives. For others, religion is their primary source of culture and identity, creating, for them, a 'higher' authority than their nationality. Businesses are now becoming more sensitive to this diversity in both operations and markets.

Operations

A business seeking to outsource production or make a direct investment will find cultural distance a challenge in many developing countries. Moreover, regions and social groups vary within a country. Minority cultures often cluster in particular regions within a country. Such a region might be attractive as a low-cost environment if these workers are typically paid less than national norms, but the firm must take account of the cultural distinctiveness of the workforce, such as a different language and behavioural norms. Where there is a sizable Muslim population, the investor must take into account the employees' need to pray regularly. Also dress codes, food requirements and religious holidays must be taken into account. A company may choose a particular region with a large population of immigrants, who may be only partially assimilated into the country's mainstream culture. Such areas may well appreciate opportunities for employment, but managers need to develop cultural awareness to build good relations with employees. Exploiting low-skilled immigrant labour is tempting to some companies with few ethical scruples, and immigrants, partly because of weak language skills, are poorly placed to complain about poor working conditions.

Some cultures accept practices such as child labour as normal, whereas most international businesses now view these practices as unethical. Moreover, child labour is in breach of international labour standards, which most MNEs support. International businesses are often confronted with weak human rights enforcement and poor working conditions in locations where they operate. Hence, managers must balance the need to adapt to different cultures with the need to uphold ethnical norms, whatever the culture. This is an aspect of their CSR profile.

Markets

Although management and marketing strategies have also tended to focus on dominant national cultures, this is now changing, as companies realize that national markets are segmented along cultural lines. An example is the Hispanic population in the US. As these consumers become more affluent, their spending power increases. Offering products and services to suit their changing needs is a growing phenomenon. While once this 'niche' market was served by Hispanic businesses, large MNEs are now realizing that they can benefit by localizing their strategies to cater for this market. Another example is the growth in services for Muslim consumers, such as Islamic financial services. Because of the Muslim prohibition on any financial transactions involving interest, products must be designed to be consistent with religious requirements. This is now a growing market (see Chapter 11), attracting global financial institutions as well as specialist Islamic providers. Niche markets sometimes evolve as they grow, becoming more internationalized. SX4.2 shows how a media organization, Al Jazeera, although initially focused on the Arab world, now looks to a global audience.

TO RECAP...

Cultural implications for operations

MNEs seeking location advantages for operations are often tempted by developing countries or poorer regions in other countries. However, they must take account of the differing cultural needs of particular groups of workers, and possible difficulties in communication.

STRATEGIC CROSSROADS

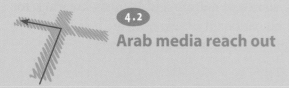

4.2 Arab media reach out

Even in remote villages across the Middle East, satellite dishes have become a common sight. Al Jazeera, the Arabic-language satellite television station based in Doha, Qatar, has become the most popular channel in the Arab world, and also one of the most widely known Arab brands internationally. It was created in 1996 from the remains of Orbit, the British Broadcasting Corporation's (BBC) attempt to bring its own brand of balanced reporting to the Arab world. Orbit shut down following a dispute with its Saudi financial backers, who disagreed with programme content. The ruler of Qatar stepped in with funding, making it clear that the station would have editorial independence over its output. Saudi investors, who have dominated Arab media in the past, are now being challenged by the rise of Qatar in the media world.

The fierce independence asserted by Al Jazeera's editor-in-chief has been its strongest asset, in a part of the world where official media organs are distrusted as being mouthpieces of the authorities. It introduced debates voicing both sides on important issues, amounting to a media revolution in the Arab world. Above all, the station seeks to reach the ordinary Arab viewer. Its editor-in-chief says of its recipe for success: 'Be accurate, factual, be there first – that's not necessarily most important – and be with the human being all the time – you don't stay at the top [by] getting the views of politicians and diplomats. You should try to get deeper into the story and try to depict how the people affected by the events or the story feel' (Symon, 25 September 2006).

Al Jazeera's coverage has angered both Saudi Arabia and the US. Nonetheless, it has expanded to 30 bureaux in diverse locations. The Al Jazeera brand now boasts sports channels, a documentary channel and a children's channel. It launched an English-language news channel in 2006, with the aim of presenting balanced and diverse perspectives on international events. Although the large cable operators in the US refuse to carry it, the new channel has signed up subscribers online and is available on YouTube, owned by Google. Al Jazeera English reaches 90 million homes worldwide, 1% of whom are in the US. It is broadcast in the UK on satellite TV through British Sky Broadcasting (BSkyB). As its English-speaking audience has increased, Al Jazeera has planned to market its brand in the UK, for example on London taxis. CNN, the original 24-hour news channel, announced in 2007 the opening of a regional hub in the Middle East.

The internet is also increasing in popularity in Gulf states, partly as a result of growing businesses with diversified interests, such as financial services. Google launched the Arabic version of its services in 2006. Seeking to tap into a fast-growing online population, estimated to number 23 million, it is offering email and a translation tool, as well as an Arabic version of Google News. This is the first unified internet platform for Arabic speakers. Facing claims that it might succumb to pressure from governments to divulge information or censor material (as it has done in China), Google claims search results in the Middle East and Africa will not be interfered with. The arrival of Arabic Google could give rise to more local Arabic websites, which could strength cross-border political, social and economic ties, emulating what Al Jazeera has done for Arab satellite television. Arabic Google, however, must contend with local rivals who are familiar with users' needs and will present competitive challenges.

Questions

- What factors have contributed to Al Jazeera's success?
- In what ways is Al Jazeera's new English service noteworthy from a cultural and business point of view?
- What factors will be significant in Arabic Google's attempt to be as successful as Al Jazeera?

Sources: Symon, F., 'How to stay at the top', *Financial Times*, 25 September 2006; Khalaf, R., 'US takes optimistic view in battle for hearts and minds in the Arab world', *Financial Times*, 15 January 2004; Boone, J., 'BBC's battle to win Arab viewers' hearts and minds', *Financial Times*, 24 June 2004; Wallis, W., and Braithwaite, T., 'Google launches Arabic version of web services', *Financial Times*, 23 June 2006; Symon, F., 'Google searches for new users', *Financial Times*, 7 August 2006; Khalaf, R., 'Al-Jazeera backs new pan-Arab daily', *Financial Times*, 31 October 2006; Edgecliffe-Johnson, A., 'Al-Jazeera English channel goes online to lure US', *Financial Times*, 4 July 2007; Luce, E., 'Al-Jazeera braves hostility to give new diversity to US', *Financial Times*, 4 August 2007;

WEB CHECK

The history of Al Jazeera's TV station and other information is at www.allied-media.com/aljazeera. Al Jazeera's English news service is at http://English.aljazeera.net.

Ethnocentric firms once assumed that their home-country products and marketing could simply be transferred to other markets. American companies such as McDonald's and Coca-Cola adopted this strategy for decades. These companies became symbols of American culture and their flagship products, the Big Mac and classic Coke, became recognizable all over the world. It was only when sales started to falter and American symbols lost their lustre that these companies reassessed their strategies. Wal-Mart, featured in CS3.2, has been in a similar position. In Brazil, it failed to take account of the fact that Brazilians like to shop in family groups, and the aisles were too narrow to accommodate them. Its exit from South Korea and Germany has demonstrated the shortcomings of replicating its retail model in overseas markets. Wal-Mart's country manager for Germany did not even speak German. A lesson from these experiences is that a polycentric approach, prioritizing an understanding of consumer cultures in different markets, is the best long-term policy for winning over consumers.

MNEs are now focusing on emerging markets, especially China and India. Market potential can be realized only by understanding and adapting to cultural differences. B&Q, the UK do-it-yourself retailer which has expanded in China, found that Chinese consumers took a rather different view of DIY activities than their Western counterparts, preferring to have others do the work for them. The ways in which the company adapted are expanded in CS4.2. Although Western companies tend to think that China's growing urban population will adopt familiar middle-class values and lifestyles, they risk failing to take account of underlying cultural dimensions, which are more deeply rooted than recent economic development might suggest. Furthermore, outside urban areas, traditional values are still the norm. China and India are highly diverse societies themselves. Both countries are a mixture of different languages, religions and ethnic groups. Both are still predominantly rural and poor. In rural regions and smaller cities, consumer markets remain weak. Here, domestic companies have an advantage, in that they are 'playing at home'. Foreign companies have found that they will not generate sales simply because of their brand. Their products and services must suit consumers' needs better than local offerings, and also compete on price.

> **TO RECAP...**
>
> **Culture's impacts on changing markets**
> Religion, language and other sources of cultural diversity within national environments are now the focus of greater attention for international companies, as they explore new markets more deeply. The emerging economies offer prospects of considerable growth, especially those of China and India, but these markets are diverse in both culture and income levels.

Conclusions

- Culture is sometimes treated as a variable which can be measured quantitatively, but the reality is that culture impacts on every aspect of international business in ways that defy quantification and may be difficult for outsiders to fathom. Business and management research has shed light on the dimensions of national cultures, such as key concepts of power distance and individualism, but it has been less helpful on the springs of culture, the social groupings which we identify with and which shape our values and attitudes. Many of these are national cultures, but they can also be ethnic or language groups or religions – all of which may cut across national boundaries.

- The culture of the business organization, including its embeddedness in its own national culture and the degree of openness to other cultures, is a factor of growing importance in international business. The expansion of subsidiaries, networks, alliances and other co-operative arrangements such as joint ventures has made the need for cross-cultural understanding imperative. At the same time, the MNE is finding new opportunities in both operations and markets which are opening up. As cultural distance widens, the risks grow, and cultural sensitivity becomes a crucial element in internationalization.

- Most of the world's societies are multicultural, and understanding the patterns of diversity and convergence within them is key to organizational success in differing national environments. The view that globalization would make distance irrelevant now seems naive. On the other hand, economic development is bringing modern consumer lifestyles to developing countries across the globe, representing a kind of convergence that proponents of globalization predicted. But these societies are evolving in ways which reflect their own national cultures and values, as well as diversity beneath the national level. Cultural diversity is increasingly intermingled with social and economic divisions, creating both challenges and opportunities for international business.

Culture and globalization
Weigh up the arguments that cultural differences are fading away against the arguments that cultural differences are still important in a globalized world. Which side in this debate do you feel is the more accurate, and why?

PAUSE TO REFLECT

Review questions

Part A: Grasping the basic concepts and knowledge

1. Describe the different facets of culture, giving an example of each that is relevant to business activities.
2. What is the significance of national identity as a source of culture?
3. Compare the importance of religion in Asian societies with that in Western societies.
4. In what aspects of work and employee relations should international managers be aware of religious sensitivities?
5. What benefits will the international manager gain from speaking the local language in the company's operations in a foreign location?
6. What is the difference between a high-context and low-context culture? Give examples.
7. What is guanxi, and why is it important in Chinese business?
8. What is the contribution of value orientation theory to our understanding of cultures?
9. What are Hofstede's culture dimensions? What correlations does Hofstede make among groups of countries, and how valid are they?
10. What insight does Trompenaars provide for international managers?
11. Contrast the ethnocentric and polycentric organization, giving examples of each.
12. What aspects of an organization form its organizational culture?
13. Describe the concept of cultural distance. How valid is it in today's world?

14. What is meant by the transnationality of a company?
15. How does economic development bring about culture change in a society? In what ways are these changes evident in rapidly growing Asian economies?
16. What are the benefits of urbanization? What are the associated problems which are being felt, particularly in developing countries?
17. Explain how the notion of cultural pluralism differs from assimilation in multicultural societies.

Part B: Critical thinking and discussion

1. Global companies and brands can claim considerable success in diverse markets. Is national culture becoming more, or less, important in the international environment, in terms of markets for consumer products?
2. The polycentric company would seem to be better adapted to international expansion than the ethnocentric one, yet most of the world's largest companies seem to be ethnocentric. How do you explain this apparent inconsistency?
3. Which organizations with distinctive cultures have featured in this chapter? Has their culture been a benefit or a drawback in terms of achieving organizational goals? (Note: read the closing case study before answering this question.)
4. Give advice to a Western business hoping to enter a joint venture with an Asian partner in an Asian country. Advise on negotiating the terms of the agreement, management arrangements and day-to-day decision-making.

Case study 4.2: DIY goes global

The thought of China's growing middle classes embracing a do-it-yourself culture presents a mouth-watering prospect for DIY companies in the US and UK. Chinese home improvement sales are growing at a rate five times that in the US. An aspect of China's new prosperity is the rapid expansion of private housing, which now comprises 70% of all new housing. Most new housing is in apartment blocks in China's big cities. Eager to cash in are DIY retailers. This market was worth $50 billion in sales in 2006. As the figure shows, the annual growth in DIY and hardware stores was over 100% in 2005. Competing against an array of local companies is B&Q of the UK, part of the Kingfisher group, which entered China in 1999. Home Depot of the US was late in following the B&Q lead, acquiring HomeWay, one of China's largest domestic DIY retailers, only in 2006.

For B&Q, any idea of transplanting its warehouse format to the Chinese market was soon swept aside when customers were found climbing 6-foot tall vertical displays to feel sink units. Chinese consumers needed to touch and handle the products, so displays were made more consumer friendly. B&Q also learned early on that new homes in China are often simply concrete shells, without floors, doors, lighting or even window frames. Moreover, most Chinese customers had little background in DIY, and little incentive to actually do the work themselves, as labour is so cheap. They have few holidays and little paid leave, in any case. The stores, therefore, started providing installation services, using local

installers. B&Q adopted a policy of relying on local managers as far as possible, rather than expatriates. This has made it easier to build relationships with local suppliers, installers and authorities, which are necessary in a market such as China, where personal relations are highly influential. It has also facili-

Figure Growth in DIY and hardware stores in China

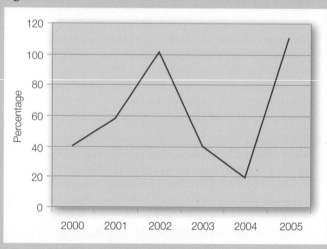

Source: Financial Times, 11 December 2006

tated an adaptation of the DIY concept to the local market. The president of B&Q China, David Wei, says that, rather than DIY, the B&Q China concept is more CIY, 'create it yourself'. They also found consumer tastes in China tended towards the ornate, leading them to stock a style of ornate home furnishings very different from what would be on offer in the UK.

In catering for Chinese tastes, B&Q are up against fierce local competition. Chinese rivals, Homemart, Home Way (now taken over by Home Depot) and Orient Home are all providing similar offerings at competitive prices. The market is fragmented, with many small local firms accounting for more than half the sector. B&Q have had to compete on price, reckoning that the consumer will be persuaded of the quality of their products over their local rivals, although 95% of B&Q's products are sourced locally.

By 2006, B&Q had grown to 49 stores in China, and has plans to double that figure. However, this will mean moving into China's second-tier cities: opportunities abound, but in these cities incomes are generally lower than in the major centres. B&Q has been evolving with changes in the market since it entered China. The target market initially had been in the middle and upper income levels, but now the market is being extended to lower levels. The company has launched a more modest service, whereby they will furnish a basic apartment for the equivalent of $6,125, half the price of a larger, more upmarket apartment. In some areas, local authorities have been clamping down on developers, ordering that most apartments be sold furnished. B&Q has adapted to this change, forming alliances with developers for interior furnishing and design. This side of the business could well expand in future, taking it even further away from the stark warehouse familiar to UK consumers. Does B&Q foresee a DIY culture developing in future in China? The company has started offering a free children's club at weekends, where children can learn basic DIY skills – skills their fathers probably could not teach them.

Home Depot approaches its Chinese expansion from a different background, and is unlikely to follow the path of B&Q. In any case, its managers are keenly aware that they will have to go through the learning process themselves. From modest beginnings in 1979, Home Depot has grown into the largest group of DIY warehouses in America, with 2,000 stores. However, it has little experience outside this market, apart from 200 stores in Canada and Mexico. Attempted expansion in Chile and Argentina ended in failure, leading to pessimism about the company's ability to internationalize. In comparison, B&Q, apart from its Chinese operations, has successfully expanded in Europe, including some 30 stores in Poland, giving it broader experience in selling in different cultures. Commenting on Home Depot's approach, B&Q said: 'They have had the attitude that if it works in Atlanta or Arkansas, it will work in Beijing or Taiwan. But if you look at the Europeans, we have had years of working across Europe and in other countries' (Rigby, 2006).

plate 4.3 New apartment blocks such as these in Shanghai offer entry into middle-class urban lifestyles for millions of Chinese, and also opportunities for businesses which cater for their needs.

Reaching saturation point in the US, Home Depot must now look for future growth through either diversification or internationalization, or both. Bob Nardelli, until recently Home Depot's CEO, took a cautious approach to international expansion. His many years at General Electric before joining Home Depot instilled in him a cautious planning-oriented approach, in marked contrast to the more entrepreneurial culture which Home Depot had had before his arrival. China was talked about for two years before the company took the plunge. The apparent dithering has frustrated Home Depot's shareholders, voicing concerns over Nardelli's remuneration package which amounted to $125 million from 2001 to 2006, plus another $121 million in share options. In January 2007, Nardelli left the company and became the CEO of Chrysler, newly independent from its former owner, Daimler of Germany.

Home Depot's purchase of the Chinese chain Home Way seemed a logical option. In contrast to B&Q, Home Depot sources only 7% of its products in China, suggesting that building supply chain links will be a priority. The acquisition presents Home Depot with an opportunity to demonstrate its international capabilities, but it will be playing catch-up to B&Q, which has demonstrated its flexibility in adapting to the Chinese market.

Questions

1 What aspects of the cultural environment in China are relevant to the DIY sector?
2 How successful has B&Q been in adapting to the tastes and needs of local consumers in China?
3 What challenges await Home Depot in its Chinese market entry?
4 Compare B&Q and Home Depot in terms of their approaches to internationalization.

Sources: Ward, A., 'Does it stack up? Why Home Depot is putting its faith in wholesale growth', *Financial Times*, 8 September 2006; Buckley, S., 'HMV's voice stays silent in China', *Financial Times*, 12 March 2005; Ward, A., 'So, how do you grow when you can't grow any more?', *Financial Times*, 11 January 2006; Buckley, N. and Liu, B., 'DIY steps back as shoppers seek home help', *Financial Times*, 10 May 2004; McGregor, R., 'China's domestic revolution helps B&Q', *Financial Times*, 2 December 2004; Dickie, M., 'Chinese consumers love B&Q's concept', *Financial Times*, 20 October 2003; Ward, A., 'Home Depot opens the door to a growing new market', *Financial Times*, 11 December 2006; Rigby, E., 'B&Q's head start in China faces threat from US group', *Financial Times*, 11 December 2006; 'B&Q stores: Renovating China's attitudes', *Business Week*, 25 April 2006.

WEB CHECK

For B&Q, go to Kingfisher's home page, www.kingfisher.co.uk. B&Q's Chinese website is www.bnq.com.cn. This is for Chinese speakers, but the cultural flavour comes through even for non-Chinese speakers. Home Depot's website is www.homedepot.com.

Further research

Journal articles

Brouthers, K. and Brouthers, L. (2001) 'Explaining the national cultural distance paradox', *Journal of International Business Studies*, **32**(1): 177–89.

Lee, K., Yang, G. and Graham, J. (2006) 'Tension and trust in international business negotiations: American executives negotiating with Chinese executives', *Journal of International Business Studies*, **37**(5): 623–41.

Luo, Y. and Shenkar, O. (2006) 'The multinational corporation as a multilingual community: Language and organization in a global context', *Journal of International Business Studies*, **37**(3): 321–39.

Triandis, H. (2004) 'The many dimensions of culture', *Academy of Management Executive*, **18**(1): 88–94.

Books

Bartlett, C., Ghoshal, S. and Beamish, P. (2007) *Transnational Management: Text and Cases*, 5th edn, Maidenhead: McGraw-Hill.

Luthans, F. and Doh, J. (2008) *International Management: Culture, Strategy and Behavior*, New York: Pearson.

THE POLITICAL AND LEGAL ENVIRONMENT

learning objectives

▷ To identify contrasting political systems and their implications for business relations
▷ To assess the sources of political risk encountered by international businesses
▷ To appreciate the changing role of governments in the business environment
▷ To understand the ways in which legal frameworks, at national, regional and international levels, impact on business activities
▷ To evaluate and respond to changes in political and legal environments which impact on international managers

Introduction

To football enthusiasts, Thaksin Shinawatra, the Thai telecommunications tycoon, is probably best known as the owner of Manchester City Football Club in the UK. However, he also headed Thailand's populist but corrupt elected government, which was overthrown by a military coup in 2006. Thaksin and his party were banned, in a rerun of a military coup in 1991. On that occasion, the army generals were soon defeated by a mass uprising leading to a new democratic government. In 2006, the military took a more conciliatory approach, promising a return to democracy. It presented a new constitution to the people, consolidating the army's authority but allowing elections for a new government. A bright yellow 194-page draft constitution was distributed to all voters. One, a fruit grower with only primary-level education, said: 'It's not easy to understand the official language. It takes a lot of time and we are very busy now collecting the fruit' (Kazmin, 2007). She, like many voters, was probably unsure what they were voting for but, above all, wished for a return to stability. The army-sponsored constitution was approved, and parliamentary elections under the system resulted in a majority for what was, in effect, the banned party of Thaksin, now under a new name and with a Thaksin associate as its head. With the army still at the helm, and bolstered by legal authority, doubts about political stability remain. This example reminds us that political and legal institutions are a mixture of formal processes and qualitative factors, and that although democracies may appear similar in form, they may differ markedly in their depth of democratic values.

Both the political system of a county and its accompanying legal system are national institutions: they spring from the nation-state as an autonomous entity, which governs its population and enacts laws to carry out its public tasks. For businesses, these institutions play a continuing role. They regulate its formation, its governance, its business activities, its relations with stakeholders and its duties to communicate with regulatory authorities and the public. When a business embarks on international expansion, far from leaving national institutions behind, it encounters new political and legal frameworks in each country it enters. Although this patchwork of national authorities might well seem dated in a globalized world, it remains an essential reality for international managers. On the other hand, regional and international frameworks are increasingly impacting on national environments. These may seem to add complexity to an already complex environment, but they represent important moves towards harmonization and co-operation among national authorities. Hence, for international businesses, understanding these evolving interactions among governments is key to global strategy.

National political systems are analysed in the first section. This broad area covers how countries are governed in terms of formal institutions, but it also covers 'grassroots' politics, such as political parties and interest groups, which shape a country's political culture and are as important to businesses as formal institutions. A subsection looks at the prospects for democracy and its implications for business. The traditional view of government 'handing down' laws to individuals and organizations is giving way to a more interactive role. Businesses are interacting directly with governments as well as grassroots organizations, creating more co-operative links. Governments now recognize the need to establish sound and transparent legal systems, on which businesses can rely, to facilitate both local enterprises and foreign investors. On the other hand, politics in many of the world's countries can be highly volatile, raising the level of political and legal risk for international business. Often, the most potentially rewarding opportunities are in developing countries, which need outside investors, but present the highest levels of risk. The last section looks at the emergence of international institutions and legal frameworks. While they do not replace national systems, they do signify to businesses that an international framework, even if fragmentary, is emerging.

> **WEB CHECK**
>
> Information about Thailand can be accessed on the World Bank's website at www.worldbank.org., where *Thailand* is listed under *Countries*.

plate 5.1 A fireworks display in Bangkok. The people of Thailand have cause to celebrate the return of civilian government, but the country's military leaders remain powerful.

Political systems

Politics is an almost universal phenomenon. Social groupings and organizations of all types accord more power and responsibility to some members than to others. The organization's politics consists of the interplay for power and status, which often takes place outside formal structures. It may be a company, a trade union, a school, a social club or even a religious grouping. What distinguishes these organizations from politics at the national level is that they are all limited to the organization itself, whereas national politics concerns the people, goals and structures which govern an entire nation-state. The political system of any state consists of the structures and processes by which it is governed. Some are formal, such as the way governments are put in place and derive legitimacy, but much is less formal, such as grassroots action on the part of citizens. We begin this section with the broad classification of formal political systems.

Political system: Structures and processes by which a nation-state is governed.

Classifying political systems

It is customary to visualize political systems on a continuum with the authoritarian system at one extreme, which is rule by dictatorship, and democracy at the other, which is based on accountability to the people. There exists neither a perfectly authoritarian state nor a perfectly democratic one, many states falling somewhere in the middle, and also varying over time. These concepts are nonetheless helpful in clarifying how political systems function. Authoritarian government, shown on the left in Figure 5.1, is the concentration of power in one or more individuals, or political party, with sole power to run the country and dictate its laws. Businesses are vulnerable, as a change in leadership could render agreements with previous leaders worthless. Authoritarian rulers, who are commonly military dictators, control the media and restrict civil liberties. Authoritarian rule existed in the former Soviet Union, which was also a planned economy controlled by the Communist Party elite. A survey conducted for *The Economist* in 2006 assessed political systems from authoritarian to democratic, based on five sets of criteria: electoral processes and pluralism; functioning of government; political participation; political culture; and civil liberties. The scores out of 10 are shown for a variety of states in Figure 5.2. On this scoring, 55 of the world's 167 independent states are authoritarian (Kekic, 2006). Covering 40% of the world's population, they are mainly in the Middle East, Africa and Asia.

Authoritarian government: Rule by one or more individuals who claim absolute power to govern a state, with no substantive accountability to its citizens.

The bottom four countries in Figure 5.2 are classified as authoritarian, with scores of 5 or under. Only one of these, North Korea, is a planned economy. The others are all emerging economies, becoming important players in the global economy. Russia and Saudi Arabia are significant oil producers, while China is important in global production networks, as well as being a major consumer of energy and raw materials. The 'market-oriented authoritarian regime' characterizes many developing countries, particularly in Asia (Plattner, 1993: 31). Political elites have shown themselves adept at guiding economic development, liberalizing where needed to attract FDI and applying controls where strategic interests are at stake. There are risks inherent in this seemingly incongruous mix. A faltering in the economy or social unrest can pose a risk to those in power, who rely on coercion and oppression, rather than consent. The populace may be content to have no political voice so long as they have jobs and prosperity, but if they do not, political instability can follow.

Figure 5.1 Features of authoritarianism and democracy

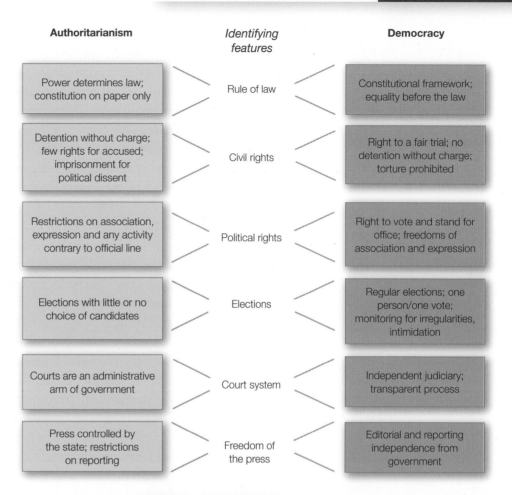

The essence of democratic government is accountability to the populace. At a minimum, this implies regular, fair and free elections, where people choose whom they wish to form the government and what policies they desire. Such a system creates winners and losers, and majority rule must be

Democratic government: Political system which, at a minimum, is based on accountability of government to the voting public, through regular, free and fair elections.

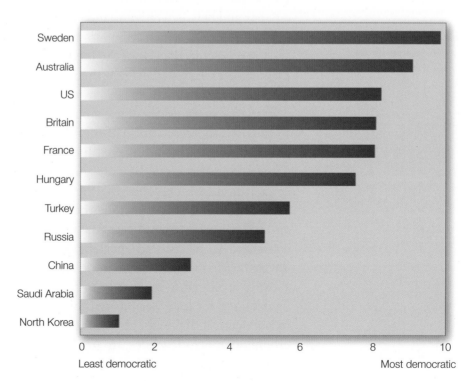

Figure 5.2 From authoritarian to democratic: selected countries

Source: Kekic, L. (2006) 'A pause in democracy's march', *The Economist: The World in 2007* data, www.theworldin.com

tempered by respect for minorities. This minimalist definition is now generally thought to be too narrow, focusing solely on the formal criterion of elections, which can be manipulated to give an outward appearance of democratic choice in otherwise authoritarian regimes (Potter, 1993). In these regimes, the mechanisms of democracy, such as parties and candidates, are controlled by the centre. Examples can be found in Russia, featured in CF5.1, as well as former Soviet republics where Russia still exerts influence. To assess democracy at a more substantive level, the extent of civil and political rights must be taken into account, as discussed in the next section.

A surge in the number of new democracies occurred over the twentieth century, as nations gained independence from colonial rule or emerged from the break-up of the Soviet Union (Huntington, 1993). There are now 82 states which can be classified as democracies at least in the minimal sense, many of which are relatively young. However, *The Economist*'s survey found considerable variation among them. Only 28 are 'full' democracies, mainly in northern Europe and North America. Sweden comes top, followed closely by other northern European states and Australia. The other 54 have weaker systems of democratic accountability, participation and civil rights. This is particularly true in states with high power distance or long histories of traditional or hereditary authority. It is sometimes suggested that the growth of economic freedom in China will eventually lead to a peaceful democratic transition, but this remains a matter of speculation (Pei, 2005). Democracy is associated with individualism and low power distance, distinguishing it from the collectivism and high power distance of authoritarian states.

Assessing democracies

Democracy is based on basic principles about relationships among individual citizens and between citizens and governmental authorities. The first of these is the rule of law, which stipulates that everyone, including government officials, is subject to the law of the land. In other words, no one is above the law. Democracies vary, however, in their adherence to the rule of law. In societies in which there are deep social and economic divisions and widespread poverty, for example, theoretical equality in law is of little avail, if the reality for many is the deprivation of life's basic needs.

Human rights, including civil and political rights, are necessary to underpin democratic processes. They are guaranteed in most of the world's written constitutions, which, following the US example, include a Bill of Rights. As Figure 5.1 shows, these include the right not to be detained without charge, and to have a fair trial. A fair trial includes the right to put one's case to the court and to be assured that the judge is unbiased. In practice, national governments in many democratic states curtail these rights where national security is judged to be at risk. In cases of suspected terrorism, suspects may be detained for long periods without charge, as national security is deemed to outweigh individuals' civil rights. These practices have been criticized as eroding democratic values. In *The Economist*'s survey of democracies, the US

TO RECAP...

Authoritarian versus democratic government

Authoritarian government rests on rule by a political elite who have power for the time being. They maintain their hold on power by prohibiting dissent, often with military force. A democratic government rests on the principle of accountability to the people, through free and fair elections. The will of the leadership dominates in an authoritarian state, while democracy relies on representative institutions such as an elected assembly.

The rule of law: Primacy of laws over the will of individuals, including both rulers and ruled.

ranked 17th, and the UK 23rd. These are more lowly rankings than might be expected, largely because of the curtailing of human rights in efforts to deter and defeat terrorism.

Where a minimal electoral democracy exists, there is a right to vote at regular intervals, but this right may provide little means of exerting influence. For citizens to have a meaningful voice, the freedom of speech and expression, as well as the right to join political parties are essential. The pluralist society, tolerating a variety of different ideologies, is the basis of democratic politics. An environment in which there are voluntary groups, including religious, cultural as well as political groups, is known as civil society. Voluntary associations are an important adjunct to participative politics. They provide a means of scrutinizing state power, providing avenues for expressing political interests and highlighting issues (Diamond, 1993: 101). Authoritarian states notoriously restrict the activities of such groups, fearing that they will breed dissent, leading to instability and unrest. On the other hand, authoritarian governments often use youth groups, trade unions and other organizations controlled by the state to mobilize support for the regime.

As Figure 5.1 highlights, civil and political rights are central to democracy. They provide institutional means for the legitimate representation of various interests, including concerns of ethnic and religious groups. In authoritarian regimes, discontent may simmer beneath the surface, and violent revolution or military coup may seem the only way to rid a country of an unwanted leader. As the opening scenario showed, Thailand experienced a peaceful military coup by the army in 2006, with the ousting of the elected prime minister, Thaksin Shinawatra. The prime minister had become authoritarian, and a flawed election earlier in the year had further undermined his democratic credentials. While many supported the coup as necessary in the circumstances, it was a setback for democracy in the country. It also sowed uncertainty among foreign investors, such as Tesco, which called a temporary halt to expansion in Thailand. FDI had been welcomed under the previous government, but the level of political risk rose with the takeover by the military.

Civil society: Voluntary groups representing cultural, religious and political diversity within a society.

TO RECAP...

Democratic society

Democracy is as much about society as government. The rule of law, encompassing both rulers and ruled, is a democratic hallmark. Without civil and political rights, pluralist political debate cannot flourish. It is important that elections are free and fair, and that citizens can trust in the validity of the outcome. Where democratic institutions are only weakly established, fragmentation and instability can result.

Quality of democracy

As more and more countries claim to be democratic, variations among countries in the quality of democracy are becoming more significant. Think of two countries with which you are familiar, and compare them according to the criteria in Figure 5.1.

PAUSE TO REFLECT

Branches of government

Whatever the political system, every government must have institutions to carry out three major functions, known as branches of government:

- The *executive* – the head of government, which usually directs an array of civil service departments to carry out central functions, such as national finances, national security and welfare policies.

- The *legislative* – those responsible for enacting the laws, often a representative assembly.
- The *judiciary* – the system of courts, whereby judges administer justice for individuals and organizations.

Concerned about the risks of democracy deteriorating into dictatorship, eighteenth-century theorists of democracy argued that the three branches should operate independently – the separation of powers (Beetham, 1991). A system of checks and balances should prevent the executive from exceeding constitutional authority through safeguards such as the need for approval of legislation by the elected body. At the same time, the independent judiciary acts as a check, should either of the other branches overstep its authority. In practice, the three branches are unlikely to be in perfect balance. Democratic systems with directly elected presidents tend to have strong executives (Linz, 1993). The US system, followed in Latin America, is a model (although the US president is not directly elected, but chosen by an electoral college). Countries with parliamentary sovereignty tend to have more circumscribed executives, vesting executive power in a prime minister who is the leader of the majority party in parliament, or a coalition of parties. The UK is an example. Following the example of France, a hybrid system has become popular, presided over by an elected president with a separate prime minister in charge of day-to-day government business. There may well be conflict between the two executives, however, and the president is the dominant figure.

Unchecked executive power is a hallmark of the authoritarian regime. In many states, both authoritarian and democratic, separation of powers is provided in the constitution, but operates imperfectly in practice. Where there is a risk to national security, the executive may assume emergency powers, deemed to be necessary in the circumstances, but extended executive powers can become entrenched. In an authoritarian state, there may be an elected assembly, but it simply rubber-stamps the laws handed down by the country's rulers. Electoral choice is usually restricted to parties and candidates approved by the ruling party, as in Russia. The degree of independence of the judiciary is indicative of the depth of checks on the executive. In authoritarian systems, it functions as an administrative arm of government, not as an independent adjudicator (see Figure 5.1). This may pose considerable risk for businesses, especially foreign ones, as they are likely to lose any dispute with authorities, regardless of the merit of their cases in law.

Separation of powers: Constitutional principle by which each branch of government – executive, legislative and judicial – has limited express authority.

TO RECAP...

Checks and balances

The three branches of government – executive, legislative and judicial – should function as counterweights to each other in a balanced government. Domination by the executive, even an elected one, provides little means for day-to-day accountability of rulers and risks slipping into authoritarianism.

COUNTRY FOCUS 5.1 – RUSSIA

Whither democracy in Russia?

With the fall of communist authoritarianism in 1990, hopes ran high in Russia that both democratic reforms and economic liberalization would bring a better life. Radical market reforms allowed private individuals to acquire state assets cheaply, creating a class of 'oligarchs' whose economic power threatened to outshine the state. Political instability ensued, and in the 1990s, the quality of life for ordinary Russians deteriorated. Vladimir Putin took office as president in 2000, renewing hope for economic growth and stability. However, Putin's background in the Soviet security services also suggested that reining in the oligarchs would be part of a broader programme of centralizing control.

Oil and gas riches have put Russia in a strong position globally, energy accounting for 40% of its GDP. The world's second largest producer of oil after Saudi Arabia, it claims 30% of the world's oil reserves and 20% of gas reserves. Yukos, the Russian oil giant, and Gazprom, the gas company formed from the former Soviet oil ministry, worked with foreign companies to explore and build capacity throughout the 1990s. The Putin leadership transformed both organizations. Yukos was broken up and sold off to state-controlled Rosneft through doubtful legal proceedings. Gazprom has been taken over by the state, which now owns 51% of its stock. Members of the government now run both companies. The two companies' productivity and exploration activities have fallen. These developments have come at a time when dependency on imported energy and questions of supply have risen up the global agenda. Europe imports 30% of its gas from Russia, through pipelines controlled by Gazprom. While claiming to be a reliable supplier, Russia has cut off supply to various neighbouring countries when

disputes arose, giving the strong impression that energy is being used as a political bargaining tool.

Russia's elected parliament, the Duma, is controlled by Putin's United Russia party, which won a landslide victory in elections in December 2007. Western observers criticized the process as neither free nor fair. Opposition parties must be approved by the government, and those which are independent have found that they are harassed and obstructed in trying to organize meetings and are denied access to the media. Putin announced he would step down as president at the end of his second term in 2008. However, he designated his successor, Medvedev, who duly won the 2008 election. Putin intends to become the prime minister, maintaining a firm grip on power. Although democrats would be dismayed, many Russians, fearful of the instability of political infighting, feel that this continuation of Putin's power ensures stability. Once hopeful of democracy's benefits, Russians are now persuaded that strong leadership is what the country needs (see figure). Russia's political leaders maintain that the country is a democracy, albeit a 'managed' democracy (Buckley, 21 April 2006). However, on most criteria, the political system has slipped backwards towards authoritarianism.

Presidential appointees have now replaced elected regional governors, and state appointments have taken over the judicial branch. The checks and balances provided in the constitution are, in practice, overridden by the executive. The state controls the three main television channels, as well as the print media. A new law allows the government to close down non-governmental organizations (NGOs) as it sees fit, as causing dissent within the country. These latter controls are seen as curtailing the institutions of civil society, on which democracy should rest. The government has also curtailed the monitoring of elections by independent observers, confining monitoring only to those observers invited by the authorities.

Figure The best kind of governance for Russia?

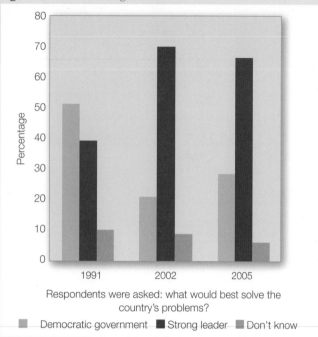

Respondents were asked: what would best solve the country's problems?

■ Democratic government   ■ Strong leader   ■ Don't know

Source: Pew Global Attitudes Project (2006) 'Russia's weakened democratic embrace', http://pewglobal.org

Russia's economy has thrived under Putin, growing at over 6% annually. The country is attracting FDI from foreign MNEs, attracted to the increased spending of Russia's growing middle classes. Moscow now has over 40 international standard shopping centres. IKEA is planning to expand beyond Moscow, opening a dozen new stores in other large cities. Negative aspects of the business climate include bureaucracy and corruption, which add to the cost of doing business in Russia. It is estimated that the bribes and other unofficial payments necessary to obtain regulatory permissions add 8.5% to the costs of any project. Foreign investors could well reason that the opportunities are so great as to outweigh these extra costs, but the growing authoritarianism could also raise doubts in their minds.

Control from the centre, both economically and politically, has aimed to quell the volatility and insecurity of the 1990s, but has led to new risks to stability. For example, serious unrest occurred in 2004 when tens of thousands of pensioners staged mass protests about changes in state benefits. The changes had been mishandled by the authorities, but, having suppressed independent sources of information such as the media and

independent legislators, the government was curiously ill-informed and in the dark about what was going wrong. Despite Putin's high personal rating in opinion polls, the rating of his government sank to 29% in 2005, with 52% of respondents saying that Russia was 'moving in the wrong direction' (Buckley and Wagstyl, 2005). There is a lingering fear that an upsurge in unrest, as occurred in Georgia and the Ukraine, could break out in Russia. Economic prosperity and rising living standards are perhaps the best guarantees of social stability. However, experts point out that Russia's economic growth has come largely from rising oil and gas prices, rather than underlying strengths. Over 40% of government revenues come from the taxes generated by the high prices of gas and oil.

Russia's businesses, both state controlled and private, have been flexing their muscles internationally. Nineteen Russian initial public offerings (IPOs), listing $22 billion on the London Stock Exchange in 2005, seemed to signal a desire to embrace market principles, although the proportion of free-floating shares in these companies is only about one-fifth. The largest IPO was Rosneft, despite its opaque governance and doubts surrounding the purchase of Yukos assets. The state, rather than shareholders, remains the ultimate force in Russian capitalism. A Russian financial expert has said: 'The market economy cannot develop within the constraints of this political system' (Ostrovsky, 2004). The government is re-establishing Russia in a prominent role on the world stage. Its rulers will be hoping that neither the Russian people nor international partners is overly concerned with an apparent shift away from democracy.

Questions

◆ In what ways has democracy gone backwards in Russia?
◆ In your view, how stable is the political system in Russia in the long term?
◆ Assess the advantages and risks for foreign investors in Russia.

Sources: Buckley, N., 'Rich rewards for riding rollercoaster', *Financial Times*, 11 October 2005; Jack, A., 'Under the cover of law and order', *Financial Times*, 19 October 2004; Buckley, N. and Wagstyl, S., 'Orange alert', *Financial Times*, 26 September 2005; Buckley, N., 'Self-confident state re-enters world stage', *Financial Times*, 21 April 2006; Ostrovsky, A., 'Russia's soaring corruption "puts investors off"', *Financial Times*, 28 November 2006; Ostrovsky, A., 'Power to Putin: but is Russia's leader too authoritarian for his own good?', *Financial Times*, 17 December, 2004; Buckley, N., 'Market reformers and former spies', *Financial Times*, 5 April 2005; Ostrovsky, A., 'The new oligarchs? Winners and losers in the Kremlin's grab for oil wealth', *Financial Times*, 7 November 2005; Parker, G., 'Moscow gas switch-off triggers urgent review', *Financial Times*, 9 March 2006; Belton, C. and Buckley, N., 'West relations suffer after "unfair" election', *Financial Times*, 4 December 2007.

WEB CHECK

For information about Russia, go to the World Bank's website at www.worldbank.org, where the *Russian Federation* is listed under *Countries*.

Politics in practice

Politics exists in every country, not just democratic ones. Authoritarian states are often ruled by a single party within which factions and allegiances to different individuals flourish. However, this vying for power usually takes place behind closed doors. In a democratic country, freedom to form political groups and express differing views is encouraged. The most obvious formal organizations are political parties, but there are many other types of formal and informal groupings, often comprising people who get together to publicize and win support for a particular cause.

In a democratic system, in theory, individuals can stand for office on their own, but in practice, they need the support and financial resources of an organized political party. An independent political party is an organization of people joined by shared political views, which puts forward candidates for public office and also aims to gain influence with government. A party is likely to have a philosophy or ideology, which unites all its members, although there are still disagreements on matters of principle within parties. It is customary to speak of parties as being to the 'right', the 'left', or the 'centre'. Although these terms are frequently used in media reporting of political news, they do not have precise meanings. Right and left in politics depends greatly on the political culture in the particular country being referred to. In general, the right represents conservative views, seeking to promote protection of property, 'law and order', family values and religious values. Conservatives in many countries, such as the UK, traditionally espouse market values and lower taxes, holding that government interference in enterprise should be kept to a minimum. These are classical liberal economic views. Many conservative parties are also associated with patriotism or nationalism. CF5.2 on France demonstrates the tension within the centre-right party between liberal and nationalist strands. While a nationalist party stresses national pride and identity, extreme nationalism can also be associated with intolerance. Nationalist views are not confined to conservative parties. Nationalism is also associated with regional parties favouring greater regional autonomy, many of which tend towards the left. Examples are in Catalonia in Spain and Québec in Canada.

Left-wing parties traditionally support a social justice agenda and a stronger state in terms of social welfare. Social democratic parties fall into this group. They are traditionally the parties associated with trade unions. The Labour Party in the UK has roots within the trade union movement, but, in recent years, has moved away from its traditional left-wing values to a more business-oriented outlook, causing tension within the party. The Democratic Party of the US is also broadly on the left, but specifically in the American context. It is traditionally the voice of the seemingly powerless (often poor) individual citizen against the might of the state, reflecting the party's historical values.

Where political systems are dominated by two major parties – the two-party system – although they roughly reflect the right and the left in political debate, both in practice are broadly based. They tend not to take strong ideological positions, preferring to portray themselves as 'all things to all people'. This way, they hope to capture the 'floating voter', who does not have strong political views either way. A risk, however, is that if politicians seem indistinguishable and speak only in broad generalities, citizens may become complacent, thinking that it does not matter whom they vote for. Turnout for elections has become low in many countries, at around 50% of the electorate or less, reflecting poorly on democratic participation. In states with a multiplicity of parties, each representing particular interests, diversity in ideology and policies is more evident. Smaller, focused parties, such as the Peasants Party in Poland, have little prospect of government on their own,

Political party: Organization of people with similar political perspectives, which aims to put forward candidates for office and influence government policies.

Two-party system: System in which two broadly based parties dominate, alternating between government and opposition, reflecting electoral fortunes.

but they can exert influence by joining a coalition government. 'Green' parties, based an environmental agenda, have been influential in this way as well.

Where there is a multiparty system, it is common for no single party to achieve a majority in the elected assembly. In this case, two or more parties form a coalition government. A coalition may also arise where a winning majority is very slender, as little as one seat. Close contests leading to a coalition government have featured in several European countries between 2005 and 2006, including Germany, Austria, Holland and the Czech Republic. Coalitions may be fragile and prone to internal conflict. Between 2005 and 2006, Poland had three different governments and five changes of finance minister. A potentially more unstable situation afflicted the Czech Republic, where elections in 2006 failed to produce a clear winner, and politicians were unable to agree on a coalition. A coalition government was finally agreed early in 2008. Any coalition eventually formed in these circumstances is likely to founder.

A broad consensus on the 'rules of the game' helps to make democracy work in the countries where it is firmly established. In these countries, the government in power accepts that it may become the opposition in the future, and does not try to keep power by, for example, changing the electoral system. In any case, the winning party may only receive 36% of the popular vote, and protecting the rights of minorities is essential to the long-term health of pluralist politics. Where the winners assume that, having had a mandate from the people, they should be able to shape all the branches of government to fit their own goals, democracy suffers. While democratic forms, such as elections, can be put in place fairly quickly, building a political culture with respect for individuals and groups with differing views is a slower process.

Many of the countries of Latin America, having endured long periods of military dictatorship, are now establishing democracies. The political cultures of these countries remain volatile, with a propensity for populist leaders who see street protests as more effective than formal institutions. In 2007, the authoritative Latinobarómetro (2007) survey of democracy in 18 Latin American countries found that about half of respondents agreed that democracy is the best form of government. This is a slight fall in overall support for democracy from the previous year. Of additional concern is the finding that only 37% of respondents were satisfied with the democracy in their country. The 2007 survey also found a fall in numbers of Latin Americans who felt the market economy was the best economic model for their country, from 62% in 2006 to 52% in 2007.

The researchers felt this perception did not necessarily reflect a leftward swing in opinion so much as a feeling that healthy economic growth in these economies was not perceived to be trickling down to the majority. Encouragingly for governments in the region, positive perceptions of lawmakers and judiciary have risen, although they do not achieve the levels of respect for the Catholic Church and the armed forces (see Figure 5.3).

Multiparty system: System in which many parties represent a wide spectrum of views, and where the government is likely to be a coalition of parties.

Coalition government: Government formed by an agreement between parties to work together, in the event of no single party commanding enough seats to form an overall majority in the elected chamber.

TO RECAP...

Plural politics

Genuinely plural politics may give rise to numerous groups and parties, from the loosely organized to the formal. They vary in their economic and social values, and many represent special interests or religious groups. Parties which veer towards the broad centre of national political culture stand a better chance of winning a governing majority than narrowly based parties. Instability can result from the political fragmentation associated with a multiplicity of small parties.

Right, left and centre
Think of your own political views on the following issues in your own country: liberal market economy; social spending by government; and the role of religion in society. Looking at your views overall, to what extent do they form a coherent philosophy which can be categorized as right, left or centre?

PAUSE TO REFLECT

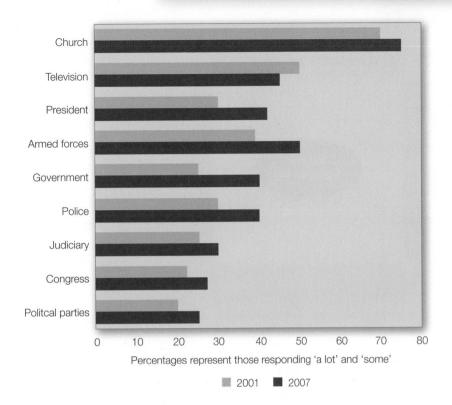

Figure 5.3 Respect for institutions in Latin America (2007)

Source: 'A warning for reformers', *The Economist*, 17 November 2007

Political risk

Political risk: Uncertainties associated with location and exercise of power within a country and from forces outside its borders.

Individual citizens and businesses alike value stability and security, as necessary conditions for achieving their goals. In any society, the centres of political power and the ways in which power is exercised affect the economic climate. Assessing their impact in terms of political risk is important for businesses, especially when contemplating investment in a new location. In this section, political risk is examined under two headings: risks arising within the national political system and risks from external factors. Risks do not always fit neatly into these categories, and in the modern world, there is increasing interaction between internal and external forces, making risk assessment more complicated, but nonetheless vital. For example, international terrorists constitute an external threat, but they may well work with disaffected groups within countries to destabilize the political system as part of their broader international objectives.

Risks within the political system

Both formal institutions and practical politics affect the business environment. Internal political risks are presented in Figure 5.4. Many concern the unpredictability of government decision-making and volatile elements in society. Physical security is a concern of all businesses, but especially those with large sites or vulnerable operations, as in the extraction industries. Issues of policing come under the general heading of 'law and order' within a society. The stable authoritarian country may seem to present fewer risks than the turbulent or fragmented democratic one. But the stability of an authoritarian state rests on coercion, while the democratic state relies on its independent institutions to provide a backdrop of stability, within which pluralist politics operate.

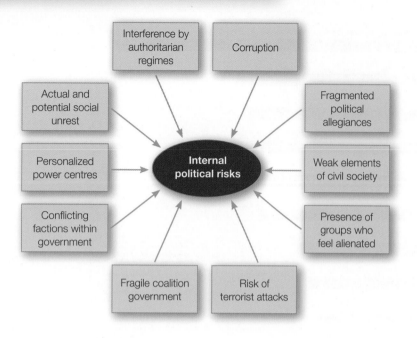

Figure 5.4 Internal political risks

A prospective investor in manufacturing may be presented with a choice among emerging markets, such as India, a Central European country or China. As discussed in Chapter 3, prospective investors look first at the country's economic environment. If GDP growth is healthy and seems to be sustainable, this constitutes a strong argument for entering the country. All three examples have healthy economic growth, developing market economies and growing consumer markets. But, in terms of political systems, they are very different. India is a democracy, but its political scene is volatile and unstable, fuelled by social and ethnic tensions, and religious strife. It also has a tradition of a strong state role in economic development, which has deterred investors in the past. The new EU states of Central Europe have formal democracies, but as yet they do not function smoothly in practice. A high turnover rate in governments and ministers militates against continuity in government policy towards businesses, which is important for investors. Corruption and bureaucracy are also obstacles in these states, which deter outsiders. Moreover, nationalist sentiment is a factor in party politics. China has pressed forward with liberal economic reforms, although its political system is authoritarian. On the surface, China seems relatively stable, and its leaders have welcomed foreign investors, but restrictions and government interference are continuing risks. Social unrest lurks beneath the surface, as prosperity has not benefited all segments of the population (see CF8.1). Even among those benefiting from globalization, there is growing disquiet about the quality of life, including levels of pollution. Without the elements of civil society, such as interest groups and other independent organizations, any display of dissent in public is stamped out by the authorities. Similarly, little heed to civil liberties and weak rule of law allow corruption to breed, which is another cause of disquiet among ordinary people who may feel helpless when up against the authorities. For companies entering the country, these are considerations which should be taken into account. They may seem to pose little threat to the country's stability, but they constitute political and legal risk.

In authoritarian states, power is often personalized. For a foreign company entering the country, making contact with the relevant individuals is necessary to smooth the way. Payments to individuals, considered to be part of the way of doing business in many emerging markets, are considered corrupt in most Western countries. Moreover, when individual office holders change, any goodwill built up with previous individuals is lost. Policies may change, and an activity which was approved previously may no longer be acceptable. Vulnerability to the apparent whims of persons in authority is one of the aspects of countries with weak rule of law. In addition, in the absence of an independent judiciary, recourse to the courts may be of little avail. The same risks arise for companies dealing with state-controlled companies in authoritarian countries, where corporate decision-making is closely linked with political power centres. These risks are highlighted in CS5.2 on Royal Dutch Shell, in connection with its activities in Russia. Shell's ownership of the Sakhalin project, legally agreed with a previous government, was rewritten in 2006 by Russia's current leadership, leaving the company little redress.

Corruption can pose a risk in almost any state. Transparency International (2007) defines corruption as 'the misuse of entrusted power for private gain'. It draws up an annual Corruption Perception Index, ranking 167 countries on a scale of 1–10, with 10 representing the least corrupt. Selected countries are shown in Figure 5.5, with their scores and rankings. Scandinavian countries top the rankings, while Russia, at 2.6, is near the bottom and China, at 4.6, is in the bottom half. Despite reforms and democratic transition, corruption remains a drawback in Central European countries, such as Hungary and Poland. Opaque bureaucracies, legacies of their communist past, are still a drawback for businesses, and also a breeding ground for corruption. Civil service jobs, required under EU law to be independent of politics, are frequently influenced by political affiliation. Established democracies also suffer from corruption, often related to donations to political parties from businesses. The relatively lowly ranking of the US in Figure 5.5 largely reflects the influence of powerful sectoral interests in political decision-making. Major companies typically contribute money to candidates and parties, with the implication that they are seeking to influence policies or gain favours. Moreover, politicians are often accused of taking corrupt payments for favours or the award of government contracts.

Organizations of all descriptions, including companies, not-for-profit organizations and interest groups, regularly lobby democratic govern-

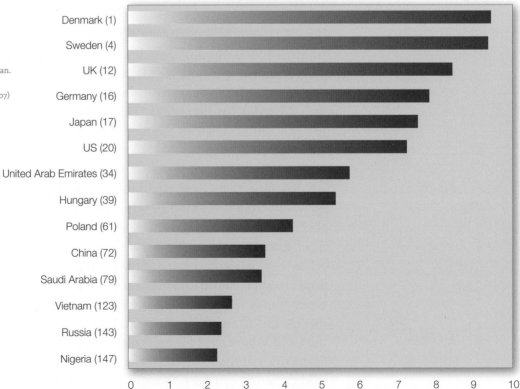

Figure 5.5 Transparency International's Corruption Perception Index, selected countries, 2007

Note: 0 = highly corrupt, 10 = highly clean. Rankings appear in brackets

Source: Transparency International (2007) Corruption Perception Index, www.transparency.org

See Transparency International's website at www.transparency.org, for a range of relevant topics.

WEB CHECK

TO RECAP...

Internal political risks

Corruption, weak rule of law and social fragmentation are among the chief risks which arise from within a political system. All are common in developing economies, to a lesser or greater extent. However, as the most economically advantageous opportunities often arise in these countries, many international businesses calculate that the risks involve extra costs, which will be outweighed by the benefits.

ments for policies and laws they wish to see adopted. As CS5.1 on online gambling shows, groups with differing perspectives can come together on a particular issue, securing favourable legislation reflecting their interests. However, while lobbying is legitimate, the payment of bribes is not, and government–business relations in many countries are tainted by scandals in this area. For the company which gains tangible benefits from its lobbying or financial contributions to politicians, the risk is that, if illegality later emerges, the company, including the individuals involved, will suffer reputational damage.

Companies doing business in countries where political risk is high must weigh up the potential benefits against the uncertainties. Keeping dealings with officials transparent and keeping records are ways of minimizing exposure to corruption. When faced with a choice of locations within a country, it is wise to avoid areas where there is a history of social and political unrest, as well as areas where local political power brokers have a grip. Local political elites can often call on their own police and military support, but for companies from outside, relying on them could be of little avail, or, at worst, make them vulnerable to becoming embroiled in internal rivalries. For physical security, companies increasingly contract commercially for protection of their sites and workforces, as CS5.2 on Royal Dutch Shell discusses.

International risks

The political environment of every country is influenced by its relations with other countries, both neighbours in its region and countries further afield, such as trading partners. As has been seen, national economies vary greatly in the size and global reach of their firms. Similarly, countries differ markedly in their political power at international level. A recognized view of international politics, known as the 'realist' view, sees relations between nation-states as based on power, in particular, economic and military power (Held, 1993). (The realist theory is discussed in Chapter 15.) Foremost among them is the US, which is the world's largest economy. During the Cold War, the US and USSR vied for global influence, building up large arsenals of weapons and flaunting military prowess. It is estimated that by the mid-1980s, world military expenditure was $1,000 billion per annum (at 1987 US dollars), which amounted to $190 for every person on earth (Held et al., 1999: 103).

With the demise of the Soviet Union and the end of the Cold War, the US has tended to view itself as the only remaining political superpower. Now, the rapid economic growth of China and the resurgence of Russia are encouraging both to raise their political profiles worldwide, based largely on their economic influence in the global economy. Developing countries in other regions are becoming pivotal, largely for resource riches. Hence relations between countries are becoming more complex than the realist view of international relations holds (Gray, 2003). With more complex relations, the threats and vulnerabilities are now more diffuse and unpredictable than in the Cold War era. As Figure 5.6 shows, international risk stems largely from insecurities in the modern world. Armed groups, private militias and organized criminals can pose threats just about anywhere. The rich and powerful

Figure 5.6 International risks

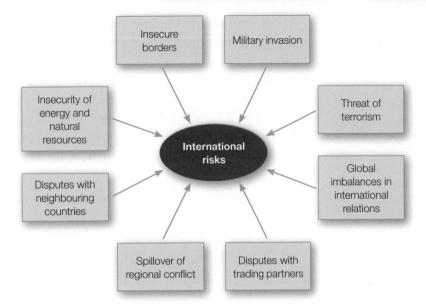

country is as vulnerable as the poor one. Indeed, some terrorists may aim to disrupt key economic or financial centres in rich countries. Some regions, such as the Middle East and Africa, where there are ongoing tensions between governments and religious groups, are prone to tip over into armed conflict and even civil war.

The threat of terrorism is now a major priority for governments throughout the world. Today's terrorists are facilitated by global communications and finance in their missions to cause fear and havoc in whatever location they choose. They have access to abundant sources of weaponry. Governments can take measures such as anti-terrorism legislation which increases police powers to detain suspected terrorists. However, they must weigh up the possible benefits in terms of national security against the incursions into human rights. In national political debate, immigration is closely linked with threats to national security. Insecure borders may constitute a weakness which terrorists can exploit, but borders cannot be made impervious, and the fluid movement of people and goods is necessary for the smooth running of legitimate transborder activities.

Energy security and guaranteed supply of natural resources such as water are also continuing concerns of governments. Indeed, some commentators argue that these issues are becoming predominant in international politics (Gray, 2003). Most governments must co-operate with others for the supply and distribution of these precious resources. Focus has fallen on Russia largely because of its oil and gas wealth, placing its authoritarian government in a potentially strong position to control investment and supply, as CF5.1 on Russia has shown. Ownership of gas pipelines has also provided a source of political leverage for Russia when dealing with countries which import its gas. China's extension of its sphere of influence in Africa owes much to the search for energy security, which Africa's resources can provide (see SX6.1). African leaders have made numerous energy and commodity agreements with the Chinese leadership, but an unstable political context on both sides could cast a shadow on their long-term viability.

TO RECAP...

External political risks

Every country is drawn into international relations with other governments, which give rise to benefits such as trade agreements and investment, but can also involve risks, such as inter-governmental disputes, which affect transborder business. Terrorist threats can arise almost anywhere. By informing themselves of a country's historical relations with other states, international managers can manage the range of possible external risks.

For international businesses, international risks are partly country specific and partly determined by fluctuating international relations between governments. Companies are reluctant to enter a country which has been a target of terrorist attacks on a regular basis, or one which has continuing territorial disputes with neighbours which lead to armed conflict. Companies may also be wary of countries which are dependent on imported energy and raw materials, which may be vulnerable to supply disputes between governments. An entire region, such as the Middle East, may be politically unstable, affecting all countries to some extent: even those which have smoothly functioning political systems are vulnerable to spillovers of regional conflict, as indicated in Figure 5.6. In some industries, such as energy, external risk is ever present. In extreme cases, oil companies have simply exited particular locations for this reason. The large oil companies, however, invest in so many countries and regions that, overall, they are able to weather such setbacks.

Is it worth the risk?

Political risks are often underestimated by companies seeking to invest in foreign locations, partly because a good deal of broad knowledge about historical and cultural dynamics is needed, and even then, there are numerous factors which could alter the initial assessment. Of the many types of risk discussed in this section, it is arguable that companies should focus on the main internal risks, corruption and the instability of the political system, because external risks, being more nebulous, are difficult to assess and guard against. Do you agree, and why?

PAUSE TO REFLECT

Case study 5.1: Online gambling's uncertain future

Gambling as a leisure activity is popular with millions of people across the globe. It is a significant element of leisure spending, generating income for diverse interests: providers of gambling services; tourism in areas where casinos are located; and governments, which benefit from licensing and from state lotteries. At the same time, gambling also arouses opposition, particularly from religious groups who view it as morally wrong, potentially addictive and leading to social problems. Nonetheless, gambling has grown in popularity, the most spectacular growth occurring in online gambling. As Figure 1 shows, growth has been dramatic and is expected to continue. However, legal setbacks in the US have impacted on prospects for the businesses which have made online gambling, particularly sports betting, their core business.

The penetration of broadband has facilitated the growth in online gambling, but the political and legal environment has been uncertain. In the US, the largest market for internet gambling (see Figure 2), the US Department of Justice has maintained that the 1961 Federal Wire Act bans any betting over telephone lines, which would include the internet. This interpretation was doubted by legal authorities, leading online betting companies to press ahead in the US market. Congressional activists, along with some large casino companies, sought to bring in specific legislation designed for the internet era, barring US banks from processing financial transactions related to online gambling. Christian conservative groups, closely linked to the Republican Party, would go further, desiring a ban on all forms of gambling. Given the popularity of the pastime, it is not clear whether a majority in Congress would support a total ban.

The separate states within the US take differing legal positions on gambling. In some, gambling in casinos is confined to riverboats in waterways or on Indian reservations, both of which are considered legally outside state jurisdiction. Indian tribes operate 350 casinos in 28 states, bringing in funds for social purposes on their reservations. Only 11 states allow commercial casinos to operate on non-Indian dry land. Nonetheless, large casino companies have invested heavily in the major commercial complexes, including Las Vegas, Nevada, home to over 100 casinos. In 2005, Americans made more than 300 million visits to casinos, double the number five years previously. Televised poker has helped to boost interest in gaming. The popularity of the televised World Poker Tour from Las Vegas has made poker the third most watched sport on American TV (after car racing and American football).

Figure 1 Estimated growth in global revenues from online gambling

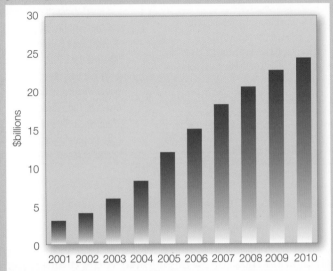

Source: Christian Capital Advisors (2005) 'Global internet gambling revenue estimates and projections', www.cca-i.com

Figure 2 The worldwide online gambling market by region

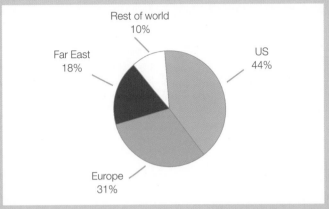

Source: Financial Times, 25 April 2005

However, the strongest growth has come in the online gambling market. While it has grown worldwide, Americans have been leading the way. In 2005, US gamblers represented nearly half the internet gambling market of $12 billion, as shown in Figure 2.

Online gambling businesses have focused on sports betting and gaming. They are mainly based 'offshore', in the Caribbean or Gibraltar, where light regulatory and tax frameworks prevail, although many are listed on the London Stock Exchange. One of these, PartyGaming, saw a huge surge in business with the introduction of its breakthrough technology for playing online poker, allowing some 70,000 players to play at the same time. Attracting 12.5 million American players, PartyGaming generated 80% of its $1 billion in revenue from the US market in 2005. Clouds were looming, however, with the arrest in 2006 of the chief executive of the UK's BetonSports, a UK citizen, in a transit lounge of Dallas airport, on his way to the company's head office in Costa Rica. This arrest had an immediate effect of sending the company's shares plummeting from 327p to 180p in London.

Antigua and Barbuda, an offshore centre, alarmed by the BetonSports arrest, took its case to the World Trade Organization (WTO) and secured a ruling against the US. The WTO found that banning the remote supply of gambling services from overseas was discriminatory because the US allowed remote gambling on horse races within the country. An estimated $21 billion in trade sanctions against the US was authorized by the WTO. In practice, these would have little effect, as Antigua and Barbuda has a population of only 83,000 and an economy 0.007% of that of the US. However, the case was important for establishing the legal principle, as well as for demonstrating that one of the world's smallest economies can take on the largest, and win.

Further arrests followed in 2006, one in New York and two in Europe, where online gambling was also proving to be popular. Joint CEOs of bwin, an Austrian betting company, were arrested by French police in Monaco, at a press conference called to announce the company's sponsorship of AS Monaco Football

Club. In France, the only legal betting is in casinos, through the state-owned lottery and under the state horse racing authority. The EU Commission has challenged the restrictive laws on gambling in many EU member states as contrary to the principle of free movement of services. In the UK, a regulatory approach has been adopted, with a new licensing system introduced by the Gaming Act 2005. While the large American casino companies had hoped for the go-ahead for large, out-of-town casino complexes in Britain, the new law is more restrictive, in response to concerns about the risks of addictive gambling.

In October, 2006, the US Congress approved legislation banning businesses operating internet gambling. Casinos (including Indian reservation casinos), online betting on horse races and online betting on state lotteries are unaffected by the new law. In one of the apparent oddities of US legislative procedure, the prohibition was 'tacked' onto a bill on a totally different topic, the Port Security Improvement Act 2006. This Act aimed to improve systems for detecting biological, chemical and nuclear weapons in containers entering US ports, which could pose terrorist threats. The core of this bill was understandably popular with legislators. Whether they would have voted for an internet gambling ban had the issue been put to them on its own, one cannot say. Critics of

plate 5.2 The bright lights of the casino sign spell excitement and a chance to win riches, but online gambling now offers a range of alternatives with excitement of their own.

the ban point out that the prohibition of alcohol in 1920 was repealed in 1933, by which time it had become clear that problem drinking and consequent social harm had actually increased rather than diminished. In 1919, the ban was at least voted on specifically. For the internet gambling companies, meanwhile, it was back to square one.

Questions

1 In what ways did the political and legal environment in the US present risks to the offshore online gambling businesses, even before the statute of 2006?

2 It is arguable that the fragmented and inconsistent legal position of gambling in the US does little to enhance respect for the law in general. Do you agree and why?

3 Contrast the different governmental approaches to gambling highlighted in this case study.

4 In your view, which governmental approach to gambling would be the best and most practicable?

Sources: Garrahan, M., 'Trying to gain trust in online gaming', *Financial Times*, 25 April 2005; Alden, E., 'Politics of US gambling makes for odd bedfellows', *Financial Times*, 27 May 2006; Garrahan, M., 'Poker's programming ace', *Financial Times*, 18 June 2005; Blitz, R., 'EC calls for fair play on gambling', *Financial Times*, 22 September 2006; Braithwaite, T., 'When the cold war suddenly got hot', *Financial Times*, 20 July 2006; Blitz, R., 'BetonSports pulls plug on US games betting operations', *Financial Times*, 20 July 2006; Blitz, R., 'Playing poker with the US Senate: $12bn industry loses a hand', *Financial Times*, 18 July 2006; Kyvig, D. (1979) *Repealing National Prohibition* (Chicago: University of Chicago Press); Beattie, A., 'WTO rules against US over online gaming', *Financial Times*, 31 March 2007.

WEB CHECK

Read about the dispute initiated by Antigua and Barbuda against the US on the WTO's website at www.wto.org. Click on *Disputes*, then *Disputes chronologically* and go to Dispute DS285, dated 13 March 2003.

Government and business

One of the aspects of globalization most often highlighted is the diminishing importance of states as sovereign players in the international environment (Kobrin, 1997). In particular, the rise in economic power of MNEs is highlighted as showing a shift away from governments as centres of power. This is a view that risks underestimating the roles played by governments in business life, which, because of their political power and resources, remain influential. Governments take in large sums of money in revenues and spend large sums in the public interest. In both roles, interactions with business are crucial. Governments may be customers, as in defence or healthcare, or they may provide subsidies to support an industry, as in farming. SX5.1 on ABC Learning provides an example of a business, childcare, built on government policy initiatives and subsidies. The broad role of national governments is outlined in Chapter 1. This section moves on to look in detail at the activities of governments in the business context.

Governments as economic players

In market economies, the liberal economic view is that governments remain on the outside, maintaining an orderly and fair environment in which private enterprises carry out transactions. In reality, governments have taken on more active roles. As highlighted in Chapter 3, even in the US, a model of economic liberalism, the state played an active part in early stages of economic development. More recently, government subsidies to some companies, such as Boeing, suggest that national strategic interests override market values in some industries. The US blocking of the takeover of the Californian oil company, Unocal, by the Chinese state-controlled oil company, CNOOC, also suggests political considerations. The US, through its influence in bodies such as the IMF and World Bank, has maintained a rather doctrinaire approach to developing economies, requiring that liberalizing reforms take precedence. However, it is evident that the development models of many countries, particularly those in South and Southeast Asia, have been premised on state guidance and state ownership of enterprises. There may be only degrees of difference between these two approaches. The listed company with private shareholders may have close ties with political leaders and government ministries, as occurred in Japan's development phase. Strategic decision-making within companies is subject to these powerful influences, although the companies were not simply taking orders: business leaders were adept at bargaining to make their voices heard (Johnson, 1982).

The fully state-owned enterprise may operate as a department of government, its employees treated as public servants. Its directors, appointed by the government, are ultimately accountable to the country's political leaders. The justification of this type of business is that it is too important strategically to be left to private enterprise. On the other hand, large public sector enterprises can be difficult for governments to manage. They have tended to become bureaucratic and inefficient in practice, swallowing huge sums in public funds. For practical reasons and because of international pressure, governments have opted for privatization, in effect raising capital by selling off a portion of the company to private investors. Such enterprises are rather hybrid in nature, with controlling stakes in the hands of government and minority private investors. As has been seen in CF5.1 on Russia, flotations of state monopolies raise questions of opaque corporate governance and the potential for politicized decision-making where authoritarian governments are the protagonists. In a market-driven democratic state, the state-controlled enterprise might seem an anomaly, but in Europe, the notion of the public stakeholder is strong, and defended as consistent with embrace of market principles (Breton, 2006). CF5.2 on France analyses this view of the role of government.

COUNTRY FOCUS 5.2 – FRANCE

Evolution or revolution in the French political environment?

France has suffered from lacklustre economic performance for a number of years, prompting politicians and citizens alike to ponder its future direction. In GDP per head, it slipped from 6th place in 1980 to 17th place in 2005, falling behind countries such as Finland and Ireland, which have become highly globalized. The French economic environment has suffered from high

Table The benefits of globalization for France

	Multinationals	Financial markets	State	Consumers	Everybody	Others
Deputies were asked: who benefits from globalization?						
UMP (Union pour un Mouvement Populaire)	25%	21.8%	3.4%	18.2%	29.6%	2.3%
PS (Parti Socialiste)	50%	50%	0%	0%	0%	0%

Source: Financial Times, 29 May 2006

unemployment, budget deficits, rampant public spending and labour market rigidities. However, French politicians are at odds on where to find solutions, highlighted in the presidential election of 2007.

President Jacques Chirac, of the centre-right UMP (Union pour un Mouvement Populaire), left office in 2007, having led the country since 1995. He had been noted for upholding statist and nationalist values, but poor economic performance and social fragmentation caused the party to rethink their underlying principles. Stepping into the political fray was Nicolas Sarkozy, who, although a member of the UMP government, had distanced himself from its record and called for changes towards a more liberal economic model. The socialists also felt the time had come for change, but emphasized social priorities, suggesting that the problem is that economic liberalism has already gone too far. As the figure shows, 85% of the French public in 2006 felt the country was going in the wrong direction, a higher proportion than in neighbouring countries.

Figure Citizens' views on the political direction of their country

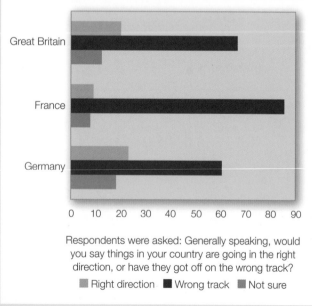

Respondents were asked: Generally speaking, would you say things in your country are going in the right direction, or have they got off on the wrong track?

■ Right direction ■ Wrong track ■ Not sure

Source: Financial Times, 19 June 2006

France's place in a globalized world has become a controversial issue. For many in France, the takeover of Arcelor by Lakshmi Mittal symbolizes the negative aspects of globaliza-

tion (see CS11.1). The new ArcelorMittal accounts for 20% of global steel production, producing three times that of the next biggest rival. Socialists point the finger at liberal reforms, while for reformers within the UMP, such as Sarkozy, the answer is to meet the challenges through more competitive businesses. The differences are apparent in the responses of the National Assembly deputies on the effects of globalization, shown in the table. UMP deputies saw more favourable effects than socialists, who were uniformly hostile.

In the election campaign, Sarkozy argued for radical changes to restore national competitiveness. He would move further towards 'neoliberal' ideas, boosting entrepreneurship and labour flexibility. Although globalization is often portrayed by the left as a threat, he urged that it should be seen more as a challenge. The country can boast a good record in start-ups, but disappointingly slow growth among new businesses, as high social costs and regulatory burden take their toll on France's small businesses. The owners of one small firm Imstar, which has been in business for 21 years providing specialist photo imaging for the biotechnology sector, express widely held views that the lack of development finance and a risk-averse culture have held back their growth. They say: 'There is no question that if we had moved to California 15 years ago, we would be a different-sized business' (Hollinger, 2006). While 25% of German SMEs export, only 5% of French SMEs do. The UMP government under Chirac brought in new policies aimed at stimulating SME growth. However, the proposal for flexible introductory employment contracts was scrapped following angry protests, indicating the difficulty faced by the government in bringing in labour reforms.

France has prided itself on its national champions, the large companies which enjoy not only economic success but a special role in French society. These are exemplified mainly by state-owned companies such as Electricité de France (EDF), the electricity supplier. A former monopoly supplier, EDF has been forced by the EU to privatize, changing itself into a registered company and opening up the energy market to competition. Within one year of the limited introduction of competition in 2004, EDF lost 10% of the open market to Suez, a rival electricity company. EDF launched an IPO in 2005, raising €7 billion for government coffers from the sale of 12.7% of the company to private investors. Employees and powerful trade unions, notably the CGT (Confédération Générale du Travail), have resisted these moves. Objections stem partly from self-interest, as public sector employees enjoy shorter hours, better pensions and early retirement schemes which other workers do not receive. Moreover, EDF has paid into a social fund largely run by the CGT, which provides numerous other benefits such as medical cover for employees. When EDF was partially privatized, the government reached an agreement with the CGT to leave the pension system untouched, transferring the liabilities to the state in return for a one-off payment. This special treatment angered many workers in other industries.

The 2007 elections were won by the UMP, Sarkozy succeeding Chirac as president. Sarkozy immediately launched into reforms to overhaul the privileged pension schemes and rigid labour market rules. Although they met resistance, the process of negotiation remained on track. On the other hand, a deteriorating economic scene, including rising consumer prices, rather tempered his reforming zeal. In an apparent shift, he announced a 'policy of civilization', emphasizing human values, social dialogue, quality of life and environmental issues. These were the very issues which had dominated the socialists' political platform in the elections. He called on economist Joseph Stiglitz to advise on ways of measuring qualitative improvements in the economy, to supplement traditional quantitative measures. The attempt to blend free-market and social values could lead to improvements in France's education system, to encourage greater innovation. He has proposed offering tax breaks to SMEs which set up profit-sharing schemes, which could represent a fairer distribu-

tion between capital and labour. It is arguable that the new social-oriented policies could, in practice, aid long-term economic performance. Sarkozy might have switched track, but has not altered his original agenda for France.

Questions

- ◆ Assess the differing approaches in French political discourse on how best to solve the country's problems.
- ◆ What indicators of France's unease with liberal economic values can be derived from the example of EDF?
- ◆ How does the issue of globalization divide French political allegiances?
- ◆ Describe the political influences on the business climate in France.

Sources: Thornhill, J., 'Rival visions: Sarkozy and de Villepin lay bare the difficult choices facing France', *Financial Times*, 12 September 2005; Munchau, W., 'Why France must relax its corporate control', *Financial Times*, 6 February 2006; Hollinger, P., 'Push for power: listing marks a tough new stage in EDF's struggle to stay out front', *Financial Times*, 15 November 2005; Hollinger, P., 'France sets free its "gazelles"', *Financial Times*, 19 October 2006; Marsh, P., 'A feel for steel: why Mittal will press home the benefits of size', *Financial Times*, 26 September 2006; Thornhill, J., 'European poll highlights French gloom on politics', *Financial Times*, 19 June 2006; Thornhill, J., 'Less exceptional: how globalisation is shifting France's political fault lines', *Financial Times*, 29 May 2006; UNDP (2006) *Human Development Report 2006* (Basingstoke: Palgrave Macmillan); Thornhill, J., 'Mission civilisatrice', *Financial Times*, 10 January 2008.

WEB CHECK

For information on France, go to the OECD's website at www.oecd.org, where *France* appears in the *Country List*.

Aiding or discouraging?

In a market economy, governments aim to encourage entrepreneurship in domestic enterprises and also to provide a hospitable business environment for foreign companies. This implies allowing businesses as much room for manoeuvre as possible. In general, businesses wish to be able to hire (and fire) staff as their needs dictate, to acquire premises relatively smoothly and to run their businesses as they see fit. Too much regulation in any of these areas is likely to be perceived by businesses as detracting from their competitiveness.

In some countries, there is little regulation, and laws may be only patchily enforced. Although this may seem advantageous for businesses, a trend is for governments to respond to the needs of stakeholders, including workers, consumers and the general public. They have become more active than ever in laying down laws for employment protection, product controls, planning procedures, pollution controls and health and safety requirements. Moreover, these measures involve putting in place regulatory bodies to monitor and enforce compliance. Most businesses recognize that some regulation is necessary, despite the burdens created, especially for small businesses.

The OECD evaluates countries on the degree of regulatory burden in product market regulation and labour market regulation. Figure 5.7 shows that there has been a marked reduction in regulation since 1998. Australia, the UK and the US are relatively lightly regulated. Heavier regulation in product markets can constitute a barrier to imports and protect home producers. This has been the case in France and Italy, but, as Figure 5.7 shows, regulation has been significantly reduced in these markets. Light regulation, while welcomed by businesses, carries risks for consumers and other businesses. It may allow aggressive firms to build up dominant market positions, consolidating their positions by acquiring competing companies. It may also leave consumers and employees vulnerable where companies have operated fraudulently. Enron, the collapsed energy trader, pursued a deliberate policy of entering markets, both individual states in the US and foreign countries, where energy trading was weakly regulated. The result following its bankruptcy was disastrous for investors, creditors and employees. It also led to the passing of the Sarbanes-Oxley Act, which imposes stricter regulation through the criminal law than most countries have in place.

Governments wishing to encourage domestic companies to expand globally can pursue various policies. An enterprise-friendly business climate will encourage entrepreneurs, including born-global firms. Many governments play a more interventionist role. Through state-owned companies, they play a direct role, or they may encourage privately owned domestic businesses by the imposition of barriers on foreign companies wishing to enter their country. In fact, both types of government intervention tend to weaken the competitive environment within the country, with the possible result that their domestic companies are not developing the tools they need strategically and operationally to compete on their own.

In countries with market economies, competition and fair business practices are the subject of legal regulation, which discourages monopolies and restrictive trade practices such as price-fixing. Anti-monopoly law is often referred to as antitrust law, following American usage. The great industrial conglomerates of late nineteenth-century America used trusts as the legal means of consolidating their economic power. The enactment of antitrust legislation around the turn of the century sought to curtail monopolists and anti-competitive practices. The zeal with which these laws are applied differs according to the political climate in any period, and the prevailing attitudes of government to big business. SX5.1 provides an example of the influence of government policies.

The EU Commission has shown considerable zest in curtailing anti-competitive activity. EU member states are subject to law on takeovers and mergers, as well as on restrictive practices. EU competition law complements national legal frameworks. Despite these efforts, monopolies or near-monopolies are still in existence, especially among state-owned enterprises. The monopolist is a firm which faces no competition, and is able to determine unilaterally the products on offer, their availability and their price. For public utilities, such as electricity, the argument may be put forward that the

Figure 5.7 Business regulation in selected countries

Note: Lower score = less regulation

Source: OECD (2005) Product Market Regulation Index, www.oedc.org

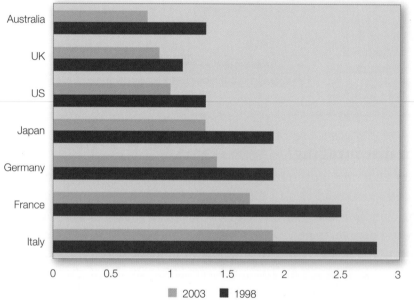

Antitrust law: Law designed to curtail monopolists and encourage competitive markets.

Monopoly: Domination by one firm of the market for particular goods or services, enabling the firm to determine price and supply.

monopoly is justified, as this area is a public good. Where the monopolist operates, the consumer is likely to be worse off than where there are competitive pressures for the customer's business. For example, consumers in Mexico, where incomes are a sixth of those in the US, pay 50% more for a phone call than US consumers would pay for the equivalent call. The reason lies in the monopolistic grip enjoyed by Telmex in Mexico's telecommunications market, in contrast to the competition in the US telecoms market.

Apart from EU competition laws for member states, regulation of monopolies and restrictive practices is the subject of national regulation. There is as yet no international framework for regulating anti-competitive practices (a topic revisited in Chapter 15). Companies which build global empires may become so dominant as to be able to control an industry. The combined size of ArcelorMittal has caused some alarm among other steel producers (see CS11.1). Microsoft dominates computer operating systems through its Windows software. Its monopolist position and restrictive practices have been the subject of anti-competitive legal actions in many countries and in the EU (see CS15.2), which the company has defended vigorously.

TO RECAP...

Business and regulation

Regulation remains mainly in the hands of national authorities, whose aims vary. While in some countries, light regulation can be seen as a location advantage, most governments have become more attentive to the needs of consumers and employees, and so impose standards in products and labour markets.

STRATEGIC CROSSROADS

5.1

Building an empire with ABC Learning Centres

Eddy Groves has become one of Australia's most successful young entrepreneurs. By the age of 40, he had built up an empire of childcare centres and amassed a huge personal fortune in the process. Following the opening of his first centre in Brisbane in 1989, the business rapidly took off. He foresaw that the market would inevitably expand as more women went out to work and needed daycare for their children (see Figure 4.11). He quickly built up the number of centres in Australia, floating the company on the Australian stock exchange in 2002. At that time it was valued at $25 million, and just four years later, it was valued at $1.2 billion. ABC Learning prides itself on the consistently high quality of its services, latest equipment and large capital investment in facilities, which smaller operations cannot match.

Crucial to the rise of ABC Learning were shifts in Australian government policy. In 1991, subsidies previously available only to community-based centres were extended to private providers. In 1997, subsidies to community centres ceased, and a system of subsidies to families was introduced, leading to an upsurge in demand. At the same time, prices climbed. The federal government pays a means-tested subsidy for each child, from $144 a week down to $24 a week for parents earning over $95,683; in addition, parents can claim a 30% tax rebate on the balance of the childcare costs. Government subsidies have grown from $200 million in 1990, to $2 billion in 2006, a growth of 14.4% per year. Privately run childcare centres have now overtaken community centres, providing 70% of childcare outside the home. Critics of this 'corporatization' of childcare say that it has gone hand in hand with rising prices (Woolrich, 2006). Whereas $100 a week might be thought reasonable by parents, some Sydney centres now charge $100 a *day*.

ABC Learning receives 44% of its income from government subsidies. It has become the dominant operator in Australia, now owning 20% of the daycare market. Acquiring rival businesses has been the main force behind the company's rapid expansion. By 2006, it had amassed 1,158 centres in Australia, its next largest rival having only 40. It owns an educational equipment company and two training colleges for childcare centre staff. Paradoxically, having facilitated the company's growth, government policies could well prove to be an obstacle to future expansion. It is likely that the Australian Competition and Consumer Commission would take a dim view of any further expansion in its core provision, on the grounds that it is verging on a monopoly in some regions. The Commission fired a warning in 2004, when ABC was made to divest some centres following the merger with Peppercorn, a former rival, on anti-monopoly grounds. In addition, ABC's efforts to expand into primary education have so far been thwarted, as Queensland legislated to retain education in the not-for-profit sector.

By the late 1990s, Groves had set his sights on expansion in the US, a market 15 times the size of Australia. Again through acquisition of existing businesses, he has quickly built up ABC Learning's market share, making it the second largest operator in the US, with 1,038 centres. Here, government subsidies are much lower than in Australia – in the region of 20–25% in comparison with over 40% in Australia. Groves remains optimistic that the US business will succeed through growing demand, because childcare is an essential service in the modern economy. He says: 'Childcare is really not a discretionary spend. Parents need to have care if they are going to work' (Marsh, 2006).

Sources: Woolrich, N., 'Concerns over ABC Learning's dominance of childcare', radio transcript, 14 March 2006, www.abc.net.au; Hills, B., 'Cradle snatcher', *Sydney Morning Herald*, 11 March 2006, www.smh.com.au; Fraser, A., 'Trading halt signals new ABC Learning expansion', *The Australian*, 14 December 2006, www.theaustralian.news.com; Marsh, V., 'Talent for nurturing a fledgling', *Financial Times*, 7 December 2006.

Questions

◆ Weigh up which factors you feel are more important in the rise of ABC Learning: entrepreneurial flair or favourable government policies. Explain your reasons.

◆ In what ways has the domination of ABC Learning in the childcare sector been a benefit or a detriment to consumers?

WEB CHECK

ABC Learning's website is www.childcare.com.au.

Regulation: who benefits?
Consider the two opposing viewpoints:
● Regulation adds to costs, wastes time and stifles the competitiveness of our country's firms in the global economy
● Regulation by our government has brought improving standards in employment and confidence in the safety of our country's products, giving us an edge in global markets, in which attention to how a product is produced is becoming increasingly crucial
Consider the validity of each of these viewpoints.
Which would you go along with?

PAUSE TO REFLECT

National legal frameworks

National legal system: System of substantive law and court structure, which is administered and enforced by state authorities.

Every business engages in a multitude of legal transactions, from simple contracts for the purchase of supplies, to more complicated contracts for the hiring of employees, to highly complex joint venture agreements. When a business decides to incorporate as a company, it undertakes numerous legal obligations and compliance requirements. The bulk of this regulation is in the national legal system of the country where its head office is located and those countries where its operations take place. Regional and local lawmaking within a country also affects its activities, and is particularly relevant in countries where decentralization and local autonomy are extensive. In the US in particular, the individual states enjoy a considerable degree of self-governance, including legislative authority and their own court systems. Wherever a firm does business, it is required to comply with the relevant laws in the same way that local companies are. It will also be affected by international law and regional legal frameworks, as Figure 5.8 indicates. Hence, a US company doing business in Germany must comply with the national and regional laws of Germany, EU law and US law, both federal and in the state of its incorporation. Much of this legislation is overlapping: there are EU as well as national laws in many areas, including employment law and health and safety. Similarly, international law overlaps with the other levels, in human rights and environmental protection, for example. We look first at national frameworks.

The legal framework in any country is closely linked to its political system, as lawmaking is a function of the country's supreme authorities. In an authoritarian

Figure 5.8 Dimensions of the legal environment

Intellectual property rights (IPR): Legal rights to the ownership and exclusive use of the products of human creativity and endeavour, such as patents for inventions, copyright for literature and music, and trademarks for corporate symbols.

state, such as a military dictatorship, the will of the leader or ruling group determines the law. There is a strong element of legal risk for companies in these countries, as the law and its application may be changed without notice. These countries also lack the separation of powers and independent judiciary, which characterize states where the rule of law prevails. Rulers of countries such as China are aware that their legal system needs upgrading in standards of fairness and impartiality. As Chapter 4 highlighted, countries which are predominantly Muslim tend to have dual systems in which both secular and religious law co-exist, and in which religious law is likely to be the ultimate authority. The oil-rich states of the Middle East emphasize the safeguards of their systems for commercial enterprises, but there remain inherent risks for Western businesses in the social and political environment, as these are traditionally closed societies with autocratic rule.

In democratic systems, the separation of powers should ensure that the three branches of government are balanced in terms of lawmaking and judicial decision-making. The democratically elected body is responsible for enacting law, and a system of independent courts applies the law impartially. At least, this is the theory. In practice, law officers in government, as well as courts and judges, may come under political pressure. If, for example, there is suspected wrongdoing in a government department, such as the paying of bribes, where does the remedy lie? Those who come forward from inside are likely to lose their jobs, and their revelations of wrongdoing, where they implicate government officers, may be covered up. The rule of law is jeopardized in these circumstances. Furthermore, because governments are enmeshed in business life, bribery may impact adversely on the business environment in the country. Corruption, therefore, poses legal as well as political risks.

A transparent legal system, where parties can enjoy impartiality in the settlement of disputes and fairness in judicial processes, is an important factor in assessing the business climate of a country. Of particular importance to business is the body of company law, which deals with the formation of companies, requirements for disclosure of company information, protection of shareholders' rights (including provision for minority rights) and corporate governance. Also important are intellectual property rights (IPR). These concern the intangible assets that a company owns and which it exploits to generate profits. The three major categories are patent, copyright and trademark. A patent, discussed in Chapter 12, may be applied for to protect a product or process of the company.

Copyright exists in literary works, music, films and software. It is not applied for, but arises automatically. With advances in media and internet technology, copyright implications have become major issues, as shown in SX5.2 on YouTube. The law in this area is evolving as new ways of generating content arise. Owners of copyright are entitled to be paid royalties for the use of their material. Much music downloading, file-sharing and self-generated content raises copyright issues which impact directly on the business models of the companies involved. The importance of the trademark has also been enhanced by the expansion of global media. The trademark is the distinctive name or logo which represents a corporate brand. It may be the brand of a product or of the company itself. Trademarks are registered, usually within the Patent Office of a country. For a company, a well-known brand is a valuable asset, which must be registered as a trademark in the countries in which it does business. Even so, some countries are notoriously lax in enforcing trademark law, allowing counterfeit brands, as well as infringement of copyright and patent, to run rife. Developing countries may be rather ambivalent in establishing and enforcing a robust system for protecting intellectual property. They realize that foreign investors require protection of their property, but they see domestic businesses thriving on the proceeds of counterfeit goods. Such goods may be both for domestic consumers and export. As their own companies start to acquire their own products and brands, they exert pressure from within to protect their own intellectual property.

STRATEGIC CROSSROADS

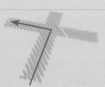

5.2

YouTube and the new internet era

YouTube, the online video-sharing website, was launched in 2005. The site grew rapidly in popularity, attracting 100 million users a day. Its founders, Chad Hurley and Steve Chen, having had experience with other web-based applications, felt it was vital to allow users to upload videos without specialist software such as media players made by Microsoft. Hence, they used the basic Flash Player found on virtually all PCs. This choice of technology helped YouTube to gain a large audience quickly. It also tempted bloggers and others who could help themselves to the site's videos, extending the potential audience. YouTube's philosophy has been that the user community decides what it wants to see, its founders describing it as 'almost the ultimate form of reality television' (Waters and Allison, 2006).

User-generated content has marked a new internet era, in which media and marketing companies, as well as internet technology companies, see both opportunities and threats. New ways of reaching audiences offer marketing potential for advertisers, but there are inherent legal risks of copyright infringement in websites which stream unlicensed copyright material. The earlier file-sharing site, Napster, caused uproar in the music industry, as media companies mounted a series of lawsuits against it for unlicensed copying of their copyright music, to which its owners had little defence. In Napster's place, legal music downloading sites have emerged, which are now a fast-growing segment of the music industry.

YouTube's founders were well aware of the risks of a repeat of Napster's troubles. YouTube's output contains much scope for copyright infringement, including copyright music, music videos, clips of film and television shows. Its approach has been to avoid acrimonious confrontation and to do deals with copyright owners, who, after all, want to use this exciting new marketplace to reach new audiences. Advertising forms the basis of such deals, by which the companies share the revenue from advertising shown alongside copyright video material. Warner, Vivendi's Universal Music and Sony BMG Music Entertainment (UK) signed deals with YouTube. Music videos, made famous in the MTV era of the 1980s, are popular once again, but now on the internet and the commercial tone has changed. MTV paid no licence fees as the companies saw the videos as promotional material. Now, the companies are collecting a licence fee and a share in advertising revenues. CBS also signed a deal with YouTube, allowing the distribution of its television content with advertising alongside, the revenues from which are also shared with YouTube. Hurley says: 'By partnering with YouTube, media companies can now have a two-way dialogue with viewers who can provide feedback about what they find entertaining' (van Duyn et al., 2006).

A year after its formation, YouTube was acquired by Google for $1.65 billion. The purchase seemed to be more about exuberance than financial logic. It follows other impulse buys by big companies: eBay's purchase of Skype for $2.6 billion and News Corporation's purchase of MySpace for $580 million. For Google, a technology company, this expansion into a sector where media companies are strong will pose challenges. The threat of lawsuits still hangs over internet videos. Developing new technology to automatically eliminate clips that infringe copyright is helping to head off damaging legal battles with copyright owners. The online community which YouTube and others have tapped into has opened doors for users and businesses alike.

Sources: Waters, R. and Allison, K., 'How to set a course for a shooting star', *Financial Times*, 9 October 2006; van Duyn, A., Taylor, P. and Waters, R., 'YouTube and Google strike music deals', *Financial Times*, 10 October 2006; Waters, R., 'YouTube gives Google chance to change tack', *Financial Times*, 11 October 2006; Chaffin, J., 'Music videos become hits all over again', *Financial Times*, 11 October 2006.

Questions
- What opportunities does YouTube offer for television and media companies?
- What copyright issues does YouTube have to deal with, and what has been their approach?

WEB CHECK

Google's corporate website is http://investor.google.com/.

Assessing legal risks

Legal risk: Uncertainties surrounding legal liabilities, their implementation in differing legal systems, and the observance of fairness and impartiality in judicial proceedings.

The complexity of the legal environment can be daunting, especially for companies from countries where business traditionally rests on personal relations. In the cultural background of these countries, directors and managers are not naturally inclined to see projects and transactions strictly in legal terms. In fact, few businesspeople anywhere find the 'fine print' of contracts very easy to fathom, often relying on professional legal advice. As markets and operations expand internationally, contractual relations become essential to the achievement of corporate goals. Companies which pay little heed to the legal dimensions of their activities may subject themselves to serious legal risk from litigation if those affected by their actions (or inaction) decide to pursue them in the relevant courts. They may also be poorly placed to bring a legal claim when they are the victims of alleged wrongdoing. It is far more prudent (and cheaper) to take precautions to comply with the law, and also to draw up contracts which minimize the risk of legal disputes arising. These precautions will also aid a firm which takes legal proceedings against another for a wrongdoing, such as breach of contract. Firms are generally reluctant to commence costly legal proceedings except as a last resort. Seeking to negotiate an agreed settlement of a dispute, or using an independent third party, as is customary in arbitration arrangements, is quicker and cheaper than legal proceedings.

A business incurs legal liability in the national legal system of countries where it locates production. Key areas where risks arise are shown in Figure 5.9. As indicated, many risks stem from weaknesses in the administration of justice and the respect for the rule of law. When disputes arise, resort to the courts can be frustrating for outsiders, as slowness and inefficiency are common problems. If the foreign company is a defendant in legal action, it is important that both civil and criminal courts are fair and impartial. Even in countries with highly developed legal systems, there may be a culture of 'home court advantage', which discriminates against foreign companies and

Figure 5.9 Legal risks in overseas locations

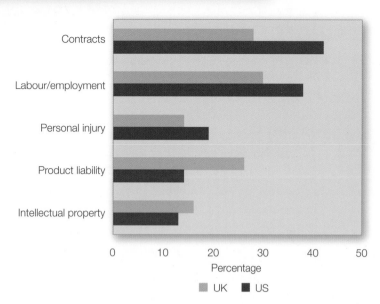

Contracts

Labour/employment

Personal injury

Product liability

Intellectual property

0 10 20 30 40 50
Percentage

UK US

Figure 5.10 Most numerous types of litigation in the US and UK (2004)

Source: *Financial Times*, 10 October 2005

which could damage the country's competitiveness in attracting international businesses. For example, empirical research in the US has shown that non-US public companies sued in US courts are more likely to lose than their US counterparts (Masters and Guerrera, 2006). Moreover, a trend is the increasing exposure of British companies to litigation in the US (Sherwood, 2005). Large companies are more likely to be the targets of litigation than small companies, generally because of the greater sums at stake and readier access to legal advice. The international law firm of Fulbright & Jaworski, in its survey of litigation trends, has found that for large US and British companies, litigation accounts for 29% of their overall legal budget (Sherwood, 2005). The bulk of proceedings are contract disputes, as shown in Figure 5.10, with labour and employment second. In both these areas, more careful attention at the negotiation stage and in efforts to find a compromise to resolve disputes would avoid much litigation.

Where the rule of law is weak, there is also likely to be a degree of corruption tolerated as normal, which both adds to costs and compromises an outside company's ethical and legal principles. It is sometimes said that lax regulation can be an attraction for companies seeking advantageous overseas locations, as they can avoid the costs associated with higher (and safer) standards of production and employment. However, adverse publicity and the tide of international public opinion are now running against this strategy. Moreover, it can prove a further risk, if a company is taken to court for its practices.

There is a distinction between the legal position of a company which sets up a wholly owned overseas subsidiary and one which subcontracts other companies to produce its products. In the first instance, it incurs direct liability for its actions. This involves liability under employment law, health and safety law and environmental law for its operations and products. Should there be a serious accident, litigation can be commenced against it in the local courts by those injured or suffering damage. Where a company outsources production to a local contractor, that contractor shoulders these liabilities. However, liability may well travel up the line to the company whose brand name appears on the products. For example, if a design or process dictated by the major company turns out to be inherently faulty or dangerous, it could be liable in negligence or product liability for the damage, despite the fact that a subcontractor was carrying out the operations.

TO RECAP...

Legal risks

Legal risks are ever-present in international business. Legal rights and obligations are at the core of market transactions. In order to manage legal risks, firms need to be alert to avenues of legal protection of their property and legal redress for wrongs they have suffered.

Legal risks in perspective
When new markets offer exciting opportunities, businesses tend to feel the potential gains outweigh the risks. When entering an emerging market with a weak legal system, what steps should a firm take to prevent possible legal setbacks?

PAUSE TO REFLECT

Regional dimensions: the EU as a supranational union

Regional economic integration has become highly significant for businesses. A business which intends to expand internationally often finds that markets and production within their home region offer the benefits of low cultural distance, as well as fewer complications for transport and distribution than networks which span the globe. Agreements between governments at regional level tend to be limited to trade and related matters (discussed in the next chapter). So far, Europe is alone in establishing deeper integration of legal and political systems. EU institutions date from the Treaty of Rome in 1956. This treaty and the numerous treaties which have followed have strengthened the role of EU institutions, impacting on the national environments of member states.

The EU has put in place an institutional framework which in many ways mirrors the three branches of national government. The main executive authority is the Council of Ministers, with a large role also played by the European Commission. However, the European Parliament has less scope for lawmaking than national legislative assemblies would have in national democratic systems. The Commission is a major source of legislation, as well as an administrative body. It has authority to issue regulations, which are directly applicable in all member states, and directives, which states are compelled to implement through national legislation. The Commission is therefore a major source of law for member states, which exists alongside national law. Where there is an overlap, EU law prevails. In the minds of many businesspeople, the EU represents unwieldy bureaucracy, creating a cumbersome tier of regulatory law. As Figure 5.8 indicates, EU lawmaking has been influential in numerous areas: employment law, consumer protection, health and safety law and environmental law. It has brought about harmonization in competition law, through its own process of notification for takeovers and mergers.

The addition of 10 new member states in 2004 was a trigger to rethink the constitutional arrangements. The structure designed in 1956 for an organization of 6 member states had become increasingly unwieldy as the number increased. With enlargement to 25 members, changes needed to be made to streamline EU processes. The considerable variation in size and wealth among the EU 25 led to adjustments in voting strength and representation in key bodies, which would give a fair share to each member state. In a draft constitutional treaty, a system of representation in the Council and European Parliament was proposed, which would allow all to play a role, but proportionally greater say would go to the larger and more populous states, with safeguards to protect smaller states. There was also a proposal for an elected president. The draft constitutional treaty needed to be ratified by all member states. In some, this was accomplished by simple vote in the legislative assembly, but in others a referendum was held. Following rejection of the constitution in referendums in France and the Netherlands, the document was shelved. Among the possible reasons for its rejection were doubts about the EU's future role as a supranational government, and 'enlargement fatigue' caused by the accession of 10 new states in 2004. In January 2007, Bulgaria and Romania joined. Meanwhile, negotiations with Turkey have

WEB CHECK

The European Parliament is at www.europarl.europa.eu. Here, numerous relevant topics can be accessed.

stalled, and other countries, mainly the Balkan states, are concerned that the window of opportunity for joining could be closing. In 2008, EU leaders again put forward the constitutional treaty, with slight alterations which were designed to ensure its acceptance by member states.

Many EU citizens are unenthusiastic about EU institutions generally, feeling that national identities and institutions better represent their interests. Many are also uneasy with further enlargement, fearing that domestic jobs may be at risk from both immigration of workers from poorer member states and the shifting of production to new member states (see Chapter 3 on the EU's economic integration). Rising nationalist sentiment in a number of countries, both within the EU and in those waiting in the wings, is perhaps an indication that national political cultures are slower to change than EU leaders had anticipated. Some commentators argue that democracy is essentially focused on a sense of community among citizens, achievable at national level and below, but unrealistic across a sprawling and culturally diverse area like the EU.

> **TO RECAP...**
> **The EU's future**
> While all would agree the EU has become unwieldy, reforming its institutions has become contentious, revealing underlying doubts about its democratic viability and its suitability to achieve its goals. Constitutional reforms will need to be more responsive to public concerns, in order to rebuild confidence in EU institutions.

> **EU enlargement at the crossroads?**
> With the accession of Romania and Bulgaria, attention has turned to Turkey and the Balkan states. Assess the arguments for and against further enlargement of the EU.
>
> *PAUSE TO REFLECT*

International organizations and law

People are accustomed to the idea of national governments as a source of law, and those in the EU have become accustomed to the EU as a source of law. Both, after all, enjoy powers stemming from the people, albeit indirectly in some cases. However, at the international level, there is no recognizable governmental apparatus; there is no lawmaking body equivalent to a national legislature. Moreover, there is no authority which can compel obedience with the powers of coercion which the sovereign state possesses. Notwithstanding, international law not only exists, but is growing in volume and impacting more than ever on international business.

The authority of international law stems from the fact that it derives from the agreement of sovereign states. When representatives of nation-states come together to build international legal frameworks, they are acting at inter-governmental level. International co-operation is often under the auspices of the UN or one of its affiliated bodies. Inter-governmental legal agreements known as 'treaties' or 'international conventions' set out the agreed provisions which the signatories intend to become part of international law. They and other countries ratify the treaty, agreeing to implement it within their borders. A country which does not ratify the treaty has no obligation to be bound by it. However, in some areas of law, such as human rights, the majority of the world's countries have become parties, as Table 5.1 shows. This indicates a widespread recognition of its legal authority as well as support for the aims of these conventions in stamping out various forms of human rights abuse.

Although enactment is an important initial step, it is sometimes observed that application and enforcement of international law are weak, due to the

> **The UN's international law website is www.un.org/law. Here there are lists of both topics (such as human rights) and institutions.**
>
> *WEB CHECK*

Table 5.1 Ratification of major human rights conventions

Convention	Number of countries which have ratified	Some notable countries which have not ratified
International Convention on Genocide	138	Japan, Indonesia, Thailand, Kenya, Nigeria
International Convention on Racial Discrimination	170	Singapore, South Korea, Malaysia
International Covenant on Civil and Political Rights	156	Singapore, Bahrain, United Arab Emirates, Cuba, China, Pakistan
International Covenant on Economic, Social and Cultural Rights	153	US, Singapore, Qatar, South Africa, Pakistan
Convention on Discrimination against Women	183	US, Iran
Convention against Torture	141	Singapore, Malaysia, Thailand, Iran
Convention on the Rights of the Child	192	US, Somalia

Source: UNDP (2006) *Human Development Report 2006* (Basingstoke: Palgrave Macmillan)

lack of any international body with powers to compel compliance. In other words, a country may ratify a convention and then ignore it in practice, without any legal repercussions. In the area of human rights, this has certainly been the case in some countries, where, despite ratifying the convention, torture and other cruel treatment or punishment have continued. On the other hand, these countries have been the target of international opprobrium, undermining international respect for their systems of justice. Moreover, a great deal of monitoring, both by UN agencies and recognized NGOs, assesses in detail the degree to which countries are complying with international law. Those which fail to meet their international obligations, as well as those which have declined to commit themselves, are targeted for criticism. International monitoring, such as the corruption index of Transparency International, benefits the countries with high scores, but damages confidence in those with low scores. The latter countries are likely to have weak rule of law in any case, not merely in the area of international law.

Implications for managers

International managers have traditionally taken the view that legal obligations extend to those which apply directly, for example, to products or operations, and which are directly enforceable by local or national authorities. International law seems remote and drafted in rather more general terms. Moreover, it does not apply directly to companies or individuals, but to countries, which are responsible for applying it. International law is often at the forefront in raising standards, setting the benchmarks which governments gradually recognize and apply. For companies, it is increasingly necessary to think in terms of these higher standards, not just because they will one day be incorporated into national law, but from a CSR perspective. For example, through national legislation, India is attempting to reduce the use of child labour, but has ratified neither of the two international conventions on the abolition of child labour. MNEs which do business in India will be aware that child labour is practised, and that its use reduces costs. However, MNEs are now aware of consumer repugnance to products made with child labour. The first of the conventions, on minimum age, was in 1973, over three decades ago. In 1973, no one could have predicted the extent that FDI and outsourcing production to low-cost countries would shape international business. The case for humane practices then was solely a moral one in many countries, but has become embodied in law at all levels since then. The case retains its moral validity, and companies are now looking at the array of ethical – not just legal – dimensions of their activities, as part of a CSR focus (see Chapter 14).

plate 5.3 Poor children in developing countries, such as these in India, are vulnerable to exploitation and the harmful effects of accidents in industrial operations.

This chapter has stressed the significance of national political and legal systems despite globalization processes. For international managers, wrongs committed in far-flung locations, which home public opinion would not have known about in earlier eras, can now come home to haunt their companies. Reputational risk of foreign operations is well known, but the risk may extend to lawsuits in the home country for harm alleged to have been committed in the overseas location. While this may seem too remote, there are cases in which it has been established that a defendant company should rightly have to answer in its home legal system, rather than simply in the courts of the country where the damage occurred. The case of the gas explosion in Bhopal, India, in 1984, in which thousands of people lost their lives, was a landmark one in this respect. Local residents in India whose health has suffered brought their claims against the American company, Union Carbide, in the US. Although establishing that this route was feasible in principle, in the event, they failed. The government of India intervened, reaching an agreement on compensation from the company, which was taken over by Dow Chemical. However, these efforts became mired in bureaucracy, and the thousands who have suffered have received little financial or medical help. In 2004, the site still had not been decontaminated, causing continuing health problems. In 2007, Ratan Tata, the Indian industrialist, offered to help to finance decontamination, with co-operation from Dow Chemical and the Indian authorities, but in practice it has proved difficult to bring the parties together. The Bhopal tragedy highlights weaknesses at national as well as international level.

In a sense, globalization, interpreted as growing interconnectedness, is having an impact on the legal dimension, which up to now had been one of the more state-centric aspects of the business environment. It is also the case that governments and law enforcement officers are co-operating in investigating crime and apprehending suspected criminals whose networks have become global. While suspected terrorists probably come top of their priorities, organized fraud and trafficking are also, unfortunately, global businesses requiring co-operative responses from national governments.

TO RECAP...

The reach of international law

While it was once thought that international law was just for states, and businesses could focus on national laws, the lines have now become more blurred. Businesses which abide by weak national laws in areas such as human rights may encounter international criticism for not heeding international standards. Therefore, an eye to international legal developments is essential for international business.

Conclusions

- Businesses interactions with political and legal actors centre mainly on national environments, those of their home country and those of countries where they do business. The national political system can be a key determinant of the manner in which enterprise activities are carried on. Although a market economy is traditionally associated with a democratic political system, among the major emerging countries such as China and Russia, authoritarian governments are guiding economic development through market reforms. Democratic systems, by contrast, set as their ideals the rule of law, free and fairly elected governments through competitive elections, and basic civil and political rights. In many countries, electoral processes exist in form, but lack the qualitative underpinnings, such as freedom of expression and a free press, which ensure genuinely pluralist politics. Whether democratic governments provide a more congenial or stable business environment than an authoritarian one partly depends on the conditions obtaining in particular countries. Where democratic institutions are shallow, and the society is divided, democracy faces an uncertain future. Some authoritarian governments may offer attractive prospects for foreign investors in liberalized environments, but the underlying role of the state casts a shadow over business relations, creating political risk.

- Political and legal risks arise in any business transactions. Businesses desire transparency and predictability in regulatory systems, and impartiality in their administration. The uncertainties stemming from weak rule of law are the major drawbacks in many legal systems. Managers may be unsure that contracts will be honoured or enforceable in the courts, and they may also fear for the legal rights in their intellectual property, on which their businesses rely. Many of the most lucrative opportunities for international business arise in countries where the rule of law is weak, and corruption is pervasive – phenomena which tend to go together. Due to pressures within countries and from outside, including the need to attract foreign businesses, governments are now concentrating on improving the legal environment for international businesses. The growing importance of regional and international lawmaking is shifting focus upwards to international standards and inviting governments and businesses to think beyond national systems, as the international legal environment becomes more interconnected.

A globalized political and legal environment?

What trends in the political and legal environment discussed in this chapter are pointing towards more integration and interconnectedness, and which trends suggest that nation-states still retain political and legal autonomy? Which of these trends do you feel is gaining the upper hand, if any?

PAUSE TO REFLECT

Review questions

Part A: Grasping the basic concepts and knowledge

1. How are political systems classified? What are the differences between an authoritarian and democratic political system? Give examples of each.
2. What is meant by the distinction between formal or 'electoral' democracy and substantive democracy?
3. What is meant by the rule of law? To what extent does it exist in actual political systems that you are familiar with?
4. What are the functions of the three branches of government? Why is it important from the perspective of accountability to have a working system of checks and balances?
5. Political parties may be categorized roughly as right, left and centre. What do these designations imply in practice? Give examples of each from a political system you are familiar with.
6. Contrast a two-party system with a multiparty political system. Which is likely to be more stable, and why?
7. What is a coalition government? Why do they often fall apart in practice?
8. What political risks arise for businesses in an authoritarian state?
9. Foreign investors often point to corruption as a negative aspect of business in many countries. What are the risks arising from corruption?
10. What are the main sources of international political risks, and what, if anything, can firms do to manage the risks?
11. What are the purposes of government regulation? What is the government's role in relation to monopolies and restrictive practices?
12. In what ways do national legal systems affect businesses operating within their territories?
13. Why is the protection of intellectual property becoming an important issue for businesses globally?
14. What are the sources of legal risk for businesses in foreign locations? What steps can they take to manage these risks?
15. What is the role of international law for businesses operating internationally?

Part B: Critical thinking and discussion

1. Authoritarian countries are often seen as more stable than democratic ones, and may thus be viewed favourably as business environments, especially if, like China, they are pursuing market policies. What are the drawbacks of doing business in an authoritarian country?
2. How do governments wield power directly in economic activities through state control? Are they a force for public good, or are they acting contrary to consumer welfare? (Look at CF5.1 and 5.2 on Russia and France respectively.)
3. A weak national legal system is sometimes perceived as a positive factor by firms, as they can feel assured that their activities will face little scrutiny from national law enforcement agencies. This is particularly the case in developing countries. What are the risks of entering countries with this motive?
4. National political and legal systems still remain distinctive within the EU. Is political union a viable goal, or should member states retain more sovereign powers?

The venerable partnership of Royal Dutch Petroleum of the Netherlands and Shell Transport and Trading of Britain dates from 1907. The two companies remained legally separate, with separate organizations and management teams meeting several times a year in 'conferences' to co-ordinate strategy. This eccentric system of corporate governance and management was called into question, however, as Shell has lost competitive ground against its major rivals. ExxonMobil and British Petroleum (BP) have grown through consolidation: Exxon acquired Mobil, and BP acquired Amoco. These acquisitions have contributed scale and global reach. Shell, by contrast, because of its dual structure, could not match its rivals in acquisitions and has rather lagged behind. It has also fallen behind in exploration activities. As Figure 1 shows, it has fallen behind competitors in finding new reserves. In addition, it was forced to lower its estimates of reserves several times in 2004. The company came to see that it needed to re-examine its governance and management structure, as well as its strategy, to become more competitive in the changing environment.

Case study 5.2:
Royal Dutch Shell
humbled but looking
to the future

Figure 1 Oil companies' reserve replacement ratio, 2001–04

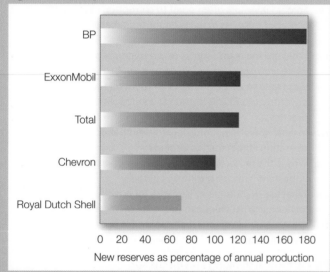

New reserves as percentage of annual production

Source: Financial Times, 28 June 2005

In 2004, the two companies reached an agreement to convert into a single company with a single board of directors and CEO. It would be registered in London, but its head office would be in the Netherlands, for tax advantages. This compromise was seen as a kind of 'political bargain', as the company is looked on as a national symbol in both countries. It is the largest company in the Netherlands. It was hoped that the new structure would help the company to make decisions more quickly, and to seize new opportunities. Jeroen van der Veer, the new CEO, took over in 2005. The aim was to change the company from its consensus-driven culture to one more suited to the changing competitive environment, with a more 'Anglo-Saxon' approach similar to those of its rivals. A Shell executive says: 'We are now a more transparent, supportive, action-oriented executive team that makes things happen' (Bickerton et al., 2005).

Like other oil companies, Shell must operate its exploration and production activities in challenging environments, including extremes of climate and terrain, as well as in countries troubled by political instability. Several decades ago, oil was relatively straight-

forward to access, but increasing demand and rising prices have meant that going into more difficult environments is a fact of life. Shell has operated in Nigeria for four decades, but still the oil-rich Niger Delta remains an area of social and political unrest, as well as criminal activity. For local inhabitants, poverty is still a major problem, as they have not benefited from the oil wealth that has been generated. Ethnic and political strife, often backed up by rival groups with their own militias, has added to the insecurity in the region. The government and state security forces have not been able to maintain stability, and widespread vandalism of pipelines, as well as looting, take their toll. Shell has had to deal with production disruption on a regular basis. It must consider its future in Nigeria. The country has reserves of gas, which can be exploited with the development of a large liquefied natural gas (LNG) project. LNG processing involves cooling the gas, to allow it to be transported by tanker, and processing it in regasification terminals at its destination. Shell has the expertise in this field, and is working in Nigeria with European partners, Total of France and Eni of Italy. Meanwhile, the company has invested in Nigerian offshore exploration and production, although these deep-sea developments have run into delays and cost overruns.

Royal Dutch Shell's largest project to date has been its investment in the Sakhalin 2 gas field, located north of Japan, off the east coast of Russia. This extreme location is rich in wildlife, as well as being a huge oil and gas field. In the early 1990s, Sakhalin Energy was formed, a company in which Royal Dutch Shell took the lead with a 55% stake, while two Japanese companies shared the remainder. In 2005, Shell announced that the massive project was some $20 billion over budget, because of rising costs as well as the diversion of a gas pipeline to accommodate the feeding ground of the rare grey whales. The cost overrun disappointed the Russian government, as its share of revenues from the finished project was contingent on the companies first recouping their costs. Shell was in a weak position. In 2006, the Russian government stepped in, forcing Shell to reduce its stake and making Gazprom the majority owner. Shell was reduced to 25%, with the two Japanese partners reduced to 12.5% each.

Figure 2 Oil reserves of leading companies, 2004

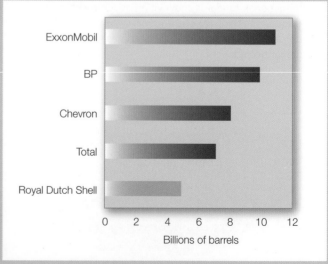

Billions of barrels

Source: Financial Times, 28 June 2005

Although the company was disappointed to lose its ownership and control, its CEO accepts that in today's world, national governments have the upper hand in dealing with natural resources. He says in respect to Bolivia's nationalization of its gas assets: 'The higher the oil and gas price is, the more national thinking you get. This is a new reality. In the end, governments are always the boss' (Hoyos and Maitland, 2006). Having had to bend to Russian pressure, Shell needs to get back to the business of finding and producing oil. It has prioritized projects that will replenish its reserves, which, as Figure 2 shows, are lower than its rivals'. It has recruited over a thousand engineers to focus on its core exploration activities. The restructuring satisfied investors that the new company is better placed competitively, but the proof will be in rebuilding reserves and production.

Questions

1 What were the causes of Shell's falling behind rival oil companies?
2 Contrast the problems Shell encounters in Nigeria with those in Russia, in terms of the political and legal environments.
3 How will Royal Dutch Shell's restructuring lead to better performance?
4 Analyse the future role of non-state-owned MNEs in the oil industry in light of growing national control over energy resources.

Sources: Catan, T., 'Elusive skills that give Shell hope', *Financial Times*, 2 November 2005; Bickerton, I., Boxell, J., Catan, T. and Tricks, H., 'Marriage after a century of cohabitation: Shell prepares for the next merger round', *Financial Times*, 28 June 2005; Burns, J. and Catan, T., 'Oil groups face rise in threats to security', *Financial Times*, 5 October 2005; Peel, M., 'Big potential profits outweigh high risks', *Financial Times*, 19 January 2005; Hoyos, C. and Maitland, A., 'Shell chief warns that Bolivia is "new reality" for oil industry', *Financial Times*, 15 May 2006; Ostrovsky, A., 'Out on a limb: how the Kremlin has been making life difficult on Sakhalin', *Financial Times*, 23 November 2006; Ostrovsky, A., 'Russia seals deal for Shell project', *Financial Times*, 22 December 2006

WEB CHECK

Royal Dutch Shell's website is www.shell.com. Go to *Investor Centre* for corporate information.

Further research

Journal articles

Dunning, J. (1998) 'An overview of relations with national governments', *New Political Economy*, **3**(2): 280–4.

Books

August, R. (2003) *International Business Law: Text, Cases and Readings*, 4th edn, London: Pearson.

Beetham, D. (ed.) (1995) *Politics and Human Rights*, Cambridge: Polity.

Donnelly, J. (2002) *Universal Human Rights in Theory and Practice*, 2nd edn, Ithaca: Cornell University Press.

Dunning, J. (ed.) (1997) *Governments, Globalization and International Business*, Oxford: Oxford University Press.

Held, D. (2006) *Models of Democracy*, 3rd edn, Cambridge: Polity.

Rose, R. (2001) *The Prime Minister in a Shrinking World*, Cambridge: Polity.

Don't forget to check the companion website at **www.palgrave.com/business/morrisonib**, where you will find web-based assignments, web links, interactive quizzes, an extended glossary and lots more to help you learn about international business.

www.palgrave.com
Companion Website

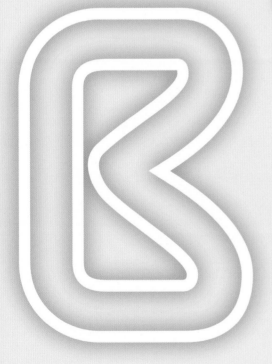

COMPETING IN THE GLOBAL MARKETPLACE

The chapters in Part 3 focus on competitive environments and strategies, from both firm and country perspectives. Chapter 6 concerns international trade and regional integration. Basic concepts and trade theories are presented and applied in the context of recent trends in global trade, together with the implications for firms and nations. In particular, Porter's theory of competitive advantage is critically examined. The theme of competitive strategies is pursued in Chapter 7, which focuses on the firm, from both strategic and organizational perspectives. Global competitive strategies are evolving in tandem with organizational adaptations as firms become more enmeshed in differing locations and organizational networks. A theme is the need to respond to local needs while maintaining a global outlook. This theme is continued in Chapter 8, on marketing. MNEs aim to adapt products and marketing strategies to local needs, but within a global strategy for the firm's products and brands. Emerging markets are increasingly targeted for their growth potential, representing some of the most challenging, as well as rewarding, new opportunities.

chapter **6**

INTERNATIONAL TRADE AND REGIONAL INTEGRATION

chapter outline

learning objectives:

▷ To appreciate the role of trade in the competitive environment for national economies, societies and firms
▷ To understand and apply key theories of international trade to a variety of contexts
▷ To identify the tools of government trade policy, and their rationale in terms of wider policy goals
▷ To assess the progress of trade agreements among countries at multilateral, bilateral and regional levels, together with their impacts on business strategy

Introduction

Once alive with fruit and vegetable production, Azerbaijan's agricultural sector deteriorated following independence in 1991, as the large Soviet-era collective farms were broken up. Agricultural workers drifted away to the city of Baku or to Russia. Into this bleak scene stepped Turkish food company, Azersun, which bought up farming land, built food-processing factories and gradually brought life back into the region's agriculture. Now, exports of preserved fruit and vegetables, tea, sugar and cooking oil are bringing prosperity and creating jobs. Azersun's president foresees a bright future for the company as demand for food increases globally. As one of the biggest non-oil investors in Azerbaijan's booming, oil-based economy, Azersun has co-operated with stakeholders in Azerbaijan to build a more diversified approach to economic development. It demonstrates the benefits of trade to societies, as well as numerous business sectors, including production, processing and distribution. This multidimensional role of trade is a theme of this chapter.

Azersun Holding's website is www.azersun.com.

WEB CHECK

Trade is the oldest type of international business, going back to ancient times. Cross-border trade has now become a routine everyday business activity, essential to wealth creation for governments and nations, as well as for businesses. Accordingly, this chapter will view trade from these differing perspectives. It begins with an overview of how trade has shaped business activities at both national and international level. Theories of trade and competition are explored for their insight into how gains from trade impact on national economies.

A major trend of the post-war period has been trade liberalization, whereby countries have reduced tariffs and other trade barriers, usually in co-operation with other countries. A series of multilateral agreements has made strides towards freer world trade, overseen by the WTO. However, recent trade tensions have led to doubt over the future of multilateralism, focusing on how governments see trade as crucial to national interests. In particular, the growing role of developing countries in trade raises questions of who benefits from trade, and who loses out. The proliferation of bilateral trade agreements signals the changing perceptions of governments on where their interests lie. We will consider the impact of these developments for firms trading internationally. Many may gain from new opportunities, while others are adversely affected by regulatory complexities. A further important dimension has been the growth in regional trade groupings and economic co-operation, which are examined in the last section. Regional free-trade initiatives, like other trade accords between countries, offer potential benefits for businesses and societies alike. However, within the international environment, there remain tensions between a desire for openness in markets and the perceived need to protect national interests.

Trade in the global economy

As highlighted in earlier chapters, growth in output and increased flows of FDI are indicators of economic prosperity. Similarly, the growing volume and value of trade around the world indicates thriving economic activity for importers and exporters. Thriving trade is also evidence of the growing interconnectedness between countries, which is a defining feature of globalization. International trade has been growing faster than GDP for many years. The nature of trade and its benefits vary greatly among countries and regions of the world. Moreover, they change over time. The wealth and power of the Italian city-states, particularly Venice, from the eleventh to the fifteenth centuries, rested on trade in a wide range of goods, from metals to peacock feathers. When its wealth declined due to shifting patterns of trade, economic and political decline soon set in (Maddison, 2001). Maintaining a leading position in global trade is a feat many businesses and governments dream of, but few countries can sustain.

Role of trade in national economies

Trade impacts on businesses, government and society, as shown in Figure 6.1. Both domestic and foreign-owned businesses stand to benefit from trade, especially if they engage directly in exporting or importing. Domestic industries, however, may struggle to compete with imports. Within society generally, consumers welcome imports, but the implications for employment are mixed, as this chapter will show. Jobs in export sectors may be

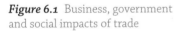

Figure 6.1 Business, government and social impacts of trade

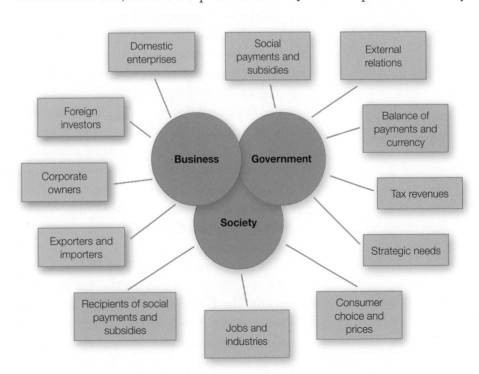

plentiful and well paid, but those in import-competing sectors may suffer. Governments are often tempted to protect local producers through subsidies, but subsidies treat only the symptoms, and not the causes, of the lack of competitiveness.

Trading transactions may be in goods or services. Trade in goods is known as merchandise trade. For a national economy, export and import data for merchandise trade give an indication of the success of the country's businesses in selling products abroad, and the demand which exists from consumers in the country for imported products. Commercial services trade includes finance, transport and technology. Merchandise as a whole can be subdivided into different sectors. The three broad categories are: agricultural products; fuels and mining products; and manufactured goods. All countries need all these products, but whether they rely on home sources or imports depends on many factors, including the natural resources of the territory and the extent to which governments seek self-sufficiency. Even if it were possible to be self-sufficient (a condition known as 'autarky'), no country in today's world aims realistically to be self-sufficient in all these areas. National decision-makers see growing trade as linked with economic growth. Questions of whether and what to produce or import have been a subject of much debate among economists, whose theories are examined in the next section. Here, we introduce the factors which represent divergence among national economies.

Countries differ in the natural endowments of their territory, including geography, climate and natural ports. The world's oil-rich countries are mostly developing economies in the Middle East, Central Asia and Africa, all of which have benefited from increased global demand, as well as recent high prices of fuel. However, reliance on a single strand of economic activity, even a lucrative one, can prove disadvantageous in the long run. Natural resources will eventually become exhausted or hard to access, and market prices can fall if there is a slump in demand.

As the opening scenario on Azerbaijan has indicated, resource-rich countries seek to diversify their economies with an eye for export potential. Oil-rich countries often opt for manufacturing or services, although much of this development has been in oil-related industries. As discussed in Chapter 3, economic development usually revolves around industrialization, which opens the possibilities for the export of manufactured goods. Manufacturing and services have the advantage that they rely heavily on human input rather than on nature and so are easier to control, giving them good long-term trade potential. Given the right investment in infrastructure, they can be exploited almost anywhere. The shift of manufacturing away from many advanced economies to developing countries is one of the features of globalized production which is shaping the trading profiles of old and new manufacturing countries.

The advanced economies of Western Europe, North America and Japan have traditionally relied on the export of manufactured goods to generate growth. The US, Germany and Japan are in the top four leading exporters, shown in Figure 6.2. With limited fuel and mining resources, these countries are net importers of fuel, a strategic need which their governments

Merchandise trade: Trade in goods, including agricultural products, fuels and mining products, and manufactured goods.

Commercial services trade: Trade in services across national borders, including financial services, business services, transport and travel.

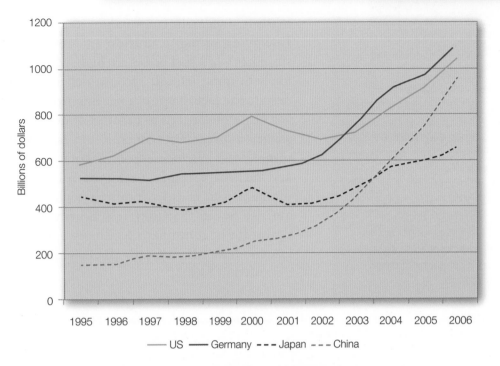

Figure 6.2 The world's leading merchandise exporting countries
Source: WTO (2007) International Trade Statistics, www.wto.org

must take into account. Of the EU countries, Germany stands out as the export leader. Featured in CF6.1 below, Germany is a high-cost economy which has maintained a strong export position in high-quality engineered products. Its concern is that its export strength has not translated into economic growth.

As manufacturing of mass-produced consumer products has shifted to low-cost locations in the developing world, the advanced economies have concentrated on high-value manufacturing and services. In both these areas, however, developing countries are also growing capacity. Latin American countries, in particular, have seen growth in services exports, and have also benefited from high prices for their mineral and oil resources. These countries are enjoying economic growth rates of over 5%, significantly higher than those of the advanced economies. The countries of Central Europe are also exploiting their advantages as low-cost locations for manufacturing and services. They are well placed to export to richer European countries, and their strengthening economies have reflected this potential.

China's export-oriented manufacturing has propelled it up the rankings of the world's largest exporters (see Figure 6.2). Consumers across the globe are likely to be buying products manufactured in China, which now dominates many sectors, including clothes and accessories, shoes, electrical appliances, audio and video equipment, mobile phones and toys. Although a net importer of fuel, it has maintained strong growth rates on the back of its manufacturing prowess. China as an exporter and importer is now crucial to business strategists as well as to governmental decision-makers around the world.

A country's balance of payments indicates the global demand at any given time for its products and services, set against the demand within its own economy for products and services from abroad. For a country with a sizable trade deficit, a worry is that its businesses are not competitive in export

The UN Conference on Trade and Development (UNCTAD) is at www.unctad.org.

TO RECAP...

Trade, development and prosperity

Governments, businesses and consumers can count the benefits of trade. Exports create wealth and generate jobs within the economy, and consumers benefit from an array of imported goods and services to buy. Thriving trade does not guarantee economic growth, but, for developing countries, growing exports are seen as necessary to development and growing prosperity.

markets, while its consumers are spending heavily on imported goods. Energy-exporting countries are among those with the highest trade surpluses when fuel prices are high, while fuel-importing countries are more likely to nurse current account deficits. China also enjoys a trade surplus, despite the fact that it is a net importer of fuel. Whether a trade imbalance is a cause of concern is a matter of debate. As noted above, most countries aspire to diversified economies, to be able to weather any sectoral downturn. China has focused on manufacturing, but its costs, including wages and fuel, have risen (see Figure 3.12), leading some businesses to shift production to cheaper locations such as Vietnam. Chinese manufacturers are also aware that they rely heavily on exports to America, where any downturn in consumer spending would adversely affect demand. Chinese leaders have dramatically increased trade with African countries, as discussed in SX6.1.

COUNTRY FOCUS 6.1 – GERMANY

Two sides of Germany's star export performance

Since overtaking the US to become the world's largest exporter of goods in 2003, Germany has maintained its stellar export performance, amounting to over €786,000 million in 2006. Exports account for 40% of GDP, and about one in every two jobs in the country. China is often cited for its export performance, its low costs giving it advantages over the advanced economies. Germany is a high-cost environment by comparison, but Germany's trade surplus is in excess of China's, as Figure 1 shows. In addition, German companies' foreign subsidiaries can now claim sales which, at €1.2 billion, exceed exports. The companies listed on the

Frankfurt Stock Exchange's Dax 30 index generate 75% of their turnover abroad.

Germany's export success story has not been mirrored in the economy as a whole, which achieved the unenviable label of 'the sick man of Europe', due to stagnant growth, high unemployment and budget deficits. Stirrings of recovery and rising corporate confidence in 2006 have been reflected in improved growth, at 2.8%. High unemployment, seemingly endemic, fell slightly from 9% in 2005 to 8.2% in 2006. However, this modest improvement came with the warning that many of the jobs are temporary or low paid. Only 26 million people out of a popula-

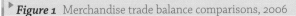

Figure 1 Merchandise trade balance comparisons, 2006

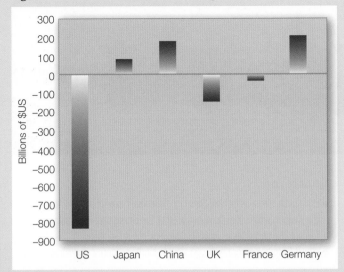

Source: *The Economist*, 27 January 2007

Figure 2 German exports by product, 2005

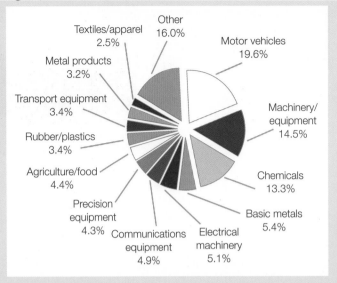

Source: Federal Statistical Office, Germany (2006) German foreign trade by product divisions, www.destatis.de

tion of 80 million are in jobs that carry full social security benefits. The reforms in healthcare and pensions, necessary to bring the budget deficit under control, cause uncertainties to persist, resulting in continued weak consumer spending. There remain lingering concerns that German companies' successes are not translating into sustainable growth at home, and are not reaching all in society. Two sides of globalization are apparent: German companies have gained, but for many ordinary Germans, globalization poses a threat. They blame globalization for the weak growth: fearing unemployment and declining income, they are disinclined to spend. Why has the national economy remained weak, and what are the prospects for the future? To answer these questions, we have to look at the nature of Germany's export success.

German companies have provided much of the engineering skill and machinery which have driven global growth. The breakdown of German exports, shown in Figure 2, features substantial shares of industrial and high-tech products, in addition to the shares of the capital-intensive engineering companies usually associated with German industry. For example, BASF is the world's largest chemical company. German machines and vehicles can be found in all the fast-growing developing economies, where they are at work building factories, fleets and infrastructure. Putzmeister, the world's largest manufacturer of concrete pumps used in the construction industry, has experienced surging global demand. Putzmeister, like other German companies, has undergone restructuring, workers accepting more flexible working and low wage growth to keep the company competitive. German companies are also becoming integrated in the global division of labour, using local subsidiaries where possible to keep costs down. Festo, which makes motors for automation technology, makes most of its components in Germany, but assembles them at its 55 foreign subsidiaries. Festo's CEO says: 'The growth is abroad but through it jobs are guaranteed in Germany. Our company lives from globalisation' (Benoit and Milne, 2006).

Germany's SMEs, known as the Mittelstand, are also contributing to export performance, although these 'hidden champions' are not in the limelight. These private companies, often family owned, are the traditional backbone of German industry. It is estimated that 98% of them are now internationalized. Many are highly specialized companies in niche markets. For example, the world's largest excavator, made by Herrenknecht in the Black Forest, was assembled in Shanghai and used to build two giant tunnels under the Yangtze River in China. Herrenknecht employs 1,500 people and has sales of €348 million, 92% of which are abroad.

Claas, another Mittelstand company, is Europe's largest maker of combine harvesters and tractors, as well as making parts for the aerospace industry. Its sales are 75% outside Germany. It is benefiting from the growth in 'mega-farms' in Eastern Europe and Russia, where the latest farm machinery is equipped with laser guidance systems and GPS receivers. Claas is working alongside farmers to help them with these innovative products. Although Claas is committed to Germany, home of its engineering expertise, it nonetheless outsources production to factories in Hungary, India and Russia. It is now benefiting from the increasing demand for biofuels such as ethanol. Its CEO is convinced that being a private company gives it the freedom to be innovative and take a long view, in investing in India and biofuels, both of which have involved taking risks.

Germany's corporate leaders have cause to be cautious about the future. Rising energy and raw materials prices are a concern, as Germany is a net importer of these products. Germany's companies have benefited from trade liberalization policies across the globe. However, signs of weakening of the WTO's multilateral trading system could lead to more protectionist policies by governments, which would impact adversely on corporate strategy. Corporate leaders remain doubtful about the domestic economy and persistent weak consumer demand. Perhaps ironically, weak domestic demand has been one of the

plate 6.1 This impressive chemical complex in Germany contributes to the country's strong position in industrial exports.

reasons why companies look abroad. German companies think first of investing abroad, not at home. Heraeus, the world's largest trader of precious metals, is indicative. In 2005, it created 779 jobs, but only 30 were in Germany. Its global workforce now numbers 10,600. Its CEO says: 'sales dropped 12% in Germany and still we hired these people. That was only possible because of globalisation' (Benoit and Milne, 2006).

Sources: Atkins, R. and Marsh, P., 'Germans hope exports will lead way to wider recovery', *Financial Times*, 11 February 2005; Benoit, B. and Milne, R., 'Germany's best-kept secret: how its exporters are beating the world', *Financial Times*, 19 May 2006; Atkins, F., 'Fizz lacks one factor', *Financial Times*, 11 December 2006; Milne, R., 'Claas act makes the right bets', *Financial Times*, 11 December 2006; 'Not what it was', *The Economist*, 10 February 2007.

Questions

◆ Explain the reasons behind German companies' export success, including the ways in which they have adapted to the changing environment.
◆ Explain the two sides of globalization evident in Germany.
◆ Why is German corporate success slow to kindle economic growth at home?

WEB CHECK

For information about Germany, go to the OECD's website at www.oecd.org, and click on *Germany* in the *Countries* list.

Patterns of global trade

In the post-war period, the world's major industrialized countries became its dominant traders, the US, Japan and Europe accounting for the bulk of world trade. The strength of these triad countries (introduced in Chapter 3) is based both on intra-regional trade as well as trade with the other two blocs. Triad countries are home to the world's largest companies, which are major trading enterprises. Much of the flow of trade among triad countries is intra-firm trade. Its extent is estimated at over a third of the total trade among triad nations (Antràs, 2003).

In recent years, this dominant triad pattern has given way to more complex patterns, as developing and transitional economies have become more active traders. Long-term trends, shown in Figure 6.3, highlight the gradual fall in North America's share from 28% in 1948 to 14.2% in 2006. This decrease is mirrored by Asia's increasing share to 27.8%. In 2006, developing countries accounted for 40% of world merchandise exports, as shown in Figure 6.4. Three processes are at work:

1 *Manufacturing* is playing an increasingly important role in developing countries (see Charlton and Stiglitz, 2005). Their export-oriented manufacturing platforms are benefiting from globalization of production. Much of this activity stems from flourishing FDI and outsourcing, often by MNEs based in the triad countries. China's surge in world trade has been the most obvious example, but many other developing countries have benefited.

2 *Advances in technology* have enabled enterprises based on service provision to locate themselves in low-cost centres far removed from clients and end users. Developing countries have benefited from these developments.

Triad: The three traditional trading centres, comprising the US, Japan and Europe.

Figure 6.3 Long-term trends in merchandise exports

Source: WTO (2007) International Trade Statistics, www.wto.org

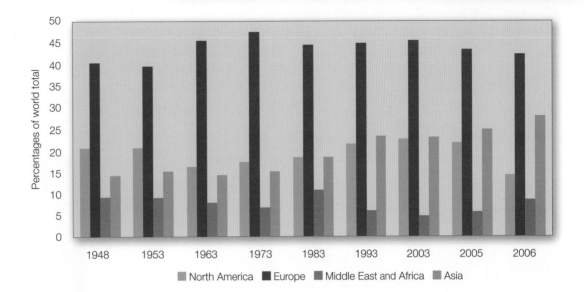

■ North America ■ Europe ■ Middle East and Africa ■ Asia

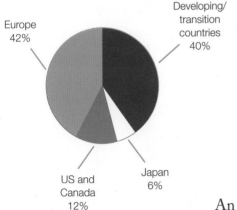

Europe 42%

Developing/ transition countries 40%

US and Canada 12%

Japan 6%

Figure 6.4 Shares of world merchandise exports ($11,783 billion), 2006

Note: Developing/transition countries = South and Central America, Mexico, Commonwealth of Independent States (CIS), Africa, Middle East and the developing countries of Asia

Source: WTO (2007) International Trade Statistics 2007, www.wto.org

TO RECAP...

Changing patterns of world trade

The triad dominance of world trade is breaking down, as newer trading countries are gaining ground. Developing and transitional economies are the main new forces in trade, many benefiting from rich natural resources and others building strong export orientations through industrialization.

Some, such as India, have been slow to develop large-scale industrial infrastructure, but have forged ahead in building service enterprises.

3 *Countries rich in oil and mineral wealth*, many of which are developing and transitional economies, have become a focus of attention, as global demand has risen. Oil is the main component of commodities trade, but copper, iron ore, steel and other products are needed for building and industrial processes worldwide. These countries have benefited from export revenues. In turn, this wealth has led to a surge in demand in their economies for imported goods, which has benefited exporters in both developing and developed countries.

An outcome of the breakdown of older trade patterns is that many more countries are now involved in international trade networks. For developing countries, trade is vital for wealth creation and economic development. However, developing countries often have weak governance and financial systems, undermined by corruption, which can impact negatively on trading partners. Advanced economies now view trade in the context of sustainable development, looking at human rights and environmental protection in relation to trading partners. For many developing countries, however, these issues are subordinated to economic goals. Concerned about energy security for its booming economy, China has agreed long-term oil supply contracts with Iran and Sudan, both of which have been the focus of international condemnation: Iran for its nuclear-testing programme and Sudan for its human rights record (see SX6.1). The growing importance of oil-rich developing and transitional economies in the emerging patterns of world trade is now drawing attention to the *context* of trade relations, including political risks and ethical issues.

The least developed countries, concentrated in sub-Saharan Africa, have tended to lose out in world markets and to fall behind the development strides of their oil-rich neighbours. The poorest countries are mainly agricultural, and they have found it difficult to access markets in developed countries. Their plight has highlighted some of the major issues facing governments, including how far to open their markets and what domestic products to protect from import competition.

STRATEGIC CROSSROADS

6.1

China turns to Africa

Tours of 15 African countries by China's leaders in the space of six months in 2006 signalled new high-level interest in the continent. Trade was at the top of their agenda, in the quest to secure the oil and other primary products needed to sustain Chinese industrial growth. In return, China exports manufactured goods, undertakes much-needed transport and infrastructure projects and offers government loans. By 2007, an estimated 800 Chinese state companies were active in Africa, winning 50% of all new public works and infrastructure contracts. Two-way trade between Africa and China has soared since 2000, as shown in Figure 1. The products traded appear in Figures 2 and 3. China's imports are dominated by fuel and other natural resources, while its exports to Africa feature a variety of consumer goods and machinery. Transport is a major export sector, encompassing vehicles of all types, along with road, rail and other infrastructure projects. Prices of most of these goods and infrastructure projects are less than would be available from Western companies. In some cases, infrastructure improvements are traded for raw material contracts. The Chinese have negotiated oil-drilling rights in Nigeria, Angola and Sudan, as well as investing in refineries and pipelines in Nigeria. China's offshore oil company paid $2.7 billion for a stake in Nigerian production, a sector which has been dominated by US and European MNEs. Africa now supplies one-third of China's oil.

There are obvious gains for African countries from their new trade relations with China, but there are also concerns that the economic benefits are not reaching ordinary people, and that poor governance is not being addressed. Growth rates in sub-Saharan Africa have nearly doubled since the surge in trade with China, from 3% per annum in 2000 to 5.8% in 2005.

Figure 1 Growth in China–Africa trade

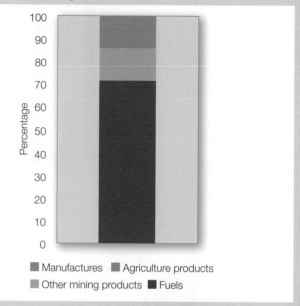

Figure 2 Chinese imports from Africa

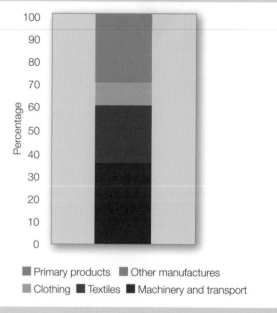

Figure 3 Chinese exports to Africa

Source: WTO (2006) *World Trade Developments in 2005*, www.wto.org

Sources: WTO (2006) *World Trade Developments in 2005*, www.wto.org; *Financial Times*, 24 January 2008

Although the leaders in the developed world are concerned that trade, loans and aid for Africa should be linked to goals such as poverty alleviation, democracy, human rights and fighting corruption, Chinese leaders make it clear that their business deals come without conditions attached. According to the Chinese president, theirs is 'a policy of non-interference in other countries' internal affairs' (Timberg, 2006). Senegal's president says: 'China's approach to our needs is simply better adapted than the slow and sometimes patronizing post-colonial approach of European investors, donor organizations and non-governmental organizations' (Wallis, 2008). The OECD's annual report on Africa in 2006 found that gains in economic growth had not as yet been matched by progress in reducing hunger and other human development goals (OECD, 2006).

The Chinese have concluded deals with Sudan, which has a poor human rights record, and Zimbabwe, whose authoritarian regime has few friends. Jobs and new business creation are needed as development priorities in most African countries, but Chinese investment has brought few jobs for local people and jeopardized local businesses in sectors now dominated by Chinese imports. The Afrobarometer (2006) public opinion survey reports that in 12 sub-Saharan African countries, only 27% of respondents expressed satisfaction with their finances in 2006, down from 31% in 2000. In South Africa and Lesotho, thousands of textile workers have lost their jobs due to Chinese imports. Although local labour would be low cost, much of the employment in infrastructure projects has gone to Chinese immigrants brought in specifically to work on Chinese-sponsored projects, some 78,000 of whom are now working in Africa. In Ethiopia, where the government has a

poor human rights record and where separatist movements are strong, Chinese investment activities have faced criticisms. One critic has said that the Chinese are 'turning into colonialists themselves. First there were the Russians, then the Americans, now it is them' (Wallis et al., 2007).

Questions

◆ Assess the benefits to each side in trade between China and African countries.
◆ Why is there cause for concern about the long-term impacts of China–Africa trade relations on economic development in Africa?

Sources: White, D., 'A spectacular resurgence', *Financial Times*, 21 November 2006; Yeh, A., 'China ventures on rocky roads to trade with Africa', *Financial Times*, 20 June 2006; WTO (2006) *World Trade Statistics 2005*, www.wto.org; Timberg, C., 'In Africa, China trade brings growth, unease', *Washington Post*, 13 June 2006, www.washingtonpost.com; Afrobarometer (2006) 2006 Survey Results, www.aftrobarometer.org.; OECD (2006) African Economic Outlook, www.oecd.org; Wallis, W., Green, M. and McGregor, R., 'China oil team in Ethiopia massacre', *Financial Times*, 25 April 2007; Wallis, W., 'Drawing contours of a new world order', *Financial Times*, 24 January 2008.

Responding to trends in global trade
What trends are evident in global trade, and how might the following players respond?
● An MNE in Europe ● The government of a developing country
● An MNE in a developing country

PAUSE TO REFLECT

International trade theories

Economists have long advanced theories to explain why and how trade works internationally, and who benefits. While some now seem outdated, the concepts still provide useful analytical tools. Further, much current thinking has its foundations in these earlier theories (Krugman, 1999).

Theories of absolute and comparative advantage

The prevailing view of governments of the late eighteenth and early nineteenth centuries was that increased exports benefited the national economy, but imports did not. Known as 'mercantilism', this outlook, which has continued to be influential, was disputed by Adam Smith and later by David Ricardo. They argued that free trade would bring increased wealth and a rising standard of living for all trading countries.

In his book, *The Wealth of Nations*, published in 1776, Adam Smith ([1776] 1950) presented what has come to be known as the 'classical theory' of international trade. He argued that a country should specialize in producing the goods in which it is has absolute advantage, that is, goods using fewer productive inputs than would be possible anywhere else. A country which can produce wheat more cheaply than it produces textiles will concentrate on wheat and import textiles from those countries which have absolute advantage in textile production. But what if one country has an absolute advantage in both textiles and wheat? In that case, the country should pursue the type of industry in which it has the greatest relative advantage over other countries.

Comparative advantage: Enjoyed by a country where production of a product involves greater relative advantages in terms of inputs than would be possible anywhere else.

Absolute advantage: Enjoyed by a country where production of a product involves using fewer productive inputs than would be possible in any other country.

This is known as the theory of comparative advantage, as set out by David Ricardo ([1817] 1973). If Country A enjoys absolute advantage in producing both textiles and wheat, it will opt to produce textiles or wheat depending on the extent of its superiority over other countries. Assume Country A produces 1 unit of wheat with 3 hours of labour, while Country B requires 10 units of labour to produce 1 unit of wheat. Further, Country A produces 1 unit of textiles with 6 hours of labour, while Country B requires 7 hours of labour. Country A should go over to producing wheat, in which it enjoys greater absolute advantage, and Country B should go over to producing textiles. Country B does not have absolute advantage in either good, but it will gain by specializing in the good in which it has the least absolute disadvantage, or comparative advantage. Once trade is opened up between the two countries, both would export excess production to the other country. Output of both goods will rise, and both countries will be better off from trade.

Smith and Ricardo did not to take into account the many differences between countries which affect their productivity and technologies. They assumed that countries will specialize in particular exportable products, not bothering to produce goods which can be imported. In the real world, most countries produce goods for export *and* home consumption, which compete against similar imported goods. These early theories also assumed that gains from trade arise from countries which are dissimilar in their technologies, whereas much of the world's trade is among countries with similar levels of technology and industrial development. Nonetheless, Smith and Ricardo demonstrated important points that we now tend to take for granted, in proving to a world steeped in mercantilism that free trade can lead to greater productivity and higher living standards for the countries involved. More-over, the scenario they depicted characterizes much trade between developed and developing countries, which has become an issue in our own era.

Factor endowment theory

Factor endowments: The labour, land, capital and natural resources of a country.

Eli Heckscher and Bertil Ohlin, two Swedish economists, turned their attention to the differences between countries and between products. They argued that every country has its own set of factors of production. Known as factor endowments, these are its labour, land, capital and natural resources, in which it has relative strengths in comparison to other countries. This concept is similar to the arguments underlying location advantages (discussed in Chapter 2). If a country is endowed with abundant natural resources, it will enjoy comparative advantage in producing goods in this sector (Ohlin, 1933). Products, too, differ according to the factors of production involved and their intensity. If more labour is needed for a product such as textiles, then the goods produced are more labour intensive. If the production of wheat requires more capital and less labour, then it is more capital intensive. The implication for trade is that a country will export the good which requires intensity in the factor with which it is relatively well endowed (its abundant factor).

Figure 6.5 The Heckscher-Ohlin-Samuelson theory

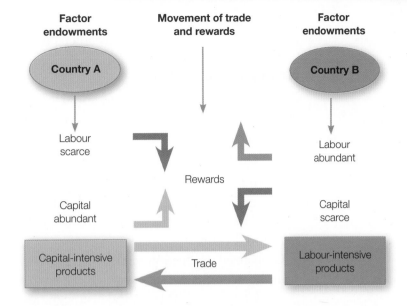

Factor-price equalization: Theory which holds that, with trade, an abundant factor of production will rise in value and a scarce factor of production will fall.

TO RECAP...

Early trade theories

Theories of comparative advantage and factor endowment focused on the conditions which characterized each country, assuming that all countries would benefit from trade, exporting products in which they had comparative advantage and importing other products. These theories take a rather static view of national economies, failing to take account of differing levels of technology and the growth of trade between countries of similar levels of development.

Further study of the effects of trade on factor prices by Paul Samuelson complemented this theory, which became known as the Heckscher-Ohlin-Samuelson theory. The factor-price equalization theorem holds that a factor of production will lose its high rewards in countries where it was scarce before trade, and gain in those where it was abundant before trade, even if the factor itself does not move between countries. Samuelson found that free trade will benefit the abundant factor and harm the scarce factor, thus creating winners and losers. Within a single economy, some groups are winners and some are losers. In Figure 6.5, Country A is labour scarce and capital abundant, while Country B is labour abundant and capital scarce. Manufacturers in A will face competitive pressures from B, where labour is more abundant, forcing down wages in A. Wages in manufacturing in B will rise, while manufacturing wages in A will fall. A's owners of capital will gain, whereas those in B will lose. Citizens in B are likely to favour trade liberalization, whereas those in A are likely to be against it. This research, therefore, seems to support protectionist policies on the part of governments.

Product life cycle theory

Vernon (1999) argued that for manufactured consumer products, there is a lifespan in which the good gradually becomes standardized and cheaper to produce. Its production shifts from the high-cost environment of the US to lower cost locations, which eventually export the product to consumers in the US. In Chapter 2, we noted that Vernon started with an assumption that all innovation originated in the US. Expressed in terms of comparative advantage, we could say that the US had comparative advantage in newly invented manufactured goods. As the good becomes more standardized and production shifts, comparative advantage shifts to the newer manufacturing countries. This theory applies to consumer products such as refrigerators and televisions, but the rather US-centric assumptions, reasonable in the 1960s, no longer hold true. Further, as highlighted earlier, new products nowadays are often launched in global markets, and manufacturing from the outset takes place in a low-cost location. Vernon's theory, however, provided insight into the links between FDI and international trade in the early stages of trends which we now identify as crucial to globalization.

Newer trade theories

Each of the theories examined so far has been found to be limited in its perspective and application. Paul Krugman (1995) has pointed out that some aspects of international trade that are observable in recent trends seem unexplained:

1 There is the rise in intra-industry trade, which is trade in similar goods between countries of similar levels of economic development. For example, the countries of the EU both export and import similar manufactured goods.

2 Globalized production tends to break down production into different steps in the value chain, each of which can be in a different geographical location (see Chapter 10). This vertical disintegration, or slicing up of the value chain, has undermined theories about skill-, capital- or technology-intensive goods, as the manufactured product consists of a series of different inputs, the labour-intensive aspects of which gravitate to low-wage locations.

3 The low-cost manufacturing countries have become major exporters. Krugman and other theorists have sought to address these trends from a theoretical perspective.

Intra-industry trade: Trade in similar goods between countries of similar levels of economic development.

Looking at the three phenomena identified by Krugman, the first, intra-industry trade, can be at least partly explained by the role of product differentiation. As consumers become more affluent and discerning, they tend to look for greater variety and to value differences between products in the same class. In goods such as vehicles, clothing, food and travel, the advanced economies offer an array of products, from basic to luxury. Some of these are home produced and some imported. The basic or standard product, such as a small car, can be contrasted with a luxury model, often with a high degree of customization. Product differentiation is facilitated by economies of scale. Economies of scale are achieved if increasing expenditures on inputs bring down the cost of producing each unit of output. Larger firms are able to spread and reduce fixed costs, using specialized workers where necessary and sourcing components globally. Economies of scale help to explain the second and third of the phenomena identified above, which are globalized production and the rise in exports from low-cost countries. The latter phenomenon is also explained by the theory of comparative advantage.

Product differentiation: Differences in attributes between products in the same class.

Economies of scale: Large scale production which results in reduction of the unit cost of products.

New trade theory also analyses global competition. It will be recalled that the classical theory assumed highly competitive markets. In today's world, many industries are dominated by a few large firms, a phenomenon known as oligopoly. Oligopolies emerge especially in industries where economies of scale are crucial, such as the oil industry. In such industries, the very large firm has obvious advantages, and smaller firms have difficulty competing. Further, the early entrant may reap increasing returns which thwart later entrants. The advantages of the early entrant are known as first-mover advantages (Lieberman and Montgomery, 1988). They can act as a barrier to entry, reinforcing the oligopolistic nature of these industries. Where a firm

Oligopoly: An industry dominated by a few very large firms.

First-mover advantages: Advantages enjoyed by the first entrant in an industry or market, which may yield increasing returns, making it harder for other entrants to follow and acting as a barrier to entry.

has first-mover advantages and economies of scale, its position may attract the attention of governments, as these benefits confer comparative advantage to the nation.

The firms in an oligopolistic industry may choose not to compete very aggressively, as all can count on a reasonable profit. They are thus tempted to agree the control of supply and pricing among themselves which can amount to anti-competitive practices. The oligopoly can be distinguished from the monopoly (discussed in Chapter 3) in that the monopolist has complete control of supply and price. If scale economies are only moderate, there is competition among firms offering differentiated products. This situation has been called monopolistic competition, whereby there is room for many producers making products in the same class. Products are differentiated from those of competitors, thus allowing each to exert some control over the price charged. Consumers enjoy choice within the class, based on differentiated products and brands.

Theories of product differentiation and monopolistic competition help to explain recent patterns of international trade. They shed light on national gains from trade and the effects of trade on different groups in society, when looked at in conjunction with the Heckscher-Ohlin-Samuelson theory. Consumers gain from increased choice, including imported and domestic products. They will also gain from the fact that international competition will tend to lower prices of domestic goods. The effect on producers has been a topic of research and debate (Davis, 1996). If they are producing for export, they will gain, as has happened in China. Workers in developed countries making goods which compete with imports will lose, although they benefit as consumers. Research has shown that in the US between 1978 and 1990, production jobs in manufacturing decreased 7.2%, whereas non-production jobs involving more skill declined 2.1% (Sachs and Shatz, 1994). Hence, there has emerged a widening gap between skilled and unskilled jobs in the US.

Monopolistic competition: Situation in which there are many producers producing products in the same class, where competition is based on product differentiation within the class.

TO RECAP...
Newer trade theories
More recent theorists have sought to explain recent patterns of international trade, including the emergence of oligopolies in some industries and the impact of the globalization of production on trade. They highlight the emergence of winners and losers from trade, both within and between countries.

Trade and globalization
In what ways do the theories of trade highlighted in this section explain processes of globalization? To what extent do the divisions between winners and losers support those who warn of the detrimental impacts of globalization?

PAUSE TO REFLECT

National competitiveness

National competitiveness has aroused growing interest in both academic and general business discourse. However, definitions differ, some with a narrow focus and some with a broader focus. Economists tend to take a narrow view, holding that the competitiveness of a national economy is its cost competitiveness, determined by unit labour costs, costs of other factors such as land, and exchange rate considerations (Thompson, 2004). Management literature has taken a broader view, taking into account individual firms and industries, each of which exists in an environmental context. Michael Porter has been an exponent of this view, which takes in the 'microeconomic' business environment. This definition is criticized by some economists for equating the competitiveness of firms with that of an entire economy. Nonetheless, the notion of environmental and institutional factors influencing national competitiveness has proved popular. Indeed, the two well-known ranking systems (discussed below) take an even broader view of the environment, including macroeconomic indicators and the political and legal environment.

Porter's theory of competitive advantage

In his book, *The Competitive Advantage of Nations* (1998a), Porter argued that the comparative advantage and factor endowment theories were too limited, and should be superseded by his new concept of competitive advantage. A firm's competitive advantages, he argues, are linked to its home-country environment, in particular to four interrelated aspects of the country's resources and industries. These four aspects he depicts as a diamond. The analysis of the country's advantages in each aspect, he argues, determines the competitive advantages of its industries and firms. In addition, Porter notes the importance of two other variables: chance and the role of national governments. These last two factors, while indirectly influential, do not carry the same weight as the determining attributes which feature in the diamond model of competitive advantage. The four sets of attributes are:

Diamond model of competitive advantage: Configuration of four sets of attributes (factor conditions, demand conditions, supporting industries and inter-firm rivalry) which, in Porter's theory, determine a nation's competitive advantage.

- *Factor conditions* – These include the country's factor endowments, or natural resources. Also included are the capabilities of its citizens, including capacity for innovation and the depth of the country's infrastructure.
- *Demand conditions* – This concerns consumer demand within the country. Included are the level of consumer demand, the types of goods and the levels of quality demanded by its domestic consumers.
- *Related and supporting industries* – Here, the focus is on clusters of suppliers and supporting industries. If they are technologically advanced, they may be internationally competitive in their own right.
- *Firm strategy, structure and rivalry* – This heading is rather an amalgam. It includes the ways in which the country's firms are organized and managed, and also the nature and extent of inter-firm rivalry within the country.

Porter's model is concerned with export performance rather than FDI, a focus which has drawn criticism from some scholars. In particular, the model tends to underestimate the role of the MNE and the extent of globalization of production (Dunning, 1993c; Rugman and Verbeke, 1993; Öz, 2000). Many important MNEs in today's world have become globalized in both their organization and activities, and cannot be said to be determined by the home-country environment. Nestlé of Switzerland is often cited as an example. In fact, in the case of multinationals from small open economies, the diamond of foreign countries may be more relevant. Rugman cites the case of Canada, whose economy is highly integrated with the US, and proposes a 'double diamond' for Canada and the US (Rugman and D'Cruz, 1993). Although the 'favourable' diamond conditions of the MNE's home country may be helpful for expansion within the region, it may not be sufficient to sustain global advantage (Rugman and Verbeke, 2004). The MNE seeks out location advantages for particular activities in numerous parts of the developing and developed world. The national diamonds of these other countries therefore become important to its global strategy, not merely to support home-based advantages.

Given the expansion of MNEs, the competitiveness of a nation should arguably be extended beyond the factors highlighted in Porter's diamond. Dunning (1993c) suggests that the role of government is crucial: national governments act both directly and indirectly in facilitating capabilities and the efficient use of resources. He also suggests that the cultural environment plays a role. This view is supported by research in the Asian context which found that, from the management perspective, institutional circumstances are more important than costs to the assessment of national competitiveness (Thompson, 2004). Porter's perspective has been described as an 'old-fashioned' one, depicting an MNE with a strong home base from which it exports competitively (Rugman and Verbeke, 1993).

However, if we broaden the range of environmental factors in Porter's diamond to include governments, institutions and cultural environment, the theory as modified remains a helpful model. It is also necessary take into account the diamonds of all relevant countries in addition to a firm's home country, to reflect the decentralized nature of MNEs in global production networks.

TO RECAP...

Competitive advantage

Porter's theory, which includes a nation's industrial structure, goes beyond the classical theories of comparative advantage, but its focus on the national characteristics of a firm's home country has been criticized for failing to take account of FDI and globalization.

Assessing the theory of competitive advantage
In what ways is Porter's theory an advance on earlier international trade theories? What criticisms can be levelled at the 'diamond' analysis, and to what extent do you feel they are valid?

PAUSE TO REFLECT

Measuring global competitiveness

Ranking the relative competitiveness of different countries is rather imprecise, as many qualitative factors are not easily measurable. Nonetheless, it has become an annual exercise, attracting the attention of the media and governments, as well as business leaders. Competitiveness indexes seem to show that government policies in both managing the economy and strengthening the institutional environment can aid the competitiveness of the country. The two organizations which compile indexes, the Institute for Management Development (IMD) and the World Economic Forum (WEF), publish annual rankings based on their own competitiveness criteria. The components in each index overlap to a large degree. The IMD criteria are economic performance, government efficiency, business efficiency and infrastructure. The IMD's aim (2007) is to assess the ability of a country to 'sustain more value creation for its enterprises and more prosperity for its people'. The WEF criteria fall under six 'pillars'. Four of these – infrastructure, macroeconomy, market efficiency and institutions – overlap with the IMD criteria. WEF's two other pillars are health and primary education, and higher education and training. They are therefore somewhat broader than the IMD's focus on 'prosperity' in mainly economic terms. The WEF ranks 117 countries, many more than the 61 ranked by the IMD.

The WEF and IMD indexes for 2007 appear in Figure 6.6. The top place is given to the US by both rankings, despite macroeconomic imbalances, noted the previous year by the WEF, when it ranked the US sixth. These imbalances include high budget deficits, high trade deficits, low levels of personal savings

The World Economic Forum's website is www.wef.org. The website of IMD is www.imd.ch. Click on *Publications*, under which there is a link to the *World Competitiveness Yearbook*.

WEB CHECK

Figure 6.6 National competitiveness rankings

Sources: WEF (2007) *Global Competitiveness Report 2007–8*, www.wef.org; IMD (2007) *World Competitiveness Yearbook* (Lausanne: IMD)

Global Competitiveness Report, 2007–08 (WEF)

1. United States
2. Switzerland
3. Denmark
4. Sweden
5. Germany
6. Finland
7. Singapore
8. Japan
9. United Kingdom
10. Netherlands
11. Korea
12. Hong Kong
13. Canada
14. Taiwan
15. Austria

Selected others:
34. China
48. India
58. Russia

Competitiveness Scoreboard, 2007 (IMD)

1. United States
2. Singapore
3. Hong Kong
4. Luxembourg
5. Denmark
6. Switzerland
7. Iceland
8. Netherlands
9. Sweden
10. Canada
11. Austria
12. Australia
13. Norway
14. Ireland
15. China Mainland

Selected others:
16. Germany
17. Finland
18. Taiwan
20. United Kingdom
27. India
43. Russia

TO RECAP...

National competitiveness
Comparing national economies on the basis of their competitiveness with each other is a rather imprecise exercise, but the rankings by leading research institutions provide insight into the relative strengths and weaknesses of different national environments, which are often cited by political and business leaders.

and high levels of personal debt. In 2007, the WEF adjusted its model somewhat, leading to less emphasis on these factors and greater emphasis on market efficiency and innovation (Giles, 2007). Switzerland and the Nordic countries rank strongly on all criteria. China's lowly WEF ranking can be attributed to weak institutions, high levels of bureaucracy and low educational levels.

Do countries or firms compete?
It is relatively easy to see how firms compete, that is, by selling products in markets. How do countries compete? With its booming economy and rising exports, China is now an economic superpower, and China's firms are highly competitive globally. Why, then, is China ranked relatively lowly in competitiveness rankings?

PAUSE TO REFLECT

Government trade policy

Free trade: Situation in which markets are allowed to operate without any government intervention.

Protectionism: Government approach to trade policy which seeks to shield domestic industries from competition from trade.

As we have seen, early trade theorists emphasized that the benefits of comparative advantage prevail where governments uphold free trade, a rather idealistic scenario in which they intervene in neither imports nor exports. In practice, governments are tempted to intervene to protect those who lose from free trade. Hence, the term protectionism is often applied to these inward-looking policies. Two factors weigh with governments. First, the steep rise in exports of consumer products from low-cost developing countries threatens competing domestic industries. Second, first-mover advantages enjoyed by a few large players in some industries, such as aerospace or nuclear power, create national comparative advantage, which governments are keen to maintain. In this section, we look first at government objectives and then at policy tools.

National interests

Government priorities in respect of trade can be grouped under several headings:

1 *National security*: National security is linked directly with defence issues, including risks from terrorism. In defence industries and technology, governments are concerned that national security is not compromised, and often give preference in procurement to national companies rather than foreign ones. How far does national security extend? US law stipulates that foreign companies or individuals may own only 25% of a US airline company, and must have two-thirds of the seats on the board. The EU has objected to this restriction, claiming that its aim is simply to create barriers to competition in the skies. The aerospace industry is of strategic importance, and is often favoured with government subsidies, as CS6.1 discusses.

2 *Strategic needs*: This area increasingly overlaps with national security. Strategic needs include food, water and energy. Historically, colonial powers saw their colonies as captive sources of strategic needs. In today's world, markets play this role, but, increasingly, governments play an active role in trade, often focusing on national strategic needs. As SX6.1 showed, Chinese leaders have sought energy security through trade deals. In a world of sovereign states, no importer can be guaranteed security by an energy supplier in another country: natural occurrences, government action and other political circumstances may intervene.

3 *Domestic employment*: Employment in domestic industries can be threatened by imports. While, in theory, governments favour free trade as beneficial to consumers, they are also concerned about domestic jobs, particularly the impact of job losses if a domestic industry becomes uncompetitive because of lower cost imports. Much of the pressure on democratic governments comes from elected representatives in the geographic areas where jobs are at risk. Using public funds to prop up local firms is costly and does not increase their competitiveness. The approach of retraining and new job creation, while applauded by governments, is not a total solution. Often, there is little public money for retraining, and many of the low-skilled workers become unemployed.

4 *Culture*: Dominant and minority cultures, including languages, ethnic and religious groups, are at the heart of a people's sense of national identity. They are shared through literature, music, film and broadcast media. The economic might of global media companies in broadcasting, newspapers, magazines and film poses a threat to smaller local producers, whose output keeps alive local culture and languages. Some governments restrict the amount of foreign content in the media and limit foreign ownership of media companies. Other policies include grants and subsidies for local content producers and broadcasters. However, government intervention in the media has a negative side. Intervening in content can descend into censorship, weakening freedom of expression and reducing consumer choice (a topic highlighted in Chapter 8 and SX15.2).

5 *Consumer protection*: Like the other principles highlighted in this section, this is capable of a broad interpretation. Consumers need to be protected

from unsafe products of all types, including food, medicines, toys and electrical goods. These products figure prominently in merchandise trade. National governments regulate health and safety standards which imports must meet. If materials used in clothing and soft furnishings make them flammable and therefore a risk, their import into most countries will be prohibited. On the other hand, governments are sometimes accused of setting safety requirements which are designed mainly to restrict imported goods. Food products have become a sensitive issue, as consumers are concerned both about the content of a product and how it is produced. Genetically modified (GM) crops and hormone-treated meat are widely exported, their producers claiming they are scientifically safe. However, many consumers object to these products, and their safety is a subject of much debate. Clear labelling would seem to be a solution, although producers have resisted. The large companies involved in GM production have argued that the objections raised against their products in some countries are simply designed to protect inefficient domestic farmers.

Tariffs and other tools of trade policy

Governments have at their disposal a number of tools to intervene in trade. The specific choice of policy instrument depends largely on the goals they hope to achieve. They may aim to control importers, or they may aim to aid home producers. The various tools are set out in Figure 6.7.

Controlling imports

Among measures aimed directly at imports are tariffs, import quotas and voluntary export restraint (VER). While a tariff can be on imports or exports, the import tariff is the commonest, levying a charge or duty on imports. Its effect is to make imported goods more expensive, encouraging consumers to purchase home-produced products. The tariff therefore benefits domestic producers. The government benefits from the revenues generated, but the consumer loses out, as the prices of foreign imported products are artificially

> **TO RECAP...**
>
> **National interests shape trade policies**
>
> Five areas of national interest impact on trade policies – national security, strategic needs, domestic employment, culture and consumer protection. Although most governments support free trade in theory, in these sensitive areas, governments often feel justified in intervening in trade on grounds of public interest.

Tariff: A charge on imports or exports, but most often, an import duty.

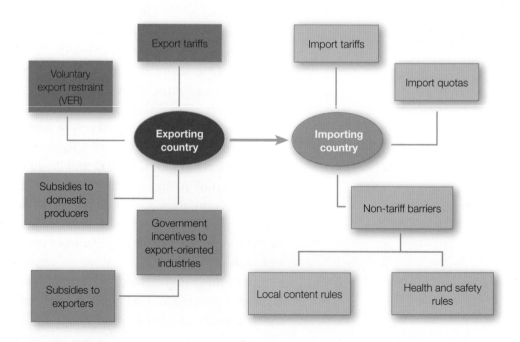

Figure 6.7 Tools of government trade policy

Import quota: Predetermined limit on the quantity of goods of a specific class that can be imported; the exporter must usually obtain a licence to export within the quota.

Voluntary export restraint (VER): Self-imposed limitation which an exporter sets on goods it exports in a particular class, usually at the behest of the importing country.

Export subsidy: Payments made by a government to producers of specific products in order to increase their production for export.

high. Similarly, the import quota protects local producers and disadvantages local consumers. The import quota sets a limit on the goods of a specific class that can be imported from a particular country. Usually, importers must apply for licences to import within these quota limits. Quotas may be set by individual countries, regional trade blocs (such as the EU) or multilaterally. Quotas have been a continuing feature of trade in textiles and clothing, as discussed in CS6.2.

The voluntary export restraint (VER) is implemented by the exporting country to curb exports voluntarily, often under pressure from governments in importing countries which fear damaging consequences to domestic industries. The self-imposed limits may be in terms of volume, value or market share. Pressures include the threat of imposing import quotas if voluntary measures are not adopted. Because it is negotiated by the parties, it is often referred to as a policy of 'managed trade'. In theory, the importing country benefits from the restrictions, but, in practice, they may be counter-productive (Zhou and Vertinsky, 2002). The US used this policy in the 1980s against Japanese car manufacturers, which were grabbing market share in the US. The policy had only limited success, as Japanese firms circumvented the restriction by building plants in the US, and upgrading the quality of their exports. As the restraint covered only small cars, they were able to manufacture small cars in the US and export the Japanese-made luxury Lexus models freely.

Governments also introduce policies which indirectly limit imports, such as local content requirements and safety regulations. Importers often take a cynical view of safety requirements, saying that their real aim is to block imports. However, there are debates about what is safe and what is not, which are not entirely resolved by available scientific evidence. In the dispute between the US and EU on hormone-treated beef, both sides cited research supporting their position: US exporters claimed that scientific research was clear that there was no risk, while research cited by the EU showed risks. Resolving such disputes is one of the tasks of the WTO, although, as we shall see, trade disputes can run on for years.

Aiding home producers

Governments may offer direct subsidies to individual producers, or incentives such as advantageous loans, tax breaks and minimum guaranteed price schemes supported by the government. Agriculture is one of the most heavily subsidized sectors globally (see Figure 6.8). The aim of most of these subsidies is to sustain local farming, much of which is small scale and inefficient. The EU's agriculture subsidy programme, the CAP, falls into this category. As was seen Chapter 3, it accounts for nearly 40% of the EU's overall budget. This type of subsidy paid directly to producers can be distinguished from export subsidies, which are linked to increasing production for export. Export subsidies are in breach of WTO rules as they distort world markets.

US farm policies have long encouraged exports. Direct payments by the government to farmers are expected to be $13.4 billion in 2008, mostly directed to the commodity crops grown for export, including cotton, rice, sugar, wheat, soya beans and rice. Subsidies are paid despite growing profits. US farm exports reached a record $82 billion in 2007, and the estimate for

Figure 6.8 Financial support for agricultural producers, 2005

Source: OECD (2006) Producer Support Index, http://www.oecd.org

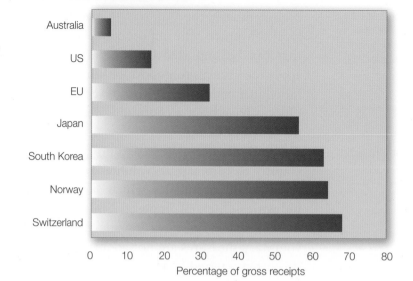

Percentage of gross receipts

TO RECAP...

Government trade policies

To curtail imports, governments use import tariffs, import quotas, VERs and various non-tariff barriers, such as safety requirements and local content requirements. Export tariffs and subsidies benefit local producers. These may be aimed at keeping alive domestic industries, but may also be used to promote exports.

2008 is $101 billion (USDA, 2008). This growth is attributed by the United States Department of Agriculture to the weak dollar and surging foreign demand. Despite WTO rules, significant reforms are unlikely, as the farm lobby is such a strong political influence in Congress. This inflexibility has been a major cause of tension in the WTO, discussed in the next section.

Case study 6.1:
Boeing and Airbus on a collision course

Boeing, the giant American aircraft maker, and Airbus, its European counterpart, are the two main competitors in the global aircraft market. In this industry, huge capital outlays, costly R&D and long timescales for new models ensure few new entrants. The outcome has been an effective duopoly, pitting the two rivals against each other for orders for new aircraft, although both companies obtain components from firms in each other's region. While Boeing is seen as a national champion in the US, Airbus is depicted as a European champion. Governments on both sides of the Atlantic have helped to fund their respective champions, but a bitter dispute has ensued, each side claiming that the other is in receipt of export subsidies which breach WTO free-trade rules. It was hoped that an amicable settlement could be reached, but prospects dimmed in 2004, when the dispute was taken to the WTO, beginning the formal process of dispute settlement. This would probably be the longest and most costly trade dispute over allegedly illegal state aid in the WTO's history.

In the large civil aircraft industry, it has been recognized that government subsidies are a fact of life. A bilateral agreement between the EU and the US in 1992 attempted to limit subsidies, spelling out the circumstances under which government aid is justifiable. 'Launch aid', to fund R&D for new models, is allowable under the agreement. The US maintains that $15 billion in launch aid received by Airbus was an illegal subsidy, giving Airbus a market advantage over Boeing. It also points to loans on preferential terms. The EU has responded that the launch aid comes within the 1992 agreement. It also maintains that the loans were on commercial terms: it borrowed €4 billion and paid back €5 billion.

In fact, it has paid 40% more than it has received in government loans since 1992.

The EU has itself launched a complaint against the US for state aid to Boeing, alleging numerous subsidies to the company. Benefits from the state of Washington, where Boeing is based, include tax breaks, tax exemptions, tax credits and infrastructure projects built exclusively for Boeing. Airbus claims these amount to $3.2 billion. It says that Boeing has also received $23 billion in subsidies through government R&D programmes. The EU argues that, overall, the generous subsidies paid to Boeing have allowed it to price its aircraft aggressively, causing loss of sales to Airbus.

In 2003, Airbus overtook Boeing to become the leading maker of big commercial jets. This was a bleak year for Boeing, as it was struck by corruption scandals involving US defence procurement contracts, followed by executive resignations. Boeing management has had to rebuild its ethical reputation as well as employee morale. Recently, it has enjoyed a resurgence under its CEO Scott Carson, who says: 'We have approached sales and the market with a very strategic view without losing sight of staying profitable' (Done and Hollinger, 2005). By 2006, Boeing seemed to be winning the competitive battle with Airbus, bringing in more orders for new planes than Airbus was achieving (see Figure 1). Boeing's new 'star' is its 787 Dreamliner, which is a medium-sized, wide-bodied, long-haul plane, capable of carrying 210–50 passengers. This new fuel-efficient aircraft has helped to swell Boeing's order book, but has suffered delays, mainly due to the innovative new materials and extensive outsourcing. Airbus's rival medium-sized, long-haul aircraft is the A350, replacing the ageing A330. The A350 has had

Figure 1 Commercial plane orders

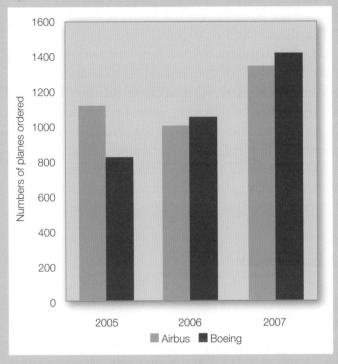

Sources: Financial Times, 17 January 2007; BBC, 2008

Figure 2 Projection of total world passenger traffic

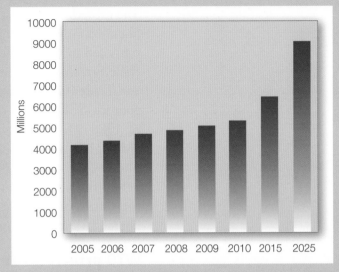

Source: Airports Council International (2007) *Global Traffic Forecast, 2006–2025,* www.airports.org/ac

to be redesigned to meet customer requirements, and its launch has been set back to 2012. Airbus has also suffered delays with its more innovative and risky project, the A380 superjumbo, the biggest commercial jetliner ever, capable of carrying 550 passengers. Boeing has no plans for a rival in this category, forecasting that the growth in passenger numbers will be accommodated mainly by more frequent services rather than by larger aircraft.

Both companies are counting on the continuing increase in air passenger traffic (see Figure 2), particularly international traffic, which is growing more quickly than domestic traffic in all regions except Asia, where low-cost, short-haul air travel is growing rapidly. Uncertainties over air travel in general include the cost of fuel, environmental pollution and terrorist threats such as the attacks in New York of 2001. Both companies have prioritized fuel efficiency in their new models, enticing carriers to buy new models to replace their older, less fuel-efficient fleet. Hence, demand for new models is likely to bring business to both manufacturers.

Airbus's competitive position has been clouded by ownership and management uncertainties. Airbus is owned by European Aeronautic Defence and Space Company (EADS), Europe's leading aerospace group. The French government holds a 17.5% stake, Daimler 22.5%, French media conglomerate Lagardère 7.5% and the Spanish government 5%. The British company

BAE Systems sold its 20% stake in 2006, although it is still involved in production. The tensions between French and German interests over where Airbus work should be located and what technology to use have troubled the company's management, and led to adverse publicity that management strife was holding up production. Airbus is looking at restructuring to regain competitiveness and better productivity.

A protracted trade dispute could be damaging to the industry and detrimental to trade relations. A probable outcome is that illegal subsidies have occurred on both sides. Although the dispute is legally between the US and EU, the two companies have become increasingly global, making the notion of 'national' products inappropriate for both. Airbus planes have more American content than some of Boeing's own: Airbus uses GE engines of the US, while Boeing uses Rolls-Royce engines of the UK. The EADS chairman says: 'national fights over national products in our industry are outdated' (Daniel, 2004). The potential damage of the dispute is summed up by BAE Systems CEO, who says: 'I am really concerned there will be no winners. If it goes the full distance the outcome will be less support for industry and the great technology created ... meaning fewer developments in the future' (Done and Hollinger, 2005). It is possible that the WTO process will encourage the parties to resume bilateral negotiations, settling the dispute by diplomacy rather than confrontation.

Questions

1   Why has a trade dispute erupted between the EU and the US over civil aircraft?
2   Assess the competitive positions of Boeing and Airbus in global markets.
3   To what extent is the notion of 'national champions' outdated?
4   Is the WTO's role enhanced or damaged by disputes such as this? Give your reasons.

Sources: Airports Council International (2007) *Global Traffic Forecast, 2006–2025,* www.airports.org/ac; Done, K., 'Airbus lags behind Boeing in orders', *Financial Times,* 17 January 2007; WTO (2007) *European Communities: Measures Affecting Trade in Large Civil Aircraft,* Dispute DS316, www.wto.org; Daniel, C., 'Airbus head dismayed by battle over subsidies', *Financial Times,* 8 October 2004; Alden, E. and Minder, R. 'Dogfight at the WTO: the US and EU step up their battle over aircraft subsidies', *Financial Times,* 8 October 2004; Done, K. and Hollinger, P., 'Cockpit crisis: will management disputes drag down Europe's aerospace champion', *Financial Times,* 15 June 2005; 'Flying dangerously', *The Economist: The World in 2007*; 'Boeing pips Airbus on 2007 orders', 16 January 2008, http://news.bbc.co.uk; Done, K., 'Jetmakers see headwinds approaching', *Financial Times,* 17 January 2008.

WEB CHECK

Boeing's website is www.boeing.com. The website of EADS is www.eads.com, which has information about Airbus.

The WTO and multilateral trade agreements

The growth in world trade in the post-war era has been facilitated by trade liberalization, bringing down tariffs and other barriers to trade which had prevailed in the protectionist era between the wars. A series of multilateral trade agreements under the framework of the General Agreement on Tariffs and Trade (GATT) was launched in 1947, with an initial membership of 50 countries. This series of agreements, culminating with the Uruguay Round of 1986–94, brought down barriers on manufactured goods significantly, although it was less successful in lowering barriers for agricultural products. The GATT was superseded by the WTO in 1995. However, it was not long before the new framework was coming under strain, raising questions over the future of both the organization and the viability of multilateral trade liberalization in general.

WTO principles and framework

Most favoured nation (MFN) principle: Principle under which a country allows imports from all countries on terms equivalent to the most preferential.

Like its GATT predecessor, the aim of the WTO is to liberalize trade among member countries. A central tenet is the most favoured nation (MFN) principle, by which a country will allow imports of products into its markets from all other members on terms equivalent to the most preferential. It cannot discriminate against any member country on trade, or give preference to any. Tariff reductions apply equally to all trading partners. The rules take account of the need for transparency and fair trading practices. Where a country feels its position had been damaged by unfair trading practices, it can take action to protect itself. For example, dumping may occur where large quantities of exported goods are sold in import markets at prices less than they would cost at home, sometimes less than their cost to produce. In these circumstances, the importing country is entitled to levy anti-dumping duties on the exporting country, in order to protect its own producers.

Dumping: The export of an inordinately large quantity of a specific class of goods in a foreign market at prices less than in their home market, which can result in 'anti-dumping' sanctions by the importing country.

There is recognition of legitimate protectionist measures, therefore, within the WTO rules. First, subsidies to local producers are not ruled out per se: subsidies may be justified to sustain local industries, but must not be used to distort international trade. Second, the rules allow importing countries to bar goods which are dangerous or a risk to health. Generally, the WTO takes into account only the product itself, and not how it was produced. Hence, objections on grounds of unethical labour standards or environmental degradation in production would not justify barring goods under WTO rules.

There is much scope for differing interpretations of these rules, as well as debate about whether the rules should be broadened to include labour and environmental criteria. One country's view of a legitimate subsidy may be viewed by others as an illegitimate competitive advantage. Similarly, countries rejecting imports on health grounds may be accused by exporters of imposing illegitimate protectionist barriers. The stringent regulations in the EU and Japan for vetting imported agricultural products are seen as effective trade barriers by some exporting countries, especially those in the developing world.

A weakness of the GATT framework was that it lacked enforcement machinery and organizational capabilities to deal with ever-widening and deepening trade issues. The WTO now has 150 members, three-quarters of them from developing countries, and it continues to grow. Vietnam, a rapidly developing trading nation, joined in 2007 (see CF9.1). The WTO has an organizational structure which the GATT lacked. Co-ordinated by a director general, policy-making takes place through a Ministerial Conference comprising trade ministers from all 150 member states, which meets every two years. The WTO has instituted a dispute resolution process whereby member countries can bring complaints of breaches of the rules by other member countries. A Dispute Settlement Body has been set up, and panels are established to deal with each dispute. A member country may seek a WTO ruling that another country is damaging its rightful trading position by breaching WTO rules. If the WTO finds that there has been a breach, the country which has suffered is authorized to take retaliatory trade sanctions against the offending country, usually the imposition of tariffs on a range of goods (see CS5.1 on online gambling).

The dispute resolution procedure has proved popular. Envisaged as likely to be invoked mainly by the major trading countries, it is increasingly being used by developing countries, concerned that they are being disadvantaged by the practices of the major trading powers. For example, Brazil won a case against the US for its subsidies of US cotton farmers. Brazil and Thailand jointly won a case against the EU for its sugar regime. The latter case reflected disquiet over the EU's preferential treatment to African, Caribbean and Pacific (ACP) developing countries' agricultural products. These cases have highlighted some of the divisive issues that now characterize world trade, testing the WTO's ability to push forward multilateral liberalization.

The Doha Round founders

Following the Uruguay Round, the continued dismantling of trade barriers has hinged on a new round of trade negotiations, the Doha Round, which commenced in 2001. Termed the 'development round', it was designed to address ways in which liberalized trade would help developing countries. Of particular attention were agriculture and textiles. Intellectual property rights and services were also on the agenda. These were all areas in which developing countries felt the world trading system was favouring the rich countries, as subsidies and tariff barriers are distorting markets (Charlton and Stiglitz, 2002). In developing countries, agriculture typically accounts for 40% of GDP and 70% of employment. Some developing countries, notably Brazil, are building capacity in modern efficient agriculture with huge export potential. They are looking to export sugar and other products to the US, as CF6.2 on Brazil highlights. However, farmers in rich countries have political 'clout' disproportionate to their actual numbers, reinforced by subsidy programmes which they defend tenaciously (Lamy, 2006).

Agriculture proved to be the major sticking point, a rift emerging between the US and the EU on reducing farm subsidies. Although accounting for only 8% of global trade, agriculture is an emotive issue. Doha negotiators set themselves ambitious targets for agriculture, hoping to achieve agreement to reduce trade-distorting domestic support by 60% and tariffs by 50%. However, the US gave little ground on its export-oriented farming subsidies, and demanded that any decrease be matched by favourable access to agricultural markets in other

TO RECAP...
Multilateralism and the WTO
Multilateral liberalization was initiated in the GATT, and continued by the WTO. The WTO has instituted a new dispute resolution process, whereby countries can seek WTO-sanctioned reprisals against trading partners in breach of its rules. Divisions among members, particularly between developing and developed countries, are straining the WTO framework.

For information on the Doha development round, go to the WTO's website at www.wto.org, and click on *Doha Development Agenda*.

WEB CHECK

countries. Such moves were resisted by rich WTO members, such as the EU, Switzerland and Japan, as well as by poorer countries, such as India and Indonesia. These countries all have frameworks in place to protect local producers.

The EU has attracted criticism for its subsidies to local farm producers and preferential arrangements for ACP countries in products such as bananas and sugar. The US and developing country exporters seek greater access to EU markets. The EU's trade minister agreed to reduce its domestic subsidies by 2013 and to phase out the preference systems. Although large exporters, such as Brazil, will benefit from the opening of markets for sugar, smaller ones, such as Mauritius, which are much less competitive, will be disadvantaged. Hence, market liberalization is tending to benefit the large developing countries, such as China, Brazil and India, while damaging the smaller poorer ones, many of which are in Africa.

For developing countries, it was unfortunate that the aims of the development round, which were linked to the urgent needs of the poorest countries, were sidelined by the hard bargaining of the rich ones. The bitterness of these protracted negotiations revealed the fragility of the multilateral trading system, casting doubts on future multilateral agreements. An increase in trade disputes between countries is a likely consequence of the disappointments of the Doha Round. Developing country exporters are continuing to pursue claims of trade-distorting barriers to their exports against the US and the EU. Moreover, the Doha talks did not address many issues that are of concern to business. These include business visa restrictions (particularly for entry into the US), the enforcement of intellectual property rights, controls on FDI and harmonizing competition law.

The growth in bilateral agreements

Given the breakdown of multilateralism, bilateral agreements are likely to become more popular. Some are 'preferential trade agreements', and some are 'bilateral investment treaties'. Agreements under both headings focus on trade and investment relations. Typically, the agreement is between a major trading power and an emerging economy, offering preferential treatment in certain sectors, but exempting sensitive sectors such as agricultural commodities. These agreements have drawbacks from a policy point of view, as well as from a practical perspective of businesses (discussed in the next subsection). Bilateral agreements are particularly favoured by the US, and are also now increasingly used by other major trading powers, such as Japan and the EU.

Bilateral deals are characteristically lopsided, the more powerful country able to slant the agreement in its favour, to the detriment of the weaker country. The poorer country is invited to give more concessions, such as the protection of foreign investments, than would feature within the WTO framework. Bilateral agreements may include conditions relating to labour and environmental standards, which do not come within the WTO framework. These are applauded by many in rich countries, but poor countries often struggle to meet them and tend to see them as barriers to trade. On the other hand, large manufacturers based in rich countries tend to be against the inclusion of labour standards in these agreements, as location advantages become diluted.

TO RECAP...

Disappointments of Doha

The aims of addressing development among the world's poorer nations were rather sidelined by attempts to achieve an agreement on agriculture, which stumbled over rich countries' reluctance to give up subsidies to farmers. Divisions among developing countries also highlighted the fragility of the world trading system.

Bilateralism rules, but who gains?

Why do bilateral agreements pose a threat to the WTO and multilateralism? If the countries entering these preferential agreements are happy to do so in their national interest, why should there be any wider cause for concern?

PAUSE TO REFLECT

TO RECAP...

Bilateralism flourishes

Bilateral trade agreements reflect the priorities and bargaining strengths of the two parties involved. The use of bilateral agreements has proliferated in an environment where multilateral trade negotiations have foundered.

COUNTRY FOCUS 6.2 – BRAZIL

Brazil becomes an agricultural superpower

In a relatively short space of time, Brazil has transformed itself into a major player in global agriculture. In a number of commodities, such as sugar, soya beans and orange juice, Brazil is challenging the more established agricultural exporters such as the US and Australia. It is also making its voice heard in trade negotiations within the WTO and at regional level. But how sustainable is Brazilian agriculture?

Agriculture in Brazil is more accurately described as 'agribusiness', as it is largely characterized by large operations over vast tracks of land. Brazil enjoys comparative advantage in agriculture, due to its combination of low-cost land, abundant water from its networks of rivers and long rainy seasons and low-cost labour. Of its total area of 851 million hectares, 280 million are suitable for farming, either for crops or pasture for animals. Brazil has another estimated 170 million hectares potentially suitable for farming, which is roughly equivalent to the entire farmland of the US currently being cultivated. By contrast, the US has no potential farmland left for future expansion. While China has a larger area of potential agriculture, its export ambitions are limited by huge domestic demand from its population, poor soil quality and dwindling water resources. Although much of Brazil's soil is also poor, investment in research and resources have led to dramatic improvements in productivity, much in the sphere of GM crops. Domestic demand among Brazil's population of 183 million is rising, but the country still has huge potential for export.

The coastal areas of Brazil have long been agricultural, but current growth is coming from the vast inland areas, such as the state of Mato Grosso do Sul, which are being converted to

Figure Growth in Brazil's agricultural exports

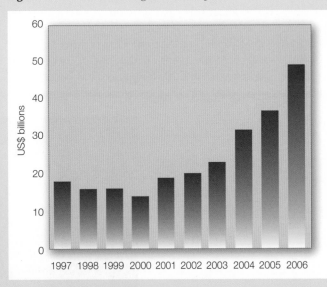

Sources: Brazilian Ministry of Agriculture (2007) 'Brazilian agricultural exports almost double in five years', 11 January, www.brazil.org.uk; Valdes, C. (2006) 'Brazil's booming agriculture faces obstacles', *Amber Waves*, **4**(5), www.ers.usda.gov

large-scale farming. Growth took off following reforms in 1999, when the government introduced incentives such as tax exemptions for farmers. It also provided financing for agricultural research and launched marketing programmes. As the figure indicates, these favourable policies produced dramatic increases in exports from 2001 onwards. Small farmers found that they could no longer compete, succumbing to large enterprises able to invest heavily. Mato Grosso's governor, himself in agribusiness, says: 'Small properties in Mato Grosso do not have viability. This has to be a scale economy, like the automotive industry. You cannot plant corn, soybeans or cotton without large properties that can be competitive on the world market. Globalisation has occurred in world farming' (Beattie, 2005). A major drawback they face is poor transport infrastructure, which adds considerably to costs, especially as distances to ports can be 1,200 miles. As infrastructure improves, they foresee greater gains in competitive advantage.

Brazil's agribusinesses have exported across the world, despite facing high tariffs in many countries, averaging 30% in the developed world. It is ranked number 1 in production and export in several commodities, as the table shows. Producers have also moved up the value chain, exporting processed products such as chicken, which carry lower import taxes in the EU. Whereas the EU imposes import taxes of 75% on raw chicken, the rate for cooked or processed chicken is only 10%. One-third of Brazil's chicken exports go to the EU, including the ubiquitous chicken tikka masala found in British supermarkets.

Brazil has become a powerful and vocal leader among developing countries, arguing for access to markets in the developed world, particularly in the WTO's Doha Round negotiations. Brazilian trade authorities have developed expertise in utilizing the WTO dispute procedure to challenge US barriers in specific commodities. They successfully brought a WTO case against the US for cotton subsidies to its farmers. Another Brazilian success was against the EU for its sugar subsidies. However, in this case, developing world interests were divided, as the sugar subsidies aided many poor ACP countries, whose producers were enjoying returns from the EU which were three times global market prices. On the other hand, the boom in clean biofuels for engines has benefited all these sugar producers. Brazil has provided Caribbean produc-

Table Brazil's position in world agriculture

Commodity	World ranking for exports	World ranking for production	Market share of global exports	Export growth rates 2000–05
Sugar	1	1	42	20
Ethanol	1	1	51	79
Coffee	1	1	26	11
Orange juice	1	1	80	4
Tobacco	1	1	29	15
Beef	1	2	24	32
Poultry	1	3	35	31
Soya beans	2	2	35	22

Source: US Department of Agriculture (2006) Foreign Agricultural Service, www.ers.usda.gov

ers with the technology to build sugar-based ethanol plants. Brazil's motives are not entirely altruistic: it can thereby export ethanol to the US via the Caribbean countries, which enjoy tariff-free access to the US.

Brazil's booming agricultural sector accounts for 30% of the country's total exports, and has contributed handsomely to the country's trade surplus, providing much-needed funds to pay off its huge debt burden. Brazil enjoys the world's largest trade surplus in agricultural products, agricultural exports accounting for two-thirds of its trade surplus of $27.5 billion in 2005. However, its agricultural superpower status is not without critics, both at home and abroad. Some Brazilian consumers complain that farmers should produce more foodstuffs for domestic consumption, rather than concentrate on commodity crops for export. There are also concerns about the environmental impact of the expansion of agricultural land. Mato Grosso is in the southern Amazon

plate 6.2 Brazil's status as an agricultural superpower owes much to its large-scale farming, such as this sugar plantation.

region, where the deforestation of the rainforest is continuing apace. US Nasa satellite images show that from 2001 to 2006, 540,000 hectares of rainforests were cleared for crops, mostly soya beans. Brazil's agribusiness association asserts that 'agribusiness is a matter of survival for Brazil', but representatives of Brazil's landless workers and small-scale farmers warn that 'their ambition is destroying nature' (Hirsch and Chu, 2005).

Sources: Valdes, C. (2006) 'Brazil's booming agriculture faces obstacles', *Amber Waves*, **4**(5), www.ers.usda.gov; Hirsch, J. and Chu, H., 'Brazil's rise as farming giant has price tag', *Los Angeles Times*, 22 August 2005; Nasa (2006) 'Expanding deforestation in Mato Grosso, Brazil', http://earthobservatory. nasa.gov; Beattie, A., 'Ethanol puts power in Brazil's tank', *Financial Times*, 16 May 2006; WTO (2006) World Trade Statistics, http://stat.wto.org; Beattie, A., 'Top of the crops: Brazil's huge heartland is yielding farms that can feed the world', *Financial Times*, 23 June 2005.

Questions

◆ What are Brazil's comparative advantages in agriculture?
◆ How is Brazil using its new status to press for liberalization in world trade?
◆ What are the concerns hanging over Brazil's future agricultural expansion?

WEB CHECK

For topics related to Brazil, see the World Bank's website at www.worldbank.org, and go to *Brazil* under *Countries*.

Business implications of recent trade developments

The benefits of multilateral agreements are both substantive and practical. In principle, they provide a harmonized set of rules which apply to trade among all trading partners, simplifying the regulatory environment for businesses and governments. International businesses of all sizes have generally favoured the liberalization of trade and a reduction in bureaucracy. By contrast, the cumulative effect of bilateralism is to produce a 'spaghetti bowl' of criss-crossing agreements. These can be particularly frustrating for international businesses. For example, a firm acquires components from three different countries, assembles a product in a fourth, and sells it in numerous markets. There could well be a dozen countries involved, with differing trading rules, depending on the nature of the goods, their source and their destination. A component may enter freely from Country A, but components from Country B may be held up because of more stringent rules. The administrative requirements, and their costs, become a growing burden. These are especially daunting for SMEs, which lack the administrative establishments of large companies, but whose growing international presence is often applauded as enlivening the competitive environment.

Many countries have opted for designated export processing zones (EPZs), which avoid the stringent and complex rules which would otherwise apply in the country. They also carry tax advantages that attract FDI. They have been key to boosting exports in China, and have been used in many other countries (see the example of Kenya in SX6.2). There are estimated to be more than 5,000 of these zones globally, employing 40 million people. Most are in manufacturing industries. While they benefit the companies which locate in these enclaves, there is debate about what benefits they offer to the country. Export zones can lead to greater liberalization in the country at large, as has happened in Ireland, but they can also be used by governments as a substitute for liberalizing their economies generally. The newer free-trade zones attempt to attract high value-added investors, often in the service sector. These investors may envisage the creation of a cluster of

Export processing zone (EPZ): Designated geographic area designed to attract export-oriented businesses through incentives such as exemption from tariffs and other trade rules which apply outside the zone.

high-tech expertise, with links to research capabilities within the country. They are able to benefit from the tax advantages and streamlined bureaucracy, but do not see themselves as fenced-off enclaves in the older mould. In this type of arrangement, the SME, in particular, is likely to find a more congenial environment.

STRATEGIC CROSSROADS

6.2

Precarious future for Kenya's export processing zones

Since 2000, Kenya's 40 EPZs have seen growing exports of textiles, bearing familiar brand names such as Lee, Wrangler and Tommy Hilfiger. EPZ enterprises have benefited from trade policies introduced in the US African Growth and Opportunity Act (Agoa) of 2000, which allowed free access to US markets for their exports until 2004, now extended to 2015. In addition, textile producers are allowed to use fabric imported from 'third parties' outside the continent. This provision initially expired in 2004, but is now extended until 2012, after which fabric must come from within the continent to benefit from Agoa. Conditions were attached to eligibility: countries had to be market-based economies; have pluralist political systems; and respect human rights, including workers' rights and the protection of children, who commonly work in the textile industry in Africa. Agoa exports are 80% oil and other fuels. The remainder are mainly textiles, Kenya being the largest producer. Kenya has benefited from this preferential status for textile exports to the US, as the larger exporters, such as China, have been restricted by import quotas under the WTO's Multifibre Agreement 1974–94, which was then replaced by the Agreement on Textiles and Clothing 1995–2005.

A hope was that Agoa would help to revitalize domestic cotton production, which had been wiped out by a lack of competitiveness in the 1990s, when global prices plummeted. Disappointingly, the cotton industry in Kenya has not revived, and the exporting firms still rely on third-country fabric, supplies of which often get held up in ports. An aim of the 2000 legislation was 'helping millions of African families find opportunities to build prosperity' (www.agoa.gov) but the reality has fallen short for the people of these sub-Saharan countries. Kenya is among the world's poorest countries, ranking 152 in the UN's Human Development Index. Over half the population live in poverty, and Kenyans have a 44% likelihood of not surviving to the age of 40. While prosperity has come to the

EPZs, it has not brought wider economic benefits, and, further, the EPZs themselves may have a precarious future.

Most of the businesses set up in Kenya's EPZs are foreign owned, mainly Indian, Sri Lankan and Bangladeshi – only 15% are locally owned. The foreign firms will stay only as long as their operations are profitable. Exports from the zones are 75% for the US, making them dependent on the US market. Kenya's cotton trouser exports to the US rose from 287,000 dozen pairs in 1998 to 3.1 million in 2004. The removal of WTO import quotas in 2005 opened the way for the large-scale producers of China and India to seize global market share. Kenyans are fearful that their textile sector will be unable to compete. The uncertainties of the investment climate had caused some owners to leave by 2005. As the figure shows, exports in 2005 fell to 20,036 million Kenyan shillings (US$280 million), or 13.1%.

In its annual report in 2005, the Kenyan Export Processing Zone Authority highlighted the problems facing textile firms, and made proposals for the future. High production costs and low productivity, largely down to weak skills and out-of-date training facilities, have damaged their competitiveness. Kenya's labour laws require that workers be given permanent jobs, while businesses argue for short-term contracts due to the cyclical

Figure Kenya EPZ exports

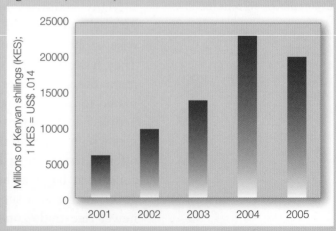

Source: Export Processing Zone Authority (2006) *Annual Report 2005*, www.epzakenya.com

nature of the industry. The authority urges reform of the labour laws, more industrial training and reform of the port procedures. In terms of strategy, it suggests that the EPZs could transform themselves into broader economic zones, including other sectors and technology parks, and it would like to see more local ownership of firms and a more favourable investment climate.

Sources: African Growth Opportunities Act (Agoa), www.agoa.gov; Export Processing Zone Authority (2006) *Annual Report 2005*, www.epzakenya.com; England, A., 'Trouble looms for Kenya as trade deal starts to unravel', *Financial Times*, 14 June 2005; BBC, 'Kenya shrinks at US textiles deadline', 4 March 2003, http://news.bbc.co.uk; UNDP (2006) *Human Development Report 2006* (Basingstoke: Palgrave Macmillan); MacDonald, S. (2006) 'The world bids farewell to the multifibre arrangement', *Amber Waves*, February, www.ers.usda.gov.

Questions

◆ Are Kenya's EPZs good examples of the benefits of EPZs? Give your reasons.
◆ What are the prospects for Kenya's EPZs in the future?

WEB CHECK

See information on Kenya on the World Bank's website at www.worldbank.org, by clicking on *Kenya* in the country list.

Regional trade and economic integration

Half or more of a country's trade is typically with other countries in its geographical region (see Figure 6.9). A major reason is the practical one that it is easier and cheaper to trade over short distances than long. Another reason is that of cultural distance (discussed in Chapter 4), in that neighbouring countries represent relatively familiar markets for businesses, in contrast to those in other continents.

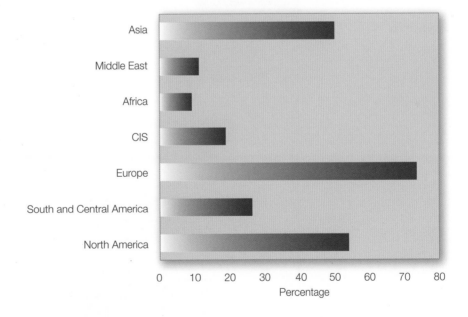

Figure 6.9 Share of intra-regional trade flows in each region's total merchandise exports, 2006
Source: WTO (2007) International Trade Statistics, www.wto.org

Regional trade agreements (RTAs): Multilateral agreements which provide for preferential trade terms between member countries.

Regional trade bloc: A group of countries within a region which aims to establish preferential arrangements for trade within the group; the bloc usually forms an organization or forum which meets regularly.

Regional trade agreements (RTAs) aim to liberalize trade within member countries in the same geographical region. The members constitute a regional trade bloc among themselves, which, while benefiting regional integration, can be seen as constituting barriers to outsiders. The WTO considers RTAs to be compatible with its multilateral approach. Much depends on member countries' visions of the purpose of the regional grouping: whether it should be limited to trade, or take in a broader integrative agenda, as the EU has done. On the other hand, as we have seen, rather narrowly focused national interests have dominated WTO negotiations, and the same perspectives are evident in regional bodies.

Regional groupings are usually categorized according to the level of economic integration they envisage, as shown in Figure 6.10. Five levels can be distinguished:

1 The *free-trade area*, whereby tariffs and other barriers are removed between member countries' trade in goods and services. Each country is responsible for its trade policies with non-member countries, as, for example, in the conclusion of bilateral agreements.
2 The *customs union*, which removes barriers to trade among member countries and also agrees common policies with respect to non-member countries.
3 The *common market*, which builds on the customs union by allowing the free movement of labour and capital among member countries, in addition to goods and services.
4 *Economic union*, which builds on the common market by introducing a common currency and common monetary and fiscal policy.
5 *Political union*, by which political processes for member countries are integrated within a political system with oversight over all member countries.

We look at each of the world's regions in turn.

Figure 6.10 Levels of regional economic integration

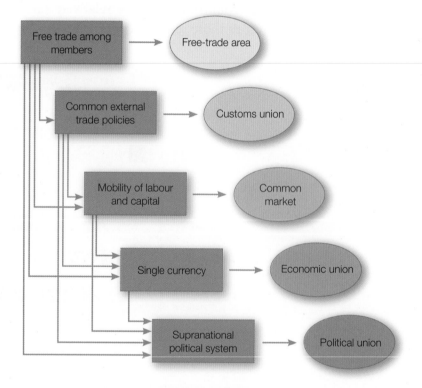

The Americas

Initiatives to liberalize trade among the countries of North and South America go back many years. Looking first at South America, although the region has a relatively high level of cultural homogeneity, efforts to deepen economic integration and build a common political identity have juddered, largely because of economic and political instability. The two major groupings have been the Andean Pact and Mercosur. The Andean Pact dates from 1969, becoming the Andean Community in 1997. Its current members are

Bolivia, Ecuador, Colombia and Peru. Chile was a founder member, but left in 1976; it has been an associate member since 2006. Other associate members are Brazil, Paraguay, Uruguay, and Venezuela, all of which are members of Mercosur. While the aim of the Andean Pact had been to establish a customs union, political instability in the 1970s set back progress, but the 1980s and 90s brought both more stable governments and renewed attempts to liberalize trade in the region.

Mercosur began life in 1988 as a free-trade pact between Argentina and Brazil, the two largest traders in South America. They were joined by Paraguay and Uruguay in 1990. While trade among member countries grew thereafter, economic instability and financial crises in Argentina and Brazil darkened prospects of forming a full customs union. A global economic upturn, especially in demand for commodities, has seen strong growth in Argentina and Brazil. These countries' trade is now mainly with other regions of the world (see Figure 6.11). Venezuela is also a strong economy globally, and the region's largest oil exporter. It joined Mercosur in 2006. Efforts to bring together Andean Community and Mercosur countries in a broad free-trade area culminated in an agreement in 2004 to create a South American Community of Nations. This initiative is stronger on broad goals than on concrete proposals, and may be seen as a response to US initiatives to construct a Free Trade Area of the Americas. A difficulty with both broad initiatives is that dominant member countries have divergent goals. Venezuela's President Chávez is less interested in free trade than in a political platform against the US, while Brazil seeks access to US markets.

The US has also pursued free trade with Central American and Caribbean countries. Following an earlier initiative, the Caribbean Basin Initiative, the US and six Caribbean countries (Costa Rica, El Salvador, Guatemala, Honduras, Nicaragua and the Dominican Republic) formed the Central American Free Trade Agreement (Cafta). In terms of trade policy, this can be described as a 'hub and spoke' pattern of trade agreement, the US forming the hub. By 2006, all the countries had ratified, but opinion is divided on whether Cafta will deliver benefits. Although industries such as textiles will benefit from access to the US market, helping these countries to compete with Chinese imports, their poor agricultural producers are vulnerable to competition from US agribusinesses. Within the US, Cafta was also controversial: businesses saw the advantages of cheap labour, but farming interests were worried that an influx of products such as sugar and rice would be detrimental.

The North American Free Trade Agreement (Nafta), dating from 1994, has been the dominant regional grouping in North America. Comprising the US, Canada and Mexico, Nafta was designed as a free-trade area, with a projected removal of

WEB CHECK

Mecosur's website is www.mercosur.int. Nafta's Secretariat, which deals with trade disputes, can be accessed at www.nafta-sec.alena.org.

Figure 6.11 Merchandise exports of Mercosur countries by destination, 2006

Source: WTO (2007) International Trade Statistics, www.wto.org

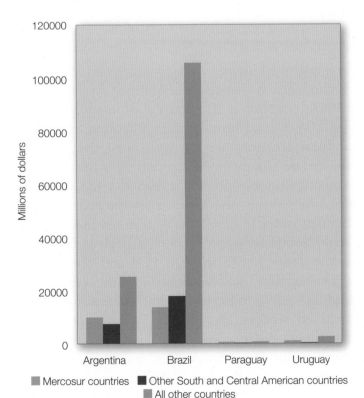

■ Mercosur countries ■ Other South and Central American countries ■ All other countries

Figure 6.12 Merchandise exports of Nafta countries by destination, 2006

Source: WTO (2007) International Trade Statistics, www.wto.org

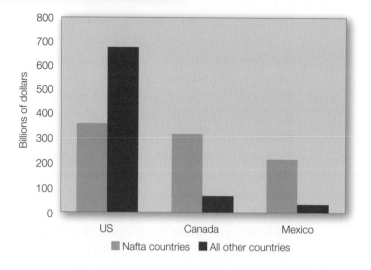

tariff barriers within 10 years, and removal of most restrictions for cross-border investment. Critics of Nafta within the US had argued that US jobs would be lost to Mexico, but US consumers stood to gain from Mexican imports. While imports from Mexico did rise, this was due in part to the trade liberalization undertaken by the Mexican government prior to 1994. Mexico has not seen the economic growth that had been expected (see CF4.2), and it has lost ground to China in exports to the US. Figure 6.12 shows the unevenness of Nafta trade flows. Canada and Mexico are heavily dependent on exports to the US, but most US exports are outside Nafta. Canada and Mexico are thus vulnerable to shifts in US trade policy and to economic downturn in the US.

Beyond Nafta

Why is the Nafta model criticized within the US and in the other member countries? What are the prospects for future regional integration of the Americas?

PAUSE TO REFLECT

Asia

Asian countries have long expressed interest in regional free-trade projects, but progress has been limited. The Association of Southeast Asian Nations (Asean) was created in 1967. It comprises 10 countries: Brunei Darussalem, Cambodia, Indonesia, Laos, Malaysia, Myanmar, the Philippines, Singapore, Thailand and Vietnam. These countries are diverse in their size, political systems and level of economic development. At one extreme is the city-state of Singapore, whose vibrant economy propels it into the top of world competitiveness rankings, while at the other extreme are the poor states of Laos and Myanmar (featured in CF14.2). Vietnam (featured in CF9.1) is catching up with the larger Southeast Asian economies, such as Indonesia and Thailand, in economic development, through FDI and outsourcing. Many play key roles in global networks, and have concluded numerous bilateral agreements with leading trading countries. In 2007, China and Asean signed a trade agreement on services liberalization, which would open Chinese markets to Southeast Asian companies in numerous sectors, including banking, IT, health, education, transport and construction.

A second group of Asian economies, the Asia-Pacific Economic Cooperation (Apec) forum, was formed in 1989. This sprawling group of 21 states and territories bordering the Pacific Ocean is not actually regional, encompassing both Asian and eastern Pacific members. Nor are all its members sovereign countries – they are referred to as 'economies'. Its members are the US, Japan, China, Hong Kong, Russia, South Korea, Thailand, Taiwan, Indonesia, the Philippines, Brunei Darussalem, Malaysia, Singapore, Papua New Guinea, Vietnam, Australia, New Zealand, Canada, Mexico, Peru and Chile. Apart from spanning a vast area, Apec's members represent 60% of global economic output, half of world trade and 2.6 billion people. Its goals have been the promotion of trade liberalization, both within Apec and with countries outside it, on a MFN basis, and co-operation on other non-trade issues through regular summits.

Apec can be described as an example of 'open regionalism', its goals more consonant with WTO's multilateralism than with bilateral agreements or more structured regional groups (Bhagwati, 2006). On the other hand, its summits are often used by members to instigate bilateral agreements. Moreover, some members wish to see Apec transformed into a regional free-trade area, the Free Trade Area of the Asia Pacific (FTAAP), eliminating barriers for members, while maintaining discrimination against non-members. Members are all part of existing regions – Asia, North America and South America – which have their own regional identities, making the notion of Apec as a region problematic. Supporters of the FTAAP see it as a 'plan B', to breathe more life into multilateral solutions following the disastrous Doha Round (Bergsten, 2006). However, the prospect of the US, China and Japan agreeing a free-trade area seems hardly more easily attainable than the Doha attempts. Critics point out that the FTAAP would seriously disadvantage non-members, particularly the EU, India and Brazil (Bhagwati, 2006), and that WTO agreement remains the best solution for world trade.

Europe

We think of the EU as the dominant regional grouping, but the European Free Trade Area (Efta), dating from 1960, is nearly as old, having been established as a free-trade area mainly for industrial goods. There are at present four member countries: Norway, Iceland, Liechtenstein and Switzerland. A number of current EU member countries, including the UK, Austria, Finland and Sweden, were members of Efta before joining the EU. Current Efta members have extensive trade links with EU countries, but have shown little enthusiasm for the deeper integration entailed in EU membership.

Despite the EU's faltering attempts to create a new constitutional framework, it remains the most integrated economically of the world's regions (see Chapters 3 and 5 for a discussion of EU institutions). For the EU 25 countries, both exports and imports are dominated by EU partners, as Figure 6.13 shows. The EU was conceived as a common market by its five founder members – Germany, France, Italy, Luxembourg and Belgium – in 1956 and was called the European Community. Even in its early years, the EU aspired to move beyond the common market to economic union and eventually political union. The aim was the free movement of people, goods, investment and services among member countries. However, progress has been uneven in all

WEB CHECK

Asean's website is www.aseansec.com. Apec's website is www.apec.org.

TO RECAP...

Asian regional integration

Asean is closer to being a regional bloc than Apec. Both have been slow to develop free-trade areas. Asean agreement with China, the regional superpower, for a possible China–Asean free-trade area would strengthen regional ties, although Asian countries have also evolved numerous bilateral agreements with their main trading partners in other regions.

WEB CHECK

The EU's website is http://europa.eu.

Figure 6.13 EU trade among member states and with major non-EU trading partners, 2006
Source: WTO (2007) International Trade Statistics, www.wto.org

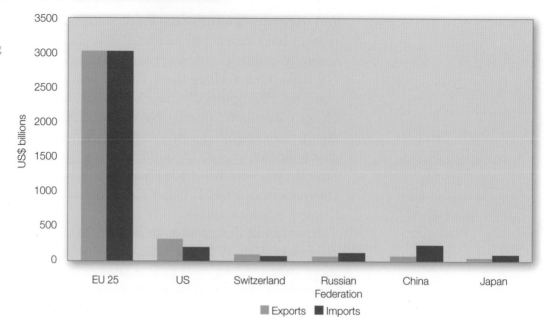

y-axis: US$ billions

Categories: EU 25, US, Switzerland, Russian Federation, China, Japan

■ Exports ■ Imports

these areas, as earlier chapters have highlighted. There are still limitations on the movement of people and financial services in particular. Measures to press ahead with economic union were contained in the Maastricht Treaty of 1991, which created the European Union. This treaty paved the way for the adoption of a common currency, the euro, and common monetary policy. The result was the establishment of the eurozone, now numbering 15 countries (see Figure 1.12).

The use of the euro and the opening of cross-border trade and investment have greatly enhanced the ability of businesses in one member country to expand into other EU countries, both in terms of markets and production. The single currency has removed the complexities and costs of exchange transactions, making it relatively simple to do business routinely in other EU countries. On the other hand, as we have seen in Chapter 3, the economies of these countries remain divergent, despite the EU Commission's continued pressing for the opening of markets to competition from other member states. There has been consolidation among firms in sectors such as banking and utilities. Nonetheless, in some countries, there remains considerable resistance to takeovers and mergers instigated by firms on other member countries. For example, the proposed merger of Italy's Autostrade with Spain's Abertis, the two largest highway companies in Europe, failed to go ahead in 2006, largely because it was blocked by the Italian government. By contrast, British Airports Authority, which runs seven airports in the UK, was taken over by the Spanish construction company, Ferrovial. In the UK's more liberal market environment, this takeover did not raise the political temperature to the degree that an equivalent takeover might have generated elsewhere in the EU.

The political aims of the Maastricht Treaty were to create an EU-wide government and parliament similar to national legislatures. It was envisaged that EU citizenship would eventually supersede national citizenship. As explained in Chapter 5, these aims have rather stalled, as has further enlargement beyond the current 27 member countries.

European economic integration
In which respects has regional integration progressed significantly, bringing benefits to EU citizens? In which respects has integration been weak, and why?

PAUSE TO REFLECT

TO RECAP...

European integration
The EU is the most economically integrated of the world's regions, most members' trade dominated by trade with other member states. Free movement of services, labour and capital remain subject to limitations, and member governments often take a national, rather than EU-wide, perspective on further integration and enlargement.

Africa

African countries are becoming more integrated in global trade, contributing to greater economic growth in many. However, economic instability and political conflicts have combined to create insecurities within many nations, which have hampered regional developments. The African Economic Community (AEC) is an umbrella organization of 53 states, designed to foster collaborative regional groupings. Of the latter, several can be highlighted, as shown in Table 6.1. The Common Market for Eastern and Southern Africa (Comesa) was formed in 1994. It comprises 20 members, of whom 13 have formed a free-trade area. The East African Community (EAC), formed in 2001, has progressed from a free-trade area to a customs union. The Economic Community of West African States (Ecowas) is also a customs union. In southern Africa, two groupings can be highlighted. The oldest, the Southern African Customs Union (SACU), has evolved since the colonial era, its members now sovereign states. The Southern African Development Community (SADC) is a broadly based inter-governmental organization aiming to foster development in its many dimensions, including trade and investment. As Table 6.1 shows, there is overlapping membership among these groupings, and much of the impetus behind them comes from the desire for governmental co-operation on pan-African issues, rather than a specific focus on trade.

Comesa's website is www.comesa.int.

WEB CHECK

Table 6.1 African regional groupings

Name	Year of formation	Members	Status
Common Market for Eastern and Southern Africa (Comesa) – 20 members	1994	Angola, Burundi, Comoros, Democratic Republic of Congo, Djibouti, Egypt, Eritrea, Ethiopia, Kenya, Kenya, Madagascar, Malawi, Mauritius, Rwanda, Seychelles, Sudan, Swaziland, Uganda, Zambia, Zimbabwe	Inter-governmental organization
Comesa Free Trade Area – 13 members	2000	Djibouti, Egypt, Kenya, Madagascar, Malawi, Mauritius, Sudan, Zambia, Zimbabwe, Rwanda, Burundi, Libya, Comoros	Free-trade area
Economic Community of West African States (Ecowas) – 15 members	1975	Benin, Burkina Faso, Cote d'Ivoire, Gambia, Ghana, Guinea, Guinea Bissau, Liberia, Mali, Niger, Nigeria, Senegal, Sierra Leone, Togo, Cape Verde	Customs union
South African Customs Union (SACU) – 5 members	1910	South Africa, Botswana, Lesotho, Swaziland, Namibia	Customs union
South African Development Community (SADC) – 14 members	1980	Angola, Botswana, Lesotho, Malawi, Mozambique, Swaziland, Tanzania, Zambia, Zimbabwe, Namibia, South Africa, Mauritius, Democratic Republic of Congo, Madagascar	Inter-governmental organization
East African Community (EAC) – 4 members	2001	Kenya, Tanzania, Uganda, Rwanda, Burundi	Customs union

African countries' exports are directed mainly towards Europe, rather than other African countries. Europe's share stood at 43% in 2005, as Figure 6.14 indicates, which represents a fall from over 50% in 2001. Exports to North America and Asia have grown, particularly trade with China, as featured in SX6.1. African trade is dominated by fuels and mining products, which are subject to price volatility. Rising prices in 2005 benefited the oil-rich countries of Nigeria and the Republic of Congo, while the poor countries of sub-Saharan Africa, dependent on agriculture, had looked to the Doha Round to provide greater access to markets in the rich countries. In the absence of either strong intra-regional blocs or multilateral agreements, bilateral agreements are proliferating.

TO RECAP...

Fragmented regional trade initiatives in Africa

The continent of Africa has seen a host of efforts to establish regional trade blocs, but most have faltered, undermined by political and economic instability. The oil-rich countries contrast with the poor countries of sub-Saharan Africa, which are dependent on agriculture. For both, bilateral agreements with trading partners outside the continent are offering hope of advantageous trade deals which can translate into economic growth.

Figure 6.14 Africa's regional exports by region, 2006
Source: WTO (2007) International Trade Statistics, www.wto.org

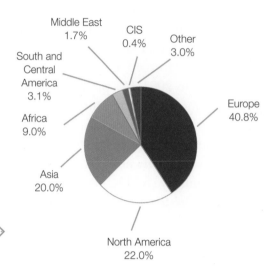

Conclusions

☐ Trade is at the heart of international business. Thanks to growing production capacity and improved communications and transport, businesses of all sizes can export and import goods and services. As firms benefit from wider markets, so consumers have also benefited from the growth in trade, bringing them greater choice and lower prices. The dominance of the triad, consisting of the US, Europe and Japan, has given way to the rise of developing countries in world trade. Despite applauding the benefits of free trade in theory, governments are wary of its impacts on their national economies and societies. Where domestic producers may struggle to compete with imported products, governments tend to adopt protectionist approaches, subsidizing the domestic industry and putting up barriers to imports. Such measures, as this chapter has shown, offer only short-term palliatives, doing little to tackle the underlying structural issues of industries failing to compete globally.

☐ Freer trade has been the objective of the WTO, taking up the principles of multilateral liberalization introduced by GATT. Although much progress has been made in reducing tariff barriers, some 'hard cases' remain, notably agricultural products, as the disappointments of the Doha Round testify. These difficulties need not spell the end of multilateralism, but they do indicate that it is rather optimistic to expect a WTO of 150 members to reach agreement on trade issues crucial to national economies. Many countries are looking closer to home, to regional groupings, to achieve liberalized trade and economic integration, but even within regions, diverse interests and political divisions emerge. The growth in bilateral trade agreements is perhaps testimony to the frailties of multilateralism. However, the spaghetti bowl of agreements poses obstacles for businesses, which seek consistency and clarity for multi-locational operations.

Trade liberalization: the wider picture

National governments tend to pursue trade policies from the narrow perspective of perceived national interests, which generates a rather protectionist approach. Choose a country you are familiar with, and make a case to the government in favour of trade liberalization which would ultimately promote national interests more effectively than protectionist policies.

PAUSE TO REFLECT

Review questions

Part A: Grasping the basic concepts and knowledge

1. What factors influence the growth of trade in a national economy?
2. Which countries form the 'triad' of trading blocs, and why have they dominated world trade?
3. What new patterns of global trade are emerging, and why?
4. What contribution to world trade is made by the least developed countries?

5. Outline the theory of comparative advantage in international trade.

6. How does factor endowment theory extend the theory of comparative advantage?

7. In what ways does product life cycle theory help to explain both FDI and international trade?

8. What contribution has new trade theory made to our understanding of recent trends in the global economy?

9. Explain what is meant by first-mover advantages.

10. What are the four aspects of Porter's 'diamond' model which determine national competitive advantage?

11. What is the role of governments in Porter's model?

12. What criteria are used to measure national competitiveness in the major indexes?

13. What aspects of national interest influence government trade policy?

14. What is the purpose of import tariffs and import quotas?

15. Why is the voluntary export restraint (VER) considered to be a rather blunt trade instrument?

16. What are the aims of subsidies for domestic producers, such as farmers?

17. Explain the aims of multilateral agreements to liberalize world trade. What is the role of the WTO in negotiating these agreements?

18. Assess the role of the WTO's dispute resolution procedure in resolving differences between countries over trade issues.

19. The growth in bilateral agreements has been a growing feature of world trade. How can this growth be explained, and what are the implications for international businesses?

20. What role do regional trade blocs play in international trade?

Part B: Critical thinking and discussion

1. Assess the trends now occurring in the pattern of world trade, which is seeing the developing and emerging economies, including the resource-rich countries, become more prominent. What are the implications for international business?

2. To what extent does Porter's 'diamond' model help to explain the developments currently taking place in world trade?

3. Why did the Doha Round of trade talks prove to be disappointing in achieving its aims? Assess the prospects for future multilateral trade agreements.

4. Compare Nafta with the EU in terms of trade, economic integration and political aims.

5. Assess the factors affecting further regional initiatives in Latin America. What are the prospects for further regional trade areas among these countries?

Case study 6.2: Piecemeal liberalization of world trade in textiles and clothing

Textiles and clothing as a sector features in countries all over the world. Besides its economic role, it has a significant cultural dimension in societies, making the sector a sensitive one for government trade policies. Unlike other types of manufacturing, wages are a greater proportion of costs than raw materials, making this industry a popular choice among developing countries in the early stages of industrialization. Many move up the value chain as they become more prosperous, but most countries retain textile and clothing manufacturing industries, even though the costs in the richer countries make them less competitive than poorer counterparts. Japan was a major exporter in the 1960s during its development phase, but it now imports almost all its clothing. China has become a powerhouse in the industry globally, its 22,000 firms employing 19 million people. Still, there are an estimated 2.7 million employees in the industry in richer countries, making this a politically sensitive industry in terms of employment, especially as the work is low skilled and often in areas with few other employment opportunities. American and European governments have long feared that floods of cheap clothing from Asia would undermine their own industries. From the 1960s onwards, therefore, developing countries targeting markets in the advanced economies have been subject to export restrictions, including import quotas and tariffs.

Globalization in clothing manufacture has seen the rich countries' MNEs, notably major brand owners and large clothing retailers, source products from low-cost economies. Costs have been reduced and consumers have reaped the benefits of cheaper imported clothes. As the US and Europe saw domestic industries struggling against imports from Asia, quota restrictions on developing country imports were set in the Multifibre Arrangement 1974–94. The result was that large producers such as China and India were limited by quotas, while smaller countries benefited, as producers sought new locations with unfilled quotas. These included Southeast Asian countries, as well as ACP countries. Firm strategy was thus dictated by the quota regime.

In the 1990s, the trend towards multilateral liberalization through the Uruguay Round included the Agreement on Textiles and Clothing (ATC) 1995–2004, which planned to end the quota system from 1 January 2005. Liberalization was meant to occur in four stages over the 10 years, to allow time for adjustments, but, in practice, quota removal was 'back loaded': 80% of the quotas for US imports remained in place until 2004. Despite this protection, US textile employment declined steadily over the 10 years, largely because firms shifted production to other locations which had preferential agreements with the US, including Mexico, which benefited from Nafta, and the Caribbean countries which were members of the Caribbean Basin Initiative (the predecessor of Cafta). As Figure 1 shows, imports into the US rose generally, benefiting consumers as prices fell. The quota system thus failed to halt the decline of uncompetitive domestic industries.

With the end of quotas in sight, low-cost Chinese producers could potentially step up exports. Western consumers anticipated more falling prices, but celebrations among Chinese producers were muted, as they knew that an import surge would be unwelcome by Western governments. China had itself taken steps to limit such a surge by imposing an export tax on its producers, but this was so low as to be of little effect. More significant was a term in China's WTO entry agreement of 2001, which allowed WTO members to impose emergency 'safeguards' against Chinese imports until 2008. The measures could be imposed before any surge actually materialized.

plate 6.3 For these textile workers in Africa, investment has brought jobs, but they are vulnerable to global competition.

By May 2005, it became clear that Chinese imports were soaring. Both the US and EU responded by imposing restrictions on China, including VERs expressed as quotas. By this time, shipments of Chinese clothing were being held up in European ports, as the new quotas had already been reached or exceeded in many categories. Some 9.8 million pullovers and 3.8 million pairs of trousers were stuck in ports, in excess of quota. Facing angry retailers whose orders had been blocked, the EU trade commissioner negotiated compromise agreements to unblock the ports, partly by using some of the 2007 quota.

Chinese producers were understandably disappointed with the protectionist 'backlash' in their main markets. Nonetheless, in 2006, Chinese imports grew in both markets (see Figure 2). Other Asian producers, such as India, Bangladesh, Indonesia and

Vietnam, however, have seen bigger increases. Partly, this represents Chinese firms shifting production to these other countries. The East Asian and sub-Saharan African countries lost position in the US market, but recouped sales in the EU. Similarly, Cafta, Bulgarian and Turkish exporters increased European exports.

Post-ATC restructuring has taken place in the context of continuing restrictions. Will liberalization proceed rapidly after

Figure 1 Clothing prices and imports to the US, 1991–2004

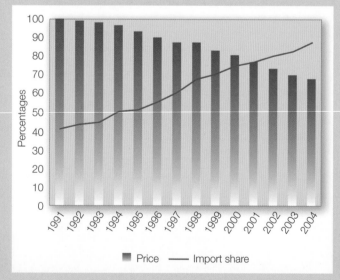

Price   —— Import share

Note: Price in 1990 = 100

Source: MacDonald, S. (2006) 'The world bids farewell to the multifibre arrangement', *Amber Waves*, February, www.ers.usda.gov

Figure 2 Imports of textiles and clothing into the US and EU, by country of origin, 2006

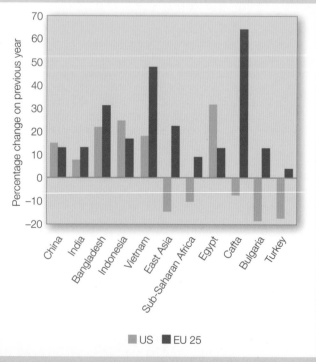

US   EU 25

Note: East Asia includes Taiwan, Hong Kong, South Korea and Macao

Source: WTO (2007) *World Trade Report 2007*, www.wto.org

2008? Even if import quotas are phased out, governments can turn to other tools of trade policy. Importing countries can continue to use WTO anti-dumping rules against China. Tariffs remain in place, clothing and textiles subject to tariffs several times higher than the 4% global average on manufactured goods. Meanwhile, the industry is evolving globally. Costs are rising in China, leading some MNEs to seek lower cost locations such as Vietnam. Many of the developing countries which benefited under the old quota system are gaining indirectly in the post-ATC era. However, they, too, are subject to global competitive pressures. The most efficient producers are increasingly turning to new technology which reduces production and distribution costs. Electronic data exchange allows retailers and manufacturers to liaise to reduce inventory costs. China is at the forefront of these developments. Notably, it achieved a 15% growth in exports to the US in 2006 (see Figure 2). These advantages have been seized by increasingly global retailers, while the rise in discount retailing in most countries confirms the importance of price sensitivities in consumer markets. Governments facing protectionist sentiment in their economies could find it is becoming more difficult to use the rather blunt instrument of managed trade policy to distort markets.

Questions

1 What protectionist barriers are common in textiles and clothing; what purposes do they serve?
2 The Agreement on Textiles and Clothing 1995–2004 was intended to liberalize world trade. To what extent has it succeeded?
3 In your view, how effective have protectionist measures been in keeping out low-cost imported clothes in rich countries?
4 Summarize the position of each of the following in relation to this case study:
   ◆ a sewing machine worker in a sub-Saharan African country
   ◆ a consumer in an EU country
   ◆ a shareholder in Wal-Mart

Sources: MacDonald, S. (2006), 'The world bids farewell to the multifibre arrangement', *Amber Waves*, February, www.ers.usda.gov; European Commission (2005) Evolution of EU textile imports from China 2004–2005, http://ec.europa.eu/trade; Harney, A., Minder, R. and Thornhill, J., 'EU warns on China exports', *Financial Times*, 27 April 2005; Minder, R., 'EU-China textiles deal comes apart at the seams', *Financial Times*, 17 August 2005; Buck, T., 'How EU textile quotas became a Chinese puzzle', *Financial Times*, 14 August 2005; De Jonquières, G., 'Lessons from the China textiles stitch-up', *Financial Times*, 30 August 2005; WTO (2007) *World Trade Report 2007*, www.wto.org.

Further research

Journal articles

Kutan, A. and Vukšić, G. (2007) 'Foreign direct investment and export performance: Empirical evidence', *Comparative Economic Studies*, **49**(3): 430–45.

Petit, P. (2006) 'Globalisation and regional integration: A comparative analysis of Europe and East Asia', *Competition & Change*, **10**(2): 113–40.

Snowdon, B. and Stonehouse, G. (2006) 'Competitiveness in a globalised world: Michael Porter on the microeconomic foundations of the competitiveness of nations, regions, and firms', *Journal of International Business Studies*, **37**(2): 163–75.

Books

Bliss, C. (2007) *Trade, Growth and Inequality*, Oxford: Oxford University Press.

Krugman, P. and Obstfeld, M. (2006) *International Economics: Theory and Policy*, 7th edn, London: Pearson.

Rivera-Batiz, L. and Oliva, M.-A. (2004) *International Trade: Theory, Strategies and Evidence*, Oxford: Oxford University Press.

Don't forget to check the companion website at **www.palgrave.com/business/morrisonib**, where you will find web-based assignments, web links, interactive quizzes, an extended glossary and lots more to help you learn about international business.

chapter 7
STRATEGY AND ORGANIZATIONS

learning objectives

▷ To examine alternative international strategies for entering new markets and choosing locations for production
▷ To identify and assess contrasting approaches to strategy formation, taking in analysis of the external competitive environment, as well as analysis of a firm's internal resources
▷ To compare differing organizational structures among MNEs, focusing on how they have evolved to adapt to the changing environment
▷ To assess the impact of national environment on the structure and behaviour of firms and networks

Introduction

Starlinger Group, an Austrian SME, is one of the thousands of 'hidden champions' of international business across the globe. A private family company based in Vienna, it is a market leader in machinery used to make woven sacks for all manner of goods, from cement to coffee beans and spices. In its 40 years of exporting, its business has grown, mirroring the growth in global markets. Almost all its machinery production goes abroad, from Brazil to Saudi Arabia. Starlinger has become a leading innovator in the sector, including new processes for recycling plastics. Its president and CEO, both women, have maintained the firm's traditional strategy of growing by acquisition. The parent company and four subsidiary companies have established offices in the US, China, Russia, India and Malaysia. These are not among Austria's traditional trading partners, and although these markets proved challenging to establish, their importance globally has justified the effort in the eyes of Starlinger's CEO, Anhelika Huemer. Her success is a story of globalization and entrepreneurship in the context of a family business, giving an indication of the diversity of today's internationalizing firms.

WEB CHECK

Starlinger's website is www.starlinger.com.

The organization which decides to spread its wings and expand internationally is undertaking a more formidable task than simply replicating an existing national strategy and enlarging its existing structure. It is aiming to succeed in unfamiliar environments with different attitudes and values, and different approaches to work and corporate life. The decision to internationalize, however, need not nowadays be a leap into the unknown. Much experience and research have shed light on the pitfalls and advantages of different environments, and on the types of organization and strategy suited to different corporate goals. This chapter aims to set out the range of strategies and organizational approaches, assessing their practical implications for firms. A theme will be changing approaches to respond to changing environments.

The chapter begins with a survey of entry strategies and the differing contexts in which they are appropriate. These options are then explored in a section on location decision-making. Large MNEs from Western countries have been at the forefront of internationalization, but SMEs are also thinking globally in increasing numbers. In addition, we now see MNEs from the developing world, particularly China and India, which are growing in confidence and strength, competing in global markets. Both internal and external factors influence strategy, and we consider key theories of competitive advantage, including Porter's five forces model, the resource-based theory of the firm and the theory based on core competencies.

Designing and adapting organizational needs to fit strategic opportunities and challenges are then considered. Organizations have evolved a number of structures designed to accommodate and foster international operations. As globalized production has become more competitive, firms have adapted through an array of networking arrangements, moving in harmony with changing strategies.

Internationalization strategy

Internationalization offers a greater variety of strategic options to the firm than are available in its home environment. There is no single best internationalization strategy. Success depends heavily on the suitability of a strategy to:

- the specific firm, given its heritage and culture
- the type of industry it is in
- the institutional and cultural environment in the foreign setting which it chooses to target.

The firm must also find a 'fit' between organizational and strategic elements. In this section, we look at how the choice of strategy is made by firms in different contexts.

Entry strategies

Entry strategies are shown in Figure 7.1 as they might be encountered by an individual firm, beginning with the decision to export, which arises mainly for manufacturing firms wishing to explore markets abroad. Traditionally, the manufacturing firm which seeks new markets begins by exporting its products to selected countries. This step involves a minimum commitment in the initial phase. No organizational presence in the foreign location is necessary, no ownership of foreign assets is involved, and there are hardly any implications for the home organization, except to set up an export department. It may use an agent in the foreign location and, if sales are healthy, it might establish a sales and marketing office there, as in the example of Starlinger in the opening vignette (see further discussion in Chapter 8 on international marketing). The firm might decide not to venture beyond this arrangement, or it may decide to set up production near to the export market, which will save on the costs of transport and distribution. German investment in the US in the closing years of the twentieth century took place only after years of operating sales and marketing subsidiaries had provided companies with the considerable knowledge of US markets (Whitley, 2001: 47).

More recently, the decision as to where to produce has been heavily influenced by the benefits of low-cost locations, from which products are transported to all the firm's markets. If its products are mass-produced goods, FDI or outsourcing in a developing or transitional economy are advantageous. These strategies involve a higher degree of interaction in the foreign location than export. Methods of internationalizing production are described in Chapter 2, where Figure 2.2 depicts the options in terms of degrees of

Figure 7.1 Internationalization strategies

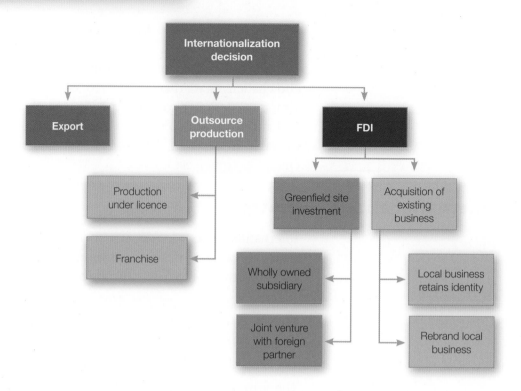

internationalization and ownership. In this chapter, we assess the organizational and strategic implications of these alternatives for particular firms and industries.

For retailers and consumer service providers, such as fast-food outlets, the franchise may be a preferred option. (See Chapter 1 and SX1.1 on McDonald's.) McDonald's operates both franchises and company-owned outlets. Whereas US outlets are overwhelmingly franchise operations, a large proportion of the foreign outlets are owned and managed by the company. Ownership gives the parent company more direct control of operations, judged to be appropriate in unfamiliar and uncertain environments.

Production in a foreign location may be carried out through an outsourcing arrangement, whereby an independent company is responsible for operations. The manufacture of mass-market consumer goods in developing countries is evidence of the popularity of this choice, especially among brand owners and retailers in the advanced economies. The manufacturing of many types of goods, as diverse as medicines and machinery, involves a licence to manufacture products subject to patent and other intellectual property (IP) protection, known as production under licence. The advantages of outsourcing are cost reductions and the relative ease with which operations can be shifted to another location. The home organization is distanced from these operations, its managers maintaining only an oversight role. Although this can be viewed as an advantage, in practice, it may become a risk in locations with weak regulatory frameworks. If there are problems such as product quality or working conditions, the brand owner may well find itself held responsible in the eyes of consumers, although the local company is legally responsible. Licensing firm-specific technology may also present a risk in countries where legal safeguards are weak.

For many companies, the flexibility, minimal commitment and major cost savings of outsourcing outweigh the risks of uncertain environments. Global

Production under licence: Process whereby the production of goods subject to patent, brand or other intellectual property rights is contracted out to another firm under terms agreed with the owner of the rights.

companies which like to control foreign operations in much the same way as those in the home country may be uneasy with this option. Similarly, highly paternalistic companies from home environments with weak institutional frameworks may wish to have greater control over foreign operations, for example by FDI through pre-existing personal ties. Companies from collaborative environments (see Whitley's classification in the later section on national variations) may not find outsourcing an attractive option, as the types of co-operative ties that underlie their corporate cultures are lacking, and the institutional environment, which would to some extent compensate, is weaker in developing countries.

FDI motives and strategies

The motives for FDI fall into four broad categories:

- *Market-related motives* – proximity to markets, actual and potential, is a powerful 'pull' factor for MNEs. This is especially true in sectors such as motor vehicles, where manufacturing involves large heavy products and transport costs and delivery times are important considerations. Many companies enter new markets by exporting, and barriers to exports are another spur to set up FDI operations close to markets. For firms well established in their home markets, there might be little scope for further growth at home, which creates a 'push' factor towards seeking markets abroad.

- *Production-related motives* – shifting production to locations where scale economies are attainable enhances efficiency. A country may have comparative advantage in low-cost labour, which brings scale economies in manufacturing of products for mass markets. It is also possible that a particular location offers technological capacities which attract investors. The investing firm often seeks network linkages which offer access to capabilities which it lacks or which complement its own capacities (Chen and Chen, 1998).

- *Resource-related motives* – seeking proximity to resources or raw materials is a traditional motive for FDI. This is associated with the internalization advantages noted by Dunning in the OLI paradigm (see Chapter 2). An example is the acquisition of plantations by Unilever, to supply raw materials, rather than to purchase them through markets.

- *Control of specific strategic assets* – this leads companies to acquire businesses, brands or other assets. They may seek to do so in markets in which competitors are already established, or where there is scope for growth which is not being exploited by local firms.

Firms seeking to internationalize through FDI can choose from a number of options, including greenfield investment, acquisition and joint venture (see Figure 7.1). The greenfield investment may take the form of a wholly owned subsidiary or a joint venture involving an equity stake. Benefits of the wholly owned subsidiary are control over operations and ownership of assets, including intellectual property rights (IPR) such as patents. In environments where arm's-length relations prevail, foreign investors are assured that, in theory, the legal environment is stable and predictable. In countries where property protection and legal institutions are weak, the paternalistic company which keeps tight personal control is likely to be prevalent among local businesses. Companies with similar management and background will be more comfortable with the weak regulation than those from countries with strong institutional and regulatory systems (Luo, 2003). FDI by Chinese companies in Africa is an example. However, many paternalistic firms will thrive only if the cultural environment supporting personal relations is similar to their home culture. Hence, a large proportion of FDI in Asia is from other Asian countries.

Companies which rely on management systems rather than co-operative personal relations may find that, in unfamiliar environments, it is preferable to enter via a joint venture, in which control can be exerted directly over the joint venture partner. CS7.2 describes how Nissan entered China in this way. The local partner is more knowledgeable about the local administrative environment and is able to guide a path through the local bureaucracy. A risk with the joint venture, however, is that the business partners must share a common strategy and mutual trust, without which the enterprise will falter. For joint ventures between Western companies and partners in developing countries, it is common for management decision-making to be entirely in the more experienced hands of the Western managers.

In recent years, large MNEs have shown a preference for acquisition of an existing business as an entry strategy. Retailers have preferred this option, which gives the investor an immediate market presence. The acquired company is a functioning business whose day-to-day operations may be little affected by the change of ownership. Centralized companies in market economies, such as the US, look at the investment as generating wealth for the parent company. They share no strategic decision-making with subsidiaries, whose managers' roles are confined to operations. Traditionally, they build few obligational ties in the local community, although this approach is now evolving (see later section on national variations among firms). Companies from environments where personal and societal relations are important take a broader view of FDI and its implications for the parent company. These companies will look for fit between their cultures and that of the acquired company, without which intra-organizational networks cannot thrive. This is the reason why European companies in the twentieth century concentrated their foreign investments in other European countries.

MNEs from transitional and developing countries are increasingly active in outward FDI. They are also playing increasing roles in global acquisition activity, suggesting that these organizations are becoming more market-oriented in strategy (Luo, 2003). The examples of outwardly focused entrepreneurial companies in CF7.1 on Poland highlights that these emerging MNEs are often well placed to manage the uncertainties that arise in weakly regulated environments similar to their own home countries. Research suggests that emerging MNEs focus on markets in their location choices for FDI (UN, 2006). SX7.1 on Weg Electric of Brazil describes how an emerging MNE from a developing country is seeking advantages offered by specific overseas locations.

TO RECAP...

FDI alternatives

Greenfield investment offers opportunities for dominant control of foreign operations, and also direct interaction with local stakeholders. Companies not aspiring to this level of engagement may opt for acquiring a foreign company, which will provide immediate market share, and whose local management can continue to take operational responsibility.

Choosing location

Locations differ in their business environments and their receptiveness to transborder businesses. The business environment comprises several dimensions, all of which impact on location decision-making of prospective firms. Figure 7.2 presents the major variables which come into consideration. The environmental dimensions featured in the top four boxes form what is known as a PEST analysis: political and legal, economic, sociocultural and technological elements. The PEST framework, however, needs to be supplemented by other aspects of the host environment which are relevant to the type of activity contemplated by the potential entrant. These are production potential and market characteristics, shown in the lower two boxes.

PEST analysis: Analysis of the political, economic, sociocultural and technological dimensions of a country, which is carried out by firms considering international expansion.

The firm seeking export markets only is mainly interested in the numbers and characteristics of potential consumers. The outsourcer is more interested in production potential and costs, as is the foreign direct investor. As FDI involves significant commitment and interaction in the location, these investors are interested in a broader range of environmental dimensions. The economic environment indicates the direction of the country in terms of economic development. These indicators also show how quickly relevant consumer markets are growing. Recall CS4.2 on DIY in China, in which a crucial element in B&Q's expansion strategy is the rising middle class. Many Western companies look to the rise in middle-class incomes in new markets (a topic considered further in Chapter 8). In most retail sectors, however, local businesses are already active and benefit from first-hand knowledge of local markets. The foreign business derives competitive advantage from its brand, systems and superior products, but may find it difficult to compete on price.

Production decisions focus on operational costs, availability of resources and numbers of skilled workers. The degree of political stability and legal protection afforded to contracts and property are important. Where the judicial system lacks independence or is very slow, the implications for

plate 7.1 Proximity to steel production, such as this foundry which supplies vital inputs, is a factor in deciding on location in many manufacturing industries.

Figure 7.2 Location decision

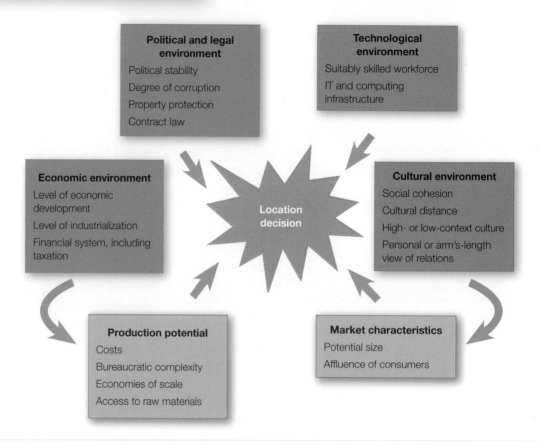

foreign investors are discouraging. Levels of bureaucratic complexity, known as 'red tape', and corruption are deterrents to much transborder business. For the company licensing the manufacture of its patented product, the protection of IP is paramount. For these companies, however, the existence of property laws may be worth little if they are only weakly enforced.

Many companies score locations on each of these dimensions, for comparative purposes. Although much data are available on some dimensions, such as the economy, countries measure data in different ways, so, even in quantitative terms, it is difficult to do exact comparisons. Other dimensions are more qualitative and more difficult to assess. Giving a country a score for social cohesion, for example, is problematic, as scoring is a rather crude instrument. Descriptive assessments in each of the dimensions give a more finely textured picture, which can aid decision-makers. Foreign direct investors are looking for a return on their investment, and must attempt to assess how locations will change in the future. While developing countries currently attract the interest of all types of foreign investor, they score poorly in many of the environmental dimensions. However, for production, they offer cost reductions which outweigh uncertainties in the political and legal spheres. For markets, emerging economies offer the largest potential growth. Investing companies are hoping that their governments are making progress in institution building as their market economies mature.

TO RECAP...

Choosing locations

A firm considering potential locations for production focuses on factors such as costs, access to resources and levels of bureaucracy. Key dimensions of the broader business environment come into play, including sociocultural factors, economic environment and political risk. These dimensions are also considered by the firm looking for new markets, as a growing economy indicates healthy demand conditions.

COUNTRY FOCUS 7.1 – POLAND

Contrasts and contradictions in Poland's business environment

As the largest of the EU accession states of 2004, Poland represents a host of opportunities for business activities at all levels. Since its emergence from communist rule in 1990, Poland has become a popular location for foreign investors, attracted by its skilled workers and wage levels only a fifth of Western European rates. Many domestic firms have also blossomed, creating jobs and meeting growing demand in consumer markets. Democratic government, combined with economic reforms and privatizations of state-owned enterprises, helped to build a stable market-oriented economy which gives businesses the confidence they seek for future growth. However, progress towards liberalization has faltered, political instability has crept in and some of Poland's endemic problems, such as cumbersome bureaucracy, have cast shadows over the business environment. A divide has emerged between the businesses and regions which have prospered and those which have not. Tensions within Polish society are reflected by tensions in the political environment, in which conservative and nationalist sentiment weighs heavily against continued momentum of the market reform processes which preceded EU accession.

Reforms pursued by Poland in the 1990s encouraged business investment by reducing red tape and lessening the regulatory burden. One successful Polish company, PKM Duda, was created in 1990 by a family of farmers who transformed themselves into entrepreneurs in the wave of start-ups which was ignited by the fall of communism. Many have successfully internationalized, as the rise in outward FDI from Poland shows (see the figure). Duda grew from a start-up to become Poland's largest meat producer, with exports around the world. As the company grew, the family gradually relinquished

Figure Poland's FDI: inflows and outflows

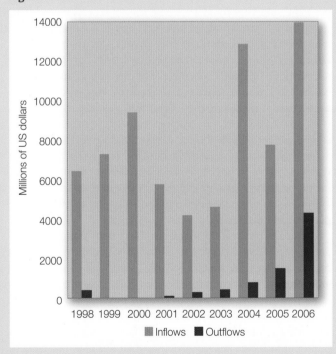

Sources: UN, *World Investment Reports 2004, 2005* and *2006* (Geneva: UN)

management control to outside professional managers, but, when Duda was listed on the Polish stock exchange in 2002, the family retained a 30% stake. Duda now has 20 subsidiaries, and is investing in Ukraine. Duda's CEO says that today Ukraine resembles Poland in the mid-1990s, growing fast and undergoing changes, but still outside the EU. Polish entrepreneurs feel they have an advantage in Ukraine because of their own similar experience. They understand the post-communist business culture, and often they can communicate without interpreters. The CEO of another Polish company, Atlas, which makes mortars and building chemicals, had a similar experience in Russia. It established a strong position in the local market and began exporting to Russia. Its CEO says: 'Our exports grew and our sales grew, and the next natural step was to invest there and to build a factory' (Anderson and Condon, 2006). He says that understanding how bureaucracy works helped in Russia: 'We understood things because we had gone through similar problems in Poland' (Anderson and Condon, 2006).

Bureaucratic and regulatory burdens remain major hurdles in Poland. In addition, economic reforms have faltered since 2000, as Polish governments have veered towards nationalist and populist policies. Political instability deepened with a series of shaky coalition governments. In the elections of 2005, no clear winning party emerged, and three governments came and went in quick succession. A coalition of conservative and nationalist parties led by the Law and Justice Party was formed in 2006. The prime minister, whose twin brother holds the office of president, seemed to take greater interest in purging the country of former communists than addressing economic and social issues. Public support soon waned, and elections in 2007 brought in a new prime minister, Donald Tusk of the liberal Civic Platform Party, which pledged renewed emphasis on economic growth. However, the conservative parties remain powerful, and Tusk must work with the conservative president.

With GDP growth at around 5.5% and FDI flowing in, the new government is confident that Poland is on the right track. Poland's level of unemployment is down from 20% to 15%, but remains one of Europe's highest. The pressure is eased largely because of the migration of workers to Western European destinations. However, their departure has left many industries, particularly the construction industry, with a shortfall in skilled workers. Only 54% of the working age population are actually in work, in contrast to the EU average of 64%. As a result, a large number of people are in receipt of state benefits including disability, unemployment and early retirement. These groups, wary of market reforms, lend support to the array of populist and nationalist political groupings.

Despite its political turmoil, Poland has been a popular destination of FDI, as the figure indicates. It has enjoyed a boom in high-tech television plants. LG Philips, the Dutch–South Korean joint venture, makes about 20% of Europe's flat-screen monitors in Poland. The country enjoys a location advantage for European markets due to its central location. Although government promises to cut red tape have not been fulfilled, investors have been philosophical. One analyst says that Poland is like Italy used to be, 'bureaucratic and sometimes corrupt, with weak government

but a dynamic economy' (Cienski and Wagstyl, 2005). On the other hand, the drawbacks have put off some investors. Toyota and PSA Peugeot Citroen decided against Poland for new car plants, opting for the Czech Republic and Slovakia. The head of General Motors' Polish division says: 'I want to make cars and not spend time in government ministries' (Cienski et al., 2004). Nonetheless, GM teamed up with a Ukrainian industrial company in a joint venture in Poland, which saw the first GM-branded car roll off the Warsaw assembly line in late 2007. The new plant employs 2,600 staff, and is seen by its president as a 'new era' in Polish carmaking (Wagstyl, 2007).

The country's dilapidated infrastructure, including poor rail and road networks, is a drawback for investors and local firms alike. Only six kilometres of new motorway was planned for 2007. The government is counting on EU funds flowing in from 2007 onwards to help rebuild infrastructure, but red tape and a shortage of building workers could lead to disappointing progress.

Tesco, the UK's largest supermarket retailer, entered Poland in 1996, and now has 44 hypermarkets. Although the presence of a hypermarket in all the major cities is welcomed by middle-class consumers, the hypermarket retailers have found Poland a difficult environment. They have not been helped by a pronouncement by the Polish finance minister in 2005 that Tesco was not the sort of investment the country needed: 'Hypermarkets like Tesco are no investment. I mean they are not vital for economic growth' (Cienski and Buckley, 2005). This ambivalence towards modern retailing is indicative of the tensions which characterize Poland. Optimism towards a new future in Europe is counterbalanced by a fear of the loss of traditional nation-based values and ways of life.

Questions

◆ What are the reasons behind the success of Poland's emerging MNEs since 1990?
◆ What tensions exist in the Polish social and political environment?
◆ Assess the attractiveness of Poland as a destination for FDI.

Sources: Anderson, R. and Condon, C., 'New promise of the old east', *Financial Times*, 11 April 2006; Wagstyl, S. and Cienski, J., 'One nation: three realities', *Financial Times*, 20 December 2006; Cienski, J., 'Polish companies look east to "re-create another Duda in Ukraine"', *Financial Times*, 4 January 2007; Cienski, J., Anderson, R. and Ward, A., 'Battle for pole in Hyundai race', *Financial Times*, 10 February 2004; Cienski, J. and Wagstyl, S., 'Poland tunes in to demand for high-tech TVs', *Financial Times*, 15 December 2006; Cienski, J. and Buckley, S., 'Tesco "not welcome" in Poland', *Financial Times*, 6 November 2005; Mackintosh, J., 'All roads point east for Europe's carmakers', *Financial Times*, 15 December 2006; UN, *World Investment Reports 2004, 2005* and *2006* (Geneva: UN); Wagstyl, S. 'Fastest growth in a decade', *Financial Times*, 12 December 2007.

WEB CHECK

Information about the Polish economy and society can be found by going to the OECD's website, www.oecd.org. Click on *Poland* in the country list.

Strategy in the changing environment

Choosing an appropriate location is only one aspect of building competitive advantage, which brings into play a range of factors relating to the firm itself. In this section, we look at a number of theories which help firms in strategic and organizational decision-making. In assessing their contributions, it is useful to note the conventional distinction between external analysis of the competitive environment and internal analysis of the firm's strengths and weaknesses. The traditional SWOT (strengths, weaknesses, opportunities, threats) analysis separates opportunities and threats (external analysis) from strengths and weaknesses (internal analysis), as shown in Figure 7.3. Theories of competitive advantage tend to be grouped accordingly; Porter's 'five forces' model is an example of an environmental approach, while firm-based models include resource-based and competence-based models. We shall look at each of these in turn.

Figure 7.3 SWOT analysis and beyond

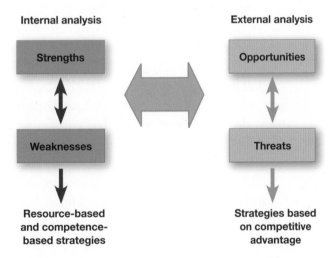

Competitive forces shaping strategy: Porter

Michael Porter (1998b: 21) asserts that 'the essence of strategy formulation is coping with competition'. He says that there are five basic forces which determine competition in any industry: customers, suppliers, potential entrants and substitute products. They can be depicted as the 'five forces model', represented in Figure 7.4.

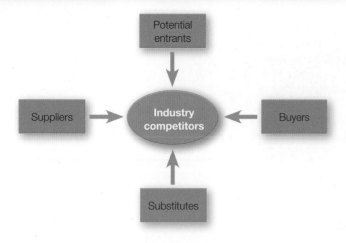

Figure 7.4 Porter's five forces model

Source: Adapted from Porter, M. (1998) *Competitive Strategy: Techniques for Analyzing Industries and Competitors* (London: Free Press)

Each of the five forces can be assessed for every industry. If there are high barriers to entry, *potential entrants* are likely to be deterred. There are several major types of entry barrier. If economies of scale are needed in the industry, potential entrants must come in on a large scale or accept that they will suffer a cost disadvantage, which will probably deter them. If product differentiation and strong existing brands already exist, new entrants will find it difficult to win market share. If large capital investment is required, as in mining, potential entrants may be discouraged.

Both *buyers* and *suppliers* may exert bargaining power in an industry, with the potential to reduce profitability. The supplier exerts power by being one of only a few possible sources, or offering a product with unique characteristics, for example to the buyer's specification. The buyer may exert power by being one of only a limited potential group of customers, for example potential purchasers of large aircraft (see the CS6.1). Alternatively, the buyer may be purchasing a standard product in large quantities. In this case, the buyer may choose among many suppliers, and is likely to choose the lowest cost product. The firm will need a low-cost product or a unique product to which customers will be attracted, despite its cost. Hence, the existence of *substitute products* will limit potential profits.

At the centre of Porter's model is *industry rivalry*. Intense rivalry will occur if there are many competitors of roughly equal size, or if the product is a basic one where there is little differentiation and it is easy for the customer to switch between products. Strategy formulation to meet competitive pressures, according to Porter, involves defining the business in order to make it less vulnerable to competition, either from existing rivals or new entrants.

Competitive strategy to cope with the five forces includes both offensive and defensive approaches. Porter distinguishes three generic strategies. They are overall cost leadership, differentiation and focus. The *low-cost position* provides a defence to all five competitive forces: it raises entry barriers because of economies of scale, and it places the firm in a favourable position in relation to strong buyers, strong suppliers and substitute products. *Differentiation* involves producing a unique product in terms of design, quality, brand or service. It has the benefit of engendering brand loyalty, shielding the firm against competitors' products. Finally, *focus* involves targeting a particular buyer group, segment or geographic area. This approach is often referred to as the 'niche' market (discussed in Chapter 8). To maximize advantage, the firm may choose markets where there are few possible substitutes or where competitors are weak.

In the last chapter, we looked at Porter's diamond model of the competitive advantage of nations. We now bring together his recommendations to MNEs for competing across locations. Global competitive advantage, he argues, is built on a consistent position across markets, integrating activities among business units. The parent company must choose the best location for each business unit, taking into account the diamond conditions for each country, which affect productivity and innovation. Some locations offer comparative advantage in low-cost labour, whereas R&D should be located where specialist skills exist. Porter stresses that although local subsidiaries naturally desire autonomy, this tendency should be resisted by central management, which must maintain a grip on global strategy. Porter (1998b: 339) urges that the national identity of the parent company should be 'inculcated in foreign subsidiaries', citing the example of Japanese companies. He claims that his recommendations for strategy integrate localization and globalization, superseding the traditional concept of comparative advantage. However, it could be argued that he tends towards global strategy, viewing foreign subsidiaries as chiefly benefiting the parent company through local operations in which they enjoy comparative advantage.

TO RECAP...

Porter's strategies for competitive advantage

Porter provides a model for assessing competitive forces within industries, which indicates to firms where the best opportunities lie and where the threat of competition is least. Internationally, he envisages global strategy as utilizing different locations for the comparative advantages they offer.

Porter and globalization

Critically assess Porter's view of global competitive advantage in terms of centre–subsidiary relations. Do you agree with Porter's recommendations for global corporate strategy, and why?

PAUSE TO REFLECT

Resource-based view of the firm

A firm's resources include assets, capabilities, organizational processes and knowledge. They can be classified in three categories: physical resources, human resources and organizational resources (Barney, 1991):

- *Physical resources* include the firm's plant and machinery, geographic location and access to raw materials
- *Human resources* include the experience, skills, knowledge, relationships and insight of its individual managers
- *Organizational resources* include its formal structure, as well as informal relations within the firm and between the firm and outsiders.

All firms have different sets of resources. An assessment of these strengths reveals which are essential to creating sustainable competitive advantage for the individual firm. Barney (1991) suggests that the firm should focus on four key attributes of the resource:

1 It must be *valuable*, in that has potential for exploiting opportunities and repelling threats.
2 It must be *rare* among the firm's competitors.
3 It must *imperfectly imitable*. For example, the innovating firm may gain first-mover advantages. The resource may also be one which derives from its unique history or culture. Where the causal links between the firm's resources and its competitive advantage are ambiguous, competitors will have difficulty imitating the successful firm's strategies, as it is not obvious which resources they should imitate. Where the successful firm's resources are complex social phenomena, they are also difficult to imitate. For example, the organizational culture may rest on personal relations among managers and with stakeholders. These are socially complex and difficult for other firms to imitate (Barney, 1986).
4 There must be *no strategically equivalent resource* which a competitor could exploit. Substitutability implies that a competitor can implement the same strategy, but from alternative resources. The two resources, Barney points

out, need not be similar, but may still constitute strategic substitutes. For example, the clear vision of a charismatic CEO is probably rare and imperfectly imitable, but a strong corporate culture may provide a competing firm with a strategic equivalent. Can a positive reputation be a source of competitive advantage? Barney suggests that it would fulfil the four criteria. As it rests on informal social relations with stakeholders, it is likely to be socially complex and therefore difficult to imitate. Some firms, he suggests, might offer contractual guarantees to customers as substitutes, but many customers might feel more assured by the firm's perceived need to maintain its reputation.

In this last attribute, the resource-based model differs significantly from models such as Porter's based on environmental determinants of a firm's performance. The latter strategy seeks imperfectly competitive industries in which the firm can gain competitive advantage. This strategy, Barney argues, neglects social welfare concerns and almost inevitably results in reduced social welfare. Social welfare benefits are more likely to be gained from resource-based strategies.

> **TO RECAP...**
>
> **Resource-based view of the firm**
>
> Every firm has its own distinctive physical, human and organizational resources. Any of these may be a source of competitive advantage if it is valuable, rare, difficult to imitate and not susceptible to substitution. Corporate culture and the firm's reputation may fall within these criteria.

STRATEGIC CROSSROADS

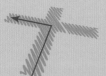

7.1

Weg Electric motors ahead in international market

Although it might seem that most manufacturing is shifting to China, emerging MNEs from other developing countries are competing in world markets. Moreover, in many specialist industries, the low-cost environment is only one factor to be considered. An example is Weg Electric of Brazil. Although Weg is a Brazilian company, its roots lie in Germany, as its three founders were descended from German immigrants to Brazil. The name 'Weg' represents the first initials of the three founders. Their engineering background steered them towards specialist manufacturing, forming Weg in 1961, to manufacture motors. The business expanded to produce a vast array of electrical equipment, motors, generators, transformers and automation systems. Eggon João da Silva, one of the three founders, became its first CEO, a post now occupied by his son. Weg has become Latin America's largest motor manufacturer, competing with much larger rivals such as General Electric, ABB and Toshiba. Weg's success lies partly in its focus on customized products to suit customer needs. It estimates that 75% of its output involves some engineering tailored to specific customers, in comparison to 50% five years ago. Responding quickly and offering a huge array of products is made feasible by its manufacturing flexibility in moving from one product to another as needed. This flexibility is facilitated by producing components in its own plants – an approach going back to the company's German heritage.

From its formation, Weg followed a strategy of self-sufficiency. In its early days, this policy was dictated by the lack of high-quality engineering suppliers in Brazil. However, the policy persisted, Weg's executives believing that it benefits them in allowing them to respond quickly to specific customers' needs. They even manufacture their own paint and copper wiring. The company now serves customers all over the world, 40% of its $1.4 billion annual sales in 2006 coming from outside Brazil. While only about 5% of its production is outside Brazil, the company is now becoming more internationalized in its strategy, making a break with its tradition. The finance director justifies this change, citing the benefits of proximity to customers: 'Making more of our products in other countries will enable us to move closer to customers' (Marsh, 2007). Since 2004, Weg has been manufacturing in China, but lower production costs are only part of the story: 'we need to be in China more than anything to learn about changes in the market [for motors and related systems] that are being driven by the rise of China as a production centre' (Marsh, 2007). Weg is also manufacturing in Argentina, Portugal and Mexico. These countries all have some cultural affinity with Brazil, but Weg also has plans to open a factory in India by 2011. The India project, like the Chinese operations, is planned to be close to its growing customer base.

Weg aims to be producing 20% of its output outside Brazil by 2012. These operations are in its own factories rather than outsourced to subcontractors, despite the general trend towards outsourcing. Hence, in both manufacturing and sourcing components, Weg has sought self-reliance. The company's culture emphasizes R&D and training as underpinning its success. Its in-house training centres, offering mechanics, electronics and chemistry, provide educational as well as training courses for Weg employees. The culture of training complements Weg's stress on R&D, on which the company spent $30 million in 2006 – four times its R&D spending in 2001. Both R&D and training enhance its strategic priorities of innovation and product development. This culture, combined with its manufacturing philosophy, has made Weg a formidable competitor to its larger rivals.

Sources: Marsh, P., 'Weg powers up from an unlikely site', *Financial Times*, 25 January 2007; Weg Electric corporate website, www.wegelectric.com; Wheatley, J., 'Brazil "must lift barriers" to investment in infrastructure', *Financial Times*, 1 March 2007; Marsh, P. 'The alloy approach: how industry in the west is learning again to compete', *Financial Times*, 12 December 2006.

Questions

◆ Describe and assess Weg's international strategy in terms of competitive advantage.
◆ Which of Weg's firm-based resources are most advantageous, and why?

WEB CHECK

Weg Electric's website is www.wegelectric.com.
See Investor Relations and Corporate Social Responsibility.

Organizational competencies

The view of the firm as a 'portfolio of competencies' also concentrates on internal analysis of the firm, but with rather more outward focus on seeking opportunities in markets. Prahalad and Hamel (1990: 81) argue that 'the real sources of advantage are to be found in management's ability to consolidate corporate-wide technologies and production skills into competencies that empower individual businesses to adapt quickly to changing opportunities'. Core competencies represent an organization's collective skill and learning in its specialist areas. These are the firm's most critical resources. They may exist across different businesses within the corporation, requiring co-ordination of skills and multiple streams of technology to unlock potential. Rather than focusing on a portfolio of *products*, these authors urge companies to look instead at their portfolio of *competencies*.

> Core competencies: An organization's collective skill and learning in specialist areas.

There are three criteria which identify the core competence:

1 It opens the door to a number of different markets. Display systems, for example, can be used in a variety of products.
2 It offers significant benefits in the end product which reaches the customer.
3 In common with the resource-based view, it is difficult for competitors to imitate.

As these criteria imply, building core competencies is a strategy for producing competitive end products. A firm may produce a winning product while not nurturing core competencies, but sustainable product leadership stems from the skills and learning which make up core competencies. Competition in core competence leadership logically precedes competition in product markets, according to these authors.

Prahalad and Hamel argue that core competencies cannot be nurtured in the diversified corporation, with its disparate semi-autonomous business units. The strategic business unit (SBU) that sees itself as the owner of its products and competencies is likely to miss opportunities which exist across product divisions. Its managers are also wary of the benefits of outsourcing and alliance strategies. The company with clear goals can benefit, but these activities may contribute little to building the skills within the company which are needed for sustained product leadership. For this reason, large pharmaceutical companies attempt to strike a balance between in-house

R&D and working with specialist SMEs. Rather than recommend specific strategies, Prahalad and Hamel (1990: 89) urge developing a company-wide 'strategic architecture', which is geared to competence building: 'a strategic architecture is a road map of the future that identifies which core competencies to build and their constituent technologies'.

The leading authors in strategic management discussed in this section have recommended global strategies for MNEs, in which head-office executives play the dominant co-ordinating roles. They differ in their perspectives on subsidiary roles. Porter would relegate them to functional limbs of the parent company. The strategists who focus on a firm's resources, including core competencies, see value as emerging across the organization and its subsidiaries, but under the visible hand of central executives.

> **TO RECAP...**
>
> **Building core competencies**
> Prahalad and Hamel single out core competencies as the key to competitive advantage. These represent the collective learning of the firm and the specialist skills of individuals within it, which, when co-ordinated across different units, will produce competitive products.

> **Management implications of strategic approaches**
> Assess the differing approaches of Porter's five forces model and the resource-based models of competitive advantage in terms of their management implications and organizational culture.
>
> PAUSE TO REFLECT

Organizational structures in the international context

For any firm, the links between its strategy, organizational structure and the business environment are fundamental. When the firm ventures across national borders, the business environment becomes more complex, and more options for structure and strategy emerge. Much management research has focused on which of these elements is the most important. For example, seminal research published by Alfred Chandler in 1962 held that strategy determines structure. As was clear even then, the expansion of international enterprises posed numerous challenges for managing people and activities in differing environments. Moreover, environmental changes highlighted the need for adaptive organizations. A variety of organizational structures has emerged as firms have expanded their international activities.

The MNE is the main organizational driver of international expansion. It may operate through a variety of organizational structures. It may wholly own subsidiaries which are closely controlled by the head office in the home country, or it may view subsidiaries as autonomous units. Alternatively, it may adopt outsourcing or franchising models to expand internationally, which involve lower levels of ownership in the foreign location. The choice of organizational structure and strategy varies with the historical background of individual companies, differing home-country environments and differing strategic objectives.

The multidivisional company

Multidivisional structure: Organizational structure characterized by separate business units based on products or geographical areas, which are co-ordinated by the parent company's head office.

In the post-war era of industrialization and international expansion, large US companies were at the forefront of internationalization, while Japan and European countries were preoccupied with reconstruction. These companies pioneered the multidivisional structure, or 'M-form', which was to become accepted as the norm for MNEs in the following decades. The emergence of the multidivisional structure was documented by the economic historian, Alfred Chandler, who focused his research on a number of well-known companies, such as DuPont and General Motors. Chandler (1962) found that when these companies diversified into different products and new markets, separate divisions or business units were needed, which could manage these operations, while overall responsibility for strategy and control was retained by the centre. Formal systems and controls predominated in relations with the divisions. The assumption is that structure followed strategy, and that new divisions can be added as the range of activities increases. Divisions can be based on products or geographic areas. Product divisions have predominated in practice, as shown in Figure 7.5. Product divisions enjoy a degree of operational autonomy and are in a position to gain first-hand understanding of foreign markets. Nonetheless, they are viewed as subordinate to the centre, which determines strategy. In addition, technology and innovation are traditionally seen as functions close to the centre.

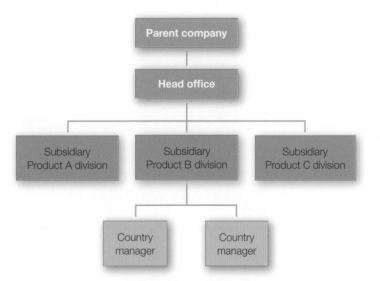

Figure 7.5 The multidivisional structure

A multidivisional structure was well suited to the consumer boom of the post-war years. As we noted in Chapter 2, this was an era driven by the mass production of standardized products, in which US companies excelled. Trade barriers were falling following the GATT, and there was little need to adapt products to national differences. Vernon's product life cycle theory, examined in Chapters 2 and 6, reflects the assumptions underlying American companies' international expansion. By 1960, US companies accounted for 59% of global FDI stock, while European companies, which had dominated in the first half of the century, saw their share slip to 33% (Bartlett and Ghoshal, 1998: 53).

Although the multidivisional model is associated with large American companies, the structure is adaptable to organizations with varying degrees of decentralization, as well as varying depth of international presence. Starlinger, the Austrian SME featured in the opening vignette, has adopted this structure. For companies in the early stages of internationalization, it is common to separate international activities into an 'international' division, based in the home country, which co-ordinates all international activities, both in products and markets. As worldwide activities grow, separate divisions can be added, for example area divisions. However, some companies, such as PepsiCo (featured in CS1.1) and Wal-Mart, have persisted with the international division, suggesting the continuing dominance of the parent company in strategy formation.

Numerous variants of the basic multidivisional model exist in practice. There is no single ideal structure, although some have emerged as more adaptable to changing environments than others. The research of Bartlett and Ghoshal highlights four models, which are set out in Figure 7.6, according to their organizational decentralization and locally responsive strategies. We look first at the three models they found to be the most common among existing companies – the international, multinational and global. The three models all have limitations in terms of organizational resilience and managerial flexibility, hence their proposal of a fourth model, the transnational company, which will be discussed in the next section.

Figure 7.6 Contrasting models of multidivisional companies

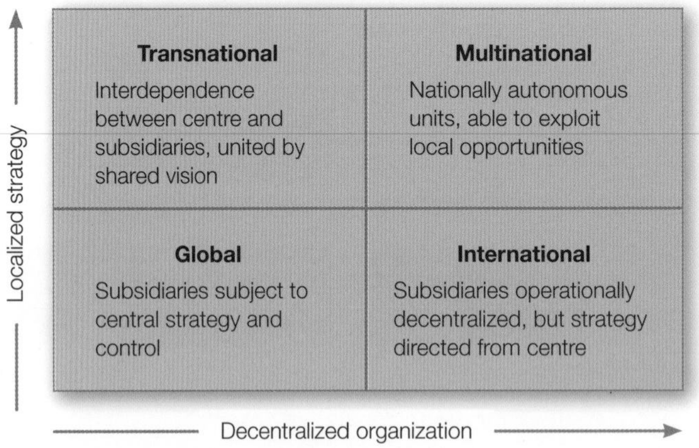

The international model is that of a 'coordinated federation' (Bartlett and Ghoshal, 1998: 57). Overall control rests with the centre, but the divisions operate as independent subsidiaries with delegated responsibilities in local operations. This is the multidivisional company observed by Chandler, controlled from the centre, but with some operational autonomy in the business units. A major limitation is its lack of localized strategy. It can be contrasted with the multinational model. Often called a 'multidomestic' model, it is a 'decentralized federation' (Bartlett and Ghoshal, 1998: 56). National subsidiaries are managed as independent units, able to adapt strategy to local conditions. Co-ordination from the centre is limited, and based on personal relationships between managers from the centre and those in subsidiary units, rather than on formal management systems. This configuration has predominated in the international expansion of many European companies, many of which were long-established family businesses. While this model benefits from local responsiveness, divisions tend to be self-contained, lacking global strategic vision from the centre.

International model: In Bartlett and Ghoshal's typology, a model of the international company based on decentralized subsidiaries.

Multinational model: In Bartlett and Ghoshal's typology, a model of the international company based on autonomous national units.

Global model: In Bartlett and Ghoshal's typology, a model of the international company based on centralized control.

Fordism: Assembly line manufacturing on a large scale, whose processes were designed for producing large volumes of standardized products.

TO RECAP...

The model multinational?

Multidivisional companies range from those in which subsidiaries have considerable latitude to those with highly centralized management structures. While the former type of structure is more locally responsive, the latter type is more oriented to global strategy.

Matrix structure: Organizational structure involving two lines of authority, such as area and product divisions.

See GE's website at www.ge.com, for an example of global product divisions. Click on *our company*, then *our businesses.*

WEB CHECK

At the opposite extreme is the global model of the international organization, which is based on strict central control of assets, resources and management. In the global company, subsidiaries have little scope for adaptation to local markets. Often, local units are simply assembly plants, utilizing components from the parent company. This model is exemplified by the industrial monoliths such as Ford in the US, which excelled in producing standardized products for global markets. Ford's vast empire became emblematic of organization and management systems known as Fordism. Fordism (discussed further in Chapter 10) was archetypal top-down management, with strict formal allocation of roles and responsibilities. While arguably well suited to the era of mass production, its inflexibility became a liability as markets became more fragmented and consumers demanded a greater range of products. Interestingly, Bartlett and Ghoshal also classify Japanese companies as examples of the global company. However, their adaptation of the model, often referred to as 'flexible mass production', incorporates flexibility, responsiveness and systems of continuous improvement, which allowed them to score considerable success in capturing global market share in industries such as motorcars and electronics. Japanese companies have also stressed the need for innovation throughout the organization as a strategic imperative. The Japanese organizational model therefore seems to demonstrate a mixture of global co-ordination and local responsiveness, which many non-Japanese MNEs have emulated.

A structure to fit the changing environment?

From the 1980s onwards, companies have sought strategies and structures to address the globalization of competition, rapidly changing technology, compressed product life cycles and a range of stakeholder relationships. Global product divisions have proved a successful structure in many companies, including GE, Siemens and Sara Lee. They allow the firm to oversee and co-ordinate operations worldwide, but they lack the local responsiveness of area divisions. A solution designed to achieve the best of both structures is the global matrix structure. In this model, shown in Figure 7.7, there are two lines of authority, global business unit managers and area managers. The model aimed to facilitate cross-functional teams. For example, teams could be formed involving product designers, engineering specialists and area specialists familiar with customers' requirements. This model was adopted by a number of firms in the 1970s, including Dow and Citibank, but most found it to be cumbersome and unworkable in practice, due to the real and potential conflict between the dual reporting channels (Bartlett and Ghoshal, 1990). ABB became the most well-known example of the matrix, but the structure became unwieldy, unsuited to large-scale projects which demanded integration and standardization (Berggren, 1996). The company abandoned the structure in favour of product divisions, as discussed in SX7.2.

STRATEGIC CROSSROADS

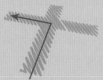

7.2

ABB's journey towards success through structural change

ABB (Asea Brown Boveri), the Swiss–Swedish electrical engineering company formed in 1833, has been at the forefront of managerial and structural innovation. The company has embraced recent radical changes in technology and changing customer needs. Finding an overall structure which will deliver success in rapidly changing markets is not easy for a company with 160,000 staff in more than 140 countries. Under its legendary CEO, Percy Barnevik, the company changed from a classic multidivisional structure to a matrix structure, radically decentralizing and giving local units greater entrepreneurial scope. One dimension of the matrix was products, organized as business areas, while the other dimension was geography. ABB was organized as a 'federation of companies' (Bartlett and Ghoshal, 1993: 28). Its 1,300 separate business units across the world were separate legal entities, in which, in the philosophy of Barnevik, each employee could take pride. The hierarchical structure of the headquarters was much reduced, as the operating companies were largely self-sufficient. Each company was allowed to retain a third of its net profits, giving frontline management a good deal of financial independence. It has been argued that, in practice, this organizational structure was dictated by the company's growth strategy, which was driven by mergers and acquisitions.

A new CEO took over in 1997, and in 1998, the complicated lines of authority and radically decentralized structure were changed in favour of a more conventional structure based on industrial divisions. However, lacklustre growth led to doubts about the company's direction. By 2000, another new CEO, Jörgen Centerman, set about restructuring the company again, aiming to refocus its strategy more on high technology, creating an 'agile, knowledge-based company' (Hall, 12 January 2001). Centerman described the new organizational goal as 'highly flexible mass customization', which would require 'common business and management processes worldwide' (Hall, 12 January 2001). ABB would become more customer focused, with separate customer segments and product segments. Customer segments included manufacturing, utilities and consumer industries, while product segments included power technology and automation technology. The new board was to include two new posts, directors of corporate processes and corporate transformation, reminiscent of Barnevik's management philosophy.

Figure ABB's revenues

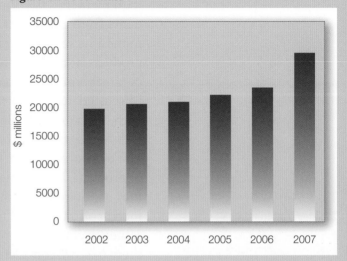

Source: ABB (2008) Financial summaries, www.abb.com

In recent years, ABB has struggled to adjust to the new global competitive environment. Its profit margins in its core businesses, power technology and transformers, have suffered, made worse by rising costs of raw materials. The transformer business has seen job losses and plant closures. ABB has its third new CEO since the departure of Barnevik. The structure is now based on five divisions: power products, power systems, automation products, process automation and robotics. Following years in which structural issues have preoccupied managers, the company has now seen improved corporate performance, with revenues up 25% in 2007 (see figure).

Questions

◆ What were the main features of the matrix structure adopted by Barnevik, and why was it eventually scrapped?

◆ In what ways did the changing organizational structure reflect the changing strategy at ABB?

Sources: Hall, W., 'ABB entrusts its future to "brain power"', *Financial Times*, 12 January 2001; Hall, W., 'ABB changes management in sweeping reorganisation', *Financial Times*, 12 January 2001; Simonian, H., 'ABB to axe 1,300 in restructuring', *Financial Times*, 1 July 2005; Bartlett, C. and Ghoshal, S. (1993) 'Beyond the M-form: Toward a managerial theory of the firm', *Strategic Management Journal*, **14**: 23–46; Berggren, C. (1996) 'Building a truly global organization? ABB and the problems of integrating a multi-domestic enterprise', *Scandinavian Journal of Management*, **12**(2): 123–37; ABB corporate website, www.abb.com.

WEB CHECK

ABB's website is www.abb.com.

Figure 7.7 The global matrix

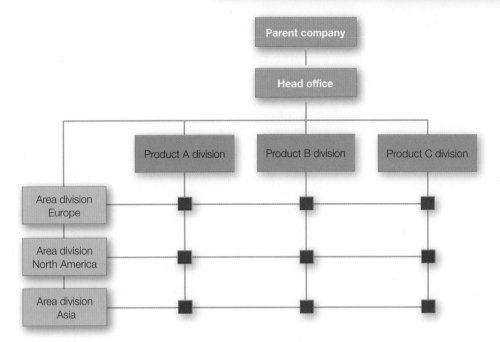

The matrix structure has been praised as an attempt to move away from the multidivisional structure towards a design and processes which are more responsive to product and geographic diversity (Bartlett and Ghoshal, 1993). In particular, it redefined management roles and responsibilities, 'away from top-down decisions to become the primary initiators of entrepreneurial action, creating and pursuing new opportunities for the company' (Bartlett and Ghoshal, 1993: 29). In this way, the structure was better able to adapt to the changing environment and global competition. Although the matrix form proved too complex in practice, the underlying principles of flexibility and devolved responsibilities represent significant advances on the traditional multidivisional structure. These principles underlie Bartlett and Ghoshal's model of the transnational structure.

The transnational model envisages separate worldwide business units co-ordinated from the centre in integrated networks. The head office has a limited role, and some of its traditional functions can be shifted to regional headquarters. Emphasis is on the processes rather than the structure, making this model stronger in managerial guidelines than in organization structures. The model aspires to combine global strategic thinking with local responsiveness. It has proved to be highly influential, its guiding principles having been taken up by a number of large companies, including Unilever (featured in CS7.1), BP (featured in CS13.1) and Nestlé. Its emphasis on networks and devolved responsibility has been influential, along with the reduced importance of the head office in business functions. However, the tendency towards decentralization can prove a drawback where global strategy is needed.

Transnational model: In Bartlett and Ghoshal's typology, the model of an international company which envisages separate business units co-ordinated from the centre.

TO RECAP...

The transnational model
The transnational structure aims to combine global co-ordination with local responsiveness. The limited role of head office, however, may lead to lack of a clear vision in terms of strategic direction.

An ideal model?
Assess the advantages of the global organization as compared to the transnational organization described by Bartlett and Ghoshal. Which model is best suited to the following MNEs, assuming each has a presence in Europe, the Americas and Asia:
- an oil company
- a hypermarket retailer
- a television manufacturer
- a brewer?

PAUSE TO REFLECT

Organizations and networks

The rethinking of organizational structures which gave rise to the global matrix and the transnational model reminded managers that structures seen as organization charts take a rather static view, and that processes and communication within the organization are equally crucial. These concerns have pointed towards a networking perspective, based more on relations than on structures. The network, as highlighted in Chapter 1, is a concept with multiple dimensions. It can be applied to the internal structure and processes of an organization. It can also apply to links between the organization and its staff with other firms. We look first at internal networks and then at inter-firm networks, including clusters.

The network organization

Networks can be viewed from both structural and relational perspectives (Dicken et al., 2001: 94). For the traditional organization, the network approach represents a change in managerial outlook. As SX7.2 on ABB points out, in modern organizations, whatever their industry, knowledge-based activities are paramount. Information and resources flow across borders as well as within the organization (see Figure 7.8). Indeed, cross-border flows take place *within* the organization. For global companies which rely on high levels of central guidance and control, the internet facilitates near-continuous communication with geographically dispersed operating units. Japanese companies were early examples of the extensive use of intranet links to co-ordinate processes. Some global companies see the internet as enabling the centre to control local operations more closely. It also facilitates the building of dialogue which allows local participation in decision-making in a more open way. The business unit a continent away can be brought much closer to the centre and to other units, allowing relations between staff to be cultivated in spite of the distances. This openness facilitates the local responsiveness that the modern MNE needs in the competitive environment. The network organization is one in which relational ties between staff in all locations are nurtured, informal as well as formal.

The notion of the network has become influential in management thinking. The network is claimed to be both a new organizational form and a new

Network organization:
Organization in which informal relational ties are nurtured, both internally and with other organizations and individuals with which it interacts.

Figure 7.8 The network organization

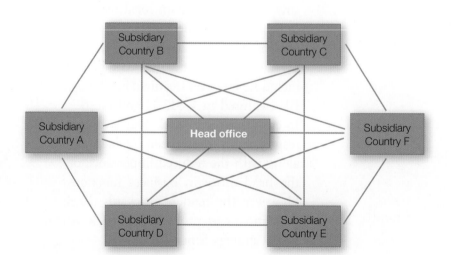

form of governance (Dicken et al., 2001: 92). These claims are somewhat overstated and, by focusing on structures, miss the genuinely transformational aspect of networks, which is in relational interactions. The transnational model incorporates principles of networks as management tools, rather than as new structures. Governance involves a blend of structures, roles and processes (see Chapter 1). The notion of the organization as a network also impacts on the way the company sees itself in the community and society. Openness, the valuing of informal relations and local voice are suggestive of a company which sees itself not simply as an economic unit, but as a social entity. One of the important implications of networking is the blurring of organizational boundaries. Relational ties emerge within the company, with suppliers and other stakeholders, and in the community. As companies increasingly find themselves having to deal with governments and other authorities, the benefit of a network approach towards the business environment becomes evident.

> **TO RECAP...**
>
> **The network organization**
>
> Relying on the internet and frequent contact to link staff in various locations, the network organization is able to co-ordinate activities across national boundaries. Its emphasis on open communication often embraces stakeholder and community ties, suggesting a responsiveness to relevant voices, from wherever they emerge.

Case study 7.1: Slimmer Unilever seeks renewed growth

Unilever is one of the few iconic companies in diversified consumer products which has remained a global powerhouse for decades. Others are its arch rival Procter & Gamble, Colgate and Nestlé. Formed with the merger of Lever Brothers of the UK and Margarine Unie of the Netherlands in 1929, the company, like Royal Dutch Shell, developed a dual corporate structure, Unilever plc and Unilever NV, listed on the London and Amsterdam stock exchanges respectively. Unlike Shell, it has resisted calls to transform itself into a single company. However, it has undergone considerable structural change in its quest to succeed against its powerful peers.

Unilever has been more highly diversified and decentralized than its rivals. Lever Brothers' founder invested in developing countries, to secure raw materials and nurture local markets for its manufactured products. As late as the 1970s, most of its profits came from West African plantations which produced vegetable oils for margarine and detergent. In addition, there were shipping lines for transporting the products and chemicals businesses which transformed them into ingredients for food and household products. The two co-chairmen, one in London and one in Rotterdam, were chiefly co-ordinators. The many decentralized subsidiaries around the world were run by national managers. Moreover, the subsidiaries themselves invested in other businesses. One, United Africa Company, invested in a variety of activities, from brewing to vehicle distribution, which had little connection with the core business. This extreme diversification inevitably led to a lack of focus. Unilever's consensual culture slowed down decision-making, causing it to miss opportunities. Meanwhile, P&G was pursuing innovation and building brands.

Weakening sales growth in 1999 (shown in Figure 1), and the need to respond to fast-moving competitors, signalled the need for streamlining and restructuring. A management review of Unilever's 1,600 brands showed that 400 were leaders or in second place in their markets, with potential to grow. In foods, they included Cornetto ice cream, Lipton's tea and Flora margarine. In home and personal care, they included Dove, Lux, Sunsilk and Pond's. The remaining 1,200 brands accounted for only 8% of turnover, and would be disposed of. The group planned to sell 100 of its 380 manufacturing sites. It shed 10% of its workforce, amounting to 55,000 jobs. A five-year 'Path to Growth' restructuring plan, launched in 2000, introduced two product divisions with responsibility for marketing its brands: foods, and home and personal care. The two new product divisions would exist alongside the regionally based business groups. The group planned acquisitions of companies which would complement its existing businesses. It bought Bestfoods of the US, the maker of Knorr soup and Hellmann's mayonnaise. It also bought Ben & Jerry's ice cream and SlimFast diet foods. The Path to Growth, perhaps optimistically, set an annual target of 5–6% growth in sales.

The new structure allowed the biggest brands to be managed centrally. The most successful were the brands in the home and

Figure 1 Unilever's growth in sales

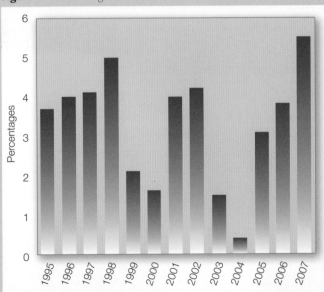

Sources: Unilever Corporate Charts 2006, www.unilever.com; Mortished, 2008

Figure 2 Group turnover by region, 2006

Source: Unilever Corporate Charts 2006, www.unilever.com

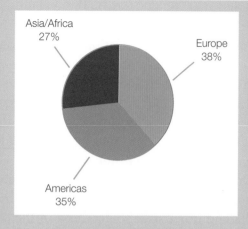

Asia/Africa 27%

Europe 38%

Americas 35%

personal care division, which were more globalized. The food brands, which are more sensitive to national differences, were less conducive to global marketing. For example, tomato soup has different tastes in the UK, the Netherlands and Germany. While the Path to Growth brought about a new focus on marketing, sales fell short of growth targets, as Figure 1 shows. The target of 5–6% growth was abandoned in 2002.

A more realistic target of 4–5% growth in sales was set in 2004. Restructuring was again in the wind, and some shareholders called for a single company structure. Less far-reaching reforms were announced. Replacing the two co-chairmen, there would be a sole CEO and a seven-strong executive team: the heads of the two product divisions and three regional heads – Europe, Americas and Asia/Africa. The two product divisions would be responsible for brands and innovation, while the three regional heads would be responsible for sales and marketing. The aim was to strike

a balance between global and local strategies. The new CEO and the more streamlined management structure would speed up the process of bringing out new brands and products. These could be launched on a worldwide basis, which, the CEO admits, 'was not easy in the past' (Wiggins, 5 May 2006). The accounting and information technology functions were outsourced, to allow the group to concentrate more on marketing. Nonetheless, 21.7% of its 212,000 worldwide workforce were still employed on its plantations in 2005.

The group is now concentrating on developing and emerging markets. Asia and Africa now account for 27% of group turnover (see Figure 2), up from 20% in 1995. Sales are also growing in Latin America. Weaker growth in Europe has been a concern. Many Unilever brands have lost ground to supermarket 'own-label' ranges. The senior managers realize that the group needs to differentiate its products to retain consumer loyalty. However, Unilever has been less innovative than its competitors. Some shareholders urge that its slow-moving approach stemmed partly from the dual company structure. Transforming the UK and Dutch companies into a single company would make it easier to acquire new businesses. However, the senior executives have rejected this radical step as being too disruptive to shareholders. Moreover, Unilever is traditionally a multicultural organization. The Dutch chairman said: 'The whole culture of Unilever is shaped around ... multiculturalism' (Wiggins, 20 December 2005). While Unilever's traditionally consensual culture could be seen as a strength, it seems to have proved a weakness in the fiercely competitive consumer markets where it operates.

Questions

1 Describe Unilever's organizational heritage in terms of its structure and culture.
2 What changes were made in the 2000 and 2005 restructuring exercises, and what were their aims?
3 Why has Unilever continued to struggle competitively in its markets?
4 What recommendations would you make to Unilever's senior management for further structural change, and why?

Sources: Tricks, H., 'Unilever House gets modern facelift, old corporate structure may be next', *Financial Times*, 5 February 2005; Wiggins, J., 'Unilever out to take rivals to the cleaners', *Financial Times*, 5 May 2006; Jones, A., 'No nimble giant: the stumbling blocks Unilever faces on its path to growth', *Financial Times*, 23 August 2004; Wiggins, J. and Burgess, K., 'Unilever disappoints as margins decline', *Financial Times*, 4 August 2006; Wiggins, J., 'Unilever to keep dual structure', *Financial Times*, 20 December 2005; Willman, J., 'Slimmer, leaner, fitter, cleaner and healthier is Unilever's stated aim', *Financial Times*, 23 February 2000; Wiggins, J., 'Unilever gains as recovery continues', *Financial Times*, 2 November 2007; Mortished, C., 'Unilever axe swings it back into black', *The Times*, 7 February 2008, http://business.timesonline.co.uk; Unilever corporate data, www.unilever.com.

WEB CHECK

Unilever's website is www.unilever.com

plate 7.2 Global brands must compete with own-brand rivals, such as these hair care products, to win over consumers.

Inter-organizational networks

MNEs have historically sought control of foreign operations through ownership and internalization, as Dunning highlights in his OLI paradigm (see Chapter 2). The result was a vertically integrated organization, where all phases of production could be controlled, thereby reducing the transaction costs associated with arm's-length contracting from a variety of suppliers. The multidivisional company has evolved away from the centralized monolithic structures which exemplified companies such as Ford. MNEs have become more outward looking and flexible, building an inter-organizational network through formal and informal relations. A firm which functions internally along network lines, with a decentralized organization and flexibility between business units, is in a position to extend network relations to actors outside the organization. Subsidiaries themselves are in a position to cultivate links with suppliers and customers (Ghoshal and Bartlett, 1990). Potential network linkages may influence firms in deciding on locations for FDI, particularly in the case of smaller MNEs and those from developing countries (Chen and Chen, 1998). The links between firms may be formal or informal, short term or enduring, and they may serve a variety of purposes, including the supply of materials and services. A variety of outside companies may thus build relational links with the organization, even exchanging staff. Globalized production takes an even broader view of external links: stages in the production process may take place in different locations, and be carried out by different companies. The outsourcing of production has now superseded the need for manufacturing subsidiaries in many industries.

The concept of the value chain can be applied to international production, in which value is created at each stage of the process. The value chain may be producer driven or buyer driven (Dicken et al., 2001: 99). In the producer-driven value chain, the transnational company co-ordinates an integrated production system, often in capital and high-tech intensive industries, such as motorcars and aircraft (see CS6.1). In the buyer-driven value chain, companies such as large retailers or brand owners co-ordinate dispersed networks of independent manufacturers. The co-ordinating organization is the main actor in a network, which may involve a number of firms in different locations (discussed further in Chapter 10). Their links are based on contracts for goods and services for a specified period. If both sides are satisfied with the outcomes, the contract may be extended. Gradually, personal relations grow, firms exchange information and co-operate on new products. The company providing the outsourced operations may look and feel like a subsidiary, but it is legally independent. There may be cross-shareholdings between them, which deepens their relations, as happens in various national business environments, including Japan and a number of European countries.

Firms may form networks in other activities besides supply linkages and production. Networks are often used to facilitate market entry or enhance marketing presence. Increasingly, R&D networks are being created, with the aim of co-operation in technological advances which will benefit all participants. As highlighted in Chapter 1, the notion of co-operation between different firms seems to run counter to that of firm rivalry. However, the

---

Inter-organizational network: Formal and informal links between separate firms which may take the form of contractual arrangements, but may also reinforce social relations between them, often based on personal ties.

Value chain: Concept which identifies the value created at each stage in a production process.

pooled research is more intensive than any single firm could afford on its own, thus reducing costs (Kogut, 2000).

In the vertically integrated organization, value-added activities are typically internalized. An alternative is the equity-based alliance, which benefits from access to wider expertise than would be accessible internally. Another is the alliance based on contractual ties, a networking arrangement which involves greater flexibility and a lower level of integration between participating firms. Companies have found that networking facilitates flexibility. A firm such as a pharmaceutical company envisages a long-term horizon, seeking to maintain its core in-house R&D activities, while working with SMEs engaged in specialist research which complements its own R&D (see Chapter 12).

The flexible giant?

The large MNE with dozens of subsidiaries spanning all continents enjoys the advantages of size, but its tendency towards bureaucracy and formal management may be drawbacks to competitiveness. How can it use inter-organizational networks to counterbalance these tendencies?

PAUSE TO REFLECT

Cluster: Group of companies and other organizations in an industry designed to bring benefits through co-operation.

Clusters

For centuries, businesses have formed groups with others engaged in the same type of economic activity, creating concentrations in particular geographic areas. With the growth of capitalist economies, the cluster is associated with 'urban agglomeration', bringing these groups of related firms into a concentrated area, providing infrastructure, communications technology and proximity to markets. Porter (1998b: 199) defines the cluster as 'a geographically proximate group of interconnected companies and associated institutions in a particular field, linked by commonalities and complementarities'. While the cluster may be in manufacturing, such as the shoe industry in northern Italy or furniture production in North Carolina in the US, the cluster also occurs in high-tech industries, in which universities and research institutions are also involved (see SX3.2 on Aviation Valley). Porter (1998b: 197) acknowledges that, with globalization, the benefits of inter-firm links in a specific geographic setting are probably waning, but suggests that the 'location paradox' of globalization comes into play: global competition, rather than reducing the traditional importance of location, can increase its importance. Specialized skills, institutions, related industries, particular groups of customers and government incentives can all be highly local. A modern example of the cluster is the export-oriented free-trade zone which has flourished in numerous developing economies (see Chapter 6). Porter argues that although businesses often import raw materials across great distances, it still pays to be part of a cluster, as the presence of numerous customers buying the same types of goods reduces risk. Many cluster firms are SMEs, which benefit from the spillover effects of close proximity to complementary businesses.

Can the cluster itself take on an international dimension? Porter's conception of the cluster as a geographical concentration has been criticized as being focused exclusively on domestic clusters. Rugman and Verbeke (2003) have proposed a new conceptualization of the transborder cluster, which extends Porter's work. They argue that one or more 'core' companies often dominate a cluster, taking on a leadership role. That company is likely to be an MNE in an FDI setting. The presence of the large MNE may attract further FDI, but there are also opportunities for local firms to become involved. They cite the shifting of R&D to foreign locations as an example, leading to linkages with local firms. The flagship firm builds relationships with participating local firms, helping them to gain greater insight into how to serve global markets.

Both Porter's more traditional view of the cluster and the concept of the transborder cluster highlight the competitive advantage which individual participating firms form through formal and informal links. The cluster also exemplifies the relationship between structure and strategy. Networking blurs the boundaries between firms, facilitating co-operative strategic initiatives. The cluster also provides a favourable environment for entrepreneurial strategies, as the example of Aviation Valley (SX3.2) showed, allowing cross-fertilization between research organizations and start-up businesses.

> **TO RECAP...**
>
> **Clusters in international business**
>
> Clusters bring together firms and other types of organization, such as research institutes, in a network environment, which benefits SMEs as well as larger firms.

National variations in firms and networks

Organization and enterprise structures are influenced by the national institutional and cultural environment in which they exist. Differences in national environments lead to the emergence of firms adapted to their home national environment, and these differences are reflected in the ways in which firms expand internationally.

Impact of national environment on the firm

Whitley (2001) identifies three broad types of business environment, which encourage different types of firm to develop:

1 *Particularistic environment*, characterized by weak formal regulatory institutions and weak legal environment. Paternalistic authority relationships prevail. China is an example.
2 *Collaborative environment*, characterized by strong institutions encouraging co-operative behaviour. Governments play a co-ordinating role, and there is a strong public training system. Germany and Japan are examples.
3 *Arm's-length environment*, also characterized by strong institutions, but these are of the formal regulatory variety, emphasizing rules and procedures. The state is more a regulator than co-ordinator. The US is an example.

The particularistic environment is likely to foster firms with strong owner control which is direct and personal. They become adept at adjusting to the uncertain and unpredictable environment, and develop flexibility as a result. Whitley describes these firms as 'opportunistic'. The collaborative environment fosters the growth of more complex organizations based on authority relationships and private property. These firms are likely to be hierarchical, but these hierarchies are co-operative, based on interdependence and linked to other institutions in society. By contrast, the pluralism of the arm's-length environment leads to firms based on units of financial control, with minimal sharing of authority among non-managerial staff and business partners. Their competencies are highly firm specific.

Whitley's three broad kinds of business environment represent ideal types. Every country is distinctive, and the characteristics he identifies exist in differing degrees in all countries. Moreover, different industries and regions vary within the national environment: institutions may well be strong at regional level and weaker at the national level. Nonetheless, these categories help us to fathom why particular types of organization flourish in the three broad types of national environment. Three broad observations can be cautiously advanced:

- Countries with weak institutional and legal frameworks are often developing countries, whose firms tend to be family based. In these firms, personal ties are all-important. Networks are likely to be built around these family and kinship ties. In today's world, companies from developing countries are expanding internationally, often under the guidance of a dominant founder or family, as in Indian companies.

- The collaborative environment encourages a view of the company not simply as a business unit, but as a social player, building relations with a range of stakeholders. The strong institutional environment in these countries provides a conducive environment for complex businesses to develop, often with the help of government guidance. German and Japanese companies fall into this category. Both hold a stakeholder perspective of the company. In both countries, employees are seen not simply as labour input, but as members of an organic whole. As a result, the principle of lifelong employment is valued, making recent restructuring involving job losses particularly painful. This process is discussed in CS7.2 on Nissan.

  In both Germany and Japan, firms are viewed as contributing to national well-being, and collaborative ties spring from the common national culture. Subsidiaries in other countries, therefore, tend to be seen as 'outsiders', making it difficult for them to blend into these relationships. Subsidiaries may be subsumed into the firm's dominant home-country culture, as has happened with Japanese subsidiaries, which are run in foreign locations as if they are Japanese firms. As noted above, this rather ethnocentric approach is combined with continuous dialogue with the corporate head office. Alternatively, the subsidiary may be left to carry on as an independent division under local management. It is notable that, although Daimler announced that its takeover of Chrysler of the US in 1998 would be a marriage of the two cultures, integration was not successful, and the Chrysler division was treated as independent. The decision in 2007 to sell off Chrysler was not entirely a surprise. Firms from collaborative environments find incremental expansion rather than takeover more successful, as relations between the head office and local managers can be nurtured over time, as in the European multinational company.

- In the more market-oriented arm's-length environment, the firm is seen as an economic entity, built on exchange transactions, both within the firm and with the external environment. Exemplified by American multidivisional companies, these firms are more focused on wealth maximization (Penrose, 1995). While the ability to generate profits is recognized as necessary for the national economy, societal goals are served only indirectly. In large American companies, as highlighted earlier, senior executives in the head office determine strategy and control the processes of implementation in other locations, whether subsidiaries or outsourced production. Like other companies in the changing environment, they see the benefits of networks for specific purposes, but these are based on formal contracts, in which the firm's independent identity is preserved. On the other hand, networks themselves build new capabilities not 'owned' by any one firm, perhaps bringing about greater appreciation of relational ties within firms (see Kogut, 2000).

COUNTRY FOCUS 7.2 – SOUTH KOREA

Bright prospects dimmed by uncertainty within South Korea's businesses

South Korea is an Asian economic success story. Over four decades of economic development have brought prosperity to its businesses and its citizens, whose average per capita income (at PPP) is now in the region of $20,000. The economy is dependent on manufacturing exports, concentrated in particular industries such as motor vehicles and mobile phones. GDP growth has faltered in recent years, as shown in Figure 1. As the country's competitiveness seems to be weakening, concern is focusing on its leading companies, which dominate export industries. South Korea may seem a role model for other Asian countries, but doubt still surrounds the soundness of its business organizations and the business environment in which they are rooted.

The business landscape in South Korea is dominated by large diversified conglomerates, the 'chaebol', which are traditional family-dominated empires. The four main chaebol are Samsung, SK, LG and Hyundai. These four groups account for 40% of the country's GDP. Controlling families typically own less than 5% of the shares in the group, but, through cross-shareholdings among the dozens of subsidiaries, they effectively control the entire group, even though they own no shares in the subsidiary companies. These subsidiaries are often run not as business

Figure 1 Growth in South Korean GDP

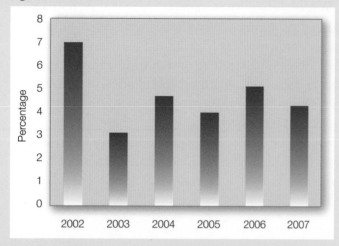

Sources: Economic data, www.economist.com; IMF World Economic Outlook, www.imf.org

entities in their own right, with their own management and shareholder responsibilities, but as vehicles of family control. A large percentage of these businesses are not viable on their own, but are kept afloat by affiliate companies who hold their shares. It is estimated that a third of the manufacturing affiliates are, in effect, 'zombie companies', producing insufficient earnings to cover the interest on their debt (Ward, 17 November 2003).

Following the Asian financial crisis of 1997–98, which exposed the weaknesses and lack of transparency of the chaebol system, the government set about reforming the system, to reduce cross-shareholdings, introduce accountability and improve corporate governance. LG has been at the forefront of reform, reorganizing its structure as a holding company with relatively independent subsidiaries. Figure 2 shows some of the major LG companies, which are all public listed companies. LG has the largest stake in each company, but shareholders are assured that each is run as a separate entity, doing away with cross-shareholdings among subsidiaries. While all subsidiaries promote the corporate brand, this new structure frees each LG company to concentrate on its core business rather than having its attention distracted by affiliates. For example, LG Electronics has formed a joint venture with Philips of the Netherlands,

becoming a global leader in flat-panel televisions. Similarly, LG Chemical, the chemicals business, sold its shares in LG Electronics and LG Securities to concentrate on its core business. Its CEO said: 'Before the spin-off we had a very complex business structure but this complexity did not bring any benefits to our shareholders. By becoming a pure chemical business, we have become easier to understand, more transparent and accountable' (Ward, 28 February 2003). Like other LG companies, LG Chemical is moving production to China. The attraction is not only cheap labour, but proximity to the company's largest potential market. South Korea's geographical and cultural proximity to China give its companies advantages in access to this fast-growing market.

Nonetheless, LG Chemical is concerned about its long-term competitiveness. It is moving towards higher value products, but mass production of basic materials still constitutes most of its sales. Ominously, it is in these core activities that China poses the greatest threat. In addition, Chinese companies are also moving up the value chain. The CEO maintains that the company is independent, with no interference from the group chairman. However, LG Corporation retains controlling stakes in all these companies, and all are headquartered in the same building as the parent company, which is 53% owned by the founder's family.

The more unreformed groups are still run as hands-on family businesses. An obstacle in the way of corporate reform has been the persisting perception within South Korea that as these groups have been responsible for South Korea's industrialization, they deserve special status as symbols of national economic strength. However, corporate scandals and criminal proceedings have embroiled members of a number of controlling families, including the heads of Samsung, SK and Hyundai Motor Corporation.

Is the business landscape in South Korea changing? About 80% of the South Korean workforce are employed in SMEs. SMEs are typically set up to supply components to chaebol companies on whom they are dependent, and are unable to do business with a company from another chaebol. SMEs with no such connections receive little encouragement or financial help from the government, export little and struggle to grow their businesses, especially where they are competing with chaebol-backed firms. An exception is Jimmy Kim, a 35-year-old American-born Korean entrepreneur. His business, Innotive, is a multimedia software company, specializing in integrating all kinds of media, including photos, videos, text, hyperlinks and music, for computers, mobile phones and other types of display screens. This is a specialist niche market, in which the large corporations own no competing businesses. Kim joined Innotive as board member, but was frustrated by its lack of sales and marketing expertise, as well as lack of capital. He orga-

Figure 2 LG holding company structure

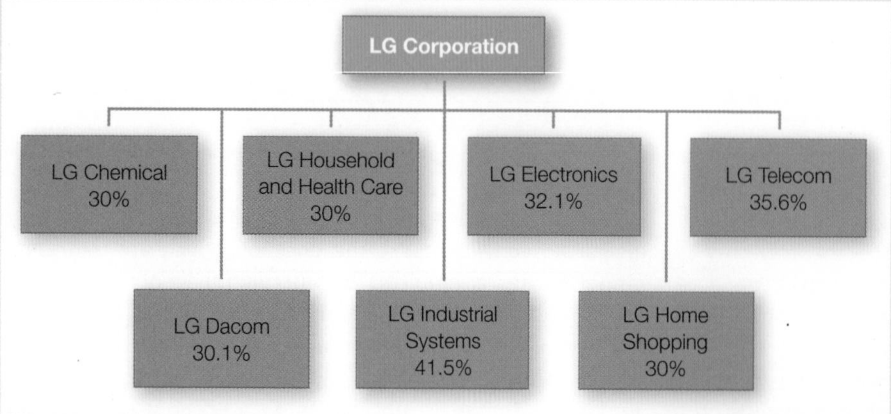

LG Corporation

LG Chemical 30%
LG Household and Health Care 30%
LG Electronics 32.1%
LG Telecom 35.6%

LG Dacom 30.1%
LG Industrial Systems 41.5%
LG Home Shopping 30%

Note: Percentages show parent company stake

Source: Financial Times, 7 April 2003

nized a management buyout and acquired the intellectual property rights, but found there were few venture capitalists willing to invest in the business. Comparing South Korea with America, he says: 'In Silicon Valley, it was: "Give me your dreams and I'll give you my money". But in Korea people would say: "Give me your house and I'll give you my money"' (Fifield, 21 September 2006). Innotive succeeded in bypassing the chaebol, and now counts among its clients Nissan, BMW, CBS TV in the US and NHK in Japan.

Although the chaebol were responsible for South Korea's successful industrialization, their continuing dominance is having an adverse effect on South Korea's competitiveness. Critics of the system urge that, to unlock the value in the separate businesses, the groups should be split up, leaving each unit to survive on its own in the marketplace. The companies could be headed by professional managers, with cross-fertilization of technology where appropriate. Such a move seems unlikely, despite the fact that family-run conglomerates are squeezing out innovative and entrepreneurial talents, such as Jimmy Kim, who are more agile in meeting the challenges of global markets.

Questions

◆ What structural and cultural features of the South Korean chaebol have raised doubts about their long-term viability?
◆ How has Jimmy Kim managed to succeed in the South Korean environment?
◆ What reforms of South Korea's organizations would you recommend, in terms of structure and strategy?

Sources: Fifield, A., 'Seoul sleepwalk: why an Asian export champion is at risk of losing its way', *Financial Times*, 19 March 2007; Ward, A., 'Changing gear to take on a superpower', *Financial Times*, 28 February 2003; Fifield, A., 'Born in the USA, making it in Korea', *Financial Times*, 21 September 2006; Ward, A., 'LG shows the way with chaebol reform model', *Financial Times*, 7 April 2003; Fifield, A., 'Chaebol chiefs display conviction to the cause', *Financial Times*, 14 December 2006; Ward, A., 'The end of a dream – or pause for breath?', *Financial Times*, 17 November 2003; Hasung, J. 'Long way to go on governance', *Financial Times*, 4 December 2006.

WEB CHECK

Access information about South Korea from the OECD's website at www.oecd.org, by clicking on *Korea* in the country list.

Firms and networks: Japanese and Korean enterprises

Japanese and Korean companies provide examples of enterprises rooted in distinctive Asian national environments, which have emerged as global companies. In both cases, their growth has mirrored the economic development taking place within the national economy. Japan was the first of the East Asian economies to set its sights on rapid economic development.

Large Japanese companies became synonymous with global competitiveness in the post-war era. Researchers analysed the basis of their success in global markets, implying that firms in other environments might, in theory, copy their successful formula (see Abegglen and Stalk, 1985). However, because the distinctiveness of the national environment played a major role, the Japanese model is perhaps more helpful in identifying the factors than as a blueprint for others to follow. The institutional environment was highly supportive, the state providing strategic guidance and necessary infrastructure development (Johnson, 1982). The Japanese company, while hierarchical in structure, is decentralized in terms of initiating decisions and is run on the basis of consensus (Whitley, 1990). This produces high levels of loyalty and commitment among staff and managers. Japanese companies became known for the principle of lifetime employment enjoyed by full-time permanent staff, and for the high degree of autonomy enjoyed by managers.

The emphasis on relational ties among Japanese firms has a long history. Before the Second World War, its leading companies had been family-dominated groups structured as holding companies (known as 'zaibatsu'). These structures were dismantled by the US occupation government. However, more informal groupings, known as keiretsu, sprang up in the post-war environment, acting like networks. Firms, banks and partner companies formed these networks. Reliance on debt financing rather than equity financing led to strong relationships with the company's main bankers. The firm would also

Keiretsu: Loose groupings of Japanese companies, usually centred on a main bank, built on cross-shareholdings and personal relations.

cultivate ties with stakeholder companies in its supply chains. Exchange of information and collaboration on new products with suppliers were beneficial to both. Companies typically had cross-shareholdings with key suppliers and with their main bank, to re-enforce the support network.

Economic downturn in the 1990s transformed a number of these traditional Japanese institutions. Lifetime employment was eroded as companies had to restructure. The banking system could not sustain the support it had traditionally given companies, thus weakening a main plank of the keiretsu system. As companies became global players, the homogeneity of corporate values and goals was compelled to give way to more diverse, market-oriented values. Japan's companies have excelled in high-tech industries, with strong global markets, which have impacted on its own organizations. Japan's companies have a long history of adaptation to both changing technology and changing markets. Their resurgence in the new millennium is indicative of these underlying strengths. CS7.2 on Nissan highlights these strengths, as well as the weaknesses of traditional institutions.

South Korean companies have experienced a more turbulent environment than their Japanese counterparts. Political instability, financial crisis and labour unrest have resulted in less strong national institutions. South Korean companies have traditionally formed around large family-dominated conglomerates known as chaebol. These are vertically integrated and traditionally controlled by the family, with much less autonomy for managers than exists in Japan. A paternalistic ethos is thus imbued, and these companies have traditionally built employee relations on mutual loyalty and commitment. The chaebol have not developed the sort of network ties that characterize Japanese keiretsu. They are closely associated with state agencies, political elites and banks, on which they depend for finance. The Asian financial crisis undermined the basis of the chaebol (see SX3.1 on Samsung). These companies are restructuring themselves along market lines, although, as CF7.2 shows, the cultural values attached to the system have been slow to change.

Chaebol: Traditional South Korean family-owned and paternalistically controlled conglomerate.

TO RECAP...
Firms and networks in Japan and South Korea
Japanese firms in the post-war era evolved informal groups, keiretsu, which linked their executives with those in their main banks and supply chain partners. These ties weakened during the economic downturn in the 1990s. South Korean companies are traditionally grouped in family-controlled conglomerates. Their traditional values have come under strain as government policies have introduced market reforms.

Organizational change

Almost all the organizations featured in the case studies in this book have wrestled with managing change. Typically, inertia has set in, managers have become complacent, innovation is at a low ebb, and competitors are gaining ground. Changes are called for – in products, markets, organizational structure and corporate culture. Changes in the management may be needed, as new people with new ideas can take a leadership role in guiding the necessary changes. However, change, vital though it is, is unsettling, disturbing routines and roles. Changes often fail to solve problems quickly, leaving morale low and shareholders discontent. Change involves not just the goals, but the manner and speed with which they are implemented. Shock therapy may be called for, but it risks backfiring in organizations with long histories of incremental changes. On the other hand, incremental changes often do not solve severe problems, as vested interests and routines remain in place. Changes in an organization with international reach are more complex than its domestic equivalent, inevitably involving different cultures and expectations.

Processes of change

Organizations are never entirely static. Changes are taking place all the time, although those within the organization are not always conscious of them. Small changes, such as altering procedure, may have implications for roles, which have a ripple effect. The organization may undergo differing degrees of change, from broad change, altering its entire direction and culture, to narrower change, rearranging business units and products. The levels of change are shown in Figure 7.9, which highlights strategic and organizational aspects. Change referred to as turnaround involves rapid deliberate change, often initiated by a new CEO. It may be an operating turnaround, which involves rationalization and cost reduction, or it may be a strategic turnaround, which repositions the company's vision and goals. This radical change affects all the levels shown in Figure 7.9. Nissan went through a turnaround orchestrated by its charismatic CEO, Carlos Ghosn, who also revamped the company's vision (see CS7.2). Revitalization, by contrast, is a slower, less radical type of change, which works gradually through the organization, through co-operation. The need for change and the actual changes depend largely on the context. Organizations in the transition economies, which have moved away from a communist system to a market environment, undergo radical changes in their culture, goals and roles of individual employees. In general, if a change of culture is contemplated, then structures, systems and people need to change in harmony. If lower level change is sufficient, then change may be piecemeal: people may be changed without altering systems.

All change begins with a conception of change, followed by a shifting of the mindset, and the implementation of the changes in practice. Change at lower levels tends to come from middle managers or staff groups, and emerges gradually. Radical change, on the other hand, is usually directed by

Turnaround: Radical change in a poorly performing organization, involving rationalization and cost reductions.

Revitalization: Gradual change aimed at refocusing an organization, usually based on co-operation among staff.

Figure 7.9 Aspects of strategic and organizational change

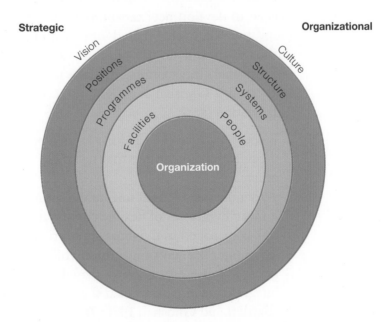

a 'focal actor' (Mintzberg and Westley, 1992). This type of change, such as restructuring, comes from the top and is managed formally. Formal change may be carried out co-operatively, or it may result in confrontation with staff. The changes instigated by Citigroup in their South Korean subsidiary, featured in CS4.1, resulted in confrontation. In practice, the catalyst for change often comes from outside the organization, for example when new owners take over. Changes which are perceived as being unilaterally imposed are sometimes resisted. The difficulties are compounded in the international sphere, as the acquired business may have a different organizational culture.

Radical change may also come about more informally from within an organization. The charismatic CEO who exerts visionary leadership may reconceive the organization's vision, bringing about radical change in its culture. As staff are accustomed to working in an organization guided by a strong shared vision, the process of change is often co-operative. Although change need not necessarily be driven by visionary leadership, successful outcomes are more likely to result from some new vision which guides the process. This applies to revitalization as well as to the more radical overhaul entailed in the turnaround (Doz and Prahalad, 1988). In the international context, this shared vision may be more critical than in a domestic company, as the MNE may well encompass a diverse range of subsidiaries, with differing organizational cultures and differing managerial styles.

Organizational change in the international context

In the 1990s, numerous large established multinational companies found that they were losing competitive edge to more agile rivals. They had become stuck in their ways, seeing growth and performance suffer. Centralized companies risked becoming too bureaucratic to be flexible, while decentralized multinationals became too dispersed to achieve unified corporate objectives. Acquisition came to be preferred by these large companies. However, they often diversified quite widely, with little attention to how the integration of these new businesses would be achieved (Hamel and Prahalad, 1989).

In the competitive environment which emerged in the 1990s, companies needed to develop new capabilities and adapt to changing technology. The innovative knowledge-based organization gained competitive advantage. Although there is no new ideal model for the era of globalization, Bartlett and Ghoshal's transnational model was designed to meet the new challenges. Bartlett and Ghoshal highlight three challenges which the international organization faces:

1 It must 'balance the diversity of perspectives and capabilities within the organization and ensure that no single management group dominates the others'.
2 To handle the different roles and responsibilities with organizational units, it must 'build a set of flexible coordination processes so that each unit and task is managed in the most appropriate manner'.
3 To counter the centrifugal force which inevitably sets in in large organizations, it must 'encourage a shared vision and personal commitment to integrate the organization at the fundamental level of individual members' (Bartlett and Ghoshal, 1998: 76).

> **TO RECAP...**
> **How change happens**
> Organizational change may be radical, as in the radical restructuring and the turnaround, which alters operations, strategy or both. Gradual change, such as revitalization, may focus on a particular aspect of the organization, such as products or roles. Formal and informal means are used to bring about change, and guidance often comes from a leader with a clear vision of the desired changes.

The second of these, flexible co-ordination processes, is both crucial and difficult when operations are spread over dispersed units. Moreover, consumer needs, competitive pressures and environmental constraints differ from one country to another. The flow of materials, products, resources and information could be managed so as to adapt to these national differences. These processes require a combination of centralized decision-making, formal processes and 'socialization', which is the building of common perspectives and values among managers. Transnational operations almost inevitably tend towards fragmentation, hence the importance of central guidance and shared vision to cope with the diversity and complexity of international operations. A further challenge is to build entrepreneurship throughout the organization, identifying opportunities and supporting initiatives. Small units, replicating SMEs, which have the latitude to be creative, are conducive to entrepreneurial cultures, but decentralization risks undervaluing the role of top management, especially in identifying global opportunities and threats.

> **TO RECAP...**
>
> **Challenges to the international organization**
> As it becomes international, the firm must balance different perspectives within its organization, allowing flexibility to respond to different organizational needs, but co-ordinating all units and fostering a shared vision. A further challenge is to encourage an entrepreneurial approach.

Conclusions

☐ The international dimension presents new opportunities and also new challenges for companies, involving their strategies, structures, relations (both internal and external) and cultures. For every company, strategy, structure and environmental factors are intertwined. The company seeking to internationalize its operations is confronted with a number of alternatives, including outsourcing and FDI options, such as greenfield investment and acquisition. The choice depends on a number of considerations, including its own goals in terms of ownership and control, its cultural affinity with foreign locations and the competitive environment which characterizes its industry. This last consideration is the focus of Porter's approach to international strategy. Porter's view of competitive advantage, which emphasizes markets and locations, lays less stress on the internal advantages a firm may possess. These resource-based advantages, including core competencies, have become a focus of strategy as the competitive environment has become more complex. The growth of emerging MNEs from developing countries is highlighting the diversity of strategies and visions in international business.

☐ Differences among MNEs in building their international presence are influenced by the national environment of their home country, and by the company's own administrative heritage. The multidivisional structure has facilitated international growth through a balance between central control and local responsiveness, varying in the degrees of responsibility entrusted to subsidiaries and other affiliates in different locations. Although global strategy would seem to point towards strong direction from the centre, in practice, highly centralized MNEs have tended to be bureaucratic and inflexible, struggling to adapt to market changes. On the other hand, highly decentralized organizations, while responsive to differing local markets, have been weakened by a lack of central co-ordination. The considerable restructuring that

MNEs have undergone in recent years has sought to balance these twin goals of global strategy and local responsiveness. The emergence of international networks, both intra-firm and inter-firm, represents a means of integrating global and local dimensions.

> **Pop loses its fizz**
> Pop, a large MNE which manufactures soft drinks and snacks, has found that its brands are being outsold by rivals, including local brands, in many markets. It has always been a highly centralized company, its product divisions designed for global markets. Advise Pop's senior management on what changes you would recommend in its strategy and organization, and how they should implement them.
>
> PAUSE TO REFLECT

Review questions

Part A: Grasping the basic concepts and knowledge

1. What are the characteristics of outsourcing as an internationalization strategy?
2. What are the leading motives for FDI? Explain each.
3. Compare greenfield investment and acquisition as alternative FDI strategies. What considerations does the firm take into account when deciding between them?
4. Which environmental factors are particularly important for the location decisions of firms seeking overseas production?
5. Compare radical and incremental change within organizations, and assess the role of leadership in each.
6. Why did a wave of corporate change and restructuring take place in the 1990s?
7. Describe Porter's five forces model. What are its implications in terms of strategy?

8. What does the resource-based view of the firm contribute to the formation of corporate strategy?

9. What are core competencies, and why are they seen as even more important than products in terms of competitive advantage?

10. Describe the multidivisional structure as a corporate model. Why is it suited to international operations?

11. Contrast the four types of multidivisional companies highlighted by Bartlett and Ghoshal, giving an example of each.

12. Why is the transnational model put forward as having advantages over the other three?

13. What are the advantages of the matrix structure, and why have companies found it difficult to implement these in practice?

14. Describe the network organization, in terms of both structure and relations.

15. What types of inter-organizational network exist, and what benefits do they offer firms in their international operations?

16. What is the role of clusters in international business?

17. What role has the keiretsu played in Japan's industrial development, and how are they indicative of Japanese business culture?

Part B: Critical thinking and discussion

1. Why have acquisitions been gaining over greenfield investments in popularity as an entry mode? Assess the role of the national environment in choosing the mode of entry, giving examples.

2. Critically assess the validity of Porter's five forces model, highlighting aspects which have attracted criticism. How could the model be improved upon?

3. MNEs from developing countries are increasing their international presence. What are their sources of competitive advantage, and what are their weaknesses in comparison with established companies from developed countries? Give examples.

4. Discuss the advantages and disadvantages of the network organization in international business. To what extent is it fair to describe it as attractive in theory, especially for its flexibility, but difficult to apply effectively in practice?

5. Distinguish between the 'particularistic', the 'collaborative', and the 'arm's-length' national environments. What types of firm are associated with each, and how are their foreign entry strategies likely to reflect their cultures?

Case study 7.2: Nissan looks beyond the turnaround

Nissan, one of Japan's leading motor manufacturers, was on the brink of bankruptcy in 1999, with debts of $17.4 billion and a plummeting share price. Into this dismal scene strode the new chief operating officer (COO), Carlos Ghosn, sent from Renault of France, which had bought a controlling stake of 37% in the weakened company. Of Brazilian, French and Lebanese descent, Ghosn's multicultural background and linguistic skills were combined with a forthright, no-nonsense approach to problem-solving. His remarkable turnaround skills and charismatic leadership style transformed Nissan, giving the company a platform for future growth under Renault oversight. In 2005, Ghosn became the CEO of both companies, leaving a new COO in charge of Nissan in Japan. What are Nissan's prospects under this new arrangement, as the global competitive environment becomes even fiercer?

As a foreigner brought in to revive Nissan, Ghosn faced an uphill task, not just because of its financial woes, but because of resistance to an outsider taking effective control of the Japanese firm. On the other hand, a leader from outside was possibly better placed to take the drastic steps needed, which a Japanese CEO would find too radical to contemplate. He had gained a reputation as a cost-cutter, and made it clear that factories and jobs would have to go – measures which ran counter to Japan's business culture of lifetime employment. He argued that it was more sensible to lose 15% of the workforce in order to save the company, than to lose 100% in the event of bankruptcy. Managers would be expected to take responsibility for meeting performance targets, and could no longer expect to be promoted simply on the basis of seniority.

The 'Nissan revival plan' designed by Ghosn focused on cost-cutting. Five factories and 21,000 jobs were lost, and non-core assets were sold. Traditional keiretsu suppliers were told that, henceforth, they would have to compete alongside outside suppliers, in another break with Japanese management culture. Nissan's rather tired designs were replaced by new ones with more consumer appeal, along with a range of new models. Improving sales, which was a priority, relied on the attractiveness of the new products and on targeting products to particular markets. The cost-cutting revival plan was followed by the 'Nissan 1-8-0 plan', representing three targets: to increase sales by 1 million units, achieve an 8% margin, and reduce debt to zero by 2005. The 8% margin and the zero debt were achieved more easily than the leap in sales. As sales in its home market had slumped, growing sales in the US and China became priorities.

Nissan was later than its rivals in entering the Chinese market, announcing a 50/50 joint venture with state-owned Dongfeng Motor only in 2002. By then, its rivals, including Honda, Toyota,

Figure 1 Nissan Motor net profits/losses

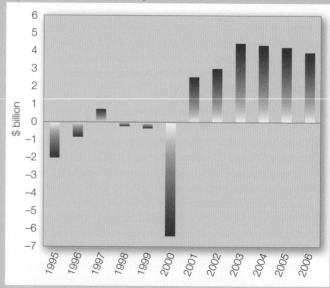

Sources: Financial Times, 7 July 2006; Nissan Annual Report 2006–7, www.nissan-global.com

Figure 2 Market shares of leading Japanese motor manufacturers in the US

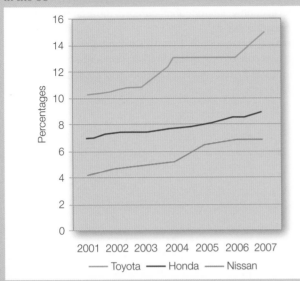

Toyota — Honda — Nissan

Note: Data for 2007 are for February 2007

Source: 'US light vehicle sales summaries', February 2007, http://wardsauto.com

plate 7.3 This dashboard of a Nissan sports car signifies one of the many global markets which Nissan is targeting.

Volkswagen, GM and Peugeot, were already established with Chinese partners, but Nissan's $1 billion investment indicated determination to catch up. The aim was to create a globally competitive player over a 10-year period. With his typical confidence, Ghosn said: 'We can move bigger, we can move better and we can move faster' (Kynge, 20 September 2002). The joint venture produced Nissan-branded cars and Dongfeng-branded commercial vehicles, achieving a good fit between the two companies. While each partner had half the seats on the board, Nissan appointed the president and took management control. It restructured and streamlined Dongfeng's operations, continuing the rationalization principles which had succeeded at Nissan.

By 2004, Nissan reported profits of $4.6 billion (see Figure 1), benefiting from a growth in sales in the US, although Nissan still trails behind rivals Toyota and Honda (see Figure 2). Nissan's new models, including the luxury Infiniti range, proved popular in the US, although it is competing directly against the well-established Toyota Lexus brand. Nissan's share price rose from Y330 in 1999 to a peak of Y1,162 in 2005. By then, Nissan was deriving 70% of its profits from the US market.

Challenges lie ahead, as the company is looking to boost sales on several fronts. It is targeting its home market, the US and other global markets, primarily China. Slowing sales in Japan and the US led to reduced profits in 2006 (see Figure 1), which caused the company to miss its targets and increased pressure for gains elsewhere. It is seeking to widen sales of its Infiniti brand in a number of markets, including the Middle East, South Korea, Japan and Europe. At the other end of the price range, competitive pressures are mounting in emerging markets, where manufacturers are focusing on small cheap cars. All motor manufacturers are confronted with rising costs of raw materials and energy, as well as issues of climate change and environmental impact. These forces in the competitive environment will present fresh challenges for the partnership of Renault and Nissan.

Nissan and Renault have gradually become more intertwined. Renault's stake in Nissan has risen to 44%, while Nissan holds a 15% stake in Renault. Ghosn took over as CEO of both companies in 2005, giving rise to an inference that the two companies would be merging. However, Ghosn strongly denied any merger intention. He said: 'Decisions for Nissan will not be taken in Paris. The empowerment of management has been a key part of Nissan's revival. Leashes are not part of the tools we use' (Ibison, 22 February 2005). He had pointed out when the cross-shareholdings were raised that merger was not intended: 'I can see all the risks of a merger. The loss of identity is a huge risk. The only thing we have is our capacity to motivate our people. How can we motivate them if they have lost their individuality? ... We have a way to develop their performance and increase their synergies but maintain their identities and focus' (Ibison, 10 May 2002). His plan was to spend 40% of his time in Japan, leaving the day-to-day running of Nissan to its Japanese COO, Toshiyuki Shiga. This heralds a new era at Nissan, in which Ghosn's strong leadership has given way to a more teamwork-oriented, consensus-driven management ethos, reminiscent of traditional Japanese corporate culture. Ghosn remains at the helm in terms of strategy, and there is a close working relationship between the two companies. Renault and Nissan are co-operating to rationalize platforms and components, and there is a constant exchange of best practices between staff, reducing purchasing and distribution costs.

Questions

1 What aspects of Japan's corporate culture had adversely affected Nissan's competitiveness?
2 What were the main elements of Nissan's revival, and what was the role of Carlos Ghosn?
3 What are the challenges facing Nissan in global markets?
4 What lessons can be learned from Nissan's case for turnaround strategy in general?

Sources: Ibison, D. and Mackintosh, J., 'The boss among bosses', *Financial Times*, 8 July 2006; Ibison, D., 'Car chief cajoles group in 180-degree somersault', *Financial Times*, 10 May 2002; Sanchanta, M., 'Nissan targets its home market', *Financial Times*, 26 April 2006; 'Ghosn in sixty seconds', *Financial Times*, 7 July 2006; Ibison, D., 'Nissan power from near-bankruptcy to zero debt in 3 years', *Financial Times*, 24 April 2003; Ibison, D., 'Ghosn hands on the baton at Nissan', *Financial Times*, 22 February 2005; Kynge, J., 'Nissan puts faith in drive into China', *Financial Times*, 20 September 2002; Nakamoto, M. 'Bonuses on empty as Nissan misses targets', *Financial Times*, 21 June 2007; Nissan Annual Report 2006–7, www.nissan-global.com.

Further research

Journal articles

Anderson, U., Fosgren, M. and Holm, U. (2007) 'Balancing subsidiary influence in the federative MNC: a business network view', *Journal of International Business Studies*, **38**(5): 802–18.

Barnett, M. (2006) 'Finding a working balance between competitive and communal strategies', *Journal of Management Studies*, **43**(8): 1753–73.

Birkinshaw, J., Morrison, A. and Hulland, J. (1995) 'Structural and competitive determinants of a global integration strategy', *Strategic Management Journal*, **16**(8): 637–55.

Brouthers, K. and Brouthers, L. (2000) 'Acquisition or greenfield start-up?' *Strategic Management Journal*, **21**(1): 89–97.

Cantwell, J. and Narula, R. (2001) 'The eclectic paradigm in the global economy', *International Journal of the Economics of Business*, **8**(2): 155–72.

Duystens, G. and Hagedoorn, J. (2001) 'Do company strategies and structures converge in global markets? Evidence from the computer industry', *Journal of International Business Studies*, **32**(2): 347–57.

chapter 8
MARKETING

learning objectives

▷ **To identify the role of marketing strategy within corporate goals and operations**
▷ **To assess appropriate market entry strategies and target markets in a variety of organizational and environmental contexts**
▷ **To appreciate the role of product markets and brands in the marketing mix for differing markets and environments**
▷ **To integrate elements of the marketing mix, including communications, pricing and distribution strategy, in international markets**
▷ **To develop awareness of ethical issues in marketing**

Introduction

Amid much fanfare, the world's cheapest car, the Tata Nano, was launched in Delhi in 2007 by legendary Indian entrepreneur, Ratan Tata. Priced at one lakh, which is Rs100,000 (about €1,700), it is about half the price of India's current cheapest car, and promises to bring car ownership within the reach of millions of Indian families, who, until now, could only afford motorcycles. Not all at the launch were enthralled by this prospect. A boom in motoring promises further congestion to India's already clogged roads and will also raise pollution levels which are already high. Tata shrugs off these concerns, as do other manufacturers who are developing their own models of the 'people's car'. Bajaj Auto, the motorbike manufacturer, is teaming up with Renault to produce a small car only slightly above the symbolic one lakh in price. But manufacturers know that any celebration of car culture in emerging markets must be seen in perspective, as environmental issues race up the motoring agenda globally. Responding to changes in today's mature markets and anticipating trends in emerging markets pose challenges and opportunities for marketing strategists, which are the focus of this chapter.

The Tata Nano is featured on the Tata Motor's website, http://tatanano.inservices. tatamotors.com.

WEB CHECK

Businesses stand or fall on the basis of the value they offer customers. The domestic company which concentrates on its home consumers builds up considerable knowledge of their needs, but must start again in international markets. International strategy involves analysing a range of potential markets to decide which products will be suitable for which markets and how best to market them. Although the potential rewards of widening markets are attractive, there are risks for firms entering markets where they have little knowledge or experience. Designing, pricing and targeting the right product for the right market has become highly competitive. Hence, the role of marketing in the organization has become critical to corporate success.

This chapter begins with an overview of marketing in the organization, assessing the customer focus which has emerged as international competitive pressures have grown. We look next at how firms choose markets for particular products. When target markets are decided, marketing strategy can be devised, including products, prices, communications and distribution. The design of the marketing mix varies according to the distinctive characteristics of each market. Customers have traditionally been viewed in transactional terms, simply as buyers. Consumers are now seen in relational terms, implying that the role of marketing is a continuing one, which builds links between customers and the company's products and brands. The notion of the consumer in society places the marketing function in cultural and social contexts. The ethical dimension of marketing, which is discussed in the last section, stems from this broader view of the role of marketing and takes a critical perspective on marketing goals and practices.

Marketing in the organizational context

Marketing as a business function has traditionally focused on the analysis of markets and provision of products targeted at particular markets. This view of marketing derives from its background in sales management, in which product planning, pricing, promotion and distribution are the relevant subfunctions (Webster, 1992). These elements are still central, but marketing is now seen more in terms of customer relations than in transactional terms. This shift reflects an evolving view of the MNE in its environment, which was highlighted in the last chapter. The large, monolithic organization, exemplified by Ford of the US, was efficient in producing standardized products for mass markets. Ford produced the first mass-market car, the Model T, which was the Tata Nano of its day, affordable by millions of ordinary Americans. But it proved incapable of adapting to consumers' wishes for greater choice. General Motors, through its network of subsidiaries, was able to offer a wider range of models, colours and features, heralding a new approach to organizational structure and also a new outlook on meeting consumer needs.

Levels of marketing

Within the MNE, marketing can be conceived at three different levels: corporate culture, competitive strategy and marketing strategy. These are shown in Figure 8.1. First, at the highest level, in the context of its *corporate culture*, the company must decide what its mission and goals are. The firm which places satisfying customer needs at the centre of its vision adopts the marketing concept. Kotler et al. (2002: 19) define the marketing concept as:

Marketing concept: An organizational focus on identifying the needs of consumers and satisfying those needs.

> the marketing management philosophy which holds that achieving organizational goals depends on determining the needs and wants of target markets and delivering the desired satisfactions more effectively and efficiently than competitors do.

The goal of satisfying customers contrasts with the 'selling concept', which focuses on products which the firm sells. This distinction is not new. It was articulated most eloquently in an article by Theodore Levitt, entitled 'Marketing myopia', published in 1960. Levitt observed that the problem faced by US railways at the time, which were losing business to other modes of transport such as roads, was that managers saw themselves in the railway business when they should have seen themselves in the transport business. They were product rather than customer oriented. He said:

> Selling is preoccupied with the seller's need to convert the product into cash, marketing with the idea of satisfying the needs of the customer by

means of the product and the whole cluster of things associated with creating, delivering, and, finally, consuming it. (Levitt, [1960] 2004: 143)

As Figure 8.1 indicates, the firm must ask itself first what customer needs it can best satisfy and who its customers are. The firm contemplating its international presence must decide which markets to enter or exit. In the large MNE which has numerous subsidiaries, marketing at this highest level focuses on the firm's overall goals. As noted in the last chapter, a shared vision is an important link among units in a multidivisional firm, in which subsidiaries may pursue a variety of different businesses.

Figure 8.1 Levels of marketing

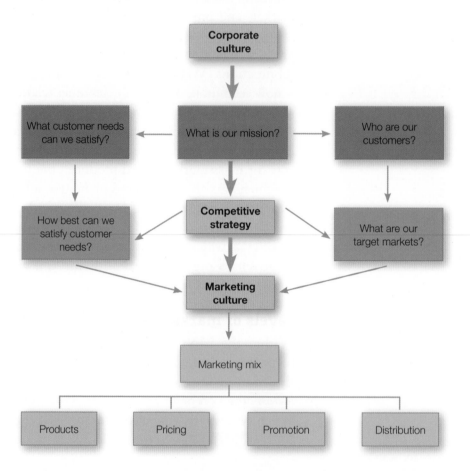

Second, a firm must decide on its *competitive strategy* in its targeted markets. Strategy may be determined at the corporate level, but in decentralized structures, managers within subsidiaries have delegated responsibility to design strategies within the firm's corporate goals. They carry out analysis of markets and devise specific strategies for market segments, targeting and positioning of the firm's products. In a customer-oriented company, decisions at this level are critical to the firm's success. Market research adds to managers' detailed knowledge of local environments. In addition, managers are likely to be involved in local networks, such as links with advertisers. These links may form a source of competitive advantage over rivals.

Third, the firm needs a *marketing strategy* to reach consumers effectively and efficiently with its products and messages. The marketing function thus implements strategic goals at the operational level. The company's strategy is implemented through the 'marketing mix': products, pricing, promotion and distribution. This level might be called the 'functional strategy', reflecting the specialist nature of the activities of marketing managers. Even at this level, however, relationships are important, as these activities are key to building the successful brand, which reflects a relationship between the company and its customers.

In a small company, the three levels of marketing may not be clearly delineated in practice, and the same people take most of the key decisions at all levels. As companies become larger and more complex organizations, variations become apparent. In a large, highly centralized company, marketing at all levels may be concentrated in the centre. Coca-Cola was traditionally such a company, even down to determining advertising for all markets. In more decentralized MNEs, while marketing at the highest level is centralized, local subsidiaries are likely to have latitude to take decisions on marketing strategy for their particular markets. In fact, centralized decision-making has been scaled back in many companies, such as Coca-Cola, in favour of more scope for local decision-making.

Global marketing strategies

In his analysis of competitive advantage, Michael Porter distinguishes three types of generic competitive strategy. These are differentiation, price and focus (see Chapter 7). These are broad strategic perspectives, describing the way firms compete globally. Similarly, in terms of marketing, there are generic strategies: the global, multidomestic and regional, shown in Figure 8.2.

Figure 8.2 Generic marketing strategies

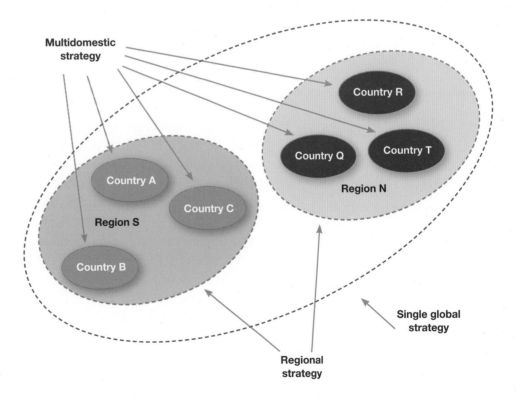

1 *The global strategy*: The single global marketing strategy is an extreme approach, assuming that consumers everywhere either have similar tastes or that tastes are converging. It follows that communications and adver-

tising can be standardized and applied globally. While this approach may still be appropriate in specific industries, it no longer resonates in consumer markets. Global strategy, however, may be advantageous where it has a particular focus, such as the product or the brand. A company may focus on a global product category, such as detergents. It co-ordinates strategy across markets within the product category, but is able to adapt the product, branding and advertising to local markets. Global product divisions have become popular among large companies in consumer markets. Similarly, a global branding strategy maintains the global brand and logo across markets, while allowing for adaptations of products in particular markets. The company thus benefits from consumers' recognition of its brands in increasingly global media such as the internet and satellite television.

2 *The multidomestic strategy*: The decentralized organization, while retaining strategic decisions on products and broad strategic principles in the head office, delegates to country subsidiaries decisions on marketing strategies to suit local markets. In consumer markets such as food, this type of strategy has been traditional (see the example of Unilever, featured in CS7.1). This strategy is appropriate for multinational companies with subsidiaries which have considerable authority to determine their own strategies.

3 *Regional and multiregional strategies*: The regional strategy is a middle way between global and multidomestic strategies. This strategy groups together the countries in a particular region, such as Europe, Asia or North America. The rationale behind the regional strategy is that there are similarities between the countries in the region. A regional strategy for distribution can lead to efficiencies, but markets may differ within regions in terms of products. Some regions comprise 20 or more diverse countries, so although this conceptual approach has appeal, in practice, country differences need to be taken into account. A standardized product across a whole region is perhaps more realistic than the global product for all markets, but is still problematic.

Even the most centralized global organizations now accept that the one-size-fits-all approach is not as responsive to consumer needs as the more adaptive multidomestic and regional strategies. Can the firm achieve the best of both worlds? It is possible to develop a global marketing strategy at the highest level while devolving marketing strategies to local decision-makers (see Figure 8.3). The company's global marketing strategy represents the broad principles which guide its strategy across its differing markets (Jeannet and Hennessey, 1998: 285). For example, it may choose to focus on global product categories, but does not attempt to standardize all elements of its marketing. Strategies at an operational level may differ from one to another, but the company sees these differences as having a logic within its broader picture. In this way, the three levels of marketing become integrated.

Global product category: Broad category of products which can be subdivided into products with distinctive features for differing markets.

TO RECAP...
Global marketing strategies
Marketing strategies range from the single global strategy for a standardized product to regional and multidomestic strategies which are adapted to different markets. The global marketing strategy may benefit from both a global perspective and adaptations for local markets, thus integrating global and local strategic considerations.

The return of global strategy?
For global companies, the pendulum seemed to swing away from global strategy towards localization. Do you feel the pendulum is now swinging back towards global strategy, and why?

PAUSE TO REFLECT

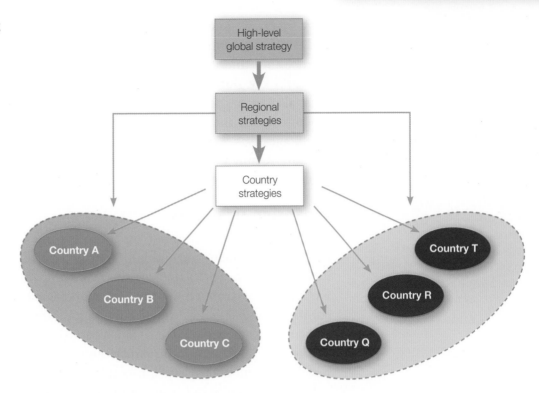

Figure 8.3 Global marketing strategy

International market expansion

In this section, we look at why and how firms seek customers for their products and services in foreign environments. The decision to enter new markets represents a strategic shift, with resource implications. Companies may decide to enter foreign markets for a variety of reasons, a common one being simply that this is what competitors are doing. Deciding which markets to enter and how to position the company's products requires extensive knowledge of the environment, as well as awareness of the risks it might present.

Why seek new markets?

Firms may take an 'opportunistic' approach to the internationalization, or they may take a more deliberate approach, planning how the new dimension will contribute towards achieving corporate goals. Seizing an opportunity which arises can prove inspired if the new market is successful, but it also represents a risk. If an impulsive decision leads to disappointment, it can be costly to exit. Of course, even companies that have put considerable research and effort into the planning can find that a particular market is not coming up to expectations. However, research and planning greatly enhance the likelihood of success.

Saturation in the home market acts as a 'push' factor towards international expansion. Firms requiring large sites may find that restrictive planning laws limit the availability of appropriate sites in home markets. To maintain its growth, the firm seeks new products and new markets, where there is more scope for growth. New markets may be countries in the same region, where the consumer markets are similar. Increasingly, firms gravitate towards the large emerging and developing economies, with their buoyant economies and greater potential for growth than the mature economies of Western Europe and America. These new markets thus exert 'pull' in attracting outside firms. As key global firms in a sector enter China and India, rivals feel they must also enter these markets, for fear of losing out. Home Depot's reluctance to enter the Chinese market when B&Q was gaining first-mover advantages was a cause of shareholder concern (see CS4.2). The company did enter China through the acquisition of an existing chain of stores, but it is playing 'catch-up'.

Expansion strategies

Expansion strategies depend on the company, its products and potential markets. A company may initially seek to build a regional strategy based on its home region. For example, European companies typically expand in the EU, benefiting from familiarity with markets and the single currency in the eurozone. The regional strategy is appropriate where customer needs are similar across the region. For Spanish companies, a logical expansion strategy has been to move into Latin American countries. This is a regional strategy, which also benefits from a common language and cultural affinity.

Many companies in consumer industries have expanded from their home region to other markets where consumer societies are similarly evolving. Hence American companies have expanded from North America to Australia, New Zealand and Western Europe. These are all countries where the business environment is stable and predictable, and where consumer markets are highly developed. Because of cultural distance, Asian markets have been seen as more challenging. A number of high-profile exits from Japan, including Carrefour of France and Boots of the UK, are indicators of the difficulties. However, the rise of China and other Asian developing countries constitutes a new spur to expand into Asia.

Focusing on developing countries or emerging markets is an appealing prospect to many companies, as they are growing quickly and consumers are eager to acquire a range of consumer goods and services. However, these countries tend to be uncertain business environments. They also differ widely in social, economic and cultural background. Government policies, while tending to become more liberalized, are unpredictable. Changes of government policy may signal a reverse towards greater restrictions on foreign companies. India is an example of mixed signals towards investors, although the size of the Indian market remains an attraction for foreign companies.

Market selection

The company which enters international markets must assess the potential of differing countries as possible markets. The screening process involves three levels of analysis: the macro-level analysis of the national environment; analysis of the consumer market in general; and micro-level analysis of factors affecting the specific product. These are depicted in Figure 8.4. We look at each in turn.

Figure 8.4 Analysis of country markets

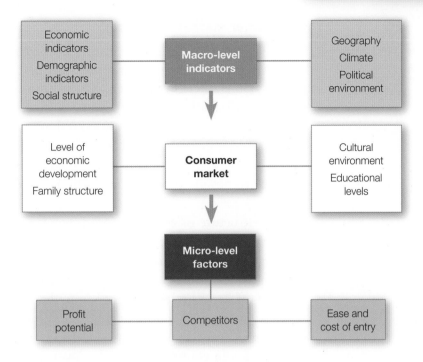

Macro-level analysis of the national environment

Assessment at the macro-level looks at geographic features, economic indicators, demographic data, social and economic structure, and the political environment. The size of the country, its geography and climate may influence the types of product that are suitable (or unsuitable), and the ease or difficulty of transporting them. Relevant economic data include GDP, GDP per capita and economic growth rates. This information is readily available from published sources, and helps to eliminate countries which are not suitable. It is not necessarily an indication of which countries *are* suitable, however. It is usually thought that if GDP per capita is below $10,000, there is too little potential for a luxury product. There may be a large and growing market among the middle classes, as in India, although GDP per capita is only $700. Demographic data show the age distribution of the population and the extent to which it is rural or urban. The world's developed economies have ageing populations. A large population of retired people may constitute a lucrative market for many products and services, such as small cars and package holidays. A country which is rapidly becoming urbanized also presents opportunities. However, as CF8.1 on China shows, unevenness of economic development can affect companies counting on prosperity spreading to rural areas.

The social and economic structure of the country indicates what types of employment are prevalent, what opportunities exist for social mobility and what role family networks play in the society. These aspects of the social structure also impact on the political environment. Political factors include levels of political instability and legal protection afforded to property, including intellectual property (such as brands). Governments may be particularly wary of foreign entrants which threaten local suppliers and jobs.

Consumer market in general

Consumer market: The aggregate of needs and desires of consumers within a country, taking into account their buying behaviour.

The consumer market in a country consists of the aggregate of needs and desires of consumers in the context of their buying behaviour and preferences. Consumers everywhere have certain essential needs to be satisfied, beyond which they seek to acquire non-essentials which make life more meaningful and pleasant. However, there are huge variations in priorities and tastes, even at the levels of basic needs. A firm considering a country as a potential market will need to know whether people will have the money to buy its products, and whether they will perceive the product as one they need.

The structure of consumption differs from country to country. In poorer countries, food, fuel and housing may account for the lion's share of an average consumer's disposable income. As countries develop economically and incomes grow, people are able to afford more goods to improve their quality of life. The level of economic development of a country is a broad indicator of a growing market for consumer products and services, such as appliances, cars, banking, fast-food meals and media products. However, consumers in countries at similar levels of development do not universally embrace all these products. Moreover, their choice of products depends on numerous social and cultural factors, including levels of education, religion and family priorities. Decision-making in family purchasing differs from country to country. In many countries, women are dominant in purchasing for the household. Market research indicates that for technology and entertainment spending, children play a role in decision-making (Carter, 2004). This seems not just to be 'pester power', but genuine involvement, representing a subtle democratization of family life.

The distinctive characteristics of a country's consumer market reflect people's expectations, as well as concerns, about their personal prosperity, as the example of Russia shows. Following the collapse of communism, the unbridled rise of capitalism in the early 1990s, although bringing riches to the very wealthy, brought deterioration in living standards for ordinary Russians. Since the advent of the new millennium, Russia has enjoyed a consumer boom. Russia's economic growth is boosting incomes of its upper middle class, but lower middle-class consumers, such as public sector workers, have prospered less. Among foreign MNEs, Metro, a German supermarket group, has established a wholesale business and three hypermarkets in Russia. IKEA, the Swedish furniture and interior design company, has gradually built up its Russian presence, confident of growth potential.

Micro-level analysis of product markets

Factors considered in a micro-level analysis include the ease of entry and its costs, the extent of competitors' presence, and the profit potential. Entering a new market through exporting is less costly than FDI. Retailers need a physical presence in the foreign market. This is less costly for a small format such as a boutique or fast-food outlet than for a large format such as a hypermarket. As the large retailing operation is a costly and complex investment, MNEs often choose the joint venture route. An anal-

plate 8.1 Shopping malls, now springing up in emerging markets, have become synonymous with modern consumer society.

ysis of competitors will show the degree of concentration and the extent to which foreign investors are active. If there are several competitors, all domestic, the foreign investor may gain competitive advantage through differentiation or possibly price, due to economies of scale which local competitors lack.

If there are already foreign firms in the market, it is likely that all are expecting it to grow in future. In this case, the firm has possibly missed an opportunity to capture market share early on. Once competitors are established, the new firm will find it difficult to seize market share from established rivals. Tesco found this to be the case when it entered Taiwan some years after Carrefour. It found the competitive environment difficult, especially with the continued popularity of local supermarkets. It exited the country in 2006, swapping its stores in Taiwan for Carrefour's stores in the Czech Republic and Slovakia, where Tesco has been the more successful.

TO RECAP...

Analysing market potential

Macro-level indicators are a starting point for analysing the market potential of a country. This profile is complemented by more detailed analysis of the consumer market in the country, which focuses on patterns of consumption. If this analysis shows market potential, the possibilities for specific product categories targeted at specific segments can then be explored.

Assessing markets

Which aspects of a country's macro-level environment and consumer market are most important for each of the following products:
● fast-food outlets ● banking services
● mobile phones?

PAUSE TO REFLECT

COUNTRY FOCUS 8.1 – CHINA

China's consumer boom takes off, but are all on board?

As Asia's fastest growing economy and home to 1.3 billion people, China has become a leading exporter to consumer markets the world over. Now, its domestic consumer market is becoming a focus of attention, providing opportunities for both local and foreign companies. Economic growth in the 9–10% range since 1994 has propelled China to seventh position in world retail markets. Increasing affluence is pulling more people into the middle class. In 2005, there were 42 million middle-class households in China enjoying annual incomes in excess of Rmb25,000 ($3,200). The number is expected to rise to 200 million by 2015. Of particular interest to retailers is the growing upper middle class, earning in the Rmb40,000–100,000 range. Middle-class consumers are concentrated in urban areas, as Figure 1 shows. Their spending power has pushed retail sales to increases of 13% annually for the past decade. Potential rewards for retailers are inviting, but they face significant challenges and uncertainties over future growth.

Foreign retailers aspiring to enter China learn early on that any preconception of China as a single market is misconceived. Disparities in income, regional differences in tastes and the sheer distances involved have all impacted on corporate strategies. Economic development has rested on industrialization, which is concentrated in the coastal areas with their growing urban populations. Cities are growing in both size and prosperity, while rural areas are still mainly poor. The urban population has risen to 40% of the total, from only 17% in 1975, and is expected to reach 50% by 2015. Average wages of urban residents doubled between 2000 and 2005. Urban residents accounted for 67% of Chinese retail sales in 2005. These increasingly affluent consumers are therefore the main target of retail-

Figure 1 Spending power of China's urban consumers

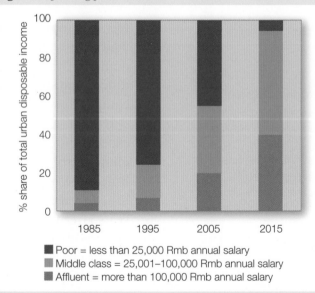

Poor = less than 25,000 Rmb annual salary
Middle class = 25,001–100,000 Rmb annual salary
Affluent = more than 100,000 Rmb annual salary

Source: Financial Times, 11 December 2006

ers in all sectors, from cars and luxury goods at the top of the scale down to clothing and food at the lower end. Hypermarket retailers now consider China a 'must' market, largely because of its potential growth. They are also encouraged by the government's lifting of the ban on foreign ownership of retailers at the end of 2004.

Among Western entrants into China's hypermarket sector are Carrefour, Wal-Mart and Tesco. There are also large Asian groups, including Vanguard, China's largest hypermarket retailer, which is based in Hong Kong and has 1,000 stores on the mainland. Carrefour is the largest and longest established Western retailer in China. Having entered China with a joint venture partner, it is now operating independently, with 90 stores in 23 cities. Despite 17 years in the country, Carrefour had a market share of only 0.6% in 2005, and its Chinese operations account for less than 3% of the group's overall sales. Carrefour cites difficulties in distribution networks, as distribution is almost all localized, inefficient and costly. Carrefour executives reason: 'In China, you do not have a national logistics systems, it is all very dislocated, so a company has to adapt to working with the local economy' (Dyer and Rigby, 2006). Wal-Mart has taken a strategic decision to invest in its own nationwide distribution network, a costly and ambitious move which, it hopes, will bring greater efficiencies in the long term. On the other hand, poor infrastructure and differing local conditions could thwart a nationwide strategy. Retailers are hoping that urbanization and rising wealth in rural areas will bring future growth, but these prospects are uncertain.

Despite rapid growth and industrialization, the bulk of China's population is still rural, amounting to 745 million people. World Bank researchers estimate that over 500 million live on less than $2 a day, a measure of 'moderate poverty' (Chen and Ravaillon, 2007). An important aspect of China's liberalization was the shift from communal farms to 'household responsibility' between 1977 and 1979, which gave farmers incentives to farm individual plots. While these reforms boosted productivity, the lack of legal property rights to their land, it later emerged, made farmers vulnerable to the appropriation of the land they farm by public sector projects and commercial developments. This has left many farming households landless and without adequate compensation. The government recognizes that rural development is now a priority, in order to maintain social stability and satisfy aspirations for a better quality of life for all socioeconomic groups. The natural propensity of Chinese people has been to save rather than spend, a tendency reinforced by worries over paying for health, housing, education and other needs. These concerns are more in evidence in poorer rural areas than in cities, where growing affluence is creating a boom in consumption. However, retailers have found that Chinese consumers are discriminating shoppers, and that cultural influences remain important.

To win market share, retailers have had to trim margins. They compete not only against other hypermarkets, but against a wealth of more traditional types of retailing such as markets. Organized retailing, through chains of stores with distribution networks, is much less developed than in Western environments, as Figure 2 shows. It is perhaps surprising, therefore, that there are over 120 hypermarkets in Shanghai, some districts having four or more. The competition creates even greater price pressures. While customers like foreign brands, they show little loyalty if prices are lower elsewhere. In Shanghai, which has reached saturation, some of these retailers are likely to withdraw, as capacity adjusts to demand. In addition, the government could compel future entrants to survey whether demand exists before approving new projects.

As they expand beyond the cities of Shanghai, Beijing and

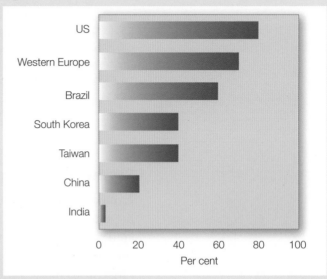

Figure 2 Penetration of organized retail

Source: Financial Times, 28 November 2006

Guangzhou, retailers are finding marked differences in tastes among consumers. Fruit and vegetables, sauces and meats are matters of local preferences. Soy sauces are favoured in the north, chilli sauces in central China and oyster sauces in the south. One preference all Chinese customers share is for very fresh food, stemming in part from experiences in previous eras when food safety standards were low. In many cases, they are reluctant to buy products which have not originated in the local district. An experienced consultant says: 'You have to get the fresh [food] right, otherwise the Chinese will not respect you' (Rigby and Dyer, 2007). This priority challenges hypermarket retailers, whose strengths are global distribution networks and economies of scale. Keeping existing customers satisfied and expanding outwards from the cities will test their adaptability in this changing market.

Questions

◆ Assess China as a potential market in terms of the three levels of analysis presented in the previous section: macro-level factors, consumer markets, and micro-level product markets.
◆ How does China's rich–poor divide impact on the growth in consumer markets?
◆ Why have hypermarket retailers flocked to China?

Sources: Lau, J., 'China market leaders are the ones to watch', *Financial Times,* 5 April 2006; McGregor, R., 'Unstoppable but unsustainable', *Financial Times,* 12 December 2006; Dyer, G. and Rigby, E., 'Wal-Mart on song in China as bid is launched', *Financial Times,* 18 October 2006; Johnson, J. and Birchall, J., '"Mom and pop" stores braced for challenge', *Financial Times,* 28 November 2006; Ward, A., 'Home Depot opens the door to a growing market', *Financial Times,* 11 December 2006; Rigby, E., 'Big chains stake out their turf in China', *Financial Times,* 13 February 2007; Sachs, J. (2005) *The End of Poverty* (London: Penguin); UNDP (2006) *Human Development Report* (Basingstoke: Palgrave Macmillan); Chen, S. and Ravallion, M. (2007) 'Absolute poverty measures for the developing world', World Bank Policy Research Paper WPS4211, www.wds.worldbank.org.

WEB CHECK

For information about China, see the World Bank's website at www.worldbank.org, and click on *China* in the country list.

Developing and emerging markets
What factors should firms prioritize when contemplating expansion into these exciting new markets? What are their disadvantages in comparison with developed countries?

PAUSE TO REFLECT

Segmentation and targeting

Even in a market with good growth potential, a firm cannot realistically hope to win over all potential consumers. It may have a single undifferentiated strategy for a standardized product, aiming to reach the maximum number of consumers. Low-cost airlines are one of the few examples of this type of strategy. However, as the discussion of consumer markets above highlighted, consumers differ in their buying power, lifestyles, location and priorities. Target marketing is aimed at particular consumers who the firm judges are most likely to purchase particular products. Targeting involves dividing consumers into different segments according to their needs and other characteristics. Particular products and appropriate ways of reaching consumers will differ from segment to segment.

For international marketing, segmentation based on differing national markets is common. However, marketers also focus on socioeconomic groups and demographic factors, which target segments across national boundaries. We consider each in turn. A *national market* is a geographic and administrative entity, whose consumers share cultural characteristics. National culture focuses on language and a shared sense of identity (see discussion in Chapter 4). It is particularly relevant in the markets for products where these elements come into play, such as food and media. Magazines, therefore, have national markets, although the same titles may have different language editions. Products such as branded food and beverages are culturally sensitive, and producers market products for national tastes. Shared national culture is also important for immigrants, who form subcultures in their new countries, as SX8.1 highlights.

Socioeconomic grouping is the second basis of market segmentation. These segments transcend national boundaries. Consumer affluence and buying behaviour may nonetheless differ from country to country. Televisions are desired by consumers everywhere, but differing levels of affluence influence the models and marketing strategy in each country. High-income groups are similar in their consumer preferences, whatever country they are in, as lifestyle is in large part a matter of income. Middle-class consumers live in similar types of accommodation and seek to furnish their houses in similar ways, wherever they live. This has been the guiding philosophy of IKEA. Luxury cars, fine jewellery and expensive holiday destinations appeal to the rich everywhere. But the firm which focuses exclusively on luxury markets risks falling sales in periods of economic downturn. Many companies, such as car manufacturers, offer a range of brands for differing income groups. Renault's Logan subsidiary produces a cheap and cheerful small car, mainly in Romania, for developing and emerging

Target marketing: Marketing aimed at satisfying the needs of a particular group of consumers.

Segmentation: Division of a consumer market into groups of similar consumers who share some key characteristics, such as socioeconomic grouping, cultural identity or demographic similarity.

markets, but has been surprised that it is selling well in established European markets. As highlighted in the opening vignette, the car market is growing swiftly in India, leading Renault to adjust its strategy by forging a joint venture with Bajaj Auto to produce an even cheaper car, rivalling the Tata Nano. India is now seen as a growing market and a manufacturing centre.

The third basis of segmentation is *demographics*. Demographic segmentation includes a number of variables, the most popular being age and gender. Young consumers in their late teens and twenties are a favourite segment of marketers. They are assumed to be free spenders on the latest products, fashion items and entertainment, whatever country they are in. Mobile phone companies target this group in particular, as do drinks companies (see CS3.1 on Heineken). In mobile phones and music players, companies target teenagers in the 13–18 age range. LG Electronics is an example, seeing this segment as setting trends which others will follow (Fifield, 2004). Given the ageing populations of most developed economies, well-off pensioners are a significant segment. These consumers are a traditional target of holiday companies selling cruises and other package holidays, but there are many other products and services which these consumers seek, such as accommodation adapted to their needs and home services. Gender is another traditional basis of demographic segmentation. Products targeted at women include clothing, magazines and cosmetics. However, in all these areas, marketers are also targeting men with products designed for their needs. Men's grooming products are a growing market, making Procter & Gamble's acquisition of the well-known brand Gillette a significant strategic move (discussed in CS8.1).

The company contemplating international markets must measure the segment attractiveness against its own business strengths before deciding which countries and which segments to target. A segment may be attractive if it is projected to grow strongly, but if it does not fit with the company's long-term goals or strengths, it will probably struggle to be competitive and capture market share. The firm may choose to target several market segments, tailoring its products and marketing mix for each. This represents a **differentiated marketing** strategy, often adopted by large MNEs. Their reasoning is that strong offerings in a number of segments will contribute to its overall strength in its product category.

By contrast, some businesses have specialized strengths, for which the relevant market is rather narrowly defined. This is known as the **niche market**. The niche market consists of a subgroup of consumers with particular specialized needs. Often the smaller company finds opportunities in niche markets which larger companies overlook. Organic products, highlighted in Chapter 13, are an example. There may well be few competitors in the niche market. Large companies may offer products in niche markets in addition to their more mainstream offerings, but their main target markets are those in which they enjoy economies of scale. Niche markets may also be specific to cultural characteristics. LG Electronics has designed its 'Qiblah' phones, which indicate the direction of Mecca for Muslim consumers. These phones are targeted at Middle East consumers. Spanish-language broadcasting in the US has formerly been considered a niche market, but, as SX8.1 shows, this market is becoming mainstream.

See LG's website at www.lge.com.

WEB CHECK

Differentiated marketing: Adapting products and marketing mix for differing target markets.

Niche market: Subgroup of consumers with specific specialized needs.

TO RECAP...

Segmentation in international markets
Segmenting according to countries is a traditional approach. Socioeconomic and demographic segments straddle national boundaries, implying more globalized strategies, although national cultural factors remain influential in much marketing decision-making.

STRATEGIC CROSSROADS

8.1

Excitement mounts as Hispanic media take to a wider stage

The Hispanic market in the US has become one of the most sought-after by media companies. The growing numbers of Hispanic consumers, as well as their youthfulness, make them an attractive market for media companies and advertisers. The Hispanic population of the US consists of Spanish-speaking people who have emigrated from Latin America, mainly Mexico, in search of employment and higher living standards than their home countries offer. Their median age is 26.7 years, placing them in the middle of the 18–34 age group, advertisers' favourite age band. While it had been expected that the numbers of Spanish speakers would decline as immigrants became assimilated, their numbers are actually growing. This is good news for media companies, which have seen their mass audiences fragmented by options such as cable television and the internet. In 2006, the US media industry expanded by 5.4% overall, but the Hispanic segment expanded by nearly double that rate, at 10.4%. Rising Hispanic audiences, whose spending power is expected to grow to $670 billion in personal income by 2020, are attracting excited attention.

The leading Spanish-language media company in the US is Univision, which owns three television networks and 69 radio stations. Founded in 1992 in Los Angeles, an 11% stake was held by Televisa, the Mexican company which is the world's largest Spanish-language media group. Televisa specializes in the 'telenovela', a melodrama format akin to the soap opera, which originated in Cuba's cigar factories, where Dickens and Balzac, both masters of emotion-laden melodramas, were read aloud to workers. The company became market leaders in creating television dramas, along with their glamorous stars, with the same efficiency of the formula-driven former Hollywood studios or Bollywood producers from India. Latin American-produced telenovelas command audiences of 2 billion, mainly in Latin America, but extending to 100 countries around the world. Univision eventually persuaded advertisers to consider its networks in the mainstream of their annual spending plans, rather than a niche. In areas with large concentrations of Hispanics, such as Los Angeles, Miami and Chicago, Univision regularly achieves larger audiences than the top English-language networks, including ABC, CBS and Fox. In 2006, Nielsen, the media research company, began measuring Univision's audiences alongside other US networks. Occasionally, its primetime ratings have beaten its larger rivals for 18–34-year-old viewers, an achievement which has sent the company's shares upwards and attracted takeover interest.

As market leader, Univision has faced competition. NBC Universal, owned by GE, bought Telemundo, a Miami-based production company, for $2.7 billion in 2002. Telemundo tackled Univision head-on with its own telenovela, *Tierra de Pasiones*. Its content is home produced, in contrast to the imported programmes of Univision. Telemundo argues that relevance to issues closer to the interests and concerns of its audiences will give it an advantage. Telemundo went so far as to establish a telenovela centre in association with a local university, to build local skills in writing the dramas, from which a pool of telenovela writers would emerge. Telemundo is also transferring material from *Tierra de Pasiones* to its websites, with accompanying advertising. Owning its content gives it flexibility and a competitive edge in the growing digital market. Telemundo also aspires to global audiences, and claims a presence in 142 markets. In 2006, it made more than $20 million selling its telenovelas to broadcasters in foreign markets such as Spain and Argentina.

Telemundo's most recent success has been in seemingly unlikely markets in Asia, including South Korea, China, Malaysia and Indonesia. Although these markets have traditionally been resistant to foreign media content, the romantic melodramas have struck a chord with viewers. The president of Telemundo International says: 'These are countries that share a lot of the same cultural values and realities. If it works in Latin America, it works in Asia' (Chaffin, 2008).

Questions
- Assess the reasons behind Univision's growth.
- How are the strategies of media firms in Spanish-language output evolving in terms of wider markets?

Sources: Chaffin, J., 'Manic for the Hispanic market', *Financial Times*, 27 June 2006; Chaffin, J., 'Hispanics warm to telenovelas with an American twist', *Financial Times*, 25 May 2006; Van Duyn, A., 'Spanish TV drama's final scene may yet need further rewrite', *Financial Times*, 28 June 2006; Chaffin, J., 'US television recognises its need to brush up on Spanish', *Financial Times*, 9 February 2006; Chaffin, J. 'Mascara melodrama eyes up Asia for the payoff kiss', *Financial Times*, 8 February 2008.

WEB CHECK

Telemundo's website is http://tv.telemundo.yahoo.com.
Univision's website is www.univision.net.

Shifting targets?
To what extent do you feel segmentation based on demographic characteristics, such as age and gender, is becoming more significant than segmentation based on national cultural differences?

PAUSE TO REFLECT

Market entry strategies

In Chapter 7, broad internationalization strategies were examined from the organizational perspective, focusing on production decisions. Here we look at entry strategies from the perspective of firms wishing to win customers in foreign markets. Market entry options, which are shown in Figure 8.5, vary with the type of product or service. For manufactured goods, companies usually consider export as a first option. Export may be indirect, through intermediaries based in the firm's home country, or direct, through intermediaries in the foreign market. Initially, a firm is likely to use agents and foreign distributors. However, as agents and distributors deal with many clients, the firm may choose to set up its own sales subsidiary in the foreign market, bypassing the intermediaries. The sales office becomes the distributor for the firm's products, holding stock, selling to buyers and engaging in marketing activities designed by the company. As it is a type of FDI, it involves a greater commitment to the location. It affords the company greater control and a better platform from which to build its new market than exporting through intermediaries.

Figure 8.5 Market entry strategies

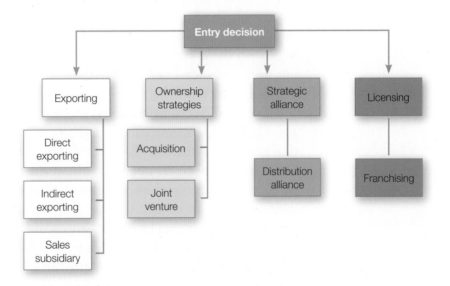

In many product categories, the firm may find production in the foreign market reduces costs. While foreign production may take the form of a greenfield operation (discussed in Chapters 2 and 7), manufacture under licence is a favoured alternative, involving less capital investment and greater flexibility. The licence is awarded by a company (the licensor) to a local producer (the licensee), giving the licensee permission to manufacture goods covered by patent or trademark, provided the terms of the licensing agreement are met. The licensee pays a royalty to the licensor, usually a percentage of sales volumes. Pharmaceutical companies use licensing agreements extensively. Food companies also use this system, as these rather low-value products are expensive to export. However, there are risks in licensing, stemming from dependence on the local partner. The quality control of the local producer may be questionable, and it may not possess the marketing skills to build market share in competition with astute rivals.

Franchising also involves licensing, but in this case, the franchisor company negotiates for an entire operation to be carried out under its name and marketing programme in the foreign location. Fast-food outlets such as McDonald's and KFC are examples. However, as highlighted in SX1.1, McDonald's has relied on managed restaurants rather than franchising in many foreign locations, a policy which is now evolving.

The advantage of ownership of assets in the foreign market is that of ultimate control over the products and marketing. Under a joint venture arrangement, the foreign entrant and a local company take equity stakes in a new company which enters the market. The hypermarkets have favoured this method of entry, dictated by legal constraints on ownership in some cases such as China, discussed in CF8.1. In developing and transitional economies, the joint venture benefits from the knowledge of the local partner and the management skills of the foreign partner. Wal-Mart has chosen an Indian firm, Bharti Enterprises, for its market debut in India. In Japan, Wal-Mart chose to purchase a stake in a Japanese retailer, Seiyu, as a low-key entry strategy. This strategy has been unsuccessful so far, as Seiyu has struggled to make profits. In the UK, Wal-Mart entered through acquisition of an existing business, ASDA, in 1999. Acquisition gives the acquirer an immediate market share, making this option attractive for companies impatient with the approach of building up a presence from scratch. ASDA has not been rebranded as Wal-Mart, but the ASDA logo now states: 'part of the Wal-Mart family'.

Strategic alliances have proved popular in some sectors. Distribution alliances link manufacturers and brand owners with companies having distribution networks already in place. For the manufacturer, the advantages are that it can reach consumers quickly, without the meticulous groundwork needed to build its own distribution network. These alliances can be equity-based joint ventures or simply contractual arrangements. General Mills, a US company which makes breakfast cereals, entered a joint venture with Nestlé, forming Cereal Partners Worldwide (CPW), a company owned equally by both partners. General Mills benefited from Nestlé's worldwide distribution network, while Nestlé benefited from General Mills' product lines, which compete against Kellogg's, the market leader. CPW is based in Switzerland and manufactures for markets outside the US and Canada.

Market entry analysis is outlined in Figure 8.6. Each possible market entry strategy has associated costs, which must be balanced against expected gains from sales. Environmental factors in the new market come into play. Political uncertainty is particularly relevant if the company has acquired ownership of assets in the foreign market, which may be jeopardized by changes in government or policies, as CF8.2 on South Africa highlights. Currency risk may affect the expected profits. The company must also consider what timescale it is contemplating for yielding the desired returns. While patience is rewarded in many markets, in others, the situation may deteriorate, often due to external factors. If the strategy fails to achieve the firm's objectives, market exit can be costly, and the company faces the unenvivable task of deciding how long to wait before abandoning its strategy, with inevitable damage to its reputation.

WEB CHECK

Cereal Partners' website is www.cerealpartners.co.uk. ASDA's website is www.asda.co.uk.

TO RECAP...

Market entry alternatives

Exporting, either directly or indirectly, is a traditional market entry strategy. For large firms, acquiring an existing business or entering a joint venture with a local partner involve ownership stakes. Licensing a foreign producer is a means of market entry which does not involve ownership of foreign assets. Strategic alliances are helpful in particular functional areas such as distribution. Decision-making must take into account costs, market potential and environmental factors.

Figure 8.6 Market entry analysis

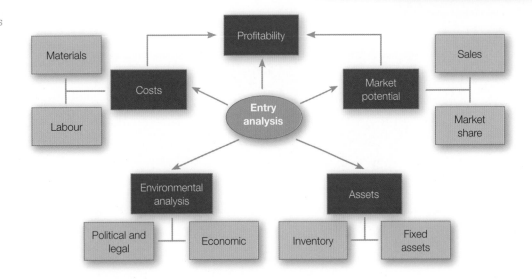

COUNTRY FOCUS 8.2 – SOUTH AFRICA

Buoyant South Africa on a wave of optimism

South Africa has become sub-Saharan Africa's most prosperous economy, its GDP four times that of neighbouring countries. Since the collapse of apartheid in 1994, democracy and economic development have bred growing optimism. Economic growth in the 3–6% range (shown in Figure 1), although not stunning in comparison to the fast-growing emerging markets, is a cause for optimism, following decades of disappointment. It has taken 25 years for real GDP per capita to recover to 1981 levels. Current GDP per head of over $6,000 ($15,000 at PPP) places South Africa in the group of middle-income countries. The economy is gradually shifting from mining and other heavy industries, on which it has traditionally depended, to service

sectors such as business process outsourcing (BPO) and tourism, which are growing globally. Figure 2 shows the breakdown of 2006 GDP growth for each sector.

Government priorities have been providing social welfare programmes and increasing participation of black South Africans in economic prosperity. A growing middle class is spending on consumer goods such as cars and new houses, and shopping at new shopping malls which are springing up all over the country, not just in the large cities. Low interest rates mean affordable mortgages and car payments, leaving consumers more money to spend on other goods.

South African consumers' spending spree has been welcome

Figure 1 South Africa's economic growth, 1984–2008

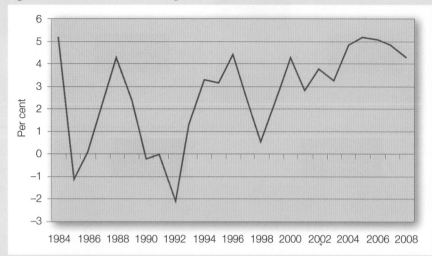

Note: Estimates for 2007 and 2008

Source: IMF (2007) World Economic Outlook, October, www.imf.org

news to banks and retailers. Barclays, the UK bank, exited South Africa in 1987, due to pressures from anti-apartheid protests. In 2005, it returned with vigour, acquiring a 56% stake in South Africa's largest retail bank, Absa. This acquisition became the single largest foreign investment in South Africa since 1994. Barclays hopes ultimately to generate 10% of its total earnings from Absa, boosting its earnings from outside the UK to one-third the total. The attractions were Absa's 7.7 million retail customers, with further potential for mortgages, credit cards and commercial property finance. With its expertise in credit cards, Barclays was especially keen to enter this market, which has ample growth potential, as only 10% of South Africans had credit cards in 2005. Absa's loans and advances rose 26% in the first year of Barclays control, and retail customers rose to 8.4 million, boding well for future growth. However, analysts have questioned the long-term viability of the South African investment. The consumer boom is offering business opportunities, but longer term prospects depend on continued economic growth, which could be affected by political risk.

Although consumption has forged ahead, South Africa's export industries have suffered from currency volatility. The currency, the rand, has doubled in US dollar terms since 2001, causing headaches for exporters, particularly manufacturers, who are important to GDP growth (see Figure 2). South Africa is in a less favourable position than the fast-growing emerging markets, such as China, which have relied on export-oriented manufacturing, although growth in high value-added services is encouraging. The strong rand has helped consumers to buy flat-screen televisions and other imported goods, but exporters have less to cheer about. Unemployment is high, at 26%, and the rate is closer to 36% if discouraged workers who have stopped looking for work are included. The economy would need to grow at over 6% annually to create enough jobs. At present, despite government training programmes, the lack of skills is holding back foreign investment as well as local businesses.

South Africa is still beset by the wide gap in incomes and quality of life between the better off classes and the 22 million very poor inhabitants, who comprise nearly half the total population. Of these, less than half have access to primary education, and some 5.5 million are suffering from HIV/Aids. Growing tax revenues are funding programmes to deal with health and deprivation, but hopes of halving poverty and unemployment by 2014 seem optimistic. The lack of skilled workers has deterred investors, but as suitably skilled candidates enter employment, prospects for bringing more citizens into salaried employment are improving.

Services are providing new jobs and growth potential. In BPO, South Africa has attracted investors such as Lufthansa, Virgin Mobile, IBM and Carphone Warehouse. South Africa offers them cost savings of about 30% compared to their home economies, as well as other benefits. The time zone, a relatively neutral accent and greater cultural affinity with northern European countries have helped to attract call-centre operations. Back-office operations are also taking off, including finance and IT. On the negative side, the costs of telecommunications are high, owing to the slowness of reforms in dismantling the state-owned monopoly provider. The numbers of candidates for BPO jobs are rising as education improves among black students. These new recruits are likely to stay in jobs longer than those in countries such as India, which has a greater supply of qualified workers. While South Africa is never likely to compete with India's high-volume BPO operations in cost savings, it is targeting niche markets in areas such as conflict resolution and HRM, in which it can build expertise.

Tourism is another growth sector which, while not offering prospects of high volumes, attracts upmarket tourists looking for stunning scenery and wildlife. Tourism's contribution to the economy has doubled since the transition to democracy in 1994. Overseas visitors number about 2 million a year, which

Figure 2 Composition of South Africa's GDP growth in 2006

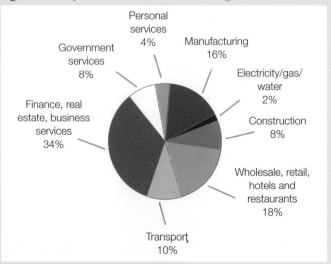

Source: Statistics South Africa, www.statssa.gov.za

should be boosted by the football World Cup in 2010. Service standards, transport and infrastructure are improving. Tourism authorities are also hoping to broaden the country's appeal, attracting younger clients who seek alternatives to beach holidays and safaris. However, they are aware that these popular types of holiday are available more cheaply in other locations, and that broadening appeal could deter the more affluent visitors. Several factors could dampen growth in tourism. Weak international air access, shortages of skilled staff and high levels of violent crime are among them.

South Africa has become a successful emerging economy, which stands out among its poorer neighbours. However, its economic landscape is one of contrasts, in which some areas are developed while others are much less developed. The bestselling product at Edcon, one of the country's largest retailers, is not flat-screen TVs or the like, but light bulbs, which have risen in demand as electricity gradually reaches into poorer communities. The less good news is that power cuts are a common phenomenon across the country, as the power generation network struggles to keep up with demand. Maintaining power to industrial and commercial customers, as well as household consumers, is one of the many challenges facing South Africa.

Questions

◆ In 2005, some criticized Barclays for its acquisition of Absa as being too risky an investment. Assess the pros and cons of the decision. Does the bank now seem to have got it right?
◆ Assess the entry decision-making process for a company from the EU considering South Africa as a possible location for its call centre.
◆ Construct a SWOT analysis of a South African company offering upmarket packages for foreign tourists.

Sources: Reed, J., 'Good times put system under strain', *Financial Times*, 6 June 2006; White, D., 'Black middle class helps fuel a spending spree', *Financial Times*, 6 June 2006; White, D., 'In defiance of gravity', *Financial Times*, 24 May 2005; Reed, J., 'Scouting for more happy customers', *Financial Times*, 6 June 2006; Reed, J., 'Swept up in a mood of optimism', *Financial Times*, 24 May 2005; Barber, L. and Russell, A., 'Softly, softly: Mbeki seeks ways to limit chaos to the north and tensions within', *Financial Times*, 3 April 2007; IMF (2006) Country report for South Africa, www.imf.org/external; Statistics South Africa (2006), www.statssa.gov.za.; Russell, A., 'A long journey', *Financial Times*, 27 June 2007; Hawkins, T., 'Out of the doldrums', *Financial Times*, 5 June 2007.

WEB CHECK

See information about South Africa by going to the World Bank's website at www.worldbank.org, and clicking on *South Africa* in the country list.

plate 8.2 The affluence of Cape Town, South Africa, seen in the modern buildings shown here, reflects the country's economic growth.

Emerging market entry
Which entry strategies are best suited to developing and emerging markets, and why? Give examples in manufactured products and in retailing.

PAUSE TO REFLECT

Products and branding

Product: Goods (tangible), services (intangible), or a combination of the two, which a firm offers to potential customers in exchange for payment, usually money.

Products and brands may have a local, national, regional or global focus. Within a product area, a company can adapt product features and marketing to national or local markets. It may also aim to build global brands, complemented by local brands or niche brands for products targeted at local markets or particular segments. Decisions on products and brands are central to marketing strategy.

Products are probably the most crucial ingredient of success in any market. The product may be a good, which is a tangible product that the consumer can physically touch, or a service, which is intangible. We tend to think of companies as specializing in one or the other, but the marketing concept, which focuses on consumer satisfaction, implies that service to the customer is an aspect of providing goods. While the traditional focus of Ford was simply to produce and sell cars, in the 1960s, GM realized that offering after-sales service was a way of winning over customers. Goods and services are therefore linked in the experience of the consumer. In some cases, there is a direct link. For example Apple's iPod music player and iTunes music downloading complement each other.

Every product has attributes which distinguish it from others in the same broad product category. These attributes or features may be crucial in appealing to certain market segments. Dyson's vacuum cleaner designed for the Japanese market is smaller and lighter than those offered in other markets, to make it suitable for small apartments (see SX2.2 on Dyson). In fact, these qualities have made it popular in other markets as well. Apart from physical attributes, the product may have intangible attributes, such as its recognition in society as a status symbol. An Indian marketing executive says of his desire to trade his motorbike for a new Tata Nano: 'A car says you are in a good position, a good career' (Johnson, 2008a).

The brand has a legal dimension and an image-creating dimension. Legally, it is a trademark or logo which distinguishes the product from similar products by other producers. When the trademark is registered, the owner has ownership rights in the form of intellectual property, which authorizes the taking of legal action against other firms which use the trademark without permission. Unfortunately, in many parts of the world, brand names and logos, although protected in theory, are weakly enforced, allowing counterfeiters to produce falsely labelled goods in large quantities. These are inevitably cheaper than the proper branded product and are usually of poor quality. Brand owners wage a constant battle against these practices, which they feel could affect legitimate sales in some markets.

Global and local dimensions

Local products and brands are the mainstay of companies which concentrate on home markets. Foreign entrants may struggle to build market share where there is strong consumer attachment to local offerings. On the other hand, if the MNE has a strong global brand, it may convey a notion of quality and prestige which will attract consumers. They will probably have to pay a premium price for the global brand, but they feel the brand is a guarantee of quality, while local products could well have inconsistent quality. In many countries, the global brand is aspirational. A Costa Rican consumer says: 'Local brands show what we are; global brands show what we want to be' (Holt et al., 2004). In areas such as pharmaceuticals, the global brand is a guarantee of safety in countries where many medicines produced by local

Brand: Trademark or logo distinguishing an organization's products from those of rivals, which is an important asset capable of legal protection.

TO RECAP...

Products and brands

In addition to providing the right product for target markets, companies aim to attract consumers by branding through trademarks.

manufacturers are unsafe and ineffective, in addition to being produced in breach of patents.

A few global brands, such as Microsoft, Coca-Cola and McDonald's, have become iconic. These brands consistently feature in global brand rankings. The top 10 from two of these ranking systems are presented in Figure 8.7. Both systems calculate financial value on the basis of brand strength in terms of consumer demand and expectations for future growth. Microsoft and Coca-Cola regularly jostle for first place. Google's swift rise to the top of the Millward Brown rankings indicates the growing power of the internet. Google is still strongly identified with the idealism of its founders, which shapes its brand image.

The brand's image-creating dimension is a source of its appeal to customers. The brand evokes a number of images in the minds of consumers, which relate to the company's reputation and values, as well as the consumer's own lifestyle, social status and values. Indeed, the consumer's aspirations to a particular lifestyle or status are perhaps more relevant: the consumer's self-image is enhanced by the brand. The company which is able to build a strong brand in the eyes of consumers builds a relationship with them which generates brand loyalty. The concept of 'brand equity' is the added value that the brand brings to the product and its owner. For this reason, brands may be worth considerable sums of money as assets in their own right. The share that brands contribute to a firm's overall value is estimated to have risen from 50% in 1980 to 70% in 2007 (Gapper, 2007).

The global brand built on quality acts as a guarantee to consumers regarding its products (Steenkamp et al., 2003). If the brand owner allows quality to suffer, the strong brand may protect it for a time but, eventually, consumers will desert the brand. Consumers also expect brand owners to maintain high standards in areas such as corporate social responsibility (Holt et al., 2004). Reporting on their CSR throughout their global operations has become common among global companies. Issues such as relations with stakeholders in local communities, employee conditions and the provision of services such as health and education for employees in developing countries are aspects of CSR, discussed further in Chapter 14.

Figure 8.7 Rankings of global brands for 2007

Sources: Interbrand, *Interbrand Best Global Brands 2007*, www.interbrand.com; Millward Brown Optimor, *Brandz Survey 2007*, www.millwardbrown.com

Millward Brown Brandz Survey				Interbrand rankings		
Brand		**Brand value $millions**	**% change on previous year**	**Brand**	**Brand value $millions**	**% change on previous year**
1	Google	66,434	77	1 Coca-Cola	66,324	−3
2	GE	61,880	11	2 Microsoft	58,709	3
3	Microsoft	54,951	−11	3 IBM	57,091	2
4	Coca-Cola	44,134	7	4 GE	57,569	5
5	China Mobile	41,214	5	5 Nokia	33,696	12
6	Marlboro	39,166	2	6 Toyota	32,070	15
7	Wal-Mart	36,680	−2	7 Intel	30,944	−4
8	Citi	33,706	9	8 McDonald's	29,398	7
9	IBM	33,572	−7	9 Disney	29,210	5
10	Toyota	33,427	11	10 Mercedes	23,568	5

A brand may benefit from associations with its country of origin. Perceptions of quality and prestige enhance the brand's image, becoming part of its brand equity. 'Made in Germany' suggests quality engineering and benefits Germany's motor manufacturers and industrial engineering companies. Italy is associated with fashion and quality in clothes and accessories, and is home to some of the most coveted brands, such as Armani and Prada. A number of Armani-label clothes, some in the top-end Armani Collezioni range, are now made in China. Although the company maintains that its stringent quality control standards remain the same, the 'made in China' label could possibly damage the firm's image. A number of luxury brands outsource manufacturing to China, and some, unlike Armani, carry no such label. LG Electronics of South Korea has launched an upmarket mobile phone under the Prada brand, extending the notion of Italian style to the mobile phone, perceived as a fashion accessory by many consumers.

Product and brand strategies

The fashion-conscious consumer seeking out the Prada-branded mobile phone represents one of many segments targeted by LG Electronics. A large company may have a portfolio of numerous products and brands, from which it chooses which brands and products are suited to different markets and segments. The global brand may be of such value that it can be extended to other products. Known as 'brand extension', this strategy relies on consumers' positive perceptions of the brand and the image it creates. For example, fashion retailers, such as Zara, extend their products to home furnishings, creating a lifestyle image consistent with the company's clothes. Jewellery and accessories are other common extensions of brands. These extensions are a means of persuading the consumer who is attracted to the brand to buy a range of other products which are associated with the same image and in the same price range.

The company may choose to differentiate its brands according to market segment. Linde, a German company which supplies forklift trucks to industrial users, has three forklift truck brands, Linde, STILL and OM Pimespo, each for a different type of forklift truck. Linde trucks are diesel powered, Still vehicles are powered with electric motors and OM Pimespo covers warehouse trucks. Each of these sub-brands is a separate division of the company. This multi-brand strategy may seem fragmented, but the company feels it does more business than it would if all the products were sold under one brand. The parent company has rationalized the parts, utilizing common parts where possible across the brands. Multiple brands may also designate different products depending on whether they are basic market entry products or more upmarket products. Car manufacturers offer numerous models in various price ranges for people with differing levels of income. Many are branded with the corporate brand, such as VW, but separate brands may be used in different markets. VW markets cars in emerging markets under the Skoda brand and also owns Audi, an upmarket brand.

A valuable brand may well form the cornerstone of a firm's international expansion. If the brand is not well known outside its home country, the firm will have to build its reputation from scratch. Alternatively, the company

Sub-brand: Brand created to serve a distinctive product or market segment under the umbrella of the firm's corporate brand.

may acquire a local company which has a strong brand and build market share on the strength of the local brand. This was the approach of Nestlé, when it acquired Rowntree of the UK. Brands such as KitKat were then added to the company's portfolio of brands.

Emerging and developing countries offer some of the most enticing prospects for market growth for consumer product companies. There are crucial differences between these markets and developed countries, in terms of income, segments and the range of appropriate products. MNEs have typically found that, although their offerings reach mass markets in developed countries, in developing countries, only a small proportion of the population is acquainted with global brands and can afford branded imported products (Dawar and Chattopadhyay, 2000). This segment may amount to only about 5% of the population. The company may reason that, as these economies are developing quickly, this proportion is likely to grow and tastes will converge with developed countries. These developments, however, may be slow to materialize. Furthermore, the assumption that these consumers will converge with Europeans or Americans might turn out to be wrong. Localizing products is an alternative, to attempt to build mass-market appeal in the developing country. Extensive knowledge of the consumer market is required, and the foreign MNE is up against knowledgeable local competitors. CS8.1 on P&G highlights the challenges of this strategy. Prices must be in the range which target consumers can afford. Unilever's Lifebuoy soap is popular in Africa, India and Indonesia. It is a basic product made from local ingredients and packaging, keeping the price low. Unilever has learned from its experience in these markets that all the elements of the marketing mix, including product, packaging, distribution and communication, must be driven by price considerations. Unilever's example indicates that strategies for emerging markets may translate from one to another.

One of the reasons that MNEs in developed consumer markets are now looking to emerging and developing markets for future growth is that the competitive environment has become intense in their home markets. Here, they rely on new and innovative products to boost sales and differentiate themselves from rivals. However, brand owners have encountered competition from supermarkets and speciality retailers who sell products under their 'own' label, or private brands. They include goods, such as food and clothing, as well as services, such as insurance. The UK has been at the forefront of this trend. Own brands are usually cheaper than the global brand and capture considerable market share in numerous product lines. Own brands accounted for 36% of retail sales in Britain by value in 2006, as seen in Figure 8.8. This share looks set to rise as consumers feel more confident of the quality of the own-brand products. Although Tesco was once perceived as working class, differentiating itself mainly

Private brand: Brands owned by supermarkets and other retailers, which are produced for sale in their outlets alone; also known as 'private labels' and 'own brands'.

Figure 8.8 Own-label share of consumer packaged goods spending
Source: Financial Times, 26 January 2006

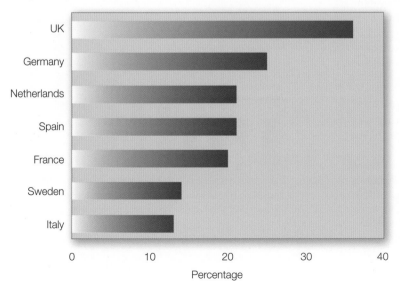

on price, it has now shifted to an emphasis on good value, whatever the price, appealing to all segments. Like other supermarkets, it has a segmented own-brand offering, with 'value', 'standard' and 'finest'.

Companies such as Unilever and P&G spend large sums on R&D, maintaining a leading role in creating new products. Their innovative products are often copied by manufacturers producing for private brands of supermarkets and multiple retailers. P&G has taken legal action against some of these producers for IPR infringement. The global brand owners argue that the own brands can never replicate the original product exactly, but the rise of their popularity with consumers suggests that they pose a real threat (Kumar and Steenkamp, 2007). In reality, retailers are building equity in their own brands. Note that Wal-Mart is ranked in seventh place in the Millward Brown rankings in Figure 8.7.

TO RECAP...

Product and brand strategies

In theory, the global brand is a strong competitor in all markets, but in practice, MNEs tend to have a portfolio of products and brands designed for differing national markets. The global brand owner faces competition from the private brands of retailers, whose products tend to be cheaper. Local producers, with their lower costs and local knowledge, offer competition to foreign entrants.

Waning of the global brand?
Global brands have faced consumer resistance in many markets, from consumers who prefer low-cost own brands and from those who object to the economic power and practices of large global companies. To what extent do you feel that the reputation of global brands is declining? Give examples.

PAUSE TO REFLECT

Procter & Gamble (P&G) started out supplying candles to the Union army in the American Civil War. The company grew into a symbol of American corporate success, its brands of consumer products featuring on the shelves of supermarkets across the globe. These include Tide laundry detergent, Crest toothpaste and Pringles crisps. P&G's strength has been innovation, offering new products and improved versions of familiar products to reflect changing consumer needs. However, the 1990s saw its innovation wane under growing bureaucracy and a complacent corporate culture, which eventually affected financial performance. In 1999, a new CEO, Durk Jager was brought in to restructure the organization. A radical restructuring ensued, sweeping away the national 'fiefdoms' of country managers and bringing in global business units based on product areas. The new product divisions would work with regional and local managers on marketing and distribution. The rapid restructuring caused considerable disruption, causing further disappointment and costing Jager his job. A.G. Lafley, who replaced him in 2000, kept the new structure, a decision which seems to have been justified by impressive earnings growth, as shown in Figure 1. The inward-looking corporate culture remained a concern when he took over. Refocusing on consumer needs and innovation has become a priority.

Under Lafley's leadership, acquisitions have helped to shape strategy and operations. The acquisition of Clairol and Wella hair care brands boosted the beauty segment, which has grown rapidly and contributes significantly to earnings. The expansion of beauty and healthcare has reflected global trends. About 40% of P&G's total staff of 110,000 employees have come from acquired compa-

Case study 8.1:
Global brands and local products light up Procter & Gamble

nies. The largest acquisition has been Gillette, bought in 2005 for $57 billion, which also owned Duracell batteries and Braun. Gillette's expertise in innovation and its global consumer relations systems were attractions for P&G, which has placed Gillette executives in key posts. Gillette also brought 22 major

Figure 1 P&G net earnings

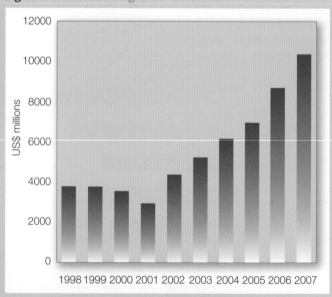

Source: P&G Annual Report 2007, www.pg.com

Figure 2 Percentages of net earnings by business unit

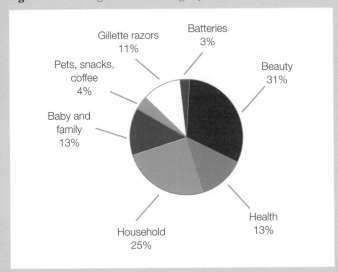

Source: P&G Annual Report 2007, www.pg.com

Figure 3 P&G's advertising expenditure

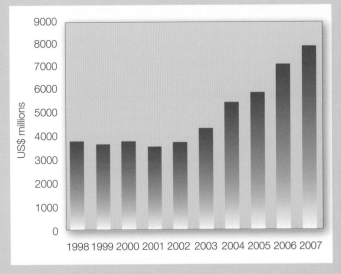

Source: P&G Annual Report 2007, www.pg.com

brands, generating over $1 billion in sales. As Figure 2 shows, Gillette and its battery business have contributed 14%, whereas pet health, snacks and coffee have contributed only 4%. These latter products, which include Iams, the pet food brand, have faced strong competition from supermarket own brands, such as Wal-Mart.

Some of the biggest challengers are private brands, as P&G's products are almost all supermarket lines. Lafley accepts that they have a role: 'A private label or a retailer brand cannot exist without branded comparison. Frankly, when we do our job well we are not very vulnerable at all to private labels, because our position broadly is middle of the market and up' (Grant, 22 December 2005). However, competition should be fair. P&G has taken legal action against Percara Enterprises and Cumberland Swan Holdings for infringement of trademark and unfair competition. These are cases where brands such as Head & Shoulders shampoo, Old Spice aftershave and Crest toothpaste feature on supermarket shelves alongside own brands designed to look similar to the P&G brand, thus possibly misleading the customer.

For P&G, advertising has been crucial, having been a pioneer in the use of mass media, particularly television. It prides itself on its constant pursuit of new ways of communicating with customers. As media options have multiplied, it has tried 'just about everything' in terms of methods and venues (Silverman, 2005). It has advertised at rock concerts and sports events. Television, it finds, is still efficient in many markets, but for beauty products, public relations are effective. Where the company has two brands in the same category, the markets and the media mix are different for each. The increasing complexity of marketing strategies and experimentation with new means of reaching consumers have led to increasing costs, as Figure 3 shows.

One of the major shifts in corporate strategy which coincided with the Gillette acquisition has been the targeting of emerging and developing economies. Of the world's 6 billion potential customers, P&G has traditionally targeted its consumer products at the world's most affluent 1 billion. These have been mainly in developed markets. The same products, such as Crest toothpaste, would be exported from the US to other countries, where they would be bought by relatively small numbers of affluent consumers. The company has now decided that serving the world's other 5 billion customers would be its next challenge. These markets, such as China and India, offer higher growth prospects than developed economies. In addition, there is a 'push' factor, in that the power of retailers in its main markets has been a source of competitive pressure. Products in these new markets need to be affordable, accompanied by appropriate marketing, and still allow these lower margin products to be profitable. The chief financial officer says: 'We've had to, in large part, create a new business model inside the company' (Grant, 15 July 2005).

A basic toothpaste and a basic laundry detergent were developed following extensive research in P&G's laboratories on particular needs in developing countries. For example, products were tested in sweltering heat and humidity, to replicate summer conditions in India. Detergents were tested on clothing stains caused by curries in India and cooking oils in China. While P&G has a central laundry laboratory in the US, 40% of P&G's R&D staff are based in their home markets, liaising with networks of P&G researchers worldwide. The company's vast expertise in science and technology research gave it an edge in product development which local producers could not match. But could these basic products compete on price with local versions? This is often a difficult test for global companies. However, P&G claims not to be perturbed by the fact that the local rival detergent in China has a 40% market share. To keep costs down, the innovation standard has changed. According to the chief technology officer: 'Prior to 2000, we were always going to deliver the absolute best, then "cost save". We have changed that to "cheaper and better"' (Grant, 16 November 2005).

Reaching consumers is another challenge in developing countries, where products must be distributed in towns and villages, often in the hinterlands, where people buy shampoo and toothpaste from kiosks. P&G has developed distribution systems in rural areas. Gillette has a stronger relationship with Western retailers in the larger cities. Here, segmentation is needed, as top-tier and middle-tier consumers can afford more expensive products. The theme which links P&G's newer markets with their established ones is satisfying consumers. Lafley says: 'Just as I believe the consumer has the power in the purchase chain, I think the consumer has the power in the consumption and media and message chain. So

Questions

1 How have acquisitions strengthened P&G's brand portfolio?
2 In what ways has P&G dealt with the challenge of supermarket own brands?
3 How have global product divisions shaped P&G strategy and culture?
4 What is P&G's product strategy in developing markets?

Sources: Grant, J., 'Check the depth of the new customer's pocket', *Financial Times*, 16 November 2005; Grant, J., 'Mr Daley's mission: to reach 6bn shoppers and make money', *Financial Times*, 15 July 2005; Buckley, N., 'The calm reinventor', *Financial Times*, 30 January 2005; Foster, L, 'Optimistic P&G hails improved outlook', *Financial Times*, 1 November 2006; Grant, J., 'Procter doctor: how Lafley's prescription is revitalising a tired consumer titan', *Financial Times*, 22 December 2005; Silverman, G., 'The soap opera makes room for racing and rock concerts', *Financial Times*, 22 December 2005; Grant, J., 'P&G launches suit against private labels', *Financial Times*, 6 May 2006; Grant, J., 'P&G learns lessons as it integrates $57 billion Gillette deal', *Financial Times*, 22 December 2005; P&G Annual Reports, 2005, 2006 and 2007, www.pg.com.

she's the boss – or he's the boss. And so the world is shifting from a "push" to a "pull"' (Grant, 22 December 2005).

WEB CHECK

The P&G website is www.pg.com.

Reaching consumers

To implement their overall competitive marketing strategy, firms use a variety of marketing tools. Having decided on its target market, the firm must reach consumers with products which satisfy their needs, appropriate communication and prices they are willing to pay. Covering all the elements at this tactical level is the term 'marketing mix'.

Marketing mix

Marketing mix: Set of co-ordinated marketing tools focusing on the four Ps (product, promotion, price and place), designed to satisfy the needs of targeted consumers.

The marketing mix can be defined as 'the set of controllable tactical marketing tools that the firm blends to produce the response it wants in the target market' (Kotler et al., 2002: 109). Four groups of variables are usually highlighted, known as 'the four Ps': product, promotion, price and place. Each of the Ps represents a number of facets, as Figure 8.9 shows.

Figure 8.9 The marketing mix

Product

The product element of the marketing mix refers to the totality of the offering to the consumer, including both goods and services. All the elements of the product offering should be consistent. If the brand is an upmarket one, presentation, design, quality and customer service should blend together. If product quality or design is found to be disappointing, consumers will feel even more let down if they have paid for a premium product. On the other hand, the low-cost basic product also needs to satisfy consumers, that is, it needs to function as described, or sales could be lost to a competitor, of which there are likely to many in mass-market products. The product may come with a guarantee or warranty from the manufacturer, which may extend to one or two years. The retailer may be part of a dealer network, which is linked with the manufacturer or even owned by the manufacturer, thus conveying to the customer the message that the firm prioritizes services and after-sales maintenance.

For many consumer goods, packaging is important, not simply as a functional aspect of the product, but as part of its image. High-quality packaging suggests a high-quality product to the consumer, important in markets such as Japan, where gift-giving is prominent in social relations and the appearance of the product is crucial. On the other hand, many consumer products companies, such as P&G, are reducing packaging to limit harm to the environment, often in response to consumer concerns.

Promotion

The second 'P' of the marketing mix is promotion, which covers all types of communication with target customers. Advertising is an important area of expenditure, as the case study on P&G highlighted. Personal contact and word-of-mouth recommendations are also important. In sectors such as industrial products and machinery, which are customized for business customers, or which involve a significant service element, personalized service may be crucial. However, even in mass-market consumer goods, if the salesperson is well informed, enthusiastic and able to help consumers by discussing particular needs, this helps to sell the product and also helps to build consumer loyalty.

Firms now have many different ways of reaching target markets through advertising. The traditional means have been television, radio and print media such as newspapers and magazines. Until fairly recently, the television commercial was a favourite vehicle, but dwindling television audiences and the rise of other media are causing firms to rethink their strategies. Digital media, including the internet and interactive cable and satellite services, offer more opportunities for advertising, tailoring the medium and messages for particular products and target consumers. The company website is now seen as a medium with several functions, including selling products, providing information and advertising. Website design is becoming a critical tool for marketing. The website may help to build relations with customers, inform them of interesting uses of the products, and get their permission to send them emails telling them about new products. The internet, it should be remembered, is accessed by only 16.9% of the world's population, consisting of the more affluent consumers (see Figure 2.11). Advertising media and messages designed in the context of developed Western societies are inappropriate in less affluent markets.

To reach consumers outside the home, advertising may appear in public spaces, including billboards, buildings and on the sides of vehicles such as taxis. These low-tech ways of reaching consumers are heavily used in developing countries, where high-tech media reach only a small fraction of the population. Sports-related advertising has become popular. This category

---

TO RECAP...

Marketing the product

The product's design and quality need to reflect expectations in its target market. The product includes its presentation, packaging and after-sales services, in addition to its functionality.

Promotion: All types of marketing communication; one of the four Ps in the marketing mix.

includes sponsorship deals with football clubs and other sports, or simply advertising at sporting events. Sports-related advertising has the added advantage of reaching a large television audience in some cases. These types of advertising require detailed planning and implementation on the ground. They are more local in their orientation than the global television campaign.

Companies have become sensitive to the need for advertising to be adapted to local environments, even when advertising a global product. Many different styles of advertising exist, and consumers react differently to different styles. The humorous message may be successful in some countries, but not in others. Celebrity endorsements may be persuasive, but the celebrity must be widely known and admired by the target consumers. For differing country markets, choosing the right magazine or newspaper, which is likely to be a local title, can be crucial to reaching the target audience. In developing countries, print media, like the internet, may reach only a small audience of relatively affluent and educated people. If the target market is broader, aiming to reach lower income consumers, billboards and other advertising in public spaces may be more appropriate. Nestlé has found that, in Brazil, local radio advertising gives better interaction with consumers than advertising on national television networks.

Pricing

Pricing strategy, the third of the four Ps, straddles different functions within the firm. Besides marketing, it also involves finance, sales and manufacturing operations. Pricing specialists are therefore in many parts of the organization, with differing perspectives. Ideally, they are co-ordinated from the centre, giving the firm a coherent pricing strategy across all brands and products. While central pricing policies would simplify strategy, differences in local markets imply that there needs to be scope for local decision-making on pricing to adapt to local market conditions.

The price of any product must take account of the costs to produce, the desired level of profits, and competitive pressures from substitute products in the market. The ability of the seller to determine price depends largely on the market. As noted in Chapter 6, the seller with a monopoly has maximum freedom to set prices in theory, but government regulations may impose restrictions. Microsoft is in the position of being a near-monopolist without regulatory intervention. Where there is monopolistic competition, there are many sellers with differentiated products, giving each more freedom to set prices than in an oligopolistic market, where there are only a few sellers offering similar products. In this type of market, a rise in price by one, if it is not followed by the other sellers, can lead to a shift away from the more expensive product.

The product will be priced differently depending on whether it is new or established in its market. The price will also vary according to the product or brand's position in the company's portfolio. The superior product with added features will have a premium price attached. However, if it is new to the market, a lower promotional price might entice customers. The pricing in this case depends partly on the nature of the market. If competitors with similar offerings abound, the question arises whether the new product can justify a premium price for its added-value features, or whether price will play a part in winning market share. These can be difficult decisions to take. A 'price floor' is largely determined by costs, and is the minimum price the firm can contemplate. A 'price ceiling' reflects demand for the product. In the middle is an 'optimum price', which is a function of the demand for the product, given the willingness and ability of consumers to buy it. The price must be high enough to generate a profit, but low enough to produce demand. Cost-plus pricing is a simple way of determining price, by calculating costs and adding a standard mark-up. By contrast, value-based pricing bases price on the perceived value of the product. In this case, the product is designed with a view to a target price rather than costs.

In every national market, there are factors which influence demand and the prices consumers are willing to pay. For this reason, it is unrealistic for a company to think in terms of a single global price. European consumers complain that many consumer goods, from Levi jeans to PlayStations, cost more in their home markets than they do in the US, even though production of these products is globalized for all markets. Companies respond by saying that the costs of marketing and distributing the products are higher in European markets. Keeping national markets separate, however, may be difficult, as individual consumers and businesses are able to buy the product in the cheapest location. If the buyer is a business, it may then resell it in the country where prices are high. Although these activities may have limited impact on overall markets, they can be more influential if the markets are neighbouring countries. This is especially true in eurozone countries, where the single currency allows consumers to see instantly how prices compare. For example, practising price discrimination between France and Germany is difficult.

The producers of luxury products for affluent consumers globally are less concerned that competitors will undercut their prices than the producers of mass-market products. The principles at work are those of elasticities. Elasticity of demand is a measure of consumer response in terms of demand to a change in price, as shown in this equation:

$$\text{Elasticity of demand} = \frac{\text{\% change in quantity demanded}}{\text{\% change in price}}$$

High elasticity of demand prevails when a small change in price produces a large change in demand, as in mass-market goods. Demand is less elastic when a large change in prices produces only a slight change in demand. Demand elasticity is greatest in markets where income levels are low. Here, the slightest change in price may cost sales, as consumers are very price sensitive. As noted above, consumers in developing countries typically have little left to spend after paying for food, fuel and accommodation. High elasticity of price prevails where price rises have a minimum impact on demand, as commonly occurs in markets where consumers are better off. Here, people have more money to spend on consumer products such as washing machines. In these markets, however, there are likely to be numerous competitors producing washing machines, causing high elasticity of demand. Thus, even in a wealthy country, a firm which raises prices significantly above those of competitors may lose sales. Companies at the premium end of the market,

Cost-plus pricing: Price based on costs plus a standard mark-up.

Value-based pricing: Price based on buyers' perceptions of value.

High elasticity of demand: Market condition in which a small rise in prices produces a significant drop in demand

High elasticity of price: Market condition in which prices can be raised with minimum adverse effect on demand for a product.

WEB CHECK

Miele's website is at www.miele.com. Note the upmarket image conveyed.

such as Miele of Germany, can justify high prices because of the superior quality of their products. Miele, whose appliances are designed to last at least 20 years, derives 30% of its sales in Germany, but is a premium brand leader in over 30 other countries. Thus, both the segment and the national environment are important in pricing strategy. McDonald's has three tiers of pricing in Europe, to cater for different budgets. Its head of European operations also recognizes national differences in economic development: 'We've got 41 countries at very different stages of development and we've got to respect that' (Wiggins, 2007).

Motorola provides an example of the effects of poor pricing strategy. Its sleak, clamshell mobile phone, the Razr, attracted consumers away from Nokia, which was compelled to rethink its strategy. Motorola's market share rose from 14% in 2003 to 22% in 2006. However, the gains came at the expense of profit margins, as the company made steep price cuts in its medium and high-end phones, while relying on increasing sales of low-end phones which had low profit margins. The effect was a loss in profitability in the handset business, which generates two-thirds of the company's revenues. The company admitted that it had got its pricing strategy wrong: 'We cannot grow at the expense of driving premium products and margins down' (Taylor, 2007). Motorola had started seeing the Razr simply as a product, allowing it to become commoditized, when it should have looked to build it as a premium brand with frequent upgrades. The CEO said: 'We need to keep the "wow" factor and enhance the customer experience' (Taylor, 2007). Motorola's experience is a lesson in the links between pricing and market strategy at the highest level.

TO RECAP...

Pricing strategy

Pricing depends on costs, level of demand and the competitive nature of the market segment. While global companies often aspire to set prices according to differing national market conditions, this policy is coming under pressure as cross-border transactions increase.

Price sensitivities

Price discrimination policies operated by global companies are becoming more widely publicized, largely thanks to the internet. Do you feel there should be greater regulatory control over the pricing of sensitive products such as medicines and essential foods, or should market considerations be allowed free rein?

PAUSE TO REFLECT

Place

Place, referring to distribution, is the fourth of the four Ps. It affects how easy or difficult it is for consumers to find products, where they can be bought and how reliable supplies are. For international operations, these can be complicated processes, involving outside firms and intermediaries, whose reliability is crucial for consistent supply. Similarly, the manufacturer may depend on a range of retailers of varying sizes and types. A distribution channel consists of all the organizations and stages that are involved in the product's journey to the hands of the consumer.

The traditional distribution channel consists of a number of independent organizations, including producers, wholesalers and retailers. These are shown in Figure 8.10. Each is a separate business which seeks to make profits on its own account. Contractual agreements between the parties govern each stage separately. An alternative is the vertical marketing system, in which the process is integrated by a dominant organization which owns or controls all the stages. This vertical integration reduces transaction costs. The dominant organization is often the producer or retailer. Alternatively, the producer may reach consumers through different channels designed to

Distribution channel: Interlinked stages and organizations involved in the process of bringing a product or service to the consumer or industrial user.

suit different products or segments. Some customers, such as business users, may require direct sales force. Consumer products may be distributed through retailers or by web-based sales. Dell Computers opted for internet sales only, bypassing intermediaries (see CS10.2). Its advantage has been that it can customize products for consumers, which has been particularly beneficial for business customers.

Figure 8.10 Distribution channels

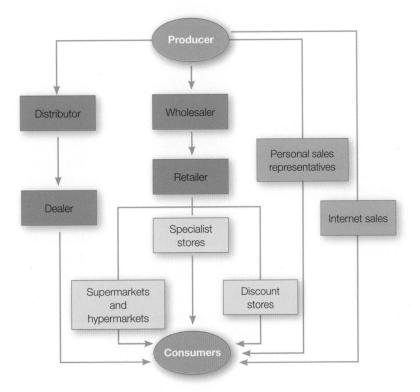

There is now enormous variety among retailers, in both size and location. The advent of the hypermarket, which sells all types of consumer product under one roof, has transformed retailing. These huge stores, of over 10,000 sq m, combine the food offerings of supermarkets with many non-food products such as clothing, appliances and electronics, often in a warehouse-type environment and at discount prices. Many conventional retailers such as supermarkets, speciality stores and department stores have struggled to compete against hypermarkets. Typically located in out-of-town malls, they attract shoppers from relatively long distances, who are happy to drive half an hour to reach them. The hypermarket usually offers services such as free parking, restaurants, travel agency, pharmacy and banking services. Hypermarkets such as Carrefour and Wal-Mart now have enormous bargaining power over producers and distributors, so achieving economies of scale. As noted earlier, hypermarkets offer their own-brand products alongside global brands. Owners of premium brands, however, sometimes feel their image suffers in the hypermarket environment, and opt for speciality shops. The choice of channel depends on the product, the brand and the target consumers.

For international marketing, channel management is crucial. Wholesalers, transport firms and other intermediaries must be co-ordinated, sometimes over long distances. Differing national environments affect how efficiently and reliably products can reach consumers. Marketing logistics concerns the co-ordinating of stages in the entire supply chain. Logistics management is discussed in Chapter 10. For the present, we highlight the marketing perspective. The aim in distribution management is to provide customers with products of the description they need, when they require them, where it is convenient for them, and with the level of service they require. Some recent trends can be highlighted. One is the growth in technology, which is transforming supply chain management. A second is the rise of specialist logistics companies which are able to offer fully integrated services. A third is the rising level of customer expectations. The car company which takes six months to deliver a car or spare parts is likely to lose business to competitors. The globalization of production has introduced global networks which offer efficiencies in production, but these benefits may be eroded unless matched by channel design and management which satisfy today's increasingly demanding consumers.

CS8.1 on P&G highlighted the growing importance of developing country markets. These environments pose challenges for distribution, as transport infrastructure is poor and consumers in rural areas may be a long way from supermarkets and other organized retail outlets. Nestlé utilizes a network of door-to-door local salespeople to deliver small packs of dairy products, biscuits and coffee to consumers in Brazil who live in poor urban areas known as 'favelas', not serviced by supermarkets. One who has been selling this way for 14 years says: 'In the *favelas*, you have to be part of the community or you just don't get in' (Wheatley and Wiggins, 2007). Nestlé has opened its 27th factory in Brazil, making products designed for low-income consumers, to be sold in neighbourhood shops and door to door.

TO RECAP...

Distribution strategy

The traditional approach to distribution, involving a series of intermediaries, is giving way to greater choice, allowing producers and manufacturers to adopt different channel strategies for different products and markets. There is a wide variety of retailing options, and direct sales through the internet or personal sales representatives offer opportunities to customize products to consumer requirements.

STRATEGIC CROSSROADS

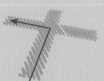

8.2

Changing attitudes to advertising to the under-12s

In 2007, Masterfoods, which makes Mars and Snickers chocolate bars, announced it was planning to stop marketing confectionary to children younger than 12 in all its markets across the world. The move represents an advance on the company's existing policy of not advertising these products to children under 6. Masterfoods is one of the world's largest owners of global brands in food services. It is a major global advertiser, although, as a private company, little corporate financial information is disclosed. The dramatic step reflected growing concern about the links between advertising and childhood obesity. It also places other large food companies in the spotlight on their advertising policies.

There are no global rules on what constitutes acceptable advertising. There is regulation at national level by governmental agencies, but standards vary greatly from country to country, depending largely on the cultural environment. For EU member states, the EU Commission is another tier of regulation. The Commission has expressed concern over the targeting of children. Many companies decide to take the initiative if they foresee compulsory rules coming into force in the near future. In addition, self-regulation through voluntary codes exists in many industries. Soft drinks companies which are members of the Union of European Beverages Association voluntarily altered their marketing policies in 2006, agreeing to halt advertising to children under 12. The UK has pursued a policy of encouraging food manufacturers to restrict their advertising of 'junk' foods to children. These are foods which are high in sugar, salt and fat and include soft drinks, crisps and confectionary.

Protecting children from junk food advertising raises practical issues. Halting television advertising aimed at children during the hours when they are likely to be watching is easier than preventing children from accessing the many websites which feature snack foods and confectionary. Websites typically offer games and other interactive activities. Requiring parental consent is an option, but parents might not want to stop their children's access to the games. In any case, children, like other consumers, can get round restrictions such as requirements to register their age.

Coca-Cola has long placed vending machines in schools, but has agreed voluntary restrictions following public pressure in the US. It is notable that the Masterfoods initiative is planned to apply globally. Nestlé and PepsiCo, which both make numerous snack foods popular with children, have no age limits on their advertising. Cadbury Schweppes does not target children under 8 globally. Kraft said in 2005 that it would phase out advertising junk food to children under 12 in the UK. Its marketing to children between 6 and 11 would focus on healthy foods. These large food companies have all introduced healthier products such as fruit juices and wholewheat snacks, in response to consumer concerns as well as possible legislation. McDonald's is now marketing heavily in China, where it targets mothers with small children. Having suffered from the US backlash against high-fat food, it is conscious of a similar risk in China, where childhood obesity is a growing urban problem.

Questions

- ◆ Why have companies re-examined their policies on advertising junk food to children?
- ◆ Assess the range of responses to the issues reflected by companies featured in this discussion.
- ◆ Do you approve the Masterfoods initiative, and why?

Sources: Ward, A., 'Coke joins battle for the brand', *Financial Times*, 21 November 2006; Dyer, G., 'Ronald helps McDonald's head off China backlash', *Financial Times*, 25 November 2006; Wiggins, J., 'Mars to pull "child" adverts', *Financial Times*, 5 February 2007; Roberts, D., Silverman, G. and Hall, B., 'Obesity fears prompt Kraft to stop targeting children with junk food ads', *Financial Times*, 13 January 2005.

WEB CHECK

See the Mars healthy eating policy at www.marshealthyliving.com. Masterfoods Europe's website is www.masterfoods-foodservice.com. Kraft provides a comprehensive website, covering brands and corporate policies, www.kraft.com.

plate 8.3 A favourite with children, but the burger is now seen as contributing to childhood obesity.

Marketing and ethics

Marketing activities impact on consumers and societies in many different ways. Businesses and consumers benefit from the huge array of products and services available worldwide. These provide day-to-day essentials such as food, and also a range of products which enhance standards of living and quality of life. However, ethical concerns are increasingly being voiced, raising firms' awareness of this dimension of their activities. Ethics concerns adherence to recognized values and principles which people in international markets generally would consider standards of right and wrong in business practices. Ethical issues include high safety standards, adherence to environmental protection principles, honesty in communications with customers and respect for the interests of employees and other stakeholders. International firms are also aware that social and cultural environments have

Figure 8.11 Overlapping spheres of ethical issues

Ethical marketing: Approach to marketing activities which prioritizes utmost fairness, safety, honesty and transparency in the interests of consumers, even in situations where the law is less stringent.

differing values. What would be considered ethical in one society, such as the paying of bribes, would not be acceptable in another. There is a growing consensus, however, on the ethical practices and values of MNEs, and on areas in which they fall beneath those standards. For example, the targeting of young people by tobacco companies would receive widespread condemnation. We will look at the broad issues of social responsibility in Chapter 14, but for now, we focus on the marketing-related aspects.

Ethical concerns in marketing are covered by law in many countries, as Figure 8.11 shows, reflecting the society's view that standards should be mandatory. Safety standards in food and other products are subject to law. Similarly, products which are potentially harmful are subject to regulation. The manufacturer or retailer (or both in the EU) will be liable for physical injury from faulty products. Products, their contents, packaging and advertising are all aspects of marketing which raise concerns in the minds of consumers and, increasingly, governments, as consumer society becomes more widespread. Advertising is increasingly regulated, to reflect social norms, as SX8.2 shows in relation to advertising to children. The sale and advertising of addictive products such as tobacco and alcoholic beverages is restricted by law. In many countries, especially in the developing world, regulation is weaker, and companies may market products more freely. As these are growing markets, opportunities abound, but MNEs which devise strategies based on targeting young consumers in developing countries might be considered to be acting unethically, even though their activities are not illegal in these markets.

The MNE's legal obligations are primarily based on national law (see Chapter 5). However, the company's broader range of stakeholders may also feel that ethical standards should influence how it generates its profits. Many consumers would now argue that abiding by legal obligations, which differ from country to country, is only one element of responsible behaviour. The firm which takes an ethical stance looks to apply high standards everywhere it operates. Large MNEs now accept that consumers expect ethical standards in marketing, not just adherence to the law. Ethical marketing focuses on issues of fairness, safety, honesty and transparency in the interests of consumers. Large global companies have become sensitive to ethical issues. Coca-Cola's flagship products, carbonated drinks, have been highlighted as contributing to obesity. Companies are also targeted over environmental issues, such as the contribution of packaging to environmental degradation (see Chapter 13).

Kotler et al. (2002: 68–73) urge that a balance should be struck between protecting consumers and allowing firms maximum freedom in their marketing activities. Businesses and consumers value freedom of enterprise and choice, but government intervention is sometimes needed in the interest of consumer protection. Areas of legislation include misleading advertising, liability for faulty or dangerous products, and regulation of high-pressure selling of products and credit deals. Such legislation features prominently in developed countries with relatively open markets. In many international markets, especially in emerging and developing countries, the institutional environment is weaker, providing limited consumer protection. On the other hand, political leaders may take a strong interventionist position in curtailing business activities and media output, especially if they feel national cultural interests are being jeopardized. In these environments, companies may face ethical dilemmas in their marketing activities. If there is little legislative protection for consumers from high-pressure selling, an ethical position would dictate that they refrain from these tactics nonetheless. Where governments routinely exert controls over content on the internet and media, a company might face the dilemma whether to proceed under the restrictions or withdraw from the market (see SX15.2).

Conclusions

◻ Marketing focuses on satisfying consumer needs with products they desire at prices they are willing to pay. While a domestic firm acquires experience of consumer needs from the outset, the firm which seeks international markets faces a more complex task of acquiring knowledge of potential markets, differing cultures and the needs of differing groups of consumers. It must also assess the strengths of existing suppliers in any potential market. Only then can country selection and entry strategy be decided upon, always bearing in mind the firm's own resources and culture. Emerging and developing countries present some of the most attractive markets in today's world, as growing incomes and changing lifestyles encompass more and more consumers. While they are attractive as markets, however, they can be uncertain business environments, in which political instability and weak legal systems may afford scant protection for contractual arrangements and property rights. Market entry through joint ventures or acquisition of a local business allows the foreign entrant to benefit from a local partner's knowledge of the cultural and business environment.

◻ The success of products and brands in differing markets depends heavily on the needs of particular groups of consumers and their perceptions of the firm – perceptions largely governed by the image of the firm's brands. Global brands were once thought to hold universal appeal, but that appeal is now rather fragmented. In many Western markets, retailers' own brands have made inroads into the market shares of global brands. In developing countries, global brands are typically associated with high quality, but it is a quality which most consumers cannot afford. MNEs seeking a wider spectrum of low-income consumers are using their innovative skills to design products specifically for these markets. Similarly, reaching consumers in developed countries through advertising and media exposure contrasts with communications in developing countries, where levels of technology are lower. In addition, the content and design of marketing messages must reflect cultural sensitivities and tastes. As companies venture deeper into new markets, ethical issues associated with products, selling methods and advertising are being voiced by consumers and other

stakeholders. Global brands have basked in high levels of brand awareness worldwide, but they are now discovering the downside of being well known, feeling the heat of consumer concerns over health, fair marketing practices and the environment.

Marketing codes of ethics
Devise a brief code of marketing ethics, consisting of the 10 principles you feel are most important in international marketing.

PAUSE TO REFLECT

Review questions

Part A: Grasping the basic concepts and knowledge

1. What are the three levels of marketing within the organization, and how do they interact to form a consistent marketing focus?
2. How does the firm's competitive strategy influence its marketing strategy?
3. Define the single global marketing strategy, and give examples of firms and products for which this strategy is suitable.
4. What are the benefits and drawbacks of a regional marketing strategy?
5. Describe 'push' and 'pull' factors in new markets.
6. How does macro-level analysis contribute to country selection for potential market entry?
7. What characteristics fall within an analysis of a country's consumer market, and why are these important in market selection?
8. Define 'segmentation'. What are the main types of segmentation in international markets?
9. Outline the main market entry strategies, and give an example of each.
10. Compare acquisition of an existing business and joint venture in terms of advantages and disadvantages from a marketing perspective.

11. What is a brand, and why have brands become crucial to companies seeking to build global markets?

12. What are the challenges facing global brands from retailers' private brands?

13. What are the benefits of having a portfolio of brands for differing segments and national markets? What are the disadvantages?

14. Describe the four 'Ps' of the marketing mix.

15. How has marketing communication changed with the growth of the internet and other media?

16. How can marketing communication be adapted for consumers in developing countries?

17. How do price elasticities affect pricing decisions in different national markets?

18. Why do firms find it difficult to operate price discrimination between different national markets?

19. What alternative distribution channels are available for a manufacturer of a consumer product such as a PC? What factors should the company consider in deciding which channel(s) to use?

Part B: Critical thinking and discussion

1. Why is China now the 'must' market for global companies? What are its drawbacks as a consumer market, and how do they differ between sectors?

2. In what ways can the global brand be described as a 'mixed blessing'? What strategies are available to promote the global brand while cultivating a localized image in consumer perceptions in different countries?

3. In what specific areas do ethical concerns impact on marketing? How does a company's stance in relation to ethical marketing influence its brand image? Give some examples.

Case study 8.2: Restoring the shine to the golden arches

The golden arches, McDonald's iconic symbol, lost their gloss in the first years of the new millennium. Symbolic of American fast-food culture, McDonald's had grown into the world's largest fast-food chain. Weakening sales in its home market and European markets led to a rethinking of the company's mission and strategy. Numerous critics generated negative publicity, from those who criticized its poor employment conditions (encapsulated in the derogative term 'McJobs'), to those who criticized its products as unhealthy. The year 2002 was a low point, when the company announced its first quarterly loss in its 47 years, Sales growth worldwide was only 1.7%, as Figure 1 shows. Its share price was down 60% from 1999. Change rose to the top of the menu, but it was several years before sales and share price recovered.

Figure 1 Sales growth of McDonald's worldwide

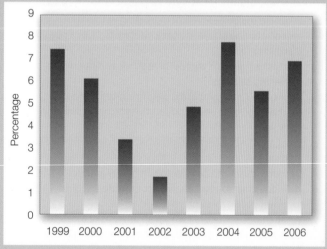

Percentage

Sources: McDonald's Annual Reports, 2004, 2005 and 2006, www.mcdonalds.com

McDonald's fall from grace was a consequence of three underlying factors. First, an expansionist strategy had focused on opening as many restaurants around the world as possible, without enough attention to quality and service. Over 2,000 new restaurants were opened each year between 1995 and 2001. The business rested on a combination of franchise and company-operated outlets, which became a model for others to follow, but

quality and performance became inconsistent (see SX1.1). Second, the traditional fast-food menu of burgers and fries was increasingly associated with obesity in the minds of consumers. Third, menus and restaurants had become tired looking and unattractive in comparison with the more pleasant and inviting chains such as Starbucks, which were gaining ground. The result was that the image of McDonald's as a brand became tarnished, losing 6% in value in Interbrand's 2003 rankings.

The new CEO, Jim Cantalupo, who took over in 2003, concentrated on improving the quality of customers' experience. The rate of opening new restaurants was slowed. The priority became boosting sales at existing restaurants. Under Cantalupo, salads were introduced to the menu, refurbishment programmes were initiated in restaurants, and marketing was given new zest. A new global advertising slogan, 'I'm lovin' it', devised by a German advertising agency, was rolled out. It was the first time that all McDonald's outlets had used the same slogan, appearing in either English or the local language in each of the 120 countries in which the company operates. The inclusion of menu items designed to cater for local tastes had always been a feature of McDonald's. Breaded meatball krokets featured on the Dutch menu at the company's first European restaurant in the Netherlands in 1971. The new strategy was to extend localization to locally designed restaurants. The golden arches, while still a visual identity, were less prominent in many city-centre locations. The company was set back by the widely publicized documentary film of 2004, *Super Size Me*, which featured a man who ate nothing but McDonald's food for a month, to the detriment of his health and waistline.

In 2005, supersize portions were scrapped, and more healthy foods were introduced. Salads, chicken, fish, fruit and yoghurt were on the menu. The introduction of premium roast coffee in 2006 helped to win back customers from Starbucks. At the same time, the company has kept its traditional burger meals, and added breakfast meals, which have proved popular. Both the breakfast products and the healthier products sell at premium prices. By 2007, the value of the brand had risen 6%, recovering from its 2003 decline. The stock price was $45, and the company announced the strongest results for 30 years.

McDonald's re-imaging as a healthy fast-food brand contrasts with rival Burger King, which has pursued a strategy of remaining faithful to its traditional menu, in the belief that this is where its brand strength lies. Has McDonald's diluted its brand's image with its refocusing and localization strategies? Its chief of marketing says: 'The business at McDonald's is much more about local relevance than a global archetype. Globally we think of ourselves as the custodian of the brand but it's all about relevance to local markets' (Grant, 9 February 2006). The brand was built on a strong core menu, and although promotions keep it to the fore, healthier and more local products now dominate in many locations. In Asia, the most popular item is Filet-O-Fish, not burgers. In Asian locations, however, it is competing with market stalls, food courts and convenience stores, which are very popular.

The company is localizing its operations through its innovative 'flexible operating platform', which is a modular kitchen which can cook different types of meal in the same restaurant. While this new equipment will enable kitchens to produce greater variety in products, it will also add to the complexity of the business. Extra investment and expertise are needed, and, for franchise businesses, innovations are often slow to be realized, given differing local circumstances. It was only in 2006 that McDonald's country heads for Europe and Asia were moved from the company headquarters in Oak Brook, Illinois, to be based in their regions. During the company's period of falling fortunes, its sales and image in Europe were particularly damaged. European revenues, as Figure 2 indicates, are 35% of the total, making upturn in these markets essential to recovery plans. Refurbishment and re-imaging were rolled out first in France, where sofas, TV screens and more upmarket interiors have combined with the new menus to improve the quality of the customer experience. The number of outlets worldwide, which reached 31,000 in 2002, has not changed appreciably since then. Emerging markets are being targeted for future growth, but strong local competitors, who are experienced in local tastes, are a greater threat in these markets than other Western branded market entrants.

McDonald's latest strategy, the Plan to Win, features five Ps: people, products, places, prices and promotions. With the addition of the people who are responsible for delivering its products, the focus is a marketing one. As a global brand, McDonald's is likely to see this asset as the source of its competitive advantage, although this strategy could well jar with its policy of appealing to local taste buds. Its CEO says: 'We're a local business with a local face in each country we operate in' (Grant, 9 February 2006).

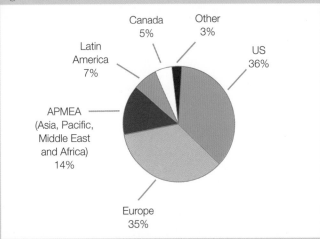

Figure 2 Share of McDonald's total revenues by geographic segment, 2005

Source: McDonald's Annual Report 2006, www.mcdonalds.com

Questions

1 What were the reasons for McDonald's losing its way in the new millennium?
2 Describe McDonald's strategy for transformation.
3 How has McDonald's combined localization with its global marketing strategy?
4 Assess the image of McDonald's as a brand. To what extent do you feel it has changed?

Sources: Valkin, V., 'McDonald's warns it will post first loss', *Financial Times*, 18 December 2002; Ward, A., 'The rise and rise of the golden arches', *Financial Times*, 27 January 2007; Grant, J., 'Golden Arches bridge local tastes', *Financial Times*, 9 February 2006; Grant, J., 'McDonald's smells new approach', *Financial Times*, 7 February 2006; McDonald's Annual Reports for 2004, 2005 and 2006, www.mcdonalds.com.

WEB CHECK

McDonald's is at www.mcdonalds.com.

Further research

Journal articles

Au-Yeung, A. and Henley, J. (2003) 'Internationalisation strategy: In pursuit of the China retail market', *European Business Journal*, **15**(1): 10–24.

Craig, C. and Douglas, S. (1996) 'Responding to the challenges of global markets: Change, complexity, competition and conscience', *Columbia Journal of World Business*, **31**(4): 6–18.

Pappu, R., Quester, P. and Cooksey, R. (2007) 'Country image and consumer-based brand equity relationships and implications for international marketing', *Journal of International Business Studies*, **38**(5): 726–45.

Walker, O. and Ruekert, R. (1987) 'Marketing's role in the implementation of business strategies: A critical review and conceptual framework', *Journal of Marketing*, **51**: 15–33.

Zott, C. and Amit, R. (2008) 'The fit between product market strategy and business model: Implications for firm performance', *Strategic Management Journal*, **29**(1): 1–26.

Books

Bradley, F. (2004) *International Marketing Strategy*, 5th edn, London: FT/Prentice Hall.

Kotler, P. (1997) *The Marketing of Nations*, New York: The Free Press.

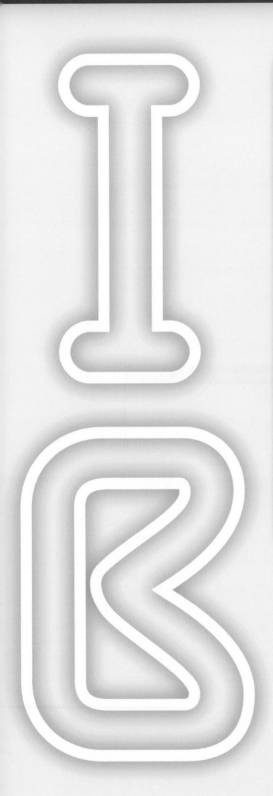

MANAGING IN THE GLOBAL ENVIRONMENT

part 4

In Part 4, the focus shifts to specific areas of management, with an emphasis on the links between strategy and practices in the international context. Chapter 9 is on HRM, which has become internationalized as MNEs have expanded beyond their home countries. International HRM stresses sensitivity to diverse social and cultural environments within a corporate HR strategy. Chapter 10 focuses on supply chain management, which has also become internationalized, as global production networks have evolved. The chapter covers global sourcing, manufacturing strategies, quality management and logistics. For companies in the global competitive environment, managing these links has posed challenges and risks, but also opportunities for building competitive advantage. Similarly, finance and accounting, covered in Chapter 11, has been transformed by global markets, presenting a liberalized environment with global capital flows. For businesses, as for regulators, the opportunities have multiplied, but numerous risks, including foreign exchange risks and capital market volatilities, have led to a heightened need for sound financial management, especially in the context of stakeholder, as well as shareholder, pressures. Chapter 12 turns to the role of innovation. For companies, innovation is key to competitive advantage, whatever the size of organization. In today's world of fast-changing technology, sustaining innovative capabilities has moved beyond traditional R&D, becoming an organization-wide focus, and touching on all dimensions of the business and its staff, including HR, financial and supply chain considerations.

chapter 9
HUMAN RESOURCE MANAGEMENT

learning objectives

▷ To appreciate the role of HRM in the international organization, highlighting links between parent companies and geographically dispersed affiliates
▷ To understand the impact of diverse cultural and institutional environments on HR policies and practices in differing locations and organizational settings
▷ To identify the ways in which relations between management and employees are evolving in the global context
▷ To gain a practical perspective on the issues arising in cross-cultural organizational environments, including teams, networks and cross-border alliances

Introduction

From small beginnings in the UK in 1993, the SG Group (formerly Stopgap), a marketing recruitment agency, has grown into an international, multimillion-pound business. Its founder, a former marketer herself, has a simple philosophy, which is to respect staff as people rather than units of labour. Work–life balance, now a prominent theme in HRM, had not been recognized in 1993, but Claire Owen, Stopgap's founder, anticipated its implications for the workplace. Flexible working hours are available to all 120 staff, 90% of whom are women. They can work the hours that suit their lifestyles, commitments and personal interests. They are free to work at home as it suits them, as long as service to the company's clients is maintained. Sixty per cent of staff work at least part of each week at home. The philosophy, which is based on trust, helps to retain staff and foster commitment to the company. It has proved extraordinarily successful in business terms, leading to a turnover of £10 million in just six years. A number of subsidiaries, including one in Australia, have been added. Although SG's flexible working model cannot be applied in all industries, the principle on which it is based is adaptable across HRM strategies, policies and practices in a variety of international contexts.

The SG Group is at www.thesggroup.co.uk.

WEB CHECK

Managing people across an entire organization, especially one with diverse geographical locations, is the formidable task of HRM. Even more challenging is the notion that, in today's competitive environment, employment is envisaged as more than simply the hiring of labour by a firm. Today's firm sees staff commitment to corporate goals as central to its competitiveness, wishing workers to feel inspired by what the company stands for. This is a major challenge, touching on people's values about economic activity and social relations generally. Even within a domestic company, these values are likely to be divergent among workers with differing lifestyles and values. In an international business, the diversity is even greater. While a firm might simply impose its home values and systems across the entire organization, it is now recognized that adapting to local differences will facilitate better management–worker relations. On the other hand, as Chapter 7 highlighted, the highly decentralized organization is not conducive to global strategic thinking. Balancing organizational and individual goals is crucial to overall corporate success.

This chapter begins with a review of the role of HRM in the international organization, analysing different organizational and strategic goals. The ethnocentric, polycentric and geocentric approaches are examined. We then look at the impact of national environments on HRM, in particular legal frameworks and cultural differences. We turn next to the elements of HR in the international context, including reward systems, recruitment, appraisal and training. Management–employee relations cut across all these elements of HR policies, and reflect diverse cultural and institutional environments. Of growing importance in international operations is the contribution of cross-cultural management skills. The transnational manager can be seen as the link between local and global strategies. The last topic is the role of HRM in international alliances, an important aspect of MNE strategy. Companies occasionally rush to form alliances which look good on paper, but disappoint in practice because of failure to think through and invest in HRM. Handled sensitively, partner companies may gain in human and performance capabilities.

HRM in the international organization

All organizations revolve around the people who carry out the work needed to achieve their goals. Even a small firm of only a few people has a division of tasks, and requires decisions to be taken on how the work is to be done, who is to do which tasks, how new staff should be brought in, and how rewards should be allocated. These aspects of the organization are historically much older than our current notion of HRM as a business function. This section examines how the theory and practice of HRM have evolved, with a focus on the growing internationalization of business.

From HRM to international HRM

Human resource management (HRM) is a range of management activities which aim to achieve organizational objectives through effective use of employees.

Personnel management: Administrative systems and processes for managing workers, including job descriptions, employee selection, rewards, training and appraisal.

Human resource management (HRM), as the name implies, sees human resources as existing alongside other types of resources, such as financial and technological. An earlier, and more limited, view of the managing of people in a business was personnel management, which consists of administrative systems and processes for managing workers, including job descriptions, employee selection, rewards, training and appraisal. HRM, by contrast, focuses on engendering employee commitment towards organizational goals and culture. In the contemporary context, HRM can be defined as 'a range of management activities which aim to achieve organizational objectives through effective use of employees' (Özbilgin, 2005: 2). Although activities such as staffing, recruitment and rewards are important, other activities such as training and development and employee relations are part of this broader view of managing people.

Two aspects of HRM distinguish it from traditional personnel management. First, it is more strategic in orientation, involved in setting and implementing corporate goals. Second, it focuses on the employee as a whole person, not simply as a worker. While personnel management had an administrative focus, which, in theory, could be implemented anywhere, the *human* focus of HRM seemed to suggest that cultural differences would need to be taken into account. This would have significant implications for companies with international operations.

From the 1980s onwards, HRM theorists increasingly recognized the strategic perspective of HRM. Some stressed that a firm's strategy should determine organizational decisions, echoing the earlier theories of Chandler (discussed in Chapter 7). This view of a 'tight fit' between structure and strategy is known as the 'matching model'. In this model, differing HRM practices stem from differing organizational cultures and strategies. The emphasis is on workers as resources which can be applied towards corporate performance. For the MNE with a multidivisional structure, a determining factor is the relationship between head office and subsidiaries. If strategy emanates entirely from the centre, HRM will reflect this. A 'softer' version of this model, known as the Harvard model, lays emphasis on the 'human' element of HRM, taking in the role of stakeholders and aspects of the environment. Recent European models also emphasize the consideration of contextual factors in HRM (Brewster, 1995). This recognition of national factors, not simply as part of the environment but as part of the model, can be seen as a step towards recognition of international HRM as distinctive. Cross-cultural elements and adaptation to differing cultural environments led to an international perspective of HRM (Budhwar and Debrah, 2001).

International HRM (IHRM) can be defined as the processes and activities of people management which involve more than one national context. This definition broadly follows that of Taylor et al. (1996). Three elements of IHRM stand out: strategic issues, environmental factors and policies and practices. These elements, shown in Figure 9.1, are interdependent. A change in one, such as a new product strategy, will impact on the others: HR systems might have to be redesigned, and local environmental factors will come into play. By the same token, a change in the environment, such as new legislation, may impact on both strategy and HR systems. For the international firm, all three elements are likely to have a cross-national perspective, adding to the complexity of HRM in international operations.

Looking at the three elements in Figure 9.1, strategic issues include the firm's need to fit HRM strategy to corporate strategy (Tatli, 2005). Also

Figure 9.1 Elements of international human resource management

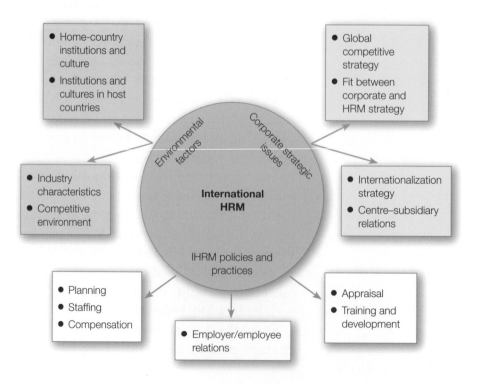

important is the firm's approach to integration and flexibility in balancing global and local issues. Environmental factors are the second element. As Figure 9.1 shows, both the home environment and the country environment of subsidiaries must be taken into account. These environmental factors influence strategic decision-making, as well as policies and practices, which form the third element. IHRM in practice is a good deal more complex than its domestic counterpart. Both national environmental differences and corporate strategic goals must be reflected in IHRM systems. Aspects of the three major elements will be examined, beginning with strategic IHRM.

Strategic issues in IHRM

The firm aims to create competitive advantage, for example by cost advantages or differentiation in products and services (Porter, 1998c). HR strategies flow from both the firm's internationalization strategy and its competitive strategy. If it has acquired another business in an overseas location, local HR systems will be in existence, and the extent of their adaptation and integration to the new owner's systems must be resolved. Greenfield projects allow investors to build systems from scratch, but local factors play a part in their design and operation. In a joint venture, the foreign partner typically takes a lead in management strategies, but the local partner's knowledge of the regulatory environment and familiarity with workplace culture give it a pivotal role.

Alignment of strategic HRM with corporate strategy involves issues of labour productivity, organizational flexibility and social legitimacy (Boxall and Purcell, 2003: 8). Cost-effective use of labour has become a competitive imperative. This explains the transfer of much manufacturing to low-wage countries, while more complex value-added activities are retained in high-wage countries. Organizational flexibility is needed in order for staff to adapt to changes, for example in technology or customer needs. However, having suitably trained staff in the right locations is only a first step. Their levels of shared corporate culture and commitment to the firm's goals are also factors in successful business strategy, as our opening vignette highlighted. The third of Boxall and Purcell's highlighted areas, social legitimacy, acknowledges the societal context of the firm's activities. These contexts vary from one location to another, often including the welfare of employees and their families. Although this can be seen as an ethical issue, it is also a business issue, impacting on stakeholder management and the firm's reputation.

Taylor et al. (1996) propose a model of strategic IHRM which is based on the resource-based theory of the firm (discussed in Chapter 7) and deals with centre–subsidiary relations. These authors suggest that successful strategy for the MNE is based not just on the parent company's resources, but on those of affiliated companies in host countries. They envisage three levels within the MNC (Taylor et al., 1996: 963):

- the parent company's resources which originate in its environment
- the parent company's resources over its lifetime
- the national and firm-level resources of affiliates.

HRM executives in the parent company benefit from the distinct range of resources, capabilities and competencies in the home country, as well as firm-specific resources. The affiliate and host country also enjoy distinct capabilities which can contribute to overall competitive advantage. How these resources are directed, however, depends in large part on the international orientation of the parent firm, as shown in Table 9.1. Taylor et al. draw on the research of Perlmutter on organizational cultures, introduced in Chapter 4. Three approaches are highlighted:

Expatriate: National of a parent company's home country, assigned to work in one of its foreign subsidiaries, usually as a secondment for a year or more

- An ethnocentric firm is likely to have highly centralized HRM policies and practices, with subsidiaries closely controlled by head office (Perlmutter, 1969). It traditionally uses expatriates, home-country nationals employed by head office, to exert parental control in subsidiary organizations (Harry, 2003).

- The polycentric firm, which adapts to local people and the local environment, is likely to be more decentralized. Its top management takes an 'adaptive' approach to HRM policies and practices, reflecting local differences among its subsidiaries. It is more inclined to trust local staff in key positions. Formal integration between staff in the headquarters and subsidiaries is low, although informal ties and communication may contribute a degree of integration in the decentralized firm (Scullian and Paauwe, 2005). In this type of MNE, implementation of company-wide strategic objectives may be problematic.

Table 9.1 Types of international orientations in MNEs

	Polycentric organization	Geocentric organization	Ethnocentric organization
Structure	Decentralized structure	Interdependence between centre and subsidiaries	Centralized structure
Strategy	Independently managed subsidiaries	Globally integrated, but locally responsive	Strategy determined at the centre
HRM: local role	Systems reflect local conditions	Local systems integrated with centre	Little adaptation to local conditions
HRM: role of HQ	Little control from the centre	Collaborative between centre and subsidiaries	Systems determined by centre

Source: Adapted from Perlmutter (1969) 'The tortuous evolution of the multinational corporation', *Columbia Journal of World Business*, 4: 9–18

Geocentrism: International approach involving collaboration between the centre and subsidiaries, and among subsidiaries.

- A third approach suggested by Taylor et al. is an 'integrative' approach to IHRM, which attempts to take the 'best' approaches wherever they occur in the MNE and use them throughout the organization. Such an approach is akin to Perlmutter's geocentric orientation. Perlmutter (1969) described this approach as one involving a collaborative orientation between centre and subsidiaries, as well as between subsidiaries. In terms of IHRM policies and practices, the integrative or geocentric approach aims to integrate local responsiveness and global strategy. Communication flows involve sharing of ideas and information at all levels, so that best practices, as well as new ideas for products or processes, can emerge from anywhere in the organization. Similarly, the aim in filling key posts is to find the best person, without regard to national background. These executives must be responsive to local differences and focused on global corporate objectives.

TO RECAP...

Strategic issues in IHRM

IHRM strategies stem from the global competitive strategy of the organization, as well as its internationalization approach. The ethnocentric firm is centralized in its decision-making and control, whereas the polycentric firm is decentralized and adaptive to local norms. The geocentric organization aims to co-ordinate global and local decision-making, seeking the best people for key posts, regardless of nationality.

National environmental factors in IHRM

A distinguishing feature of IHRM is the divergent national environments in which the MNE operates, which impact on both corporate and HRM strategy. The national environment covers a range of factors relevant to HRM. We will divide them into two broad areas, the cultural environment and the institutional environment, set out in Figure 9.2.

Cultural environment

A number of theories used to compare national cultures were examined in Chapter 4. These theories should be applied cautiously, bearing in mind the risk of stereotyping national cultures. Hofstede's cultural dimensions provide helpful tools, although it should be noted that the research is now rather dated. Hofstede (1994: 36) found that companies which originate in countries of large power distance tend to be centralized and hierarchical, with large differences in status between the senior staff and ordinary workers. Subordinates have little say in management. Asian businesses with paternalistic family structures fall into this category. Where power distance is small, subordinates and superiors have more open channels of communication and greater mutual respect. In general, countries with small power distance tend to be more individualistic, while countries with large power distance are more collectivist. In the more individualist environment, employees as individuals enjoy rights and responsibilities, usually based on a contract of employment. That contract covers a range of legally binding terms, including compensation, holidays, hours and location of employment.

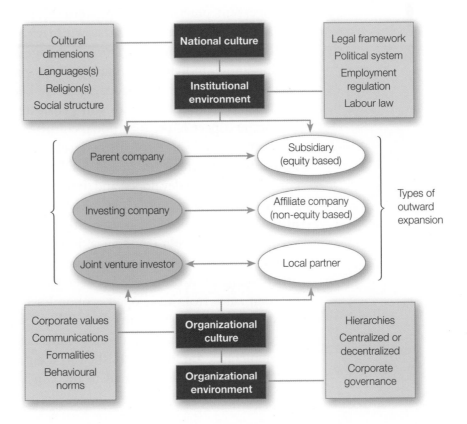

Figure 9.2 Cultural and institutional environments of IHRM

In the collectivist environment, the employee is subsumed within the organization. Details of salaries and job descriptions matter less than how the person fits in with others, creating a harmonious whole. The overseas expansion of Japanese companies showed the strength of this outlook in terms of corporate goals. But this type of organizational culture may pose problems for the management of subsidiaries, especially those in more individualistic countries. In practice, Japanese companies have adapted to differing national environments. Although their widely acclaimed management practices are cited as crucial to their corporate success, these practices have become modified in foreign subsidiaries. Some, such as lifetime employment, have also been relaxed in the domestic environment, as Japanese firms struggled to regain competitiveness in the 1990s. The Japanese emphasis on decision-making through consensus is adaptable to more individualist environments, and is consistent with recent trends towards greater employee involvement in Western companies. CS7.2 on Nissan indicated that notions of individual empowerment and performance-based rewards are altering the corporate culture, partly brought about by the alliance with Renault.

Three areas of cultural influence which have been identified in research are religious influences (such as Islam and Hinduism), traditional cultural influences (such as Confucianism, African traditional practices) and Western influences (both colonial and modern) (Budhwar and Debrah, 2005). India, for example, presents a combination of religious cultures, traditional cultural influences such as caste, and the legacy of bureaucracy from British colonial rule. Confucian belief in hierarchy is prevalent in many Asian countries, including Taiwan, South Korea and China. The relational networking practices of guanxi in China have become integrated into management practices. The Western MNE from an individualist culture faces challenges in imposing its own HRM systems in new environments. MNEs have been the instigators of change in developing countries, introducing more individualist management practices. For example, reward linked more closely to performance has become more common. On the other hand, traditional values still permeate social relations, which are an important aspect of organizational culture.

Emerging multinationals from developing and transitional economies are becoming prominent in global FDI, including acquisitions of existing companies in both developed and developing countries. Many of these newer MNEs are based in more collectivist cultures with traditions of large power distance. Furthermore, many are either state owned or with a strong state involvement. Chinese companies, in particular, have been active in global markets. These firms are gaining experience in managing subsidiaries in other countries. A difference between these firms and earlier surges in FDI by companies from developed economies is that these are from countries which are still industrializing themselves. Some are in the relatively early stages of building managerial and financial expertise. Others, such as Indian conglomerates, are long established in their own countries. These emerging MNEs tend to be less attuned to the concerns that preoccupy more indi-

TO RECAP...

The cultural environment of IHRM

National cultures of both parent and subsidiary firms influence HR policies and practices. A familiar pattern has seen Western firms from individualist cultures expanding into developing countries with more collectivist cultures, where Western HR practices must be adapted. IHRM is also adapting to the expansion of emerging multinationals from developing countries.

vidualist and lower power distance cultures. They tend to be dominated by owners, such as dominant families. Weak corporate governance and little attention to shareholder and other stakeholder interests are indicative of the national environments in these countries, where institutions and legal frameworks are still developing.

How culture bound is HRM?

HRM theory and practice have been products of the Anglo-American cultural environment. Do you feel they are losing their relevance as MNEs become more internationalized? Or do they have universal relevance, needing only modification in different environments?

PAUSE TO REFLECT

National institutional environment

The national institutional environment of a country consists mainly of its formal public institutions, such as the legal framework, judicial system and political system. Also important are the groups and organizations which are more limited in scope and authority, but play supportive roles, often as regulatory bodies. These include professional bodies, trade unions, consumer groups and charitable organizations. Networks of formal and informal groups are influential in both regulatory and welfare functions. Employment law, health and safety law and labour relations law are all relevant aspects of the institutional environment of HRM. Employment law itself covers a wide range of work-related issues. They include protection from unfair dismissal, rights in respect of redundancy, the right to maternity leave and the right not to be discriminated against on grounds of race, ethnicity, gender, religion or age. National social security systems provide benefits for unemployment and disability, as well as pensions. Many governments stipulate a national minimum wage, as an aspect of social welfare policies.

The more developed economies, which are home to the most MNEs, generally have the most highly developed institutional environment. They include Western Europe, the US and Japan. As we have seen, the social welfare laws and institutions differ from country to country (see Chapter 3). In European countries, especially the Scandinavian countries, the state has played a strong role in employment protection (see CF9.2 on Sweden). This protection comes at a cost, funded from both public and corporate coffers. As case studies in this book have shown, employers in high-cost economies have felt compelled by competitive pressures to locate operations in lower cost environments. The US is also a high-cost environment, but here, the role of government in employment protection is less, and many of the costs of employee pensions and health benefits have been shouldered by employers (see CF2.1). This situation has become unsustainable as health costs have spiralled. Japan's MNEs have played a strong traditional role in social welfare, extending to housing, holidays and a range of benefits in kind for employees. Their approach differs considerably from their US counterparts, however. Japanese organizational culture has tended to look on employees as family members, whose welfare is integral to the corporate mission. This approach, too, is waning, as Japanese companies have taken on more non-regular workers (see CF1.1).

Developing and transitional economies are in the process of building institutional frameworks. While their low-cost environments are largely attributable to lower wages, a major factor is their less developed systems of worker protection, with their associated costs. The bulk of the world's manu-facturing jobs are now located in developing countries. Large power distance and low individualism characterize many of these economies, the effects of which are weak employee voice in management and poor working condi-tions, with little protection for individual employees. For Western MNEs, these low-cost environments have appeal, but stakeholders in MNEs' home countries often object to their dual standards. In addition, developing coun-tries are facing internal pressures to improve labour standards, as CF9.1 on Vietnam indicates.

As MNEs from developing and transitional economies become more active players in international business, new scenarios are emerging in rela-tions between the centre and subsidiaries, in terms of HRM. The emerging MNE is typically from an environment where institutions are weak, and personal and family powers are strong. When it acquires a business in a developed country where institutions and employment protection are strong, it has little choice but to adapt to the legal requirements for employment law in the host country. Indian companies which have taken over European firms are examples. Where it acquires a business in a developing country, however, it faces little such pressure, as these countries are normally content simply to see the economic benefits. Its shareholders and other stakeholders in its home environment are also likely to focus on the economic benefits, as CF9.1 on Vietnam shows in the case of Korean foreign investors. This is also the case with Chinese investment in Africa. Chinese firms investing abroad face less domestic scrutiny of their treatment of workers in developing coun-tries than Western companies face in *their* African operations. The Chinese firm, therefore, is able to devise global HR strategies for subsidiaries in developing countries, whereas local concerns and local stakeholders are a greater preoccupation of Western MNEs.

TO RECAP...

National institutional environments

National institutions, formal and informal, offer protection for human rights and working conditions. They are more established in the developed world, reflected in the costs incurred by employers. In the developing world, weak institutions may be seen as a location advantage, but Western companies in these environments may be accused by home-country stakeholders of exploiting dual standards.

Don't forget to check the companion website at **www.palgrave.com/business/morrisonib**, where you will find web-based assignments, web links, interactive quizzes, an extended glossary and lots more to help you learn about international business.

www.palgrave.com
Companion Website

COUNTRY FOCUS 9.1 – VIETNAM

Vietnam: what about the workers?

When American troops left Vietnam in 1975, the war-torn country was beset by poverty. Since then, Vietnam has transformed its agrarian economy, becoming one of Asia's leading success stories in industrialization. Its rapid economic development culminated in admission to the WTO in 2007. This remarkable achievement has been guided by the communist-led government, which can point to economic growth of about 8% annually. Rises in GDP per capita, shown in Figure 1, have accompanied a significant reduction in poverty and improved living standards. Liberal market reforms have opened the country to private capital, largely from foreign investors. These investors are concentrated in manufacturing in export industries. With one million new workers entering the workforce each year, Vietnam has looked to job creation in industries such as textiles, which attract foreign investors. It is also attracting more high-tech firms. Intel is building a $1 billion semiconductor assembly and testing plant. Vietnam's availability of young, diligent workers is a source of comparative advantage. Wage levels are generally lower than those in China. In China, new employment laws are strengthening employment contracts, providing employment protection and giving trade unions more say in employment practices (although the trade unions are under the control of the Communist Party). Vietnam's communist-led development has followed the Chinese example thus far. Will its employment environment evolve similarly?

Vietnam has poured resources into state-owned industries, which represent 38% of GDP. Key sectors, such as telecommunications and banking, are state dominated. Spurred by

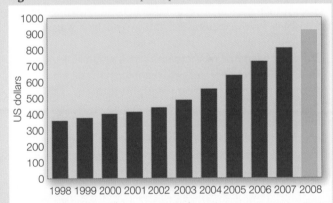

Figure 1 Vietnamese GDP per capita

Note: Estimate for 2008

Source: IMF (2007) World Economic Outlook 2007, www.imf.org.

market reforms, state entities have become active in the newer sectors, such as service industries, retail, resorts and property development. The ownership structure of these entities is opaque. Corporate governance, like other aspects of the institutional environment, revolves around links to the party. Nonetheless, Vietnam now has a thriving capital market and stock exchange. WTO terms commit the government to large-scale privatizations, although privatizations have tended to be smaller firms which are not in strategic sectors. Foreign capital has been channelled into export industries. However, foreign investors are often disappointed by the lingering legacies of state planning. Bureaucratic state machinery, endemic corruption and poor infrastructure are among the pitfalls awaiting investors. Corruption adds considerably to the costs of investing companies, putting a squeeze on other costs, such as wage demands. Although the government, stung by corruption scandals, has attempted to weed out corrupt officials, Transparency International's Corruption Perception Index indicates that Vietnam is actually getting worse, having fallen for the fourth year running, down to 123rd position in 2007, a drop of 12 places from the previous year.

Figure 2 Inward flows of FDI to Vietnam

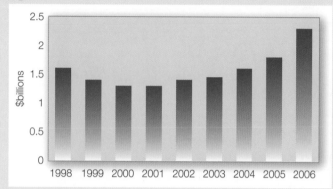

Source: UN (2007) World Investment Report 2007 (Geneva: UN)

Despite the drawbacks of the institutional environment, investors continue to flock to Vietnam, as Figure 2 shows. A rise in exports following WTO entry could test the country's ability to meet demand. There is competition to find and retain skilled workers and also to find managers and executives. Some Vietnamese employees and managers, frustrated by the difficulties of the business climate and low wages, have emigrated to more highly paid jobs abroad.

Nike has been one of Vietnam's most significant investors, coming to the country in 1995. Nike's operations are subcontracted to other companies, mainly Korean and Taiwanese. About 160,000 workers are employed in these operations, making Nike shoes and apparel. Vietnamese-produced goods account for 30% of Nike's global supply and 9% of Vietnam's manufactured exports. Nike has faced criticism for low wages, poor working conditions and oppressive working practices in these outsourcing factories. Respiratory illnesses are particularly common in the textile industry. A low point was a report by an independent auditor in 1997, showing poor safety conditions. The company has introduced monitoring, but has been criticized for 'systemic' abuses, such as long hours and unpaid wages (Birchall, 2007). The foreign owners of these factories have direct responsibility for the employees. Korean owners, in particular, arouse cultural tensions with local people, as the Koreans sided with the US during the Vietnam War. Although owners from Asian countries have a cultural affinity with the Vietnamese workers, the relatively large power distance and authoritarian management style have led to insensitivity to local cultural differences.

Worker unrest and strikes have drawn the government's notice to employment conditions in the export sector. It has increased the minimum wage, but this has only partially satisfied workers, who point to poor working conditions and long hours, in some cases, 70 hours a week. Under the current system, the employment relationship is not simply between the employee and the company. Workers face three layers of authority in negotiating issues such as wages, working hours, rest periods and social insurance – the state, the owners and the state-controlled labour unions. Although there is a legal right to strike, it pertains only to the state-controlled trade unions. As these strikes are not officially sanctioned, workers face dismissal. Independent trade unions are illegal, and the state-controlled unions are linked to political leaders, keen to appease foreign owners in order to retain jobs within the country.

Some analysts suggest that political reforms are ultimately needed, which would result in sounder, more efficient institutional structures. In one indication of political reform, Vietnam now has a National Assembly of elected representatives. Although dominated by the Communist Party, it has not been the rubber stamp type of body which some predicted, instead witnessing quite vociferous criticism of officials. Freedom of religion and association, like freedom of speech, are constrained, giving the country a weak human rights profile consonant with its weak employment rights. While the Communist Party enjoyed a sense of legitimacy as it rebuilt the country in the 1980s, many Vietnamese people are now questioning its competence for sustainable economic development. On a practical level, corruption and state bureaucracies are damaging the country. There is a fear that if costs rise or labour disputes disrupt production, investors will relocate, repeating the familiar tendency of globalization. Vietnam's leaders have seen the opportunities presented by globalization and market values, but have held on to the principle of ultimate state control of the economy. It is perhaps ironic that the roots of communist ideology lie in workers' struggles against capitalist oppressors. Meanwhile, China's new employment laws are meeting resistance from American MNEs, who say that they will discourage foreign investors, many of whom are shifting production to Vietnam.

plate 9.1 Work in the industrial plant in the background contrasts with traditional agricultural work in the nearby rice paddy.

Kazmin, A., 'In Beijing's footsteps: how a still wary Hanoi is forsaking ideology for trade', *Financial Times*, 8 January 2007; Transparency International (2007) Corruption Perception Index, www.transparency.org; Kazmin, A., 'Corruption crisis throws shadow over Vietnam's Communist Party congress', *Financial Times*, 18 April 2006; Birchall, J., 'Nike to focus on workers' rights', *Financial Times*, 21 May 2007.

Questions

◆ Describe the main features of Vietnam's institutional environment. How do these factors impact on the work environment and labour relations?

◆ What are the attractions of Vietnam for foreign investors?

◆ What are the prospects for better employment protection and improved labour relations in Vietnam?

WEB CHECK

For information about Vietnam, see the World Bank's website at www.worldbank.org and click on *Vietnam* in the country list.

Sources: Kazmin, A., 'Investors return to challenges of Vietnam', *Financial Times*, 17 November 2006; Kazmin, A., 'Socialist legacy stops Vietnam from realising its full IT potential', *Financial Times*, 24 April 2006; Dyer, G., 'China's labour debate spurs war of words for US interests', *Financial Times*, 3 May 2007;

Race to the bottom?

What means are available for improving working conditions and security of employment for workers in developing countries? Will improving conditions and wages inevitably result in investors moving operations elsewhere? Give some country examples.

PAUSE TO REFLECT

IHRM policies and practices

HR planning: Process of devising systems for all aspects of HR, including selection, recruitment, compensation and appraisal of staff, within the strategic goals of the organization.

We have outlined a number of factors which come into play in the formation of IHRM policies and practices. The strategy and resources of both parent company and overseas subsidiaries are influential. Environmental factors in the company's home environment, as well as those of its overseas operations, are also influential. In this section, we look at how these influences translate into specific policies. HR planning refers to the overall process of devising a co-ordinated system for the different subfunctions of HRM, which are staffing, compensation, appraisal, training and employee relations. HR planning in the international firm is more complex than in a domestic firm, as it must assess the need for staff in a number of different locations, as Figure 9.3 shows. For the MNE, the co-ordination of subfunctions between the centre and the decentralized business units is a major challenge.

Staffing

Staffing: Processes for selecting and allocating staff to particular posts within the organization, in keeping with corporate goals.

Parent-country national (PCN): National of the home country of a parent company, who takes on a management role in foreign operations.

Staffing concerns the process by which staff are designated for particular roles within the organization. Staffing policies are crucial to the MNE, as the co-ordination of operations in different locations depends on having competent and motivated staff. Every company requires a range of staff, from senior managers down to operational staff. In ethnocentric organizations, the staffing of key positions is often centralized in the parent company's headquarters, reflecting a cultural bias towards the home country. Sending parent-country nationals (PCNs) to establish an expatriate oversight of foreign locations has been a favoured policy of MNEs, used to ensure that head-office policies and procedures are followed to the letter (Schuler et al., 2002). This ethnocentric approach to staffing runs the risk that the firm

Figure 9.3 International HR planning

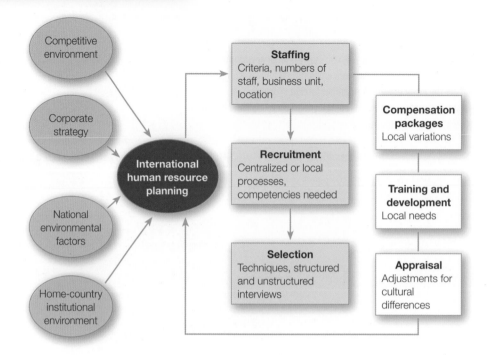

will build only a weak understanding of local culture, tending to underestimate the specific cross-cultural competencies needed for international operations. Rising costs of selection, training, relocation and repatriation have led companies to look for alternative policies. Furthermore, expatriates are not always welcome in host countries. Indonesia has introduced a policy of limiting expatriates employed by foreign banks. Leading foreign banks have expressed disquiet, saying that halting the import of foreign bankers could damage the country's economic development, as there is a shortage of local skilled bankers. Reflecting a situation which is not uncommon in developing countries generally, the HSBC country manager for Indonesia says: 'A lot of the skills we need to manage our various businesses just aren't here yet' (Aglionby, 2007).

Nonetheless, MNEs rely heavily on host-country nationals (HCNs). At the operational level, HCNs are the norm, recruited for their job-specific skills. HCN managers are also important in supervisory roles, especially where local language and communication skills are involved. These managers form links between the local workforce and corporate headquarters, which can be crucial for workplace relations, as well as performance. The role of PCNs has evolved, often being called in for specific tasks, such as initiating a new operational process, organizational restructuring roles and management oversight (Schuler et al., 2002). The polycentric approach is to rely on HCNs, as they are familiar with the culture and language, and are likely to have the relevant business contacts. Their disadvantage is that they may be less effective in co-ordination between head office and subsidiary. Many companies aim to develop a group of global managers with cross-cultural skills, who can improve the overall co-ordination of global operations (discussed in a later section). This type of manager would have both local sensitivity and global outlook. Often, a third-country national (TCN) fits this profile, which is akin to that envisaged by Perlmutter in the geocentric organization.

Host-country national (HCN): National of the host country of a foreign investor, who is employed either by the parent company directly or by the partner organization in the host country.

Third-country national (TCN): Person employed by a parent company to work in its foreign operations, who is neither a national of the parent's home country nor the host country.

Recruitment and selection are important aspects of staffing. The firm must decide what criteria are applied, both to job descriptions and personnel specifications. Nowadays most companies aim to recruit people who are best suited for the particular job, that is, on grounds of merit, rather than subjective criteria or family connections (known as 'nepotism'). However, in many cultural environments, nepotism is still influential. There are legal obligations associated with recruitment in most countries, although they differ in how rigorously they are applied. Most countries' laws prohibit discrimination against applicants and employees on grounds of race, ethnic group or gender. In the UK, the relevant provisions are in the Sex Discrimination Act 1975 and the Race Relations Act 1976. In addition, indirect discrimination is also prohibited. For example, discrimination against part-time employees has been found to be indirectly discriminatory, as a large proportion of part-timers are women. Similarly, all EU member states are bound by a directive which stipulates that women are entitled in law to equal pay for work of equal value to men. Another piece of antidiscrimination legislation is the Disability Discrimination Act 1996, which prohibits discrimination against disabled people who would be able to do the particular job with reasonable adjustment to the working conditions.

Recruitment by MNEs for people to work in various country locations must encompass a range of criteria besides education and qualifications. Cross-cultural skills, language skills and communication skills are important for international assignments and for any post where there is a diverse workforce. Enthusiasm for working in a multicultural environment is also important for motivation, as CS9.1 on L'Oréal shows. Cross-cultural skills are more highly valued in polycentric organizations than in ethnocentric ones. Ideally, these skills are combined with management competencies which fit with the firm's strategy. For example, IBM is shifting from a sales focus to a broader customized service. Therefore, liaising with customers comes high in its set of competencies.

Selection processes aim to find the candidates who fit the criteria best and who will perform successfully in the job. No selection process can provide a perfect correlation between assessment of the candidate and future performance. Recruitment methods are influenced by environmental factors, which may have a discriminating effect on applicants in minority groups (Kyriakidou, 2005). Tests provide measurements of skills, but, for qualitative aspects, interviews are widely used. Interviews may be either structured or unstructured. Structured, competency-based interviews have greater predictive validity than the traditional unstructured interview (Yeung and Brittain, 2001). More systematic behavioural interviews pose questions about past behaviour, combined with an assessment of competencies.

Compensation

Compensation covers a range of rewards which the employee receives. While we tend to think mainly of monetary rewards, non-monetary rewards, such as job satisfaction, are also important and vary depending on the cultural context. Monetary rewards include wages, salaries and benefits, which form a pay package. The pay system needs to meet a number of criteria. It must be

---

WEB CHECK

The EU's Employment, Social Affairs and Equal Opportunities home page is http://ec.europa.eu/employment_social. Policies in all areas are covered, and a *Quick Guide* provides an outline.

TO RECAP...

International staffing
Staffing policies reflect a firm's international strategy and degree of local decision-making. While the use of expatriates has been a traditional means of oversight and control, increasing reliance on nationals of the host country or a third country suggests greater internationalization of staffing policies. Similarly, an emphasis on cross-cultural competencies is increasingly recognized as essential for integration of international operations.

designed to achieve organizational goals, such as delivering quality products to customers while keeping down labour costs. It should attract and retain suitably qualified people. It must motivate employees in all parts of the organization. It must also be perceived as fair between employees who work in different parts of the organization.

In designing reward structures, MNEs must bear in mind the organization's HR strategy as well as its competitive strategy, looking to achieve a 'fit' between them. Parent companies based in Europe and America, where the individual contract of employment is the cornerstone of the employment relationship, focus mainly on monetary reward systems. Performance-related pay, which links financial reward directly with performance, is an example. Under performance-related pay schemes, the employee receives payments for accomplishing specific tasks or targets, in addition to basic salary or wages. However, employers increasingly recognize that the one-size-fits-all type of reward structure is unsatisfactory in the context of diverse groups of employees and the needs of individual employees. Employees seek a range of benefits to suit their own personal goals in the context of work–life balance. An opportunity to work at home is appreciated by some workers, as the opening vignette on SG Group showed. There, it was found that a customized package makes the employee feel more valued as a person by the employer, probably leading to greater commitment to the firm.

Flexibility and adaptation to employee needs can be extended to the firm's employees in different countries, but firms must bear in mind that motivation and incentives are culturally sensitive. Employees in Asia, where paternalistic values are influential, may be motivated by non-monetary rewards, such as loyalty and trust shown by management. In many countries, women are increasingly working outside the home and hence value benefits such as childcare. Although part of a reward package, this benefit reflects a more welfare-oriented cultural environment, as in Sweden (see CF9.2). Pensions and healthcare are becoming important issues for staff, varying according to the provisions of state schemes in differing countries (Tieman, 2004). In the example of GECAD, featured in SX9.1, the majority of employees turned down the offer of jobs with higher pay at Microsoft, to stay with the small, innovative firm, which offered greater job satisfaction. In Asian cultures, motivation is based more on relationship needs than an individual's urge to achieve. Hence, monetary rewards linked to employee performance risks being out of tune with cultural values (Zhou and Martocchio, 2001). While accommodating country preferences, rewards need to motivate all employees, whatever their location. An additional factor for the firm which employs expatriates is that of the substantial disparity which can occur between the salary of PCNs and that of HCNs or TCNs, which can create distinctions which inhibit smooth relations. US MNEs, for example, tend to reward expatriates according to home-country entitlements, reflecting an ethnocentric approach (Schuler et al., 2002).

Reward systems in US and UK firms have traditionally been based on the assumption that pay is the chief motivating factor for workers. It has been

Reward system: Comprehensive system of monetary and non-monetary rewards provided for staff in return for the work they perform for the organization.

Performance-related pay: Payments made to employees in addition to salary, which are for specific tasks performed or targets met.

Work–life balance: Allocation of time and commitment between work and personal life, which reflects the personal needs of the employee.

TO RECAP...
Cultural dimensions of compensation
Compensation based on monetary reward is appropriate in Western individualist cultural environments, where employees are primarily motivated by financial gains. In more group-oriented cultures, motivation is more relational, indicating that non-monetary factors play an important role in employees' expectations. Flexible benefits are increasingly valued by Western employees, suggesting that 'money isn't everything'.

argued that with economic development, national cultures which tended traditionally towards collectivism are becoming more individualistic and more attuned to monetary rewards. China is an example of a country where this trend can be observed, although foreign-owned enterprises are more market oriented than state-owned enterprises (Bratton and Gold, 2007: 98). The growth in market-oriented HR practices is often seen as evidence of 'convergence', stemming from globalization (Chaing and Birtch, 2005). Research suggests that, although changes in HR practices are occurring, their impact is filtered through differing national cultures, suggesting that cultural diversity among different locations remains a live issue for IHRM (Bratton and Gold, 2007: 106).

Rewarding workers in diverse environments
Assume that you are the HR director for a parent company based in the UK, with subsidiaries in the US and China. What factors will you take into account when designing reward systems for these differing locations?

PAUSE TO REFLECT

Appraisal

Employees everywhere accept that there is a need for their work to be monitored, and that decisions about their performance can affect their job prospects, compensation and development opportunities. However, there is little consensus on how these processes should be carried out. In theory, performance review helps both organizations and employees to be more effective. It helps to identify training needs and provides career guidance. It should identify employees who are performing poorly, and also encourage those who have been outstanding. However, formal systems, such as annual interviews, often become bogged down in bureaucratic procedures, in which managers and employees alike feel little is gained. The process may even be associated with a lowering of morale and motivation if it leads to criticisms which employees feel are unfair.

Just as reward systems are becoming more cognizant of individual and cultural sensitivities, appraisal systems are becoming more tailored to the individual's needs and personal development. A developmental approach takes account of not just the feedback from a person's manager, but from other sources such as colleagues and clients. The process may be a continuing one, building up a picture gradually. Formal systems of assessing individual performance are likely to be of less benefit in cultural environments which are dominated by relationships rather than measurements of individual performance. MNEs would find it simpler to adopt a common appraisal format for all business units around the globe, but such a system would not reflect the differing values attached by divergent cultures to types of work and reward. On the other hand, MNEs do need ways of identifying those in far-flung business units who would be suitable candidates for managerial careers across the organization. The MNE parent company aims at achieving a balance between culturally sensitive appraisals of local employees and facilitating the development of global managers (discussed below).

Appraisal: Process of analysing an employee's work achievement and potential for further development.

TO RECAP...
Appraisal
Appraisal systems aim to assess worker performance for a number of purposes, including identification of staff performing poorly, working in positions unsuited to their skills, and showing potential for greater responsibilities. MNEs with staff in diverse locations require flexible appraisal systems which incorporate the cultural sensitivities of local employees.

Training and development

Training and development: The building of competencies and skills of individual employees, to enable them to improve work performance and achieve organizational goals.

MNEs with operations in multiple locations face particular challenges in enabling employees to work effectively across cultures. Training and development represents a traditional subfunction of HRM, dealing with the building of skills and competencies in individual employees. Traditionally, training is the narrower of the two concepts, addressing the particular skill needs of individuals, while development focuses on the broader context of the organization. However, training is now seen more in the development context, which includes the strategy of the organization and the individual employee's personal development. Individual competencies are addressed in the context of organizational goals. Socialization in the company's culture and ways of doing things is part of this process. It includes the company's values, language and rituals, which help to bond staff, wherever they are located. It may take place through training and also through informal relations with other employees. Socialization can be a sensitive issue for the MNE, as these processes are rooted in a company's home culture. Socialization activities transplanted from the parent company, especially if they are competitive in nature, may not be appreciated in distant subsidiaries where individual assertiveness is frowned on.

Socialization: Processes, both formal and informal, by which employees become imbued with a company's culture and norms of behaviour.

Parent company HRM strategy lies behind HR development policies. As with other subfunctions discussed in this section, the firm's overall strategy is a beacon, balancing global integration along with local responsiveness. For centralized organizations, global integration is dominant, while for firms with a multidomestic strategy, local firms take their own decisions about the competencies needed and the type of training and development to design. The transnational company, described by Bartlett and Ghoshal (1998), aims to balance these two perspectives. Each subsidiary is considered to be unique in its requirements, but its programmes must be designed collaboratively with head office. Managers are key to integrating the various subsidiaries. They are able to work with people across national borders, while retaining a focus on both corporate strategy and operations. The firm which focuses on learning rather than a mechanistic training approach is better able to meet the challenges of new technology.

Developing skills in the workforce has become a major factor in competitive advantage, stressed in the resource-based theory of the firm and the core competency approach to strategy. The national environment is influential in the fostering of an educated and skilled workforce, which, for countries looking to attract FDI, can be a location-specific advantage. Low skill levels in many developing countries have attracted investors in industries with low-skill requirements, but tend to hold back the growth of higher value-added industries, inhibiting FDI in these industries. South Africa is an example, as discussed in CF8.2. Corporate strategy in India's IT and outsourcing companies depends crucially on availability of staff with appropriate skills (discussed in CS9.2). Skills shortages could potentially jeopardize their expansion plans.

TO RECAP...

Training and development in the international context

Accessing the right skills and competencies in the right place at the right time poses a complex set of challenges for MNEs. Individual employee needs for training and development must be assessed in the context of the particular business unit and the overall needs of the organization. Development is increasingly viewed as critical to employee commitment and organizational performance.

L'Oréal, the Paris-based cosmetics group, is a company a lot of people would like to work for. It receives more than 400,000 job applications annually, only 1,800 of which are offered jobs. Three-quarters of applicants apply online, and the company is experimenting with applications via the virtual world of the Second Life website. Processing all these applications is a mammoth undertaking, which the HR executives take very seriously. They look for people who like working in a multicultural environment, living in different places and taking on new challenges. Twenty candidates are interviewed for every one appointed. L'Oréal's vice president for HR, Geoff Skingsley, says: 'If you're an unambitious stay-at-home, don't waste your time sending a CV to L'Oréal. The group has an extraordinary policy of staff development and international mobility' (Tiemen, 28 April 2005). Skingsley himself has worked in four countries in 18 years. Of the company's global workforce of 52,000, 11,500 are in France. R&D is concentrated in France, where there are also eight production plants. Because of French employment protection legislation, it is difficult to fire employees, making it especially important to hire the right people. The company's aim is 'to have a body of people who are diverse. The fundamental principle that underpins it is that, if you have people with a variety of backgrounds in a team, they will develop more ideas and come up with surprising solutions' (Tiemen, 28 April 2005).

Innovation has been a source of competitive advantage for L'Oréal. Its chairman has said: 'We live or die by our ability to innovate, and everyone in the company knows that. By doing so, we encourage people to feel they are empowered to take risk' (Tieman, 18 November 2005). Nearly 3,000 researchers are employed by the company, and it applies for 500 patents a year. To consumers, L'Oréal is best known for its portfolio of brands, including Lancôme, Garnier, Maybelline and Vichy. It acquired Body Shop in 2006, marking a departure into retailing, but executives stress they were not specifically looking to purchase a retailer, but to add to its products in ways which reflect consumer needs. The Body Shop's fair trade policies, marketing and product development convinced them that the purchase would enhance its core strategy of building brands in beauty products, including hair care, skin care and perfumes. The strategy has delivered healthy sales growth and profits (see Figure 1).

L'Oréal's HR strategy emphasizes career development. It aims to move managers every three or four years, to provide new challenges, either to different countries or to new roles, depending on the individual employee. Some employees wish to acquire new skills, while others seek to apply existing skills to a different brand. The policy of providing fresh challenges is perceived as key to improved corporate performance. The company's range of brands offers abundant variety. Consumer brands are the largest group, but there are also luxury brands such as Armani perfumes, professional products such as Redken, 'active' cosmetics such as La Roche Posay, as well as the Body Shop. The company has found that membership of a team which develops a brand provides motivation for employees. Remuneration for employees

Case study 9.1:
Look good and feel good with L'Oréal

in France is performance related, giving them an opportunity to earn an extra three months' pay in bonuses.

Western Europe is L'Oréal's largest market, generating nearly half its sales, as shown in

Figure 1 L'Oréal's operating profits

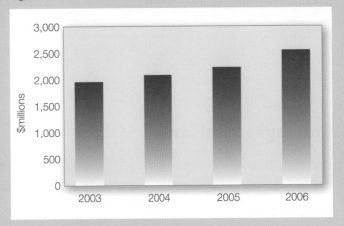

Source: L'Oréal Annual Reports 2005, 2006, www.l'oreal-finance.com

Figure 2. With sluggish consumer spending in Europe, the company is refocusing its strategy on emerging markets and on anti-ageing products, as these have considerable growth potential. Sales growth in Russia in 2005 was up 44%. Eastern Europe as a whole grew 22%. L'Oréal has pursued a strategy of organic growth from a long-term perspective, reflecting its two dominant shareholders. The family of the founder, who started the company in 1909, still controls 27.5% of the shares, and Nestlé controls 26.4%. The outgoing chairman said in 2005: 'I'd like to think there are three things that people recognise: we are unwavering in our strategy, we have a long-term approach to

Figure 2 L'Oréal's sales by region, 2006

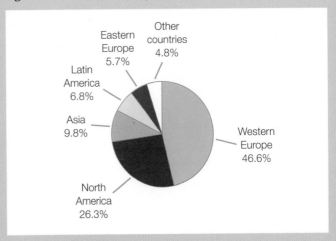

Source: L'Oréal Annual Report 2006, www.l'oreal-finance.com

everything we do, and we attempt to reconcile performance and the interests of all our stakeholders' (Tiemen, 18 November 2005). There is a suggestion that L'Oréal might wish to acquire Giorgio Armani, the fashion house, as it already owns the licence to sell Armani perfumes. Such a move would

mark a change of strategy, but could well look an attractive possibility.

Employee relations

Employee relations: Practices which involve managers and workers in workplace communication and decision-making.

Employee relations refers broadly to practices which involve managers and employees in workplace communication and decision-making. An outline of the main types of employee relations is shown in Figure 9.4. These relations may be direct, between workers and managers, or representative, through intermediary bodies such as trade unions. Firms are unlikely to have all the channels indicated in the diagram, but most have one or more. Parent companies may choose to play the dominant role in employee relations, but often, local managers play an important role, both in direct communication with workers and through local representatives, as indicated by the broken lines in Figure 9.4. **Industrial relations** focuses mainly on relations between managers and worker organizations. We shall begin this section with the broad types of employee involvement, followed by industrial relations.

Industrial relations: Processes by which managers and worker organizations deal collectively with work-related issues such as terms and conditions of employment.

Employee involvement

There are two broad approaches to employee involvement: management-led initiatives and structures which give employees the right of direct participation (see Figure 9.4). In the first group, managers retain ultimate decision-

Figure 9.4 Employee relations in the MNE

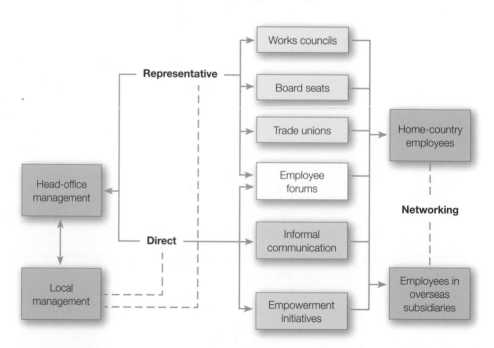

making authority. These initiatives fall under the general heading of 'empowerment'. Employee empowerment rests on the principle that employees themselves should have authority to take decisions, either individually or collectively, and should have adequate control over the resources to carry them out. The use of self-managing teams is an example, whereby employees take responsibility for decisions and performance. Sweden is noted for this approach, discussed in CF9.2. It is also practised successfully in SMEs, where the corporate culture focuses on innovation and employee identification with corporate goals, as shown in SX9.1 on GECAD. Employee involvement is more difficult to implement in large organizations with bureaucratic systems, as managers are likely to resist any erosion of their power. In this type of organization, employee involvement must evolve gradually and on a consensual basis. Large companies sometimes pay lip service to empowerment, although, in practice, core systems do not change. A half-hearted initiative may leave a lingering loss of trust, undermining the aims of boosting employees' sense of involvement.

The second group of activities give employees rights to participate directly in decision-making. Works councils are an example. They are mandatory consultative committees, organized at workplace level, which serve as channels of information and give employee representatives rights in personnel matters and other affairs of the company. Works councils are widespread in Europe, and have been at the forefront of German industrial relations, as part of Germany's philosophy of co-determination in corporate governance. In the UK, works councils exist in only 19% of workplaces. New EU legislation on consultation could possibly stir greater interest in these structures.

The cultural and institutional environments of the particular location, as well as the organizational culture of the parent firm, are influential forces in employee relations. In the EU, the Information and Consultation Directive of 2005 has required member states to bring in legislation compelling employers to provide information to employees and to consult them in a range of decisions, such as business strategy and possible redundancies. In much of Europe, legislation requires formal worker representation on corporate boards (see Chapter 1 and CF9.2 on Sweden). In the UK, there is no formal requirement for employee representation. Hence, for the UK, the new legislation represents a substantial step towards mandatory consultation. It applies initially only to large companies, but is being extended to companies employing 50 or more people. One could argue that it reflects a belief that companies perform better when employees are well informed and have a say in the decisions which affect them. The legislation does not require setting up workplace representative forums. Communication could be direct with each employee through email. The employee forum can be organized as a vehicle for direct communication. However, in some situations, the use of representatives to speak on behalf of employees is helpful.

AstraZeneca, the Anglo-Swedish pharmaceutical company, has long used elected forums and union representatives for consultation. Its HR director says: 'We benefit from the skills and experience of our representatives and the trust that has been built up' (Clegg, 2005). This approach is indicative of the Swedish emphasis on employee participation. By contrast, evidence

Employee empowerment: Policy of devolving to employees, individually or in teams, authority to take decisions and control work processes.

Works council: Representative bodies organized at workplace level, which give employees rights to information and consultation in personnel and other business-related issues within the firm.

suggests that a majority of employees in the UK are sceptical about the consultation process, feeling that their voice has little effect as 'management has already made up its mind' (Donkin, 2005). For example, if the company has decided to outsource their jobs to a low-cost location, they might see consultation as a sham.

AstraZeneca's website is www.astrazeneca.com. Click on *Careers* for HR policies and practices, including *People, culture & values*.

WEB CHECK

STRATEGIC CROSSROADS

9.1
GECAD reinvents itself

With the fall of communism in Romania in 1990, employment opportunities were limited, and business start-ups had little access to finance. In this unlikely environment, a group of IT entrepreneurs sprang up, developing such high-quality antivirus software that the world soon took notice. One of these was Radu Georgescu, whose company, GECAD, developed the RAV reliable antivirus software in 1994. By 2003, it had built a distribution network spanning 60 countries, protecting 10 million users. Several other Romanian companies also built successful IT businesses, with few resources and little business experience. SOFTWIN funded its early development by providing outsourcing services, first for European customers, and later for North American and Japanese customers. SOFTWIN's owner points to two reasons for its success. The first is a long tradition of strength in mathematics. The second was the presence of a thriving virus production industry in neighbouring Bulgaria in the 1990s, which spurred Romanian IT programmers to develop protective software, as they were always the first to suffer from new viruses.

Romanian IT entrepreneurs inevitably attracted the interest of large IT companies. Between 2004 and 2006, 10 Romanian software companies were bought out. GECAD was acquired by Microsoft in 2003, in a deal worth millions of dollars, which Georgescu shared with the employees. Today, every Microsoft operating system includes GECAD technology. In addition to the money, GECAD's managers and developers were all offered jobs at Microsoft's headquarters in Redmond, Washington, in the US. This chance-of-a-lifetime offer was taken up by only 10% – a remarkable outcome, considering the trend among young Romanians to immigrate to countries with higher pay. All the rest, including all the managers, stayed with Georgescu, even though they were barred by the deal from continuing in the antivirus business. Georgescu feels the reason they stayed was that they preferred the challenges of building new products themselves, rather than becoming submerged in a large

organization. He says: 'People are as loyal to you as you are to them' (*Financial Times*, 2 March 2007).

GECAD set about rebuilding a new IT business from scratch. The company now has three separate businesses. AXIGEN produces mail server software. GECAD ePayment is an online payment system, and there is also an IT security services business. The three new product areas, like the company's antivirus software, are building a global client base. Georgescu himself remains the owner and chairman, but has no executive role. He shuns the idea of an executive office, preferring to sit at an ordinary workstation. He shifts to a different station every two months. He is concerned that Romania is becoming an outsourcing location for foreign investors, attracted to the low-cost advantages. Wipro, one of India's largest outsourcing companies, opened a BPO centre in Romania in 2007, aiming to recruit 1,000 workers. However, this kind of work will not nurture the type of creative talent that has gained Romania global respect in software development. A GECAD employee says of the group: 'We are a group where people do matter more than procedures. Each of us, no matter what position ... in the Gecad group, daily evaluates situations and takes decisions. We do not act like machines' (GECAD, 2007). IT outsourcing, moreover, is likely to follow the well-worn path of shifting to a lower cost location as wages rise. The GECAD example shows that innovation and employee involvement are a surer route to attracting and retaining highly skilled employees.

Questions
◆ What are the key elements in GECAD's business success?
◆ Describe the corporate culture of GECAD. How can its employee involvement and commitment be replicated in larger organizations?

Sources: Cane, A., 'Why security software is increasingly labelled "made in Romania"', *Financial Times*, 8 November 2006; 'The value of staff loyalty', *Financial Times*, 2 March 2007; Leahy, J., 'Tata unit set to double foreigners on staff', *Financial Times*, 2 November 2007; GECAD (2007) GECAD corporate website, www.gecad.com.

WEB CHECK

Gecad's website is www.gecad.com.

Industrial relations

As an area of employee relations, industrial relations tends to have confrontational overtones, largely because of the historical legacy of labour conflicts between management and trade unions. The history of organized labour dates back to the early period of industrialization in Western countries, when the key industries were manufacturing and mining. Owners were often hostile to these new organizations which agitated for workers' rights and had an aura of subverting managerial authority. The labour landscape has changed dramatically since then, and so have the outlooks of managers and employees in the industrialized world. Most now see the importance of dialogue and co-operation, but confrontations do still occur. In developing and transitional countries where employee involvement is weaker and working conditions are often poor, industrial relations can be turbulent.

Independent trade union: A self-governing organization of workers, independent of employer or other controls, which exists to gain better terms and conditions of employment for its members.

An independent trade union, also referred to as a 'labour' union, can be broadly defined as an organization of workers which aims to gain better terms and conditions of employment for its members. This definition includes worker organizations which are not independent, such as those organized by the employer. Enterprise unions in Japan are an example. It also includes those in communist states, which are overseen by the Communist Party. Vietnam is an example, highlighted in CF9.1. These worker organizations are not free, and must be distinguished from independent trade unions which exist in pluralist social and political environments.

In the shift from manufacturing to services which has taken place in the industrialized world, trade unions in many countries have shown a reluctance to adapt to the changing needs of members. It could be argued that the gains which the early unionists fought for, such as the minimum wage, are now in place in most countries. Some unions are responding to recent trends in employment, such as increasing numbers of part-time and women workers, and increasing numbers of public sector workers. Trade union membership has broadly declined in most countries, as shown in Figure 9.5. Sweden, which has high levels of membership, is exceptional in recording a rise. The decline has occurred mainly in private sector jobs. The density of union membership among women is now equal to or higher than that of men in Canada, the UK, Ireland, Sweden, Norway and Finland (Visser, 2006). This reflects greater participation rates in the workforce and the growing importance of trade unions in public sector employment. Part-time workers are considered part of the 'normal' workforce in Sweden, Norway and the Netherlands, where there are growing numbers of part-time workers joining unions (Visser, 2006).

Despite the globalization of production, trade unions have not internationalized in response to the changing patterns of employment. The trade union landscape is therefore rather fragmented, as unions remain focused on national issues and national systems. Their organizational structures, cultures and bargaining practices differ considerably from country to country. Collective bargaining, still one of their most important functions, may take place at enterprise level or national level; it may involve individual employers or employer associations. Legal frameworks of industrial relations also differ

Figure 9.5 Trade union density in selected countries

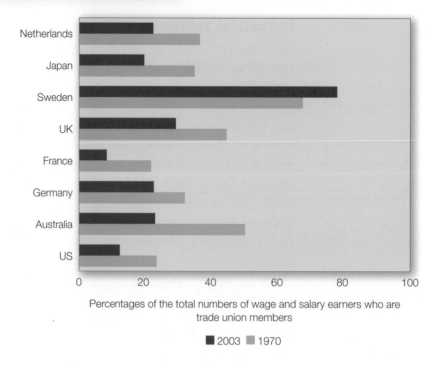

Percentages of the total numbers of wage and salary earners who are trade union members

■ 2003   ■ 1970

from country to country. In many countries, strikes and other forms of industrial action are constrained by legal rules. These legal frameworks apply to domestic companies and foreign-owned companies alike.

MNEs which operate in a number of different countries are obliged to adhere to the industrial law in each country. In practice, they tend to go beyond this minimal requirement, broadly accepting industrial relations norms in host countries, even when they conflict with the company's stance in its home country. US MNEs have tended to take a hostile view of trade unions, largely because of their confrontational legacy. Where they are able to establish subsidiaries in a union-free environment, they are likely to take the opportunity (O'Hagan et al., 2005). In Ireland, where there is no legal obligation on employers to recognize or negotiate with trade unions, most US-owned subsidiaries do not recognize trade unions. On the other hand, Wal-Mart, which operates a strong anti-union stance in the US, recognizes trade unions at its outlets in China. Some developing and transitional economies, eager to attract FDI, see their business-friendly environments with limited trade union recognition rights as enhancing their location advantages. However, worker unrest can break out if conditions are poor, as CF9.1 on Vietnam showed, causing disruption and a sharp deterioration in industrial relations.

Some of the aspects of the changing environment which affect IHRM in general can be highlighted in the case of employee relations. These include the globalization of production, the widening reach of MNEs and the economic power represented by global companies. MNEs may close units and shift operations with relative ease, using the threat of closure as a strong bargaining tool, against which workers and their representative organizations have little sway. Against this rather gloomy scenario, it can be pointed out that companies are increasingly persuaded that involving workers in the decisions which affect them improves performance and wins approval from all stakeholders. Wal-Mart has used its buying power to improve labour

TO RECAP...

Employee relations

Both formal and informal means of involving employees in the decision-making processes of the organization are now seen as valuable elements of HRM. For international operations, differing legal and cultural environments shape management–employee relations. Firms which seek out weak regulatory environments for international operations may face criticism from stakeholders.

standards in a factory in the Philippines (Birchall, 2007). Here, workers were dismissed by the Korean factory owners because they went on strike to force the management to allow the setting up of a trade union with collective bargaining rights (to which they are legally entitled). Wal-Mart refused to place new orders until the workers were reinstated and talks towards setting up a union were established. Wal-Mart has stopped short of demanding that the workers have collective bargaining rights, but its intervention suggests its sense of ethical responsibility.

The future of trade unions

Argue for or against the following statement, giving your reasons: 'Trade unions ceased to be relevant in the globalized economy.'

PAUSE TO REFLECT

COUNTRY FOCUS 9.2 – SWEDEN

Sweden's evolving social model

Sweden, along with other Scandinavian countries, regularly features near the top of competitiveness league tables (see Figure 6.6). The features which propel these countries up the table include sound public and private institutions, a stable macroeconomic environment, and high-quality healthcare and educational systems. In Sweden, the high standard of living, generous welfare state and strong state presence in corporate life are hallmarks of the 'social model' of capitalism. It has been preserved by a consensus between the government, leading businesses and labour unions. In recent years, however, there have been signs of a weakening belief in the social

model, triggered largely by the high costs of social benefits, high taxation and spiralling pensions bill to pay for Sweden's ageing population. Economic growth has slowed (see Figure 1), and Sweden compares unfavourably with other countries on entrepreneurial activity (see Figure 1.3). Political and business leaders point to the need for the private sector to boost productivity and create jobs, and for the government to trim back the state welfare system. In short, the call is for a shift towards market reforms.

Sweden has long embraced egalitarian values, in both the workplace and society generally. Swedes' dislike of social hierarchy is mirrored in the political environment. The dominant political party in Sweden has been the Social Democrats, who have governed for 65 of the last 74 years. Successive governments have upheld state ownership, which extends from strategic industries such as airlines and telecommunications to a range of other industries, including alcoholic drinks, pharmacies, casinos and stock exchanges. For example, V&S, founded in 1917, is 100% state owned, and has become one of the world's largest alcoholic beverages companies. Its best-known global brand is Absolut Vodka. The prospect of the privatization of V&S, which seemed unthinkable a few years ago, is now being contemplated.

Besides the state, the other dominant force in Swedish business is the family empire of the Wallenbergs, which includes among its many businesses Ericsson, ABB, AstraZeneca pharmaceuticals, Scania trucks and Electrolux, the world's leading maker of white goods (Ericsson features in SX1.2, and ABB in SX7.2). The fifth generation of Wallenbergs is now at the helm. The large companies in the Wallenberg portfolio have had close ties with the government, and have benefited from Sweden's tax structure. Their control of these public companies provides boardroom stability and a long-term perspective. They are noted for having stood by their companies in hard times, when, in more market-oriented economies, they would have been vulnerable. On the other hand, their paternalism and privileged position have become anachronistic in an era of more open markets.

In 2006, Swedish voters elected the centre-right alliance led by the Moderate Party, to form the government, marking an apparent disenchantment with the social model. As part of their electoral platform, the moderates promised reforms to tackle high unemployment by slimming down benefits programmes and cutting taxes, so that companies could afford to hire more people. Another of their electoral planks was the need to slim down state ownership. The new prime minister, Fredrik Reinfeldt, said: 'The state should not own companies if the ownership doesn't have an obvious strategic role' (Ibison, 2007). The new government is proceeding slowly with privatizations. While its philosophy favours free-market policies, there is a risk that if state assets are sold to foreign owners, Swedish jobs could be under threat of outsourcing to lower cost locations.

For employees, the Swedish social model represents an employee-oriented organizational environment. Sweden is among the most generous and equitable nations in providing job-related education and training. Men and women in all age groups can expect similar entitlements. Workers aged 55–64 can expect roughly similar entitlement to training as those in the 25–34 age group, making lifelong learning a reality in Sweden.

Employee participation combines with a relaxed and consultative management style to give the Swedish workplace an egalitarian corporate culture. Sweden comes top in femininity in Hofstede's rankings, indicating a concern with good working relationships, employment security, quality of life and co-operation. Legislation has provided for works councils. In addition, Sweden has followed the German principle of co-determination in corporate governance, which entitles workers to board seats, although the Swedish board is a single tier, rather than the two-tier German system. For a company with 25 or more employees, there is entitlement to one representative on the board, and for 1,000 or more employees, three representatives. In most large Swedish companies, the head of HRM is a member of the board.

Decentralized decision-making is a feature of the Swedish organization which is often cited as central to competitiveness. Autonomous work groups, pioneered at Volvo, have considerable authority to elect their own supervisors, schedule and inspect their own work. Known as the 'Volvo approach', this empowerment of teams fosters a co-operative ethos, which engenders commitment. Swedish MNEs also pursue strategies of decentralization in relation to subsidiaries, valuing localized decision-making, and local managers' knowledge of political and cultural issues which affect the organization.

Figure 2 Average hours worked per annum, per person in employment, includes part-timers

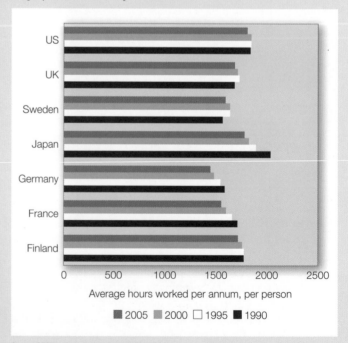

Source: OECD statistics (2007), http://stats.oecd.org

Figure 1 GDP growth

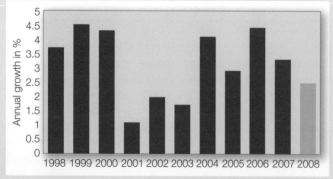

Note: Estimate for 2008

Source: IMF (2007) World Economic Outlook, www.imf.org

Underlying the employee-centredness of the organization is the belief that the worker who is happy at work and has plenty of time for other interests will benefit the company in terms of job performance. Swedes were early advocates of paternity leave from work. Swedish workers typically enjoy a range of non-monetary rewards designed to satisfy individual employees' needs. They have also been advocates of the need for employees to find their own work–life balance. Working long hours is the cultural norm in some countries, and is taken to indicate employee commitment. In Sweden, efficiency at work is highly valued, but having a good balance between work and life is also a priority. As Figure 2 indicates, hours worked per annum have fallen in most countries since 1990, but Swedes actually worked longer hours in 2005 than in 1990 (1587 in 2005 compared to 1561 in 1990). Balancing work and family life, along with flexible hours, makes it easier for women to pursue career development. In common with other Scandinavian countries, Sweden has taken steps to increase the representation of women on boards and in executive positions. Women account for 23% of the directors in major Swedish companies.

The election of the centre-right alliance on a platform of rolling back the state does not imply a desire to jettison the Swedes' distinctive social and consensus. Reforms to the welfare and tax systems, which have been a heavy burden on small businesses, are aimed at creating new jobs and encouraging young and growing companies. They are evolutionary than revolutionary.

Questions

◆ Describe the main characteristics of Sweden's social model of capitalism.
◆ Why is Sweden ranked highly in global competitiveness?
◆ What policies and practices designed to foster employee participation traditionally feature in Swedish organizations?
◆ What employment changes are taking place under the centrist government?

Sources: Ibison, D., 'Swedish business breaks its political silence', *Financial Times*, 31 August 2006; Ibison, D., 'Model change: how Sweden is to shed its vast state holdings', *Financial Times*, 22 January 2007; Brown-Humes, C., 'Can the next Wallenberg generation maintain its status and influence?', *Financial Times*, 12 July 2004; Penttila, R., 'Leisure is the vital ingredient in Nordic success', *Financial Times*, 18 January 2007; Hofstede, G. (1991) *Cultures and Organizations* (London: HarperCollins); V&S Group (2007) V&S Employment, www.vsgroup.com; OECD statistics, http://stats.oecd.org; OECD (2007) *Education at a Glance 2007*, www.oecd.org.

WEB CHECK

See information on Sweden by accessing the OECD website at www.oecd.org, and clicking on *Sweden*. V&S is at www.vsgroup.com/.

Managing across cultures

An MNE's competitiveness rests on its global strategy and its ability to co-ordinate activities in different locations. Managers with global and local competencies are key players in the transnational organization and its network of linked organizations, many of which are local. Both organizational and individual capabilities are involved (Adler and Bartholomew, 1992). The organization needs to design and implement IHRM systems which identify and nurture these competencies.

The transnational manager

The transnational organization takes in the full spectrum of its international units when making decisions, looking at the business from a global perspective rather than a parent company perspective. The polycentric company benefits from local responsiveness, but decentralization and local autonomy for business units may lead to little harnessing of inter-unit synergies. The transnational organization aims to benefit from these interactions through more responsive HR management systems. Cultural diversity among the different units, often seen by ethnocentric companies as an obstacle to be overcome, is perceived as an opportunity to develop competitive strengths. Diversity can therefore become a resource. Including representatives of many cultures among the company's executives and managers is an indication of a move away from home-country dominance. However, a multiplicity of different nationalities does not produce a transnational perspective if all simply represent their own cultural backgrounds. Much depends on the skills of managers in working with, communicating with, and learning from, people of different cultures.

The use of expatriates represents a stage in the development of international management expertise. Although the expatriate must utilize cross-cultural skills, these are generally limited to the location of the assignment. The expatriate is selected for assignment to a specific country, with its distinctive cultural environment, whereas the transnational manager is adept at understanding a range of cultures. Selecting the right people for international assignments, and assessing their performance, has been a focus of IHRM research (Schuler et al., 2002). Firms look for a mixture of knowledge, skills and abilities, including:

- Interpersonal skills, including the ability to work with others and co-ordinate activities
- Knowledge of the foreign language of the targeted country
- Ability to adjust to foreign business practices
- Technical competence
- Ability to adapt to a different social and cultural environment.

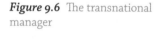

Transnational manager: Manager able to understand and adapt to a range of cultural environments.

Figure 9.6 The transnational manager

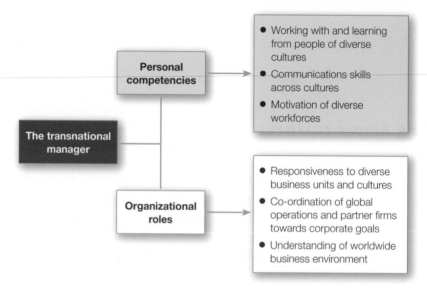

Prior to taking up the international assignment, the expatriate is given relevant training for the specific tasks ahead, and for adapting to the new environment. Training and cultural acclimatization will improve the likelihood that the expatriate will successfully complete the foreign assignment. As the above list shows, the qualities which the expatriate manager possesses are similar to those of a transnational manager. Interpersonal skills are perhaps the most important. The transnational manager's skills, however, cover a broader spectrum of cultures and a wider range of managerial competencies, as shown in Figure 9.6. Rather than focus on the single assignment, followed by a repatriation programme in the home country, cross-cultural interaction is a career-long mission. Moving among the firm's various overseas locations, and dealing with partner firms in various networks, the transnational manager transcends the 'us-and-them' mindset which characterizes the traditional expatriate. For the transnational manager, there is no home-country bias: interactions with colleagues of all cultures are on an equal footing.

TO RECAP...

The transnational manager

The transnational manager develops a range of competencies across different cultures, such as communication and motivation. In addition, the transnational manager is able to co-ordinate disparate units into a coherent whole, while retaining local responsiveness.

plate 9.2 Teamworking leads to greater understanding across cultural and organizational boundaries.

Cross-cultural teams

Teamwork, as well as individual endeavour, is valuable for organizational success. A team may be set up for a specific short-term purpose, such as a project team. A team which is set up as part of the firm's strategy, such as innovation, may have a longer time frame. The team may be internal to the company, or one involving partner firms in strategic alliances.

Teamworking within a single organization can help to give employees an understanding of how different perspectives can contribute to enhanced performance. This is especially true if the team is cross-functional, consisting of people from different departments, such as finance, marketing and HRM. In this situation, a culturally diverse workforce will bring further dimensions to understanding different perspectives. For the MNE with operations in different countries, the diversity in approaches and organizational strategies is even greater. In some companies, these differences have been seen as obstacles to overcome, for example by imposing a strong corporate culture to unify a diverse workforce. In Intel, the US semiconductor company, meetings are structured and run in the same way, according to company guidelines, regardless of the cultural differences of staff (Holbeche, 1999: 191). This approach is designed to reduce possible conflict from cross-cultural differences. An alternative approach is to tap this diversity as a creative spur. Ericsson has taken this approach, setting up cross-cultural teams which reflect the globalization of its business.

In societies with more collectivist cultures, working in teams may come naturally, while in more individualist societies, teamworking skills are more acquired than natural. People of a similar cultural background may find it easier to structure a team activity and set about dealing with the tasks than a multicultural team. In the culturally diverse team, how to deal with a variety of backgrounds, attitudes and expectations may lead to a slowness in addressing the tasks. Some members will focus mainly on the task, while others will focus on the process, including social relations among members.

However, once such a team reaches a consensus on purpose, roles and methods of decision-making, they are likely to come up with more imaginative solutions than the homogeneous team.

In setting out tasks and roles, people from low- and high-context cultures have differing approaches (see Chapter 4). Those from low-context cultures, such as the US and Germany, wish to see plans of meetings structured in detail, along with roles of individuals. The team leader is chosen as a facilitator, with interpersonal and cross-cultural skills. In high-context cultures, relationships are more important than detailed timetables, which members may find frustrating. In these cultures, which are typically more hierarchical and have larger power distance, the team leader plays a stronger role in guiding discussion. The multicultural team must identify and decide how to resolve their different approaches, to form a way of working which builds on the strengths of each. As organizations become more transnational, the experience of staff in working in multicultural teams helps to build the cross-cultural competencies which, at the organizational level, become core competencies.

TO RECAP...
Cross-cultural teams
Teamworking among people with different cultural backgrounds can be within the organization and across organizational boundaries. Building the understanding and trust between members which leads to successful teamworking helps to create cross-cultural competencies.

Cross-cultural teams
What are the challenges of working in a cross-cultural team? Based on your own experience of cross-cultural teams, make a list of suggestions for enabling them to function smoothly, so that all feel involved in the decision-making.

PAUSE TO REFLECT

IHRM in international alliances

International alliances have become a common feature of the international business landscape. Their popularity stems largely from the potential benefits they offer in terms of learning and transferring both knowledge and competencies (Schuler et al., 2002). However, HRM considerations, which are crucial to the success of these alliances, are often underestimated. Here we examine the HRM aspects of international joint ventures and acquisitions, for lessons in how to improve their chances of success.

International joint ventures

International joint venture: Formal agreement between two or more organizations in different countries, to form a new organization, in which each normally has a share in the equity.

The participants in an international joint venture are typically the two parent companies from different countries, and the organization they create. In the equity-based joint venture (introduced in Chapter 1), each parent company takes a stake in the ownership of the new firm. In general, the firm with the dominant share enjoys greater control over the joint venture firm. The joint venture may be created to do business in the home country of one of the parent companies, or in a third country. Retailers often enter overseas markets via a joint venture with a local partner. In these cases, there is sometimes friction between the local partner, whose ideas for the new firm are based on local knowledge, and the foreign firm, whose ideas are based on greater management experience. Each must be open to the suggestions of the other partner if the venture is to be a success. If the joint venture is a manufacturing company, such as Sony Ericsson, the Japanese–Swedish joint venture, the aim is to carry out operations in a number of countries, with a view to building global markets. The complementary strengths of the two parent companies contribute to the competitive advantage of the joint venture. Several sets of organizational and individual relations affect its success, and where there are tensions or conflicts over goals and processes, performance could be adversely affected. The following relations can be highlighted:

- *Relations between the two parents* – Relations between the partners are critical, especially in the formative stage. Their divergent corporate and national cultures will have implications for the structure and strategy of the new firm. HR policies and practices in the new firm may be a blend of both, or reflect the dominant partner. In any case, means should be agreed for settling any conflicts which arise.
- *Relations between the new firm and the environment* – The culture and institutions of the country in which it operates influence HR policies. The country is likely to be that of one of the parent companies, but need not be. If a third country, then local staff will be critical.
- *Relations between each parent and the new firm* – Each parent will want a say in the recruitment and selection of senior staff. When the new firm is up and running, both parent firms wish to see that operations conform to agreed terms, bringing benefits to each organization involved.

As it becomes established, the new firm takes on its own distinctive strategy and organizational culture, to which its HR policies contribute. Staffing and HR development foster the firm's own competencies, which complement those of its parent companies. Managers must be able to interact with the differing company cultures of each parent (Buckley et al., 2002). Ultimately, a 'hands-off' approach by the parents, trusting the new firm to take decisions it judges best, can lead to greater success (Schuler et al., 2004). Transfer of new knowledge to the parents and to other business units in the parents' networks is one of the goals of joint ventures, and HR systems need to be designed to support these knowledge flows. It is not surprising that research into the skills needed by joint venture partners reveals that flexibility, openness to discussion and the ability to listen and compromise are cited by managers as the most crucial. Known as 'diplomatic' skills, they complement the need for cultural sensitivity. Selection procedures which emphasize these skills are important, and these skills can be enhanced through training which focuses on the management skills needed in co-operative arrangements.

International mergers and acquisitions

Mergers and acquisitions (M&As) across national borders have become prominent in companies' internationalization strategies. While MNEs from developed countries have been the main drivers of M&A activities in the past, companies from the developing world are now becoming active as well, acquiring businesses in developed as well as developing regions. In 2006, the value of overseas acquisitions by Indian companies, at $22.4 billion, was roughly double that of acquisitions by foreign firms in India, at $11.3 billion (Leahy, 2007). The globalization of capital markets has facilitated increased activity in markets for corporate control (discussed in Chapter 11). Here we focus on the HRM aspects of these cross-border

TO RECAP...

International joint ventures

The successful international joint venture can bring benefits to parent firms, creating knowledge and expanding international presence. In time, it gains its own organizational identity and competencies, which complement those of its parents. Achieving the right balance between control and autonomy requires co-operation and trust between the parent firms.

deals. Handling the implications for the people affected is crucial to the successful 'marriage' of two firms, but often, in the frenzy of a takeover, these aspects receive too little attention.

A merger is an agreement between two organizations to combine into one, on roughly equal footing. The new entity sometimes takes a new name, but often takes the names of the merged companies, as in GlaxoSmithKline, the pharmaceutical company formed from GlaxoWelcome and Smith KlineBeecham, each of which was itself formed by a merger. As consolidation in the pharmaceutical industry shows, larger companies, with their larger resources, are more able to conquer global markets than smaller ones. Genuine mergers of equals are rare, as there is usually a dominant company and a weaker one. The creation of DaimlerChrysler in 1998 was described as a 'merger' at the time, but was actually a takeover of Chrysler by Daimler. Hopes were high that the two companies could merge their distinctive strengths to become a more formidable player in global markets. After a brief turnaround in the early years of the new millennium, the financial weaknesses of Chrysler, especially $18 billion in healthcare liabilities to workers, ultimately proved insoluble. In 2007, it was sold to a private equity firm (discussed further in Chapter 11).

A takeover or acquisition involves one company buying another outright, or acquiring a controlling stake in the acquired company. Often the target company is happy with the deal offered, and takeover terms are agreed amicably. Many takeovers, however, are 'hostile', in that the target company is not in favour of the takeover, or wishes to be taken over by a different firm, with which its directors feel greater empathy. A number of reasons for M&As can be highlighted:

- To enter new markets
- To acquire new technology or innovative capacity
- To diversify, to achieve economies of scale
- To achieve greater vertical integration.

It is often the case that the target company is perceived to be underperforming and poorly managed, offering an opportunity for new owners to improve performance. In this case, shareholders of the target company may welcome the takeover, as a spur to management changes which will unlock greater shareholder value.

The degree of integration which results from a takeover varies with the organizations themselves and their reasons for the alliance. Figure 9.7 shows three levels of integration. The acquired company may retain its strategic and organizational autonomy (bottom-left quandrant). This is often the case when the acquired company is a well-known brand. An example is the proposed acquisition of Puma by the French luxury group, PPR, which owns a portfolio of luxury brands, including Gucci. At the opposite extreme is full assimilation of the acquired company (top-right quadrant). This may be the aim if the acquirer takes over a rival firm in the same industry, with a view to realizing cost reductions. The third possibility is that of a co-ordinated partnership (bottom-right quandrant), whereby the distinctive culture and strengths of the acquired company remain, but strategies are meshed with

Merger: Agreement between two or more companies to form a new company, in which the constituent companies are subsumed.

Acquisition: Purchase of the whole of the capital of a company, or a controlling stake, which amounts to a change of ownership.

Figure 9.7 Degrees of integration in acquired organizations

that of the new owner. This may occur where a firm acquires a business with special expertise in a related business, which it sees as a growth area in the future. It may also occur where the local knowledge and skills of employees in the acquired business are integrated into the larger organization, as shown in SX9.2 on Austrian banks.

STRATEGIC CROSSROADS

9.2
Austrian banks look eastwards

Following the collapse of communist regimes in Central and Eastern Europe, the banks were in disarray, heavily indebted, inefficient, and in need of rebuilding to underpin the emerging market economies in these new states. Austria's three main banks seized the opportunities for expansion, acquiring banks all over the region, and expanding their customer base. Erste Bank, Raiffeisen International and Bank Austria Creditanstalt (BA-CA) have focused their internationalization strategies eastwards partly because their historical and cultural affinities place them in an advantageous position to understand and work in the local cultures. The CEO of Raiffeisen says: 'Much of Austria is a mix of former east Europeans. We have a common history and a common destiny' (Simonian, 2007). Raiffeisen and BA-CA were early entrants into these countries, having set up greenfield operations to serve Austrian exporters during communism. Erste was originally a savings bank, and began acquiring banks in Central and Eastern Europe only in the 1990s. Both Raiffeisen and BA-CA are now developing retail banking services for growing numbers of consumers and SMEs. Most of the local banks which have been taken over by

new Austrian owners were formerly state owned and inefficient, with archaic IT systems. Modernization has involved restructuring, as well as integration of the acquired banks into the parent companies' organizations.

The Austrian parent banks stress that sensitivity to local cultures has helped them to utilize the abilities of staff in the acquired banks. Sensitivity in management appointments has helped the new owners to win the confidence of local employees, even when radical changes are taking place. A board member of BA-CA says: 'We've always wanted to have local management. If we have expatriates, it's only to complement the locals' (Simonian, 2007). Erste has acquired 10 banks, in Slovakia, the Czech Republic, Hungary, Croatia, Slovenia, Serbia and Romania. The parent company recognized that, because of historical Czech–Austrian tensions, local employees might be unhappy with an Austrian in charge of Ceska Sporitelna, their Czech acquisition. Erste opted for an American, who had no experience in the region, but had experience in retail banking, restructuring and post-merger integration. From a loss in 1999, the Czech bank made €310 million in profits in 2006. Raiffeisen now has 30 locally hired Eastern Europeans working at its Vienna headquarters in senior positions.

Austria's bankers now have their sights set on Ukraine and Russia. In these countries, they face more domestic and international competitors, but they feel that they have first-mover advantages in the region, because of their experience in Central and Eastern Europe. Raiffeisen has turned to the skills of specialists from earlier acquisitions to help in the more recent deals. The demand for consumer banking, mortgages and financing for SMEs is growing in all these markets. The Austrian banks offer a unique combination of turnaround expertise and experience in cross-cultural management. They have been transformed from domestic companies to powerful regional players.

Sources: Frey, E., 'Sights set further to east', *Financial Times*, 20 November 2006; Simonian, H., 'Austrian trio with an eye for eastern opportunity', *Financial Times*, 3 May 2007; Accenture (2006) 'Erste Bank Group outsources procure-to-pay processes to Accenture', http://accenture.tekgroup.com.

Questions

◆ What are the reasons behind the acquisition strategies of the Austrian banks?
◆ Describe the Austrian banks' IHRM policies and practices in integrating acquired banks.

WEB CHECK

Raiffeisen Bank is at www.rzb.at. Erste Bank is at www.sparkasse.at/ertebank/group. Bank Austria Creditanstalt is at www.ba-ca.co.

The HRM implications of acquisitions vary with the levels of integration envisaged. Much turns on whether a restructuring is involved that will affect staffing in both organizations. If assimilation is the aim, the acquiring firm may slim down operations with a view to cost savings. Employees in firms taken over tend to worry above all about their jobs disappearing in the reconfigured business. Companies may tend to see issues of downsizing in isolation, when they ought to be looking at the broader necessity of restructuring (Schuler et al., 2005: 227). If restructuring is needed, it is less painful if dealt with early on, so that staff are not left in the dark. The new owners have every interest in retaining the best people, but these high-flyers may well depart if kept waiting during a period of insecurity. It is also important for changes in organization and staffing to be explained fully to staff, helping to put in place communication channels which will build commitment to the new organizational arrangements.

In cross-border acquisitions, the new owners must be sensitive to the existing culture in the acquired company, regardless of the level of integration ultimately envisaged. The example of the Austrian banks' expansion showed the benefits of acting expeditiously and taking cultural sensitivities into account. If the new business is to be assimilated, its employees may be apprehensive that the new owners will place their own managers in key posts. Addressing cultural sensitivities early on and acknowledging that they will be taken into account in HR policies will pave the way for an integration of the two cultures. Integrating two businesses often takes longer than anticipated, largely because the executives who agreed the deal underestimated the impact on individual employees. A restructuring involves new roles and responsibilities, which impact on managers and employees alike. Training and development can be built into the integration process.

In today's global environment, many companies seek M&A activity as a fast-track route to internationalization, acquiring companies in different parts of the world at a rapid rate. Companies from developing and transitional countries have become active in international M&A activities, as Figure 9.8 shows. Moreover, the deals have got bigger. Many of the acquirers are underpinned by significant state ownership or control, which provides the necessary funding from public coffers, in contrast to the more limited streams of funding enjoyed by privately owned companies. Favoured sectors are resources

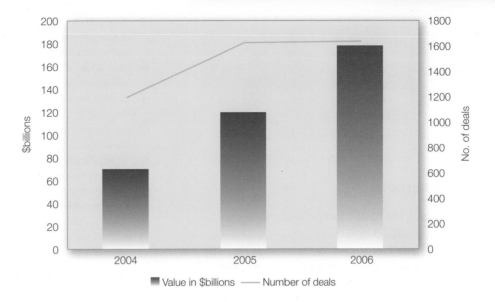

Figure 9.8 Foreign acquisitions by emerging market companies

Source: Financial Times, 29 November 2006

and energy, reflecting the concerns of political leaders about national strategic interests. The owners and other stakeholders in these companies, therefore, may have a rather different profile from the traditional shareholder profile in privately owned companies. Corporate governance structures and managerial skills are less developed than in Western counterparts. Their view of employees and other stakeholders tends to diverge from that prevailing in more established market economies. These companies lack the experience of Western counterparts in managing alliances. Research has indicated that acquisitions by Chinese companies which require integration have had only mixed success (Larsen, 2006). As changes in corporate ownership and direction evolve, it is likely that a focus on IHRM, which has been developed largely in the advanced economies, will become more widespread. This trend is discussed in CS9.2 on the expansion of Indian outsourcing companies.

Conclusions

- ❑ Managing people from diverse cultural backgrounds and national environments is the formidable task of international HRM. To add to the challenge, the modern firm demands not simply a diligent workforce, but one made up of workers who identify with corporate goals, and managers who prioritize employee needs and personal goals. While it was once thought that Western HR policies and practices were transferable across cultures, the more recent view is more tentative. As market forces penetrate economies, especially in developing countries, HR issues are rising up the corporate agenda. HR functions, including selection, compensation, appraisal, and training and development, must take account of differing cultural contexts. Designing and implementing systems which accord with aspirations of local workers can benefit corporate performance, helping to achieve corporate goals.

- ❑ Cross-cultural competencies are increasingly seen as a core resource within the firm, forming a cornerstone of its competitive advantage in global markets. Whereas firms have

traditionally seen relations between parent firm and subsidiary as central to strategy, the current global competitive environment presents numerous other organizational options which present both opportunities and challenges. MNEs' internationalized production, carried out by independent contractors, offers opportunities to reduce costs and achieve economies of scale, but working arrangements and conditions in low-cost environments seldom measure up to the standards of MNEs' home countries. Diffusion of responsibility in international operations can militate against improving HRM practices. In international joint ventures, partner firms take direct ownership and responsibility, but relations are often bumpy, as cultures collide. Acquisitions have proved popular as a market entry strategy, among MNEs from both the developed and developing world. The integration of HR policies and practices, taking account of local differences, is crucial to the success of these alliances. Strategies conceived in the boardroom depend on people working together to achieve common goals, a test which should ensure the centrality of IHRM in corporate strategy.

Evolving IHRM

How is IHRM evolving in response to:
- the changing organizational environment
- globalization
- changing expectations of employees?

PAUSE TO REFLECT

Review questions

Part A: Grasping the basic concepts and knowledge

1. Define international HRM (IHRM) and explain how it is distinguishable from HRM in the national context.
2. How does IHRM differ in polycentric, geocentric and ethnocentric organizations?
3. Assess the strengths of the integrative model of strategic IHRM.
4. In what ways does the national cultural environment impact on IHRM?
5. Define the roles of host-country nationals (HCNs), parent-company nationals (PCNs) and third-country nationals (TCNs) in each of the elements of HR planning: staffing, recruitment and selection.
6. What is meant by 'work–life balance', and why has it become important in designing HRM policies?
7. What elements must be taken into account when designing a reward structure in an international context?
8. What are the functions of the appraisal system, and how is it affected by cultural differences?
9. How can training and development help to 'socialize' an employee into the company's ways of doing things, despite national cultural differences across a firm's diverse locations?
10. How is the management of employee relations influenced by differences in national environments? Give examples.
11. What is the role of the independent trade union, and how is it evolving in the international environment?
12. How is the role of expatriates evolving as an element of IHRM strategy?
13. To what extent is the transnational manager a key role in international business?
14. What is meant by 'cross-cultural competencies', and how can they be cultivated through teamworking?
15. What are the distinctive characteristics of independence, assimilation and collaborative partnership as HR strategies following an acquisition or merger?

Part B: Critical thinking and discussion

1. In what ways does IHRM contribute to the MNE's overall competitive strategy?
2. Examine differences in the national institutional environment between developed and developing countries, and assess the implications for HRM.
3. The international joint venture is recognized for its potential in achieving competitive advantage in new markets, but poses HRM challenges which are often underestimated. What are the challenges and how can they be resolved?
4. What IHRM issues arise in the cross-border merger or acquisition? In what circumstances should the acquirer look to integrate, or alternatively, keep distinctive, the acquired organization?

Case study 9.2:
Shifting centre of gravity for Indian outsourcing companies

India has prospered as an offshore location for outsourcing services since the 1990s, when its skilled IT workers and low-wage environment began to attract the attention of firms from high-cost Western countries. Indian companies built reputations in software development, and later branched out into other activities which were suitable for outsourcing, including financial services and call centres. Leading Indian outsourcing companies are Tata Consultancy Services (TCS), Infosys and Wipro Technologies, all of which have expanded rapidly. For these companies, India's pool of low-cost, skilled workers has been the chief source of competitive advantage. These firms are now looking further afield to provide a wider range of services and a more customer-oriented approach for global clients. TCS has expanded the range of services it offers, branching out from IT services to IT infrastructure and BPO, including banking and finance, insurance and call centres. This shift in strategy involves moving beyond the offshore model, to become more geographically dispersed and facilitate greater interaction with customers and their environments. HRM strategies are shifting in tandem, focusing on hiring staff of differing nationalities and with language skills, to speak to customers in their own language. However, these companies see this strategic move as complementary to their established model, rather than a radical departure.

TCS is the oldest and largest of India's IT outsourcing companies. It is one of the three main businesses of the Tata conglomerate, India's largest private sector group. Along with Tata Steel and Tata Motors, these Tata companies have all become global players. Tata Steel's 2006 purchase of Corus, the Anglo-Dutch steel producer, for $13.1 billion, became the biggest Indian takeover of a foreign company in history. The UK is one of TCS's largest outsourcing markets (see Figure 1), and it also operates within the UK, reflecting its new focus on interaction with customers. It operates a BPO centre in Peterborough, for Pearl insurance company, for whom it performs a range of services, including processing life insurance and pension policies. TCS owns the software platform for this operation, affording it an advantageous position for attracting more UK clients.

Geographically, TCS began to diversify in 2002, setting up development centres near its major markets, in locations where labour was relatively cheap and which benefited from the same time zone as its customers. This is known as 'near-shore outsourcing', or 'near-sourcing', benefiting from geographical proximity to customers, shown in Figure 2. For most outsourcing companies,

Figure 1 TCS revenues by geographic segment, 2006

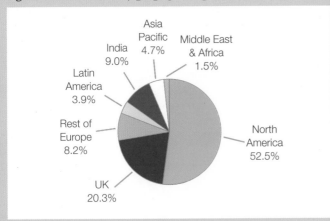

Source: TCS Annual Report, 2006–7, p. 74, www.tcs.com

Figure 2 TCS's global strategy

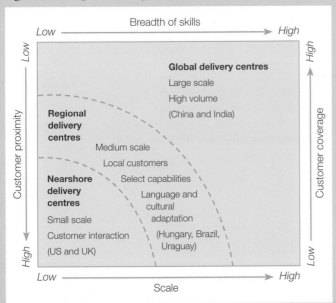

Source: Adapted from the TCS Annual Report, 2006–7, p. 51, www.tcs.com

the largest market is the US, followed by Europe. Centres in Latin America and the Caribbean can serve US customers. Centres in Eastern Europe can serve Western Europe, and centres in India and China can serve Japan and South Korea. However, TCS denies the notion that the new strategy is a combination of 'an India-centric delivery model with near-shore centres' (TCS, 2007). Instead, its aim is to achieve a more globally integrated model, with services delivered in the most efficient way to meet customers' needs. For example, it operates BPO delivery centres in four cities in India, Eastern Europe, the UK and Chile.

TCS envisages its new global strategy as having three prongs, as shown in Figure 2. High-volume, standardized services are provided in India. India is also home to some of TCS's advanced research centres. However, many services are offered regionally or locally, depending on client needs. Its CEO says: 'We are talking about a model in which we retain a large workforce in India but where increasingly our focus is on building up compe-

tence in local markets, so we can be greater use to customers' (Marsh, 2007). Of TCS's 85,000 employees, a third are based outside India. There are 10,000 in the US, the largest market, and several thousand in the other main regions. The bulk of these are Indian nationals employed overseas, but the company is increasingly hiring local staff, as well as gaining locally based staff through acquiring companies. The TCS head of global HR says that the company is coming under increasing demand from clients to provide staff with local language skills. By 2007, 9.6% of the company's total employees were overseas nationals, representing 67 different nationalities. TCS has developed a new HR programme called the Corporate Growth Initiative, designed to integrate staff of the acquired companies and improve employee communications. The stated aim is to create 'a single organizational value system among all employees' (TCS, 2007). This is perhaps a tall order for a company which has increased its sales and its staff fivefold in six years. In the last quarter of 2006, TCS acquired 100 new people *a day*. In addition to the centres in India, the company has training centres in the US, China, Hungary and Uruguay.

Also recognizing the need for local expertise, Infosys recruits graduates in the US, UK and other countries, who are given intensive training programmes at its centres in India, after which they are sent back to their home countries. Here, they are employed delivering Infosys's specialist services. Infosys's CEO says: 'Our whole endeavour is to go from just being perceived as an outsourcing company to somebody who can be a trusted transformation partner for our clients' (Leahy, 28 November 2006).

TCS's employment structure is similar to that adopted by global manufacturing companies. Jobs are allocated between low-cost and high-cost centres to reflect where specific skills are needed and where it is important for staff to be near to the customers. Thus, staff in high-cost countries, who are referred to as 'consultants' by TCS, are there to interact with customers in their own language. The numbers of TCS consultants has multi-

plate 9.3 India's expertise in IT, exemplified by the IT professionals pictured here, is now being expanded into a range of business services in global markets.

plied 10 times in the last five years. While costs are high, these consultants are considered essential, as they are positioned to generate business in the main markets. In these markets, TCS and other Indian companies are competing against some of the largest outsourcing companies, such as IBM and Accenture. The competition is not likely to

Questions

1 How are Indian outsourcing companies changing their global strategies?
2 What are the IHRM implications of TCS's new global strategy?
3 How are recruitment, training and development evolving in the Indian outsourcing companies, to reflect new global strategies?
4 What challenges face TCS and other Indian outsourcers in integrating their rapidly expanding, as well as multicultural, workforce?

Sources: Marsh, P., 'A new twist to India IT outsourcing', *Financial Times*, 31 January 2007; Leahy, J., 'Tata unit set to double foreigners on staff', *Financial Times*, 2 November 2006; Leahy, J., 'India's IT groups start move to "near-sourcing"', *Financial Times*, 2 November 2006; Leahy, J., 'Unleashed: why Indian companies are setting their sights on western rivals', *Financial Times*, 6 February 2007; Leahy, J., 'Programmers' passage to India', *Financial Times*, 28 November 2006; TCS (2007) Annual Report, 2006–7, www.tcs.com.

overawe the Indian outsourcers, who have taken on successive challenges with relish.

WEB CHECK

Tata Consulting Services' website is www.tcs.com.

Further research

Journal articles

Birkinshaw, J., Bresman, H. and Håkanson, L. (2000) 'Managing the post-acquisition integration process: How the human integration and task integration processes interact to foster value creation', *Journal of Management Studies*, **37**(3): 395–425.

Bjorkman, I., Stahl, G. and Vaara, E. (2007) 'Cultural differences and capability transfer in cross-border acquisitions: The mediating roles of capability complementarity, absorptive capacity, and social integration', *Journal of International Business Studies*, **38**(4): 658–72.

Haslberger, A. (2005) 'The complexities of expatriate adaptation', *Human Resource Management Review*, **15**: 160–80.

Johnson, J., Lenartowicz, T. and Apud, S. (2006) 'Cross-cultural competence in international business: Toward a definition and model', *Journal of International Business Studies*, **37**(4): 525–43.

Books

Guirdham, M. (2005) *Communicating Across Cultures at Work*, Basingstoke: Palgrave Macmillan.

Scullion, H. and Linehan, M. (2005) *International Human Resource Management*, Basingstoke: Palgrave Macmillan.

Don't forget to check the companion website at **www.palgrave.com/business/morrisonib**, where you will find web-based assignments, web links, interactive quizzes, an extended glossary and lots more to help you learn about international business.

chapter 10
SUPPLY CHAINS

learning objectives

▷ To identify the key elements of international supply chains and the interrelationships, appreciating variations among sectors and environments
▷ To be able to evaluate supply chain strategies in action, from make-or-buy decisions to manufacturing and distribution options
▷ To appreciate the transformation in manufacturing brought about by the principles of lean production and continuous improvement
▷ To understand the increasingly important role of quality in all elements of the supply chain, including the impact of differing national environments
▷ To assess the development of transport and logistics in the context of consumer markets, as well as community and environmental impacts

Introduction

A freight train pulling into Pardubice station near Prague in the Czech Republic one day in June 2007 was hardly unusual. But this was no ordinary train. It had carried its cargo of computer components from Shenzhen in China over 8,000 km across Central Asia. European Rail Shuttle (ERS), part of the AP Moller-Maersk group, claims that this was the first consignment of imported goods from China to have made the journey by train, echoing the old Silk Road of medieval times, with its images of camels carrying Asian silks to Europe. Was this a one-off event or the start of a new Silk Road trade route? ERS's 17-day journey took half the time the typical sea journey would take, but the train could carry only 1% of the volume of a modern container ship. A new Silk Road project, combining a road and rail network across Central Asia, is being planned through co-operation among Central Asian governments. Although most of China's manufacturing is concentrated in the coastal areas, industries are slowly moving to more remote central and western regions, pushed largely by rising costs, especially wages. From inland centres, most exports travel long distances to coastal ports for shipment by sea. A new Silk Road could benefit both these inland manufacturers and the regions which have lagged behind in development. The unfolding story of the new Silk Road is essentially one of improving supply chains in a changing competitive environment, which is the focus of this chapter.

Central Asian economies have joined in the Central Asian Regional Economic Cooperation (Carec). Read about these developments on the website of the Asian Development Bank, www.adb.org/carec.

WEB CHECK

The processes of production and delivery of products to consumers are increasingly across national borders. From the sourcing of raw materials to the delivery of the product to the end consumer, numerous international locations are linked together through networks of different organizations. Both the organizations and the stages in the process form global supply chains. This transformation of production is at the heart of MNEs' competitive strategy. Through a strategic approach to managing supply chains, they are able to reduce costs, improve quality and gain flexibility to respond to changing consumer needs. However, the successful integration of all stages and suppliers into a seamless whole depends to a large extent on the contributory strengths of each element and the nature of the relations between the various players. MNEs are increasingly focusing on utilizing suppliers' expertise and technology to enhance competitive advantage.

The chapter begins with an overview of the strategic role of supply chain management. We then examine the range of strategies available to MNEs, in the context of varying industrial, organizational and environmental factors. Global sourcing and the transformation of manufacturing processes are highlighted as the major forces shaping supply chain strategy. Improving quality and reliability has been a shared goal of all players. Although Japanese companies have been to the fore in quality initiatives, quality management has now permeated all international business activities. The logistics function links the entire process. The changing strategic and organizational aspects of logistics are indicative of the new integrative approach to managing global supply chains. However, strains within transport systems and infrastructure, as well as concerns about the environment, are raising global issues which touch on all aspects of supply chain planning.

plate 10.1 This 1876 photograph shows China's first railway train, setting out from Shanghai towards Woosung on the Yangtze River.

Supply chain management in theory and practice

Original equipment manufacturer (OEM): A somewhat misleading term, which designates a focal manufacturer in a supply chain, who assembles the final products destined for end consumers.

In Chapter 1, we introduced the business function of operations, defined as the process of making and delivering goods or services, which, in the context of international business, crosses national boundaries. A traditional way in which operations are depicted is as a pipeline, with the focal company in the middle, as shown in Figure 10.1. 'Upstream' activities are the supply of raw materials, usually by purchase from another firm. Production and assembly take place within the focal organization, often referred to as the original equipment manufacturer (OEM), although this term is somewhat misleading, as the OEM need not manufacture all the components itself. The firm then contracts for 'downstream' activities, such as logistics and warehousing, with other firms. Traditionally, each of the firms involved attempts to obtain the best deal it can with other organizations. Market transactions at each stage involve transaction costs, including renegotiating

Figure 10.1 The external supply chain

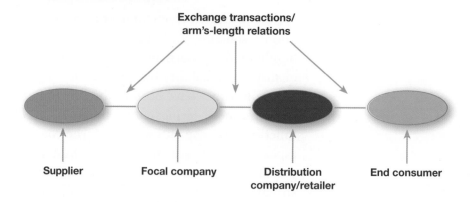

with continuing suppliers and contracting with new ones. Market relations also involve uncertainties, as they entail relying on outside firms over which the manufacturing firm has no control.

Internalization is a means of overcoming market vicissitudes. Transaction costs can be reduced, as internal relationships among subsidiaries replace external exchange transactions. As the OLI paradigm shows, ownership and internalization advantages ensure stability of supply and control over supply (see Chapter 2). The vertically integrated firm is shown on the left in Figure 10.2. Ford, the legendary example, owned its own steel mills and even owned a railway which brought raw materials to its River Rouge factory (Drucker, 1990). While vertical integration was envisaged as reducing transaction costs, it became evident that the costs of internalization were also significant. The ownership of all manner of assets, combined with the bureaucracy associated with managing all the processes involved, made the fully integrated company a cumbersome, inflexible organization. It was well suited to producing standardized products in large quantities, but lacked flexibility to respond to changing markets. Competitive pressures forced companies to reconsider their strategies.

Figure 10.2 Different types of supply chain

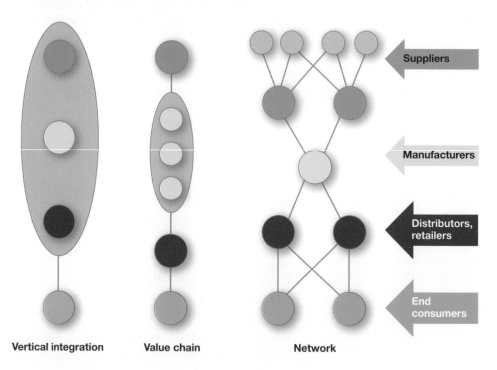

Evolution of supply chain management

A theoretical antecedent of the supply chain was Porter's concept of the value chain (see Chapter 7), shown in the middle in Figure 10.2. It is defined as 'a system of interdependent activities, which are connected by linkages' (Porter, 1998b: 78). Linkages exist where one link or activity affects others in the chain, in terms of cost or effectiveness. Trade-offs may be needed. For example, paying more for high-quality raw materials may result in lower after-sales service. Porter envisaged the value chain as internal to the company, but said that the company's value chain may become interdependent with those of its suppliers. Supply chain management (SCM) as a term dates from the early 1980s, when it was used mainly in connection with logistics, focusing on materials flow, inventory and transportation, often in the context of an individual firm. It was soon recognized that this rather limited operational focus was part of a larger picture, involving the integration of numerous processes, complex relationships and varying strategies. Supply chain management can be defined as the integration of all the business processes involved in the sourcing, production and delivery of goods and services to end consumers.

Relational and strategic aspects of the reconceptualized SCM can be highlighted:

Supply chain management (SCM): The integration of business processes which encompass all stages of the production process for goods or services, from the supply of raw materials to the delivery of the product to the end consumer.

- *The growth of networks* – The notion of a 'chain' implies a streamlined process of a series of one-to-one relations. Although the chain was envisaged as taking place within a single firm, a firm may be part of a number of supply chains: they may have many customers and alternative suppliers, as the network configuration in Figure 10.2 shows. Hence, relations are 'many-to-many' (Vollmann et al., 2000). Suppliers may be ranked as 'tier-one' suppliers, who make components, and 'tier-two' suppliers, who supply material to tier-one suppliers. Inter-organizational relations have become as crucial as intra-organizational links. These relations emphasize longer lasting partnerships than the arm's-length transactions that traditionally characterize inter-firm relations. However, these sets of relationships are not static, and power may move from one firm to another within a network.
- *Growth of co-operation between firms* – The supplier-buyer model gave way to a more complex behavioural pattern between firms as the integration of business processes evolved. The exchange of information between firms allows for quicker responses to buyers' needs, such as design and packaging. In new product development, the time to market can be reduced by SCM. Whereas companies once thought of profit generation from each transaction, SCM has encouraged them to look at the bigger picture, whereby all firms in the chain gain from co-operation. This has been described as a 'win–win' situation.
- *The re-examination of resource positioning and competencies* – As highlighted in Chapters 7 and 9, every firm faces the issues of deciding what its core competencies are, in which it will invest, and which competencies are not core and can be divested. The manufacturing company, for example, may outsource design and components, but

TO RECAP...

Supply chain management

Supply chain management has evolved from an operational concept to a broad strategic focus, in which business processes are integrated and linked to an array of suppliers and customers.

choose to assemble and test the products itself. It may also handle end user relationships, as it may gain vital information from customers. This is a pattern common in the electronics sector, where new product development is costly.

Supply chain strategies

Supply chain strategies seek to provide the best value to the consumer at the most competitive price. Strategies vary according to the type of product, consumer expectations and type of supply chain. A product can be designated by its phase in its life cycle: introduction, growth, maturity or decline. Products may also be classified as a simple product, such as a grocery item, or a complex product, such as a car. In supply chains such as those for groceries sold in supermarkets, most products are mature, volumes are high and demand is predictable. These characteristics of the market are the chief factors in the strategic decision-making of large supermarket retailers. Long-term planning is possible, and firms invest heavily in distribution, including IT and automation technology. In a sector such as fashion apparel, also a simple product, the life cycle is compressed, and the window of opportunity is small, therefore the supply chain must be able to respond quickly to satisfy demand. However, keeping too much stock at the point of sale is risky, as fashion items can command the full price for only a limited period before they are superseded by newer lines. On the other hand, the high margins and the prospect of large sales of a popular item (especially impulse sales) encourage firms to keep large stocks near the retail outlets. Inventory planning is therefore precarious. Supply chain strategy seeks quick response from distribution centres and requires tight co-ordination.

In sectors where products are simple, such as fashion apparel and groceries, there are clear benefits in improving efficiency in downstream activities such as distribution. In these sectors, value delivered to the end customer is largely reliant on instant availability of the desired product at the right price. Products which are expensive and complex, involving a number of manufacturing processes, such as a car, have more complex supply chains. In these products, strategies focus on improvements in design, sourcing, subassembly and manufacturing, rather than downstream activities. Value to the consumer is created through quality, choice and after-sales service. Hence, strategies focus on these aspects of complex supply chains.

A supply chain may be described as efficient, agile or lean, depending on the type of product and the volumes involved:

Efficient supply chain: Ability to process and move high volumes of goods quickly and at the lowest possible cost.

- The efficient supply chain is exemplified by groceries. These products are akin to commodities and are sold in high volumes. Large retailers compete on price, and margins are low. The aim in designing and improving supply chains is efficiency, which has been driven by retailers rather than producers (discussed in the logistics section below). Moving large volumes of goods quickly and at the lowest possible cost is the aim of the efficient supply chain.

Agile supply chain: Ability of firms in a supply chain to respond quickly to frequent changes in consumer preferences and levels of demand.

- The agile supply chain is exemplified by fashion apparel, where demand is difficult to forecast. Companies focus on manufacturing and design, and require flexibility to respond to changing fashion. Short product life cycle, high volatility and high levels of impulse purchases make it difficult to predict demand (Bruce and Daly, 2004). All partners in the agile supply chain must be able to react to fluctuations in demand. In the agile operation, minimal lead times are required and the sharing of information between partners is crucial. Garment manufacturers have been attracted to China and other Asian countries because of their low costs, but the distances to Western markets make it difficult to operate agile supply chains. Production in China may be appropriate for clothing manufacturers of standard products, which are more akin to commodities. For latest fashion trends, firms such as Zara use supply chain design more akin to lean manufacturing. Zara sources raw materials in low-cost countries and does much of the manufacturing in its home region in Spain, close to consumer markets (discussed in CF10.1 on Spain). In addition, its high-tech SCM of downstream activities gives it agility which is the envy of rival firms.

Lean supply chain: Integrated approach which emphasizes the elimination of waste at every stage in the supply chain.

- The lean supply chain, exemplified by complex manufactured products, aims to eliminate waste, and is associated closely with lean manufacturing (discussed below). Competitive advantage rests on the integration of design, sourcing and manufacturing, often between partner firms with whom close relational ties are established. For complex products, therefore, the firm's supply chain strategy reflects its overall business strategy. The lean supply chain shares characteristics of the agile and efficient strategies described above. Efficient systems reduce costs by shortening lead times and reducing inventories. Agile systems allow firms to respond quickly to changes in the market and changes in the supply network.

TO RECAP...
Efficient, agile and lean supply chains
The efficient supply chain seeks to move goods in large volumes quickly and at the lowest possible cost. The agile supply chain is more responsive to changes in demand and environmental changes. The lean supply chain aims to improve efficiency and flexibility, focusing on simplifying processes and eliminating waste, including time.

Beyond the fragmented supply chain
In what ways have new co-operative frameworks aided supply chain strategies in serving customers more quickly and with greater responsiveness to changing demand, despite growing internationalization? Give examples.

PAUSE TO REFLECT

Don't forget to check the companion website at **www.palgrave.com/business/morrisonib**, where you will find web-based assignments, web links, interactive quizzes, an extended glossary and lots more to help you learn about international business.

www.palgrave.com
Companion Website

COUNTRY FOCUS 10.1 – SPAIN

Globalization's changing fortunes in Spain

Spain is commonly seen as one of globalization's success stories. In the decade from 1994 to 2004, more than €100 billion flowed into the country in FDI, attracted by low wage bills and proximity to European markets. Sustained economic growth saw the economy expand 40% over the decade. From virtually no motor industry in the early 1990s, Spain became the world's sixth largest car producer. Tourism prospered, accounting for 12% of Spain's GDP and 11% of employment. Coastal resort developments, targeted mainly at the mass holiday market, helped to swell the profits of construction and property industries, which are dominated by some of Spain's largest companies. Banking, construction and tourism sectors saw stunning growth. The improvement in Spain's business environment owed much to its political transformation from military dictatorship to democracy in the 1970s, followed by EU membership in 1986. As one of the poorer EU members, Spain was entitled to EU structural funds for building infrastructure and services. This investment added to the attractiveness of Spain for foreign investors.

As Spanish wages and costs rose, the country's location advantages diminished. It also became more expensive as a tourist destination. The annual increase in the number of tourists was slowing by 2003, as Spanish resorts lost out to cheaper destinations in Turkey and North Africa. In 2004, the accession of poorer countries to the EU meant a shift of much EU funding away from Spain to these new member states. Construction companies affected by the phasing out of EU funds sought to diversify and expand abroad. Manu-

Figure 1 Spain's FDI inflows and outflows

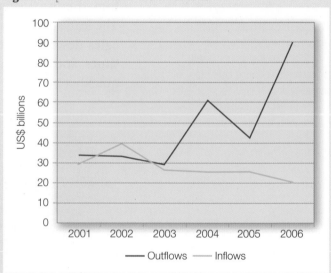

Source: OECD (2007) Trends and recent developments in foreign direct investment, www.oecd.org

facturing jobs tended to migrate to the new EU member states to the east. As Figure 1 shows, FDI inflows have fallen in the new millennium. The biggest threats to Spanish manufacturing were posed by the rise of China and India, where manufacturing costs easily undercut those in Spain. Sectors such as textiles, clothing and footwear, which are traditional industries in Spain, succumbed to low-cost imports, while the manufacturing of complex products such as cars was shifting to the new EU states to the east. How could Spain respond?

The cry of *deslocalización* became common in Spain, as foreign investors closed factories and shifted production to cheaper locations. More than 40 MNEs either closed or sold factories in Spain between 2002 and 2005. Carmakers and components manufacturers figure prominently among the departures. Ford, Honda and VW have moved some production to Eastern Europe, with the inevitable ripple effect felt in supply chains. In 2006, it was estimated that the number of tier-one suppliers would halve, to about 30 in next decade, while their numerous tier-two suppliers would be whittled down from thousands to hundreds. US components manufacturer, TRW, controlled by Blackstone, the private equity group, moved production of airbags and seat belts to Poland to save on costs. Delphi's closure and sale of its factory near Cadiz in southern Spain was highlighted in the opening vignette in Chapter 2. Hewlett-Packard shifted production of its desktop and large format printers from its factory near Barcelona to Singapore. However, the company retained the Barcelona site, and converted it into an R&D centre, which now employs more people than the manufacturing facility employed. VW has also opened a new car design centre near Barcelona. These new jobs are more highly skilled, reflecting a change the Spanish government would like to see replicated all over the country. But moving up the manufacturing ladder to more high-value activities poses challenges.

Underinvestment in education, training and R&D have combined to deter foreign investors who require skilled workforces, while rising wages and low productivity deter companies in low-end manufacturing. On the other hand, an influx of immigrants, many from North African and Latin American countries, has provided new workers willing to take low wages. Of a total population of 43 million, immigrants account for 7%. Economists warn that, with tourism and construction tending to contract, sustaining economic growth is problematic. Spain's government has remained optimistic. Relatively low wages, good infrastructure and proximity to European markets remain attractive to investors. Entrepreneurial, scientific and creative enterprises are indicative of a willingness to adapt to changing realities. Many Spanish textile companies have shifted production to China, Morocco or Eastern Europe, but Zara, the international fashion retailer, has demonstrated how 'old' industries can be transformed.

Zara's parent group, Inditex, is run by one of Spain's leading entrepreneurs, Amancio Ortega. From its beginnings in a haberdashery shop in the relative backwater of Galicia in northwest Spain, Ortega has built a fashion empire worth €13 billion, employing 50,000 people. Tackling the seemingly unavoidable problems of long delivery times and surplus stock held at retail outlets, he revolutionized supply chains in the clothing industry. Over half Zara's output is manufactured locally. New designs can be on display in shops in three weeks, in contrast to the six-month delay typical in the fashion industry for getting new lines to retailers. Logistics technol-

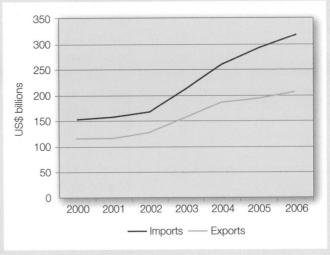

Figure 2 Spain's imports and exports of goods

Source: WTO (2008) International Trade Statistics, www.wto.org

ogy enables inventory to be supplied as needed on a just-in-time basis, reducing inventory costs. Zara's new business model for fashion industry supply chains created a revolution in the industry.

Spain has seen a widening trade deficit, as shown in Figure 2, indicating its waning competitiveness in exports. However, its large companies have prospered, becoming world players, propelled largely by acquisitions (see Figure 1). High-profile purchases of foreign firms include Banco Santander's purchase of the UK bank, Abbey National, and the purchase of BAA (British Airports Authority) by construction and infrastructure company, Ferrovial. Spanish companies' outward expansion is responding to globalization's challenges, which its manufacturing companies cannot match.

Questions

◆ What factors accounted for Spain's attractiveness for foreign investors in the 1990s?

◆ Why has Spain's competitiveness waned in the new millennium?

◆ In what sectors can Spain compete globally, and why?

◆ What are the lessons of Spain's experiences in sustaining the benefits of globalization?

Sources: Mulligan, M., 'New boldness that makes Spanish business stand out', *Financial Times*, 14 June 2005; Mulligan, M., 'Factory closures hit unskilled workers', *Financial Times*, 14 June 2005; Crawford, L., 'Beacon of hope in a hard-pressed sector of the economy', *Financial Times*, 14 June 2005; Wolf, M., 'Pain will follow years of economic gain', *Financial Times*, 21 June 2007; Crawford, L., 'Modernised nation faces uncharted territory', *Financial Times*, 21 June 2007; Mulligan, M., 'Investing in Spain: automotive companies in drive to become clusters of excellence', *Financial Times*, 25 October 2006; Mulligan, M., 'Redundant manufacturing base rises from the ashes', *Financial Times*, 21 June 2007; OECD statistics for Spain, www.oecd.org.

WEB CHECK

See information about Spain by going to the OECD's website at www.oecd.org, and clicking on *Spain* in the country list. Inditex, the owner of Zara and numerous other brands, is at www.inditex.com.

Global sourcing

Global sourcing: Processes of co-ordinating and integrating design and supply of goods between suppliers and purchasers in different locations worldwide.

From an operational perspective, acquiring raw materials and components has tended to be viewed as the 'purchasing' function, having a tactical focus. In more recent supply chain thinking, this function is conceived more broadly as sourcing. Global sourcing as a concept differs from international purchasing, in that it has become strategic in character, becoming more integrated with other elements in the supply chain (Brown and Cousins, 2004). The firm must address issues of sourcing and possible supply partners in the context of its overall competitive strategy.

Make or buy?

Whether already engaged in production or contemplating a new manufacturing enterprise, the firm must address basic questions of what it should be doing in-house and what it should buy from external suppliers:

- Which activities should we carry out ourselves, and which activities should we not be carrying out?
- If we seek specialist provision of a product or activity from another firm, what are we looking for in the other firm, and how should the relationship be structured and managed?
- How would the specialist provider fit in with our existing links to suppliers and customers?

Sourcing options are presented in Figure 10.3. The firm which aims to be completely self-sufficient is represented in the top-left circle. The vertically integrated company seeks control of all stages of the supply chain, whether in the home country or from wholly owned subsidiaries in foreign countries. For a complex product, there may be thousands of parts. Probably no firm in the modern environment would purport to source all its own raw materials and make all its own components in the manner of Ford in the 1920s. Large

Figure 10.3 Make-or-buy decisions

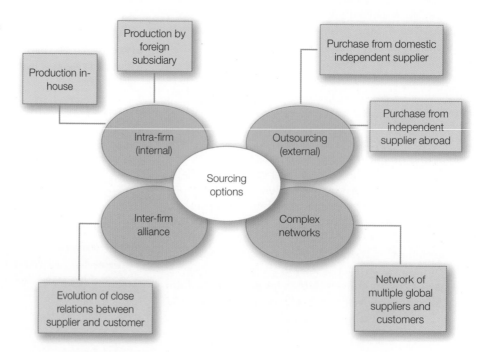

US car manufacturers have traditionally exemplified this strategy, but, spurred by the loss of competitive edge, have turned increasingly to outsourcing from external suppliers. In 1980, 87% of the parts in a Ford car were made by Ford. By 2005, the percentage was 40% (Brown et al., 2005: 221). Suppliers are often in low-cost countries. The strategic choice as seen by these manufacturers is between in-house production and external sourcing through arm's-length transactions. This internal versus external dichotomy can be contrasted with the more co-operative approaches of alliance and network strategies (the lower two circles in Figure 10.3).

Outsourcing to external suppliers is shown in the top-right circle of Figure 10.3. This option is essentially based on exchange transactions. The prospect of cost savings is a major influence in choosing this option. A firm may be able to purchase an item from a supplier who is able to achieve significant economies of scale through volume production, particularly in a low-cost location. The firm which outsources an item it had been making itself also benefits from reduced overheads and bureaucracy.

There are three areas of risk associated with the decision to outsource, which a firm must carefully consider:

1 The firm which decides to outsource an activity stands to lose that competency. It then becomes dependent on the outsourcing company. If the outsourcing company fails, this may jeopardize production in its customers' factories.

2 There may be shifts in power over the long term in the supply chain, which are difficult to predict at the time the decision is taken. For example, the outsourcing company may itself become a powerful player in its specialism, eventually able to exert control over client companies. In outsourcing to Japanese aerospace companies, such as Mitsubishi, Boeing effectively underwrote the Japanese companies' burgeoning technological expertise. These Japanese companies now have considerable power within the Boeing supply chain, which, at the outset of the subcontracting agreement 25 years ago, Boeing would not have foreseen (Mills et al., 2004). (This point was raised in CS6.1.)

3 As sourcing has become increasingly global, there are risks that environmental factors, such as political risk, may have adverse impacts. Responding to global competitive pressures, firms seek cost advantages far afield, creating complex supply networks which cross numerous national boundaries, often dealing with companies they are not familiar with. Communication systems have been facilitated by the internet, but, in terms of negotiations and contracts, there is considerable scope for misunderstanding between firms of differing cultural backgrounds (see discussion in Chapter 4). Improved transportation systems have facilitated the reliable flow of materials, but these systems can come under strain (see later section in this chapter). Political instability or labour unrest may disrupt supply chains. In addition, political change may trigger a shift in policy which is detrimental to the business environment.

The firm must assess the risks, and possibly have other sources of supply as alternatives, as SX10.1 on Bosch highlights.

The bottom-left circle of Figure 10.3 shows the option of inter-firm alliances, in which the participating companies work closely with each other. Japanese companies have evolved this type of supply chain strategy, reliant on ties within inter-firm networks, or keiretsu (see Chapter 7). US companies lost manufacturing competencies in the activities which they outsourced to external suppliers on an arm's-length basis, whereas Japanese companies have sought to strengthen ties with suppliers. Although these companies are legally independent, they have close ties with the manufacturer (OEM), and are often located in the immediate vicinity of assembly facilities. This allows both organizations to benefit from the cost savings of low inventory, just-in-time systems (discussed later in this chapter). These 'satellite' companies are typically involved in the design of new products, where their specialist innovative expertise is a source of competitive advantage for the manufacturer. A result has been the integration of R&D and production skills between the companies. Large Japanese companies have arguably benefited from their management of supply chains, avoiding the risks attached to outsourcing. The sharing of knowledge and expertise with external suppliers brings potential benefits in the reduced time to market and represents a more complex relationship than the exchange transaction represented by purchasing from an external supplier.

The bottom-right circle in Figure 10.3 represents the more recent network approach to supply chains. While all participating firms are independent, their multiple links with external firms allow them to become more competitive through co-operation. Three benefits can be highlighted:

1 Early supplier involvement can reduce the time to market of new products. Improved information flow can help to predict demand more accurately, reducing excess inventory.
2 Value enhancement can be achieved through co-operation between supplier and customer. The specialist expertise of the supplier may bring innovation and the ability to customize for different end consumers. Indeed, as SX10.1 on Bosch shows, the supplier may be the source of key innovations.
3 The firm which establishes ties with a supplier in another country gains valuable knowledge of that country and its ways of doing business. This experience may benefit it in terms of markets for its products, as well as opportunities to form other supply chain ties. This global sourcing approach represents a flexible view of make-or-buy decision-making, in which sourcing decisions depend on organizational and environmental factors which are constantly changing.

TO RECAP...

Make or buy?

To make or buy does not consist of the simple alternatives they might appear to be. Some firms have tended to see purchasing from an external source as the sole alternative to making a product in-house. However, close relations between supplier and customer, through inter-firm alliances and networks, lead to more integrated supply chains and the blurring of organizational boundaries.

Make-or-buy decisions in context
Look again at the sourcing options presented in Figure 10.3. Which companies, in terms of national and corporate culture, are likely to choose which option(s), and why? The companies may be either types of firms or real ones.

PAUSE TO REFLECT

Global sourcing strategies

In recent years, firms in many sectors as diverse as electronics, textiles and motor vehicles have decided to source globally. The overwhelming reason is the cost savings. The more complex the end product, however, the greater the challenges of global sourcing. The decision-making process must take into account a number of factors, which will have a long-term impact on its own manufacturing competencies. Longer and more costly transport must also be taken into account, as the opening vignette showed. Legal and regulatory import restrictions, which differ according to the country of origin, come into play. Exchange rate and currency fluctuations can be crucial.

The firm which has decided to source its supplies globally must decide which country, which suppliers, and how to structure the relationship. These issues are set out in Figure 10.4, which also highlights the role of the firm's strategic goals in the decision-making process. If cost efficiency is the main goal, then a low-cost location is the obvious choice. However, for companies making complex products, factors such as quality and reliability are also important. For this reason, carmakers have been decidedly more cautious than textile companies. The traditional view is that labour-intensive activities, which involve standard technology, are the obvious choices for outsourcing. Suppliers to carmakers must become involved in more collaborative relations over a longer period than those in textiles or electronics.

Carmakers have built up ties with reliable suppliers either in their home country or close to home. For example, US carmakers have sourced in Mexico, and European manufacturers turn to Central and Eastern Europe. Until recently, they have been reluctant to take advantage of the lower cost alternatives from China and India. However, the quality of component manufacturing in these countries is improving, and their domestic car markets are booming. Some of the large tier-one global components suppliers, such as Bosch (featured in SX10.1), Denso and TRW Automotive, are now alert to the possibilities. These companies have become adept at

Figure 10.4 Global sourcing decisions

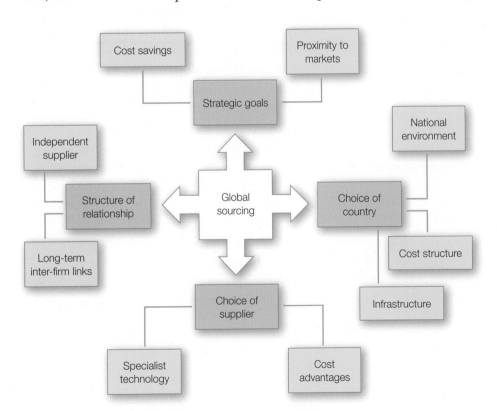

buying parts from low-cost suppliers which they incorporate into components for delivery to final assembly plants.

The growth in global sourcing has proceeded hand in hand with a revision of companies' product policies. If core components can be standardized and simplified, they may be used in a number of different models, and they may also be suitable for manufacture in a low-cost country. Companies which are highly competitive globally have tended to reduce the number of parts. The Japanese company, Canon, is an example. It has sought to produce a camera which will have features that customers everywhere in the world desire, such as good picture quality. It then went about designing a camera which would satisfy consumers, but with standardization of parts (Kotabe, 1998).

The manufacturer may decide to make adjustments in its own processes to enable it to fit in with the capabilities and limitations of low-cost suppliers. For example, a firm's engineers may redesign a part to reduce its technical complexity, enabling it to be manufactured abroad by an outsourcer. Alternatively, the firm can focus on developing the supplier's capabilities, enabling it to manufacture more technically complicated parts in the low-cost country. This involves keeping experienced engineers in the location, which entails extra costs. However, building a longer term relationship with these suppliers can pay dividends. In 1999, Toyota helped Indian suppliers to build steering components. This involved sending Japanese workers to India to teach the techniques which would result in improved quality. The results over the next four years were remarkably successful. The defects were cut from 1,000 for every 1,000,000 parts to fewer than 50, which is roughly equivalent to the defect rate of established Toyota suppliers (Bergmann et al., 2004). This is just one component, and the company would not have the resources in terms of skilled people with the language and technical skills to replicate this success for large numbers of parts. Toyota thus faces challenges in maintaining high levels of quality globally, as discussed in CS10.1. There is also the risk that proprietary technology will fall into the hands of a firm which will become a competitor in the future.

How can a high-cost manufacturing company maintain its competitive advantage while taking advantage of global sourcing? The company which outsources to an independent contractor simply to achieve cost efficiencies, without looking at its overall strategy, risks losing manufacturing competencies and innovative capacity. A spectacular example was IBM in the 1980s. Although it had guarded its own proprietary technology in the past, when it decided to produce PCs, it chose microprocessors from Intel and operating software from Microsoft. These supply deals allowed it to gain market share quickly. However, Intel and Microsoft were able to supply other companies as well, creating opportunities for smaller PC companies to undercut IBM and eat into its market share. It struggled in the PC sector, eventually selling out to Chinese company, Lenovo (see CS2.2).

TO RECAP...
Global sourcing
Global sourcing helps firms to achieve greater integration with suppliers, benefiting from cost reductions and efficiency gains. However, longer term impacts on strategy must be considered, as firms must guard against the dilution of core competencies, innovative capacity and proprietary technologies.

STRATEGIC CROSSROADS

10.1

Bosch steers a steady course in changing vehicle markets

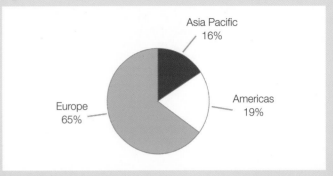

Figure Bosch's global sales ($36 billion) by region, 2006

Asia Pacific 16%

Americas 19%

Europe 65%

Source: Bosch company data, www.bosch.com

From its modest beginnings in 1886, Robert Bosch GmbH, based in Stuttgart, Germany, has become the world's largest supplier of automotive components. In its 150-year history, it has witnessed a transformation in the manufacturing of vehicles, automotive technology, and relations between suppliers and vehicle manufacturers. Manufacturers are constantly raising standards in terms of technology, quality and customer satisfaction. Staying at the forefront of these developments, Bosch has enhanced its market position as a tier-one supplier. Concurrently, global sourcing has become a competitive reality, reflecting cost reduction priorities across the automotive industry. Bosch has expanded to 300 subsidiaries in 50 countries, generating 74% of its sales outside Germany in 2006, with China now the focus of expansion. What are the keys to the company's longevity and continuing success? Bosch's executives highlight the focus on innovation as a core competency. They also point to the fact that Bosch is a private company owned by a foundation, which ensures stability, long-term thinking and financial flexibility. Critical to its commercial success have been the company's internationalization strategy and value-enhancing network alliances.

Bosch has prided itself on its long history of innovation. Having been a pioneer in diesel fuel injection systems, it has pursued a strategy of incremental innovation, coupled with expansion in its range of products. It has diversified from car parts to central-heating boilers, household appliances and industrial machinery. These other divisions account for 35% of its sales worldwide, and the company would like to see this share rise to 50%, reducing its dependence on car parts. In 2004, Bosch overtook Delphi, the troubled US company, to become the world's largest car components manufacturer. The comparison between Bosch and Delphi is instructive. Delphi remained dependent on GM and the US market, and became weighed down with unsustainable labour costs. Bosch is more internationalized as well as more diversified. While its sales are predominantly European (see figure), it is seeking to reduce this share to 50%. It has a broad base of customer companies, further distinguishing it from Delphi. The head of Bosch's vehicle division, Bernd Bohr, says: 'With the changing market on the manufacturers' side the challenge is to win with the winners. That is the key' (Milne and Wihofszki, 14 August 2005). While it is building capacity in Asia, it would like to develop ties with Toyota and Hyundai, although both have been reluctant to deal with foreign suppliers.

A changing pattern of interaction has characterized the car components industry, described by Bosch as a process of 'co-evolution' between suppliers and manufacturers. Bosch sees network alliances as crucial to its innovative and market successes, as different organizations have complementary core capabilities. Bosch supplies different injection systems to different customers, who compete with each other for market share. Bosch engineers are able to transfer learning from one to the other, facilitating improvements in both. New products are often the result of customer initiatives, and Bosch has staff located with customers, to become involved in applications. Much of the current R&D is in software, for which it has a software development centre in Bangalore, India.

While Bosch has gained a reputation for quality and reliability in supplying upmarket brands such as BMW and Mercedes, Bosch's product strategy encompasses the full spectrum of vehicles. It is supplying ABS brakes and engine management systems to the low-cost Logan, made by Renault in Romania. For high-volume components, Bosch aims to have two manufacturing plants, to ensure that, if there is a problem at one, the other can continue supply. This also allows the two to contribute to each other's learning, reinforcing Bosch's emphasis on continuous learning and knowledge links within and across organizations in supplier networks.

Car plants in Europe have been moving eastwards to countries where costs are lower, such as Slovakia and the Czech Republic. Moves further east, into Russia and Ukraine, are also occurring. Bosch and other tier-one suppliers have responded to these shifts. A major challenge is the rise of China and India in both vehicle manufacturing and components. In these markets, Bosch is competing against up-and-coming local components manufacturers, who are eager to move up the value chain. India's largest auto components maker, Bharat Forge, states that it wants to 'become an integral part of the development chain not just the supply chain' (Yee and Reed, 2007). Bharat Forge gained nearly half its sales from Europe in 2006. Its strategic goals are to diversify its products into other sectors such as energy, and to do business with a broad range of customers in different countries across the globe. It is perhaps not surprising that these goals almost exactly mirror those of Bosch.

Questions

◆ What changes in global supply chains are exemplified by Bosch?
◆ What challenges face Bosch in the changing environment?

'Technology advances and exports fuel Bosch growth', *Financial Times*, 14 August 2005; Griffiths, J., 'Bumpy ride is far from over', *Financial Times*, 28 September 2006; Milne, R., 'Bosch takes the long view', *Financial Times*, 25 September 2006; Yee, A. and Reed, J., 'Bharat Forge aims at overseas takeovers', *Financial Times*, 1 June 2007; Bosch company data, www.bosch.com.

Sources: Kash, D. and Anger, R. (2005) 'From a few craftsmen to an international network of alliances: Bosch diesel fuel injection systems', *International Journal of Innovation Management*, **9**(1):19–45; Milne, R. and Wihofszki, O., 'Bosch warns on risk-aversion', *Financial Times*, 3 April 2007; Milne, R., 'Bosch targets growth in low-cost cars', *Financial Times*, 2 March 2006; Milne, R. and Wihofszki, O.,

WEB CHECK

Bosch company information is at www.bosch.com.

Sourcing in the era of globalization
In what ways do sourcing decisions of MNEs exemplify the processes of globalization, and what aspects of sourcing indicate the importance of localization?

PAUSE TO REFLECT

Global manufacturing strategies

Mass manufacturing in its early days was epitomized by Ford's gigantic River Rouge factory, which housed the first moving assembly line. Fordist mass production (defined in Chapter 7) entailed complex machinery designed to produce standardized products, staffed by semi-skilled workers trained to do simple repetitive tasks. This type of production was inflexible and costly. Large inventories were stored at the assembly plant 'just in case' they were needed. Switching to new product lines or modifying existing ones was difficult and time-consuming. For employees, this type of work was monotonous and low in job satisfaction, resulting in labour conflict with employers.

The need for flexibility in manufacturing was a major factor in the demise of Fordist manufacturing. New thinking focused on flexible mass production, allowing manufacturing systems to produce a greater variety of products, giving rise to the term mass customization. The Japanese are usually credited with these developments, although they can be traced back to Western engineers, including the American, William Deming. Deming's ideas made little impact in his home country, but Japanese firms saw their potential in the 1950s and 60s (Deming, 1986). The aims were to be able to produce a range of products for differing customers' needs, and to change to new products with minimum disruption, while maintaining the benefits of mass production. Whereas Fordist production was based on 'production-push', mass customization was based on 'demand-pull' (Dicken, 2003: 365).

Mass customization: Production of a diversity of products utilizing mass-production techniques.

plate 10.2 Advances in the factory production line combine the benefits of mass manufacturing and customization.

Mass production and flexible mass production are compared in Figure 10.5. As indicated, flexible manufacturing involves much more than redesigning machinery and systems. Both inventory management and employee involvement have undergone radical changes, as we reveal in the next section.

Flexible manufacturing: Manufacturing processes based on machines, tasks and co-ordination systems which are adapted to achieve both volume and variety.

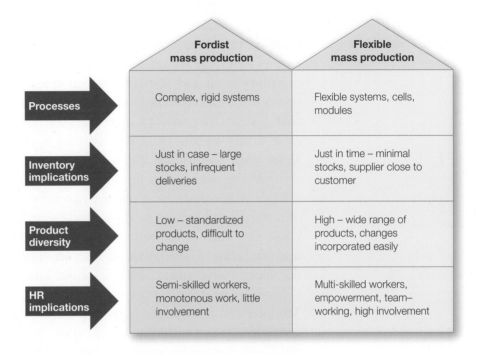

Figure 10.5 Fordist mass production compared to flexible mass production

Flexible manufacturing processes

When designing manufacturing processes, the goals include improving efficiency, reducing costs, incorporating flexibility, maintaining quality, promoting innovation and, most importantly, keeping a focus on the needs of the end consumer. The principles and practices of flexible manufacturing have made huge strides in realizing these objectives. Flexibility and constant adaptation of processes are aided by simplification and discipline in operating practices. Simplification has been achieved partly by reducing the number of parts in complex products such as cars, as noted in the last section. Technology has brought solutions in terms of economies of scale and reliability. New flexible equipment can allow customized products to be produced, enabling products to be manufactured in small batches. Manufacturers aim to achieve reductions in set-up time, simplifying the workplace environment. These simplified systems are able to reduce throughput times.

Manufacturing cells: Arrangement of workers into teams, each of which has responsibility for manufacture and inspection of a specific product or component.

A key aspect of the flexible manufacturing system is the creation of manufacturing cells, by which a product's production is concentrated in a 'cellular' layout, where a group of workers function as a team, often set up in a 'U' shape. As each operator is close to the others, a sense of ownership of the process is encouraged. From the HR standpoint, members are empowered by this team configuration. For employees in modern car manufacturing, skill levels and a focus on corporate goals have transformed jobs. From the manufacturing standpoint, a focus on continuous improvement improves performance. Cells have become incorporated into production systems, improving the efficiency of assembly line production.

Lean production: Systems and techniques of production enabling companies to reduce waste, leading to greater flexibility in production processes and products.

Reducing waste has been the guiding principle of lean production, conceived by Taiichi Ohno for Toyota, and now adapted in diverse industries across the globe. The Toyota Production System aims to reduce or eliminate waste within the factory environment. Waste is broadly defined as including not just materials and products, but lost time in which machinery stands idle. The production system is based on a continuous flow, which in turn relies on the management of inventory. Just-in-time (JIT) manufacturing ensures that there is a continuous flow of materials, with low work-in-process inventory levels and shorter production lead times. Unlike the just-in-case principle of earlier mass production, JIT systems can achieve reductions in costs because they do not require huge levels of inventory. The system requires clear timely signals from downstream operations to upstream operations about what to produce and when. The exact components needed should arrive at the workstation just at the time they are required. A JIT system is suitable where there are repetitive operations demanding a continuous flow of materials. It has been used successfully in the car and computer industries. Close proximity of the supplier to the assembly plant aids in managing JIT manufacturing. Close strategic partnerships with long-term suppliers, as developed by Japanese companies, contribute to the success of JIT systems.

Just-in-time (JIT) manufacturing: System of production which relies on a continuous flow of materials.

Modular strategy has been another innovation in flexible manufacturing. Modular components or parts can be standardized, allowing them to be configured into a variety of products or services, known as modular manufacturing. Production costs are thereby reduced, and the variety of customized end products is increased. Modular strategies involve both product design and production. The impetus towards modularity may be consumer driven or production led. In the computer industry, consumer demand has led to the creation of products which are compatible, with standardized interfaces between modules. The power of the module suppliers has grown, as the earlier example of Intel shows. By contrast, in the car industry, modular production has been driven by the need of manufacturers to reduce complexity. The production of a car can be broken down into separate elements, which can be manufactured independently and are often outsourced. Suppliers have thus become centres of design and technology expertise themselves.

Modular manufacturing: Strategy of designing and using a component in a variety of end products.

Agile manufacturing: The ability to respond and adapt to continuous change in the design, production and delivery of products.

In consumer markets, reducing costs while offering a wide range of products is a source of competitive advantage, as is the ability to adapt quickly to changing demand and circumstances. Responsiveness in supply chains was highlighted earlier as a feature of the agile supply chain. This approach is also applicable in production, in that agile manufacturing allows the firm to respond quickly to changing demand (Brown et al., 2005: 132). Agile manufacturing can be seen as a further development of the processes associated with lean production. The firm which operates lean production processes with low inventory requirements should be able to respond quickly to changes in demand. However, like lean production, there are numerous elements involved in making the strategy successful. Technological innovation, information-sharing within the supply chain, and a workforce culture which fosters creative involvement throughout the organization are all elements of the agile manufacturing strategy.

TO RECAP...
Manufacturing beyond Fordism
Modern flexible manufacturing systems have benefited from the use of technology to simplify and automate processes, reduce levels of inventory and organize workers more effectively than the early assembly lines made famous by Ford. Lean manufacturing has reduced wastage and improved quality, while agile manufacturing and mass customization have improved responsiveness to changing markets and facilitated product variety.

COUNTRY FOCUS 10.2 – SLOVAKIA

Slovakia counts the gains from foreign investors

Slovakia, or the Slovak Republic as it is officially known, is among Europe's smaller and poorer countries. GDP per capita was just over $10,000 in 2006. Formerly part of Czechoslovakia, it became a separate republic in 1993. Economic growth made slow progress under the semi-authoritarian rule and inward-looking policies of Vladmir Meciar's government which followed. However, the reforming government of Mikulas Dzurinda from 1998 to 2006 brought privatizations and the opening of the economy to foreign investors. New industries were built on the ashes of the old heavy industries of the past, providing jobs and prosperity. EU entry in 2004 brought the prospect of funding for infrastructure and other projects. Foreign investors have flocked to Slovakia, lured largely by the country's low wages, which are one-quarter those of the euro-zone. Car manufacturers and components makers have been at the forefront, but electronics companies, including manufacturers of flat-screen televisions, have also been prominent. Slovakia's location at the heart of Europe has been an attraction. Also appealing has been the new flat tax rate of 19% for corporation tax.

As Figure 1 shows, greenfield FDI has soared. In the 1990s, Volkswagen became the first major carmaker to set up a factory in Slovakia. It produced 238,000 cars in its Bratislava factory in 2006. PSA Peugeot Citroen and Kia, the South Korean carmaker, established greenfield factories in 2006. The Czech Republic, with a 100-year history in car production and well known for Skoda, has been the leader in the sector in Central Europe, but Slovakia has been catching up. The Czech Republic made 850,000 cars in 2006. It could be overtaken by the three Slovakian carmakers, which are aiming to produce

Figure 1 Number of greenfield FDI projects in Slovakia and the Czech Republic

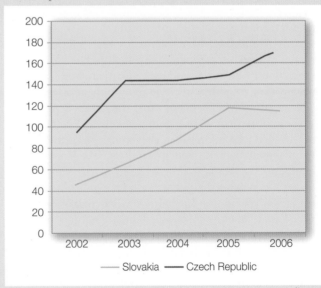

Source: UN (2007) *World Investment Report 2007* (Geneva: UN)

850,000 cars annually by 2010, nearly three times the number produced in 2005. Their plants are located in the western half of the country, which is close to the large European markets, reducing delivery times and avoiding import taxes. Kia's country manager for Slovakia says: 'If we try to do everything from South Korea, we cannot know what exactly European customers want' (*The Economist*, 2007). Kia also has an eye on the Russian market. Apart from the attractions of low wages, these companies have been attracted by the relatively high levels of skills in Slovakia, a legacy of the country's long manufacturing history.

A wave of suppliers has followed these global carmakers. VW's former Slovakia chairman has said: 'We employ 9,000 people but a further 30,000 work at the companies that supply us and that goes for the other two carmakers too' (Krosnar, 2007). Many South Korean firms have arrived, aiming to supply Kia as well as Hyundai, its parent company, located just across the border in the Czech Republic. Visteon has two Slovakian factories manufacturing just-in-time components for Kia and PSA. Slovakia's automotive sector is estimated to employ 95,000 workers.

Have local companies benefited from the backward linkages brought by FDI? Matador is a rarity among Slovak companies: a tyre maker privatized in the 1990s, which has remained independent and become successful internationally. At the time of privatization in 1994, the company had limited resources and R&D capacity. It chose to enter a joint venture with Continental of Germany, producing tyres for the Central and Eastern European markets, a business which now produces 2.2 million tyres a year. Matador's technical director, the son of the owner, negotiated a joint venture with a division of Gazprom of Russia in 1995 to produce tyres in Omsk, Russia, for the growing market there. In 2004, Matador diversified into metal car parts, hoping to benefit from the arrival of Peugeot and Kia in Slovakia. It opted for axle parts, as they are the nearest parts to tyres and would bring synergies in R&D. They now supply pressed and welded parts to VW's assembly plan in Bratislava, as well as Skoda Auto and Audi. In 2005, Matador formed a separate joint venture with a South Korean company to produce door frames for Kia in Slovakia and Hyundai in the Czech Republic. Skoda Auto has now started up production in India, and, not surprisingly, Matador is contemplating a nearby operation producing parts.

FDI has surged in Slovakia, while the Czech Republic has lost some of its lustre, as Figure 2 shows. FDI is providing much-needed jobs in Slovakia, alleviating the relatively high level of unemployment, which stands at 12%. However, the manufacturing jobs are concentrated in the west of the country, whereas in the poorer eastern regions, unemployment affects one in five. In the areas where manufacturing is concentrated, labour shortages are emerging due to lack of skills and emigration, as skilled workers seek better paid jobs in other EU countries. The growing competition for skilled workers has pushed up wages, and staff turnover rates are rising quickly, leading to low staff loyalty to the newly established companies. There is a high level of temporary workers in supplier plants, raising quality concerns. In a country where

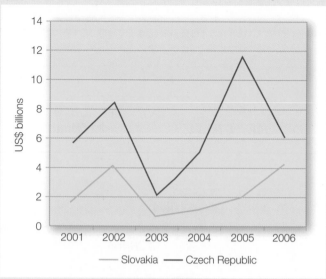

Figure 2 Inflows of FDI into Slovakia and the Czech Republic

Source: OECD (2007) Trends and recent developments in foreign direct investment, www.oecd.org

labour mobility is notoriously low, the components companies have resorted to bussing in workers from long distances.

There are concerns that Slovakia's economic growth has been too rapid, exacerbating the division between the booming west and poor east of the country. A risk is that rising wage levels and skill shortages will make the country less competitive. Elected in 2006, the new government is looking to improve education and social programmes, especially in the east of the country. While not pursuing further privatizations, it is content with the liberalized business environment.

Questions

◆ What are the reasons for Slovakia's recent surge in FDI?
◆ How sustainable is Slovakia's current economic growth? What are the underlying concerns?
◆ How has Slovakia benefited from globalization, and how well placed is it to capture future benefits from globalization?

Sources: Anderson, R., 'Industry shrugs off political shock', *Financial Times*, 20 February 2007; Anderson, R., 'Reaping the rewards of openness', *Financial Times*, 20 February 2007; Krosnar, K., 'Welcome to the Detroit of the east', *Financial Times*, 20 February 2007; Cienski, J., 'Slovak bank chief pours cold water on fears of overheating economy', *Financial Times*, 29 May 2007; Condon, C. and Cienski, J., 'Eastern Europe hit by shortage of workers', *Financial Times*, 5 June 2007; OECD (2007) Trends and recent developments in foreign direct investment, www.oecd.org; *The Economist*, 'Vroom', 23 June 2007, p. 72.

WEB CHECK

For information on Slovakia, go to the OECD's website, www.oecd.org, and click on *Slovak Republic*.

Consumer-driven manufacturing strategies
Outline the ways in which the following innovations in production are driven by the goal of consumer satisfaction: lean production, mass customization, modular strategies, and agile manufacturing.

PAUSE TO REFLECT

The shifting geography of manufacturing

The spectacular rise of Japanese manufacturers was a major feature of changing industries in the second half of the twentieth century. In 1960, the US manufactured more than half of global car production. By 2000, this share had fallen to 14%. Japan's share in 1960 was 1.3%, and by 2000, it had risen to 20.5%. Japan's growth in global market share was achieved with little overseas production until the 1980s. Nissan built its first overseas plant (at Sunderland in the UK) in 1986, and Toyota built its first European plant in 1992. This expansion marked a change of strategy, whereby production was shifted to be near major markets, partly to get round import barriers. Since then, these companies have located manufacturing and supply links in or near their major markets.

At the outset of this section on global manufacturing, we highlighted the corporate goals shared by all manufacturing companies. They included efficiency, cost reductions, quality, innovative capacity and, ultimately, consumer satisfaction. These factors all influence decisions concerning where to manufacture. A firm may choose to outsource manufacturing to firms in low-cost locations, through licence agreements. However, quality and innovation could well suffer if the process is not controlled by the brand owner.

At the opposite extreme, the company which manufactures at home has greater ownership of assets and more control over the processes than it would in manufacturing abroad, but costs are likely to be high, so this strategy is only appropriate for a limited range of products. A firm in a high-cost country could well manufacture high-end products in its home environment, while outsourcing low-end ranges in low-cost environments. Canon, the Japanese digital camera and office equipment company, is an example. It makes high-end copiers in Tokyo, customizing them for customers' needs, while it assembles low-end models near Shanghai in China. Canon's chairman says: 'It's very important for us to maintain manufacturing in Japan. Product development and manufacturing go hand in hand, and Japan is where communication between the two takes place' (Hayashi, 2007). Canon's foreign-made products were 39% of sales in 2006, down from 42% in 2004. Sharp assembles flat-panel televisions in five factories around the world, but the LCD panels are made only in Japan, to reduce the risks of its intellectual property being stolen. Maintaining flexibility in manufacturing capabilities is especially important for firms with a high exposure to the uncertain environments in developing countries. Further, rising wages and other costs in developing countries can weaken their comparative advantage over time.

TO RECAP...

Location factors in manufacturing

Manufacturers consider a number of factors in deciding where to manufacture and which products to manufacture in which locations. They include costs of labour, including skilled labour, proximity to suppliers, proximity to major markets, level of technology involved, and the risks to their intellectual property in some countries.

The manufacturing supply chain

In what ways have changes in manufacturing processes and changes in supplier relationships with OEMs impacted on decisions about where to manufacture?

PAUSE TO REFLECT

Quality management

Quality management principles and practices have accompanied developments in mass manufacturing. Growing awareness of health and safety issues has given impetus to these developments. These issues concern products, processes, workers, consumers and the impact on the physical environment. Practices are influenced by the corporate and national environments. The quality of the item supplied by a supplier affects the manufacturing process and the quality of the goods which eventually find their way to the customer. For early mass manufacturers, product quality was a matter for an inspection department, where staff inspected finished products. This approach of treating quality as a staff function had inherent limitations. For example, a defect in a part supplied by an external supplier may not be apparent, or a shortcoming in the assembly process could be overlooked. It was also limited in the sense that it focused solely on objective, measurable criteria. While quality control mechanisms remain a crucial element, quality in the modern context can be defined more broadly in terms of customer satisfaction: does the product or service satisfy the customer's needs and expectations? Furthermore, quality is now seen in the context of the entire supply chain, not simply as an organizational issue. Five forces have led to this broader view of quality (Juran, 1995):

- The complexity and precision of products, which depend on the quality of each element and on consistency in the manufacturing process.
- Threats to health and the environment, which have increased with the growth in mass manufacturing and the growth in factory output generated.
- Legislation in the areas of consumer protection and health and safety.
- Growing consumer awareness and involvement in quality issues.
- The rise of quality as an aspect of international competitive pressure.

The newer approach views quality as akin to a management philosophy. Pervading the entire organization, it becomes part of the workplace culture. Much of the modern thinking on quality management is linked to the aspects of flexible mass production developed by Japanese manufacturers, as discussed in CS10.1 on Toyota. They include employee empowerment, teamworking and JIT inventory systems. Kaoru Ishikawa introduced the concept of total quality control as a system which involved all workers in analysing problems. The notion of quality circles was one of his innovations. The quality circle consists of a small group of people who meet regularly in the workplace, identifying problems and discussing solutions. Quality circles are closely associated with the philosophy of continuous improvement, or kaizen (Imai, 1986). Continuous improvement encompasses all staff in the organization, who maintain a constant focus on ways in which products and processes can be improved. The linking of continuous improvement and quality crystallized in modern approaches to quality. These include systems based on total quality management and, more recently, six sigma.

Total quality management

Total quality management (TQM) is an approach to quality which encompasses an entire system and all staff (see Figure 10.6). Its focus is customer satisfaction, and it is conceived as an organization-wide approach. TQM as a strategy implies changes to design, production and delivery of products. It also has HR implications, as employee participation is needed to

---

Quality: Degree to which a product or service meets the needs and expectations of customers.

Quality circle: Small group of workers which meets regularly to identify problems and discuss solutions.

Continuous improvement: Process which strives constantly to find creative ways in which problems can be solved and processes improved, involving all workers in the organization.

TO RECAP...

Quality management

Quality management has evolved from a functional approach to a broader management philosophy, which involves the entire organization and supply chain.

Total quality management (TQM): Approach to quality which commits the entire organization to continuous improvement principles and extends to supply chain partners.

achieve improvements in the products and production processes. The company which adopts this approach faces numerous challenges in achieving the necessary integration. They include high levels of communication between staff, as well as a widespread knowledge of processes and techniques. The leadership of senior staff and facilitators in TQM techniques is an important factor. Continuous improvements are sought in all areas, including processes, training, automation and inventory reduction (see Figure 10.6). As continuous improvement aims to reduce defects and improve processes, cost reductions in production are likely to result, in addition to higher quality.

Figure 10.6 Elements of total quality management

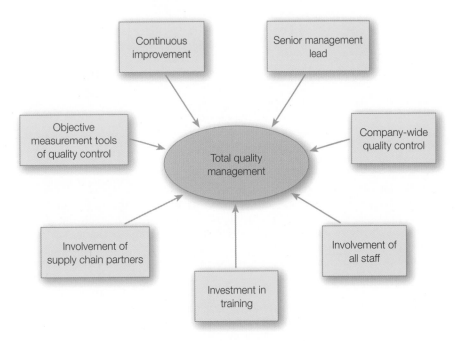

The TQM approach must be linked to business strategy overall. TQM strategies can be designed to fit the firm's competitive strategy. If a high-quality product in global markets is the main aim, the focus will be engineering and design systems. If the firm is seeking cost reductions above all, continuous improvement, JIT, automation and upstream supplier links will be the focus. Quality is critical in both types of strategy, but the quality evaluation will differ depending on factors such as price, service and the firm's reputation. TQM makes demands on every employee to think in terms of continuous improvement, which implies substantial investment in training and education. TQM represented a transformation in thinking about quality in the broader management context. Although developed by Japanese companies, it has proved to be transferable to diverse environments. However, differing cultural and institutional environments, as well differing organizational environments, influence the extent to which it can make dramatic changes in processes and work culture, as CS10.1 on Toyota shows.

TO RECAP...

TQM

TQM is an organization-wide approach to quality, which is closely associated with the aims of a firm's overall business strategy. The approach relies on the implementation of continuous improvement among all staff and supply chain partners.

Formed in the nineteenth century, Toyota was originally a loom works. It was not until 1936 that its first cars were produced. By then, Ford had built 20 million cars and had become famed for its model of mass manufacturing. Toyota developed its own 'lean' manufacturing model, known as the Toyota Production System (TPS). The new system was based on the principles of elimination of waste and continuous improvement (kaizen). Toyota's lean production principles became the new global model of car production and the benchmark for quality. As rival carmakers have gradually implemented these principles, does Toyota risk losing its competitive advantage? Toyota executives see their continuing success as founded in their unique approach to employee knowledge and involvement, which is more difficult for rivals to replicate than techniques. However, Toyota's rapid global expansion has entailed adapting its production system to diverse local conditions, where staff learning and commitment are not so developed, raising questions about Toyota's ability to maintain its competitive edge in quality.

When Toyota started making cars, it adopted the assembly line principle pioneered by Ford. However, given Japan's small domestic market, production had to be designed for flexibility, allowing different models to be assembled on a common system. It developed flexible manufacturing to ensure that components were delivered just in time to be processed. The aim was zero stock, as in-process stock was seen as wasteful. Similarly, production would ideally be in smooth, uninterrupted flows, with no in-process buffers. Staff were constantly on the lookout for ways to improve processes, leading to a reduction in defects and cost savings. If a defect was spotted, the line could be stopped and the problem investigated, thereby limiting the damage and disruption. Continuous improvement relies heavily on staff. Becoming imbued with the 'Toyota way' was time-consuming, taking up to 15 years. Employees must be constantly attentive to see how processes might be simplified and improved, although they were under the inevitable pressure of assembly line work to keep the flow continuous.

Changes were gradually introduced into the TPS, from 1990. The major change was the division of assembly lines into segments, each allocated a set of tasks associated with a module. Each had a quality control station at the end, and there were buffers separating segments. Workers assigned to a segment gained a sense of teamwork and accomplishment. They also felt less pressured than in the past, allowing them to think more deeply about quality improvements. This change has reflected an emphasis on the self-development of workers. Toyota's approach has continued to be to improve production in small steps rather than great leaps, emphasizing continuous learning and problem-solving at all levels of the organization, which defines the Toyota way. The steady stream of small improvements has been a hallmark of Toyota in production processes, bringing benefits of better quality and cost savings.

While Toyota had its sights on building market share in foreign markets, particularly the US, it was relatively slow in locating production overseas. It embarked on overseas production in the 1980s, with 'transplants' of its Japanese factories which were adapted locally. Its first US factory was in Kentucky in 1988. As Figure 1 indicates, overseas production has grown, although in 2006, 60.7% of global production was in Japan. Local sourcing has become company policy, ensuring reliability of JIT supply chains and reducing costs. Key suppliers are either subsidiaries

Case study 10.1: Toyota goes global

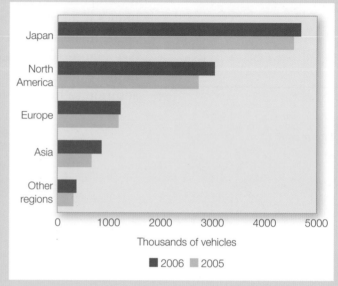

Figure 1 Toyota production by major region

Thousands of vehicles

■ 2006 ■ 2005

Source: Toyota Annual Report 2006, www.toyota.co.jp

or firms with which the company has relational ties. Its US corporate president, Jim Press, says: 'We are a global company, but we have to apply our global lessons locally and to localize production' (Schiffers, 2007). In the US, Toyota's models proved popular for their build quality and durability, which were superior to those of domestic rivals. North American sales are now a third of its total global sales (see Figure 2). It has seven factories in the US. All are non-unionized and located outside the traditional motor industry region of Detroit, which is a labour union stronghold. The Tundra pick-up truck is the first Toyota vehicle totally designed and manufactured in the US, at the company's new assembly plant in Texas.

Toyota's success in the US is partly explained by the weakness of US car manufacturers, which have undergone painful restructuring to deal with spiralling costs and lacklustre domestic sales. In the first three months of 2007, Toyota overtook GM in global car sales, selling 2.35 million vehicles, compared to the 2.26 sold by GM. Shrugging off the landmark achievement, a Toyota

Figure 2 Toyota's total sales and North American share

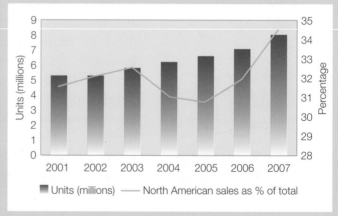

■ Units (millions) —— North American sales as % of total

Source: Financial Times, 10 May 2007

spokesman said: 'Our goal has never been to sell the most cars in the world. We simply want to be the best in quality. After that, sales will take care of themselves' (BBC, 24 April 2007). In contrast to US carmakers, which have internationalized through acquisition, Toyota has tended to expand organically, maintaining its clear focus rather than becoming embroiled in the difficulties of integrating acquired companies. Its most recent international expansion is in China, where it faces formidable rivals in GM and VW, which are longer established. However, entering China only in 2002, Toyota built up production quickly. Production in Asia rose 29% in 2006 (see Figure 1). Toyota is increasingly sourcing its cars for the Chinese market from local suppliers, either local companies or Japanese component manufacturers in the country.

In 2005, a massive recall of 1.4 million cars for repairs and a recall of 380,000 Lexus and Highlander vehicles in 2006 were a blow to Toyota management and threatened to dent

the company's reputation for quality. The recalls coincided with strides made by rival carmakers such as Hyundai in building stronger reputations for quality. A 'back to basics' campaign was launched by Toyota executives, concerned that essential principles had been overlooked in the company's rapid global expansion. New staff in diverse locations were picking up the techniques of lean production, but lacked the depth of understanding of continuous improvement. New training centres were set up, and 'mother' plants in Japan were designated to teach new workers and managers how the system should work. While Toyota has worked to refocus on quality, it is aware that making its system work in differing environments is a major challenge for the future, as its rivals are narrowing the gap.

Questions

1 Explain the key features of the Toyota Production System, stating the ways in which it was innovatory?

2 What have been the challenges faced by Toyota in developing a successful global strategy?

3 Why does Toyota risk losing its competitive advantage as it expands globally?

Sources: Benders, J. and Morita, M. (2004) 'Changes in Toyota Motors' operations management', *International Journal of Production Research*, **43**(3): 433–44; Schiffers, S., 'Toyota, an all-American company?', BBC, 12 January 2007, www.bbc.co.uk; BBC, 'Toyota "world's largest carmaker"', 24 April 2007, www.bbc.co.uk; Nakamoto, M., 'Bumpy road ahead for Toyota', *Financial Times*, 10 May 2007; Mackintosh, J., 'Toyota's steady speed leaves rival's big ideas for dust', *Financial Times*, 12 June 2003; Simon, B. and Reed, J., 'Toyota shifts Prius drive into top gear', *Financial Times*, 8 January 2007; Mackintosh, J., 'Toyota strives to steer back towards quality', *Financial Times*, 13 July 2006; Kotabe, M. (1998) 'Efficiency vs. effectiveness orientation: A comparison of U.S. and Japanese multinational companies', *Academy of Management Executive*, **12**(4): 107–19; Toyota Corporation, Annual Report 2006, www.toyota.co.jp.

WEB CHECK

Toyota's global corporate website is www.toyota.co.jp

Six sigma

Six sigma: A quality control system which focuses on improvements in measurable performance through cost reductions and elimination of defects.

Six sigma is a system of quality control pioneered by Motorola in the 1980s. It is more focused on reducing costs than TQM. Six sigma stresses the importance of design, elimination of defects and process performance. It is sometimes seen as more of a business strategy than a system of quality control (Maguad, 2006). From a quality perspective, it brings together a package of quality tools for statistical measures of product performance. While none of these was new at the time, their integration in an overall business strategy created a powerful programme. From the strategy perspective, six sigma's emphasis on processes involving the whole organization gives it an affinity with the philosophy of lean production. Four processes are involved:

1 Change management is needed to introduce a system of measurement and accountability for results.

2 Innovation is needed to design products which meet customers' expectations.

3 Problem-solving entails examining all aspects of the operation, from design to analysis and control.

4 Project management demands that staff remain focused on analysing and improving performance and eliminating defects.

Information about six sigma can be found at www.isixsigma.com.

WEB CHECK

TO RECAP...

Six sigma

Six sigma represents an approach to quality management based on analysing and improving performance, with the aid of a variety of quality measurement tools. It is particularly associated with eliminating defects and reducing costs.

For these processes to succeed, 'champions' must be designated within the organization, supported by HR and training programmes. Six sigma has proved popular with managers, largely because of its focus on reducing costs and shortening product cycle times. A more recent variation known as 'lean six sigma' aligns this approach more closely with lean production, with its stress on satisfying customer expectations.

International quality standards

Quality standards may be set by industry bodies, national bodies or companies themselves. As companies become more active internationally, they perceive the need to demonstrate their quality credentials to potential suppliers and customers. A company may designate its own quality standards, which enhance its reputation in the competitive environment. However, external accreditation offers an outward sign of its commitment which is more objective. The growing number of companies seeking external accreditation indicates that both improvement in quality performance and the visible labels of quality assurance standards are becoming more important in international business.

International standards are set by the Geneva-based organization, the International Organization for Standardization (ISO). It has devised two main sets of standards, which overlap to some extent. ISO 9000 standards are for general quality assurance, and the ISO 1400 series applies to environmental management. These standards offer a means for companies to apply voluntarily for their structures and process to be assessed. Any company in any location can apply, service providers as well as producers of goods. The assessment of applicant firms is carried out by independent auditors, and firms are certified by bodies accredited by the ISO (not by the ISO itself). Although obtaining ISO certification can be a time-consuming and costly process, the company which gains ISO certification is in an advantageous position to obtain lucrative international contracts. The assurance of uniformity of standards has grown in importance as supply chains have become more internationalized. Hence, if existing suppliers to an MNE are ISO 9000 certified, any new firm hoping to join them will have to be similarly certified in order even to be considered.

ISO 9000 dates from the 1980s, when three levels of standards were designed. The first, ISO 9001, was a set of standards for firms which design, develop, produce, install and service products. Levels 2 and 3 (ISO 9002 and ISO 9003) were designed for firms with a more limited range of activities. Following a revision in 2000, the new standards are known as ISO 9000:2000. There is now only one comprehensive set of standards, ISO 9001:2000, which applies to all firms, with separate provisions for design, manufacturing and service activities. Despite the new name, they are still generally referred to as 'ISO 9000 standards'. Key concepts of quality assurance and stakeholder expectations are incorporated, combining a management focus with the setting of technical standards. There are four headings: management responsibility; resource management; product or service realization; and measurement, analysis and improvement. For each of these, documentation and record-keeping are of utmost importance. These stringent requirements place responsibility on every member of the organization to take an active role in quality issues. Although it is expensive to provide and maintain the documentation required, the expense is likely to be justified in terms of new business that ISO certification helps the firm to attract. Moreover, the quality management processes encouraged are not simply a matter of paperwork. The firm's quality management processes will benefit from continuous improvement, improved communications and a renewed focus on customer requirements. As with other approaches to quality management, the ultimate goal is to satisfy customers.

ISO 9000: Internationally recognized quality standards, for which companies can apply to be certified by bodies accredited by the ISO.

The ISO's website is www.iso.org.

WEB CHECK

TO RECAP...

ISO standards

ISO standards provide a means for companies to apply and meet internationally recognized quality standards, in both manufacturing and services. Although the certification process is costly, it is perceived as a valuable aspect of quality assurance, and is increasingly recognized in international business.

Quality management in differing environments

Environmental differences between countries affect production systems, sensitivity to quality issues, quality management processes and consumer expectations. Three main factors have caused increased awareness of these differences by MNEs:

1 Supply chains have become more internationalized, bringing into networks countries of varying levels of economic and technological development, including developing countries.
2 MNEs have increasingly outsourced production to developing countries. Although standardized products and products for emerging markets have been the obvious candidates, outsourcing production of high-tech products has become possible as developing countries' industries move up the value chain. While one-third of all mobile phone handsets were outsourced in 2007, it is expected that, by 2010, half of all handsets will be manufactured by outsourcers (*Financial Times*, 2007).
3 As product life cycles shorten, MNEs now seek to market new products in numerous national markets simultaneously, including developed and emerging markets.

The themes of quality management highlighted in this discussion so far include the importance of HR development, a focus on customer satisfaction and the incorporation of quality management into the strategic goals of the organization. As TQM became influential, these themes were emphasized, most prominently in Japan and other industrialized countries. A number of aspects of the national environment can be highlighted, but we focus here on the sociocultural and institutional environments, as these are influential in both the human and technological facets of quality management.

The cultural environment influences perceptions of work and achievement, as well as the attitudes of workers and managers towards each other. Also rooted in cultural heritage are people's views of the role of the company in society. The Japanese worker traditionally identifies closely with the firm's goals, which provides strong motivation. Worker empowerment and teamwork have featured in Japanese quality management. The worker from a Western cultural environment is more individualistic than the Japanese worker, but individual goals are also strong motivators, which Western HR development policies foster. Low power distance and worker empowerment also underpin HRM in Western countries. Continuous improvement relies on active worker involvement and responsibility, which helps to explain why Japanese quality management practices have been successful in Western environments. In Japan, South Korea and Western industrialized countries, the value of education and training is prioritized by governments and businesses. Also, a large middle class is the mainstay of consumer society, in which educated consumers demand high levels of quality in products and services.

By contrast, in many developing countries, education is weaker and not universal in society. Training provision by both governments and businesses, while viewed as important in principle, is likely to be poorly resourced. As noted in CF8.2 on South Africa, the lack of skilled workers has proved to be a stumbling block in attracting FDI. Middle-class consumers in developing countries, although growing in number, still tend to be outnumbered by a large rural population, where poverty and lack of education are major problems. Developing countries, especially those in Asia, incline towards high power distance and hierarchical organizations. In these environments, the training of workers and the development of management staff to implement quality systems pose particular challenges, as cultural values are incompatible with worker empowerment. In India, while resources have gone into the computing and high-tech sector, the level of education in rural areas is low. Here, social structures, employment patterns and authority structures make it difficult to implement programmes which require workers to think independently about processes (Prasad and Tata, 2003). In addition, a cultural tendency to view actions and events in a segmented way, rather than holistically, is an impediment to introducing quality control measures.

High power distance and traditional authority structures, common in developing countries, make it difficult to bring about changes in the work culture in a factory or service context. The challenge for managers in these countries is to design quality management systems which can be implemented to take account of cultural influences, rather than attempting to import programmes which seem incompatible with cultural values, and could be counterproductive (Hui et al., 2004). For example, where workers are uncomfortable with empowerment, authoritative relations built on trust between managers and subordinates could be used to alter behaviour patterns (Hui et al., 2004).

Weak institutional environments in most developing countries constitute significant drawbacks in improving quality standards. For consumers in these countries, foreign products are often seen as guarantees of higher quality than local equivalents. The foreign product costs more, but, especially for products such as medicines, the foreign branded product is perceived as safer. China has been the source of many goods, from food products to toys, which pose risks to health and safety. Harmful goods may enter domestic markets or be exported. McDonald's has become so concerned about the quality of local supplies in China that it has taken proprietary control of the entire supply chain, producing all its own ingredients. Raising quality standards involves tightening up the regulatory environment as well as improving manufacturing processes. The Chinese government announced it had shut down 180 food factories on safety grounds in the first half of 2007, signalling that it is taking quality seriously.

TO RECAP...

Cultural dimensions of quality management

Quality control systems and TQM have achieved results in developed countries where levels of education and training are high. Also influential has been the personal involvement of workers and guidance from managers. In developing countries where these systems and values are only weakly developed, quality systems are evolving, but processes are influenced by cultural values, which must be taken into account.

Quality in the competitive environment

Today's consumers expect high levels of quality and durability in products, but they also want low prices. Critically evaluate the effects of price competition on quality. To what extent are manufacturers and service providers tempted by a strategy of focusing on price to the detriment of quality? Give examples.

PAUSE TO REFLECT

Logistics

Logistics: Management of processes for moving materials and products within a supply chain.

Logistics as a function concerns the flow of materials and products in the supply chain, in both upstream supply activities and downstream activities, by which finished products reach the end consumer. To function efficiently, the different links in the supply chain must be co-ordinated so that goods of the right description flow smoothly, reaching the customer when and where they are needed. Numerous links must be co-ordinated, from suppliers to customer firms, from manufacturers to distributors, retailers and end consumers. All the links involve transport. The short journey from the supplier to the assembly plant nearby must be timed to the second in a JIT system. At the opposite extreme, the sea journey of thousands of kilometres travelled by manufactured goods from China to end consumers in Western countries takes over a month. We look first at how logistics has evolved in the global environment, and then at transport issues.

Global logistics management

Logistics traditionally conjures up images of large warehouses bulging with goods and large amounts of paperwork to keep track of them. The modern supply chain, however, emphasizes the integration of activities and exchange of information, so that goods can flow as and when needed. Moving materials continuously in frequent, reliable deliveries as they are required reduces the costs of handling and lessens the need for large inventories to be stored in warehouses. In some cases, goods travel direct from the manufacturer to the retailer or end customer. These processes are made possible by linking computer systems to gather, transmit and share data. JIT systems implemented by suppliers rely on the continuous provision of data, as discussed earlier in this chapter. Downstream activities also utilize these principles, through continuous replenishment, whereby inventory is replenished quickly and order cycles are reduced. Whereas logistics was formerly viewed as a fragmented set of discrete activities, including various modes of transport and warehousing, MNEs are now looking for more integrated logistics solutions, with higher levels of customization for their needs. As logistics has become increasingly international, the companies with international capabilities, as well as the ability to handle huge volumes, have seen strong growth. DHL Logistics, a division of Deutsche Post, is an example, which has grown rapidly by acquisition, increasing its international capabilities.

DHL Logistics is at www.dhl.com. Click on *global website* for company information.

WEB CHECK

Much of the impetus in revolutionizing distribution activities has come from powerful buyers such as large retailers. In the US, Wal-Mart has worked with producers in devising an 'efficient consumer response' system, whereby all parties work together to satisfy consumers 'better, faster, and at less cost' (cited in Mills et al., 2004: 1022). Similar arrangements have been initiated in Europe, where powerful retailers, such as Auchan and Tesco, are influential. The following features of these arrangements between large producers and retailers can be highlighted:

- Reduction of inventories
- Reduction of cycle time in the distribution channel
- Elimination of paper transactions

- Streamlining of product flow
- Satisfaction of consumers with the products they want, including a varied assortment, promotions and new products.

These producer–retailer arrangements signal more collaborative relations between the different organizations in the supply chain, in contrast to the rather adversarial relations of arm's-length transactions in earlier eras. Success depends heavily on the sharing of information among partners, as well as integrating systems throughout the entire supply chain. Indeed, the tight co-ordination that is required needs specialist 'interface managers', with cross-functional skills, to achieve smooth supply chain integration. Hence, SCM in downstream activities has organizational, informational and managerial facets.

Some retailers and consumer goods companies in developed countries are shifting downstream activities to China, close to manufacturing centres. Goods can be sorted, labelled and packed into containers in the right quantities for different customers by logistics companies. Some goods are even placed in display units before being packed. They are then sent from the port where they dock to the individual shop, cutting out the need for distribution centres in the destination. For retailers, the shifting of these distribution and sorting activities to China represents an opportunity to reduce costs.

Transport in the changing environment

Supply chains depend on the physical movement of materials and goods from one place to another – the greater the distance, the more complicated and risky the journey. For international supply chains, the main modes of transport are ships, road freight haulage, rail freight and air freight. In addition, ports, airports, terminals and depots are critical links in the process. These transport and infrastructure industries represent an array of different owners, both public and private, with differing perspectives and differing national environments. Global companies seeking to integrate supply chains must deal with a host of independent transport and infrastructure organizations, among which there has tended to be little co-ordination. Political and economic factors are influential in global trade. As Chapter 6 showed, the protectionist policies of governments impact on international trade, affecting manufacturers and transport companies. Shipping and logistics can amount to a significant share of costs, as Figure 10.7 shows.

The growth in trade and extended supply chains have created challenges for transport systems across the world. The boom in exports from China to distant consumer markets increased demand for transport services and infrastructure, as highlighted in the opening vignette. Shipping companies, such as Maersk, featured in SX10.2, must assess what capacity will be needed in the long term. Although China has rapidly increased port capacity to handle exports, the building of new port and infrastructure facilities in destination countries has involved long lead times. Moreover, links by road and rail from ports must be simultaneously developed, to prevent bottlenecks in ports. Hence, transport systems face challenges in adjusting to variations in demand and routes. We look at the two most popular modes of transport, by water and overland.

TO RECAP...

Logistics management

As logistics has become more international, the smooth integration of links in the supply chain has become more important. Formerly necessitating numerous independent organizations, modern logistics companies aim to provide a seamless, efficient and reliable service, which can be customized for customers.

Figure 10.7 Breakdown of costs for goods imported into the US from China

Source: *Financial Times*, 16 November 2004

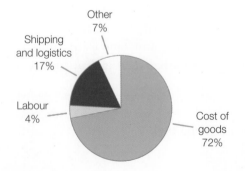

plate 10.3 The advent of the container revolutionized shipping and necessitated the building of specialist container ports.

By water

Transporting goods by sea and inland waterways has taken place since ancient times. This type of travel seems slow by current standards, but it enjoys cost and environmental advantages over quicker alternatives. Whereas sea journeys in earlier generations could be precarious and unpredictable, modern shipping and navigation have greatly reduced the risks and improved safety. A major factor in globalization's advance was the containerization of freight. The container, invented in 1956, is a strong metal box of a standard size, which facilitates the safe handling of quantities of goods. Container shipping has dramatically reduced the costs of ocean shipping – a factor which was crucial to growth in trade volumes. Much shipbuilding shifted to ships designed to take containers. A new breed of supership, capable of carrying 8,000 containers, was a further innovation, highlighted in SX10.2. However, these very large ships have caused headaches in ports where berths were not designed for them. The traditional pattern of dealing with containers has been to move the full container from the docks to destinations inland and to bring it back with goods destined for export. Trade imbalances have caused this pattern to break down, however, as the volumes from China to destination ports far exceed volumes travelling the reverse journey, leaving thousands of empty containers in ports. These imbalances are shown in Figure 10.8, on Long Beach port facilities, where East Asian trade makes up more than 90% of shipments.

The two large US west coast ports, Long Beach and Los Angeles, which handle 45% of all US container traffic, have struggled to cope with the increase in traffic. In 2002, a strike by the dock workers' union shut down US west coast ports for 11 days. It took 100 days to clear the backlog of cargo. These ports seized up in 2004 – a crisis caused by congestion – sending shivers through JIT supply chains. Labour disputes have also led to congestion, as dock workers and their unions have been reluctant to bring in changes

Figure 10.8 Container trade at the Port of Long Beach

Note: TEU = twenty-foot equivalent units, the standard industry measure

Source: Port of Long Beach, TEU Summaries, www.polb.com

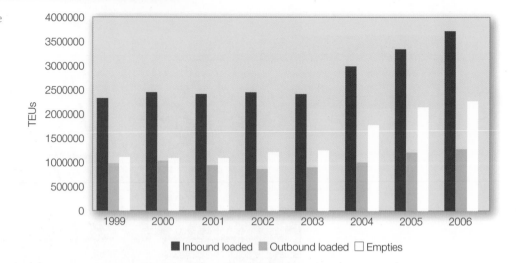

to working conditions and new technology designed to speed up dockside processes. Bad weather also causes hold-ups. These examples demonstrate the vulnerability of systems which come under strain, as a backlog can quickly build up.

STRATEGIC CROSSROADS

10.2
Maersk encounters bumpy seas

A.P. Moller Maersk, the Danish conglomerate, is the world's largest shipping company and the global leader in container shipping. Dating back to 1904, the company has traditionally operated in a number of sectors. Besides shipping, it has had interests in oil and gas exploration, banking, airlines, supermarket retailing and IT services. In recent years, Maersk has shed some of these non-core businesses, to focus on what its owners consider to be its core activities, which are shipping and energy. It sold its IT business and its airline interests, but remains diversified, retaining its supermarkets and banking interests. In all, it owns over a thousand companies, and it operates as a joint venture partner in a number of activities, particularly in container terminals.

Maersk has aimed to achieve vertical integration in its shipping activities, enabling it to control as much as possible of the container shipping supply chain. Besides its shipping business, Maersk Lines, it owns shipbuilders, terminals and logistics companies. This integration has enabled it to offer a flexible and seamless service to customers, in contrast to companies which deal with multiple external providers. In expanding and integrating these activities, its aim has been to pursue scale, increasing the size of the business as well as the capacity of its ships. It owns the world's largest container ship, the Emma Maersk, which is 397 m long and 56 m wide. Maersk has been the leader in the trend towards bigger ships, believing that

more capacity is the best way to improve efficiency. Maersk's terminal business, APM Terminals, has expanded to 45 ports in 28 countries, mostly in the main trading regions: 14 are in the US, 8 in China and 8 in Europe. Although the parent company stresses that APM Terminals is run independently, Maersk Lines' ships are their biggest customer.

China's export surge brought increased volumes and healthy revenues to the companies able to cope with the increased demand. Consolidation has occurred in the shipping industry, the largest operators seeking acquisitions of smaller rivals. Maersk acquired Sealand, in 1999. It became more ambitious in 2005, buying Anglo-Dutch operator, P&O Nedlloyd, at the time the world's third largest shipping company, for €2.3 billion. Maersk's shipping business was already much larger than its nearest rival, the Mediterranean Shipping Company (MSC), but, with the two acquisitions, its capacity became more than twice that of MSC. Maersk had had difficulties integrating Sealand, but it had even greater difficulties integrating P&O Nedlloyd. Integration strains, including IT systems problems, affected corporate performance in 2006. Furthermore, in 2006, global shipping capacity outstripped demand: capacity grew by 17%, while demand grew at half that rate. Integration problems and slowing demand caused Maersk to suffer substantial losses in its container shipping division, as shown in the figure. The company's annual profits were bolstered by other divisions, particularly energy exploration. However, corporate health depended on recovery in the container business, and, with a number of new ships being built, the company recognized that it had been unrealistic in forecasts of increased demand. Jacques Saadé, the president and founder of Marseilles-based

Figure Maersk net profits by division in 2006

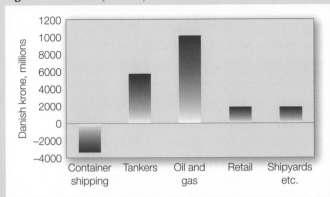

Source: A.P. Møller-Mærsk A/S Annual Report 2006, www.maersk.com

CMA CGM, the third largest container shipping line, questioned the wisdom of Maersk's takeover of P&O Nedlloyd. He felt it was too big to be absorbed, and that smaller acquisitions are the better long-term strategy.

Maersk was forced to rethink the strategy of 'bigger means better', given the uncertainties of the global trading environment. In many companies, especially one as large as Maersk, whose revenues nearly equal those of Microsoft, shareholders might have expressed concerns about senior management. Maersk, although a publicly listed company on the Copenhagen Stock Exchange, is controlled by the founding families, who hold 75% of the voting shares. The company is thus protected from the sort of shareholder criticisms which public companies typically face. Nonetheless, in 2007, the company brought in a new CEO, the first outsider appointed to the post in its history. A restructuring has followed, splitting the container business into three divisions: Maersk Line, the logistics business and ERS (highlighted in the opening vignette). The new management is confident it is finally steering its container business back into profit.

Questions

◆ Critically assess Maersk's approach to the strategic crossroads it has faced.

◆ In your view, is Maersk's ownership structure, which is based on private control, a benefit or a detriment in terms of strategic direction?

Sources: MacCarthy, C., 'Danish group quietly shifts focus to ships and energy', *Financial Times*, 9 August 2005; Wright, R., 'Building the engines of globalisation: the story of shipping giant Maersk', *Financial Times*, 3 October 2006; Wright, R., 'Fraught times for freight as an industry tries to box clever', *Financial Times*, 26 April 2006; Wright, R., 'CMA CGM chief looks forward to smooth sailing', *Financial Times*, 1 July 2007; A.P. Møller-Mærsk A/S Annual Report 2006, www.maersk.com; Wright, R., 'Møller-Maersk begins shake-up', *Financial Times*, 5 December 2007; Wright, R., 'Maersk Line chief defends restructuring', *Financial Times*, 6 December 2007.

WEB CHECK

See Maersk's website at www.maersk.com.

Waterborne transport is more fuel efficient and less pollutant than other modes of transport, but river networks are underutilized in much of the world. Barge traffic is growing in China at a rate of 35% a year, and enjoys an advantage in the concentrated manufacturing area of the Pearl and Yangtze Rivers. In Europe, river transport is highly developed, carrying 40% of inland container freight. By contrast, in the US, only a small fraction of freight travels by river, despite the fact that the Mississippi River and its tributaries, running from the Gulf of Mexico to the Great Lakes, are within easy reach of 60% of US consumers. The Osprey Line, a Texas-based shipping company, is running river boats loaded with containers in the Mississippi River network, building container terminals along the routes. The Mississippi's ageing infrastructure, with its 215 locks in varying states of repair, make this an unattractive prospect for many businesses. It is slow compared to road freight, but much cheaper. The journey from New Orleans to Memphis by truck takes 8 hours at a cost of $40 a tonne, while the journey by river barge takes 72 hours and costs $5 a tonne. Attracting even a small percentage of freight to the river takes pressure off crowded roads, and simply returning empty containers to ports is a useful activity. Calls for government funding for infrastructure improvement along the Mississippi have become more vocal as the benefits of river haulage have received more serious attention.

Overland

Road and rail haulage have come under strain with rising demand for cross-border transport. Road haulage carries 78% of freight in the US. As the highways become choked and communities become more sensitive to the environmental issues involved in building more roads, attention has turned to rail freight. The railways were instrumental in America's industrialization in the nineteenth century. The rail network peaked at 610,000 km in 1920, and since then has shrunk to 277,000 km. Still, 16% of freight is carried by rail in the US. While investment is needed, rail operators, which are all listed companies, are in a difficult position. Owning the track as well as the rolling stock, they would face huge capital expenditure for long-term infrastructure improvement, and, like shipping companies, fear shrinking returns from overcapacity. Railways in Europe are a mixture of state-owned and public companies, and infrastructure improvements have been funded to a greater extent from public funds. Cross-border rail traffic in Europe has been frustrated by differing national systems, mainly state owned, and different train control systems. Efforts to introduce a single system, the European Rail Traffic Management System, have been slow, and, even when introduced, have not proved totally interoperable, which has been frustrating for freight services companies. Standardization of rolling stock is also needed. The opening of rail freight markets to competition is gradually leading to the transport of more shipping containers by rail. Road networks in Europe have come under strain from traffic congestion, especially in mountainous areas. Some European countries, including Austria, Switzerland and Germany, have systems of road charging for trucks on some key routes.

In developing countries, poor road and rail networks, combined with inefficient equipment, make transport precarious and also costly. Inland regions of China and India have less well-developed transport infrastructure than coastal areas. The Chinese government and private investors are improving infrastructure. Inefficient state-owned companies have maintained strongholds in transport, which is slowly giving way to more responsive operators. Since 2006, foreign logistics companies have been allowed to own all the shares in trucking companies in China. A Japanese operator stepped in quickly to introduce a new service providing parts deliveries to Toyota dealers in China. A new Silk Road network, consisting of six road/rail corridors across Central Asia, offers the prospect of better infrastructure for exporters (see opening vignette). It is being aided by development funds from large donors such as the World Bank and UN Development Programme.

Lack of infrastructure investment in India is generally acknowledged to be holding back economic development, and it is becoming an important political issue (Wright, 2007). The frustration caused by poor roads and traffic congestion is largely attributed to underinvestment (highlighted in the opening vignette in Chapter 8, which featured the Tata Nano). Lethargic and bureaucratic state-owned companies are a major factor. In poorer developing countries in Africa, goals of increasing trade are often hampered by inadequate port facilities, poor infrastructure and high costs.

For manufacturers and logistics companies, uncertainties and delays add to costs. While air freight has gained in volumes, it is costly, and usually only feasible for high-value cargo. Moreover, expensive investments in transport infrastructure will lead to higher charges. As JIT systems depend on reliability of deliveries, companies are adapting the model to more localized production, as CS10.1 on Toyota showed.

TO RECAP...

Transport alternatives

Water transport, whether inland or on the high seas, offers benefits of fuel efficiency and less damaging environmental impacts than other types of transport. For logistics companies, which increasingly aim to offer an integrated service including warehousing and distribution, road transport is a crucial element. Port facilities and other transport infrastructure differ widely across the globe. The smooth flow of goods in supply chains remains subject to uncertainties, both natural and manmade.

Transport and globalization
In what respects has transport been a
facilitator of globalization? What are the impacts,
on both exporting and importing countries, of the
huge variations in transport infrastructure, and
associated costs, in today's world?

PAUSE TO REFLECT

Conclusions

☐ Henry Ford is often remembered for offering consumers any colour of car, so long as it was black. The modern consumer expects a choice of model, customized equipment, competitive prices, high levels of quality, and, as if these demands were not enough, rapid delivery. MNEs have developed flexible manufacturing systems, capable of delivering customized products, while keeping costs down. Innovations such as lean production and JIT processes, pioneered by Japanese companies, have transformed manufacturing globally. These developments entailed organizations visualizing supply chains as interdependent elements, through which materials and products should, ideally, flow smoothly. Entering strategic thinking only in the 1980s, supply chain management, taking in each stage in the sourcing, production and delivery of goods, is now seen as critical to corporate success. Compelled to rethink questions of what to make and what to buy from outsiders, the firm must look at where its own core competencies lie, and where it might gain competitive advantage by relying on others. Sourcing materials and parts, especially for complex products such as cars, has been transformed by the rapid growth in global suppliers, most recently in low-cost emerging economies.

☐ Flexible manufacturing and global sourcing, although appearing to be the ideal strategy, match up uneasily in practice: the dependability of supplies is inclined to decrease as the distance increases. Japanese companies have traditionally sourced from suppliers in the near vicinity of assembly plants, often through an inter-firm alliance. Sourcing a component from a distant supplier entails risks, from transport hold-ups as well as uncertainties about reliability and quality. Expectations of quality have risen enormously, as have expectations that firms will respond quickly to changing markets. These expectations, similarly, test global supply chains. The nearby supplier can respond instantly to changing demand in JIT systems, or make changes instantly if quality problems are spotted. The distant supplier is not so well placed, and is probably dealing with much larger quantities of goods. Strategies for integration of supply chains rely increasingly on technology, for information exchange, ordering and tracking. However, supply chains are not static, and a problem in a complex network will have knock-on effects down the line. Logistics and transport are elements vulnerable to disruption and delays, particularly in the light of a multiplicity of providers and disparities in infrastructure in different countries. While scale has increased and costs have fallen in the era of globalization, achieving seamless integration has proved an elusive goal. Vertical integration, so often criticized for its inflexibility, has advantages after all, as Henry Ford might remind MNEs if he were around today.

Rethinking supply chains
Inflexible vertically integrated supply
chains gave way to more flexible, less costly
alternatives. Global sourcing also offers opportunities to
reduce costs. However, the changing environment and changing
markets are causing firms to rethink supply chain strategies.
What specific factors would you highlight as important in
today's environment, and what strategic responses
would you recommend? Give examples
from different sectors.

PAUSE TO REFLECT

Review questions

Part A: Grasping the basic concepts and knowledge

1. Taking an overview of the manufacturing supply chain, what are the distinct activities involved?
2. What benefits are perceived to arise from the vertical integration of a supply chain?
3. What are the advantages of the networked supply chain in the global environment?
4. Contrast the three types of supply chain – efficient, agile and lean – citing the advantages of each.
5. What factors come into play in the 'make-or-buy' decision-making process?
6. What are the risks associated with outsourcing?
7. How have Japanese companies benefited from the use of inter-firm alliances as a supply chain strategy?
8. Discuss the pros and cons of global sourcing for the manufacturer of a complex product.
9. In what ways did flexible manufacturing represent an advance on Fordist manufacturing?
10. Summarize the chief tenets of lean production.
11. What are the advantages and disadvantages of JIT production systems?

12. How has the concept of quality management evolved into a broader management approach?

13. Explain what is meant by TQM. Why are HRM implications particularly important?

14. What is the object of internationally recognized quality standards?

15. How have logistics evolved to meet the needs of global supply chains?

16. Examine how container shipping transformed transport by sea, including both the advantages and disadvantages.

Part B: Critical thinking and discussion

1. How have the internationalization strategies of MNEs influenced the evolution of SCM?

2. Assess the advantages and disadvantages of lean production strategies in global supply chains.

3. Assess the benefits to emerging economies from global sourcing and manufacturing strategies of MNEs; and the risks these strategies pose for the parent company.

4. What challenges are posed by differing cultural environments in quality management? Give examples.

5. Assess the challenges and risks currently facing logistics management in international operations.

Case study 10.2: Dell makes changes to regain competitiveness

Dell, the computer company founded by Michael Dell in the 1980s, became renowned for its application of lean manufacturing principles and efficient SCM. Becoming a public company in 1989, Dell soared ahead in PC sales during the boom of the late 1990s, selling mainly to business customers, attracted by its low prices. Its business model was based on the cost advantages of selling direct to consumers via the telephone and internet. The bursting of the dot.com bubble in 2000 saw slowing sales growth and falling prices. By lowering prices and squeezing margins, the company was able to surge ahead of its main US rival, Hewlett-Packard, in PC sales in 2002. However, the price war between the two rivals was taking its toll. Dell's main source of competitive advantage, low prices, was slipping away, but Dell was reluctant to alter its business model.

Dell's model of lean production in the manufacture of PCs was a radical departure from the norms in the industry when Michael Dell set up his PC business as a college student in Texas. Derived from Japanese flexible manufacturing precedents, it uses principles of continuous improvement and JIT processes. While most companies have a backlog of orders and large stocks of inventory, Dell works on the build-to-order model, holding a minimum of stock. One of Dell's selling points has been its ability to customize the product for the individual customer. The goods are ideally built within a short time of the order being placed. The process depends on integrated and highly responsive suppliers, as only a few days' stock are held at any given time. In some factories, components come straight from the container truck into the assembly line. On the other hand, with a myriad of different customer wishes to satisfy, stocks of components must be available, either at Dell premises or with logistics providers who store supplier-owned products, adding an extra 10 days' supply. Making the supply chain work smoothly requires fully integrated technology, including automation of order processing and parts management. It has also been important for Dell to keep manufacturing processes simple, so that production can be increased to cope with a surge in demand.

In the direct selling model, for which Dell became famous, low prices and customer service are the main attractions for customers. However, the company's position has weakened in both respects. Competitors, including HP, Acer and Lenovo (IBM's former PC arm), have improved manufacturing and supply chain

efficiencies, eroding Dell's price advantage. Dell has prided itself on its direct contact with customers, which keep it in touch with their changing needs, and responding quickly with changes in products. However, in the 2000s, Dell slipped in customer service rankings, particularly in the US. It had no exciting product to match the IBM Thinkpad, for example. In addition, customer support was suffering, as customers often felt let down by weak service at call centres. Dell responded by moving its manufacturing head, Dick Hunter, to customer services, to rebuild confidence. In addition, it announced a $100 million investment in customer service in 2006. Dell's largest market is the US, which accounts for more than half its sales. A restructured HP has made cost reductions and regained competitiveness, which helped it to overtake Dell in US market share in 2006, while Dell's market share fell (as shown in Figure 1).

To grow sales beyond its highly competitive home market, Dell has expanded internationally, targeting emerging markets such as China, where it has two factories. However, the direct sales model is not necessarily suitable to the differing cultural environments. The Chinese consumer who buys directly expects a relationship with the seller, whereas the Dell model is essentially a direct *sales* model. Dell has often considered retail sales as a means of improving growth, but has been reluctant in the past, as the large stocks needed run counter to the company's philosophy of lean supply chains. Furthermore, it has argued that the

Figure 1 Dell's market share in the US

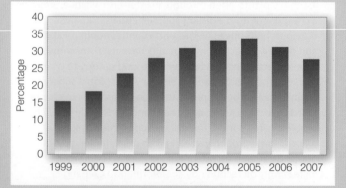

Source: Dell Inc. (2007) Financial history, www.dell.com

direct model is better suited to business customers, who account for 85% of the company's sales. However, in a shift of policy, it is now selling through Wal-Mart in the US and Carphone Warehouse stores in the UK. It has also linked up with retailers in Japan and China, to sell desktop and notebook computers. Dell said of its retailing moves: 'We're committed to finding new ways to reach more customers and this is one example' (Allison and Nuttall, 2007). However, it has suffered from weaker revenue growth, especially in the Americas, which accounts for 62% of its revenues (see Figure 2).

Although Dell has admitted lapses in customer services, it has tended to look at aggressive pricing and weakening demand in business markets as the main causes of its waning fortunes. Gradually, the company has recognized the inherent limitations of its product range and direct selling methods. Dell has diversified its products, expanded into indirect sales and started building up computer services for the complex needs of business customers. In all these areas, its rivals enjoy long head starts. HP and IBM have been offering services for years. Dell is contemplating acquiring an experienced services company, to build capacity quickly. Traditional retail businesses have expanded into internet sales and services, whereas Dell, the pioneer in direct PC sales, has reversed the process, moving from direct to indirect sales to foster growth. Dell's future was somewhat clouded for much of 2006 and 2007, due to a scandal over possible misconduct and accounting errors, investigated by the US Securities and Exchange Commission. The company admitted altering sales accounts to meet

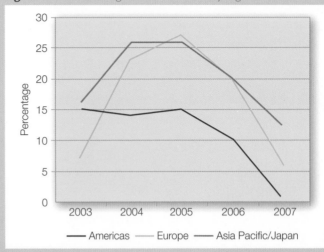

Figure 2 Dell's annual growth in revenues by region

Source: Dell Inc. (2007) Financial history, www.dell.com

Questions

1 What were the manufacturing and supply chain innovations which Dell pioneered in PCs?
2 How did Dell's competitive advantage become eroded, and how did the company respond?
3 Assess the strength of Dell's original business model for global markets in the current environment.
4 What changes have been made by Dell, and what further changes would you make, to regain competitiveness?

Sources: Ody, P., 'Bespoke aims for mass production', *Financial Times*, 20 June 2001; Waters, R., 'Dell aims to stretch its way of business', *Financial Times*, 13 November 2003; Morrison, S., 'A low-cost pioneer's high-end ambitions', *Financial Tilmes*, 19 December 2002; Morrison, S., 'It's gloves off in the computer business', *Financial Times*, 8 June 2004; Allison, K., 'Patience with Dell is starting to wear thin', *Financial Times*, 25 July 2006; Allison, K., 'Dell to target indirect sales', *Financial Times*, 17 May 2007; Allison, K., 'Dell to cut 10% of workforce, *Financial Times*, 31 May 2007; Allison, K. and Nuttall, C., 'Dell to sell its computers at Wal-Mart', *Financial Times*, 25 May 2007; Dell investor relations website, www.dell.com; Allison, K., 'Dell to lower writedowns in restated earnings', *Financial Times*, 20 October, 2007.

targets between 2003 and 2007, and was compelled to restate earnings for the four years. Michael Dell, having spent several years in the background, returned to take the helm as CEO in 2007. Amid concerns that sales are slowing generally in the sector, the company is looking to its founder to steer its new strategy.

WEB CHECK

Dell's website is
www.dell.com

Further research

Journal articles

Boyd, D., Spekman, R., Kamauff, J. and Werhane, P. (2007) 'Corporate social responsibility in global supply chains: A procedural justice perspective', *Long Range Planning*, **40**(3): 341–56.

Hong, J., Easterby-Smith, M. and Snell, R. (2006) 'Transferring organizational learning systems to Japanese subsidiaries in China', *Journal of Management Studies*, **43**(5): 1027–58.

Kotabe, M., Parente, R. and Murray, J. (2007) 'Antecedents and outcomes of modular production in the Brazilian automotive industry: a grounded theory approach', *Journal of International Business Studies*, **38**(1): 84–106.

Stuart, F. and McCutcheon, D. (2000) 'The manager's guide to supply chain management', *Business Horizons*, **43**(2): 35–44.

Books

Womack, J., Jones, D. and Roos, D. (1990) *The Machine That Changed the World*, New York: Rawson Associates.

Zinkgraf, S. (2008) *Six Sigma: The First 90 Days*, London: Pearson.

chapter **11**
FINANCE AND ACCOUNTING

chapter outline

▷ **Introduction**
▷ **Overview of global financial markets**
▷ **The international monetary system**
   Evolution of the international monetary system
   The determination of exchange rates
   Financial crises and their lessons
▷ **Managing foreign exchange**
   Foreign exchange transactions
   Currency risk strategy
▷ **Global capital markets**
   Stock exchanges
   Bond markets
▷ **International corporate finance**
   Balancing equity and debt
   Cross-border mergers and acquisitions
   The roles of hedge funds and private equity
▷ **International accounting issues**
   Diversity in accounting standards
   Translation of financial statements
   Progress towards harmonization
   The changing regulatory environment
▷ **Conclusions**

learning objectives

▷ **To gain an overview of the principles and workings of the international monetary system**
▷ **To become familiar with foreign exchange risks, and the tools available to manage them**
▷ **To understand the role of global financial markets in international business**
▷ **To evaluate the corporate financing options which allow firms to function internationally, together with their impacts on decision-makers, shareholders and other stakeholders**
▷ **To highlight key international accounting issues which impact on businesses at the international level and in diverse national environments**

Introduction

Debenhams, the department store chain, is well known to consumers across Britain, and also in the 16 countries where it has branched out. In recent years, it has made headlines not so much for its fashion brands as for its corporate financing changes. A public listed company, it was bought out in 2003 by a group of private equity investors, who took it private. They put in £600 million themselves and financed the remainder by debt, constituting a £1.1 billion burden on the company. To pay off the huge debt, the new management sought greater efficiencies in the business: staff numbers were cut; cash flow was improved by having more frequent sales to shift stock; better deals were obtained from suppliers; and expenditure on store refurbishments slowed to a trickle. These measures produced impressive growth in sales in the short term, encouraging the private equity owners to relist the company in 2006, retaining a 35% stake themselves. The successful IPO, valuing the business at £1.68 billion, earned them more than three times the £600 million they had invested, making Debenhams one of Europe's most lucrative buyouts. Meanwhile, signs of deterioration in the business were becoming apparent. Sales were flagging, key staff had departed, and the tired appearance of stores compared unfavourably with rivals such as Marks & Spencer. Three profits warnings ensued, and shares in the newly refloated company fell. Private equity had promised to improve performance and add value, but in this case, the beneficiaries were the buyout groups, who were accused of taking value out of the business for short-term profits. Their controversial role has raised questions of accountability in the rapidly changing world of global finance, which is a theme of this chapter.

Businesses are constantly engaged in financial decision-making and activities, which affect the organization and its stakeholders. Managers must decide how to raise the capital to achieve the firm's goals, how to deliver products or services which will sell sufficiently to generate a profit, and how to invest in further value-generating activities. For the international firm, success or failure depends heavily on having the financial framework in place which will ensure that cross-border transactions and investments will generate maximum returns while guarding against the risks of foreign exchange transactions. The growing complexity of international operations has been accompanied by greater exposure to financial risk. Despite the globalization of financial flows, finance and accounting are among the most closely regulated business functions, mainly in national regulatory frameworks. This chapter looks at financial and accounting issues which affect international business in the context of national and international frameworks.

The chapter begins with an overview of the global financial environment. The international monetary system is then discussed, assessing its strengths and limitations in terms of the stability which is needed to facilitate international business activities. For business operations across national boundaries, managing foreign exchange risk is a crucial area of expertise, which must be viewed in the light of the firm's overall financial strategy. Capital markets are discussed next, highlighting the options available to companies for raising capital and borrowing. We then turn to corporate finance from the managerial perspective, examining the ways in which firms seek finance internationally, and the risks associated with each. The changing landscape of corporate ownership and control are discussed, highlighting mergers and acquisitions, as well as the role of private equity. Lastly, we focus on international accounting issues. Although harmonization in accounting practices and standards is a trend, underlying national environments point to a continuing divergence in the way standards are applied in practice.

WEB CHECK

Debenhams is at www.debenhams.com. Here, the IPO prospectus can be accessed. One of the private equity groups involved, CVC Capital Partners, is at www.cvc.com.

plate 11.1 For quality-conscious retailers, upgrading the appearance of stores and maintaining the flow of new product lines, although costly, help to maintain customer satisfaction and boost sales.

Overview of global financial markets

Individuals and organizations of all types raise funds and make investments. The range of financial choices and their specific functions have grown enormously in recent decades. In earlier generations, investors looked no further than banks for investment, seeking safe ways in which to hold funds and not expecting much in the way of return. Now, most seek growth and customization to particular needs. Deposits have given way to a transactions orientation. In 1980, bank deposits made up 42% of all financial securities, but this share had fallen to 27% by 2005 (Wolf, 2007b). Figure 11.1 presents an overview of international financial markets, including the types of investment they offer. These investments, which are discussed in detail in later

Securities: Financial instruments of ownership, debt obligation or future rights, which can be traded.

sections, all fall under the general heading of securities. Securities traditionally refer to instruments of ownership of shares or debt agreements, such as bonds. However, they also cover newer types of investment known as 'derivatives'. Capital markets facilitate the raising of capital and borrowing. While commodities markets, dealing in products such as metals, are centuries old, derivatives are relatively recent. Foreign exchange markets are by far the largest market, facilitating every type of international business transaction.

Figure 11.1 Overview of global financial markets

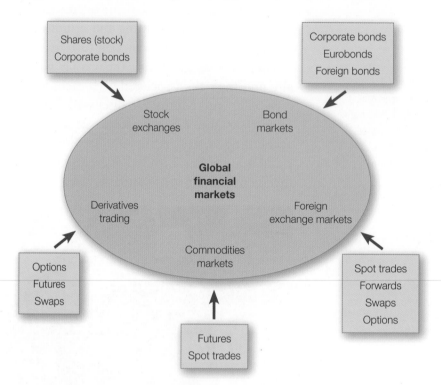

The international monetary system

The growth in global capital markets can be attributed largely to liberalization in national financial systems, which opened the way for growth in cross-border financial flows. Another factor has been advances in computing and the internet, which carry out cross-border transactions easily and quickly. Along with greater opportunities has come greater exposure to foreign exchange risk, encompassing both commercial enterprises and national governments. Maintaining monetary stability at the international level rests heavily on international initiatives and governmental co-operation. Some governments allow their currencies to be bought and sold without limits – known as convertibility. These are 'hard' currencies, which are said to be fully convertible. The currencies of the developed world generally fall into this category, while 'soft' currencies, usually associated with developing countries and less stable economies, are not fully convertible.

Convertibility: The extent to which a government allows its currency to be bought and sold freely by both residents and foreigners.

Evolution of the international monetary system

International business relies on cross-border financial flows. Businesses in the current era have become accustomed to dealing with currency fluctuations, whereas earlier eras saw exchange rates controlled by international consensus.

The gold standard system lasted from 1870 to 1914, and encompassed all the major trading countries. It coincided with Britain's dominance in trade, and is categorized as an era of financial globalization (Held et al., 1999: 198). However, it was marked by less global financial convergence than might be supposed. It was based mainly in Europe and yet, even within Europe, national authorities differed in their policies, for example in setting national interest rates. The instability of the First World War brought the gold standard era to a close, to be replaced by monetary instability and a lack of clear financial leadership. Despite the uncertainties, global capital flows and FDI were growing, and more countries around the world were participating.

As the Second World War was drawing to a close, the Bretton Woods agreement of 1944 ushered in a new era, in which it was hoped that monetary stability and financial flows would be resumed. National monetary autonomy would be maintained, but every currency would have a fixed exchange rate linked to the US dollar, which was itself fixed in terms of gold at $35 an ounce. The new system reflected the fact that the US was now the world's strongest economy. At the centre of the Bretton Woods agreement was the creation of the International Monetary Fund (IMF) to oversee the global financial system, monitoring national economies and providing loan facilities for countries with balance of payments difficulties. Strains within the new system emerged from the 1960s onwards.

The communist countries, representing a significant block of states, were excluded from the Bretton Woods system, highlighting the tensions which existed in the Cold War era. In the 1950s, Soviet authorities with dollar funds deposited them in Western European banks, where they became labelled 'eurodollar' funds and grew rapidly. Other currencies joined them, creating a huge 'eurocurrency' market, which, because it was dealing in foreign currencies, escaped national regulation. American MNEs operating in Europe also made use of this market. As the eurocurrency market prospered, the US saw inflation combined with a growing trade deficit, giving rise to speculation against the dollar. By 1971, the dollar's link with gold was severed, signalling the end of the Bretton Woods era. The final blow was the first of several oil crises in 1973. The Organization of Petroleum Exporting Countries (Opec), which is a producers' cartel, imposed limits on oil production and raised the price of oil fourfold, in the first of a number of steep rises. The rises resulted in huge transfers of funds from the oil-importing states to the oil-exporting states, much of it flowing into large banking institutions. Global financial flows increased, enveloping a wider range of countries than hitherto, many of which were developing countries seeking funding for economic development. Hence, the breakdown of the Bretton Woods system resulted in a more dispersed and fragmented monetary system. Exposure to risks also mounted, for both investors and national financial systems.

The determination of exchange rates

Following the collapse of the Bretton Woods system, there was greater flexibility in the setting of exchange rates, leading to concern by the IMF about threats to overall stability. It recognizes a number of categories of exchange rate framework, which are shown along a diagonal in Figure 11.2, ranging

TO RECAP...

From fixed exchange rates to volatility
The gold standard and the Bretton Woods system attempted to fix exchange rates, but both broke down from external strains and internal lack of cohesion.

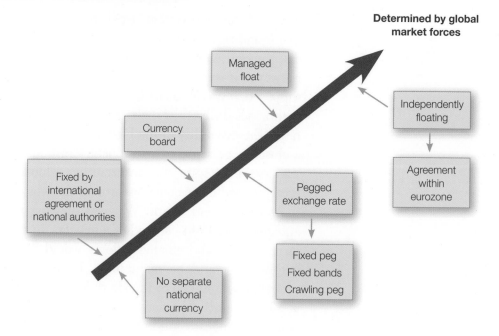

Determined by global market forces

Managed float

Currency board

Independently floating

Fixed by international agreement or national authorities

Pegged exchange rate

Agreement within eurozone

No separate national currency

Fixed peg
Fixed bands
Crawling peg

Figure 11.2 From fixed to floating exchange rates: international diversity

Pegged exchange rate: Linking the exchange rate of a currency to another currency, often with some degree of movement allowed.

Currency board: Framework whereby a country guarantees conversion of its currency into another currency, supported by reserves of the backup currency.

from a fixed rate to a free-floating currency. Only 25 of the IMF's 187 member states have independently floating currencies, whereby the value of the currency is allowed to float against other currencies in the market (see Figure 11.3). The IMF classifies eurozone countries under 'no separate tender', a category covering countries which have no currency of their own. The euro, as used by all eurozone countries, is a free-floating currency, supervised by the European Central Bank.

A large number of countries have a managed float, whereby the government may intervene if necessary, but there is no predetermined path. India and Russia fall into this category. The pegged exchange rate, some form of which exists in 63 countries, links a currency to that of another currency, usually the US dollar or the euro. In most cases, the peg may be a 'conventional' one, allowing very little movement. Alternatively, it may be more flexible, allowing movement within fixed bands or wider bands, in what is known as a 'crawling' peg. A crawling pegged exchange rate exists in China.

The currency board is an arrangement whereby the country guarantees that it will convert the currency into another currency, often the dollar, at a fixed exchange rate, backed up by sufficient reserves in the other currency. This arrangement is similar to a fixed exchange rate, with the additional requirement of sufficient dollar reserves to back the issuance of currency. Countries with currency boards include Hong Kong, Bulgaria and Estonia. Argentina adopted a currency board in 1989, linking the currency to the dollar, but abandoned it in 2001, following prolonged financial crisis and a bail-out from the IMF. Under the currency board arrangement, a government's inability to manage monetary policy independently, which effectively gives the US control over the country's interest rates, is a drawback, especially when the country's currency comes under pressure.

Given the diversity of national approaches to exchange rates, the IMF urges countries to run their exchange rate policies in ways that promote international financial stability. In 2007, it set out new criteria for governments to follow, implying that it might intervene if it judges they are straying

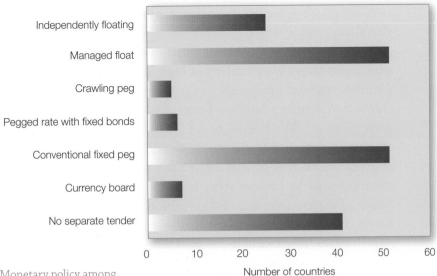

Figure 11.3 Monetary policy among IMF member states, 2006

Source: IMF (2006) Monetary policy framework, www.imf.org

from its guidelines. The three criteria can be phrased negatively: governments are warned not to allow 'fundamental exchange rate misalignment', not to accumulate excessive reserves, and not to intervene in manipulating the currency (Guha, 2007). We look at each in turn:

1 *Currency misalignment*: this refers to a situation in which a country's currency is set too high or too low in relation to market perceptions. For example, if a country's currency is undervalued, its exporters have an advantage over trading partners. The US has complained that China's currency, which is pegged to the dollar, is undervalued. Because of the importance of the US economy, the dollar is a favoured currency in international business. Oil is priced in dollars, as are commodities generally. However, the dollar has steadily declined in value against other major currencies for several years (see Figure 11.4). While beneficial for American exporters, the weak dollar is disadvantageous for foreign creditors and companies exporting to America. In 2007, Opec expressed concern on behalf of its 12 members, noting that the purchasing power of their oil revenues had fallen by nearly a third (Blas, 2007a). These countries

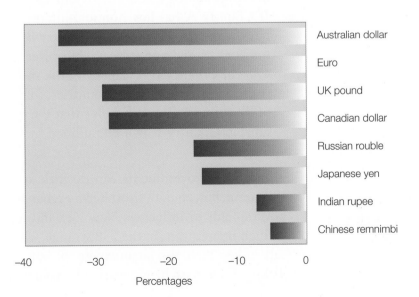

Figure 11.4 The US dollar's decline against other major currencies, 2002–06

Source: Financial Times, 6 December 2006

were therefore reluctant to increase production and cut prices, although global demand was rising. Moreover, Opec members in the Middle East and northern Africa were increasing trade with European countries, whose currencies were trading at high levels against the dollar.

2 *Excessive reserves*: foreign exchange reserves in a number of countries have climbed to dizzying heights. From 2001 to 2004, global currency reserves grew from $2,000 billion to $4,700 billion. The central bank of every country is responsible for currency policy decisions. Central banks hold reserves, which may be in gold or a mix of currencies, aiming to hold sufficient reserves to protect their own currency. Two-thirds of the world's currency reserves are held by six countries: China, Japan, Taiwan, South Korea, Russia and Singapore. Following the Asian financial crisis, Asian governments accumulated considerable reserves as a means of protection against future vulnerabilities. By 2007, China was estimated to hold $1,400 billion in reserves. Although the US dollar has been the favoured currency, central banks are now diversifying into other currencies, and also investing in other asset classes. 'Sovereign wealth funds', which have been created by governments for investment purposes, are becoming active in global markets (these are discussed in Chapter 15).

3 *Non-intervention*: while governments have the authority to intervene in the country's currency, they are reluctant to do so. As national financial systems have become more open to outside investors, and residents are able to invest abroad, currencies may become caught up in global financial markets. Inflation and interest rates impact on a country's currency – a relationship that is highlighted in the linked theories known as the Fisher effect and the international Fisher effect (IFE). The Fisher effect relies on the distinction between the nominal interest rate, which is the rate actually offered by lenders, and the real interest rate, which is the return following adjustment for inflation. A country's 'real' interest rate is arrived at by subtracting its rate of inflation from its nominal interest rate. The implication is that, over time, a country's real interest rates would be expected to be unchanged, as nominal interest rates rise and fall in harmony with inflation rates. In the international sphere, where there are free flows of capital among countries, investors are looking for advantageous returns. If Country A has low nominal interest rates and Country B has higher rates, investors will invest in Country B, assuming a wish to repatriate the funds as capital and interest. However, demand is likely to push up the value of Country B's currency in the short term. If investors sell or repatriate funds to their home countries, this could lead to lowering the value of B's currency. The IFE holds that the gain from higher nominal interest rates in Country B will be nullified by Country B's exchange rate in the long run.

Individual governments can do little to influence exchange rates in the long term, but, equally, short-term exchange rate movements are difficult for governments to influence. New Zealand has attracted investors because of its high interest rate, in the 7–8% range, which contrasts with Japan's interest rate of less than 1%. Japan's many personal savers, who account for 30% of Tokyo's foreign exchange market by volume and value, have invested heavily

International Fisher effect (IFE): Theory which holds that gains in nominal interest rates will be nullified by movements in exchange rates over the long term.

Real interest rate: A country's interest rate adjusted for inflation, by subtracting the inflation rate from the nominal interest rate (which is that actually offered by lenders).

The IMF's website is www.imf.org.

WEB CHECK

in New Zealand. They have been joined by international speculators, who borrow in Japan and invest in New Zealand, in what is known as the 'carry trade'. This demand causes the New Zealand dollar to rise while the Japanese yen has fallen. The Reserve Bank of New Zealand intervened in 2007, selling NZ dollars to halt the currency's rise against the yen and US dollar, but the intervention had little effect.

Impacts of exchange rate policies
In what ways does a country's exchange rate policy impact on the following:
● Businesses within its borders which carry out international transactions
● Foreign trading partners
● Investors (both foreign and domestic)?

PAUSE TO REFLECT

Financial crises and their lessons

In the post-Bretton Woods era, national financial systems have become integrated through global financial markets. In addition, more countries have become enmeshed in global finance, including many developing countries. Increased financial flows offer opportunities for the financing of economic development, but can be volatile, posing risks for systems which are growing rapidly. Both external and internal factors come into play, as shown in Figure 11.5. In the 1990s, emerging countries, with their high growth rates and newly liberalized economies, attracted investors in large numbers, but these flows went into reverse at the first signs of underlying weakness, causing financial crisis in a number of countries. Although there were local differences, there were common factors: a currency crisis; a debt mountain, of both public and private debt, often in dollars; and a banking crisis. The first was in Mexico in 1995, where the currency, the peso, was pegged to the dollar. In the early 1990s, Mexico was experiencing severe inflation, causing price rises in exports to the US, but the government refused to lower the exchange rate. A result was a huge trade deficit, amounting to 6% of GDP. The policy of defending the peso's peg against the dollar encouraged foreign investors, but also attracted

Figure 11.5 Internal and external factors in the Asian financial crisis

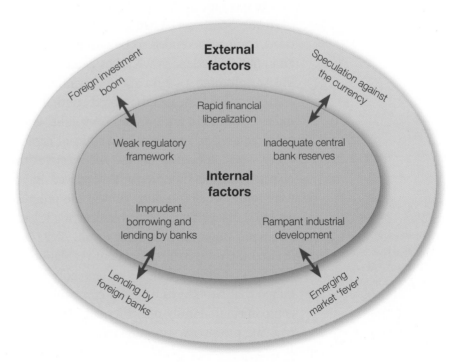

currency speculators, sensing an imminent devaluation. The government intervened, buying pesos and selling dollars, but ran out of foreign currency reserves and devalued the peso in 1994. The IMF, in conjunction with the Bank for International Settlements (BIS, the central bankers' bank) and the US government, put together an aid package. The IMF insisted on stringent monetary policies and cuts in public spending as part of the package, establishing the precedent of imposing austerity measures for countries in financial distress.

The IMF's greatest challenge came in the Asian financial crisis of 1997, which struck several Southeast Asian countries, affecting Thailand, Indonesia and South Korea the hardest. These countries, like Mexico, had enjoyed export-led economic development. Infrastructure and industrial projects were financed largely by borrowing, often in dollars from large international institutions. As in Mexico, local currencies were pegged to the dollar. The crisis struck first in Thailand, where speculators took positions against the Thai currency, the baht. Although the government tried to defend the currency, it was forced to abandon the dollar peg, which precipitated a fall of 55% in its value against the dollar. This move effectively doubled the funds needed to cover the dollar-denominated debt, leading to a debt crisis combined with a currency crisis. As investors fled, the IMF was called in to stop the financial meltdown. The flight of investors from Thailand produced a domino effect, reflecting investors' perceptions that similar problems existed in other Southeast Asian industrializing economies. Other countries in the region were forced to devalue, as the 'contagion' spread. Indonesia also suffered from huge dollar-denominated debt and a falling currency. Here, the IMF imposed a package of austerity measures, including rises in interest rates, cutbacks in government spending and increases in taxes. These reforms were intended as solutions, but the effect was to worsen the crisis (Stiglitz, 2002: 97). Unemployment went up as businesses went bankrupt and banks closed. Poverty tripled, affecting almost a quarter of the Indonesian population. Social unrest and political crisis ensued, culminating in the overthrow of the government in 1998. An interim government followed by a new democratic system pledged to reform emerged from the crisis.

In the Southeast Asian countries which suffered worst from the financial crisis, companies tended to be family business empires with close ties to banks and political leaders, in what has been termed 'crony capitalism'. Untying these links to promote a sound and independent financial system was the aim of the IMF, but, given the deeply rooted cultural heritage, it was unrealistic to expect radical changes in basic values overnight, as SX11.1 on APP illustrates. Banks were required to have a certain ratio of capital to their outstanding loans and other assets, known as 'capital adequacy'. Although achievable as a long-term objective, in the short term, this proved impossible. Many Indonesian banks were forced to close, which slowed the progress of recovery. The IMF has now accepted that mistakes were made, saying it had 'badly misgauged the severity' of economic downturn (Borsuk et al., 1999). Southeast Asian countries have learned the need for independent regulation of the banking sector, but ownership and control of companies generally is still dominated by elites. It is estimated that two-thirds of listed companies in the region, and nearly all private companies, are family run (Plender, 2007). Although these economies are now enjoying prosperity, structural weaknesses still affect the financial environment.

TO RECAP...

Averting national financial crisis

Liberalized financial markets and flows of inward investment can create strains on currencies and banking systems, especially in emerging economies where regulatory institutions are weak. A sound banking sector and monetary policy framework help to maintain confidence in the currency and in the economy.

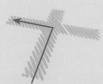

STRATEGIC CROSSROADS

11.1
Has APP learned the lessons of Asia's financial crisis?

APP (Asia Pulp and Paper) is the world's tenth largest paper company, producing more than 7 million tonnes of paper and pulp each year. The fortunes of APP, the centrepiece of the Widjaja family empire, have mirrored the financial ups and downs of Indonesia and other Asian economies. Coming to Indonesia from mainland China in the 1930s, the Widjajas built up businesses in paper, real estate and banking, through the family company Sinar Mas. They began listing their companies in the 1990s, benefiting from the wave of foreign investment which flowed into Indonesia. In contrast to the corruption and favouritism endemic in Indonesia, the Sinar Mas businesses were perceived as more market driven and therefore favoured by investors, a view bolstered by APP's New York Stock Exchange (NYSE) listing. However, the company accumulated massive debts and succumbed to the Asian financial crisis. In 2001, it announced it would not be repaying $14 billion in bonds, making it the largest ever corporate debt default in emerging markets. Angry creditors, among them major international banks, tried to pursue APP in Indonesia's courts for several years, but failed to recover the debts, even though they were confident the company had funds or could have restructured the debt. The 2006 court judgment, which relieved the company of the debt, was considered indicative of the country's weak legal system, constituting a warning to investors that the corrupt institutional environment remains a risk in Indonesia. Of the 180 countries which appear in Transparency International's Corruption Perception Index, Indonesia ranks a lowly 143.

Notwithstanding financial uncertainties, the Widjajas have expanded in the region, focusing on mainland China, where they have long had business links. Here, they have 17 businesses and 20 tree plantations, employing 20,000 workers. Debts in the Chinese operations in 2003, which amounted to $2 billion, became a concern to creditors. They hired the firm KPMG to report on the status of the company's finances in China, but KPMG were given no access to information. China has also been seen as a possible destination of the missing funds owed to other APP creditors. Creditors have urged that independent management of the businesses is needed, to ensure transparency and principles of sustainability in managing the forests. However, the family has resisted the call for outside managers. The latest in the line of family leaders, armed with a US education, including an MBA degree, is looking to a bright future for his family's empire.

Despite its debt default, APP has been able to obtain funding privately from hedge funds and is considering going back to public capital markets. In 2007, it was encouraged by the successful listing of a Widjaja family business on the Singapore stock exchange, for which the equity of $540 million was raised in just half a day. APP might consider listing the Chinese operations on a Chinese stock exchange, assuming China opens its exchanges to foreign companies. Would international investors buy APP shares or bonds as enthusiastically as they did in the 1990s? Some would not, especially those nursing losses. However, APP has a growing presence in China, with considerable potential for further growth. These factors, along with its Chinese connections, would help to lure new investors.

Questions

◆ In what ways is APP illustrative of the structural weaknesses in Indonesia that contributed to the financial crisis?

◆ How has APP been able to rebuild its businesses despite its record-breaking debt default? What lessons are there in the APP story so far for would-be investors in the future?

Sources: Guerin, B., 'APP confronts its paper tigers', *Asia Times*, 27 February 2003; Aglionby, J., 'Victory for APP in bonds court case', *Financial Times*, 4 November 2006; Aglionby, J., 'APP bonds ruling faces challenge', *Financial Times*, 16 April 2007; Lucas, L., 'APP ponders return to capital markets', *Financial Times*, 28 June 2007; Transparency International (2006) *Corruption Perception Index 2007*, www.transparency.org.

WEB CHECK

APP's website is www.asiapulppaper.com.

The Asian financial crisis and beyond
Assess the relative importance of external and internal factors to the Asian crisis. How can other emerging economies take lessons from the structural issues which have been highlighted as contributory factors?

PAUSE TO REFLECT

Managing foreign exchange

The foreign exchange market facilitates the conversion of funds from one currency to another. Foreign exchange has traditionally been seen as a service for cross-border business transactions and investments. International firms constantly encounter foreign exchange issues: between suppliers and customers in different countries, and between the MNE parent and a foreign subsidiary. Revenues may arise in foreign countries, and the receiving company will wish to convert these funds into its own currency. Exchange rates are constantly changing, introducing a degree of risk in these transactions. Such risks can be managed with the aid of a hedge, which insures against adverse currency movements. Foreign exchange business falls into two broad categories:

Hedge: A financial tool or arrangement which insures a firm against adverse currency movements in its international financial activities.

1 Businesses insuring or hedging against these risks, which all international companies incur.
2 Businesses dealing in foreign exchange as a financial activity in its own right, with speculative implications.

Although these two types of activity have differing aims, they rely on the same types of transaction.

Foreign exchange transactions

Foreign exchange transactions can be spot trades, forwards, swaps or options. The spot contract is a transaction determined by the exchange rate between the two currencies at the time of the deal on a particular day, and is settled in a few days. Exchange rates vary from minute to minute, and even a slight variation may alter a large deal by considerable sums. If a business must pay a foreign supplier on a particular day, a spot deal involves risks. A forward contract will be helpful in these circumstances. This is a derivative product, which depends on the value of another asset, in this case, cash. Derivatives offer a variety of means to mitigate exposure to risk, whether from interest rates, currency, commodity prices or loan default. Cadbury, featured in CS11.2, deals with 40,000 suppliers around the world, many in volatile commodities markets. It therefore relies on forward contracts. An attraction is that the initial outlay is only a fraction of the notional value of the instrument. Many are traded on exchanges, but the most rapid growth has been in over-the-counter (OTC) contracts, which are agreed by the parties without using an exchange.

Spot contract: Transaction in which the terms, including the exchange rate, are agreed and performed almost immediately.

Derivative: Financial instrument whose value is dependent on another asset class, such as stock.

The forward or futures contract is a contract to carry out a specific transaction on a designated date in the future. The paying firm may contract to purchase the foreign currency 30 days ahead at a fixed rate. The forward exchange rate represents the trader's expectations of how strong the two currencies will be against each other in 30 days' time. For example, a European firm might owe a Brazilian supplier 100,000 real. Assuming a current rate of 1 real = €.40, it would require €40,000. A trader might offer a 30-day forward rate of 1 real = €.41. While this would involve paying €41,000, which is €1,000 more than today's spot rate, it would protect the firm if the real were to appreciate significantly against the euro in the 30 days. On the other hand, if the real depreciates to €.38, the firm is locked into the less

Forward or futures contract: Contract to carry out a particular transaction on a designated date in the future.

advantageous rate. In this case, the option may offer a more effective hedge. The foreign exchange option gives the firm the right, but not the obligation, to purchase the currency at a specific exchange rate, thus protecting itself against a rising currency. The option must be paid for, by a premium on the rate. The option is a marketable asset, which can be sold, and the most the firm would lose is the premium paid for it.

The foreign exchange swap is a combination of a spot transaction to sell funds in a given currency and a forward transaction to buy the funds back at a future date. This type of swap transaction is useful for the firm which is holding funds in a foreign currency which it does not need now, but will need in order to make a payment at a future date. The swap allows it to insure itself against appreciation of the foreign currency in the interim. Currency swaps are often used in debt markets, in which a company may swap a loan at a less advantageous rate for one in a different currency at a more advantageous rate.

The use of derivatives has grown dramatically in recent years, as Figure 11.6 shows. The BIS estimates that the face value of all derivatives contracts stands at $450,000 billion, which represents a fourfold increase from 2000 (Tett, 2007). The growth far outstrips the growth in cash markets, on which derivative products are based. The proportion of derivatives contracts conducted on exchanges is only about one-fifth the size of the OTC sector. The rise in derivatives indicates an increase in innovative financial instruments for managing risk, but the speed of their growth has led to concern that strategies are becoming too risky, especially in the context of a largely unregulated environment.

Foreign exchange option: Financial instrument which gives the firm the right, but not the obligation, to purchase currency at a particular exchange rate.

Swap: Financial instrument which allows a firm to customize terms to its advantage by swapping them with another party.

TO RECAP...
Foreign exchange transactions
The use of derivatives, such as forward contracts, options and swaps, has become common, as companies seek to hedge risks of exposure to currency volatility.

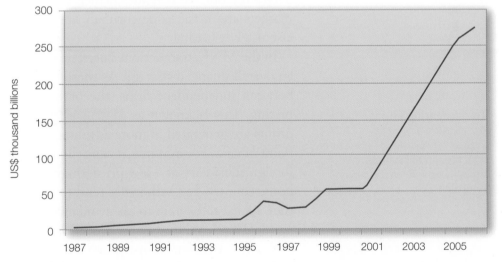

Figure 11.6 Amounts outstanding on interest rate and currency swaps
Source: Financial Times, 19 June 2007

Currency risk strategy

When a company agrees to buy or sell in a foreign currency, a currency risk is incurred, as the payment can rise or fall depending on currency fluctuations. This is known as 'transaction risk'. If the buyer has more market power than the seller (for example in the case of a large retailer), then the invoice currency could be the buyer's, which leaves the seller with currency risk. If the seller has greater market power and determines the currency, then the buyer is exposed to currency risk, because the buyer firm may have to pay more in local currency than it had anticipated. This situation also represents a risk for the seller, known as a 'credit risk': if the buyer is adversely affected by currency movements, there is a risk the firm will not pay at all. A hedging strategy may be used in these situations, but firms need to remember that the hedging devices themselves involve transaction costs, as they rely on derivatives. The company may also lose the benefit of any currency movement in its favour. It must therefore look carefully at the types of transactions to hedge and how much. Companies may adopt a policy of partial hedging, tolerating a level of risk, or hedging to protect themselves from only the most extreme outcomes.

Hedging is an aspect of risk management, and has been more heavily used as companies have become exposed to greater international risks. Hedging decisions should be taken along with other financial decisions, looking at the impact on corporate value and cash flows. In theory, hedging should reduce the cost of capital, offsetting the costs of the hedging devices. The company which is heavily indebted, relying on cash flows to service its debts, will calculate the likelihood of losses and the amounts which are tolerable, and may well hedge accordingly.

Companies which are routinely involved in foreign exchange transactions may look for longer term strategies to build a 'natural' hedge. For example, where the MNE subsidiary deals in the local currency, this offsets the effects of currency movements. Both these approaches are highlighted in CS11.2 on Cadbury. The MNE which adopts a global sourcing policy must consider currency risk implications. The company may ensure that there is a balance between costs and revenues, which is made easier if sourcing, assembly and markets are in the same currency area, such as the eurozone. This policy is also used by Cadbury.

In the MNE, transactions between subsidiaries can be managed as part of an overall financial strategy. As these transactions are not arm's-length deals between independent firms, the parent company has scope to adjust the pricing. This is known as transfer pricing, and is a way of ensuring that profits are generated in more advantageous locations from a tax and finance point of view. For example, it can sell products from the home country to the foreign subsidiary at a low price, thereby reducing the profits earned in the home country. Tax authorities tend to take a dim view of these strategies, as they appear to be akin to tax avoidance. However, as taxation is governed at national level, MNEs can seek location advantages. Manipulation of transfer prices by the parent company can undermine the authority and incentives of managers in subsidiaries, as the prices set by the MNE's head office are likely to mask their true performance. For example, when a subsidiary is ordered to charge a lower price for a product sold to a fellow subsidiary than it would to an arm's-length customer, its revenues suffer. Its financial position is thus weakened artificially, while its fellow subsidiary appears healthier due to the manipulation of transfer pricing.

Transfer pricing: Pricing of products traded internally within the MNE, such as between subsidiaries, often with the aim of maximizing financial benefits to the parent company.

TO RECAP...
Currency risk strategy
The MNE manages relations with suppliers and subsidiaries, seeking advantageous ways of balancing revenues and costs in particular currency areas. An example is transfer pricing.

Global capital markets

Capital markets serve a variety of interests, both direct players and indirect beneficiaries. Direct players include companies, governments, financial intermediaries and investors. Indirect beneficiaries are communities and whole societies which benefit from funds generated in capital markets. In earlier eras, financial activities have centred on equities and debt transactions, but new types of financial product and new players are now adding to the complexity and diversity of global financial markets.

Stock exchanges

Equities: Shares, also known as 'stock', in a registered company.

Equities represent investment in the ownership of public companies, fulfilling companies' need for capital and investors' desire to own shares. Trading in equities is handled by the world's stock exchanges, which supervise the listing of companies and their compliance with listing rules. Although the domestic market of the exchange accounts for the majority of listings, the leading stock exchanges have become internationalized, listing many foreign companies, as Figure 11.7 shows. Investors have gained an appetite for foreign shares as well. Governments may use capital controls to protect domestic financial systems, by preventing foreign investment and preventing local investors from investing abroad. However, many markets have gradually opened up, attracting foreign investors as well as foreign listings. Of the exchanges shown in Figure 11.7, only the Chinese exchanges operate strict controls. The two exchanges in New York, the NYSE and the Nasdaq, which lists more technology-oriented companies, are key players, with numerous foreign listings. The London Stock Exchange (LSE) is the largest European exchange, attracting numerous foreign IPOs.

Many stock exchanges have themselves become public companies, competing with each other in global markets and giving rise to takeover moves. Euronext, the European cross-border exchange, merged with the NYSE Group in 2007. The combined NYSE Euronext has a share of over a

The NYSE is at www.nyse.com. The LSE is at www.londonstockexchange.com. The Nasdaq is at www.nasdaq.com

WEB CHECK

Figure 11.7 Number of listed companies on major stock exchanges, 2006

Source: World Federation of Exchanges (2007) Statistics, www.world-exchanges.org

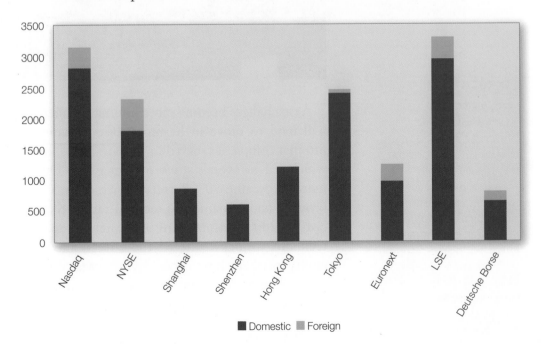

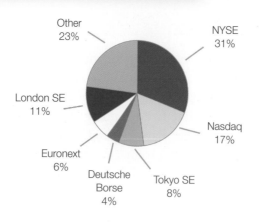

Figure 11.8 Leading exchanges' shares of total share trading by value, 2006

Note: Global total = US$69,829,943.7 millions

Source: World Federation of Exchanges (2007) Statistics, www.world-exchanges.org

third of global share trading (see Figure 11.8). Stock exchanges are influenced by environmental factors. These include the macroeconomic environment in the country in which the exchange is located, the soundness of its quoted companies, and global trends in particular sectors. The prominence of the NYSE in global trading is such that any prolonged falls are likely to affect other exchanges, such as the LSE. One reason is that UK companies have many subsidiaries and operations in the US. On the other hand, local factors may cause rises and falls not mirrored elsewhere. Growing exchanges in emerging markets are attracting predominantly local companies and investors.

plate 11.2 Shares can rise and fall frequently, even in the course of a single day, tracked by trading screens in the many stock exchanges now established around the world.

TO RECAP...

Equity markets

Equity markets provide the infrastructure for trading in listed companies. Companies benefit from a rise in their market value, while shareholders see gains in share values. Institutional investors such as pension funds rely to a large extent on equities to fund their liabilities. Stock exchanges have become more internationalized, attracting foreign investors and listings from foreign companies.

As exchanges become more internationalized, it has been argued that they will tend to move in harmony (Goetzmann et al., 2001). Investment in internet companies soared in the late 1990s, seeing huge rises in share prices, which led to overall stock market gains. During this boom period, stock markets became 80% correlated, which was an unusually high correlation, brought about mainly by sectoral rather than country factors. The bubble burst in 2000, causing many of the new companies to collapse in value. Other technology stocks suffered the effects, and many investors shifted out of equity markets into other investments. As equities fell, country factors became more important. Similarly, investors became more critical in evaluating sectors and individual companies (Hargreaves, 2003).

COUNTRY FOCUS 11.1 – HONG KONG

Hong Kong thrives from Chinese connections

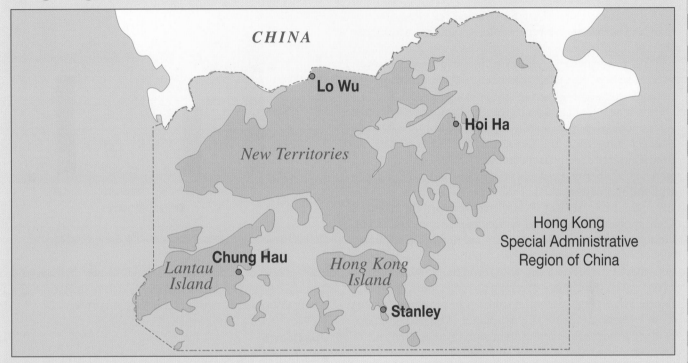

Hong Kong was one of Asia's leading business and financial centres under British colonial rule, noted for its open market and entrepreneurial environment. The return of the territory to Chinese sovereignty in 1997 posed the question of whether its liberal environment would be in jeopardy under its new communist rulers in Beijing. Hong Kong was assured that its way of life and economy would be allowed to continue under its status of Special Administrative Region (SAR). The executive in the new system of government is chosen in a method controlled by Beijing, through an 'election committee'. In the legislature, the Legislative Council, there is a democratic element: 25 of the 60 seats were open to direct elections in 1998, rising to 30 in 2004. Twenty-five of the directly elected seats are held by pro-democracy parties, which have been vocal in calls for further democratic reforms. There is thus a political divide between pro-Beijing and pro-democracy advocates. However, democratic advocates have urged that the SAR needs democracy to protect the rule of law. Hong Kong suffered economic downturn in the years following the Asian financial crisis, but has recovered its economic dynamism, benefiting from its strategic position close to the mainland's surging economy, with which it has a historical cultural affiliation. On the other hand, its long-established Western links are becoming gateways to international capital markets for the mainland's burgeoning companies. Hong Kong's economy is now dominated by financial and other services, as Figure 1 shows.

The Hong Kong Stock Exchange (HKSE) has attracted IPOs from mainland Chinese companies, as well as from Hong Kong and Taiwanese groups whose main operations are on the mainland. These mainland enterprises constitute nearly half

Figure 1 Hong Kong's GDP by sector

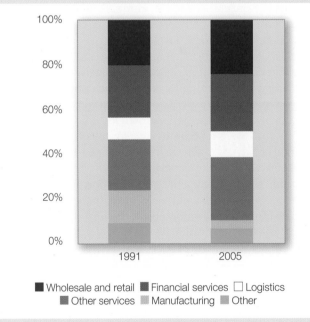

Source: The Economist (2007) Special Report on Hong Kong, 30 June

the companies listed on the HKSE and half its market capitalization. The largest of the IPOs have been privatizations of state-owned enterprises, with listings in both Shanghai and Hong Kong. In 2006, it exceeded New York, coming second only to London, in the value of IPO capital raised (see Figure 2). In 2006, the listing of the Industrial and Commercial Bank of China (ICBC), worth $21.9 billion, became the largest ever

IPO. Like other listings of mainland companies, ICBC remains state controlled: the IPO represented only a 17% stake, which places minority shareholders in a weak position. Beijing authorities are anxious for businesses to choose mainland exchanges over Hong Kong for listings. With hundreds of mainland businesses aspiring to IPOs, it would seem inevitable that the mainland exchanges will grow rapidly while the HKSE will see fewer listings. However, mainland companies in various sectors, including manufacturing, construction and mining resources, continue to opt for Hong Kong.

The Chinese mainland exchanges, having languished in the early 2000s, rose dramatically in 2006, adding 76% in value between June 2005 and October 2006. This rise has been driven by retail demand from ordinary Chinese investors, who were unable to invest outside the country and were unhappy with the 2% interest paid on bank deposits. From the perspective of companies seeking IPOs, the drawbacks of the mainland exchanges are the weak legal system, burdensome and unpredictable regulations, and government interference. By contrast, the HKSE has attracted numerous international asset managers, whose funds form a substantial and more stable investor base. In 2007, the Chinese government announced a significant reform, relaxing capital controls which have prevented citizens from investing outside the mainland. Hong Kong enjoys distinct advantages as an environment, including the rule of law, free press, open markets, transparency, capital mobility and a fully convertible currency. One banker specializing in Hong Kong listings says: 'Many companies still look to overseas listings in places such as Hong Kong because of the benefits associated with perceived higher corporate governance standards' (Tucker, 2007).

Is there likely to be a convergence between Hong Kong and mainland China financial centres? Although they remain far apart, they are becoming increasingly integrated, and Hong Kong's continued prosperity as a financial centre depends increasingly on Chinese business activity. China's WTO accession in 2002 gave a boost to this source of business, as a lowering of barriers to foreign investment gathers pace, including acquisitions on the mainland. Hong Kong has played an important role in opening the gates of opportunity to international companies with ambitious China strategies. It has thus benefited from globalization's reach into mainland China. On the other hand, its location advantages of a stable and open environment are clearly part of its attractiveness to interna-

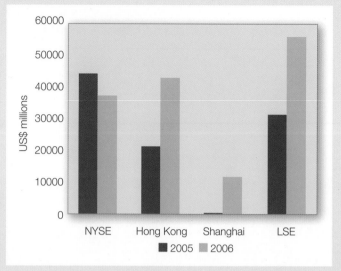

Figure 2 Value of IPOs in selected exchanges

Source: World Federation of Exchanges (2007) Equity raised by IPOs, www.world-exchanges.org

tional investors. Convergence could result in mainland exchanges becoming more open, in which case Hong Kong could find its competitive advantage slipping away.

Questions

◆ How has Hong Kong benefited as a financial centre from its links to mainland China?

◆ What are Hong Kong's competitive advantages as a financial centre? Are these likely to be eroded?

◆ Are further democratic reforms necessary for Hong Kong's open economy to continue to flourish?

Sources: Tucker, S., '$1bn IPOs opt for listings in Hong Kong', *Financial Times*, 18 June 2007; Mitchell, T. and Dyer, G., 'Another door opens: how China is ushering its biggest bank to market', *Financial Times*, 25 October 2006; Mitchell, T., 'One country, two systems and its limits', *Financial Times*, 29 June 2007; Mitchell, T., 'Odd bed-fellows and alliances in both camps', *Financial Times*, 24 October 2006; Mitchell, T., 'Ten years on, democracy is still a distant promise', *Financial Times*, 29 June 2007; Tucker, S., 'A battle for hearts and wallets', *Financial Times*, 24 October 2006; *The Economist*, Special Report on Hong Kong, 30 June 2007.

WEB CHECK

Information about Hong Kong can be accessed by going to the IMF website, www.imf.org. Under *Country Information*, click on *Hong Kong*.

Globalization and stock markets
Contrast the stock markets described in this section in terms of their internationalization. Assess the extent to which stock markets at present are indicative of globalization trends or, alternatively, more local factors. Give examples.

PAUSE TO REFLECT

Bond markets

Loan capital is a traditional way of raising money, and also provides numerous investment opportunities. The bond or debenture is a marketable security. The company which sells the bond is the issuer. It issues the bond for a fixed period which carries a fixed rate of interest. The investor is paid interest as well as the face value. While a dividend paid to shareholders may vary, or not be paid at all in lean years, the bondholder is entitled to regular interest payments. The fixed income is thus appealing to many investors, although inflation may constitute a future risk. A benefit of corporate bonds for the company is that long-term finance is made available at relatively attractive rates. Another advantage is less exposure to equity markets, which is a benefit during periods of stock market volatility. Between 2000 and 2004, issuance of bonds doubled, from $2,379 billion to $4,858 billion (Tett and Tassell, 2005). Pension funds held 60% of their investments in equities in 1999, but, by 2004, this was down to 50% (shown in Figure 11.9).

Bond: A type of loan security issued by organizations for a fixed period, with interest payable to the lender.

Figure 11.9 Shifting investments of worldwide pension funds
Source: Financial Times, 10 October 2005

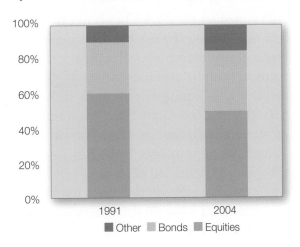

In recent years, international bonds have become popular, as companies have looked beyond national borders for efficient ways of raising capital. The international bond is an instrument issued by or to overseas lenders (creditors). There are two types of international bond: the foreign bond and the eurobond. The foreign bond is issued outside the country of the organization and denominated in the currency of the issuing country. The countries which are attractive are those with low interest rates, which in recent years have been obtainable chiefly in Japan and Switzerland. Foreign bonds are issued mainly by public authorities, large multinationals and financial institutions. Brazil issued its first bond denominated in its own currency in 2005. This 10-year bond raised the equivalent of about $1.5 billion from investors, mainly in the US and Europe. While many investors might have shied away from the bond because of the local currency risk, the issue was a sign of confidence in Brazil's economy. The eurobond may be issued by a variety of entities, including large companies and sovereign governments. The eurobond may be denominated in any currency and sold to investors in many capital markets except that of the currency in which it is denominated. Whereas dealings in shares on stock exchanges are regulated by national regulatory authorities, eurobonds, which are denominated in a foreign currency, fall outside national regulation.

Foreign bond: Bond issued outside the country of the issuing organization, denominated in the currency of the issuing country.

Eurobond: Bond issued in countries outside that of the currency in which it is denominated.

TO RECAP...
Global bond markets
Loan capital is required by large organizations – governments as well as companies – around the world. Bonds offer investment opportunities which contrast with equities, as regular interest payments are guaranteed, as well as the return of capital at the end of the fixed term.

International corporate finance

The finance function in business has historically been cast in a supportive role, focusing on the company's accounts and financial statements. In recent years, however, finance has taken on a wider and more central role. Areas such as regulatory compliance, risk management and performance measurement have become increasingly important in the competitive environment. Financial considerations are crucial to strategic decisions across the company. They apply to decisions such as resource allocation and decisions whether to outsource a function or keep it in-house. For the MNE with numerous subsidiaries in different countries, financial decisions are key to the functioning of the subsidiary in its relations with the parent company. With the expansion of global capital markets, local financing alternatives come increasingly into the frame for corporate decision-makers.

Balancing equity and debt

Debt/equity ratio: Expression of the balance between debt financing and equity financing for a particular company.

All companies must raise funds to carry out their activities. Equity financing (through issuing shares) and debt financing (through borrowing) are the two broad means available to all companies. The balance between equity and debt financing can be expressed as the debt/equity ratio, which is the firm's debt divided by its equity. For example, if the firm's debt is €5,000, and its equity €10,000, its debt/equity ratio is expressed as 0.5. The higher the ratio, the greater the reliance on debt, known as 'leverage' in finance terminology. Where the ratio of over 1, the firm's debts exceed its equity. In some countries, such as Japan and Germany, debt financing by banks has been the norm, whereas in the US, equity finance has been preferred, resulting in lower debt/equity ratios. However, debt financing of buyout activities has resulted in a trend towards greater reliance on debt, discussed later in this chapter. As a general rule, where levels of equity finance are high, shareholder concerns are paramount, whereas for the highly leveraged company, creditor concerns are to the fore. Corporate governance frameworks tend to follow these capital arrangements. In countries where debt financing is prevalent, banks have traditionally played a monitoring role, often taking equity stakes in debtor companies. A recent trend has been the weakening role of German banks, along with reductions in their equity stakes, taking Germany closer to the more shareholder-oriented models prevalent in the US and UK.

Public and private companies differ in the ways in which they finance their activities, as well as in their ownership structures. A comparison is set out in Figure 11.10, which shows that while there are formal likenesses, the players are different. In particular, holders of the public company's equity are much more dispersed than in the private company. For both types of company, an advantage of the corporate form over the unincorporated business (highlighted in Chapter 1) is that the company takes on a separate legal identity from its owners, who are its shareholders. Shareholders who invest in a company enjoy 'limited liability', which means that their liability for the company's debts is limited to the amount they have invested in its equity. The shareholder hopes to be paid 'dividends' by the company, which are paid from its profits in a given year. It has no obligation to pay dividends. Shareholders in a private company often take their remuneration as dividends, while those in public companies may content themselves with the prospect of a dividend, but count more on a rise in market value of their shares.

Those who loan money to a company, public or private, are legally entitled to interest payments, which are deductible in calculating profits. Debt financing is therefore considered to have an advantage for tax purposes. However, servicing high levels of debt may constitute financial risk (discussed below). A company may issue corporate bonds, but usually only large companies do so. Corporate bonds are normally handled through investment banks, and entail rules of disclosure similar to listing rules in equity markets, along with scrutiny by a ratings agency such as Moody's, which will give the company a credit rating. Given these complexities, most companies choose to borrow from banks.

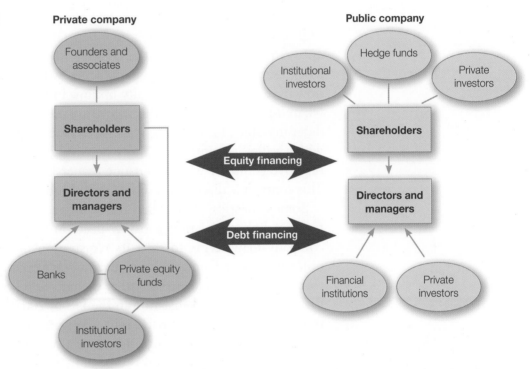

Figure 11.10 A comparison of equity and debt financing for private and public companies

The private company is usually funded by only a few shareholders, often members of the same family, each of whom has a substantial portion of the equity, as well as a direct interest in the company. A private company faces fewer regulatory requirements regarding disclosure of its affairs than the public company. From the enterprise point of view, the private company is closely controlled by 'insider' owners and managers. It is often argued that this gives the private company agility as well as stability to think long term, in contrast to public companies, in which ranks of diverse shareholders with short-term perspectives keep an eye on quarterly results. Private companies featured in this book illustrate this point well (they include Heineken in CS3.1 and Bosch in SX10.1). A drawback of the private company is its limited ability to borrow money, which often hinges on guarantees given by the owners, despite their formal limited liability (SX2.2 on Dyson illustrates this point). This is a common complaint of SMEs. For larger private companies, debt financing has become much more accessible in recent years, mainly as a result of the growth in private equity funds (discussed below).

It has long been the pattern that private companies turn themselves into public companies in order to access greater resources in both equity and debt markets. To realize these benefits, the company takes the further step of listing on a stock exchange, becoming a 'quoted' company through an IPO (see Chapter 1). As Figure 11.10 shows, it will acquire an array of new shareholders, and it stands to see its value rise through trading, which in turn enhances its ability to access debt financing. However, 'outside' investors, especially hedge funds, have short-term gains in mind. Moreover, shareholders and managers have differing perspectives. The issuance of shares and share options to managers, which has become common, is designed in part to better align management and shareholder interests (see Chapter 14 for a further discussion).

In addition to shareholder scrutiny, the public company commits itself to high levels of regulatory oversight. Financial reporting and corporate governance requirements apply in the country where it is registered. Listing on a stock exchange also involves compliance with the exchange's rules. MNEs now have a wide range of equity options in respect of where to register and where to list their shares. The regulatory environment may either attract or deter investors, for differing reasons. A strict regime may attract companies which value its safeguards and extensive disclosure requirements, while a secretive company with an opaque ownership structure would be deterred. This contrast is discussed in CF11.2 on Dubai.

Some countries, often called 'offshore' locations, offer comparative advantages of light regulation and low taxation (see SX14.1 on Accenture). A company may decide to shift its registration or stock exchange listing in order to benefit from offshore advantages. Some companies have delisted from the NYSE and listed on other exchanges, following the introduction of the Sarbanes-Oxley legislation in the US in 2002. A more radical step is to transform the company back into a private company. This may seem an unlikely strategy, as the shareholders must all be bought out, but private equity funds specializing in this type of buyout have gained ground in recent years. Both delistings and buyouts are discussed later in this chapter.

The MNE's subsidiaries are registered in the country in which they are located. Equity and debt funding of local companies at local level are ways of hedging foreign exchange risk. This strategy, which creates local financial ties, is a means of establishing good relations with the government, which can be helpful if there are policy shifts against foreign businesses. When governments restrict foreign companies in their ability to remit profits back to their home country, the funds must be used locally, for example reinvesting in local operations. As banking and financial systems in emerging economies become more established, the cost of local currency bond issues is likely to be competitive. VW, for example, has issued peso bonds in Mexico. Although low-cost funding in emerging markets carries risks, these risks have diminished, and the IMF has actively encouraged local corporate bond issues (IMF, 2004).

TO RECAP...

Debt and equity financing

Corporate preferences for debt or equity financing are linked to ownership and governance structures in national environments. In economies with open markets for shareholder participation and control, equities are a favoured way of raising capital, whereas in more closed, more narrowly controlled markets, debt financing is preferred, usually through banks. Private companies, especially SMEs, have fewer capital-raising options than public companies: their shares are not traded, and debt financing is more limited.

Cross-border mergers and acquisitions

The acquisition of existing businesses has been a favoured means of MNE international expansion. An acquisition strategy commonly stems from the perceived need to expand quickly in markets where the company has little presence or knowledge. In some global industries, companies are driven by the desire for global market share, which leads to consolidation among a few large players. The oil industry and the shipping industry are examples (see CS5.2 and SX10.2). Cross-border acquisitions have become a feature of modern capitalism. Companies from the advanced economies have been the largest players, but those from emerging economies are becoming more active in M&A markets (see Figure 11.11). In an acquisition, the acquiring company takes over the target company, which may be a public or private company, usually by acquiring a controlling share of the stock. If it is a private company, the process is fairly straightforward, as the owners are bought out.

Figure 11.11 Cross-border mergers and acquisitions by companies in developed and developing economies

Source: UNCTAD (2006) Cross-border M&A sales by region and economy of purchaser, www.unctad.org

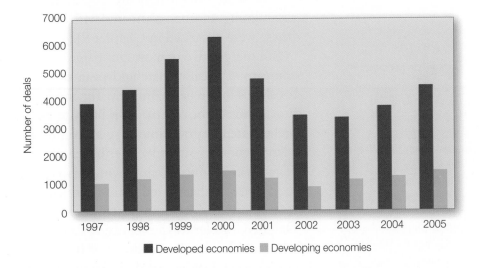

The acquisition of a public listed company is more complex, and involves more complex financial arrangements which depend on the company law of the country or state (in federal systems such as the US) of the target company. In general, the would-be acquirer makes an offer to the board of the target company, which may be a cash offer for shares or a mixture of cash and shares in the acquiring company. If the board approves, the offer is likely to be approved by the shareholders. If the board disapproves, the offeror company may well raise the offer, to make it more attractive. But if the board disapproves in principle, the offer may become 'hostile', and the offeror company may bypass the board and make the offer directly to the shareholders. Although rare, there have been instances of hostile takeovers succeeding. The Vodafone takeover of Mannesmann in Germany in 2000 is an example. In this case, the high proportion of foreign shareholders, amounting to 70% of the total, accepted the bid. However, a criminal case against the former Mannesmann directors for taking illegal bonuses led to a bitter aftermath, in which many in Germany questioned the rise of shareholder value over traditional stakeholder concerns. In fact, hostile offers have been on the increase, as determined would-be acquirers are not deterred by negative responses from target companies. The Mittal takeover of Arcelor is the example featured in CS11.1. In takeovers such as this, which involve public companies with large market shares, competition authorities may postpone proceedings in order to investigate if the combined enterprise would constitute abuse of a dominant position (see discussion of competition law in Chapter 5).

High levels of M&A activity are associated with periods of rising markets, such as the late 1990s and the years from 2003 onwards. The share price of the target company tends to rise, due to a 'bid premium', which is the difference between the share price before and after the bid. The bid premium may be 15% in a friendly acquisition, but double that in a hostile one. Shares in acquiring companies tend to slump from the time they initiate a takeover. This is partly because of the cost of the bid, whether successful or not. It is also the case that shareholders in the acquiring company perceive that their shares (and dividends) will be 'diluted' by an enlarged shareholder base in the case of share offers. They are also aware of the difficulties associated with assimilating another company, with the attendant costs and uncertainties (these were discussed in Chapter 9).

In a merger, two or more companies come together as equals to form a new company. Typically, shareholders in the 'old' companies change their shares for shares in the new company. The merger is less common than the acquisition, as one of the companies is likely to be dominant. Mergers are sometimes orchestrated by governments, who combine small players in an industry into a larger company, in order to enhance competitiveness. During Japan's period of rapid economic development, this type of state-sponsored consolidation took place in heavy industries and chemicals (Johnson, 1982). In more market-oriented environments, takeovers predominate. The formation of DaimlerChrysler was announced as a merger, but was more akin to an agreed takeover. The different cultures of the two companies did not become integrated, and Chrysler was sold to a private equity purchaser in 2007.

TO RECAP...
M&A strategies in perspective
Companies from both developed and developing countries have become more ambitious in their M&A strategies as their international expansion plans have accelerated. For the acquirer, finding suitable target companies and appropriate funding are usually more readily achieved than the long-term task of integrating acquired companies, especially those with different corporate cultures.

Don't forget to check the companion website at **www.palgrave.com/business/morrisonib**, where you will find web-based assignments, web links, interactive quizzes, an extended glossary and lots more to help you learn about international business.

www.palgrave.com
Companion Website

Lakshmi Mittal, the Indian steel magnate, built a business empire which became the world's largest steel producer. His strategy rested mainly on shrewd acquisitions of both plants and sources of raw materials such as coal mines, often in the developing world. His bid for Arcelor, the European steelmaker, in 2005, represented a change of strategy, partly because the target company was the second largest in the industry and also because it was Western European. Arcelor was viewed as a European champion. Its shareholders, managers and other stakeholders resisted a takeover. In the battle which followed, Mittal was compelled to raise his offer and make other concessions, but for many, the outcome left a bitter legacy.

The global steel industry in the 1990s offered Mittal opportunities to buy cheaply several outdated, formerly state-owned plants in post-communist countries, including Poland, the Czech Republic, Romania and Ukraine. In 1995, he bought a virtually derelict plant in Kazakhstan, which was transformed into a showcase steel mill. He also bought stakes in Chinese operations. The late 1990s saw low steel prices and difficult trading conditions for steelmakers. From 2001 onwards, growing Chinese demand led to rising steel prices globally, which Mittal was well positioned to benefit from. By the time of the Arcelor bid, Mittal had businesses in 14 countries on four continents, employing 220,000 workers. Mittal Steel, the parent company, was registered in the Netherlands and listed on the Euronext in Amsterdam and the NYSE. It was 98% owned by Mittal and his family, who also dominated the board of directors, which was divided between classes of directors, with differing rights attached to each class. The unusually structured board had class A directors, which included Mittal and his family members, no class B directors, and six independent class C directors, with limited rights (see Chapter 14 for a further discussion of these issues). Several of the nominally independent directors had business links with Mittal. Mittal himself was both chairman and CEO. The parent company was a holding company, with no business of its own. All the assets and operations were in the subsidiaries, locally registered companies with their own boards of directors. Only one, Mittal Steel South Africa, is a quoted company. Transparency of accounts and governance of the subsidiaries became issues of concern during the takeover battle for Arcelor.

Case study 11.1:
Sparks fly in Mittal Steel's takeover of Arcelor

Arcelor was formed only in 2001, in a merger of three existing steel companies: Arbed of Luxembourg, Usinor of France and Aceralia of Spain. Arcelor was registered in Luxembourg, and set about restructuring the operations in Europe, while expanding into lower cost locations such as Brazil. Improved financial results followed from the merger and restructuring. Arcelor's strong presence in Western Europe and skills in producing high-quality steel made it an attractive target. Mittal's bid of €18.1 billion for Arcelor, launched in January, 2006, was immediately met with hostility by Arcelor shareholders, but sent the share price rising, as Figure 1 shows. Mittal dropped his plan to hold a majority of the merged company, and suggested that he

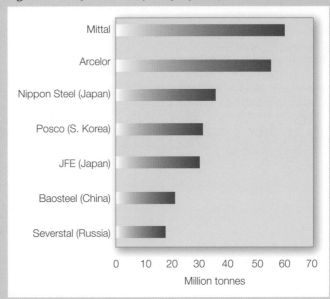

Figure 2 Steel production by company, 2005

Source: Financial Times, 27 June 2006

would be willing to reduce his control. As a defence to the bid, Arcelor directors sought an alternative merger, with Severstral of Russia, which would act as a 'white knight' to fend off Mittal. However, Arcelor shareholders were not persuaded that this deal would be to their advantage, as 38% of the new business would end up in the hands of the Russian steel oligarch, Alexei Mordashov. Mittal raised his bid to €22.7 billion and then to €26.9 billion, a sum 43% more than the original offer. This improved offer, which was accepted in June, gave shareholders the equivalent of €40.4 per share. This was structured as 13 Mittal shares for every 12 Arcelor shares they held, plus €12.55 cash. Hence, over two-thirds of the price was in Mittal shares, leaving lingering concern about shareholder rights in the new entity.

In terms of payment, the deal looked attractive to Arcelor shareholders, and they were also reassured that Mittal had dropped his insistence on controlling the majority of the company. However, he

Figure 1 Movement of Arcelor share price, 2006

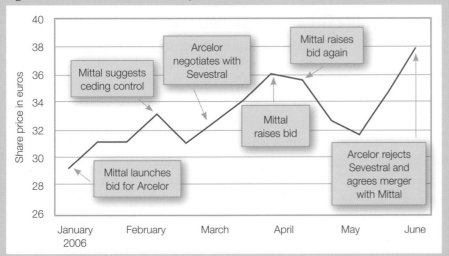

retained 43.4% of the new company, named ArcelorMittal, in which he owns 10 times more stock than any other shareholder. Mittal said he would step down as CEO, giving way to an Arcelor executive. However, within months, Mittal had taken over as CEO himself. Despite the new name of the company, which suggests a merger, this was a takeover by Mittal, who, despite reducing his ownership stake in the parent company, remains the dominant owner and is also in control of management decision-making. The new company's register includes former Arcelor shareholders, among whom are hedge funds and other activist groups, who, within a year of the takeover, were questioning the governance and launching legal actions against Mittal.

With their different cultures and management traditions, the task of integration is challenging. The Indian entrepreneur's autocratic style has been effective in less regulated environments with weak institutions and limited attention to employee and stakeholder values. Moreover, Arcelor's employees number 100,000, a large number to be integrated

by the acquiring company, especially one with a different corporate culture.

ArcelorMittal now dominates the global steel industry, as Figure 2 shows. It is larger than the next three largest companies combined, and is positioned to gain even greater efficiencies. The presence of such a huge company is likely to spark further consolidation, as rivals feel their positions threatened. Mittal himself aims to carry on expanding. He says of his takeover of Arcelor: 'What we've done puts us ahead of the competition by many years. We are a new benchmark for the industry and I'd like to see other players move forward as well through their own consolidation efforts' (Marsh, 26 September 2006). His view is that a smaller group of global companies would be better able to control supply and prices, while reducing costs and increasing sales, thus avoiding the market volatilities which have affected the steel industry in the past.

Questions

1   What were the hurdles Mittal had to overcome in his hostile bid for Arcelor?
2   Assess the shareholder and stakeholder perspectives in the takeover battle and in the new company.
3   What competitive advantages are now enjoyed by ArcelorMittal in global markets?

Sources: Marsh, P., 'An ambitious man of steel', *Financial Times*, 4 February 2006; Marsh, P., 'A feel for steel: why Mittal will press home the benefits of size', *Financial Times*, 26 September 2006; Marsh, P., 'Deal finalised in a palace, but sealed in an airport', *Financial Times*, 27 June 2006; Plender, J., 'Mittal kingdom: why governance may be an impediment in the pursuit of Arcelor', *Financial Times*, 28 April 2006; Marsh, P., 'Arcelor succumbs to Mittal', *Financial Times*, 26 June 2006; Saigol, L., 'Investors challenge Arcelor Mittal on terms', *Financial Times*, 13 June 2007.

WEB CHECK

ArcelorMittal's website is www.arcelormittal.com.

Winners and losers in battles for corporate control

Takeover situations can be viewed from a number of different perspectives. What issues are raised for each of the following groups, and how likely is each to gain from a takeover:
- Shareholders of the acquiring/acquired company
- Managers of the acquiring/acquired company
- Employees of the acquiring/acquired company?

PAUSE TO REFLECT

The roles of hedge funds and private equity

Hedge funds and private equity groups have become active players in global finance, impacting on capital markets and also playing key roles in corporate finance. Although they pursue different strategies, both types of fund are privately controlled, raising money from wealthy investors, which is invested in a variety of assets by expert fund managers, in the hope of producing higher returns than straightforward investments such as equities. Both are perceived as rather aggressive players in global finance. We examine how these rather secretive funds operate and assess their widespread influence in international business.

Hedge funds

Hedge fund: Investment fund managed by an individual or firm, which is active in all types of securities markets; noted for skills in achieving short-term gains for investors.

Hedging as a kind of insurance is a common aspect of overall business strategy. By contrast, the hedge fund is a specialist investment vehicle which is active in equities and bonds as well as derivatives trading. In UK and US markets, where they are most active, hedge funds now account for half of equity and bond trading. Hedge fund managers have delivered returns above those in conventional equity markets, and have attracted considerable inflows of funds. In periods of falling equity markets, such as the slump in 2001, hedge funds became popular with a broad spectrum of investors. By 2006, the money invested in hedge funds was estimated at $1,400 billion globally (Figure 11.12).

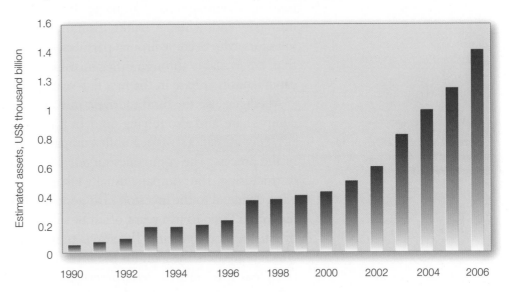

Figure 11.12 Growth in hedge funds

Source: Financial Times, 27 April 2007

Hedge funds have produced good returns for investors, but the targeted companies are usually less enthusiastic. Many derivatives allow the investor to take a position on a company's shares without having full ownership, making it difficult for companies to trace the ownership of their shares. Typically, they 'go short' on a company's shares, selling shares they do not own, in the hope that they will fall in value. They then buy them back at a lower price, realizing a gain. These transactions do not have to be disclosed to the company, and the hedge fund can build up a stake in secret. From this platform, hedge funds often become activist shareholders, seeking to influence corporate strategy, and exerting influence especially in takeover situations. This role is illustrated CS11.2 on Cadbury. These initiatives are often unwelcome, as the hedge fund manager's perspective tends to be short-term gain. Warren Buffet, the American hedge fund manager, became a thorn in the side of a number of large companies, including Coca-Cola. His objection to the company's purchase of Quaker Oats in 2001, which was then acquired by PepsiCo, is now seen as a strategic blunder (see CS1.1). Hedge funds have become active in loan markets, often taking on a role which was formerly the preserve of banks. Banks have traditionally accepted the risk of loans on their books, but the growth of derivatives allows banks to 'securitize' debt, selling these new products on to investors, thus dispersing the risk. Hedge funds have been active in these new securities.

Private equity

Private equity fund: Investment fund managed on behalf of wealthy investors, usually structured as a partnership and lasting a fixed number of years.

Private equity funds have been active since the 1970s, when they operated mainly as venture capital funds, providing finance for SMEs, particularly young and innovative businesses. They have only recently become more mainstream in corporate finance. In 1997, they accounted for less than 4% of the total value of M&A deals, but by 2006, their share had risen to a quarter (Larsen, 2007). Before looking at their role, it is necessary to look briefly at how these funds are structured. In most cases, one or more individuals, who become the fund's managers, set up a limited liability partnership (LLP), with a limited life of 10 years. As it is not a company, it escapes company regulation. The managers, who are the general partners, set about raising capital for the fund in a campaign of signing up investors, who may be pension schemes, university endowments, banks, insurance companies and rich individuals. The investors, who become limited partners, are typically looking for higher returns than are available through other investments. The fund reaches the end of its capital-raising phase in the first few years, and is then said to be closed.

Managers use the fund to invest in companies, usually buying a controlling equity share, and also relying on debt financing – an arrangement known as a leveraged buyout (LBO). Public companies are taken into private ownership in the process. The companies targeted tend to be ones which they feel need restructuring. The company usually takes on more debt, which may be used to pay a dividend to the investors. The general manager sells or moves the companies on in three to five years, often by selling to another private equity fund or by relisting the company. The aim is to make a profit on the sale of the equity, which represents the gain for the investors. General partners generate income from fees and from 'carried interest', based on the performance of the fund.

Some funds combine in a consortium to make large buyout offers. One of the largest acquisitions has been the Texas utility provider, TXU, for $44 billion in 2007. Buyouts of ailing car manufacturer DaimlerChrysler and component manufacturers Delphi and Visteon were negotiated in 2007. Less obvious as buyout targets have been Alliance Boots, the UK chemist chain, and J. Sainsbury, the supermarket chain. However, these deals' success depends crucially on the investment and interest rate climate. The major private equity funds, such as Blackstone and KKR (Kohlberg Kravis Roberts), have benefited from low interest rates, but the heavy reliance on debt makes this business model risky in an environment of rising interest rates. In these circumstances, banks must tighten their lending policies, in what is termed a 'credit crunch', affecting businesses and consumers alike. Difficulties in obtaining low-cost lending, as occurred in 2007, impact strongly on both private equity buyout and hedge fund activities.

A number of criticisms have been levelled at both hedge funds and private equity funds. The combination of high debt levels and short time frame in which companies must improve performance places pressure on the managers of bought-out companies and runs a high risk of failure, especially if there is an economic downturn. The downside of private equity is highlighted in the opening vignette on Debenhams. Most people would praise the venture capital role of private equity in helping to finance start-ups and other SMEs, but many people balk at taking private well-known public companies with thousands of employees, many of whom stand to lose their jobs in the ensuing radical restructuring. Taking companies private removes them from regulation and governance requirements of public companies. Critics in Germany have been particularly vocal, calling the funds 'locusts', bent on asset-stripping (Smith, 2007). One

Leveraged buyout (LBO): Purchase of a controlling stake in a company, financed by borrowing.

Blackstone's website is www.blackstone.com.

WEB CHECK

partner in a buyout firm has put it this way: 'We have a great corporate governance advantage' (Guerrera and Politi, 2007). Funds defend themselves robustly, saying their focus on delivering better performance and shareholder value benefits companies in the long term, and generates long-term job creation.

By 2007, Blackstone owned businesses with estimated annual revenues of $87 billion and more than 400,000 employees. Its widely ramified financial empire also includes hedge funds. That year, both Blackstone and KKR announced they were launching IPOs, perhaps sensing that financing and regulatory constraints were in the offing. This strategic shift will bring these major players into the strict regulatory framework of quoted public companies. An emerging trend is the growth in government players operating through sovereign wealth funds, which are active in private equity investment, both as investors and fund managers (see discussion in Chapter 15). An example of the latter is discussed in CF11.2 on Dubai. In 2007, China announced it was investing $3 billion of its massive foreign exchange reserves in Blackstone, seeking to diversify its reserves out of US Treasury bonds. The growth and influence of private equity funds have attracted the concerns of governments in the open markets where these funds are active investors. The funds' secretiveness, lack of accountability and escape from regulation sit uneasily with the concept of open markets. Initiatives to introduce voluntary codes of practice or mandatory regulation are being debated in the US and European countries (Bruce, 2007).

TO RECAP...

The roles of hedge funds and private equity

These funds have developed astute global scanning skills, seeking out returns for investors and fund managers which outperform conventional investments such as equities and bonds. Their 'activist' approach has impacted on target companies, most radically in the case of private equity buyout, usually accompanied by heavy debt burdens. Because of their reliance on debt financing and loan securities, these funds carry risks when borrowing becomes more expensive and less readily available.

COUNTRY FOCUS 11.2 – DUBAI

Dubai looks beyond oil wealth

Dubai is one of the seven self-governing emirates within the United Arab Emirates (UEA), a federation of Arab Gulf states. Although oil wealth has been important to its economy, its direct importance is now diminishing as the emirate's oil and gas are now nearly exhausted. Sheikh Mohammed bin Rashid Al Maktoum, Dubai's ruler and a prominent figure in the world of horse racing, is now focusing on economic diversification. The economy is now dominated by services, as the figure shows, with trade, transport and construction to the forefront. The government under Sheikh Mohammed sees the greatest future growth in financial services, making Dubai an international financial and investment centre.

Figure Dubai's GDP by sector

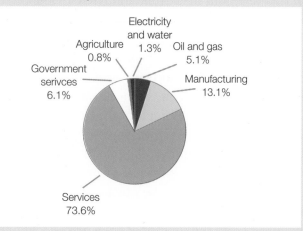

Note: Services includes trade, construction, transport, storage, real estate and business services, restaurants and hotels, social and personal services, and domestic services

Source: Dubai Government (2007) Dubai Strategic Plan 2015, http://egov.dubai.ae

Dubai has benefited from its location by offering financial services for oil-rich neighbours to invest their petrodollars. It now hopes to extend its range to more international investors. An outward-looking international approach has helped to create a favourable business climate, offering a currency pegged to the dollar and no capital controls. This approach is in marked contrast to neighbours such as Saudi Arabia, which is closed to foreigners. Free-trade zones have been set up, which welcome foreign companies, avoiding the UAE requirement that all companies must be majority owned by a UAE national.

The Dubai International Finance Centre (DIFC) has attracted investment banks offering project finance, banking and asset management. They also offer specialist Islamic finance – financial products which are Sharia compliant. The main difference between Islamic finance and conventional finance is the prohibition on interest. However, innovative products have been designed to use profits to replicate products in conventional markets. An Islamic bond pays coupon profits instead of interest. Customized equity investments are available, adding to the range of Islamic financial products in this growing market. Both equities and bonds, including Islamic bonds, are traded in Dubai's new stock exchange.

In 2005, Dubai created the Dubai International Financial Exchange. There are no restrictions for foreign investors, and the exchange is regulated by the Dubai Financial Services Authority (DFSA), modelled on its London counterpart. This is in contrast to the opaque regulatory environment which prevails in other Arab states. With strong economic growth, huge infrastructure projects and a thriving property market, the region is likely to attract international issuers and investors over time, but its progress has been slow. Local companies are possibly deterred by the strict regulatory framework. Luring international investors is also posing challenges. Companies in the region are largely dominated by ruling families and government agencies which they control. They are perceived as having opaque management and weak governance structures, which could deter foreign investors, despite the high standards imposed by the DFSA. The instability of the Middle East generally and the tension between the US and Iran in particular are also causes of uncertainty.

Dubai Ports World (DP World), one of Dubai's leading companies and a subsidiary of Dubai World Group, had an unwelcome brush with negative US sentiment in 2005. From its origins as Dubai's port authority, DP World has grown into the world's third largest container terminal operator, largely through acquisitions. Its purchase of P&O, the UK ports and ferries operator, proved controversial in the US. Members of Congress proposed legislation to block DP World's takeover of P&O's five US ports on the grounds that it threatened national security. Initially determined to go through with the takeover, DP World eventually backed down and sold the US ports. The other 44 ports obtained in the takeover included those in India and China, which are seen as vital to the company's strategy of increasing business in Eastern export-led economies.

Dubai investors continue to pursue opportunities internationally. Istithmar World Capital, the Dubai World Group's investment subsidiary, has taken at 2.7% stake in the UK's Standard Chartered Bank and a 2.3% stake in Time Warner. Although a government investment agency, it is hoping to attract other investors, particularly among Dubai's oil-rich neighbours looking to invest petrodollars. Istithmar seeks to emulate the success of private equity groups in the US and UK. It sees its investments in sectors such as media as longer term and more 'patient' than private equity groups. In contrast, Dubai International Capital (DIC), an investment fund owned by Sheikh Mohammed, seems closer to the private equity model. DIC bought Tussauds Group, famous for its waxworks museums, from a private equity firm in 2005 for £800 million, and sold it a year later to Blackstones for £1.3 billion in cash. DIC retains a 20% interest in the company. It also owns the Travelodge hotel chain in the UK. These Dubai investors have shown a preference for UK investments, many sensing they would not be welcome in the US.

Dubai's economic development has been led by Sheikh Mohammed, through companies owned by the sheikh or the government. This concentration of political and economic power reflect the emirate's traditional values and social structures, which co-exist with foreign cultures which have become increasingly important in modern Dubai. The population is mainly made up of foreign residents, from construction workers to skilled professionals, on whom the economy depends. Local citizens make up only 15% of the population of 1.4 million. Poor living and working conditions for the thousands of Indian construction workers have led to violent protests, attracting the world's media. Workers have demanded the right to organize in unions, as well as better conditions. The government has responded to a limited extent, concerned about future unrest. Both NGOs and foreign governments have raised the issues of forced labour and human trafficking, which could impact on the government's position in future free-trade agreements.

As Dubai is transforming itself into an economy focused on services, its strategic location and twenty-first-century infrastructure and facilities give it advantages globally and within the region. Its investment funds, awash with oil wealth, are influential in global finance. However, internal tensions and regional instability still hang over the emirate's charge to become a global financial centre.

Questions

◆ What are Dubai's strengths as a regional financial centre?
◆ In what ways do environmental factors impact on potential issuers and investors in Dubai's stock exchange?
◆ How is private equity as a model being used by Dubai funds?

Sources: Khalaf, R., 'Dubai plays large role on world stage', *Financial Times*, 27 November 2006; Tett, G., 'Trades lag hopes at DIFX', *Financial Times*, 27 November 2006; Khalaf, R., 'Oil fuels new confidence', *Financial Times*, 27 November 2006; Kerr, S., 'Pressure mounts to improve labour conditions', *Financial Times*, 24 July 2007; Kerr, S., 'Pillars of economic success', *Financial Times*, 24 July 2007; Drummond, J., 'Raft of bourses crowds market', *Financial Times*, 24 July 2007; Wright, R., Yeager, H. and Kirchgaessner, S., 'DP World chief defiant over ports as House rejects Bush compromise', *Financial Times*, 9 March 2006; Dubai Government (2007) Dubai Strategic Plan 2015, http://egov.dubai.ae.

WEB CHECK

For information about Dubai, see the IMF's website at www.imf.org. Under *Country Information*, click on the *UAE*. Information about Dubai as a financial centre is available here.

plate 11.3 Dubai's ambitious waterfront construction projects reflect its aspirations as a global financial centre.

The good, the bad and the risky
Hedge fund and private equity fund managers argue that their active investment strategies stir up complacent incumbent managers, acting as a catalyst to achieve better performance and long-term value creation. If this represents the 'good', what are the 'bad' and 'risky' aspects of their activities?

PAUSE TO REFLECT

International accounting issues

Accounting is one of the core business functions, providing quantitative financial information on an organization's activities, assets and liabilities, which is vital to corporate strategists and investors. In today's world, as we have seen in this chapter, complex transactions, innovative financial products and organizational complexity have created challenges as well as opportunities for finance managers. Equally, financial complexity creates challenges in quantifying and presenting relevant information. Businesses have historically been obliged to adapt to national differences in accounting standards in their international operations. It is generally agreed that harmonization and simplification would help to facilitate cross-border operations, but numerous issues reflect the depth of diversity. In this section, we look at the major current issues affecting businesses, regulators and stakeholders in international companies.

Diversity in accounting standards

Accounting is a vital function for all businesses, whether registered companies or unincorporated businesses. For unincorporated businesses, balance sheets and profit and loss accounts are of interest mainly to the owners, investors and the relevant tax authorities. Private companies and partnerships are generally required to file annual financial reports with national regulators, but face no public disclosure requirements, as their capital is not traded in public markets. Listed companies are subject to the highest levels of disclosure and financial reporting regulation. The information they provide is crucial to the smooth functioning of capital markets. Corporate decision-makers, investors and regulators rely directly on this information in making judgments, and members of the broader community are indirectly affected by financial information, as participants in pension funds, employees and consumers. The position of the auditor is crucial in providing independent monitoring of the company's financial information, which helps to assure the public of accuracy and objectivity. When it emerges that companies have been falsifying or misrepresenting their financial situation, as in the Enron and Parmalat scandals, public confidence is set back. Investors, including individual and institutional investors, are looking for international opportunities for financial gain. However, national differences in accounting standards and regulation can pose considerable risk.

Every country has its own distinctive accounting practices. These practices underlie the country's accounting standards, which are the rules designed to achieve consistency in the calculation and presentation of financial statements. Diversity among national accounting standards stems from a number of factors, presented in Figure 11.13.

The cultural environment covers a number of variables relevant to accounting traditions. Of Hofstede's cultural dimensions (discussed in

Auditor: Professional accountant appointed by a company to prepare its annual accounts in accordance with applicable regulatory rules, and from an independent perspective.

Figure 11.13 Influences on national accounting practices

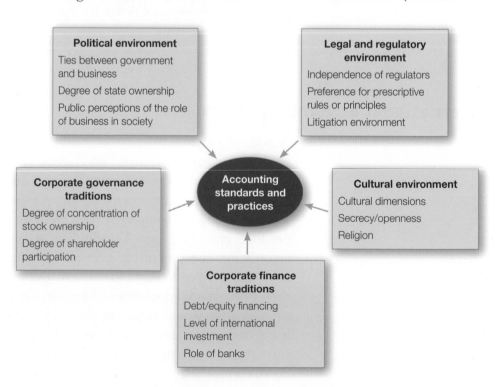

Chapter 4), power distance and individualism are relevant. Large power distance and low individualism are often linked in countries where business elites are dominant. In countries with insider-dominated corporate cultures, secrecy tends to predominate over openness. A range of countries fall into this category, including Asian, Latin American and some Continental European ones. Muslim financial systems also fall into this category, as discussed in CF11.2 on Dubai. Countries with small power distance and high individualism, such as the US and the UK, have traditions of open capital markets and wider shareholder participation. In these countries, openness and transparency are more highly valued. These countries also have similar corporate governance traditions, with strong equity markets and high levels of international investment. Countries in which debt financing is the norm give greater influence to banks and less to equity markets. These factors are reflected in accounting standards. Where banks are critical, financial reporting addresses debt issues and takes a banking perspective. Where shareholders are dominant, financial reporting emphasizes key shareholder concerns, such as profits and investments. If a company has numerous shareholder constituencies, including international shareholders, their concerns are inevitably diverse, many taking a short-term view. Companies in this environment are tempted to take a rather optimistic view of their financial position.

In Figure 11.13, the political and regulatory environments appear in separate boxes, although they are linked in practice. In countries where the government plays an active role in business, including state ownership, businesses are likely to come under considerable political influence. In this environment, regulators are closely linked to government. China is an example, as SX11.2 shows. This type of environment can be a deterrent to international investors. In countries where governments play a more limited role, such as the US and the UK, regulators are expected to be independent. It is also expected that financial reporting rules will provide objective and unbiased information for the broad investing public, including international investors. However, divergence on the nature of regulation has created a divide between countries which seem to share the same goals of transparency and accuracy in financial reporting.

In the US, the generally accepted accounting principles (GAAP) are based on prescriptive rules, whereas European systems are based more on principles. In the latter type of system, there is more scope for judgment and flexibility in interpretation, providing, in the views of advocates, more useful information to outsiders. The rules-based system lends itself to lengthy, legally correct results, which provide sound evidence for defence lawyers, a major concern in the US, where litigation is common. This approach is less helpful to investors and the general public. US practitioners and regulators now recognize that the high priority on reducing litigation risk has resulted in too great a swing away from providing clear information which investors need. However, moves towards a principles-based system have been slow. Meanwhile, the many European companies which list in the US are required to provide financial reports which conform to US standards.

TO RECAP...

Diversity in accounting practices and standards

Accounting practices reflect differing business practices in diverse national environments. These influences include culture, political and legal systems, and patterns of business ownership. International investors are likely to be attracted to markets which are open and transparent, rather than those in which the government and other powerful stakeholders are highly influential.

Translation of financial statements

For an MNE with subsidiaries in different countries, accounts must be prepared in the local currency for each subsidiary and 'translated' into the currency of the MNE's home country. The parent company then prepares 'consolidated accounts' in its home-country currency. This process involves a risk associated with changing foreign exchange rates, known as translation risk. If there is a fall in the value of the foreign currency in relation to the home currency, this reduces the apparent value of the foreign subsidiary's equity and its profits, leaving a negative translation exposure. Conversely, if the foreign currency rises in value, this is reflected in the consolidated accounts. Currency translation can be achieved by either the current rate method or the temporal method.

The current rate method uses the exchange rate on the date of the balance sheet to translate from the foreign subsidiary's currency into the home currency of the company. This could be misleading, as transactions reported are likely to have taken place when different exchange rates applied. The temporal method takes the exchange rate which applied when a transaction actually took place. Transactions on many different days are likely to show many different exchange rates. As a result, the balance sheet will balance in the foreign currency, but may not balance in the home currency. For this reason, the use of a single exchange rate may seem preferable, suggesting that the use of the current rate method should be chosen. In some cases, the foreign subsidiary may use the currency of the parent company in most of its operations. If this is the case, the temporal method gives a more accurate picture.

Progress towards harmonization

Efforts to harmonize international accounting standards have been spearheaded by the International Accounting Standards Board (IASB). Its aim has been to produce a set of harmonized rules which will be acceptable to national regulators everywhere, making the process of preparing accounts cheaper and providing clear information which users everywhere can understand. Under harmonized rules, users are assured that the same definitions and treatment of income and assets are being applied, whatever the country. The IASB has produced the International Financial Reporting Standards (IFRS), which replaced national accounting standards in the EU in 2005.

Changing over from accounts prepared according to GAAP to IFRS rules has caused some initial consternation for companies. Although the IFRS rules are intended to give a more accurate and informative picture, they generally lead to a less rosy one. The following is a summary of their implications in specific areas:

- *Financial instruments, including derivatives* – Financial instruments must be measured at 'fair value' with gains and losses in the profit and loss account, even though these instruments are inherently volatile. AstraZeneca, the pharmaceutical company, announced that, as a consequence, it would be reviewing its use of currency hedges.

Translation risk: Risk associated with the translation of accounts prepared in a local currency into the currency of the home country of an MNE.

TO RECAP...

Translation risk

MNEs with subsidiaries in different countries aim to reduce risks associated with currency fluctuations of accounts prepared in various local currencies. Using a single exchange rate is often preferable.

International Financial Reporting Standards (IFRS): International accounting standards, designed to harmonize reporting standards in different countries, which are gradually supplanting national accounting standards.

- *Treatment of mergers, acquisitions and joint ventures* – The accounts must recognize assets and liabilities in proportion to ownership stakes. Under UK GAAP, joint ventures appeared in the accounts as 100% owned by the company, although, in reality, a partner had a stake.

- *Treatment of leases* – Companies such as airlines, retailers and restaurants use leases which allow them to operate aircraft or premises without owning them. Recording them as assets, companies have not been forced to reveal the long-term debt incurred. Under IFRS, these long-term debts must appear on the balance sheet. For companies with large numbers of leases, this change produces a significant rise in debt on the financial statement.

- *Employee benefits including share options* – The cost of these benefits must be treated as operating expenses in the profit and loss account. These benefits include pension funds, which, in some cases, are in deficit.

- *Accounting for subsidiaries and business segments* – Reportable segments must be based on the company's organizational structure and reporting system, preventing the company from hiding poor results which might otherwise stand out. Accounts for all subsidiaries, both domestic and foreign, must be included in consolidated accounts. Special purpose entities, commonly used to remove certain transactions off balance sheet, must also be included.

A consequence of the changes brought about by the IFRS is an apparent rise in debt and other liabilities on the balance sheet. These consequences can be far-reaching, as debt/equity ratios are affected, and are likely to be reflected in changes in market perceptions and share price. Vodafone, one of the first large companies to report under the new IFRS rules, revealed a rise of 27% in net debt, from £8.7 billion under UK accounting standards to £11.1 billion under IFRS. The company pointed out that the differences reflected presentational changes rather than a fundamental increase in debt (Jopson, 2005). Among the chief causes of the apparent rise was its 77% stake in a joint venture with an Italian company, which had appeared in earlier accounts as if it was 100% owned by Vodafone, ignoring the stake owned by the Italian partner.

In addition to EU states, Australia, New Zealand and numerous other countries have adopted the IFRS. In 2007, India announced aims to achieve IFRS convergence by 2011, becoming the 103rd country to do so. The total number is expected to rise to 150 by 2011 (IASB, 2007). Although the IFRS is not accepted in the US, the IASB and the Financial Accounting Standards Board, the US authority, are working together to bring the US rules closer to the IFRS. Even if all the world's companies and regulators agree on a single harmonized system, differences would remain from country to country, as business practices and cultural factors influence accounting practices in different countries (Salter and Niswander, 1995).

WEB CHECK

The website of the IASB is www.iasb.org.

TO RECAP...

Harmonization

Under harmonized IFRS rules, which use the same definitions and the same treatment of income and assets, the aim is to produce an accurate and informative picture of a company's finances, whatever the country.

STRATEGIC CROSSROADS

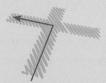

11.2
Cultural revolution in Chinese accounting

China's transition from a planned economy to a market-based one is being accompanied by an equally radical shift in accounting practices. Until the 1990s, China's accounting system was based on the rigid Soviet system, known as 'fund-based' accounting, which focused on how state funds were being used and what was being produced. Business experiences of Western businesspeople in the early 1990s revealed that Chinese counterparts saw only output value of goods produced. One recalls: 'you could make 17,000 green fridges, and even if they were piled up in the warehouse and you had no chance of selling them, you'd account for them as sales revenue' (Jopson, 8 December 2006). The shift to fundamental concepts of Western accounting, such as cash flow, profit margins, assets and liabilities, has had to be learned from scratch. The process has been likened to a 'cultural revolution'. Although not as turbulent as the painful upheaval of the Maoist Cultural Revolution in the 1960s, a fundamental shift in ways of thinking about businesses is involved.

Formed in 1998, China's National Accounting Institute (NAI) is leading the way in 're-educating' the country's accountants, to prepare them for the introduction of accounting rules modelled on international standards. Its rationale is that China's economic development and role in the global economy demand that businesses are run on the basis of accurate records about their performance, assets and liabilities. The 1,200 companies listed on the exchanges in Shanghai and Shenzhen have had to apply these standards since 1 January 2007. The injection of $27 million from the World Bank to the NAI is indicative of the importance of these changes. Like regulatory frameworks everywhere, the real tests will be how they are applied and enforced.

The new accounting rules being adopted are not IFRS standards, but are aligned with them. A major difference is the treatment of transactions with 'related parties', such as from one subsidiary to another. These must be reported under IFRS, but China exempts transactions with state-controlled entities from this provision. Given the pervasiveness of the state in Chinese business, the lack of this information could substantially affect levels of disclosure. Furthermore, there are concerns about weaknesses in disclosure and governance generally among Chinese businesses, even in an environment where basic standards are internationally recognized. The manipulation of accounts to give too optimistic a picture in advance of listing, to cover up bad loans or fraud, is a worry to investors everywhere, but particularly in environments with a legacy of poor disclosure. The stock markets of Shanghai and Shenzhen are gradually easing restrictions on foreign ownership of shares, which should rise from the 2006 limit of 2%. FDI flows into China reached $72.4 billion in 2005, a rise of 19% on 2004. These investors with equity positions are looking for improvements in transparency and enforcement of accounting standards. Much depends on the state regulatory authority, the China Securities Regulatory Commission. Investors would like to see it play a strong independent role, to bolster market confidence, but independent regulation still has a long way to go in China.

Questions

◆ Why has the legacy of the old accounting system proved an obstacle in learning modern accounting principles in China?
◆ Even with the adoption of international accounting standards, what challenges remain in Chinese accounting practices?

Sources: Jopson, B., 'Number crunchers line up for boot camp', *Financial Times*, 8 December 2006; Jopson, B., 'Experts warn of China's "blind spot"', *Financial Times*, 31 December 2006; Jopson, B., 'After the abacus: China's accounting switch holds perils as well as promise', *Financial Times*, 4 July 2006.

The changing regulatory environment

The nature and extent of regulation varies among exchanges and is subject to national law and regulatory frameworks, including corporate governance requirements. As companies have become more complex financially and increased their international exposure, the regulatory environment has come under the spotlight. The corporate scandals of Enron and WorldCom in the US revealed worrying deficiencies in financial reporting and corporate governance in these companies. Enron's financial statements substantially overstated earnings and concealed considerable off-balance sheet debt, despite outward compliance with accounting standards. Meanwhile, senior executives and their families personally enriched themselves from company dealings. Enron's auditors, Arthur Andersen, had effectively become insiders, working with Enron executives rather than advising them independently. Moreover, Andersen was making more money from its management services to Enron than it was making from auditing services, compromising its independence. The Enron board, although consisting of directors who were nominally independent, in fact had financial links with the company, thereby detracting from its ability to monitor the senior executives objectively.

In the wake of Enron, the Sarbanes-Oxley Corporate Reform Act of 2002 was passed by the US Congress. Included in its provisions were a revision of disclosure rules for off-balance sheet debts and a requirement that incentive-based compensation be disclosed. Of more significance for internal control processes was the requirement that CEOs and chief financial officers (CFOs) certify annual reports, backed up with stringent criminal penalties for reckless certification. Details of internal controls had to be included in annual reports from 2005 onwards (Section 404), along with separate opinions by auditors on their effectiveness in combating fraud. The costs of compliance with the new legislation have proved to be onerous. Foreign companies listed in the US have expressed concern at having to comply with the more stringent control mechanisms, and a number have delisted from US exchanges. BASF, the German chemicals company, announced it could save $6.8 million a year by delisting from the NYSE, focusing its market on the Frankfurt exchange. Its CFO said: 'We will have ... significantly less complexity, especially in reporting' (Wiesmann, 2007). Although Sarbanes-Oxley was intended to eliminate false reporting and fraudulent practices, there have been fears that more regulatory hurdles are not necessarily the solution. Those determined to abuse almost inevitably find ways to meet formal compliance requirements while finding new ways of evading them.

As in the case of IFRS rules, in order to be effective, the changes must go deeper than the legal formalities, engendering changes in corporate culture. Legislation in itself is insufficient to bring about such changes (Morrison, 2004). Changes in corporate values and responsibilities would seem to be a greater long-term safeguard. Companies have become more involved in wider reporting of social and environmental initiatives of their activities, placing this information in their annual reports. Known as 'triple bottom line' reporting, it includes financial, social and environmental reporting. Their corporate citizenship credentials, however, are often viewed as separate from business activities. Enron is an example, holding itself out as exemplary in corporate citizenship. This subject is discussed in greater detail in the final part of this book. For present purposes, it is perhaps encouraging to note that a wider view of the company's role in society, beyond the profit-focused model, is creeping into the regulatory environment. The implication is that shareholders and other stakeholders are focusing on a variety of moving targets, all of which they expect to see reported candidly in company reports.

TO RECAP...

The changing regulatory environment

International business partners, investors and other stakeholders require full and accurate financial data in order to take decisions regarding investments and operations in different countries. However, corporate failures in a highly regulated environment such as the US show the limits of regulation per se, and the need for an approach which is less mechanistic and more based on values of responsible reporting.

Conclusions

◻ Whereas in the past, finance as a function was envisaged as subordinate to core business activities, it has now become central in corporate decision-making. This ascendancy is linked to internationalization of investment and operations. Wider opportunities for international financial strategies offer possibilities undreamt of in previous generations, but also greater exposure to risk and market volatility. International expansion has been encouraged by national governments which have liberalized their financial systems and welcomed foreign investors. With relative ease, companies may list on foreign stock exchanges, attract international investors and access debt facilities from a host of global providers. The finances of subsidiaries located in foreign countries can be managed through various hedging arrangements to minimize foreign exchange risk, and the improving financial systems in emerging economies facilitate the localization of financing foreign operations. These benefits provide the means to manage currency risk and associated political and legal risk. On the other hand, the globalization of financial markets has brought interdependence and the risk that any market turmoil will create ripple effects across the globe.

◻ As the competitive environment has become globalized, corporate finance has become swept up in competitive pressures to deliver ever-improving financial performance. These pressures crystallize in takeovers and buyouts, often triggered by private equity and hedge funds, and leading to increased levels of debt. Despite the globalization of capital markets, regulatory systems are predominantly national in scope. Regulatory bodies are becoming increasingly aware of the need for consistency and transparency across national borders, as evidenced by moves towards the harmonization of international accounting standards. The IFRS is now impacting on corporate reporting the world over, even in countries which have not adopted it. Although focusing on convergence in the reporting of financial data, the IFRS has broader implications for financial decision-making and corporate governance. Investors, creditors and managers are thus becoming better able to scrutinize a company's financial position and assess strategic options in rapidly changing markets.

IFRS and beyond
What trends are evident in the changing regulatory environment, which impact on MNEs? To what extent are these changes constraints on their activities or beneficial in their value-creating activities?

PAUSE TO REFLECT

Review questions

Part A: Grasping the basic concepts and knowledge

1. In what ways was the Bretton Woods agreement designed to foster international monetary stability?
2. What factors precipitated the break-up of the Bretton Woods system?
3. Countries may determine exchange rates in a variety of ways. What are the advantages and disadvantages of the pegged exchange rate?
4. What is the role of the IMF in maintaining exchange rate stability?
5. Examine the role of government policy in influencing exchange rates in light of the international Fisher effect.
6. Assess the relative influence of external and internal factors in causing the Asian financial crisis of 1997.
7. Define the major types of foreign exchange transaction used in international business, and specify the types of transaction in which each is appropriate.
8. Why have derivative products grown in popularity? Assess the pros and cons of their availability from the perspective of the finance executive of an MNE.
9. What is the role of hedging as a currency risk strategy for the non-financial company?
10. How have stock exchanges become globalized despite their national regulatory roles?
11. Explain the differences between equity markets and bond markets.
12. What is meant by equity financing, and why do some companies tend to rely more on debt financing? Give examples.
13. How does a takeover differ from a merger?
14. What is the role of hedge funds in global financial markets, and why are they controversial?
15. Explain the role of private equity in international finance.
16. What are the sources of diversity in international accounting practices? How do these differences impact on divergent accounting standards?
17. What is meant by 'translation risk' in accounting, and how do international businesses overcome it?
18. What changes are being introduced by the new International Financial Reporting Standards (IFRS)? Give examples of how they impact on international business.
19. What trends are observable in the changing regulatory environment internationally? In your view, are these changes advantageous or disadvantageous to a firm's competitiveness?

Part B: Critical thinking and discussion

1. To what extent has the rise in derivatives trading, combined with the securitization of debt, led to an uncertain international financial environment?
2. What are the differences between a friendly takeover and a hostile takeover of a company? What risks are associated with a hostile takeover?
3. Assess the impact of differing national regulatory environments for international financial flows.
4. Examine the ways in which a private equity groups invest and manage companies. Compare the positive and negative aspects of a private equity buyout.

Cadbury Schweppes is one of the world's leading companies in confectionary and beverages. Formed through the merger of Cadbury's confectionary business and Schweppes beverages in 1969, the two companies separately go back over 200 years. Cadbury Schweppes serves consumers in 200 countries with a large portfolio of brands, including Dairy Milk chocolate and numerous local brands. It is a world leader in chocolate and confectionary products, ranking either first or second in 22 of the top 50 confectionary markets in the world. Acquisitions have played a major part in its strategy. The acquisition of Dr Pepper and 7-Up helped it to establish itself in the American beverage market. However, it has faced fierce competition from the two giants, Coca-Cola and PepsiCo. It sold its European beverages business to Blackstone and Lion Capital private equity groups in 2006, for £1.26 billion, to concentrate on its core confectionary business in the region. (Its UK beverages had been sold to Coca-Cola in 1999.) Acquiring Adams chewing gum business in 2002 has helped to boost confectionary profits, benefiting from the growing sales of chewing gum.

Overall, Cadbury Schweppes gains 60% of its revenues from confectionary and 40% from beverages. Following the European beverages disposal, its structure was based on four regional operating units, shown in Figure 1. Of these, Americas Beverages was the most profitable in 2006, while Europe, the Middle East and Africa were rather flat. In part, this reflects normal expectations of lower profit margins in confectionary than in beverages, but additional factors were a product recall and an accounting scandal. Accounting irregularities in Nigeria were damaging to profits, and the company took a majority holding in Cadbury Nigeria as a result. The other major setback was a product recall of Dairy Milk and six other products in the UK, due to the presence of salmonella in the production system. The company was fined by the Food Standards Authority. Both are indicative of the types of risk incurred in international business. Health and safety are particularly important in food production, and widely dispersed operations create challenges in maintaining quality.

Overlaying the regional units are six global functions, which are represented by teams in each region. The functional teams, espe-

Case study 11.2:
A sweet future for Cadbury Schweppes?

cially global commercial and global supply chains, are responsible for co-ordinating global strategy within the regions. The parent company's operations are carried out in its many diverse subsidiaries throughout the world, a legacy of the two companies' long history and policy of growing by acquisitions. In 2003, it announced a cost-cutting programme called Fuel for Growth, in which it aimed to close a fifth of its 133 factories worldwide, Figure 2 shows the regional breakdown of its 94 production sites in 2006. Acquired businesses have been allowed considerable local autonomy, in management, finance and brands. This decentralization, however, has made it difficult for head office to gain efficiencies which it needs to compete in global markets. Cadbury Schweppes also relies on independent bottling companies which produce beverages under licence. It acknowledges there are risks inherent in this arrangement, as quality and control of processes cannot be guaranteed. It has pursued a policy of buying out many of these bottling companies. The company's complex operating structure is cited as part of the reason that its profit margins are relatively low. Its margin in confectionary in 2006 was 10%, and in beverages 21%. Cadbury Schweppes executives would like to see confectionary margins of 15%, which is the average in the confectionary industry.

Registered in the UK and listed on the LSE, 80% of Cadbury Schweppes' revenues and profits are generated outside the UK. It deals in dozens of currencies, using a number of hedging devices. For transactional currency exposure, it relies on forward exchange contracts to hedge exposure in trading activities. Its policy is to hedge specifically identified transactions, using financial instruments which refer to actual assets and liabilities or firm commitments. These include interest rate swaps, cross-currency interest rate swaps and forward rate contracts. These derivatives, it stresses in its *Annual Report and Accounts 2006*, are used in the normal course of its business. This sets it apart from the use of hedging strategies for speculative purposes. As the company is a purchaser of commodities such as cocoa, sugar and aluminium, it is exposed to fluctuations in commodity prices. It uses forward contracts to give it firm prices in these markets. It also relies on derivatives in debt financing. Of its borrowings, amounting to £2,909 million in 2005, 75% were either at fixed rates or converted to fixed rates by interest rate swaps. Its financial policy in respect

Figure 1 Contribution to revenue and profits of Cadbury Shweppes' regional units, 2006

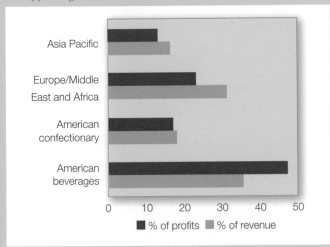

Source: Cadbury Schweppes *Annual Report and Accounts 2006*, www.cadburyschwppes.com

Figure 2 Cadbury Schweppes' production assets by region, 2006

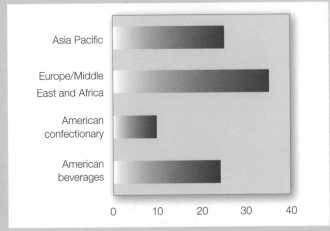

Source: Cadbury Schweppes *Annual Report and Accounts 2006*, www.cadburyschwppes.com

to subsidiaries is to structure borrowings to the trading cash flows that service them, thus enjoying a natural hedge against currency risk.

The translation of balance sheets and results poses translation risks. The company does not hedge translation exposure and earnings, as it views the benefits to be only temporary. As confectionary revenues in 2006 were 32% from emerging markets, translation risk is a continuing issue.

In recent years, Cadbury Schweppes has restructured to slim down its sprawling businesses, and considered whether it should withdraw altogether from beverages to concentrate on its core confectionary business. The arrival of Nelson Peltz, an activist shareholder and hedge fund manager, in 2006 seemed to galvanize the company into thinking about disposal of the Americas Bever-

ages unit. Although he acquired only 3% of the company's equity, the expectation was that strategic changes would occur, and the share price immediately rose, having been lacklustre over the previous year. Concentration on the core confectionary business might cheer investors, but they are looking for improved profit margins, which indicate further restructuring is needed. In these circumstances, a takeover is a possibility. The presence of an activist shareholder possibly makes this more likely, suggesting that managers of the new Cadbury, minus Schweppes, will not have long to improve performance.

Questions

1 In what respects is Cadbury Schweppes' complex structure impairing its competitiveness?
2 What are the main risks faced by the company in its international operations?
3 How has it reduced risk in its foreign exchange activities?
4 Why did Cadbury Schweppes become a possible takeover target?

Sources: Cadbury Schweppes *Annual Report and Accounts 2006*, www.cadburyschweppes.com; Griggs, T., 'Cadbury's profits rise in spite of product recall', *Financial Times*, 5 August 2006; Jones, A., 'Cadbury to slash 10% of workforce in shake-up', *Financial Times*, 28 October 2003; Wiggins, J., 'Cadbury plans to cut 7,800 jobs and drop "Schweppes"', *Financial Times*, 20 June 2007; Wiggins, J., 'Cadbury's strategy unlikely to keep takeover approach at bay', *Financial Times*, 20 June 2007.

WEB CHECK

Cadbury Schweppes' website is www. cadburyschweppes.com.

Further research

Journal articles

Filatotchev, I. and Toms, S. (2006) 'Corporate governance and financial constraints on strategic turnarounds', *Journal of Management Studies*, **43**(3): 407–33.

Kwok, C. and Tadesse, S. (2006) 'National culture and financial systems', *Journal of International Business Studies*, **37**(2): 227–47.

Books

Allen, F. and Gale, D. (2007) *Understanding Financial Crises*, Oxford: Oxford University Press.

Glyn, A. (2006) *Capitalism Unleashed*, Oxford: Oxford University Press.

Obstfeld, M. and Taylor, A. (2004) *Global Capital Markets: Integration, Crises and Growth*, New York: Cambridge University Press.

Pilbeam, K. (2005) *International Finance*, 3rd edn, Basingstoke: Palgrave Macmillan.

Don't forget to check the companion website at **www.palgrave.com/business/morrisonib**, where you will find web-based assignments, web links, interactive quizzes, an extended glossary and lots more to help you learn about international business.

chapter **12**
INNOVATION AND STRATEGY

chapter outline

▷ **Introduction**
▷ **The elements of innovation**
▷ **Theories of innovation in international business**

  Theories of competitive advantage of the firm

  Innovation in the context of economic development

▷ **Innovation in the national environment**

  Nations and innovative capacity

  Impacts of technology transfer in host countries

▷ **Innovation and the organization**

  The born-global firm

  The research-intensive MNE

  Broadly focused MNE innovation strategies

▷ **Co-operative innovation strategies**
▷ **Managing innovation**

  Creating new ideas inside the firm

  Managing external sources of innovation

  Managing intellectual property rights

▷ **Conclusions**

learning objectives

▷ **To identify the elements of innovation essential to global competitiveness**
▷ **To apply theories of innovation in the organizational and national contexts to gain a deeper understanding of the dynamics of innovation processes**
▷ **To appreciate national environmental differences in the creation and dissemination of new products and technologies, including the role of FDI and government policies**
▷ **To understand the strategies and practices involved in managing innovation in differing types of international organization, highlighting the role of IP in the research-intensive company**

Introduction

M. Torres, a small engineering company in Pamplona, northern Spain, looks like many other SMEs from the outside, its business having been built up by its founder, Manuel Torres. But Torres' talent for continued innovation in diversified industries makes the company stand out. His first business was in the paper industry, in which, after only three years, his designs for new machinery were being exported to five continents. He then turned to the aerospace industry, soon counting Boeing and Airbus among his clients. Such was Torres' confidence that, when the company had only 70 staff, he approached Boeing with his idea for a flexible design system, which was soon implemented on the Boeing 777. More recently, he has turned his talents to the environment, which he sees as offering huge opportunities for innovation. The company is now a leader in wind energy, drawing on technology developed for the aerospace industry. His latest innovation is a desalination plant powered by wind energy, to meet the problem of the growing scarcity of drinking water, an issue close to home in the dry regions of Spain, and also one which is becoming global. New desalination plants, he anticipates, could play a role in sustainable development in African countries. M. Torres is an unusual company, but its guiding philosophy of seeking solutions to needs, both present and future, is one which is at the heart of all innovation.

M. Torres' website is www.mtorres.com

WEB CHECK

Companies' competitiveness depends heavily on innovation to meet the changing needs of customers. In addition to goods and services designed to meet their needs, today's demanding consumers expect the latest technology, high quality, dependability and competitive prices. Product life cycles have shortened dramatically, posing challenges for managers to acquire and maintain leads in innovative technology. The company which achieves success with a new product can no longer afford to be complacent, as competitors are inevitably coming up with rival offerings to tempt consumers: they might perform better, cost less, look more attractive, or incorporate more customizable features. Large companies with well-known brands once thought that their size, global reach and large R&D budgets would ensure them continued market dominance, but, increasingly, world-beating innovations are springing up from small creative enterprises such as M. Torres. Moreover, the developed country dominance of technological innovation is giving way to a more dispersed scene, as individuals and firms from developing countries are unleashing new creativity. Creating a new, market-winning product or technology in this competitive environment poses new challenges, but also offers huge potential rewards. This chapter aims to illuminate the innovation process in international business, including environmental, strategic, organizational and managerial dimensions.

We begin by identifying the key elements of innovation. Next we look at theories of innovation in the context of firms, industries and national economies. We then focus on national differences in innovation, including cultural and institutional factors which impact on R&D in different locations. Technology transfer has become an important force in developing and emerging economies, closely associated with FDI and manufacturing under licence. With globalization, opportunities for technology transfer abound, but gains are unevenly shared. We uncover why some countries and firms benefit more than others. Managing innovation, both within the firm and in relation to external partners, is key to maximizing innovation potential. Once considered a specialized function, innovation is now recognized as a potent dimension of corporate culture which permeates the entire organization. Innovation is closely linked with entrepreneurship and is fostered by different strategies and policies depending on the size of the firm and industry. The research-intensive firm can be distinguished from the more broadly focused innovative organization. We highlight the crucial role of intellectual property (IP) rights, such as patents, copyrights and trademarks. Managing, protecting and defending IP assets in differing environments has become a major challenge for international business, highlighting issues of ownership and cooperation in sustaining competitive advantage.

plate 12.1 Green energy from wind turbines is rising up the agenda for both governments and innovative technology companies.

The elements of innovation

Innovation: New or improved product or way of doing things, which aims to contribute to value creation for the organization.

Innovation covers a wide range of activities, varying in their depth of organizational impact. Innovation can be defined as any new or improved product or way of doing things, which aims to contribute to value creation for the organization. Not all new ideas or changed procedures are valuable as innovations. The test is whether the new idea can be translated into enhanced value which consumers desire. For example, a new flavoured carbonated drink may be innovative, but if it proves unpopular with consumers, it does little to enhance the company's innovative reputation. By comparison, the sports drink was a successful innovation, which resulted in a number of competing brands launched by beverage companies eager for a share of the new market.

The elements of innovation are shown in Figure 12.1. An innovation may consist of the invention of a totally new product, which requires operational and HR changes. This radical innovation can be distinguished from incremental innovation, such as a series of minor improvements in an existing production process. Incremental innovation is associated with the philosophy of continuous improvement in production processes (discussed in Chapter 10). Much innovation is technology driven, especially radical innovations. **Technology** may be broadly defined as the systematic application of scientific knowledge to practical purposes. Important innovations may take place in non-technology activities. A new means of marketing communication, such as community activities, is an example. Moreover, technological innovations require cross-functional co-ordination to transform them into improved market performance. As Figure 12.1 shows, the elements of innovation are interrelated. The launch of a new product, for example, involves consumer research and cross-functional teams including marketing specialists.

Technology: Systematic application of scientific knowledge to practical purposes.

Figure 12.1 Elements of innovation

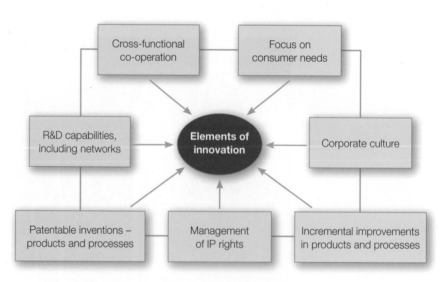

Invention: New product or process which represents a technological leap forward and is capable of industrial application.

Patent: Intellectual property right for inventions, which is granted by patent authorities for a term of years, following rigorous examination; it gives the patent holder the right to exploit the product or process commercially, or licence others to do so, on payment of royalties.

New and improved products and services are a source of competitive advantage. **Inventions** represent radical innovation, which may have a revolutionary impact in an industry. An example is Bosch engineers' diesel fuel injection system (see SX10.1). An invention is a new product or process which represents a distinctive leap forward in technology and has industrial application. Inventions are important as industrial property, and may be protected in IP law by the patent. **Patents** are valuable intangible assets, particularly in industries such as engineering, machinery manufacturing and pharmaceuticals. Application for a patent for a specific invention normally takes place at national level, and may require a long process of painstaking examination, to satisfy patent authorities that the invention is truly novel and represents a genuine leap in technology. Once granted, the patent entitles the patent holder to exclusive rights to manufacture the product, or to licence another firm to do so, on payment of royalties to the owner. For a company with a portfolio of patents, enforcing them against infringers who manufacture copies without permission can be a costly and time-consuming activity, and difficult to pursue in countries with weak institutional frameworks. The MNE which boasts a steady stream of patent applications and income generation from successful patented products is likely to enjoy competitive advantage in its sector.

The MNE's activities in patenting new products are likely to rely on one or more R&D units within the organization or with associated organizations. R&D provides the science and technology research which is necessary to generate new products. These may become patentable inventions or more modest innovations which nonetheless help the company to improve its offerings. A modest improvement that leads to a new feature which can enhance a brand can be a highly successful innovation. Although Bosch has benefited from ground-breaking inventions, it has built on innovation success by continuous development and refinement, meeting changing consumer needs through a stream of incremental improvements.

Innovation goes to the heart of corporate culture, permeating the whole organization, not simply R&D departments. Fostering innovative thinking and creativity is closely associated with entrepreneurial firms, often small companies which have been built around the founder's vision. Engendering this culture is a challenge for larger, more established companies which have become set in their ways. Similarly, when the start-up grows into a more bureaucratic organization, such as Microsoft, it, too, might struggle to maintain the entrepreneurial culture in which its innovative ideas have flourished.

TO RECAP...

What is innovation?

Innovation concerns both new products and ways of doing things, *and* the organizational and cultural environment in which new ideas can be transformed into successful products. Innovation may come from the R&D department of a large organization or a small entrepreneurial firm. Transforming new ideas into value-creating products and services is the key to successful innovation.

Elements of innovation

Of the elements of innovation featured in Figure 12.1, which are the most important for each of the following types of firm, and why?
● Fast-food restaurant, with global franchise structure ● Aircraft manufacturer
● Internet retailer
● Pharmaceutical company

PAUSE TO REFLECT

Theories of innovation in international business

Innovation is a factor in the competition between firms, regions and nations. The firm with a capacity to innovate is in a better position to compete in markets than one which lacks innovative capacity. Theories of the organization, such as the resource-based view of the firm and Porter's theory of competitive advantage, stress innovation as an influential factor. It also features as an ownership advantage in Dunning's OLI paradigm. For regions and nations, innovative capacity is an aspect of the environment which helps us to understand why and how they differ in their development. Some theorists see innovation in the context of stages of economic development of a country. We examine these schools of thought in turn.

Theories of competitive advantage of the firm

Innovative capacity, for example a strong R&D department, is an internal resource unique to the firm. In resource-based theories of competitive advantage (discussed in Chapter 7), the firm with a valuable, imperfectly imitable resource is well placed to gain sustainable competitive advantage (Barney, 1991: 108). Knowledge is a resource, and innovative firms develop organizational capabilities to integrate the specialist knowledge of individuals into organizational competences (Conner and Prahalad, 1996). The firm which is first with new technology gains first-mover advantages, not just in the technology itself, but in winning customers and gaining reputation. However, customer loyalty and a firm's reputation are difficult to sustain in competitive markets, suggesting that innovative capacity is more valuable to the firm over time.

In a similar vein, innovation constitutes a core competence of the organization (Prahalad and Hamel, 1990). Prahalad and Hamel (1990: 83) are adamant that: 'Cultivating core competence does *not* mean outspending rivals on R&D.' They cite the examples of Japanese company, Canon, which spent less on R&D than its US rival Xerox, but still managed to surpass Xerox in worldwide market share. They highlight Japanese companies' ability to draw on competencies in their networks of affiliated companies at lower costs than companies which adopt costly vertical integration strategies. Canon became astute in integrating only aspects of the supply chain which supported core competencies. This sourcing and production strategy envisages a value chain which focuses on customer satisfaction.

Michael Porter envisages the competitive advantage of the firm as emanating from the organization and performance of activities such as operations, logistics and marketing, in a value chain. He argues that competitive advantage stems in part from how well the firm manages the links within the value chain, as well as links with suppliers, distributors and retailers. However, Porter (1998a: 45) also recognizes the role of innovation, defined broadly as both new technology and small process changes, in creating competitive advantage. He stresses that in international markets, innovations may anticipate consumer trends, such as emphasis on product safety. Competitive advantage thus accrues to companies which devote resources to R&D ahead of their rivals, as highlighted in SX12.1 on Martek Marine. For Porter (1998a: 43–7), innovation involves some discontinuity, creating a new situation in which further innovation is unleashed. Any of the following may be catalysts:

- *New technology* – A new product, such as the flat-screen television, is an example, which creates a new paradigm for the industry.
- *New or shifting buyer needs* – When buyers develop new needs, such as a need for convenience food, firms may gain competitive advantage by creating new value chains to meet changing demand.
- *New industry segment* – A new specialized industry segment may be created, which leads to further innovations in the value chain, such as new ways to reach consumers. Porter cites the forklift truck industry as an example. Another is the container shipping industry, which, as SX10.2

showed, gave rise to new logistics arrangements, new ship designs and new port designs.

- *Shifting input costs or availability* – Where inputs such as labour, raw materials or transportation undergo a significant change, competitive advantage can be gained by arranging value chains to optimize benefits from the opportunities. Shifts in global production represent an example of this means of gaining competitive advantage.

- *Changes in government regulations* – Changes in national laws, such as product standards, environmental controls and trade rules, may lead to innovations which yield competitive advantage. Many firms seek technological innovation in anticipation of changing regulations, to be in a position to take early advantage.

Although Porter recognizes the contribution of R&D and market research, which are more extensive in large companies, he acknowledges that innovations often emerge from small companies. The national environment is important in determining the directions which companies take, the resources and skills available to them, and the pressures for change they face.

TO RECAP...

Innovation in competitive markets

Successful firms have nurtured innovative capacities within their organizations and in inter-firm networks, maintaining a focus on their core competencies in the markets in which they compete. They are alert to changes in technology in their industries, customer demands and government regulation, seeing opportunities to reconfigure value chains to gain competitive advantage.

STRATEGIC CROSSROADS

12.1

Martek Marine rides the waves of innovation

Martek Marine, based in Rotherham in the UK, is an SME specializing in safety, environmental and monitoring systems for the shipping industry. Formed in 2000, its three founders had all worked for a large manufacturer in the industry, but had become frustrated by their employer's lack of vision in failing to spot opportunities for new products to address regulatory changes in marine operations. In setting up Martek, their goal was to anticipate rising standards in safety and pollution regulations by developing innovatory products ahead of global competitors. For a start-up which had only £6,000 at the outset, this was an ambitious goal. The complementary strengths of its three founders helped to make it a reality. Paul Luen was an engineer, Mike Pringle was a sales and marketing specialist and Steve Coulson was a hydrographic surveyor with additional marketing expertise. The company now exports to 60 countries, through 18 overseas sales agencies, which were developed in less than four years.

Understanding the legal environment of shipping has been crucial to Martek's success. The shipping industry is regulated internationally through a framework of shipping conventions overseen by the International Maritime Organization (IMO). These conventions are amended regularly, creating a continuing need for new products. Whereas in international law

generally, ratification by member countries may take many years, in shipping law, the procedure has been modified to one of 'tacit acceptance'. This procedure allows for amendments to take effect two years from their communication to member countries. It is thus predictable when compliance will be required for each new rule. Not content with this time frame, Martek's executives take an even longer view, monitoring minutes of IMO meetings to find out what trends are emerging. Paul Luen says: 'We have our ear very close to the ground' (Tyrell, 2007). It has developed the ability to anticipate what will be required a few years down the line, designing products in excess of current specifications, to ensure they are ahead of competitors. Luen also feels that, as an SME, Martek has been able to move more swiftly than larger rivals.

Its first product, TempSafe, was a temperature monitoring system for pump rooms. Besides complying with the latest legislation, it was designed to be cheaper than rival systems, with some added features to tempt customers. Costs were kept down by building as much as possible of the system from standard components. TempSafe's success ensured that Martek generated healthy sales in its first year. Some of the revenues were invested in a database and marketing tools. An aggressive marketing strategy, contacting potential customers directly, has been key to winning sales. While maintaining a focus on technical compliance, market research has aided them in designing products which also take into account customer needs.

The International Convention for the Safety of Life at Sea

(SOLAS) has been amended many times, requiring improvements in safety standards, in which Martek is taking a lead. Its patented Bulksafe system for detecting and monitoring the ingress of water in cargo holds was the first to be approved under new regulations in 2003. Following consultation with naval architects, ship operators and ordinary crew, they designed a system which is simple, relatively cheap, easy to install and corrosion proof.

Martek prides itself on the fact that its entire workforce is focused on 'shared ownership of business goals' (www.martek-marine.com), and participate in an employee share scheme. It has an open management style and corporate culture, and practises principles of continuous improvement (kaizen). It has achieved ISO 9001:2000 accreditation. The company also has a strong outward focus towards stakeholders. It has built up relations with key suppliers, through contractual collaboration agreements. Its business is run on principles of social,

ethical and environmental responsibility. This covers a range of activities from using environmentally friendly products to taking students for vocational work experience.

Questions

- ◆ What are the key elements of Martek's approach to innovation, and in what ways is its innovation strategy linked to entrepreneurship?
- ◆ What are the core competencies of Martek, and what are its sources of competitive advantage?

Sources: Tyrell, P. (2007) 'A well-plotted course to success', *Financial Times*, 4 January 2005; Martek Marine website, www.martek-marine.com; IMO website, www.imo.org.

WEB CHECK

Martek Marine's website is www.martek-marine.com.

Innovation in the context of economic development

This section focuses on the impact of changes in innovation at the level of the nation. It is helpful to recall Porter's diamond model of national competitive advantage in Chapter 6. The four determinants are factor endowments (such as labour skills, natural resources, energy resources, capital and infrastructure), demand conditions, related and supporting industries, and firm strategy, structure and rivalry. Porter classified innovation under factor endowments. However, as Dunning (1993c) has pointed out, governments and foreign investors all play roles in innovation and economic development, which Porter tends to underestimate. International business activity contributes to a nation's accumulation of technology, helping to drive its economic development (Narula, 1993).

Changes in the economic activities of a country's people come about because of some break with the past. Joseph Schumpeter (1942: 83) saw this process as one of 'creative destruction', whereby radical changes in technology bring about qualitative changes. Capitalist economic development, he argued, relies on continuous introduction of new products, new methods of production, new markets and new forms of industrial organization. Capitalist development can be broken down into various stages of growth, which have been explored by a number of theorists (see Dunning, 1993a).

A four-stage process, outlined in Figure 12.2, gives an indication of the key features of the development process which characterizes many recent developing countries. The development path varies from country to country, and no country follows a pattern exactly as depicted in this outline. However, the four-stage outline does show the elements of development which they share to a greater or lesser extent. As can be seen, innovation is crucial to the process. Indigenous innovation capacities interact with innovation-driven investment from FDI, particularly in stage 3. There are qualitative

Figure 12.2 Stages of development (change)

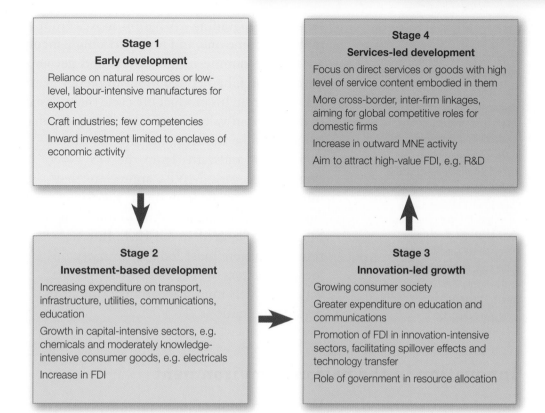

Stage 1
Early development

Reliance on natural resources or low-level, labour-intensive manufactures for export

Craft industries; few competencies

Inward investment limited to enclaves of economic activity

Stage 2
Investment-based development

Increasing expenditure on transport, infrastructure, utilities, communications, education

Growth in capital-intensive sectors, e.g. chemicals and moderately knowledge-intensive consumer goods, e.g. electricals

Increase in FDI

Stage 3
Innovation-led growth

Growing consumer society

Greater expenditure on education and communications

Promotion of FDI in innovation-intensive sectors, facilitating spillover effects and technology transfer

Role of government in resource allocation

Stage 4
Services-led development

Focus on direct services or goods with high level of service content embodied in them

More cross-border, inter-firm linkages, aiming for global competitive roles for domestic firms

Increase in outward MNE activity

Aim to attract high-value FDI, e.g. R&D

leaps between all these stages, and the capacity of a nation to move to more innovative-intensive stages depends largely on its factor endowments and government policies.

Government policies vary in orientation. An import substitution policy is more inward oriented, whereas export-oriented policies are more outward oriented. These different approaches affect national innovative capacity and organizations. Trade policies are also influential. A country which takes a protectionist stance will develop differently from one with few trade restrictions. The country pursuing export-led industrialization usually welcomes FDI. Examples are China and Vietnam. Countries which pursue import substitution strategies are less welcoming to FDI, seeking to retain control over economic development. An example is India. The path of China's development would seem to reflect the stages in Figure 12.2 more closely than India's, although both are among the world's leading developing countries. It is notable that India has had much lower levels of FDI, and has only recently become more open to foreign investors (see CF2.2). India's development has focused less on manufacturing and more on high-tech services, rather bypassing stage 2 in Figure 12.2. China is now becoming more discerning in welcoming FDI, looking for technology gains which will benefit local industries, a shift which is highlighted in stage 3.

Theories based on stages of growth have been criticized as reflecting a Western capitalist model, implying that developing countries' economies and cultures will converge with Western advanced economies (Sachs, 2000). Porter (2000: 20) speaks of economic progress as a 'process of

TO RECAP...

Innovation and economic development

For nations, innovation represents a break with the past, which opens doors to greater productivity and prosperity. The catalyst for innovation is often FDI, which affords opportunities to developing countries to access technology and value-creating processes. Theories of innovation through stages of economic development show how external influences, government policies and indigenous industries interact to create and sustain innovative capacity.

successive upgrading'. A nation moves from a low-income economy to a middle-income one, and finally to a high-income one. To reach the level of advanced economy, it must invest and develop innovative capacity. As we have seen in Chapter 4, notions of modernization can be rather ethnocentric. Vernon, in his product life cycle theory, assumed that American values were tantamount to what it meant to be modern, and that all innovations spread outwards from the US. Now, even ethnocentric MNEs appreciate that innovation can flourish in a variety of cultural environments. An example is Singapore, featured in CF12.1. International managers must look at a variety of location factors which help to shape the ways in which innovation transforms firms, regions and nations.

How does innovation spearhead prosperity?
In stage-based theories of economic development, how and to what extent does innovation play a role at *each* stage in shifting a country to a higher stage of development? Give examples.

PAUSE TO REFLECT

Innovation in the national environment

We tend to think of innovation, especially technological breakthroughs, as the product of talented individual inventors or entrepreneurial firms, which stand out from ordinary, less visionary counterparts. Creative people and firms, however, do not simply spring forth from the air. They emerge in contexts, both organizational and geographical. At firm and national level, crucial factors play a part in identifying, nurturing and directing creative potential. In a later section we look at how organizations can build innovative capacity. In this section, we look at innovation in differing national environments.

Nations and innovative capacity

Nation-specific factors have been recognized as critical to technological innovation capacity. From the 1980s, the notion of the 'national system of innovation' was used to explain the post-war technological success of Japan (Archibugi and Michie, 1997). It will be recalled from Chapter 10 that Japan was at the forefront of post-Fordist flexible manufacturing. A country's national innovation system is determined by a number of factors, as shown in Figure 12.3.

National spending on R&D by both firms and governments is an important indicator of levels of innovation, and also contributes to economic growth (UN, 2006: 103). R&D expenditure as a percentage of GDP in different countries is shown in Figure 12.4. All these countries saw rises between 1975 and 2006. Switzerland, Sweden and Japan have maintained their leading positions, but Finland has seen the most dramatic rise. While formal R&D systems are influential, so too are linkages – between firms, universities and other research centres. Simply spending more on R&D does not seem to be decisive in ensuring diffusion and productivity gains (Freeman, 1997: 32). Every country has strengths and

Figure 12.3 The national innovation system

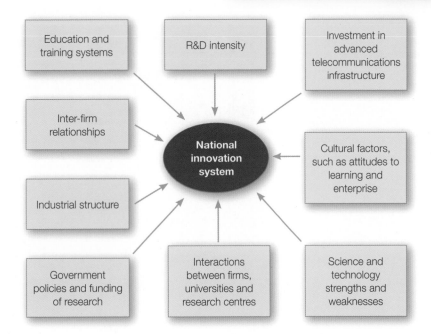

weaknesses in particular fields of science and technology. The world's leading countries in formal R&D expenditure differ considerably in their research strengths, as Figure 12.5 shows. While the US and Japan are strong in most of the main research-intensive sectors, other countries are more concentrated in their specialisms. Over 60% of Switzerland's R&D expenditure is in pharmaceuticals. Singapore, featured in CF12.1, is building expertise in biomedical research, aided by government funding and policy initiatives.

Figure 12.4 Gross domestic expenditure on R&D as a percentage of GDP in selected countries

Note: For 1975, Germany refers to Western Germany (the Federal Republic of Germany)

Source: OECD (2007) Main Science and Technology Indicators, www.oecd.org

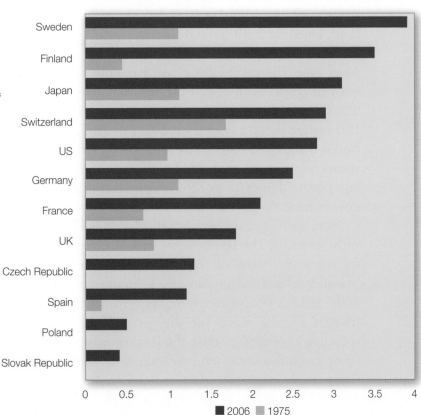

Figure 12.5 The top seven countries in R&D: breakdown in sector, 2006

Source: UK Department of Trade and Industry (2007) The R&D Scoreboard 2006, www. innovation.gov.uk

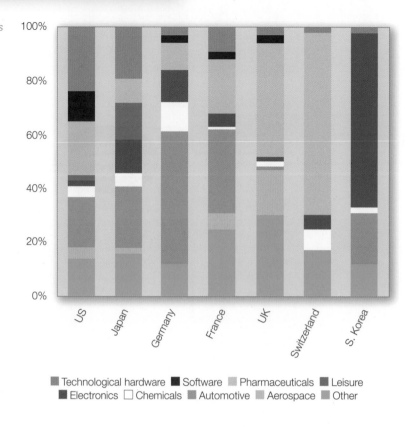

Industrial structure is influential in innovation. The presence of very large companies usually ensures high levels of business investment in R&D. In some industries, such as pharmaceuticals, new products take years to come to market, encountering numerous hurdles, such as clinical trials and testing, along the way. This industry is dominated by large companies and high levels of R&D spending. Many are based Switzerland, boosting Switzerland's overall R&D investment. Where there are many competing domestic firms, pressures to innovate are intense, while weak domestic competition will have the opposite effect. Countries may wish to attract high-tech FDI, but they must have suitable infrastructure and skills within the domestic workforce to benefit from the investment. If these are weak, a country is likely to attract lower technology FDI, and find it difficult to rise up the technology ladder. Singapore's development shows unevenness, with strong infrastructure but weaker innovation skills among the domestic workforce, presenting challenges for businesses and government.

There are huge gaps between the developed and developing world in innovative capacity. The 10 countries with the largest R&D expenditure account for more than 86% of the world total. For developing countries, simply 'opening up' and waiting for new technologies to flow in is not enough (UN, 2006: 101). A firm's strategy and government policies play roles. Technology transfer can be aided (or discouraged) by government policies. Public spending is needed to raise the level of infrastructure and skills, but developing countries are often constrained by limited revenue-raising possibilities, with the exception of those rich in natural resources.

Finally, cultural factors are relevant. A culture which values entrepreneurial activity is conducive to innovation (see Figure 1.3). However, for radical innovations in sectors where formal R&D is vital, other aspects of culture also come into play, highlighting the multidimensional nature of innovation. Formal R&D flourishes in countries with strong educational achievement in science and technology. The highly entrepreneurial cultures are not always those strongest in scientific education. Japan is among the latter, but it has relatively low levels of individual entrepreneurial activity. Notwithstanding, Japanese organizations have built strong reputations in innovation and R&D. Toyota consistently ranks among the top companies in patent applications, indicating the benefits of strong R&D combined with the practices of continuous improvement, which emphasize harmony rather than individualism (Pilling, 2005). R&D leading to radical innovations requires researchers with high educational attainment in science and technology subjects, while entrepreneurial innovators are frequently people with less inclination towards formal education.

COUNTRY FOCUS 12.1 – SINGAPORE

Singapore strives to climb the innovation ladder

Since its independence in 1965, the city-state of Singapore has become one of Asia's outstanding examples of economic development. This small state, of only 699 sq km, which is home to 4.5 million people, now boasts per capita GDP at $32,030. It has transformed itself into high-tech manufacturing hub and financial centre, rivalling Hong Kong. Linchpins of Singapore's development model have been a strong government role and the promotion of FDI. Improvements in infrastructure, low taxation and a sound legal system, including strong IP rights, have lured foreign investors. Singapore trails its regional rival,

Hong Kong, in attracting FDI (see figure). There are now some 14,000 MNEs and affiliates with operations in Singapore. It is in the top 10 rankings in global competitiveness reports compiled by the WEF and IMD (see Figure 6.6). Aware of growing competition from China and India in research-intensive sectors, the government is now focusing on innovation as a source of future competitive advantage. However, decades of reliance on FDI and skilled foreigners have impacted on national innovation capacity. Another factor is the rather repressive political and social environment, which deters local creative individuals, and contrasts markedly with the liberalism shown towards foreign investors. Moreover, rising inequality and the beginnings of political instability pose risks for Singapore's hitherto stable society.

Figure FDI inflows to Singapore and Hong Kong

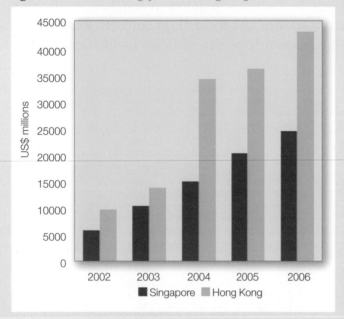

Sources: UN, World Investment Reports 2005 and 2007 (Geneva: UN)

Singapore's political system is dominated by a single party, the People's Action Party (PAP), whose legendary leader, Lee Kwan Yew, was prime minister from 1959 to 1990. Lee is credited with prioritizing social goals of universal education, healthcare and poverty reduction. High-quality education became one of the features of Singapore which helped to attract the FDI. Although prosperity was growing, citizens became accustomed to the erosion of civil society, with state restrictions on the media, religious groups and political opposition. Lee Kwan Yew is still influential, as a 'minister mentor', while the prime minister since 2004 has been his son, Lee Hsien Loong.

PAP dominance cracked slightly in 2004, with two of the 84 parliamentary seats going to opposition politicians. This disenchantment with the establishment is perhaps indicative of divides within Singapore society. Inequality has risen; the income of the poorest 20% fell 15% between 1998 and 2003, threatening the social cohesion which has underpinned economic development. Political dissent is now surfacing on the internet, through blogs, chat rooms and podcasts, which

criticize the Lee family and the government. One of their targets has been Temasek Holdings, the state-owned investment agency founded in 1974 and now headed by the wife of the prime minister.

One of Singapore's attractions for foreign investors in research-intensive industries has been its IP protection, which is the strongest in the region. MNEs are assured that their patents, trademarks and copyrights will be robustly enforced, with oversight of the regulatory system from the government. Its bilateral free-trade agreement (FTA) with the US in 2003 gave protections to US drug companies which go well beyond the WTO's multilateral agreements. The WTO policy is designed to strike a balance between IP protection and availability of drugs needed by developing countries. This is being eroded by bilateral agreements between the US and its trading partners. The FTA also allows for extended duration of US-owned patents, to compensate companies for regulatory delays incurred when applying for their original patents. While US companies clearly gain from this FTA, manufacturers and innovators in the host country face new restrictions on their access to technology.

The US–Singapore FTA has provided a policy backdrop for the Singapore government's aims to create an innovation centre for biomedical research. Known as Biopolis, it complements the country's long-standing strength in pharmaceutical manufacturing. Government funding of $3 billion has gone into the building of state-of-the-art research facilities and the hiring of leading scientists from abroad. Its liberal rules on stem cells, including the cloning of human embryos for research, are the key to its attractiveness. Singapore has three universities, five polytechnics and numerous research institutes. However, local academic research is limited, and local skilled researchers are mostly in lowly positions. Singapore lacks a major domestic drug company.

In a survey of businesses conducted by researchers at the National University of Singapore, 90.6% of respondents expressed concerns over obtaining innovators (Wong et al., 2005). Asked what characteristics would be most helpful, creativity and open-mindedness were the most common replies. In high-tech industries, 81.3% of respondents in the survey said the lack of skills or ability hampered their innovation. However, only 19.6% said they would look in the local labour market, while a majority (52.4%) said they had used people from elsewhere. Many young, educated Singaporeans are emigrating to better jobs in less restrictive countries. Meanwhile, the government is easing the social restrictions. It is planning two new casinos to improve its lifestyle image, but, like other government policies, it seems to be targeted at attracting well-to-do foreigners. It is launching a programme to attract educated foreign workers from elsewhere, hoping to add 2 million to the population by 2020. However, this policy has been criticized as jeopardizing the chances of talented local people.

For young people looking for employment, working for a foreign MNE or in the public sector looks easier and more attractive than forming their own business. However, to remain competitive, the country needs both entrepreneurial businesses and home-nurtured innovation. Government policies have been ambivalent: it has prioritized education, but its favourable treatment of foreign MNEs has discouraged local entrepreneurs and innovators, weakening national innovation capacity. Rising inequality and disenchantment with the long-ruling political establishment are creating uncertainties in society, which threaten to disrupt social cohesion.

Questions

◆ In what ways has Singapore's economic development model weakened national innovative capacity? Does a lack of home-grown innovators matter?

◆ How sustainable is Singapore's combination of a market economy and authoritarian political rule?

◆ What recommendations would you make to the Singapore government to maintain global competitiveness?

Sources: Wong, P., Ho, Y. and Singh, A. (2005) 'Singapore as an innovation city in East Asia: An exploratory study of the perspectives of innovative industries', World Bank Policy Research Working Paper no. 3568, April 2005; Burton, J., 'Singapore goes back to its roots for skilled staff', *Financial Times*, 2 August 2007; Burton, J., 'Straits under strain: why inequality is centre stage in Singapore's election', *Financial Times*, 4 May 2006; Burton, J., 'Singapore detains opposition leader after election', *Financial Times*, 8 May 2006; Burton, J., 'Singapore aims to be a biotechnology hub', *Financial Times*, 10 June 2005; UN, World Investment Reports 2005 and 2007 (Geneva: UN); US Trade Representative (2003), The US-Singapore FTA, www.ustr.gov.

WEB CHECK

For information about Singapore, click on *Singapore* in the country list on the IMF's website, www.imf.org.

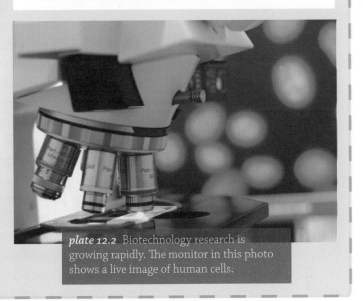

plate 12.2 Biotechnology research is growing rapidly. The monitor in this photo shows a live image of human cells.

> **Innovation: can policies really make a difference?**
> It is often said that innovators, like entrepreneurs, are 'one-off', creative individuals who are 'born, not bred'. Hence, policies can ultimately have little impact in raising a country up the innovation ladder. Do you agree or disagree with this view, and why?
>
> *PAUSE TO REFLECT*

Impacts of technology transfer in host countries

Industrialization involves the adoption of new technologies which are transformed through capital investment and organizational changes. The difference between developing and developed countries is often referred to as the 'technology gap', as the developing countries have limited access to the technologies which can lead to higher value industries. Hence, they seek technology transfer from external sources. Technology comprises both 'codified' and 'tacit' components. Codified knowledge consists of the tangible elements such as designs, specifications and machinery, which are often the subject of licence agreements. Tacit knowledge includes the skills and organizational arrangements with which to produce new products. A blueprint represents more than its outward appearance, as understanding how it was designed is integral to understanding how it can be copied and adapted. Knowledge as well as technology can be seen as ownership advantages which are complex and, to a significant extent, tacit (Kogut and Zander, 2003).

Technology transfer typically involves transfer from companies in the developed world to host countries in industrializing and developing coun-

Codified knowledge: Tangible elements of knowledge, such as products, designs and specifications.

Tacit knowledge: Intangible elements, such as skills and know-how, which help in the understanding and application of the tangible elements.

tries. However, late industrializing countries, such as Japan, South Korea and Taiwan, have themselves become sources of the transfer of manufacturing technology to other countries. The greater the tacitness of the technology, the more difficult it is for host countries to benefit from its transfer. A country's absorptive capacity depends crucially on the relevant knowledge and skills of the labour force, as local people must have competence in applying the technology in operations.

Technology transfer occurs through differing channels, or 'modes', shown in Table 12.1. These are capital goods imports, licensing, FDI, strategic alliances and joint ventures. *Capital goods imports* offer limited scope for technology benefits and depend on embodied technology. Imports of machinery and equipment which embody advanced technology have played a role in Hong Kong and Singapore. The transfer of tacit components is not easily facilitated in imports of capital goods. Therefore, high levels of technological expertise, as possessed by Hong Kong and Singapore, are needed to convert this embedded technology to commercial advantage. *Technology licensing* has played an important role in the early phase of industrialization in South Korea, India, Brazil and Japan. In this arrangement, a firm acquires a licence to use technology, including the payment of royalties and fees to the owner. In its post-war development period in the 1950s and 60s, Japanese firms gained access to technology through licences from foreign owners, negotiated by government departments, mainly the Ministry of International Trade and Industry (MITI), which also controlled imports (Johnson, 1982; Francks, 1992). MITI's policy of suppressing imports of finished goods and allowing duty-free imports of modern technology and machinery greatly aided the development agenda (Johnson, 1982: 217). MITI negotiated for the import of a single version of heavy machinery, together with a licence to produce copies. More recently, South Korea has demonstrated the potential of licensing for the host country. South Korea's spending on licences for technology imports grew tenfold from 1982 to 1991, its period of rapid economic growth (Mowery and Oxley, 1997).

Table 12.1 Channels of technology transfer

Mode	Description	Benefits for host country	Drawbacks for host country
Capital goods imports	Import of machinery and equipment with embodied technology	Useful in early industrialization; limited technological skills needed to operate	Limited potential for furthering the technology locally
Technology licensing	Host firm obtains a licence from owner of technology, and pays royalties and fees to owner	Greater potential for local users than embodied technology; spillover effects possible	Often older technology than FDI; may offer little scope for innovation and interaction with owner
FDI	Equity investment, such as wholly owned subsidiary; often greenfield site	Opportunities for local skilled workers and managers to work alongside inward investor; spillover effects; local supplier involvement; more advanced than licensed technology	Competition created may be detrimental to local producers in the same industry
Joint venture and strategic alliance	Two or more partners agree to a shared project, with equity contribution in the case of a joint venture	Pooling of technology, know-how and management expertise; reliable enforcement of IP rights attracts partners with key technology	Partner who owns the key technology may guard ownership tightly, especially in a weak legal environment

As technological advancement has gathered pace, *FDI* has become an important technology transfer. In this situation, the foreign investor usually undertakes capital investment, such as a greenfield project, including skilled managers from its head office. Local staff employed in these operations gain skills and knowledge from 'learning by doing', which help them to adapt products for local markets and to develop products themselves. The extent to which they gain innovative capacity depends on the country's education, training and indigenous research levels. Spillover effects include linkages with local firms, for supplies and services. As Chapter 10 highlighted, suppliers often develop technological specialisms in conjunction with foreign investors, benefiting both partners. Foreign investors, however, have become wary of their core technology finding its way to firms which then become competitors. On the other hand, Japanese FDI in the US, for example in car manufacturing, is an example of innovation gains from studying consumer markets at first hand and responding to consumer needs.

Joint ventures and *strategic alliances* also provide opportunities for both partners. However, in these arrangements, as in FDI, the benefits for foreign investors and local hosts depend on relations between the partners. SX12.2 illustrates the ways in which two foreign firms formed a strategic alliance to bring technological solutions to Indian customers.

For joint ventures in developing countries, the technology tends to be on the side of the more technologically advanced partner. Foreign car manufacturers in China have found that, as Chinese firms acquire two or more joint venture partners, their commitment to any given project may be uncertain. In the worst circumstances, technology may leak to local competitors. These situations pose the greatest risk that proprietary technology will be jeopardized. The legal protection afforded to IP is likely to be weakly enforced, especially when the aggrieved firm is a foreign company. An independent legal system based on the rule of law is an important aspect of the business environment for potential foreign entrants, as CF12.2 shows. Developing countries now recognize that the legal system, including IP protection, is crucial in their quest to reap gains from FDI in high-tech industries. Bypassing proprietary technology by seeking open technological solutions is another possibility available in some sectors, as the case of Amadeus indicates.

> **TO RECAP...**
>
> **Channels of technology transfer**
>
> Technology transfer takes place through the import of capital goods, licensing, FDI, and joint ventures and strategic alliances. The host country hopes to gain not just specific technology, but the capacity for further innovation which will lead to gains for local firms. However, its absorption capacity depends on the capacities within its national innovation system. Attracting FDI in high-tech and complex industries also depends on the levels of legal protection for intellectual property.

STRATEGIC CROSSROADS

12.2

Amadeus strikes a new chord with customers

Amadeus started life in 1987 as a reservations platform organized by three European airlines, Air France, Iberia and Lufthansa. It grew to become a publicly listed global distribution system (GDS) company, serving a customer base of mainly traditional travel agents, but, in 2005, was sold to two private equity funds. Its core business was distributing travel providers' products to travel agencies and airline offices. Rapid changes taking place in the travel industry include the rise of online retail travel agents, direct online booking by airlines and the growth of low-cost carriers. Travel has become the largest e-commerce category. These changes have undermined the roles of local travel agents and the legacy carriers, compelling Amadeus to re-examine its business. Amadeus responded by broadening its range of services in online travel and improving services through technological innovation. Although it considered abandoning its core business, as some of its competitors had done, Amadeus decided that improving the technology and expanding into new geographical areas would provide continuing scope for growth. Online booking is rapidly eroding the role of the travel agent, but in Africa, South America and India, travel agents are likely to remain important players for many years.

India presented the greatest opportunity, but also posed challenges. Here, the online travel retail market is growing rapidly, and is expected to increase by 271% between 2005 and 2010. There are wide gaps between services available in the cities and those in rural areas. Few Indians have internet access in their homes, but India's urban residents are flocking to internet cafes, which are popular in the large cities. Deregulation of the airline sector in 2003 has aided the boom, leading to rapid growth in private carriers. In four years, seven new airline companies have taken to the skies, competing with the two state-run carriers, which decided to merge in 2007. State-run and private carriers alike now offer retail internet booking systems. Not to be left behind, Indian Railways now has high-speed trains and internet booking, further eating into the business of travel agents.

With its vast network of 487 airlines, as well as car rental companies, hotels and cruise lines, Amadeus embarked on an initiative to offer Indian travel agents a package of services, allowing them to book complete customized holidays for clients, on a new internet-based system which would dramatically reduce their telecoms costs. The travel agents were mostly small traditional businesses. They felt that personalized contact with the client was their major advantage, and they were inherently sceptical of new technology. They needed to be persuaded of cost benefits and new services they could offer clients. Amadeus showed them how the new system would work, deciding to focus mainly on the cost benefits. They were duly won over, but there remained technological hurdles.

Amadeus aimed to reach India's 20,000 travel agents, many in rural areas with no internet access at the outset of the project in 2004. It brought in BT Global Services as a technology partner. BT took the view that becoming acquainted with the various parties was key to the collaboration. Its experts visited the Amadeus data centre in Germany, met suppliers and had discussions with the travel agents themselves, to see how they worked. Dealing with four different ADSL providers in India and setting up satellite dishes for agents outside any ADSL network was painstaking, but even the remote agents are now connected to the ADSL network. In three years, the online system has proved a success with agents. Amadeus is now planning a 'virtual call centre' which will allow agents to access immediately the travel history of any existing customer, helping them to offer a more personalized service.

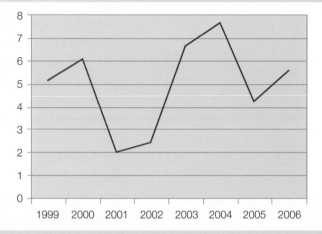

Figure Amadeus's percentage growth in bookings

Note: Number of bookings in 1999 was 372 million

Source: Amadeus website, www.amadeus.com

Travel agents everywhere are struggling to retain customers and win back customers who have migrated to retail online booking. By offering more customized services over a vast range of options, Amadeus is reckoning that there is still a potential market for local travel agents. Its global bookings grew 5.5% in 2006, as shown in the figure. Further growth depends largely on designing its portfolio of services in tandem with continuing improvement in travel technology. It is now increasingly utilizing open technology, in order to develop innovative solutions more quickly, often in conjunction with partner firms. Through continuing involvement with Indian travel agents, Amadeus's R&D and technology portfolio remain firmly focused on customer needs in a rapidly changing travel industry.

Questions

◆ How is Amadeus responding to the rapidly changing travel industry?
◆ Assess the benefits of the new internet-based system to the two Western companies and to the host society.

Sources: Mulligan, M. and Saigol, L., 'Amadeus buy-out takes travel group full-circle', *Financial Times*, 17 January 2005; Nairn, G., 'A flying relationship', *Financial Times*, 13 July 2007; Yee, A., 'Online travellers gain the personal touch', *Financial Times*, 9 November 2005; Amadeus website, www.amadeus.com; *Financial Press*, 'Indian airlines to merge operations from July 15', 11 May 2007, www.financialexpress. com; Euromonitor International (2007) 'India leads growth in online travel sales in Asia', 14 March 2007, www.euromonitor.com.

WEB CHECK

The Amadeus website is www.amadeus.com.

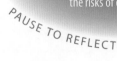

The technology gap
What steps can national authorities in developing countries take to bridge the technology gap? What are the risks of overreliance on FDI?

PAUSE TO REFLECT

Innovation and the organization

Although all firms recognize the importance of innovation, there is little consensus on the best strategies for generating new ideas and transforming them into successful products. Innovation is often seen as shrouded in mystery. Why do some organizations and people come up with world-shattering inventions and others do not? It could be a matter of accident or good luck – the inventor stumbles on a good idea. Much invention does happen in this haphazard way, but most CEOs now believe that it takes much more than good ideas. Strategy and organizational arrangements, as well as creative people, facilitate the process. There is now a growing consensus on at least one issue, which is that innovation involves the whole of the organization, not just the people in R&D and new product design. Much of the diversity in approaches stems from the differences between industries, companies and national environments: a policy which is successful in inspiring new ideas in one company may flop in another. Innovation strategy and management must fit in with the company's overall competitive strategy and corporate culture.

In this section, we look at how differing strategies emerge in differing types of organization. Shown in Figure 12.6, they are the innovative SME which internationalizes early in its life, the large research-intensive MNE which is active in new product innovation, and the MNE which takes a multipronged approach to innovation. Figure 12.6 indicates the main sources of innovation and their outputs. For many companies, a key strategic choice is whether to rely on innovations generated in-house or to buy in technology from other firms, possibly buying the firm outright. A recent trend has been the growth in inter-firm co-operative strategies. Often cited as indicating the globalization of R&D, this trend is examined in a separate section.

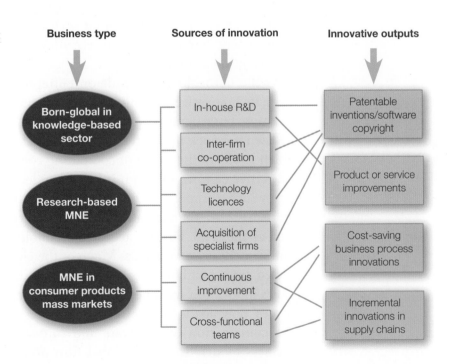

Figure 12.6 Innovation in different types of international business

The born-global firm

In high-tech sectors, new businesses are now likely to seek international markets early in their life. These 'born-global' businesses tend to be both innovative and entrepreneurial, usually centred on a charismatic founder or co-founders, as in the case of Google. These start-ups may spring from any country. They lack the organizational structures and physical resources of large firms, and rely on knowledge-based capabilities and innovative flair in product markets. They become focused at an early stage on foreign markets. Their internally created products are designed for global markets from the outset, but they do not rely solely on in-house innovation. Thanks to their entrepreneurial flair, they are adept at spotting the potential of other firms' innovations, and adapt to new technology and markets.

Internet and IT companies are to the fore, benefiting from the globalization of markets and production. Knight and Cavusgil (2004: 129) refer to their 'international entrepreneurial orientation' and 'international marketing orientation'. As the internet becomes more widespread and accessible, companies in all sectors rely on email and the internet for sourcing, transactions, transport and communications. The internet has become influential in marketing, presenting opportunities for internet companies to sell advertising. Google has expanded its advertising potential by buying YouTube (see SX5.2). Google has evolved a strategy of combining both in-house innovation and acquisition. Its innovative outputs are largely in the area of intellectual property, mainly software, which is copyright. Copyright is easily copied by infringers, and internet companies often become embroiled in copyright disputes. Searching constantly for innovations, Google has hired computer scientists at an impressive rate, with suitable rewards. Larry Page, Google's co-founder, announced a hiring spree in 2007, adding 1,548 new staff in one quarter, despite having no specific projects in mind for them to work on. The rise in costs resulting from this influx dampened profits, but Page was simply convinced that Google needed to 'scale up' (Waters and Nuttall, 2007). Investors in other sectors might have been critical of the management, but an element of eccentricity makes Google stand out as an unconventional company.

As the born-global depends on entrepreneurial and innovative advantages, its innovative capabilities can become dulled as it grows older, larger and more bureaucratic. Newer born-globals, with the enthusiasm of youth, are keen to knock them off their pedestals. Apple is an example of company which is 'old' in the world of computing companies, but has maintained its innovative culture, although it has struggled to win market share in products which compete with the industry giant, Microsoft. Steve Jobs, its charismatic co-founder and CEO, has trusted in exciting new products, such as the iPod, but has acquired technology and ideas from outside, to complement its own talents. Much of the electronics of the iPod was engineered by a neighbouring company in Silicon Valley, PortalPlayer. The iPod's innovation went beyond the hardware, however. Jobs' negotiation of iTunes' downloads with record companies was crucial to iPod's success. The combination of hardware and software amounted to an innovative business model. The born-global firm often starts life with a focus on a

WEB CHECK

Apple's website is www.apple.com.

unique product. As the firm matures, it must evolve a competitive strategy which supports its core competency in innovation. This involves organizational capabilities, responsiveness to changing markets, product adaptations, marketing and distribution.

The research-intensive MNE

The MNE which has internationalized gradually, creating its own innovative products, is closer to the conventional model of the international business. Such companies evolve a strong corporate culture of innovative excellence, based on an array of successful products and brands. They spend considerably on R&D, including background science and technology research. They also spend heavily on marketing, using global marketing strategies with adaptations of products and marketing communications for differing national markets. Organizationally, these companies are usually multidivisional, with numerous subsidiaries and affiliated companies in dispersed locations. Because they tend to be bureaucratic and process driven, this type of company is vulnerable to competition from smaller, younger companies, which are more agile and creative. Smaller companies, however, tend to lack the research depth and marketing resources of the established MNEs, a point highlighted in CS12.2 on the pharmaceutical industry. The 20 largest companies ranked by R&D spending are listed in Table 12.2, which shows that the predominant sectors are automotive, pharmaceuticals and electronics.

Table 12.2 The world's 20 largest companies by R&D spending, 2006

Rank	Company	R&D expenditure, 2006 (£ billion)	Sector	Country
1	Ford	4.7	Automotive	US
2	Pfizer	4.3	Pharmaceuticals	US
3	General Motors	3.9	Automotive	US
4	DaimlerChrysler	3.9	Automotive	Germany
5	Microsoft	3.8	Software	US
6	Toyota	3.7	Automotive	Japan
7	Johnson & Johnson	3.7	Pharmaceuticals	US
8	Siemens	3.5	Electronics	Germany
9	Samsung Electronics	3.2	Electronics	South. Korea
10	GlaxoSmithKline	3.1	Pharmaceuticals	UK
11	IBM	3.1	Technology hardware	US
12	Intel	3.0	Technology hardware	US
13	Novartis	2.8	Pharmaceuticals	Switzerland
14	Volkswagen	2.8	Automotive	Germany
15	Matsushita Electric	2.8	Electronics	Japan
16	Sanofi-Aventis	2.8	Pharmaceuticals	France
17	Nokia	2.7	Technology hardware	Finland
18	Sony	2.6	Electronics	Japan
19	Roche	2.5	Pharmaceuticals	Switzerland
20	Honda	2.3	Automotive	Japan

Source: UK Department of Trade and Industry (2007) The R&D Scoreboard 2006, www.innovation.gov.uk

For pharmaceutical companies, R&D leading to new medicines is a core competence. The process of research, testing, patenting and obtaining regulatory approval in numerous markets is costly and time-consuming. The costs for a single prescription drug can reach nearly $1 billion. Large pharmaceutical companies are some of the world's largest R&D spenders. They depend on a pipeline of new drugs, but most have a few 'blockbuster' drugs which generate the bulk of their profits. Pfizer has relied heavily on Lipitor, a cholesterol medicine, which generated $12.9 billion in sales in 2006, making it the world's bestselling drug and generating 27% of Pfizer's revenues. Pfizer executives are conscious that they need replacements for this profit stream, but there are growing competitive and legal threats to patent ownership. These are discussed in CS12.2. Uncertainty in patent protection in many emerging markets is a risk for all research-based companies.

Having traditionally located R&D activities in their home countries, research-intensive MNEs have begun to look further afield for talented scientists, often in lower cost locations. This globalization of R&D has brought benefits. Specialist research units in differing locations may operate semi-autonomously, outside the bureaucracy of the central management, and in a more relaxed environment. Co-ordination from the centre is necessary, as much research spans different specialist areas. Novartis, the Swiss pharmaceutical company, has decentralized its R&D, a trend highlighted in CF12.2 on Switzerland. Novartis relies on experienced scientists from its Basle headquarters to travel to dispersed research laboratories, co-ordinating and encouraging an internal flow of knowledge.

Pharmaceutical companies have been active in M&A markets. As the last chapter indicated, consolidation generally takes place in environments of escalating costs and the search for scale economies. Large companies are constantly on the lookout for small specialist firms with expertise in specific areas. A breakthrough medicine can transform company fortunes for a small start-up company, such as a biotechnology company. Most SMEs lack the resources to exploit their inventions. The MNE may acquire the company, or, alternatively, they may simply buy the product's patent, or obtain a licence to exploit it commercially.

WEB CHECK

For information on Pfizer's R&D, go to its home page at www.pfizer.com, and click on *Research & Development*.

TO RECAP...

MNEs and breakthrough innovations

MNEs in sectors driven by new product innovation have found competitive pressures growing in tandem with the globalization of markets. The costs of R&D and the uncertainty of protecting IP have led to consolidation among large companies, while there remains potential for SMEs with creative flair, often by selling or licensing technology to a larger company.

COUNTRY FOCUS 12.2 – SWITZERLAND

Is Switzerland losing its competitiveness in innovation?

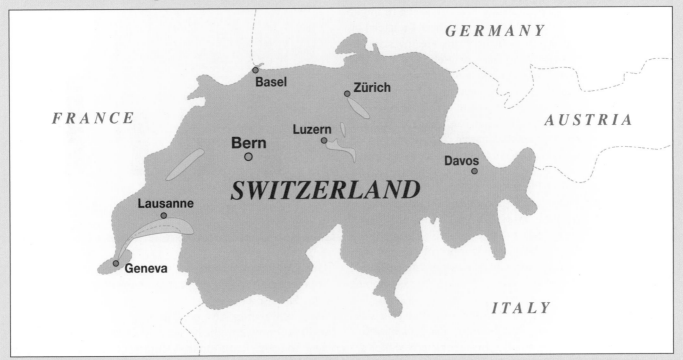

Switzerland has long enjoyed prestige as a centre of international business. Its prosperous, open economy and stable democratic political system have provided an institutional framework, supported by sound financial and regulatory systems. One of Switzerland's strengths has been its high-quality education, complemented by excellence in science and technology R&D, especially in pharmaceuticals, chemicals and electronics. Its research-intensive MNEs in these sectors have helped to propel Switzerland up the competitiveness league tables. Now, other European countries, such as Sweden and Finland, are charging forward in innovation, causing concern that Switzerland could be losing its competitiveness. Somewhat worryingly for the Swiss, economic growth has been stagnant for 15 years, and, as Figure 1 indicates, forecasters predict little improvement.

Switzerland is the world's oldest democracy. It prides itself on its federal political system, based on lean central government with considerable decentralized authority residing in the 26 cantons, each with its own parliament. Relationships between these power centres can be complex, calling for co-ordination and making efficiencies difficult to achieve. Federal government spending has been rising, particularly to fund healthcare and pensions for an ageing population. Not in the EU, Switzerland is surrounded by EU member states, which are its main trading partners, and with whom it has bilateral trade agreements. The Swiss have been proud of their independent position, voting only in 2002 to join the UN. However, they are finding that their somewhat sheltered domestic economy is hampering economic growth. Lack of competition in domestic sectors has become a concern, as is the discouraging environment for entrepreneurial SMEs.

Figure 1 Switzerland's real GDP growth

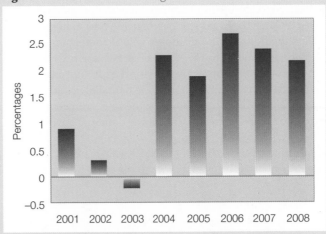

Note: Forecasts for 2007 and 2008

Source: The Economist, Switzerland profile, 19 January 2006, www.economist.com

Switzerland's traditional strength has been in its research-intensive global companies, such as Novartis and Roche. The country's higher education system, while small in size, is strong in basic science. Companies and government authorities have prioritized basic research. Swiss firms spend 10% of their R&D budgets on in-house basic research. Public funding for R&D has been channelled mainly into basic science centred in academic institutions. This has tended to neglect the applied science which is central to innovation. In science/industry co-operative agreements, for example, the government funding goes entirely to the academic partner. This system is now perceived as too rigid, underestimating the need for industrial input into innovation. Moreover, government spending on R&D has diminished as public spending has been diverted to social security programmes. Switzerland's R&D strengths are mainly in pharmaceuticals and electronics. Swiss MNEs in these sectors have reduced their domestic spending on R&D, choosing to invest abroad, as Figure 2 shows. This strategy is largely explained by the forces of globalization as Swiss firms are investing in research capabilities nearer to large markets. Most of this funding is targeted at European and American affiliates, but investment in Asia now rising. The weakening in domestic R&D, particularly in business-focused research, is now perceived as damaging competitiveness, especially in contrast to Sweden and Finland, which have been more dynamic. The number of US patents obtained by Swiss residents, taken as an indication of innovation, has decreased slightly since 1990, while Finns have tripled their number (see Figure 3).

Despite its well-known MNEs, most firms in Switzerland are small – 90% of firms have fewer than 10 full-time employees. Although it is recognized that entrepreneurial SMEs have much innovation potential, the business environment has not been favourable to them. High costs, including start-up costs and financing, have deterred many small firms. However, biotech SMEs have seized the opportunities presented by close proximity to global pharmaceutical companies for research collaboration and product development. There is also collaboration between SMEs and the universities. In some cantons, SMEs are given incentives, such as cheap sites and lower tax rates for new firms. By 2006, there were 137 biotech companies and 81 biotech suppliers operating in Switzerland. About one in every three IPOs on the Swiss stock exchange is now in life sciences.

Perhaps ironically, the country whose companies, such as Nestlé, have been at the forefront of globalization is waking up to a weakening competitive position at home. Innovative performance has declined during the period of economic stagnation, and SMEs, which should be the spur to entrepreneurial expansion, have tended to drift in the domestic environment,

Figure 2 R&D expenditure of MNEs in their home countries and in foreign affiliates

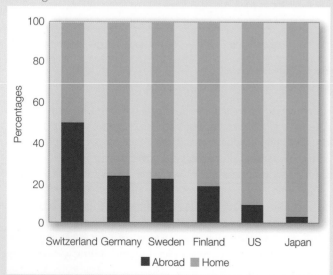

Source: OECD (2006) *Review of Innovation Policy: Switzerland* (Paris: OECD)

Figure 3 Numbers of patents granted by US Patent and Trademark Office to inventors resident in Finland, Sweden and Switzerland

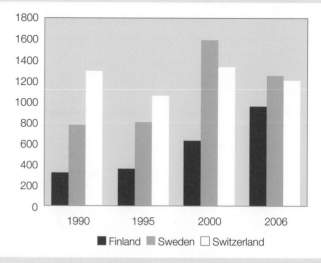

Source: US Patent and Trademark Office (2006) Patent Counts by Country/State and Year, www.uspto.gov

finding little encouragement from innovation policy-makers. The lack of direct public support for innovation in the business sector has also been a factor. Similarly, Switzerland's applied science universities have been underestimated as a source of business innovation, being labelled as second best to basic science research institutions. A shifting of the balance to more applied research and greater encouragement of SMEs would aid businesses to become more competitive globally.

Many of the co-operative R&D agreements funded within the EU framework are open to Swiss participation, and, indeed, these links are vital for Swiss innovation. However, managing these activities is difficult for Swiss participants as the country is not in the EU. Switzerland has been proud of its independence and its strong scientific tradition. Reforms are now needed to retain competitiveness and improve economic growth, but the rather fragmented political system tends to militate against a strong national innovation policy. Decentralization, a bulwark of Swiss democracy, is a factor which can be seen as a strength, but also a weakness.

Questions

◆ What are the strengths and weaknesses of Switzerland's innovation system?
◆ Why has Switzerland lost momentum in innovation?
◆ What reforms are needed within Switzerland to maintain competitiveness in innovation?
◆ Comment on the view that Switzerland represents the paradox of an inward-looking domestic economy and outward-looking MNEs.

Sources: Beck, B., 'A special case', *The Economist*, 12 February 2004; *The Economist*, Switzerland profile, 19 January 2006; Hall, W., 'Tough year and no recovery in sight', *Financial Times*, 4 December 2002; Davoudi, S., 'Biotechs flock to join drugs industry with Swiss listing', *Financial Times*, 17 July 2007; OECD (2006) *Review of Innovation Policy: Switzerland* (Paris: OECD).

WEB CHECK

For information about Switzerland, go to the OECD's website, www.oecd.org, and click on *Switzerland* in the country list. Novartis is at www.novartis.com, where there is a link to *R&D*.

Broadly focused MNE innovation strategies

Even in research-intensive industries, MNEs are broadening their innovation focus beyond new products, and also seeking new ideas from outside. This multipronged strategy is apparent in the consumer products sectors, in which competition is dominated by a few large companies, such as P&G and Unilever. Competition in food and consumer products is not simply between the brands, but increasingly between the global brands and retailers' private labels (see Chapter 8, including CS8.1 on P&G). P&G's ability to keep ahead of the private labels rests on its core competence in innovation, but the company is moving away from an in-house approach to a more open approach. It has cut back its own R&D spending and invested in new product ideas from outside. One-third of its product ideas now come from outside. Some of these come from acquiring the companies which own the technology. P&G has refocused on its core brands, incorporating bought-in new ideas, such as the Crest Spin-Brush toothbrush. The Crest brand has been strengthened by the acquisition. P&G's marketing skills and resources were far greater than those of the small company which invented the SpinBrush. P&G still employs about 7,900 R&D staff (compared to 12,000 at Pfizer), and its CEO remains adamant that the new strategy is not one of 'outsourcing innovation', but retaining a strong core of research expertise (Buckley, 2005).

In global markets, especially in mass-produced consumer goods, innovation may be found in marketing, finance or distribution departments. Often called 'business process innovation', this type of innovation is about finding new ways of working which better meet consumers' needs and also reduce costs. This concept is related to quality theories, particularly continuous improvement and six sigma (see Chapter 10). Innovations taken individually may not seem significant, but cumulatively, they can transform a process. Incremental innovation can be beneficial in adapting to new markets or improving supply chain management. Wal-Mart is credited with innovations in supply chain management, such as 'cross-docking', by which manufacturers of consumer goods deliver products direct from their factories to retail outlets, thus reducing costs and improving response times. As noted in Chapter 10, Tesco's Chinese suppliers are able to pack goods in display units for shipping in containers, allowing them to be delivered straight to stores. Although Chinese manufacturers have built their business models on cheap labour, many have pursued innovations in sourcing and product design, enhancing their competitive advantage. The unsettling message for competitors in other parts of the world is that business process innovation is becoming even more important, especially in the growing consumer markets in emerging economies. Incremental innovation in product differentiation is also a source of competitive advantage. The firm whose products and processes reduce damaging environmental impacts, for example, is building competencies for a sustainable future. This type of firm is likely to rely on both a strong research focus and lower profile incremental innovations which cumulatively deliver significant improvements.

Incremental innovation: Approach to innovation based on a series of small improvements in an existing product or service.

TO RECAP...
Broadly focused innovation strategies
Seeking new ideas from outside and fostering incremental innovations in all aspects of the firm's activities can contribute to competitive advantage.

Innovation strategies adapt to changing markets
In what ways are innovation strategies increasingly driven by customer pull, rather than technology push? Give examples.

PAUSE TO REFLECT

Co-operative innovation strategies

The firm with in-house depth in R&D enjoys ownership advantages. The commercial exploitation of its own patents provides channels for direct feedback to its scientists and engineers on customer perceptions and possible improvements. The firm is thus well placed to sustain its core competencies. This traditional model of innovation, however, is seen as inadequate in many markets. It is costly and inflexible. The firm cannot employ specialist scientists in all relevant research areas, and acquiring wholly owned subsidiaries in different locations for their specialist expertise is costly. An 'in-between' option of collaborative agreements is a means of keeping to the forefront of innovation in several markets simultaneously. While once viewed as a second-best option, inferior to ownership, collaboration is now seen as bringing benefits which are equally valuable. Globalization is often cited as the cause of this changing perspective (Narula and Duysters, 2004). A number of trends can be highlighted:

- Increasing competition in crucial markets, such as consumer goods
- Prioritization of reducing costs in production and supply chain activities
- Increasing R&D costs, especially for firms with centralized R&D
- Shortening product life cycles, as well as shortening technology life cycles
- Increasing complexity of products, especially those with many components
- Increasing integration of sectors which were once separate, such as media and telecommunications.

Collaboration between firms is not new, but it has become increasingly international. Its popularity as a strategic choice, among firms of all sizes and in a variety of activities, signals a shift to more outward-looking strategies. It also marks a shift away from hierarchical firms towards more flexible organizations and networks. As we have seen, companies are not averse to acquiring technology from external sources, through licensing or acquisition. Co-operative R&D agreements involve working with other firms to a greater extent. Although goals and motives differ among firms, added flexibility, lower risk and cost reductions are key aims which they share.

The potential benefits and risks are shown in Figure 12.7. The sharing of the risk and cost of developing new technology can help to speed up the introduction of new products, benefiting all partners. There are two aspects of sharing new technology R&D:

1 Firms may seek complementary specialisms which other firms possess.
2 They may form alliances with competitors in the same research, speeding up the process.

If firms decide to go it alone, the process is slower, and each is duplicating much of the work of the other. What is more, neither can be certain of being first with a successful outcome. By co-operating, both stand a better chance of success, although they will have to settle for sharing the plaudits with a rival. They can reason that in research with uncertain outcomes, 'half a pie' is better than none at all (Narula and Duysters, 2004). Their distinctive innovative competencies will still come into play in designing, producing and adapting products for particular markets.

Co-operative R&D agreement: Agreement between organizations to work on specific research projects, sharing knowledge and expertise.

Figure 12.7
Potential benefits
and risks of
co-operative R&D
agreements

Potential benefits

- Sharing fixed costs and gaining economies of scale in R&D
- Speeding up introduction of new technology
- Sharing financial risks
- Accessing complementary knowledge
- Learning new technology

Co-operative R&D agreements

Risks

- Disagreement on objectives among partners
- Differences in culture and ways of working
- Uncertainty over IP rights, even leakage of core firm-specific technology
- Dulling of core competencies
- Loss of control over specific R&D

The success of an alliance strategy depends partly on the relations between the partners, as Figure 12.7 shows. If they disagree on objectives or do not work well together, perhaps because of a clash of corporate cultures, the co-operative project is jeopardized. Many collaborations which look promising on paper stumble because of poor working relations and lack of trust. In these situations, opportunism may set in. For firms which bring many ownership-specific assets and knowledge to the alliance, a risk is that their technology may be leaked. On the other hand, firms which closely guard their core technology, for fear that partners might take it for their own purposes, offer little potential benefit for alliance partners. Hence, the balance must be struck between give and take, ensuring that each partner has a stake in making it work. Ideally, each side should perceive that the investment in resources is balanced by a potential benefit for the firm.

Co-operative agreements cover differing organizational arrangements and goals. They vary from fluid collaborations involving numerous participants to highly integrated agreements involving equity ownership. Equity and non-equity agreements are shown in Figure 12.8. The choice of agreement depends on the strategic goals of the partners. The joint venture (discussed in Chapter 7) may be designed to pursue collaborative research. A possible risk is that ownership of new technology might pass to the joint venture company. This could be a good thing for development goals in the host country, but the partner company which contributed the bulk of the core research capability might feel aggrieved. A partner may license the joint venture to use its technology, thus retaining ownership advantages, as Figure 12.8 indicates. The Sony Ericsson joint venture has proved successful, combining the complementary technological expertise of the two companies – Sony on the media side and Ericsson on the telecommunications side.

A non-equity agreement is a less risky alternative if core technology needs to be guarded. As Figure 12.8 shows, there are numerous options. The joint research agreement is popular among companies with complementary specialist research competencies. For example, Whirlpool, which manufactures washing machines, has collaborated with P&G, which makes a variety of detergents and fabric conditioners. Whirlpool's vice president has said: 'When choosing partners for strategic alliances, we focus on parallel industries. Products that are used with our products, that rely on our products – those that really get us to touch the consumer – help us to innovate. Fabric, chemical and food manufacturers are the companies that make products that touch our customers' (Johnson, 2004).

Sony Ericsson's website is www.sonyericsson.com. Click on *corporate home* for corporate information.

WEB CHECK

Figure 12.8 Equity and non-equity R&D agreements

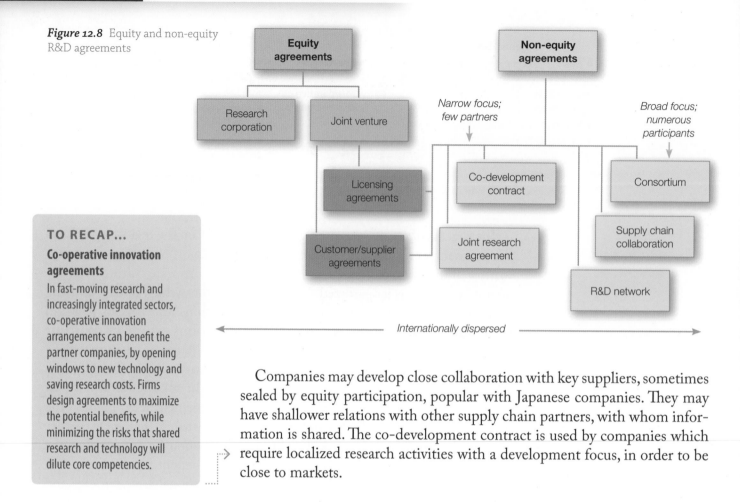

Companies may develop close collaboration with key suppliers, sometimes sealed by equity participation, popular with Japanese companies. They may have shallower relations with other supply chain partners, with whom information is shared. The co-development contract is used by companies which require localized research activities with a development focus, in order to be close to markets.

Managing innovation

Most managers probably feel that their company 'could do better' in innovation. Simply telling existing staff to be more innovative is ineffective, and managers are often unsure what needs to be done to generate new ideas. One of the first lessons they learn is that they can only create better systems and conditions in which innovation can flourish; they cannot actually make it happen. Innovation can come from external as well as internal sources, which are interdependent, as shown in Figure 12.9. Managing innovation therefore requires oversight of how the relevant policies and activities blend into a coherent whole.

Creating new ideas inside the firm

A corporate culture of openness to new ideas fosters innovation. Large organizations tend to become bureaucratic and inward looking, bogged down by procedures. Employees in this environment are focused on roles and responsibilities. They are not encouraged to think creatively, just follow directions from above them in the hierarchy. Indeed, people who stand out as individualists with new ideas and a willingness to ask awkward questions are often seen as misfits in the large organization. However, this type of person is likely to be more innovative, as disruption of the status quo is a key aspect of innovation. Hence, hiring people who do not fit the corporate culture could help to generate new ideas. But this step in itself is only a start.

Figure 12.9 Internal and external aspects of managing innovation

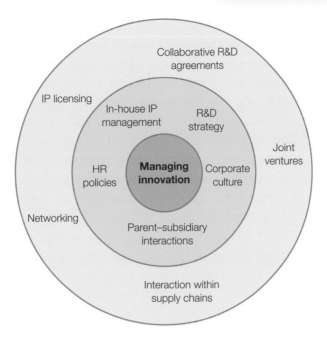

A culture of receptiveness to new ideas must follow, or the fledgling creative talent will soon be thwarted by the entrenched bureaucracy and vested interests in powerful positions.

On the other hand, large numbers of creative employees can pose challenges for HR managers. As highlighted earlier, Google has rapidly increased its workforce, from 2,292 in 2004 to 13,786 by July 2007, aiming to obtain the very best scientific and creative talent available. A workforce dominated by creative and intense people can be unsettling and chaotic. Google's HR director says: 'We kind of like the chaos' (*The Economist*, 1 September 2007). Not all employees like this environment, which is outwardly informal, but can feel uncomfortable to some, especially for new employees who are given little idea of where they are to work and what they are meant to do. He goes on: 'Creativity comes out of people bumping into each other and not knowing where to go' (*The Economist*, 1 September 2007). However, the creation of new ideas inside the company has been disappointing. Its big innovations, such as YouTube, have been acquisitions. Employees are tempted to leave the company when they have served long enough to take up their share options, as happened to Microsoft in the 1980s, often to move to a newer firm.

Long-term innovation capacity within the organization involves a constant willingness to change – in products, ways of doing business and organizational structure. M. Torres, featured in the opening vignette, is an example of an SME in which the stream of innovations comes almost entirely from within the firm. It is often said that the adaptive organization aims to make its current thinking obsolete before competitors do it for them (Hamel and Prahalad, 1994). The surest way to sustain innovation is to build core competencies which nurture innovation and, importantly, transform new ideas into added value. A work environment which fosters a problem-solving approach in individuals and teams allows new ideas to flourish. If each individual and team is imbued with organizational goals and feels a responsibility to meet the challenges posed by competitors, this becomes a powerful motivating force. HR systems need to support this approach, providing, for example, suitable rewards for those whose ideas have brought success.

There are differences in managing R&D as opposed to non-technological innovation. Organizations with huge R&D budgets, such as Novartis or Intel, rely on 'technology push' to systematize research. Companies which rely on proprietary technology gain advantage from their exclusivity, and tend to internalize core R&D. They need new products based on cutting-edge research, backed up by patents covering essential elements, to prevent competitors from utilizing their technology. However, it is becoming harder to guarantee advantages flowing from ownership-specific technology assets. As product life cycles become shorter and technology becomes standard in a short space of time, competitors can tap into technology in markets, making it difficult for originators to sustain a technological lead. Research-intensive companies, therefore, focus on building the competencies which will sustain innovation, which are more difficult for competitors to replicate than individual technologies. The example of Kodak in CS12.1 shows the speed at which technology can make a business model obsolete.

Many companies now perceive that competitive advantage in non-technological innovation is therefore becoming more important. Much of this type of innovation is 'customer pull' innovation, focusing on the 'how' rather than the 'what' of innovation. It can be in elements of the business model which surround the core technology, such as manufacturing, logistics, marketing and finance. Dell (discussed in CS10.2) built core competencies on customization and interaction with the client. When customer relations deteriorated, its competitive advantage began to evaporate. Having in place adaptable systems and processes which can encourage the opportunities for more customer-oriented innovations creates competitive advantage which is potentially more sustainable than that based on new products which soon become industry standard.

TO RECAP...

Creating innovation from within

Building and maintaining core competencies in innovation helps to sustain competitive advantage. Many companies are broadening from research-based innovation to non-technological innovation, which is less dependent on proprietary assets.

Case study 12.1: Kodak – a new business model for the digital age

In just a few years, Eastman Kodak witnessed the global collapse of its traditional film and camera business, which was swept away by digital cameras. Although disruptive innovation is an inevitable feature of business, the rise of digital cameras has been remarkably rapid, destroying a multibillion-dollar film industry. Following the introduction of digital cameras into consumer markets in 1999, Kodak realized that its 125-year-old business would have to adapt to the new technology, but the new cameras were expensive, and it reckoned on continuing healthy profits from its traditional business. In particular, it assumed that there would be little change in China and other emerging markets for many years. This misjudgment brought the company to the brink of ruin. It belatedly launched a strategy to reinvent Kodak as a digital company, realizing time was swiftly running out.

Kodak became best known for its iconic little yellow boxes of celluloid film, which became one of the world's most profitable consumer products. Film, paper and chemicals were the core of the business. In this highly capital-intensive industry of a few players, profit margins could be over 50%. From the introduction of expensive digital cameras in late 1999, sales of film started to plummet. They dropped 10% annually after 2000, falling 30% in 2004. Yet, in 2003, Kodak still operated a global network of factories producing film and employing 69,000 people, a reduction of only 700 from the previous year. Alarm signals started to sound in 2004, as the company could see that its film business, which accounted for 70% of its sales, was rapidly evaporating. A new CEO, Antonio Perez, who arrived in 2005 from Hewlett Packard, was faced with a crisis (see figure). He immediately called for job cuts and reductions in manufacturing capacity by about two-thirds. A strategy for the transformation of the business was launched. It would be difficult for Kodak to make up the time lost, and it had to compete against entrenched camera and electronics makers such as Sony, HP, Canon and Nikon. Late in joining the revolution, it needed to formulate a digital strategy from scratch. Most important, it would need to quickly build up

Figure Kodak's net earnings

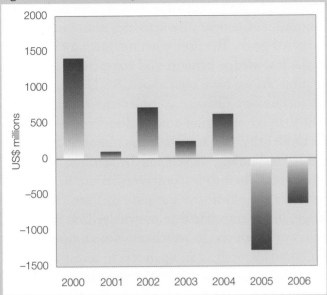

plate 12.3 Digital cameras, which have fallen rapidly in price, have transformed family photo-taking.

Source: Kodak Annual Report 2006, www.kodak.com

a range of products to generate profits which would offset the losses being incurred in its traditional business. This was a mammoth challenge in a market with formidable competitors, where margins were much thinner than it had become accustomed to in traditional photographic products.

Although the situation looked bleak, there were some causes for optimism. Kodak was a respected brand, especially in the US market. It introduced digital cameras aimed at this market, including holiday-makers and families wanting products in the low-to-middle price range. Kodak's researchers had been active in digital technology for 20 years, accumulating a portfolio of IP rights. Perez was keen to turn these underexploited assets into products which would enhance the brand. Kodak became one of the first companies to spot a gap in the market for consumers to turn their stored pictures into prints quickly, easily and cheaply. Given his background at Hewlett Packard, with its strength in printers, Perez saw the benefits of a range of printing products to complement paperless pictures. Kodak has pioneered easy-to-use home printers with 'docking' facilities for cameras. It also introduced self-service kiosks in shops and an online printing service. Acquiring several print companies has helped to build up the digital printing supply chain quickly. Consumables such as thermal printing paper will not take the place of its little golden boxes, but the new range of printing products has helped to boost the proportion of pictures which consumers print.

Diversification has played a part in Kodak's transformation strategy. Digital commercial printing and medical imaging are both growth areas globally. These are not entirely new areas to Kodak, as the company has a long history in supplying X-ray laboratories and Hollywood film studios. It is now looking to expand into providing hospitals with image archiving software. GE Healthcare and Siemens are big players in this market, but Kodak feels that the growth potential is so great that it can compete successfully. It has opened a medical imaging centre in Shanghai.

Kodak is hoping that its China strategy will now contribute to the turnaround, having failed in the past to see how Chinese consumer behaviour was changing. In the 1990s, Kodak launched 8,100 franchised Kodak Express shops in China, assuming that Chinese consumers would use their film-processing machines. However, Chinese consumers have embraced digital cameras more rapidly than anyone predicted, and the machines are already obsolete. The shops are now selling digital cameras, but many are selling other brands, despite their Kodak franchise. In place of the American who had been in charge of Kodak's China operations, there are now Asian executives, but the place of the Kodak Express shops in the new China strategy looks uncertain.

Kodak's survival plan has been fashioned largely on new products and services designed for the digital age. The company has learned not to be complacent about the spread of new technology. It has also grasped the need for continuing innovation. The stand-alone digital camera is leading to further innovations in technology, allowing consumers to share and display images on different media, such as mobile phones and the internet. Kodak has formed a partnership with Motorola, the US mobile phone maker, to share technology for taking images from mobile phones more easily. Kodak reported a small profit in 2007, but shareholders are not yet rejoicing.

Questions

1 What were Kodak's failings in innovation strategy which led to it being left behind?

2 In what ways does its new strategy stem from its long-standing business strengths, and in what ways it is breaking with its past?

3 How would you assess Kodak's core competencies as sources of competitive advantage in the future?

Sources: Yee, A., 'Great pictures, but where are the profits?', *Financial Times*, 1 September 2005; Roberts, D., 'A shot at a digital future', *Financial Times*, 27 September 2004; Morrison, S., 'Kodak struggles to adapt to digital world', *Financial Times*, 25 April 2005; Allison, K., 'Kodak struggles with late entry to the digital age', *Financial Times*, 2 August 2006; Yee, A., 'Banishing the negative: how Kodak is developing its blueprint for a digital transformation', *Financial Times*, 26 January 2006; Dickie, M., 'China rejects its role in a corporate escape plan', *Financial Times*, 26 January 2006.

WEB CHECK

Kodak's website is www.kodak.com.

Managing external sources of innovation

Co-operation with outsiders can benefit companies in both new technology and non-technological innovation. Co-operative activities must be designed and managed to achieve desired goals. The firm must maintain a clear focus on strategic goals and on the knowledge benefits and competencies it seeks to gain from any co-operation. As we have seen above, R&D collaboration can open windows to new technology. Often, a complementarity of competencies is of greater benefit than co-operation among direct competitors, as corporate goals are easier to identify and any clash in cultures is less of an obstacle. However, accessing technology developed by another company depends on skills on both sides. When their competencies are in different areas, each company must have the absorptive capacity to learn from both tacit and codified knowledge, and to translate this knowledge into the development of new technologies or products. Researchers with an openness to other research areas and methods, as well as an openness to research contributions from outside the company are more likely to foster fruitful collaborations than those with narrow specialisms and methods. Skills are needed in assimilating outside contributions and learning while maintaining a company focus.

An openness to external sources of innovation is also a prerequisite for value gains from external sources in non-technological areas. Ideas may emerge from any one involved in a supply chain, including suppliers, distributors and customers. Customer-focused innovation may be highly local in character, and opportunities often emerge through working with network partners. Companies with limited resources for R&D cannot compete with the large companies on inventions and new technology, but customer-focused, non-technological innovation offers abundant opportunities to gain competitive advantage. Companies headquartered in developing countries, which serve local markets and markets in other developing countries, show creativity in meeting customers' needs, often focusing innovative talents on making do with poor infrastructure, reducing costs, and offering products adapted to local needs at low prices for poor customers.

Cemex, the Mexican cement manufacturer, is an example of this approach. Its extensive consumer research found that in many developing countries, cement is viewed as a consumer product (Sull and Ruelas-Gossi, 2004). Cemex's research showed that building improvements meet not just the consumer's desire for more space, but an urge to create something of value for future generations. Advertising was thus adapted to reflect these social values. The notion of cement as an aspirational product might strike consumers in developed economies as strange, but, for Cemex, helping people to build a legacy for future generations of their families was key to a series of further innovations, including novel ways for families to finance building work. These new ideas also highlight the entrepreneurial dimension of innovation.

WEB CHECK

Cemex's website is www.cemex.com, where all aspects of the global business, including its sustainability policy, can be found.

TO RECAP...

Managing external sources innovation

The ability to assimilate technology and ideas from outside sources, while maintaining a focus on corporate goals, is increasingly seen as integral to sustaining core competencies in innovation.

The innovation culture

What aspects of corporate culture are most important for fostering innovation, and how can managers implement changes towards rejuvenating companies which have fallen behind more innovative rivals?

PAUSE TO REFLECT

Managing intellectual property rights

Managing intellectual property rights (IPR) is a rather specialized aspect of innovation, which is important in competitive markets for a wide range of companies, not just research-intensive ones. In most countries, it is a matter of public policy that inventors be rewarded with proprietary rights in the form of IPR, arming the inventor with a right to sue infringers and providing incentives to potential inventors. As we have seen, countries with weak IP protection raise uncertainties for foreign investors and companies which seek foreign partners to manufacture under licence. IPR cover a number of types of property. For research-intensive companies which produce new products and processes, patents are vital. However, there are other complementary resources which are more widespread, such as copyright and trademark. Managing the range of IPR in an integrated manner enables the company to gain the greatest benefit from these assets. While all have legal and technical dimensions which must be appreciated, taking too narrow a viewpoint on IPR is a mistake. Bill Gates, the founder of Microsoft, highlights the challenges: 'It is no longer simply the legal department's problem. CEOs must now be able to formulate strategies that capitalise on and maximise the value of their company's intellectual property assets to drive growth, innovation and cooperative relationships with other companies' (Gates, 2004). Lawyers, R&D managers, marketing specialists and senior management all play roles in managing IP. Although international harmonization is taking place, IPR remain essentially national in orientation. A consequence is that the legal implications become more complex as the firm's products become more widely available globally. Hence, an awareness of country environments as well as differing legal frameworks is necessary.

The main IPR are shown in Figure 12.10. The patent is the grant of an exclusive right to exploit an invention, which can be either a product or process, for a limited period, in return for detailed revelations of how it works to regulatory authorities, usually a national patents office. The invention must be new and not obvious to those versed in the technology. The period of grant may be up to 20 years. As a type of property, the patent can be

Figure 12.10 The main intellectual property rights

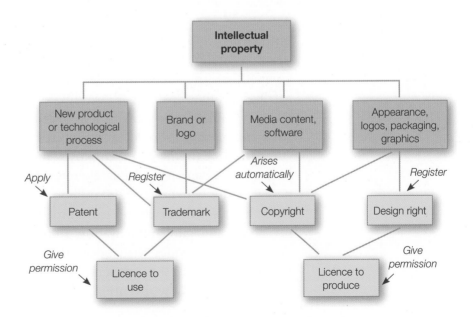

Copyright: Property of the author in a literary, musical, dramatic or artistic work, including software.

Trademark: Distinctive logo or brand applied to a product, which can be registered with national authorities, legally prohibiting its use without permission of the owner.

Design right: Appearance of a product, including packaging and symbols, which can be registered with national authorities, prohibiting its use without the owner's permission.

bought and sold, or licensed to someone else to produce the product. Copyright is the property which resides in literary, musical and artistic works. It includes films and broadcast media. In contrast to patents, which must be applied for, copyright arises automatically. Importantly for technology companies, software is classified as copyright, while hardware is classified as patentable. There is overlap, however, where software is embedded in hardware, recognized in the software patent. Media companies' main assets are in copyright. Owners may give permission for copying, receiving royalty payments in return.

Trademark relates to a distinctive logo or brand applied to a company's products. Trademarks must be registered, usually at a national patent office, and may last indefinitely, so long as the firm is actively using the mark. As with other IPR, the owner is legally entitled to stop others from using the mark without permission. This may be difficult in countries with weak IP protection. Design right is a broad category, covering the appearance of most industrial and handicraft products. It refers to a product's 'look and feel', rather than the product itself. It also includes logos, packaging and graphic symbols such as computer icons. Registering design in the EU became simpler with the harmonized European Design Directive in 1998, which was implemented in 2001. The registered design lasts 25 years, and the process is cheaper and simpler than trademark registration.

As Figure 12.10 shows, there is overlap between the different types of IPR. For a new product, several rights are likely to be involved, including one or more patents, a brand, packaging and possibly software. If a company incorporates software from another company, it must obtain permission from the copyright owner. For example, the Apple iPhone uses Google software. Co-ordinating the many rights, including applications and permissions, poses challenges for IP managers.

IP managers must master both internal and external aspects of IP assets. Internally, patents must be filed for new products. Even when patents are granted, the firm usually has only a limited time in which to exploit the new technology fully. Competitors are invariably working through the process to find ways of producing the same outcomes without infringing patents. Moreover, patents are often challenged by competitors, involving both firms in costly litigation. Firms in research-intensive sectors must devote resources to studying existing patents for information about what competitors are doing, in order to learn from them and also to avoid infringing others' patents. Rewarding employee inventors is an important issue, as employees hold the tacit knowledge on which the firm relies. Incentives and rewards should be structured to retain these inventors in the company. In extreme cases, employee inventors have sued their employers because they were not adequately rewarded for their inventions. One Japanese inventor won nearly $200 million from his former employer. EU legislation has also addressed this issue, broadening the basis on which employee inventors can claim compensation. Implemented in the UK by the Patents Act 2004, it provides that, once an invention is patented, the employee inventor can claim for compensation on the basis of 'outstanding benefit' which flows from the invention, a broader test than that in the old legislation of 1977, under which benefits flowing only from the patent could justify special compensation.

Time is of the essence in the exploitation of new patents, leading many firms to consider licensing the technology to others. Some firms like to keep exploitation in-house, but the more pragmatic approach is probably to look to outsiders to win market share in more markets more quickly. Using external firms can also help to build brand recognition, as international licensing helps to raise awareness of the brand in international markets. A company may be averse to licensing these firm-specific assets for others to produce, as some control over the commercial exploitation is lost. Much depends on the careful selection of partners and the monitoring of their activities, as any lapses in quality can damage the company and the brand. A balance must be found between what activities to keep in-house and what activities to contract others to do. Defending patents and other IPR has become a costly exercise, as patent challenges through litigation have become widespread (see CS12.1 on the pharmaceutical industry).

> **TO RECAP...**
> **Managing IPR**
> Intellectual property is an important element in the firm's portfolio of assets, crucial in research-intensive companies. Given the limited duration of patents, managers must seek to gain maximum competitive advantage from the exclusivity conferred by law, pursuing global opportunities, such as licensing, before the technology is superseded.

Conclusions

☐ Innovation encompasses both a distinctive corporate culture and a range of activities which spur firms and individuals to come up with new ideas which can be translated into new and better products. Radical innovations include ground-breaking inventions which are capable of shifting an entire industry, but gradual improvements to refine and adapt existing products, while less revolutionary, can have profound impacts on a firm's competitive position. These effects can become amplified as firms extend their reach in international markets.

☐ The small, creative firm, often with a 'born-global' perspective, is the source of many new ideas, but translating them into new products usually requires either benefiting from considerable entrepreneurial skill and determination on the part of the owners, or catching the attention of a large company with the resources to penetrate global markets. Large companies face challenges in maintaining a culture of openness to new ideas, as organizations tend to become more bureaucratic with age and size. Large and small companies look to in-house and external sources of new ideas. Possibilities abound for the alert manager as well as for the R&D specialist. Firms linked in global supply chains, in which information and ideas are commonly shared, offer much scope for improving ways of doing things. Innovation strategies, once rooted in technology push forces, are being transformed to consumer pull approaches. This focus does not imply that technology and R&D have taken a back seat, but that R&D activities are integrated into the firm's overall strategy of competitive advantage: the new product, new brand and new marketing strategy are now seen as interdependent, each element crucial to satisfying customer needs.

☐ Innovation can spring from any company or individual anywhere in the world. In inventions of new products and technology dependent on R&D resources, the developed world has long been dominant. The concentration of IPR in these advanced countries has played an important role in the ability of their MNEs to maintain innovation leads. Is the globalization of production and markets leading to the globalization of innovation? All countries have distinctive innovation capacity, rooted in their sociocultural environment, their education systems, levels of scientific and technological research, industry structure and links between businesses and other research activities, such as universities. Government policies are crucial in public support for education and science, and in encouraging young entrepreneurial businesses to bring new ideas to fruition. For developing countries, rising up the innovation ladder can be slow and halting, especially in a context of economic and political instability, which is often a consideration. Historically, developing countries have relied on processes of technology transfer, most recently from FDI, to boost innovative capacity. These processes have produced dramatic transformations of national economies, for example, in Southeast Asia. At the same time, MNEs from the developed countries are awakening to the innovation potential in different locations, whether in subsidiaries or research partnerships. The growth of co-operative R&D is perhaps a key indicator of the changing competitive landscape, encompassing a wide range of organizations in diverse locations.

Globalization of innovation?
Assess the evidence and arguments for and against the view that innovation is becoming globalized. In your view, are the most convincing arguments on the 'yes' or 'no' side of the debate?

PAUSE TO REFLECT

Review Questions

Part A: Grasping the basic concepts and knowledge

1. Identify the elements of innovation, and give a brief summary of each.
2. What is the role of innovation in theories of competitive advantage? In what way can innovation be a core competence?
3. Theories of economic development highlight innovation as a driver. What types of innovation are relevant in each of the four stages which appear in Figure 12.2?
4. What are the key factors in a country's national innovative capacity?
5. For developing countries, what steps are needed to raise innovative capacity?
6. Explain the difference between tacit and codified knowledge in the technology transfer process.
7. Why is FDI usually cited as the most effective means of technology transfer from the point of view of the host country?
8. Describe the main features of the innovation approach of the born-global firm.
9. What is meant by an incremental innovation strategy, and how can it deliver competitive advantage?
10. Explain why co-operative innovation strategies have gained in popularity with MNEs.
11. What are the organizational implications of co-operative R&D agreements, including the risks?
12. How can a company foster the creation of new ideas from within the firm?
13. What are the main IPR for protecting innovations, and how are they acquired?
14. What is the difference between technology push and customer pull innovations?
15. How can a company best manage external sources of innovation to maximize the gains in terms of its own corporate goals?
16. What is the role of licensing of patented products or processes in international business, and what considerations must be borne in mind when deciding what firms should be granted licences?

Part B: Critical thinking and discussion

1. In what ways can government policies help to build innovative capacity, and how do the policy choices differ in relation to different stages of economic development?
2. Why is the large, research-intensive MNE, such as a pharmaceutical company, finding the global competitive environment increasingly tough? (Read CS12.2 before answering.)
3. For the large MNE, assess the relative merits of keeping R&D in-house or acquiring new ideas from external sources.
4. What role is played by SMEs in breakthrough innovations, and how does it differ in differing national environments (give examples from this chapter)?
5. Explain why managing IPR is becoming more multifaceted in the international competitive environment.

Case study 12.2:
Is innovation under threat in the pharmaceutical industry?

The global pharmaceuticals industry is undergoing seismic changes, affecting companies, governments and consumers. From the industry perspective, the former chief executive of Pfizer, the world's largest research-based pharmaceutical company, highlights a 'serious paradox'. He says that 'the potential for [medical] breakthroughs has never been better, but the operating environment has never been more difficult' (Jack and Bowe, 2005). In theory, the industry should be rejoicing. Medical science is advancing in exciting ways, making new therapies possible as a result of mapping of the human genome. Demand for drugs is increasing globally, as people are living longer and more countries are widening access to medicines. In addition, spending on medicines is perceived by all as more efficient than dealing with illnesses through hospitalization and surgery. On the other hand, it is estimated by experts that it could be many years before understanding of the genome translates into more effective medicines. The large pharmaceutical companies have seen thinning pipelines of new products, increased costs, a tougher competitive environment and a more stringent regulatory environment. Moreover, in an era of health consumerism, there is a debate on whether the high prices and patent monopolies of the large drug companies are in the public interest.

All pharmaceutical companies, from start-ups to global giants, seek innovative new medicines which they can protect through patents and which translate into market winners. Of the numer-

ous obstacles along the way, a major one is cost, which tends to deter small – and, increasingly, medium-sized – companies. While much cutting-edge research is taking place within SMEs, they are being hunted by larger companies who either take them over or negotiate licensing deals to take their fledgling products to market. It has been estimated that, taking into account setbacks along the way, a new medicine which reaches the market has probably cost over $1 billion. National regulatory approval must be obtained in each country where the drug is planned to be launched. Meeting differing national safety standards, including issues of side effects, can be time-consuming and costly. The time lapse between patent application and launch has lengthened, thereby shortening the period in which the company can recoup its expenses through sales before patents expire.

The regulatory environment has become highly litigious, especially in the US. A company with a patented medicine can expect challenges to its patents from very early on in the patenting process, any one of which, if successful, can dent its patent protection and thus its profits. Legal challenges may also be mounted against its testing process, which can force the removal of a drug from the market. Merck was forced to withdraw Vioxx, its anti-inflammatory treatment, after indications that it created a risk of heart attack. This move had knock-on effects on competitors, forcing them to withdraw similar products or, like Pfizer, place new health warnings on those still available. In 2005,

Merck faced over 500 lawsuits from patients, relatives, regulators, health insurance companies and investors.

Pfizer, with a net income of $9 billion on sales of $53 billion, would seem to have had few worries in 2005. However, shares plummeted one-third in the course of the year, and the CEO lost his job. One of Pfizer's greatest headaches, like other companies in the industry, is the rise of generic manufacturers. These are companies which manufacture drugs whose patents have expired or are expiring, and offer them in markets at much lower prices than the 'originator' company, whose branded drug then suffers sharp decreases in sales. These companies have become increasingly aggressive, challenging patents to find market openings, and setting up the manufacture of generic products before the patent expiry of the branded drug. Pfizer's cholesterol drug, Lipitor, has seen depleting profits as a result of generic challenges, long before patent expiry in 2009. The chief protagonist in this case has been Ranbaxy of India, which feels it should be legally entitled to produce the drug before that expiry. Generic manufacturers also launch 'at-risk' products before the outcome of their patent challenges, in order to be first to benefit if they are successful in their court battle. The head of Novartis says: 'It disturbs me that the branded pharmaceutical industry is having to spend millions a year just to defend itself ... A patent is society's reward for innovation and it needs to be protected' (Jack, 22 November, 2005).

Teva, an Israel-based company and generics market leader, had revenues of $5 billion in 2005, on a par with Merck. Generics manufacturers have become thorns in the sides of the R&D-intensive pharmaceutical companies, accused of undermining incentives to innovate. Generics are increasing their market share globally (see figure), now representing 54% of drug sales by volume in the US, the world's largest pharmaceuticals market. Generics find favour with government health authorities, health insurers and retail consumers who must pay for their own prescriptions. The aggressive growth of the generics sector is bringing price pressures to bear on brand owners. At the same time, health authorities and private health insurance companies are assessing the clinical and cost-effectiveness of each drug before authorizing it. In the US, private health insurance companies, who control considerable budgets in the absence of a comprehensive national health service, are sensitive to effectiveness and price.

National health authorities operate health technology assessments, which create additional hurdles before treatments can win approval. In the EU, these mechanisms vary between countries, each one maintaining control over its own health policy. The German authorities enforced price cuts on payments by the state health system for Lipitor, and Poland has imposed 13% price cuts on hundreds of brands of imported medicines. The Polish health minister acknowledged protectionism, arguing it was justified as local generics manufacturers stood to gain. This apparent 'health nationalism' has become an additional element in the battle between the brand owners and generics manufacturers. CEOs

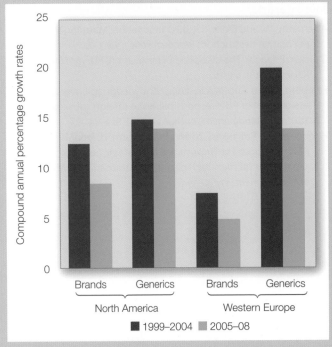

Figure Growth in value of pharmaceutical markets

Source: Financial Times, 22 November 2005

of the large drug companies warn that these moves are damaging to innovation, denying patients access to newer generations of medicines. Facing the threats to their profits and future R&D expenditure, they are pursuing a number of strategies to meet the generics threat.

Four of the major drug companies (GlaxoSmithKline, Sanofi Aventis, Pfizer and Novartis) have developed their own generics businesses, producing 'authorized generics' of their own drugs. Novartis sees no contradiction in this pre-emptive strategy, asserting that it is a way of maintaining market share before competitors move in on drugs with expired patents. They have also launched new patents to gain further protection for drugs, by making modifications and improvements. For example, shifting from a tablet to a capsule would qualify for a fresh patent, effectively extending the monopoly. Generics manufacturers and health authorities bemoan this strategy, but recognize the competitive pressures on the originator companies.

The core competence of the large research-based pharmaceutical companies remains innovation. In 2006, Pfizer's expenditure on R&D was over $7 billion, amounting to 15.7% of its $48 billion in revenues. It fears that the difficult operating environment is undermining its capacity to develop the medicines of the future.

Questions

1 What challenges are intensifying for the research-based pharmaceutical companies?
2 To what extent are these challenges unfair, in your view, and why?
3 How are the pharmaceutical companies responding to the more adverse operating environment?
4 Is innovation threatened by the more competitive environment, or has competition actually stimulated innovation?

Sources: Jack, A., 'The price of pain: how governments are striving to keep a lid on drug costs', *Financial Times*, 9 May 2006; Jack, A. and Bowe, C., 'Shock treatment: drugs companies seek new remedies to restore growth', *Financial Times*, 21 April 2005; Jack, A. and Cienski, J., 'Novartis chief warns on drugs nationalism', *Financial Times*, 3 July 2006; Jack, A., 'Patently unfair? Makers of branded drugs struggle to counter the generic onslaught', *Financial Times*, 22 November 2005; Jack, A., 'One pill makes you larger: a wave of pharma mergers as new drug costs soar', *Financial Times*, 5 October 2005; Pfizer Corp., Annual Report 2006, http://media.pfizer.com.

WEB CHECK

GlaxoSmithKline's website is www.gsk.com.

Further research

Journal articles

Abernathy, W. and Clark, K. (1985) 'Innovation: Mapping the winds of creative destruction', *Research Policy*, **14**: 3–22.

Drucker, P. (2002) 'The discipline of innovation', *Harvard Business Review*, **80**(8): 95–102.

Feinberg, S. and Gupta, A.K. (2004) 'Knowledge spillovers and the assignment of R&D responsibilities to foreign subsidiaries', *Strategic Management Journal*, **25**(8–9): 823–45.

Hagedoorn, J., Roijakkers, N. and Kranenburg, H. (2006) 'Inter-firm R&D networks: The importance of strategic network capabilities for high-tech partnership formation', *British Journal of Management*, **17**: 39–53.

Oxley, J. and Sampson, R. (2004) 'The scope and governance of international R&D alliances', *Strategic Management Journal*, **25**(8–9): 723–49.

Teng, B.-S. (2007) 'Corporate entrepreneurship activities through strategic alliances: A resource-based approach toward competitive advantage', *Journal of Management Studies*, **44**(1): 119–42.

Books

Smith, D. (2005) *Exploring Innovation*, Maidenhead: McGraw-Hill.

Trott, P. (2008) *Innovation Management and New Product Development*, 4th edn, London: Pearson.

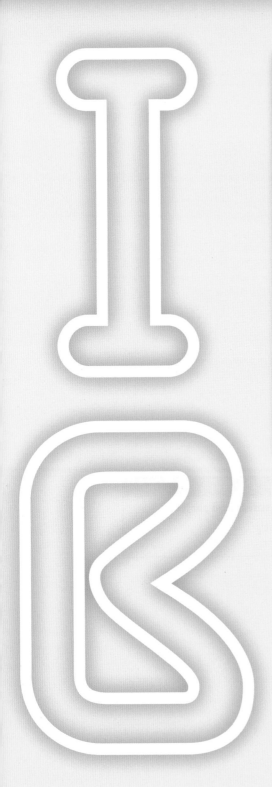

In Part 5, we highlight some global issues confronting business strategy and operations, focusing on business and governance perspectives on managing them in the changing competitive environment. Chapter 13 concentrates on the ecological challenges, including pollution, climate change and environmental degradation. As these issues gather urgency, they are rising up the agenda for strategists, from global and local perspectives. Environmental management has become central to CSR, which is the subject of Chapter 14. In this chapter, the role of the company in society is critically examined in the context of global issues. We look at why and how companies are responding to social and environmental challenges, rethinking their strategies and stakeholder relations. This discussion leads into Chapter 15 on global governance. Themes of globalization and governance are examined in light of evolving rule-making patterns, in which businesses, governments and international organizations interact. A redefining of regulatory frameworks is creating new roles and new responsibilities. This rather fluid situation creates uncertainties, but it also offers opportunities for businesses in both enterprise and governance initiatives.

chapter 13
Ecological challenges for business and society

chapter 14
Corporate social responsibility

chapter 15
Global governance

ECOLOGICAL CHALLENGES FOR BUSINESS AND SOCIETY

learning objectives

▷ To identify the changes taking place in the ecological environment, and their impacts on human well-being
▷ To understand the role of international business in environmental change, in the context of industrialization and economic development
▷ To appreciate the evolving role of national governments and international co-operation in responding to the diverse impacts of climate change
▷ To assess the function of environmental management in a firm's strategy and practice, in developed and developing countries
▷ To critically examine the role of consumers in environmental protection

Introduction

In the spring of 1989, an oil tanker straying miles off course hit a reef in Prince William Sound, Alaska, releasing 10.8 million gallons of crude oil into the sensitive coastal environment. The *Exxon Valdez* disaster caused devastation to marine and coastal ecosystems, and wrecked the economy of what was a fishing community, destroying the livelihoods of thousands of local people. ExxonMobil (the two companies merged in 1999), the ship's owner, has only grudgingly accepted liability, maintaining that the cause of the accident was poor navigation by the ship's captain. The company was legally compelled to pay $2.1 billion in clean-up costs and $1 million in fines to the Alaskan and US federal governments, with provision for later payments if more clean-up was needed. By 2006, these authorities found there were still toxic remains of the oil and 'substantial loss of habitat' (McNulty, 2006). They asked for a further $92 million, which ExxonMobil refused to pay. In actions over their ruined livelihoods, over 32,000 residents brought claims against Exxon, winning damages of $5 billion in 1994. Exxon paid none of this award to these victims, but, instead, chose to pursue legal appeals through the US court system, culminating in a Supreme Court case in 2008, when the damages were reduced to $507.5 million by the Supreme Court. But, 19 years later, 20% of the fishermen have died, and the remaining reflect on nearly two decades of alternating hope and despair.

The *Exxon Valdez* case highlights themes which run through this chapter. First, there are the long-term impacts of environmental pollution caused by human activity, together with the weakness of accountability systems to deal with the physical damage as well as harm to humans. Second, it highlights the issue of businesses' acceptance of responsibility for the impact of their activities on the environment. Industrialization, infrastructure development, transport links and energy production have been central to global economic growth. These activities have all had profound impacts on the ecological environment, affecting our continued enjoyment of life and that of future generations. This chapter examines these impacts, looking at what processes are taking place, what we should be doing about them, and who should take responsibility for dealing with the problems and alleviating future harmful effects.

We begin by identifying the elements of the natural environment. They include the air, land and seas, as well as ecosystems and climate. These elements interact in ways which scientists are learning more about as time goes by. It has become clear that the shift from agricultural to industrial production has been the major factor in accelerating environmental degradation. Expanding scientific knowledge and greater awareness of the damaging changes taking place have led to new strategies on the part of businesses, as well as government action at national and international levels. On the other hand, national governments, especially in emerging economies, are keen to promote industrialization for its economic benefits, despite fears about environmental degradation and climate change. Are the goals of modern consumer society compatible with society's wishes to rein in environmental harm? Businesses hold many of the answers. International businesses, large and small, are responding with innovation, management initiatives and a focus on environmental performance.

Elements of the natural environment

Ecology: The relationship between organisms and their environment, including the changes in their distribution and numbers.

Ecosystem: A complex set of relationships among living organisms and the habitat which sustains them.

Biodiversity: A variety of living organisms and species co-existing in the same habitat.

The natural environment has long been a subject of study, by scientists and amateur enthusiasts alike. They look not just at individual organisms, but at the relationship between organisms and their environment, traditionally referred to as ecology. A widening interest in ecology has led to the study of the distribution and abundance of organisms, as well as the broad relationships among organisms in their habitats, known as ecosystems. An ecosystem is complex, consisting of living creatures such as people, plants, animals and microorganisms, and also the water, soil and air which sustain them. If all the elements of the ecosystem are in balance, it is said to be 'sustainable', indicating that each organism is able to reproduce itself. Usually, such an ecosystem will exhibit biodiversity, which is a variety of living organisms and species co-existing in the same habitat. Ecosystems constantly undergo changes, many of them natural or climatic, but, increasingly, changes are due to human activity, such as building factories, roads and cities. We tend to think of an ecosystem as an area such as a forest, with its distinctive wildlife and habitat. The concept now covers new phenomena, such as the 'urban ecosystem' and the 'global ecosystem'. Although the latter might seem far-fetched, it is now recognized that spatially separated places and actions can share a common ecosystem. This insight is most potently demonstrated with the global phenomenon of climate change.

Figure 13.1 shows three broad areas of environmental concern: climate change, pollution and natural resources. The issues listed under each of these headings are interrelated. For example, climate change impacts on water and forest resources. Environmental indicators can be monitored, providing data on how these changes are taking place and what their impacts are. This monitoring can help governments and businesses in strategic decision-making.

Changes in earlier eras took place gradually, but environmental changes in the last half-century have occurred at a much more rapid rate than in any previous comparable period in history (UNEP, 2005). The causes are largely due to processes associated with human activity, including industrialization, increased use of land for agriculture and rising energy demands. Govern-

Figure 13.1 Environmental indicators

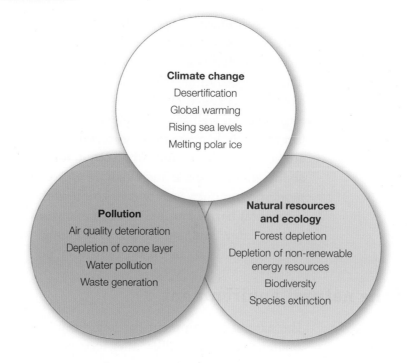

TO RECAP...

Global interactions in the natural environment

The natural environment includes all living organisms, as well as natural resources such as soil, water and air. The ways in which human, plant and animal life interact with their environments are part of sensitive ecosystems.

ments and citizens have tended to see the economic benefits and improvements in human well-being as outweighing the loss of natural ecosystems. However, it is now evident that the effects of environmental degradation are impacting in detrimental ways on societies.

The changing environment and societies

The post-war period has seen huge improvements globally in human well-being. Life expectancy has increased, infant mortality has decreased and progress has been made in controlling diseases which have ravaged populations in the past. Famines have become less frequent. More people than ever have access to clean drinking water. Quality of life in terms of education, equal opportunities and the enjoyment of cultural goods has increased. Although these achievements are undoubtedly good news, there are underlying concerns that improvements in human well-being are beginning to look unsustainable, as environmental degradation, climate change and depletion of natural resources occur.

Industrialization and its social impacts

Economic activity increased sevenfold between 1950 and 2000 (UNEP, 2005). The main processes at work were industrialization, urbanization and population growth. The world's population doubled to 6 billion in this period, adding 2 billion in the past 25 years. Processes linked to industrialization are shown in Figure 13.2, together with the economic and social changes, and environmental impacts.

Factory production, as opposed to craft production, provides the means to increase output greatly, with accompanying efficiencies and economies of scale. Demand rises for raw materials such as steel and other metals, chemicals, energy and improved transport. These developments were first seen in

Figure 13.2 Industrialization and its impacts

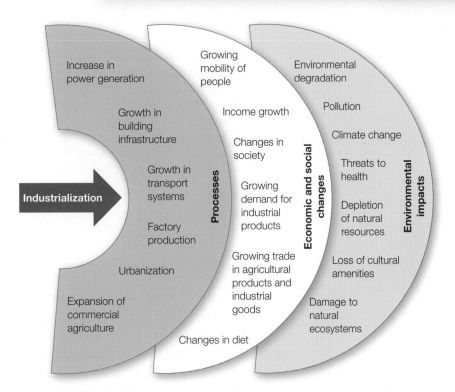

the early industrializing countries of Europe, followed by America. Industrialization was accompanied by urbanization, enabling workers to live near employers' factories. This proximity, however, made them vulnerable to pollution of the air and water from both industrial processes and poor urban infrastructure. In this era, the impacts and threats were mainly local. Only in the second half of the twentieth century did the spread of industrial systems bring environmental degradation extending across national borders. The capitalist economies of the West, which continued to increase output, were joined by the planned economies of the USSR and its satellite states, which pursued rapid industrialization.

Industrial production is now a common feature of economic life around the world. Mass production brings the benefits of rising output, wealth creation and rising incomes. Average income per person doubled between 1950 and 2000, mainly because of the wealth generated by industrialization. There followed changes in social relations, working life and patterns of consumption (see Figure 13.2). As urban workers' incomes rise, the share of their income spent on food declines, and the share spent on industrial goods and services rises. The staple diet of rural life, dependent on rice and wheat, gives way to more processed foods, more fats and higher meat consumption. The Chinese ate 20 kg of meat per capita in 1980, but by 2007 they were eating 50 kg per capita. Growing populations and expanding urban areas make growing demands on agriculture. Changes in land use, mainly converting land to farmland, have been directly responsible for altering ecosystems, deforestation and other outcomes shown in Figure 13.2. Resulting environmental degradation and pollution now threaten the improved well-being which economic development brought about.

TO RECAP...

Industrialization and environmental degradation

Both capitalist and state-run enterprises have exploited the potential of industrial production, with ever-expanding industrial complexes, rising needs for energy and other resources and, most recently, increased use of large-scale transport systems. Environmental degradation, often considered a price worth paying, is now seen in a more critical perspective, largely because of threats to human well-being.

The right to development?
Developing countries are loath to accept a
need to put the brakes on economic development
for the sake of environmental concerns. They argue that
they are as entitled as the earlier industrializing
economies to pursue their own growth strategies. Do
you agree with them, and why?

PAUSE TO REFLECT

Pollution

Pollution: Release of harmful
substances from a source through
air, soil or water.

Pollution refers to the release of harmful substances which are transmitted through air, soil or water from the point where they were released. Poor air and water quality now affects much of the world, posing risks to health as well as the environment. Some pollution results from natural events, such as the eruption of a volcano, or hurricane damage. However, most is attributable to deliberate human activity. Furthermore, most pollution can be traced to industrialization and related processes, such as growing transport networks and weakly regulated urbanization.

Air quality is measured by determining the concentration of particulate components. They include road dust, vehicle exhaust, coal dust and metal particles from industrial operations. A standard measure, PM10, enables comparisons to be made between different locations. According to the World Health Organization (WHO), even low levels of PM10 (particles of 10 micrometres or less in diameter) are potentially harmful to health, but concerns arise where levels are over 20 per cubic metre of air (WHO, 2006a). The health effects of air pollution include respiratory diseases, cardiovascular diseases and chronic bronchitis. Urban dwellers in developing countries are among the worst affected by pollution, in air and water quality, as well as water shortages. About 90% of China's cities suffer from polluted water, and many also suffer from water shortages. China's cities, along with Cairo (see CF13.1 on Egypt), are also the worst affected by poor air quality, as shown in Figure 13.3.

Transboundary pollution: Pollution
which extends across national
boundaries, sometimes great
distances from the source.

Acid rain: Contamination caused by
the accumulation of pollutants in
atmospheric water, mainly from the
burning of fossil fuels, which, when
it falls as rain, causes harm to plant
and animal life.

Pollution was once considered a purely local issue, but scientists can now monitor the dispersal of pollutants, revealing their potential to cause harm a long way from the point of origin. This is known as transboundary pollution. Among the most damaging is acid rain, which is mainly caused by sulphur dioxide and nitrogen oxides, which are generated by the burning of fossil fuels. Acids are dissolved in atmospheric water, producing sulphuric and nitric acids. These are carried by winds, and are capable of travelling long distances. Lakes and rivers have been the chief casualties of acid rain, with declines in fish, plants and insects. The acidification of forest soils also results, damaging trees.

To meet energy demands, the growing nuclear industry has found converts within many national governments. While nuclear power gener-

Figure 13.3 Air pollution in selected cities
Source: World Bank (2007) 'Pollution in China', www.worldbank.org

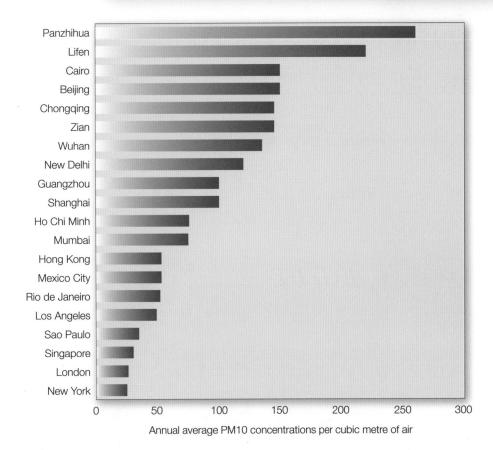

Annual average PM10 concentrations per cubic metre of air

ation has the advantage of being cleaner than coal in terms of emissions, the nature of the radioactive fuel and its by-products raises new risks and produces a new range of pollution problems. The uranium used as fuel must be mined, processed and transferred to power stations. The process of generation is itself complex and dangerous. Risks include the escape of radioactive materials into the environment, emissions of radioactive water and gases from the processing plants, and lingering radioactivity from nuclear waste. The potential harm can be catastrophic, as radioactivity can rapidly kill humans, animals and plants, spreading transboundary pollution over a large area. The Chernobyl disaster at a Russian nuclear power station in 1986 vividly demonstrated the risks, especially in countries where environmental laws and safety standards are weak or poorly enforced.

Accountability for pollution
What are the difficulties in making countries accountable for pollution which causes harm outside their national borders? What are the solutions?

PAUSE TO REFLECT

COUNTRY FOCUS 13.1 – EGYPT

Is Egypt balancing environmental and economic agendas?

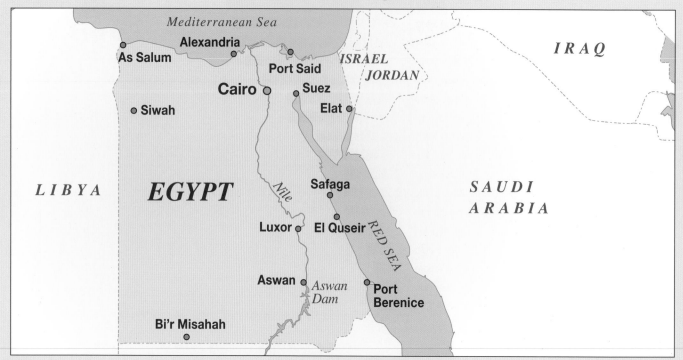

Egypt, an Arab republic, is striving to become a beacon of economic development in the Middle East, a region of the world which has suffered continuing political instability and religious conflict. Egypt has some distinct advantages, including gas and oil riches, low-cost labour and a thriving tourism sector. After a period of stagnation in the new millennium, the economy has been growing (see Figure 1), both from new local enterprises and foreign investment. Egypt faces huge socio-economic and environmental challenges. Its growing population of 79 million people, more than half of whom are under 25, is packed into only 6% of the country's land area. They are concentrated in teeming cities with high unemployment, worsening poverty and some of the world's worst pollution problems. The authoritarian political regime retains state control of major industries such as energy. The gap between the growing masses of urban poor and the affluent, living in outlying gated communities, is potentially destabilizing.

Although Egypt now has an elected parliament, political power remains concentrated in the executive, under the leadership of President Hosni Mubarek and the ruling National Democratic Party, which has governed the country for half a century. Religious political parties are banned and dissident groups are suppressed. Nonetheless, the Muslim Brotherhood, the most organized opposition force, has considerable popular support. It now claims 88 seats in the 444-seat parliament, up from 17 in 2000. This increase in support is partly due to anti-US sentiment and the rise of Islamic movements generally in the Middle East, but mainly due to its social programmes, including health and education, especially in poor urban areas.

Figure 1 Egypt's GDP growth

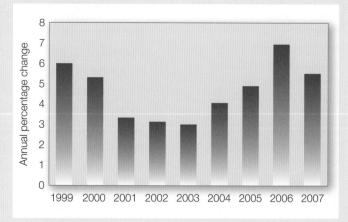

Note: IMF estimate for 2007

Source: *Financial Times*, 13 December 2006

Cairo is home to 17 million people, and grows by an estimated 200,000 new residents every year. This has resulted in unregulated growth in informal slum areas, where air pollution and contaminated water pose risks to health, especially in children. Cairo's poor air quality, among the world's worst, is caused by a combination of factors, including unregulated car emissions, urban industrial operations and the open air burning of waste. Privately owned lead smelters, which burn scrap metal, are largely unregulated and, despite their pollutant operations, have proliferated in the urban landscape. Although cement is one of the most polluting of all industries, there are numerous cement plants in the city. As Cairo is located on the edge of the desert, it is subject to desert dust, consisting of mineral particles and dirt which mix with industrial emissions. These form long-lasting clouds over the city, absorbing sunlight and trapping pollutants. The dry, hot, desert climate exacerbates the harmful effects of emitted carbon dioxide, sulphur dioxide and nitrogen oxides.

The Egyptian government has tried to move heavily polluting activities out of densely populated areas, but this is only partially effective. Egypt is 92% dependent on fossil fuels. Besides the risks to health, pollution is causing environmental degradation and economic loss. Acid deposition damages buildings, including ancient monuments. It also reduces crop yields. Agriculture is crucial to Egypt's economy, not only for its growing population, but for export. It is estimated that the cost of environmental degradation is 3.2–6.4% of GDP per annum. Egypt's government first introduced environmental protection laws in 1994, and has strengthened regulatory powers with the creation of an environmental affairs agency. Institutional difficulties pose challenges for broad strategies to clean up the environment. In particular, the country presents a contrast between a cumbersome state bureaucracy and an informal sector, largely off the radar of formal regulation.

Increasing global demand for oil and gas has benefited Egypt, attracting foreign energy companies. Egypt has become the world's sixth largest exporter of liquefied natural gas. The government sees both economic and environmental gains in the energy sector: increased revenues and industry initiatives which help it to switch to cleaner fuels. However, the energy companies have been frustrated by a combination of high costs in reaching Egypt's unusually deep gas deposits and government subsidies to consumers within the country. The subsidies have been reduced, partly to help control huge budget deficits, but there are concerns that rising fuel and food prices will lead to social and political unrest. Absolute poverty (defined as living on less than $1 a day) rose from 16.7% of the population in 1999 to 23% in 2003, following the period of weak growth.

Government reforms introduced in 2004, which were aimed at improving the business environment, seem to be successful. Industrial development is bringing new jobs to Egypt, especially in sectors such as textiles, furniture, white goods and food processing. Due to cheap labour and subsidized energy, foreign investors have seized opportunities, as FDI inflows reveal (see Figure 2). Turkish textile companies have set up, followed by other textile companies, forming a textiles cluster, including spinning, weaving and dyeing plants. Companies from Switzerland, Italy and Pakistan have joined the cluster. Egypt's strategic location makes it a platform for exports to Europe, an advantage in competing with China for manufacturing operations. These industries are bringing low-skilled jobs to Upper Egypt, where poverty is worst. A growing concern, however, is that Egypt's withdrawal of water from the Nile, on which it is relies almost totally for fresh water, is unsustainable, given the demands of a growing population,

Figure 2 Egypt's FDI inflows

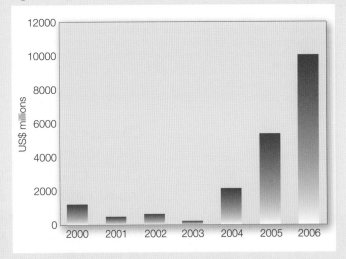

Sources: UN, World Investment Reports, 2006 and 2007 (Geneva: UN)

together with growing agricultural, industrial and tourism sectors. Egypt's drawing from the Nile is subject to political co-operation with Ethiopia. In 2007, there was a rise in social unrest and strikes by textile workers over rising food prices and water shortages.

Tourism accounts for over a tenth of Egypt's GDP, and is seen as crucial to economic growth. One of the world's oldest civilizations, Egypt offers a host of ancient monuments, such as the pyramids, but it is now looking to attract a broader range of tourists to its beach and golf resorts. Few countries can compete with the range of activities offered, from desert safaris to diving to look at coral reefs. However, the country's tourist attractions are also under threat from pollution and environmental degradation. The limestone of ancient monuments suffers severe erosion, and the coral reefs are also being eroded. Increased development on the Red Sea coast, with new roads and airports, contributes to Egypt's growth in greenhouse gas emissions, which have risen 21% since 1990. Egypt is an exempted country under the Kyoto Protocol, but would be affected by any new international convention which increased the obligations on developing countries.

The Egyptian government is hoping that the latest surge in economic growth will be sufficient to maintain political stability, but it has done little to tackle directly the environmental problems of the cities, which are coupled with long-standing social and economic issues.

Questions

◆ What are the main factors in the environmental deterioration of Cairo?

◆ In what ways do Egypt's environmental problems impact on its economic ambitions?

◆ What recommendations would you make to the Egyptian government to develop the tourism sector while protecting the environment?

◆ How do Egypt's urban problems, including poverty as well as poor living conditions, take on a political dimension which could threaten the government?

Sources: Wallis, W., 'Breaking the mould of inertia', *Financial Times*, 23 November 2004; Wallis, W., 'Cairo inhabitants driven further apart', *Financial Times*, 13 December 2006; England, A., 'A force to be reckoned with', *Financial Times*, 13 December 2006; Saleh, H., 'Exports emerge as bright spot in the economy', *Financial Times*, 7 December 2005; UN (2004) *Millennium Development Goals: Second Country Report on Egypt* (Geneva: UN); World Bank (2007) *Urban Development in the Middle East and North Africa*, www.worldbank.org; UNDP (2006) *Human Development Report 2006* (Basingstoke: Palgrave Macmillan).

WEB CHECK

For information on Egypt, see the World Bank's website at www.worldbank.org, and click on *Egypt* in the country list.

Climate change

Climate change: Global rise or fall in temperatures, whether natural in causation or caused by human activity.

Global warming: Global rise in temperatures, impacting on all forms of life and ecosystems.

Climate change is broadly defined by the UN Intergovernmental Panel on Climate Change (IPCC) as 'any change in climate over time, whether due to natural variability or as a result of human activity' (UNEP, 2007: vol. 2, p. 21). In the present era, climate change takes the form of global warming, from rising global air and ocean temperatures. Global warming is known to be caused mainly by the damaging build-up of a number of 'greenhouse gases', particularly CO_2, which deplete the ozone layer of the earth's atmosphere. The build-up in greenhouse gases has been caused mainly by the surge in emissions from industrialization, energy generation and transport. Climate change is global in its causes and its consequences. It thus differs essentially from air pollution, as climate change impacts are independent of where in the world the greenhouse gases are emitted (HM Treasury, 2006).

The earth has warmed 0.7° C since 1900. As Figure 13.4 shows, concentrations of greenhouse gases are rising, increasing the pace of global warming.

plate 13.1 Blame for the rise in greenhouse gas emissions rests heavily on coal-burning power stations.

Figure 13.4 Rising levels of greenhouse gases

Source: HM Treasury (2006) Stern Review on the Economics of Climate Change, www.hm-treasury.gov.uk

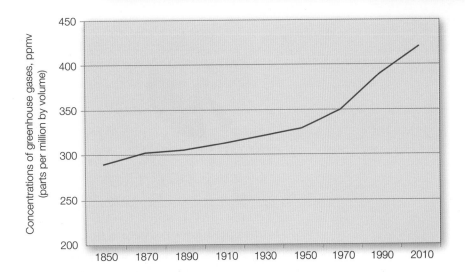

The IPCC's website is www.ipcc.ch.

WEB CHECK

The UN IPCC predicts that global temperature will have risen 3° C by 2100, although it states that the rise could be anywhere in the band 2–4.5° C, depending on uncertainties of the unfolding processes and steps taken to reduce emissions (UNEP, 2007). CO_2 emissions are likely to increase by 55% between 2004 and 2030, or 1.7% a year (IEA, 2006). If this annual growth rate continues, concentrations would be more than treble preindustrial levels by 2100 (HM Treasury, 2006). The impact on societies, the environment and economic life would be devastating.

Global warming is causing the polar icecaps to melt and sea levels to rise, threatening coastal regions worldwide. Extreme weather events, such as droughts, floods, storm surges and extremely high sea levels are becoming more frequent and intense. Coastal regions thus suffer doubly, from rising sea levels and vulnerability to storm damage. Countries affected include low-lying Asian countries, such as Vietnam, Bangladesh, India and parts of China. Most of Bangladesh is less than 10 m above sea level, so rising seas of an estimated 1.5 m would submerge 16% of the country, affecting 17 million people. Food and water scarcity, leading to health risks, are likely outcomes, which will be more severe in the poorest regions, where levels of resources and technology are low. Desertification, floods and extreme storms are making agriculture problematic, especially in developing countries.

Rising land temperatures will be of benefit in some countries, such as those in northern Europe, in which they help to offset the damaging effects of cold to human health. Here, a greater variety of crops will be possible, but the warmer temperatures will be conducive to more pests and diseases, substantially wiping out the benefits of the rise in temperatures. Key wheat-exporting countries, including Australia, Canada and Argentina, have experienced severe droughts attributable to climate change, which is a factor in rising wheat prices (see CF13.2 on Australia).

Scientists fear that if global temperatures rise by 4° C, 'feedback' effects take place, which would increase the rate of warming. For example, the permafrost, the layer of soil which is permanently frozen, is melting, releasing methane, a greenhouse gas twenty times stronger than carbon dioxide. If the rising temperatures cause the Amazon rainforest to die, the forest, which absorbs carbon from the atmosphere at present, would shift to

Figure 13.5 Global CO$_2$
emissions, 2006

Source: Netherlands Environmental
Assessment Agency (2007) 'China now no. 1
in CO$_2$ emissions', www.mnp.nl

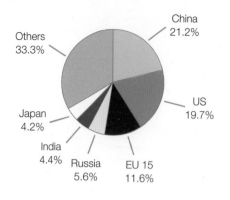

producing carbon dioxide. In general, as soils warm, the biological activity in them increases, generating more carbon dioxide, thus contributing to global warming.

Developed economies and rapidly growing emerging economies tend to have the highest emissions. The US and China are the two largest emitters, as Figure 13.5 shows. The US has per capita CO$_2$ emissions of over 20 tonnes per annum, whereas in China, per capita CO$_2$ emissions are only about 4 tonnes. Emissions are rising in both countries, however, but more rapidly in China. China's CO$_2$ emissions have risen from about 12% of the global total in 2000 to over 20% in 2006.

Figure 13.6 Greenhouse gas
emissions per capita in EU, 2004

Source: European Environment Agency (2006)
Greenhouse gas emission trend and projections
in Europe 2006, http://reports.eea.europa.eu

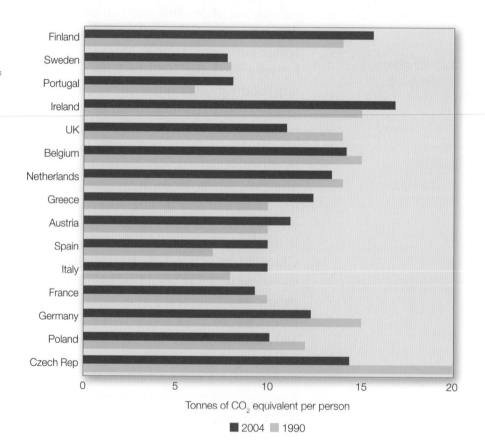

TO RECAP...

Causes and impacts of climate change

The build-up of greenhouse gases in the atmosphere is the chief cause of global warming, which is resulting in climate change. Climate change is capable of causing devastating consequences, likely to be most severe in the poorer countries and among the poorest inhabitants in each country affected.

Average annual emissions per capita in the EU 25 in 2004 were 10.9 tonnes of CO$_2$ equivalent. However, there are variations from country to country, as Figure 13.6 shows. Although EU policies have asserted the need to reduce emissions, in some countries, they have risen. These include Ireland, Spain, Italy, Austria and Finland. A range of national government policies have been influential in reducing emissions, as the next section highlights.

**Mitigating
climate change impacts**
The world's poor countries have levels of
greenhouse gas emissions that are a small fraction of those
of the developed and industrializing countries, yet they are likely
to suffer the worst effects from climate change. What, if
anything, can be done, and should the big emitters bear
some of the responsibility?

PAUSE TO REFLECT

Governance and the environment

National governments bear responsibility for the oversight of a country's safety and well-being. Many take an active role in industrialization, often through state-owned enterprises. Governments are often rather ambivalent about environmental protection, reluctant to stifle growth while aware of the risks to ecosystems and human health. In the face of climate change and transboundary pollution, the policies of national governments are complemented by international co-operation, which exerts collective pressure on individual governments.

National governments

National governments have a number of legal and policy tools at their disposal with which they can safeguard the environment within their borders. In the past, governments have tended to be more reactive than proactive in dealing with environmental protection. Industrial development has tended to take priority, as governments are above all concerned to create employment and economic prosperity. They have prioritized boosting power generation, and allowed modification of water courses and the depletion of underground water, to serve urban populations and industrial needs. However, natural resource depletion combined with pollution lead to long-term damage, especially when climate change is taken into account.

In an environment of weak environmental protection, businesses are not necessarily inclined to reduce factory emissions into the air, and have often allowed waste to flow into waterways. When pollution reaches levels harmful to human health, or rivers become depleted of fish, governments respond. Similarly, urbanization often proceeds in a haphazard way, with little planning, as CF13.1 showed. The consequence can be urban sprawl, including risks to health and environmental damage. Governments now realize that environmental protection frameworks which can prevent damage are more effective and efficient than piecemeal measures to remedy harms which have occurred. The most common areas of national regulation are:

- Legal controls on emissions into the air, soil and waterways, with penalties, often fines administered through the courts, for violations, as part of the country's criminal law.
- Provision of legal means for civil claims for damages to be brought against polluters.

- Planning systems which supervise urban development and land use, including agricultural land and forests.
- Systems for the control of waste disposal from all sources, including industrial plants and individual householders.
- Planning systems which assess the environmental impacts of new industrial and transport infrastructure, including airports.

Developed countries are likely to have policies in all these areas. Developing countries may aspire to these goals, but lack the resources or institutional framework to implement them. Even in countries which have legal provisions in all these areas, enforcement is often lax. Fines for pollution are sometimes treated by companies as merely an expense, failing to change behaviour. Fines are also inadequate in putting right environmental wrongs. For example, even when a specific source of effluent into a river is stopped, it may be a long time before river life is restored. Urban development and planning regulation are areas of corruption in many countries, leading to unlawful development and the flouting of environmental safeguards.

In developing countries, environmental priorities are likely to focus on providing access to clean water and sanitation. At the start of the new millennium, over 1 billion people lacked access to clean water and 2.6 billion lacked access to improved sanitation. One of the UN's Millennium Development Goals is to reduce these numbers by half, but progress is slow, and could be jeopardized by extreme events associated with climate change (see Chapter 15).

In the developed world, the above list would be thought by many not to go far enough. There are additional areas of environmental concern which many governments are addressing. A national government with 'greener' policies would look at the following additional policies, and would also incorporate incentives to encourage changed behaviour patterns:

- Legal requirements that new products must contain a proportion of recyclable components.
- Compulsory recycling programmes for a range of products.
- Legal requirements that factories and power generators must use the cleanest materials and technology available.
- The introduction of targets for the reduction of CO_2 emissions.
- Emissions trading schemes, whereby polluting companies can buy credits from those which are less polluting.
- Use of taxation policies to encourage environmental protection, such as higher taxation of gas-guzzling cars, duties on fuel, taxation of air travel.
- An 'environmental tax' on companies whose industries are heavily polluting.
- Restrictions on the use of private motor vehicles in city centres with high levels of air pollution, coupled with subsidies for cleaner urban transport such as trams and bicycles.
- Government funding for R&D into clean technology.
- House-building regulations which include energy efficiency requirements, such as wall and roof insulation.

Many governments now have at least some of these green policies. The EU has taken a lead in this regard, with recycling directives and an emissions

Emissions trading scheme: Scheme whereby a company buys credits to offset its greenhouse gas emissions from companies which are less polluting.

trading scheme which is compulsory for the most polluting industries, including power generation, steel-making and cement manufacturing. The EU emissions trading scheme can be distinguished from voluntary schemes undertaken by a wide range of companies, which are discussed in the next main section. The EU Commission has announced it will legislate for reductions in CO_2 emissions from new cars by 2012 (discussed in CS13.2). In the other areas, such as taxation and spending, which are national matters, European countries, especially Germany, have been to the forefront. Authorities in other parts of the world might consider these measures too restrictive on companies and individuals, hampering national competitiveness. They might also be wary that curbs on consumer behaviour would be unpopular with the electorate in democratic countries.

Some governments, such as that of the US, have promoted the development of clean technology, while resisting restrictions on emissions and taxation of polluting activities. A trend is for individual states in the US to introduce stronger green policies than exist under federal law and government policy. California has set an example, which over 20 other states have followed. The California plan is to require carmakers to reduce emissions in new cars and light trucks by 30% of 2002 levels by 2016. However, the state authorities face legal challenges by motor manufacturers, who have argued that they would suffer financially and consumer choice would be reduced (*The Economist*, 22 September 2007).

TO RECAP...

The role of national governments in environmental protection

National governments often juggle priorities which conflict with each other. They wish to encourage businesses and yet impose controls where necessary to protect the natural environment from degradation and keep pollution at levels which do not risk human health or ecosystems. Most governments adopt environmental protection policies, but they differ in their depth of commitment, resources and enforcement.

Setting an example or stifling competitiveness?
What are the reasons behind the differing policy approaches to climate change by different national governments? Distinguish between:
• developed and developing countries
• differing approaches among developed economies

PAUSE TO REFLECT

International co-operation

With international co-operation, global issues can be tackled collectively and slow-moving national governments can be encouraged to play a role. International co-operation is the most appropriate means of dealing with transboundary pollution and climate change. The principle that the polluter is liable for damage caused has long been accepted in transboundary pollution cases. The 'polluter pays' principle was reinforced by the UN's Conference on Environment and Development at the Rio Summit (informally known as the Earth Summit) in 1992. However, holding governments or commercial companies accountable for damage caused in another jurisdiction is difficult to achieve in practice, as there are limits to the jurisdiction of national courts, and the International Court of Justice deals only with disputes between states. Bringing a case for harm alleged to be caused by pollution against a foreign company can be difficult, especially when the damage occurs in developing countries. Often pollution cases are lopsided: the victims are poor people in poor countries, while the polluters are large MNEs with huge resources to defend legal cases. The weak legal systems in developing countries often provide little redress to local victims, but suing in the home country of the foreign company is complex, requiring proof that the cause of the accident or incident was directly linked to the head office's activities, rather than local causes. Residents in a community in Ecuador were successful in pursuing Texaco, a US oil company, in the US courts for the dumping of crude oil, by using international human rights law. The US Supreme Court has subsequently limited the broad use of human rights claims by non-US residents. The Bhopal case in India (discussed in Chapter 5) is another example of the difficulties and complexities of seeking legal redress for pollution damage which has a cross-border dimension.

The UN has taken the initiative in encouraging sustainability as an environmental principle. The Rio Declaration on Environment and Development of 1992 acknowledged states' rights to development, but with the qualification that development should be sustainable. The concept of sustainable development dates from a UN report on environment and development of 1987, known as the Brundtland Report. Sustainable development was defined as 'development that meets the needs of the present without compromising the ability of future generations to meet their own needs' (UN, 1987). The UN Framework Convention on Climate Change dates from 1992, following the first of the IPCC's reports. Further negotiations led to a treaty, the Kyoto Protocol of 1998, which set targets for reductions in greenhouse gas emissions. The aim was that emissions by developed countries would be reduced to 5% below 1990 levels by 2008–12. Developing countries were exempted because of their need for economic growth and because their emissions per capita were low in comparison to developed countries. A provision, known as the 'clean development mechanism', was introduced to help developing countries reduce emissions. Under this process, governments in developed countries can finance projects, such as renewable energy projects, which count towards the developed countries' reduction targets. Despite the refusal of the US to ratify the Kyoto Protocol, the treaty received the necessary ratifications to become international law in 2005.

With the Kyoto Protocol due to expire, debate has shifted to its replacement. The IPCC's fourth report has emphasized the urgent need of collective action on global warming by mandatory reductions in emissions. Meanwhile, the main developing countries have powered ahead economically, increasing their emissions significantly in the process. Developing countries will account for three-quarters of the increase in global CO_2 emissions between 2004 and 2030, China alone accounting for 39% of the rise (IEA, 2006). However, China, India and other developing countries continue to maintain that they should not have to meet targets for emissions reductions. They argue that the developed world should bear the brunt of reductions as their activities are most responsible for the present state of affairs. They also assert that they should be entitled to the same opportunities for economic growth as the earlier industrializing countries enjoyed. China has urged that, as it is the 'factory of the world', rich countries have effectively offloaded their emissions by offshoring manufacturing industries and buying back finished goods (Harvey, 2007).

Two factors are now weighing with national governments:

Sustainable development: Development that meets the needs of the present without compromising the ability of future generations to meet their own needs.

1 The damaging impacts of climate change can lead to social, economic and political fallout for governments. Protests against pollution are an indication of the disquiet.

2 There are now compelling economic arguments for reducing emissions. The Stern Report calculated that the cost of reducing emissions if action is taken quickly would be about 1% of global GDP, but the cost could rise to 5–20% if no action is taken (HM Treasury, 2006). Once damage has occurred to human well-being, ecosystems and natural resources are difficult, sometimes impossible, to put right, whereas resources spent on prevention of disaster are more efficient.

Uncertainty over the possibilities of international agreement on mandatory emissions targets sends ambiguous signals to businesses which are considering their strategies for investment and operations. MNEs with operations in several countries continue to be subject to different regulations in each, with considerable divergence in standards. In those where standards are lower, there is uncertainty over the levels of future controls. The UN's executive secretary on the Climate Change Convention has urged that clarity of the regulatory position is essential for businesses to engage in the necessary long-term planning. For this reason, an increasing number of businesses are supporting binding cuts, which provide firm targets on which to base decision-making.

TO RECAP...
International co-operation edging forward
Legal proceedings against polluters across national borders seldom achieve satisfactory conclusions. Years of legal wrangling often end in stalemate, and the clock cannot be turned back when damage to ecosystems and human health have occurred. Governments are gradually being persuaded of the need to impose regulations, providing a degree of certainty for MNEs' planning horizons.

Benefiting from international divergence?
Some national governments have been notably reluctant to embrace environmental goals, for fear of jeopardizing national competitive advantage. Others have embraced environmentalism in theory, but done little to impose targets in the short term. What strategy would you recommend to businesses, both domestic firms and foreign investors, in these countries? Should they take a strong environmental position to set an international example, or seek competitive advantage from the lack of regulation?

PAUSE TO REFLECT

Don't forget to check the companion website at **www.palgrave.com/business/morrisonib**, where you will find web-based assignments, web links, interactive quizzes, an extended glossary and lots more to help you learn about international business.

www.palgrave.com
Companion Website

COUNTRY FOCUS 13.2 – AUSTRALIA

How sustainable is Australia's export boom?

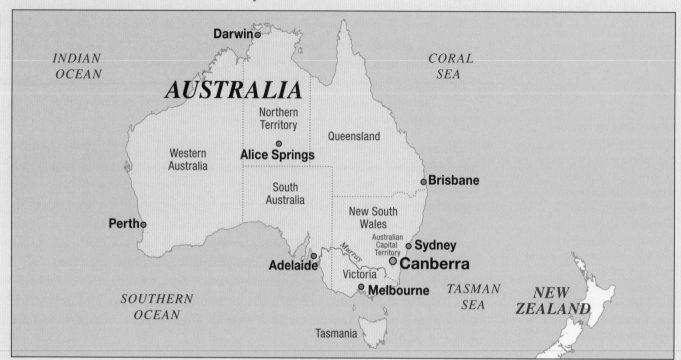

Australia has been basking in prosperity from increasing global demand for its exports of mining and agricultural products. For coal and mineral exports, it has long benefited from proximity to the dynamic economies of Asia, first Japan and then China. Now, India is becoming its fastest growing market. Australia's agriculture has prospered from export growth in global markets, making it the world's sixth largest agricultural exporter. Australia's major exported products are shown in Figure 1. These export industries are now the subject of debate on sustainability in the new context of climate change and the depletion of natural resources. In particular, coal, which is by far its largest export product, is targeted because of its greenhouse gas emissions.

Many of the world's economies see China as a threat, but for Australia, China presents opportunities due to its growing demand for primary products. China is Australia's second largest trading partner, now linked in a bilateral free trade agreement. Their trading strengths are complementary, Australia supplying key natural resources, while importing manufactured goods from China. China is the largest customer of Melbourne-based BHP Billiton, the world's largest diversified mining company, which supplies Chinese customers with increasing volumes of coal, iron ore, oil, copper and other metals. As a result, its profits have more than quadrupled since 2003, to over US$13.7 billion in 2007. The company is now eyeing India's potential growth. India's imports from Australia are growing rapidly, up 30% between 2005 and 2006.

Coal is Australia's largest export and also the source of 80% of the country's energy needs. Australia's emissions per capita are the highest of any major economy, but the total for its

Figure 1 Australia's largest export products

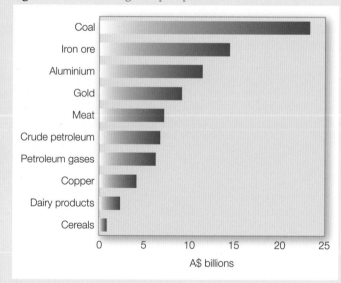

Source: Australian Department of Foreign Affairs and Trade (2007) Exports of Primary and Manufactured Products 2006, www.dfat.gov.au

population of 20 million amounts to only 1.4% of the world total. Australia's Liberal-National coalition government did not sign the Kyoto Protocol, and took a robust stance, arguing that the protocol would 'cost us jobs and damage our industry', in the words of Prime Minister John Howard (Johnston, 2005). A new Labour government, elected in 2007, has reversed this policy, agreeing to targeted emissions reductions.

Australia is the driest inhabited continent on earth (only Antarctica is drier). Extreme drought associated with climate change is seriously affecting its agricultural sector. In 2007, Australia suffered severe drought. Crucial to the country's water supply is its largest river, the Murray River, flowing into the Murray-Darwin Basin, serving farmers, industry and residents. Irrigation and pasture for livestock consume almost 80% of the basin's flows. The river is degenerating from over-exploitation and pollution, which, combined with higher temperatures and lower rainfall, have dramatically reduced its flows. Hardly any water from the Murray River reaches the sea. A result is that rivers and soil which are already salty are becoming more saline.

Australians' average water use per person per day is one of the world's highest, and two and a half times that of a UK resident (UNDP, 2006). It is said that Australia is the world's biggest exporter of 'virtual water', embedded in farm produce. It takes 10,000–13,000 litres of water to produce 1 kilo of beef. As 70% of the country's water supply is used for agriculture, this sector is coming under the spotlight. Agricultural exports account for a quarter of the total of the country's total exports. Australia's main farm exports are from 'dryland' farming, such as wheat and cattle, which rely on rainwater. As Figure 2 shows, Australia is a major global wheat exporter. Crops requiring irrigation, representing 23% of the total, include rice and fruit. Environmentalists now question whether both dryland and irrigated farms are sustainable in light of water scarcity. In particular, rice-growing for export, while highly efficient, is criticized, as the fields are submerged in water six months of the year.

Some critics argue that Australia's agricultural export industry is essentially unsustainable, and that the water it currently absorbs would be better utilized in industries and for city dwellers, who suffer extreme limits on water use at present. One rice farmer says: 'If you are on a level 5 [the highest] water restriction and can't wash your car and you see some crocodile down the river growing rice, I can see why you would get cranky' (Beattie, 2007). Expensive recycling and desalination plants are being built to provide for the cities' needs. Trade in

plate 13.2 The parched banks of Australia's depleted Murray River tell a sad story of overuse and drought.

water has been implemented, whereby farmers can sell their water allocation either for a year or permanently. It has been suggested that farmers could sell their water allocations to cities, or the government could buy out the farmers' rights and leave river systems to recover environmental health. This would require changes in the law which would be unpalatable to rural residents.

Although commodities dominate Australia's trade, services are becoming important, with education and tourism to the fore. These sectors are boosted by the increasing numbers of students and tourists from Asia, who help foster better cross-cultural understanding within Australia. These developments are welcome indications of diversification, but it is arguable that other sectors, especially high-tech innovation, could potentially contribute more to wealth creation than they are at present. Chinese FDI in Australia is growing, as Chinese firms see opportunities to gain greater stakes in their supplier industries. However, outward flows of FDI from Australia to Asia remain modest. Australia has traditionally looked to ties with the US, the UK and other European countries. Now, with nearly half of Australia's exports destined for Asia and the growth of China as a rival 'superpower' to the US, Australia's position is more ambivalent. Moves towards greater Asian integration are following Asian trade links. There is a growing awareness that reliance on the export of natural resources looks increasingly problematic, as overexploitation of resources and climate change take their toll.

Figure 2 The world's top 10 wheat exporters

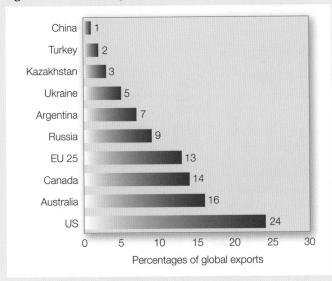

China 1
Turkey 2
Kazakhstan 3
Ukraine 5
Argentina 7
Russia 9
EU 25 13
Canada 14
Australia 16
US 24

Percentages of global exports

Source: Financial Times, 4 September 2007

Questions

- Why is Australia's mining sector, although highly profitable at present, considered precarious in terms of long-term growth?
- Assess Australia's current problems of water scarcity and the measures being taken to solve them.
- Why has Australia been unwilling to sign the Kyoto Protocol, and what are the prospects for the country joining in future international mandatory emissions reduction targets?
- In your view, what are the prospects for Australia diversifying its economy, and shifting to a more environmentally sustainable strategy?

▶ **Sources:** Marsh, V., 'Australia's Howard sets his sights on Asia', *Financial Times*, 2 April 2005; Marsh, V. and Mallet, V., 'Asian markets have crucial role', *Financial Times*, 28 October 2004; Tucker, S., 'Lucky Country prospers riding the commodities wave', *Financial Times*, 29 November 2005; Tucker, S., 'Resources boom may mask problems', *Financial Times*, 29 November 2005; Johnston, T., 'We'll take our own approach to cutting harmful emissions', *Financial Times*, 29 November 2005; Marsh, V., 'Far-flung mining operations', *Financial Times*, 28 October 2004; Beattie, A., 'Thirsty work', *Financial Times*, 24 May 2007; *The Economist*, 'The big dry', 28 April 2007; UNDP (2006) *Human Development Report 2006* (Basingstoke: Palgrave Macmillan; BHP Billiton (2007) Annual Report 2007, http://bhpbilliton.com; Australian Department of Foreign Affairs and Trade (2007) Exports of Primary and Manufactured Products 2006, www.dfat.gov.au.

WEB CHECK

For information about Australia, go to the OECD's website at www.oecd.org, and click on *Australia* in the country list. BHP Billiton's website is www.bhpbilliton.com, where there is a link to *Sustainable Development*.

Business strategy and sustainability

Despite mixed signals from governments, many firms are taking environmental concerns more seriously in their strategies and policies. Figure 13.7 shows the main factors in corporate environmental strategy, including regulation, costs and ethical concerns. As Figure 13.7 indicates, these influences are interrelated. For example, corporate values are influenced by customer concerns as well as ethical principles. In some cases, firms see specific opportunities in innovation and technology which reduce pollution, conserve energy or result in more environment-friendly products. However, these opportunities may only be abundant where government regulation is driving change. International businesses face a welter of different national regulatory systems, with varying degrees of environmental protection. Although less regulated locations offer cost advantages, many companies now view environmental concerns as global, implying the raising of standards in all locations, even where not legally required. This stance is increasingly likely to be driven by customer and broader stakeholder pressures.

Figure 13.7 Determinants of corporate environmental strategy

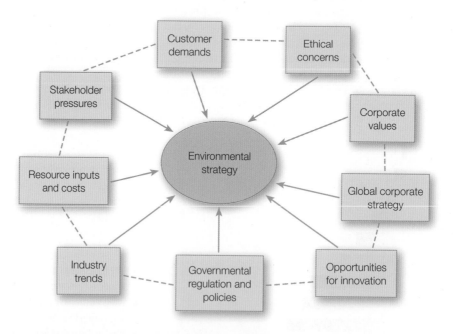

Ecology's role in business strategy

Operational costs are a major concern for businesses. If the operation is a factory which generates pollution, the firm might decide that, in the absence of regulation, expensive clean technology to reduce emissions would be unjustified, as it reduces the firm's competitiveness. In this situation, no firm has the incentive to improve its environmental impact, and there are likely to be few firms carrying out R&D into cleaner technology, as there would be too few customers. For there to be a shift from this way of thinking, environmental concerns must be seen as an imperative rather than an 'extra'. When a government legislates to require reductions in greenhouse gas emissions, all firms in the country must comply, and firms whose business provides such specialist technology will gain customers. As we have seen, however, governments are reluctant to take such bold moves. Reasoning in ways similar to that of individual firms, countries fear being perceived as too costly in terms of regulation and therefore uncompetitive internationally. Without legislative compulsion, why would a firm seek to improve its environmental performance?

The assumption held by many firms is that environmental performance is a cost, weighing down competitiveness with little obvious economic benefit. However, the risk for businesses is that if they fail to act on environmental impacts, their future may be bleak, as the planet's resources are running out and the human costs are rising. Businesses have tended to look mainly at short-term gains, paying little heed to long-term harm. However, failing to take a long view of markets' productive capacity and externalities is one of the well-known pitfalls of business strategy generally. It could be argued that, given the extreme conditions and events associated with climate change, business models for the future will need to be radically adjusted to ensure survival.

Capitalism has thrived on processes of 'creative destruction', as new technologies replace the old, and firms which are unable to adapt go to the wall. Today's challenge may be couched in terms of sustainability, introduced above in the context of sustainable development. For businesses, sustainability implies using natural resources to generate profits in ways which do not lead to irrevocable destruction of resources or ecosystems, or cause damage to human well-being. This argument is sometimes referred to as the 'business case' for environmentalism. It rests on the principle that businesses essentially act from economic, rather than altruistic or ethical movies. Carbon trading is an example of this approach, resting as it does on economic incentives. Environmentalists, however, tend to argue that the business case is too weak to achieve the radical shifts in behaviour needed to stem global warming.

Ethics and environmental strategies

For some companies, making environmental protection a priority is considered the right way to pursue its business, irrespective of costs and differing levels of national regulation. This is the basis of an ethical strategy. It is closely associated with principles of corporate social responsibility (CSR), discussed in the next chapter. An ethical approach commits the company to high standards of behaviour in every respect, not simply environmental performance.

Some companies aim to be 'carbon neutral'. A number of companies, including Marks & Spencer, BSkyB and HSBC have taken the route of

TO RECAP...

The 'business case' for protecting the environment

The potentially devastating effects of climate change are threatening the sustainability of many current business models, compelling firms to make long-term adjustments to their strategies in order to remain profitable in a world of environmental constraints.

Carbon neutrality: Policy of reducing emissions to a minimum and then offsetting the remaining emissions through activities which directly contribute to environmental protection.

Carbon offsetting: Policy whereby a firm invests in green projects, often in developing countries, which are the equivalent of the firm's greenhouse gas emissions.

carbon neutrality. First, they reduce their emissions from energy use and transport, and then offset the remaining emissions. Carbon offsetting rests on the principle of paying for emissions by investing in projects such as planting forests on deforested land or building wind farms. This approach has been adopted by Reckitt Benckiser, which makes laundry detergents and other products which are potentially damaging to the environment. Carbon offsetting schemes rest on a voluntary market in emissions trading which is unregulated, unlike the EU's official trading schemes. Environmentalists are wary of the lack of verification associated with these unofficial schemes operating in developing countries. A Voluntary Carbon Standard produced by the International Emissions Trading Association goes some way to achieve consistency of standards and ensure that the projects actually yield improvements in emissions which would not otherwise have occurred.

Many companies risk falling foul of the gap between 'rhetoric and reality', if they boast of green credentials which are not followed through in practice, leaving them exposed to accusations of hypocrisy. They may even face greater scrutiny than counterparts which do not have strong environmental principles. Environmentalists are among the harshest critics of business, and environmental NGOs are responsible for much of the information and publicity which reaches the public on green issues. Groups such as Greenpeace and Friends of the Earth raise awareness of environmental issues, and have become noted for their scepticism of business motives. Nonetheless, many have formed partnerships with MNEs, in efforts to promote sustainability goals.

Chiquita, the US banana company, which has been criticized for its poor record on environmental and labour rights in Latin America, has formed a partnership with the Rainforest Alliance. Unilever, the consumer goods company, has worked with Greenpeace. These initiatives might be viewed as mere public relations activities on the part of the MNEs. On the other hand, consumers are becoming more conscious of environmental performance. They are also becoming better informed, due to the availability of environmental data from NGOs and inter-governmental sources. The company which takes initiatives to communicate with consumers on its environmental performance is taking something of a risk. If it suffers a setback, the critics are likely to be vociferous. However, it would probably feel that the policy of winning consumer confidence can withstand minor setbacks. BP, featured in CS13.1, has taken a strong environmental position in communicating with the public, but suffered reputational damage from a series of disasters. Recovering from an environmental disaster depends heavily on having policies in place and communicating with stakeholders on how they will be implemented in practice.

Marks & Spencer launched a 'Look behind the label' campaign, inviting consumers to scrutinize its environmental performance. The policy covers every aspect of the business, including sourcing fish from sustainable sources, treatment of animals and use of chemicals. Its head of corporate responsibility stresses: 'Across a supply chain of 2,000 factories, 10,000 farms and tens of thousands of workers, you can never be perfect all the time, so don't pretend you are. But do talk about how much it matters to you and your core

Chiquita's website is www.chiquita.com. Here there is a link to the company's *Corporate Responsibility*.

WEB CHECK

standards' (Murray, 2006). Communicating an ethical stance to stakeholders and the wider public is an important aspect of its environmental strategy. Transparency and willingness to accept scrutiny are needed, but with numerous suppliers and contractors involved, possible shortcomings may arise, despite monitoring systems.

TO RECAP...

Ethics and environmentalism

Taking a strong ethical stance on the environment entails looking at every aspect of a company's activities, to assess and reduce damaging environmental impacts. This approach goes beyond adhering to legal requirements, and is likely to be costly in financial terms. However, it can bring significant reputational benefits where policies and communication strategies are carefully focused.

Economic and ethical strategies coming together?

In what ways does the business case for environmentally sustainable objectives either diverge or converge with the ethical argument?

PAUSE TO REFLECT

Case study 13.1:
BP's green strategy takes a battering

In the late 1990s, BP embarked on a new environmental strategy. In 1997, it became the first large oil company to warn of the dangers of global warming and the use of fossil fuels, distinguishing itself sharply from competitors, notably ExxonMobil, which resisted such a strategy. The following year, the BP motto was changed to 'Beyond Petroleum', and the company's emblem was changed to a green-and-yellow sun-like symbol. The company began investing in alternative energy, including solar technology. BP also extolled social ideals, including human rights, which were an important consideration for MNEs with operations in developing countries. Investors responded favourably, but BP risked becoming an easy target for critics who saw the stance as being more motivated by marketing and political considerations than genuine commitment.

An explosion at a BP oil refinery in Texas City in 2005, which killed 15 people and injured more than 170, was the beginning of a disastrous period in the company's history. The refinery, which had been acquired by BP as one of several acquisitions in the late 1990s, was subjected to a cost-cutting programme, beginning with a 25% budget cut in 1999. The refinery manager said Texas City 'was a big old, rundown and dirty refinery and people were desperate for hope … they did the best they could' (McNulty, 19 March 2007). Investigations carried out by the US Chemical Safety Board (CSB) after the disaster revealed a record of mechanical failures and poor safety standards. Worryingly for the company, investigators also found organizational failings. Training and staffing budgets had been cut. Workers who complained of safety risks (referred to as 'whistleblowers') even feared retaliation by supervisors for reporting safety deficiencies. Spending cuts had not taken enough account of safety implications. One of the CSB's recommendations was that BP appoint an additional non-executive director with specific professional safety expertise in refinery operations.

The investigation by the CSB into the Texas City explosion also criticized the federal agency in charge of regulation, the Occupational Safety and Health Administration (OSHA). The records had shown that in the 20 years the OSHA had been inspecting the site, 10 incidents had occurred and weaknesses should have been

apparent, leading to a comprehensive investigation. However, no such investigation occurred. Although three workers had died in an accident at the site in 2004, the OSHA did not undertake an inspection that year. BP was found by the CSB to have lobbied successfully in Texas against environmental monitoring controls and equipment upgrades. Investigations found that the company estimated it had thereby saved $150 million, but the CSB found that key upgrades might have prevented the Texas City explosion. BP had been considered the 'greenest' of the oil companies, and, it seems, was able to convince regulators that it did not need tough controls.

BP's second major disaster came in 2006, when an oilfield in Prudhoe Bay, Alaska, had to be shut down due an oil spill of 270,000 gallons of oil from severe corrosion in a pipe. Although BP was not the major owner of the site, it was responsible for maintenance and operations, and thus attracted the strongest criticism. The 38-year-old Prudhoe Bay oilfield was North America's largest, located in an area of ecological sensitivity and extreme environmental conditions, including frequent blizzards in the long winter. Again, inadequate funding and slack monitoring were indicated as causes of the corrosion. Although BP maintained that its testing of the pipeline did not show corrosion, tests conducted after the accident showed numerous locations where repairs or replacements were needed. BP faced both criminal action from the US Department of Transport and also legal action by the Alaskan regulator, both of which resulted in fines.

Extreme weather also played a role in BP's third high-profile disaster, the delayed repairs of its new Thunder Horse platform in the Gulf of Mexico following hurricane damage in July 2005. The world's largest floating platform listed heavily in Hurricane Dennis, leading engineers to fear it would be lost. It was righted, but repairs to underground infrastructure were slower than anticipated, delaying the start of production. As Figure 1 shows, a number of oil companies suffered losses in production from hurricanes in the Gulf in 2005. The losses amounted to 8% of the Gulf's annual oil production and 6% of its annual gas production. Climatologists believe that the rising temperatures of the sea surface are leading to more severe storms. In 2005, Hurricane

Figure 1 Loss of oil production from the Gulf of Mexico's hurricanes in 2005

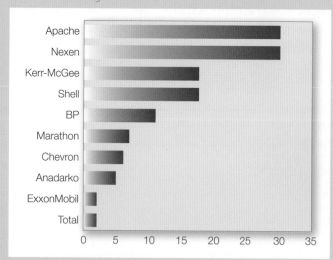

Note: Companies listed are those worst affected. Losses from shutdowns are shown as percentages of worldwide production for each company

Source: Financial Times, 5 October 2005

Figure 2 BP net profits

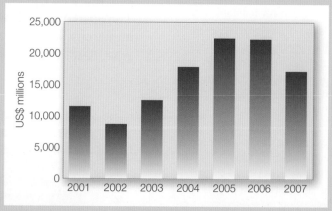

Sources: BP Annual Reports 2001–06; Statement of 2007 Results, www.bp.com

Katrina caused more damage to coastal refineries than offshore installations, while two other hurricanes damaged mainly offshore rigs and platforms. BP had no insurance to cover the damage or interruption to its business. Following its acquisitions of three rival oil companies in the late 1990s, BP decided that, because of its size, production losses in one region could be compensated by increasing production in another. This policy of 'self-insurance', however, was re-examined in light of the three accidents in quick succession which affected production for the American market.

In 2007, BP had to revise its projected production forecasts, to 18% less than anticipated the previous year. After several years of growth, its profits were down 22% in 2007, as Figure 2 shows. Senior managers have embarked on a fundamental rethinking of BP's organization and operations. Executives have looked at the experience of Exxon, which suffered a severe blow to its reputation after the *Exxon Valdez* oil spill (see the opening vignette of this chapter). Exxon reviewed its entire approach to safety and concluded that a centralized approach was the best way to ensure consistent safety standards. BP's decentralized structure, composed of numerous business units and profit centres, was seen as part of the problem. In a more centralized structure, the senior management would be in a better position to implement improved safety policies and procedures across the whole company, whatever the location. However, the investigations following the Texas City explosion and Prudhoe Bay spillage indicated that a change of management culture was needed, including training and empowerment of staff with safety responsibilities. BP had sought to create a new environmental strategy, staking its reputation on environmental and social principles. However, it failed to appreciate the implications of its high ideals for its operations across the entire organization, and it faces an uphill task in regaining public confidence.

Questions

1   To what extent was BP to blame for each of the three disasters?
2   What regulatory failures are highlighted in the case study?
3   What lessons should MNEs learn from BP's environmental strategy of the late 1990s, which was criticized as a mere marketing device?
4   What recommendations would you make to BP executives for a new strategy which will regain public confidence?

Sources: McNulty, S., 'BP paints grim picture of Texas refinery before blast', *Financial Times,* 19 March 2007; Hoyos, C., 'BP battles to clear its Augean stables', *Financial Times,* 20 September 2006; Hoyos, C., 'Green ideals now provide fuel for taunts', *Financial Times,* 20 September 2006; Catan, T. and Hoyos, C., 'BP spells out losses from hurricanes', *Financial Times,* 5 October 2005; McNulty, S., BP fought off Texas safety controls, *Financial Times,* 5 March 2007; McNulty, S. and Hoyos, C., 'Long history of complaints over BP field', *Financial Times,* 8 August 2006; Harvey, F., 'Katrina: "first taste of a bitter cup"', *Financial Times,* 10 October 2005; Hoyos, C., 'I must learn from what happened at BP America', *Financial Times,* 24 July 2006; BP Annual Reports 2001–6, www.bp.com; BP Statement of 2007 Results, www.bp.com.

WEB CHECK

BP's website is www.bp.com, where there is a link to *Environment and Society.*

Competitive advantage and environmental strategies

The traditional view of competitive advantage is that there is an inherent conflict between ecological and economic concerns (Porter, 1998b: 351). Reducing or preventing pollution and environmental degradation are seen as costs which result in higher prices and reduced competitiveness. As ecological sustainability becomes a strategic concern, companies are in a position to gain first-mover advantages with ecologically oriented strategies (Shrivastava, 1995). Companies respond with innovations in clean technology and innovative ways to become more resource efficient. These measures can often reduce costs, which can add up to considerable annual savings. Porter (1998b: 359) cites the example of 3M, which was compelled by regulation to reduce solvent emissions. The company was able to avoid solvent-based coatings altogether by coating products with water-based solutions. This shift also eliminated the need to obtain regulatory approval for solvent-based coatings. In fact, 3M, based in the US, has pursued policies designed to improve efficiency and reduce waste independently of regulatory pressures, which have not been as stringent in the US as in some other countries. Since the 1970s, when oil prices surged, the company has operated its Pollution Prevention Pays (3P) programme. 3M's manager of environmental initiatives and sustainability estimates that huge savings have resulted from these projects (Harvey, 2006b). The 3P programme has also engaged employees to find energy savings in all aspects of the business. The company has benefited from first-mover advantages in environmental protection, which has contributed to competitive advantage.

The resource-based theory of the firm (discussed in Chapter 7) can be widened to encompass the notion of core competencies based on new capabilities of firms in managing within ecological constraints (Banerjee, 2002). Sustained competitive advantage can thus emerge from 'natural-resource-based' competencies (Hart, 1995). Examples are the opportunities to develop new technological solutions for emissions reduction and other aspects of environmental degradation. Proactive organizations, often SMEs in research-intensive activities, pursue innovations in a variety of sectors, including waste recycling, renewable energy sources and crop varieties which need less water. For these companies, government policies can be crucial. New technology is typically more expensive for the customer, especially in the early stages, and if government funding is available, customers, particularly business customers, are more inclined to commit resources. The Danish company Vestas Wind Systems is one of the world's leading builders of wind turbines. Dominating the global market for the biggest turbines, it is expanding in China and the US, but it closed a factory in Australia due to lack of support from the Australian government. With Australia's change of government in 2007, greener policies could present new opportunities.

For companies in sectors that are less directly linked to the environment, sustainability is increasingly being seen as part of a firm's broad competitive strategy. Although 3M's environmental strategy has been clearly based on business principles, this approach is now becoming similar to the ethical stance. Most companies present their environmental policies in terms of sustainability and responses to climate change, but for some, the environment is elevated to a core strategy. A driving force has been the emergence of consumers who are more engaged in environmental issues, and who are seeking products and services with sustainability credentials. They include health-conscious consumers, who are adding to the growth in sales of organic foods, as SX13.1 on Whole Foods Market shows. They are not only concerned about where their food comes from, but also issues such as chemical additives. Many of these greener products come at premium

WEB CHECK

3M's website is www.3m.com.

prices, making them accessible mainly to more affluent consumers in the developed world. As climate change gains greater awareness among people everywhere, environmental concerns are becoming more mainstream in consumer purchasing as well as in corporate strategy (see last section of this chapter).

Nonetheless, there are many companies that operate without regard to the risks posed by climate change. A survey of Asian companies in 2007, which looked at a number of issues related to corporate governance, found that most paid no attention to their environmental impact (Asian Corporate Governance Association, 2007). The survey covered 582 companies in 11 countries. Only 58% of the respondent companies answered the questions in the 'clean and green' section at all. Questions included whether they had staff assigned to address green issues and whether they had set emissions reductions targets. The lowest response rates were from Indonesia (22%), followed by China (31%), and 64% of the total scored zero on this section. Large Japanese, Taiwanese and South Korean companies, by contrast, scored in the region of 80% or more. Arguably, these latter companies are more attuned to investor and consumer concerns. On the other hand, manufacturing companies in Indonesia and China are integrated into the supply chains of global MNEs, whose managers would be in a position to exert pressures for raising standards.

TO RECAP...

Competitive advantage and environmental issues

Making environmental performance an aspect of a company's competitive advantage entails a strategy of product differentiation which relies on customers' perceived needs and desires to purchase environmentally friendly products and services, often at premium prices.

Deriving competitive advantage from environmental goals
Assess the benefits and risks of a competitive strategy based on environmental performance, giving examples from specific firms.

PAUSE TO REFLECT

Environmental management in practice

The company which bases its corporate strategy at least in part on environmental performance is committed to a comprehensive review of its activities and products. Environmental management involves assessing and monitoring environmental impacts in all locations worldwide, and continually improving processes in ways which improve environmental performance in all its operations. In this section, we highlight the ecological challenges and the processes by which managers can address them.

Identifying and responding to the challenges

The major environmental changes which businesses need to address are water scarcity, climate change, depletion of natural resources, habitat change, biodiversity loss and overexploitation of the oceans. These changes affect businesses to a greater or lesser extent depending on the types of activity they engage in. Loss of biodiversity and habitat change are often highly localized, impacting on communities with concentrated industrial operations. These communities are also likely to suffer from poor air quality. As global supply chains expand, transport and logistics industries have exerted pressures for new transport networks and infrastructure to accommodate their growing fleets. However, new roads, depots and airports, like factories, impact on ecosystems and biodiversity.

Water scarcity is a trend which affects virtually all businesses and societies, not just agriculture. The manufacture of products from cars to semiconductors uses huge amounts of water. The use of fresh water exceeds long-term sustainable supply by 5–20%, leading to the unsustainable mining of underground water in order to keep manufacturing processes running. As competition for water increases, costs will rise. Operations heavily dependent on water need to become more efficient in the use of water, but there are also opportunities for innovation in processes and materials.

Figure 13.8 Identifying and responding to environmental impacts

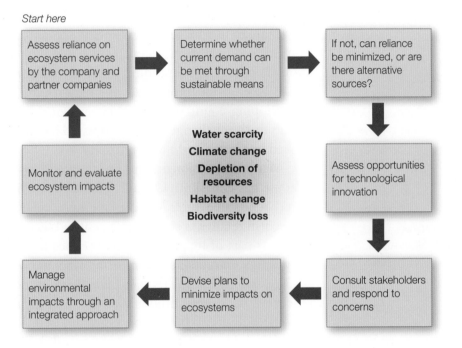

Figure 13.8 sets out step by step the process of identifying and responding to environmental impacts of a company. A first step for business managers is to identify and understand the ecosystems affected by their business, including the activities of suppliers and affiliated firms. This task may be more complex than it seems, as managers must acquire an understanding of the environmental impacts of partner firms, which might be in a range of different locations, facing a diversity of risks. The firm must take into account the entire life cycle of products, including possible problems with discarded products and the potential for recycling. Firms sometimes find that they do not have the expertise to assess, let alone manage, all these issues. The assessment must include an evaluation of whether the current demands of the firm and partner firms for raw materials and energy are sustainable from an environmental perspective. Managers must take into account existing government regulations and new regulations which can be reasonably anticipated. If the firm is operating in a number of countries, it must assess how to approach a myriad of standards.

Seizing opportunities

Ecological changes are presenting important opportunities for innovation. The UK engineering company Tanfield took a far-sighted decision in 2004

TO RECAP...

Identifying environmental challenges

International firms must assess how their activities impact on ecosystems, taking into consideration activities throughout their supply chains. They must also consider differing national standards and anticipate regulatory changes.

to buy Smith Electric Vehicles, which had a plan to develop environmentally friendly electric vans and trucks, for delivery and maintenance activities. In 2007, Tanfield won a contract for delivery vehicles with supermarket retailer, Sainsbury's. A listed SME, it saw its share price rise from 10p at the time of the acquisition to 180p by the time the contract with Sainsbury's was concluded (Oakley, 2007).

Industrial agriculture, or 'agribusiness', has acquired a poor reputation for soil damage, the destruction of forests and the overuse of water from unsustainable sources. All these issues can now be alleviated through technological advances. Systems to use irrigation water more frugally are available, as are systems to use sensors for reducing the amounts of fertilizer needed. There are also conservation systems which combine agriculture and forest management, aiding reforestation. Consumer concerns over unsustainable agriculture have given impetus to organic farming, as highlighted in SX13.1. In developing countries, with their growing populations and precarious agriculture, the challenges being addressed include developing crop strains which need less water and fewer nutrients.

Many international firms are now addressing the need to reduce greenhouse gas emissions. Options include switching to cleaner fuels such as gas and renewable fuels such as biofuels, solar and wind power. IKEA, the Swedish retailer, is switching its entire UK company car fleet to hybrid vehicles, as part of its programme to reduce its carbon dioxide emissions by 9% by 2010. Carmakers are meeting demand with a range of green models, discussed in CS13.2. IKEA's plan does not include its fleet of delivery trucks serving its stores, although it is experimenting with electric vehicles for home deliveries. Increasing efficiency reduces CO_2 emissions and can be achieved in operations, transport and buildings. Businesses can recycle supplies and use new technologies which reduce the consumption of water per unit of output.

Monitoring environmental performance

Measuring emissions and disclosing them publicly is a first step towards setting targets for reductions. In 2007, Wal-Mart announced its aim to measure and reduce greenhouse gas emissions throughout its supply chain, for everything from beer to vacuum cleaners. As the world's largest retailer, with huge power over suppliers, it is in a position to bring about dramatic changes throughout the supply chain, also impacting on competitors. It aims to design a reporting system which would cover its supplier base of more than 60,000 companies. Wal-Mart embarked on a new environmental strategy in 2005, targeting packaging and the chemicals used by suppliers.

Monitoring and measuring environmental performance is crucial for the organization and all its stakeholders. Performance measurement tools can be adapted to apply to a variety of different processes in different businesses. As new projects come on stream or new opportunities arise, the means of assessing and monitoring environmental impacts are then in place. If targets are met, staff are assured that the business is making progress. With increasing

TO RECAP...

Responding to environmental concerns

As companies become more conscious of the environmental impacts of their operations, they are addressing the need to reduce pollution, reduce reliance on limited resources and curtail the environmental degradation associated with their activities. For international businesses, environmental concerns may be local, such as damage to ecosystems, and global, such as the need to reduce emissions. Many companies are seizing opportunities for innovative solutions to environmental concerns.

scientific knowledge and rising expectations, targets and performance may well have to be altered. The flexibility to adapt to new situations is an aspect of the environmental awareness which should become part of corporate culture. Traditionally, the environment was grouped with health and safety in functional terms. Now, it is becoming central for all functional areas, increasingly influencing financial management.

Companies frequently turn to third-party verification of environmental performance. These assessors have specialist expertise, and their independence lends greater credibility to the monitoring process than in-house assessments. A number of bodies now offer certification systems, by which a company's products and services must meet standards set across a whole industry. Certification aims to assure consumers that a firm's products meet independent standards. Like third-party verification, certification is international in its scope, allowing global comparisons to be made. Certification is now available across a wide range of goods and services, including forestry products, food and tourism. On the other hand, certification can backfire if either the certifying organization or the company whose products are certified are perceived to fall beneath expected standards. Environmentalists warn that consumers can be misled into thinking that products are from sustainable sources, when, in fact, standards vary considerably.

Social and environmental impacts now feature regularly in companies' annual reports. They take their place alongside financial reporting in what is known as triple bottom line reporting. In these reports, managers identify and assess the risks faced by the company from environmental uncertainties and resource constraints globally. They set out how the company is managing its operations in sustainable ways. Institutional investors such as pension funds have taken a keen interest in environmental reporting. In America, a group made up of investors, NGOs and representatives from state governments petitioned the Securities and Exchange Commission (SEC) in 2007, pointing out that companies ought to be telling investors how climate change is affecting their business, which is directly relevant to future profits. These institutional investors, who control about $40 trillion in investments, are in a strong position to bring about changes in the way that companies disclose risks stemming from climate change.

As yet, the reporting of greenhouse gas emissions is not required of listed companies on stock exchanges. However, from 2005, UK companies have been required to submit an operating and financial review in their annual reports. Both government guidance and investor concerns are leading to greater disclosure of environmental impacts on the business. There are no standard measurements which are recognized, but the environment ministry recommends measurements of CO_2 and methane emissions and the company's record on waste and water use. It is left to the company to decide whether to measure carbon emissions per employee, per unit of output or per unit of turnover. Increasing focus on disclosure, making comparisons across companies easier, is likely to come with growing concerns about climate change.

Third-party verification: The use of independent specialist bodies for the measurement of a firm's environmental performance.

Triple bottom line reporting: Corporate reporting focusing on social and environmental aspects of the company, in addition to traditional financial information.

Triple bottom line reporting is also important in assessing the social impacts of the firm's business. This is the focus of the next chapter, but it should be noted here that there is considerable overlap between social and environmental concerns:

1 Social responsibility encompasses managing environmental performance. As we have seen, industrial activities are linked to processes such as pollution which affect people's well-being.

2 Social responsibility implies altering the organization's behaviour to achieve social values, beyond legal obligations. Business initiatives are setting environmental standards such as emissions reductions which are more demanding than the current law in many countries. While there is a business case for anticipating future regulations, these firms are also responding to stakeholder concerns and authoritative evidence of the long-term damage to societies and ecosystems caused by climate change.

STRATEGIC CROSSROADS

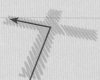

13.1

Whole Foods Market: more than a niche player

Texas-based Whole Foods Market is a fast-growing supermarket chain with a difference, specializing in organic fruit and vegetables, fish from sustainable sources and meat from animals raised in compassionate conditions. Perishable products accounted for 67% of its total retail sales in 2006. It also sells other food and beverages, dietary supplements, household products, personal care products and organic cotton clothing. Natural and organic food is usually considered a niche market, catered for by small outlets with a limited range of products, often run by family firms. When Whole Foods Market was formed in 1980, it resembled this type of traditional wholefoods retailer, but its youthful founders envisaged a larger layout similar to a supermarket, calling their first store SaferWay, a take-off on the familiar Safeway supermarkets.

John Mackey, the charismatic CEO and co-founder, embraced an ethical and stakeholder-centred philosophy as well as an overtly capitalist business strategy, based on expansion by acquisitions. From 1984, the company set about acquiring smaller health and natural food stores across the US. It expanded rapidly, listing on the Nasdaq exchange in 1992. In 2002 it expanded into Canada, and in 2004 it acquired seven Fresh & Wild stores in the UK. Its store in central London, on the site of the old Barker's department store, covers 80,000 sq ft, with a restaurant seating 350 people. It most ambitious acquisition has been the takeover of its chief US rival, Wild Oats Markets, a public listed company. However, the process proved difficult, resulting in damage to its reputation, as well

as that of its CEO. The US Federal Trade Commission blocked the $.5 billion takeover on anti-competitive grounds, but, on appeal, federal judges allowed it to go ahead, on the grounds that the competition in organic retailing has now widened to include mainstream supermarkets such as Wal-Mart and Safeway. Meanwhile, an investigation by the SEC revealed that Mackey had been posting anonymous messages on an online financial message board, which was thought to be inappropriate behaviour for an executive of a public company.

As consumers become more concerned about the health and environmental aspects of food and other products, Whole Foods Market is tapping into a lucrative market. Its US stores generate twice the profit per square foot of any other supermarket, indicating that consumers are willing to spend premium prices for ethically and environmentally friendly products. Each store generates average annual sales of $22 million. As the figure shows, sales have grown rapidly. The acquisition of Wild Oats added another 110 stores to its portfolio, which would bring the total to nearly 300. The number of employees, or 'team members', as they are known within the company, has grown from 19 in 1980 to 43,000. They enjoy higher-than-average pay for the sector, together with free health insurance, but the company has taken a robust stance against trade union membership, which the founders object to on libertarian principles.

The CEO, although cultivating a rather hippy appearance, has pursued a shrewd marketing strategy designed to strike a chord with affluent consumers. The appearance of the stores, with natural wood interiors and attractive displays of fresh produce, alongside brochures explaining the sources of the food and how it has been processed, gain the shoppers' confidence. Fish are certified by the Marine Stewardship Council,

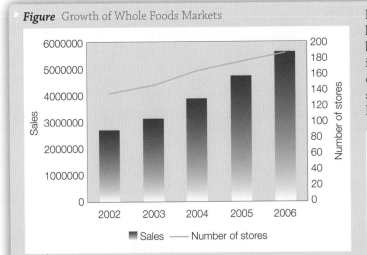

Figure Growth of Whole Foods Markets

Source: Whole Foods Market Annual Report 2006, www.wholefoodsmarkets.com

an independent body which certifies that fisheries are run on a sustainable basis. It sells no GM products, and no products with artificial colours or preservatives. Its motto is 'Whole Foods, Whole People, Whole Planet'. Its size and growing dominance in the sector, however, could be considered threatening to local and regional foods, which have been a concern of the organic movement.

According to its Annual Report for 2006, Whole Foods Market aspires to become an international brand. The company has introduced a range of private labels, with three corporate brands. Although it would no longer seem to be a niche player, its North America president says: 'We have always considered ourselves alternative even as we got bigger' (BBC, 2007). Its size and behaviour, however, are testing its ethical and stakeholder values.

Questions
◆ Assess Whole Foods Market's business strategy in light of its ethical principles, in particular discussing whether its size and values are compatible.
◆ Why has Whole Foods Market grown so popular with consumers? What are its prospects in international markets?

Sources: Murray, S., 'Where customers fork out for high quality', *Financial Times*, 14 October 2004; BBC (2007) 'Whole Foods – a retail phenomenon', 6 June, www.news.bbc.co.uk; Birchall, J., 'Whole Foods CEO apologises for gaffe', *Financial Times*, 18 July 2007; Martin, A., 'Judge sides with Whole Foods on deal for Wild Oats', *New York Times*, 17 August 2007, www.nytimes.com; Whole Foods Market Annual Report 2006, www.wholefoodsmarket.com.

WEB CHECK

Whole Foods Market is at www.wholefoodsmarket.com, where its environmental philosophy can be found.

Environmental reporting from the investors' perspective

Why are investors becoming increasingly focused on companies' environmental impacts, and what types of disclosure are most crucial in the following types of international business:
● Global brand of sportswear with outsourced manufacturing in developing countries
● Food retailer which sources fresh produce from many different countries, including developing countries
● Global steel-making company?

PAUSE TO REFLECT

Shared responsibilities: businesses and governments

The aims of businesses and governments are often depicted as being in conflict. Businesses desire maximum freedom to carry out the goals of the enterprise, while government regulation acts as a constraint. In the global competitive environment, MNEs tend to gravitate towards countries with the friendliest regulatory frameworks. However, in terms of environmental protection, these stereotypical roles are ceasing to reflect reality. Governments increasingly acknowledge the need to address climate change, although they are often reluctant to impose regulations. Meanwhile, many businesses have taken leads in innovative solutions within government frameworks which offer incentives. We look here at how these interactions are working in two crucial areas: energy needs and waste management.

Meeting energy needs

As societies become industrialized, their energy needs rise. Industrial production, transport and urban lifestyles all depend on energy. The growth in GDP is mirrored by energy consumption: global GDP rose nineteenfold from 1900 to 2001, and consumption of commercial energy rose eighteenfold (Wolf, 2006b). Governments are now addressing the dual issues of depletion of non-renewable energy resources and climate change. Although coal has been predominant in energy generation, its drawbacks are that it is non-renewable, and it causes acid rain and carbon dioxide emissions. Oil reserves are also becoming depleted, compelling oil companies and governments to seek reserves which are more difficult and expensive to access. As Figure 13.9 shows, energy industries are the largest source of greenhouse gas emissions within the EU. Reducing reliance on fossil fuels is therefore indicated for a sustainable energy policy. Governments and businesses are looking at a more diversified array of energy sources, including hydroelectric, gas and nuclear power. Nonetheless, coal remains significant, especially in developing countries.

The view of the UK government is that future energy needs will come from a diversity of sources, seen in Figure 13.10. It envisages an increase in nuclear energy, mainly due to its low carbon footprint and security of supply (UK Department of Business, Enterprise and Regulatory Reform, 2006: 113). This represents a shift in policy. Until recently, there had been little enthusiasm for replacing Britain's ageing nuclear power stations, which have undergone decommissioning over a number of years. Gas is also favoured for its cleaner power generation than coal, and is projected to grow in importance, although, like coal, it is now reliant on imported supplies.

In 2004, the UK relied on coal combustion for 34% of its energy, and in Germany, coal accounted for half its electricity generation. Due to EU environmental protection legislation, a third of the UK's power plants must close no later than 2015. The gap created by the closure of old coal-fired and nuclear power stations must be filled. Companies are in a strong position to influence this decision-making. Encouraged by government policies, many have invested in R&D in clean technology.

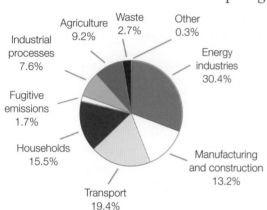

Figure 13.9 Share of total greenhouse gas emissions in the EU 25 countries by sector, 2004

Source: European Environment Agency (2007) *Europe's Environment: the Fourth Assessment*, www.eea.europa.eu

Figure 13.10 Shifting sources of power generation in the UK

Source: UK Department for Business, Enterprise and Regulatory Reform (2006) *Energy Review 2006*, www.dti.gov.uk

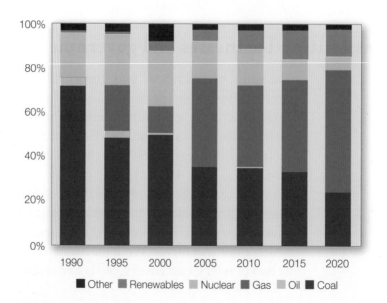

Creating cleaner coal-fired power stations relies on three means of reducing emissions. These are:

1 To achieve efficiency, advances in clean technology allow continued reliance on the burning of fossil fuels.
2 Making use of biomass in conjunction with coal is an option which could reduce emissions without radical modifications to existing plants.
3 Carbon capture and storage, also known as 'carbon sequestration', involves capturing carbon and sulphur before they reach the atmosphere, and storing them in safe reservoirs, often underground or in the sea. Much of the R&D has been carried out by oil companies. Drawbacks are the risks of leakage from these sites, and the legal prohibition on the dumping of industrial waste at sea. Depleted oil and gas fields in the North Sea can be used as potential storage sites, but international co-operation is needed to clarify the legal liability of these projects.

All three methods depend on regulatory frameworks to ensure safety of transport and storage.

Nuclear power is now perceived as central to a low carbon economy. New nuclear power plants are likely to be built and run by specialist companies such as EDF. The UK government has expressed a wish to help the process along by streamlining the planning and licensing of nuclear power plants, and possibly offering incentives such as tax credits. Such incentives, while not outright subsidies, encourage companies to embark on these vast long-term projects. Environmentalists are concerned that not enough emphasis is being given to renewables. Companies in the renewables sector, including wind generation and biofuels, also see opportunities for growth. They can argue that the costs and safety risks of nuclear power are major drawbacks. On the other hand, technological improvements are reducing the risks, producing less waste than older nuclear plants. Although still very costly, they are cheaper to build than their predecessors.

Biofuels are also enjoying a renaissance, thanks to their green credentials. Biomass is any organic matter derived from plants or animals. These materials are traditional sources of fuel for burning. Biofuels are carbon neutral: the carbon dioxide emitted from burning is balanced by the carbon dioxide the plant absorbs while growing. Ethanol is a type of biomass produced from grain or sugar. Growing crops for biofuel production is now a big business globally. Brazil is the leader in this sector, producing ethanol by distilling sugar cane. Brazilians see ethanol exports as a money-spinner, but they have been thwarted by import tariffs in their largest potential market, the US. US farmers produce ethanol from maize (corn), wheat and other grain. They are heavily subsidized by the federal government. Some biofuel companies make biodiesel from oil-bearing crops such as soya, palm oil and rapeseed. Brazil's ethanol represents an apparently attractive option to fossil fuels, but there are fears that growing more sugar cane, palm oil and other crops for biofuel is depleting the rainforests and pushing aside other crops that are needed for food. Globally, grain prices are rising, due to demand for food as well as demand from the biofuel industry (see further discussion in Chapter 15). Another consideration is that the price of maize doubled in 2006, causing concerns over the viability of biofuel production.

Carbon capture and storage: Process of removing carbon dioxide from the burning of fossil fuels and storing it deep underground.

A company which specializes in carbon capture technology is the Norwegian company, Sargas, whose website is www.sargas.no.

WEB CHECK

Biofuels: Fuels derived from organic matter, seen as an alternative to fossil fuels.

TO RECAP...
Meeting energy needs
The goal of most governments is a shift away from fossil fuels, which are non-renewable and polluting, towards cleaner energy generation. Renewable sources, such as wind and solar power, are being expanded, and there is a resurgence of interest in nuclear power, despite its costs and safety risks. Biofuels are viewed as a green alternative to fossil fuels, but crops grown for biofuel must compete with food crops.

Energy security
Environmental concerns are one set of factors which weigh with governments in designing energy policies, but there are others. For example, a thriving coalmining sector employs a large workforce which would be out of work if the mine closes. Assess the relative importance of all the factors which governments take into account in designing energy policies.

PAUSE TO REFLECT

Waste and recycling

The richer a society is, the more waste is generated – from industrial processes, urban living and increased volumes of packaging. It was once considered adequate to set aside landfill sites in conjunction with incineration, to deal with all types of rubbish. This policy is now recognized as short-sighted and dangerous, as both produce greenhouse gas emissions, landfill releasing methane and incineration releasing CO_2 and other gases such as toxic dioxins. Although municipal authorities have borne the brunt of dealing with waste, regulation at national and EU level has led to changes in policies towards more enlightened ways of treating and recycling waste.

In 1975, the EU issued its first waste directive, which set out a hierarchy of treatment methods, shown in Figure 13.11. This has been followed by others on specific issues such as landfill, recycling and hazardous waste. The EU has also followed up with regimes for producer responsibility for specific types of product. By 2020, half of all EU municipal waste and 70% of construction waste must be recycled. By 2025, it will be prohibited to landfill materials which could be recycled, including paper, wood, glass, plastic, textiles and metal. Not all member states have embraced these directives wholeheartedly, partly because of the extra burdens placed on businesses and consumers. Germany has taken a leadership role, but other countries are now undergoing a change of culture towards one of recycling and reducing emissions. The US has been slow to adopt rules which would reduce landfill and increase recycling, but individual states are doing so, in an effort to cut the Americans' world record for household waste, which is an annual 737 kg per person.

The tightening of regulations has opened up opportunities for waste management companies to expand their geographic reach and diversify their activities, to deal with waste treatment in specific sectors. One of these initiatives is to treat waste as a source of renewable energy. These projects both get rid of waste and act as a substitute for fossil fuel. Although they have a poor image and raise safety fears in the minds of the public, waste-to-energy plants are

plate 13.3 Paper recycling has become an important growth industry globally, due to resource constraints and environmental pressures.

Figure 13.11 Hierarchy of waste treatment methods

now clean enough to be sited in city centres. Waste management is now seen as an essential element in governments' climate change agendas.

Regulatory systems which adopt producer responsibility are compelling managers to look at the full life cycle costs of products, including maximizing the potential for recycling. In some companies, recycling has become a high-profile activity. Nike's Reuse-a-Shoe programme utilizes old trainers to create sports surfaces such as basketball and tennis courts and the Considered Boot is a sustainable line of shoes. Nike has found that using fewer materials and keeping designs simple make recycling easier. As metals become more expensive, recycling electronic equipment to extract small amounts of metal becomes worthwhile. Computer manufacturers have examined the ways in which their machines are made, as recycling computer hardware is a growing problem. Most of the millions of PCs that are manufactured end up in landfill sites, but new restrictions on landfills have made recycling an imperative. Among the 700 different materials which make up a PC are heavy metals and other pollutants which are dangerous in landfill. HP has been at the forefront in seeking ways to design PCs that contain safer materials for easier recycling. Discarded equipment, if it can be recycled so that materials can be extracted, can yield materials which can be sold or reused, re-entering the supply chain. Some individual US states, such as California, have adopted an alternative to the producer responsibility principle, charging an advanced recycling fee on producers of products, collectable at the point of purchase. The funds are used by the state for recycling.

TO RECAP...

Changing perceptions of waste and recycling

Governments, businesses and consumers are becoming better informed about ways of dealing with waste which minimize environmental impacts. Innovation in waste recovery, recycling and waste-to-energy technologies are providing opportunities for businesses, which now see waste management as a global business.

STRATEGIC CROSSROADS

13.2

Customer-led packaging innovation from Huhtamaki

The office worker rushing to buy a gourmet coffee from a coffee shop probably does not think much about the disposable cup and lid provided, but for Huhtamaki, this quintessentially modern product poses challenges which help to determine the direction of its global business. A Finnish company founded in 1920, Huhtamaki was originally a confectionary manufacturer, before diversifying into a variety of businesses, including pharmaceuticals. Gradually, these businesses were whittled down, and packaging became its core industry. That strategic decision having been taken, the company built up manufacturing capacity quickly, acquiring 14

packaging companies from 1997 to 2001. Packaging facilities tend to be located near customers, and Huhtamaki's expansion has therefore followed markets. It now has 66 manufacturing sites in 36 countries. Emerging markets are its fastest growing markets, as shown in the figure. These markets are expected to grow 9.5% between 2004 and 2009, while markets in developed countries will grow only 2.4%. To meet demand, Huhtamaki has opened new production facilities in China and India, with their growth in purchasing power and modern retail outlets. Its largest markets remain in the developed world, where consumer priorities are convenience, quality and safety in packaging. In addition, environmental issues are rising up the agenda: What materials are used? How energy efficient is production? Are they recyclable?

Packaging for food in single-use containers has traditionally relied on plastics. However, as plastics are petroleum based,

Figure Global consumer packaging market

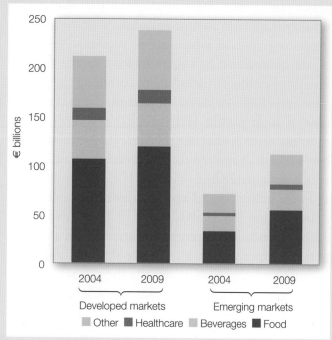

€ billions

Developed markets   Emerging markets

■ Other ■ Healthcare ■ Beverages ■ Food

Note: 2009 figures are estimates

Source: Huhtamaki Annual Report 2006, www.huhtamaki.com

packaging has become a growing contributor to municipal waste in the world's cities. Huhtamaki's environmental goals are to minimize natural resource depletion, increase efficiency in processing, and reduce waste generation, including emissions into the air. Its view of sustainable packaging is that environmental impacts should be minimal. Bioware sustainable packaging is totally compostable and biodegradable. It has been adopted by environmentally conscious retailers such as Marks & Spencer. Huhtamaki's moulded fibre packaging is designed as a strong packaging for fresh foods. It is made entirely from recycled materials, paper scrap and fibre.

Packaging is recognized as important to the consumer's enjoyment of a product. It is also an element in the marketing and brand recognition of a product. Manufacturers and retailers are constantly seeking new packaging solutions which are distinctive to their products and brands. The environmental dimension of their choice of packaging is an aspect of their corporate strategy, and is also designed to attract today's environmentally conscious consumers. A challenge for Huhtamaki is to develop packaging which offers improvements for the consumer over traditional plastic while also being environmentally sustainable.

they raise environmental problems: they do not decompose in landfill sites, the manufacturing process releases harmful emissions, and oil is a non-renewable resource. Researchers have looked at the whole life cycle of packaging, seeking sustainable alternatives. At the same time, they are aware that manufacturers and retailers need to keep the costs of packaging down to a small proportion of the overall product.

Huhtamaki has responded with innovations designed to meet the needs of consumer convenience as well as environmental goals. Busy lifestyles and urbanization have been factors in the changing packaging industry. People consume more food and beverages on the go, which implies not just dishes and trays but disposable cutlery as well. They also buy convenience foods to microwave at home in the packaging. A proliferation of

Questions

◆ What are the challenges posed for designing packaging to suit modern lifestyles and protect the environment?
◆ Huhtamaki's fastest growing markets are in emerging economies, where cost is likely to be a bigger factor than environmental concerns. How should its environmental strategy be framed in these markets?

Sources: Scott, M., 'Solution is in shoppers' hands', *Financial Times*, 18 April 2007; Scott, M., 'Where there's muck there's brass', *Financial Times*, 18 April 2007; Goldstein, N. and Olivares, C. (2007), 'What's what and who's who in compostable products', *In Business*, **29**(4): 16–17; Huhtamäki Oyj, Annual Report 2006, www.huhtamaki.com.

WEB CHECK

Huhtamaki's website is www.huhtamaki.com.

Focus on consumers

Although businesses around the world have committed themselves to changes in response to environmental concerns, the issues of what changes are needed in consumer behaviour and how to bring them about are vexing. Households are responsible for 15.5% of EU greenhouse gas emissions, as shown in Figure 13.9. Consumers in modern industrial societies tend to take for granted an array of modern appliances and electronic goods, one or more cars for work and leisure, and the ability to travel widely by air at relatively low cost. Consumers in industrializing countries are emulating those in the older industrialized economies, rapidly acquiring the same types of goods and services, enjoying travel and leisure activities. For international businesses, growing markets in these countries, including Brazil, Russia, India and China (sometimes referred to as the BRIC countries), are now providing the greatest opportunities for growing sales of virtually all consumer products, from beverages to televisions. Industrialization, mass consumer markets, urbanization and global transport are taking a toll on the environment. Pollution, poor air and water quality, degraded ecosystems and dwindling natural resources are undermining the quality of life that consumers everywhere have assumed would forever accompany increasing wealth.

Consumers in Western countries have become accustomed to messages exhorting them to adopt greener lifestyles, but most are not willing to change their behaviour in radical ways, as CS13.2 highlights. The ethical consumer, using a bicycle instead of a car and forgoing foreign holidays, remains in a minority. For most, the throwaway culture prevails, in which machines are discarded not because they are broken, but because their owners wish to have the latest model. It was estimated that in 2005, Americans owned nearly 3 billion electronic products, from mobile phones to TVs, all of which were soon to be superseded by newer, sleeker models with more features, but also creating environmental problems.

Nonetheless, consumers are increasingly concerned about the environment. They exert pressure on companies whose products they buy to be more environmentally friendly, demand newspapers made from recycled paper, and want fish from sustainable sources. Products such as organic food inevitably cost more than industrially processed food, and while affluent consumers with strong ethical principles are willing to pay, the majority are not. Research by the EU Commission in 2006 showed that, although 85% of citizens feel their governments should invest more in renewable energy, 59% were unwilling to pay more (European Commission, 2006). This represents a *rise* from 54% in 2002, although climate change has received considerable public attention in the intervening years. The percentage of those unwilling to pay more was 70% in the new EU member states, which are emerging economies.

The notion of sustainable consumption is not new. In 1987, the Brundtland Report said that 'living standards that go beyond the basic minimum are sustainable only if consumption standards everywhere have regard for long-term sustainability' (UN, 1987). Business leaders in the EU have urged that strengthening consumer commitment is now needed to balance industry's efforts. However, governments are reluctant to take politically unpalatable measures. As 50% of emissions come from buildings, governments could introduce new standards to make new buildings, including housing, more energy efficient. However, the prospect of additional costs feeding through to house prices is a deterrent. Similarly, raising duties on petrol and transport is unpopular. Aircraft fuel enjoys exemptions from both VAT and excise duty. Growing air travel is one of the fastest rising sources of CO_2 emissions, yet governments collectively support these exemptions. When the UK government announced above-inflation rises in petrol duty in 2000, blockades on the roads caused by lorry drivers led the chancellor of the exchequer to drop the planned rise. Consumers' reluctance to change their habits of consumption, especially if financial cost is involved, is posing policy challenges for governments, which are becoming more urgent as climate change impacts on societies. Governments are gradually imposing emissions targets for new cars, but, as CS13.2 shows, the cleaner vehicle is not the first choice of most consumers.

TO RECAP...

Changing consumer behaviour

Consumers are becoming more conscious of environmental concerns, but are often reluctant to accept changes perceived as detrimental to their lifestyles and purchasing behaviour. Companies selling premium products such as organic foods are enjoying expanding markets, as affluent consumers seek alternative products on health as well as environmental grounds. Mandatory rules, as in recycling requirements and controls on car emissions, are gradually bringing about changes.

Conclusions

☐ Industrialization, urbanization and improved transport have brought economic benefits and improvements to human well-being across the globe. However, these processes have also led to environmental degradation and climate change, threatening the prospects of future generations to reap similar benefits. Many harmful effects are localized, impairing the living conditions and natural environment of communities. Concentrations of air and water pollution are now recognized as causing ill health, threatening future gains in well-being which economic development makes possible. Of the challenges facing the planet, climate change is the most pervasive, including rising sea levels, floods, drought and extreme weather events. Reducing emissions of greenhouse gases, largely resulting from the burning of fossil fuels, is recognized as key to curbing climate change impacts. Responses to environmental concerns by national governments have been mixed. Many have taken policy steps to curtail emissions, while others remain focused on economic growth. The Kyoto Protocol of 1998 called on the major economies in the developed world to abide by targets to reduce emissions, while refraining from including developing countries in such a regime. However, developing countries are now in the spotlight, in particular China and India, with their rapidly increasing greenhouse gas emissions.

☐ International businesses with operations in diverse locations must focus on a variety of environmental impacts, which are increasingly recognized in global corporate strategy. While regulation is a driver in some countries, in others, such as developing countries, motivations stem from principled concerns about sustainable development, as well as perceived risks to future financial performance. Environmental strategies entail possible changes in operations and sourcing, performance targets and monitoring. Although operational changes and rising costs for scarce resources present a gloomy picture, the opportunities for innovation and efficiency gains have spurred many forward-thinking companies to devise creative solutions which can be a source of competitive advantage. Stakeholders, including investors and consumers, have taken a growing interest in corporate 'green' credentials, but are only gradually recognizing the implications for changes in their own patterns of consumption. Legislation is biting in some areas, such as waste recycling, and in others, the hope is that business innovations are producing cleaner alternatives which meet consumers' expectations, without the need to make painful changes to lifestyles.

Reality check for the consumer

The consumers in developing countries who are seeing rising incomes are eager to buy into modern consumer lifestyles. This lifestyle is now taken for granted by consumers in the developed world. Is it right to force consumers to change their behaviour, for example by restricting people to one foreign holiday per year? Should consumers in the developed world bear the brunt of changes, or should governments in the developing world also take steps to halt the rise of unsustainable consumption?

PAUSE TO REFLECT

Review questions

Part A: Grasping the basic concepts and knowledge

1. Define 'ecosystem', and state how environmental indicators impact in an ecosystem.
2. What are the major social impacts of industrialized production?
3. Why is transboundary pollution particularly difficult to control and prevent?
4. What is global warming, and what are its main causes?
5. Explain the impacts of climate change, and the implications for societies.
6. What factors do national governments take into consideration when framing environmental policies? What are the main areas of legislation?
7. On what grounds did the Stern Report recommend action by national governments to deal with climate change?
8. What were the aims of the Kyoto Protocol? Why has international co-operation become more problematic since it was agreed in 1998?
9. Define 'sustainable development'. Why has this concept been difficult to 'sell' to developing nations?
10. What are the main determinants of an environmental strategy for business, and how do they differ between companies?
11. What is the 'business case' for adopting an environmental protection strategy?
12. What is meant by 'carbon neutrality', and why is this concept being adopted as a strategic goal by businesses?
13. How can an environmental strategy enhance competitiveness within the framework of a resource-based view of the firm?
14. In what ways can anticipated environmental constraints lead to innovation and new business opportunities? Give examples.
15. In what ways does environmental monitoring pose difficulties for businesses? How does third-party verification represent a step forward?
16. Outline the policy issues involved for governments in how to meet future energy needs while reducing greenhouse gas emissions.
17. What innovative developments in waste recycling and disposal are being taken up by companies as part of a whole life cycle approach to their products?
18. How can consumers be persuaded that changes in their behaviour are needed, in order to achieve environmental sustainability?

Part B: Critical thinking and discussion

1. Environmentalists are sometimes accused of advocating turning the clock back on economic development. Is this a fair or unfair depiction, and why?
2. Pollution in some regions, in particular in urban areas of developing countries, is at such high levels that people's well-being is impaired and ecosystems are being destroyed. How, if at all, can national governments, who have contributed to the pollution by their industrialization policies, be persuaded to change their policies?
3. Climate change is usually referred to as an example of a global environmental issue, but countries tend to take a national perspective on the impacts. What changes in thinking are

needed, in order for national authorities to co-operate in, for example, reducing emissions?

4. How is the competitive landscape changing, favouring companies which seek to gain competitive advantage from environmental policies?

5. Environmental monitoring for companies is still in the early stages, but the perceived need for transparency and disclosure is growing. How should companies in the following industries respond:
- car manufacturing
- the passenger airline industry
- banking?

Case study 13.2: Who's driving the green car?

The need to reduce CO_2 emissions has now been acknowledged by all the world's major car manufacturers. They have varied in their responses, some becoming early pioneers of new technology, while others have joined the bandwagon belatedly. Their varying strategies reflect ambivalence about which technology to focus on and their perceptions of the markets for greener vehicles. Regulators are closing in on traditional vehicles with high emissions, but consumers must be persuaded of the benefits of the new vehicles. The green car typically costs more and is more complicated to operate, posing challenges for manufacturers who are investing heavily in green technology.

One of the major drivers of innovation has been government pressure on manufacturers to reduce the emissions in new vehicles. Cars' average emissions of CO_2 in 2007 were 160g per km driven. The European Commission aims to reduce this level to 120g by 2012. This would be a significant reduction, requiring costly investment in new technologies, pushing up the price of new vehicles. It would also imply focusing on small cars, which are more fuel efficient than larger, heavier models. California, which is noted for its proactive approach to reducing emissions, is demanding that a proportion of all new cars should have alternative technology. Could the days of the large sports utility vehicles (SUVs) and light trucks favoured by American motorists be numbered? The rising cost of fuel and insecurity of foreign supplies could help to persuade motorists to opt for one of the greener vehicles available.

Manufacturers have targeted the twin goals of reducing emissions and achieving greater fuel efficiency. The table lists alternative technologies with their advantages and disadvantages. Hybrid vehicles, although pioneered by Honda, are closely associated with Toyota, which has become the market leader. Its first hybrid model, the Prius, was launched in 1997. In 2006, it sold 325,000 hybrids, including Prius, Lexus and Camry models (see the figure). This is only 4% of the 8.8 million cars it sold in total. Purchasers were mainly urban dwellers concerned about climate change and not deterred by the high price. Hybrids have enjoyed a tax credit from US federal authorities, which, to the disappointment of Toyota, was reduced in 2007. The hybrid car achieves 30% savings in fuel costs, but this does not compensate for the higher cost of the car unless the price of fuel rockets. While hybrids have gained Toyota plaudits for its green credentials, other manufacturers note that some, such as the luxury Lexus, actually have relatively high fuel consumption. In 2009, Toyota is launching a full-size Tundra pick-up truck able to run on 85% ethanol, in a bow towards American consumer demand for larger vehicles, despite their weaker green credentials.

German manufacturers have invested in improved technology for petrol and diesel cars, reducing CO_2 emissions to levels which undercut hybrids in some cases. VW introduced a clean diesel version of the Golf in 2007, with emissions of just 119g per km, down from the 135g per km of the previous Golf. Citroen is introducing the C-Cactus hybrid diesel, made from largely recycled or recyclable materials. Its light weight, 1,306 kg, helps it to achieve emissions of just 78g per km. The small car, while the environmentalist's choice, does not necessarily excite consumers, however. Toyota sees its new model SUVs and pick-ups as key to building market share in America, and, along with US car manufacturers, has lobbied against restrictions on emissions, through its membership of the Alliance of Automobile Manufacturers. Honda and Nissan have not joined the Alliance.

American manufacturers are also investing in green technology, although they have been rather later in introducing new greener models. General Motors has produced a concept car, the Volt

Table Alternative green technologies

Type	Description	Advantages	Disadvantages
Hybrid	Combination of electric motor, battery and internal combustion engine	Reduced reliance on fossil fuel; many models of car available	High initial outlay
Plug-in hybrid	Plug-in battery which can be charged from a household power socket	Lower fuel consumption than hybrids	Limited distance before needing to be recharged
Natural gas	Compressed natural gas (CNG) or liquefied petroleum gas (LPG) stored in pressurized tank	Significantly lower CO2 emissions than petrol; conventional engine can be refitted for gas	Limited availability of gas; less fuel efficient than petrol
Flex fuel	Engine designed to run on petrol or a blend with up to 85% ethanol	Little modification needed to conventional engines; established technology	20–30% less fuel efficient than petrol-only use
Clean diesel	Improved diesel engine with reduced CO2 emissions	Significant reductions in emissions, rivalling hybrids; cars less expensive to buy than hybrids	Reliance on fossil fuel

Figure Toyota's sales of hybrid cars

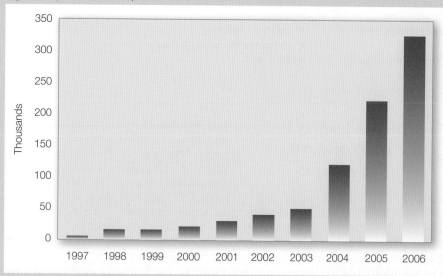

Source: *Financial Times*, 26 July 2007

electric car, which runs on plug-in batteries. This car will not be produced until 2010. A challenge is to produce a battery light enough to fit easily into a normal car, while giving enough power to go a reasonable distance. The aim of the Volt is to travel 65 km on battery power alone. With this type of vehicle, much depends on developing improved car batteries. In Japan, Panasonic and Matsushita have formed a joint venture, in which Toyota has a 60% stake, to advance plug-in technology.

As car manufacturers traditionally enjoy their largest profit margins on their luxury models, a shift to smaller, more fuel-efficient cars could pose a threat for companies such as Germany's luxury carmakers.

BMW's fleet overall has one of the highest average fuel emissions levels. Like its rivals, it is introducing a small car with low emissions. The impact of future EU carbon-cutting regulations on the luxury segment is not necessarily as bleak as it might seem. Perhaps ironically, these companies could stand to benefit. Prestige German manufacturers have high R&D budgets and enviable histories of innovations in safety and new technology. The tighter rules will push up prices, giving greater scope for profit margins. Long popular in America, SUVs are growing in popularity in Europe, despite their poor environmental image. In contrast to their American counterparts, the new SUVs are often cleaner diesel versions, although their green credentials are not their chief appeal. BMW sums up consumer sentiment: 'While CO_2 emissions aren't at the top of the shopping list, they can only become more and more important to consumers' (Reed, 10 September 2007).

Staunch environmentalists are sceptical of the green car, urging that more radical changes in behaviour are needed, such as a shift away from the private motorcar to clean public transport. Most governments favour this policy, but shy away from banning cars except in congested city centres with localized pollution problems. Mandatory restrictions on emissions are acting as a spur to innovative manufacturers, providing opportunities to gain competitive advantage in the new environmentally conscious era.

Questions

1 What factors are influencing the move towards greener cars?
2 Of the alternative technologies in the development process, which in your view holds at the greatest long-term prospect, and why?
3 Would you agree with the view that there is a conflict between manufacturers desire to go green and their desire to sell more cars?
4 Toyota has brandished its green credentials, but is criticized by other manufacturers. Why?

Sources: Reed, J., 'Toyota to accelerate sales of hybrids', *Financial Times*, 8 July 2007; Simon, B. and Reed, J., 'Toyota puts on the pressure in hybrid car race', *Financial Times*, 26 July 2007; Simon, B. and Reed, J., 'The "Teflon kimono" starts to show signs of wear and tear', *Financial Times*, 26 July 2007; Reed, J., New vehicles carry a lot of manufacturers' hopes', *Financial Times*, 11 September 2007; Reed, J. and Simon, B., 'Carmakers look for the rewards in tighter rules', *Financial Times*, 11 September 2007; Mackintosh, J., 'Brussels emissions crusade drives small car production', *Financial Times*, 11 March 2005; Mackintosh, J. and Milne, R., 'Hybrid makers yearn to fuse green credentials with profit', *Financial Times*, 20 September 2005; Reed, J., 'European market for the SUV refuses to run out of road', *Financial Times*, 10 September 2007.

Further research

Journal articles

Aragón-Correa, J. and Rubio-López, E. (2007) 'Proactive corporate environmental strategies: Myths and misunderstandings', *Long Range Planning*, **40**(3): 357–81.

Blackman, A., Lyon, T. and Sisto, N. (2006) 'Voluntary environmental agreements when regulatory capacity is weak', *Comparative Economic Studies*, **48**(4): 682–702.

Earnhart, D. and Lizal, L. (2006) 'Pollution, production and sectoral differences in a transition economy', *Comparative Economic Studies*, **48**(4): 662–81.

Wagner, M. (2007) 'Integration of environmental management with other managerial functions of the firm: Empirical effects of drivers of economic performance, *Long Range Planning*, **40**(6): 611–28.

Wilson, H. (2006) 'Environment, democracy and the green state', *Polity*, **38**(2): 276–94.

Books

Barrow, C. (2006) *Environmental Management for Sustainable Development*, London: Routledge.

Hanley, N., Shogren, J. and White, B. (2006) *Environmental Economics*, 2nd edn, Basingstoke: Palgrave Macmillan.

chapter 14
CORPORATE SOCIAL RESPONSIBILITY

learning objectives

▷ To define CSR and related concepts in the context of theories which examine the role of the firm in society
▷ To assess the strategic implications of CSR for international business
▷ To appreciate the changing role of philanthropy internationally, along with the rise of diverse social enterprises in the not-for-profit as well as for-profit sectors
▷ To assess corporate governance structures and processes in light of CSR principles
▷ To examine supply chains and global production in terms of CSR and stakeholder impacts
▷ To assess trends in CSR reporting, highlighting impacts on consumer and other stakeholder groups

Introduction

The humble cotton T-shirt might not seem to constitute a statement of corporate values, but for UK clothing retailer, Marks & Spencer, it represents a commitment to fair trade policies, which aim to aid farmers in some of Africa's poorest countries. The Fairtrade mark ensures that cotton farmers receive a guaranteed price, as well as social development projects for their communities, such as education and healthcare. Now expanding its international division, Marks & Spencer has become a major purchaser of fair trade cotton. It aims to have sold 20 million Fairtrade T-shirts and other garments by 2008. Fair trade is only one of its 'five pillars' of CSR, the others being climate change, waste reduction, sustainable sourcing and health. The company's integration of environmental, fair trade and well-being goals into its CSR approach brings reputational benefits which, it hopes, will translate into competitive advantage, as consumers increasingly take these issues into account in their everyday shopping. Marks & Spencer's policies reflect a growing approach to CSR, which rests on both business and ethical grounds, as this chapter highlights.

Marks & Spencer's website is www.marksandspencer.com. The Fairtrade Foundation's website is www.fairtrade.org.uk.

WEB CHECK

The company's role in society, formerly seen as essentially economic, is now giving way to a broader view, extending to questions of how the business is run from an ethical perspective. This broader perspective, referred to as 'corporate social responsibility' (CSR), focuses on underlying values and goals which impact on all aspects of the business, including environment, production, HRM, finance and marketing. Along with the related concepts of corporate citizenship and stakeholder management, CSR offers a view of the company and its managers as interacting with multiple players in society, including consumers, government authorities, non-governmental organizations (NGOs) and communities. CSR has gathered momentum as the trends of globalization and the increasing power of large MNEs have been perceived more critically.

The chapter begins by defining CSR and related concepts. We next examine CSR theories and their implications for management practices, with a particular focus on the international dimension. As earlier chapters have highlighted, international businesses are often confronted by tension between diverse national cultural and institutional environments, as well as by issues raising ethical principles which crosscut diverse cultures.

CSR can represent a radical shift in corporate strategy, or an adjunct to existing strategy. Philanthropy has long been recognized as a means of furthering social and moral values – indeed, long before CSR as a term existed. In our era, both global and local trends have emerged. Philanthropy has become international in its horizons, reflecting a growing awareness of the social role of business. The multiplicity of stakeholders is the subject of the next section, on accountability and ethical behaviour. In it, we examine corporate governance from the stakeholder perspective. We then look at the position of shareholders as owners, contrasting their influence with that of executives. This tension between owners and managers has been a perennial theme in management debate, and is key to the firm's responsiveness to multiple stakeholders, notably in supply chains. Employees are recognized as stakeholders of the MNE, but workers engaged in outsourced manufacturing have a more ambiguous relationship. This has become one of the most emotive subjects in the CSR context. For many people, the vision of poorly paid Asian workers working in sweatshop conditions is the enduring image of what is bad about globalization. We therefore examine how CSR is changing corporate policies on global operations. In addition to monitoring, one of the more obvious changes is the growth in reporting of social performance, which is reviewed in the last section.

Corporate social responsibility (CSR) and related concepts

Business activities are woven into the societies in which they take place. Notions of the role of business vary over time and across cultures. In countries where family firms and paternalism are prominent, the firm is perceived as part of the social fabric and the embodiment of cultural values. Although the firm is based on economic activities, employees in Asian family firms feel themselves to be members of a family more than operatives in an economic enterprise. Where market economies and capitalist ownership structures have become dominant, firms, although still often family dominated in many cases, are focused on the economic purpose of the business, to generate profits for the owners.

Where owners take a hands-on role in managing the business, as in the typical SME, there is often a feeling of shared goals and social values between owner/managers and employees. However, when companies grow into large, impersonal organizations, owners, especially if they are dispersed investors, become distanced from managers, who have tended to become more professionally focused. In turn, employees, hired for particular skills under contracts of employment, form another distinct set of interests, separate from those of owners and managers. The company thus becomes rather fragmented in terms of the interests of owners, managers and workers, each group looking to foster self-interested economic goals. This economic orientation of the company, characteristic of firms in market economies, represents the antithesis of the socially oriented firm whose goals coincide with those of the society from which it springs.

It is in the context of a divergence – even conflict – between economic and social values that CSR has emerged. Concerns over the role of business enterprises in capitalist societies have been voiced for many years. The accumulation of wealth and economic power in privately owned corporations has been questioned, particularly in democratic societies with egalitarian ideals

(Galbraith, 1958). In their influential book *The Modern Corporation and Private Property* (1932), Berle and Means were concerned about the power of industrial oligarchies, and they projected that, by 1950 in the US, 200 corporations would control 70% of total economic activity, even though share ownership was becoming more dispersed (Bratton, 2001). Writing in 1963, Joseph McGuire expressed the view that firms have social responsibilities in addition to their economic role of making profits for shareholders:

> The idea of social responsibilities supposes that the corporation has not only economic and legal obligations, but also certain responsibilities to society which extend beyond these obligations. (McGuire, 1963: 144)

This notion of the company as having social responsibilities provided the basis for a rethinking of the role of the company in society, now encapsulated in the concept of CSR. CSR can thus be defined as an approach to the firm which takes in economic activities, legal obligations and social responsibilities. While many welcome this broader view of the role of the firm in society, it has also aroused objections from those who feel that businesses are best at focusing on profit-making, leaving social concerns for individuals, families, government agencies and charitable institutions. The economist Milton Friedman (1970) famously argued that 'the business of business is business', and that companies best serve society by profit generation and shareholder primacy.

Defining the nature and extent of social responsibilities has been one of the challenges associated with CSR, in both theory and practice. The notion of 'responsibility' suggests that obligation arises, but in a broad social context, it is difficult to identify specific obligations. Moreover, a theme of CSR literature has been that CSR is voluntary (Thompson, 2005). Companies espousing CSR voluntarily undertake activities beyond their legal obligations, thus apparently contradicting the view that CSR involves social 'obligation'. A number of related concepts have been drawn into the debate. We highlight the three most important here, as shown in Figure 14.1: ethics, corporate citizenship and stakeholder interests. First, CSR is closely associated with ethics in business, based on the premise that a company may be abiding by the letter of the law, but its behaviour could still be condemned on moral grounds. For example, a company which outsources manufacturing to companies which employ children of 14 is within national law in some countries, but Western consumers may well object on ethical grounds.

Figure 14.1 Corporate social responsibility and related concepts

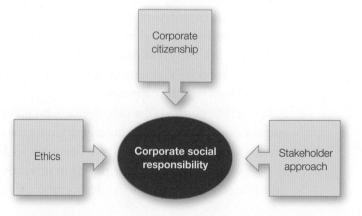

Corporate citizenship: The concept that companies, like individuals, have the legal and moral duties attached to citizenship.

Second, CSR is sometimes equated with corporate citizenship, a concept which evokes the status of individual citizens as members of nation-states. Corporate citizenship, however, is used in a variety of contexts, outlined below:

- The company can be seen as analogous to the individual citizen. Beyond the citizen's legal duties, such as the duty to pay tax and obey the law, are the moral responsibilities of the good citizen, such as helping neighbours in distress and aiding authorities in investigating crime. This view of corporate citizenship is similar to that of CSR. Of course, an individual is usually a citizen of only one country, whereas the company may operate in a number of different societies, in each of which it undertakes to abide by local laws and social expectations. Although these aims seem clear, they may be difficult to apply in practice, especially in developing countries with weak rule of law and social instability, as CF14.1 on Nigeria illustrates.

- The concept of the 'global corporate citizen' has been invoked to cover those obligations that go beyond the country-specific ones, but this term is rather abstract. It can be argued that 'acts-citizenship' could apply to companies, suggesting that they act in ways that show civic virtue wherever they operate (Thompson, 2005). Perhaps in the area of climate change, a truly global issue (discussed in Chapter 13), the notion of a global corporate citizen would be relevant.

- For some companies, especially in America, 'corporate citizenship' has become the preferred term to cover philanthropic donations and activities, discussed below and featured in SX14.1 on Accenture. This narrow definition of corporate citizenship is common among companies whose business strategy is focused on shareholder wealth maximization.

The third concept of 'stakeholder interests' can arguably provide a conceptual tool for international CSR, as stakeholders encompass shareholders, employees and customers in diverse locations. It will be recalled from Chapter 1 that a stakeholder can be any group or interest that affects or is affected by the company. Social responsibility in this framework would imply taking into consideration all the interests which impact on the company globally. This approach has the benefit of allowing managers to put 'names and faces' on identifiable groups (Carroll, 1991: 43). However, it may be less helpful in aiding corporate decision-makers to make judgments between conflicting interests of stakeholders in different locations (Pedersen, 2006).

Tensions arise where social and economic considerations conflict. Many large companies now address CSR and stakeholder issues routinely, seeking to be good corporate citizens in their various locations. Moreover, investors and employees have a range of divergent priorities themselves, among which, besides wealth maximization, are social goals and sustainability. In CF14.1, we see the difficulties which arise for companies seeking to be socially responsible in an unstable environment of multiple stakeholders with differing agendas.

TO RECAP...

CSR and related concepts

CSR takes a view of the business enterprise which combines economic, legal and social responsibilities. Legal and social obligations are more complex in the international context in which MNEs operate. The company can be envisaged as a corporate citizen in each location, while the notion of stakeholder interests aids in visualizing the distinct constituencies which impact on the company.

COUNTRY FOCUS 14.1 – NIGERIA

Sharing the benefits of oil wealth in Nigeria

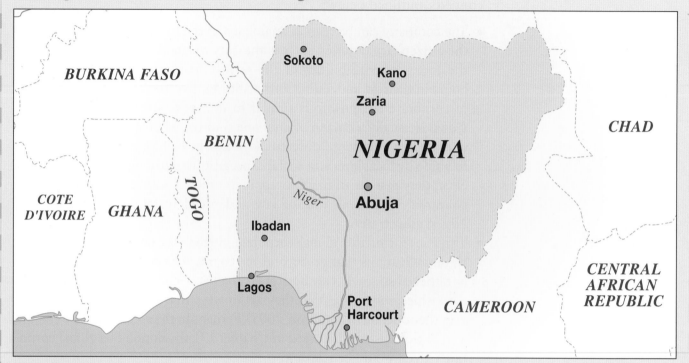

As Africa's largest oil producer, Nigeria is dependent on wealth generated from oil, which accounts for 95% of its exports. Rising production of liquefied natural gas is also playing a part in the country's resource-dependent economy. These benefits multiply as natural resources become scarcer and security of supply becomes a global issue. With Africa's largest population, of 141 million people, Nigeria is hoping that resource wealth will deliver economic development and social welfare to all its people. Unfortunately, Nigeria's record of poor governance has turned the advantage of resources into what has been termed the 'resources curse' (Murdy, 2006). The country's management of its natural resources has been blighted by corruption, political instability and ethnic conflict. Overcoming these problems involves co-operation between government, investing companies and community groups.

Following the end of military rule in 1999, a new democratic system based on federalism promised stability. To some extent, these hopes have borne fruit, although presidential and local elections have been marred by fraud, violence and vote-rigging. The economy has grown at around 5% per annum, as shown in Figure 1. Much of this growth is attributed to renewed vigour in financial services and agriculture, which are helping to boost GDP per capita, as shown in Figure 2. FDI, formerly concentrated in the oil industry, is now increasing in non-oil sectors. Nonetheless, the economy remains dependent on oil, which accounts for 80% of government receipts. Thanks to rising oil prices, the country has now paid off 90% of its $36 billions in foreign debt and has $47 billions in reserves. The

Figure 1 Nigeria's GDP growth

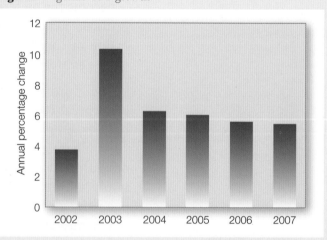

Source: *Financial Times*, 12 July 2007

benefits of oil wealth are not evenly shared. Poverty is widespread: 92% of the population are below the $2-a-day poverty line, and life expectancy at birth is only 46.5 years. The bulk of the population lack access to adequate sanitation and drinking water. Reducing corruption and improving health, education and transport are key to improving well-being in the future.

Although the central government is now functioning more effectively, delivering welfare to ordinary people is hampered by corruption at state and regional levels. Nigeria's federal system gives the 36 states considerable power over resources and public spending. Having been designed to accommodate the country's many ethnic and religious groups, decentralization has in fact contributed to instability which threatens national unity. In the oil-rich Niger Delta, armed militant groups and criminal gangs have taken much power into their own hands. These groups have diverse goals which blur the line between criminal and legitimate activities. Some claim to be fighting for development and social benefits for the poor communities of the delta, who they feel have been excluded from the oil wealth. However, many are engaged in the theft of oil from pipelines, resulting in loss of production, thought to be about a quarter of overall output. Militant leaders are able to equip themselves with arms from the proceeds, and gain personally from deals with elected politicians, which tend to be tainted by corrupt payments.

Figure 2 Nigeria's GDP per capita

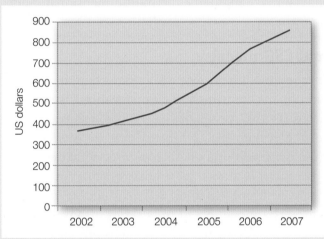

Source: Financial Times, 12 July 2007

Foreign oil and gas companies, mainly from Europe and the US, have invested heavily in Nigeria over the years, playing a vital role in exploration and production. Its main investors are Royal Dutch Shell, ExxonMobil, Chevron, Total and Agip. They have welcomed the democratic transition, but continue to encounter a range of difficulties, especially a lack of security for their employees. The Nigerian army and police forces are ill equipped and trained to guarantee security. The government seconds police officers to the oil companies, who pay and train them, but they are hardly a match for the militant groups who are in the ascendancy in vast swathes of low-lying terrain in the delta region, crisscrossed by waterways. Dealing with militants therefore remains a fact of life for the oil companies. Royal Dutch Shell has devised a new policy to offer as many contracts as possible to the local communities, as a way of lessening the hostility between local people and foreign companies. Local businesses which stand to benefit are those engaged in barge and boat leasing, maintenance, catering and transportation work. The policy is risky, as local firms can be entwined with militant groups. The task of vetting all contractors for links with militants is crucial, and there is the risk of inadvertently awarding contract work to firms with militant

links. Nonetheless, Royal Dutch Shell is hoping that this gesture of good faith towards the community will persuade militants to give them full access to the oilfields and reduce the number of attacks on installations.

An alternative strategy for foreign oil companies is to exploit oil deep under the sea off Nigeria's coast. In offshore locations, militants are less obstructive, but the engineering costs associated with drilling in deep water are higher than onshore. Deals negotiated between the government and the oil companies in the 1990s, when the price of oil was in the region of $20 a barrel, allowed them a generous period of initial production to cover investment costs before they started sharing revenues with the government and paying taxes. In 2007, the Nigerian government, like governments of other oil-rich countries, demanded that these contracts be amended to terms more favourable to itself, reflecting rises in the price of crude oil to $90 a barrel. This policy also applies to offshore contracts, which are attracting new investors, such as state-owned oil companies from Asia, especially China. These new investors are establishing stakes in oil resources in order to secure supplies for their home economies. Nigeria offers rights for the exploitation of new oil reserves in exchange for investment in refineries, railways, power plants and rural telephony. These infrastructure projects, particularly power generation, are desperately needed for Nigeria's future economic development. On the other hand, it is feared that the new Asian investors have less concern for host community stakeholders' interests. One Nigerian entrepreneur, whose company builds power plants to service businesses, has felt sufficiently optimistic about the economy's prospects to acquire Costain West Africa, a subsidiary of Costain, the UK construction company. The country needs more local entrepreneurs in this mould to justify optimism about economic growth and prosperity for all Nigeria's people.

Questions

◆ List the different stakeholders which foreign oil and gas companies in Nigeria must take into account.
◆ Summarize the claims of each of the stakeholder interests listed in Question 1, and make recommendations for dealing with each.
◆ Assess Royal Dutch Shell's community policy in terms of CSR.

Sources: Wallis, W., 'Recovery has failed to reach the poor', *Financial Times*, 12 July 2007; Wallis, W., 'Highest stakes for a generation', *Financial Times*, 12 July 2007; Mahtani, D., 'Delta militants cause oil jitters', *Financial Times*, 16 May 2006; McGreal, C., 'Ruling party named winner in disputed Nigerian election', *Guardian*, 24 April 2007; Mahtani, D., 'Loosening ties with the West', *Financial Times*, 16 May 2006; Mahtani, D., 'A badly flawed exercise in democracy', *Financial Times*, 12 July 2007; White, D. and Mahtani, D., 'Politics get in way of reform', *Financial Times*, 16 May 2006; UNDP, *Human Development Report 2007* (Basingstoke: Palgrave Macmillan); Green, M., 'Nigeria threatens renegotiation of contracts with big oil groups', *Financial Times*, 24 October 2007; Murdy, W., 'Mining companies can help lift the resources curse', *Financial Times*, 25 August 2006.

WEB CHECK

For information about Nigeria, go to the World Bank's website at www.worldbank.org, and click on *Nigeria* in the country list.

> **CSR and stakeholder interests**
>
> In what ways do the concepts of CSR and stakeholder interests overlap? In what ways can a CSR approach help international managers to evaluate and take decisions regarding the conflicting demands of multiple stakeholders?
>
> PAUSE TO REFLECT

Theories of CSR

The concepts at the heart of CSR have been woven into a number of theories, which aim to clarify the strategic implications of CSR for corporate decision-making and behaviour. We highlight the multidimensional model of CSR and the stakeholder theory.

The multidimensional CSR model

CSR recognizes that the economic dimension, while important, is complemented by non-economic dimensions which encompass social issues. The economic role can depicted as the centre of a set of concentric circles (Committee for Economic Development, 1971). Alternatively, it can be envisaged as a continuum of responsibilities, with economic activities at one extreme, moving through legal obligations, to voluntary activities such as philanthropy at the opposite extreme (Steiner, 1975). Building on these theories, Carroll (1991) devised a model based on a series of boxes shaped like a pyramid. Shown in Figure 14.2, Carroll's four dimensions are:

1 *Economic responsibilities*, including profits, products and jobs.
2 *Legal responsibilities*, envisaged by Carroll as a 'social contract' between business and society, whereby firms abide by relevant laws and regulations and, in return, enjoy legal safeguards for operations, such as contract enforcement and protection of patents.
3 *Ethical responsibilities*, which Carroll (1991: 41) envisages in terms of stakeholders' expectations of moral behaviour. He observes that values and norms change over time, and advises companies to keep in tune with the concerns of consumers and investors.
4 *Philanthropic activities*, which he identifies as good corporate citizenship. Philanthropy (discussed later in this chapter) consists of funding and activities directed towards some social purpose. Carroll acknowledges that for many companies, philanthropic giving represents enlightened self-interest. Indeed, for many companies, CSR is equated with charitable activities, which are perceived as separate from the firm's economic activities (see the SX14.1 on Accenture as an example).

Carroll's third level, the ethical dimension, is distinctive, making this model of CSR stronger than the minimalist formulation which focuses on philanthropy. Carroll draws on stakeholder theory to aid in understanding, analysing and managing the groups and interests which the firm must take

Figure 14.2 A multidimensional
CSR model

Source: Based on Carroll, A. (1991) 'The pyramid
of corporate social responsibility: Toward the
moral management of organizational
stakeholders', *Business Horizons,* **34**: 39–48

into account. These are also shown in Figure 14.2. He identifies five major
stakeholder groups: owners (shareholders), employees, customers, local
communities and society at large. Responding to their numerous claims is
not, he admits, a 'win–win' situation, but represents 'a legitimate and desir-
able goal for management to pursue to protect its long-term interests'
(Carroll, 1991: 43). Carroll urges that the model aims to create a greater role
for ethical considerations in management, but couches these mainly in stakeholder terms, highlighting the need to identify opportunities and threats
posed by stakeholders. He is thus, perhaps unwittingly, veering towards the
business case for CSR, discussed in a later section.

Stakeholder theories

As Carroll's model showed, a stakeholder approach is helpful in identifying
specific aspects of social responsibility. Some theorists have devised stakeholder theories which go further, providing a framework for assessing and
responding to stakeholder interests. Mitchell et al. (1997) propose a theory of
stakeholder salience, offering a set of criteria by which to evaluate and compare
stakeholder impacts, actual and potential, on the company. The three criteria
are power, legitimacy and urgency. A stakeholder may have *power*, such as
economic resources, to impose its will on corporate managers. Wal-Mart as a
customer has power, for example, over supplier companies. *Legitimacy* is the
extent that the stakeholder's claim is based on legal or moral grounds, and
urgency indicates how pressing it is for the company to act instantly. Stakeholders display these attributes in differing degrees. Mitchell et al. point out
that legitimacy has tended to dominate much stakeholder discourse, giving it
a normative underpinning, whereas their three-pronged analysis of saliency is
broader. Although they argue that the moral dimension is recognized, advocates of CSR might be unsettled by the implication that the powerful stakeholder is able to influence the company, whereas the legitimate stakeholder
who lacks power is less influential (Morrison, 2003).

Figure 14.3 Dimensions of stakeholder engagement

Source: Based on Pedersen, E. (2006) 'Making corporate social responsibility operable: How companies translate stakeholder dialogue into practice', *Business and Society Review*, **111**(2): 137–63

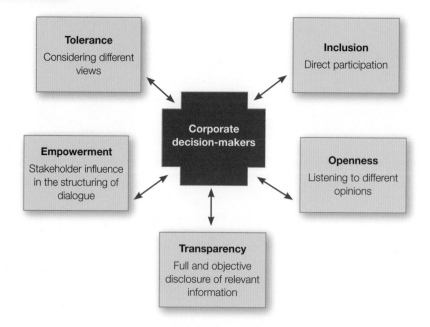

Management interaction with stakeholders is the focus of Pedersen's theory (2006). He urges the need for participatory dialogue in assessing stakeholder claims, identifying five levels of engagement, as shown in Figure 14.3. This theory recognizes differing types of dialogue and differing depths of participation. Some stakeholders participate directly, and others exert influence by voicing their opinions. Where different views are voiced, the company should show tolerance and openness to all the different viewpoints. For example, both sides in a conflict between profit generation and fairness to a group of workers should be explored openly.

Empowerment is another consideration for managers: in what ways and to what degree should shareholders and employees influence the structure of the dialogue? As we will see in the discussion of accountability later in this chapter, both groups tend to have little direct influence in the large MNE. Finally, transparency is an important dimension of stakeholder management, which underlines all the other dimensions. Full, fair and timely disclosure of information by the MNE on social and environmental impacts is a necessary basis for meaningful dialogue with stakeholders. Pedersen's theory emphasizes that stakeholder dialogue based on openness to all points of view is a way of resolving the incompatible interests which inevitably arise in stakeholder management.

Internationalizing the theories

CSR and stakeholder theories become more complex when the international dimension is taken into account. An international firm interacts with diverse societies, each of which has stakeholder interests. The MNE which co-ordinates activities in numerous countries faces differing legal systems in each, with differing legal responsibilities. Moreover, obedience to the law is an ambiguous concept in itself. Typically, the law provides that individuals and firms must take 'reasonable care' in areas such as health and safety, which is subject to varying interpretations, especially in different cultural environments. Reasonable care in respect of working conditions for a highly

TO RECAP...

CSR and stakeholder theories

The multidimensional model of CSR holds that the company has ethical responsibilities beyond the economic and legal responsibilities which are generally seen as central to business enterprises. The ethical dimension involves assessing and responding to stakeholder groups and interests, which are often incompatible. Dialogue, transparency and openness aid managers in stakeholder management.

skilled worker in an advanced economy is different from the same requirement for a low-skilled worker in a developing country, especially one who is only semi-literate. Companies are often accused of double standards, locating low-skilled work in low-cost environments where regulation is weak. The company is shielded by the fact that legal actions for wrongs against workers are rare in these environments (see CF9.1 on Vietnam). Companies are also free to locate activities or register their companies in particular countries for the tax benefits they enjoy, as the example of Accenture shows. Although not legally wrong, this device can be perceived as tax avoidance, which many regard as morally wrong. It is frowned on by political authorities, who design specific legislation to curtail tax avoidance arrangements. The MNE is also able to gain financial advantages by opting for one country over another because of its more friendly financial system. These practices are generally accepted as aspects of directors' duties to maximize shareholder wealth.

For production, outsourcing or market entry, country selection can take on an ethical dimension, in addition to business criteria. There may be a persuasive case for entering a country on economic grounds, such as access to resources, but if the government is a military dictatorship, ethical concerns may arise. If a foreign company is already doing business in the country when a military dictator takes over, it may well decide to pull out. These points are discussed in CF14.2 on Myanmar. In many cases, the situation is not as straightforward as it might seem. Many of the world's governments are authoritarian, with little or no democratic accountability, but foreign companies do business in them nonetheless. China, Russia and Middle Eastern countries are some examples highlighted in this book. Many companies find these countries offer stability which is sometimes lacking in pluralist political systems (see Chapter 5). Social and political instability makes doing business difficult, as seen in CF14.1 on Nigeria. Countries rich in natural resources inevitably attract foreign investors. Stakeholder management is more difficult and sensitive in situations where there are numerous governmental, social and political groups with conflicting sectional interests and claims to legitimacy.

Stakeholder theory in the international arena also highlights conflicts of interest between the home country and foreign operations, as well as between foreign locations. Workers and communities in locations with little voice and weak legal rights are overshadowed by those with greater power. For the international manager weighing up stakeholder interests, Pedersen's approach would seem to be especially relevant, as dialogue can help to foster understanding of divergent points of view in a cross-cultural environment.

COUNTRY FOCUS 14.2 – MYANMAR (BURMA)

Is doing business in Myanmar compatible with CSR?

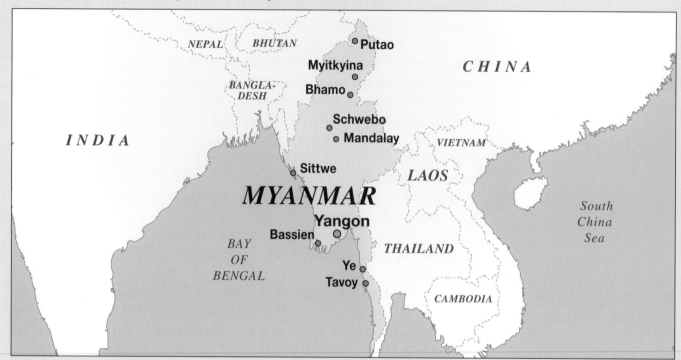

In the autumn of 2007, people all over the world saw images on their televisions of Burmese soldiers attacking civilians, including Buddhist monks, in the streets of Myanmar's cities, where hardship had reached crisis proportions. For some Western companies, this marked the turning point in doing business in Myanmar, persuading them to suspend operations until the country's military regime ceases its repressive practices and turns its attention to the welfare of citizens. Unease with the military government is even reflected in the name of the country. Myanmar's military rulers changed the country's name from Burma in 1989, but it is still referred to as Burma by many foreign governments and the global media, including the BBC.

Myanmar is one of Southeast Asia's largest countries, covering an area larger than Germany and Poland combined. Richly endowed with natural resources and in a strategic location, it should be enjoying economic growth and prosperity on a par with its Southeast Asian neighbours. In fact, it is among the world's least developed countries. GDP per capita, shown in Figure 1, is significantly lower than that of its Asian neighbours. Its population of 52 million have long suffered from widespread poverty and poor healthcare, reflected in a lowly ranking of 132 in the UN's Human Development Index. The lack of reliable statistics poses obstacles for the assessment of social conditions. It is clear, though, that poor healthcare, which is estimated to account for just 3% of national government spending, has led to rises in diseases such as malaria and tuberculosis, while military spending amounts to a huge 40% of the national budget. Myanmar's controversial military regime has also been criticized for human rights abuses,

including the forced labour of its citizens and use of child soldiers. Should foreign investors stay away, and should importers refuse to buy Burmese exports?

Figure 1 Comparative GDP per capita, 2007

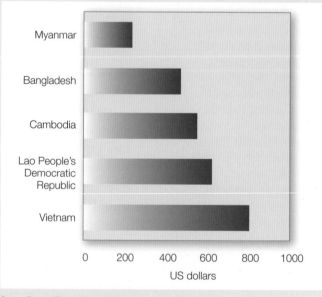

Source: Financial Times, 12 September 2007

Burma celebrated independence from British colonial rule in 1948 by instituting a democratic government, which sought to represent its culturally diverse society and to promote economic development. The country became a major exporter of rice and teak, as well as oil, gas and numerous minerals. It is a leading source of gemstones, especially rubies. An army coup in 1962 ushered in the military dictatorship, based on socialist ideology and central economic planning. Economic mismanagement led to deepening poverty, culminating in a violent uprising in 1988. Market-oriented reforms were then introduced, and democratic reforms were announced. Opportunities for FDI opened up, through joint ventures between foreign investors and newly created state-owned enterprises controlled by the military rulers and their business associates. The market reforms, however, served to mask a reality which strengthened the generals' grip on the country's main business sectors, including manufacturing, mining, construction, timber, tourism and retail.

Promises of democratic reforms led to disappointment. Free elections for an assembly were held in 1990, the first for nearly forty years. The National League for Democracy (NLD) received an estimated 80% of the total votes, but elected members were never allowed to take their seats. Aung San Suu Kyi, the NLD leader, was placed under house arrest. In 1997, the US announced economic sanctions against Myanmar, which barred future investment and banned imports from the country, although Burmese gemstones could be imported via third countries. The EU followed suit with an arms embargo and other sanctions, but stopped short of investment restrictions. Oil companies Total of France and Chevron of the US continued to operate in Burma, but have been criticized for co-operation with the generals, especially for the use of forced labour in the building of pipelines. FDI continued to flow into the country, but has declined in recent years (see Figure 2).

Figure 2 Flows of FDI into Myanmar

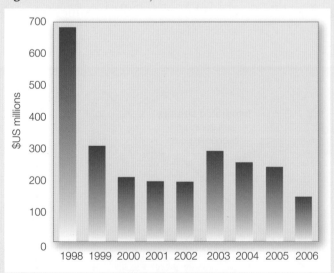

Source: UN, World Investment Reports, 2005, 2006 and 2007 (Geneva: UN)

Following the violent suppression of protestors in 2007, the issue of international firms' relations with the military regime resurfaced. Sanctions imposed by the US, the UK and Australia had gradually been tightened, but it was clear that Myanmar's neighbours, especially India and China, had continued to do 'business as usual' with the regime. For a number of Western companies, CSR concerns and risk of reputational damage weighed heavily. Timbmet, the UK's largest importer of hard-

plate 14.1 These highly revered Buddhist monks are important in Burmese culture and society, which have been strained to breaking point by the harsh military regime.

woods, decided to stop sourcing from Myanmar, its corporate responsibility director stating: 'we judged that trading with Burma was not responsible' (Kazmin, 27 October 2007). He noted that the firm was unable to verify the legality of either the environmental or labour conditions of Burmese suppliers. Cartier decided to stop sourcing gems mined in Myanmar, the sale of which earns annually a total of $300 million for the junta. Rolls-Royce decided to stop servicing aircraft engines for the state airline, Myanmar Airways.

These firms have taken the decision to withdraw from Myanmar on ethical rather than legal grounds, although future tightening of sanctions by the US, Australia and the UK could impose further legal restrictions. Chevron and Total have not divested their stakes in the Yadana gas field and its pipeline, arguing that withdrawal would generate a windfall for the generals and lead to less scrupulous investors moving in. For oil companies with large investments in infrastructure, the decision to withdraw from a country is more complex and radical than the decision of a jeweller to stop sourcing gems. Given the severe economic and political instability afflicting Myanmar, a quick return to business as usual seems a long way off. Democratic reforms, as promised in the elections of 1990, would help to restore legitimacy, but the deep vested economic interests of the generals and their business friends will be difficult to shift, continuing to pose ethical issues for foreign businesses.

Questions

◆ Summarize the CSR case against doing business in Myanmar.
◆ What factors would persuade businesses to resume operations in Myanmar?
◆ Do you agree or disagree with Total and Chevron's stance in respect to Myanmar, and why?

Sources: Malinowski, T. (2007) 'No longer the generals' Burma', *Washington Post*, 21 October 2007; Oehlers, A. (2004) 'Sanctions and Burma: Revisiting the case against', *Burma Economic Watch*, www. econ.mq.edu.au; Jagan, L. (2002) 'Analysis: Burma's economic crisis', BBC News, 15 March 2002, www. bbc.co.uk; UNDP (2007) *Human Development Report 2007* (Basingstoke: Palgrave Macmillan); Human Rights Watch (2007) *Sold to be Soldiers: the Recruitment and Use of Child Soldiers in Burma*, **19**(15C), 30 October; Kazmin, A., 'Burma's junta warned of growing anger', *Financial Times*, 6 December 2007; Kazmin, A., 'The junta's exports lose their sparkle', *Financial Times*, 27 October 2007; Kazmin, A., 'Surge in dissent spurs crackdown by Burma's junta', *Financial Times*, 12 September 2007; Human Rights Centre of the University of California, Berkeley (2007) Burma Report 2007, www.hrcberkeley.org; UN World Investment Reports, 2005, 2006 and 2007 (Geneva: UN).

WEB CHECK

For information about Myanmar, go to the World Bank website at www.worldbank.org, and click on *Myanmar* in the country list.

CSR and international corporate strategy

Companies around the world are aware of a rising tide of public opinion which encourages them to take more seriously the social and environmental impacts of their operations. Their responses are influenced by the cultural and administrative history of the individual firm, including its ownership structure and investor interests. It is arguable that as a company's shareholder base becomes more international, its stakeholder horizons will also become more internationalized. This section examines how CSR can be adopted by companies and shape strategy in international business. Four alternative approaches are shown in Figure 14.4. For two of them, CSR is an addition to economic goals, while for the other two, CSR becomes integral to corporate strategy.

Figure 14.4 Corporate stategy and CSR

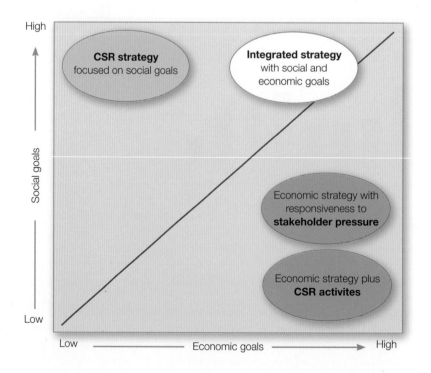

Bolted-on CSR

In Figure 14.4, strategies are indicated according to the strength of economic and social goals. All companies are social institutions, and therefore have some social dimension in their strategies, if only to abide by minimal legal obligations such as the duty to pay workers. Companies which prioritize economic goals may take up CSR through engagement in charitable and community activities or respond to stakeholder pressures. Both these orientations are below the diagonal in Figure 14.4, as they do not impact on the core business and thus do not represent a strategic approach to CSR. These activities may help to foster good community relations, sometimes prompted by negative publicity that has damaged the company's reputation in the past (see CS14.2 on Nike). Philanthropy can be broadly defined as the giving of resources to particular recipients deemed worthy of the gift, with no expected material return. Individuals and organizations of all types engage in philanthropy (discussed below). The firm which donates to charities often sees these activities as enhancing the firm's business reputation.

Philanthropy: Donation of resources to recipients deemed to be good causes in the eyes of the donor, with no expected material return.

In recent years, corporate philanthropy has become more sophisticated, targeted at specific projects and internationally diversified. Instead of simply giving money to charities, many companies set up foundations to engage in more proactive investments, a move adopted by Google, through its foundation, Google.org. Foundations may partner local organizations in developing countries, providing active guidance to achieve results in areas such as health and education. This is a more targeted approach to philanthropy than simply making cash donations. These developments reflect the global perspective of today's large companies and also the large sums now channelled into charitable giving. These activities are typically described as 'corporate citizenship activities'. They are an adjunct to the business, often resonating with shareholders, but subsidiary to the essential economic goals of the business, as SX14.1 shows. Enron is an extreme example of the compartmentalization of corporate citizenship activities. Its directors pursued an aggressive and risky financial strategy, which eventually brought down the company through fraudulent trading and investments. At the same time, Enron had an impeccable corporate citizenship profile in terms of philanthropy. Nonetheless, thousands of stakeholders, including investors, employees and creditors, suffered as a result of the Enron collapse.

Responding to stakeholder pressures is a second approach to CSR. This approach also starts from the assumption that the company is essentially devoted to economic goals. However, directors recognize that they use resources from society, and that their activities can have negative impacts such as pollution (Husted and Salazar, 2006). Directors respond not out of a sense of responsibility to society, but from the need to mitigate the effects of negative stakeholder impacts as they arise in the firm's operations. This type of firm sees stakeholder interests as a potential impediment to achieving corporate goals, and responds only when it is pressurized into doing so. This is thus a reactive approach, taking an instrumental view of stakeholders' roles. Companies which outsource manufacturing in developing countries often view local operations in this perspective.

STRATEGIC CROSSROADS

14.1
Accenture's corporate citizenship profile

Accenture is a successful company in satisfying growing global demand for management consultancy, technology services and outsourcing. It is involved in a range of sectors, including communications technology, IT services, financial services and government services. The company's origins lie in the consultancy division of the accounting firm, Arthur Andersen, from which it separated in 1989, to form Andersen Consulting, although it retained links with its former parent as both were part of Andersen Worldwide, registered in Switzerland. Tension between Andersen Consulting and the consultancy activities of Arthur Andersen led Andersen Consulting to become independent in 2000, taking the new name of Accenture. Although based in the US, Accenture became incorporated in the offshore haven of Bermuda. It listed on the NYSE, launching an IPO in 2001. The company has two classes of shares: common shares (traded publicly) and those held by founders and partners (voted as a block).

Since its IPO, Accenture has grown quickly, especially in outsourcing and government contracts for large projects, which have attracted considerable publicity, not all of it favourable. In 2002, the US Congress queried Accenture's entitlement to take on federal government contracts because of its reincorporation in a tax haven country. The US Congress is also concerned that the company's outsourcing activities have seen huge growth in client services in low-cost countries such as India, China and the Philippines, to the apparent detriment of jobs in the US. By 2006, its global outsourcing staff had grown to 48,000, an increase of 31% on 2005; 23,000 of these workers were in India. The company has been awarded large contracts in the UK, including the National Insurance Recording System for HM Revenue and Customs. Accenture was a prime contractor in the sweeping modernization of the NHS computer system, a project worth £12.4 billion, which aimed to integrate general practitioners, hospitals and other NHS organizations. Following three years of work and an investment of £260 million in the NHS project, Accenture felt compelled to pull out, due to delays stemming particularly from one of its key software providers. The pull-out left a legacy of uncertainty over the management of the massive project, damaging the company's reputation in one of its largest markets. Accenture directors were forced to announce the write-off of $450 million to its shareholders.

Accenture's motto is 'High performance. Delivered'. 'High performance' is defined as 'outperforming peers in revenue growth, profitability and total return for shareholders' (*Annual Report 2006*). The company prides itself on its corporate citizenship, focusing on charitable activities. It has a record of corporate philanthropy, setting aside 5 million shares at the time of the IPO to form Accenture Foundations, to fund charitable donations worldwide. They include grants to charities, disaster relief and volunteer work by employees on specific projects. Accenture staff seconded on volunteer development work further their own personal development and gain an understanding of development issues on the ground. Can this lead to a concern for social and environmental responsibility on the part of their employers? Accenture's Annual Reports of 2005 and 2006 make no mention of CSR, and mention stakeholders only in the context of creating value through high performance. The company provides no social or environmental reporting in respect of its operations. On the other hand, Accenture is clearly proud of its corporate citizenship record, highlighting in the *Annual Report 2006* a computer-based training system for nurses in Kenya. NHS patients and staff in the UK, as well as Accenture's ordinary shareholders, might have cause to question Accenture's views of responsibility to stakeholders.

Questions
◆ Which of the theories of CSR and stakeholder management best fits Accenture, and why?
◆ Summarize Accenture's approach to corporate citizenship.
◆ In your view, is Accenture a good corporate citizen, and why?

Sources: Stewart, A., 'Accenture', in Understanding Philanthropy, *Financial Times*, 16 December 2005; Murray, S., 'A donation worth more than money', Understanding Global Philanthropy, *Financial Times*, 11 December 2007; Cross, M., 'Not what the doctor ordered', *Guardian*, 6 April 2006, www.guardian.co.uk; McCue, A., 'Accenture pulls out of £12.4 billion NHS IT project', 28 September 2006, www.silicon.com; Accenture, Annual Reports 2005 and 2006, www.accenture.com.

WEB CHECK

Accenture's website is www.accenture.com. Go to *About Accenture*, where there is a link to *Corporate Citizenship*.

CSR as public relations?
A minimal approach to CSR sees social goals as voluntary charitable activities that enhance the firm's reputation. What are the risks of reputational backlash if firms with this approach suffer from negative publicity, such as reports of sweatshop conditions or corruption? Give examples.

PAUSE TO REFLECT

Strategic CSR

A CSR-focused strategy is the highest level in terms of social goals, representing an unequivocal commitment to corporate CSR. This approach places social and environmental responsibilities at the heart of corporate goals. In contrast to the integrated strategy, which weighs up business and social goals, this strategy pursues social goals regardless of cost. It is associated with 'altruism', a principle in ethical philosophy denoting unselfish concern for others. Directors take the view that social goals are the benchmarks for right or wrong in the conduct of the business globally. This type of company is stronger than any of the others in social outputs, but this model is unlikely to appeal to many firms. The social enterprise funded largely through philanthropy, discussed in the next section, is an example of this model.

The final approach, the integrated strategy, is that of the strategic social investor. It falls roughly on the diagonal in Figure 14.4, representing a balance between social and economic goals. Directors in this type of company see the benefits of stakeholder engagement and social investment, but may also feel a moral responsibility to stakeholders. One of its perceived strengths is that it offers a business case for CSR which resonates with managers. The business case for CSR stresses that strategic CSR can improve corporate performance as well as being socially responsible. CS14.1 on GrupoNueva exemplifies this approach. Stakeholder participation is important in this approach. Among the benefits which might result are strategic interaction with governments, for example if funding and expertise are available for social and environmental initiatives. Another is the opportunity to differentiate products (McWilliams, 2001). A further possible benefit is the ability to attract highly qualified and motivated staff committed to social goals. There are costs involved, such as the need to provide training programmes. However, GrupoNueva found that the benefits are likely to lead to improved financial performance.

It is arguable that the overall level of social outputs would be increased to a greater extent by appealing to firms to adopt an integrated strategy rather than appealing to them on ethical grounds, as the enlightened self-interest approach is likely to have more widespread appeal (Husted and Salazar, 2006). The UK review of company law (discussed in the section on corporate governance) recommended high standards in business conduct on reputational, not ethical, grounds, appealing to enlightened self-interest. The integrated CSR strategy is also consonant with recommendations on sustainability highlighted in the last chapter. As the Stern Report illustrated, the costs incurred to mitigate the impacts of climate change at an early stage are less than the costs and adjustments which will arise as impacts deepen (HM Treasury, 2006).

TO RECAP...

Integrated or bolted-on CSR?

Companies can be differentiated according to the depth of their social, stakeholder and ethical commitments. For some, social investment is an adjunct to the business, and shareholder concerns predominate. For the CSR-focused company, social goals are at the heart of the enterprise, permeating culture and strategy. More common is the company which incorporates social and economic goals in an integrated strategy, balancing stakeholder impacts across international operations.

Don't forget to check the companion website at
www.palgrave.com/business/morrisonib, where you will find
web-based assignments, web links, interactive quizzes, an
extended glossary and lots more to help you learn about
international business.

www.palgrave.com
Companion Website

A Latin American company which specializes in wood and cement products would probably not come to mind as exemplary for its CSR and triple bottom line reporting. But GrupoNueva, as its name implies, is a new departure in a region where poor working conditions, weak environmental standards and lack of transparency are common. The group was founded by a billionaire philanthropist, Stephan Schmidheiny, whose vision of combining business goals with social responsibility has become GrupoNueva's guiding philosophy. Based in Chile, the group now comprises two companies: Masisa, an integrated forestry and wood products company registered as a public company in Chile, and Plycem, a company specializing in cement products for building. Amanco, a subsidiary specializing in water systems for building and agricultural irrigation, was sold by GrupoNueva in 2007. In 2003, the founder donated his majority shareholding in the parent company to a charitable trust, the Viva Trust. Dividends paid to the trust are used to fund social, educational and environmental projects in Latin America, particularly among the poorer sections of society.

GrupoNueva integrates its business strategy with ethical, social and environmental goals. Far from viewing CSR as negatively impacting on profitability, its founder asserts that this approach is the best means of creating value in the long term: 'a company that manages its business in a responsible way, with consideration for its own employees, its neighbours, for society and for the environment will be more profitable, much more economically solid than the irresponsible company' (GrupoNueva Sustainability Report 2006). The company's business principles are legal compliance, ethical conduct, workers' rights and respect for the natural and social environment. Its strong anti-corruption stance distinguishes it from many companies in Latin America, where opaque business and political links are common. Its principles are aligned closely with risk management. Its managers argue that the company is better placed to meet the challenges of environmental disasters and consumer pressures than companies focused exclusively on economic goals.

The group's business strategy emphasizes market leadership, profitability and low-cost production. Its success can be seen in its growth in net sales, up 20% in 2006 (see Figure 1). While most of its customers are in Latin America, it also has customers in the

Case study 14.1: GrupoNueva blends performance and social responsibility

US and Europe, as Figure 2 shows. Its high environmental standards of sourcing wood and managing forests on a sustainable footing helps to win over environmentally conscious consumers and also helps to build Masisa's brand reputation in global markets. At the same time, it maintains a strong focus on poor communities, in markets and social causes.

The needs of poor people and their communities form a thread running through the GrupoNueva philosophy. It views those at the bottom of the pyramid, living in low-income communities, as both a challenging market and a priority for the responsible company. The company aims to be generating 10% of its sales from these communities by 2010. Projects to date include a new line of furniture for low-cost housing in Chile, which Masisa hopes will reach as many as 50,000 families by 2010. The basic furniture pack, comprising six pieces of furniture, sells for only $130, as compared with $400 that the six pieces would cost separately in ordinary retail outlets. In Guatemala, a drip irrigation system for small farmers has been pioneered by Amanco. Financing arrangements, which have been an obstacle for poor families, have been developed in conjunction with the Inter-American Development Bank, the World Bank and the Soros Foundation. Farmers participating in the scheme have seen dramatic improvements in production and quality of their crops.

Implementing GrupoNueva's CSR principles depends heavily on the training and commitment of its employees. The company recognizes responsibility for the 17,600 people who work in its operations, whether 'direct' or 'indirect' employees who are employed by contractors, for example in forestry plantations. Nearly all these workers, including indirect employees, have participated in business principles training workshops, which emphasize the principles of ethics, eco-efficiency and social responsibility. Among these principles are internationally recognized human rights, including the right of trade union membership and collective bargaining. Its employees have been asked to come up with ideas for new products to appeal to low-income consumers. Twelve out of a total of 246 suggestions were pursued by the company, one of which was the irrigation system in Guatemala discussed above. GrupoNueva's HR policies for appointing managerial staff prioritize appointing multifunctional people in all key positions, aligning incentives with the company's priorities, and building a culture of strong values combined with performance.

Figure 1 GrupoNueva's net sales

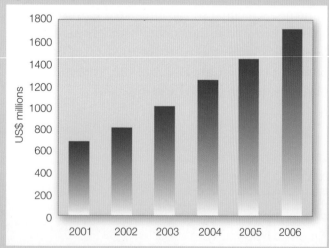

Source: GrupoNueva, Financial data, www.gruponueva.com

Figure 2 GrupoNueva's markets, 2006

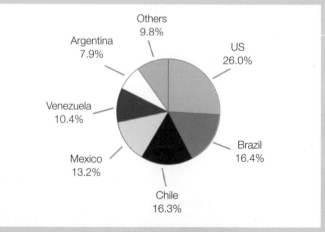

Source: GrupoNueva (2007) Financial data, www.gruponueva.com

The company operates in some areas with indigenous populations. In these areas its policies rest on cultural sensitivity as well as development needs, taking into account that these communities are often poor. In Venezuela, Masisa works among the Kariña people, promoting their language and traditions, but also providing a new water system. Where the traditional land rights of indigenous people overlap with the company's forestry plantations, its approach is one of dialogue and negotiation with local communities.

GrupoNueva's stakeholder approach to strategy and management practices is reflected in its corporate governance principles. However, it is a private company, its shares are not publicly traded, and its stakeholders do not participate directly in governance. Does this detract from its CSR princi-ples? The group argues that its board of directors is imbued with the company's business principles, vision and triple bottom line strategy, which ultimately creates value for its shareholders (mainly the Viva Trust) and other stakeholders. Masisa earned a top-five ranking for corporate governance in Latin America in the Investor Relations Global Rankings in 2006. These rankings assess transparency, management accountability, director independence and election processes, minority shareholder protection and shareholder voting systems.

Questions

1 In what ways does GrupoNueva combine CSR with goals of maximizing profitability?
2 How does the company's focus on poor communities fit in a CSR strategy?
3 In what ways do GrupoNueva's HR policies enhance its reputation for corporate responsibility?

Sources: GrupoNueva (2006) Sustainability Report, at www.gruponueva.com; Webb, T. (2007), 'Latin America: Time to be bold and reach new markets', Ethical Corporation, 12 January, www.ethicalcorp.com; Maitland, A., 'A new frontier in responsibility', *Financial Times*, 29 November 2004; Investor Relations Global Rankings 2006, *MZ Bulletin* (2007) no. 24, www.irglobalrankings.com.

WEB CHECK

GrupoNueva is at www.gruponueva.com.

The business case for CSR
Summarize the business case for CSR. Why is this approach perceived as a diluted version of CSR by critics with strong ethical positions, and how would you meet their objections?

PAUSE TO REFLECT

Philanthropy and social entrepreneurship

Social purposes are served through not-for-profit and for-profit organizations. Increasingly, philanthropy and voluntary work are being combined with a business orientation, furthering social and environmental aims.

Changing role of philanthropy

Philanthropy is widespread, filling needs which are often overlooked by governments. Religious organizations play a strong social role in many societies (recall the example of the Muslim Brotherhood in CF13.1 on Egypt). Individual philanthropy has long been practised by founders of business empires such as Rockefeller and Ford. The Ford and Rockefeller foundations, for example, supported agricultural research into new strains of wheat and rice for developing countries, which contributed to the 'green revolution' of the 1960s and 1970s. Some philanthropists, such as Cadbury and Rowntree in the UK, took a proactive approach to social causes not dissimilar to corporate citizenship initiatives today. However, these rather paternalistic nineteenth-century antecedents have given way to more co-operative philanthropic activities.

Philanthropists are less likely nowadays to make a one-off donation of money than to take an active interest in particular causes and organizations which they support. As the donors are usually successful businesspeople,

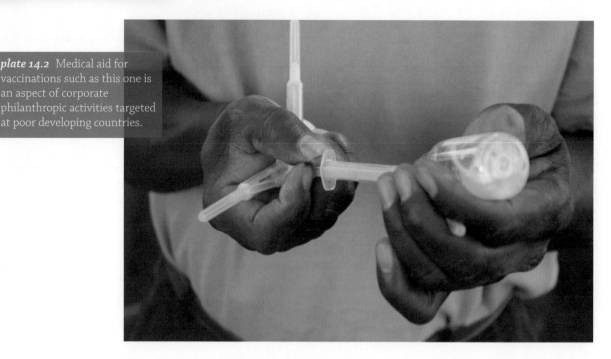

plate 14.2 Medical aid for vaccinations such as this one is an aspect of corporate philanthropic activities targeted at poor developing countries.

their business aptitude can be advantageous, although it might be argued that business goals are so different from human development goals that they are possibly not ideally suited to this new role. Social and cultural changes have played an important part in the changing role of philanthropy.

The US has the highest levels of philanthropy, both corporate and individual. US donors gave away nearly US$300 billion in 2006, up from US$260 billion the previous year (Giving USA Foundation, 2007). Individual giving accounts for 75% of this sum, far overshadowing corporate philanthropy. The leading individual donors are successful businesspeople, often founders who have amassed vast private fortunes. Rising executive pay and rising stock markets (to which executive pay is linked, as discussed below) help to account for rising levels of giving. Bill Gates, the co-founder of Microsoft, has invested US$35 billion from his personal fortune in a foundation which focuses on public health and diseases in the developing world. The Gates Foundation's funds rose to a total of US$66 billion in 2007, making it the world's largest charity. This rise was due mainly to a single donation of US$31 billion from fund manager Warren Buffet. Under US law on charities, the foundation must disburse at least 5% of its funds each year to remain tax exempt and to be relieved of making other payments to the government.

Foundations and other charities have generally welcomed the injection of funds and a business approach, but doubts about current trends have emerged:

- the role of the donors in setting the agenda, who lack experience and expertise in delivering social services in developing countries
- the ability of agencies in the developing world, in terms of organization and skilled staff, to make use of large lump sums
- the foundations' lack of accountability mechanisms
- a possible diminishing of official government aid.

Philanthropists, corporate and individual, favour some causes over others, as Figure 14.5 shows. Gates is unusual in favouring a somewhat overlooked

The Bill & Melinda Gates Foundation is at www.gatesfoundation.org.

WEB CHECK

Figure 14.5 Types of recipient organization receiving the greatest shares of US donations, 2006

Source: Giving USA Foundation (2007) *Giving USA 2007*, www.aafrc.org

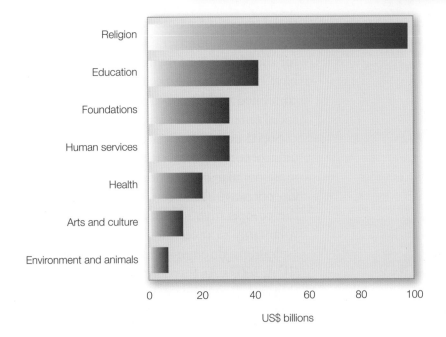

cause, but the bulk of US charitable giving flows to religious and other groups, already well off, rather than the poor. Some voluntary workers in official aid organizations express a concern that governments might point to the activities of private philanthropists as a reason for scaling back official aid programmes. From a CSR perspective, it could be argued that questionable business strategies and practices have facilitated the accumulation of multibillion-dollar personal fortunes of executives in the first place (see CS15.2 on Microsoft). Their firm's stakeholders, including employees, customers, business partners and communities, might feel aggrieved that ethical principles guiding charitable giving by its billionaire executives are not matched by ethical practices in the ways their firm's profits have been generated. Uneasiness surfaced in 2007, when Goldman Sachs, the investment bank, moved to set up a new charitable foundation to receive portions of record pay-outs of over $50 million each to its senior executives. Goldman already had a charitable foundation, founded in 1999, but the new one, Goldman Gives, seems to have been created specifically to counter the adverse publicity its executive remuneration had attracted (White, 2007).

Business leaders turn philanthropists
Business leaders who have accumulated fortunes from their firms seem to be smitten by an urge to give it away in order to make the world a better place. Is this a sign that ethical principles are rising up the social agenda, or an indication of the failures of public authorities in both rich and poor countries to focus on social welfare issues?

PAUSE TO REFLECT

Social enterprises

Social enterprise: A business formed for social objectives, in which revenues from trading in goods or services are largely reinvested for its social purposes.

Social enterprises have been described as a 'third sector' between charities and businesses run for profit (Cabinet Office, 2007). Charities operate under regulatory restrictions which limit the activities they can engage in, in return for tax advantages. Social enterprises represent a more flexible type of organization. The social enterprise can be defined as 'a business with primarily social objectives whose surpluses are principally reinvested for that purpose or in the community, rather than being driven by the need to maximise profit for shareholders or owners' (Cabinet Office, 2007). Some social enterprises have charitable status, but most have an enterprise orientation which is combined with social aims. Some charities wishing to trade set up separate social enterprises to carry out trading activities in goods or services.

Social enterprises can take a variety of legal forms. While many remain unincorporated associations, some form registered companies. One of the most popular options internationally is the co-operative. The International Co-operative Alliance (ICA), an umbrella body dating from 1895, defines the co-operative identity as 'an autonomous association of persons united voluntarily to meet their common economic, social and cultural needs and aspirations through joint-owned and democratically-controlled enterprise' (ICA, 2007). As this definition indicates, the co-operative has open member-ship and all participate in its activities and its democratic governance. Concern for the community is one of the guiding principles of the co-operative, which can focus on a variety of sectors and types of activity, from agriculture and banking to tenant or housing co-operatives. Migro, Switzerland's largest supermarket chain, is a co-operative. Co-operatives are usually registered as entities under specific statutes within each country (or individual state in the US). The registration confers limited liability on the particular co-operative, which is regulated within a national framework.

For all social enterprises, the need to sustain social goals is paramount. American billionaires have been active in promoting social enterprises. Jeff Skoll, Ebay's first president, has adopted a philanthropic approach which supports people starting up enterprises to deal with social issues such as poverty reduction. The 'venture philanthropist' is a new breed of donor, willing to commit funds to worthy enterprises. The Skoll Foundation urges that the social entrepreneur needs innovation, a market orientation and a social objective (Jack, 2007). It has supported Riders for Health, an organi-zation created by two British motorbike enthusiasts who created a logistics network for distributing medicines to remote locations in the developing world. It is estimated that there are 55,000 social enterprises in Britain (Cabinet Office, 2007).

Although the social enterprise has considerable potential, long-term viability can be precarious. Governance and accountability can give rise to tension between the key players, including donors, employees, volunteers and benefici-aries. All are motivated by passion for the cause, but oversight and monitoring tend to be weak and efficiency can suffer (Kogut, 2005). Poor governance and weak control over finances can sometimes lead to individuals making personal gains at the expense of the organization. Lack of transparency can add to problems of attracting donors or investors. Some have been able to find a number of investors, diversifying their financial support, but others look to governments to fund their continued work. The investor in such an enterprise is one who seeks a return based on the achievement of social objectives rather than profits. However, measuring results poses another challenge. Without recognized ways of measuring and analysing performance, social enterprises are unlikely to be able to attract more mainstream investors.

Co-operative: Voluntary organization in which all participate to achieve common goals in a community, usually regulated within a national framework.

WEB CHECK

For information on social enterprises, go to the Cabinet Office website at www.cabinetoffice.gov.uk. Click on *Third Sector*, then *Office of the Third Sector website*, then *social enterprises*.

Social entrepreneur: Person whose creative talent and business flair are directed towards an enterprise focused on achieving specific social goals.

TO RECAP...

Philanthropy and social enterprises

Giving to good causes and working in enterprises which serve mainly social purposes contribute to social and environmental activities around the world. Many of these organizations fill a gap in government and business provision, such as delivering goods and services to remote areas in developing countries.

How to succeed in a social enterprise
List the elements which you feel are most important to the long-term success of a social enterprise, in order of importance.

PAUSE TO REFLECT

Accountability and ethical behaviour

The scandals of Enron in the US and Parmalat in Europe revealed fraudulent and unethical behaviour at the heart of companies which had been outwardly in compliance with the law, thus undermining public confidence in corporate systems. Some of the issues highlighted in the aftermath of these corporate collapses were the weakness of boards in monitoring managers, a lack of transparency in decision-making and spiralling rewards for executives which went largely unchecked. Companies commonly adopt codes of ethical behaviour in addition to CSR goals, but the code is of little practical effect in the absence of an ethical culture which pervades the entire organization. Similarly, global companies also adopt codes of conduct in relation to supply chains, including contracted manufacturers and employees. Much international attention from shareholders and consumers is now focusing on how companies translate statements of principle into higher standards of accountability and ethical behaviour.

Diversity in corporate governance

Corporate governance (introduced in Chapter 1) determines the structures and processes by which directors are answerable for their running of the company. Reflecting the prevailing view of the company's role in society, these mechanisms shape corporate decision-makers' outlook on social responsibility. In a shareholder-centred model of corporate governance, such as in the US and the UK, directors are answerable legally to shareholders for their actions and decisions; stakeholders other than shareholders play no direct role in formal governance. Duties to other stakeholders such as employees are recognized in employment protection legislation, but these duties are not part of company law or corporate governance structures. In stakeholder-oriented structures such as those in large German companies, employees are represented on the supervisory boards, giving them a direct say in company strategy, through co-determination. Their voices must be balanced against the voices of owners and managers, as CS1.2 highlighted.

A stakeholder orientation is also associated with Japan, although the Japanese system is rather different from either the market model of the Anglo-American type or the stakeholder model of the European type. Although they have formal governance structures on American lines, large Japanese companies are imbued with a culture which takes a broad social perspective on the role of the company. Shareholders have tended to play a more passive role than those in more market-oriented economies, and directors see corpo-

Co-determination: Principle by which employees are represented in governance structures along with shareholders.

rate and societal goals as fused, rather than potentially incompatible. For large Japanese companies, therefore, a CSR approach is inherent in corporate culture, but there are two provisos. First, as in other high-context cultures, Japanese corporate governance has tended to be weak in disclosure and transparency, relying on behind-the-scenes negotiation and decision-making (Nakamoto, 2007). CSR initiatives in Japan have emphasized the need for fuller reporting of social and environmental impacts. Second, Japanese companies have tended to be ethnocentric in terms of central direction, regarding foreign operations and their stakeholders more in instrumental terms rather than subject to a participatory role in management. The 'social' in the Japanese CSR approach has therefore centred on national social values rather than a plurality of social values in international operations.

Is globalization impacting on these differing national corporate governance perspectives? If there is a gradual convergence taking place, one would expect to see market-oriented governance taking on more CSR or stakeholder interests, and stakeholder-oriented governance becoming more open to market considerations. To some extent, we can see both these trends occurring. First, looking at the changes taking place in the stakeholder-oriented systems, these are more open to market forces and shareholder activism. In Germany, the strong voice of trade unions on supervisory boards is now being criticized as disproportionate in relation to other stakeholders, including shareholders. In Japan, corporate restructuring has resulted in a more market-oriented approach, and outside investors are gaining influence on boards (see CF1.1).

Second, for companies following the Anglo-American model, CSR is making an impact on management, but has not brought about radical changes in governance structures. The OECD's *Principles of Corporate Governance*, which were approved by member governments as international benchmarks, recognize the role of stakeholders insofar as they are established in law in different countries (OECD, 2004). In some, they participate in governance; in others, their legal position is more ambiguous. The OECD's principles stress that in all cases, stakeholders should have access to information and be free to communicate their concerns (OECD, 2004: 21). The UK *Combined Code on Corporate Governance* makes no mention of stakeholders other than shareholders (FRC, 2006). However, largely because of lobbying from environmental and stakeholder groups, recent revisions to UK company law have incorporated references to stakeholders. These are incorporated in the Companies Act 2006 (DBRR, 2006).

The cornerstone of the duty of directors is to act in the best interests of the company itself, which is generally taken to mean focusing on the shareholders, whose interest is in wealth maximization. However, shareholder value is not always best served by short-term attention to the financial bottom line, and co-operative relationships, which might entail short-term costs, could bring benefits in the longer term (House of Commons Library, 2006). Two approaches were considered by lawyers reviewing the existing law. The 'pluralist' approach would imply giving more voice to stakeholders, slackening shareholder control, but possibly entailing conflicts between interests which could damage the efficiency of the company. A second

WEB CHECK

For resources on corporate governance, see the OECD's website, and click on *Corporate Governance* under Topics.

approach, which was adopted, was that of 'enlightened shareholder value', which entails:

> the need for the company to foster business relationships with employees, suppliers and customers, the need to have regard to the impact of its operations on communities and the environment, and the need to maintain a reputation for high standards in business conduct. (House of Commons Library, 2006)

The revised law recognizes CSR as a management issue, rather than a matter of governance, leaving in place the shareholder model of governance, albeit with a more complex stakeholder agenda.

Corporate governance and CSR
In your view, should CSR and stakeholder interests be part of corporate governance structures, and why?

PAUSE TO REFLECT

Shareholder perspectives

For companies in market economies, the guiding principle of governance is that shareholders are the major stakeholder group whom managers must satisfy. In practice, the relationship between shareholders and managers can be fraught. Many shareholders are rather passive investors, content to allow managers to run the business. For small investors, there is little choice, as they lack the resources to exert influence, by, for example, nominating a candidate for the board (which could be prohibitively expensive). Large institutional investors, such as pension funds, have also traditionally been acquiescent. Where inactive investors account for half or more of the company's shares, as is common, managers are likely to be given a free rein to run the business as they see fit. But whose interests will they actually serve? Whether managers can be trusted to seek shareholders' interests or are naturally inclined to seek their own self-interest (above all, the need to keep their jobs) is one of the key issues that is debated (see Letza et al., 2004). On the assumption that they are naturally self-interested, it has become common for managers to acquire shares in the company they manage, better aligning their interests with shareholders and providing an incentive to improve corporate performance. Whether this policy works is discussed in the next subsection.

Active investors, as well as many government policy-makers, seek improved and transparent governance, with greater representation of shareholder and other stakeholder interests. Shareholders with substantial stakes, such as activist hedge funds, are often highly assertive, especially when they feel managers are underperforming. Pension funds are also becoming more active as investors, and these funds see CSR implications as impacting on their investment decisions. An example is CalPERS (the California Public Employees Retirement System), which controls an investment portfolio of over US$250 billion. The appointment of independent members (known as 'non-executive' directors) to boards is now recognized as contributing to higher standards of governance, helping to prevent a board being controlled by either management interests or dominant shareholders. However, the presence of outside directors is not a panacea. Looking at Nike, featured in

CS14.2, 10 of the 12 board members are nominally independent, but the dominant shareholder controls the appointment of most of the directors.

The right to appoint and dismiss directors is one of the most important of shareholders' rights. Although they generally have the right to vote for board members, in practice, there are no candidates except those selected by managers, and these management nominees are almost always elected. In Europe, a director must receive a majority of votes to be elected, although there is no requirement for a 'one share, one vote' principle to operate (discussed below). In the US, shareholders have no right to vote *against* a candidate. They may either vote *for* a recommended candidate or abstain. The abstentions are not counted, so the managers' choice of candidate will be elected, even though abstentions (known as 'withheld votes') were in the majority. Some US companies, such as Pfizer, have adopted a rule that if withheld votes form the majority, the director elected must resign. The SEC has proposed reforms to make it easier for shareholders to submit their own candidates. Such proposals are supported by active investors, but strong resistance expressed by many powerful business and political leaders dims the prospect of reform (Grant, 2007). The apparent message to directors is: 'Directors, you are hired by management, not by shareholders' (Eckbo, 2004). Nike represents an extreme example of this situation, as ordinary shareholders have no vote at all for three-quarters of the board's members, and for the three they elect, abstentions are not counted.

Although democratic principles point to 'one share, one vote', control mechanisms, such as multiple voting shares and priority shares, are commonly adopted by companies. In Nike's case, B shares carry limited voting rights, whereas A shares, 90% owned by the founder, vote three-quarters of the board.

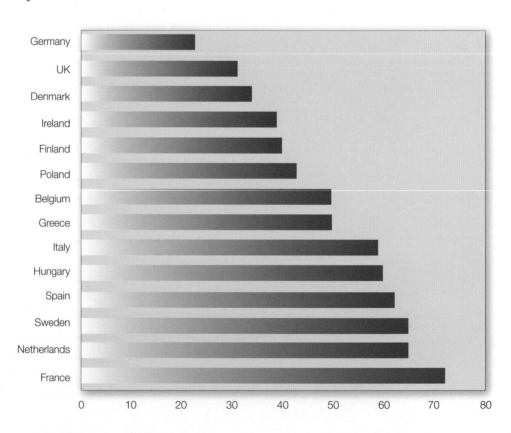

Figure 14.6 Percentage of companies with control-enhancing mechanisms

Source: European Corporate Governance Institute (2007) *Proportionality between Ownership and Control of EU Listed Companies,* www.ecgi.org

Control-enhancing mechanisms are widely available in EU countries, as shown in Figure 14.6. Multiple voting schemes are available in 53% of EU countries. Supporters of democratic reforms argue that the weighting given to certain shareholders protects managers favoured by entrenched interests, weakening the monitoring role which shareholders are meant to perform. The EU's internal market commissioner pressed for reform in 2005, but by 2007 had retreated. An underlying fear of democratic reforms is that they would benefit activist shareholders such as hedge funds and buyout groups, who have become skilful at putting pressure on managements, sometimes disproportionate to their holdings. These investors, as Chapter 11 highlighted, take a short-term view of gains from their stakes, which could jeopardize long-term strategy. Another factor which weighed against democratic reform was that, although investors rated companies with unequal systems less highly than those without, performance seemed not to be affected (ECGI, 2007).

One share, no vote
In what ways do companies fall short of the democratic principles expected of political systems? If the company performs well financially, does it matter that control-enhancing mechanisms are in place? What type of corporate governance would be consistent with ethical and other CSR considerations?

PAUSE TO REFLECT

Executive power and rewards

Executives are entrusted with responsibilities for formulating the firm's strategy, committing its resources and overseeing its operations. Just as there may be little effective check on their activities, there is little check on their pay. US executives saw a sixfold increase in executive pay between 1980 and 2003 (see CF2.1). It has been argued that this rise mirrors the increase in market capitalization of American companies, whether small, medium or large. Technological change is another factor cited, whereby new economy companies grow larger much more quickly than those of earlier generations. Globalization is cited as a driver in the growth of firms generally and the growth of high-tech companies in particular (Guha et al., 2006). Research has shown, however, that executive rewards have grown out of proportion to growth in company size, performance or industry classification (Bebchuk and Grinstein, 2005). Had executive pay grown in line with these three measures, it would have been half the actual size it had reached by 2003. The median remuneration for CEOs of FTSE 100 companies reached £2.4 million in 2006. The equivalent figure for the 200 top CEOs in the US was US$8.4 million, an 8% rise on the previous year. For executives of financial services companies, reward packages are US$30–35 million (Guha et al., 2006).

Salary forms a small portion of executive pay, only 10% in the US (see Figure 14.7). Stock options have become a favoured type of remuneration, giving the executive the right to purchase stock at a designated price, normally the closing price on the date of the grant of the options. Many American companies have been caught up in scandals involving manipulation of the timing, especially the backdating of stock options to a date when the shares were trading at a lower price than the date of the grant. As of 2007, the SEC was investigating 170 cases of backdating. In all, some 850

Stock option: Right to buy shares at a set price and within a specific time period.

CEOs representing 10% of all US companies are estimated to have been involved in backdating (Bebchuk and Peyer, 2007). Both old economy and new economy companies are affected, but those more likely to be involved are those with few independent directors and CEOs of long tenure, who are in a strong position to influence boards. Steve Jobs, CEO of Apple, is an example. He was awarded backdated stock options amounting to half a billion dollars by a board meeting which never took place. Performance-linked rewards are typically packaged in long-term incentive plans (LTIPs), including conditional awards of shares based on perform-ance (see Figure 14.7). LTIPs form 15% of compensation packages in the US, whereas in the UK, they account for 38%. Links of pay to performance are therefore weaker in the US than in the UK, perhaps due to the right of shareholders to vote on the matter in the UK.

In the US, shareholders have no say in the award of executive remuneration (usually referred to as 'compensation'), which is a matter for the board. In the UK, Australia, Sweden and the Nether-lands, shareholders have a vote on executive remuneration, although it is not binding on the board. It has been argued that the relatively weak position of shareholders in US corporate law has led to unchecked executive power (Bebchuk, 2005). Boards are meant to represent shareholders' interests, but in two-thirds of American companies, the CEO is also the chairman and is therefore strongly placed to influence board deci-sions. Board members are typically home-country nationals and current or former executives themselves. Nike's 12 board members in 2007 were all American and included current or former executives of Microsoft, Apple, IBM, Gap, Starbucks and FedEx. Although these directors are all inde-pendent, there is an in-built leaning towards a management perspective.

High-profile cases of executives receiving lavish rewards despite poor corporate performance have led to criticisms of the system as a whole. Bob Nardelli was rewarded with a severance package of US$210 million in 2007, despite deteriorating share performance during his tenure in the offices of chairman and CEO of Home Depot. Research carried out on the FTSE 100 companies indicates that pay and long-term corporate performance are only weakly correlated (PricewaterhouseCoopers, 2007). Disparity between super-star incomes and those of average citizens draws criticism. American business leaders also face criticism over corporate practices which, while legal, are perceived as unethical. The Sarbanes-Oxley legislation of 2002 introduced stronger penalties for accounting fraud and stricter liability of directors for oversight, but did not touch broad principles of corporate governance.

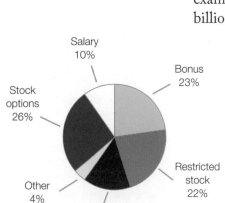

Figure 14.7 Breakdown of executive compensation in the US
Source: Financial Times, 29 August 2006

TO RECAP...

Executive rewards

Rising executive pay has become associated with performance measures such as share price. While remuneration reflecting global corporate success is generally applauded, companies are criticized for designing reward systems which maintain large payouts despite weak performance. In systems where corporate law leaves executives largely unchecked by shareholder scrutiny, excessive rewards are now widely perceived as ethically untenable and damaging to corporate reputation.

Executive pay
It is sometimes claimed that executives are the superstars of the corporate world, thus justifying superstar pay similar to that of sports and entertainment celebrities. Do you agree or disagree with this analogy, and why?

PAUSE TO REFLECT

Supply chains and employees

Employees are a key stakeholder group. When employed directly by a company, they are considered primary or internal stakeholders. For the modern MNE, employee status and degrees of organizational control may be complex, as illustrated in Figure 14.8. Employees hired directly by the MNE in its home country tend to be higher managerial or technological staff, although some of these, such as researchers, may not be full-time employees of the company. In Figure 14.8, the staff in foreign locations are manufacturing staff. Only those hired by the majority-owned subsidiary in country B are closely linked to the MNE parent company. In these subsidiaries, the MNE parent can influence HR policies and practices. At the opposite extreme, employees in countries C and D are employed by other companies, or even employment agencies. Where there are two intermediaries between the MNE parent and the manufacturing worker, head office is in a weak position to control or monitor what is happening in the factories making its branded products. Outsourced manufacturing and other activities have produced economic efficiencies for MNEs, but generally weakened CSR standards, particularly in developing countries. Some of the main issues are health and safety, job insecurity, poor treatment of workers and unpaid overtime.

Figure 14.8
Employees directly and indirectly connected to the MNE

Note: Employees include full time, part time and temporary

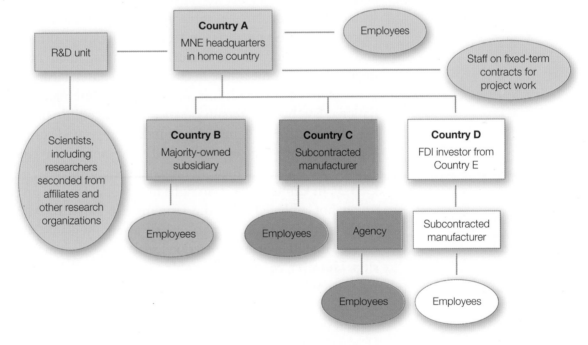

CSR in the employment context focuses on both legal and ethical dimensions. Legal frameworks in international business can be complex. Local, national and international law apply, often overlapping (see Chapter 5). Through the International Labour Organization (ILO), a body affiliated to the UN, a number of international conventions cover almost all aspects of the work environment. These conventions represent international consensus on labour standards, and have also become part of domestic law in many countries. The ILO (2006: 10) defines international labour standards as 'rules that govern how people are treated in a working environment'. They cover the following:

International labour standards: Rules agreed by the ILO on working conditions and the treatment of workers.

- *Health and safety* – protection, training and enforcement of health and safety frameworks appropriate for the industry
- *Employment rights* – including the right to be paid for work carried out; right to terms of employment; right to redundancy payment and payment for unfair dismissal where national law provides
- *Human rights* – including rights of human dignity and freedom from abuse; freedom of association and the right to collective bargaining; non-discrimination in employment; prohibition of child labour; and prohibition of forced or compulsory labour.

International conventions cover all these aspects of employment, and national law provides for implementation, enforcement and redress for breaches. In some countries, these minimum standards are not recognized, and in others, although recognized in law, they are weakly enforced in practice. As a minimal position, MNEs may opt to abide by national law, while a stronger CSR policy would observe international standards. An obstacle to higher CSR standards is the weak control exerted by MNEs over subcontractors which are legally independent. They have persuasive powers over these companies, but may acquiesce with contractors' practices unless forced to take action when mistreatment of workers emerges. Poorly paid workers in developing countries are vulnerable to harsh management practices. Immigrants and women, in particular, are vulnerable to exploitation. Worker organizations representing their interests are frequently lacking. Although MNEs arrange auditing to take place in factories producing their branded goods, some owners have become astute in covering up abuses, falsifying audit records.

Freedom of association is recognized in international conventions and national law, but workers in practice may have little prospect of representation or collective bargaining by an independent trade union, due to the policies of local owners as well as MNE parent companies who adopt an anti-union stance in their home countries. Wal-Mart is an example (see CS3.2). In China, there is no right for a worker to join an independent trade union not affiliated with the Communist Party. In Mexico, 'maquiladora' workers who work in foreign-owned assembly plants should, in theory, be covered by employment protection legislation, which includes union membership. However, companies are able to avoid the legislation by using employment agencies to hire workers. The agency becomes the workers' employer, giving both the MNE parent company and the plant owner little direct control over workers and working conditions. Computer companies such as IBM and Dell, which have outsourced assembly to contract manufacturers, have been in this position (see country C in Figure 14.8). The contracted company uses an agency to employ staff. A report by the Catholic development charity Cafod (2004) drew attention to mistreatment of workers in Mexican assembly plants, which led to calls for greater control of suppliers.

The OECD (2001) published its *Guidelines for Multinational Enterprises*, which emphasizes a range of recommended policies for international operations. They include:

- Contribute to economic, social and environmental progress with a view to achieving sustainable development

- Respect the human rights of those affected by their activities consistent with the host government's international obligations
- Support and uphold good corporate governance principles
- Encourage, where practicable, business partners, including suppliers and subcontractors, to apply principles of corporate conduct compatible with the guidelines
- Abstain from any improper involvement in local political activities.

It is common for global companies to set out their standards in voluntary codes, but these codes almost always refer to national law, rather than international labour standards. A risk is that fine-sounding principles are not followed up in practice, as SX14.2 demonstrates. In the computer industry, individual companies dealt with this issue by devising a common code. Each had had a corporate code of conduct for suppliers, but following the Cafod report, the Electronic Industry Citizenship Coalition (EICC, 2005) adopted a common electronic industry code of conduct. This code covers the following headings: labour; health and safety; ethics and management systems. As of 2007, 30 companies had signed up to the code. The code espouses the principles of human rights, safe working conditions, fair treatment of employees and freedom of association. Although encouraging participants 'to go beyond legal compliance, drawing on internationally recognized standards', the code adopts local law as the standard. The reference to 'drawing on' international standards is indicative of the non-binding approach, which favours collaboration and co-operation. In 2007, the EICC took steps towards increasing reporting and the use of third-party auditors, as well as greater collaboration with NGOs. These steps recognize the scepticism of consumers, who have become accustomed to stories of 'sweatshop' conditions in outsourced manufacturing (see CS14.2).

WEB CHECK

For international labour standards, see the ILO's website at www.ilo.org.

plate 14.3 Fair trade initiatives, such as fair trade coffee production pictured here, have contributed to CSR strategies.

Agricultural and extraction industries have also raised CSR issues. Cadbury acquires commodities such as cocoa beans through numerous intermediaries, with no direct contact with the actual producers in West Africa and other regions. Fair trade initiatives, highlighted in the case of Marks & Spencer in the opening vignette, attempt to address the weaknesses of poor producers in developing countries. Cadbury has a human rights and ethical trading policy, in an attempt to monitor working conditions, health and safety, and employment conditions in the supply chain. For the extractive industries, CSR has raised broad issues of governance within societies, especially those with widespread poverty. These issues are discussed in SX14.2 on Anglo American, which has committed itself to CSR, but has appeared to compromise its principles in practice. Mining and oil companies often provide healthcare, education and village projects to improve living conditions. These activities bring genuine benefits, but serve to highlight the contrast between villages where relevant workers live and the rest. Voluntary initiatives by companies (and also charitable activities) cannot take the place of governments, which are responsible for the overall welfare of citizens.

STRATEGIC CROSSROADS

14.2

Anglo American's CSR principles under fire

Mining companies confront a number of sensitive CSR issues. Extraction operations are inherently dangerous, cause direct environmental damage and often take place in unstable political and social environments, especially in developing countries. Anglo American plc, the world's second largest mining company, has long faced all these issues. It has adopted a set of CSR policies to address these impacts, holding itself out as an example to the industry. In 2003, Anglo American launched a toolbox, known as the Socio-Economic Assessment Toolbox (SEAT) to help managers understand and deal with the effects of their operations on local communities. SEAT is divided into five stages:

- Profile operations in the host community
- Engage with the full range of stakeholders
- Identify the impacts of operations, and the community's key development issues
- Develop a management plan to mitigate the negative aspects and maximize the benefits, while also addressing the broader development issues
- Produce a report in conjunction with stakeholders.

The toolbox is designed to be helpful in a variety of differing operations, recognizing the highly localized nature of mining operations. However, the company's activities have been the subject of adverse reports, casting doubt on the depth of its CSR principles.

Founded by the Oppenheimer family in South Africa in 1917, Anglo American is now a UK-listed plc with a number of subsidiaries and affiliated companies. A restructuring of its numerous diversified businesses has taken place, leading to a refocusing on its core mining activities. The company suffered from lapses in safety and a series of fatal accidents in its South African operations in 2006. There have also been allegations that the relocation of local inhabitants to make way for mining operations has involved little consultation. A further complaint was that the settlements to which they were moved had inadequate water and sanitation facilities. Adding to the adverse publicity, the South African government has accused the company of slowness in implementing black empowerment laws, which require the company to allocate a sizable portion of its equity to local partners. Cynthia Carroll, the new CEO appointed in 2007, set about negotiating numerous agreements to comply with the law, and mending relations with the South African government.

AngloGold Ashanti (AGA), an Anglo American affiliate, has licences to operate gold mines in the Democratic Republic of Congo (DRC), which contains some of Africa's richest gold fields. Having endured years of civil war, the country still suffers from violent conflict between armed groups fighting over control of mining areas, the riches from which provide funds for their activities. These groups and their warlords have a documented history of human rights atrocities, particularly in the northeast area of the country, which is rich in gold. AGA and other MNEs have been active in this region despite allegations that they were knowingly dealing with warlords. Human Rights Watch concluded that AGA and other MNEs engaged in resource exploitation were contributing to the continued conflict, with its damaging impacts on human well-being for the people of the DRC. A UN panel of experts produced four reports on the situation, naming 85 companies in connection with breaches of the OECD's guidelines for MNEs. In 2003, the UN Security Council imposed an arms embargo on dealing with named groups, which forbids direct or indirect assistance, whether military or financial.

Two warlords from the northeast region of the DRC are in the custody of the International Criminal Court in The Hague, where prosecutions are underway for war crimes and crimes against humanity, which would include 'those who direct mining operations ... even if they are based in other countries' (Human Rights Watch, 2005). Could AGA or its parent Anglo American be implicated? In 2006, Anglo American reduced its stake in AGA from 54% to 42%. Anglo American referred to AGA in 2006 as an 'independently managed subsidiary' (www. angloamerican.co.uk). The company's Interim Report for 2007 stated that it is looking to sell its remaining stake. The parent is attempting to distance itself from association with AGA, but its directors might not escape legal entanglement, and doubts about its commitment to CSR remain.

Questions

◆ Describe Anglo American's approach to CSR in terms of its policies.

◆ In what ways do Anglo American's operations in practice depart from its CSR principles and the OECD's guidelines for MNEs?

◆ What recommendations would you make to Anglo American to deal with human rights and other allegations associated with its African operations?

Sources: Mathiason, N., 'Fresh allegations tarnish a glittering year for Anglo', *Observer*, 22 April 2007; Human Rights Watch (2005) *The Curse of Gold*, http://hrw.org; Murray, S., 'SEAT process to the rescue', *Financial Times*, 29 November 2004; Carroll, R., 'Multinationals in scramble for Congo's wealth', *Guardian*, 22 October 2002; Rice, X., 'Congolese warlord accused of massacre placed in ICC custody', *Guardian*, 19 October 2007; Curtis, M., 'Painful extraction', *Guardian*, 3 August 2007; Anglo American plc, www.angloamerican.co.uk; Anglo American plc, *Annual Report 2006* and *Interim Report 2007*, www.angloamerican.co.uk; UN (2003) *Report of the UN Panel of Experts on the Illegal Exploitation of Natural Resources and Other Forms of Wealth from the Democratic Republic of Congo*, S/2003/1027; O'Connell, D., 'Cyclone Cynthia shakes up Anglo', *The Sunday Times*, 2 March 2008, http://business.timesonline.co.uk.

WEB CHECK

Anglo American's website is www.angloamerican.co.uk, which has a link to *Corporate responsibility*.

CSR and globalization
In what ways do globalized production and global supply chains pose challenges for international CSR? Can they be overcome, in your view, or is globalization essentially at odds with CSR principles?

PAUSE TO REFLECT

Reporting CSR

Monitoring and reporting CSR performance go hand in hand. Only by transparency and disclosure can companies be assessed on their CSR records. Moreover, firms which stress their CSR credentials strengthen their position in terms of competitive advantage by the use of social reporting or social audit. Companies may adopt triple bottom line reporting, including social and environmental as well as financial performance (see CS14.1). Governments encourage this move, although for most companies, it represents a voluntary initiative.

Countries differ in their legal reporting requirements. The Netherlands, Denmark and Norway require environmental reporting. In France, directors must mention social and environmental matters in their reports. In the UK, regulations require companies to provide an operating and financial review (OFR) with information on environmental impacts and other non-financial information necessary for investors to understand the company's position. Although the focus is on shareholders, stakeholder and CSR issues increasingly fall within this category. This information may be rather sketchy, and falls short of a thorough report on CSR and sustainability. The number of companies producing non-financial reports is growing, as shown in Figure 14.9. The number of reports which use external verification is also growing, reaching 300 by 2003 (CorporateRegister, 2004). Of the world's regions, companies in Europe are the most likely to produce non-financial reports: 54% of the total between 2001 and 2003 were European companies. Asian and Australasian companies accounted for 25%; companies from the Americas accounted for 19%; and African and Middle Eastern companies, 2%. The majority of the American companies reporting were from North America. Latin American companies accounted for only 5% of the American total.

Figure 14.9 Growth in non-financial reporting by companies

Source: CorporateRegister (2004) 'Towards transparency: progress on global sustainability reporting, 2004', www.CorporateRegister.com

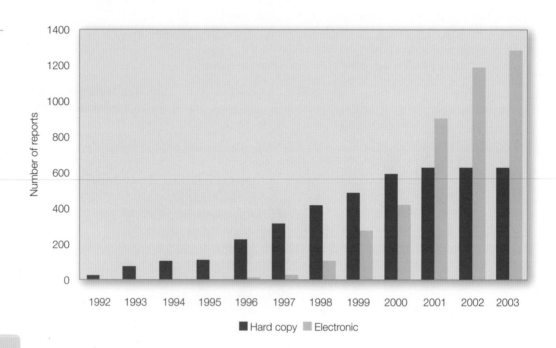

Hard copy ■ Electronic

TO RECAP...

CSR reporting

Although CSR reporting is young, companies are increasingly feeling the need to provide stakeholders with non-financial aspects of corporate performance, including social and environmental impacts. As more companies take up the challenge, guidelines are emerging, which aid businesses and consumers in assessing companies' social relationships across global operations, as well as the environmental sustainability of their operations.

The focus of reports and the information presented vary considerably. Environmental reporting is commoner than other areas of reporting, as Figure 14.10 shows. Broadly focused CSR reports can lead to a better understanding of the company's risk profile, which is of benefit to investors and other stakeholders. Vague statements received by sceptical readers do not benefit companies as much as data on social performance. On the other hand, data obtained through social audits of factories in developing countries are susceptible to falsification by factory owners, fearful of losing valued contracts from brand owners, but also under pressure to reduce costs. The Global Reporting Initiative (GRI), a UN-backed organization, has produced detailed guidance on CSR reporting (GRI, 2006). While its recommendations are rather daunting in the comprehensive detail they prescribe, many companies have taken up the challenge, as Figure 14.10 indicates.

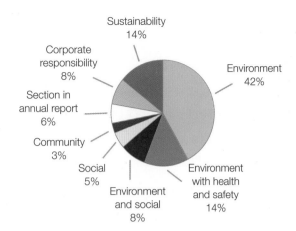

Figure 14.10 Types of non-financial report issued by companies, 2001–03

Note: Percentages of a total of 3,637 hard copy and PDF reports

Source: CorporateRegister (2004) 'Towards transparency: progress on global sustainability reporting, 2004', www.CorporateRegister.com

Conclusions

☐ Companies are forces in all the societies in which they either operate directly or direct operations of others. Corporate leaders in Western market economies have traditionally seen their role chiefly in economic terms, as one of wealth creation for the company's shareholders, within the legal constraints imposed by national law. This view is now challenged by a broader view of the company in society, encapsulated in the concept of CSR, which takes into account the social and environmental dimensions of the company's activities. CSR principles also imply that companies' impacts should be assessed on ethical as well as legal criteria. A stakeholder approach serves to assess these wider impacts. Beyond shareholders, companies interact with an array of stakeholders, including employees, consumers, communities and governments. However, approaches to CSR and stakeholder participation vary greatly. For some companies, CSR represents a bow to stakeholder considerations, without entailing a shift in competitive economic strategy. For these companies, philanthropic activities are often viewed as a means of satisfying a company's social obligations. For other companies, CSR represents an opportunity to remodel strategy on socially and environmentally sustainable principles. This more radical approach, perhaps more costly in the short term, is viewed by many companies as generating sustainable competitive advantage in the future.

☐ CSR has both governance and management implications. Most governance structures are wedded to shareholder primacy, although in some national settings, stakeholders, especially employees, have a voice in governance. Given the traditional focus on maximization of shareholder value prevalent in market-based economies, it is perhaps ironic that shareholders have little say in governance processes in most companies. Boards of directors are charged with monitoring managers and safeguarding shareholders' interests, but are often dominated by the executive interests they should be monitoring, or by dominant shareholders. Although directors' legal obligations to non-shareholding stakeholders receive scant acknowledgement in corporate governance systems, they are being increasingly recognized in management policies. Importantly, as globalization has deepened, workers in supply chains and contract manufacturing plants are now recognized as stakeholders. Although MNEs have tended to view national law as the extent of their legal obligations, adherence to international labour standards and moral obligations to a wider range of stakeholders are increasingly demanded. Moreover, investors and consumers are often at the forefront in demanding broader and deeper CSR commitment, as well as higher levels of transparency and disclosure of social impacts through reporting mechanisms. International managers, whether reluctantly or enthusiastically, are now taking CSR seriously.

The future of CSR
In your view, are companies becoming more committed to CSR principles, or simply more adept at wrapping existing competitive strategies in CSR terminology? (CS14.2 is relevant to this debate.)

PAUSE TO REFLECT

Review questions

Part A: Grasping the basic concepts and knowledge

1. Describe the changes that have taken place in perceptions of the role of the company in society.
2. Define CSR, and explain each of the three key aspects.
3. What is meant by 'corporate citizenship', and how does it impact on CSR?
4. Why does the stakeholder approach interact closely with CSR?
5. Describe Carroll's three-dimensional model of CSR. What are its strong points in helping us to understand CSR strategies?
6. How can CSR theories be expanded to apply to international business?
7. What are the distinguishing features of a CSR strategy which integrates economic and social goals?
8. Why is a bolted-on CSR approach often criticized by proponents of strategic CSR?
9. How does strategic philanthropy differ from straightforward charitable giving? In what ways is philanthropy becoming more engaged with recipient organizations?

10. What drawbacks can be highlighted in the new approaches to philanthropy?

11. Define 'social enterprise' and give an example with which you are familiar.

12. What are the doubts which surround the long-term viability of social enterprises, and how can they be resolved?

13. What advantages and disadvantages are associated with stakeholder-oriented corporate governance? Cite examples from Japan and Germany.

14. What principles form the basis of the Anglo-American model of corporate governance? How is UK law changing to reflect stakeholder interests?

15. From the shareholder's perspective, what are the weaknesses in corporate governance, particularly voting arrangements?

16. Why has executive pay become prominent as an issue in corporate governance, and what are the wider implications for CSR?

17. In what ways is CSR reshaping strategies in supply chains which rely on outsourced manufacturing, in relation to legal and ethical considerations?

18. Why is non-financial reporting, including triple bottom line reporting, an element of the CSR agenda? Which countries are to the forefront?

Part B: Critical thinking and discussion

1. Analyse the essential conflict between the CSR approach to corporate strategy and the view that the economic role of the business is all that matters. How are the differences between these two views becoming blurred by the 'business case' for CSR?

2. Stakeholder management is often praised in principle, but criticized as unworkable in practice. To what extent is this a fair criticism, and how can stakeholder management be made more effective in practice?

3. CSR concepts and theories have evolved mainly in the Anglo-American context. How can they be applied when multiple societies, differing legal frameworks and diverse cultures are involved?

4. To what extent do strategic philanthropy and social enterprises represent new directions in CSR, or simply fringe developments?

5. Managers tend to feel they know best how to run companies and produce the greatest returns for shareholder value. Many shareholders feel that boards, which should represent their interests as owners, are, in practice, biased towards managers. Assess the apparent conflict between managers and shareholders on issues of accountability and corporate control.

6. CSR, corporate citizenship and stakeholder interests are now commonly used by companies as a means to enhance their business reputations, featuring especially in public relations materials. In practice, many adopt the terminology without adopting CSR as a strategy and culture. To what extent does this pervasiveness of 'buzz words' detract from genuine changes in strategy on the part of many companies?

Nike is one of the world's most recognizable brands. Since its beginnings in Oregon in the US in 1968, it has become the global leader in sportswear, its reputation resting especially on its branded trainers and other footwear which bear its iconic logo. Because of its huge array of branded products and 35% share of the global retail market in branded trainers, we tend to think of Nike as a manufacturer. In fact, its core business focuses on design, development and marketing, employing 30,000 people, mainly in the US. Its footwear and apparel are manufactured almost entirely outside the US, by independent contract manufacturers operating in some 36 countries and employing over 800,000 people in 2007. Two-thirds of Nike footwear is made in China and Vietnam. Its strategy is to use outsourced, low-cost production to manufacture products with a high reputation for quality, at premium prices. Often cited as an example of globalization, the strategy has proved highly successful, generating revenues in 2007 in excess of US$16 billion (see Figure 1). Other ingredients of Nike's success are huge spending on advertising (nearly $2 billion in 2007) and paying athletes and other sportspeople to endorse its products (accounting for $40 million in 2007). Nike's high media profile has given rise to controversy, with criticisms of working conditions in the factories which make its products. The company acknowl-

Case study 14.2: Nike's evolving CSR strategy

edges that this is the key issue in its industry, and has embarked on CSR initiatives, but how does its CSR measure up?

From 1992, Nike has implemented a code of conduct for contract factories. This code espouses principles of international labour

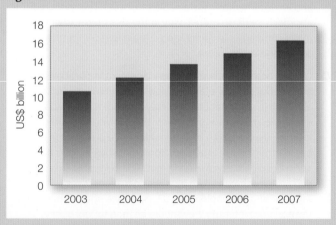

Figure 1 Nike's net revenues

US$ billion

2003 2004 2005 2006 2007

Source: Nike *Annual Report 2007*, www.nikebiz.com

standards and requires factories to abide by local law. Chief among these principles are health and safety regulations; pay due to workers; and controls on overtime required of workers. Enforcement of these standards, however, is notoriously difficult in light of pressures on factory owners to keep costs down and meet deadlines. Nike's response to critical reports in the 1990s was to improve monitoring of factories, using third-party monitors to improve compliance. It staunchly defended its commitment to corporate responsibility, gaining much media attention. However, it also attracted a hostile critic, Mike Kasky, who launched legal proceedings against it in 1998 for engaging in what was, in effect, commercial advertising, while claiming protection of the US Constitution which guarantees free speech for individual citizens. Nike had used press releases and letters to editors of journals and newspapers to defend its labour practices. Although Nike lost in the California Supreme Court, stalemate ensued in the appeal process which followed. The two sides reached an agreement in 2003 to end their legal battle, with Nike volunteering to donate US$1.5 million to the Fair Labour Association, which monitors working conditions in contract factories.

During an understandable withdrawal from the media limelight, Nike rethought its CSR policies. Appointing a corporate responsibility committee at board level in 2001 was part of its new approach, which was presented in a full *Corporate Responsibility Report* in 2004. This report states that corporate responsibility is important to deliver value to the company's five core stakeholder groups: 'consumers, shareholders, business partners, employees and the community' (p. 9). It goes on to mention its 'direct' stakeholders, who are 'consumers, employees, governments, retailers, athletes and athletic associations, suppliers and workers in our supply chain' (p. 13). 'Indirect' stakeholders cited were academics, media, trade unions and NGOs. The report presents findings of monitoring carried out in its factories, which show that chief areas of concern are health and safety, and employment terms, including wages and working hours (see Figure 2). The report also announces an intention to give 3% of pre-tax profits to non-profit organizations, including cash, products and services. The Nike Foundation, set up in 2005, is one of Nike's main philanthropic channels, concentrating on alleviating poverty and gender inequality in developing countries.

A shorter corporate responsibility report, focusing on strategy, appeared in 2005. It states that 'systemic change for workers' is now needed, going beyond the standard risk and reputation approach usually taken, to a more holistic strategy (Global Corporate Responsibility Strategy, 2005). It announced aims to end 'excessive overtime' in the factories by 2011, and to design education programmes for workers on freedom of association, including the right to join independent trade unions. Both goals could be difficult to achieve in practice, as indicated by the lengthy time frame. The first involves changes in design and planning processes, as factories are often faced with sudden increases in orders or design variations. The second

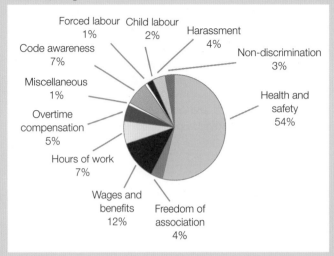

Figure 2 Audit findings on compliance in 40 Nike contract factories, 2003

Source: Nike *Corporate Responsibility Report 2004*, www.nikebiz.com

aim, freedom of association, is restricted by law in China and Vietnam, both of which ban independent trade unions.

Has Nike evolved into a company with CSR at its centre? The company's annual reports for 2006 and 2007 make no mention of either corporate responsibility or stakeholders, although a vice president and a committee of corporate responsibility appear in lists of officers and committees at the end. Under 'risk factors', it is stated briefly that non-compliance with its code by contractors could pose a risk to its reputation.

Similarly, Nike's corporate governance reflects little influence by multiple stakeholders. The share structure consists of class A and class B shares. Nike's founder, Philip Knight, owns 90% of the A shares, which are not tradable. Knight was CEO until his retirement in 2004, and remains chairman of the board. The B shares, which are tradable and listed on the NYSE, represent the 19,600 ordinary shareholders. The B shareholders have limited voting rights. Nike's board comprises 12 members: 9 are elected by class A shareholders, and 3 by class B. Ordinary shareholders have no say over executive rewards. Nike paid its CEO over $6 million in total remuneration in 2007. That year, its five top executives earned a total of $22,331,749 in remuneration, including stock options.

Nike has encountered political as well as legal tension in recent years. The American Jobs Creation Act of 2004 reflects fears of legislators over outsourced jobs. As a result, Nike had to repatriate $500 million of foreign earnings in 2006.

Questions

1 How has Nike's CSR approach changed over the years?
2 Assess Nike's current approach to CSR and stakeholder management. Has it undergone 'systemic change', or less radical changes?
3 Critically evaluate Nike's corporate governance in terms of CSR.

Sources: Waldmeir, P., 'Judges opt out of Nike free speech case', *Financial Times*, 27 June 2003; Murray, S., 'Nike makes the step to transparency', *Financial Times*, 13 April 2005; Birchall, J., 'Nike to promote workers' rights', *Financial Times*, 30 May 2007; Company documents at www.nikebiz.com: Annual Reports 2006 and 2007; *Corporate Responsibility Report 2004*; Global Corporate Responsibility Strategy 2005; Proxy Statement 2007.

WEB CHECK

Nike's corporate information is at www.nikebiz.com. Here there is a link to *Nike responsibility*.

Further research

Journal articles

Donaldson, T. (1996) 'Values in tension: Ethics away from home', *Harvard Business Review*, **74**(5): 48–62.

Husted, B. and Allen, D. (2006) 'Corporate social responsibility in the multinational enterprise: Strategic and institutional approaches', *Journal of International Business Studies*, **37**(6): 838–49.

McWilliams, A., Siegel, D. and Wright, P. (2006) 'Corporate social responsibility: Strategic implications', *Journal of Management Studies*, **43**(1): 1–18.

Scherer, A. and Palazzo, G. (2007) 'Toward a political conception of corporate responsibility: Business and society seen from a Habermasian perspective', *Academy of Management Review*, **32**(4): 1096–120.

Windsor, D. (2006) 'Corporate social responsibility: Three key approaches', *Journal of Management Studies*, **43**(1): 93–114.

Books

Strange, R. (ed.) (2008) *Corporate Governance and International Business*, Basingstoke: Palgrave Macmillan.

Don't forget to check the companion website at **www.palgrave.com/business/morrisonib**, where you will find web-based assignments, web links, interactive quizzes, an extended glossary and lots more to help you learn about international business.

chapter 15
GLOBAL GOVERNANCE

learning objectives

▷ To identify the processes and players shaping global governance mechanisms
▷ To highlight the global challenges encountered by international business, governments and civil society, particularly in the areas of human well-being, climate change and risks to security
▷ To gain an overview of the shifts taking place in international markets, including the growing influence of sovereign players
▷ To assess the impacts of international rule-making for businesses operating in differing national environments
▷ To appreciate the links between CSR strategic approaches and engagement in global governance networks, highlighting the ethical dimensions for international business

Introduction

In a stampede to obtain bottles of discounted cooking oil at a Carrefour hypermarket in western China in 2007, 3 people were killed and 31 injured. Inflation in food prices, acutely felt by Chinese consumers, has become a global issue, impacting on societies worldwide. The poorest countries, unable to afford rising import prices, risk food insecurity. The tragic incident in China was a reminder of two phenomena. First, it demonstrates the interconnectedness of the actions and policies of numerous players, including governments, producers and corporate decision-makers. Second, it reveals the paucity of overarching frameworks and institutions for solving the problems of human suffering. The subject of this chapter, global governance, concerns emerging mechanisms shaping cross-border business and meeting global challenges, such as climate change, poverty and risks to security. National governments and international organizations have long been influential, but, increasingly, MNEs are taking part in setting norms.

The chapter begins by defining global governance and identifying the organizations which take part directly and indirectly. We also look at relevant theories of international politics, which underpin evolving governance mechanisms. We go on to highlight the challenges confronting today's decision-makers. They include climate change, disparities in human well-being and threats to security, such as war and terrorism. As will be seen, one theme is that in all these areas, inequalities in wealth, power and international influence are factors which have created global divides among countries and peoples.

We then examine the roles of MNEs and governments. Although we think of the former as 'private' players and the latter, 'public', in fact, their roles are becoming blurred. Many MNEs have become so powerful as to dwarf governments. At the same time, wealthy governments and state-owned companies are becoming increasingly active in the world's markets. Both trends pose challenges for international regulation. The section on international rule-making focuses on three contrasting aspects of international business in which national and international rule-making are evolving: global finance, competition and the internet. In all three, there is a tension between national law and evolving international rule-making. Has the time come to bring in some regulatory control at international level? And if so, how can it be achieved realistically? Although no powerful player, whether company or government, welcomes restrictions on its activities, it might perceive that the existence of a stable set of rules, driven by consensus, is preferable in the long term to the insecurities of a weakly governed environment. Global governance could therefore pose opportunities rather than threats.

Global governance

Global governance: Evolving transnational processes of regulation and standard-setting by governmental and non-governmental agents.

The term global governance might suggest a system of worldwide rule-making. This would be partially true, in that there is a great deal of rule-making taking place internationally. However, far from resembling a coherent system, it emerges from numerous sources, formal and informal, public and private. In this section, we take an overview of these processes, including differing theoretical interpretations.

Definition and scope

The word 'governance' has come into use only recently, in tandem with globalization. Governance can be distinguished from 'government' in the traditional sense. Government denotes a rule-making entity with an identifiable structure, which has authority to make and enforce its rules, backed up by coercive powers. Governance also denotes authoritative rule-making, but with a focus on processes rather than structures, encapsulated in the notion of 'governance without government' (Underhill and Zhang, 2006). Cross-border relationships and agreements among governmental and non-governmental bodies create rules which are recognized as legitimate. Global governance can thus be defined as evolving transnational processes of rule-making and standard-setting by governmental and non-governmental players. Governance can be likened to a network, in contrast to the traditional view of government as a hierarchical structure. It is perhaps difficult to conceive of systems of rules which emerge through informal and fluid structures and practices, rather than formal law-making. The key attribute linking these differing types of authority is that organizations and individuals feel an obligation to comply.

The emergence of governance mechanisms with global spheres of authority reflects the interconnectedness and interdependence associated with globalization. As Chapter 5 pointed out, there is no global government with overarching powers to legislate for all of us on the lines of a 'superstate'. Nonetheless, in many areas, rule-making is a burgeoning phenomenon internationally, as shown in Figure 15.1. Within each, specific issues can be identified. Some are regulatory in nature, such as market regulation and shipping rules, which aid international businesses in cross-border transactions, investment and operations. Others reflect global challenges, including terrorism and poverty. While these latter issues might not seem directly relevant to businesses, in fact, they impact on the business environment, entailing risk management strategies. These issues are addressed by a variety of organizations and through numerous mechanisms, discussed in the next section.

TO RECAP...

What is global governance?
In contrast to the hierarchical structures of state governments, global governance covers a range of processes taking place at international level, which address areas of concern to us all, including economic, political, social, environmental and communications.

Figure 15.1 Dimensions of global governance

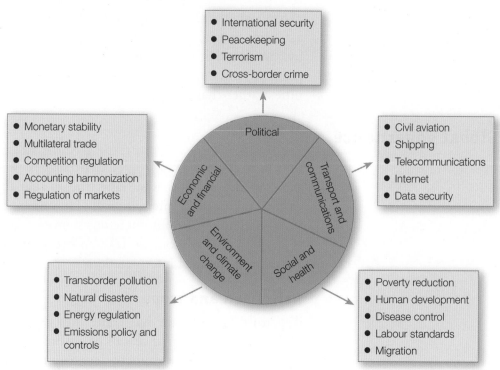

Actors and processes

The types of organization that feature in global governance range from formal government structures to informal groupings. The main types of organization are shown in Figure 15.2. There is overlap among these bodies and an organization may be party to a number of collectivities. In the postwar period, a variety of inter-governmental and non-governmental organizations has emerged. The UN has been the most prominent, as the body of treaties and international conventions attest. They are overseen by UN organizations, such as the United Nations Environment Programme (UNEP) and the International Labour Organization (ILO) (see Chapters 13 and 14 respectively). Typically, international bodies focus on particular issues and sectors where professional expertise is needed. A number have been discussed in this book, including the IMF's role in the international monetary system and the WTO's role in multilateral trade agreements. Governments join numerous alliances such as Opec, which co-ordinates policy among its 12 member countries. Its collective policies are influential in global governance.

For-profit business enterprises cover a variety of organizations, including ones in which national governments are important shareholders or important customers (discussed below). MNEs now typically participate in numerous networks and industry bodies which set standards and agree procedures. An example is the electronic industry code of conduct, highlighted in the last chapter. It has also become common, especially for MNEs with a strategic CSR focus, to form alliances with local civil society organizations and international organizations. Companies are able to benefit from the specialist knowledge of NGOs in these collaborations, which is particularly relevant in areas such as the environment (see Chapter 13). SX15.1

Civil society organizations: Voluntary groups representing cultural, religious and political diversity within a society.

Figure 15.2 Types of organization in global governance

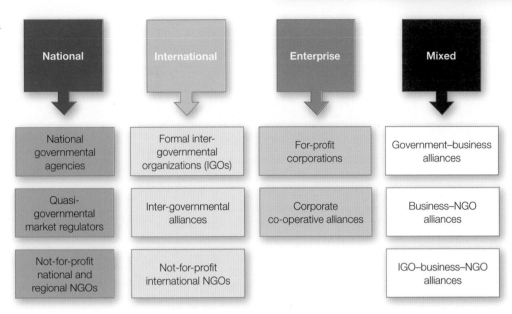

shows an example of an innovative project involving the UN, business and civil society in combating diseases in Africa.

The emergent process is thus a complex and multilayered governance, in which all parties seek aims such as consistent and standardized systems across national borders. Apart from rule-making, organizations carry out monitoring and review. With numerous different parties and interests, often representing conflicting aims and values, international negotiation can frequently be tense and lead to frustration, as evidenced by the WTO's Doha Round (see Chapter 6). Negotiations at the international level, whether between governments or firms, virtually always involve inequality among the players. Factors such as economic power and control over strategic resources give some parties the scope to exert their own interests over others without these advantages. On the other hand, even the powerful see their long-term prosperity as contingent on settled rules perceived by all as legitimate. Theories of global governance help us to understand the motives and behaviour of the various players, as well as the vexing issue of how to achieve co-ordinated action to deal with some of the world's pressing challenges.

TO RECAP...

Actors and processes of global governance

Global governance is multilayered, encompassing both formal and informal processes. State and non-state actors are prominent, the latter category featuring businesses and NGOs.

Governance as networking
In what ways do co-operative groupings differ from hierarchical structures in terms of rule-making and setting norms? What are the advantages and disadvantages of governance as opposed to government?

PAUSE TO REFLECT

Don't forget to check the companion website at **www.palgrave.com/business/morrisonib**, where you will find web-based assignments, web links, interactive quizzes, an extended glossary and lots more to help you learn about international business.

STRATEGIC CROSSROADS

15.1

Product Red: a new business model in the making?

Launched in January 2006, Product Red was the brain child of U2 singer Bono and Bobby Shriver, a Californian music and media promoter. Media attention was assured, as both are well-known personalities, Bono as a musician and campaigner for aid to Africa, and Shriver as a nephew of John F. Kennedy. They aimed to raise large sums of money from big companies for the UN Global Fund to Fight AIDS, Malaria and Tuberculosis, founded in 2001. Their idea was to create a brand, Product Red, which would be licensed to companies for use on a range of consumer products, part of the proceeds from which would go to the Global Fund. It was important for them to attract global brands to the scheme, as only these large companies could raise the large sums of money envisaged. Product Red is itself a registered company, whose business is simply licensing its logo. As it does not actually make anything, its strength lies in the brand image and its ethical associations, aided by the celebrity of its founders. As a sub-brand, Red can enhance the brand reputation of companies which sign licence agreements.

Companies were somewhat hesitant in coming forward, perhaps doubting the extent of the appeal to 'conscience consumers', who are now presented with an increasing array of ethical consumption options. Nonetheless, a steady flow, if not a torrent, of large companies have signed up. Known as 'partners', they include Apple (with a red iPod), Nike (with its Converse brand), Emporio Armani, Gap, American Express, Motorola and Hallmark, the greeting card company. These companies welcome the opportunity to launch an ethical product, reaching a wider market than they attract with their existing product ranges. However, the Red products are marginal for these companies. Red does no marketing itself, relying on the partner companies. There is a risk that, without prominent marketing, sales will be thin. Gap gives half its profits from its Red clothes to the cause. Both Gap and Nike are keenly aware of CSR issues, having had negative publicity for their outsourced manufacturing practices. Although Gap's Red T-shirts are made in Africa, sourcing and manufacture are not the major issues for Red licensing. The business model is therefore distinguishable from other ethical models such as fair trade initiatives. In fact, the Fairtrade Foundation of the UK has welcomed Red, as another approach for ethical business.

Based in Geneva, the Global Fund describes itself as a partnership between governments, civil society, the private sector and communities. It operates 'as a financial instrument, not an implementing entity' (The Global Fund, 2008), using local

Table Money received by the Global Fund as of January, 2008

Contributor	Contribution in US$ millions
US	2,539.6
France	1,164.6
Italy	1,008.2
UK	668.5
Japan	662.6
European Commission	728.6
Germany	403.1
Canada	431.4
Netherlands	321.5
Sweden	277.9
Russia	105.2
China	10.0
The Gates Foundation	350.0
Product Red and partners	53.6

Source: The Global Fund (2008) Pledges and contributions, www.theglobalfund.org

health experts and facilities. It funds programmes for treating patients needing antiretroviral therapy, reducing the transmission of HIV, and training healthcare workers. Working within local communities, it hopes to strengthen underlying health systems. It has become the world's largest channel for contributions from rich countries towards combating Aids. Its contributors are mainly governments (see table), but it is aware that pledges by governments are often slow to materialize. With commitments to increase the number of Aids patients being treated, it is anxious to attract more money. Its director welcomes corporate philanthropy, but realizes that companies, like governments, can decide to give the money to another cause. The director says: 'We need flows to be sustainable' (Beattie, 27 January 2007). Total sums raised now amount to over $9 billion. The contribution of Product Red and its partners is over $53 million. This sum is dwarfed by the largest contributions from governments, but many governments, such as China, have contributed much less. As more Red partners join, it has the potential to grow into a more significant and predictable source of funds. Bobby Shriver said of Red's guiding principle: 'Red is not a charity. It is simply a business model' (Beattie, 27 January 2007).

Red is dependent on continuing to sign up major global brands with products which appeal to consumers. Ethical consumers are on the increase, but there are several global issues which might seem more compelling, such as climate change. Product Red is hoping that consumers worldwide will recognize that Aids in Africa, and its close association with poverty, is not just an African tragedy, but a human one.

Sources: Beattie, A., 'Spend, spend, spend. Save, save, save', *Financial Times Magazine*, 27 January 2007; Beattie, A., 'Challenges ahead for Bono's brand', *Financial Times*, 1 December 2007; The Global Fund (2008) 'How the Global Fund works', www.theglobalfund.org; The Global Fund (2008) Pledges and contributions, www.theglobalfund.org.

Questions

◆ What is the basis of Product Red's business model, and what is the role of each of the key organizations involved?

◆ In your view, what are the prospects for growth for Product Red as a company? Could its model be copied by other firms?

WEB CHECK

Product Red's website is www.joinred.com.
The Global Fund is at www.theglobalfund.org.

Theories of global governance

Global governance is intertwined with the politics of international relations. Three influential theories are presented here (see Table 15.1). Realism and liberal institutionalism have both developed into schools of thought which share the same basic assumptions. A third theory focuses on global citizenship.

Table 15.1 Three theories of global governance

Theory	Major institutions	Basis of international co-operation	Power relations
Realism	Sovereign states	Promotion of national interests	Power politics at international level
Liberal institutionalism	States, MNEs, international institutions	Shared goals and growing international focus	Market orientation with regulation; goal of controlling power politics
Global citizenship	Emerging democratic institutions at global level	Notion of universal citizenship	Based on need rather than power

The realist school

The realist school of thought on international relations is the oldest of the theories presented here. Its primary focus is the sovereign nation-state, and its primary tenet is that states are always motivated by self-interest. As clashing interests bring them into conflict with each other, their main concern is national security. In this anarchic environment, the most powerful, often backed by military might, prevail. However, the powerful hardly feel secure, as other power-seeking nations are never far away. Advocates of this view argue that states join international institutions and co-operate with other states in pursuit of their own self-interest. They also recognize the role of non-state players such as MNEs. It has been suggested that large corporations have become so powerful as to eclipse the power of states, but realists believe that, in the end, the state always has the upper hand in both political and economic spheres (Gilpin, 2002).

In the world picture of the realist theorist, international stability will prevail if there is a single dominant power, a situation known as 'hegemony'.

Stability of a sort is also possible where there is a balance of power among states, as occurred in the Cold War period, in which two ideological blocs, represented by communism and liberal democracy, vied for supremacy. Following the end of the Cold War, the US became the dominant economic and political player. The US supported institutions which served perceived national self-interest and showed little enthusiasm for those, such as the UN and the WTO, which rested on principles of multilateralism. The US supported the UN at its inception in 1945, on condition that clear statements of national sovereignty were included in the Charter, but American policy became more unilateral and nationalist in the following decades. Intervention in other countries' affairs came to be seen as justifiable in terms of national self-interest. Historical research shows that the US has mounted 30 'invasions, interventions and regime changes' in other countries since the end of the Second World War (Johnson, 2006: 19). This list excludes minor military operations, and also excludes the wars in Iraq and Afghanistan. Described as a new sovereigntist approach, this aggressive foreign policy holds that global governance mechanisms pose a threat (Ruggie, 2004).

The rapid economic development of emerging economies is leading to new centres of economic power in trade, manufacturing and finance. An example is resource-rich Kazakhstan, featured in CF15.1. Concerned about the increasing global insecurity which accompanies the shifting balance of power, many realists believe that global and regional institutions can play a role in reconciling conflicting national interests, benefiting all in the long term (Gilpin, 2002). The next theory we consider, the liberal institutionalist, shares this belief, but takes it further than realist theories.

New sovereigntist approach: Approach to international relations which emphasizes state sovereignty and views international law and multilateral agreements as threats to sovereignty.

plate 15.1 Gleaming buildings in Kazakhstan's new capital, Astana, point to the country's global ambitions.

COUNTRY FOCUS 15.1 – KAZAKHSTAN

Kazakhstan seeks a new role on the international stage

Bordering Russia to the north, China to the east and the Caspian Sea to the southwest, with its links to the Mediterranean, Kazakhstan enjoys an unrivalled strategic position. When vast reserves of oil and gas are taken into consideration, it is not difficult to see why the strategic importance of this central Asian country has rocketed in recent years. Part of the former Soviet Union, it became an independent state in 1991, although within the CIS (Commonwealth of Independent States). President Nursultan Nazarbayev, now 68, led the transition to independence and has held office since 1989. He sought to create a distinctive Kazakh state, steering a new course between the political superpowers. Russian ties remain strong, however. A third of the country's population of 13 million are ethnic Russians, and economic links with Russia have been instrumental in the development of the resource riches, including the crucial pipelines taking the country's oil northwards.

In the new millennium, Kazakhstan reached annual GDP growth rates of 9–10%, largely from the oil and gas wealth, which form 70% of the country's exports. With the help of FDI, new oil and gas fields are expected to triple output within a decade, placing the country among the top 10 energy producers. Moreover, as it is both outside Russia and outside Opec (the cartel of oil-producing countries which controls 60% of remaining global oil reserves), Kazakhstan has an advantage for oil importers in the West. In addition to pipelines leading north to Russia, new pipelines are taking oil west from the Caspian to the Mediterranean, and east across Kazakhstan to China. China's national oil company (CNPC) paid a premium

price of over $4 billion for PetroKazakhstan in 2005, to secure oil assets, linked to a pipeline running to China. Western oil companies entered contracts with the Kazakh government in the 1990s, to develop new sites. A consortium led by Eni of Italy has developed the offshore Kashagan oilfield in the Caspian Sea, and the Tengiz oilfield development has been led by Chevron of the US (see map).

Figure 1 Kazakhstan's GDP growth

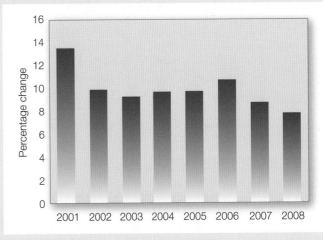

Source: IMF (2007) World Economic Outlook Database, www.imf.org

Although the American giant ExxonMobil was keen to take the lead of the Kashagan project, the Kazakh government instead chose Eni, partly as a counterbalance to the American-led Tengiz development. Cost overruns and delays have caused friction among the Western partners and with the Kazakh government. KazMunaiGaz, the Kazakh state oil company, was a minor participant in the initial contract in 1997. The US government has pressed the case for ExxonMobil, offering Kazakhstan technical and financial aid in exchange for the replacement of Eni by ExxonMobil as the lead company. In a deal agreed at the end of 2007, the stakes of the four Western partners were reduced by 2%, to 16.8% each, with compensation. KazMunaiGaz's stake was increased from 9.26% to 16.8%. The government was in a strong position to take the lion's share, but instead opted for a co-operative solution based on equal stakes, with the implication that the Kazakh government would have a greater say. The dispute left the project further behind, and multiparty co-operation is needed to meet the deadline of producing oil by 2011.

The government is counting on increasing oil revenues to fund public spending. It has spent lavishly on prestige projects, including a space programme and a new, showpiece capital city, Astana. However, it has come under pressure to increase spending on social welfare, including education and health. GDP per capita is rising (see Figure 2), and new wealth is evident, but there are concerns that it is not being spread across society. Although Nazarbayev has pursued market reforms, his regime has been authoritarian. He has channelled wealth and power to his family and associates, who have become ruling oligarchs. The country became a one-party state in 2007, as the president's party won all the seats in the parliament. Furthermore, Nazarbayev has bypassed the constitution, intending to stand for president indefinitely.

country as a growing force in global governance, in a position commensurate with its new economic prominence. Kazakh companies have been active in seeking a higher international profile in capital markets, listing on the LSE. Kazakhmys, the country's largest copper mining company, has a primary listing on the LSE, attracting the interest of European investors. Nazarbayev is hoping to join the WTO in 2008, and has campaigned for chairmanship of the Organization for Security and Co-operation in Europe (OSCE). The OSCE is an oversight body for security, democracy and human rights. One of its roles, for example, is monitoring elections. Chairmanship would be considered a diplomatic prize for the former Soviet republic, but one which might seem unlikely, given the country's poor human rights record and weak democratic credentials. The OSCE could put Kazakhstan's bid for chairmanship on hold, keeping open the prospect of the post at a later date. As a one-party state, it would not satisfy OSCE democratic criteria, but the prospect of a leadership role might prompt democratic reforms. Having withdrawn from attempts to monitor elections in Russia because of lack of co-operation, the OSCE is concerned that it is seen as having a pro-Western bias in assessing democratic development. Its 56 members are encouraged to see a former Soviet republic put itself forward as a candidate for the chairmanship.

Kazakhstan will face challenges in making the transition from a pivotal resource-rich country to an international political player. It will also face challenges at home, as new contenders for power line up to succeed Nazarbayev, along with movements pressing for democratic reforms.

Figure 2 Rising GDP per capita in Kazakhstan

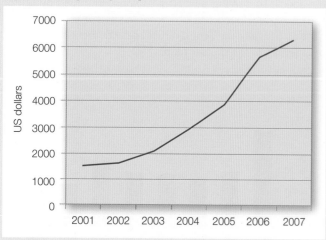

Source: IMF (2007) World Economic Outlook Database, www.imf.org

The president is aiming to make Kazakhstan one of the world's 50 most competitive countries. He envisages the

Questions

◆ Explain Kazakhstan's role as 'power broker' in the changing balance of power between the world's large economies.
◆ What global governance organizations and processes are referred to in this country focus feature? Explain the significance of each in global governance.
◆ What are Kazakhstan's long-term prospects of pursuing both sustainable economic development and an international political role?

Sources: Wagstyl, S. and Gorst, I., 'Securing stability on the steppes', *Financial Times*, 27 June 2007; Gorst, I., 'A pragmatic reliance on Russia – for now', *Financial Times*, 27 June 2007; Betts, P., 'Kazakhstan plays a deft hand in the global oil game', *Financial Times*, 27 November 2007; Gorst, I., 'Kazakhs seek more control of Kashagan', *Financial Times*, 7 September 2007; Gorst, I. and Wagstyl, S., 'Kazakhstan to be offered deal on chairing watchdog', *Financial Times*, 27 November 2007; Crooks, E. and Gorst, I., 'Energy groups are battered but not beaten', *Financial Times*, 15 January 2008.

WEB CHECK

For information about Kazakhstan, see the World Bank's website, at www.worldbank.org, and click on *Kazakhstan* in the country list.

Liberal institutionalism

Liberal institutionalism has become the major rival to realism. The liberal tradition generally rests on values of democracy in the political sphere and markets in the economic sphere. At the international level, these values are promoted more through international co-operation than power politics, with its overtones of conflict and insecurity. It is believed that international institutions which create new norms and incentives can be imbued with legitimacy transcending national power centres. The advocates of this view believe that it is possible to progress towards international governance, which will make power politics and wars seem increasingly irrational (McGrew, 2002). This view might seem rather idealistic, but the increasing interdependence of states and widening of multilateral co-operation can be taken as evidence that state players now perceive their roles as more co-operative than self-interested (Keohane, 1984). International institutions have been demonstrated to provide benefits and reduce uncertainties for national players: they 'empower governments rather than shackle them' (Keohane, 1984: 13).

Some argue that the liberal perspective might succeed in taming power politics, but not necessarily transcending it (McGrew, 2002). A number of non-democratic states have gained power on the global stage. The rise in numbers of countries aspiring to become liberal democracies is encouraging, but in many cases, their democratic institutions are weak (see Chapter 5). Liberals are concerned that many international institutions, such as the WTO and the IMF, are dominated by the most powerful states and lack democratic credibility themselves. Where these institutional forces are linked to globalization, they can lead to a backlash. International governance to date has shown itself to be weak in reducing insecurity and poverty. Sub-Saharan African countries in particular have fallen behind in economic and human development. As yet, the hope that globalization would bring benefits through trade and FDI has not been realized. Leaders of poor countries would probably view global governance as simply another way of saying that the rich are able to dictate their own terms.

Global citizenship

The third theory looks beyond both realism and liberal institutions, to governance whose basis of legitimacy transcends states and governments. The notion of citizenship is usually associated with the sovereign state, although the concept of the corporate citizen has become recognized (see Chapter 14). The idea of a global citizen stretches the concept even more, as the whole world is envisaged as a kind of community. Embracing a cosmopolitan view of democracy, advocates believe that citizenship is multilayered. A person can be a citizen of a state, and also a citizen at regional and global levels. We highlighted climate change as a global issue, but advocates of global citizenship highlight others in addition, such as disease control, human rights and global security. Accountability and transparency of institutions at the global level are essential to reflect democratic responsiveness to the full range of stakeholders. Inherent in this vision of global governance is a criticism of existing inter-governmental institutions, which tend to be weighted heavily towards their more powerful members.

Global citizenship: Extension of the notion of citizenship from the state to the entire world, involving global rights and responsibilities.

Another weakness of existing governance which is implied in this theory is a perceived failure of market-based institutions to deal with global challenges such as poverty (Held, 2006). This theory thus espouses goals closer to those of social democracy than liberal democracy. In answer to critics who object that the idealistic vision of a universal community is unattainable and unworkable, advocates point out that states are already embedded in networks of power-sharing. They argue that the traditional view of state sovereignty held by realists is long outdated. Moreover, the growing scope and depth of international rule-making suggests that the vision of all of humanity sharing one world is not as fanciful as it might seem. Indeed, in the area of human rights, international lawmaking has markedly progressed (see Chapter 5).

Assessing the theories
Which of the three theories described most closely represents your views on global governance? Which of the three would be best at solving global problems?

PAUSE TO REFLECT

Meeting global challenges

Many issues once thought to be essentially national are increasingly recognized as having global implications which demand global solutions. Assessing the scale and depth of impacts is gradually proceeding, but designing and implementing the means for collective problem-solving has resulted in a patchwork of initiatives, with varying degrees of international consensus and commitment. Global issues have been discussed in earlier chapters as they relate to international business. In particular, the environment and climate change have been discussed in Chapter 13, and international political risk has been discussed in Chapter 5. Here we focus specifically on meeting the challenges of global peace and security, human well-being and climate change.

Peace and security

We live in an uncertain world, where violent conflicts, terrorism and criminal activities are everyday news headlines. Figure 15.3 shows the types of threat along with the governance mechanisms which have emerged to deal with them. In the 1990s, over a third of the world's countries were directly or indirectly affected by serious societal warfare (Ruggie, 2004). Of these, two-thirds endured armed conflicts of seven or more years. Military arsenals and nuclear stockpiles are growing. Although nuclear power is viewed as a legitimate clean alternative to fossil fuel, the use of nuclear materials, especially in environments with poor safety systems and weak record-keeping, creates concerns. In 2006 alone, 250 incidents of unauthorized possession or criminal activity involving nuclear materials were reported, indicating a 'persistent problem' (UN News Service, 2007). With the risk of terrorism in the post-9/11 world, there arises the possibility of a terrorist attack on a nuclear power station, which could well occur in a weakly protected environment.

Under the auspices of the UN, the post-war period witnessed unprecedented strides towards building a new global environment of peace and

Figure 15.3 Meeting the challenges to peace and security

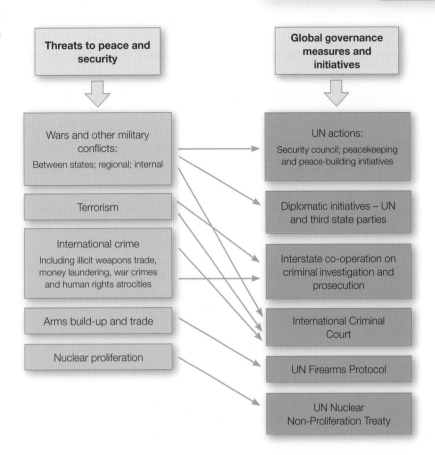

security. A host of treaties, most important of which is the UN Charter, set out principles limiting the use of force and protecting human rights. The role of the UN in preventive diplomacy, peacekeeping and peace-building has been instrumental in containing and resolving conflicts, but durable success is difficult to achieve, as the example of the Democratic Republic of Congo (featured in SX14.2) shows.

The Nuclear Non-Proliferation Treaty, aimed at controlling the proliferation of nuclear weapons, came into force in 1970 and has been ratified by 187 nations. Its three pillars are disarmament, non-proliferation and the peaceful use of nuclear energy. In recent years, however, reviews of its provisions have led to a weakening in this consensus. A gap between the nuclear and non-nuclear states seemed unbridgeable at the review meeting in 2005. The non-nuclear states called on the nuclear powers, most notably the US, to reduce their arsenals, but met with refusal. At the opposite end of the arms spectrum, a major obstacle in settling violent conflicts around the world has been the growth in small arms and light weapons. There are an estimated 600 million handguns, pistols, submachine guns and light missiles in circulation globally, and a thriving trade is encompassing an increasing number of developing countries (World Economic Forum, 2006). It is a lamentable fact that the weapons trade contributes to conflict and insecurity in developing countries, where living conditions are precarious in any case, adding to the human misery of both inhabitants and millions of refugees. A landmark treaty, the UN Firearms Protocol, which is the first ever global firearms treaty, was adopted by the UN General Assembly in 2001, by a vote of 153 in favour and 1 against (the one being the US). The Protocol

TO RECAP...

Threats to peace and security
Despite UN peacekeeping and peace-building initiatives, violent conflicts are often difficult to resolve, contributing to regional and global insecurities. Terrorism and international crime are facilitated by funds and weapons, which in today's globalized environment are readily available. UN efforts to fashion treaty agreements to control weapons and nuclear proliferation have achieved some successes, but they are not accepted by all member states.

came into legal force in 2005, with the 40th ratification. By 2007, 78 countries had signed, including China, the world's third largest exporter of weaponry. However, the two largest weapons-exporting countries, the US and Russia (in that order), had not.

The somewhat mixed picture of efforts by UN bodies to control conflict and sponsor agreement on disarmament led the World Economic Forum to record some slight improvement in global peace and security in its Global Governance Report, from a score of 2/10 in 2005 to 3/10 in 2006 (World Economic Forum, 2006).

Threats to security
What are the main global threats to security in today's world, in your view? How adequate are the mechanisms in place for dealing with them, and how could they be improved?

PAUSE TO REFLECT

Human well-being

Income, living conditions, health and education are areas of concern which once centred mainly on families. In the twentieth century, it came to be appreciated that these are societal issues, for which states bear either direct or indirect responsibility for people living within their borders. Gradually, these issues have come to be perceived as extending beyond national borders. The fact that 45% of the world's population lives below the line of 'moderate' poverty and that this percentage has grown in the current era of globalization are now seen as issues for us all. More to the point for international business, private sector businesses are crucial in poverty alleviation, as they are largely responsible for driving economic growth. Although disparities in well-being among different regions have always existed, the gaps among developing countries have opened up new divides. Successful developing countries, such as China, have made progress in reducing poverty, while the poorest developing countries have fallen behind.

Major aspects of human well-being are outlined in Figure 15.4, together with global governance mechanisms. The threats to human well-being are interrelated. Poverty is a major issue which impacts on all the others, its impacts extending beyond basic lack of income. World Bank researchers using standard measures of poverty are able to assess changes over time in all the world's regions. Absolute poverty is defined as living on less than $1 a day. This is a category prevalent only in developing countries. People living below this line struggle to survive. They lack sufficient food, safe drinking water, sanitation and shelter. Moderate poverty is defined as living on between $1 and $2 a day. In this category, basic needs are met, but little more. People in this category may well lack access to sanitation. For most of the period since 1990, the proportion of people living in moderate poverty has risen (Chen and Ravallion, 2007). Although not as urgently at risk as those living in absolute poverty, they remain extremely vulnerable to risks from disease and poor living conditions.

At the UN Millennium Summit of world leaders in 2000, the UN announced a set of Millennium Development Goals (MDGs), which are targeted at developing countries. Most of these are social goals, and others, such as environmental and technology goals, promise benefits to societies as

Absolute poverty: Defined by the World Bank as living on less than $1 a day.

Moderate poverty: Living on between $1 and $2 a day.

Figure 15.4 Improving human well-being

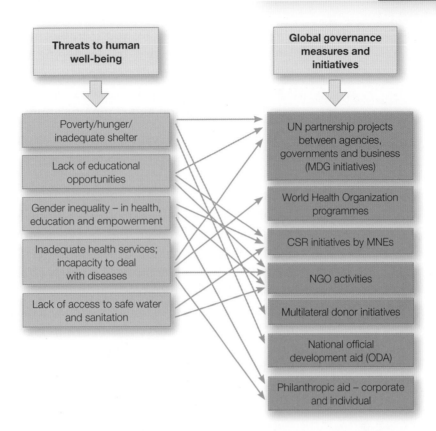

a whole. Using 1990 as a base line, the MDGs set ambitious goals to be achieved by 2015 (UNDP, 2002). Some of the goals contain a number of related targets. The goals and targets are set out below:

1 Halve the proportion of people living on less than $1 a day and suffering from hunger
2 Ensure that children everywhere, boys and girls alike, complete primary education
3 Eliminate gender inequality in schools
4 Reduce infant and under-five mortality rates by two-thirds
5 Reduce maternal mortality ratios by three-quarters
6 Halt and begin to reverse the spread of Aids, malaria and other major diseases
7 Integrate principles of sustainable development into country policies, and reverse loss of environmental resources, including:
   • Halve the proportion of people without safe drinking water and basic sanitation
   • Achieve a significant improvement in the lives of at least 100 million slum dwellers
8 Develop a global partnership for development, including:
   • Develop rule-based, predictable systems in finance, trade, governance and poverty reduction
   • Address the problems of the least developed countries, including trade, debt relief and official development aid (ODA)
   • Address the needs of landlocked and small island developing countries
   • Take measures to reduce debt to sustainable levels, through international and national means

- Develop strategies for youth employment
- Target drugs needed by developing countries, through co-operation with pharmaceutical companies
- Working with the private sector, make vital technologies available, especially information and communications.

As the list of MDGs shows, a combination of UN, multilateral, corporate, NGO and philanthropic projects bear responsibility, both collectively and as individual players (see also Figure 15.4). A business initiative was also announced at the summit, consisting of a coalition of companies, Business Action for Africa, to foster pro-growth policies and investment, as part of the UN Global Compact. This initiative brought together business leaders, civil society leaders and development experts.

At the halfway point, in 2007, the UN (2007b) had to report that progress had been slow and the goals were unlikely to be met. The proportion of the world's population living on less than $1 a day fell from 28% in 1990 to 21% in 2001. Progress is uneven, as shown in Figure 15.5. Eastern and Southeast Asian countries have made significant progress, but progress has been slow in sub-Saharan Africa, which is the most seriously affected region (see CF15.1 on Burkina Faso).

Figure 15.5 Proportion of people living on less than $1 a day in selected regions

Source: UN (2007) *The Millennium Development Goals Report* (New York: UN)

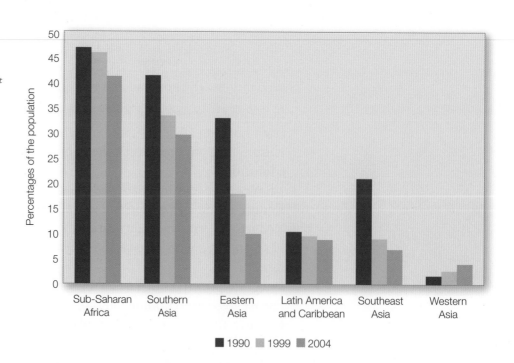

Four MDGs (4–7) are associated with health. Although the fight against HIV/Aids has received global attention, there has been only modest progress in halting its spread. By the end of 2006, 39.5 million people worldwide were living with HIV, up from 32.9 million in 2001. The number dying from Aids has also increased, from 2.2 million in 2001 to 2.9 million in 2006. Sub-Saharan Africa accounts for 63% of the people living with HIV. The UN's Global Fund to Fight AIDS, Tuberculosis and Malaria is the leading initiative, discussed in SX15.1.

The UN's website dedicated to the Millennium Development Goals is www.un.org/millenniumgoals.

WEB CHECK

plate 15.2 This Indian woman is among India's millions of inhabitants struggling to survive on less than $1 a day.

Preventing and fighting diseases depend heavily on improving water and sanitation. Unsafe water is the commonest cause of illness among the poor. Half the population of Africa, Asia and Latin America suffer from diseases linked to unsafe water. In 2005, 1 billion people lacked access to safe drinking water, and 2 billion lacked basic sanitation. The MDG of providing basic sanitation for half the developing world is unlikely to be met. East Asian, Southeast Asian, West Asian, North African and Latin American countries are likely to meet the target, but South Asian and sub-Saharan African countries are not.

As Chapter 14 highlighted, philanthropy has long formed part of a CSR agenda, and some MNEs, such as Nike, now focus strategic philanthropy on human development goals in the developing world. Despite the co-operative efforts of the UN, large donors and numerous corporate and NGO initiatives, progress on the key MDGs of poverty, hunger and disease has been disappointing in sub-Saharan Africa, where problems are most acute. African countries are now enjoying growth rates of nearly 6%, suggesting that economic development is taking off. However, poor governance, lack of infrastructure and risks to internal insecurity have posed obstacles to progress. Integrated efforts by donor organizations and recipient authorities, together with improvements in basic infrastructure, are needed to deliver aid effectively. It has been recommended that, for long-term benefits, technology transfer (the eighth MDG) and preferential trade deals by the developed world are more effective than pouring in aid (Collier, 2006). These issues are highlighted in CF15.1 on Burkina Faso.

TO RECAP...

Improving human well-being

The UN's Millennium Development Goals (MDGs) have set targets for reducing poverty and achieving other aims for the poorest people in the developing world by 2015. However, by the midway point, these targets looked unlikely to be met in many countries. Building basic infrastructure systems, such as safe water and sanitation, are key to achieving a number of goals such as alleviating poverty and fighting disease.

Making poverty history?
Is this an achievable goal or merely an ideal? Who are the key players in a position to bring sustainable reductions in poverty in the poorest countries, and what types of action would be most effective?

PAUSE TO REFLECT

COUNTRY FOCUS 15.2 – BURKINA FASO

Staying poor or building a new future: Burkina Faso

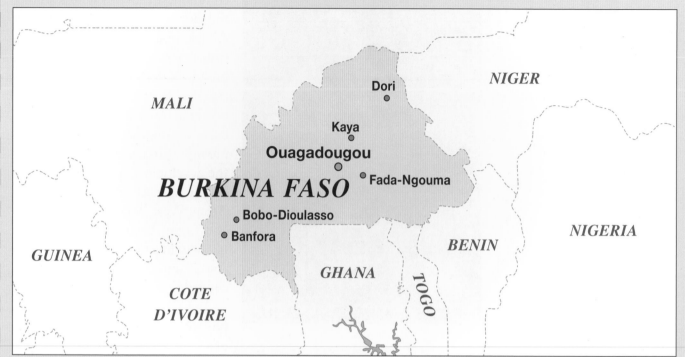

More than half of Burkina Faso's population of 14 million people live on less than $1 a day. One of the world's poorest countries, GDP per capita is about $500, and its Human Development Index ranking is 176 out of 177 countries (UNDP, 2007). Life expectancy is only 51 years. Geography and history have not been kind towards this landlocked western Africa country. It has been embroiled for years in regional conflict and insecurity, much of it associated with illegal trade in diamonds and arms. The economy is dominated by agriculture, but producers are dependent on neighbouring countries for access to ports for their agricultural exports. Its main export, cotton, accounts for a third of the economy and over 80% of exports. Falling cotton prices globally, combined with the high costs of overland transport, have had devastating economic and human effects. The government blames much of the suffering of its small-scale farmers on the support and subsidies afforded to American cotton farmers, whose exports have distorted world trade. Its president delivered a speech to the WTO in 2003, on behalf of Burkina Faso and other poor African cotton-producing countries, highlighting their plight to the international community. He said that African producers should be allowed to benefit from their comparative advantage, in that US production costs are twice those of African producers. The US government, he said, pays $3–4 billion a year to its cotton farmers, amounting to $56,000 per farmer. US subsidies are 60% higher than Burkina Faso's entire GDP.

A former French colony, Burkina Faso became independent in 1960, but political conflict and coups in the early decades of independence held back development. President Blaise Compaoré seized power from a socialist government in 1987, and embarked on a policy of liberalization and market reforms. These policies were warmly welcomed by the IMF and the World Bank, who persuaded donors to boost aid to the country. Donors still pay half the government's annual budget. International aid has helped to reduce poverty and provide schools as well as build infrastructure such as roads. The government is hoping that, with stability returning to the region, foreign investment will follow, helping the country to diversify its economy away from agriculture. However, doubt hangs over the country's long-term political stability. Compaoré has maintained tight control through a single dominant political party, stifling the fragmented opposition voices. He has been the architect of the country's development policies as well as a unifying force in this multicultural and multilingual society. It is feared that instability could ensue when he steps down, especially if poverty cannot be reduced significantly.

Mining is a sector which offers prospects for exploitation. Burkina Faso has not enjoyed the natural resource wealth of some of its neighbours, such as Mali and Ghana, which are rich in gold and attract FDI (see figure). In Burkina Faso, a gold-mining industry has existed for a long time, most of it carried out by artisan miners, who work in a dangerous, unregulated environment, generating low levels of output. In 2003, the government introduced a new mining code, which cut corporation tax and exempted companies from tax before the commencement of production. In the gold rush which followed, 20 MNEs asked for exploration permits. Four are starting production in 2008, with another four to follow in

Figure Comparative FDI inflows

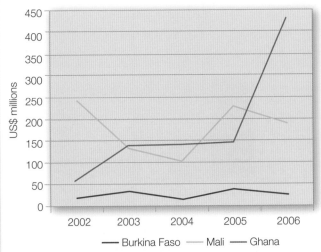

Source: UN, World Investment Reports 2005, 2006 and 2007 (Geneva: UN)

of premium prices, compensating them for the difficulties encountered in this type of production. For example, crops are vulnerable to pests, which must be controlled without the use of pesticides. A seemingly unlikely buyer has emerged in the form of Victoria's Secrets, the upmarket lingerie retailer, whose owner has signed a preliminary agreement with Burkina Faso's cotton growers' union. Farmers are not as yet rejoicing. Only a small fraction of the country's 2.5 million cotton workers are in the organic sector. The organic market is small, and growers feel that reviving the conventional sector will be the best guarantee of a sustainable industry in future. The difficulties of reaching agreement in the WTO's Doha Round do not bode well for the least developed countries' cotton exports. A growing worry is that Burkina Faso, like other poor developing countries dependent on agriculture, will be more severely affected by climate change than higher income countries. Events such as drought and flooding, which can wipe out production, are predicted to become more frequent.

2009. There is also the prospect that uranium mining could be viable, for which 30 foreign companies have asked for exploration permits. The prospect of a mining boom is enticing, but the government is aware of the need to regulate new industries. The new mining code requires foreign companies to invest in training local technicians. The government is keen that the funds raised from the mining sector will be turned into sustainable growth, with involvement of local stakeholders. The director of a mine run by Gold Fields of South Africa is working with village chiefs, NGOs and artisan miners to build community ties, which it hopes will form the pattern for future development.

The prospects for a revival of the cotton industry look bleak. A hope is that investment will flow into processing industries which help to add value, to offset the high costs of electricity and transport of goods to ports in Ivory Coast, Togo or Ghana. A niche market in organic cotton has offered some hope for revival. Organic growers have been bolstered by the prospect

Questions

- ◆ What are the factors contributing to Burkina Faso's precarious economic position and extreme poverty?
- ◆ What steps are being taken to foster development and reduce poverty in Burkina Faso?
- ◆ In what ways is Burkina Faso indicative of the plight of poor developing countries generally?

Sources: World Bank (2007) World Development Indicators 2007, www.worldbank.org; Green, M., 'In search of a better way of life', *Financial Times*, 18 September 2007; Green, M., 'The hardest battles are yet to be fought', *Financial Times*, 18 September 2007; Fontennella, J., 'Hopes pinned on a new generation', *Financial Times*, 18 September 2007; Williams, F., 'African countries challenge US subsidies', *Financial Times*, 10 June 2003; UN (2007) *World Investment Report 2007* (Geneva: UN); UNDP (2007) *Human Development Report 2007* (Basingstoke: Palgrave Macmillan).

WEB CHECK

Information on Burkina Faso can be found on the World Bank's website, www.worldbank.org. Click on *Burkina Faso* in the country list.

Climate change

The eighth Millennium Development Goal covers environmental sustainability and climate change. The report in 2007 highlighted the continued deforestation and loss of biodiversity of both land and seas (UN, 2007b). By then, a total of 20 million sq km of land and sea had been declared protected areas. This is a vast area, twice the size of China, but much of it is weakly managed in terms of conservation. Regrettably, only a tenth (2 million sq km) is marine ecosystems, even though these areas are particularly vulnerable, suffering from depleted fish stocks and the precariousness of coastal livelihoods. As Figure 15.6 shows, CO_2 emissions continue to rise globally, growing more rapidly in the large developing economies. Companies in the developed world have taken initiatives towards reducing greenhouse gas emissions, encouraged by carbon trading schemes (see Chapter 13).

Figure 15.6 Emissions of carbon dioxide (CO_2), 1990 and 2004
Source: UN (2007) *The Millennium Development Goals Report* (New York: UN)

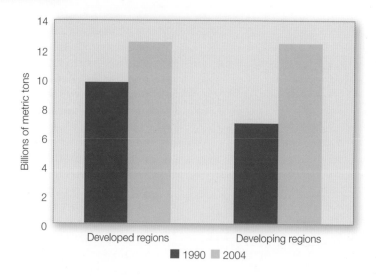

The split among countries on a possible successor to the Kyoto Protocol, so-called 'son of Kyoto' legislation, reveals a familiar problem in the business context. A company (or country) will enjoy the benefits of stabilizing global warming even if it took no steps to bring it about. In this situation, each is counting on others to act, and the result could be that no one is willing to act. In that case, the situation will be much worse than it would be if each had taken steps in the beginning.

Efforts to achieve international co-operation highlight the continued relevance of realist theories of international relations. However, concerted action is contributing to solving the global challenges highlighted in this section, suggesting that there is a tendency towards the liberal institutional perspective among many countries. The shift of public opinion in the US is indicative. Half of US states have adopted 'son of Kyoto' legislation. Governments in developed countries are key players in the concerted efforts to deal with problems in the developing world. Aid and trade are the focus of much of this activity, discussed in the following section.

TO RECAP...

Concerted action on climate change

Although there is a growing consensus on the damaging impacts of climate change, agreement on global goals and the means to achieve them are elusive. National economic self-interest is perceived by some governments as being jeopardized by capping emissions, but a shift in perspective to global economic sustainability is leading many governments to accept that changes in behaviour are imperative.

Global citizenship and climate change
In what ways can self-interested national governments be persuaded by global citizenship arguments to accept emissions targets and other changes in behaviour to combat climate change?

PAUSE TO REFLECT

Development issues: aid and trade

Aid from rich donor countries to developing countries, either bilaterally or in multilateral projects, provides direct assistance. This aid is typically targeted at poverty alleviation, health and education, but can come packaged with other terms such as a trade deal, which tends to favour the donor country. Debt relief is an important element for heavily indebted poor countries. In the long term, however, economic growth is the driver of poverty reduction. Building economic capacity is required, which is not necessarily the focus of aid packages. Governments in the developing world need long-term policies to improve well-being and economic prosperity, based on the sustainable use of resources and social priorities. They are frequently constrained by conditions set by donor countries and organizations. Among the most common are structural reforms based on economic liberalization and democratic institutions, which are not always suitable in unstable economic and political environments. It is notable that the aid philosophy of China is not based on this liberal economic outlook, but is nonetheless criticized as favouring the stronger country's interests (see SX6.1).

States in the developed world offer official development assistance (ODA) towards poverty alleviation and other MDGs. The UN recommends a target of 0.7% of gross national income (GNI) to be allocated to ODA, but most rich countries fall short of this target (see Figure 15.7). The G8 summit at Gleneagles in Scotland in 2005 addressed the 'global development challenge', specifically the plight of Africa, which received much media attention (The G8 Gleneagles, 2005). The G8 leaders looked at a mixture of aid measures, debt cancellation and trade deals, promising an aid package of $50 billion to Africa. They also promised debt relief for the highly indebted poor countries and greater contributions to the World Bank. These promises, however, carried no guarantee that the funding would be forthcoming, or that the funds promised would be 'new', rather than money diverted from other programmes. At the G8 summit two years later, in 2007, the $50 billion package was reaffirmed as a goal, but all the countries except Canada had fallen behind in delivering the promised assistance (Williamson, 2007).

Official development assistance (ODA): Funds and other types of government aid provided to foreign countries, often as part of an aid package which also includes trade provisions.

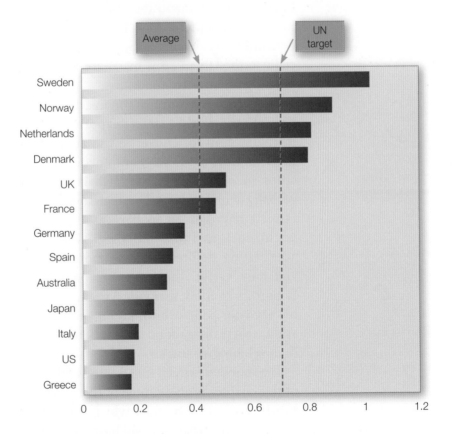

Figure 15.7 Official development assistance as percentage of GNI, 2006

Source: OECD (2006) 'Final ODA Flows in 2006', www.oecd.org

The Doha Round of WTO negotiations was intended to focus on development issues, but became mired in stalemate as rich trading blocs were reluctant to lower trade barriers (see Chapter 6). Moreover, multilateral liberalization jeopardizes poor countries that have enjoyed preferential trade deals in the past. To compensate, the EU has introduced the 'Everything But Arms' (EBA) initiative for the least developed countries, and the US has implemented the African Growth and Opportunity Act (Agoa), featured in SX6.2. Both schemes have limitations: the EBA applies only to the poorest countries, and the Agoa is also restrictive and time constrained. The least developed countries account for just 1% of the EU's imports, largely because poor transport and infrastructure make it difficult for these countries to take advantage of the opportunities. Opening rich country markets to all least developed, heavily indebted and sub-Saharan African countries would help considerably to create jobs and promote growth.

Recent trends in agricultural trade have highlighted the problems faced by the poorest countries. Three-quarters of the world's poor live in rural areas, mainly in countries whose economies are dominated by agriculture. Industrialized countries have traditionally used trade-distorting measures which favour their own producers, helping to displace the agricultural exports of developing countries which are unable to compete. A result was that investment in farming and agriculture, including public spending, declined in these poorer countries. Many poor countries which once exported food have become food importers. A long era of falling global food prices now seems to be drawing to a close, as prices of key crops such as wheat, rice and maize are rapidly rising, amid increasing demand. Two factors can be high-lighted. First, demand for meat is rising among the growing middle classes in China and India. As 8 kg of grain are needed to produce 1 kg of beef, demand for grain surges. Second, the subsidies being paid to farmers, especially in the US, to grow maize for ethanol biofuel are resulting in decreased planting of crops for food.

One-third of America's maize harvest now goes into ethanol produc-tion. As the world's largest exporter of maize, America now uses more of its maize crop for conversion to ethanol than it exports as food. Further-more, biofuel subsidies have encouraged farmers to switch from growing crops such as soya beans to maize, leading to rises in soya bean prices globally, which adversely affect soya bean-importing countries. American farmers have gained, as have food-exporting countries in the developing world, such as India and Brazil. An effect in Brazil, however, has been accelerating deforestation, as more areas are cleared to grow soya beans and raise cattle. The losers are poor people in countries which are net importers of food, many in Africa. Rising food prices leave large numbers of very poor people, both urban and rural inhabitants, in a precarious situ-ation, especially as food accounts for 50% or more of household spending in developing countries.

The stampede which killed three Chinese shoppers, described at the outset of this chapter, is an example of the impacts of food price inflation. The UN's World Food Programme, which feeds 90 million of the world's poorest people, warned that it would have to cut back its food aid operations in 2007 because of rising costs (Blas, 2007b). Some governments impose price controls on food to help consumers, but market-distorting policies can discourage farmers, who fear their returns will be squeezed, especially in the context of rising costs. An unfortunate effect of government price controls tends to be shortages of supply in ordinary shops, while a 'black' market commanding inflated prices caters for those able to afford them.

A recent WTO initiative, Aid for Trade, aims to promote trade-related development, allowing developing countries to gain greater capacity to benefit from trade. Aid for Trade is broadly defined. It includes trade policy and regulations, trade development, the building of trade-related infrastructure and the building of productive capacity. The latter category covers a range of activities, from improvements in agriculture, to banking and business services. It also includes programmes for sustainable development. Donors contribute through bilateral and multilateral arrangements. These projects are based on the principle of country ownership, in that the governments in recipient countries must have clear trade and growth strategies.

These diverse projects are difficult to measure in terms of equivalent ODA, and many, such as the building of economic infrastructure, are aimed at broad improvements in the recipient countries, not just trade capacity. Although total ODA rose in the period from 2002 to 2005, aid for trade declined as a percentage of the total from 35% in 2002 to 32% in 2005. Aid from OECD countries towards building economic infrastructure has declined since the 1990s. Partly this is because donor countries assumed that public–private partnerships would fill the gaps, but this has not generally occurred (WTO/OECD, 2007). Aid for building productive capacity has increased, and aid to social sectors, such as education and health, has increased. However, there has been less support for trade investment and employment projects. Major recipients of aid for trade are shown in Table 15.2. As can be seen, Asian developing countries received larger volumes of funding, but these represented smaller proportions of GNI than aid for trade funding to poorer countries, which are mainly in sub-Saharan Africa.

Although infrastructure and capacity-building funding by OECD countries has declined, the major developing countries are raising their aid and trade profiles. China has stepped up its efforts to offer assistance and loans to developing countries, many in Africa, largely as part of agreements to secure access to resources. India is also making the transition from recipient to donor, phasing out aid and boosting its own aid, especially to Africa. For example, it has extended $40 million to Angola for a railway project managed by Indian Railways. Although China has attracted international notice for its acquisition of oil assets in Sudan, India's state-owned oil company has made similar deals out of the public glare. However, the wisdom of India's shift in policy has been questioned by development experts (Johnson, 2008b). India is home to one in three of the world's poorest people and 40% of all undernourished children. Some 400 million Indians live on less than $1 a day. India can be considered a 'swing state', key to achieving the MDGs by 2015. Cutbacks in aid from richer countries could jeopardize these targets, but, with an economic growth rate of 9%, India is, in theory, well placed to meet them. Of crucial importance are its wealth of private sector enterprises, numerous active NGOs and a democratic political system. India's shift in policy is largely motivated by a desire to become more self-reliant. It aspires to be a global power and is seeking a permanent seat on the UN Security Council, alongside China, which has had a permanent place from the beginning. This trend towards outward-

Table 15.2 The highest recipients of aid for trade, 2002–05

Country	US$ millions	Percentage of GNI
Zambia	173	13.9
Nigeria	185	7.6
Tunisia	188	1.4
Burkina Faso	192	11.6
Senegal	196	8.5
Bolivia	210	6.4
Uganda	215	14
Ghana	228	10.6
Madagascar	250	18.7
Mozambique	275	20.1
Morocco	277	1.3
Kenya	295	4.0
Philippines	313	0.5
Tanzania	315	12.2
Thailand	341	0.1
Pakistan	342	1.5
Sri Lanka	416	5.1
Ethiopia	474	17.1
Egypt	507	1.0
Bangladesh	624	2.1
China	708	0.1
Indonesia	1052	0.9
India	1387	0.2
Vietnam	1391	3.7

Source: WTO/OECD (2007) *Aid for Trade at a Glance 2007: 1st Global Review*, www.oecd.org

TO RECAP...

Development promoted by aid and trade

Rich countries have tended to focus aid to poor countries on health and education, while improving trade regimes and funding economic development projects have received less attention. The latter policies are arguably more effective in fostering economic growth to ensure long-term poverty reduction. Much responsibility lies with developing country governments to ensure clear trade and development strategies.

looking policies by emerging economies reflects a shift in influences in the global economy, with implications for global governance, as the following section examines.

Do aid and trade work for Africa?

What types of aid are most effective for economic development in poor African countries? What types of trade deals benefit the African countries which rely on agricultural exports, and why are multilateral agreements so difficult to achieve?

PAUSE TO REFLECT

Shifting influences in global markets

As we found in Chapter 6 on trade, sovereign states hold diverse views on the role of government in the economy, which are reflected in trade and development policies. For states with high levels of government ownership and control of strategic industrial sectors, global expansion is seen as both enhancing the state's position in international relations and benefiting from market gains. Sovereign players are thereby gaining in global influence. Their influence can be potent in sectors such as energy, when they take control of assets and production formerly controlled by large Western MNEs. In this section, we consider the implications of shifts in power in global governance.

New sovereign economic players

An economist writing in the *Financial Times* has said: 'Globalisation was supposed to mean the worldwide triumph of the market economy. Yet some of the most influential players are turning out to be states, not private actors' (Wolf, 2007b). All governments raise money and spend it according to their priorities. Democratically accountable governments are usually constrained by elected assemblies to disperse public funds according to social and other priorities. In a recent trend, which has been described as economic nationalism, state-owned or state-controlled companies are increasingly active in acquisitions, both at home and in global markets. The energy sector is an example, reflecting the growing importance of energy security globally. The seven largest state-owned energy companies (from Saudi Arabia, Russia, China, Iran, Venezuela, Brazil and Malaysia) control over 10 times the oil and gas reserves of the four major Western oil companies (ExxonMobil, Shell, BP and Chevron) (Hoyos, 2007). State-controlled companies in some cases decide to launch IPOs, becoming listed companies. As listed companies, they dwarf some of the largest Western companies. Figure 15.8 presents a comparison of approximate

Economic nationalism: The growth and expansion of state-owned and state-controlled companies, aimed at promoting national economic power in global markets.

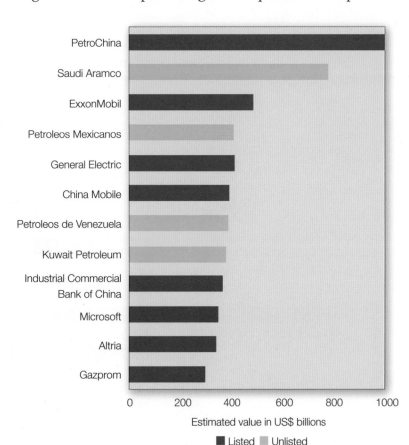

Figure 15.8 The world's largest listed and unlisted companies, 2006

Sources: *Financial Times*, 15 December 2006, 8 November 2007

Sovereign wealth fund: Fund held by a sovereign state, often from accumulated reserves, which may be invested in global markets, often through a state-owned investment company.

values of the world's largest companies. The value of unlisted companies, such as Saudi Aramco, can only be estimated, as data are not disclosed. For listed companies, market value fluctuates as shares are traded, and a surge in value, as has occurred on the Shanghai Stock Exchange, may owe more to demand than to underlying value. It should also be borne in mind that listed companies differ markedly in the portion of tradable shares; only 2% of PetroChina's shares are traded.

Sovereign wealth funds

In recent years, Asian central banks and petrodollar investors have become the two of the largest new forces in global finance. The McKinsey Global Institute (2007) highlights these new investors as the new 'power brokers', along with private equity groups and hedge funds. Petrodollar investors are in the oil-rich countries, mainly in the Middle East. They fall into two groups: 60% are sovereign wealth funds of the oil-exporting countries, and 40% are wealthy private individuals.

Asian central banks are also a growing force, having accumulated huge current account surpluses due to their success in export-oriented manufacturing. Wealth held in official reserves is being diversified, while investment funds and investment corporations are being created to manage the funds. Singapore has long pursued this policy, through the Government of Singapore Investment Corporation (GSIC) and Temasek Holdings. The influence of national players in global finance has given rise to some criticisms and concerns, mainly arising from their size, lack of transparency and possible political agenda, examined below.

Size

The amounts under sovereign management were estimated at about $2,500 billion in 2007, and could soar to $12,500 billion by 2015 (McKinsey Global Institute, 2007). The largest are shown in Figure 15.9. Their investment poli-

Figure 15.9 The world's largest sovereign wealth funds
Source: Financial Times, 30 July 2007

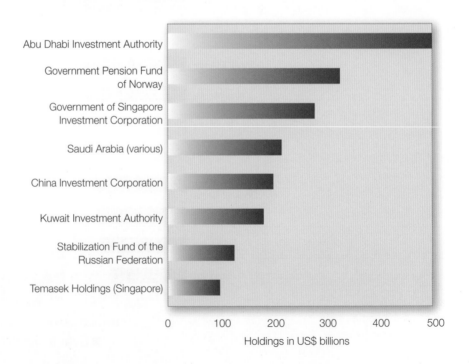

Holdings in US$ billions

cies have been marked by a willingness to take risks, investing in a range of assets, including equities, property, private equity funds, hedge funds and emerging markets. These companies often build up a portfolio (see CF11.2 on Dubai).

Lack of transparency

Sovereign wealth funds and state-controlled investment companies are often accused of lack of transparency. A notable exception is the Norwegian fund, which is the largest equity owner in Europe, holding 3,500 investments, which are all listed on its website. Most sovereign funds do not submit themselves to the rules of disclosure and corporate governance which ordinary private sector companies routinely comply with. Executives are typically ministers or associates of ministers, and governance is secretive. Singapore's funds reveal little information on investment policies or assets. The IMF has recommended to Singapore that greater transparency is needed to strengthen public confidence, but the government has traditionally viewed its secrecy as an advantage (Burton, 2007). In global markets, however, lack of transparency can bring disadvantages. If investment policies are not made public, comments or rumours can lead to uncertainty and volatility in markets. This is one of the reasons that, in countries where disclosure is expected, sovereign investors are sometimes unwelcome, especially if they wish to purchase a large stake in a domestic company.

Non-commercial agenda?

Investments by sovereign wealth funds can trigger political alarm in the country of destination, and can be interpreted as a means of spreading political influence. As noted in the CF11.2 on Dubai, Dubai Ports Authority was compelled to sell the five US ports it acquired as part of its purchase of P&O. Kuwait acquired a stake of over 20% in BP in 1988, but was required by the British government to reduce its holding to 9.9%. The US vets potential purchasers of American companies, under rules applied by the Committee on Foreign Investment in the US (see CS2.2). Germany has also considered this policy, as a way of blocking investors in sensitive industries. France and Germany were undisturbed by the Dubai ruling family's purchase of a stake in the European Aeronautic Defence and Space Company (EADS), but are more sceptical about the prospect of Gazprom buying energy assets in Europe, as there is a suspicion of an underlying move to exert political influence (see CS15.1). The European Commission has the power to regulate investment, but is committed to open markets. The idea of the 'golden share' owned by the government, through which it can veto a foreign state-owned investor, is a possible device for deterring unwelcome takeovers. A re-examination of competition policy is taking place at national and European level, and international competition policy is also being debated, as discussed below.

Sovereign wealth funds and state-controlled companies have existed for many years, but have grabbed the limelight recently, due to globalization and rising energy prices. When high-profile Western banks, such as UBS and Citigroup, saw the value of their investments eroding as global credit markets

---

WEB CHECK

The website of the GSIC is www.gic.com.sg. The website of the Abu Dhabi Investment Authority is www.adia.ae.

TO RECAP...

Sovereign players in global markets

The increasing influence of active sovereign wealth funds is being watched by governments and companies around the world. These entities are becoming active investors in markets, but their opaque structures and government control have led to doubts about their long-term policies.

slumped in 2007, a number of sovereign wealth funds stepped in to inject capital. Unaccustomed to being in the spotlight, these players are facing questions over their policies and behaviour in markets. Their responsiveness could help to determine the extent of their future impacts. Many have origins in emerging economies with authoritarian or semi-authoritarian governance systems. International trends in global finance have been towards greater transparency and accountability, which are likely to run counter to the tendencies of these national players.

Case Study 15.1: Gazprom – an ordinary company?

Just as pro-Western parties were on the verge of seizing power from Ukraine's Russia-friendly prime minister in the 2007 elections, Gazprom, the Russian gas giant, issued a warning that it might cut off gas supplies to the country unless certain demands were met. This apparently political gesture was not without precedent. An earlier stand-off in 2005 had resulted in the cut-off of supplies to Ukraine. As most of Europe's gas imports from Russia come via Ukraine, a new wave of shivers shot through Europe's gas markets. At that time, both the Russian president and Gazprom's CEO suggested that if Europe blocked Gazprom's westward expansion, they would shift to Asia and the US as alternative markets. Gazprom presents itself as a normal commercial company, and its deputy CEO says that the incident in 2005 was commercially, not politically, motivated. But its history, ownership and political ties suggest the strong influence of the Russian political leadership.

Gazprom came into existence in 1989, with the renaming of the Soviet Union's Ministry of Gas. Market reforms in the 1990s saw the privatization of gas and oil, allowing business leaders to buy state assets advantageously and spearhead development of Russia's natural resource wealth. Growing wealth became concentrated in these privatized entities, creating a class of powerful business oligarchs. Their prospects for expansion were good in the new market environment, and democratic reforms were progressing (see CF5.1). However, a financial crisis occurred in 1998, when the country defaulted on its debt, undermining economic progress and threatening political stability. Vladimir Putin restored strong central government, and also brought privatized assets increasingly back under state control. The Russian government gradually built up its share in Gazprom stock, culminating in the purchase of $7.5 billion in shares, to increase its stake from 39% to just over 50%, thus giving it control. Effectively, the government already had control, as the shares had been held as treasury stock. But the money paid to Gazprom, which arrived late in 2005, was already earmarked to buy the oil company Sibneft from the oligarch Roman Abramovich and other partners. Further acquisitions followed, raising Gazprom's market capitalization dramatically (shown in Figure 1), and making it one of the world's largest energy companies.

Gazprom controls of a quarter of the world's gas reserves. Although styling itself as a 'national champion', it now sees itself as having progressed to become a global energy business, accord-

ing to its CEO, Alexei Miller. To what extent is its strategy now determined by business considerations? Historically, Gazprom has been constrained by its political masters. It was forced to subsidize exports to Russia-

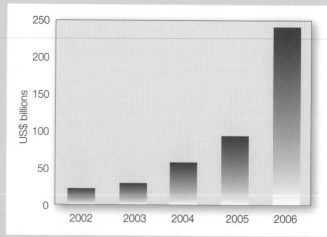

Figure 1 Gazprom's growth in market capitalization

Source: Gazprom (2007) Gazprom in Figures 2002–06, www.gazprom.com

friendly neighbours, Ukraine being the largest. When Ukraine and Georgia steered closer to the West, Gazprom raised prices. Ukrainians faced steep prices rises of 40% in 2006. Prices for gas piped to Georgia have doubled. Gazprom has enjoyed no such pricing freedom at home, where it has been subjected to government price controls. Its sales of gas to power generators account for 37% of domestic sales, and retail consumer business accounts for only 15%. Profitability is limited in both segments because of price controls. The company has thus turned to export markets, mainly in Europe, as a source of profits. European countries import a quarter of their gas supplies from Russia. In 2005, Germany imported 35% of its oil and 32% of its gas from Russia. Fears over reliability of supply have clouded possible future deals for growth in these markets, particularly in the retail consumer markets. As Figure 2 shows, exports to these markets have decreased.

Despite the potential for growth in productivity from exploiting its vast gas reserves, Gazprom's exploration and development of new fields has progressed slowly. It has focused on diversifying

Figure 2 Breakdown of Gazprom's gas exports by volume

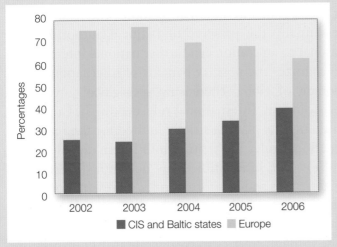

Source: Gazprom (2007) Gazprom in Figures 2002–06, www.gazprom.com

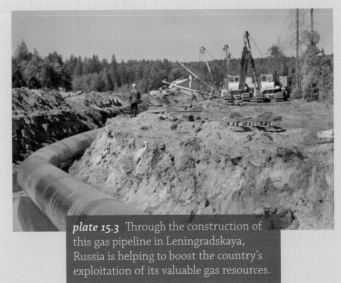

plate 15.3 Through the construction of this gas pipeline in Leningradskaya, Russia is helping to boost the country's exploitation of its valuable gas resources.

into energy markets and power generation. In a deal struck with EON in 2006, Gazprom acquired a Hungarian retail gas supply business in return for giving EON a 25% stake in its large Siberian gas field. Other such deals could be in short supply, however. In 2007, the EU Commission announced plans to restrict non-European companies' access to energy assets in the EU. Gazprom's exports to the EU are welcome, but its control of pipelines and power grids is more controversial. The EU Commission has sought to 'unbundle' the EU energy market, which consists of energy transmission, distribution and supply businesses. The Commission has proposed that the same unbundling conditions should apply to outside investors. For Gazprom, with its close ties to the Russian government, however, such a break-up would be inconceivable.

Looking further afield, Gazprom announced a massive investment in Nigeria, where it is seeking to become a major player. In a deal with the Nigerian president in 2008, it gained access rights to Nigeria's huge gas reserves, promising investment in energy infrastructure in return. China is already in control of most of Nigeria's gas fields, leaving Gazprom the difficult task of exploration for further fields. Exploiting Nigeria's gas reserves would involve building plants for producing liquefied natural gas (LNG),

which could be shipped to Europe and elsewhere. The shift of focus to Nigeria could be interpreted as an attempt to seize opportunities offered by the Nigerian government to open up to non-Western investors. The company will need to apply both technical and management expertise in this notoriously difficult environment. Violence has been a problem at the country's one existing LNG plant, delaying plans by Western MNEs to build more. Can Gazprom succeed where the others have failed? A Nigerian official has commented: 'Gazprom is saying, "We're better than Shell or any other company that has exploited you for the past 50 years"' (Green, 2008). Executives of Western multinationals might have doubts about the wisdom of the Nigeria strategy on both commercial and risk assessment criteria. Although the focus on international expansion can be justified, Gazprom has tended to be weak in keeping costs and spending under control. Gazprom's ordinary investors would also be concerned that its productivity and exploration activities look rather lacklustre compared to Western oil companies. Nigeria could be a stern test.

Questions

1 In what ways is Gazprom different from a company whose investors are chiefly interested in shareholder returns?
2 To what extent do you feel Gazprom has become increasingly influenced by Russian political aspirations on the world stage?
3 Why are European governments wary of Gazprom?

Sources: Wagstyl, S., Olearchuk, R., Belton, C. and Buckley, N., 'Gazprom puts on display of political muscle', *Financial Times*, 3 October 2007; Benoit, B. and Thornhill, J., 'Fear that gas supply gives Russia too much power over Europe', *Financial Times*, 12 January 2005; Catan, T. and Ostrovsky, A., 'Gazprom rejects EU pipeline demand', *Financial Times*, 30 May 2006; Ostrovsky, A., Condon, C. and Hoyos, C., 'Gazprom gains access to Hungary market', *Financial Times*, 14 July 2006; Green, M., 'Gazprom plans Africa gas grab', *Financial Times*, 5 January 2008; Walsh, C., 'Is Gazprom driven by politics or profit?', *Observer*, 18 December 2005; Belton, C., 'Gazprom hurt by costs', *Financial Times*, 6 December 2007; Gazprom website, www.gazprom.com.

WEB CHECK

Gazprom's website is www.gazprom.com.

States as new economic forces
In what ways are states nudging MNEs as forces driving global investment? How is this trend affecting international business?

PAUSE TO REFLECT

Trends and issues in international rule-making

Recalling the differing theories of international relations, the realist envisages rule-making as essentially the preserve of national authorities, but recognizes that international co-operation can further national interests. The liberal institutionalist recognizes the positive benefits of international rule-making, and the proponent of global citizenship sees global governance eventually becoming transcendent. International rule-making has a place in all these perspectives, although its place is strictly limited for the realist. At the highest level, international rules are written into international law. As Chapter 5 pointed out, however, international law does not displace state sovereignty. International treaties and less formal rules represent 'horizontal' rule-making, rather than hierarchical structures which would threaten domestic structures. The EU is an example, whereby countries which retain sovereign authority agree through treaties to co-operate in EU institutions. The tendency worldwide is towards a proliferation of rule-making activity, both formal and informal, to which governments and businesses willingly subscribe, often as a result of extensive consultation. In this section, we highlight some of the main areas in which trends and issues impact on international business. These are global finance, competition and the internet.

Global finance

The globalization of financial markets (discussed in Chapter 11) has given rise to a multilayered regulatory environment. There is no global central bank, global securities and exchange commission or global derivatives regulator. The growth of hedge funds and derivatives trading, which have expanded rapidly, has raised concerns of global financial instability. Regulation at the global level is divided among national and international bodies, as shown in Figure 15.10. National regulators, such as securities and exchange commissions, remain paramount, but international mechanisms and private sector agencies are becoming active as well. The global character of financial flows suggests that state regulators are not appropriate, but national governments are reluctant to cede authority to supranational bodies. Transgovernmental networks, such as the OECD, play an important role. For example, the OECD partnered the WTO in devising guidelines for the Aid for Trade initiative discussed earlier. The OECD has itself taken on a rule-making function. An example is the Anti-Corruption Convention of 1997. The Financial Action Task Force, formed in 1989, is based on co-operation between national and international agencies to detect money-laundering activities, trace the assets of criminals and confiscate laundered money. It currently has 34 state members, as well as regional groups. It has also been extended to non-bank institutions.

The oldest supranational agency in global finance is the Bank for International Settlements (BIS) dating back to 1930. Its aim is to foster co-operation among central banks, providing a forum for dialogue and also guidance on national supervision. The BIS, which now has 45 central banks as members, is instrumental in cross-national financial flows. The Basel Committee on Banking Supervision is its oversight body. The Basel II Accord, which was

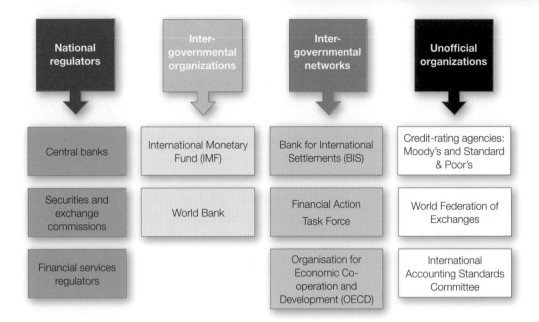

Figure 15.10 Global financial governance

updated in 2006, provides a framework for bank regulation, including the stipulation of capital adequacy rules for national authorities to implement through their own regulatory systems.

Non-official mechanisms figure strongly in financial governance. The World Federation of Exchanges is an example. In the developing bond markets, where harmonization of standards is important, a number of agencies have emerged. Bond-rating agencies, such as Moody's Investors Service and Standard & Poor's, exercise significant authority, even over national governments. The International Accounting Standards Committee has taken a lead in accounting and auditing standards in international business (see Chapter 11).

Global governance may seem weak in the face of threats of instability and volatility. The Bretton Woods institutions, the IMF and World Bank, have been active in policy-making rather than governance. Their roles, which were established in a world of dominance by developed countries, are now being re-examined. Financial crises, foreign exchange volatility and, more recently, volatility in credit derivatives markets suggest that global financial institutions are in need of reform. Three issues, in particular, have emerged:

- A cause of concern is the development of financial activities which have little link with the 'real world', becoming an end in themselves, rather than serving the needs of populations for productivity and greater prosperity. For example, most foreign exchange transactions and derivatives trading are pursued as ends in their own right.
- There is little public accountability or democratic responsiveness in global finance. Technocrats and civil servants fall naturally into their own ways of thinking, tending towards a culture of secrecy, in contrast to an outward-looking culture of accountability. Reformers who subscribe to the global citizenship or cosmopolitan views of governance argue for institutions to address questions of social equity and democracy in global finance. They see an 'emerging legitimacy deficit of financial governance' (Underhill and

The IMF's website is www.imf.org. The BIS website is www.bis.org.

WEB CHECK

Zhang, 2006: 4). On a more modest and pragmatic level, it is urged that greater co-ordination among national regulators is needed (Rogoff, 2007).

- Decision-making and representation in inter-governmental institutions are heavily weighted in favour of the developed world. The 24 directors on the IMF's executive board roughly represent regions – European countries elect 8; the Americas, 6; Asia, 5; North Africa and the Middle East, 3; but the remaining 43 countries in Africa elect only 2. Even when developing countries have equal representation, they can seldom raise the teams of expert negotiators and support staff that developed country delegations command. Although they are stakeholders in the processes of dealing with global problems, they have little role in the institutions and strategies which affect them (Held, 2006).

Competition

The growth of large businesses with huge economic power and wide geographical spread has been a feature of globalization. Competition policy has traditionally been a matter for national governments, whose focus is the domestic competitive environment and national welfare. Aspects of competition which are subject to controls are monopolies (antitrust law), cartels and anti-competitive practices. These phenomena are often linked. For example, independent companies which dominate a market may form a cartel to fix prices. Their influence can be considerable, adding 25% or more to the final price of goods subject to the cartel's actions (Jenny, 2003). Most developed economies have enacted competition law to prohibit these practices, and also to refer proposed mergers to scrutiny if they would create a monopoly (see Chapter 5). Whereas firms engaged in anti-competitive practices would be caught by competition law and institutions in their home jurisdictions, they have long engaged in such practices in international markets, where there is no equivalent regulator. In some cases, countries even exempt cartels aimed exclusively at foreign markets from national competition law, as the export cartel is seen as enhancing national competitiveness. Developing countries, which tend not to have competition law and enforcement mechanisms, are weakly placed to combat these practices. A significant proportion of goods imported by the poorest developing countries are affected by these anti-competitive practices (Jenny, 2003). The OECD and the WTO have considered the introduction of international competition rules through multilateral agreement, which would apply to protection of international competition. Their aims would be:

- to set down core principles of transparency and fairness
- to attempt to introduce/strengthen competition institutions in developing countries
- to offer technical assistance and capacity-building to participating countries
- to bring competition issues within the WTO dispute settlement process.

These proposals, which would offer the core of a governance framework for competition, were in the Doha Declaration, but have not as yet been adopted. Although a competition chapter is common in bilateral agreements, efforts to reach multilateral agreement have failed. The US has been at the forefront of opposition to the WTO proposals, on grounds that they would constitute binding international rules. Instead, following the recommendations of the International Competition Advisory Committee, the International Competition Network was launched in 2001. It is aimed mainly at the harmonization of national competition rules, remaining concerned with national welfare issues. It does not directly address issues of international competition, which the WTO proposals would do (Budzinski, 2004).

Many countries have anti-monopoly legislation in place, but their competition offices typically function with a handful of staff on a limited budget, and are ill equipped to take on large global companies with far greater resources. The global company, even if it is fined or compelled to make changes to its behaviour, suffers little economic loss. In some national environments, large domestic companies, either state controlled or deemed to be national champions, are deliberately sheltered from anti-competitive scrutiny. The EU has taken a strong stance against monopolists and anti-competitive practices, in accordance with its foundation principles of promoting a single market. Member states which attempt to shelter national champions from takeovers inevitably attract objections from the EU competition commissioner. The competition commissioner's longest running case, however, has been against Microsoft, featured in CS15.2.

WEB CHECK

For resources on competition, go to the EU's website at http://europa.eu. Under *Activities*, click on *Competiton*.

TO RECAP...

Governance of global competition

Competition policy remains essentially based in national regulatory systems. An exception is the EU, which has shown determination is tackling monopolies and anti-competitive practices among member states. A WTO initiative aimed at building a global framework for addressing competition has faced opposition from the US.

Global competition rules

Although the WTO has jurisdiction over unfair trading practices, as yet, it has no capacity to deal with monopolies and anti-competitive practices, which are types of unfair competition which can have similar impacts on trade. What are the arguments in favour of a set of global competition rules, and what obstacles stand in the way of achieving multilateral agreement?

PAUSE TO REFLECT

The internet

The eighth MDG includes improved access to the internet. By the end of 2005, only 15% of the world's population were using the internet. There are huge disparities in internet access (see Figure 15.11). In the developed world, 50% of people have access; in the developing world, only 9%; and in the least developed countries, only 1%. Internet technology offers huge benefits for businesses and societies. Businesses are enabled to compete globally, expanding production and markets. For societies, the internet presents new opportunities for individual citizens in social interaction, consumer choice and access to information. The internet also provides new means to participate in civil society and engage in dialogue with authorities. Although the potential benefits and opportunities would seem to be incontrovertible, the internet also carries risks. Businesses daily encounter new threats to online security, and many, especially media companies, suffer from IPR infringements. Governments, especially authoritarian ones, tend to see the internet as a threat. National governments have traditionally retained legal authority to regulate communications technology, but their authority does not extend beyond national borders. There is no global internet regulator, but there are governance mechanisms emerging, in which businesses and NGOs are active. In this section, we look at the trends and issues.

Figure 15.11 Number of internet users per 100 of population, 2002 and 2005

Source: UN (2007) *The Millennium Development Goals Report* (New York: UN)

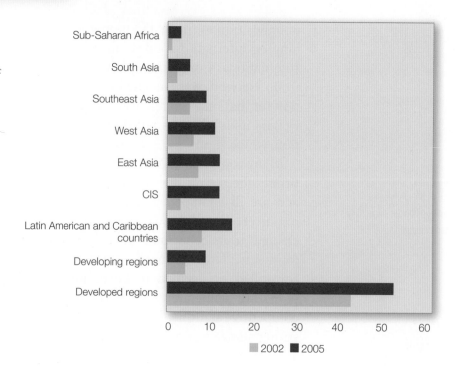

The business perspective

One of the effects of this digital divide is that businesses in the developed world are the more likely to be integrated in global production networks and markets.

Consider the ways in which the internet affects business activities and builds global competitive advantage. Globalized production, sourcing, distribution and logistics all depend on the internet. Marketing and dealing with customers are increasingly carried out via the internet, especially for business customers. For knowledge-based businesses, such as IT and software companies, IP rights are key assets (see Chapter 12). Yet, despite the vision of global products for global markets, national systems of regulation are the foundation of property rights. Many would urge that national legal authorities can never succeed in taming the internet, as the battle is 'lost in advance' (Brousseau, 2004). Businesses rely on the protections offered through IP law at national level to protect their inventions, software and brands. Where national law is weak or enforcement is lax, their operations can be affected by unlawful copying, piracy and counterfeiting.

Media companies which depend on copyright protection for their content have been particularly vulnerable to infringement. The revolution in downloading media content and mobile communications is challenging copyright holders, whose permission is needed for copying, along with payment of royalties (see SX5.2). These issues are being resolved through collaboration and agreement by the main corporate players, such as content providers and mobile phone networks. The International Federation of the Phonographic Industry (IFPI), a global association for the recording industry, is active in attempts to control illegal downloading. Its efforts have been boosted in France by the introduction of a new scheme to stamp out internet piracy, which has brought together the IFPI, film industry, internet service providers (ISPs) and government. This co-ordinated regulation based on agreement

Resources in international internet regulation can be found on the OECD's website at www.oecd.org, by clicking on *Information and Communications Technology* in the topics list.

WEB CHECK

among the key players could be a model of evolving governance mechanisms, in the absence of formal global institutions. The OECD plays a role which shades from the advisory to the rule-making. It provides guidance to national authorities in areas such as data protection, the legal recognition of digital signatures and telecommunications standards. Thus, especially among countries in the developed world, there is growing inter-governmental co-ordination.

Implications for society

Societies are becoming increasingly interconnected as the internet expands. With unprecedented access to information, people are better informed than ever, as consumers, investors and citizens. Active interest in global issues and the rising profiles of NGOs owe much to online information sources. Recall that social and environmental reports are increasingly becoming available online (see Figure 14.9). On the other hand, threats to security, often connected to criminal activities, are a major headache for businesses, governments and individuals, causing both financial losses and impairment of operations, which are difficult to quantify. Security technology, specializing in filtering and preventing virus attacks, has been a growth sector (see SX9.1). Advances in filtering technology have made it possible to detect copyright infringement, which most would consider a legitimate use, but filtering technology can be used for more controversial purposes, such as censoring content, which raises ethical issues for business and governments. These are illustrated in SX15.2.

Although the internet is perceived as open and global, transcending national borders, it is perhaps ironic that the 'bordered internet' is becoming a reality for both governments and businesses (Goldsmith and Wu, 2006). As access is widening to include more members of society, national concerns are becoming more evident in the control of content. Businesses are able to cater for differences in language, interests and values, which help them to satisfy customers. More problematic, governments can use filtering technology to impose controls on internet use and content within national borders. The physical infrastructure of networks is local assets owned by telecommunications companies which operate as ISPs. Government controls are usually imposed via ISPs. In 2008, the British government announced an intention to require ISPs to filter extremist websites which promote terrorism. The government was particularly concerned that vulnerable young people could be radicalized by such websites (Watson, 2008). Although the government justified this measure, such controls would curtail freedom of expression, which is enshrined in international law as well as the UK's domestic Human Rights Act. There is already a good deal of anti-terrorist legislation on the statute books in Britain, as elsewhere, aimed at guarding national security. How far does national security extend, and to what extent is a government justified in curtailing expression to protect its citizens? As Table 5.1 showed, most countries have signed up to the two main UN conventions on human rights. Nonetheless, countries with authoritarian governments habitually curtail freedom of expression and political dissent. For governments, controlling access and censoring internet content for a whole country are difficult to achieve in practice. Individual users have become adept at

plate 15.4 The internet depends on complex infrastructure, as seen in this photo of an IT professional working with internet cables.

TO RECAP...

Emerging internet governance

Governments tend to be ambivalent towards the internet, valuing the economic integration it brings, but concerned that national security could be jeopardized. Although the internet was once envisaged as sweeping away national borders and ushering in the global society, widening access is being counterbalanced by fragmentation along national lines.

bypassing controls. China has been faced with something of a dilemma – wishing to control political dissent, but desiring to promote the internet to foster economic growth. China's approach, which is designed to manage internet use, is discussed in SX15.2.

STRATEGIC CROSSROADS

15.2

China welcomes the internet, but on its own terms

For ordinary Chinese citizens, the internet represents a unique and exciting new world of communication and social interaction. Internet chat rooms, blogging and social networking enable people to communicate on a scale never enjoyed before, and certainly not envisaged by the country's Communist Party leadership. The number of internet users is growing (see figure). Although 170 million is still a small fraction of the population, the growing number of mobile phone subscribers, estimated at 430 million, is adding to the trend. However, growing internet popularity has been accompanied by growing apparatus of state censorship.

The Communist Party leaders' primary concern is social and political stability, and political dissent is perceived as the main threat. Firewalls are used to block external websites, such as news sites and particular news items which could be interpreted as dangerous. They also target internal web activity deemed harmful. Realizing they cannot totally control the internet, the authorities seem to have opted to tolerate social and entertainment uses, but have gone to considerable lengths to stamp out any perceived threats to party rule. Sometimes,

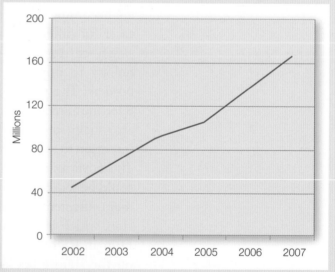

Figure Number of internet users in China

Source: Financial Times, 13 November 2007

however, the distinction between social and political is blurred, as social sites can be used as a tool to organize people and exchange views which are critical of the government. The internet is inherently difficult for national authorities to manage, but the Beijing authorities are devoting much time and effort to proving it can be done.

Bureaucracy pervades all aspects of life in China. There are now about 12 different government bodies dealing with supervision of the internet, under the oversight of the Ministry of Information Industry. There are nine government-licensed internet access providers, which sell internet access to ISPs. Internet content providers (ICPs) must also be licensed. Foreign companies are active as ICPs and ISPs, often in joint ventures, and all must co-operate with the authorities. Many Western companies operate in China, including Microsoft, Google and Yahoo, which are all American companies. The strategic decision to enter China was fraught in each case, as they realized it involved compromising ethical principles, including freedom of expression. In Congressional hearings in the US in 2006, instigated as a result of public criticism, they argued that they see their presence as bringing about more open communication in the future. This argument has not convinced everyone, and these firms risk reputational damage, both at home and in China, as many Chinese businesses had hoped that a strong stand by these global companies would help in applying pressure to the government for more openness.

It is reported by Human Rights Watch that Google has itself become the censor, not the victim of state and ISP censorship, as Google's own staff produce the 'block list' for filtering content and blocking search results. Controversially, Cisco of the US has supplied Beijing with powerful internet control tools. Yahoo has faced criticism for co-operating with the Chinese authorities to track down dissidents. Yahoo also uses staff who monitor conversations in chat rooms and report suspect participants to the Chinese authorities. Yahoo argues that it has given control over what is done under its brand name in China to its Chinese partner, Alibaba. Its CEO also says that the company is behaving legally: 'To be doing business in China, or anywhere else in the world, we have to comply with local law ... I do not like the outcome of what happens with these things, but we have to follow the law' (Goldsmith and Wu, 2006). On the other hand, the suppression and imprisonment of dissidents have received considerable adverse international media attention, especially in the run-up to the Beijing Olympics of 2008. Although China considers the issues internal only, the international community views human rights as a global issue, which could come back to haunt the Beijing-compliant Western companies.

Questions

◆ In your view, is China's approach to managing the internet justified, and is it sustainable in the long term?

◆ Do you agree or disagree with the Western companies which have agreed to comply with China's censors?

Sources: Bristow, M., 'Web dissent on the rise in China', BBC news, 16 October 2007, http://news.bbc.co.uk; Thompson, B., 'Daily reality of net censorship', BBC news, 17 October 2007, http://news.bbc.co.uk; Dickie, M., 'China learns to click carefully', *Financial Times*, 13 November 2007; Waters, R., Dickie, M. and Kirchgaessner, S., 'Evildoers? How western internet groups thrive behind the great firewall of China', *Financial Times*, 15 February 2006; Goldsmith, J. and Wu, T. (2006) 'Digital borders', *Legal Affairs*, January/February, www.legalaffairs.org; Human Rights Watch (2006) *Race to the Bottom*, www.hrw.org.

The internet untamed?
Although the internet promotes greater freedom of expression and access to information for people, both as consumers and as citizens, it is constrained in many ways. What are the major constraints, and how do they impact on international business? To what extent are governments justified in controlling internet access and content?

PAUSE TO REFLECT

Corporate social responsibility (CSR) and global governance

Companies participate in international networks which engage in rule-making and sign up to standards and principles which have been set through intergovernmental bodies. These co-operative activities need not suggest a specifically CSR agenda, but, in fact, much rule-making related to international business has a CSR dimension. An example is the Global Reporting Initiative, explained in the last chapter. MNEs are often confronted with higher international than national standards, for example in labour and human rights. In this respect, CSR strategies recognize the legitimacy of global rule-making, which is often ahead of national legislators in raising standards. Companies which have operations in developing countries have increasingly recognized a social role in addition to their primary economic role. Many companies, especially those in the oil and extractive industries, have become embroiled in conflict zones, where operations are precarious and vulnerable. In these regions, the rule of law is weak and national institutions are unstable. Fragile political leadership strives to balance the interests of numerous stakeholders, many international, while grappling with widespread social unrest and poverty. In countries such as Nigeria (featured in CF14.1), companies become providers of services such as health and education, which are generally associated with nation-states. However, they recognize that there is a business case for improving conditions for workers, as well as a moral case, in that all are stakeholders in the collective goal of improving well-being and, with it, prosperity.

One of the CSR initiatives which has attracted attention in a number of Western consumer markets is the fair trade initiative, promoted by the Fairtrade Foundation. Featured in the opening vignette of Chapter 14, it is based on the principles of sustainable agriculture and the belief that producers of agricultural products should be entitled to a reasonable return, which is often lacking in volatile markets and numerous intermediaries. For consumers, products with the fair trade logo offer a guarantee that producers have had a fair deal, for which they are willing to pay a premium price. Fair trade schemes also provide other benefits such as education. Although fair trade products are considered a niche market, their growing popularity has attracted the attention of the larger companies such as Marks & Spencer, aware that consumer demand is growing.

Companies have been active in initiatives connected to the MDGs, cited above. Many of the goals for Africa cannot be achieved without business partnership. Business opportunities abound, involving engagement with local decision-makers and civil society organizations. The UN's Global Compact, launched in 2000, was part of the millennium project, involving UN agencies, companies and civil society organizations in partnership activities and dialogue. It is based on shared goals and principles, including human rights, labour rights, environmental sustainability and anti-corruption. These principles, however, form neither a regulatory regime nor a voluntary code. The Global Compact can more accurately be described as a 'learning network' (Brinkmann-Braun and Pies, 2007). It has grown into the world's largest corporate citizenship initiative, with more than 3,000 participants. As it has grown, the co-ordinating organization has evolved a governance structure. A 20-member Global Compact board was established in 2006, consisting of 12 members from business, 2 from labour, 4 from civil society and 2 from the UN. It also operates through inter-agency co-operation with the UNEP and UNDP.

Having been criticized for its lack of enforcement and monitoring mechanisms, the Global Compact introduced annual reporting from 2003 onwards, suggesting that companies use the GRI guidelines. In 2007, 927 submitted reports, representing less than half the 3,000 participants. For the future, an aim of the organization is to recruit more companies from China, India, Russia, Brazil and other emerging economies. The weak representation of participants from the developing world is indicative of many CSR and global governance initiatives. The tension which cuts across national priorities, corporate economic goals and global concerns presents an ever-changing dynamic for international business.

Fair trade initiatives: Initiatives by companies, often under the Fairtrade trademark, which guarantee a reasonable return to producers and provide other benefits for producer communities.

The Fairtrade Foundation's website is www.fairtrade.org.uk.

WEB CHECK

The UN Global Compact is at www.unglobalcompact.org.

WEB CHECK

TO RECAP...

CSR and global governance

Many global governance networks and rule-making mechanisms reflect CSR goals, such as labour and environmental standards. Companies are active both as participants in the formulation of standards and their application in particular sectors. The UN's Global Compact has engaged companies and civil society organizations in projects within the broad range of the MDGs.

Conclusions

☐ Global governance represents evolving processes of rule-making and norm-setting, together with organizational frameworks for implementation. Diverse participants are active in governance mechanisms, including governments, businesses, inter-governmental organizations and NGOs. In contrast to rule-making by sovereign states, international governance processes typically involve participants devising frameworks for self-regulation with which all agree to comply. They address areas of common concern, including the environment, social issues, communications, and economic and political issues. Key global challenges which can be highlighted are risks to peace and security, poverty and climate change. Reaching agreement on common goals and the means to achieve them is often elusive where sovereign states are concerned. Governments are inclined to see national self-interest in a rather competitive context, fearing that any relinquishing of authority to a 'higher' international level will detract from their autonomy. Many governments now appreciate that co-operative frameworks to deal with global problems actually enhance national potential through co-operative efforts which both alleviate the problems and create a more stable international environment.

☐ Tensions with governance processes stem particularly from the changing power relations among countries. The era of globalization is witnessing a rise in economic power on the part of the large developing countries and the resource-rich nations, which are becoming more influential in international trade and FDI. As their economic power translates into international political influence, they are gaining stronger positions in global markets, especially through the expansion of state-controlled companies and sovereign wealth funds. It is perhaps a paradox that globalization seems to have bred a rise in economic nationalism. Have processes of global governance slipped backwards, or is there merely realignment among the key actors? The global citizenship approach to governance holds that international co-operation is needed to deal with global issues, and that participation of all stakeholders – large and small, poor and rich – is the only sustainable approach to global challenges. Many governments would find this notion unpalatable, but MNEs are increasingly taking a more outward-looking stance, from both a self-interested and CSR-oriented point of view. As global governance increasingly encompasses corporate and NGO players, in addition to government authorities, the tensions remain evident, but emerging solutions may be in sight.

CSR merging with global governance?

In what ways are CSR strategies compatible with global governance initiatives? In what ways are MNEs in a position to exert pressure on governments to co-operate more at international level, and should they be doing so, in your view? Give your reasons.

PAUSE TO REFLECT

Review questions

Part A: Grasping the basic concepts and knowledge

1. Define 'global governance' and explain how the concept differs from 'government' in the usual sense.
2. How do the roles of inter-governmental organizations differ from NGOs and other civil society organizations, in terms of global governance?
3. What are the basic principles held by the realist school of thought on international relations? To what extent do realists advocate international institutions?
4. In what ways is the global citizenship perspective consistent with processes taking place in the era of globalization, and in what ways is it inconsistent?
5. What are the main risks to peace and security, and how are global governance mechanisms meeting the challenges?
6. What issues are highlighted by the Millennium Development Goals?
7. Why have some regions shown greater progress in reducing poverty than others?
8. What are the main problems which have held back development in sub-Saharan Africa?
9. What difficulties stand in the way of international agreement to set emissions reduction targets? In what ways is public opinion shifting?
10. What is the reasoning behind giving aid to poor countries in the form of official development assistance (ODA)?
11. How does Aid for Trade differ from traditional ODA? Give examples.
12. From the host country's perspective, what are the drawbacks of ODA?
13. Why has trade become a key development issue for developing countries?
14. How do state-owned companies and sovereign wealth funds differ from traditional MNEs?
15. How are sovereign players making an impact in global markets, and why are they causing concern?
16. What are the governance mechanisms which regulate financial markets?
17. Why is international rule-making in global financial markets said to be in need of reform?
18. What is the argument for a regulatory framework to scrutinize monopolies and anti-competitive practices at the global level?
19. In what ways is the internet, despite being a global network, becoming more subject to national regulation?
20. How does a CSR strategy interact with participation in global governance networks?

Part B: Critical thinking and discussion

1. Global governance processes are multiplying and encompassing a diverse range of players. However, it could be argued that they are mainly discussion platforms, and that the strong economic players, both companies and nations, are still the dominant forces. Do you agree or disagree with this view, and why?
2. To what extent is the dominant position of the US being challenged at present? Which countries and regions represent the greatest challenges, and why?
3. African countries are now seeing growth rates in the region of 6%, largely because of the benefits of natural resource wealth.

Although this is beginning to look like a 'success story', what are the factors which suggest that economic prosperity and human development have a long way to go?

4. Russia, India and China are all investing in African countries, with packages of aid, trade and infrastructure projects. How does this trend impact on Western governments which give aid and debt relief, usually with conditions attached; and Western MNEs, many of which have long operated in Africa?

5. What recommendations would you make as global governance principles to be applied to sovereign wealth

funds and state-owned companies which are active foreign investors?

6. MNEs increasingly see the developing world as their biggest growth markets in the future. How should an MNE with a CSR strategy apply CSR principles to new markets in developing countries such as India, Russia and China? Looking at the two country focus features in this chapter, how would the foreign MNE devise a CSR strategy for entering Kazakhstan or Burkina Faso?

Case study 15.2: Microsoft versus competition authorities: and the winner is…

Microsoft, the American software giant, has a long history of battles with competition authorities, having defended lawsuits in the US, Japan, South Korea and the EU. Commanding 90% of the global market for its Windows operating system, its legal entanglement is possibly not surprising. However, given the company's huge resources in comparison with those of most national regulators, Microsoft has had a tendency to treat anti-competitive claims against it as of little substantial threat. The company is one of the world's best-known brands and Bill Gates, its billionaire founder, is an iconic example of the successful entrepreneur, lauded especially in America. US legal battles, although protracted, left Microsoft's strategy and practices roughly intact. The more bruising battles have been against the EU competition authorities, who have struck at two practices in particular – bundling applications software with the Windows operating system and limiting interoperability with other firms' systems and applications.

These two issues were the focus of antitrust lawsuits in the US. In 2000, a US federal judge found that Microsoft had failed to abide by its obligations under an agreement reached with the court in 1995, and should be broken up into two companies. The company won an appeal, avoiding this punishment. A new agreement reached in 2002 was much weaker, requiring it to disclose information about its operating system. By this time, the European Commission's competition officials were looking into complaints by Sun Microsystems that, because of Microsoft's failure to divulge information, its servers would not work smoothly with Windows. A second complaint was about the bundling of Microsoft's Media Player software with Windows, which was claimed to prejudice companies such as RealNetworks, who offered rival products. The allegation was that these practices were in breach of Article 82 of the EU Treaty, which prohibits abuse of a dominant market position.

Competition authorities generally hope to reach a negotiated agreement over complaints, under which the firm agrees to change its behaviour. For both sides, this solution is quicker and less costly than court proceedings. Negotiations between Microsoft and the competition officials, however, proved frustrating for both sides. The company showed no sign of accepting any significant constraints on its practice of integrating elements into the Windows package. Its lawyers argued that this would undermine its entire business model, on which its success was built. The competition officials refused to budge on the unbundling requirement. In March 2004, the competition commissioner issued a formal ruling finding Microsoft guilty of abusing its dominant market position, and fined it a record €497 million. It was ordered

to offer a version of Windows without Media Player to PC manufacturers, and to offer information to rivals to allow their server systems to work with Windows software. Microsoft decided to appeal against the ruling, to the European Court of First Instance, and also applied to have the sanctions suspended until the court could hear the case. In December 2005, however, the court refused to suspend the sanctions, and Microsoft was ordered to implement the Commission's ruling immediately. It was also threatened with a daily fine of €2 million. Another fine, of €280.5 million, followed for failing to comply with the March 2004 ruling. Meanwhile, the South Korean Fair Trade Commission decided against Microsoft in a similar legal action, ordering it to sell a version of Windows without the Media Player and instant messaging software. The company appealed against this decision.

In 2007, the European appeal case was heard in the Court of First Instance, which came down strongly on the side of the competition commissioner, on both the illegal bundling and refusal to supply interoperability information. Microsoft could have appealed against this decision to the European Court of Justice (ECJ), but decided to admit defeat, agreeing at last to comply with the March 2004 ruling. It would allow open-source software developers access to interoperability information for work-group servers, which would benefit businesses and other large organizations. The competition commissioner said: 'It is

Figure Microsoft's net annual income

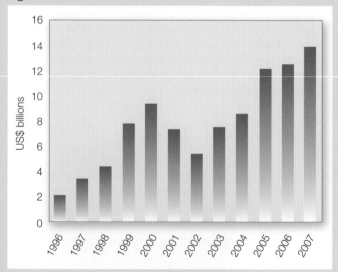

Source: Microsoft (2007) Annual Report 2007, www.microsoft.com

regrettable that Microsoft has only complied after a considerable delay, two court decisions and the imposition of daily penalty payments' (Bounds and Dixon, 2007). The company had set aside €1.6 billion to cover fines. The costs of its four firms of lawyers, although astronomical, would make little dent in its finances (see figure).

By the time of the 2007 decision by the ECJ, all the companies which had complained about Microsoft's monopolistic behaviour had settled with the company for agreed sums of compensation, thought to amount to €4.3 billion. However, the importance of the case goes well beyond the complaints of the rival companies in the original lawsuit. Lawyers for the European Committee for Interoperable Systems, a group of rival companies, hailed the decision as a victory for competition and consumers. The *Financial Times* (24 April 2006) stated that Microsoft's practices have 'hurt innovation and undermined healthy competition', but concluded that markets, rather than regulators, would be better at restoring competition. However, it is arguable that the consumer lost out in markets where Microsoft Windows used its dominant position to restrict choice. The EU decision against Microsoft was criticized by the head of the antitrust division of the US Justice Department, who claimed it would harm consumers 'by chilling innovation and discouraging competition' (Buck, 18 September 2007).

The launch of Microsoft's Vista operating system and the new Office suite of applications in 2006 raised further competition issues. EU authorities are launching fresh probes into the dominance of Office software, as well as possible illegal linking of its Internet Explorer system to the Windows operating system. They feel that now the legal principles are established, they can challenge the aspects of the company's technology which are more central to its business. The ongoing case has implications for other companies. As technological innovations move away from the desktop PC model to more internet-based and mobile applications, the competitive landscape is shifting. Microsoft has responded with a range of internet-based services, but it took the more radical step of launching a takeover bid for Yahoo in 2008. Google is approaching dominance in the search business in many countries, thus attracting the interest of competition regulators, as has already happened in South Korea.

Microsoft has continued to prosper, its revenues in 2007 topping $51 billion, which is greater than the GDP of most of the world's *countries*. However, economic power alone does not win legal battles in environments which observe equality before the law. The EU regulators have gained the upper hand against Microsoft on points of competition law. Representing 27 countries, the Commission is more strongly placed than national regulators to challenge monopolistic behaviour. The EU competition unit feels that it has won an important battle for competition and consumer choice, but foresees further conflicts ahead.

Questions

1. Why was Microsoft accused of abuse of a dominant market position by competition authorities, and what are the remedies?
2. Who were the winners in the long-running legal battle to date between the EU and Microsoft: the EU, Microsoft, consumers, rival companies or nobody?
3. In your view, should there be a global competition authority with agreed rules to apply, and why?
4. How is the competitive environment shifting in computer and internet technology, and which companies are in the strongest position?

Sources: Buck, T., 'Forcing Windows open', *Financial Times*, 20 April 2006; Buck, T., 'Windows shutdown', *Financial Times*, 21 April 2006; Buck, T., 'Microsoft braced for courtroom climax', *Financial Times*, 14 September 2007; Bounds, A. and Dixon, L., 'Microsoft admits defeat in EU battle', *Financial Times*, 23 October 2007; Buck, T., 'Microsoft suffers stinging defeat', *Financial Times*, 18 September 2007; *Financial Times*, 'Microsoft: no time to fight the last war', 24 April 2006; Microsoft Corp. Annual Report 2007, www.microsoft.com.

WEB CHECK

Microsoft's website for investor relations is at www.microsoft.com/msft.

Further research

Journal articles

Lotz, A. (2007) 'Global democracy: Diverse representation or states-plus?', *Polity*, **39**(1): 125–36.

Scherer, A., Palazzo, G. and Baumann, D. (2007) 'Global rules and private actors: Toward a new role of the TNC in global governance', *Business Ethics Quarterly*, **16**: 505–32.

Schwab, K. (2008) 'Global corporate citizenship', *Foreign Affairs*, **87**(1): 107–18.

Books

Archibugi, D., Held, D. and Kohler, M. (eds) (1998) *Re-Imagining Political Community: Studies in Cosmopolitan Democracy*, Cambridge: Polity.

Collier, P. (2007) *The Bottom Billion*, New York: Oxford University Press.

Sands, P. (2006) *Lawless World*, London: Allen Lane.

Stiglitz, J. (2007) *Making Globalization Work: The Next Steps to Global Justice*, London: Penguin.

Stiglitz, J. and Charlton, J. (2007) *Fair Trade for All: How Trade Can Promote Development*, Oxford: Oxford University Press.

Don't forget to check the companion website at **www.palgrave.com/business/morrisonib**, where you will find web-based assignments, web links, interactive quizzes, an extended glossary and lots more to help you learn about international business.

Epilogue

This journey through international business began with an Indian firm which is expanding internationally in a sector long considered the preserve of Western MNEs and their global brands. Evolving its own distinctive model of the fast-food outlet, Café Coffee Day is indicative of the changing competitive landscape, which features an array of new players from differing cultural backgrounds jostling the established MNEs. Adapting to this changing environment is a formidable challenge facing today's international manager, as the real-life examples featured in this book have shown. In industries ranging from childcare to steelmaking, we have encountered management and market changes which are now shaping international business. At the forefront are forces associated with globalization, but frequently, and perhaps paradoxically, localization is a crucial strategic element. Recall the following examples:

- Globalized production networks rely on location advantages of different countries, maintaining an ability to shift production as other locations become more advantageous.
- Country differences remain potent in markets, especially consumer markets. Global companies have learned the lessons, adapting products and marketing strategies, as well as acquiring local brands.
- Country-specific factors are crucial in financial markets, even though global financial flows are one of the defining characteristics of globalization.
- The quintessential global medium, the internet, is adapting to local differences: new technology allows international companies to cater for national preferences, but it also allows governments to impose controls, such as the filtering of content.

The growing diversity of international economic players is evident not only in the growth of MNEs from emerging and developing countries, but in the rise of sovereign players, mainly governments, often acting through listed companies. To a great extent, the rise of sovereign players reflects the comparative advantage of their respective countries, for example in natural resources and energy. Although many westerners hold that the role of states in markets should be one of cautious intervention, state authorities in most countries may wear several hats – as regulator, owner, investor and customer. More active state authorities in all these capacities are a feature of the changing competitive reality for businesses. For companies in strategic industries, such as energy and mining, evolving governance structures imply a refocusing of corporate culture towards shared responsibilities with governments, especially in resource-rich regions. Although this might seem to represent a departure from the purely economic view of the company, it points to an emerging reality of today's world, in which companies are viewed in terms of their social and environmental impacts.

It has become almost commonplace for companies of the developed world to boast of their social responsibility credentials. For some companies, CSR represents a rethinking of corporate strategy to accord with social and ethical goals, while for others, economic goals remain paramount. Which is the better strategy? All companies classified as 'for profit' exist to create value for their owners. However, as we have repeatedly seen, value creation is an elusive goal: today's winning formula can quickly be overtaken by new competitors and changing markets. Sustaining competitive advantage over the long term is the ultimate goal, but many underlying assumptions are now being eroded, including the continued availability of low-cost energy, water, raw materials and labour. As we have seen, the ravages of climate change, coupled with the depletion of resources and financial constraints, are redefining competitive advantage. Notwithstanding, unrestrained economic growth has been the hallmark of emerging economies, especially China and India. Besides bringing prosperity to their home economies, their growth has been good news economically for many other countries, developed and developing alike. Consumers everywhere now enjoy low-cost imported manufactured goods, and resource-rich countries are enjoying booming exports due to rampant demand from China. But China cannot import clean air and water, both of which have been depleted by breakneck industrialization, the negative consequences of which are now dawning on the Chinese people.

One might hope that growing wealth would lead naturally to social and environmental benefits for whole societies, but nowhere has this happened without targeted policies by governments and companies, either through legislation or co-operation. For governments, whether elected or not, the risk of social instability is overriding, threatening to wipe out economic gains and jeopardize the business organizations behind them. International businesses are fortunate in that they are able to redesign strategies and relocate as opportunities open (and close) in different countries. But as their stakeholders range across many societies, they have been compelled to think about global as well as local issues, while many governments have tended to see issues through nation-centred spectacles. The breakthrough inventions and innovations which improve human well-being as well as generate economic gains are largely down to creative people with entrepreneurial vision. The good news is that these talented individuals are emerging from all quarters of the globe, and in today's connected world, they can make their voices heard.

appendix 1
Atlas

1	Netherlands	7	Slovenia	13	Serbia
2	Belgium	8	Croatia	14	Albania
3	Luxembourg	9	Slovakia	15	Macedonia
4	Switzerland	10	Hungary	16	Moldova
5	Czech Republic	11	Bosnia & Hercegovina	17	Armenia
6	Austria	12	Montenegro	18	Azerbaijan

THE WORLD

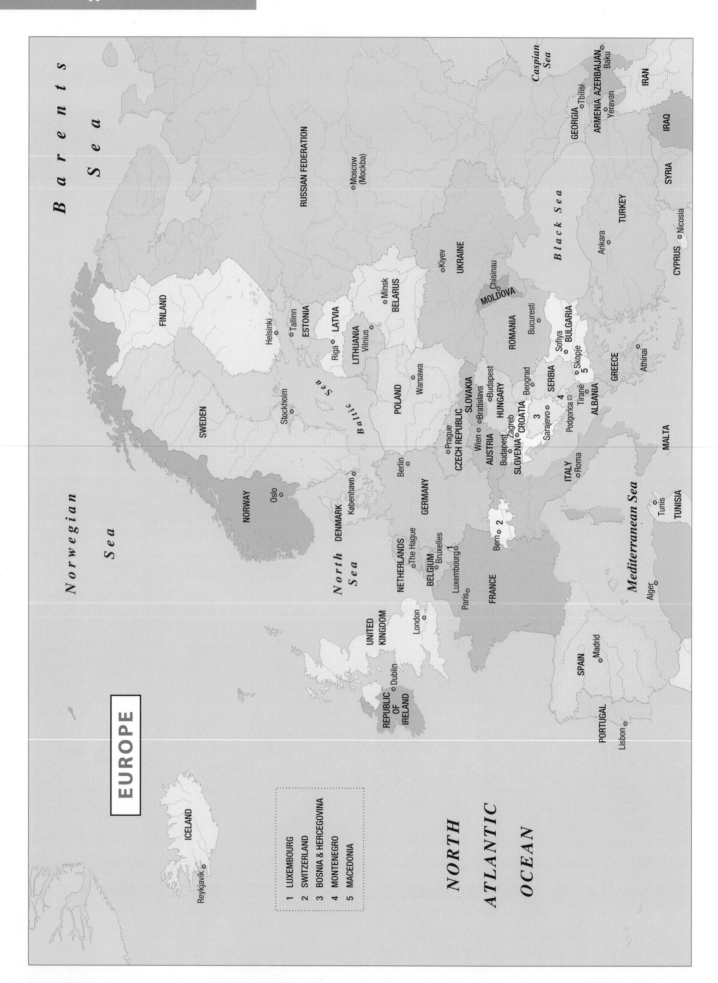

EUROPE

1 LUXEMBOURG
2 SWITZERLAND
3 BOSNIA & HERCEGOVINA
4 MONTENEGRO
5 MACEDONIA

ICELAND

Reykjavik

NORTH
ATLANTIC
OCEAN

Norwegian
Sea

Barents Sea

FINLAND

Helsinki

SWEDEN

Stockholm

NORWAY

Oslo

DENMARK
København

North
Sea

NETHERLANDS
The Hague

BELGIUM
Bruxelles

Luxembourg

Paris

FRANCE

Bern 2

GERMANY

Berlin

Prague
CZECH REPUBLIC

Wien
AUSTRIA
Budapest
SLOVENIA
Zagreb
CROATIA

UNITED
KINGDOM

London

REPUBLIC
OF
IRELAND

Dublin

RUSSIAN FEDERATION

Moscow
(Mockba)

ESTONIA
Tallinn

LATVIA
Riga

LITHUANIA
Vilnius

Minsk
BELARUS

POLAND
Warsawa

Baltic Sea

Kyiv
UKRAINE

Chisinau
MOLDOVA

ROMANIA
Bucuresti

Beograd
SERBIA

SLOVAKIA
Bratislava
HUNGARY
Budapest

Sarajevo
3
4
Podgorica
Tirane
ALBANIA

BULGARIA
Sofiya

Skopje
5

ITALY
Roma

Black Sea

GREECE
Athinai

MALTA

Mediterranean Sea

Tunis
TUNISIA

Alger

SPAIN
Madrid

PORTUGAL
Lisbon

GEORGIA
Tbilisi

ARMENIA AZERBAIJAN
Yerevan   Baku

Caspian
Sea

IRAN

IRAQ

SYRIA

TURKEY
Ankara

CYPRUS Nicosia

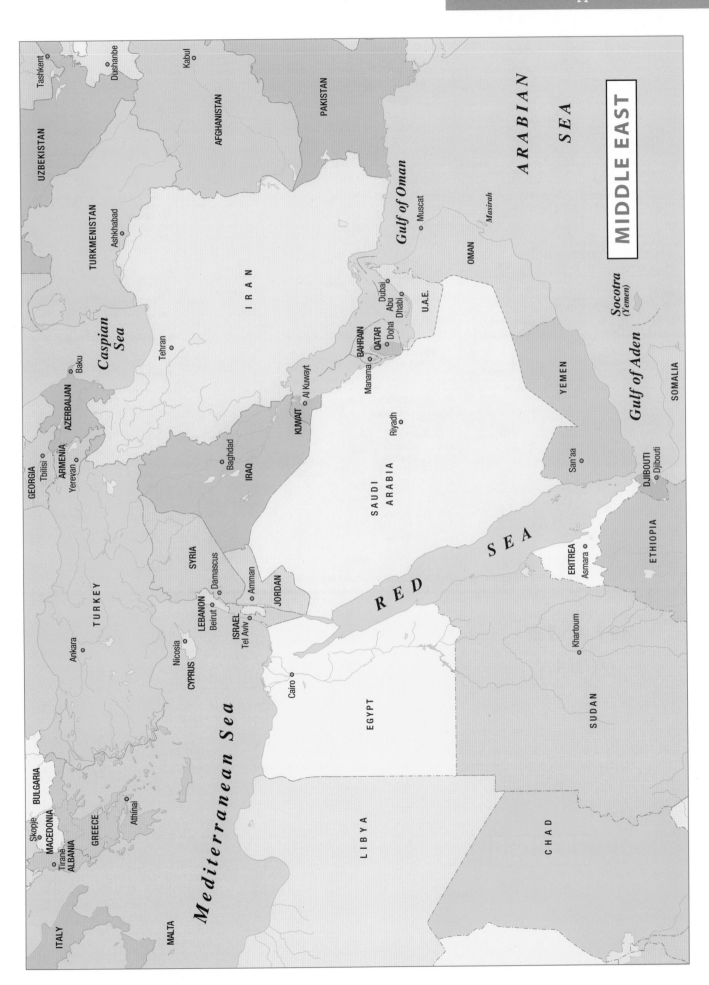

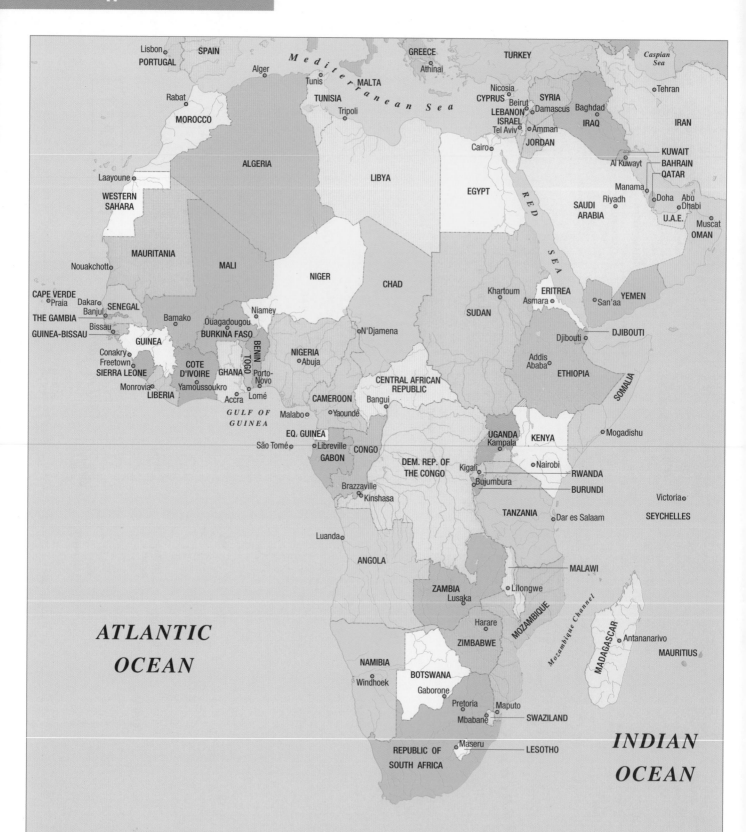

AFRICA

GUATEMALA
San Salvador
EL SALVADOR
Tegucigalpa
NICARAGUA
Managua
San José
COSTA RICA
PANAMA
Panama City

CARIBBEAN SEA

ST. LUCIA
ST. VINCENT &
THE GRENADINES
GRENADA
Caracas
VENEZUELA

BARBADOS
Bridgetown

TRINIDAD
& TOBAGO
Port of Spain

COLOMBIA
Bogotá

Georgetown
GUYANA
Paramaribo
SURINAME
Cayenne
FRENCH
GUIANA

Quito
ECUADOR

PERU

Lima

BRAZIL

Brasilia

La Paz
BOLIVIA

Sucre
(Legal Capital)

PARAGUAY

Asunción

SOUTH AMERICA

SOUTH
PACIFIC
OCEAN

CHILE

ARGENTINA

Santiago

Buenos Aires

URUGUAY

Montevideo

SOUTH
ATLANTIC
OCEAN

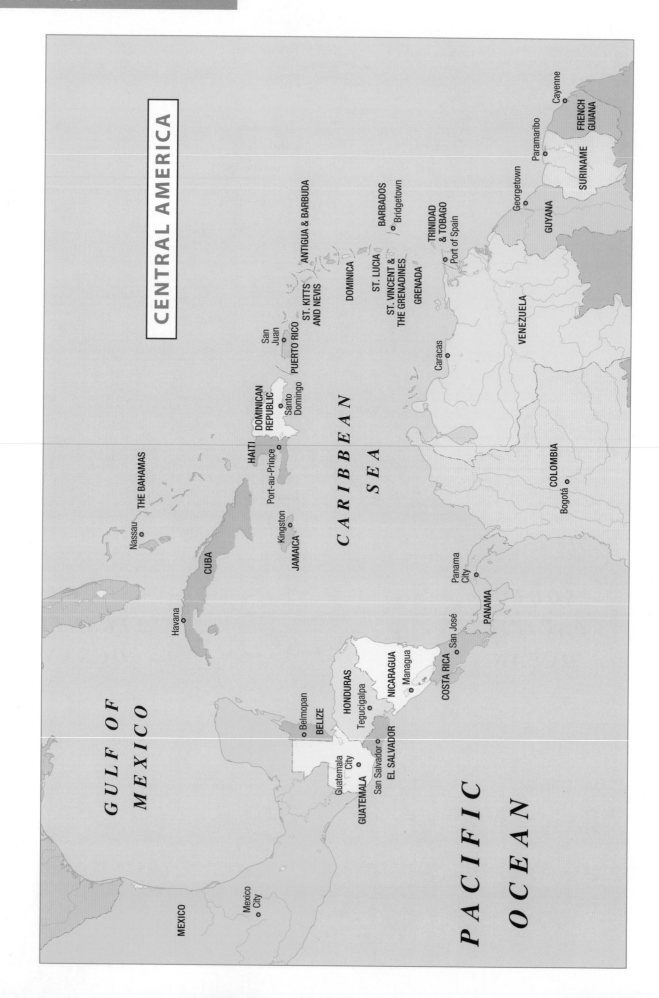

CENTRAL AMERICA

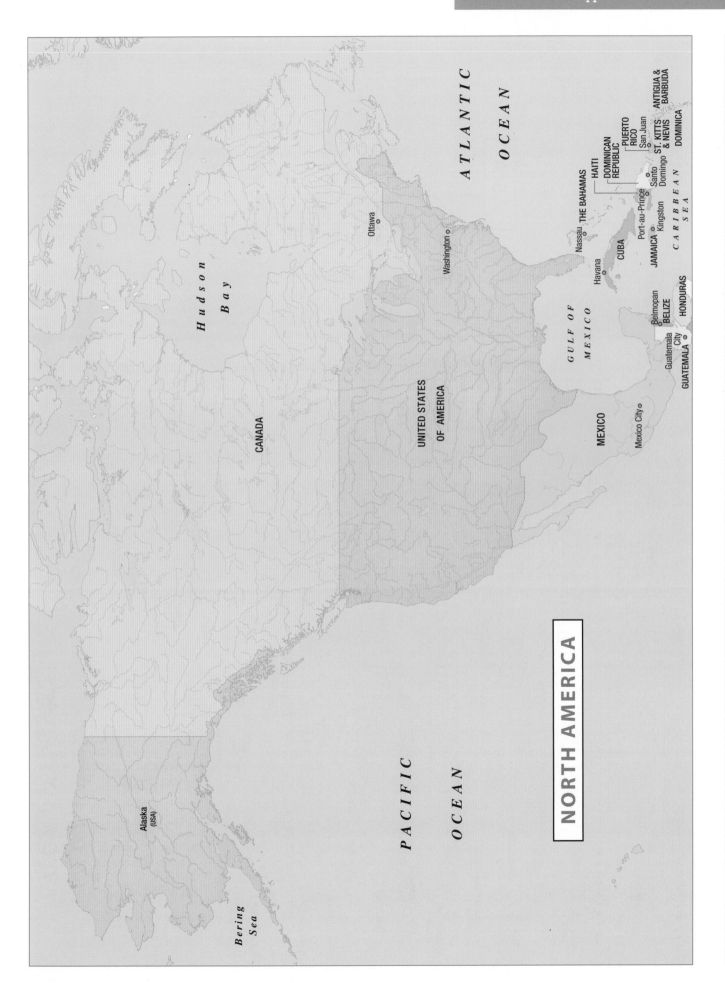

NORTH AMERICA

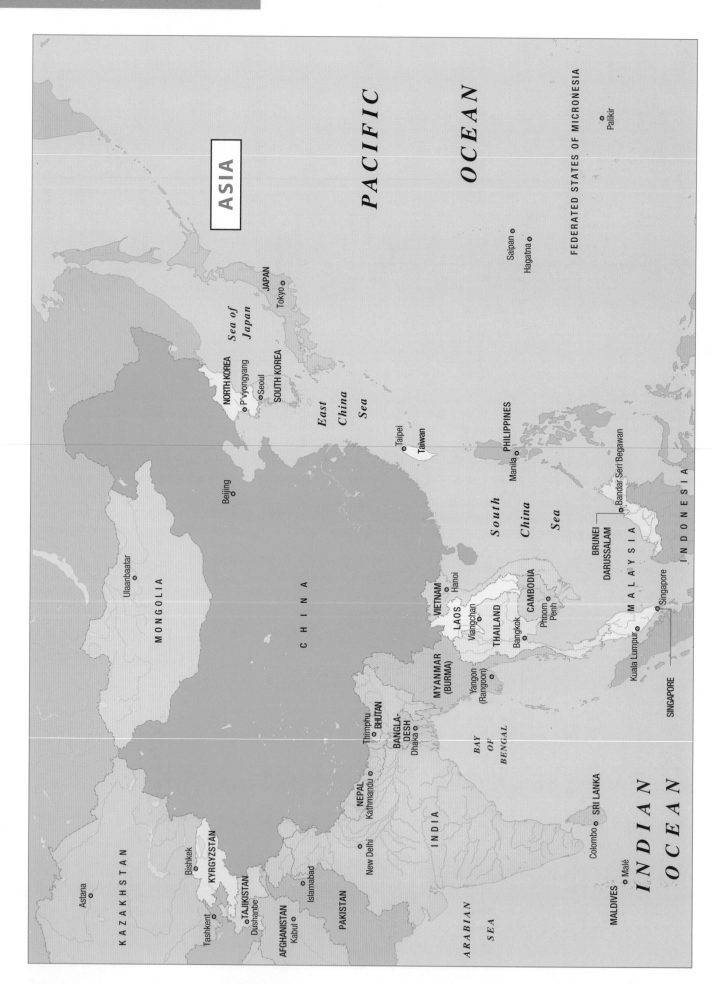

ASIA

PACIFIC

OCEAN

FEDERATED STATES OF MICRONESIA

Palikir

Saipan

Hagatna

JAPAN

Sea of Japan

Tokyo

NORTH KOREA

P'yongyang

Seoul

SOUTH KOREA

East China Sea

Beijing

Taipei

Taiwan

PHILIPPINES

Manila

South China Sea

Bandar Seri Begawan

BRUNEI DARUSSALAM

MALAYSIA

INDONESIA

Ulaanbaatar

MONGOLIA

C H I N A

VIETNAM

Hanoi

LAOS

Viangchan

THAILAND

Bangkok

CAMBODIA

Phnom Penh

Singapore

SINGAPORE

Kuala Lumpur

MYANMAR (BURMA)

Yangon (Rangoon)

Thimphu

BHUTAN

BANGLA-DESH

Dhaka

BAY OF BENGAL

NEPAL

Kathmandu

I N D I A

New Delhi

SRI LANKA

Colombo

KAZAKHSTAN

Astana

Bishkek

KYRGYZSTAN

Tashkent

TAJIKISTAN

Dushanbe

AFGHANISTAN

Kabul

Islamabad

PAKISTAN

MALDIVES

Malé

ARABIAN SEA

I N D I A N

O C E A N

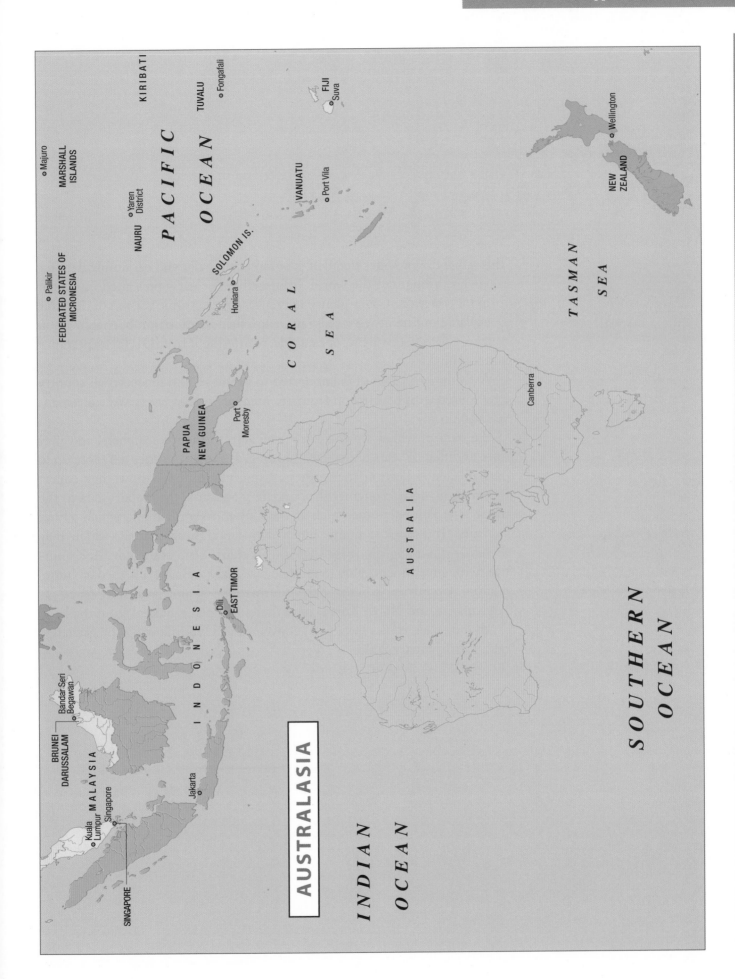

AUSTRALASIA

KIRIBATI

TUVALU   ○ Fongafali

FIJI
Suva ○

○ Majuro

MARSHALL
ISLANDS

PACIFIC

OCEAN

NEW
ZEALAND

○ Wellington

VANUATU

○ Port Vila

○ Palikir

FEDERATED STATES OF
MICRONESIA

NAURU

Yaren
District ○

TASMAN

SEA

SOLOMON IS.

Honiara ○

CORAL

SEA

PAPUA

NEW GUINEA

Port ○
Moresby

Canberra
○

Bandar Seri
Begawan

BRUNEI
DARUSSALAM

I N D O N E S I A

AUSTRALIA

EAST TIMOR

Dili ○

Jakarta ○

Kuala M A L A Y S I A
Lumpur ○ Singapore ○

SINGAPORE

SOUTHERN

OCEAN

INDIAN

OCEAN

appendix 2
Country data at a glance

This appendix provides detailed geographical, social and economic data for countries throughout the world. Information is clearly presented in tabular form for convenient, at-a-glance reference. An electronic version of the table is available online at www.palgrave.com/business/morrisonib, enabling you to manipulate the data by, for example, reordering it by GDP, life expectancy and so on.

With the exception of data referred to in the second footnote, all country data is used with permission from *The Statesman's Yearbook* (www.statesmans yearbook.com).

The data provided are the latest available to their researchers, and may refer to different years under each heading, as some countries are more up to date in data collection than others. Countries differ in how they collect information, how frequently they update it and how they report data to the many international bodies such as the UN and World Bank, which gather statistics. This book contains much data from these sources, which may therefore differ slightly from that in this chart. Data is included for countries with governments able to provide reasonably reliable, up-to-date information. Countries where such information is not available (such as Afghanistan and North Korea) have therefore been excluded from the list.

All monetary values have been converted to US$ following the exchange rate as at 1 January 2008.

COUNTRY	GEOGRAPHICAL		SOCIAL						ECONOMIC							
				Life expectancy (years)					GDP			Industrial structure (% of GDP)			Trade balance	
	Capital	Area (km²)	Population projection 2010 (millions)	M	W	Urban population (%)	HDI world rank	Adult literacy rate (%)	Total GDP (US$ billions)	GDP per capita (US$ at PPP)	Real GDP growth rate (%)	Industry (%)	Agriculture (%)	Services (%)	Import (US$ millions)	Export (US$ millions)
Albania	Tirana	28,748.0	3.25	75.4	75.4	43.8	68	98.7	9.1	5,316	5.0	18.9	25.3	55.7	1,485.0	330.0
Algeria	Algiers	2,381,741.0	35.42	69.8	72.4	58.8	104	69.8	114.7	7,062	3.6	52.7	10.0	37.3	13,322.0	24,469.0
Angola	Luanda	1,246,600.0	18.50	39.3	42.3	14.0	162	66.8	44.0	2,335	18.6	65.2	8.1	26.7	5,832.0	13,475.0
Antigua and Barbuda	St John's	442.0	n/a	70.0	75.0	37.8	57	95.0	1.0	12,586	12.2	21.7	3.7	74.6	336.0	45.0
Argentina	Buenos Aires	2,780,400.0	40.74	70.7	78.2	90.1	38	97.2	214.1	14,280	8.5	21.3	10.7	57.3	13,119.0	29,566.0
Armenia	Yerevan	29,743.0	2.99	68.0	74.7	64.5	83	99.4	6.4	4,945	13.3	35.1	25.9	39.0	1,302.2	712.2
Australia	Canberra	7,703,354.0	21.36	78.5	83.3	75.0	3	99.0*	768.2	31,794	2.5	10.9	33.1	56.0	131,422.0	111,381.0
Austria	Vienna	83,858.0	8.44	76.0	81.8	65.8	15	99.0	322.4	33,700	3.1	29.7**	1.6	68.6	119,090.0	116,017.0
Azerbaijan	Baku	86,600.0	8.67	63.2	70.5	51.5	98	98.8	20.1	5,016	31.0	37.8	13.1	49.1	2,626.4	2,591.7
Bahamas	Nassau	5,382.0	0.30	66.5	73.0	89.4	49	95.5	4.3	n/a	3.4	n/a	n/a	92.0	1,977.0	401.0
Bahrain	Manama	720.0	0.80	73.1	75.9	90.0	41	87.7	13.0	21,482	7.6	42.8	n/a	56.6	5,404.0	6,613.7
Bangladesh	Dhaka	147,570.0	166.64	62.1	63.7	24.3	140	41.1	62.0	2,053	6.4	26.4	22.7	50.9	11,157.1	8,150.7
Barbados	Bridgetown	430.0	0.30	71.4	78.5	51.7	31	99.7	3.0	17,297	3.9	16.0	4.0	80.0	1,397.0	252.8
Belarus	Minsk	207,600.0	9.53	62.3	74.0	70.9	64	99.7	36.9	7,918	9.9	37.0	11.8	51.2	9,092.0	8,021.0
Belgium	Brussels	30,528.0	10.52	75.7	82.0	97.2	17	99.0*	392.0	32,119	3.0	26.9	1.3	71.8	277,718.0	289,757.0
Belize	Belmopan	22,964.0	0.30	69.5	74.5	51.0	80	76.9	1.2	7,109	5.8	19.7	15.1	65.2	660.4	268.2
Benin	Porto-Novo	112,622.0	9.87	53.2	54.7	54.6	163	33.6	4.8	1,141	3.8	14.3	36.0	49.7	818.7	540.8
Bhutan	Thimphu	46,650.0	0.70	61.7	64.2	8.5	133	47.0	0.9	1,969	11.0	39.4	33.7	26.9	188.3	97.7
Bolivia	Sucre	1,098,581.0	10.03	62.0	66.2	64.2	117	86.9	11.2	2,819	4.6	21.5	12.2	66.3	2,191.8	2,810.4
Bosnia & Hercegovina	Sarajevo	51,129.0	3.94	71.4	76.8	54.4	66	94.6	11.3	7,032	6.0	27.5	11.9	60.6	4,518.7	1,115.0
Botswana	Gaborone	581,730.0	1.95	35.9	36.7	49.4	124	78.9	10.3	12,387	2.6	45.6	2.5	51.9	2,107.5	2,975.5
Brazil	Brasília	8,514,877.0	198.98	66.6	74.6	83.0	70	88.4	1,068.0	8,402	3.7	19.1	5.8	75.1	62,782.0	96,475.0
Brunei	Bandar Seri Begawan	5,765.0	0.40	74.2	77.3	76.1	30	92.7	5.1	28,161	0.4	71.6	0.9	27.5	1,812.0	7,593.5
Bulgaria	Sofia	110,994.0	7.47	68.9	75.6	69.8	53	98.2	31.5	9,032	6.1	25.6	10.7	63.7	18,312.3	11,835.2
Burkina Faso	Ouagadougou	270,764.0	16.10	46.8	48.2	17.8	176	24.8	6.2	1,213	5.9	18.0	31.0	50.9	8,555.6	382.7
Burundi	Bujumbura	27,834.0	9.55	42.6	44.5	10.0	167	58.9	0.8	699	5.1	19.4	49.3	31.3	130.0	37.5
Cambodia	Phnom Penh	181,035.0	15.22	52.4	59.8	18.6	131	73.6	7.2	2,727	10.8	28.0	35.6	36.4	3,193.3	2,475.5
Cameroon	Yaoundé	475,440.0	19.66	45.1	46.5	51.4	144	67.9	18.3	2,299	3.8	19.1	44.2	36.7	2,902.0	3,195.2
Canada	Ottawa	9,984,670.0	33.80	77.4	82.4	80.4	4	99.0	1,251.5	33,375	2.8	27.0	2.0	71.0	227,240.0	264,078.0
Cape Verde	Praia	4,033.0	0.60	67.0	73.2	55.9	102	75.7	1.1	5,803	5.8	16.4	10.7	72.8	278.0	41.8
Central African Republic	Bangui	622,984.0	4.59	38.4	40.1	57.3	171	48.6	1.5	1,224	3.8	22.3	56.5	21.2	247.0	181.0
Chad	N'Djaména	1,284,000.0	11.72	42.5	44.7	25.0	170	25.5	6.5	1,427	0.5	15.4	38.7	45.8	450.0	233.0

COUNTRY	GEOGRAPHICAL		SOCIAL						ECONOMIC							
	Capital	Area (km²)	Population projection 2010 (millions)	Life expectancy (years) M	Life expectancy (years) W	Urban population (%)	HDI world rank	Adult literacy rate (%)	GDP Total GDP (US$ billions)	GDP per capita (US$ at PPP)	Real GDP growth rate (%)	Industrial structure (% of GDP) Industry (%)	Agriculture (%)	Services (%)	Trade balance Import (US$ millions)	Export (US$ millions)
Chile	Santiago (administrative), Valparaíso (legislative)	756,096.0	17.13	74.8	80.9	87.0	40	95.7	145.8	12,027	4.0	34.5	8.9	56.6	23,006.0	32,025.0
China	Beijing	9,572,900.0	1,351.51	69.9	73.5	43.9	81	93.3	2,668.1	6,757	11.1	51.1	15.4	33.5	791,461.0	968,936.0
Colombia	Bogotá	1,141,748.0	47.89	69.3	75.4	76.4	75	94.2	135.8	7,304	6.8	30.2	13.9	55.9	12,077.0	12,303.0
Comoros	Moroni	1,862.0	0.90	61.1	65.4	35.0	134	56.2	0.4	1,993	1.2	11.9	40.9	47.2	58.7	0.4
Congo, Democratic Republic of the	Kinshasa	2,344,798.0	69.01	42.1	44.1	31.8	168	65.3	8.5	714	5.1	12.1	57.1	30.8	2,056.0	1,813.0
Congo, Republic of the	Brazzaville	341,821.0	4.00	50.7	53.2	53.5	139	82.8	7.4	1,262	6.1	63.3	6.3	30.4	691.0	2,289.0
Côte d'Ivoire	Yamoussoukro	322,460.0	20.38	45.2	46.7	54.9	166	48.1	17.5	1,648	0.9	20.4	26.2	53.4	4,167.7	6,902.1
Croatia	Zagreb	56,542.0	4.53	71.4	78.4	59.0	47	98.1	42.7	13,042	4.8	29.3	8.9	61.8	16,589.0	8,024.0
Cuba	Havana	110,861.0	11.26	75.5	79.2	75.7	51	96.9	n/a	n/a	2.6	27.0	5.0	68.0	5,251.0	1,665.0
Cyprus	Nicosia	9,251.0	0.90	76.1	81.1	69.2	28	96.8	15.4	22,805	3.7	n/a	n/a	n/a	5,814.1	1,197.9
Czech Republic	Prague	78,866.0	10.20	72.9	79.1	74.3	32	99.0	141.8	20,538	6.4	39.6	3.7	56.7	76,342.0	78,135.0
Denmark	Copenhagen	43,094.0	5.50	76.5	80.2	85.4	14	99.0	275.2	33,973	3.5	26.5	2.6	70.9	87,284.5	98,201.0
Djibouti	Djibouti	23,200.0	0.90	51.6	54.0	83.6	149	65.5	0.8	2,178	3.2	20.5	3.6	75.8	238.8	59.1
Dominica	Roseau	750.0	0.10	71.0	76.0	72.0	71	94.0	0.3	5,643	4.0	21.0	18.6	60.4	115.3	44.4
Dominican Republic	Santo Domingo	48,137.0	10.20	63.9	71.0	59.3	79	87.7	30.6	8,217	10.7	32.9	11.8	55.2	8,882.5	5,183.4
East Timor	Dili	15,410.0	1.27	54.5	56.6	7.7	n/a	n/a	0.4	n/a	-2.9	n/a	n/a	n/a	n/a	n/a
Ecuador	Quito	272,045.0	13.80	71.4	77.3	61.8	89	91.0	40.8	4,341	3.9	28.3	9.0	62.6	7,492.0	7,813.0
Egypt	Cairo	1,001,450.0	79.50	68.4	72.8	52.2	112	56.1	107.5	4,337	6.8	34.8	16.5	48.7	12,866.0	7,701.0
El Salvador	San Salvador	21,041.0	7.10	67.8	73.9	59.4	103	79.7	18.3	5,255	4.2	30.0	8.7	61.0	5,948.8	3,329.6
Equatorial Guinea	Malabo	28,051.0	0.60	42.6	43.9	48.0	127	84.2	8.6	15,073	-5.2	86.0	8.9	5.0	3,234.4	5,557.6
Eritrea	Asmara	121,100.0	5.30	51.8	55.7	20.0	157	56.7	1.1	1,109	2.0	25.0	12.9	62.1	538.0	520.0
Estonia	Tallinn	45,227.0	1.30	65.6	77.0	69.5	44	99.8	16.4	15,478	11.2	21.0	4.0	75.0	7,602.5	5,299.3
Ethiopia	Addis Ababa	1,127,127.0	89.57	46.6	48.7	15.7	169	41.5	13.3	1,055	9.0	13.3	47.7	39.0	1,455.0	480.2
Fiji Islands	Suva	18,333.0	0.90	65.7	70.1	51.7	92	93.2	2.8	6,049	3.6	27.0	16.2	56.8	1.4	0.8
Finland	Helsinki	304,112.0	5.30	75.3	82.3	62.7	11	99.0	209.4	32,153	5.5	31.0	3.0	66.0	69,147.6	77,125.8
France	Paris	543,965.0	62.50	75.9	83.0	76.3	10	99.0	2,230.7	30,386	2.2	24.9	2.7	72.4	363.6	358.8
Gabon	Libreville	267,667.0	1.39	53.7	55.2	83.7	119	71.0	9.5	6,954	1.2	46.4	7.6	46.0	1,349.4	4,128.9
The Gambia	Banjuk	10,689.0	1.85	54.3	57.1	22.2	155	37.8	0.5	1,921	6.5	14.2	25.8	60.0	160.1	111.0

COUNTRY	GEOGRAPHICAL Capital	Area (km²)	SOCIAL Population projection 2010 (millions)	Life expectancy (years) M	W	Urban population (%)	HDI world rank	Adult literacy rate (%)	ECONOMIC GDP Total GDP (US$ billions)	GDP per capita (US$ at PPP)	Real GDP growth rate (%)	Industrial structure (% of GDP) Industry (%)	Agriculture (%)	Services (%)	Trade balance Import (US$ millions)	Export (US$ millions)
Georgia	Tbilisi	69,700.0	4.30	66.6	74.3	52.5	96	99.0	7.6	3,365	9.4	24.3	20.6	55.0	1,041.6	583.4
Germany	Berlin	357,116.0	82.37	76.2	81.8	88.1	22	99.0	2,906.7	29,461	2.7	29.6	1.2	69.2	1,075,552.0	13,17,531.0
Ghana	Accra	238,533.0	24.89	56.3	57.3	45.4	135	54.1	12.9	2,480	6.2	24.3	36.0	39.7	4,297.3	2,784.6
Greece	Athens	131,957.0	11.22	76.8	81.7	60.9	24	91.0	245.0	23,381	4.3	22.4	7.3	70.3	44,856.0	13,671.0
Grenada	St George's	344.0	0.10	66.0	69.0	40.7	82	96.0	0.5	8,021	0.7	22.6	7.5	69.8	233.2	59.7
Guatemala	Guatemala City	108,889.0	14.38	63.6	71.0	46.3	118	69.1	35.3	4,568	4.9	19.3	22.5	58.2	7,189.1	3,429.5
Guinea	Conakry	245,857.0	10.30	53.4	54.1	34.9	160	29.5	3.3	2,316	2.2	36.6	24.2	39.1	688.4	725.6
Guinea-Bissau	Bissau	36,125.0	1.85	63.2	46.2	34.0	175	39.6	0.3	827	2.7	13.1	62.4	24.5	65.3	65.0
Guyana	Georgetown	214,999.0	0.73	60.0	66.1	37.6	97	98.6	0.9	4,508	5.1	28.6	30.8	40.6	563.1	494.9
Haiti	Port-au-Prince	27,700.0	10.06	50.8	52.4	37.5	146	51.9	5.0	1,663	2.2	16.4	27.1	56.5	1,115.8	333.2
Honduras	Tegucigalpa	112,492.0	7.53	65.8	69.9	54.4	115	80.0	9.2	3,430	6.0	30.6	13.4	56.0	3,921.8	1,533.9
Hungary	Budapest	93,030.0	9.94	68.6	76.8	65.2	36	99.3	112.9	17,887	3.9	31.2	4.3	64.5	58,290.0	55,368.0
Iceland	Reykjavik	102,819.0	0.31	78.9	82.8	92.8	1	99.0*	15.9	36,510	4.2	22.7	8.2	69.1	5,030.8	3,115.3
India	New Delhi	3,166,285.0	1220.18	61.8	65.0	28.3	128	64.8	906.3	3,452	9.7	26.6	22.7	50.7	0.6	0.5
Indonesia	Jakarta	1,890,754.0	239.60	64.9	68.8	45.5	107	87.9	364.5	3,843	5.5	44.2	17.1	38.7	35,652.0	58,773.0
Iran	Tehran	1,648,195.0	74.28	71.9	69.0	66.6	94	77.0	222.9	7,968	4.7	40.6	11.7	47.7	15,207.0	28,345.0
Ireland	Dublin	70,273.8	4.53	75.1	80.3	59.9	5	99.0*	222.7	38,505	5.7	41.2	3.3	55.5	78,375.7	137,810.0
Israel	Jerusalem	22,072.0	7.27	77.6	81.7	91.6	23	96.9	123.4	25,864	5.2	2.0	16.0	82.0	38,473.0	36,585.0
Italy	Rome	301,277.0	59.03	76.9	83.1	67.4	20	98.5	1844.7	28,529	1.9	27.3	2.6	70.1	341.3	352.2
Jamaica	Kingston	10,991.0	2.76	69.0	72.5	52.2	101	87.6	10.5	4,291	2.5	29.1	5.5	65.3	3,179.6	1,309.1
Japan	Tokyo	377,915.0	127.76	78.5	85.5	65.8	8	99.0*	4,340.1	31,267	2.2	27.6	1.4	71.0	565,850.0	632,246.0
Jordan	Amman	89,342.0	6.45	69.9	72.9	79.1	86	89.9	14.2	5,530	6.3	25.9	2.2	71.9	5,069.2	2,766.1
Kazakhstan	Astana	2,724,900.0	15.76	57.8	69.0	55.9	73	99.0*	77.2	7,857	10.7	38.6	8.6	52.8	8,408.7	12,926.7
Kenya	Nairobi	582,646.0	40.65	48.1	46.3	39.3	148	73.6	21.2	1,240	6.1	19.0	16.9	64.1	3,708.3	17,987.7
South Korea	Seoul	99,585.0	48.67	73.3	80.6	80.3	26	97.9	888.0	22,029	5.0	33.8	3.6	62.6	224,463.0	253,845.0
Kuwait	Kuwait City	17,818.0	3.05	75.2	79.5	96.2	33	93.4	7,566.0	26,321	5.0	59.7	0.0	40.3	16,252.0	22,427.0
Kyrgyzstan	Bishkek	199,900.0	5.50	62.7	71.1	34.0	116	98.7	2.7	1,927	2.7	23.3	37.7	39.0	717.0	581.7
Laos	Vientiane	236,800.0	6.17	53.4	55.9	20.7	130	68.7	3.4	2,039	7.6	23.5	50.3	26.2	534.6	319.6
Latvia	Riga	64,589.0	2.24	65.8	77.0	68.0	45	99.7	20.1	13,646	11.9	24.7	4.7	70.6	4,054.0	2,284.0
Lebanon	Beirut	10,452.0	4.23	69.8	74.2	87.5	88	86.5	22.7	5,584	1.0	21.0	11.7	67.3	9,397.0	1,747.0
Lesotho	Maseru	30,355.0	2.04	34.6	37.7	18.0	138	81.4	1.5	3,335	7.2	43.1	16.3	40.6	736.0	354.8
Liberia	Monrovia	99,065.0	4.31	40.0	43.0	45.0	n/a	38.3	0.6	n/a	7.8	5.0	77.0	18.0	268.1	103.8
Libya	Tripoli	1,759,540.0	6.53	71.6	76.2	86.2	56	81.7	50.3	10,335	5.6	64.0	5.3	30.6	7.6	13.9
Lithuania	Vilnius	65,200.0	3.34	66.6	77.8	66.8	43	99.6	29.8	14,494	7.5	31.2	7.1	61.7	12,017.5	8,636.3
Luxembourg	Luxembourg	2,586.0	0.48	74.9	81.0	91.8	18	100.0	41.4	60,228	6.0	20.5	0.6	78.9	19,792.5	14,385.6

| COUNTRY | GEOGRAPHICAL | | SOCIAL | | | | | | ECONOMIC | | | | | | | |
	Capital	Area (km²)	Population projection 2010 (millions)	Life expectancy (years) M	W	Urban population (%)	HDI world rank	Adult literacy rate (%)	GDP — Total GDP (US$ billions)	GDP per capita (US$ at PPP)	Real GDP growth rate (%)	Industrial structure (% of GDP) — Industry (%)	Agriculture (%)	Services (%)	Trade balance — Import (US$ millions)	Export (US$ millions)
Madagascar	Antananarivo	587,041.0	21.30	54.1	56.8	26.6	143	70.6	5.5	923	4.9	14.4	31.7	53.8	603.0	486.0
Malawi	Lilongwe	118,484.0	15.04	39.8	39.6	16.3	164	61.0	2.2	667	7.9	14.9	36.7	48.4	288.9	265.1
Malaysia	Putrajaya (administrative), Kuala Lumpur (legislative and financial)	329,847.0	27.92	70.9	75.6	63.8	63	88.7	148.9	10,882	5.9	47.3	9.2	43.5	92,220.0	107,722.0
Maldives	Malé	298	0.32	67.1	66.1	28.8	100	97.2	0.9	5,261	19.1	15.0	7.0	78.0	414.3	152.0
Mali	Bamako	1,248,574.0	13.51	47.2	48.5	32.2	173	26.4	5.9	1,033	5.3	29.7	34.2	36.1	988.3	927.8
Malta	Valletta	246.0	0.40	75.9	80.8	91.6	34	92.3	5.6	19,189	3.3	26.2	2.8	71.0	4,186.5	3,101.1
Mauritania	Nouakchott	1,030,700.0	3.36	54.3	51.1	38.3	137	51.2	2.7	2,234	11.4	29.4	20.8	49.8	418.0	330.3
Mauritius	Port Louis	800.0	1.29	68.8	75.7	43.3	65	84.3	6.4	12,715	3.1	30.2	6.2	63.6	2,301.2	1,850.4
Mexico	Mexico City	1,964,375.0	110.29	72.6	77.5	75.5	52	90.3	839.2	10,751	4.8	26.5	4.0	69.5	196,810.0	187,999.0
Moldova	Chişinău	33,848.0	3.71	63.9	71.3	36.1	111	96.2	3.3	2,100	4.0	23.2	24.1	52.7	1,038.1	659.8
Mongolia	Ulan Bator	1,565,008.0	2.71	62.1	66.1	56.8	114	97.8	2.7	2,107	8.6	15.9	29.7	54.4	680.2	524.0
Montenegro	Podgorica	13,812.0	0.60	n/a	n/a	n/a	n/a	n/a	2.3	n/a	n/a	n/a	n/a	n/a	n/a	n/a
Morocco	Rabat	458,730.0	32.38	67.5	71.9	57.4	126	52.3	57.3	4,555	8.0	30.3	16.1	53.6	10,900.0	7,839.0
Mozambique	Maputo	799,380.0	22.64	41.1	42.7	35.6	172	46.5	8.5	1,242	7.6	28.9	26.6	44.5	1,849.7	1,503.9
Namibia	Windhoek	825,112.0	2.16	47.6	49.0	32.4	125	85.0	6.4	7,586	4.6	31.1	10.6	58.3	1,250.5	1,071.6
Nepal	Kathmandu	147,181.0	29.90	61.2	62.0	15.0	142	48.6	8.1	1,550	2.8	21.7	40.7	37.5	1,812.5	763.6
The Netherlands	The Hague (seat of government), Amsterdam (nominal)	41,528.0	16.50	76.9	81.4	65.8	9	99.0*	657.6	32,684	2.9	25.9	71.4	2.7	392,490.0	442,833.0
New Zealand	Wellington	270,534.0	4.29	76.8	81.3	85.9	19	99.0*	103.9	24,996	1.8	23.0	8.0	69.0	24,884.6	22,663.9
Nicaragua	Managua	131,812.0	5.83	67.3	72.1	57.3	110	76.7	5.4	3,674	3.7	25.0	18.0	57.0	1,636.4	605.1
Niger	Niamey	1,186,408.0	15.79	44.3	44.4	77.8	174	14.4	3.5	781	5.2	39.6	7.4	43.3	488.5	351.8
Nigeria	Abuja	923,768.0	158.31	43.1	43.6	46.6	158	66.8	114.7	1,128	5.6	43.8	31.2	25.0	11,096.0	23,657.0
Norway	Oslo	323,802.0	4.79	78.1	82.7	77.8	2	99.0	311.0	41,420	2.8	38.3	1.8	59.9	60,270.5	102,288.0
Oman	Muscat	309,500.0	2.77	72.7	75.7	77.6	58	74.4	24.3	15,259	5.9	53.2	2.1	44.7	7,873.0	13,345.0
Pakistan	Islamabad	796,096.0	173.35	62.8	63.2	34.1	136	48.7	128.8	2,370	6.9	22.9	23.6	53.4	16,735.0	13,352.0
Panama	Panama City	75,001.0	3.51	72.3	77.4	57.2	62	91.9	17.1	7,605	8.1	13.8	5.7	80.5	4,817.7	1,021.8
Papua New Guinea	Port Moresby	462,840.0	6.71	54.9	56.0	13.2	145	57.3	5.7	2,564	2.6	39.4	27.2	33.4	932.4	1,812.9
Paraguay	Asunción	406,752.0	6.46	68.7	73.2	57.2	95	91.6	9.1	4,642	4.3	28.4	22.0	49.6	2,390.0	2,319.3
Peru	Lima	1,285,216.0	28.89	67.5	72.6	73.9	87	87.7	93.3	6,039	7.6	30.1	10.1	59.8	7,818.0	8,940.0
Philippines	Manila	300,076.0	93.00	68.3	72.5	61.0	90	92.6	116.9	5,137	5.4	32.5	14.7	52.8	33,975.0	34,383.0

COUNTRY	GEOGRAPHICAL		SOCIAL						ECONOMIC							
	Capital	Area (km²)	Population projection 2010 (millions)	Life expectancy (years) M	Life expectancy (years) W	Urban population (%)	HDI world rank	Adult literacy rate (%)	GDP Total GDP (US$ billions)	GDP per capita (US$ at PPP)	Real GDP growth rate (%)	Industrial structure Industry (%)	Agriculture (%)	Services (%)	Trade balance Import (US$ millions)	Export (US$ millions)
Poland	Warsaw	312,685.0	37.90	70.8	79.4	61.8	37	99.7	338.7	13,847	6.2	30.5	3.1	66.4	10,390.0	90,900.0
Portugal	Lisbon	91,947.0	10.73	73.9	80.6	54.6	29	92.5	192.6	20,410	1.3	28.0	4.0	68.0	43,710.0	30,490.0
Qatar	Doha	11,493.0	0.89	71.2	76.0	92.0	35	81.7	28.5	27,664	10.3	70.7	0.4	28.9	3,654.3	10,990.1
Romania	Bucharest	238,391.0	21.15	67.8	75.0	54.6	60	97.3	121.6	9,060	7.7	38.1	13.1	48.8	16,487.0	13,876.0
Russia	Moscow	17,075,400.0	140.32	59.0	72.1	73.3	67	99.4	986.9	10,845	6.7	34.0	5.7	60.3	96,307.0	183,452.0
Rwanda	Kigali	25,314.0	10.60	42.1	45.6	18.5	161	64.0	2.5	1,206	5.3	21.5	41.9	36.6	233.3	67.2
Samoa	Apia	2,830.8	0.19	67.2	73.3	23.3	77	98.7	0.4	6,170	2.3	25.0	40.0	35.0	258.4	95.3
Saudi Arabia	Riyadh	2,149,690.0	26.42	10.1	73.9	87.6	61	79.4	309.8	15,711	4.3	52.0	5.2	42.8	29,637.1	71,474.6
Senegal	Dakar	196,722.0	13.31	54.5	56.9	49.6	156	39.3	8.9	1,792	2.1	21.6	15.0	63.4	2,065.0	1,257.0
Serbia	Belgrade	88,361.0	n/a	n/a	n/a	n/a	n/a	n/a	31.8	n/a	5.7	n/a	n/a	n/a		
Seychelles	Victoria	232.0	0.08	72.0	77.0	50.0	50	91.9	0.8	16,106	3.5	30.0	2.9	67.1	470.5	236.8
Sierra Leone	Freetown	71,740.0	6.19	39.4	42.1	38.8	177	29.6	1.4	806	7.4	31.6	52.6	15.7	188.0	34.6
Singapore	Singapore City	682.3	4.59	76.7	80.6	100.0	25	92.5	132.2	29,663	7.9	30.4**	0.0	69.6	231,302.0	265,555.0
Slovakia	Bratislava	49,034.0	5.40	70.4	78.2	57.5	42	99.6	55.0	15,871	8.3	28.6	4.0	67.4	29,260.0	27,780.0
Slovenia	Ljubljana	20,273.0	2.00	72.7	80.0	50.8	27	99.7	37.3	22,273	5.7	31.9	2.3	65.8	13,854.0	12,767.0
Solomon Islands	Honiara	28,370.0	0.53	61.6	63.0	16.5	129	62.0	0.3	2,031	6.1	n/a	n/a	n/a	62.6	56.0
South Africa	Pretoria (administrative), Cape Town (legislative), Bloemfontein (judicial)	1,219,090.0	49.28	46.8	50.2	56.9	121	86.0	255.0	11,110	5.0	31.0	3.8	65.2	26,713.0	31,085.0
Spain	Madrid	492,592.0	45.11	75.9	83.2	76.5	13	99.0*	1,224.0	27,169	3.9	30.1	3.4	66.5	249,984.0	184,154.0
Sri Lanka	Kotte (administrative and legislative), Colombo (commercial)	18,797,257.0	19.58	67.9	75.6	21.1	99	91.1	27.0	4,595	7.4	26.3	20.5	53.2	6,004.8	5,133.2
Sudan	Khartoum	2,505,810.0	41.23	54.9	57.9	38.9	147	58.8	37.6	2,083	11.8	18.3	42.5	39.2	2,152.8	1,949.1
Suriname	Paramaribo	163,820.0	0.47	65.9	72.6	66.7	85	88.0	1.6	7,722	5.5	19.6	11.1	69.3	740.0	782.2
Swaziland	Mbabane (administrative), Lobamba (legislative)	17,363.0	1.16	32.1	32.9	23.6	141	79.2	2.6	4,824	2.1	49.8	15.7	34.5	1,034.6	955.2
Sweden	Stockholm	450,295.0	9.24	82.7	78.3	83.4	6	99.0*	384.9	32,525	4.5	28.2	1.8	70.0	736,510.0	903,866.0
Switzerland	Berne	n/a	7.57	78.6	83.7	73.4	7	99.0*	379.8	35,633	3.2	26.5	1.2	72.3	138,778.0	147,388.0

COUNTRY	GEOGRAPHICAL		SOCIAL						ECONOMIC							
				Life expectancy (years)					GDP			Industrial structure (% of GDP)			Trade balance	
	Capital	Area (km²)	Population projection 2010 (millions)	M	W	Urban population (%)	HDI world rank	Adult literacy rate (%)	Total GDP (US$ billions)	GDP per capita (US$ at PPP)	Real GDP growth rate (%)	Industry (%)	Agriculture (%)	Services (%)	Import (US$ millions)	Export (US$ millions)
Syria	Damascus	185,180.0	21.43	71.6	75.1	50.2	108	82.9	34.9	3,808	3.3	29.3	23.5	47.1	5,935.0	5,561.0
Tajikistan	Dushanbe	143,100.0	7.07	61.0	66.3	24.8	122	99.5	2.8	1,356	7.0	24.0	24.3	51.7	822.9	699.1
Tanzania	Dodoma	942,799.0	43.54	45.5	46.3	35.4	159	69.4	12.8	744	6.2	16.1	44.7	39.2	1,511.3	902.5
Thailand	Bangkok	513,115.0	65.13	66.3	73.8	32.0	78	92.6	206.2	8,677	5.0	42.7	9.3	48.0	84,983.0	96,107.0
Togo	Lomé	56,785.0	7.12	52.4	56.3	64.8	152	53.0	2.2	1,506	2.0	18.5	38.1	43.3	754.5	597.7
Tonga	Nuku'alofa	748.0	0.10	71.0	73.5	33.5	55	98.5	0.2	8,177	1.3	15.1	28.5	56.3	73.4	18.1
Trinidad and Tobago	Port of Spain	5,128.0	1.35	66.9	73.0	39.2	59	98.5	19.9	14,603	12.0	45.7	1.3	53.0	3,911.7	5,204.9
Tunisia	Tunis	164,150.0	10.66	71.2	75.4	63.7	91	74.3	30.3	8,371	5.4	29.3	10.3	60.4	12,114.0	9,679.0
Turkey	Ankara	780,580.0	77.70	66.5	71.1	66.3	84	88.3	402.7	8,407	6.1	29.1	13.4	57.5	51,203.0	35,761.0
Turkmenistan	Ashgabat	448,100.0	5.16	58.3	66.8	45.4	109	98.0	10.5	5,938	9.0	41.0	21.3	37.7	1,785.0	2,506.0
Uganda	Kampala	241,548.0	34.04	46.9	47.6	12.3	154	93.9	9.3	1,454	5.4	21.5	31.0	47.5	1,113.5	480.7
Ukraine	Kyiv	603,700.0	45.17	60.1	72.5	67.3	76	99.4	106.1	6,848	7.1	38.2	15.3	46.5	29,691.0	33,432.0
United Arab Emirates	Abu Dhabi	83,600.0	4.73	76.4	80.8	85.1	39	77.3	104.2	25,514	9.4	51.0	3.5	45.5	32,841.0	48,172.6
UK	London		61.52	76.7	81.2	89.1	16	99.0*	2345.0	33,238	2.8	26.6	1.0	72.4	422,583.0	489,477.0
USA	Washington, DC	3,794,083.0	314.69	67.1	74.7	21.0	12	99.0*	13,201.8	41,890	2.9	26.0	2.0	72.0	1,673.5	906.0
Uruguay	Montevideo	176,215.0	3.37	71.7	79.0	92.5	46	97.7	19.3	9,962	7.0	26.8	9.4	63.8	2,990.2	3,021.3
Uzbekistan	Tashkent	447,400.0	28.58	63.4	69.8	36.7	113	99.3	17.2	2,063	7.3	21.6	34.7	43.7	2,712.0	2,988.0
Venezuela	Caracas	916,445.0	29.05	70.0	75.9	87.6	74	93.0	181.9	6,632	10.3	43.0	2.6	54.4	13,732.0	26,656.0
Vietnam	Hanoi	332,934.0	90.85	68.6	72.6	25.8	105	92.7	60.9	3,071	8.2	38.5	23.0	38.5	17,760.0	16,706.0
Yemen	Sana'a (legislative and administrative), Aden (commercial)	555,000.0	24.48	59.3	61.9	25.7	153	49.0	19.1	930	4.0	41.5	11.4	47.1	3,858.6	4,675.7
Zambia	Lusaka	752,612.0	12.63	37.9	36.9	35.9	165	79.0	10.9	1,023	5.2	26.1	22.2	51.7	1,253.0	930.0
Zimbabwe	Harare	390,757.0	13.76	37.3	36.5	35.0	151	90.0	5.0	2,038	-4.8	23.8	17.4	58.8	1,779.0	1,609.0

Notes:

*At least 99%.

**Source of data on industrial structure: The Economist Newspaper (2008) *Pocket World in Figures*, London: Profile Books.

Glossary

Absolute advantage Enjoyed by a country where production of a product involves using fewer productive inputs than would be possible in any other country.

Absolute poverty Defined by the World Bank as living on less than $1 a day.

Accounting and finance for international businesses Budgeting, costs and raising finance, any or all of which arise in more than one country, and involve more than one regulatory authority.

Acid rain Contamination caused by the accumulation of pollutants in atmospheric water, mainly from the burning of fossil fuels, which, when it falls as rain, causes harm to plant and animal life.

Agile manufacturing The ability to respond and adapt to continuous change in the design, production and delivery of products.

Agile supply chain Ability of firms in a supply chain to respond quickly to frequent changes in consumer preferences and levels of demand.

Aid for Trade WTO initiative by which aid is directed at capacity-building and other developments in recipient countries.

Alliance Co-operative arrangement between two or more different organizations for a particular purpose, which offers benefits to participating organizations while retaining their individual identity.

Alliance capitalism Capitalist market model which rests heavily on relational ties among firms, through cross-shareholding and personal ties.

Antitrust law Law designed to curtail monopolists and encourage competitive markets.

Appraisal Process of analysing an employee's work achievement and potential for further development.

Acquisition Purchase of the whole of the capital of a company, or a controlling stake, which amounts to a change of ownership.

Assimilation In societies, process by which a minority culture gradually acquires the language and culture which predominates in a country.

Auditor Professional accountant appointed by a company to prepare its annual accounts in accordance with applicable regulatory rules, and from an independent perspective.

Authoritarian government Rule by one or more individuals who claim absolute power to govern a state, with no substantive accountability to its citizens.

Balance of payments The total credit and debit transactions between a country's residents and those of other countries over a given period.

Biodiversity A variety of living organisms and species co-existing in the same habitat.

Biofuels Fuels derived from organic matter, seen as an alternative to fossil fuels.

Bond A type of loan security issued by organizations for a fixed period, with interest payable to the lender.

Born-global firm Entrepreneurial firm which adopts a global focus and commitment to international operations from the start.

Brand Trademark or logo distinguishing an organization's products from those of rivals, which is an important asset capable of legal protection.

Buddhism Asian religion based on the teachings of Buddha.

Business process outsourcing (BPO) The shifting of particular business functions or processes to a specialist company, usually for cost savings.

Carbon capture and storage Process of removing carbon dioxide from the burning of fossil fuels and storing it deep underground.

Carbon neutrality Policy of reducing emissions to a minimum and then offsetting the remaining emissions through activities which directly contribute to environmental protection.

Carbon offsetting Policy whereby a firm invests in green projects, often in developing countries, which are the equivalent of the firm's greenhouse gas emissions.

Chaebol Traditional South Korean family-owned and paternalistically controlled conglomerate.

Christianity Monotheistic religion based on belief in Jesus Christ, whose teachings are in the Bible.

Civil society Voluntary groups representing cultural, religious and political diversity within a society.

Civil society organizations Voluntary groups representing cultural, religious and political diversity within a society.

Climate change Global rise or fall in temperatures, whether natural in causation or caused by human activity.

Cluster Group of companies and other organizations in an industry, designed to bring benefits through co-operation.

Coalition government Government formed by an agreement between parties to work together, in the event of no single party commanding enough seats to form an overall majority in the elected chamber.

Co-determination Principle by which employees are represented in governance structures along with shareholders.

Codified knowledge Tangible elements of knowledge, such as products, designs and specifications.

Commercial services trade Trade in services across national borders, including financial services, business services, transport and travel.

Comparative advantage Enjoyed by a country where production of a product involves greater relative advantages in terms of inputs than would be possible anywhere else.

Confucianism Ancient Chinese ethical and philosophical system based on the teachings of Confucius.

Consumer market The aggregate of needs and desires of consumers within a country, taking into account their buying behaviour.

Continuous improvement Process which strives constantly to find creative ways in which problems can be solved and processes improved, involving all workers in the organization.

Convertibility The extent to which a government allows its currency to be bought and sold freely by both residents and foreigners.

Co-operative Voluntary organization in which all participate to achieve common goals in a community, usually regulated within a national framework.

Co-operative R&D agreement Agreement between organizations to work on specific research projects, sharing knowledge and expertise.

Copyright Property of the author in a literary, musical, dramatic or artistic work, including software.

Core competencies An organization's collective skill and learning in specialist areas.

Corporate citizenship The concept that companies, like individuals, have the legal and moral duties attached to citizenship.

Corporate governance A company's decision-making structure and processes at the highest level, by which its directors are responsible to its owners and other stakeholders.

Corporate social responsibility (CSR) The approach of the business enterprise which takes in economic activities, legal obligations and social responsibilities.

Cost-plus pricing Price based on costs plus a standard mark-up.

Cultural distance In the business context, the degree to which a firm is unfamiliar with the culture of a foreign business location.

Cultural melting pot Mixture of cultures to form a new and distinctive culture, often in a new setting, such as the 'settler' societies of the US and Australia.

Cultural pluralism The recognition of separate cultures within a society.

Culture Shared, learned values, norms of behaviour, means of communication and other outward expressions which distinguish one group of people from another.

Currency board Framework whereby a country guarantees conversion of its currency into another currency, supported by reserves of the backup currency.

Debt/equity ratio Expression of the balance between debt financing and equity financing for a particular company.

Democratic government Political system which, at a minimum, is based on accountability of government to the voting public, through regular, free and fair elections.

Derivative Financial instrument whose value is dependent on another asset class, such as stock.

Design right Appearance of a product, including packaging and symbols, which can be registered with national authorities, prohibiting its use without the owner's permission.

Developed country Country whose economy has become industrialized and technologically advanced.

Developing country Country in the process of industrialization and building technological capacity.

Diamond model of competitive advantage Configuration of four sets of attributes (factor conditions, demand conditions, supporting industries and inter-firm rivalry) which, in Porter's theory, determine a nation's competitive advantage.

Differentiated marketing Adapting products and marketing mix for differing target markets.

Direct and indirect taxes Direct taxes are paid by individuals and companies on their earned and unearned income. Indirect taxes are incurred for goods and services at the point of delivery.

Distribution channel Interlinked stages and organizations involved in the process of bringing a product or service to the consumer or industrial user.

Dumping The export of an inordinately large quantity of a specific class of goods in a foreign market at prices less than in their home market, which can result in 'anti-dumping' sanctions by the importing country.

Eclectic paradigm Dunning's theory of FDI, based on ownership advantages, location advantages and internalization.

Ecology The relationship between organisms and their environment, including the changes in their distribution and numbers.

Economic development Process of change in economic activities and organizations of a country.

Economic growth An economy's increase in total income over time, usually shown as an annual percentage change.

Economic nationalism The growth and expansion of state-owned and state-controlled companies, aimed at promoting national economic power in global markets.

Economies of scale Large-scale production which results in reduction of the unit cost of products.

Ecosystem A complex set of relationships among living organisms and the habitat which sustains them.

Efficient supply chain Ability to process and move high volumes of goods quickly and at the lowest possible cost.

Emerging economy or market Fast-growing developing or transition economy.

Emigration The movement of people out of a country.

Emissions trading scheme Scheme whereby a company buys credits to offset its greenhouse gas emissions from companies which are less pollutant.

Employee empowerment Policy of devolving to employees, individually or in teams, authority to take decisions and control work processes.

Employee relations Practices which involve managers and workers in workplace communication and decision-making.

Entrepreneur Individual who, having identified a new business opportunity, assembles the necessary resources and creates a new business.

Entrepreneurship Attributes associated with business start-ups, including identifying opportunities, pursuing innovative ideas, and willingness to undertake manageable risks.

Equities Shares, also known as 'stock', in a registered company.

Equity Total shares in the registered company.

Ethical marketing Approach to marketing activities which prioritizes utmost fairness, safety, honesty and transparency in the interests of consumers, even in situations where the law is less stringent.

Ethnic grouping People drawn together by sense of common identity, sense of belonging, and a shared history, including a belief in common descent (real or mythical).

Ethnocentrism Perspective of individuals and organizations completely imbued with their own culture, to the exclusion of differing cultures.

Eurobond Bond issued in countries outside that of the currency in which it is denominated.

European Union (EU) Regional European economic union, comprising 27 member states.

Eurozone EU member states which are members of the European Monetary Union (EMU).

Executive directors Officers employed by the company, who are in charge of day-to-day management.

Expatriate National of a parent company's home country, assigned to work in one of its foreign subsidiaries, usually as a secondment for a year or more.

Export processing zone (EPZ) Designated geographic area designed to attract export-oriented businesses through incentives such as exemption from tariffs and other trade rules which apply outside the zone.

Export subsidy Payments made by a government to producers of specific products in order to increase their production for export.

Factor endowments The labour, land, capital and natural resources of a country.

Factor-price equalization Theory which holds that, with trade, an abundant factor of production will rise in value and a scarce factor of production will fall.

Fair trade initiatives Initiatives by companies, often under the Fairtrade trademark, which guarantee a reasonable return to producers and provide other benefits for producer communities.

FDI inflows Value of FDI which flows into a recipient country from all foreign investors.

FDI outflows Value of all foreign direct investments made by a country's firms over a period, usually a year.

FDI stock Accumulated value of all foreign investments within a country.

First-mover advantages Advantages enjoyed by the first entrant in an industry or market, which may yield increasing returns, making it harder for other entrants to follow and acting as a barrier to entry.

Flexible manufacturing Manufacturing processes based on machines, tasks and co-ordination systems which are adapted to achieve both volume and variety.

Fordism Assembly-line manufacturing on a large scale, whose processes were designed for producing large volumes of standardized products.

Foreign bond Bond issued outside the country of the issuing organization, denominated in the currency of the issuing country.

Foreign direct investment (FDI) Investment by an organization in a business in another country with a view to establishing production in the host country.

Foreign exchange option Financial instrument which gives the firm the right, but not the obligation, to purchase currency at a particular exchange rate.

Forward or futures contract Contract to carry out a particular transaction on a designated date in the future.

Franchise A commercial agreement by which a business (the franchisee) is allowed to use the brand, products and business format of another business (the franchisor), in return for payment of agreed fees between the two parties.

Free trade Situation in which markets are allowed to operate without any government intervention.

Geocentrism International approach involving collaboration between the centre and subsidiaries, and among subsidiaries.

Global citizenship Extension of the notion of citizenship from the state to the entire world, involving global rights and responsibilities.

Global governance Evolving transnational processes of regulation and standard-setting by governmental and non-governmental agents.

Globalization Increasing and deepening interactions between individuals and organizations across the globe.

Globalization of markets The melding of national markets into a single global market; applies to standardized products, such as industrial goods and commodities, but for most consumer products, national markets remain distinct.

Globalization of production Trend in manufacturing industries, in particular, of shifting operations to countries where conditions and environment are more advantageous for the firm than they are in its current location; usually involving cost reductions.

Global model In Bartlett and Ghoshal's typology, a model of the international company based on centralized control.

Global product category Broad category of products which can be subdivided into products with distinctive features for differing markets.

Global sourcing Processes of co-ordinating and integrating design and supply of goods between suppliers and purchasers in different locations worldwide.

Global warming Global rise in temperatures, impacting on all forms of life and ecosystems.

Greenfield investment FDI which involves the investor in setting up an operation from scratch in a new location.

Gross domestic product (GDP) Value of the total economic activity within an economy, including domestic and foreign producers.

Gross national income (GNI) Total income from all final products and services produced within a country; includes foreign income earned by the country's residents.

Guanxi Personal relations which establish trust and mutual obligations necessary for business in China.

Hedge A financial tool or arrangement which insures a firm against adverse currency movements in its international financial activities.

Hedge fund Investment fund managed by an individual or firm, which is active in all types of securities markets; noted for skills in achieving short-term gains for investors.

High-context culture Culture in which information is conveyed nonverbally, often relying on personal understandings of meanings.

High elasticity of demand Market condition in which a small rise in prices produces a significant drop in demand.

High elasticity of price Market condition in which prices can be raised with minimum adverse effect on demand for a product.

Hinduism Polytheistic religion whose followers are concentrated in India.

Host-country national (HCN) National of the host country of a foreign investor, who is employed either by the parent company directly or by the partner organization in the host country.

HR planning Process of devising systems for all aspects of HR, including selection, recruitment, compensation and appraisal of staff, within the strategic goals of the organization.

Human resource management (HRM) A range of management activities which aim to achieve organizational objectives through effective use of employees.

International Financial Reporting Standards (IFRS) International accounting standards, designed to harmonize reporting standards in different countries, which are gradually supplanting national accounting standards.

Immigration The movement of people into a country.

Import quota Predetermined limit on the quantity of goods of a specific class that can be imported; the exporter must usually obtain a licence to export within the quota.

Income inequality The extent to which the members of a population do not all enjoy equal shares in the country's income.

Incremental innovation Approach to innovation based on a series of small improvements in an existing product or service.

Independent trade union A self-governing organization of workers, independent of employer or other controls, which exists to gain better terms and conditions of employment for its members.

Industrial relations Processes by which managers and worker organizations deal collectively with work-related issues such as terms and conditions of employment

Inflation The persistent rise in the general level of money prices.

Initial public offering (IPO) Process by which a company becomes a public company, inviting prospective investors to subscribe for its shares for the first time.

Innovation New or improved product or way of doing things, which aims to contribute to value creation for the organization.

Invention New product or process which represents a technological leap forward and is capable of industrial application.

Intellectual property rights (IPR) Legal rights to the ownership and exclusive use of products of human creativity and endeavour, such as patents for inventions, copyright for literature and music, and trademarks for corporate symbols.

Inter-governmental organization (IGO) Grouping of representatives of sovereign states formed to foster international co-operation to tackle particular global issues.

International business Any business activity across national borders, including exporting and importing, manufacturing, service provision and retailing; also refers to the organization itself which engages in cross-border business.

International Fisher effect (IFE) Theory which holds that gains in nominal interest rates will be nullified by movements in exchange rates over the long term.

International HRM (IHRM) Processes and activities of people management which involve more than one national context.

International joint venture (IJV) Formal agreement between two or more organizations in different countries, to form a new organization, in which each normally has a share in the equity.

International labour standards Rules agreed by the ILO on working conditions and the treatment of workers.

International marketing Function by which an organization assesses and meets the needs of consumers outside its home market, for its products.

International model In Bartlett and Ghoshal's typology, a model of the international company based on decentralized subsidiaries.

International operations Process by which the firm makes and delivers its goods or services across national borders.

Inter-organizational network Formal and informal links between separate firms which may take the form of contractual arrangements, but may also reinforce social relations between them, often based on personal ties.

Intra-industry trade Trade in similar goods between countries of similar levels of economic development.

Islam Monotheistic religion based on the teachings of the prophet Muhammad, as revealed in the Koran; followers are referred to as Muslims.

ISO 9000 Quality standards, for which companies can apply to be certified by bodies accredited by the International Organization for Standardization.

Joint venture A formal arrangement between two or more organizations, which may be based in different countries, which results in the formation of a new entity in which each invests.

Judaism Ancient monotheistic religion, predominant in the modern state of Israel.

Just-in-time (JIT) manufacturing System of production which relies on a continuous flow of materials.

Keiretsu Loose groupings of Japanese companies, usually centred on a main bank, built on cross-shareholdings and personal relations.

Labour productivity Calculation which divides output by the hours worked per person.

Lean production Systems and techniques of production enabling companies to reduce waste, leading to greater flexibility in production processes and products.

Lean supply chain Integrated approach which emphasizes the elimination of waste at every stage in the supply chain.

Legal risk Uncertainties surrounding legal liabilities, their implementation in differing legal systems, and the observance of fairness and impartiality in judicial proceedings.

Leveraged buyout (LBO) Purchase of a controlling stake in a company, financed by borrowing.

Liberal market economy Capitalist economic system, in which supply and demand, as well as prices, are determined by free markets for goods and services.

Location advantages Factor endowments of a particular country or area within a country, which offers specific benefits to the potential foreign investor.

Logistics Management of processes for moving materials and products within a supply chain.

Low-context culture Culture in which information is conveyed predominantly by explicit expression.

Macroeconomics Study of whole economic systems, in particular, national economies.

Manufacturing cells Arrangement of workers into teams, each of which has responsibility for manufacture and inspection of a specific product or component.

Marketing concept An organizational focus on identifying the needs of consumers and satisfying those needs.

Marketing mix Set of co-ordinated marketing tools focusing on the four Ps (product, promotion, price and place), designed to satisfy the needs of targeted consumers.

Mass customization Production of a diversity of products utilizing mass-production techniques.

Matrix structure Organizational structure involving two lines of authority, such as area and product divisions.

Merchandise trade Trade in goods, including agricultural products; fuels and mining products; and manufactured goods.

Merger Agreement between two or more companies to form a new company, in which the constituent companies are subsumed.

Microeconomics Study of economic activity at the level of individuals and enterprises.

Moderate poverty Defined by the World Bank as living on between $1 and $2 a day.

Modular manufacturing Strategy of designing and using a component in a variety of end products.

Monopolistic competition Situation in which there are many producers producing products in the same class, where competition is based on product differentiation within the class.

Monopoly Domination by one firm of the market for particular goods or services, enabling the firm to determine price and supply.

Monotheistic religion Religion based on belief in one god.

Most favoured nation (MFN) principle Principle under which a country allows imports from all countries on terms equivalent to the most preferential.

Multidivisional structure Organizational structure characterized by separate business units based on products or geographical areas, which are co-ordinated by the parent company's head office.

Multinational enterprise (MNE) An organization or set of organizational relations co-ordinating business activities across national borders.

Multinational model In Bartlett and Ghoshal's typology, a model of the international company based on autonomous national units.

Multiparty system System in which many parties represent a wide spectrum of views, and where the government is likely to be a coalition of parties.

National budget balance The extent to which public spending exceeds receipts from taxes and other sources.

National culture Culture, including a sense of identity and belonging, which distinguishes and unites people, linking them to a territorial homeland, usually a nation-state.

National government Formal institutions by which sovereign lawmaking authority is exercised in a country.

National legal system System of substantive law and court structure, which is administered and enforced by state authorities.

Network Broad category of both intra-firm and inter-firm links. They may involve individuals, teams and whole organizations.

Network organization Organization in which informal relational ties are nurtured, both internally and with other organizations and individuals with which it interacts.

New sovereigntist approach Approach to international relations which emphasizes state sovereignty and views international law and multilateral agreements as threats to sovereignty.

Niche market Subgroup of consumers with specific specialized needs.

Non-executive directors Officers who sit on the board as independent directors, not employed in management positions.

Non-governmental organization (NGO) Voluntary organization formed by private individuals for a particular shared purpose.

Nonverbal communication Gestures and facial expressions which convey meaning within a particular linguistic context.

Official development assistance (ODA) Funds and other types of government aid provided to foreign countries, often as part of an aid package which also includes trade provisions.

Offshoring Contracting out of a business process to another country, the main motivation usually being to benefit from its low-cost environment.

Oligopoly An industry dominated by a few very large firms.

Organizational or corporate culture Values and practices of an organization in relations with its stakeholders.

Original equipment manufacturer (OEM) A somewhat misleading term, which designates a focal manufacturer in a supply chain, who assembles final products destined for end consumer.

Outsourcing Shifting of an operation or process by one organization to another, under a contractual agreement, usually designed to reduce costs for the organization shedding the activity.

Ownership advantages Resources specific to the firm, such as technology, managing skills and marketing skills.

Parent-country national (PCN) National of the home country of a parent company, who takes on a management role in foreign operations.

Patent Intellectual property right for inventions, which is granted by patent authorities for a term of years, following rigorous examination; it gives the patent holder the right to exploit the product or process commercially, or license others to do so, on payment of royalties.

Pegged exchange rate Linking the exchange rate of a currency to another currency, often with some degree of movement allowed.

Performance-related pay Payments made to employees in addition to salary, which are for specific tasks performed or targets met.

Personnel management Administrative systems and processes for managing workers, including job descriptions, employee selection, rewards, training and appraisal.

PEST analysis Analysis of the political, economic, sociocultural and technological dimensions of a country, which is carried out by firms considering international expansion.

Philanthropy Donation of resources to recipients deemed to be good causes in the eyes of the donor, with no expected material return.

Planned economy Economic system in which the supply and price of goods and services are controlled by central planning authorities of the state.

Political party Organization of people with similar political perspectives, which aims to put forward candidates for office and influence government policies.

Political risk Uncertainties associated with location and exercise of power within a country and from forces outside its borders.

Political system Structures and processes by which a nation-state is governed.

Polycentrism Perspective of individuals and organizations which recognizes their own culture as one among many, and strives to understand differing cultures.

Pollution Release of harmful substances from a source through air, soil or water.

Polytheistic religion Religion based on belief in numerous gods or other deities.

Portfolio investment Financial investment in an overseas company without a view to obtaining control over management decision-making.

Private brand Brands owned by supermarkets and other retailers, which are produced for sale in their outlets alone; also known as 'private labels' and 'own brands'.

Private company Registered company in which shares are not tradable and which is subject to lower levels of public disclosure of information than the public company.

Private equity fund Investment fund managed on behalf of wealthy investors, usually structured as a partnership and lasting a fixed number of years.

Privatization The process of converting a state-owned entity into a company in which private investors are invited to buy shares.

Product Goods (tangible), services (intangible), or a combination of the two, which a firm offers to potential customers in exchange for payment, usually money.

Product differentiation Differences in attributes between products in the same class.

Production under licence Process whereby the production of goods subject to patent, brand or other intellectual property rights is contracted out to another firm under terms agreed with the owner of the rights.

Promotion All types of marketing communication; one of the four Ps in the marketing mix.

Protectionism Government approach to trade policy which seeks to shield domestic industries from competition from trade.

Public company Registered company in which all or a portion of shares are tradable, usually on a stock exchange; subject to a high level of public disclosure of corporate information.

Quality Degree to which a product or service meets the needs and expectations of customers.

Quality circle Small group of workers which meets regularly to identify problems and discuss solutions.

Real interest rate A country's interest rate adjusted for inflation, by subtracting the inflation rate from the nominal interest rate (which is that actually offered by lenders).

Refugee A person forced to leave his or her own country, for any of a number of reasons, including natural disaster and civil war.

Regional trade agreements (RTAs) Multilateral agreements which provide for preferential trade terms between member countries.

Regional trade bloc Group of countries within a region which aims to establish preferential arrangements for trade within the group; the bloc usually forms an organization or forum which meets regularly.

Registered company Entity formed through registration with national authorities, which enjoys legal status separate from the owners and limited liability for the company's obligations.

Remittances Money sent back to home countries by migrant workers.

Research and development (R&D) Science and technology directed towards new and improved products and processes.

Reward system Comprehensive system of monetary and non-monetary rewards provided for staff in return for the work they perform for the organization.

Rule of law Primacy of laws over the will of individuals, including both rulers and ruled.

Securities Financial instruments of ownership, debt obligation or future rights, which can be traded.

Segmentation Division of a consumer market into groups of similar consumers who share some key characteristics, such as socioeconomic grouping, cultural identity or demographic similarity.

Separation of powers Constitutional principle by which each branch of government – executive, legislative and judicial – has limited express authority.

Six sigma A quality control system which focuses on improvements in measurable performance through cost reductions and elimination of defects.

Social cohesion Shared sense of belonging to a society despite cultural differences.

Social enterprise A business formed for social objectives, in which revenues from trading in goods or services are largely reinvested for its social purposes.

Social entrepreneur Person whose creative talent and business flair are directed towards an enterprise focused on achieving specific social goals.

Social market economy Capitalist economic system which seeks to combine a market approach with social justice priorities.

Socialization Processes, both formal and informal, by which employees become imbued with a company's culture and norms of behaviour.

Sovereign wealth fund Fund held by a sovereign state, often from accumulated reserves, which may be invested in global markets, often through a state-owned investment company.

Spillover effects Opportunities for local firms to benefit from FDI, gaining technological competence which generates new local businesses and technological capacities.

Spot contract Transaction in which the terms, including the exchange rate, are agreed and performed almost immediately.

Staffing Processes for selecting and allocating staff to particular posts within the organization, in keeping with corporate goals.

Stakeholder Individual, organization or interest which affects the company or is affected by the company.

Stock option Right to buy shares at a set price and within a specific time period.

Structural unemployment Loss in jobs due to changes in technology or shifting of operations to another location.

Sub-brand Brand created to serve a distinctive product or market segment under the umbrella of the firm's corporate brand.

Subculture Culture which distinguishes a minority grouping in a state where a different national culture is dominant.

Supply chain management (SCM) The integration of business processes which encompass all stages of the production process for goods or services, from the supply of raw materials to the delivery of the product to the end consumer.

Sustainable development Development that meets the needs of the present without compromising the ability of future generations meet their own needs.

Swap Financial instrument which allows a firm to customize terms to its advantage by swapping them with another party.

Tacit knowledge Intangible elements, such as skills and know-how, which help in the understanding and application of the tangible elements.

Target marketing Marketing aimed at satisfying the needs of a particular group of consumers.

Tariff A charge on imports or exports, but most often, an import duty.

Technology Systematic application of scientific knowledge to practical purposes.

Third-country national (TCN) Person employed by a parent company to work in its foreign operations, who is neither a national of the parent's home country nor the host country.

Third-party verification The use of independent specialist bodies for the measurement of a firm's environmental performance.

Total quality management (TQM) Approach to quality which commits the entire organization to continuous improvement principles and extends to supply chain partners.

Trademark Distinctive logo or brand applied to a product, which can be registered with national authorities, legally prohibiting its use without permission of the owner.

Training and development The building of competencies and skills of individual employees, to enable them to improve work performance and achieve organizational goals.

Transboundary pollution Pollution which extends across national boundaries, sometimes great distances from the source.

Transfer pricing Pricing of products traded internally within the MNE, such as between subsidiaries, often with the aim of maximizing financial benefits to the parent company.

Transition economy A country which is changing its economy from a state-planned system to a market-based one.

Translation risk Risk associated with the translation of accounts prepared in a local currency into the currency of the home country of an MNE.

Transnational manager Manager able to understand and adapt to a range of cultural environments.

Triad The three traditional trading centres, comprising the US, Japan and Europe.

Triple bottom line reporting Corporate reporting focusing on social and environmental aspects of the company, in addition to traditional financial information.

Turnaround Radical change in a poorly performing organization, involving rationalization and cost reductions.

Two-party system System in which two broadly based parties dominate, alternating between government and opposition, reflecting electoral fortunes.

Urbanization The process of large-scale shift from a rural to urban environment.

Value chain Concept which identifies the value created at each stage in a production process.

Value-based pricing Price based on buyers' perceptions of value.

Voluntary export restraint (VER) Self-imposed limitation which an exporter sets on goods it exports in a particular class, usually at the behest of the importing country.

Work–life balance Allocation of time and commitment between work and personal life, which reflects the personal needs of the employee.

Works council Representative bodies organized at workplace level, which give employees rights to information and consultation in personnel and other business-related issues within the firm.

References

Abegglen, J. and Stalk, G. (1985) *Kaisha: The Japanese Corporation* (New York: Basic Books).

Aglionby, J. (2007) 'Indonesia seeks to curb expat bank jobs', *Financial Times*, 2 May.

Anderson, B. (1991) *Imagined Communities* (London: Verso).

Antràs, P. (2003) 'Firms, contracts, and trade structure', *The Quarterly Journal of Economics*, **118**(4): 1375–418.

Archibugi, D. and Michie, J. (1997) 'Technological globalisation or national systems of innovation?' in Archibugi, D. and Michie, J. (eds) *Technology, Globalisation and Economic Performance* (Cambridge: Cambridge University Press) pp. 1–23.

Asian Corporate Governance Association (2007) Corporate Governance Watch 2007, www.acga-asia.org.

Atkins, R. and Williamson, H. (2004) 'Germany puts extra hours into keeping domestic jobs', *Financial Times*, 30 June.

Banerjee, S. (2002) 'Corporate environmentalism: The construct and its measurement', *Journal of Business Research*, **55**: 177–91.

Barkema, H., Bell, J. and Pennings, J. (1996) 'Foreign entry, cultural barriers and learning', *Strategic Management Journal*, **17**(2): 151–66.

Barney, J. (1986) 'Organizational culture: Can it be a source of sustained competitive advantage?' *Academy of Management Review*, **11**(3): 656–65.

Barney, J. (1991) 'Firm resources and sustained competitive advantage', *Journal of Management*, **17**(1): 99–120.

Bartlett, C.A. and Ghoshal, S. (1990) 'Matrix management: Not a structure, a frame of mind', *Harvard Business Review*, **90**(4): 138–45.

Bartlett, C.A. and Ghoshal, S. (1993) 'Beyond the M-form: Toward a managerial theory of the firm', *Strategic Management Journal*, **14**: 23–46.

Bartlett, C.A. and Ghoshal, S. (1998) *Managing Across Borders: A Transnational Solution*, 2nd edn (London: Random House).

Bebchuk, L. (2005) 'The case for increasing shareholder power', *Harvard Law Review*, **118**: 833–917.

Bebchuk, L. and Grinstein, Y. (2005) 'The growth of executive pay', *Oxford Review of Economic Policy*, **21**: 283–303.

Bebchuk, L. and Peyer, U. (2007) 'Lucky CEOs', Harvard Law School discussion paper no. 566, www.law.harvard.edu.

Beetham, D. (1991) *The Legitimation of Power* (Basingstoke: Macmillan – now Palgrave Macmillan).

Berggren, C. (1996) 'Building a truly global organization: ABB and the problems of integrating a multi-domestic enterprise', *Scandinavian Journal of Management*, **12**(2): 123–37.

Bergmann, M., Mangaleswaran, R. and Mercer, G. (2004) 'Global sourcing in the auto industry', *McKinsey Quarlerly*, special edition, pp. 42–51.

Bergsten, F. (2006) 'Plan B for world trade: Go regional', *Financial Times*, 16 August.

Berle, A. and Means, G. (1932) *The Modern Corporation and Private Property* (New York: Macmillan).

Betts, P. (2006) 'The capitalist divide on either side of the Rhine', *Financial Times*, 7 July.

Bhagwati, J. (2006) 'Why Asia must opt for open regionalism on trade', *Financial Times*, 3 November.

Birchall, J. (2007) 'Sacked Manila factory workers hit at Wal-Mart', *Financial Times*, 16 April.

Blas, J. (2007a) 'Falling US dollar puts pressure on the buying power of Opec nations', *Financial Times*, 24 July.

Blas, J. (2007b) 'Global hunger set to worsen, FAO warns', *Financial Times*, 18 December.

Borsuk, R., Goad, G. and Phillips, M. (1999) 'IMF admits errors in Asian crisis, but defends its tight-money policy', *Wall Street Journal*, 20 January.

Boxall, P. and Purcell, J. (2003) *Strategy and Human Resource Management* (Basingstoke: Palgrave Macmillan).

Bratton, J. and Gold, J. (2007) *Human Resource Management*, 4th edn (Basingstoke: Palgrave Macmillan).

Bratton, W. (2001) 'Berle and Means reconsidered at the century's turn', *The Journal of Corporation Law*, **26**: 737–70.

Breton, T. (2006) 'It is the stakeholders' duty to assess mergers', *Financial Times*, 6 February.

Brewster, C. (1995) 'Towards a European model of human resource management', *Journal of International Business Studies*, **26**: 1–22.

Brinkmann-Braun, J. and Pies, I. (2007) 'The Global Compact's contribution to global governance revisited', discussion paper no. 2007-10, Martin-Luther-Universität, Halle-Wittenberg, http://ssrn.com.

Brousseau, E. (2004) 'Property rights on the internet: Is a specific institutional framework needed?', *Economics of Innovation and New Technology*, **13**(5): 489–507.

Brown, S. and Cousins, P. (2004) 'Supply and operations: Parallel paths and integrated strategies', *British Journal of Management*, **15**(4): 303–20.

Brown, S., Lamming, R., Bessant, J. and Jones, P. (2005) *Strategic Operations Management*, 2nd edn (Oxford: Elsevier).

Bruce, M. and Daly, L. (2004) 'Lean or agile: A solution for supply chain management in the textiles and clothing industry?', *International Journal of Operations & Production Management*, **24**(2): 151–70.

Bruce, R. (2007) 'New pressure on private equity to go public', *Financial Times*, 15 February.

Buckley, N. (2005) 'The power of original thinking', *Financial Times*, 14 January.

Buckley, P., Glaister, K. and Husan, R. (2002) 'International joint ventures: Partnering skills and cross-cultural issues', *Long Range Planning*, **35**: 113–34.

Buckley, P. and Ghauri, P. (2004) 'Globalisation, economic geography and the strategy of multinational enterprises', *Journal of International Business Studies*, **35**(2): 81–98.

Budhwar, P. and Debrah, Y. (2001) 'Rethinking comparative and cross national human resource management research', *International Journal of Human Resource Management*, **12**(3): 497–515.

Budhwar, P. and Debrah, Y. (2005) 'International HRM in developing countries', in Scullion, H. and Linehan, M. (eds) *International Human Resource Management* (Basingstoke: Palgrave Macmillan) pp. 259–78.

Budzinski, O. (2004) 'The international competition network: Prospects and limits on the road towards international competition governance', *Competition & Change*, **8**(3): 223–42.

Burton, J. (2007) 'Singapore's wealth fund flattered by imitation', *Financial Times*, 5 September.

Cabinet Office (2007) 'Social enterprise background', www.cabinetoffice.gov.uk.

Cafod (Catholic Agency for Overseas Development) (2004) *Working Conditions in the Electronics Industry*, www.cafod.org.uk.

Carroll, A. (1991) 'The pyramid of corporate social responsibility: Toward the moral management of organizational stakeholders', *Business Horizons*, **34**: 39–48.

Carter, M. (2004) 'Advertising for families acting under the influence', *Financial Times*, 26 October.

Castells, M. (2000) *The Rise of the Network Society*, 2nd edn (Oxford: Blackwells).

Cecchetti, S. (2006) 'Core inflation is an unreliable guide', *Financial Times*, 12 September.

Chaing, F. and Birtch, T. (2005) 'A taxonomy of reward preference: Examining country preferences', *Journal of International Management*, **11**(3): 357–75.

Chen, S. and Ravallion, M. (2007) 'Absolute poverty measures for the developing world, 1981–2004', World Bank policy research working paper, no. WPS4211, http://econ.worldbank.org.

Chandler, A. (1962) *Strategy and Structure: Chapters in the History of the Industrial Enterprise* (Cambridge, MA: MIT Press).

Charlton, A. and Stiglitz, J. (2005) 'A development-friendly prioritisation of Doha round proposals', *World Economy*, **28**(3): 293–312.

Chen, H. and Chen, T. (1998) 'Network linkages and location choice in foreign direct investment', *Journal of International Business Studies*, **29**(3): 445–68.

Cienski, J. (2006) 'Exodus of Polish workers leaves vacuum for others', *Financial Times*, 29 August.

Clegg, A. (2005) 'Why it pays to put the workers in the picture', *Financial Times*, 6 April.

Collier, P. (2006) 'Africa's three main problems and how to fix them', *Financial Times*, 21 December.

Committee for Economic Development (1971) *Social Responsibilities of Business Corporations* (New York: Committee for Economic Development).

Conner, K. and Prahalad, C. (1996) 'A resource-based theory of the firm: Knowledge versus opportunism', *Organization Science*, **7**(5): 477–501.

CorporateRegister (2004) 'Towards transparency: Progress on global sustainability reporting, 2004', www.CorporateRegister.com.

Dana, L. (2000) 'Culture is of the essence in Asia', Mastering Management, *Financial Times*, 27 November.

Davis, S., Haltiwager, J. and Schuh, S. (1996) *Job Creation and Destruction* (Cambridge, MA: MIT Press).

Dawar, N. and Chattopadhyay, A. (200) 'The new language of emerging markets', *Financial Times*, 13 November.

DBRR (Department of Business, Enterprise and Regulatory Reform) (2006) Companies Act 2006, www.dti.gov.uk.

De Jonquieres, G. (2006) 'China's industrial policy should think small', *Financial Times*, 7 September.

Deming, W. (1986) *Out of the Crisis* (Cambridge, MA: MIT Press).

Diamond, L. (1993) 'Three paradoxes of democracy', in Diamond. L. and Plattner, M. (eds) *The Global Resurgence of Democracy* (Baltimore: The Johns Hopkins University Press) pp. 95–107.

Dicken, P., Kelly, P., Olds, K. and Yeung, H. (2001) 'Chains and networks, territories and scales: Towards a relational framework for analysing the global economy', *Global Networks*, **1**(2): 89–112.

Dicken, P. (2003) *Global Shift*, 4th edn (London: Sage).

Dollar, D. (2004) 'Globalization, poverty, and inequality since 1980', World Bank policy research working paper, no. 3333, http://econ.worldbank.org.

Donkin, R., (2005) 'Hopes for an improved dialogue in the workplace', *Financial Times*, 31 March.

Doz, Y. and Prahalad, C. (1988) 'A process model of strategic redirection in large complex firms: The case of multinational corporations', in Pettigrew, A. (ed.) *The Management of Strategic Change* (Oxford: Basil Blackwell) pp. 63–83.

Drucker, P. (1990) 'The emerging theory of manufacturing', *Harvard Business Review*, **68**(3): 94–102.

Dunning, J. (1993a) *Multinational Enterprises and the Global Economy* (Wokingham: Addison Wesley).

Dunning, J. (1993b) *The Globalization of Business* (London: Routledge).

Dunning, J. (1993c) 'Internationalizing Porter's diamond', *Management International Review*, **33**(2): 7–15.

Eckbo, E. (2004) 'CEO elections out of shareholders' control', *Financial Times*, 17 August.

EICC (Electronic Industry Citizenship Coalition) (2005) 'Electronic Industry Code of Conduct', Version 2, www.eicc.info.

ECGI (European Corporate Governance Institute) (2007) *Proportionality between Ownership and Control of EU Listed Companies*, www.ecgi.org.

Fifield, A. (2004) 'Sheer adrenalin for LG Electronics' image', *Financial Times*, 16 December.

Financial Times (2007) 'Handset outsourcing', *Financial Times*, 20 June.

Francks, P. (1992) *Japanese Economic Development* (London: Routledge).

FRC (Financial Reporting Council) (2006) *The Combined Code of Corporate Governance 2006*, www.frc.org.uk.

Freeman, C. (1997) 'The "national system of innovation" in historical perspective', in Archibugi, D. and Michie, J. (eds) *Technology, Globalisation and Economic Performance* (Cambridge: Cambridge University Press) pp. 24–49.

Freeman, R.E. (1984) *Strategic Management: A Stakeholder Approach* (Boston, MA: Pitman).

Friedman, M. (1970) 'The social responsibility of business is to increase its profits', *New York Times Magazine*, 13 September, pp. 32–3.

Friedman, T.L. (1999) *The Lexus and the Olive Tree* (New York: HarperCollins).

Galbraith, K. (1958) *The Affluent Society* (New York: Houghton Mifflin).

Gapper, J. (2007) 'Companies feel benefit of intangibles', *Financial Times*, 23 April.

Gates, B. (2004), cited in Sherman, A., 'How to protect your property', *Financial Times*, 12 November.

Gerlach, M. (1992) *Alliance Capitalism: The Social Organization of Japanese Business* (Berkeley: University of California Press).

Ghemawat, P. (2001) 'Distance still matters' *Harvard Business Review*, **79**(8):137–46.

Ghoshal, S. and Bartlett, C. (1990) 'The multinational corporation as an interorganizational network', *Academy of Management Review*, **15**(4): 603–25.

Ghoshal, S. and Bartlett, C. (1995) 'Building the entrepreneurial corporation: New organizational processes, new managerial tasks', *European Management Journal*, **13**(2): 139–55.

Giles, C. (2007) 'Economists' rule change puts US on top of world', *Financial Times*, 1 November.

Gilpin, R. (2002) 'A realist perspective on international governance', in Held, D. and McGrew, A. (eds) *Governing Globalization* (Cambridge: Polity Press) pp. 237–48.

Giving USA Foundation (2007) *Giving USA 2007*, www.aafrc.org.

Global Entrepreneurship Consortium (2007) *Global Entrepreneurship Monitor 2006*, www.gemconsortium.org.

Goetzmann, W., Li, F. and Rouwenhorst, K.G. (2001) 'Long-term market correlations', NBER working paper no. W8612, http://papers.ssrn.com.

Goldsmith, J. and Wu, T. (2006) 'Digital borders', *Legal Affairs*, January/February, www.legalaffairs.org.

Gray, J. (2003) *Al Qaeda and What it Means to be Modern* (London: Faber and Faber).

GRI (Global Reporting Initiative) (2006) *Sustainability Reporting Guidelines*, Version 3, www.globalreporting.org.

Guerrera, F. and Politi, J. (2007) 'Life on the other side', *Financial Times*, 24 April.

Guha, K. (2007) 'IMF plans currency crackdown', *Financial Times*, 19 June.

Guha, K., Guerrera, F., Callan, E. et al. (2006) 'Gilded age: How a corporate elite is leaving middle America behind', *Financial Times*, 21 December.

Hakansson, H. and Ford, D. (2002) 'How should companies interact in business networks?', *Journal of Business Research*, **55**: 133–9.

Hall, E.T. (1976) *Beyond Culture* (New York: Doubleday).

Halliday, F. (2000) 'Global governance: Prospects and problems', in Held, D. and McGrew, A. (eds) *The Global Transformations Reader* (Cambridge: Polity Press) pp. 431–41.

Hamel, G. and Prahalad, C. (1989) 'Strategic intent', *Harvard Business Review*, **67**(3): 63–78.

Hamel, G. and Prahalad, C. (1994) *Competing for the Future* (Boston, MA: Harvard Business School Press).

Hargreaves, D. (2003) '"A sense of protectionist fervour": Why are stock markets signalling a retreat from globalisation?', *Financial Times*, 22 April.

Harry, W. (2003) 'Expatriates', in Tayeb, M. (ed.) *International Management* (Harlow: Pearson) pp. 282–306.

Hart, S.L. (1995) 'A natural-resource-based view of the firm', *Academy of Management Review*, **20**(4): 874–907.

Harvey, F. (2006a) 'An inhuman race: How the lure of the city is rapidly swelling the world's slums', *Financial Times*, 7 August.

Harvey, F. (2006b) 'Survival in a changing world', FT Sustainable Business, *Financial Times*, 9 October.

Harvey, F. (2007) 'Yo, Kyoto', *Financial Times*, 2 October.

Hayashi, Y. (2007) 'Japan adds factories at home', *The Wall Street Journal*, 12 June.

Held, D. (1993) 'From city-states to a cosmopolitan order?' in Held, D. (ed.) *Prospects for Democracy* (Cambridge: Polity Press) pp. 13–25.

Held, D. (2006) 'Reframing global governance: Apocalypse soon or reform!', *New Political Economy*, **11**(2): 157–76.

Held., D., McGrew, A., Goldblatt, D. and Perraton, J. (1999) *Global Transformations: Politics, Economics and Culture* (Cambridge: Polity Press).

HM Treasury (2006) *Stern Review on the Economics of Climate Change*, www.hm-treasury.gov.uk.

Hofstede, G. (1994) *Cultures and Organizations: Software of the Mind* (London: HarperCollins).

Hofstede, G. (1996) 'Images of Europe: Past, present and future', in Joynt, P. and Warner, M. (eds) *Managing Across Cultures: Issues and Perspectives* (London: International Thomson Business Press) pp. 147–65.

Hofstede, G. (1999) 'The business of business is culture', in Buckley, P. and Ghauri, P. (eds) *The Internationalization of the Firm*, 2nd edn (London: International Thomson Business Press) pp. 381–93.

Holbeche, L. (1999) 'International teamworking', in Joynt, P. and Morton, B. (eds) *The Global HR Manager* (London: CIPD) pp. 179–206.

Hollinger, P. (2005) 'France bets all on picking winners', *Financial Times*, 24 June.

Holt, D., Quelch, J. and Taylor, E. (2004) 'How model behaviour brings market power', *Financial Times*, 23 August.

House of Commons Library (2006) 'The Company Law Reform Bill', House of Commons Research Paper 06/30, www.parliament.uk/commons.

Hoyos, C. (2007) 'The new seven sisters: Oil and gas giants that dwarf the west's top producers', *Financial Times*, 12 March.

Hui, M., Au, K. and Fock, H. (2004) 'Empowerment across cultures', *Journal of International Business Studies*, **35**(1): 46–60.

Hunter, J. (2003) 'Determinants of business success under "hypocapitalism": Case studies of Russian firms and their strategies', *Journal of Business Research*, **56**: 113–20.

Huntington, S. (1993) 'Democracy's third wave', in Diamond, L. and Plattner, M. (eds) *The Global Resurgence of Democracy* (Baltimore: The Johns Hopkins University Press) pp. 3–25.

Huo, Y. and McKinley, W. (1992) 'Nation as a context for strategy: The effects of national characteristics on business-level strategies', *Management International Review*, **32**(2): 103–13.

Husted, B. and Salazar, J. (2006) 'Taking Friedman seriously: Maximizing profits and social performance', *Journal of Management Studies*, **43**(1): 75–91.

Hutchinson, K., Quinn, B. and Alexander, N. (2005) 'The internationalisation of small to medium-sized retail companies: Towards a conceptual framework', *Journal of Marketing Management*, **21**: 149–79.

Hymer, S. (1975) 'The multinational corporation and the law of uneven development', in Radice, H. (ed.) *International Firms and Modern Imperialism* (Harmondsworth: Penguin) pp. 37–62.

IASB (International Accounting Standards Board) (2007) 'India announces convergence with IFRS for public entities from 2011', 24 July, www.iasb.org.

ICA (International Co-operative Alliance) (2007) 'Co-operative identity, principles and values', www.ica.coop/coop/principles.html.

IEA (International Energy Agency) (2006) *World Energy Outlook 2006*, www.worldenergyoutlook.org.

Ietto-Gillies, G. (2003) 'The role of transnational corporations in the globalisation process', in Michie, J. (ed.) *Handbook of Globalisation* (Cheltenham: Edward Elgar) pp. 139–49.

ILO (International Labour Organization) (2006) *Core Labour Standards Handbook*, www.ilo.org.

Imai, M. (1986) *Kaizen* (Singapore: The Kaizen Institute).

IMD (International Institute for Management Development) (2007) *World Competitiveness Yearbook* (Lausanne: IMD).

IMF (International Monetary Fund) (2004) *Global Financial Stability Report* (Washington, DC: IMF).

Jack, A. (2007) 'Beyond charity? A new generation enters the business of doing good', *Financial Times*, 5 April.

Jeannet, J.-P. and Hennessey, H.-D. (1998) *Global Marketing Strategies*, 4th edn (Boston: Houghton Mifflin).

Jenny, F. (2003) 'Competition law and policy: Global governance issues', *World Competition*, **26**(4): 609–24.

Johanson, J. and Vahne, J.-E. (1999) 'The internationalization process of the firm: A model of knowledge development and increasing foreign market commitments', in Buckley, P. and Ghauri, P. (eds) *The Internationalization of the Firm: A Reader*, 2nd edn (London: International Thomson Business Press) pp. 43–54.

Johanson, J. and Wiedersheim-Paul, F. (1999) 'The internationalization of the firm: Four Swedish cases', in Buckley, P. and Ghauri, P. (eds) *The Internationalization of the Firm: A Reader*, 2nd edn (London: International Thomson Business Press) pp. 27–42.

Johnson, C. (1982) *MITI and the Japanese Miracle* (Stanford: Stanford University Press).

Johnson, C. (2006) *Nemesis* (New York: Metropolitan Books).

Johnson, E. (2004) 'Harnessing the power of partnerships', *Financial Times Mastering Innovation*, 8 October, pp. 4–5.

Johnson, J. (2008a) 'Environmentalists fear cost as Tata brings motoring to the masses', *Financial Times*, 9 January.

Johnson, J. (2008b) 'Western donors wrestle with the contradictions of rising India', *Financial Times*, 23 January.

Jopson, B. (2005) 'Debt rises up the agenda as IFRS brings balance sheets into focus', *Financial Times*, 16 June.

Jorde, T. and Teece. J. (1989) 'Competition and cooperation: Striking the right balance', *California Management Review*, **31**(3): 25–37.

Juran, J. (1995) *A History of Management for Quality: The Evolution, Trends, and Future Directions of Managing for Quality* (Wisconsin: ASQC Quality Press).

Kanbur, R. and Lustig, N. (1999) 'Why is inequality back on the agenda?', paper at the World Bank Conference on Development Economics, Washington, DC, 28–30 April.

Kazmin, A. (2007) 'Calling the shots', *Financial Times*, 16 August.

Kekic, L. (2006) 'A pause in democracy's march', *The Economist: The World in 2007*, pp. 93–4.

Keohane, R. (1984) *After Hegemony* (Princeton: Princeton University Press).

Kluckhohn, F. and Strodtbeck, F. (1961) *Variations in Value Orientations* (Westport, CT: Greenwood Press).

Knight, G. and Cavusgil, S. (2004) 'Innovation, organizational capabilities, and the born-global firm', *Journal of International Business Studies*, **35**(2): 124–41.

Kobrin, S. (1997) 'The architecture of globalization: State sovereignty in a networked global economy', in Dunning, J.

(ed.) *Governments, Globalization and International Business* (Oxford: OUP) pp. 147–71.

Kogut, B. (2000) 'The network as knowledge: generative rules and the emergence of structure', *Strategic Management Journal*, **21**: 405–25.

Kogut, B. (2005) 'Who good causes need governance reform', Mastering Corporate Governance, *Financial Times*, 10 June, pp. 6–8.

Kogut, B. and Singh, H. (1988) 'The effect of national culture on the choice of entry mode', *Journal of International Business Studies*, **19**(3): 411–32.

Kogut, B. and Zander, U. (2003) 'Knowledge of the firm and the evolutionary theory of the multinational corporation', *Journal of International Business Studies*, **34**(6): 625–45

Kotabe, M. (1998) 'Efficiency vs. effectiveness: Orientation of global sourcing strategy: A comparison of US and Japanese multinational companies', *Academy of Management Executive*, **12**(4): 107–19.

Kotler, P., Armstrong, G., Saunders, J. and Wong, V. (2002) *Principles of Marketing*, 3rd European edn (London: Prentice Hall Europe).

Kumar, N. and Steenkemp, J.-B. (2007) *Private Label Strategy: How to Meet the Store Brand Challenge* (Boston: Harvard Business School Press).

Kozul-Wright, R. (1995) 'The myth of Anglo-Saxon capitalism: Reconstructing the history of the American state', in Chang, H.J. and Rowthorn, R. (eds) *The Role of the State in Economic Change* (Oxford: Clarendon Press) pp. 81–113.

Krugman, P. (1995) 'Growing world trade: Causes and consequences', Brookings Papers on Economic Activity, **1**: 327–77.

Krugman, P. (1999) 'Was it all in Ohlin?', October, http://web.mit.edu/Krugman.

Kyriakidou, O. (2005) 'Operational aspects of international human resource management', in Özbilgin, M. (ed.) *International Human Resource Management* (Basingstoke: Palgrave Macmillan) pp. 103–24.

Lafontaine, F. (1999) 'Myths and strengths of franchising', in Mastering Strategy, *Financial Times*, 22 November.

Lamy, P. (2006) 'Doha's final deadline', *The Economist: The World in 2007*, p. 150.

Larsen, P. (2006) 'Emerging markets bite back', *Financial Times*, 29 November.

Larsen, P. (2007) 'Private equity bids keep on growing', *Financial Times*, 28 March.

Latinobarómetro (2007) Latin American democracy survey, www.latinobarometro.org.

Leahy, J. (2007) 'Unleashed: Why Indian companies are setting their sights on western rivals', *Financial Times*, 7 February.

Lee, Y. and Gordon, R. (2005) 'Tax structure and economic growth', *Journal of Public Economics*, **89**(5–6): 1027–43.

Letza, S., Sun, X. and Kirkbride, J. (2004) 'Shareholding versus stakeholding: A critical review of corporate governance', *Corporate Governance*, **12**(3): 242–62.

Levitt, T. ([1983]1995) 'The globalization of markets', in Ghauri, P. and Prasad, S. (eds) *International Management: A Reader* (London: Dryden Press) pp. 21–32.

Levitt, T. ([1960] 2004) 'Marketing myopia', *Harvard Business Review*, **82**(7/8): 138–49.

Leys, S. (1978) *Chinese Shadows* (Harmondsworth: Penguin).

Lieberman, M.B. and Montgomery, D.B. (1988) 'First-mover advantages', *Strategic Management Journal*, **9**: 41–58.

Liebreich, M. (2007) 'How to save the planet: Be nice, retaliatory, forgiving & clear', New Energy Finance White Paper, www.newenergyfinance.com.

Linz, J. (1993) 'Perils of presidentialism', in Diamond, L. and Plattner, M. (eds) *The Global Resurgence of Democracy* (Baltimore: The Johns Hopkins University Press) pp. 108–26.

López, H. and Fajinzylber, P. (2006) *Close to Home: The Development and Impact of Remittances in Latin America*, World Bank Report, www.worldbank.org/lac.

Luce, E. (2006) 'Out on a limb: why blue-collar Americans see their future as precarious', *Financial Times*, 3 May.

Luce, E. and Merchant, K. (2004) 'The logic is inescapable: Why India believes commercial imperatives will help it beat the offshoring backlash', *Financial Times*, 28 January.

Luo, Y. (2003) 'Market-seeking MNEs in an emerging market: How parent-subsidiary links shape overseas success', *Journal of International Business Studies*, 34: 290–309.

Maddison, A. (2001) *The World Economy: A Millennial Perspective* (Paris: OECD).

Maguad, B. (2006) 'The modern quality movement: Origins, development and trends', *Total Quality Management*, **17**(2): 179–203.

Mallet, V. (2006) 'Welcome to megacity', *Financial Times*, 5 August.

Masters, B. and Guerrera, F. (2006) 'Foreign companies faring worse in US law courts', *Financial Times*, 13 December.

McAleese, D. (2001) *Economics for Business* (Harlow: Pearson Education).

McGrew, A. (2002) 'Liberal internationalism: Between realism and cosmopolitanism', in Held, D. and McGrew, A. (eds) *Governing Globalization* (Cambridge: Polity Press) pp. 267–89.

McGuire, J. (1963) *Business and Society* (New York: McGraw-Hill).

McKinsey Global Institute (2007) *The New Power Brokers: How Oil, Asia, Hedge Funds, and Private Equity Are Shaping Global Capital Markets* (San Francisco: McKinsey & Company).

McNulty, S. (2006) 'Exxon resists claim for more oil spill cash', *Financial Times*, 1 June.

McWilliams, A. (2001) 'Corporate social responsibility: a theory of the firm perspective', *Academy of Management Review*, **26**(1): 117–28.

Mills, J., Schmitz, J. and Frizelle, J. (2004) 'A strategic review of supply networks', *International Journal of Operations & Production Management*, **24**(10): 1012–36.

Mintzberg, H. and Westley, F. (1992) 'Cycles of organizational change', *Strategic Management Journal*, **13**: 39–59.

Mitchell, R., Agle, B. and Wood, D. (1997) 'Toward a theory of stakeholder identification and salience: Defining the principle of who and what really counts', *Academy of Management Review*, **22**(4): 853–86.

Morrison, J. (2003) 'Corporate citizenship: More than a metaphor?' *The Journal of Corporate Citizenship*, **10**: 89–102.

Morrison, J. (2004) 'Legislating for good corporate governance: Do we expect too much?' *The Journal of Corporate Citizenship*, **15**: 121–33.

Mowery, D. and Oxley, J. (1997) 'Inward technology transfer and competitiveness', in Archibugi, D. and Michie, J. (eds) *Technology, Globalisation and Economic Performance* (Cambridge: Cambridge University Press) pp. 138–71.

Murray, S. (2006) 'A deafening silence', in FT Sustainable Business, *Financial Times*, 9 October, p. 2.

Nakamoto, M. (2007) 'TSE head hits out at standards of governance', *Financial Times*, 22 November.

Narula, R. (1993) 'Technology, international business and Porter's "diamond": Synthesizing a dynamic competitive development model', *Management International Review*, **33**(2): 85–107.

Narula, R. and Duysters, G. (2004) 'Globalisation and trends in international R&D alliances', *Journal of International Management*, **10**: 199–218.

Oakley, D. (2007) 'Rush into green arena raises bubble fears', *Financial Times*, 16 October.

OECD (Organization for Economic Co-operation and Development) (2001) *Guidelines for Multinational Enterprises* (Paris: OECD).

OECD (2004) *Principles of Corporate Governance* (Paris: OECD).

O'Hagan, E., Gunnicle, P. and Morley, M. (2005) 'Issues in the management of industrial relations in international firms', in Scullion, H. and Linehan, M. (eds) *International Human Resource Management* (Basingstoke: Palgrave Macmillan) pp. 156–78.

Ohlin, B. (1933) *International and Interregional Trade?* (Cambridge, MA: Harvard University Press).

Ohmae, K. (1995) *The End of the Nation State* (London: HarperCollins).

Osborn, R. and Hagedoorn, J. (1997) 'The institutionalisation and evolutionary dynamics of interorganizational alliances and networks', *Academy of Management Journal*, **40**(2): 261–78.

Öz, Ö. (2002) 'Assessing Porter's framework for national advantage: The case of Turkey', *Journal of Business Research*, **55**(6): 509–15.

Özbilgin, M. (2005) 'Introducing international human resource management', in Özbilgin, M. (ed.) *International Human Resource Management* (Basingstoke: Palgrave Macmillan) pp.1–13.

Patten, C. (1998) *East and West* (Basingstoke: Macmillan – now Palgrave Macmillan).

Pauly, L. and Reich, S. (1997) 'National structures and multinational corporate behaviour: Enduring differences in the age of globalization', *International Organization*, **51**(1): 1–30.

Pedersen, E. (2006) 'Making corporate social responsibility operable: How companies translate stakeholder dialogue into practice', *Business and Society Review*, **111**(2): 137–63.

Pei, M. (2005) 'Time to reflect on how far China has to go', *Financial Times*, 19 January.

Pei, M. (2006) *China's Trapped Transition* (Cambridge, MA: Harvard University Press).

Penrose, E. (1995) *The Theory of the Growth of the Firm*, 3rd edn (Oxford: Oxford University Press).

Perlmutter, H. (1969) 'The tortuous evolution of the multinational corporation', *Columbia Journal of World Business*, **4**: 9–18.

Perlmutter, H. (1995) 'The tortuous evolution of the multinational corporation', in Ghauri, P. and Prasad, S. (eds) *International Management: A Reader* (London: Dryden Press) pp. 3–14.

Pew Global Attitudes Project (2002) *Among Wealthy Nations … US Stands Alone in its Embrace of Religion*, http://pewglobal.org.

Pilling, D. (2005) 'Creative models shaped by education', *Financial Times Special Innovation Report*, 8 June, pp. 6–8.

Plattner, M. (1993) 'The democratic moment', in Diamond, L. and Plattner, M. (eds) *The Global Resurgence of Democracy* (Baltimore: The Johns Hopkins University Press) pp. 26–38.

Plender, J. (2007) 'Corporate groups are pressed to reduce their opacity', *Financial Times*, 2 July.

Porter, M. (1998a) *The Competitive Advantage of Nations* (Basingstoke: Macmillan – now Palgrave Macmillan).

Porter, M. (1998b) *On Competition* (Boston, MA: Harvard Business School Publishing).

Porter, M. (1998c) *Competitive Strategy: Techniques for Analyzing*

Industries and Competitors (with new introduction) (New York: Free Press).

Porter, M. (2000) 'Attitudes, values, beliefs and the microeconomics of prosperity', in Harrison, L. and Huntington, S. (eds) *Culture Matters* (New York: Basic Books) pp. 14–28.

Potter, D. (1993) 'Democratization in Asia', in Held, D. (ed.) *Prospects for Democracy* (Cambridge: Polity Press) pp. 355–79.

Prahalad, C. and Hamel, G. (1990) 'The core competence of the corporation', *Harvard Business Review*, **68**(3): 79–91.

Prasad, S.B. and Ghauri, P. (1995) 'A network approach to probing Asia's invisible business structures', in Ghauri, P. and Prasad, S.B. (eds) *International Management: A Reader* (London: The Dryden Press) pp 285–92.

Prasad, S. and Tata, J. (2003) 'The role of socio-cultural, political-legal, economic, and educational dimensions in quality management', *International Journal of Operations & Production Management*, **23**(5): 487–521.

PricewaterhouseCoopers (2007) *Executive Compensation Review of the Year 2007*, www.pwc.co.uk.

Ricardo, D. ([1817] 1973) *Principles of Political Economy and Taxation* (London: Dent).

Rogoff, K. (2007) 'No grand plans, but the financial system needs fixing', *Financial Times*, 8 February.

Ruggie, J. (2004) 'American exceptionalism, exemptionalism and global governance', Harvard University Research Working Paper Series, no. RWP04-006, http://ssrn.com.

Rugman, A. and D'Cruz, R. (1993) 'The "double diamond" model of international competitiveness: The Canadian experience', *Management International Review*, **33**(2): 17–39.

Rugman, A. and Verbeke, A. (1993) 'Foreign subsidiaries and multinational strategic management: An extension and correction of Porter's single diamond framework', *Management International Review*, **33**(2): 71–84.

Rugman, A. and Verbeke, A. (2003) 'Multinational enterprises and clusters: An organizing framework', *Management International Review*, **3**: 151–69.

Rugman, A. and Verbeke, A. (2004) 'A perspective on regional and global strategies of multinational enterprises', *Journal of International Business Studies*, **35**: 3–18.

Rugman, A. and Verbeke, A. (2005) 'Towards a theory of regional multinationals: A transaction cost economics approach', *Management International Review*, **45**(1): 5–17.

Sachs, J. (2000) 'Notes on a new sociology of economic development', in Harrison, L. and Huntington, S. (eds) *Culture Matters* (New York: Basic Books) pp. 29–43.

Sachs, J. and Shatz, H. (1994) 'Trade and jobs in US manufacturing', Brookings Papers on Economic Activity, issue 1, no. 00072303 (Washington, DC: Brookings Institute).

Salter, S. and Niswander, F. (1995) 'Cultural influence on the development of accounting systems internationally: A test of Gray's (1988) theory', *Journal of International Business Studies*, **38**(2): 379–97.

Sapir, A. (2005) 'Globalisation and the reform of European social models', paper at ECOFIN conference, Manchester, 9 September, www.bruegel.org.

Schuler, R., Budhwar, P. and Florkowski, G. (2002) 'International human resource management: Review and critique', *International Journal of Management Reviews*, **4**(1): 41–70.

Schuler, R., Jackson, S. and Fendt, J. (2005) 'Managing human resources in cross-border alliances', in Scullion, H. and Linehan, M. (eds) *International Human Resource Management* (Basingstoke: Palgrave Macmillan) pp. 202–35.

Schumpeter, J.A. ([1942] 1975) *Capitalism, Socialism and Democracy* (New York: Harper & Row).

Scullion, H., and Paauwe, J. (2005) 'Strategic HRM in multinational companies', in Scullian, H. and Linehan, M. (eds) *International Human Resource Management* (Basingstoke: Palgrave Macmillan).

Sherwood, B. (2006) 'Large companies "targeted" for legal action', *Financial Times*, 10 October.

Shrivastava, P. (1995) 'The role of corporations in achieving ecological sustainability', *Academy of Management Review*, **20**(4): 936–60.

Silver, S. (2005) 'Problems lie in wait for controversial trade deal', *Financial Times*, 14 March.

Smith, A. ([1776]1950) *An Inquiry into the Nature and Causes of the Wealth of Nations* (London: Methuen).

Smith, A.D. (1991) *National Identity* (Harmondsworth: Penguin).

Smith, P. (2007) 'Secretive sector steps into the glare of publicity', *Financial Times*, 24 April.

Steenkamp, J.-B., Batra, R. and Alden, D. (2003) 'How perceived brand globalness creates brand value', *Journal of International Business Studies*, **34**(1): 53–65.

Steiner, G. (1975) *Business and Society*, 2nd edn (New York: Random House).

Stiglitz, J. (1989) *The Economic Role of the State* (Oxford: Basil Blackwell).

Stiglitz, J. (2002) *Globalization and its Discontents* (London: Allen Lane).

Stiglitz, J. (2003) 'Dealing with debt', *Harvard International Review*, **25**(1): 54–9.

Sull, D. and Ruelas-Gossi, A. (2004) 'The art of innovating on a shoestring', *Financial Times*, Mastering Innovation, 24 September, p. 11.

Swann, C. (2005) 'Broadening appeal lifts sector', *Financial Times*, 8 June.

Tatli, A. (2005) 'Strategic aspects of international human resource management', in Özbilgin, M. (ed) *International Human Resource Management* (Basingstoke: Palgrave Macmillan) pp. 82–102.

Taylor, P. (2007) 'Motorola falls victim to its own success', *Financial Times*, 19 March.

Taylor, S., Beechler, S. and Napier, N. (1996) 'Toward an integrated model for strategic international human resource management', *Academy of Management Review*, **21**(4): 959–85.

Terkel, S. (1980) *American Dreams: Lost and Found* (New York: New Press).

Tett, G. (2007) 'No turning back the revolution', *Financial Times*, 28 May.

Tett, G. and Tassell, T. (2005) 'A swing into bonds: Why equities are losing their allure for global investors', *Financial Times*, 10 October.

The Economist (2007) 'Vermont takes on Detroit', 22 September, p. 54.

The Economist (2007) 'Inside the Googleplex', 1 September, p. 58.

The G8 Gleneagles (2005) The Gleneagles Communiqué, www.g8.gov.uk.

Thompson, E. (2004) 'National competitiveness: A question of cost conditions or institutional circumstances?', *British Journal of Management*, **15**: 197–218.

Thompson, G. (2005) 'Global corporate citizenship: What does it mean?' *Competition & Change*, **9**(2): 131–52.

Tieman, R. (2004) 'There's more to life than money', *Financial Times*, 28 April.

Transparency International (2007) Corruption Perception Index, www.transparency.org.

Trompenaars, F. (1994) *Riding the Waves of Culture* (New York: Irwin).

Tu, W.-M. (2000) 'Multiple modernities: A preliminary inquiry into the implications of East Asian modernity', in Harrison, L. and Huntington, S. (eds) *Culture Matters* (New York: Basic Books) pp. 256–66.

Tucker, S. (2006) 'China told to refine governance' *Financial Times*, 17 April.

Tuschke, A. and Sanders, G. (2003) 'Antecedents and consequences of corporate governance reform: The case of Germany', *Strategic Management Journal*, **24**: 631–49.

Underhill, G. and Zhang, X. (2006) 'Norms, legitimacy, and global financial governance', World Economy & Finance Working Paper Series (London: Birkbeck, University of London).

UK Department for Business, Enterprise and Regulatory Reform (2006) *Energy Review 2006*, www.dti.gov.uk.

UN (1987) *Report of the World Commission on Environment and Development: Our Common Future* (The Brundtland Report), www.un-documents.net.

UN (2001) *World Investment Report 2001* (Geneva: UN).

UN (2005) *World Investment Report 2005* (Geneva: UN).

UN (2006) *World Investment Report 2006* (Geneva: UN).

UN (2007a) *World Investment Report 2007* (Geneva: UN).

UN (2007b) *The Millennium Development Goals Report* (New York: UN).

UNDP (United Nations Development Programme) (1998) *Globalization and Liberalization* (New York: UNDP).

UNDP (2002) *Human Development Report 2002* (New York: UNDP).

UNDP (2004) *Human Development Report 2004* (New York: UNDP).

UNDP (2005) *Human Development Report 2005* (New York: UNDP).

UNDP (2006) *Human Development Report 2006* (Basingstoke: Palgrave Macmillan).

UNEP (United Nations Environment Programme) (2005) *Millennium Ecosystem Assessment*, www.millenniumassessment.org.

UNEP (2007) *Fourth Assessment Report of the Intergovernmental Panel on Climate Change*, www.ipcc.ch.

United Nations News Service (2007) 'Illicit trafficking, theft of nuclear materials "a persistent problem", UN agency reports', 12 September, www.un.org/News.

USDA (United States Department of Agriculture) (2008) Newsroom News Release no. 0051.08, 21 February, www.usda.gov.

Vernon, R. ([1966]1999) 'International investment and international trade in the product cycle', in Buckley, P. and Ghauri, P. (eds) *The Internationalization of the Firm: A Reader* (London: International Thomson Business Press) pp.14–26.

Visser, J. (2006) 'Union membership statistics in 24 countries', *Monthly Labor Review*, **129**(1): 38–50.

Vollmann, T., Cordon, C. and Raabe, H. (2000) 'Supply chain management', Part 8, Mastering Management (London: Financial Times).

Wagstyl, S. (2007) 'Lies haunt a reformer's grip on power', *Financial Times*, 25 October.

Wallace, P. (2004) 'The English patient', *The Economist: The World in 2005*, p. 34.

Wallis, W. (2005) 'Evangelicals see opportunity in Promised Land', *Financial Times*, 16 July.

Waters, R. and Nuttall, C. (2007) 'Hirings soar, profits fall … but it's "just Google being Google"', *Financial Times*, 23 July.

Watson, R. (2008) 'Internet terrorism crackdown', BBC News, 18 January, www.news.bbc.co.uk.

Webster, F. (1992) 'The changing role of marketing in the corporation', *Journal of Marketing*, **56**: 1–17.

Wheatley, J. and Wiggins, J. (2007) 'Little by little Nestle aims to woo Brazil's poor', *Financial Times*, 20 February.

White, B. (2007) 'Goldman's charity dims bonuses glare', *Financial Times*, 22 November.

Whitley, R. (1990) 'Eastern Asian enterprise structures and comparative analysis of forms and business organization', *Organization Studies*, **11**(1): 47–74.

Whitley, R. (2001) 'How and why are international firms different? The consequences of cross-border managerial coordination for firm characteristics and behaviour', in Morgan, E., Kristensen, P. and Whitley, R. (eds) *The Multinational Firm* (Oxford: Oxford University Press) pp. 27–68.

WHO (World Health Organization) (2006a) *Air Quality Guidelines 2006*, www.who.int.

Wiesmann, G. (2007) 'BASF to save €5m a year in NYSE delisting', *Financial Times*, 2 August.

Wiggins, J. (2007) 'Burger, fries and a shake-up', *Financial Times*, 27 February.

Williams, F. (2005) 'Concerns grow over deal to help poor states', *Financial Times*, 15 December.

Williamson, H. (2007) 'G8 split over Africa and pledges', *Financial Times*, 6 June.

Wolf, M. (2006a) 'China should stick to trial and error', *Financial Times*, 7 June.

Wolf, M. (2006b) 'Why the energy revolution will power ahead', *Financial Times*, 28 June.

Wolf, M. (2007a) 'The new capitalism', *Financial Times*, 19 June.

Wolf, M. (2007b) 'We are living in a brave new world of state capitalism', *Financial Times*, 17 October.

World Bank (2004) *World Development Report 2004* (Washington, DC: The World Bank).

World Bank (2006) *World Development Report 2006* (Washington, DC: The World Bank).

World Economic Forum (2006) *Global Governance Initiative Annual Report 2006*, www.wef.org?

Wright, R. (2007) 'A failure to keep up with the times', *Financial Times*, 27 March.

WTO/OECD (2007) *Aid for Trade at a Glance 2007: 1st Global Review*, www.oecd.org.

Yamin, M. (1991) 'A critical re-evaluation of Hymer's contribution to the theory of the transnational corporation', in Pitelis, C. and Sugden, R. (eds) *The Nature of the Transnational Firm* (London: Routledge) pp. 57–71.

Yeung, R. and Brittain, S. (2001) 'Beyond the interview', Mastering People Management, *Financial Times*, 12 November.

Zhou, J. and Martocchio, J. (2001) 'Chinese and American managers' compensation award decisions: A comparative study', *Personnel Psychology*, **54**(1): 115–45.

Zhou, D. and Vertinsky, I. (2002) 'Can protectionist trade measures make a country better off? A study of VERs and minimum quality standards', *Journal of Business Research*, **55**: 227–36.

Zimmerer, T., Scarborough, N. and Wilson, D. (2007) *Essentials of Entrepreneurship and Small Business Management*, 5th edn (New Jersey: Prentice Hall).

Index of business organizations

Index of people

Subject index